CONTENTS

work against literacy, or does it redefine what it means to be literate in the twenty-first century?

to take another look at a subject that no one can claim to understand fully, not even those who have found themselves in the thick of battle.

Steingraber, diagnosed with a type of cancer known to be caused by exposure to environmental carcinogens, returns to her childhood home to explore the local industrial landscape. A scientist by training, Steingraber traces the use of DDT in World War II and its subsequent use by the agricultural industry, mapping these developments on to the geography of the countryside that surrounds her home.

Now that genetic technology has moved off the pages of science fiction novels and into research labs, who will control it? The government? The medical community? Religious conservatives? Stock argues for a genetic free market in which parents have the right to enhance their progeny in any way they want—and can afford.

The term *divided consciousness* refers to those times when we withdraw mentally from the world around us. Daydreams and other forms of subjective escape often help us to keep our mental balance by shutting out events when they threaten to be overwhelming. But when does our power to shut things out begin to close the door on sanity itself?

Anyone who watches the presidential debates or listens to talk radio can see that Americans love to argue. But the truth is that the winner in any debate may prove to be mistaken, while the loser may fail to communicate information that everyone could benefit from hearing. According to linguist Deborah Tannen, there has to be a better way.

Technological innovations happen in response to problems, but each innovation ends up producing a series of new problems in turn—which require new innovations, which produce new problems once again, apparently ad infinitum. Is all of this change self-defeating? While admitting that technology has "revenge effects," Edward Tenner makes the case that progress is no illusion.

Losing one's sense of self or having an empty self is typically imagined to be a fate worse than death. But Robert Thurman, an expert on the Buddhism of Tibet, argues that we have misjudged the experience of "no self," which is not a dark corridor to oblivion, but the road to what he calls "infinite life."

What it means to have a self has changed over the course of the past thirty years. While Baby Boomers set out to change the world, Generation Me seeks out fun as the highest value and promotes self-esteem as the greatest good. Drawing on data taken from 1.3 million young people, Twenge argues that this obsessive focus on the self is not just bad for society, it's also bad for the individual.

THEMATIC CONTENTS

What should a college or university ask beginning students to think and write about? Our goal is to have our students engage with the most pressing problems of our time—problems that resist easy answers and that need to be explored in ways that move across the boundaries that separate the disciplines. In the process of crossing these boundaries, each of us has to invent our own ways of thinking and writing. We offer the follow thematic combinations to illustrate how this creative work might be pursued.

Making Sense of Violence

World Religion and World Secularity

Education: Learning, Conforming, and Knowing

The Future of The Environment: Evolution and Human Ingenuity

Medical Practice and the Arts of Healing

Gender

Art and the Making of Meaning

Economics and Justice

Culture and Performance

Democracy in the Age of Globalization

PREFACE

This book probably differs from most you have encountered, at least those that you have encountered in school. Generally, the books taught in school tell students how to think, but ours has a different purpose. We wanted to put in your hands a book that would require you to make connections for yourself as you think, read, and write about the events that are likely to shape your future life.

Although the articles and essays assembled here deal with subjects as diverse as the global increase in ethnic violence and the practice of Tibetan meditation, the book is not really "about" violence or meditation or any of the other subjects explored by the readings we have selected. Instead, this book is about the need for new ways of thinking, and it does not pretend that those ways of thinking are widely practiced today. Our world has seen more change in the last hundred years than it had seen in the previous thousand. From the media we get daily reports on subjects that our great-grandparents might have found incomprehensible: breakthroughs in cloning; mergers of U.S. firms with Japanese or German partners; a global treaty on biological weapons; a new account of the universe in the first seconds after the Big Bang; the melting of the polar icecaps; legislation to extend health-care benefits to same-sex couples. Such events are truly without precedent.

Never before have people faced uncertainty in so many different areas. Will the Internet be a negative influence, contributing to the forces that have pulled apart the family unit, or will it strengthen our neighborhoods and communities? Will the global economy create widespread unemployment and environmental decline, or will it usher in an era of undreamed-of prosperity and peace? Will encounters between different cultures, long separated by geography, lead to a new renaissance, or must such meetings always end in balkanization and violence? Unlike the questions posed by the standard textbook, the answers to these questions aren't waiting for any of us in the teacher's edition. Not even the best educated and the most experienced among us can foresee with certainty how the life of our times will turn out. If our problems today are much more sweeping than those encountered by humankind before, they are also more complex. Globalization is not just an issue for economists, or political scientists, or historians, or anthropologists: it is an issue for all of them—and us—together. The degradation of the biosphere is not just an ecological matter, but a political, social, and cultural matter as well.

The uniqueness of our time requires that we devise new understandings of ourselves and of the world. One purpose of this book is to provide a forum for these understandings to emerge. It may seem strange, perhaps, that we would have such lofty goals in a course for undergraduates. Surely the experts are better equipped to respond to issues of the sort our world now confronts than are beginning students in our colleges and universities. But this assumption may be unjustified. While the forms of expertise available today clearly have great value, most of the current academic disciplines were created more than a century ago, and the divisions of knowledge on which they are based reflect the needs of a very different society. It is worth remembering, for example, that in 1900 cars were a new technology, and airplanes and radios had yet to be invented. Scientists still debated the structure of the atom. The British Empire dominated three-fourths of the globe, and "culture" meant the traditions of Western Europe's elite, never more than one-tenth of one percent of the population of that region. In a certain sense, the current generation of college students, teachers, and administrators needs to reinvent the university itself, not by replacing one department or methodology with another, but by forging broad connections across areas of knowledge that still remain in relative isolation.

New Humanities for New Times: The Search for Coherence

Some readers of this book will be surprised by the absence of material from the traditional humanities: poems and plays, photographs of paintings and statues, excerpts from great works of philosophy such as Plato's *Republic* and Descartes's *Discourse on Method*. Clearly, no one should leave Aristotle or Shakespeare or Toni Morrison unread. And anyone unfamiliar with Leonardo da Vinci, Frida Kahlo, Thelonious Monk, and Georgia O'Keeffe has missed a priceless opportunity. Yet this book has grown out of the belief that the humanities today must reach further than in centuries past. Without intending to do so, traditional humanists may have contributed to the decline of their own enterprise. One could even argue that the humanities have seen their principal task as the preservation of the past rather than the creation of the future. Humanists have often left real-world activities and concerns to other fields, while devoting themselves to passive contemplation, aesthetic pleasure, and partisan critique. Consequently, most people outside the university have come to consider the humanities as something closer to entertainment, wish fulfillment, or a covert form of politics, while regarding the sciences as the only real truth.

The humanities today must be understood in a new way: not as a particular area of knowledge but as the human dimension of *all* knowledge. Engineering may lie outside the traditional humanities, but it enters the domain of the New Humanities when we begin to consider the unexpected consequences of technological innovation, as Edward Tenner does in his observations on the consequences of the automobile. When we define the humanities in this way, it may come as a surprise that some of our society's foremost humanists work in fields quite far removed from the traditional humanities. Oliver Sacks, one of the writers in this collection, is a world-renowned neurologist whose case histories have served both to open up the mysteries of the human brain and, at the same time, to humanize: patients suffering from a wide array of mental illnesses, brain injuries, and neurological disorders. And Devra Davis, an expert in epidemiology, is working to get the chemical, pharmaceutical, food, and health care industries to change their business practices to safeguard society from the effects of environmental toxins.

The New Humanities, as represented by this book, promote change in another way as well: they invite us to take knowledge obtained at the university beyond the confines of the university itself. In a certain sense, this means that we all must become our own best teachers: we must find in our own lives—our problems, values, dreams, and commitments—an organizing principle that cannot be found in a curriculum. The great, unspoken secret of the university is that the curriculum has no center: specialization makes sure of that. Historians write primarily for historians; literary critics for other critics. As we shuttle back and forth between these specialized disciplines, the only coherence we gain is the coherence we have constructed for ourselves. Under these conditions, what the New Humanities can teach us is a different way of using knowledge, a way of thinking that synthesizes many different fields of study.

Specialized learning in the disciplines typically deals with the "how," but it often leaves unanswered the "why." There has never been a course called "Life 101," and given the complexity of our world, such a course would have to be without end. But something important will be missing if we leave the "why" questions unexplored. Should we continue to pursue a technological utopia? Does modern science mean the end of religion? Is social inequality an acceptable price to pay for economic growth? Any attempt to answer these questions requires specialized knowledge, yet knowledge alone is not enough. Because a cogent, well-informed case can be made on either side of almost every issue, the source of our ultimate commitments must reach deeper. We might say that the "why" questions shape these commitments because they address our most basic and most personal relations to other people and to the world. In different ways, these questions ask us how we choose to live. No expert can choose on our behalf, because no expert can live our lives for us or define what our experiences should mean to us.

The coherence missing from the curriculum is not a quality of knowledge but of our own lives. In itself, no amount of learning can produce a sense of coherence. That sense arises, instead, from a creative and synthetic activity on our part as we interact with the world. Again and again, we need to make connections between discrete areas of knowledge and between knowledge and our personal experience. This coherence is never complete because there is always something more to learn that remains unconnected, but we might think of coherence, not as a goal reached once and for all but as an ideal worth pursuing continuously. Of course, cynicism and fragmentation are always options, too, and they require no special effort. One could easily live as though nothing and no one mattered, but in such a case, learning and living become exercises in futility. The New Humanities offer a better path.

Knowledge in Depth and Knowledge of the World

As everyone understands, formal education has been carefully designed to keep the disciplines separate. In economics classes, we typically read economics; in history classes, we typically read history. This approach allows information to be imparted in small, efficiently managed packages. We can divide, say, biology from chemistry, and then we can divide biology into vertebrate and invertebrate, and chemistry into organic and inorganic. We start with the general and move to the particular: ideally, we learn in depth, with increasing mastery of details that become more and more refined. At the end of the semester, if everything goes well, we can distinguish between an ecosystem and a niche, a polymer and a plastic, a neo-Kantian and a neo-Hegelian. We can contrast Hawthorne's treatment of the outsider with Salinger's, or we can explain the debate about whether slavery or states' rights actually caused the Civil War.

Knowledge in depth is indispensable. But it can also create a sense of disconnection, the impression that education is an empty ritual without real-world consequences beyond the receipt of a grade and the fulfillment of a requirement. In the classroom, we learn to calculate sine and cosine without ever discovering how these calculations might be used and why they were invented. Searching for symbols in a poem or a short story becomes a mental exercise on par with doing a crossword puzzle. Instead of reflecting on why events have happened and how they get remembered and recorded, we refine our ability to recapitulate strings of dates and names. At its worst, learning in depth can produce a strange disconnect: the purpose of learning becomes learning itself, while activity in the real world becomes incidental, even difficult to imagine. As students reach the final years of high school, they may understand vaguely that they ought to know *Hamlet,* and should be able to identify *The Declaration of Independence* and explain how photosynthesis has influenced the shape of leaves, but in response to an actual tragedy, an environmental disaster, or a real-life legal crisis, they might feel unqualified to speak and unprepared to act.

College-level learning can offer an escape from this predicament by giving students greater freedom to choose what they will study, and in many cases the subjects they choose are closely related to their real-world objectives. But even with this newfound freedom, the problem of disconnection crops up in other ways. After years of hard work, a student who has mastered electrical engineering may still leave college poorly informed about the globalized, commercial environment in which most engineers now do their work. Students well versed in Renaissance drama or the history of World War I may find their own lives after graduation much more difficult to explain. For some people, this problem of disconnection may arise long before graduation. One who sets out to memorize facts from, say, a social psychology textbook may find that these facts grow increasingly stale. Easily memorized one day, they are quickly forgotten the next. The risk of knowledge in depth is that we lose our sense of the larger world and we forget that a field like psychology, for all its current sophistication, began with tentative and somewhat clumsy questions about the mind. Ironically, the more we treat an area of knowledge as a reality in itself, the less we may be able to understand and use what we have supposedly learned.

There is another kind of knowledge that we begin to create when we ask ourselves how our learning pertains to the world outside the classroom. This line of questioning is more complex than it might initially seem because the larger world is never simply out there waiting for us. All knowledge begins as a knowledge of parts and fragments, even our knowledge of the private lives we know in most detail. Each of our private lives may seem complete, in itself, just as a field like psychology can seem to explain everything once we are immersed in its methods and its facts. But this sense of completeness is an illusion produced by the limits of our perspective. Beyond the reach of what we know here and now, nothing seems to matter. We begin to get a glimpse of the larger world, however, only when we shift our focus from one reality to another: only then do we discover the deficiencies in our previous ways of thinking, and only then are we able to think in new and different ways. This movement from the known to the unknown is the essence of all learning; indeed, the most successful learners are generally those who have developed the highest tolerance for not knowing—those who continue to question and explore issues beyond their own areas of specialization, entertaining alternatives that others might find unimaginable.

Knowledge itself can be defined in many ways: as a quantity of information, as technical expertise, as cultivated taste, as a special kind of self-awareness. And as varied as these definitions may appear, they share an underlying principle. Whatever the form knowledge may take, it always emerges from a process we might call *connecting*. The eighteenth-century English scientist Sir Isaac Newton, who first understood the complex relations between force, mass, and acceleration, may have been inspired by connecting his scientific work with his deeply held religious convictions about the rational perfection of God and His Creation. Many other notable thinkers likewise found inspiration through connection. Roughly two hundred years after Newton's discoveries had sparked a technological revolution, a young lawyer born in India, Mohandas K. Gandhi, drew on Henry David Thoreau's *Civil Disobedience,* written in support of abolitionists just before the Civil War, to launch a campaign of passive resistance against the racist government of South Africa. Two years before Gandhi spent his first term in jail as a political prisoner, a French artist and intellectual, Marcel Duchamps, shocked the art world with a painting—*Nude Descending a Staircase*—inspired by scientific photographs of athletes in motion. Whether we are talking about physics or political systems, epidemiology or aesthetics, knowledge by its very nature brings together disparate worlds of thought and action.

Creative Reading: From Explicit to Implicit

The selections in this book are intended for creative reading. The humanities should do more than convey information or give professors a chance to demonstrate their brilliance. After all, studies have consistently demonstrated that we retain little of what we have been taught unless we put that knowledge to use. At its best, education should offer beginners the chance to practice the same activities that more accomplished thinkers engage in: beyond receiving knowledge, beginners should participate in the making of knowledge. The articles and chapters collected in this book offer many opportunities for such participation. All of the selections are challenging, some because they are long and complex, some because they draw on specialized disciplines, and some because they open up unusual perspectives. These are not readings that lend themselves to simple summaries and multiple-choice answers. Instead, they require discussion—they were written to elicit activity and response.

It is important not to think of essays such as these as truths to be committed to memory or arguments to be weighed and then accepted or rejected. It might be more useful to see them in much the same way we now see Internet sites. Every site on the Internet is linked to countless others by the connections that Web authors and programmers have forged. As a result of their cumulative efforts, one site links us to another and then to the next, on and on for as long as we care to go. In some ways, even the most useful and informative written texts are less sophisticated than the simplest Web sites, and the Internet can transform the labor of many days—sifting through periodicals and rummaging through the library stacks—into the work of a few hours. Yet the Web also has limitations that the printed word does not. The Web, after all, can show us only those pathways that someone has already made semipermanent. By contrast, *all* connections to the printed text are *virtual* connections: any text can be linked to any other text in a web of inquiry and analysis potentially much vaster than the Internet itself. When we surf the Internet, we find only what others want us to find, but the connections we personally forge between one text and the next may truly be uncharted terrain.

Texts can be connected to other texts in any way a reader finds helpful and credible. But the ideas set forth in a text also offer a potential network of connections waiting to be made. Of course, every text has an explicit dimension: the words on the page in their most literal form and the order in which ideas are presented. Because of this explicit content, it is possible to memorize and repeat, more or less verbatim, the information that a text provides. We might try to remember, for example, all the members of the "alphabet army" Pietra Rivoli discusses in "Dogs Snarling Together: How Politics Came to Rule the Global Apparel Trade." Yet the meaning of a text is something more than what the words on the page explicitly state. A text becomes meaningful only through the implicit connections it motivates. To understand a text, as opposed to simply repeating it, is to move back and forth from the explicit to the implicit until an interpretation takes shape. In Rivoli's case, what matters more than the particular figures she mentions is the overall direction of global trade in the twentieth century—a direction that involves the members of the "alphabet army" she discusses, but is not determined by that army alone.

Remember that these implicit dimensions are always virtual. An essay on the politics of AIDS, for example, may not be explicitly related to an article on bicycles in West Africa. But between them a connection could still be made, an important and original one. While some connections might seem potentially more fruitful and easily forged than others, improbable connections have sometimes revealed enormous vistas of knowledge. In practice this means that the most creative readers are also those most willing to take constructive risks, exploring connections that others have overlooked. At the same time, a connection must be credible, and the more sustained that connection becomes—the more deeply and widely it extends across the details of the texts at hand—the more persuasive the interpretation that arises from it.

The most basic form of interpretation starts when we connect one part of a text with other parts. Consider, for example, the first sentence of Jonathan Boyarin's "Waiting for a Jew." "My story begins in a community," he writes, "with an illusion of wholeness." Needless to say, this statement can stand alone, but it also serves as a point of departure. Practically every detail that follows in Boyarin's account can be connected in some way to this key phrase "the illusion of wholeness." Sometimes the experiences he recalls may appear to underscore the word *illusion*, confirming the irreparable loss of the community in which he had grown up. But other moments in his narrative might speak directly to *wholeness*—to the persistence of communities of shared belief in the midst of a larger, unbelieving world. Explicitly, of course, Boyarin's text makes no such point, but implicitly the point is waiting to be made, and by making it we become interpreters of the text.

When we read for content, we are reading to preserve the knowledge made by others. But when we read for implicit connections, we become cocreators with the authors themselves. To recapitulate some portion of

Boyarin's narrative might help us pass a quiz or defend a point of view in the context of a debate, but when we use Boyarin's narrative as an opportunity to make connections of our own, we join in the same questioning that started him on his path. The purpose of such reading is not to get the "right answer" but to understand more fully the world in which we live, a process literally without end. In this sense, the best interpretations leave the texts behind as they move forward, toward other questions and other texts.

Connective Thinking: The Search for a Shared Horizon

Much of formal education promotes mimetic, or imitative, thinking: we learn to reproduce information already collected and organized by someone else. Mimetic thinking presupposes the adequacy of knowledge in its present state. But what happens when we discover that our knowledge leaves something out? Perhaps the lecture in English class this afternoon contradicted a point made yesterday in anthropology class. Or perhaps an assigned article has described an aspect of the social world in a manner that we find inaccurate or disconcerting. On occasions like these, when we encounter the limits or defects of knowledge, mimetic thinking cannot help us; instead, we are obliged to think connectively—to think *across* domains of knowledge rather than thinking from within them.

Sometimes connective thinking happens in response to crisis. The complex body of knowledge we call immunology, for example, has advanced rapidly in an effort to counter the spread of HIV and AIDS. So, too, a growing crisis in farming, caused by the overuse of pesticides, has spurred extensive research in plant genetics. But whether or not real-world crises bear down on us, the construction of knowledge of any kind necessarily produces contradictions. In "Meat and Milk Factories," Peter Singer and Jim Mason describe their visit to the factory farm of an Iowa pig producer and the farmer's defense of his business practices. Even if we don't share Singer and Mason's concerns about the ethical treatment of animals, few readers would doubt the truthfulness of the evidence they present. And fewer still would question their ability to put together a compelling argument: their account is well written, carefully researched, and coherently organized. It is precisely the coherence of their case, however, that limits its value for readers. At best, Singer and Mason can only offer us one perspective—their own.

As soon as we have read more than a single text, we encounter discontinuous images and perspectives of the world that we must somehow reconcile. Precisely because most accounts are more or less true to the perspectives they adopt, the way out of this discontinuity seldom lies with a blanket rejection of one perspective or another, a simple "right" or "wrong." Instead, the most constructive and creative response is to search for a larger shared horizon, a new way of thinking that is broad enough in scope to do justice to both accounts. This search is not quite the same as "compare and contrast." After all, we can endlessly compare and contrast details that are relatively trivial and that do not bridge the gaps between texts. A shared horizon, on the other hand, is more inclusive than either text alone and often connects them on the level of implications, not explicit claims. And once a shared horizon presents itself, the connections we make gradually prompt us to explore questions we raise—and answer—for ourselves.

When an observer of world events like Amy Chua contemplates the rise of ethnic violence, she proposes that different societies may need to follow different routes to economic and political development. On the other hand, Bryan Caplan, an economist, argues that the self-interest that drives both local and global capitalism tends to encourage socially beneficial behavior. Confronting these two disparate positions, we are bound to be puzzled about their possible connections. Do the two arguments simply contradict one another? If they do, then perhaps you will find Chua's reasoning more persuasive, or you will favor Caplan's position. However, no two essays simply exist in a state of contradiction. To a greater or lesser extent they will also confirm and complement one another. We might assume, as Caplan does, that everyone stands to benefit from reading the world through the lens of economics. Conversely, we might prefer to believe, along with Chua, that differences of culture and history need to be respected. But what if that history is one of colonization and local oppression? The point of connective thinking is not to say "yes" to one writer and "no" to the other. Nor is it to declare blithely that we all have a right to our personal opinions. Instead, connective thinking allows us to explore the many ways in which the two discussions might fit together, forming a whole that is greater than the sum of its parts.

Connective thinking is creative and independent in a way that mimetic thinking can never be. No matter how ably we summarize the views of Chua and Caplan, this is not the same as connecting them within the context of a larger question or debate. Yet these connections are never waiting for us fully formed already: there is always the need for a leap of imagination. Chua's primary concern is the alleviation of global instability, the burden of which often falls most heavily on minorities and "outsiders." Caplan's goal is to establish that the study of economics reveals that the market works, in general, to encourage socially beneficial behaviors. At first, when we consider these differences, no shared horizon may present itself, but we can push our thinking farther. The best advice is not to stop at what the authors have said but to ask about the implications of their ideas—to ask how the issues they have raised might have an impact on us personally and how they might affect both our society and our world. Chua and Caplan may appear to be miles apart at first, but a shared horizon might begin to open up when we contemplate the possibility that a global market might serve to draw global attention to local inequities, or when we recognize that both authors share a basic commitment to an improved social situation and to an increase in human happiness.

Writing to Tell, Writing to See

Mimetic thinking goes hand in hand with writing to tell—writing for the purpose of demonstrating mastery over an existing body of information. In American schools, the classic example of writing to tell is the venerable book report. Like mimetic thinking, writing to tell has its appropriate place. Connective thinking calls, however, for writing of a different kind, which might be described as writing to see. In this case, the writer has to do something more than recount the knowledge of others; like connective thinking, it is an active pursuit in which the writer takes that knowledge somewhere new. In the act of writing to tell, people give answers. In the process of writing to see, we start with a question inspired by others and go on to explore what they have left unexplored; we engage in the kind of writing that higher education at its best can foster: exploratory writing, writing to see. A good example of such writing is "The Mind's Eye," by Oliver Sacks. Because Sacks is a neurologist—an Oxford-trained physician and a professor of medicine—we might have expected him to present some of the answers he has found in his four decades of research. Instead he begins with a question, one that seems startling in its simplicity: "to what extent are we . . . shaped, predetermined, by our brains, and to what extent do we shape our own brains?" In his attempt to think through the question he has posed, Sacks might have drawn on research by other specialists in fields like chemistry, genetics, and neuroanatomy. He might have taped electrodes to the heads of volunteers or studied their brains with an MRI machine. But instead, the sources Sacks decides to work with are books written by people who have adapted to blindness in a surprising variety of ways.

It may have been the case that the question Sacks poses—do our brains shape us, or do we shape our brains?—has followed him from the earliest years of his medical practice. But he may have formulated the question only after he had read the books he refers to in his essay. What seems certain, no matter how his project began, is that Sacks realized sooner or later that these books called into doubt much that he had once assumed about the development of the brain. On the one hand, his training led him to believe that the tasks handled by the different areas of the brain were essentially fixed after childhood. On the other hand, accounts by people who had lost their sight strongly suggest that brains can rebuild themselves—that brains are capable of significant change, even far into adulthood. We cannot know exactly what inspired Sacks to write, but surely one powerful motive was the discontinuity between his old assumptions and the new evidence.

Discontinuity is where the most valuable and valued writing starts. From time immemorial, teachers of English have told their students to begin the task of writing only after they know clearly what they want to say. These instructions have always expressed more fantasy than truth. Typically, a position—a thesis or argument—will remain fairly vague until we have done a great deal of preliminary writing. Discontinuities lead us to the search for a shared horizon, and from this shared horizon our own questions come. Then, provided we are willing to push far enough, a coherent position begins to emerge, not all at once in a grand vision but cumulatively, with one insight building on the next. At some point, as these insights begin to cohere, we recognize the direction of our thoughts, a direction that writing itself has revealed. We write and then we see where our writing has taken us. Only then are we in a position to convey our discoveries to others in a well-crafted presentation.

In order for Sacks to become a source for our own writing, we need to start with a question his work leaves unresolved. If human brains are inherently as flexible as he suggests, then why do people usually seem so similar in their outlooks and behavior? Could it be that education, and not nature or evolution, has made us all the same? If at some point in the future we abolish formal schooling, would our mental lives become far less uniform than they are now? Of course, each of us is free to conclude that human nature will never change, regardless of our brains, and in that case we might choose to brush aside the implications of Sacks's ideas. But these ideas might also prompt us to rethink a number of our presuppositions. If events in our lives are actually capable of changing the structure of our brains, then perhaps we are doing serious damage to ourselves when we spend countless hours glued to television shows that routinely push their viewers into emotions like envy, anger, and contempt. Could it be that we need to care for our mental health much as we care for our bodies through diet and exercise? As we set out to explore questions of this kind, we might also draw on Martha Stout's discussion of the way the brain responds to psychological trauma. Or we might make some fruitful connections to Robert Thurman's thoughts about the pursuit of wisdom. Ultimately, through our reading and thinking, we might start to develop a position of our own.

Developing a Position

A position is not exactly an argument in the ordinary sense of the word. In everyday speech, the term *argument* suggests an adversarial stance: we might argue for, or against, William Greider's ideas about worker-owned businesses. "Making an argument" tends to mean deciding ahead of time what you think about an issue and then finding "support" to back up your points. There is, however, another way. Instead of simply ratifying an existing belief, each of us can use the readings to formulate a position of our own. To do so is to imagine ourselves in a different way, not as combatants but as participants in an ongoing conversation. Even if we read a writer with distaste, what matters most are the questions raised, not the answers given. Precisely because the search for a position begins with some degree of uncertainty, it requires a willingness on our part to suspend judgment and to pursue ideas wherever they might lead. It is important to remember that this pursuit does not require complete assent or unwavering commitment. We can always explore ideas that we eventually reject. The proper spirit for writing to see might be described as exploratory and experimental.

An experiment involves a "dialogue" between projection and revision. First, we imagine or "project" an outcome based on our prior knowledge and experience. We make an educated guess about the conclusion we will probably draw from our reading of an author or authors. Perhaps we start with the claim that Chris McCandless, the young man whose travels and death Jon Krakauer retraces, was spoiled and self-deceiving. Yet when we turn to Alexander Stille's account of alternative attitudes toward the natural world, our opinion of McCandless may grow less clear. As we write, our thinking may appear to lose its way and we may realize, after three or four pages, that we have contradicted ourselves. Perhaps McCandless's actions now seem justified, even commendable. Instead of treating this change in our position as a failure or a lapse, we should appreciate its value as a discovery, which we could make only after a great deal of hard work. And rather than return to our original stance, we should revise what we have written in order to present a revised position. But revision, too, involves experiment and discovery. The point of a new draft is never simply to change a position: the point is also to explain how and why the position has changed.

The Spirit of the New Humanities

Because we can learn from everything, no one should fear making mistakes. We should never forget that the greatest thinkers of every age have often been refuted later, whereas ordinary people have sometimes lived more wisely than they were given credit for. Not so long ago, the best-educated Europeans believed that all celestial bodies beyond the moon were eternal and changeless. The learned taught that matter in every form could be reduced to the basic elements of earth, air, fire, and water. Medical experts sternly warned against the perils of regular bathing and eating whole grains. In sexual reproduction, men were supposed to contribute the blueprint, while women provided the raw material. One could spend a lifetime enumerating the follies that have passed for knowledge. And when we pause to consider such a checkered history, we might decide that education is itself a folly.

But maybe not. Instead of expecting knowledge to be true once and for all, we might try to see it as pragmatic and provisional, always subject to revision given further evidence or new circumstances. In our society today, the sciences may offer the best example of this experimentalist attitude, but some philosophers and artists of every generation have also refused the twin consolations of dogmatism and disillusionment. In the years ahead, our society will face many challenges—environmental, social, cultural, economic, and political—that are sure to seem overwhelming. Given the high level of uncertainty that has become a constant feature of our lives, people may be drawn to ideologies that promise truths exempt from all revision and insulated from the challenges of diversity. If this book does nothing else, we hope that it will offer an alternative more compatible with the values espoused by the readings we have chosen: trust in the world, and trust in ourselves.

Web Site

For details on the companion Web site www.newhum.com, please refer to the inside cover. This Web site provides many helpful materials for both students and instructors.

Acknowledgments

We would like to express our deep appreciation to the following colleagues for their support and suggestions:

Dan Bauer, Georgia College and State University; Tisha Bender, Rutgers University; Manuel Betancourt, Rutgers University; Lynn Z. Bloom, University of Connecticut, Storrs; Barbara B. Booker, Pasco-Hernando Community College; Kirk Branch, Montana State University; John C. Brereton, Boston Athenaeum; Susan E. Carlisle, Boston University; Suzanne Diamond, Youngstown State University; Melora Giardetti, Simpson College; Alfred E. Guy, Jr., Yale University; Andrew Haggerty, Broome Community College; Paul Hammond, Rutgers University; Susanmarie Harrington, Indiana University–Purdue University, Indianapolis; Jessica Hedges, Rutgers University; Deborah H. Holdstein, Governors State University; Deborah Kirkman, University of Kentucky; Thomas C. Laughner, University of Notre Dame; Jennifer Lee, University of Pittsburgh; Jenna Lewis, Rutgers University; Gina L. Maranto, University of Miami; Trinyan Mariano, Rutgers University; Stephen M. North, SUNY Albany; Judith Gatton Prats, University of Kentucky; Thomas Recchio, University of Connecticut; Tony Spicer, Eastern Michigan University; Roberta J. Stagnaro, San Diego State University; Gordon P. Thomas, University of Idaho; Anna Tripp, California State University, Northridge.; Mark Vareschi, Rutgers University; and Paul Yeoh, Rutgers University.

R.E.M.
K.S.

DAVID ABRAM

DAVID ABRAM IS an ecologist, anthropologist, and philosopher, but it is work on magic that has most shaped his research on the connections among the environment, human experience, and modes of perception. After the magic trick has been performed, Abram believes, we are left "without any framework of explanation. We are suddenly floating in that open space of direct sensory experience, actually encountering the world without preconceptions, even if just for a moment." How would our thinking about the earth and our place on it change if we could suspend our preconceptions about our own central importance? This is the question that Abram brings to the fields of ecopsychology and environmental philosophy.

"The Ecology of Magic" is drawn from Abram's book, *The Spell of the Sensuous: Perception and Language in a More-than-Human World*, which explores our perception of the natural world and the way we use language and symbols to process our experience. In "The Ecology of Magic," Abram describes his travels through Sri Lanka, Indonesia, and Nepal to study the lifeways of magicians and healers. Over the course of his research, Abram came to see the role of traditional magicians and healers as bridging the gap between humankind and nature; "the shaman or sorcerer," he tells us, "is the exemplary voyager in the intermediate realm between the human and the more-than-human worlds."

Abram could be characterized as just such a voyager. After receiving his doctorate in philosophy from SUNY at Stony Brook, he and his wife founded the Alliance for Wild Ethics, an organization that focuses on raising ecological awareness. When asked to explain why he draws so heavily on academic discourse and continues to write for an academic audience when his thinking has taken him in such unconventional directions, Abram answered that his goal in writing *The Spell of the Sensuous* was "to bridge the gap between the world of the

Abram, David. "The Ecology of Magic." *The Spell of the Sensuous*. New York: First Vintage Books, 1997. 3–29.

Quotations come from Scott London's interview with David Abram for the National Public Radio series, *Insight & Outlook* <http://www.scottlondon.com/interviews/abram.html>. For the *Utne* citation, please see <http://www.coejl.org/speakers/abram_d.php>.

imagination—the kind of magical world of these indigenous, traditional societies—and the world of academia, the intelligentsia, and the scientific elite. But I didn't want to do that just by writing a scholarly or scientific analysis of indigenous, animistic ways of thinking. I wanted to do the opposite. I wanted to do an animistic analysis of rationality and the Western intellect, and to show that our Western, civilized ways of thinking are themselves a form of magic." For his efforts, the *Utne Reader* designated him one of a hundred visionaries currently transforming the world.

The Ecology of Magic
A Personal Introduction to the Inquiry

Late one evening I stepped out of my little hut in the rice paddies of eastern Bali and found myself falling through space. Over my head the black sky was rippling with stars, densely clustered in some regions, almost blocking out the darkness between them, and more loosely scattered in other areas, pulsing and beckoning to each other. Behind them all streamed the great river of light with its several tributaries. Yet the Milky Way churned beneath me as well, for my hut was set in the middle of a large patchwork of rice paddies, separated from each other by narrow two-foot-high dikes, and these paddies were all filled with water. The surface of these pools, by day, reflected perfectly the blue sky, a reflection broken only by the thin, bright green tips of new rice. But by night the stars themselves glimmered from the surface of the paddies, and the river of light whirled through the darkness underfoot as well as above; there seemed no ground in front of my feet, only the abyss of star-studded space falling away forever.

I was no longer simply beneath the night sky, but also *above* it—the immediate impression was of weightlessness. I might have been able to reorient myself, to regain some sense of ground and gravity, were it not for a fact that confounded my senses entirely: between the constellations below and the constellations above drifted countless fireflies, their lights flickering like the stars, some drifting up to join the clusters of stars overhead, others, like graceful meteors, slipping down from above to join the constellations underfoot, and all these paths of light upward and downward were mirrored, as well, in the still surface of the paddies. I felt myself at times falling through space, at other moments floating and drifting. I simply could not dispel the profound vertigo and giddiness; the paths of the fireflies, and their reflections in the water's surface, held me in a sustained trance. Even after I crawled back to my hut and shut the door on this whirling world, I felt that now the little room in which I lay was itself floating free of the earth.

Fireflies! It was in Indonesia, you see, that I was first introduced to the world of insects, and there that I first learned of the great influence that insects—such diminutive entities—could have upon the human senses. I had traveled to Indonesia on a research grant to study magic—more precisely, to study the relation between magic and medicine, first among the traditional sorcerers, or *dukuns,* of the Indonesian archipelago, and later among the *dzankris,* the traditional shamans of Nepal. One aspect of the grant was somewhat unique: I was to journey into rural Asia not outwardly as an anthropologist or academic researcher, but as a magician in my own right, in hopes of gaining a more direct access to the local sorcerers. I had been a professional sleight-of-hand magician for five years back in the United States, helping to put myself through college by performing in clubs and restaurants throughout New England. I had, as well, taken a year off from my studies in the psychology of perception to travel as a street magician through Europe and, toward the end of that journey, had spent some months in London, England, exploring the use of sleight-of-hand magic in psychotherapy, as a means of engendering communication with distressed individuals largely unapproachable by clinical healers.[1] The success of this work suggested to me that sleight-of-hand might lend itself well to the curative arts, and I became, for the first time, interested in the relation, largely forgotten in the West, between folk medicine and magic.

It was this interest that led to the aforementioned grant, and to my sojourn as a magician in rural Asia. There, my sleight-of-hand skills proved invaluable as a means of stirring the curiosity of the local shamans. For magicians—whether modern entertainers or indigenous, tribal sorcerers—have in common the fact that they work with the malleable texture of perception. When the local sorcerers gleaned that I had at least some rudimentary skill in altering the common field of perception, I was invited into their homes, asked to share secrets with them, and eventually encouraged, even urged, to participate in various rituals and ceremonies.

But the focus of my research gradually shifted from questions regarding the application of magical techniques in medicine and ritual curing toward a deeper pondering of the relation between traditional magic and the animate natural world. This broader concern seemed to hold the keys to the earlier questions. For none of the several island sorcerers that I came to know in Indonesia, nor any of the *dzankris* with whom I lived in Nepal, considered their work as ritual healers to be their major role or function within their communities. Most of them, to be sure, *were* the primary healers or "doctors" for the villages in their vicinity, and they were often spoken of as such by the inhabitants of those villages. But the villagers also sometimes spoke of them, in low voices and in very private conversations, as witches (or "lejaks" in Bali), as dark magicians who at night might well be practicing their healing spells backward (or while turning to the left instead of to the right) in order to afflict people with the very diseases that they would later work to cure by day. Such suspicions seemed fairly common in Indonesia, and often were harbored with regard to the most effective and powerful healers, those who were most renowned for their skill in driving out illness. For it was assumed that a magician, in order to expel malevolent influences, must have a strong understanding of those influences and demons—even, in some areas, a close rapport with such powers. I myself never consciously saw any of those magicians or shamans with whom I became acquainted engage in magic for harmful purposes, nor any convincing evidence that they had ever done so. (Few of the magicians that I came to know even accepted money in return for their services, although they did accept gifts in the way of food, blankets, and the like.) Yet I was struck by the fact that none of them ever did or said anything to counter such disturbing rumors and speculations, which circulated quietly through the regions where they lived. Slowly, I came to recognize that it was through the agency of such rumors, and the ambiguous fears that such rumors engendered in the village people, that the sorcerers were able to maintain a basic level of privacy. If the villagers did not entertain certain fears about the local sorcerer, then they would likely come to obtain his or her magical help for every little malady and disturbance; and since a more potent practitioner must provide services for several large villages, the sorcerer would be swamped from morning to night with requests for ritual aid. By allowing the inevitable suspicions and fears to circulate unhindered in the region (and sometimes even encouraging and contributing to such rumors), the sorcerer ensured that *only* those who were in real and profound need of his skills would dare to approach him for help.

This privacy, in turn, left the magician free to attend to what he acknowledged to be his primary craft and function. A clue to this function may be found in the circumstance that such magicians rarely dwell at the heart of their village; rather, their dwellings are commonly at the spatial periphery of the community or, more often, out beyond the edges of the village—amid the rice fields, or in a forest, or a wild cluster of boulders. I could easily attribute this to the just-mentioned need for privacy, yet for the magician in a traditional culture it seems to serve another purpose as well, providing a spatial expression of his or her symbolic position with regard to the community. For the magician's intelligence is not encompassed *within* the society; its place is at the edge of the community, mediating *between* the human community and the larger community of beings upon which the village depends for its nourishment and sustenance. This larger community includes, along with the humans, the multiple nonhuman entities that constitute the local landscape, from the diverse plants and the myriad animals—birds, mammals, fish, reptiles, insects—that inhabit or migrate through the region, to the particular winds and weather patterns that inform the local geography, as well as the various landforms—forests, rivers, caves, mountains—that lend their specific character to the surrounding earth.

The traditional or tribal shaman, I came to discern, acts as an intermediary between the human community and the larger ecological field, ensuring that there is an appropriate flow of nourishment, not just from the landscape to the human inhabitants, but from the human community back to the local earth. By his constant rituals, trances, ecstasies, and "journeys," he ensures that the relation between human society and the larger society of beings is balanced and reciprocal, and that the village never takes more from the living land than it returns to it—not just materially but with prayers, propitiations, and praise. The scale of a harvest or the size of a hunt are always negotiated between the tribal community and the natural world that it inhabits. To some extent every adult in the community is engaged in this process of listening and attuning to the other presences that surround and influence daily life. But the shaman or sorcerer is the exemplary voyager in the intermediate realm between the human and the more-than-human worlds, the primary strategist and negotiator in any dealings with the Others.

And it is only as a result of her continual engagement with the animate powers that dwell beyond the human community that the traditional magician is able to alleviate many individual illnesses that arise *within* that community. The sorcerer derives her ability to cure ailments from her more continuous practice of "healing" or balancing the community's relation to the surrounding land. Disease, in such cultures, is often conceptualized as a kind of systemic imbalance within the sick person, or more vividly as the intrusion of a demonic or malevolent presence into his body. There are, at times, malevolent influences within the village or tribe itself that disrupt the health and emotional well-being of susceptible individuals within the community. Yet such destructive influences within the human community are commonly traceable to a disequilibrium between that community and the larger field of forces in which it is embedded. Only those persons who, by their everyday practice, are involved in monitoring and maintaining the relations *between* the human village and the animate landscape are able to appropriately diagnose, treat, and ultimately relieve personal ailments and illnesses arising *within* the village. Any healer who was not simultaneously attending to the intertwined relation between the human community and the larger, more-than-human field, would likely dispel an illness from one person only to have the same problem arise (perhaps in a new guise) somewhere else in the community. Hence, the traditional magician or medicine person functions primarily as an intermediary between human and nonhuman worlds, and only secondarily as a healer.[2] Without a continually adjusted awareness of the relative balance or imbalance between the human group and its nonhuman environ, along with the skills necessary to modulate that primary relation, any "healer" is worthless—indeed, not a healer at all. The medicine person's primary allegiance, then, is not to the human community, but to the earthly web of relations in which that community is embedded—it is from this that his or her power to alleviate human illness derives—and this sets the local magician apart from other persons.

The primacy for the magician of nonhuman nature—the centrality of his relation to other species and to the earth—is not always evident to Western researchers. Countless anthropologists have managed to overlook the ecological dimension of the shaman's craft, while writing at great length of the shaman's rapport with "supernatural" entities. We can attribute much of this oversight to the modern, civilized assumption that the natural world is largely determinate and mechanical, and that which is regarded as mysterious, powerful, and beyond human ken must therefore be of some other, nonphysical realm *above* nature, "supernatural."

The oversight becomes still more comprehensible when we realize that many of the earliest European interpreters of indigenous lifeways were Christian missionaries. For the Church had long assumed that only human beings have intelligent souls, and that the other animals, to say nothing of trees and rivers, were "created" for no other reason than to serve humankind. We can easily understand why European missionaries, steeped in the dogma of institutionalized Christianity, assumed a belief in supernatural, otherworldly powers among those tribal persons whom they saw awestruck and entranced by nonhuman (but nevertheless natural) forces. What is remarkable is the extent to which contemporary anthropology still preserves the ethnocentric bias of these early interpreters. We no longer describe the shamans' enigmatic spirit-helpers as the "superstitious claptrap of heathen primitives"—we have cleansed ourselves of at least *that* much ethnocentrism; yet we still refer to such enigmatic forces, respectfully now, as "supernaturals"—for we are unable to shed the sense, so endemic to scientific civilization, of nature as a rather prosaic and predictable realm, unsuited to such mysteries. Nevertheless, that which is regarded with the greatest awe and wonder by indigenous, oral cultures is, I suggest, none other than what we view as nature itself. The deeply mysterious powers and entities with whom the shaman enters into a rapport are ultimately the same forces—the same plants, animals, forests, and winds—that to literate, "civilized" Europeans are just so much scenery, the pleasant backdrop of our more pressing human concerns.

The most sophisticated definition of "magic" that now circulates through the American counterculture is "the ability or power to alter one's consciousness at will." No mention is made of any *reason* for altering one's consciousness. Yet in tribal cultures that which we call "magic" takes its meaning from the fact that humans, in an indigenous and oral context, experience their own consciousness as simply one form of awareness among many others. The traditional magician cultivates an ability to shift out of his or her common state of consciousness precisely in order to make contact with the other organic forms of sensitivity and awareness with which human existence is entwined. Only by temporarily shedding the accepted perceptual logic of his culture can the sorcerer hope to enter into relation with other species on their own terms; only by altering the common organization of his senses will he be able to enter into a rapport with the multiple nonhuman sensibilities that animate the local landscape. It is this, we might say, that defines a shaman: the ability to readily slip out of the perceptual boundaries that demarcate his or her particular culture—boundaries reinforced by social customs, taboos, and most importantly, the common speech or language—in order to make contact with, and learn from, the other powers in the land. His magic is precisely this heightened receptivity to the meaningful solicitations—songs, cries, gestures—of the larger, more-than-human field.

Magic, then, in its perhaps most primordial sense, is the experience of existing in a world made up of multiple intelligences, the intuition that every form one perceives—from the swallow swooping overhead to the fly on a blade of grass, and indeed the blade of grass itself—is an *experiencing* form, an entity with its own predilections and sensations, albeit sensations that are very different from our own.

To be sure, the shaman's ecological function, his or her role as intermediary between human society and the land, is not always obvious at first blush, even to a sensitive observer. We see the sorcerer being called upon to cure an ailing tribesman of his sleeplessness, or perhaps simply to locate some missing goods; we witness him entering into trance and sending his awareness into other dimensions in search of insight and aid. Yet we should not be so ready to interpret these dimensions as "supernatural," nor to view them as realms entirely "internal" to the personal psyche of the practitioner. For it is likely that the "inner world" of our Western psychological experience, like the supernatural heaven of Christian belief, originates in the loss of our ancestral reciprocity with the animate earth. When the animate powers that surround us are suddenly construed as having less significance than ourselves, when the generative earth is abruptly defined as a determinate object devoid of its own sensations and feelings, then the sense of a wild and multiplicitous otherness (in relation to which human existence has always oriented itself) must migrate, either into a supersensory heaven beyond the natural world, or else into the human skull itself—the only allowable refuge, in this world, for what is ineffable and unfathomable.

But in genuinely oral, indigenous cultures, the sensuous world itself remains the dwelling place of the gods, of the numinous powers that can either sustain or extinguish human life. It is not by sending his awareness out beyond the natural world that the shaman makes contact with the purveyors of life and health, nor by journeying into his personal psyche; rather, it is by propelling his awareness laterally, outward into the depths of a landscape at once both sensuous and psychological, the living dream that we share with the soaring hawk, the spider, and the stone silently sprouting lichens on its coarse surface.

The magician's intimate relationship with nonhuman nature becomes most evident when we attend to the easily overlooked background of his or her practice—not just to the more visible tasks of curing and ritual aid to which she is called by individual clients, or to the larger ceremonies at which she presides and dances, but to the content of the prayers by which she prepares for such ceremonies, and to the countless ritual gestures that she enacts when alone, the daily propitiations and praise that flow from her toward the land and *its* many voices.

All this attention to nonhuman nature was, as I have mentioned, very far from my intended focus when I embarked on my research into the uses of magic and medicine in Indonesia, and it was only gradually that I became aware of this more subtle dimension of the native magician's craft. The first shift in my preconceptions came rather quietly, when I was staying for some days in the home of a young "balian," or magic practitioner, in the interior of Bali. I had been provided with a simple bed in a separate, one-room building in the balian's family compound (most compound homes, in Bali, are comprised of several separate small buildings, for sleeping and for cooking, set on a single enclosed plot of land), and early each morning the balian's wife came to bring me a small but delicious bowl of fruit, which I ate by myself, sitting on the ground outside, leaning against the wall of my hut and watching the sun slowly climb through the rustling palm leaves. I noticed, when she delivered the fruit, that my hostess was also balancing a tray containing many little green plates: actually, they were little boat-shaped platters, each woven simply and neatly from a freshly cut section of palm frond. The platters were two or three inches long, and within each was a little mound of white rice. After handing me my breakfast, the woman and the tray disappeared from view behind the other buildings, and when she came by some minutes later to pick up my empty bowl, the tray in her hands was empty as well.

The second time that I saw the array of tiny rice platters, I asked my hostess what they were for. Patiently, she explained to me that they were offerings for the household spirits. When I inquired about the Balinese term that she used for "spirit," she repeated the same explanation, now in Indonesian, that these were gifts for the spirits of the family compound, and I saw that I had understood her correctly. She handed me a bowl of sliced papaya and mango, and disappeared around the corner. I pondered for a minute, then set down the bowl, stepped to the side of my hut, and peered through the trees. At first unable to see her, I soon caught sight of her crouched low beside the corner of one of the other buildings, carefully setting what I presumed was one of the offerings on the ground at that spot. Then she stood up with the tray, walked to the other visible corner of the same building, and there slowly and carefully set another offering on the ground. I returned to my bowl of fruit and finished my breakfast. That afternoon, when the rest of the household was busy, I walked back behind the building where I had seen her set down the two offerings. There were the little green platters, resting neatly at the two rear corners of the building. But the mounds of rice that had been within them were gone.

The next morning I finished the sliced fruit, waited for my hostess to come by for the empty bowl, then quietly headed back behind the buildings. Two fresh palm-leaf offerings sat at the same spots where the others had been the day before. These were filled with rice. Yet as I gazed at one of these offerings, I abruptly realized, with a start, that one of the rice kernels was actually moving.

Only when I knelt down to look more closely did I notice a line of tiny black ants winding through the dirt to the offering. Peering still closer, I saw that two ants had already climbed onto the offering and were struggling with the uppermost kernel of rice; as I watched, one of them dragged the kernel down and off the leaf, then set off with it back along the line of ants advancing on the offering. The second ant took another kernel and climbed down with it, dragging and pushing, and fell over the edge of the leaf, then a third climbed onto the offering. The line of ants seemed to emerge from a thick clump of grass around a nearby palm tree. I walked over to the other offering and discovered another line of ants dragging away the white kernels. This line emerged from the top of a little mound of dirt, about fifteen feet away from the buildings. There was an offering on the ground by a corner of my building as well, and a nearly identical line of ants. I walked into my room chuckling to myself: the balian and his wife had gone to so much trouble to placate the household spirits with gifts, only to have their offerings stolen by little six-legged thieves. What a waste! But then a strange thought dawned on me: what if the ants were the very "household spirits" to whom the offerings were being made?

I soon began to discern the logic of this. The family compound, like most on this tropical island, had been constructed in the vicinity of several ant colonies. Since a great deal of cooking took place in the compound (which housed, along with the balian and his wife and children, various members of their extended family), and also much preparation of elaborate offerings of foodstuffs for various rituals and festivals in the surrounding villages, the grounds and the buildings at the compound were vulnerable to infestations by the sizable ant population. Such invasions could range from rare nuisances to a periodic or even constant siege. It became apparent that the daily palm-frond offerings served to preclude such an attack by the natural forces that surrounded (and underlay) the family's land. The daily gifts of rice kept the ant colonies occupied—and, presumably, satisfied. Placed in regular, repeated locations at the corners of various structures around the compound, the offerings seemed to establish certain boundaries between the human and ant communities; by honoring this boundary with gifts, the humans apparently hoped to persuade the insects to respect the boundary and not enter the buildings.

Yet I remained puzzled by my hostess's assertion that these were gifts "for the spirits." To be sure, there has always been some confusion between our Western notion of "spirit" (which so often is defined in contrast to matter or "flesh"), and the mysterious presences to which tribal and indigenous cultures pay so much respect. I have already alluded to the gross misunderstandings arising from the circumstance that many of the earliest Western students of these other customs were Christian missionaries all too ready to see occult ghosts and immaterial phantoms where the tribespeople were simply offering their respect to the local winds. While the notion of "spirit" has come to have, for us in the West, a primarily anthropomorphic or human association, my encounter with the ants was the first of many experiences suggesting to me that the "spirits" of an indigenous culture are primarily those modes of intelligence or awareness that do *not* possess a human form.

As humans, we are well acquainted with the needs and capacities of the human body—we *live* our own bodies and so know, from within, the possibilities of our form. We cannot know, with the same familiarity and intimacy, the lived experience of a grass snake or a snapping turtle; we cannot readily experience the precise sensations of a hummingbird sipping nectar from a flower or a rubber tree soaking up sunlight. And yet we do know how it feels to sip from a fresh pool of water or to bask and stretch in the sun. Our experience may indeed be a variant of these other modes of sensitivity; nevertheless, we cannot, as humans, precisely experience the living sensations of another form. We do not know, with full clarity, their desires or motivations; we cannot know, or can never be sure that we know, what they know. That the deer does experience sensations, that it carries knowledge of how to orient in the land, of where to find food and how to protect its young, that it knows well how to survive in the forest without the tools upon which we depend, is readily evident to our human senses. That the mango tree has the ability to create fruit, or the yarrow plant the power to reduce a child's fever, is also evident. To humankind, these Others are purveyors of secrets, carriers of intelligence that we ourselves often need: it is these Others who can inform us of unseasonable changes in the weather, or warn us of imminent eruptions and earthquakes, who show us, when foraging, where we may find the ripest berries or the best route to follow back home. By watching them build their nests and shelters, we glean clues regarding how to strengthen our own dwellings, and their deaths teach us of our own. We receive from them countless gifts of food, fuel, shelter, and clothing. Yet still they remain Other to us, inhabiting their own cultures and displaying their own rituals, never wholly fathomable.

Moreover, it is not only those entities acknowledged by Western civilization as "alive," not only the other animals and the plants that speak, as spirits, to the senses of an oral culture, but also the meandering river from which those animals drink, and the torrential monsoon rains, and the stone that fits neatly into the palm of the hand. The mountain, too, has its thoughts. The forest birds whirring and chattering as the sun slips below the horizon are vocal organs of the rain forest itself.[3]

Bali, of course, is hardly an aboriginal culture; the complexity of its temple architecture, the intricacy of its irrigation systems, the resplendence of its colorful festivals and crafts all bespeak the influence of various civilizations, most notably the Hindu complex of India. In Bali, nevertheless, these influences are thoroughly intertwined with the indigenous animism of the Indonesian archipelago; the Hindu gods and goddesses have been appropriated, as it were, by the more volcanic, eruptive spirits of the local terrain.

Yet the underlying animistic cultures of Indonesia, like those of many islands in the Pacific, are steeped as well in beliefs often referred to by ethnologists as "ancestor worship," and some may argue that the ritual reverence paid to one's long-dead human ancestors (and the assumption of their influence in present life), easily invalidates my assertion that the various "powers" or "spirits" that move through the discourse of indigenous, oral peoples are ultimately tied to nonhuman (but nonetheless sentient) forces in the enveloping landscape.

This objection rests upon certain assumptions implicit in Christian civilization, such as the assumption that the "spirits" of dead persons necessarily retain their human form, and that they reside in a domain outside of the physical world to which our senses give us access. However, most indigenous tribal peoples have no such ready recourse to an immaterial realm outside earthly nature. Our strictly human heavens and hells have only recently been abstracted from the sensuous world that surrounds us, from this more-than-human realm that abounds in its own winged intelligences and cloven-hoofed powers. For almost all oral cultures, the enveloping and sensuous earth remains the dwelling place of both the living *and* the dead. The "body"—whether human or otherwise—is not yet a mechanical object in such cultures, but is a magical entity, the mind's own sensuous aspect, and at death the body's decomposition into soil, worms, and dust can only signify the gradual reintegration of one's ancestors and elders into the living landscape, from which all, too, are born.

Each indigenous culture elaborates this recognition of metamorphosis in its own fashion, taking its clues from the particular terrain in which it is situated. Often the invisible atmosphere that animates the visible world—the subtle presence that circulates both within us and between all things—retains within itself the spirit or breath of the dead person until the time when that breath will enter and animate another visible body—a bird, or a deer, or a field of wild grain. Some cultures may burn, or "cremate," the body in order to more completely return the person, as smoke, to the swirling air, while that which departs as flame is offered to the sun and stars, and that which lingers as ash is fed to the dense earth. Still other cultures may dismember the body, leaving certain parts in precise locations where they will likely be found by condors, or where they will be consumed by mountain lions or by wolves, thus hastening the reincarnation of that person into a particular animal realm within the landscape. Such examples illustrate simply that death, in tribal cultures, initiates a metamorphosis wherein the person's presence does not "vanish" from the sensible world (where would it go?) but rather remains as an animating force within the vastness of the landscape, whether subtly, in the wind, or more visibly, in animal form, or even as the eruptive, ever to be appeased, wrath of the volcano. "Ancestor worship," in its myriad forms, then, is ultimately another mode of attentiveness to nonhuman nature; it signifies not so much an awe or reverence of human powers, but rather a reverence for those forms that awareness takes when it is *not* in human form, when the familiar human embodiment dies and decays to become part of the encompassing cosmos.

This cycling of the human back into the larger world ensures that the other forms of experience that we encounter—whether ants, or willow trees, or clouds—are never absolutely alien to ourselves. Despite the obvious differences in shape, and ability, and style of being, they remain at least distantly familiar, even familial. It is, paradoxically, this perceived kinship or consanguinity that renders the difference, or otherness, so eerily potent.[4]

Several months after my arrival in Bali, I left the village in which I was staying to visit one of the pre-Hindu sites on the island. I arrived on my bicycle early in the afternoon, after the bus carrying tourists from the coast had departed. A flight of steps took me down into a lush, emerald valley, lined by cliffs on either side, awash with the speech of the river and the sighing of the wind through high, unharvested grasses. On a small bridge crossing the river I met an old woman carrying a wide basket on her head and holding the hand of a little, shy child; the woman grinned at me with the red, toothless smile of a beetle nut chewer. On the far side of the river I stood in front of a great moss-covered complex of passageways, rooms, and courtyards carved by hand out of the black volcanic rock.

I noticed, at a bend in the canyon downstream, a further series of caves carved into the cliffs. These appeared more isolated and remote, unattended by any footpath I could discern. I set out through the grasses to explore them. This proved much more difficult than I anticipated, but after getting lost in the tall grasses, and fording the river three times, I at last found myself beneath the caves. A short scramble up the rock wall brought me to the mouth of one of them, and I entered on my hands and knees. It was a wide but low opening, perhaps only four feet high, and the interior receded only about five or six feet into the cliff. The floor and walls were covered with mosses, painting the cave with green patterns and softening the harshness of the rock; the place, despite its small size—or perhaps because of it—had an air of great friendliness. I climbed to two other caves, each about the same size, but then felt drawn back to the first one, to sit cross-legged on the cushioning moss and gaze out across the emerald canyon. It was quiet inside, a kind of intimate sanctuary hewn into the stone. I began to explore the rich resonance of the enclosure, first just humming, then intoning a simple chant taught to me by a balian some days before. I was delighted by the overtones that the cave added to my voice, and sat there singing for a long while. I did not notice the change in the wind outside, or the cloud shadows darkening the valley, until the rains broke—suddenly and with great force. The first storm of the monsoon!

I had experienced only slight rains on the island before then, and was startled by the torrential downpour now sending stones tumbling along the cliffs, building puddles and then ponds in the green landscape below, swelling the river. There was no question of returning home—I would be unable to make my way back through the flood to the valley's entrance. And so, thankful for the shelter, I recrossed my legs to wait out the storm. Before long the rivulets falling along the cliff above gathered themselves into streams, and two small waterfalls cascaded across the cave's mouth. Soon I was looking into a solid curtain of water, thin in some places, where the canyon's image flickered unsteadily, and thickly rushing in others. My senses were all but overcome by the wild beauty of the cascade and by the roar of sound, my body trembling inwardly at the weird sense of being sealed into my hiding place.

And then, in the midst of all this tumult, I noticed a small, delicate activity. Just in front of me, and only an inch or two to my side of the torrent, a spider was climbing a thin thread stretched across the mouth of the cave. As I watched, it anchored another thread to the top of the opening, then slipped back along the first thread and joined the two at a point about midway between the roof and the floor. I lost sight of the spider then, and for a while it seemed that it had vanished, thread and all, until my focus rediscovered it. Two more threads now radiated from the center to the floor, and then another; soon the spider began to swing between these as on a circular trellis, trailing an ever-lengthening thread which it affixed to each radiating rung as it moved from one to the next, spiraling outward. The spider seemed wholly undaunted by the tumult of waters spilling past it, although every now and then it broke off its spiral dance and climbed to the roof or the floor to tug on the radii there, assuring the tautness of the threads, then crawled back to where it left off. Whenever I lost the correct focus, I waited to catch sight of the spinning arachnid, and then let its dancing form gradually draw the lineaments of the web back into visibility, tying my focus into each new knot of silk as it moved, weaving my gaze into the ever-deepening pattern.

And then, abruptly, my vision snagged on a strange incongruity: another thread slanted across the web, neither radiating nor spiraling from the central juncture, violating the symmetry. As I followed it with my eyes, pondering its purpose in the overall pattern, I began to realize that it was on a different plane from the rest of the web, for the web slipped out of focus whenever this new line became clearer. I soon saw that it led to its own center, about twelve inches to the right of the first, another nexus of forces from which several threads stretched to the floor and the ceiling. And then I saw that there was a *different* spider spinning this web, testing its tautness by dancing around it like the first, now setting the silken cross weaves around the nodal point and winding outward. The two spiders spun independently of each other, but to my eyes they wove a single intersecting pattern. This widening of my gaze soon disclosed yet another spider spiraling in the cave's mouth, and suddenly I realized that there were *many* overlapping webs coming into being, radiating out at different rhythms from myriad centers poised—some higher, some lower, some minutely closer to my eyes and some farther—between the stone above and the stone below.

I sat stunned and mesmerized before this ever-complexifying expanse of living patterns upon patterns, my gaze drawn like a breath into one converging group of lines, then breathed out into open space, then drawn down into another convergence. The curtain of water had become utterly silent—I tried at one point to hear it, but could not. My senses were entranced.

I had the distinct impression that I was watching the universe being born, galaxy upon galaxy. . . .

Night filled the cave with darkness. The rain had not stopped. Yet, strangely, I felt neither cold nor hungry—only remarkably peaceful and at home. Stretching out upon the moist, mossy floor near the back of the cave, I slept.

When I awoke, the sun was staring into the canyon, the grasses below rippling with bright blues and greens. I could see no trace of the webs, nor their weavers. Thinking that they were invisible to my eyes without the curtain of water behind them, I felt carefully with my hands around and through the mouth of the cave. But the webs were gone. I climbed down to the river and washed, then hiked across and out of the canyon to where my cycle was drying in the sun, and headed back to my own valley.

I have never, since that time, been able to encounter a spider without feeling a great strangeness and awe. To be sure, insects and spiders are not the only powers, or even central presences, in the Indonesian universe. But they were *my* introduction to the spirits, to the magic afoot in the land. It was from them that I first learned of the intelligence that lurks in nonhuman nature, the ability that an alien form of sentience has to echo one's own, to instill a reverberation in oneself that temporarily shatters habitual ways of seeing and feeling, leaving one open to a world all alive, awake, and aware. It was from such small beings that my senses first learned of the countless worlds within worlds that spin in the depths of this world that we commonly inhabit, and from them that I learned that my body could, with practice, enter sensorially into these dimensions. The precise and minuscule craft of the spiders had so honed and focused my awareness that the very webwork of the universe, of which my own flesh was a part, seemed to be being spun by their arcane art. I have already spoken of the ants, and of the fireflies, whose sensory likeness to the lights in the night sky had taught me the fickleness of gravity. The long and cyclical trance that we call malaria was also brought to me by insects, in this case mosquitoes, and I lived for three weeks in a feverish state of shivers, sweat, and visions.

I had rarely before paid much attention to the natural world. But my exposure to traditional magicians and seers was shifting my senses; I became increasingly susceptible to the solicitations of nonhuman things. In the course of struggling to decipher the magicians' odd gestures or to fathom their constant spoken references to powers unseen and unheard, I began to *see* and to *hear* in a manner I never had before. When a magician spoke of a power or "presence" lingering in the corner of his house, I learned to notice the ray of sunlight that was then pouring through a chink in the roof, illuminating a column of drifting dust, and to realize that that column of light was indeed a power, influencing the air currents by its warmth, and indeed influencing the whole mood of the room; although I had not consciously seen it before, it had already been structuring my experience. My ears began to attend, in a new way, to the songs of birds—no longer just a melodic background to human speech, but meaningful speech in its own right, responding to and commenting on events in the surrounding earth. I became a student of subtle differences: the way a breeze may flutter a single leaf on a whole tree, leaving the other leaves silent and unmoved (had not that leaf, then, been brushed by a magic?); or the way the intensity of the sun's heat expresses itself in the precise rhythm of the crickets. Walking along the dirt paths, I learned to slow my pace in order to *feel* the difference between one nearby hill and the next, or to taste the presence of a particular field at a certain time of day when, as I had been told by a local *dukun,* the place had a special power and proffered unique gifts. It was a power communicated to my senses by the way the shadows of the trees fell at that hour, and by smells that only then lingered in the tops of the grasses without being wafted away by the wind, and other elements I could only isolate after many days of stopping and listening.

And gradually, then, other animals began to intercept me in my wanderings, as if some quality in my posture or the rhythm of my breathing had disarmed their wariness; I would find myself face-to-face with monkeys, and with large lizards that did not slither away when I spoke, but leaned forward in apparent curiosity. In rural Java, I often noticed monkeys accompanying me in the branches overhead, and ravens walked toward me on the road, croaking. While at Pangandaran, a nature preserve on a peninsula jutting out from the south coast of Java ("a place of many spirits," I was told by nearby fishermen), I stepped out from a clutch of trees and found myself looking into the face of one of the rare and beautiful bison that exist only on that island. Our eyes locked. When it snorted, I snorted back; when it shifted its shoulders, I shifted my stance; when I tossed my head, it tossed *its* head in reply. I found myself caught in a nonverbal conversation with this Other, a gestural duet with which my conscious awareness had very little to do. It was as if my body in its actions was suddenly being motivated by a wisdom older than my thinking mind, as though it was held and moved by a logos, deeper than words, spoken by the Other's body, the trees, and the stony ground on which we stood.

Anthropology's inability to discern the shaman's allegiance to nonhuman nature has led to a curious circumstance in the "developed world" today, where many persons in search of spiritual understanding are enrolling in workshops concerned with "shamanic" methods of personal discovery and revelation. Psychotherapists and some physicians have begun to specialize in "shamanic healing techniques." "Shamanism" has thus come to connote an alternative form of therapy; the emphasis, among these new practitioners of popular shamanism, is on personal insight and curing. These are noble aims, to be sure, yet they are secondary to, and derivative from, the primary role of the indigenous shaman, a role that cannot be fulfilled without long and sustained exposure to wild nature, to its patterns and vicissitudes. Mimicking the indigenous shaman's curative methods without his intimate knowledge of the wider natural community cannot, if I am correct, do anything more than trade certain symptoms for others, or shift the locus of disease from place to place within the human community. For the source of stress lies in the relation *between* the human community and the natural landscape.

Western industrial society, of course, with its massive scale and hugely centralized economy, can hardly be seen in relation to any particular landscape or ecosystem; the more-than-human ecology with which it is directly engaged is the biosphere itself. Sadly, our culture's relation to the earthly biosphere can in no way be considered a reciprocal or balanced one: with thousands of acres of nonregenerating forest disappearing every hour, and hundreds of our fellow species becoming extinct each month as a result of our civilization's excesses, we can hardly be surprised by the amount of epidemic illness in our culture, from increasingly severe immune dysfunctions and cancers, to widespread psychological distress, depression, and ever more frequent suicides, to the accelerating number of household killings and mass murders committed for no apparent reason by otherwise coherent individuals.

From an animistic perspective, the clearest source of all this distress, both physical and psychological, lies in the aforementioned violence needlessly perpetrated by our civilization on the ecology of the planet; only by alleviating the latter will we be able to heal the former. While this may sound at first like a simple statement of faith, it makes eminent and obvious sense as soon as we acknowledge our thorough dependence upon the countless other organisms with whom we have evolved. Caught up in a mass of abstractions, our attention hypnotized by a host of human-made technologies that only reflect us back to ourselves, it is all too easy for us to forget our carnal inherence in a more-than-human matrix of sensations and sensibilities. Our bodies have formed themselves in delicate reciprocity with the manifold textures, sounds, and shapes of an animate earth—our eyes have evolved in subtle interaction with *other* eyes, as our ears are attuned by their very structure to the howling of wolves and the honking of geese. To shut ourselves off from these other voices, to continue by our lifestyles to condemn these other sensibilities to the oblivion of extinction, is to rob our own senses of their integrity, and to rob our minds of their coherence. We are human only in contact, and conviviality, with what is not human.

Although the Indonesian islands are home to an astonishing diversity of birds, it was only when I went to study among the Sherpa people of the high Himalayas that I was truly initiated into the avian world. The Himalayas are young mountains, their peaks not yet rounded by the endless action of wind and ice, and so the primary dimension of the visible landscape is overwhelmingly vertical. Even in the high ridges one seldom attains a view of a distant horizon; instead one's vision is deflected upward by the steep face of the next mountain. The whole land has surged skyward in a manner still evident in the lines and furrows of the mountain walls, and this ancient dynamism readily communicates itself to the sensing body.

In such a world those who dwell and soar in the sky are the primary powers. They alone move easily in such a zone, swooping downward to become a speck near the valley floor, or spiraling into the heights on invisible currents. The wingeds, alone, carry the immediate knowledge of what is unfolding on the far side of the next ridge, and hence it is only by watching them that one can be kept apprised of climatic changes in the offing, as well as of subtle shifts in the flow and density of air currents in one's own valley. Several of the shamans that I met in Nepal had birds as their close familiars. Ravens are constant commentators on village affairs. The smaller, flocking birds perform aerobatics in unison over the village rooftops, twisting and swerving in a perfect sympathy of motion, the whole flock appearing like a magic banner that floats and flaps on air currents over the village, then descends in a heap, only to be carried aloft by the wind a moment later, rippling and swelling.

For some time I visited a Sherpa *dzankri* whose rock home was built into one of the steep mountainsides of the Khumbu region in Nepal. On one of our walks along the narrow cliff trails that wind around the mountain, the *dzankri* pointed out to me a certain boulder, jutting out from the cliff, on which he had "danced" before attempting some especially difficult cures. I recognized the boulder several days later when hiking back down toward the *dzankri*'s home from the upper yak pastures, and I climbed onto the rock, not to dance but to ponder the pale white and red lichens that gave life to its surface, and to rest. Across the dry valley, two lammergeier condors floated between gleaming, snow-covered peaks. It was a ringing blue Himalayan day, clear as a bell. After a few moments I took a silver coin out of my pocket and aimlessly began a simple sleight-of-hand exercise, rolling the coin over the knuckles of my right hand. I had taken to practicing this somewhat monotonous exercise in response to the endless flicking of prayer-beads by the older Sherpas, a practice usually accompanied by a repetitively chanted prayer: *"Om Mani Padme Hum"* (O the Jewel in the Lotus). But there was no prayer accompanying my revolving coin, aside from my quiet breathing and the dazzling sunlight. I noticed that one of the two condors in the distance had swerved away from its partner and was now floating over the valley, wings outstretched. As I watched it grow larger, I realized, with some delight, that it was heading in my general direction; I stopped rolling the coin and stared. Yet just then the lammergeier halted in its flight, motionless for a moment against the peaks, then swerved around and headed back toward its partner in the distance. Disappointed, I took up the coin and began rolling it along my knuckles once again, its silver surface catching the sunlight as it turned, reflecting the rays back into the sky. Instantly, the condor swung out from its path and began soaring back in a wide arc. Once again, I watched its shape grow larger. As the great size of the bird became apparent, I felt my skin begin to crawl and come alive, like a swarm of bees all in motion, and a humming grew loud in my ears. The coin continued rolling along my fingers. The creature loomed larger, and larger still, until suddenly, it was there—an immense silhouette hovering just above my head, huge wing feathers rustling ever so slightly as they mastered the breeze. My fingers were frozen, unable to move; the coin dropped out of my hand. And then I felt myself stripped naked by an alien gaze infinitely more lucid and precise than my own. I do not know for how long I was transfixed, only that I felt the air streaming past naked knees and heard the wind whispering in my feathers long after the Visitor had departed.

I returned to a North America whose only indigenous species of condor was on the brink of extinction, mostly as a result of lead poisoning from bullets in the carrion it consumes. But I did not think about this. I was excited by the new sensibilities that had stirred in me—my newfound awareness of a more-than-human world, of the great potency of the land, and particularly of the keen intelligence of other animals, large and small, whose lives and cultures interpenetrate our own. I startled neighbors by chattering with squirrels, who swiftly climbed down the trunks of their trees and across lawns to banter with me, or by gazing for hours on end at a heron fishing in a nearby estuary, or at gulls opening clams by dropping them from a height onto the rocks along the beach.

Yet, very gradually, I began to lose my sense of the animals' own awareness. The gulls' technique for breaking open the clams began to appear as a largely automatic behavior, and I could not easily feel the attention that they must bring to each new shell. Perhaps each shell was entirely the same as the last, and *no* spontaneous attention was really necessary. . . .

I found myself now observing the heron from outside its world, noting with interest its careful high-stepping walk and the sudden dart of its beak into the water, but no longer feeling its tensed yet poised alertness with my own muscles. And, strangely, the suburban squirrels no longer responded to my chittering calls. Although I wished to, I could no longer focus my awareness on engaging in their world as I had so easily done a few weeks earlier, for my attention was quickly deflected by internal, verbal deliberations of one sort or another—by a conversation I now seemed to carry on entirely within myself. The squirrels had no part in this conversation.

It became increasingly apparent, from books and articles and discussions with various people, that other animals were not as awake and aware as I had assumed, that they lacked any real language and hence the possibility of thought, and that even their seemingly spontaneous responses to the world around them were largely "programmed" behaviors, "coded" in the genetic material now being mapped by biologists. Indeed, the more I spoke *about* other animals, the less possible it became to speak *to* them. I gradually came to discern that there was no common ground between the unlimited human intellect and the limited sentience of other animals, no medium through which we and they might communicate with and reciprocate one another.

As the expressive and sentient landscape slowly faded behind my more exclusively human concerns, threatening to become little more than an illusion or fantasy, I began to feel—particularly in my chest and abdomen—as though I were being cut off from vital sources of nourishment. I was indeed reacclimating to my own culture, becoming more attuned to its styles of discourse and interaction, yet my bodily senses seemed to be losing their acuteness, becoming less awake to subtle changes and patterns. The thrumming of crickets, and even the songs of the local blackbirds, readily faded from my awareness after a few moments, and it was only by an effort of will that I could bring them back into the perceptual field. The flight of sparrows and of dragonflies no longer sustained my focus very long, if indeed they gained my attention at all. My skin quit registering the various changes in the breeze, and smells seemed to have faded from the world almost entirely, my nose waking up only once or twice a day, perhaps while cooking, or when taking out the garbage.

In Nepal, the air had been filled with smells—whether in the towns, where burning incense combined with the aromas of roasting meats and honeyed pastries and fruits for trade in the open market, and the stench of organic refuse rotting in the ravines, and sometimes of corpses being cremated by the river; or in the high mountains, where the wind carried the whiffs of countless wildflowers, and of the newly turned earth outside the villages where the fragrant dung of yaks was drying in round patties on the outer walls of the houses, to be used, when dry, as fuel for the household fires, and where smoke from those many home fires always mingled in the outside air. And sounds as well: the chants of aspiring monks and adepts blended with the ringing of prayer bells on near and distant slopes, accompanied by the raucous croaks of ravens, and the sigh of the wind pouring over the passes, and the flapping of prayer flags, and the distant hush of the river cascading through the far-below gorge.

There the air was a thick and richly textured presence, filled with invisible but nonetheless tactile, olfactory, and audible influences. In the United States, however, the air seemed thin and void of substance or influence. It was not, here, a sensuous medium—the felt matrix of our breath and the breath of the other animals and plants and soils—but was merely an absence, and indeed was constantly referred to in everyday discourse as mere empty space. Hence, in America I found myself lingering near wood fires and even garbage dumps—much to the dismay of my friends—for only such an intensity of smells served to remind my body of its immersion in an enveloping medium, and with this experience of being immersed in a world of influences came a host of body memories from my year among the shamans and village people of rural Asia.

I began to find other ways, as well, of tapping the very different sensations and perceptions that I had grown accustomed to in the "undeveloped world," by living for extended periods on native Indian reservations in the southwestern desert and along the northwestern coast, or by hiking off for weeks at a time into the North American wilderness. Intermittently, I began to wonder if my culture's assumptions regarding the lack of awareness in other animals and in the land itself was less a product of careful and judicious reasoning than of a strange inability to clearly perceive other animals—a real inability to clearly see, or focus upon, anything outside the realm of human technology, or to hear as meaningful anything other than human speech. The sad results of our interactions with the rest of nature were being reported in every newspaper—from the depletion of topsoil due to industrial farming techniques to the fouling of groundwater by industrial wastes, from the rapid destruction of ancient forests to, worst of all, the ever-accelerating extinction of our fellow species—and these remarkable and disturbing occurrences, all readily traceable to the ongoing activity of "civilized" humankind, did indeed suggest the possibility that there was a perceptual problem in my culture, that modern, "civilized" humanity simply did not perceive surrounding nature in a clear manner, if we have even been perceiving it at all.

The experiences that shifted the focus of my research in rural Indonesia and Nepal had shown me that nonhuman nature can be perceived and experienced with far more intensity and nuance than is generally acknowledged in the West. What was it that made possible the heightened sensitivity to extrahuman reality, the profound attentiveness to other species and to the Earth that is evidenced in so many of these cultures, and that had so altered my awareness that my senses now felt stifled and starved by the patterns of my own culture? Or, reversing the question, what had made possible the absence of this attentiveness in the modern West? For Western culture, too, has its indigenous origins. If the relative attunement to environing nature exhibited by native cultures is linked to a more primordial, participatory mode of perception, how had Western civilization come to be so exempt from this sensory reciprocity? How, that is, have we become so deaf and so blind to the vital existence of other species, and to the animate landscapes they inhabit, that we now so casually bring about their destruction?

To be sure, our obliviousness to nonhuman nature is today held in place by ways of speaking that simply deny intelligence to other species and to nature in general, as well as by the very structures of our civilized existence—by the incessant drone of motors that shut out the voices of birds and of the winds; by electric lights that eclipse not only the stars but the night itself; by air "conditioners" that hide the seasons; by offices, automobiles, and shopping malls that finally obviate any need to step outside the purely human world at all. We consciously encounter nonhuman nature only as it has been circumscribed by our civilization and its technologies: through our domesticated pets, on the television, or at the zoo (or, at best, in carefully managed "nature preserves"). The plants and animals we consume are neither gathered nor hunted—they are bred and harvested in huge, mechanized farms. "Nature," it would seem, has become simply a stock of "resources" for human civilization, and so we can hardly be surprised that our civilized eyes and ears are somewhat oblivious to the existence of perspectives that are not human at all, or that a person either entering into or returning to the West from a nonindustrial culture would feel startled and confused by the felt absence of nonhuman powers.

Still, the current commodification of "nature" by civilization tells us little or nothing of the perceptual shift that made possible this reduction of the animal (and the earth) to an object, little of the process whereby our senses first relinquished the power of the Other, the vision that for so long had motivated our most sacred rituals, our dances, and our prayers.

But can we even hope to catch a glimpse of this process, which has given rise to so many of the habits and linguistic prejudices that now structure our very thinking? Certainly not if we gaze toward that origin from within the midst of the very civilization it engendered. But perhaps we may make our stand along the *edge* of that civilization, like a magician, or like a person who, having lived among another tribe, can no longer wholly return to his own. He lingers half within and half outside of his community, open as well, then, to the shifting voices and flapping forms that crawl and hover beyond the mirrored walls of the city. And even there, moving along those walls, he may hope to find the precise clues to the mystery of how those walls were erected, and how a simple boundary became a barrier, only if the moment is timely—only, that is, if the margin he frequents is a temporal as well as a spatial edge, and the temporal structure that it bounds is about to dissolve, or metamorphose, into something else.   ■

NOTES

1. This work was done at the Philadelphia Association, a therapeutic community directed by Dr. R. D. Laing and his associates.

2. A simple illustration of this may be found among many of the indigenous peoples of North America, for whom the English term "medicine" commonly translates a word meaning "power"—specifically, the sacred power received by a human person from a particular animal or other nonhuman entity. Thus, a particular *medicine person* may be renowned for her "badger medicine" or "bear medicine," for his "eagle medicine," "elk medicine," or even "thunder medicine." It is from their direct engagement with these nonhuman powers that medicine persons derive their own abilities, including their ability to cure human ailments.

3. To the Western mind such views are likely to sound like reckless "projections" of human consciousness into inanimate and dumb materials, suitable for poetry perhaps, but having nothing, in fact, to do with those actual birds or that forest. Such is our common view. This text will examine the possibility that it is civilization that has been confused, and not indigenous peoples. It will suggest, and provide evidence, that one perceives a world at all only by projecting oneself into that world, that one makes contact with things and others only by actively participating in them, lending one's sensory imagination to things in order to discover how they alter and transform that imagination, how they reflect us back changed, how they are different from us. It will suggest that perception is *always* participatory, and hence that modern humanity's denial of awareness in nonhuman nature is borne not by any conceptual or scientific rigor, but rather by an inability, or a refusal, to fully perceive other organisms.

4. The similarity between such animistic world views and the emerging perspective of contemporary ecology is not trivial. Atmospheric geochemist James Lovelock, elucidating the well-known Gaia hypothesis—a theory stressing the major role played by organic life in the ceaseless modulation of the earth's atmospheric and climatic conditions—insists that the geological environment is itself constituted by organic life, and by the products or organic metabolism. In his words, we inhabit "a world that is the breath and bones of our ancestors." See, for instance, "Gaia: The World as Living Organism," in the *New Scientist*, December 18, 1986, as well as *Scientists on Gaia*, ed. Stephen Schneider and Penelope Boston (Cambridge: M.I.T. Press, 1991).

■ *QUESTIONS FOR MAKING CONNECTIONS WITHIN THE READING* ■

1. David Abram's essay begins with a description of his travels in eastern Bali and ends with his return to the United States. What happens to Abram during the course of his travels? When he says, "I began to *see* and to *hear* in a manner I never had before," what does he mean?

2. Abram tells us that one cannot become a shaman without "long and sustained exposure to wild nature, to its patterns and vicissitudes." What is "wild nature"? How does it differ from the kinds of nature one finds in a city, a suburb, or a state park? How does Abram's experience of "wild nature" differ from the experience one might have in each of these places?

3. As Abram reflects on the differences between how he felt when he was in Indonesia and how he felt on his return to the United States, he considers the possibility that Westerners might have "a real inability to clearly see, or focus upon, anything outside the realm of human technology, or to hear as meaningful anything other than human speech." What is it that Abram would like for us to focus on instead?

■ *QUESTIONS FOR WRITING* ■

1. In "The Ecology of Magic," Abram describes how his travels made him "a student of subtle differences." What does it mean to become such a student? What does one notice? And why is it important to notice such things?

2. As Abram sees it, there is a qualitative difference between the ways Westerners experience nature and the ways shamans experience nature. And yet, somehow, Abram himself was able to transcend the difference and access these other ways of feeling. What made it possible for Abram to do this? Could anyone have the experiences Abram describes?

■ *QUESTIONS FOR MAKING CONNECTIONS BETWEEN READINGS* ■

1. In "The Mind's Eye," Oliver Sacks asks, "to what extent are we—our experiences, our reactions—shaped, predetermined, by our brains, and to what extent do we shape our own brains?" By phrasing the question in this way, Sacks asks us to consider "to what extent" the brain shapes experience *and* experience shapes the brain. Drawing on Abram's discussion of sensuous experience and shamanism for your examples, respond to Sacks's question. Is the relationship between the shaping power of the brain and the power of personal experience one of relative equality? Is the brain itself largely responsible for who we are and how we experience the world, or is sensuous experience more decisive?

2. Abram defines humanity in the following way: "We are human only in contact, and conviviality, with what is not human." Gregory Stock has a very different view, however. In arguing for self-selected human enhancement, he makes the following prediction: "As we consciously transform ourselves, we will become no less human than we became tens of thousands of years ago when we embarked upon a course of self-domestication and began, quite unconsciously, to self-select for the human qualities that enable us to live and work together effectively." How do you imagine that humanity will be defined in the future? Will we still need nature to see ourselves as human? In concrete terms, discuss how the idea of humanity might be transformed if the course of human history follows the divergent paths described by Abram and Stock.

LEILA AHMED

LEILA AHMED, THE author of *A Border Passage: From Cairo to America—A Woman's Journey*, has spent her life contending with issues of identity. Coming of age in Cairo during a period of political tumult, Ahmed witnessed the transformation of Egypt from a British colony into a sovereign Arab nation. The multilingual, multicultural family life that she knew—English and French were spoken at home, and a cosmopolitan Yugoslavian nanny introduced her to many different cultures through language and food—came increasingly into conflict with the young Egyptian nation's attempts to carve out a discrete cultural identity. Ahmed found herself struggling in particular with the "living Islam" she inherited from the women in her family and the strict, patriarchal "official Islam" that was woven into the self-understanding of the Egyptian nation.

Drawn from *A Border Passage*, "On Becoming an Arab" charts the emergence of the Arab League as a political association. It also provides a record of Ahmed's conflicted feelings as she is told that she is an Arab and that this identity supersedes her prior understanding of herself as an Egyptian. For Ahmed, her experience is representative of how the process of developing an Arab identity "unsettled and undercut the old understanding of who we were and silently excluded people who had been included in the old definition of Egyptian" (244). Writing the book, and this section in particular, was a way for Ahmed to come to "understand the history [she]'d lived through." As Ahmed's personal and political history demonstrates, markers of identity are neither perfectly separate nor completely intertwined, but rather always in play.

Ahmed left Egypt to pursue her education and to fashion her identity as a scholar at Cambridge University's Girton College; she has since been elected a lifetime member of Clare Hall at Cambridge. After receiving her doctorate in 1981, she taught Near Eastern studies at the University of Massachusetts-Amherst. She continues to cross borders in her academic career, having been

Ahmed, Leila. "On Becoming an Arab." *A Border Passage: From Cairo to America—A Woman's Journey*. New York: Farrar, Straus and Giroux, 1999. 243–70.

Quotations come from "On Becoming an Arab" as well as an interview with Ahmed available at <http://us.penguingroup.com/static/rguides/us/border_passage.html>.

appointed the first ever professor of women's studies at Harvard Divinity School, where she currently teaches as the Victor S. Thomas Professor of Divinity. Prior to writing *A Border Passage*, Ahmed published her influential work, *Women and Gender in Islam,* which focuses on the range of relationships that Muslim women have to the Islamic religion.

■ ■

On Becoming an Arab

I remember the very day that I became colored.

—ZORA NEALE HURSTON

The teacher called on me to read. I started haltingly. She began interrupting me, correcting me, quietly at first but gradually, as I stumbled on, with more and more irritation, leaving her desk now to stand over me and pounce on every mistake I made. She was an irascible woman, and I had not prepared my homework.

"You're an Arab!" she finally screamed at me. "An Arab! And you don't know your own language!"

"I am not an Arab!" I said, suddenly furious myself. "I am Egyptian! And anyway we don't speak like this!" And I banged my book shut.

"Read!"

I sat on stonily, arms folded.

"Read!"

I didn't move.

She struck me across the face. The moment afterward seemed to go on forever, like something in slow motion.

I was twelve and I'd never been hit before by a teacher and never slapped across the face by anyone. Miss Nabih, the teacher, was a Palestinian. A refugee.

The year was 1952, the year of the revolution. What Miss Nabih was doing to me in class the government was doing to us through the media. I remember how I hated that incessant rhetoric. *Al-qawmiyya al-Arabiyya! Al-Uraba! Nahnu al-Arab!* Arab nationalism! Arabness! We the Arabs! Even now, just remembering those words, I feel again a surge of mingled irritation and resentment. Propaganda *is* unpleasant. And one could not escape it. The moment one turned on the radio, there it was: military songs, nationalistic songs, and endless, endless speeches in that frenetic, crazed voice of exhortation. In public places, in the street, it filled the air, blaring at one from the grocery, the newsstand, the café, the garage, for it became patriotic to have it on at full volume.

Imagine what it would be like if, say, the British or French were incessantly told, with nobody allowed to contest, question, or protest, that they were now European, and only European. European! European! European! And endless songs about it. But for us it was actually worse and certainly more complicated. Its equivalent would be if the British or French were being told that they were white. White! White! White! Because the new definition of who we were unsettled and undercut the old understanding of who we were and silently excluded people who had been included in the old definition of Egyptian. Copts, for example, were not Arab. In fact, they were Copts precisely because they had refused to convert to the religion of the Arabs and had refused, unlike us Muslims, to intermarry with Arabs. As a result, Copts (members of the ancient Christian church of Egypt) were the only truly indigenous inhabitants of Egypt and as such, in our home anyway and in the notion of Egypt with which I grew up, Copts had a very special place in the country. In the new definition of us, however, they were included as speakers of Arabic but they were not at the heart of the definition in the way that we were.

But of course the people who were most directly, although as yet only implicitly, being excluded by the redefinition were the Jews of Egypt, for the whole point of the revolutionary government's harping insistence that we were Arab, in those first years following the founding of Israel, and following the takeover of Egypt's government by New Men with a new vision and new commitments, was to proclaim our unequivocal alignments: on the side of the Palestinians and Arabs and against Israel, against Zionism. Ever since, this issue has been the key issue determining the different emphases Egypt's leaders have placed on its identity. If they have proclaimed insistently and emphatically (as Nasser did) that we were Arab, it has meant that we would take a confrontational, unyielding line on Israel and that we would "never deal with the Zionists." If we were Egyptians above all (Sadat), then we could talk, negotiate.

Our new identity proclaimed openly our opposition to Israel and Zionism—and proclaimed implicitly our opposition to the "Zionists" in our midst, Egyptian Jews. For although explicitly Zionism was distinguished from Jewishness, an undercurrent meaning "Jewish" was also contained in the word. The word "Arab," emerging at this moment to define our identity, silently carried within it its polar opposite—Zionist/Jew—without which hidden, silent connotation it actually had no meaning. For the whole purpose of its emergence now was precisely to tell us of our new alignments and realignments in relation to both terms, Arab and Jew.

Jews and Copts were not, to me, abstractions. They were people my parents knew and saw and talked about, and they were my brothers' friends and my sister's and my own, including my best friend, Joyce. I am sure I sensed these insidious, subterranean shifts and rearrangements of our feelings that this new bludgeoning propaganda was effecting, or trying to effect, in us. And I am sure that this, as well as the sheer hatefulness of being endlessly subjected to propaganda, was part of the reason I so much disliked and resisted the idea that I was an Arab.

Nor was it only through the media that the government was pressuring us into acceptance of its broad political agenda and coercing us into being Arab. For this was the era, too, of growing political repression and of the proliferation of the *mukhabarat*, the secret police—the era when political opponents and people suspected of being disloyal to the revolution were being jailed or disappearing. In this atmosphere, being disloyal to the revolution and to the Arab cause (being, as it were, un-Arab) became as charged and dangerous for Egyptians as being un-American was for Americans in the McCarthy era.

The propaganda worked on me and on others. To question our Arabness and all that our Arabness implied became unthinkable. Only despicable, unprincipled traitors would do such a thing. And it is with this complicated legacy that my own sense of identity as Egyptian and as Arab is entangled.

The following pages recount a personal odyssey through the politics, emotions, and history of our becoming Arab. For no matter how carefully I examined my memories and feelings, they remained opaque until I took this journey into history and into the history of the world of my childhood. These pages both describe the information that I discovered and pieced together—some of it quite surprising and even shocking to me—and trace the process and voyage of discovery itself and my new understandings of my past.

Thinking back to the incident with which I began this chapter, I asked myself what this scene between me and Miss Nabih told me about my parents and family, from whom, certainly, I got my understanding of what it meant to be Egyptian. Why was it that I was so stubborn, so convinced that I was Egyptian and not Arab, definitely not Arab? Presumably this was what my parents thought, but why? Was this a class issue? Were they part of some elite milieu which imagined they were Egyptian while "the masses" knew all along that they were Arabs? When, in fact, did Egyptians become Arab—or have we always been Arab?

The answer to this question, which I assumed I would find simply by looking up a book or two on the history of Egypt, actually took quite a lot of detective work, for it was not clearly or fully addressed in any of the books where I had expected to find it. It felt as if I had embarked in search of some esoteric secret. In the last few years there has begun to be a scholarship piecing together the history of the rise of Arab nationalism, but as regards Egypt, it is a history as yet only barely sketched in.

The story, anyway, begins in Syria, in the late nineteenth century, where the idea of an Arab identity and Arab nationalism first arose. Prior to this, "Arab" had referred throughout the Middle East only to the inhabitants of Arabia and to bedouins of the region's deserts. It was among the Christians of Syria, and in particular among a group of Syrian men who had attended French missionary schools, that the idea of Arab nationalism first appeared, in part as a movement of literary and cultural revival and in part as a way of mobilizing both Christian and Muslim Syrians to throw off the domination of the Islamic Ottoman Empire.

Egyptians, who in that era were preoccupied with getting rid of the British, not the Ottomans, were either uninterested in or positively hostile to this strange Syrian idea of an Arab identity. Mustapha Kamil, the leading nationalist of the day in Egypt, strongly pro-Ottoman and pro-Islamic, denounced Arab nationalism as an idea invented and fomented by the Europeans to hasten the destruction of the Ottoman Empire. And paranoid though Kamil's notion sounds, there may have been some truth to it. Historical records suggest that British officials were indeed already encouraging and supporting the idea of Arabism even before World War I (that they did so during the war is well known).

Well into the first decades of this century, neither the self-defined new Arabs nor the Egyptians themselves thought that this new identity had anything to do with Egyptians. For example, in 1913 an Arab conference was organized in Paris. When an Egyptian who was attending as an observer asked permission to speak, he was refused on the grounds that the floor was open only to Arabs.

During World War I, the idea of Arab nationalism emerged again as an important idea—and again as an idea mobilizing people against the Turks and their Islamic Empire. This time it took the form of the British-instigated "Arab revolt," led by T. E. Lawrence. (The fact that this famous revolt was led by an Englishman makes obvious, of course, Britain's political interest in promoting Arabism as a way of fighting the Ottoman Empire and bringing about its final dissolution.) Once more, as with the Syrian form of Arab nationalism, not only were Egyptians not part of this movement, they were, if anything, inclined to be sympathetic to the other side. For one thing, this Arab movement now involved mainly the Arabs of Arabia and nomadic tribal Arabs, people whom Egyptians regarded as even more different from themselves than the Syrians. The distinction between settled and nomad is, in the Middle East, one of the fundamental divides. For Egyptians it is a distinction that has marked off their society from that of "the Arabs" (Arabians, nomads) since the beginning of their civilization.

In addition, these Arabs were fighting *with* the hated British, the oppressors of Egypt, and *against* the Islamic Empire and the caliph of Islam.

Egypt's Khedive Abbas had been sent into exile by the British for his open sympathies with the Turks and the Islamic Empire, and so also had the leader of the Nationalist Party, Mohamad Farid. The Egyptian writer Naguib Mahfouz, in his novel *Bain al-Qasrain (Palace Walk)*, set in World War I, portrays his characters, the "common folk" of Egypt, as praying for the return of Abbas and for the Turks to "emerge victorious" and as declaring that "the most important thing of all is that we get rid of the "English nightmare" and that the caliphate return to its former glory. Aware of popular sentiment in Egypt, the British took care to represent the Arab revolt to Egyptians as a rebellion not against the caliph but against the "impious, godless" Young Turks who were oppressing "the Arabs."

At the end of the war the British invited the leaders of the Arabs to the Versailles conference but refused to permit the Egyptian leaders to attend. Still, the Arabs reaped no benefits. In a series of treaties the European powers (Britain and France) dismantled the Ottoman Empire and distributed among themselves its former territories. For the British, having induced the Arabs to fight with them against the Turks by promising them independence, had also signed a secret treaty with the French (the Sykes-Picot agreement) undertaking to divide between them after the war "the spoils of the Ottoman Empire." Formalizing their control over the territories that they had just captured from the Ottomans, France took Syria and divided it into two countries, Lebanon and Syria, and Britain took Iraq and Palestine. Britain was, of course, already occupying Egypt. Similarly the Balfour Declaration, promising Palestine, a land obviously with its own inhabitants, to people living elsewhere—designating it a national homeland for the Jews—had been issued earlier, in 1917, when the British first captured Palestine. (There were, of course, Jews as well as Muslims and Christians among the population of Palestine when the British captured it, but it was not out of concern for Palestinian Jews that the British now declared Palestine a homeland for the Jews but rather—as is well known—in response to the desires and hopes of European Jewry for a homeland in Palestine.)

Some of this I knew already. I knew about T. E. Lawrence and the Arab revolt, and I had known in a general way that Arab nationalism was a recent idea. But only now, putting together the Christian and missionary-inspired origins of Arab nationalism in Syria and the use the British made of the idea to mobilize the "Arabs" against the Ottomans, did I realize the extent to which Arab nationalism had emerged as a way of opposing the Islamic Empire. And only now did I realize the extent to which Egypt had not only *not* been Arab but actually had been mostly on the opposite side to that of the Arabs. The exiled khedive and political leaders of Egypt supported the Ottomans and hated the British, and so apparently did the "masses." And even the modernizing intellectuals, who wanted political independence from the Ottomans, had all their cultural, intellectual, and personal ties with Turks and with Istanbul, which many of them regularly visited.

And so already my understanding of Egypt and its relation to the Arabs was beginning to shift. Already I was beginning to feel that the world was not as I had assumed it to be and its seas and continents not after all where I had thought they were. Still, whatever internal shifts and readjustments were involved for me in what I had learned thus far, they were nothing to the geologic shifts and turmoil and upheaval that I would find myself flung up or cast down by as I read on, trying to piece together what happened next—and reading now about the history of the Jews in Egypt and about Egypt's relations to Zionism and the Palestinians.

Eventually things would calm down. Eventually I would come to see that these facts, too, were part of the history of Egypt and that after all they fitted quite intelligibly into that history. But to begin with, with almost every new detail I learned I found myself precipitated into a state of general agitation, my feelings running the gamut of shock, disbelief, shame, despair, and exhilaration—why exhilaration?—and finally, finally understanding. Physically I could not sit still, I could only read a paragraph or two at a time, at least whenever I stumbled upon one or the other of these, to me, completely mind-blowing facts. I'd jump up and walk and walk, repeating to myself whatever it was I'd just read. Egyptians, I'd be rushing around saying to myself, joined their Zionist friends in Cairo and Alexandria to celebrate the Balfour Declaration? There were Zionist associations in Cairo and Alexandria then? It was okay in Egypt to be a Zionist? The governor of Alexandria, Ahmad Ziyour Pasha—later prime minister of Egypt—went to a party in the city celebrating the Balfour Declaration that culminated in their sending a telegram to Lord Balfour to thank him?

Hours and hours and days of this, then, would be interspersed with enormous, crashing, paralyzing anxieties at the very thought of writing about Arabness. There was no question I couldn't do it. I'd just have to leave it out. Just forget it—Arab, not Arab—just forget it. It was much too complicated. How could I possibly deal with all this history?

The first Jewish flag to fly over Jerusalem after its capture by the British was made in Egypt? Joseph Cicurel of the house of Cicurel (a department store I remembered from my childhood, the Harrods of Cairo) had had it made in his Alexandria workshops. Cicurel was president of the Zionist association of Cairo. And at the same time he was an Egyptian nationalist? He was also a trustee of the Bank of Egypt, the bank founded by the Muslim nationalist Talaat Harb with the object of wresting control of the Egyptian economy from Europeans and placing it in Egyptian hands. The same was true of Leon Castro, the vice president of the same Zionist association and likewise an Egyptian nationalist. A member of the Wafd, the party leading the struggle for independence from the British, he was also a friend and staunch supporter of Saad Zaghloul, leader of the Wafd and *the* hero of the Egyptian nationalist struggle.

On and on, more such extraordinary facts about Egyptians' relationship to Zionism—and also to the Palestinians. The Egyptian government sent a

representative—we are now in 1925—to the celebrations for the inaugura-
tion of the Hebrew University in Jerusalem. This representative was none
other than Ahmad Lutfi al-Sayyid, the editor of *al-Jarida*, the paper that
shaped the political consciousness of a generation of Egyptians—my father's
generation—and the man who would later facilitate women's entry into the
Egyptian University. In the late 1920s and early 1930s, when Palestinians
began publishing a paper in Egypt advocating their cause, the Egyptian
government several times closed the paper down and banned the publication of "Palestinian propaganda." And in the wake of conflict over the Wail-
ing Wall and Muslim fears about rights of access to the al-Aqsa mosque, also
in the early 1930s, it even banned the invocation of the name of Palestine in
mosques on Fridays. Meanwhile several Zionist papers continued publication and Zionism was not banned.

Reading such facts as these and observing my own feelings and the paralyzing anxiety I felt at the mere thought of writing about such things, I
came to conclude that this sort of information did not ordinarily figure in
history books on Egypt precisely because, according to the political alignments of our day, alignments that we consider to be entirely obvious and
natural, they seemed so shamefully unpatriotic, and so disloyal and unfeeling toward the Palestinians.

In the ensuing days I would begin to understand how it was that Egyptian attitudes had been so profoundly different from what they are today, and
I would come to understand also my own connection to that past and the
ways in which it was interwoven with my own early life. But even then,
even when I'd understood all this, I would still find myself completely
stalled and unable to imagine how I could possibly write about these things.

Still feeling totally paralyzed, I began to analyze my paralysis as a product probably of my having internalized the taboos against questioning Arabness that had been part, after all, of my adolescence. But this insight—if it
was an insight—did me no good. I was still perfectly capable of silencing
myself without any external prohibitions.

Quite a number of remarkable Egyptians, I discovered along the way,
had been suspected or accused of being either too pro-Jewish, too conciliatory, and too weak on Zionism or deficient in their Arabness or their loyalty
to Arabness. Among those whose actions or words or positions one way or
another laid them open to such charges were Saad Zaghloul, hero of Egyptian nationalism. And Taha Husain and Tewfik al-Hakim and Naguib
Mahfouz, three of Egypt's finest writers. Major figures in the country's history. The equivalent in American terms would be to find that Harry Truman,
William Faulkner, F. Scott Fitzgerald, and Eugene O'Neill had all been suspected of un-American inclinations. And of course there was Anwar Sadat,
gunned down in part for his retreat—and all that such a retreat implied—
from Nasser's position as to Egypt's fundamental Arabness.

But knowing this made no difference either. Nothing unfroze me.

Then one evening as I was walking home, something began to shift. I am not sure quite why or how things began to change but I know that the shift was connected to, or, more exactly, was the direct outcome of, the preceding perfectly pleasant but uneventful few hours. I was in Cambridge for the year on a fellowship (it was here that I pursued and pieced together this history) and had gone out to hear a talk by the Lebanese novelist Hanan al-Shaykh. She'd come down from London to speak at the Oriental Studies Faculty. Hanan was already there when I arrived and rose to greet me, which took me by surprise: we had met only once, briefly and in a crowd, and I hadn't expected her to recognize me. It had felt good, I realized, sitting down and looking around me, to be recognized and to be greeted in the way that, in the world in which I had once lived, one automatically greeted people—or at least other women. The room was more crowded than it had been for the previous lecturers. Aside from Tareef and Bassim, who were the professors at the Oriental Faculty, and some students, the audience did not seem the usual academic crowd that I'd seen at other lectures. Hanan's reputation had clearly drawn out from wherever they were in their separate spaces a good number of the town's Arab and, I guessed from their looks, specifically Lebanese community. There were several older people there, many of them women, living, for whatever reason, in this exile. Here now to honor one of their own, to take pride in her, to listen to her words—and to remember.

Hanan, a slight, beautiful woman, began to read in a clear, soft voice and the room fell quiet, a look of intentness and pleasure and anticipation already on people's faces. Her paper, about how she became a writer, was full of evocations of the streets and cafés of Beirut, and of its dusty, cluttered, narrow bookshops, and of her youthful discoveries of the classics of contemporary Arabic literature, and of poetry read and heard and ideas exchanged under the apple trees. It began, almost at once, to work its enchantment. As the minutes passed, the faces around me grew perceptibly happier, mellower, more relaxed. Even Bassim and Tareef, sitting facing me on either side of her—dear colleagues both but men who, as I knew, were somewhat skeptical of the fame of Arab women writers—were looking mellow and happy and relaxed. They had clearly been won over.

I found myself thinking enviously that this was what I would like to be writing, something that would affirm my community in exile. Something that would remind its members of how lovely our lives, our countries, our ways are. How lovely our literature. What a fine thing, whatever it is people say of us, what a fine thing it is, in spite of them all, to be Arab; what a wonderful heritage we have. Something that would sustain them. Sustain us. What wouldn't I give, I sat there thinking, listening to her quote Arab poets, to have had that in my past, all that wealth of Arabic literature that nurtured her as writer; what wouldn't I give now to have all those poets and writers to remember and write about and remind people of? I loved the lines she was quoting—but I appreciated them, I realized, only the way I might the poetry of a foreign tongue that I only somewhat knew. They did not have for me the resonances of lines learned long ago. Nor, of course, since they were in literary Arabic, did they have the charge and redolence and burdened evocativeness of a language spoken in childhood and youth and in love and anger and just in the ordinary moments of living. But on the other hand they didn't have that wealth and redolence for her, either. Even though she clearly loved the literature and language and was herself a fine Arabic writer, for her too it was a language she had not spoken in childhood and did not speak now. Nobody speaks literary Arabic—or maybe just some pedant somewhere.

We went afterward—Hanan, Tareef, Bassim, Zeeba (another colleague), and I—for drinks at King's. The mood of the lecture stayed with us, our talk pleasant, relaxed, easy. At some point Hanan asked me what I was working on. I was vague, evasive, guilty. I even lied a little. "I'm looking at Egypt's history," I said, "twentieth century." And then for the rest of the evening I felt guilty, sitting there like a Judas among these friends. I felt like a betrayer. Was it even imaginable that I could have responded, sitting there among them—two Lebanese, one Palestinian, one Iranian, three of the four of them having been made homeless one way or another by Israeli aggression or by some spin-off of that conflict—was it conceivable that I could say, "Well, actually I am looking into this whole question of the Arabness of Egyptian identity, I am trying to really look at it, deconstruct it. You see I remember . . ." It was completely unimaginable, impossible, inconceivable.

I felt like a betrayer.

Coming out onto King's Parade, afterwards, the night suddenly balmy, the street almost empty though it wasn't that late, people's voices carrying clear, loud, the way they do sometimes on summer nights—but not usually now, in winter, winter on the point of turning to spring—I walked on homeward, down Senate House Passage and along the narrow road onto the bridge. There was a crescent moon over the trees in a deep, deep sky.

I did feel kin, of course, and I did feel that I was among people who were, in some quite real sense, my community. But was this because of "Arabness"? Was I, for instance, really likely to feel more kin, more at home, with someone from Saudi Arabia than with someone, say, from Istanbul? I doubted it. (Saudis speak Arabic, Turks don't.) This, though, was not the issue now. I realized that my feelings of being completely prohibited from writing about Arabness were not, or not only, a response to old prohibitions or a fear of breaking some mental taboo internalized in adolescence. No, my fear that I would, in this act of unraveling, cross over the line into betrayal was about real, not abstract betrayal. I'd been so set on this act of unraveling, this taking apart of the notion of Arabness. It had seemed to me so essential, so necessary to understanding what it was that I'd lived through, and essential and necessary also to freeing myself from the unbearable lies that I'd forever felt trapped in. Essential and necessary in one sense, and yet to proceed would inevitably, as it now felt, take me over the line into betrayal. And so, thinking about it now, from the context of having been with people I liked and felt in some sense kin with, I wondered what it could possibly matter, when weighed against the reality of people's being driven from their homes or penned into impossible lives, that I had felt myself coerced into being something that I did not feel I was. A small, trivial nothing of a detail to put up with as a way of conveying to them solidarity and support.

But I am not here to betray, I said, waiting at the traffic lights. Had I said it out loud? I looked around—there was nobody there anyway.

I am not here to betray. I just do not want to live any longer with a lie about who I am. I don't want any longer to live with lies and manipulations, I can't stand to be caught up like this forever in other people's inventions, imputations, false constructions of who I am—what I think, believe, feel, or ought to think or believe or feel.

But how—if I don't directly address this—how will I ever free myself from lies?

If I didn't live where I live, I thought to myself, if I were still living in Egypt, I probably wouldn't feel that it was so absolutely necessary to extricate myself from this enmeshment of lies. In Egypt the sense of falseness and coercion would be there in a political sense, but at least in ordinary daily life I'd be just another Egyptian, whereas in the West it's impossible for me ever to escape, forget this false constructed Arabness. It's almost always somehow there, the notion that I am Arab, in any and every interaction. And sometimes it's quite grossly and offensively present, depending on how bigoted or ignorant the person I am confronting is.

But this is a problem, I realized now, arising out of *their* notion of Arab, the Western, not the Arab, notion of Arab. So there are two different notions of Arab that I am trapped in—both false, both heavily weighted and cargoed with another and silent freight. Both imputing to me feelings and beliefs that aren't mine. They overlap in some ways, but they are not, I am sure, identical. But this was a piece of the puzzle—the fact that there were two different notions of Arab—that for the moment I would have to defer figuring out.

Anyway, the long and short of it is that I am not here to betray. I am taking apart the notion of Arabness and following out the history of when and how we became Arab just to know—not with the object of, or as code for, the betrayal of anybody. For Egyptians to debate or question their Arabness ("search" for their identity) is usually code, as I realize now, for debating the extent of our responsibility toward the Palestinians. And it is accordingly read by Arabs and by Egyptians as a covert way of advocating either support for or abandonment of the Palestinians. But my own exploration of the question here is not code for anything. My sole object here is only to see things, as clearly and exactly as I know how, for what they are. And to free myself of lies.

And so in any case one reason that Zionism was permitted to be overtly present in Egypt in the late 1920s and early 1930s and that prominent members of the government and of the governing classes were sympathetic to Zionism was that Egyptians seemed not to know what is obvious to us in hindsight—that making Palestine into a homeland for the Jews would eventually entail the expulsion and dispossession of the Palestinians. There had as yet been no large-scale immigration of Europeans to Palestine and, at the end of the 1910s and through most of the 1920s, when troubles broke out intermittently in Palestine the government and media in Egypt typically reacted by exhorting the Jews and Muslims and Christians of Palestine to work together to find a peaceful solution, offering themselves as mediators, and worrying that this reprehensible interreligious, intercommunal violence would spread to their own country. Because of this last concern, newspapers (or at least some newspapers) and the government responded to news of outbreaks of violence in Palestine by reiterating their own total commitment to preserving religious pluralism, and the government in addition took such measures as banning Palestinian "propaganda"—in fear that interreligious hostilities and in particular anti-Jewish violence, as yet unknown in Egypt, would spread to their own land.

For, as of 1918, the modernizing intellectuals and their party, the Wafd, had begun to become the uncontested political leaders of the nation. And in the early twenties their political goals and platform—democracy, a constitution guaranteeing, among other things, the rights of the individual, pluralism, and an implicit secularism committed to the equal rights of all Egyptians, regardless of religion—won the support of the nation in a landslide election that carried small villages as well as major cities. These goals, conceived and defined by the country's political and intellectual leadership, received the endorsement of the populace as a whole.

Egypt's experiment in democracy would be conducted under difficult circumstances. The British, refusing to grant Egypt complete independence, retained important powers and sometimes interfered outright in the democratic process, at one point later forcing Egypt's king, literally at gunpoint (surrounding his palace with their tanks), to appoint the prime minister they wanted. The king, for his part, plotted to wrest power back from the government to himself. Despite these difficulties the country did make political progress and there were even some exhilarating times and significant achievements, among them the promulgation of a constitution in 1923, article 3 of which granted equal rights to all Egyptians, "without distinction of race, language, or religion." The same principles were reiterated in Egypt's Nationality Laws, which went into effect in 1929 with the formal dissolution of the Ottoman Empire and the replacement of Ottoman citizenship with a brand-new nationality, the Egyptian nationality. These principles and a commitment to Egypt as a multireligious community were furthermore made clear and visible to all in the composition of the government.

When, in 1924, Zaghloul became Egypt's first elected prime minister, Jews as well as Copts served in his cabinet—and indeed both Jews and Copts would continue to serve in the Egyptian government in the following decades.

As all this shows, then, not only was the country's political leadership deeply committed to the goal of preserving Egypt as a pluralist society; in addition, Jews were integrally part of the community of Egypt and of its political and cultural leadership, and they were the friends and colleagues and co-workers of Muslim and Coptic Egyptians. Then there were other factors, too, influencing how Egyptians related to the issue of Palestine. Most obviously, there were no Palestinians then (or very few) in Egypt and certainly there was no historical community of Palestinians as there was a historical Jewish community. In this era about half the Jewish community of Egypt—a community of about 75,000—were Egyptian Jews. The rest were recent immigrants from other territories of the Ottoman Empire and from Europe. (These latter often looked down on the local Jewish community, particularly the Jewish working classes, who were indistinguishable in culture and ways from working-class Muslims and Copts. Middle- and upper-class Jews, like Copts and Muslims of their class, were fast becoming Europeanized.)

And then finally there was the fact that Egyptians at this point did not (and at any class level) see themselves as Arab or as having any special connection with the Arabs, nor did they think that they had any particular interest in or special responsibility for what transpired in Palestine.

Egyptian attitudes began to shift toward a sympathy with the Palestinians in the thirties, as the situation in Palestine began to change when, with the rise of Fascism in Europe, European Jewish immigration to Palestine increased enormously. Palestinian political activism also increased. Through the thirties Palestinian strikes and rebellions against the British and their struggles with Zionists were constantly in the news. By the late thirties the Palestinians had won the sympathies of Egyptians. Fund-raisers and various other events in support of Palestine and in aid of Palestinian relief were held at all class levels, including by Huda Shaarawi's Feminist Union, among the first associations to organize a regionwide conference in support of the Palestinians.

Most important, in terms of publicizing the situation of Palestinians and mobilizing popular support for them, the Muslim Brotherhood, dedicated to instituting an Islamic government in Egypt and to freeing all Muslim lands from imperialists, vigorously took up the Palestinian cause. It began to hold protest demonstrations on Balfour Day and to address the issue of Palestine in Friday sermons.

It was these sorts of activities that, as I mentioned earlier, the government had been attempting to suppress, out of its commitment to a pluralist Egypt and its desire to prevent the spread of interreligious strife. And the government continued through the thirties to try to suppress inflammatory pro-Palestinian activities and to keep Egypt out of direct involvement in the question of Palestine. This was the position assumed not only by the Wafd when it was in power but by the several governments formed by different parties in this era. This view represented, in other words, the consensus position of the governing classes across party lines. And so a rift began to form in Egypt on the issue of Palestine, not on the matter of sympathy for the Palestinians but as to what Egypt's political involvement should be: a rift, initially, not so much between the governing classes and the "masses" as between the government and governing classes on the one hand and the Brotherhood on the other.

Through the thirties the demonstrations the Brotherhood organized grew steadily more massive, and they began to take the direction that the government had, all along, feared they would take. In 1936, the Brotherhood called for a boycott of Jewish businesses. In the same year, the first anti-Jewish graffiti to be reported in Egypt appeared in Port Said. In 1938, police clashed with Brotherhood demonstrators—some of whom were shouting "Down with the Jews"—and tried to prevent them from entering the Jewish quarter of Old Cairo.

It was in the thirties that a few intellectuals—two or three men to begin with, all of whom had links with the Arabs—began to express the idea that Egypt should align itself with the Arabs and regard itself as Arab. But it was probably the emphasis the Muslim Brotherhood now placed on this idea that helped spread it most effectively. While the government had emphasized Egypt's heritage as quintessentially and indissolubly multicultural (Pharaonic, Mediterranean, and Islamic, as they put it in those days) as a way of legitimizing its determined emphasis on pluralism as a fundamental goal for this country, the Brotherhood countered by asserting that Islam and only Islam constituted Egypt's defining identity. It was Islam, they declared, that had saved Egypt from its pagan past (thereby conveniently erasing from history the fact that the majority of Egyptians had been Christian at the time of the Muslim invasion)—an Islam brought to the country, they stressed, by the Arabs. All Egyptians, therefore, and all Muslims owed a particular debt to the Arabs and had an obligation to help liberate Arab lands from infidel imperialists.

By the end of the thirties the popularity of the Palestinian cause and the growing influence of the Brotherhood were forcing the government and dominant political parties to slant their message differently. In 1939, a prominent member of the Wafd made headlines by writing an article declaring "Egypt is Arab!"

Through World War II overt political activism and demonstrations were banned under the Emergencies Act. When they resumed after the war, the pro-Palestinian demonstrations organized by the Muslim Brotherhood took the course of ever greater intercommunal tensions and anti-Jewish violence that the government and the different political parties had all along feared. Huge demonstrations held on Balfour Day in 1945 and again in 1947 spilled over into violent attacks on Jews and now on any other group deemed "foreign." Jewish, European, and Coptic shops were looted, and synagogues and Catholic, Greek Orthodox, and Coptic churches and schools vandalized. One synagogue was set on fire.

The unraveling of that old world and its society are just dimly part of the fabric of my own memories.

I remember being at play in the garden one dusk when the news came that al-Na'rashi, the prime minister, had been shot. *"Atalu al-Na'rashi!"* They killed al-Na'rashi! "They," I know now, were the Muslim Brothers. There was somberness then in our home. My parents, I believe, knew the Na'rashis. But not only somberness—there was something electric, still there even now in my memory, about how they uttered the words and how they spoke of this death. Now I imagine them saying to one another, the adults, living through these crises and troubled times, what next for the country, what next?

And I remember the midnight-blue paper on the windows, purplish when the daylight came through it, during the 1948 war with Israel, and being woken in the night and taken downstairs to the entree, a room with no windows and only a heavy glass and ironwork door, where everyone was gathered in the darkness, talking, listening to the bombs fall.

This was a few months before the assassination of Na'rashi (al-Nuqrashi)—as the history books, not my memory, tell me.

And then, in retaliation for Na'rashi's murder, Hasan al-Banna, the founder of the Muslim Brotherhood and its Supreme Guide, was gunned down. This I do not remember. The Muslim Brotherhood, by now an enormously powerful organization in the country with a vast membership and its own secret military units, was engaged through the forties in a terrorist and counterterrorist war with the political establishment. Al-Banna died in the hospital to which he was brought and where, by order of King Farouk, he was given no medical treatment.

It was by order of Farouk, too, that Egypt went to war with Israel. After the United Nations resolution to partition Palestine and Israel's declaration of statehood in 1948, the Egyptian political establishment—both government and opposition—had favored a cautious response, a verbal, not a military, response. But Farouk harbored dreams, now that the Ottoman Empire was gone, of having himself declared caliph of Islam. He worried that, if Egypt did not go to war now, King Abdullah of Jordan, who had declared that Jordan would go to war, would reap glory on the battlefield and put an end to his own dreams. And so, pre-empting the Egyptian government's decision and in violation of the constitution, he ordered military units to cross into Palestine. After the fact, the government hastily convened a meeting to bestow a semblance of legality on the king's orders. The opposition, however, and in particular the Liberal Constitutionalists—who (as the history books put it), out of a "narrow Egyptian secular nationalism" were "most impervious to Palestinian appeals"—were fiercely critical of this government action.

But of course it was not that Farouk had been pervious to Palestinian appeals. Nor was it only Farouk for whom from now on taking up the Palestinian cause was essentially an avenue to the fulfillment of his political ambitions. While Na'rashi was making speeches cautioning against a hasty military response, Hasan al-Banna was declaring in mosques the Muslim Brotherhood's readiness for a jihad against the Zionists. But he, too, was in reality furthering his own cause. In the forties the Brotherhood, historians have speculated, had a trained secret army of about 75,000 men. But they reportedly sent to the Palestine campaign just 600. The movement was hoping, say historians, to reserve most of its secret units for its Egyptian war—its war on the cities of Egypt.

By this point, that is, Palestine and the Palestinian cause had begun to be what they have been ever since in the politics of the Arab world: an issue that the Middle East's villains and heroes would use to manipulate people's sympathies and to further their own political ends and fantasies of power—with what costs or benefits to the Palestinian people only the Palestinians themselves can say.

Where did my parents stand in all this? I don't know. I was too young and do not remember. It would be quite impossible for me to have grasped what they said enough to be able to say, now, they said this or believed that.

And yet also now I think I know.

But the evidence I have is so vague, so insubstantial, so inconclusive. Some things I do know and do remember beyond a shadow of a doubt. For instance, I know that they definitely did not like the Muslim Brothers. I don't remember any particular thing that they said about them, but I remember this as a general feeling. And I remember that a man who was a relative by marriage (a younger man beholden in some way, looking in some way to my father) was a Muslim Brother and that he emerged from prison at some point (still, now, in the days of King Farouk) and that he had tuberculosis and that he came to our house and that my father, making clear to him (and evidently to all of us) his total disapproval of his politics, helped him get treatment.

I don't remember in any way that I would now be able to reproduce what my parents were saying as they lived through these wrenching times in the history of Egypt. But I was there, obviously, and heard them talk and no doubt in some sense absorbed what they were saying. And they *were* people who talked politics. Over lunch when my father came home from work and on weekends when we were home from school and joined our parents. Over tea and the papers in the early morning, sitting in my mother's huge bed, where we half listened to them talk. What exactly was the content of that grief and somberness that descended over our home and the feeling of charged tension that I remember when Na'rashi was shot? What exactly did they say to each other? And what did they say when al-Banna was shot—and allowed to die, untreated, by order of the king?

That's another thing I incontrovertibly know and remember: they did not like King Farouk.

And what did they say when there were riots in Egypt and attacks on synagogues and churches? And what did they say as we sat in the dark in the entree, listening to the sound of distant bombs and anti-aircraft fire and then a nearer, louder, more frightening explosion? What were they saying about the war with Israel? Could they have been among those who condemned the king for getting us into this war? Could they have been among those who, like the government opposition, condemned the government for "lending any semblance of legitimacy" to the king's action? Could they have been among those who, like the Liberal Constitutionalists, out of a "narrow Egyptian secular nationalism" opposed the war? Could they have been among those "impervious to Palestinian appeals" who believed that Egypt should not go to war with Israel? Could they have been among those for whom grief about what was happening to Egypt overrode and took priority over what was happening to the Palestinians?

Though I do not remember their words, I would have picked up the import of what they were saying, and their attitudes would certainly have shaped my responses to whatever I encountered at school.

Including, of course, Miss Nabih.

I did not know, until I read into this history and learned what I have here set down, that there had been Egyptians—perfectly ordinary, decent, upright, principled citizens of Egypt, not disloyal, unpatriotic, unfeeling people—who believed in something else, some other idea of Egypt and its society and future, and who openly argued against getting involved in supporting the Palestinians and going to war with Israel.

My parents were the people that they were. Of the class that they were, the milieu that they were, the era that they were. And they had the feelings and beliefs about Egypt that they had, and the hopes for Egypt that they had. Not indifference toward the Palestinians and their sufferings, nor commitment to some "narrow Egyptian secular nationalism," but quite simply loyalty to their own community and to the people—Copts, Jews and Muslims—who made up that community had been what my parents had steadfastly held on to and had refused to be moved from. Loyalty to their actual community—over and above some fictive, politically created community that the politicians ordered them to be loyal to. And, yes, their overall position reflected too their particular hopes for Egypt, and their commitment to what we today call "pluralism." But "pluralism" after all is merely a modern version of what had been, in another world, another era, their tradition and heritage, from generation to generation to generation, in Cairo and Alexandria and Spain and Morocco and Istanbul.

And so this, then, had been the source of those moments of inexplicable exhilaration in the midst of turbulence—my beginning to glimpse finally what had been the history and prehistory of my own conflicted feelings. They taught me so well, instilled in me so deeply their notion of what it was to be Egyptian, that I still mourn and am always still and all over again filled with an enormous sense of loss at the thought of the destruction of the multireligious Egyptian community that I knew. And still now news of intercommunal violence in Egypt and of attacks on Copts (there are no Jews now) and of attacks on Muslims too, of course—but it is the Copts who are the beleaguered community—is almost the bleakest news I know of coming out of there.

In 1941, Anthony Eden, the British foreign minister, proposed the creation of an Arab League, to include Egypt. This British proposal precipitated an intense debate that polarized Egyptians. Was Egypt Arab? Mediterranean? Pharaonic? Britain had put forward the idea as a counterproposal to an idea that Iraq had been advancing: the creation of a federated Arab state, to consist of Iraq, Syria, Jordan, and Palestine. Such a federation, should it occur, could lead to the rise of a formidable new power in the Middle East, and this was something Britain did not want. It was something Egypt did not want, either. As the region began to adjust to the disappearance of Turkey as the center of empire and the newly emergent countries began to vie for regional dominance, Egypt—at that point the richest, most developed and most populous nation in the region—had no intention of ceding power and influence to Iraq or Jordan or to any federation of these. Thus, in 1943, the Egyptian government agreed to the British proposal and the Arab League was formed in 1945.

And so here we are in 1945, and Egypt, for reasons of regional strategy, officially becomes an Arab country, although not as yet exclusively Arab, as it would become under Nasser. And again, curiously, Britain played the role of instigator, and of midwife, as it were, to the birth of yet another Arab nation. Once more, as with its leadership of the Arab revolt, Britain's purpose in urging Egypt to define itself as Arab was, of course, the furtherance of British political interests.

It was as if we had become Arab, and all the region gradually had become Arab (when, once, only Arabia had been Arab), because the Europeans saw us as Arabs—all of us as just Arabs. And because, to serve their own political interests and in pursuit of their own ends—the dismantling of the Ottoman Empire, the acquisition of new colonial territories, retaining control of territories under their mandate—it was strategically and politically useful to them, in this particular era in history, to define us, and to have us define ourselves, as Arabs. And gradually over this era we had all complied, imagining this, correctly or not, to be in our own interest, too.

The Europeans were defining us and we, falling in with their ideas, agreed to define ourselves as Arab in the dictionary sense: "a member of the

Semitic people of the Arabian peninsula; a member of an Arabic-speaking people." But the Europeans were also defining us as Arab in quite another sense. Just as with the word "African"—"a native or inhabitant of Africa; a person of immediate or remote African ancestry; esp: Negro"—there is no trace in the dictionary definition of the word's pejorative connotations. There is nothing here of what anyone who has heard of O. J. Simpson or *The Bell Curve* or who knows anything about American history *knows* what that word means. This is the case also with the word "Arab," which similarly comes, in European tongues, internally loaded in the negative.

Such words carry within them entire landscapes, entire histories.

The European powers defined us as "Arab" in this other sense by what they did. They defined us as "Arab" in this sense when they made an agreement with Sheikh Abdullah and those who fought alongside Lawrence, promising them independence—and then broke the agreement. They defined us as "Arab" at the Peace conferences of Versailles and Sèvres when they dealt with Middle Eastern territories as mere spoils of the Ottoman Empire, to be divided between France and Britain as booty, bargaining with one another for this bit or that, drawing lines and borders on their maps with little concern for the people and lands they were carving up. And they defined us as "Arab" when they designated an already inhabited land as a homeland for people living, then, elsewhere. They defined us as "Arab" when they led Egyptians to believe that in return for neutrality during the war they would get independence—and failed to keep their promise and exiled leaders and fired on demonstrators who dared protest. They defined us as "Arab" when they set aside the results of elections and forced the appointment of their chosen prime minister.

"Arabs" meant people with whom you made treaties that you did not have to honor, arabs being by definition people of a lesser humanity and there being no need to honor treaties with people of lesser humanity. It meant people whose lands you could carve up and apportion as you wished, because they were of a lesser humanity. It meant people whose democracies you could obstruct at will, because you did not have to behave justly toward people of a lesser humanity. And what could mere arabs, anyway, know of democracy and democratic process?

Until now, all who had come to this land of Egypt—Greeks, Romans, Arabs, Turks—had known that they were coming to a place of civilization. All, until now, had come knowing that they had as much to learn here as to teach, as much to take, in terms of knowledge and ways of understanding and of living, as to give. That, until now, was how it had been.

The Europeans began writing their meaning of the word "arab" freely and indiscriminately all over the Middle East from about 1918 on, when the region as a whole fell into their hands. Prior to this, during their rule in Egypt, that meaning of the word had occasionally surfaced—at Dinshwai, for instance— but it had not been the dominant, consistent hallmark of their conduct.

And so in those years they scribbled their meaning of "arab" all over the landscape, in their acts and in the lines they drew on maps, tracing out their meaning in a script at once cryptic and universal: as cryptic and universal as the mark of a snake or the trail of deer on a blank page of snow.

And in time, quite soon, their meaning of the word "arab" would enter our meaning of it, too. Not etymologically, in the way that dictionaries trace meanings through transformations from word to word to word. No. It entered it corrosively, changing it from within, as if the European meaning were a kind of virus eating up the inside of the word "Arab," replacing it with itself— leaving it unchanged on the outside. Think of what it did to the words "African," "Africa": somehow, somehow, loading those words in the negative.

The European meaning of "arab," then, hollowed out our word, replacing it entirely with itself. Except that now ours is their meaning of the word "arab" in reverse. Like "black" and "Black," as in "Black is beautiful."

It is this sense of "arab," the European sense, with its cargo of negativities, that I, living in the West, so often encounter and feel myself trapped in. This is the meaning of "arab," still very much alive, still very much around, that prompted me, for instance, to quickly hide my Arabic newspaper in my shopping bag so that people would not know I was Arab—and so react to me, possibly, in some bigoted fashion, as people all too commonly do when they discover I am Arab. Like the man—more extreme than usual—who spat at me on the bus in Cambridge when I was a student: smiling at first, asking me if I was Israeli, and then, leaning toward me, seeing that the medallion I wore was after all Arabic, spitting right at me. And it is the meaning of "arab" that is there in my students' understanding when, as they grow more at ease with me, they disarmingly reveal that they would never have thought of calling me an Arab until I had called myself one, because, until then, they had thought the word was an insult. And it is there in the countless microaggressions (as the noted author and legal scholar Patricia Williams calls them) that ordinarily and daily are part of the fabric of living for those of us in the West who belong to a "race" charged, in this culture, in the negative.

And it is there in the meanings threading Western books and films and newspapers and so on. I, like many I know who are Arab, never go to a film in which I know that Arabs or Muslims figure. Naturally—why would I want to subject myself to the lies and racism that all too often are part of such things? This goes, too, for popular books on Arabs—their very popularity is usually an index of the fact that they are filled with bigotries and dehumanizations masquerading as truth.

But it would be another generation, not my parents' generation, not the generation who had grown up admiring European civilization, who would come to see clearly and to decipher for themselves what it was that the Europeans had scrawled across the landscape.

Nasser, born in 1917 and coming to consciousness, then, entirely after the watershed year of 1918, was perhaps among the first to figure out (for he was, whatever his flaws, an astute man) the meaning of what they had traced there—and to respond to it by crystallizing the identity "arab" into its obverse, "Arab," although even he, as I discovered to my surprise, fully grasped that he was Arab only a few years before I got slapped for not knowing that I was Arab. For Nasser seems to have understood that he was Arab precisely by intently studying the marks and runes the imperialists had made upon the landscape. Reflecting himself on when it was exactly that he understood that he was Arab, he singles out the study of the recent history of the region, and above all (he repeatedly returns to this) the history of Palestine, as critical to his understanding of himself as an Arab. He wrote in his *Philosophy of the Revolution:* "As far as I am concerned I remember the first elements of Arab consciousness began to filter into my mind as a student in secondary school, when I went out with my fellow schoolboys . . . every year as a protest against the Balfour Declaration whereby England gave the Jews a national home usurped unjustly from its legal owners. When I asked myself at the time," Nasser goes on, "why I left my school so enthusiastically and why I was angry for this land which I never saw I could not find an answer except the echoes of sentiment." Gradually "a form of comprehension" began when he studied "the Palestine campaigns and the history of the region in general" in military college, and finally that comprehension crystallized "when the Palestine crisis loomed on the horizon."

"When I asked myself . . . why I was so angry." Anger, as Nasser's own choice of words makes clear, was the key emotion in the early formation of his nascent identity as an Arab.

Spring is here.

The crocuses are out on the Backs. Rivulets of blue, all along the pathways, vividest, vividest blue, and gashes and splashes of it on the verges and under the trees.

Why then, walking through this, did I suddenly feel this sense of loss—measureless, measureless loss—sweep through me?

And so that, O my daughter, is what happened. That, in those years, is what happened to us.   ■

■ *QUESTIONS FOR MAKING CONNECTIONS WITHIN THE READING* ■

1. How many definitions of the word *Arab* does Ahmed provide in "On Becoming an Arab"? Construct a chart that tracks the changes in the meaning of *arab* and *Arab* over time. Why did Ahmed reject the name in the 1950s and why does she accept it now?

2. Ahmed states repeatedly in her piece that she is "not here to betray." One could argue that repeating this declaration is a clear sign that Ahmed is concerned that she will be read as betraying someone or some cause. Whom is she worried about betraying? And why does she feel that

her search for her own identity might appear to justify the charge of betrayal?

3. What role does Palestine play in Ahmed's project of defining the contemporary meanings of *Arab* and *Egyptian*?

■ *QUESTIONS FOR WRITING* ■

1. Ahmed describes her project as "a personal odyssey through the politics, emotions, and history of our becoming Arab." Why does she include emotions as part of her project? Where do you see emotion surfacing in her argument? Are there places where you would say that emotions are shaping her argument? What role should the emotions play in research on the formation of the self in history?

2. Ahmed's story begins with a slap and ends with "a sense of loss—measureless, measureless loss. . . ." What would you say Ahmed has learned by the end of her odyssey? Is her lesson one that applies to people generally or only to expatriates?

■ *QUESTIONS FOR MAKING CONNECTIONS BETWEEN READINGS* ■

1. In Ahmed's narrative, she documents the changing meaning of *Arab* over time, pointing to a moment when the word "silently carried within it its polar opposite—Zionist/Jew—without which hidden, silent connotation it actually had no meaning." Later in her account, Ahmed reports that "[t]he European meaning of 'arab' hollowed out our word, replacing it entirely with itself." Does Ahmed find herself caught in one version of the "argument culture" that Deborah Tannen describes in "The Roots of Debate in Education and the Hope for Dialogue"? What roles do conflict and dialogue play in the identity formation of an individual? A nation?

2. Both Ahmed and Jonathan Boyarin are concerned with locating the self in time, and both are concerned with memory and loss. Their methods for pursuing their shared interests diverge, however, as do their writing styles and their conclusions: Ahmed closes with "a sense of loss—measureless, measureless loss . . ." while Boyarin ends with "the marginal redemption of one Jew." How do you account for these differences? What might those who are not Jews or Arabs learn from the journeys of these two writers? Write an essay where you discuss what, if anything, can be learned from reading about another's search for identity.

ANDREW J. BACEVICH

FOR MOST CITIZENS, patriotism takes the form of either service or dissent. In his years of professional and personal experience as a participant and student of the military, Andrew J. Bacevich has engaged in both. After graduating from the U.S. Military Academy at West Point, he served in Vietnam from 1970 to 1971. While still in the army, Bacevich earned his doctorate in American diplomatic history from Princeton University. He retired from military service at the rank of colonel and has taught at Boston University as a professor of international relations and history since 1998. He is also a prominent and authoritative critic both of the U.S. occupation in Iraq, which he calls "immoral, illicit, and imprudent," and of the expanding American militarism more generally.

The New American Militarism: How Americans Are Seduced by War, a book-length treatment of the issues Bacevich begins to explore in "The Real World War IV," is an indictment of American foreign policy across the ideological spectrum. He charts the swift evolution that brought America from the antimilitary skepticism of the Vietnam era to the widespread contemporary belief that martial activity is the solution to both domestic and international problems. During this forty-year period, "political leaders, liberals and conservatives alike," he writes, "became enamored of military might. Militarism insinuated itself into American life."

In May 2007, Bacevich lost his son, a first lieutenant in the Army and also named Andrew J. Bacevich, to the Iraq war; he responded to this loss with a moving *Washington Post* editorial called "I Lost My Son to a War I Oppose. We Were Both Doing Our Duty." Though he is a self-described "Catholic conservative," Bacevich continues to make known his criticism of American military intervention across a wide range of publications and forums, in defiance of easy

---

Bacevich, Andrew. "The Real World War IV." *Wilson Quarterly* 29(1) (Winter 2005): 36–61.

Quotations come from "Warheads," a *San Diego Union-Tribune* review of Bacevich's book, available at <http://www.signonsandiego.com/uniontrib/20050327/news_lz1v27war.html>; "Rescinding the Bush Doctrine," an editorial by Bacevich in the *Boston Globe*, available at <http://www.boston.com/news/globe/editorial_opinion/oped/articles/2007/03/01/rescinding_the_bush_doctrine/>; "Seduced by War," an interview with Bacevich that appears in *Bostonia* and is available at <http://www.bu.edu/alumni/ bostonia/2004/winter/war/index.html>.

ideological categorization. As an author, Bacevich argues that both liberals and conservatives are complicit in the growing gap between American values and American foreign policy. As a citizen, Bacevich is a living testament to the complexity of political belief and affiliation, and an example of how an active American public can live out its patriotism and "think realistically of other ways of achieving our purposes in the world" beyond a commitment to military aggression.

■   ■

The Real World War IV

In the eyes of its most impassioned supporters, the global war on terror constitutes a de facto fourth world war: The conflict that erupted with the attacks on the World Trade Center and the Pentagon is really a sequel to three previous conflicts that, however different from one another in terms of scope and duration, have defined contemporary history.

According to this interpretation, most clearly articulated by the neoconservative thinker Norman Podhoretz in the pages of *Commentary* magazine, the long twilight struggle between communism and democratic capitalism qualifies as the functional equivalent of World War I (1914–18) and World War II (1939–45). In retrospect, we can see that the East-West rivalry commonly referred to as the Cold War was actually World War III (1947–89). After a brief interval of relative peace, corresponding roughly to the 1990s, a fourth conflict, comparable in magnitude to the previous three, erupted on September 11, 2001. This fourth world war promises to continue indefinitely.

Classifying the war on terror as World War IV offers important benefits. It fits the events of September 11 and thereafter into a historical trope familiar to almost all Americans, and thereby offers a reassuring sense of continuity: We've been here before; we know what we need to do; we know how it ends. By extension, the World War IV construct facilitates efforts to mobilize popular support for U.S. military actions undertaken in pursuit of final victory. It also ratifies the claims of federal authorities, especially those in the executive branch, who insist on exercising "wartime" prerogatives by expanding the police powers of the state and circumscribing constitutional guarantees of due process. Further, it makes available a stock of plausible analogies to help explain the otherwise inexplicable—the dastardly events of September 11, 2001, for example, are a reprise of the dastardly surprise of December 7, 1941. Thus, the construct helps to preclude awkward questions. It disciplines.

But it also misleads. Lumping U.S. actions since 9/11 under the rubric of World War IV can too easily become an exercise in sleight of hand. According to hawks such as Podhoretz, the chief defect of U.S. policy before 9/11 was an excess of timidity. America's actual problem has been quite the reverse.

The key point is this. At the end of the Cold War, Americans said "yes" to military power. Indeed, ever since Vietnam, Americans have evinced a deepening infatuation with armed force, soldiers, and military values. By the end of the 20th century, the skepticism about arms and armies that informed the American experiment from its founding had vanished. Political leaders, liberals and conservatives alike, became enamored of military might. Militarism insinuated itself into American life.

The ensuing affair has had a heedless, Gatsby-like aspect, a passion pursued in utter disregard of any likely consequences. Few in power have openly considered whether valuing military power for its own sake or cultivating permanent global military superiority might be at odds with American principles.

To the extent that some Americans are cognizant of a drift toward militarism by their country, the declaration of World War IV permits them to suppress any latent anxiety about that tendency. After all, according to precedent, a world war—by definition, a conflict thrust upon the United States—changes everything. Responsibility for world wars lies with someone else: with Germany in 1917, Japan in 1941, or the Soviet Union after 1945. Designating the several U.S. military campaigns initiated in the aftermath of 9/11 as World War IV effectively absolves the United States of accountability for anything that went before. Blame lies elsewhere: with Osama bin Laden and Al Qaeda, with Saddam Hussein and his Baath Party thugs, with radical Islam. America's responsibility is to finish what others started.

But this militaristic predisposition, evident in the transformation of American thinking about soldiers, the armed services, and war itself since Vietnam, cannot of itself explain the rising tide of American bellicosity that culminated in March 2003 with the invasion of Iraq. We must look as well to national interests and, indeed, to the ultimate U.S. interest, which is the removal of any obstacles or encumbrances that might hinder the American people in their pursuit of happiness ever more expansively defined. Rather than timidity or trepidation, it is unabashed confidence in the strength of American arms, combined with an unswerving determination to perfect American freedom, that has landed us in our present fix.

During the 1980s and 1990s, this combustible mix produced a shift in the U.S. strategic center of gravity, overturning geopolitical priorities that had long appeared sacrosanct. A set of revised strategic priorities emerged, centered geographically in the energy-rich Persian Gulf but linked inextricably to the assumed prerequisites for sustaining American freedom at home. A succession of administrations, Republican and Democratic, opted for armed force as the preferred means to satisfy those new priorities. In other words, a new set of strategic imperatives, seemingly conducive to a military solution, and a predisposition toward militarism together produced the full-blown militarization of U.S. policy so much in evidence since 9/11.

The convergence between preconditions and interests suggests an altogether different definition of World War IV—a war that did not begin on 9/11, does not have as its founding purpose the elimination of terror, and does not cast the United States as an innocent party. This alternative conception of a fourth world war constitutes not a persuasive rationale for the exercise of U.S. military power in the manner pursued by the administration of George W. Bush, but the definitive expression of the dangers posed by the new American militarism. Waiting in the wings are World Wars V and VI, to be justified, inevitably, by the ostensible demands of freedom.

Providing a true account of World War IV requires that it first be placed in its correct relationship to World War III, the Cold War. As the great competition between the United States and the Soviet Union slips further into the past, scholars work their way toward an ever more fine-grained interpretation of its origins, conduct, and implications. Yet as far as public perceptions of the Cold War are concerned, these scholars' diligence goes largely unrewarded. When it comes to making sense of recent history, the American people, encouraged by their political leaders, have shown a demonstrable preference for clarity rather than nuance. Even as the central events of the Cold War recede into the distance, the popular image of the larger drama in which these events figured paradoxically sharpens.

"Cold War" serves as a sort of self-explanatory, all-purpose label, encompassing the entire period from the mid-1940s through the late 1980s. And since what is past is prologue, this self-contained, internally coherent, authoritative rendering of the recent past is ideally suited to serve as a template for making sense of events unfolding before our eyes.

From a vantage point midway through the first decade of the 21st century, the commonly accepted metanarrative of our time consists of three distinct chapters. The first, beginning where World War II leaves off, recounts a period of trial and tribulation lasting several decades but ending in an unambiguous triumph for the United States. The next describes a short-lived "post–Cold War era," a brief, dreamy interlude abruptly terminated by 9/11. The second chapter gives way to a third, still in the process of being written but expected to replicate in broad outlines the first—if only the United States will once again rise to the occasion. This three-part narrative possesses the virtues of simplicity and neatness, but it is fundamentally flawed. Perhaps worst of all, it does not alert Americans to the full dimensions of their present-day predicament. Instead, the narrative deceives them. It would be far more useful to admit to a different and messier parsing of the recent past.

For starters, we should recognize that, far from being a unitary event, the Cold War occurred in two distinct phases. The first, defined as the period of Soviet-American competition that could have produced an actual World War III, essentially ended by 1963. In 1961, by acquiescing in the erection of the Berlin Wall, Washington affirmed its acceptance of a divided Europe. In 1962, during the Cuban Missile Crisis, Washington and Moscow contemplated the real prospect of mutual annihilation, blinked more or less simultaneously, and tacitly agreed to preclude any recurrence of that frightening moment. A more predictable, more stable relationship ensued, incorporating a certain amount of ritualistic saber rattling but characterized by careful adherence to a well-established set of routines and procedures.

Out of stability came opportunities for massive stupidity. During the Cold War's second phase, from 1963 to 1989, both the major protagonists availed themselves of these opportunities by pursuing inane adventures on the periphery. In the 1960s, of course, Americans plunged into Vietnam, with catastrophic results. Beginning in 1979, the Soviets impaled themselves on Afghanistan, with results that proved altogether fatal. Whereas the inherent resilience of democratic capitalism enabled the United States to repair the wounds it had inflicted on itself, the Soviet political economy lacked recuperative powers. During the course of the 1980s, an already ailing Soviet empire became sick unto death.

The crucial developments hastening the demise of the Soviet empire emerged from within. When the whole ramshackle structure came tumbling down, Andrei Sakharov, Václav Havel, and Karol Wojtyla, the Polish prelate who became Pope John Paul II, could claim as much credit for the result as Ronald Reagan, if not more. The most persuasive explanation for the final outcome of the Cold War is to be found in Soviet ineptitude, in the internal contradictions of the Soviet system, and in the courage of the dissidents who dared to challenge Soviet authority.

In this telling of the tale, the Cold War remains a drama of compelling moral significance. But shorn of its triumphal trappings, the tale has next to nothing to say about the present-day state of world affairs. In a post-9/11 world, it possesses little capacity either to illuminate or to instruct. To find in the recent past an explanation of use to the present requires an altogether different narrative, one that resurrects the largely forgotten or ignored story of America's use of military power for purposes unrelated to the Soviet-American rivalry.

The fact is that, even as the Cold War was slowly reaching its denouement, World War IV was already under way—indeed, had begun two full decades before September 2001. So World Wars III and IV consist of parallel rather than sequential episodes. They evolved more or less in tandem, with the former overlaid on, and therefore obscuring, the latter.

The real World War IV began in 1980, and Jimmy Carter, of all people, declared it. To be sure, Carter acted only under extreme duress, prompted by the irrevocable collapse of a policy to which he and his seven immediate predecessors had adhered—specifically, the arrangements designed to guarantee the United States a privileged position in the Persian Gulf. For Cold War–era U.S. policymakers, preoccupied with Europe and East Asia as the main theaters of action, the gulf had figured as something of a sideshow before 1980. Jimmy Carter changed all that, thrusting it into the uppermost tier of U.S. geopolitical priorities.

From 1945 through 1979, the aim of U.S. policy in the gulf region had been to ensure stability and American access, but to do so in a way that minimized overt U.S. military involvement. Franklin Roosevelt had laid down the basic lines of this policy in February 1945 at a now-famous meeting with King Abd al-Aziz Ibn Saud of Saudi Arabia. Henceforth, Saudi Arabia could count on the United States to guarantee its security, and the United States could count on Saudi Arabia to provide it preferential treatment in exploiting the kingdom's vast, untapped reserves of oil.

From the 1940s through the 1970s, U.S. strategy in the Middle East adhered to the military principle known as economy of force. Rather than establish a large presence in the region, Roosevelt's successors sought to achieve their objectives in ways that entailed a minimal expenditure of American resources and, especially, U.S. military power. From time to time, when absolutely necessary, Washington might organize a brief show of force—in 1946, for example, when Harry Truman ordered the USS *Missouri* to the eastern Mediterranean to warn the Soviets to cease meddling in Turkey, or in 1958, when Dwight Eisenhower sent U.S. Marines into Lebanon for a short-lived, bloodless occupation—but these modest gestures proved the exception rather than the rule.

The clear preference was for a low profile and a hidden hand. Although by no means averse to engineering "regime change" when necessary, the United States preferred covert action to the direct use of force. To police the region, Washington looked to surrogates—British imperial forces through the 1960s, and, once Britain withdrew from "east of Suez," the shah of Iran. To build up the indigenous self-defense (or regime defense) capabilities of select nations, it arranged for private contractors to provide weapons, training, and advice. The Vinnell Corporation's ongoing "modernization" of the Saudi Arabian National Guard (SANG), a project now well over a quarter-century old, remains a prime example.

By the end of 1979, however, two events had left this approach in a shambles. The first was the Iranian Revolution, which sent the shah into exile and installed in Tehran an Islamist regime adamantly hostile to the United States. The second was the Soviet invasion of Afghanistan, which put the Red Army in a position where it appeared to pose a direct threat to the entire Persian Gulf—and hence to the West's oil supply.

Faced with these twin crises, Jimmy Carter concluded that treating the Middle East as a secondary theater, ancillary to the Cold War, no longer made sense. A great contest for control of the region had been joined. Rejecting out of hand any possibility that the United States might accommodate itself to the changes afoot in the Persian Gulf, Carter claimed for the United States a central role in determining exactly what those changes would be. In January 1980, to forestall any further deterioration of the U.S. position in the gulf, he threw the weight of American military power into the balance. In his State of the Union address, the president enunciated what became known as the Carter Doctrine. "An attempt by any outside force to gain control of the Persian Gulf region," he declared, "will be regarded as an assault on the vital interests of the United States of America, and such an assault will be repelled by any means necessary, including military force."

From Carter's time down to the present day, the doctrine bearing his name has remained sacrosanct. As a consequence, each of Carter's successors has expanded the level of U.S. military involvement and operations in the region. Even today, American political leaders cling to the belief that skillful application of military power will enable the United States to decide the fate not simply of the Persian Gulf proper but of the entire greater Middle East. This gigantic project, begun in 1980 and now well into its third decade, is the true World War IV.

What prompted Jimmy Carter, the least warlike of all recent U.S. presidents, to take this portentous step? The Pentagon's first Persian Gulf commander, Lieutenant General Robert Kingston, offered a simple answer when he said that his basic mission was "to assure the unimpeded flow of oil from the Arabian Gulf." But General Kingston was selling his president and his country short. What was true of the three other presidents who had committed the United States to world wars—Woodrow Wilson, FDR, and Truman—remained true in the case of Carter and World War IV as well. The overarching motive for action was preservation of the American way of life.

By the beginning of 1980, a chastened Jimmy Carter had learned a hard lesson: It was not the prospect of making do with less that sustained American-style liberal democracy, but the promise of more. Carter had come to realize that what Americans demanded from their government was freedom, defined as more choice, more opportunity, and, above all, greater abundance, measured in material terms. That abundance depended on assured access to cheap oil—and lots of it.

In enunciating the Carter Doctrine, the president was reversing course, effectively renouncing his prior vision of a less materialistic, more self-reliant democracy. Just six months earlier, this vision had been the theme of a prescient, but politically misconceived, address to the nation, instantly dubbed by pundits the "Crisis of Confidence" speech, though, in retrospect, perhaps better called "The Road Not Taken."

Carter's short-lived vision emerged from a troubled context. By the third year of his presidency, economic conditions as measured by postwar standards had become dire. The rates of inflation and unemployment were both high. The prime lending rate was 15 percent and *rising*. Trends in both the federal deficit and the trade balance were sharply negative. Conventional analysis attributed U.S. economic woes to the nation's growing dependence on increasingly expensive foreign oil.

In July 1979, Carter already anticipated that a continuing and unchecked thirst for imported oil was sure to distort U.S. strategic priorities, with unforeseen but adverse consequences. (When Carter spoke, the United States was importing approximately 43 percent of its annual oil requirement; today it imports 56 percent.) He feared the impact of that distortion on an American democracy still reeling from the effects of the 1960s. So on July 15 he summoned his fellow citizens to change course, to choose self-sufficiency and self-reliance—and therefore true independence. But the independence was to come at the cost of collective sacrifice and lowered expectations.

Carter spoke that night of a nation facing problems "deeper than gasoline lines or energy shortages, deeper even than inflation or depression." The fundamental issue, in Carter's view, was that Americans had turned away from all that really mattered. In a nation once proud of hard work among strong, religious families and close-knit communities, too many Americans had come to worship self-indulgence and consumption. What you owned rather than what you did had come to define human identity. But according to Carter, owning things and consuming things did not satisfy our longing for meaning. Americans were learning that piling up goods could fill the emptiness of lives devoid of real purpose.

This moral crisis had brought the United States to a historic turning point. Either Americans could persist in pursuing "a mistaken idea of freedom" based on "fragmentation and self-interest" and inevitably "ending in chaos and immobility," or they could opt for "true freedom," which Carter described as "the path of common purpose and the restoration of American values."

How the United States chose to deal with its growing reliance on foreign oil would determine which of the two paths it followed. Energy dependence, according to the president, posed "a clear and present danger" to the nation, threatening the nation's security as well as its economic well-being. Dealing with this threat was "the standard around which we can rally." "On the battlefield of energy," declared Carter, "we can seize control again of our common destiny."

How to achieve this aim? In part, by restricting oil imports, investing in alternative sources, limiting the use of oil by the nation's utilities, and promoting public transportation. But Carter placed the larger burden squarely in the lap of the American people. The hollowing out of American democracy required a genuinely democratic response. "There is simply no way to avoid sacrifice," he insisted, calling on citizens as "an act of patriotism" to lower thermostats, observe the highway speed limit, use carpools, and "park your car one extra day per week."

Although Carter's stance was relentlessly inward looking, his analysis had important strategic implications. To the extent that "foreign oil" refers implicitly to the Persian Gulf—as it did then and does today—Carter was in essence proposing to annul the growing strategic importance attributed to that region. He sensed intuitively that a failure to reverse the nation's energy dependence was sure to draw the United States ever more deeply into the vortex of Persian Gulf politics, which, at best, would distract attention from the internal crisis that was his central concern, but was even more likely to exacerbate it.

But if Carter was prophetic when it came to the strategic implications of growing U.S. energy dependence, his policy prescription reflected a fundamental misreading of his fellow countrymen. Indeed, as Garry Wills has observed, given the country's propensity to define itself in terms of growth, it triggered "a subtle panic [and] claustrophobia" that Carter's political adversaries wasted no time in exploiting. By January 1980, it had become evident that any program summoning Americans to make do with less was a political nonstarter. The president accepted this verdict. The promulgation of the Carter Doctrine signaled his capitulation.

Carter's about-face did not achieve its intended political purpose of preserving his hold on the White House—Ronald Reagan had already tagged Carter as a pessimist, whose temperament was at odds with that of the rest of the country—but it did set in motion a huge shift in U.S. military policy, the implications of which gradually appeared over the course of the next two decades. Critics might cavil that the militarization of U.S. policy in the Persian Gulf amounted to a devil's bargain, trading blood for oil. Carter saw things differently. On the surface the exchange might entail blood for oil, but beneath the surface the aim was to guarantee the ever-increasing affluence that underwrites the modern American conception of liberty. Without exception, every one of Carter's successors has tacitly endorsed this formulation. Although the result was not fully apparent until the 1990s, changes in U.S. military posture and priorities gradually converted the gulf into the epicenter of American grand strategy and World War IV's principal theater of operations.

"Even if there were no Soviet Union," wrote the authors of NSC-68, the spring 1950 U.S. National Security Council document that became the definitive statement of America's Cold War grand strategy, "we would face the great problem of the free society, accentuated many fold in this industrial age, of reconciling order, security, the need for participation, with the requirement of freedom. We would face the fact that in a shrinking world the absence of order among nations is becoming less and less tolerable." Some three decades later, with the Soviet Union headed toward oblivion, the great problem of the free society to which NSC-68 alluded had become, if anything, more acute. But conceiving the principles to guide U.S. policy turned out to be a more daunting proposition in World War IV than it had been during any of the three previous world wars. Throughout the 1980s and 1990s, U.S. policymakers grappled with this challenge, reacting to crises as they occurred and then insisting after the fact that their actions conformed to some larger design. In fact, only after 9/11 did a fully articulated grand strategy take shape. George W. Bush saw the antidote to intolerable disorder as the transformation of the greater Middle East through the sustained use of military power.

Further complicating the challenge of devising a strategy for World War IV was the fundamental incompatibility of two competing U.S. interests in the region. The first was a steadily increasing dependence on oil from the Middle East. Dependence meant vulnerability, as the crippling oil shocks of the 1970s, administered by the Organization of Petroleum Exporting Countries (OPEC), amply demonstrated. As late as World War II, the United States had been the world's Saudi Arabia, producing enough oil to meet its own needs and those of its friends and allies. By the end of the 20th century, with Americans consuming one out of every four barrels of oil produced worldwide, the remaining U.S. reserves accounted for less than two percent of the world's total. Projections showed the leverage of Persian Gulf producers mushrooming in the years to come, with oil exports from the region expected to account for between 54 and 67 percent of world totals by 2020.

The second U.S. interest in the region, juxtaposed against Arab oil, was Israel. America's commitment to the security of the Jewish state complicated U.S. efforts to maintain cordial relations with oil-exporting states in the Persian Gulf. Before the Six-Day War (1967), the United States had tried to manage this problem by supporting Israel's right to exist but resisting Israeli entreaties to forge a strategic partnership. After 1967, that changed dramatically. The United States became Israel's preeminent international supporter and a generous supplier of economic and military assistance.

The Arab-Israeli conflict could not be separated from World War IV, but figuring out exactly where Israel fit in the larger struggle proved a perplexing problem for U.S. policymakers. Was World War IV a war of blood-for-oil-for-freedom in which Israel figured, at best, as a distraction and, at worst, as an impediment? Or was it a war of blood-for-oil-for-freedom in which the United States and Israel stood shoulder to shoulder in a common enterprise? For the first 20 years of World War IV, the American response to these questions produced a muddle.

During his final year in office, then, Carter initiated America's new world war. Through his typically hapless and ineffectual effort to rescue the Americans held hostage in Iran, he sprinkled the first few driblets of

American military power onto the surface of the desert, where they vanished without a trace. The rescue effort, dubbed Desert One, remained thereafter the gold standard for how not to use force, but it by no means curbed America's appetite for further armed intervention in the region. Ronald Reagan gave the spigot labeled "military power" a further twist—and in so doing, he opened the floodgates. Although Carter declared World War IV, the war was fully, if somewhat haphazardly, engaged only on Reagan's watch.

Reagan himself professed to be oblivious to the war's existence. After all, his immediate preoccupation was with World War III. For public consumption, the president was always careful to justify the U.S. military buildup of the 1980s as a benign and defensive response to Cold War imperatives. All that the United States sought was to be at peace. "Our country has never started a war," Reagan told the annual Veterans of Foreign Wars convention in 1983. "Our sole objective is deterrence, the strength and capability it takes to prevent war." "We Americans don't want war and we don't start fights," he insisted on another occasion. "We don't maintain a strong military force to conquer or coerce others."

This was, of course, at least 50 percent bunkum. During the Reagan era, with the first stirrings of revived American militancy, defense and deterrence seldom figured as the operative principles. In fact, the American military tradition has never viewed defense as anything other than a pause before seizing the initiative and taking the fight to the enemy.

Partisan critics saw Reagan's muscle flexing as the actions of a reckless ideologue unnecessarily stoking old Cold War tensions. Viewing events in relation to Vietnam and the Cuban Missile Crisis, they forecast dreadful consequences. Reagan's defenders, then and later, told a different story: Having intuitively grasped that the Soviet system was in an advanced state of decay, Reagan proceeded with skill and dexterity to exploit the system's economic, technological, and moral vulnerabilities; the ensuing collapse of the Soviet empire proved conclusively that Reagan had gotten things right. Today neither interpretation, Reagan as trigger-happy cold warrior or Reagan as master strategist, is especially persuasive. Assessing the military record of the Reagan years from a post–9/11 perspective yields a set of different and arguably more relevant insights.

Looking back, we can see that the entire Reagan era was situated on the seam between a world war that was winding down and another that had begun but was not yet fully comprehended. Although preoccupied with waging the Cold War, Reagan and his chief advisers, almost as an afterthought, launched four forays into the Islamic world, with mixed results: the insertion of U.S. Marine "peacekeepers" into Lebanon, culminating in the Beirut bombing of October 1983; clashes with Libya, culminating in punitive U.S. strikes against targets in Tripoli and Benghazi in April 1986;

the so-called tanker war of 1984–88, culminating in the commitment of U.S. forces to protect the flow of oil from the Persian Gulf; and American assistance throughout the 1980s to Afghan "freedom fighters," culminating in the Soviet army's ouster from Afghanistan. These actions greatly enhanced the ability of the United States to project military power into the region, but they also emboldened the enemy and contributed to the instability that drew Reagan's successors more deeply into the region.

The nominal stimulus for action in each case varied. In Lebanon, the murkiest of the four, Reagan ordered marines ashore at the end of September 1982 "to establish an environment which will permit the Lebanese Armed Forces to carry out their responsibilities in the Beirut area." This was a daunting proposition, given that Lebanon, divided by a civil war and variously occupied by the Syrian army, the Israeli Defense Forces, and (until its recent eviction) the Palestinian Liberation Organization, possessed neither an effective military nor an effective government and had little prospect of acquiring either. Vague expectations that a modest contingent of U.S. peacekeepers camped in Beirut might help restore stability to Lebanon motivated Reagan to undertake this risky intervention, which ended disastrously when a suicide bomber drove into the marine compound, killing 241 Americans.

In the case of Libya, Muammar al-Qaddafi's declared intention of denying the U.S. Sixth Fleet access to the Gulf of Sidra, off Libya's coast, had led to preliminary skirmishing in 1981 and again in March 1986. But it was Qaddafi's support for terrorism and, especially, alleged Libyan involvement in the bombing of a Berlin disco frequented by GIs that prompted Reagan to order retaliation.

In the tanker war, Reagan was reacting to attacks perpetrated by both Iran and Iraq against neutral shipping in the Persian Gulf. Since 1980, the two nations had been locked in an inconclusive conflict. As that struggle spilled over into the adjacent waters of the gulf, it reduced the availability of oil for export, drove up insurance rates, and crippled merchant shipping. An Iraqi missile attack on the USS *Stark* on May 17, 1987, brought things to a head. Iraq claimed that the incident, which killed 37 sailors, had been an accident, and offered compensation. The Reagan administration used the *Stark* episode to blame Iran for the escalating violence. In short order, Kuwaiti supertankers were flying the Stars and Stripes, and U.S. forces were conducting a brisk campaign to sweep Iranian air and naval units out of the gulf.

In the case of Afghanistan, Reagan built on a program already in existence but hidden from public view. In July 1979, the Carter administration had agreed to provide covert assistance to Afghans resisting the pro-Soviet regime in Kabul. According to Zbigniew Brzezinski, Carter's national security adviser, the aim was to induce a Soviet military response, thereby "drawing the Russians into the Afghan trap." When the Soviets did invade, in December 1979, they became bogged down in a guerrilla war against the U.S.-backed mujahideen. Reagan inherited this project, initially sustained it, and then, in 1985, greatly stepped up the level of U.S. support for the Afghan resistance.

At first glance, these four episodes seem to be all over the map, literally and in terms of purpose, means, and outcome. Contemporaneous assessments tended to treat each in isolation from the others and to focus on near-term outcomes. "After the attack on Tripoli," Reagan bragged, "we didn't hear much more from Qaddafi's terrorists." Nonsense, replied critics, pointing to the suspected Libyan involvement (since confirmed) in the bombing of Pan American flight 103 in December 1988 and in the midair destruction of a French DC-10 nine months later. When a ceasefire in 1988 ended the fighting between Iran and Iraq, Secretary of Defense Caspar Weinberger assessed U.S. involvement in the tanker war as a major achievement. "We had now clearly won," he wrote in 1990. With several hundred thousand U.S. troops deploying to the gulf that very same year to prepare for large-scale war, Weinberger's claims of victory seemed, at best, premature.

To be sure, Reagan himself labored to weave together a comprehensive rationale for the various military actions he ordered, but the result amounted to an exercise in mythmaking. To listen to him, all these disparate threats—Soviet leaders pursuing global revolution, fundamentalists bent on propagating Islamic theocracies, Arab fascists such as Libya's Qaddafi and Syria's Hafez al-Assad, fanatical terrorists such as Abu Nidal—morphed into a single conspiracy. To give way to one element of that conspiracy was to give way to all, so the essential thing was to hold firm everywhere for peace.

Further muddying the waters were administration initiatives seemingly predicated on an assumption that no such overarching conspiracy against peace actually existed, or at least that selective U.S. collaboration with evil-doers was permissible. The Reagan administration's notorious "tilt" toward Saddam Hussein in the Iran-Iraq War, offering intelligence and commercial credits to the region's foremost troublemaker—perhaps the final U.S. effort to enlist a proxy to secure its Persian Gulf interests—provides one example. Such opportunism made a mockery of Reagan's windy pronouncements regarding America's role as peacemaker and fed suspicions that the president's rhetoric was actually intended to divert attention from his administration's apparent strategic disarray.

Considered from a post-9/11 vantage point, however, Reagan-era uses of force in Lebanon, Libya, Afghanistan, and the tanker war do cohere, at least in a loose sort of way. First, and most notably, all four initiatives occurred in the greater Middle East, hitherto not the site of frequent U.S. military activity. Second, none of the four episodes can be fully understood except in relation to America's growing dependence on imported oil. Although energy considerations did not drive U.S. actions in every instance, they always loomed in the background. Lebanon, for example, was not itself an oil exporter, but its woes mattered to the United States because instability there threatened to undermine the precarious stability of the region as a whole.

The four episodes constituting Reagan's Islamic quartet were alike in one other way. Although each yielded a near-term outcome that the administration touted as conclusive, the actual results turned out to be anything but. Rather, each of the four pointed toward ever-deepening American military engagement.

The true significance of Reagan's several interventions in the Islamic world lies not in the events themselves but in the response they evoked from the U.S. national security apparatus. A consensus emerged that, in the list of pressing U.S. geopolitical concerns, the challenges posed by the politically volatile, energy-rich world of Islam were eclipsing all others, including the size of the Soviet nuclear arsenal and the putative ambitions of the Soviet politburo. Given the imperative of meeting popular expectations for ever-greater abundance (which meant importing ever-larger quantities of oil)— Jimmy Carter's one-term presidency having demonstrated the political consequences of suggesting a different course—the necessary response was to put the United States in a position to determine the fate of the Middle East. That meant forces, bases, and infrastructure. Only by enjoying unquestioned primacy in the region could the government of the United States guarantee American prosperity—and thus American freedom.

From the outset, *dominance* was the aim and the driving force behind U.S. actions in World War IV—not preventing the spread of weapons of mass destruction, not stemming the spread of terror, certainly not liberating oppressed peoples or advancing the cause of women's rights. The prize was mastery over a region that leading members of the American foreign-policy elite, of whatever political persuasion, had concluded was critically important to the well-being of the United States. The problem, at its very core, demanded a military solution.

In March 1984, Donald Rumsfeld, out of power but serving as a Reagan administration troubleshooter, told Secretary of State George Shultz that Lebanon was a mere "sideshow." The main show was the Persian Gulf; instability there "could make Lebanon look like a taffy pull." According to Shultz's memoir, *Turmoil and Triumph* (1993), Rumsfeld worried that "we are neither organized nor ready to face a crisis there." In fact, the effort to reorganize was already under way. And here is where Reagan made his most lasting contribution to the struggle to which Jimmy Carter had committed the United States.

Seven specific initiatives figured prominently in the Reagan administration's comprehensive effort to ramp up America's ability to wage World War IV:

• The upgrading in 1983 of the Rapid Deployment Joint Task Force, the Persian Gulf intervention force created by Carter after the Soviet incursion

into Afghanistan, to the status of a full-fledged regional headquarters, U.S. Central Command.
- The accelerated conversion of Diego Garcia, a tiny British-owned island in the Indian Ocean, from a minor U.S. communications facility into a major U.S. forward support base.
- The establishment of large stocks of supplies and equipment, preloaded on ships and positioned to facilitate the rapid movement of U.S. combat forces to the Persian Gulf.
- The construction or expansion of airbases, ports, and other fixed locations required to receive and sustain large-scale U.S. expeditionary forces in Egypt, Saudi Arabia, Oman, Kenya, Somalia, and other compliant states.
- The negotiation of overflight rights and agreements to permit U.S. military access to airports and other facilities in Morocco, Egypt, and elsewhere in the region to support the large-scale introduction of U.S. troops.
- The refinement of war plans and the development of exercise programs to acclimate U.S. forces to the unfamiliar and demanding desert environment.
- The redoubling of efforts to cultivate client states through arms sales and training programs, the latter administered either by the U.S. military or by American-controlled private contractors employing large numbers of former U.S. military personnel.

By the time Ronald Reagan retired from office, the skids had been greased. The national security bureaucracy was well on its way to embracing a highly militarized conception of how to deal with the challenges posed by the Middle East. Giving Reagan his due requires an appreciation of the extent to which he advanced the reordering of U.S. national security priorities that Jimmy Carter had barely begun. Reagan's seemingly slapdash Islamic pudding turned out to have a theme after all.

Those who adjudge the present World War IV to be necessary and winnable will see in Reagan's record much to commend, and may well accord him a share of the credit even for Operations Enduring Freedom and Iraqi Freedom. It was Reagan who restored the sinews of American military might after Vietnam, refashioned American attitudes about military power, and began reorienting the Pentagon toward the Islamic world, thereby making possible the far-flung campaigns to overthrow the Taliban and remove Saddam Hussein. George W. Bush pulled the trigger, but Ronald Reagan had cocked the weapon.

Those who view World War IV as either sinister in its motivation or misguided in its conception will include Reagan in their bill of indictment. From their perspective, it was he who seduced his fellow citizens with promises of material abundance without limit. It was Reagan who made the fusion of military strength with American exceptionalism the centerpiece of his efforts to revive national self-confidence. It was Reagan's enthusiastic support of Afghan "freedom fighters"—an eminently defensible position in the context of World War III—that produced not freedom but a Central Asian power vacuum, Afghanistan becoming a cesspool of Islamic radicalism and a safe haven for America's chief adversary in World War IV. Finally, it was Reagan's inconclusive forays in and around the Persian Gulf that paved the way for still-larger, if equally inconclusive, interventions to come.

Throughout the first phase of World War IV, from 1980 to 1990, the United States viewed Iran as its main problem and even toyed with the idea that Iraq might be part of a solution. Washington saw Saddam Hussein as someone with whom it might make common cause against the mullahs in Tehran. During the second phase of World War IV, extending through the 1990s, Iraq supplanted Iran as the main U.S. adversary, and policymakers came to see the Iraqi dictator as their chief nemesis.

Various and sundry exertions ensued, but as the U.S. military profile in the region became ever more prominent, the difficulties with which the United States felt obliged to contend also multiplied. Indeed, instead of eliminating Saddam, the growing reliance on military power served only to rouse greater antagonism toward the United States. Actions taken to enhance Persian Gulf stability—more or less synonymous with guaranteeing the safety and survival of the Saudi royal family—instead produced instability.

Phase two of the war began in August 1990, when Saddam Hussein's army overran Kuwait. From the U.S. perspective, Saddam's aim was clear. He sought to achieve regional hegemony and to control, either directly or indirectly, the preponderant part of the Persian Gulf's oil wealth. Were Saddam to achieve those objectives, there was every likelihood that in due course he would turn on Israel.

So after only the briefest hesitation, the administration of George H. W. Bush mounted a forthright response. At the head of a large international coalition, the nation marched off to war, and U.S. forces handily ejected the Iraqi occupiers and restored the Al-Sabah family to its throne. (Bowing to American pressure, Israel stayed on the sidelines.) Its assigned mission accomplished, the officer corps, led by Colin Powell, had little interest in pressing its luck. The American army was eager to scoop up its winnings and go home.

The elder President Bush dearly hoped that Operation Desert Storm might become a great historical watershed, laying the basis for a more law-abiding international system. In fact, the war turned out to be both less and more than he had anticipated. No new world order emerged from the demonstration of American military prowess, but the war saddled the United States with new obligations from which came yet more headaches and complications.

Saddam survived in power by brutally suppressing those whom the Bush administration had urged to rise up in opposition to the dictator. After first averting its eyes from the fate of the Iraqi Shiites and Kurds, the administration eventually found itself shamed into action. To protect the Kurds (and to prevent Kurdish refugees from triggering a military response by neighboring Turkey, a key U.S. ally), Bush sent U.S. forces into northern Iraq. To limit Saddam's ability to use his army as an instrument of repression, the Bush administration, with British support, declared the existence of "no-fly zones" across much of northern and southern Iraq. In April 1991, Anglo-American air forces began routine combat patrols of Iraqi airspace, a mission that continued without interruption for the next 12 years. During his final weeks in office, Bush initiated the practice of launching punitive air strikes against Iraqi military targets.

Thus, in the year that followed what had appeared to be a decisive victory in Operation Desert Storm, the United States transitioned willy-nilly to a policy that seemed anything but decisive. As a result of that policy, which the Bush administration called "containment," the presence of substantial U.S. forces in Saudi Arabia and elsewhere in the Persian Gulf, initially conceived as temporary, became permanent. A contingent of approximately 25,000 U.S. troops remained after Desert Storm as a Persian Gulf constabulary—or, from the perspective of many Arabs, as an occupying army of infidels. As a second result of the policy, the United States fell into the habit of routinely employing force to punish the Iraqi regime. What U.S. policymakers called containment was really an open-ended quasi-war.

This new policy of containment-with-bombs formed just one part of the legacy that President Bush bequeathed to his successor, Bill Clinton. That legacy had two additional elements. The first was Somalia, the impoverished, chaotic, famine-stricken Islamic "failed state" into which Bush sent U.S. forces after his defeat in the November 1992 elections. Bush described the U.S. mission as humanitarian, and promised to have American troops out of the country by the time he left office. But when Clinton became president, the troops remained in place. The second element of the legacy Clinton inherited was the so-called peace process, Bush's post–Desert Storm initiative aimed at persuading the Arab world once and for all to accept Israel.

President Clinton was unable to extract from this ambiguous legacy much of tangible value, though not for want of trying. During his eight years in office, he clung to the Bush policy of containing Iraq while ratcheting up the frequency with which the United States used violence to enforce that policy. Indeed, during the two final years of his presidency, the United States bombed Iraq on almost a daily basis. The campaign was largely ignored by the media, and thus aptly dubbed by one observer "Operation Desert Yawn."

In the summer of 1993, Clinton had also ratcheted up the U.S. military commitment in Somalia. The results proved disastrous. After the famous Mogadishu firefight of October 1993, Clinton quickly threw in the towel, tacitly accepting defeat at the hands of Islamic fighters. Somalia per se mattered little. Somalia as a battlefield of World War IV mattered quite a bit. The speedy U.S. withdrawal after Mogadishu affirmed to many the apparent lesson of Beirut a decade earlier: Americans lacked the stomach for real fighting; if seriously challenged, they would fold. That was certainly the lesson Osama bin Laden drew. In his August 1996 fatwa against the United States, he cited the failure of U.S. policy in Lebanon as evidence of America's "false courage," and he found in Somalia proof of U.S. "impotence and weaknesses." When "tens of your soldiers were killed in minor battles and one American pilot was dragged in the streets of Mogadishu," crowed the leader of Al Qaeda, "you left the area, carrying disappointment, humiliation, defeat, and your dead with you."

From Mogadishu onward, the momentum shifted inexorably in favor of those contesting American efforts to dominate the gulf. For the balance of the Clinton era, the United States found itself in a reactive posture, and it sustained a series of minor but painful and painfully embarrassing setbacks: the bombing of SANG headquarters in Riyadh in November 1995; an attack on the U.S. military barracks at Khobar Towers in Dhahran in June 1996; simultaneous attacks on U.S. embassies in Kenya and Tanzania in August 1998; and the near-sinking of an American warship, the USS *Cole*, during a port call at Aden in August 2000.

To each of these in turn, the Clinton administration promised a prompt, decisive response, but such responses as actually materialized proved innocuous. The low point came in late August 1998, after the African embassy bombings. With the United States combating what Bill Clinton referred to as "the bin Laden network," the president ordered cruise missile strikes against a handful of primitive training camps in Afghanistan. For good measure, he included as an additional target a Sudanese pharmaceutical factory allegedly involved in the production of chemical weapons. Unfortunately for Clinton, the training camps turned out to be mostly empty, while subsequent investigation cast doubt on whether the factory in Khartoum had ever housed any nefarious activity. Although the president spoke grimly of a "long, ongoing struggle between freedom and fanaticism," and vowed that the United States was "prepared to do all that we can for as long as we must," the operation, given the code name Infinite Reach, accomplished next to nothing, and was over almost as soon as it began. The disparity between words and actions—between the operation's grandiose name and its trivial impact—spoke volumes. In truth, no one in the Clinton White House had a clear conception of what the United States needed to do—or to whom.

Finally, despite Clinton's energetic and admirable contributions, the peace process failed to yield peace. Instead, the collapse of that process at Camp David in 2000 gave rise to a new cycle of Palestinian terrorist attacks and Israeli reprisals. An alienated Arab world convinced itself that the United States and Israel were conspiring to humiliate and oppress Muslims.

Just as the Israeli Defense Forces occupied Gaza and the West Bank, so too did the U.S. military seemingly intend to occupy the Middle East as a whole. In Arab eyes, the presence of U.S. troops amounted to "a new American colonialism," an expression of a larger effort to "seek control over Arab political and economic affairs." And just as Israel appeared callous in its treatment of the Palestinians, so too did the United States seem callous in its attitude toward Iraqis by persisting in a policy of sanctions that put the burden of punishment not on Saddam Hussein but on the Iraqi people.

The end of the 1980s had found the Reagan administration engaged in a far-reaching contest for control of the Middle East, a de facto war whose existence Reagan himself either could not see or was unwilling to acknowledge. Ten years later, events ought to have removed any doubt as to whether the circumstances facing the United States qualified as a war, but the Clinton administration's insistence on describing the adversary as disembodied "terrorists" robbed those events of any coherent political context. In the manner of his immediate predecessors, Clinton refused to concede that the violence directed against the United States might stem from some plausible (which is not to imply justifiable) motivation—even as Osama bin Laden outlined his intentions with impressive clarity. In his 1996 declaration of jihad, for example, bin Laden identified his objectives: to overthrow the corrupt Saudi regime that had become a tool of the "Zionist-Crusader alliance," to expel the infidels from the land of the Two Holy Places, and to ensure the worldwide triumph of Islam. But his immediate aim was more limited: to destroy the compact forged by President Roosevelt and King Ibn Saud. A perfectly logical first step toward that end was to orchestrate a campaign of terror against the United States.

For Clinton to acknowledge bin Laden's agenda was to acknowledge as well that opposition to the U.S. presence in and around the Persian Gulf had a history, and that, like all history, it was fraught with ambiguity. In the Persian Gulf, the United States had behaved just like any other nation, even as it proclaimed itself democracy's greatest friend. For decades it had single-mindedly pursued its own interests, with only occasional regard for how its actions affected others. Expediency dictated that American policymakers avert their eyes from the fact that throughout much of the Islamic world the United States had aligned itself with regimes that were arbitrary, corrupt, and oppressive. The underside of American exceptionalism lay exposed.

In the annals of statecraft, U.S. policy in the Persian Gulf from FDR through Clinton did not qualify as having been notably harsh or irresponsible, but neither had it been particularly wise or enlightened. Bin Laden's campaign, however contemptible, and more general opposition to U.S. ambitions in the greater Middle East, developed at least in part as a response to earlier U.S. policies and actions, in which lofty ideals and high moral purpose seldom figured. The United States cannot be held culpable for the maladies that today find expression in violent Islamic radicalism. But neither can the United States absolve itself of any and all responsibility for the conditions that have exacerbated those maladies. After several decades of acting as the preeminent power in the Persian Gulf, America did not arrive at the end of the 20th century with clean hands.

Years before 9/11, bin Laden understood that World War IV had been fully joined, and he seems to have rejoiced in the prospect of a fight to the finish. Even as they engaged in an array of military activities intended to deflect threats to U.S. control of the Persian Gulf and its environs, a succession of American presidents persisted in pretending otherwise. For them, World War IV remained a furtive enterprise.

Unlike Franklin Roosevelt, who had deceived the American people but who understood long before December 7, 1941, that he was steadily moving the United States toward direct engagement in a monumental struggle, the lesser statesmen who inhabited the Oval Office during the 1980s and 1990s, in weaving their deceptions, managed only to confuse themselves. Despite endless assertions that the United States sought only peace, Presidents Reagan, Bush, and Clinton were each in fact waging war. But a coherent strategy for bringing the war to a successful conclusion eluded them.

Even as it flung about bombs and missiles with abandon, the United States seemed to dither throughout the 1990s, whereas bin Laden, playing a weak hand, played it with considerable skill. In the course of the decade, World War IV became bigger and the costs mounted, but its resolution was more distant than ever. The Bush and Clinton administrations used force in the Middle East not so much as an extension of policy but as a way of distracting attention from the contradictions that riddled U.S. policy. Bombing *something*—at times, almost *anything*—became a convenient way of keeping up appearances. Thus, despite (or perhaps because of) the military hyperactivity of the two administrations, the overall U.S. position deteriorated even further during World War IV's second phase.

George W. Bush inherited this deteriorating situation when he became president in January 2001. Bush may or may not have brought into office a determination to finish off Saddam Hussein at the first available opportunity, but he most assuredly did not bring with him a comprehensive, ready-made conception of how to deal with the incongruities that plagued U.S. policy in the greater Middle East. For its first eight months in office, the second Bush administration essentially marked time. Apart from some politically inspired grandstanding—shunning an international agreement to slow global warming, talking tough on North Korea, accelerating plans to field ballistic missile defenses—Bush's foreign policy before 9/11 hewed closely to the lines laid down by his predecessor. Although Republicans had spent the previous eight years lambasting Clinton for being weak and feckless, their own approach to World War IV, initially at least, amounted to more of the same.

Osama bin Laden chose this moment to begin the war's third phase. His direct assault on the United States left thousands dead, wreaked havoc with the American economy, and exposed the acute vulnerabilities of the world's sole superpower.

President Bush's spontaneous response to the events of 9/11 was to see them not as vile crimes but as acts of war. In so doing, he openly acknowledged the existence of the conflict in which the United States had been engaged for the previous 20 years. World War IV became the centerpiece of the Bush presidency, although the formulation preferred by members of his administration was "the global war on terror."

When committing the United States to large-scale armed conflict, presidents have traditionally evinced a strong preference for explaining the stakes in terms of ideology, thereby distracting attention from geopolitics. Americans ostensibly fight for universal values rather than sordid self-interest. Thus, Franklin Roosevelt cast the war against Japan as a contest that pitted democracy against imperialism. The Pacific war was indeed that, but it was also a war fought to determine the future of East Asia, with both Japan and the United States seeing China as the main prize. Harry Truman and his successors characterized the Cold War as a struggle between a free world and a totalitarian one. Again, the war was that, but it was also a competition to determine which of two superpowers would enjoy preponderant influence in Western Europe, with both the Soviet Union and the United States viewing Germany as the nexus of conflict.

During its preliminary phases—from January 1980 to September 2001—World War IV departed from this pattern. Regardless of who happened to be occupying the Oval Office, universal values did not figure prominently in the formulation and articulation of U.S. policy in the Persian Gulf. Geopolitics routinely trumped values in the war. Everyone knew that the dominant issue was oil, with Saudi Arabia understood to be the crown jewel. Only after 9/11 did values emerge as the ostensible driving force behind U.S. efforts in the region—indeed, throughout the greater Middle East. On September 11, 2001, World War IV became, like each of its predecessors, a war for "freedom." To this theme President George W. Bush has returned time and again.

In fact, President Bush's epiphany was itself a smoke screen. His conversion to the church of Woodrow Wilson left substantive U.S. objectives in World War IV unaltered. Using armed might to secure American preeminence across the region, especially in the oil-rich Persian Gulf, remained the essence of U.S. policy. What changed after 9/11 was that the Bush administration was willing to pull out all the stops in its determination to impose America's will on the greater Middle East.

In that regard, the administration's invasion of Iraq in March 2003 can be said to possess a certain bizarre logic. As part of a larger campaign to bring the perpetrators of 9/11 to justice, Operation Iraqi Freedom made no sense at all and was probably counterproductive. Yet as the initial gambit of an effort to transform the entire region through the use of superior military power, it not only made sense but also held out the prospect of finally resolving the incongruities bedeviling U.S. policy. Iraq was the "tactical pivot"—not an end in itself but a way station. "With Saddam gone," former counter-terrorism official Richard Clarke has written in *Against All Enemies* (2004), "the U.S. could reduce its dependence on Saudi Arabia, could pull its forces out of the Kingdom, and could open up an alternative source of oil."

Pulling U.S. forces out of Saudi Arabia did not imply removing them from the region; a continuing American troop presence was necessary to guarantee U.S. access to energy reserves. But having demonstrated its ability to oust recalcitrants, having established a mighty striking force in the center of the Persian Gulf, and having reduced its susceptibility to the oil weapon, the United States would be well positioned to create a new political order in the region, incorporating values such as freedom, democracy, and equality for women. A Middle East pacified, brought into compliance with American ideological norms, and policed by American soldiers could be counted on to produce plentiful supplies of oil and to accept the presence of a Jewish state in its midst. "In transforming Iraq," one senior Bush administration official confidently predicted, "we will take a significant step in the direction of the longer-term need to transform the region as a whole."

Bush and his inner circle conceived of this as a great crusade, and, at its unveiling, a clear majority of citizens also judged the preposterous enterprise to be justifiable, feasible, and indeed necessary. At least two factors help to explain their apparent gullibility.

The first is self-induced historical amnesia. Shortly after 9/11, Deputy Secretary of State Richard Armitage growled that "history starts today." His sentiment suffused the Bush administration and was widely shared among the American people. The grievous losses suffered in the attacks on the World Trade Center and the Pentagon had rendered irrelevant all that went before—hence the notable absence of interest among Americans in how the modern Middle East had come into existence, or in the role the United States had played since World War II in its evolution. The events of 9/11 wiped the slate clean, and on this clean slate the Bush administration, in quintessential American fashion, fancied that it could begin the history of the greater Middle East all over again.

There is a second explanation for this extraordinary confidence in America's ability to reorder nations according to its own preferences. The progressive militarization of U.S. policy since Vietnam—especially U.S. policy as it related to the Middle East—had acquired a momentum to which the events of 9/11 only added. The aura that by 2001 had come to suffuse American attitudes toward war, soldiers, and military institutions had dulled the capacity of the American people to think critically about the actual limits of military power. And nowhere had those attitudes gained a deeper lodgment than in the upper echelons of the younger Bush's administration. The experiences of the previous 30 years had thoroughly militarized the individuals to whom the president turned in shaping his global war on terror, formulating grand statements, such as his *National Security Strategy of the United States of America,* and planning campaigns, such as the invasions of Afghanistan and Iraq. Theirs was a vision, writes James Mann in *The Rise of the Vulcans* (2004), of "a United States whose military power was so awesome that it no longer needed to make compromises or accommodations (unless it chose to do so) with any other nation or groups of countries."

As the epigraph to his book *Why We Were in Vietnam* (1982), Norman Podhoretz chose a quotation from Bismarck: "Woe to the statesman whose reasons for entering a war do not appear so plausible at its end as at its beginning." For the architects of the global war on terror—George W. Bush, Dick Cheney, Donald Rumsfeld, Condoleezza Rice, and Paul Wolfowitz—it's too late to heed the Iron Chancellor's warning. But the outsized conflict that is their principal handiwork continues.

As this is written, the outcome of World War IV hangs very much in the balance. American shortsightedness played a large role in creating this war, and American hubris has complicated it unnecessarily, emboldening the enemy, alienating old allies, and bringing U.S. forces close to exhaustion. Yet like it or not, Americans are now stuck with their misbegotten crusade. God forbid that the United States should fail, allowing the likes of Osama bin Laden and his henchmen to decide the future of the Islamic world.

But even if the United States ultimately prevails, the prospects for the future will be no less discouraging. On the far side of World War IV, a time we are not now given to see, there wait others who will not readily concede to the United States the prerogatives and the dominion that Americans have come to expect as their due. The ensuing collision between American requirements and a noncompliant world will provide the impetus for more crusades. Each will be justified in terms of ideals rather than interests, but the sum of them may well doom the United States to fight perpetual wars in a vain effort to satisfy our craving for limitless freedom.   ■

■ *QUESTIONS FOR MAKING CONNECTIONS WITHIN THE READING* ■

1. Bacevich asserts that he will provide "a true account of World War IV," one that places it in "its correct relationship to World War III, the Cold War." How does Bacevich's account differ from Norman Podhoretz's? What makes Bacevich believe that his version is the true one?

2. Traditionally, history is understood as an objective account of the past grounded in the facts. Bacevich, though, sees all history "as fraught with ambiguity." Where do you see evidence in Bacevich's account of such ambiguity? Is it possible to be objective while presenting a version of history that acknowledges ambiguity? Does Bacevich's self-described "messier" narrative produce a version of history that is more believable, more accurate, or just more confusing?

3. Bacevich begins by defining "the ultimate U.S. interest" as "the removal of any obstacles or encumbrances that might hinder the American people in their pursuit of happiness ever more expansively defined." He concludes with the prospect of "perpetual wars" fought "in our vain effort to satisfy our craving for limitless freedom." The "pursuit of happiness ever more expansively defined" and the pursuit of "limitless freedom" seem like attractive goals, but Bacevich is troubled by them for reasons he doesn't state outright. How could America's pursuit of happiness and freedom have negative consequences? If these aren't the goals that should be driving American foreign policy, what are the alternatives?

■ *QUESTIONS FOR WRITING* ■

1. Bacevich does not conceal his dissatisfaction with American foreign policy and with the American citizenry in general. For example, he argues that "a clear majority of citizens" saw "the preposterous enterprise [of the invasion of Iraq] to be justifiable, feasible, and indeed necessary." If Americans really held this view, what made it so appealing? Why does Bacevich think that leaders from both parties have seized "opportunities for massive stupidity" over the past 40 years? What would change if people accepted Bacevich's position on the root cause of the current endless war on terror?

2. What is the difference between viewing the events of September 11 as "vile crimes" rather than as "acts of war"? What would have been gained by seeing September 11 as a crime? What would have been lost? Given Bacevich's reading of the past, would it have been possible for America's leaders or the American public to accept the representation of September 11 as a "crime"? What do you think would it have taken to make this view of September 11 the dominant view?

■ *QUESTIONS FOR MAKING CONNECTIONS BETWEEN READINGS* ■

1. In "A World on Edge," Amy Chua argues that "market-dominant minorities are the Achilles' heel of free-market democracy" because their success inspires resentment that leads to instability and violence. Given

Chua's assessment, is it advisable for the United States to abandon the "progressive militarization of U.S. policy since Vietnam," as Bacevich recommends? If the United States began to support a great degree of international cooperation, would this approach serve to defuse tensions created by class differences and economic inequalities, or might it actually worsen those tensions by making America's wealth and power even more frustratingly obvious? Is the solution to the problem Chua has identified to be found in Bacevich's analysis of the U. S. role in shaping the current global unrest?

2. Throughout his essay, Bacevich offers a view of Americans and their leaders as settling for answers that are simple, straightforward, and ill-informed. At one point, he says both groups have "a demonstrable preference for clarity rather than nuance." William Greider, on the other hand, has great faith in the leadership potential of American employees. "[D]oes anyone doubt that, if employees acquired such self-governing powers, the terms of work would be reformed drastically in American business? Or that, it they owned the enterprise together, the rewards and risks would be reallocated in more equitable ways?" What leads Bacevich and Greider to have such opposed views on the preferences and the potentials of Americans? Do they bring these views to their arguments or do their views arise out of their research? Are these views of the average American fictions or descriptions of reality?

JONATHAN BOYARIN

JONATHAN BOYARIN IS an anthropologist and an ethnographer who has studied the lifestyle and culture of Jews all over the world. Though anthropology originally emerged as a way for outsiders to study and understand foreign cultures, the anthropology that Boyarin practices is of a different sort: he is providing an insider's view of cultures and traditions that are, in some ways, his own. Thus, Boyarin's fieldwork on Jewish identity and tradition in Paris, New York, and Jerusalem is not simply descriptive; it has been pursued in the interests of both defining and preserving Jewish culture. Boyarin's research has led him to participate in the effort to revive the Yiddish language, both as an advocate and as a translator, and to provide an historical and scholarly record of the role that Jewish intellectuals and religious leaders have played in the development of Western civilization. And it has also led him, as "Waiting for a Jew" chronicles, to invent a "funky Orthodox" Jewish identity for himself.

Considered one of America's most original thinkers about Jewish culture, Boyarin has written extensively about the roles that history, memory, and geography have played in the formation of Jewish identity. In *A Storm from Paradise: The Politics of Jewish Memory* (1992), *Thinking in Jewish* (1996), *Palestine and Jewish History: Criticism at the Borders of Ethnography* (1996), and *Powers of Diaspora* (2002), Boyarin asks his readers to consider whether or not there is such a thing as an "essential" Jewish identity. (Identity, for Boyarin, is a family enterprise; he co-wrote the last of these books with brother Daniel Boyarin, who is also a student of Jewish culture past and present.) While the notion that there is an essential, unchanging self at the core of every human being has fallen out of favor in academic circles, Boyarin bids his readers to recognize that identity does not serve the same function for marginalized groups that it serves for dominant groups. As Boyarin puts it in *Remapping Memory: The Politics of TimeSpace* (1994), "For people who are somehow part of a dominant group, any assertions of essence are ipso facto products and reproducers of the system of domination. For subaltern groups, however, essentialism is resistance, the insistence on the 'right' of

Boyarin, Jonathan. "Waiting for a Jew: Marginal Redemption at the Eighth Street Shul." *Thinking in Jewish*. Chicago: University of Chicago Press, 1996. 8–34.

the group actually to exist." As "Waiting for a Jew" documents, answering the question "Who are you?" is not as simple as it might seem, for the answer requires that one first consider the histories, traditions, and communal life experiences that have made the notions of "an identity" and "one's own identity" possible.

Waiting for a Jew
Marginal Redemption at the Eighth Street Shul

My story begins in a community, with an illusion of wholeness. I am between the age when consciousness begins and the age of ten, when my family leaves the community and my illusion is shattered. Our family lives on the edge of the Pine Barrens in Farmingdale, New Jersey, along with hundreds of other families of Jewish chicken farmers who have come from Europe and New York City in several waves, beginning just after World War I.

Among the farmers are present and former Communists, Bundists, Labor Zionists, German refugees who arrived in the 1930s, and Polish survivors of concentration camps. These, however, are not the distinctions I make among them as a child. Johannes Fabian has shown us that when we write ethnography we inevitably trap those about whom we write into a hypostatic, categorical, grammatical "present" (Fabian 1983). An autobiographer has the same power over the memory of himself and those he knew in prior times as the fieldworker who later obliterates the narrative aspect of his encounter with his subjects—the power to deny their autonomy in hindsight.[1] Those of the farming community whom I will later remember, I know therefore by their own names and places: my grandparents closer to Farmingdale proper; the Silbers off on Yellowbrook Road, with a tree nursery now instead of chickens; the Lindauers, stubbornly maintaining an egg-packing and -distribution business, while others find different ways to earn a living.

My child's world is not exclusively Jewish, nor am I brought up to regard it as such. Across our road and down a few hundred yards is a tiny house built by Jewish farmers when they first came to settle here. It is now, incredibly, occupied by a black family of ten. Next to them lives an equally poor and large white family. Shortly before we leave Farmingdale, the old Jew in the farm next to ours passes away, and the property passes to a Japanese businessman. The young men he hires live in the farmhouse, growing oriental vegetables on the open field and bonsai in a converted chicken coop, and they introduce me to the game of Go. The nearest Jewish household is that of my great-uncle Yisroel and his wife Helen, the third house to the right of ours.

Yet we are near the heart of Jewish life in Farmingdale. Half a mile—but no, it must be less—down Peskin's Lane (the name my grandfather Israel Boyarin gave to what was a dirt road in the 1930s) is the Farmingdale Jewish Community Center, on the next plot of land after Uncle Yisroel's house. Just past the community center is the farm that once belonged to my father's uncle Peskin, the first Jew in Farmingdale. Fifteen years after Peskin's death, the bodies of two gangsters were found buried on the farm. The local papers noted: "Mr. Peskin was not available for comment."

Our own farm consists of eleven acres. Facing the road is the house my grandfather built, with a large front lawn and an apple tree in back. Farther back, four large chicken coops mark the slope of a hill ending in our field, behind which woods conceal the tiny Manasquan River. The field, well fertilized by chickens allowed to scratch freely on it during the day, is leased each summer by a dirt farmer who grows corn. My father has joined the insurance agency begun by my mother, and they have gotten rid of the birds. The coops stand empty by my fourth birthday. One day, though, while a friend and I chase each other through the coops in play, we are startled by a pair of chickens. Their presence in the stillness and the faint smell of ancient manure is inexplicable and unforgettable. Thus, on the abandoned farm, my first memories are tinged with a sense of traces, of mystery, of loss. Do all who eventually become anthropologists have this experience in some form, at some time in their early lives?

My mother's turn to business is wise: chicken farming as the basis for the community's livelihood is quickly becoming untenable. Nor is it surprising, as she had given up a career as a chemist to come live with my father on the farm—thus taking part in the process of Jewish dispersal from the immigrants' urban centers, which in the last quarter of the century would be mirrored by a shrinking of Jewish communities in small towns and a reconsolidation of the Orthodox centers. My mother's father, an Orthodox Jew from a leading Lithuanian rabbinical family, has struggled to learn English well and has gone into the insurance business himself. After his death, my mother tells me that he had originally resisted her desire to marry the son of a Jewish socialist, but he consented when he met my father's father's father, a Lubavitcher Hasid named Mordechai.

My grandfather's concern for his daughter's future as an observant Jew was well founded. The Sabbath is marked in our family only on Friday nights: by my mother's candle-lighting, and her chicken soup in winter; by the challah; by the presence of my grandfather. We do not keep kosher, nor do we go to shul on *shabbes*.

The Jewish Community Center—with its various functions as social and meeting hall, synagogue, and school—is nevertheless a focus of our family's life. Most of the ten or so other children in these classes I see at other times during the week as well, either in public school or playing at one another's homes. I am there three times each week, first for Sunday school, and then for Hebrew school on Tuesday and Thursday afternoons. This odd distinction is no doubt a practical one, since some parents do not choose to send their children three times a week. But since Sunday school was first a Christian institution, it also reflects an accommodation to Christian church patterns, as evidenced by the fact that Sundays are devoted to teaching stories of the Bible. One Sunday school teacher we have in our kindergarten year captivates me with his skill in making these stories come to life, as when he imitates the distress of an Egyptian waking up to find his bed covered with frogs.

Another teacher, a young woman with a severe manner and a heavy black wig, the wife of a member of the Orthodox yeshiva in Lakewood, later causes general misery because of her inability to understand children, although I will eventually appreciate the prayers she teaches us to read. One time I come in to Hebrew school immediately after yet another in a series of martyred family dogs has been run over in front of our house. Her attempt to comfort me is like some malicious parody of Talmudic reasoning: "You shouldn't be so upset about an animal. If a chicken and a person both fell down a well, which one would you save first?"

In addition to this somewhat haphazard religious training, there is the local chapter of Habonim, the Labor Zionist Youth Organization, to which my older brother and sister belong. I tag along and am tolerated by their peers. Once I am given a minor role in a stage performance by the chapter. Though I am too young to remember quite what it is about, the phrase *komets-aleph:aw* stands in my memory.

Later I will learn that this phrase occurs in a famous and sentimental Yiddish folksong. It is the first letter of the Hebrew alphabet, the first thing countless generations of Jewish children have been taught. Here is an unusual case in which a traditional lesson—how to pronounce the alphabet—is successfully inculcated in the secularized framework of a dramatic performance about the traditional setting. Perhaps this is because of the necessary rehearsals, in which I must have heard, as the song puts it, "once more, over and over again, *komets-aleph:aw*." The memory reinforces my later preference for this older, European pronunciation of the Hebrew vowels, my sense of the Israeli *kamets-aleph:ah* as inauthentic.

Also memorable at the Jewish Community Center is the annual barbecue run by the Young Couples' Club. Though my father will assure me in an interview years later that its association with the Fourth of July was purely a matter of convenience, the atmosphere is certainly one of festival, even including "sacrifices" and "altars": My father and his friends set up huge charcoal pits with cement blocks, and broil vast amounts of chicken; corn is boiled in aluminum garbage cans to go with it.[2] For the children, a Purim-like element of riotous excess is added: This one time each year, we are allowed to drink as much soda as we want. One year "wild," blond-haired Richie L., whose parents have a luncheonette booth for a kitchen table and an attic filled with antiques, claims to drink fourteen bottles, thus adding to the mystique he holds for me.

But it is the days when the Community Center becomes a synagogue that leave the strongest impression on my memory. There must be services every Saturday morning, but I am completely unaware of them. What I will remember are the holidays: Purim, Rosh Hashanah, Yom Kippur, Simchas Torah, and a crowd of people who just a few years later will never be there again. On the fall holidays, the shul is full of movement, impatience, noise, and warmth. Except for a few moments such as the shofar blowing, we children are free to come and go: By the steps in front, tossing the juicy, poisonous red berries of a yew that was planted, I am told, in memory of my brother Aaron, whom I never knew; inside the main doors, to look left at Walter Tenenbaum wrapped in a *tallis* that covers his head, standing at a lectern by the Ark of the Torah as he leads the service, or to look right, along the first long row of folding chairs for our fathers; thence a few rows back to where our mothers sit separately from the men, although unlike most synagogues that look and sound as traditional as this one, there is no *mekhitse*, no barrier between women and men; and finally out through the side door and down a flight of wooden steps to the monkey bars, into the ditch where one miraculous day we found and drank an intact bottle of orange soda, or into the kitchen, social room, and classroom in the basement. Once each year we children are the center of attention, as we huddle under a huge tallis in front of the Ark on Simchas Torah to be blessed.

In classic ethnographies of hunting-and-gathering groups, landscapes are described as personalized, integral elements of culture. This was true of the landscape of my childhood friendships, which today is as obliterated as any *shtetl* in Eastern Europe. Any marginal group in mass society may be subject without warning to the loss of its cultural landscape, and therefore those who are able to create portable landscapes for themselves are the most likely to endure.

The Jews have been doing so for thousands of years; the Simchas Torah tallis can stand in front of any Ark, and the original Ark, in the biblical account, was itself transported from station to station in the desert. Yet the members of a community are orphaned when the naïve intimacy of a living environment is torn away from them. Such a break appears often in Jewish literature—significantly with the emphasis not forward on the beginning of adulthood, as in the European *Bildungsroman*, but rather on the end of childhood.[3]

I suddenly discover the distance between the world and myself at the end of August in 1966. When my parents pick me up from camp, they take me to a new house. For the last time, we attend high holiday services in Farmingdale. It is the only time we will ever drive there, and our family's friends no longer join us during the afternoon break on Yom Kippur for a surreptitious glass of tea and a slice of challah. Farmingdale is no longer home, and though our new house is only ten miles away, it is another world.

We live now in an almost exclusively white, middle-class suburb with many Jews, but our older, brick house is isolated on a block of working-class cubes. While neighbors my age play football in our yard, I often retreat to my room and console myself with sports books for preadolescents. My new and bewildering sense of marginality leads me to develop an exquisite self-consciousness. It is manifested in an almost constant internal dialogue, which keeps me company and will interfere with my adolescent sexuality.

Ostracism is often the fate of a new kid on the block, and it may last longer when his family is Jewish and his home better than those on either side. There is a custom in this part of New Jersey of tolerating petty vandalism on "mischief night," the night before Halloween. Pumpkins are smashed, and we, along with other unpopular families on the block, have the windows of our cars and house smeared with soap. One Halloween I wake up to see graffiti chalked in bold letters on the sidewalk in front of our house: "Jon the Jew, a real one too." My father summons the kids next door—whom we suspect of being the authors—to scrape the words off the sidewalk, as I burn with shame.

He and I never discuss the incident, but later I will compare it with a memory of Freud's: As a child, he was walking with his father, when a gentile knocked his father's hat off. Rather than confronting the man, Freud's father meekly bent over to pick up the hat, and his son's humiliation persisted into adulthood (Bakan 1958; D. Boyarin 1997). The moral is that a victim is likely to view any response as adding insult to injury. In my case, as my father asserts the American principle of equality and "teaches a lesson" to my occasional and vindictive playmates by forcing them to erase what they have written, I feel as though he is inviting them to write the words again, this time making me watch my own degradation.

The new synagogue my parents join is only a partial refuge. It exemplifies the difference between a shul and a temple. Everything in Farmingdale had faced inward: little concern was paid for praying in unison, and though the *shammes* would bang his hand on the table for silence, he was seldom heeded; even the cantor was alone with God, facing away from everyone else, rather than performing for the congregation. Calling a synagogue a temple, by contrast, is doubly revealing. On the one hand, it indicates a striving for the majesty of the ancient House in Jerusalem. On the other hand, just like the English term used to designate it, its trappings are borrowed from the Christian world, down to the black robes worn by the rabbi and cantor.

These robes lack the warm mystery of Walter Tenenbaum's tallis. The responsive readings of Psalms in English seem ridiculously artificial to me from the first. And my mother, who still comes only on the holidays though I sometimes drag my father to temple on Friday nights, complains of the rabbi's long-winded sermons and yearns aloud for the intimate conversations along the back wall of the Farmingdale Jewish Community Center.

Unlike some, I do not leave the synagogue immediately after my bar mitzvah. I teach the blessings of the Haftorah to two reluctant boys a year younger than me. I briefly experience religious inspiration, and for perhaps two weeks put on *tefillin* every morning. But the atmosphere is hollow, and the emptiness breeds cynicism in me in my teens.

The coldness of the building itself is symptomatic of the lack of sustenance I sense there. The pretense and bad taste of modern American synagogues are well-known yet puzzling phenomena that deserve a sociological explanation of their own. Even the walls of the temple are dead concrete blocks, in contrast to the wood of the Farmingdale Jewish Community Center. Services are held in a "sanctuary," unlike the room at the Community Center where activities as varied as dances and political meetings were conducted when services were not being held. Aside from any question of Jewish law, there is a loss of community marked by the fact that everyone drives to the temple rather than walking. It is a place separated from the home, without the strong and patient webs spun by leisurely strolling conversations to and from a shul.

Most generally, the temple is victim to the general alienation of the suburbs. What happens or fails to happen there is dependent on what the people who come there expect from each other. Those who belong (there are vastly more "members" than regular attendees) seem bound primarily by a vague desire to have Jewish grandchildren. The poor rabbi, typical of Conservative congregations, seems hired to be a stand-in Jew, to observe all the laws and contain all the knowledge they don't have the time for. They are not bound to each other by Jewish religious ways, nor do they share the common interests of everyday life—the same livelihood or language—that helped to make a complete community in Farmingdale.

I go off to college and slowly discover that my dismissal of Judaism leaves me isolated, with few resources. I had realized my individual difference on leaving Farmingdale. Now, much more removed from a Jewish environment than ever before, I become aware of my inescapable Jewishness. In the small northwestern college of my dreams, everyone around me seems "American" and different, though I have never thought of myself as anything but American. Even in the humanities curriculum on which the school prides itself, Jewish civilization is absent. It is as though Western cultural history were just a triumphant straight line from the Greeks to Augustine and Michelangelo (with his horned Moses and uncircumcised David), confusion setting in at last only with Marx and Freud.

Five years too late to benefit me, a Jewish Studies position will in fact be established at the college. Such positions are usually funded by Jewish individuals or organizations, and hence they represent the growing acculturation (not assimilation) of Jews into American academic life. The fact that they are regarded as legitimate by the academic community, however, is part of a reintegration of Jewish thought into the concept of Western humanities. Jewish ethnographers can contribute to this movement—for example, by elucidating the dialectic of tradition and change as worked out in communities facing vastly different historical challenges. We may then move beyond efforts to explain the explosive presence of Jews in post-Enlightenment intellectual life as a result of their "primitive" encounter with "civility" (Cuddihy 1974) to explore how the Jewish belief that "Creation as the (active) speech or writing of God posits first of all that the Universe is essentially intelligible" (Faur 1986: 7) provided a pathway from Torah to a restless, unifying modern impulse in the natural and social sciences.

Such notions are far beyond me as an undergraduate. At my college in the 1970s, the social scientists in their separate departments strive to separate themselves from their "objects of study"; the humanists treasure the peace of their cloisters; the artists, knowing they are intellectually suspect, cultivate a cliquish sense of superiority; and there is none of the give-and-take between learning and everyday experience that I have come to associate with the best of Jewish scholarship.

I find a friend, a Jew from Long Island, and we begin to teach each other that we need to cultivate our Jewishness. We discuss the "Jewish mentality" of modern thinkers, and paraphrasing Lenny Bruce's category of the *goyish*, sarcastically reject all that is "white." "I am not 'white,' " my friend Martin proudly postures, "I am a Semite." Meanwhile, reflecting on my own dismissal of suburban Judaism, I decide not to end willingly an almost endless chain of Jewish cultural transmission. I stake my future on the assumption that a tradition so old and varied must contain the seeds of a worthwhile life for me, and decide to begin to acquire them through study.

Besides, my reading as a student of anthropology leads me to reason that if I concentrate on Jewish culture, no one will accuse me of cultural imperialism (see Gough 1968). No doubt others in my generation who choose to do fieldwork with Jews are motivated by similar considerations. Jewish anthropologists as a class are privileged to belong to the world of academic discourse, and to have an entrée into a variety of unique communities that maintain cultural frameworks in opposition to mass society.

Something deeper than Marxist critiques of anthropology draws me to Yiddish in particular. Before I left Farmingdale, my best friend had been a child of survivors from Lemberg. I remember being at his house once, and asking with a sense of wonder: "Ralph, do you really know Yiddish?"

Ralph told me that although he understood the language—which his parents still spoke to him—he had never learned to speak it. Still, I was impressed that he knew this secret code. And now that I am finished with college and looking to find my own way home, Yiddish seems to be the nearest link to which I can attach myself. It is the key to a sense of the life of the *shtetl*, that Jewish dreamtime that I inevitably associate with my lost Farmingdale.

The Farmingdale community has, by this point, completely disintegrated: Virtually no Jews in that part of New Jersey earn their living as chicken farmers anymore. Many of those who have gone into business have moved to nearby towns like Lakewood. The Torah scrolls of the Community Center have been ceremoniously transferred to a new synagogue near housing developments on the highway between Farmingdale and Lakewood. I have never considered becoming a chicken farmer myself.

So, when I finish my college courses, without waiting for graduation, I flee back to New York. "Flee": No one chases me out of Portland, Oregon, God forbid! "Back": The city, though a magnet and a refuge, has never been my home before. Yet for three years I have shaped my identity in opposition to the "American" world around me, and I have reverted, along with my close friends, to what we imagine is an authentic New York accent—the "deses" and "doses" that were drilled out of my parents' repertoire in the days when New York public school teachers had to pass elocution exams.

Rejecting suburban Judaism, belatedly pursuing the image of the sixties' counterculture to the Pacific Northwest, and self-consciously affecting a "New York Jew" style were all successive attempts to shape a personal identity. In each case, the identity strategy was in opposition to the prevailing conventions of the immediate social order. Similarly, opposition to their parents' perceived bourgeois complacency may underlie the involvement of young people with Judaism. Yet as Dominique Schnapper has noted (1983), for young, intellectual Jews becoming involved in Jewish religion, politics, or culture, there can be no question of canceling out prior experience and "becoming traditional." In fact, this is true even of the most seemingly Orthodox and insular Jewish communities. There is a difference between learning about great rabbis of the past through meetings with Jewish graybeards who knew them, and through reading about their merits in the Williamsburg newspaper *Der Yid*.

Of course, not only Jews are in the position of reconstituting interrupted tradition (cf. Clifford 1986: 116 ff.). But since they have been in the business of reshaping tradition in a dialogue with written texts for thousands of years, Jews may benefit more directly than others from learning about what other Jews are doing with their common tradition. It is conceivable that individuals may choose to adopt traits from other communities or even join those communities based on what they read in ethnographies. Whether such cultural borrowings and recombinations are effected in an "authentic" manner will depend less on precedent than on the degree of self-confident cultural generosity that results.

Arriving in New York, I adopt a knitted yarmulke, although my hair still falls below my shoulders. I immediately begin a nine-week summer course in Yiddish at Columbia, and it seems as though the language were being brought out from deep inside me. When I go to visit my parents on weekends, my father remembers words he'd never noticed forgetting. When I take the IRT after class back down to the Village, it seems as if everybody on the train is speaking Yiddish. Most important for my sense of identity, phrases here and there in my own internal dialogue are now in Yiddish, and I find I can reflect on myself with a gentle irony that was never available to me in English.

Then, after my first year in graduate school, I am off to Europe the following summer, courtesy of my parents. I arrive at the Gare du Nord in Paris with the address of a friend and without a word of French. I am spotted wearing my yarmulke by a young North African Jew who makes me understand, in broken English, that he studies at the Lubavitch yeshiva in Paris. He buys me a Paris guidebook and sets me on my way in the Metro. At the end of the summer, this meeting will stand as the first in a set of Parisian reactions to my yarmulke which crystallize in my memory:

—The reaction of the generous young Trotskyist with whom my friend had grown close and with whom I stayed for two weeks: She could see the yarmulke only as a symbol of Jewish nationalism and argued bitterly that it was inherently reactionary;

—Of a young North African Jew, selling carpets at the flea market at Clignoncourt, who grabbed my arm and cried, "*Haver! Haver!* Brother Jew!";

—Of another young man, minding a booth outside one of the great department stores, who asked me if I were Orthodox, and interrupted my complicated response to explain that, although he was Orthodox himself, he was afraid to wear a yarmulke in the street;

—Of an old man at the American Express office who spoke to me in Yiddish and complained that the recent North African migrants dominated the Jewish communal organizations, and that there was no place for a Polish Jew to go.

Those first, fragmentary encounters are my fieldwork juvenilia. In assuming the yarmulke, I perhaps do not stop to consider that neither my actions nor my knowledge match the standards that it symbolically represents. But it works effectively, almost dangerously, as a two-way sensor, inducing Jews to present themselves to me and forcing me to try to understand how I am reflected in their eyes.

Externally, I learn many things about the situation of French Jewry. From the patent discomfort my non-Jewish Trotskyist friend feels at my display of Jewish specificity, I gain some sense of the conflicts young French Jews—coming out of the universalist, antihistorical revolutionary apogee of May 1968—must have felt years later when they first began to distinguish themselves from their comrades and view the world from the vantage point of their specific history. From the young street peddlers, I learn about how much riskier public proclamation of oneself as a Jew is perceived as being in Paris than in New York, and a concomitant depth of instant identification of one Jew with another. My meeting with the old Polish Jew at the American Express office hints at the dynamics of dominant and declining ethnic groups within the Jewish community, so vastly different from those dynamics in the United States.

Internally, I begin to understand that an identifiably Jewish headcovering places its own claims on the one who wears it. The longer it stays put, the more its power to keep him out of non-kosher restaurants grows. More important, people want to know who he is as a Jew. And if he does not know, the desire for peace of mind will spur further his effort to shape an identity.

Returning from Paris, I find an apartment at Second Avenue and Fifth Street in Manhattan. I tell people, "After three generations, my family has finally made it back to the Lower East Side." In fact, none of my grandparents lived on the East Side for a long time after immigrating, even though my mother tells me she regrets having missed the Yiddish theater on Second Avenue during her girlhood. By the time I move in, there is no Yiddish theater left. The former Ratner's dairy restaurant on Second Avenue, where, I'm told, Trotsky was a lousy tipper, is now a supermarket. Though sometimes one still sees a white newspaper truck with the word *Forverts* in lovely blue Hebrew letters on its side drive by late at night, this neighborhood has been the East Village since the sixties, and I think of it as such.

A new friend, who devotes his time to a frustrating effort to rescue Lower East Side synagogues, tells me of a shul still in use on an otherwise abandoned block east of Tompkins Square Park. Though my friend has never been inside, he is sure that I will be welcomed, since such an isolated congregation must be looking for new blood.

The place is called the Eighth Street Shul, but its full name is Kehilas Bnei Moshe Yakov Anshei Zavichost veZosmer—Congregation Children of Moses and Jacob, People of Zavichost and Zosmer. It is owned by a *landsmanshaft* (hometown society) founded by émigrés and refugees from two towns in south central Poland. No one born in either town prays regularly at the shul now, and only one or two of the congregants are actually members of the society.

The shul is located in the center of what New York Latinos call "Loisaida"—an area bounded by Avenue A on the east, Avenue D on the west, Houston Street on the south, and Fourteenth Street on the north. Once the blocks up to Tenth Street were almost exclusively Jewish, and on nearly every one stood a synagogue or a religious school. Now two of those former synagogues stand abandoned, several more have become churches, and the rest have disappeared.

Eighth Street is a typical and not especially distinguished example of turn-of-the-century Lower East Side synagogue architecture.[4] It consists of five levels. The lowest contains a cranky and inadequate boiler. The second is the *besmedresh* or study room, which was destroyed by a suspicious fire in August 1982. The third level is the main sanctuary, long and narrow like the tenements among which it was tucked when it was built. Two rows of simple pews are separated by an aisle, which is interrupted in the center of the room by the raised table from which the weekly Torah portion is read. At the very front is the Ark, surrounded by partially destroyed wooden carvings that are the most artistic aspect of the shul. The walls are decorated with representations of the traditional Jewish signs for the zodiac; the two in front on the left have been obliterated by water damage from the leaky roof. Covering most of this level, with roughly an eight-foot opening extending toward the back, is the women's gallery. The gallery is constructed in such a way that it is easier for women sitting on opposite sides of the opening to converse with one another than to see what the men are doing downstairs. Finally, upstairs from the women's gallery is an unused and cramped apartment that was once occupied by the shul's caretaker. In the roof behind it, an opening that was a skylight until there was a break-in is now covered with a solid wooden framework, allowing neither light nor vandals to enter.

Avenues B and C, which mark off the block, were once lively commercial streets with mostly Jewish storekeepers. There were also several smaller streets lined with tenements, right up to the edge of the East River. When the FDR Drive was built along the river, all the streets east of Avenue D disappeared, the tenements on the remaining available land were replaced by municipal housing, and the stores declined rapidly. During the same years, a massive middle-class housing cooperative, funded by a government mortgage, was built along Grand Street one mile to the south. Many of the remaining Jewish families moved into those houses, leaving virtually no Jews in the immediate area of the Eighth Street Shul.

Yet a minyan has continued to meet there every Saturday morning, with virtually no interruptions, throughout the years of the neighborhood's decline, while the block served as the Lower East Side's heaviest "shopping street" for hard drugs. It has lasted into the present, when buildings all around it are being speculated upon and renovated by both squatters and powerful real estate interests. It appears that until recently the main reason for this continuity was a felicitous rivalry between two men who were unwilling to abandon the synagogue because their fathers had both been presidents of it at one time. Perhaps if there had been only one, he would have given up and made peace with his conscience. Perhaps if the two men had naturally been friends they could have agreed to sell the building and officially merge their society with another still functioning further south in the neighborhood. If they had been able to agree on anything besides continuing to come to the shul, the shul might not have survived this long.

The first time I walk in, a clean-shaven, compact man in his sixties— younger than several of the congregants, who number perhaps seventeen in all—hurries forward to greet me. What's my name? Where do I live? Where am I from originally? And where do I usually go to pray on shabbes? His name is Moshe Fogel, and he sees to it that I am called to the Torah, the honor accorded any guest who comes for the first time, without asking any questions as to his level of religious observance. Later, an older member explains to me: "Once upon a time, you wouldn't get called to the Torah unless you kept kosher and observed shabbes." Now, Moish prefers simply to leave those matters undiscussed.

The history of the East Side as a place where all types of Jews have lived together reinforces his discretion. Externalities such as proper or improper clothing are not essential criteria for participation. This is true of the entire Orthodox community on the East Side and has even become part of its mystique. Rabbi Reuven Feinstein, head of the Staten Island branch of the East Broadway-based yeshiva, Tifereth Jerusalem, noted in a recent speech the common reaction in Boro Park and other thriving Orthodox centers to the nonconformist dress of East Side visitors: "It's okay, you're from the East Side." The president at Eighth Street still wears a traditional *gartl* when he prays, a belt worn over his jacket to separate the pure from the base parts of his body, and no one has suggested that such old customs are out of place today. But partly because the older members at the Eighth Street Shul walked through the East Village in the 1960s and knew there were many young Jews among the longhairs—even if they were horrified at the thought—they were willing to include in the minyan a young man in the neighborhood who, when he first came, wore dreadlocks under a Rastafarian-style knitted cap. It is also doubtless true that at that time there was no other Orthodox synagogue anywhere that he would have contemplated entering.

By contrast, it is impossible for any Jew raised in the middle of secular society (including a Jewish anthropologist) to join a traditionalist community without giving up major parts of his or her identity. The ways in which a researcher of contemporary Hasidic life "becomes a Hasid" are much more dramatic than the way in which one becomes a regular at Eighth Street—but they are probably more transient as well. In order to gain the confidence of the traditionalist communities, the fieldworker has to give the impression, whether implicitly or explicitly, that he or she is likely eventually to accept their standards in all areas of life (Belcove-Shalin 1988). All one has to do at Eighth Street is agree to come back—"a little earlier next time, if possible."

Two things will draw me back to join this congregation, occasionally referred to as "those holy souls who *daven* in the middle of the jungle." The first pull is the memory of Farmingdale: the Ashkenazic accents and melodies (though here they are Polish, whereas Walter Tenenbaum had prayed in his native Lithuanian accent); the smell of herring on the old men's breath and hands; the burning sensation of whiskey, which I must have tasted surreptitiously at the conclusion of Yom Kippur one year in Farmingdale.

The second thing that draws me, though I do not come every week, is a feeling that I am needed and missed when I am absent. It's hard for me to get up early on Saturday mornings, after being out late Friday nights. It still seems like a sacrifice, as though I were stealing part of my weekend from myself. If I arrive in time for the *Shema*, about half an hour into the service, I congratulate myself on my devotion. The summer before I marry, in 1981, I hardly come at all. When I go with my brother to meet Moshe Fogel at the shul and give him the provisions for the kiddush I am giving to celebrate my upcoming wedding, I tell Dan that I usually arrive "around nine-thirty," to which Moish retorts: "Even when you used to come, you didn't show up at nine-thirty!" Though he says it with a smile, a message comes through clearly: If I want to claim to belong, I should attend regularly and arrive on time. Although I am always welcome, only if I can be counted on am I part of the minyan. The dependence of Jews on each other—a theme running through biblical and rabbinic literature—is pressingly literal at Eighth Street.

Meanwhile, my feelings about Paris coalesce into a plan. I know I want to live there for a time, but only if I will be among Jews. Since I am at the point in my graduate school career when I must find a dissertation topic, I decide to look for fieldwork situations with Jews in Paris. I make an exploratory visit with my fiancée, Elissa. Will she agree to a pause in her own career to follow me on this project? Will the organizations of Polish Jewish immigrants whom I have chosen to study be willing to have me study them?

The answer is yes to both questions. Speaking Yiddish and appearing as a nice young Jewish couple seem to be the critical elements in our success. We are invited to sit in on board meetings, negotiations aimed at the reunification of societies split by political differences for over half a century. I am struck by the fact that these immigrants seem so much more marked by their political identification than the East European Jews I've met in New York. Also, I am impressed at the number of societies remaining in a country that has suffered Nazi occupation and that historically has shown little tolerance for immigrant cultural identifications.

But I am drawn not so much by the differences between these Yiddish speakers and those I know in New York as by encountering them in an environment that is otherwise so foreign. Speaking Yiddish to people with whom I have no other common language confirms its legitimacy and reinforces the sense of a distinctive Jewish identity that is shared between generations. I go for a trial interview of one activist, who is disappointed that I didn't bring "the girl," Elissa, along with me. When he discovers to my embarrassment that I have been secretly taping the interview, he is flattered.

Just before leaving Paris, Elissa and I climb the steps of Sacré Coeur. The cathedral itself is an ungracious mass, and the city looks gray and undifferentiated below us. I experience a moment of vertigo, as if I could tumble off Montmartre and drown. Part of my dream of Paris, "capital of the nineteenth century," is an infantile fantasy of becoming a universal intellectual—

to be free both of the special knowledge and of the limitations of my knowledge that follow on my personal history. Yet I know I cannot come to Paris and immediately move among its confident, cliquish intellectual elite. Even less will I ever have contact with that "quintessentially French" petite bourgeoisie typified by the stolid Inspector Maigret. My first place will be with the immigrants, whose appearance, strange language, and crowded quarters provided material for unkind portraits by Maigret's creator, Simenon, in the 1930s.[5] If I am unable to come to see Paris as they have seen it, if I cannot make out of a shared marginality a niche in the city for myself, I will be lost, as much as the "lost generation," and in a most unromantic way.

During the two years between our decision to spend a year in Paris and the beginning of that year, I attend the Eighth Street Shul more and more regularly, and Elissa occasionally joins me. Gradually, my feelings when I miss a week shift from guilt to regret. One shabbes, waking up late but not wanting to miss attending altogether, I arrive just in time for the kiddush, to the general amusement of the entire minyan. One February morning I wake up to see snow falling and force myself to go outside against my will, knowing that on a day like this I am truly needed.

Other incidents illustrate the gap in assumptions between myself and the other congregants. I try to bring friends into the shul, partly because it makes me more comfortable, and partly to build up the congregation. A friend whose hair and demeanor reflect his love of reggae music and his connections with Jamaican Rastafarians comes along one Yom Kippur. We reach the point in the service when pious men, remembering the priests in the days of the Temple, descend to their knees and touch their foreheads to the floor. Since no one wants to soil his good pants on the dirty floor, sheets of newspaper are provided as protection. Reb Simcha Taubenfeld, the senior member of the congregation, approaches my friend with newspaper in hand and asks in his heavy Yiddish accent: "Do you fall down?" The look of bewilderment on my friend's face graphically illustrates the term "frame of reference."

Another week, the same friend, failing to observe the discretion with regard to the expression of political opinions that I have learned to adopt at shul, gets into a bitter argument over the Palestinian question. Fishel Mandel, a social worker and one of the younger members of the congregation, calls me during the week to convey the message that "despite our political differences, your friend is still welcome."

After our wedding, I attend virtually every week. When Elissa comes, she is doubly welcome, since the only other woman who attends regularly is Goldie Brown, Moish Fogel's sister. Though Goldie doesn't complain about being isolated in the women's gallery one flight above the men, she seconds Elissa's suggestion that a mekhitse be set up downstairs. The suggestion gets nowhere, however: It would entail displacing one of the regular members of the congregation from his usual seat, and though there is no lack of available places (I myself usually wander from front to back during the course of the service), he refuses to consider moving.

I reason that I will have more of a voice concerning questions such as the seating of women if I formalize my relationship to the shul by becoming a member. My timid announcement that I would like to do so meets with initial confusion on the part of the older members of the society present. Then Fishel, ever the mediator and interpreter, explains to me that the shul is not organized like a suburban synagogue: "There's a *chevra*, a society, that owns the shul. In order to join, you have to be *shomer mitzves*, you have to keep kosher and strictly observe the Sabbath."

I drop my request. Shiye the president reassures me with a speech in his usual roundabout style to the effect that belonging to the chevra is a separate question from being a member of the minyan: "They send their money in from New Jersey and Long Island, but the shul couldn't exist without the people that actually come to pray here."

Meanwhile, our plans to go to Paris proceed. Our travel plans become a topic for discussion over kiddush at shul. One of the older, Polish-born members tells us for the first time that he lived in Paris for nine years after the war. We ask him why he came to America, and he answers, "*Vern a frantsoyz iz shver* [It's hard to become a Frenchman]," both to obtain citizenship and to be accepted by neighbors.

At the end of the summer, we expect to give a farewell kiddush at the shul. A few days before shabbes, I get a phone call from Moish Fogel: "Don't get things for kiddush. We won't be able to daven at Eighth Street for a while. There's been a fire. Thank God, the Torah scrolls were rescued, but it's going to take a while to repair the damage." It is two weeks after Tisha B'Av, the fast commemorating the destruction of the Temple in Jerusalem.

Leaving New York without saying goodbye to the shul and its congregation, we fly overnight to Brussels and immediately *shlep* (the word "drag" would not do the burden justice) our seven heavy suitcases onto a Paris train. Arriving again at the Gare du Nord, I think of the thousands of Polish Jews who were greeted at the station in the twenties and thirties by fellow immigrants eager to hire workers. As soon as we get off the train, Elissa immediately "gets involved," demanding the credentials of two men who claim to be policemen and attempt to "confiscate" a carpet two Moroccan immigrants are carrying. Upon Elissa's challenge, the "policemen" demur.

We practice our French on the cab driver: I explain to him why we've come to Paris. He warns us that we shouldn't tell strangers we're Jewish. It is only a few weeks since the terrorist attack on Goldenberg's restaurant, and no one knows when the next anti-Semitic attack may come. I reply that if I hadn't said we were Jewish, we wouldn't have found out he was a Jew as well, adding that in New York the names of taxi drivers are posted inside the cabs. He says he wouldn't like that at all.

So we receive an early warning that ethnicity in Paris is not celebrated publicly as it is in New York, nor are ethnic mannerisms and phrases so prevalent as a deliberate element of personal style. This is the repressive underside of marginality. It appears wherever the individual or community think it is better not to flaunt their distinctiveness, even if they cannot fully participate in the host culture. It leads to suspicion and silence, to the taxi driver's desire for anonymity.

Arriving at our rented apartment, we meet our neighbor Isabel, who will be our only non-Jewish friend during the year in Paris, and who later explains that meeting us has helped dispel her prejudices about Jews. Over the next few days, we introduce ourselves to Jewish storekeepers in the neighborhood: Guy, the Tunisian kosher butcher; Chanah, the Polish baker's wife; Leon, the deli man from Lublin, who insists he didn't learn Yiddish until he came to Paris.

We have a harder time finding a synagogue where we feel at home. For Rosh Hashanah and Yom Kippur, we have purchased tickets at one of the "official" synagogues run by the Consistoire, the recognized religious body of French Jewry set up under Napoleon. Most synagogues run by the Consistoire are named after the streets on which they're located. Meeting a Hasid on the street, I ask him whether he happens to know when Rosh Hashanah services begin at "Notre Dame de Nazareth." He grimaces and makes as if spitting: "Don't say that name, *ptu ptu ptu!*"

The synagogue is strange to us as well. Most of the crowd seems if anything more secular than most American Jews, who go to the synagogue only on the high holidays. Many teenagers wear jeans or miniskirts. Because of the fear of terrorism, everyone is frisked on entering. Inside, the synagogue is picturesque with its nineteenth-century pseudo-Moorish motifs; when it was built, Offenbach was the choirmaster. Yet it is as religiously dissatisfying as the suburban American temple I used to attend. The services seem to be conducted in a traditional manner, but it is hard to tell from among the noisy throng in back. The shammes, as a representative of the government, wears a Napoleonic hat, and the rabbi delivers his sermon from a high pulpit.

After Yom Kippur, I think idly about the need to find a more comfortable shul, and when I hear about an East European-style minyan within walking distance, I consider going on Simchas Torah. Watching television reports of terrorist attacks on Simchas Torah in other European capitals, I am consumed with shame at my own apathy, and thus I walk a kilometer or two to find the synagogue on the rue Basfroi the following shabbes.

Going in, I am first shown into a side room, where men are reciting incomprehensible prayers with strange and beautiful melodies. Eventually I realize that they are North African Jews, and I venture into the main room to ask, "Is there an Ashkenazic minyan here?"

The man I ask replies in French, "We're not racists here! We're all Jews!" at which his friend points out:

"The young man spoke to you in Yiddish!" Continuing in Yiddish, he explains that while everyone is welcome in the main synagogue, the services there are in fact Ashkenazic, and so some of the North African men prefer to pray in their own style in the smaller room.

Gradually I settle in, though I have trouble following the prayers in the beginning. Remembering a particular turn in the melody for the reader's repetition of the Amidah that the president at Eighth Street uses, I listen for it from the cantor here at the rue Basfroi, and hear a satisfying similarity in his voice. I feel like a new immigrant coming to his landsmanshaft's shul to hear the melodies from his town.

Throughout our year in Paris, I attend this synagogue about as frequently as I had gone to Eighth Street at first. Although the congregation is not unfriendly, no one invites me home for lunch, partly out of French reserve, and perhaps also because it is clear that I'm not very observant. I feel "unobservant" here in another sense: I do not register the vast store of information obviously available here about the interaction of religious Jews from different ethnic backgrounds. It escapes me, as though I were "off duty." In contrast to my feelings at Eighth Street, I am not motivated by the desire to make myself a regular here. And this is not my fieldwork situation: Nothing external moves me to push my way through socially, to find out who these people really are and let them see me as well.

The Jews I encounter in the course of my research belong to an entirely different crowd. The landsmanshaftn to which they belong are secular organizations. If I wanted to observe the Sabbath closely, it would be difficult for me to do my fieldwork. The immigrants hold many meetings on Saturdays, including a series of *shabbes-shmuesn*, afternoon discussions at which the main focus this year is the war in Lebanon.

I mention to one of my informants that I sometimes go to the synagogue. "I admire that," he responds. "I can't go back to the synagogue now. I've been away too long; it's too late for me." Toward the end of the year, we invite an autodidact historian of the immigrant community to dinner on Friday night and ask him to say the blessing over the challah. "I can't," he refuses, and will not explain further. Though his intellectual curiosity has led him to become friendly with us, and he is considering doing research on the resurgence of Orthodoxy among French Jews, his critical stance vis-à-vis his own secularist movement is insufficient to allow him to accept this religious honor. Enjoying the possibilities offered by marginality is sometimes impossible for those who are neither young nor well educated and who have often been deceived in their wholehearted commitments.

Throughout the year, Elissa has been growing stricter regarding *kashres*. She refuses to eat nonkosher meat and will order only fish in restaurants. She articulates our shared impression that Jewish secularism has failed to create everyday lifeways that can be transmitted from generation to generation, and that any lasting Judaism must be grounded in Jewish law and learning. Before parting for the summer—she to study Yiddish at Oxford, I to Jerusalem, to acquire the Hebrew that I will need to learn about Jewish law—we discuss the level of observance we want to adopt on our return to New York, but we come to no decision.

Elissa and I meet at the end of the summer in Los Angeles, for the bar mitzvah of her twin cousins. I am uncomfortable riding on shabbes; after spending an entire summer in Jerusalem, for the first time, it seems like a violation of myself. The roast beef sandwich I eat at the reception is the first nonkosher food I've eaten since leaving Paris.

Thus, without having made a formal declaration, I join Elissa in observing kashres (save for occasional lapses that I call my "*treyf* of the month club" and that become less and less frequent), and she joins me in keeping shabbes, albeit with some reluctance. Preparing to fulfill a promise made in a dream I had while in Paris, I take a further step: At the beginning of November, I begin attending daily services at another East Side shul and thus putting on tefillin again. One of my mother's cousins at the Telshe Yeshiva in Cleveland—whom I have never met—told me in the dream that I would always be welcome there, and I responded that if I got there, I would put on tefillin every day from then on. Later in November, Elissa and I fly to Cleveland for the weekend. Though we are welcomed warmly, it is clear that the rabbis and *rebetsins* at the yeshiva hoped for something more Jewish from me, the great-grandson of the Rosh Yeshiva's second wife, Miriam.

We return to the Eighth Street Shul as well, which has been secured and repaired sufficiently to make it usable once again. There are changes. Old Mr. Klapholz, with whom I hardly had exchanged a word, has passed away. Fishel's uncle Mr. Hochbaum, a congregant for half a century, no longer attends, since he is unable to walk all the way from Grand Street. On the other hand, my long-haired friend has moved into the neighborhood and attends regularly. Two of the younger members of the congregation have small children now, and they must go to a shul where there are other children for their son and daughter to play with. In February, our oldest member passes away, and after Shavuot, another member moves to Jerusalem. Two more young men eventually begin coming regularly and bring along their infant children. Now, in June 1986, the shul has thirteen regular male attendees. I am no longer free to sleep late on Saturday mornings, and fortunately I no longer want to.

All of this, to the extent it is of my own making, is the result of a search to realize that fragile illusion of wholeness which was destroyed when my family and almost all the others left Farmingdale. I will hazard a guess that Jewish anthropologists—perhaps anthropologists in general—are motivated by a sense of loss. Yet the seamless image of community is inevitably a child's image. We cannot regain what is lost, if only because it never existed as we remember it. Nothing in society is quite as harmonious as it seemed to me then, and I later learned about bitter political struggles that had taken place in Farmingdale, just as they had among the immigrants in Paris.

Our strategy, rather, should be to attempt to understand what it is we miss and need, which is available in still-living communities in another form. The image of wholeness which we share is foreshadowed by communities all of us stem from, however many generations back, and it can serve as a guide in the search for the reciprocal relationships of autonomous adulthood.

Anthropology is a tool for mediating between the self and the community. It has helped me to come to belong at the Eighth Street Shul: to withhold my opinions when it seems necessary, without feeling the guilt of self-compromise; to accept instruction and gentle reprimands with good humor; to believe it is worthwhile preserving something that might otherwise disappear. But belonging at Eighth Street does not mean that I have dissolved myself into an ideal Orthodox Jew. If I attempted to do so, I would be unable to continue being an anthropologist. If I fit into any category, it may be what my friend Kugelmass calls the "funky Orthodox": that is, those who participate in the community but whose interests and values are not confined to the Orthodox world. In fact, there are no ideal Orthodox Jews at Eighth Street; it is our respective quirks that provide the *raison d'être* of this haphazard but now intentional once-a-week community.

The fact that I have found a religious community that needs me because of its marginality and will tolerate me because of a generosity born of tradition is what I mean by the marginal redemption of one Jew. Likewise, if the shul survives, it will be because of its very marginality, because of the many individuals who have recognized the creative possibilities of a situation that demands that they create a new unity, while allowing each of them to retain their otherness. Isn't this the dream of anthropologists? Whether attempting to communicate knowledge between different Jewish communities, or between communities much more distant in tradition and empathy, we are messengers. We spend our own lives in moving back and forth among the worlds of others. As we do so, in order to avoid getting lost along the way we must become cultural pioneers, learning to "get hold of our *trans*cultural selves" (Wolff 1970: 40). Communities on the edge of mass society, or even on the fringes of ethnic enclaves, seem to be among the most congenial fields in which to do so.

Let me finish with a parable:

Two Jews can afford to be fastidious about the dress, comportment, and erudition of a third. It gives them something to gossip about and identify against. Ten healthy Jews can have a similar luxury; an eleventh means competition for the ritual honors. It's nine Jews who are the most tolerant, as I learned one forlorn shabbes at Eighth Street. It was almost ten o'clock, and there was no minyan. Since everyone seemed content to wait patiently, I assumed that someone else had promised to come, and asked, "Who are we waiting for?"

"A *yid*," our oldest member replied without hesitation.

Eventually a Jew came along.   ■

NOTES

1. Compare Pierre Bourdieu's critique of the structuralist theory of "reciprocal" gift exchange: "Even if reversibility [i.e., the assumption that gifts entail counter-gifts of equivalent value] is the objective truth of the discrete acts which ordinary experience knows in discrete form and calls gift exchanges, it is not the whole truth of a practice

which could not exist if it were consciously perceived in accordance with the model. The temporal structure of gift exchange, which objectivism ignores, is what makes possible the coexistence of two opposing truths, which defines the full truth of the gift" (1977:6).

Similarly, in a narrative such as this one, because I, as author, already know the ending, it may seem as though each successive element fits into those that precede and follow it in such a way that their necessity is perfectly known. Actually my aim is to show how the background that nurtured me shaped in part my unpredictable responses to situations that in themselves were historically rather than culturally determined. See my conclusion, where I refer to one of the communities I now participate in as "haphazard but intentional."

2. Even if it was no more than a matter of convenience, this annual event demonstrates Jonathan Woocher's point that American Jewish "civil religion expects Jews to take advantage of the opportunities which America provides, and to use them to help fulfill their Jewish responsibilities" (1985:161).

3. This may seem an outrageously loose claim, and I am quite willing to be proven wrong by literary scholars. But compare the conclusion of James Joyce's *Portrait of the Artist as a Young Man:*

> Mother is putting my new secondhand clothes in order. She prays now, she says, that I may learn in my own life and away from home and friends what the heart is and what it feels. Amen. So be it. Welcome, O life! I go to encounter for the millionth time the reality of experience and to forge in the smithy of my soul the uncreated conscience of my race. (1968:252–53)

with the end of Moshe Szulsztein's memoir of a Polish Jewish childhood:

> When the truck was already fairly far along Warsaw Street and Kurow was barely visible, two more relatives appeared in a great rush, wanting to take their leave. These were my grandfather's pair of pigeons. The pigeons knew me, and I knew them. I loved them, and perhaps they loved me as well . . . But the truck is stronger than they are, it drives and drives further and further away from Kurow. My poor pigeons can't keep up, they remain behind . . . Before they disappear altogether from my view I still discern them within the distant evening cloud, two small flying silver dots, one a bit behind the other. That, I know, is the male, and the second, a bit in front, is the female. (1982:352)

4. For photographs of Eighth Street and other Lower East Side shuls, both surviving and abandoned, see Fine and Wolfe (1978).

5. "In every corner, in every little patch of darkness, up the blind alleys and the corridors, one could sense the presence of a swarming mass of humanity, a sly, shameful life. Shadows slunk along the walls. The stores were selling goods unknown to French people even by name" (Simenon 1963: 45).

REFERENCES

Bakan, David. 1958. *Sigmund Freud and the Jewish Mystical Tradition.* Princeton, N.J.: Van Nostrand.

Belcove-Shalin, Janet. 1988. "Becoming More of an Eskimo." In *Between Two Worlds: Ethnographic Essays on American Jews.* Pp. 77–98. Ithaca, N.Y.: Cornell University Press.

Bourdieu, Pierre. 1977. *Outline of a Theory of Practice.* Cambridge: Cambridge University Press.

Boyarin, Daniel. 1997. *Judaism as a Gender.* Berkeley and Los Angeles: University of California Press.

Clifford, James. 1986. "On Ethnographic Allegory." In *Writing Culture: The Poetics and Politics of Ethnography,* edited by James Clifford and George Marcus. Pp. 98–121. Berkeley and Los Angeles: University of California Press.

Cuddihy, John. 1974. *The Ordeal of Civility: Freud, Marx, Lévi-Strauss and the Jewish Struggle with Modernity.* New York: Basic Books.

Fabian, Johannes. 1983. *Time and the Other.* New York: Columbia University Press.

Faur, José. 1986. *Golden Doves with Silver Dots.* Bloomington: Indiana University Press.

Fine, Jo Renée, and Gerard Wolfe. 1978. *The Synagogues of New York's Lower East Side.* New York: Washington Mews Books.

Gough, Kathleen. 1968. "Anthropology and Imperialism." *Monthly Review* 19: 12–27.

Joyce, James. 1968 (1916). *Portrait of the Artist as a Young Man.* New York: Viking Press.

Schnapper, Dominique. 1983. *Jewish Identities in France: An Analysis of Contemporary French Jewry,* translated by Arthur Goldhammer. Chicago: University of Chicago Press.

Simenon, Georges. 1963. *Maigret and the Enigmatic Left,* edited by Daphne Woodward. New York: Penguin Books.

Szulsztein, Moshe. 1982. *Dort vu mayn vig iz geshtanen.* Paris: Published by a Committee.

Wolff, Kurt. 1970. "The Sociology of Knowledge and Sociological Theory." In *The Sociology of Sociology,* edited by Larry T. Reynolds and Janice M. Reynolds. Pp. 31–67. New York: David McKay.

Woocher, Jonathan. 1985. "Sacred Survival." *Judaism* 34 (2): 151–62.

■ *QUESTIONS FOR MAKING CONNECTIONS WITHIN THE READING* ■

1. When Jonathan Boyarin describes his childhood in Farmingdale, New Jersey, he takes us into a world of Jewish traditions and references that may be unfamiliar to some readers: indeed, Boyarin's essay is concerned, in part, with tracing the author's efforts to grow more familiar with and gain a greater understanding of his own traditions. In the process, he describes many different kinds of Jews: an Orthodox Jew, a Jewish socialist, a Lubavitcher Hasid, an observant Jew, Zionists, and Jews who have been acculturated into American academic life, to name a few. What are the differences between the groups that Boyarin identifies? Why is he drawn to one group more than another?

2. "Waiting for a Jew" opens with the statement, "My story begins in a community . . . ." What is the difference between an essay and a story? Why has Boyarin elected to tell his fellow anthropologists a story? What are the major events or pieces of this story? Is this a story that has a point? A moral? An argument?

3. The subtitle Boyarin has selected for his essay is "Marginal Redemption at the Eighth Street Shul." What is "marginal redemption"? What is it that gets redeemed in "Waiting for a Jew"?

■ *QUESTIONS FOR WRITING* ■

1. "[O]n the abandoned farm," Boyarin writes, "my first memories are tinged with a sense of traces, of mystery, of loss. Do all who eventually become anthropologists have this experience in some form, at some time in their early lives?" In posing this question, Boyarin suggests that there might be a connection between anthropology and a sense of loss. What might this connection be? In what ways has Boyarin's own research been shaped by this sense of loss?

2. Boyarin believes that "[a]ny marginal group in mass society may be subject without warning to the loss of its cultural landscape, and therefore those who are able to create portable landscapes for themselves are the most likely to endure." What is the difference between a "cultural landscape" and a "portable landscape"? At the end of Boyarin's story, what kind of landscape does he inhabit?

■ *QUESTIONS FOR MAKING CONNECTIONS BETWEEN READINGS* ■

1. Leila Ahmed and Jonathan Boyarin can both be considered insiders, part of the very cultures they are studying. Are they both insiders in the same way, though? What difference does it make whether a culture is studied by insiders or outsiders? Write an essay in which you explore what it means to be a member of a culture. Consider the role that self-reflection plays in either establishing or limiting memberships in the cultures that Ahmed and Boyarin describe.

2. In "The Myth of the Ant Queen," Steven Johnson argues that complex systems have an intelligence of their own. And he suggests that as such systems develop, the individuals involved—whether humans or ants— may remain largely oblivious to the larger patterns of change. Individuals may assume they are doing one sort of thing, but the system as a whole is doing something else. Does Boyarin appear to share this way of thinking? Is culture also a complex system that unfolds in directions the individual actors might not always control or even understand fully? When we look at cultural change as exemplified by Boyarin's religious odyssey, does that change appear to be directed by a "unified, top-down" intelligence, or does it take place from the bottom up, as a result of individual choices made by many different people? Are some cultures, institutions, and religions organized differently—that is, in a more top-down way?

BRYAN CAPLAN

MANY OF THE significant upheavals in the history of the modern society have arisen from attempts by marginal groups to win voting rights. Americans in particular are so fond of the "one person, one vote" style of democracy that exporting it is a cornerstone of foreign policy. Letting the public have a voice in the shape of government—whether through the election of representatives or through direct referenda—is seen as a countervailing force to the influence of industry and other special-interest groups driven by greed. This belief in the supremacy of the democratic form of government is bolstered by the long-standing assumption that rational decision-making motivated by self-interest will, in the end, produce the best decisions for society as a whole.

Bryan Caplan, an economist who teaches at George Mason University, challenges these and other assumptions that have traditionally supported our faith in democracy. While "most social scientists assume that voters' errors balance out," leading to the best outcomes on average, Caplan insists in *The Myth of the Rational Voter: Why Democracies Choose Bad Policies* that this is "just wishful thinking" by democratic fundamentalists. He challenges the prevailing belief in the "wisdom of crowds" by claiming that the public is led by biased assumptions to support policies that are detrimental to popular well-being. "In theory," he writes, "democracy is a bulwark against socially harmful policies. In practice, however, democracies frequently adopt and maintain policies that are damaging. How can this paradox be explained?" The problem, in Caplan's view, is that while "most people resist even the most basic lessons of economics," they nevertheless cling firmly to strong, emotionally motivated opinions on economic policy. The public as a whole "suffers from anti-market bias" that leads to emotionally satisfying but otherwise irrational and detrimental outcomes.

Caplan, Bryan. *The Myth of the Rational Voter.* Princeton, NJ: Princeton University Press, 2007.

Quotations come from Caplan's own site, <http://www.bcaplan.com/cspan.pdf>; an excerpt from "The Myth of the Rational Voter: Why Democracies Choose Bad Policies" that appears on the CATO Institute site, <http://www.cato.org/pub_display.php?pub_id=8262l>; "Special-Interest Secret," a *Wall Street Journal* editorial by Caplan, available at <http://online.wsj.com/article_email/SB117893365787300771-lMyQjAxMDE3NzE4MjkxMzIzWj.html>; an interview with Caplan on Australian radio, transcribed online at <http://www.abc.net.au/rn/counterpoint/stories/2007/1967721.htm>; and "Dumbocracy in America," an interview with Caplan available at <http://www.tcsdaily.com/article.aspx?id=061907A>.

If, as Caplan suggests, "the majority can be wrong" and "democracy is not sacred," what should the consequences be for both domestic and foreign policy? Can voters be educated to make better economic policy decisions, or should a council of studied economists be empowered "to declare legislation to be uneconomical and strike it down in the same way the Supreme Court strikes down restrictions on free speech as unconstitutional?" If both Republicans and Democrats—and bipartisan coalitions—all generate economically unsound policies, how much emphasis should the United States and other democracies continue to place on the will of the majority? And if the public is prone to irrational decision-making when it comes to national policy, is it time to reconsider the prospects of self-governance in other areas of human endeavor as well?

"Market Fundamentalism" Versus the Religion of Democracy

The trouble with the world is that the stupid are cocksure
and the intelligent are full of doubt.

—BERTRAND RUSSELL[1]

Economists perennially debate each other about how well the free market works. They have to step outside their profession to remember how much—underneath it all—they agree.[2] For economists, greedy intentions establish no presumption of social harm. Indeed, their rule of thumb is to figure out who could get rich by solving a problem—and start worrying if no one comes to mind. Most noneconomists find this whole approach distasteful, even offensive. Disputes between economists are quibbles by comparison.

Out of all their contrarian views, nothing about economists aggravates other intellectuals more than their sympathy for markets. As Melvin Reder aptly states, comprehension of mainstream economics "tends to generate appreciation of the merits of laissez-faire even when that appreciation does not extend to acceptance."[3] Left to their own devices, "normal" intellectuals could spend their careers cataloging human greed and the evils that flow from it. But economists stand in their midst, a fifth column, using their mental gifts to defend the enemy.

The hostility that economists provoke is evident from all the name-calling. Karl Marx, the classic poison pen, accused Ricardo and his fellow classical economists of "miserable sophistry," of suffering from "the obsession that bourgeois production is production as such, just like a man who believes in a particular religion and sees it as *the* religion, and everything outside of it only as *false* religions." For Marx, economists are apologists for the bourgeoisie, who "set up that single, unconscionable freedom—Free Trade" and replaced the feudal era's "exploitation veiled by religious and political illusions" with "naked, shameless, direct, brutal exploitation."[4] Rosa Luxemburg, in her essay "What is Economics?" proclaims with disgust that

> The bourgeois professors serve up a tasteless stew made from the leftovers of a hodge-podge of scientific notions and intentional circumlocutions—not intending to explore the real tendencies of capitalism, at all. On the contrary, they try only to send up a smoke screen for the purpose of defending capitalism as the best of all possible orders, and the only possible one.[5]

Modern detractors continue to oscillate between calling economists hired intellectual guns of the rich and a coven of conservative ideologues. But the more sophisticated critics protest that they object to certain brands of economics, not the whole field. For instance, Robert Kuttner's "quarrel is with a utopian—really, a dystopian—view of markets, not with economists as a breed."[6] But he takes back with one hand what he gives with the other, accusing "self-described liberal" economists of "dismantling much of the case for a mixed economy." If liberal Democratic economists are beyond the pale, who is not?

The Charge of Market Fundamentalism

"Market fundamentalism" is probably the most popular insult against economics these days. The world listened when billionaire George Soros declared that "Market fundamentalism . . . has rendered the global capitalist system unsound and unsustainable."[7] Robert Kuttner has a handy summary of what market fundamentalism amounts to:

> There is at the core of the celebration of markets a relentless tautology. If we begin, by assumption, with the premise that nearly everything can be understood as a market and that markets optimize outcomes, then everything comes back to the same conclusion—marketize! If, in the event, a particular market doesn't optimize, there is only one possible inference: it must be insufficiently marketlike.[8]

He insists, moreover, that this fault is not limited to a right-wing fringe: "Today, the only difference between the utopian version and the mainstream version is degree." Indeed, "As economics has become more fundamentalist, *the most extreme version of the market model has carried the greatest political, intellectual, and professional weight.*"[9] Even worse, economists' fundamentalism overflows into the policy arena:

> American liberals and European social democrats often seem unable to offer more than a milder version of the conservative program—deregulation, privatization, globalization, fiscal discipline, but at a less zealous extreme. *Few have been willing to challenge the premise that nearly everything should revert to a market.*[10]

Joseph Stiglitz joins the chorus against market fundamentalism, happily discarding the guarded professorial prose of his Nobel prize-winning research:

> The discontent with globalization arises not just from economics seeming to be pushed over everything else, but because a particular view of economics—market fundamentalism—is pushed over all other views. Opposition to globalization in many parts of the world is not to globalization per se . . . but to the particular set of doctrines, the Washington Consensus policies that the international financial institutions have imposed.[11]

Market fundamentalism is a harsh accusation. Christian fundamentalists are notorious for their strict biblical literalism, their unlimited willingness to ignore or twist the facts of geology and biology to match their prejudices. For the analogy to be apt, the typical economist would have to believe in the superiority of markets virtually without exception, regardless of the evidence, and dissenters would have to fear excommunication.

From this standpoint, the charge of "market fundamentalism" is silly, failing even as a caricature. If you ask the typical economist to name areas where markets work poorly, he gives you a list on the spot: Public goods, externalities, monopoly, imperfect information, and so on. More importantly, almost everything on the list can be traced back to other economists. Market failure is not a concept that has been forced upon a reluctant economics profession from the outside. It is an *internal* outgrowth of economists' self-criticism. After stating that markets usually work well, economists feel an urge to identify important counterexamples. Far from facing excommunication for sin against the sanctity of the market, discoverers of novel market failures reap professional rewards. Flip through the leading journals. A high fraction of their articles present theoretical or empirical evidence of market failure.

True market fundamentalists in the economics profession are few and far between. Not only are they absent from the center of the profession; they are rare at the "right-wing" extreme. Milton Friedman, a legendary libertarian, makes numerous exceptions, on everything from money to welfare to antitrust:

> Our principles offer no hard and fast line how far it is appropriate to use government to accomplish jointly what is difficult or impossible for us to accomplish separately through strictly voluntary exchange. In any particular case of proposed intervention, we must make up a balance sheet, listing separately the advantages and disadvantages.[12]

When Friedman prefers laissez-faire, he often openly acknowledges its defects. He has no quasi-religious need to defend the impeccability of the free market. For example, his discussion of natural monopoly states:

> [T]here are only three alternatives that seem available: private monopoly, public monopoly, or public regulation. All three are bad so we must choose among evils. . . . I reluctantly conclude that, if tolerable, private monopoly may be the least of the evils.[13]

Friedman is far more market-friendly than the average economist. But a "market fundamentalist"? Hardly. He recognizes numerous cases where market performance is poor, and does not excommunicate less promarket colleagues for heresy.

If neither the typical economist nor Milton Friedman himself qualifies as a market fundamentalist, who does? The only plausible candidates are the followers of Ludwig von Mises and especially his student Murray Rothbard. The latter does seem to categorically reject the notion of suboptimal market performance:

> Such a view completely misconceives the way in which economic science asserts that free-market action is *ever* optimal. It is optimal, not from the personal ethical views of an economist, but from the standpoint of the free, voluntary actions of all participants and in satisfying the freely expressed needs of the consumers. Government interference, therefore, will necessarily and always move *away* from such an optimum.[14]

Both Mises and Rothbard have passed away, but their outlook—including Ph.D.s who subscribe to it—lives on in the Ludwig von Mises Institute. But groups like these have basically given up on mainstream economics; members mostly talk to each other and publish in their own journals. The closest thing to market fundamentalists are not merely outside the mainstream of the economics profession. They are *way* outside.

Popular accusations of market fundamentalism are plain wrong. Yes, economists think that the market works better than other people admit. But they acknowledge exceptions to the rule. The range of these exceptions changes as new evidence comes in. And it is usually economists themselves who discover the exceptions in the first place.

Democratic Fundamentalism

> In wide areas of life majorities are entitled to rule, if they wish, simply
> because they are majorities.
>
> —ROBERT BORK, *The Tempting of America*[15]

The disparity between economists' open-mindedness and the charge of market fundamentalism is so vast that it is hard not to speculate about the motives behind it. I sense a strong element of projection: accusing others of the cognitive misdeeds one commits oneself. Take "creation scientists." Faculty and researchers of the Institute for Creation Research follow a party line: "The scriptures, both Old and New Testaments, are inerrant in relation to any subject with which they deal, and are to be accepted in their normal and intended sense."[16] You can hardly get less scientific. Yet a standard debating tactic of creation scientists is to insist that "evolutionary theory, along with its bedfellow, secular humanism, is really a religion."[17] Creationists' attacks on the objectivity of mainstream evolutionists seem to stem from their sense of scientific inferiority to their opponents.

Similarly, the most vocal opponents of "market fundamentalism" are themselves often believers in what can accurately be called "democratic fundamentalism." Its purest expression is the cliché, attributed to failed 1928 presidential candidate Al Smith, that "All the ills of democracy can be cured by more democracy."[18] In other words, *no matter what happens,* the case for democracy remains untouched. Victor Kamber has a book called *Giving Up on Democracy.*[19] The title's rhetorical power stems from the widespread belief that democracy has to be the answer. You can complain about democracy, but you cannot "give up" on it. Indeed, many admire its flaws. As Adam Michnik exclaims, "Democracy is gray," but "Gray is beautiful!"[20]

A person who said, "All the ills of markets can be cured by more markets" would be lampooned as the worst sort of market fundamentalist. Why the double standard? Because unlike market fundamentalism, democratic fundamentalism is widespread. In polite company, you can make fun of the worshippers of Zeus, but not Christians or Jews. Similarly, it is socially acceptable to make fun of market fundamentalism, but not democratic fundamentalism, because market fundamentalists are scarce, and democratic fundamentalists are all around us.

Everyone from journalists and politicians to empirical social scientists and academic philosophers is willing to publicly profess his democratic fundamentalism without embarrassment. At the end of a book cataloging his decades of disappointment with American politics, William Greider still cheerfully writes:

> After thirty years of working as a reporter, I am steeped in disappointing
> facts about self-government. Having observed politics from the small-town
> courthouse to the loftiest reaches of the federal establishment, I know quite

a lot about duplicitous politicians and feckless bureaucracies, about gullible voters and citizens who are mean-spirited cranks. These experiences, strangely enough, have not undermined my childhood faith in democratic possibilities, but rather tended to confirm it.[21]

What—if anything—*would* undermine Greider's "childhood faith"? The post-1992 political direction was probably not a dramatic improvement in his eyes. But you can bet that his faith is as vibrant as ever. If an economist waxed poetic about his childhood faith in the free market, he would be tagged a market fundamentalist, and his credibility would plummet.

Perhaps we should expect no better of journalists, however talented their writing. But one would hope that empirical social scientists would strive harder for objectivity, or at least feel social pressure to keep their faith to themselves. Yet democratic fundamentalism is not hard to find there either. To take only one example, Pranab Bardhan rigorously analyzes the causal relationship between democracy and development.[22] But before he gets down to business, Bardhan not only virtually admits to democratic fundamentalism, but presumes his readers to be democratic fundamentalists too! "Most of us, ardent democrats all, would like to believe that democracy is not merely good in itself, it is also valuable in enhancing the process of development." Unfortunately, the empirical literature testing this claim is "rather unhelpful and unpersuasive. It is unhelpful because it usually does not confirm a causal process and the results go every which way." Despite the shortage of empirical support, Bardhan gratuitously ends with an affirmation of faith: "I remain an incorrigible optimist for the long-run healing powers of democracy."[23] How many scholars would survey an expansive literature on market performance, admit that the evidence is too mixed to draw any conclusion, then speak of the "long-run healing powers of capitalism"? They would be too embarrassed—and should be.

Democratic fundamentalism is also evident in analytic philosophy, legendary for its guarded skepticism. Normative political theorist Ian Shapiro is a prime example. He objects to the notion of "some 'bird's eye' standpoint, existing previously to and independently of democratic procedures, by reference to which we can evaluate the outcomes they produce."[24] In plain language, democracy is right by definition, for there is no extra-democratic standard of right and wrong.

This is an admittedly uncharitable reading. Like most philosophers, Shapiro quickly qualifies his position, affirming that political principles must be defended on "consequentialist grounds." But he then qualifies his qualification, leaving his democratic fundamentalism intact. "The difficulty then becomes that the desirability of the consequences in question is *debatable,* suggesting that they should have to vie for support with other values and policies. Like it or not, democracy rears its head in the very definition of justice."[25] This is one of the baldest rigged juries in the history of philosophy: Democracy must be judged by its consequences, but the only way to judge its consequences is by a vote!

Lest someone dare to assert that the consequences of a policy are not "debatable," Shapiro elsewhere rules out the possibility. Highly technical matters might be beyond debate, but not questions of substantive democratic interest:

> In certain (though not all) circumstances one can reasonably act on the advice of an airplane pilot, an auto mechanic, an architect, or a physician without understanding its rationale or even being interested in it. But the idea that there is an analogous political expertise reasonably prompts suspicion.[26]

Why?

> Most minimally, the suggestion that there is political expertise is suspect because there are few reasons to believe that there is in fact much of it. What is typically billed as knowledge about the world of politics seems so meager, and is so regularly undermined by events, that people who set themselves up as political experts often give off the whiff of snake oil.[27]

By now, sweeping rejections of expert opinion should be painfully familiar, but it is still odd for a noted political expert to belittle the idea of political expertise. If Shapiro does not consider himself an expert, why does he bother writing books? Anyone who grades final exams in political science courses has seen for himself that disparities in political knowledge are real and large. If that is not good enough, there is plenty of empirical evidence about political knowledge, none of which Shapiro bothers to challenge.[28]

But isn't he right about the experts being "regularly undermined by events"? It depends on how strictly you grade them. If the "experts" are less than impressive, try comparing them to laymen. Moreover, much of the experts' bad press can be explained by selection: Sensible experts and questions with well-established answers get less coverage than cranks and controversy.

Shapiro is slightly more hesitant to make a sweeping dismissal of economics. But democratic fundamentalism triumphs in the end:

> It would be foolish not to recognize that economists, for instance, often have esoteric knowledge (perhaps less than they think they have) about the workings of the economy that is relevant to democratic deliberation about it. But because decisions about the limits of the market sphere and the structure of its governance are linked to the controversial exercise of power, they are inescapably political; thus economic policy making should never be ceded to professional economists. They must persuade lay representatives, in non-technical terms, if we are to be bound by their advice.[29]

Perversely, then, the *more* irrational the electorate is, the *less* of a say economists have. If a lay audience will listen to reason, economists wield some influence. But a stubbornly wrongheaded lay audience is entitled to do whatever it likes: "Economic policy making should *never* be ceded to professional economists."[30] If this is not democratic fundamentalism, what is?

In his research on "sacred values," psychologist Philip Tetlock observes that "people often insist with apparently great conviction that certain relationships and commitments are sacred and that *even to contemplate* trade-offs with the secular values of money or convenience is anathema."[31] In the modern world, democracy is one of the best examples; the faithful equate minor deviations with total apostasy, and condemn sinful thoughts as harshly as wicked deeds.

A standard rhetorical tactic is to equate modest reductions in the role of government with the elimination of government regulation altogether. Robert Kuttner tells us that "in the emblematic case of airline regulation, what began under President Carter as 'regulatory reform' quickly evolved into a drive for complete deregulation."[32] Apparently, the Federal Aviation Administration's continuing regulation of safety does not count. A similar ploy is to equate mere *talk* of cutting government with doing it. Richard Leone of the Twentieth Century Fund alleges that "faith in idealized market structures also has spawned a political jihad intent upon stripping away the community and government safeguards against market abuses and imperfections. . . . Democrats and moderate Republicans are stumbling all over each other to prove their conversion to the one true faith of laissez-faire economics."[33] Strangely, the laissez-faire jihad failed to push federal spending as a percentage of GDP below 18%—and most of the decline during the 1990s clearly stemmed from the end of the Cold War.[34]

In the end, apologists for democracy often fall back on Winston Churchill's slogan, "Democracy is the worst form of government, except all those other forms that have been tried from time to time."[35] On the surface, this sounds like mature realism, not democratic fundamentalism. But Churchill's maxim is an all-or-nothing rhetorical trick. Imagine if an economist dismissed complaints about the free market by snapping: "The free market is the worst form of economic organization, except all the others." This is a fine objection to communism, but only a market fundamentalist would buy it as an argument against moderate government intervention. Churchill's slogan is every bit as weak. Just because dictatorship is disastrous, it hardly follows that democracy must have free rein. Like markets, democracy can be limited, regulated, or overruled. Contramajoritarian procedures like judicial review can operate alongside democratic ones. Supermajority rules allow minorities to thwart the will of the majority. Twisting a marginal trade-off into a binary choice is fundamentalism trying to sound reasonable.

Will the Real Fundamentalism Please Stand Up?
The Case of the Policy Analysis Market

A major story broke on July 28, 2003.[36] Senators Ron Wyden and Byron Dorgan demanded that the Department of Defense end funding for an obscure program, the Policy Analysis Market (henceforth PAM). Still in its preliminary stage, the program's aim was to create online betting markets for questions of national security. PAM traders could profit by—among other things—correctly predicting the number of Western terror casualties. Critics quickly labeled it the "Terror Market" scheme. Wyden and Dorgan condemned it without reservation:

> Spending taxpayer dollars to create terrorism betting parlors is as wasteful as it is repugnant. The American people want the Federal government to use its resources enhancing our security, not gambling on it.[37]

Television and newspaper coverage was almost entirely unfavorable—and so was public opinion. Could the PAM's backers be too blind to see that it gave a financial incentive for terrorism? Was there any more egregious case of market fundamentalism? The Secretary of Defense killed the program on July 29—*one day* after the publicity began. John Poindexter, head of the Information Awareness Office, had to offer his resignation the next day. After two months, all funding for the office was terminated. So much for bureaucratic inertia.

Then a funny thing happened. Other media—published less frequently and aimed at more sophisticated audiences—followed up on the Terror Market story. They delved into the rationale of the project, and talked to its creators about possible flaws in its design. Several lessons emerged.[38]

First, there is a large body of empirical evidence on the predictive accuracy of speculative markets, on everything from horse-racing to elections to invasions. "Put your money where your mouth is" turns out to be a great way to get the well informed to reveal what they know, and the poorly informed to quiet down. No system is perfect, but betting markets outperform other methods of prediction in a wide variety of circumstances. The PAM was inspired not by ivory tower theorizing, but by the proven success of betting markets in other areas.

Second, the amount of money on the PAM table was very small. Individual bets were limited to a few tens of dollars. The idea that these paltry sums would motivate additional terrorism is ludicrous. Terrorists who wanted to profit from their attacks could make a lot more money by manipulating normal financial markets—shorting airline stocks and such. Incidentally, the 9/11 Commission found that did not happen either.[39]

Third, the program was shut down so quickly that there was no time to verify the accusations. According to Robin Hanson, my colleague and one of the brains behind the PAM, "During that crucial day, no one from the government asked the PAM team if the accusations were correct, or if the more offending aspects could be cut from the project."[40] The creators had anticipated and already addressed the obvious objections, but opponents were too inflamed to listen. Constructive criticism was in short supply, to say the least; the goal was to kill the program, not improve it.

Last, the PAM experience raised a dilemma for those who embrace the "wisdom of crowds." Surowiecki forcefully defends the merits of decision markets like the PAM. But he also affirms that "there's no reason to believe that crowds would be wise in most situations but suddenly become doltish in the political arena." As long as there *is* a right answer, "Democracy's chances of adopting good policies are high."[41] How then can Surowiecki account for the public's extreme hostility to the PAM? If decision markets and democracy both work well, the PAM should be popular.[42]

If the critics studied the PAM more thoroughly, they would have been angrier still. A key feature was the ability to make *conditional* bets. You could wager, for example, on the number of Western terrorist casualties *if* the United States invades Iraq, and the number *if* it does not. Comparing the price of those two bets would reveal whether the market thinks an invasion will make us more or less safe from terrorist attacks. In short, betting markets could second-guess not only political leaders, but public opinion itself. This is bound to rub democratic fundamentalists the wrong way.

Overall, the creators of the PAM were far from market fundamentalists. They built on a solid body of evidence, thought carefully about potential problems, and were open to criticism. Their plan was to test the program out on a small scale, work out the bugs, and gradually expand it.

Almost the opposite holds for opponents. They did not question the track record of predictive betting markets. Apparently, they knew nothing about it and did not care to learn. Despite the obvious failures of traditional intelligence in recent years, they were convinced that the best policy was more of the same. Listen to Wyden and Dorgan:

> The example that you provide in your report would let participants gamble on the question, "Will terrorists attack Israel with bioweapons in the next year?" Surely, such a threat should be met with intelligence gathering of the highest quality—not by putting the question to individuals betting on an Internet website.[43]

Surely? How do they know? At minimum, the PAM would have raced betting markets against old-fashioned intelligence gathering. But democratic fundamentalists did not want to put their antimarket dogma to the test.

Private Choice as an Alternative to
Democracy and Dictatorship

Undemocratic politics is not the only alternative to democratic politics. Many areas of life stand outside the realm of politics, of "collective choice." When the law is silent, decisions are "up to the individual" or "left to the market." If the term were not preempted, private choice could be called "the Third Way," the alternative to both democracy and dictatorship.

For most of human history, religion was a state responsibility. The idea that government could have no established religion was inconceivable. All that has changed; now individuals decide which religion, if any, to practice. Verbal gymnastics notwithstanding, this depoliticization is undemocratic. The majority now has as little say about my religion as it would under a dictatorship; in both cases, the law ignores public opinion. Before the 1930s, similarly, many areas of U.S. economic life were undemocratically shielded from federal and state regulation.[44] The market periodically trumped democracy, on everything from the minimum wage to the National Recovery Administration. And unless you are a democratic fundamentalist, you have to be open to the possibility that this was all for the good.

Fervent partisans of democracy often grant that democracy and the market are substitutes. As Kuttner puts it, "The democratic state remains the prime counterweight to the market."[45] Their complaint is that the public has less and less say over its destiny because corporations have more and more say over theirs. To "save democracy," the people must reassert its authority.

Fair enough. Though their opponents greatly overstate the extent of privatization and deregulation, these policies take decisions out of the hands of majorities and put them into the hands of business owners. But the critics rarely wonder if this transfer might be desirable. They treat less reliance on democracy as automatically objectionable.

This is another symptom of democratic fundamentalism. If all that an economist had to say against a government program were, "That's government intervention. Government is supplanting markets!" he would be pigeonholed, then marginalized, as a market fundamentalist. But when an equally simplistic cry goes up in the name of democracy, there is a sympathetic audience. It is logically possible that clear-eyed business greed makes better decisions than confused voter altruism. Why not at least compare their performance, instead of prejudging?

The complaint that we are "losing democracy" is especially weak when we bear in mind that this is not a binary choice between unlimited democracy and pure laissez-faire. Just because *some* democracy is beneficial or necessary, it scarcely follows that we should not have *less*. Consider deregulation of the television and radio spectrum. Democratic fundamentalists find the idea offensive because it ends democratic oversight.[46] But it is hard to see the value of democracy in the entertainment industry. Premium networks like HBO demonstrate that the profit motive, uninhibited by majority preferences, is a recipe for high-quality, creative programming. Democratic fundamentalism holds back the rest of the industry.

Most democratic enthusiasts recognize that free markets are a substitute—albeit a self-evidently undesirable one—for democracy. A few take the more extreme position that the notion of depoliticized choice is incoherent.[47] This position is best expressed in the work of Ian Shapiro, who criticizes the "implausible notion that a scheme of collective action is an alternative to a scheme of private action."[48] "Were it possible somehow for society to 'not undertake' collective action," defects in collective decision-making "might amount to a prima facie argument against all collective action."[49] But in fact, private action is "parasitic" on collective action:

> The institutions of private property, contract, and public monopoly of coercive force . . . were created and are sustained by the state, partly financed by implicit taxes on those who would prefer an alternative system. The real question, for democrats, is not "whether or not collective action?" but whether or not democratic modes of managing it are superior to the going alternatives.[50]

This argument is seriously flawed.

First, even if private action presupposes the existence of collective action, it remains feasible to eschew collective action *in some or most areas*. Just because a doctor's treatment keeps you alive hardly shows that you have to grant him absolute authority over your whole life. You can heed his advice if your survival depends on it, and otherwise do as you please. Similarly, suppose we grant that private action is a parasite on the body of government. It does not follow that the host must have final say across the board. Indeed, a presumption against collective action is compatible with the view that private action depends upon government: What better reason could there be to overrule the presumption than that private action could not otherwise survive?

Second, Shapiro's argument can be readily reversed. Collective decision-making is "parasitic" on the wealth created by the market economy. It would be hard to have an orderly vote if businesses had not fed, clothed, housed, and transported the electorate and candidates. Does this reveal an internal contradiction in every regulation? Hardly.

Last, it is not true that private action is inherently parasitic or dependent upon collective action. The existence of the black market proves that property rights and contracts are possible without government approval. That is why one drug dealer can meaningfully tell another, "You stole my crack" or, "We had a deal." Indeed, the black market shows not only that property and contract can persist without the government's support, but that they can survive in the face of its determined resistance.

Contrary to naysayers, there is no conceptual flaw in prescriptions to rely more on private choice and less on collective choice. The proposal is quite intelligible. In fact, the counterarguments are so weak that their popularity seems to be another symptom of democratic fundamentalism. People want to rule alternatives to democracy out of court, to avoid putting their faith to the test.

Voter Irrationality, Markets, and Democracy

Critics of the economics profession are right about one thing. Economists *really do* subscribe to a long list of views that are unpopular, even offensive. Perhaps most offensive is economists' judgment that markets work considerably better than the general public thinks. That judgment is the foundation of economists' promarket outlook, the so-called Washington Consensus. . . .

No matter how well you think markets work, it makes sense to rely on markets *more* when you grow more pessimistic about democracy. If you use two car mechanics and discover that mechanic A drinks on the job, the natural response is to shift some of your business over to mechanic B, whatever your preexisting complaints about B.

Should my [argument] push you toward democratic pessimism? Yes. Above all, I emphasize that voters are irrational. But I also accept two views common among democratic enthusiasts: That voters are largely unselfish, and politicians usually comply with public opinion. Counterintuitively, this threefold combination—irrational cognition, selfless motivation, and modest slack—is "as bad as it gets."[51]

If public opinion is sensible, selfishness and slack prevent democracy from fulfilling its full promise. But if public opinion is senseless, selfishness and slack prevent democracy from carrying out its full threat. Selfishness and slack are like water rather than poison. They are not intrinsically injurious; they *dilute* the properties of the systems they affect. Thus, when the public systematically misunderstands how to maximize social welfare—as it often does—it ignites a quick-burning fuse attached to correspondingly misguided policies. This should make almost anyone more pessimistic about democracy.

The striking implication is that even economists, widely charged with market fundamentalism, should be more promarket than they already are. What economists currently see as the optimal balance between markets and government *rests upon an overestimate of the virtues of democracy*. In many cases, economists should embrace the free market in spite of its defects, because it still outshines the democratic alternative.

Consider the insurance market failure known as "adverse selection." If people who want insurance know their own riskiness, but insurers only know average riskiness, the market tends to shrink. Low-risk people drop out, which raises consumers' average riskiness, which raises prices, which leads more low-risk customers to drop out.[52] In the worst-case scenario, the market "unravels." Prices get so high that no one buys insurance, and consumers get so risky that firms cannot afford to sell for less.

Economists often take the presence of adverse selection as a solid reason to deviate from their laissez-faire presumption.[53] But given the way that democracy really works, the shift in presumption is premature. Given public opinion, what kind of regulation is democracy likely to implement? The essence of the adverse selection problem is that insurers do not know enough to charge the riskiest consumers the highest premiums. But how would a person with antimarket bias see things? The last thought on his mind would be, "If only insurance companies could identify the riskiest consumers and charge them accordingly." Reflected in the fun-house mirror of antimarket bias, the "obvious" problem to fix is *higher rates for riskier people,* not the imperfect match between risks and rates.

The fact that regulation *could* help correct the adverse selection problem— for example, by making everyone buy insurance—is therefore a weak argument for regulation. Given the public's antimarket bias, democracy will probably force companies to charge high-risk clients the same as everyone else. The basic economics of insurance tells us that this makes the adverse selection problem worse by encouraging low-risk consumers to opt out. But basic economics is what the public refuses to accept. It does not take a market fundamentalist to recognize that it may be prudent to muddle through with the imperfections of the free market, instead of asking the electorate for its opinion.

Even among economists, market-oriented policy prescriptions are often seen as too dogmatic, too unwilling to take the flaws of the free market into account.[54] Many prefer a more "sophisticated" position: Since we have already belabored the advantages of markets, let us not forget to emphasize the benefits of government intervention. I claim that the qualification needs qualification: Before we emphasize the benefits of government intervention, let us distinguish intervention designed by a well-intentioned economist from intervention that appeals to noneconomists, and reflect that the latter predominate. You do not have to be dogmatic to take a staunchly promarket position. You just have to notice that the "sophisticated" emphasis on the benefits of intervention mistakes theoretical possibility for empirical likelihood.

In the 1970s, the Chicago school became notorious for its "markets good, government bad" outlook. One could interpret my work as an attempt to revive that tradition. Many of its arguments were flawed, even contradictory. If people were as uniformly rational as Chicago economists assumed, government policy could not stay bad for long. George Stigler eventually pulled the rug out from under Milton Friedman by saying so.[55] But flawed arguments can still lead to a true conclusion; Stigler was a better logician, but Friedman had greater insight. Placed on a foundation of rational irrationality, perhaps the Chicago research program that Friedman inspired can live again.

Correcting Democracy?

The main upshot of my analysis of democracy is that it is a good idea to rely more on private choice and the free market. But what—if anything—can be done to improve outcomes, *taking the supremacy of democracy over the market as fixed?* The answer depends on how flexibly you define "democracy." Would we still have a "democracy" if you needed to pass a test of economic literacy to vote? If you needed a college degree? Both of these measures raise the economic understanding of the median voter, leading to more sensible policies. Franchise restrictions were historically used for discriminatory ends, but that hardly implies that they should never be used again for any reason. A test of voter competence is no more objectionable than a driving test. Both bad driving and bad voting are dangerous not merely to the individual who practices them, but to innocent bystanders. As Frédéric Bastiat argues, "The right to suffrage rests on the presumption of capacity":

> And why is incapacity a cause of exclusion? Because it is not the voter alone who must bear the consequences of his vote; because each vote involves and affects the whole community; because the community clearly has the right to require some guarantee as to the acts on which its welfare and existence depend.[56]

A more palatable way to raise the economic literacy of the median voter is by giving *extra* votes to individuals or groups with greater economic literacy. Remarkably, until the passage of the Representation of the People Act of 1949, Britain retained plural voting for graduates of elite universities and business owners. As Speck explains, "Graduates had been able to vote for candidates in twelve universities in addition to those in their own constituencies, and businessmen with premises in a constituency other than their own domicile could vote in both."[57] Since more educated voters think more like economists, there is much to be said for such weighting schemes. I leave it to the reader to decide whether 1948 Britain counts as a democracy.

A moderate reform suggested by my analysis is to reduce or eliminate efforts to increase voter turnout. Education and age are the two best predictors of turnout. Since the former is the strongest predictor of economic literacy, and the latter has little connection with it, the median voter's economic literacy exceeds the median citizen's. If "get out the vote" campaigns led to 100% participation, politicians would have to compete for the affection of noticeably more biased voters than they do today.[58]

Most worries about de jure or de facto changes in participation take the empirically discredited self-interested voter hypothesis for granted.[59] If voters' goal were to promote their individual interests, nonvoters would be sitting ducks. People entitled to vote would intelligently select policies to help themselves, ignoring the interests of everyone else. There is so much evidence against the SIVH, however, that these fears can be discounted. The voters who know the most do not want to expropriate their less clear-headed countrymen. Like other voters, their goal is, by and large, to maximize social welfare. They just happen to know more about how to do it.

Since well-educated people are better voters, another tempting way to improve democracy is to give voters more education. Maybe it would work. But it would be expensive. . . . A cheaper strategy, and one where a causal effect is more credible, is changing the curriculum. Steven Pinker argues that schools should try to "provide students with the cognitive skills that are most important for grasping the modern world and that are most unlike the cognitive tools they are born with," by emphasizing "economics, evolutionary biology, and probability and statistics."[60] Pinker essentially wants to give schools a new mission: rooting out the biased beliefs that students arrive with, especially beliefs that impinge on government policy.[61] What should be cut to make room for the new material?

> There are only twenty-four hours in a day, and a decision to teach one subject is also a decision not to teach another one. The question is not whether trigonometry is important, but whether it is more important than statistics; not whether an educated person should know the classics, but whether it is more important for an educated person to know the classics than elementary economics.[62]

Last but not least on the list of ways to make democracy work better is for economically literate individuals who enjoy some political slack to *take advantage of it* to improve policy.[63] If you work at a regulatory bureau, draft legislation, advise politicians, or hold office, figure out how much latitude you possess, and use it to make policy better. Subvert bad ideas, and lend a helping hand to good ones. As Ronald Coase says, "An economist who, by his efforts, is able to postpone by a week a government program which wastes $100 million a year . . . has, by his action, earned his salary for the whole of his life."[64] As Bastiat emphasizes, the voter who acts on his biased judgments is not just hurting himself. If you employ your political wiggle room to improve policy, you are doing your part to tame a public nuisance.

Economics: What Is It Good For?

> Our primary mission should be to vaccinate the minds of our undergraduates against the misconceptions that are so predominant in what passes for educated discussion about international trade.
>
> —PAUL KRUGMAN, *"What Do Undergrads*
> *Need to Know About Trade?"*[65]

Most of the preceding remedies suffer from a catch-22. Once you use up your political slack, the only way to curtail the political influence of the economically illiterate to is convince them it is a good idea. However, if you were persuasive enough to do *that*, you could "cut out the middleman" and directly convince them to start voting more sensibly. Persuasive resources are scarce. Is there anything that can be done, holding constant the persuasive resources of the economics discipline and "allied forces"?[66] Is there any way to make better use of their time? I believe there is.

Economists have a reputation for being unwilling to give definite answers and unable to reach a consensus. Harry Truman famously longed for a "one-handed economist," who could not say "on the one hand, on the other hand." Paul Samuelson added, "According to legend, economists are supposed never to agree among themselves. If Parliament were to ask six economists for an opinion, seven answers would come back—two, no doubt, from the volatile Mr. Keynes!"[67]

Both economists and their detractors know these stereotypes are dead wrong. But for once, however, economists themselves are largely to blame for the misunderstanding. When economists choose between communicating (*a*) nothing, or (*b*) simplified but roughly accurate conclusions, they strangely seem to prefer (*a*). When you have an *entire semester* with a group of students, they forget all but the main points. If you fail to hammer a few fundamental principles into your students, odds are they will take away nothing at all. Yet in the dozens of economics courses I have taken, the professors rarely took their constraint seriously. Many preferred to dwell on the details of national income accounting, or mathematical subtleties, or the latest academic fad.

I know from experience that professors have an enormous amount of slack. They can drastically change the content and style of their courses at low cost. So to the question, "How can teachers of economics make better use of their time?" I answer that they should strive to channel the spirit of the original one-handed economist, Frédéric Bastiat.

It makes no difference if "teacher of economics" is your official job description. Everyone who knows some economics—professors, policy wonks, journalists, students, and concerned citizens—has opportunities to teach. Each of us should begin, like Bastiat, by contrasting the popular view of a topic with the economic view. Make it obvious that economists think one thing and noneconomists think something else. Select a few conclusions with profound policy implications—like comparative advantage, the effect of price controls, and the long-run benefits of labor-saving innovation—and exhaust them. As Bastiat advises, "We must . . . present our conclusions in so clear a light that truth and error will show themselves plainly; so that once and for all victory will go either to protectionism or free trade."[68]

Economists who follow Bastiat's advice help their colleagues as well. A stereotype—that they fail to offer definite conclusions—handicaps economists. Being *counterstereotypical* not only makes you more persuasive and influential as an individual. It also undermines the stereotype, making economists more persuasive and influential as a profession.

At first, many feel uncomfortable being a one-handed economist. But anyone can do it. Spend less time qualifying general principles. Except at the best schools, introductory classes should be almost qualification free—

there is too much nonsense to unlearn to waste time on rare conditions where standard conclusions fail. Most of the exceptions taught in introductory classes can be profitably deferred to intermediate courses; most of the exceptions taught in intermediate courses can be profitably deferred to graduate school. The best students will understand if you tell them, "Those questions will be addressed in more advanced courses." For the rest, you must respect the Laffer Curve of learning: They retain less if you try to teach them more.

To take an example that is likely to be controversial, economists do a bad job teaching students about competition.[69] Textbooks usually say, "Competition works *as long as . . .*" and then list the many strong assumptions of perfect competition. Many texts are wrong on technical grounds: Perfectly competitive assumptions are *sufficient* conditions of efficiency, not necessary ones.[70] But they also deserve censure for failing to emphasize that even imperfect competition defies the cliché that "businesses charge whatever they like." Indeed, students' casual equation of greedy motives and bad outcomes is overstated for *monopolies*. Like competitive firms, monopolies have an incentive to reduce costs, cut their prices when costs fall, and look over their shoulder for potential competition. It is more important for students to understand that self-interest often encourages socially beneficial behavior, than to understand that this mechanism falls short of perfection. Antimarket bias almost ensures that they will not forget the market's shortcomings.

At this point, a fair challenge to pose is: If people's views about economics are so irrational, how is persuasion possible? My answer is that irrationality is not a barrier to persuasion, but *an invitation to alternative rhetorical techniques.* Think of it this way: If beliefs are, in part, "consumed" for their direct psychological benefits, then to compete in the marketplace of ideas, you need to bundle them with the right emotional content. There is more than one way to make economics "cool," but I like to package it with an undertone of rebellious discovery, of brash common sense. Who does not side with the child in the Hans Christian Andersen fable who exclaims, "The Emperor is naked!"? You might be afraid of alienating your audience, but it depends on how you frame it. "I'm right, you're wrong," falls flat, but "I'm right, the people outside this classroom are wrong, and you don't want to be like *them*, do you?" is, in my experience, fairly effective.

Yes, these techniques can be used to inculcate fallacies as well as insight. But there is no intrinsic conflict with truth. You can actually get students *excited* about thinking for themselves on topics where society disapproves, as Ralph Waldo Emerson does in his essay "Self-Reliance." He paints truth-seeking as not merely responsible, but heroic:

> The nonchalance of boys who are sure of a dinner, and would disdain as much as a lord to do or say aught to conciliate one, is the healthy attitude of

human nature. How is a boy the master of society; independent, irresponsible, looking out from his corner on such people and facts as pass by, he tries and sentences them on their merits, in the swift, summary way of boys, as good, bad, interesting, silly, eloquent, troublesome. He cumbers himself never about consequences, about interests; he gives an independent, genuine verdict.[71]

Bastiat, similarly, makes logic and common sense appealing by ridiculing those who lack them. Take his famous Candlemakers' Petition:

We are suffering from the ruinous competition of a foreign rival who apparently works under conditions so far superior to our own for the production of light that he is *flooding the domestic market* with it at an incredibly low price; for the moment he appears, our sales cease, all the consumers turn to him. . . . This rival . . . is none other than the sun.

[I]f you shut off as much as possible all access to natural light, and thereby create a need for artificial light, what industry in France will not ultimately be encouraged?[72]

The petition does more than teach economics. It turns protectionism into a joke. In the process, Bastiat depicts economists not as pedants, but as the life of the intellectual party. Without compromising his intellectual integrity, Bastiat makes readers' desire to think well of themselves work in his favor.

If you do not have a full semester to enlighten your audience, my advice becomes more relevant still. The less time you have, the more important it is to (1) highlight the contrast between the popular view and basic economics in stark terms; (2) explain why the latter is true and the former is false; and (3) make it fun.

When the media spotlight gives other experts a few seconds to speak their mind, they usually strive to forcefully communicate one or two simplified conclusions. They know that is the best they can do with the time allotted to them. But economists are reluctant to use this strategy. Though the forum demands it, they think it unseemly to express a definite judgment. This is a recipe for being utterly ignored.[73] If you are one voice in a sea of self-promotion, you had better speak up clearly when you finally get your chance to talk.

Admittedly, economists have less latitude on television than in class. If a reporter interviews you about the trade deficit, but you keep changing the subject to comparative advantage, the interview might not be aired, and you reduce your chance of being interviewed again. But it is worth testing the limits of the media's tolerance. It is not so off-putting to preface any mention of the trade deficit with a short disclaimer: "Trade deficits, contrary to popular opinion, are not a bad thing. Whenever the trade deficit goes up, people always want to 'do something' about it, but they're wrong—like all trade, international trade is mutually beneficial, whether or not there is a trade deficit." Maybe you could tack on an amusing example too: "I run a huge trade deficit with Wegmans Supermarket—I buy thousands of dollars of its groceries, but Wegmans buys nothing from me—and it is nothing to worry about." If you cannot steer the conversation away from the latest numbers, at least steal a little time to put the numbers in perspective.

Outlets like newspaper columns and blogs lie somewhere between television sound bites and semester-long courses. You have more slack in print or online than on TV. But you still have to heavily simplify. I know one economist who intentionally writes columns with fewer words than the editor requests. That way, he explains, it is hard for newspapers to cut his favorite parts—which he evidently suspects copy editors are likeliest to hate.

There is much to learn from Bastiat's approach to economic education. But that is only the beginning.[74] Bastiat puts economic education in a broader context. Economists study the world, but are also a part of it. Where do they fit in? Bastiat's answer is "the refutation of commonplace prejudices." To use modern terminology, economists supply the public good of correcting systematically biased beliefs. Their main task: "clearing the way for truth . . . preparing men's minds to understand it . . . correcting public opinion . . . breaking dangerous weapons in the hands of those who misuse them."[75]

Economists already do some of this by instinct. It is hard to be sure, but in the absence of generations of economic education, changes like falling tariffs and privatization would probably have happened on a smaller scale, or not at all.[76] But economists are in a peculiar situation: They correct public opinion not because market forces *drive* them to, but because market forces *grant* them the wiggle room to perform this function, if they are so inclined. This means that a great deal depends on the profession's morale—how enthusiastically it accepts its responsibility.

One of the main factors that has undermined the profession's morale in recent decades is the marginalization of the idea of systematically biased beliefs about economics. If it really is the case that voters on average correctly understand economics before they hear word one, *who needs economists?* What social function do they serve?

This is not an impossible question to answer. Professional economists could devote themselves to reducing the variance of public opinion, to narrowing dispersion due to random errors. In so doing, they would attain Keynes's ambition: for economists to become "humble, competent people on a level with dentists."[77]

Such professional humility is dangerous. Economists who compare themselves to dentists will basically accept their society as it is. This would be fine if reducing variance were the only task for economists to perform. But in the real world, economists are the main defense against the systematic errors that are the foundation for numerous bad policies. If they look the other way, these mistakes go largely unchecked. Nothing is more likely to make economists desert their posts, to deter them from performing their vital function, than a misguided humility.

Economists should not forget that they have made mistakes in the past, and will again. We should all admit our limitations. But there are two kinds of errors to avoid. Hubris is one; self-abasement is the other. The first leads experts to overreach themselves; the second leads experts to stand idly by while error reigns.

Conclusion

Along with market fundamentalism, economists are often accused of arrogance. In a way, then, I am playing into the critics' hands. I advocate neither market fundamentalism nor arrogance, but we should quit trying so hard to avoid the impression of either. There is no reason to be defensive. Economists have created and popularized many of the most socially beneficial ideas in human history, and combated many of the most virulent. If they were self-conscious of their role in the world, they could do much more. ■

NOTES

1. Brainy Quote (2005a).
2. Colander (2005) shows that the degree of consensus perceived by the latest generation of economists has substantially increased.
3. Reder (1999: 236).
4. Tucker (1978: 461; 460; 475).
5. Waters (1970: 249).
6. Kuttner (1997: 37).
7. Soros (1998: 20).
8. Kuttner (1997: 6).
9. Kuttner (1997: 6, 9; emphasis added).
10. Kuttner (1997: 7; emphasis added).
11. Stiglitz (2002a: 221).
12. Friedman (2002: 32).
13. Friedman (2002: 28).
14. Rothbard (1962: 887). Even at the libertarian extreme of the economic profession, however, the charge of "market fundamentalism" does not exactly fit. On closer reading, Rothbard only makes the agnostic claim that the effect of government intervention on social welfare is ambiguous because every act of government hurts at least one person (Caplan 1999: 833–35).
15. Bork (1990: 139).
16. Shermer (2002: 142).
17. Shermer (2002: 143).
18. Eigen and Siegel (1993: 115).

19. Kamber (1995).

20. Bardhan (1999: 109).

21. Greider (1992: 407).

22. Bardhan (1999).

23. Bardhan (1999: 93; 109).

24. Shapiro (1996: 9).

25. Shapiro (1996: 9; emphasis added).

26. Shapiro (1996: 128).

27. Shapiro (1996: 128).

28. See e.g. Somin (2004), Delli Carpini and Keeter (1996), Dye and Zeigler (1996), Bennett (1996), Smith (1989), and Neuman (1986).

29. Shapiro (1996: 129).

30. Robert Bork (1990: 36–58) actually takes a more fundamentalist position than Shapiro. Bork largely accepts the economists' view of the world. But if economics and the public disagree, he maintains that judges should *still* side with the public.

31. Tetlock (2003: 320; emphasis added).

32. Kuttner (1997: 37).

33. Kuttner (1997: xi–xii).

34. Council of Economic Advisers (2005: 304).

35. Eigen and Siegel (1993: 109).

36. For an in-depth discussion, see Hanson (2005).

37. Wyden (2003).

38. For further discussion, see Hanson (2006), and Wolfers and Zitzewitz (2004).

39. National Commission on Terrorist Attacks Upon the United States (2004: 171–72, 499).

40. Hanson (2006).

41. Surowiecki (2004: 270).

42. My story is that decision markets are more reliable than public opinion because markets charge for biased beliefs, and democracy does not. Surowiecki interestingly observes that play-money markets are less accurate than real-money markets, but still work fairly well because "status and reputation provided incentive enough to encourage a serious investment of time and energy" (2004: 20). But how well would they work if status and reputation depended on the *orthodoxy*, not the *accuracy*, of one's beliefs?

43. Wyden (2003).

44. See e.g. Gillman (1993).

45. Kuttner (1997: 7).

46. See e.g. McChesney (1999).

47. See e.g. Shapiro and Hacker-Cordón (1999), Shapiro (1999, 1996), and Holmes and Sunstein (1999).

48. Shapiro (1996: 8).

49. Shapiro (1996: 37). Shapiro is responding to Riker and Weingast's concerns about cyclical and strategic voting, but his objection is clearly much more general.

50. Shapiro and Hacker-Cordón (1999: 6).

51. For further discussion, see Caplan (2002a).

52. Akerlof (1970).
53. For doubts about the role of adverse selection in insurance markets, see Chiappori and Salanie (2000), Cawley and Philipson (1999), and Hemenway (1990)·
54. See e.g. Stiglitz (2003, 2002a).
55. Stigler (1986).
56. Bastiat (1964b: 57–58).
57. Speck (1993: 175).
58. By way of comparison, Citrin, Schickler, and Sides (2003) conclude that 100% participation would at most mildly help the Democratic Party.
59. See e.g. Caplan (2001), Sears and Funk (1990), and Citrin and Green (1990).
60. Pinker (2002: 235).
61. On debiasing, see Fischhoff (1982).
62. Pinker (2002: 236).
63. See Tullock (1999) and Harberger (1993).
64. Coase (1999: 44).
65. Krugman (1996: 118).
66. For further discussion, see Tollison and Wagner (1991).
67. Samuelson (1966: 1628).
68. Bastiat (1964a: 5).
69. For further discussion, see Pashigian (2000).
70. For example, price can be driven down to marginal cost by Bertrand competition and contestable monopoly, not just perfect competition.
71. Emerson (n.d.: 42).
72. Bastiat (1964a: 56–57).
73. For further discussion, see Caplan (2002b).
74. For an appreciation of Bastiat's political economy, see Caplan and Stringham (2005).
75. Bastiat (1964a: 121).
76. On this question, see Frey (2002, 2000).
77. Keynes (1963: 373).

REFERENCES

Akerlof, George. 1970. "The Market for 'Lemons': Quality Uncertainty and the Market Mechanism." *Quarterly Journal of Economics* 84(3): 488–500.

Bardhan, Pranab. 1999. "Democracy and Development: A Complex Relationship." In Ian Shapiro and Casiano Hacker-Cordón, eds., *Democracy's Value*. Cambridge: Cambridge University Press: 93–111.

Bastiat, Frédéric. 1964a. *Economic Sophisms*. Irvington-on-Hudson, NY: Foundation for Economic Education.

———. 1964b. *Selected Essays on Political Economy*. Irvington-on-Hudson, NY: Foundation for Economic Education.

Bennett, Stephen. 1996. " 'Know-Nothings' Revisited Again." *Political Behavior* 18(3): 219–33.

Bork, Robert. 1990. *The Tempting of America*. New York: Free Press.

Caplan, Bryan. 1999. "The Austrian Search for Realistic Foundations." *Southern Economic Journal* 65(4): 823–38.

———. 2001. "Libertarianism Against Economism: How Economists Misunderstand Voters and Why Libertarians Should Care." *Independent Review* 5(4): 539–63.

———. 2002a. "Sociotropes, Systematic Bias, and Political Failure: Reflections on the Survey of Americans and Economists on the Economy." *Social Science Quarterly* 83(2): 416–35.

———. 2002b. "Economic Illiteracy: A Modest Plea Against Humility." *Royal Economic Society Newsletter* 119: 9–10.

Caplan, Bryan, and Edward Stringham. 2005. "Mises, Bastiat, Public Opinion, and Public Choice: What's Wrong With Democracy." *Review of Political Economy* 17(1): 79–105.

Cawley, John, and Tomas Philipson, 1999. "An Empirical Examination of Information Barriers to Trade in Insurance." *American Economic Review* 89(4): 827–46.

Chiappori, Pierre-Andre, and Bernard Salanie, 2000. "Testing for Asymmetric Information in Insurance Markets." *Journal of Political Economy* 108(1): 56–78.

Citrin, Jack, and Donald Green. 1990. "The Self-Interest Motive in American Public Opinion." *Research in Micropolitics* 3: 1–28.

Citrin, Jack, Eric Schickler, and John Sides. 2003. "What If Everyone Voted? Simulating the Impact of Increased Turnout in Senate Elections." *American Journal of Political Science* 47(1): 75–90.

Coase, Ronald. 1999. "Economists and Public Policy." In Daniel Klein, ed., *What Do Economists Contribute?* New York: New York University Press: 33–52.

Colander, David. 2005. "The Making of an Economist Redux." *Journal of Economic Perspectives* 19(1): 175–98.

Council of Economic Advisers. 2005. *Economic Report of the President.* Washington, DC: U.S. Government Printing Office.

Delli Carpini, Michael, and Scott Keeter. 1996. *What Americans Know About Politics and Why It Matters.* New Haven: Yale University Press.

Eigen, Lewis, and Jonathan Siegel, eds. 1993. *The Macmillan Dictionary of Political Quotations.* New York: Macmillan.

Emerson, Ralph. n.d. *Essays.* New York: Grosset and Dunlap.

Frey, Bruno. 2000. "Does Economics Have an Effect? Toward an Economics of Economics." Institute for Empirical Research in Economics Working Paper No. 36.

———. 2002. "Do Economists Affect Policy Outcomes?" Working Paper Series, Institute for Empirical Research, University of Zürich.

Friedman, Milton. 2002. *Capitalism and Freedom.* Chicago: University of Chicago Press.

Gillman, Howard. 1993. *The Constitution Besieged: The Rise and Demise of Lochner Era Police Powers Jurisprudence.* Durham, NC: Duke University Press.

Greider, William. 1992. *Who Will Tell the People?* New York: Simon and Schuster.

Hanson, Robin. 2005. "The Policy Analysis Market (and FutureMAP) Archive." URL http://hanson.gmu.edu/policyanalysismarket.html.

———. 2006. "Decision Markets for Policy Advice." In Eric Patashnik and Alan Gerber, eds., *Promoting the General Welfare: American Democracy and the Political Economy of Government Performance.* Washington, DC: Brookings Institution Press, forthcoming.

Harberger, Arnold. 1993. "Secrets of Success: A Handful of Heroes." *American Economic Review* 83(2): 343–50.

Hemenway, David. 1990. "Propitious Selection." *Quarterly Journal of Economics* 16(4): 1063–69.

Holmes, Stephen, and Cass Sunstein. 1999. *The Cost of Rights: Why Liberty Depends on Taxes.* New York: Norton.

Kamber, Victor. 1995. *Giving Up on Democracy: Why Term Limits Are Bad for America.* Washington, DC: Regency.

Keynes, John Maynard. 1963. *Essays in Persuasion.* New York: Norton.

Krugman, Paul. 1996. *Pop Internationalism.* Cambridge: MIT Press.

Kuttner, Robert. 1997. *Everything for Sale: The Virtues and Limits of Markets.* New York: Knopf.

McChesney, Robert. 1999. *Rich Media, Poor Democracy: Communication Politics in Dubious Times.* Urbana: University of Illinois Press.

National Commission on Terrorist Attacks Upon the United States. 2004. *The 9/11 Commission Report.* URL http://www.9–11commission.gov/report/911Report.pdf.

Neuman, W. Russell. 1986. *The Paradox of Mass Politics: Knowledge and Opinion in the American Electorate.* Cambridge: Harvard University Press.

Pashigian, B. Peter. 2000. "Teaching Microeconomics in Wonderland." George J. Stigler Center for the Study of Economy and the State Working Paper No. 161.

Pinker, Steven. 2002. *The Blank Slate: The Modern Denial of Human Nature.* New York: Viking.

Reder, Melvin. 1999. *Economics: The Culture of a Controversial Science.* Chicago: University of Chicago Press.

Rothbard, Murray. 1962. *Man, Economy, and State: A Treatise on Economic Principles.* Los Angeles: Nash.

Samuelson, Paul. 1966. "What Economists Know." In *The Collected Scientific Papers of Paul A. Samuelson.* Vol. 1. Cambridge: MIT Press: 1619–49.

Sears, David, and Carolyn Funk. 1990. "Self-Interest in Americans' Political Opinions." In Jane Mansbridge, ed., *Beyond Self-Interest.* Chicago: University of Chicago Press: 147–70.

Shapiro, Ian. 1996. *Democracy's Place.* Ithaca, NY: Cornell University Press.

———. 1999. *Democratic Justice.* New Haven: Yale University Press.

Shapiro, Ian, and Casiano Hacker-Cordón. 1999. "Reconsidering Democracy's Value." In Ian Shapiro and Casiano Hacker-Cordón, eds., *Democracy's Value.* Cambridge: Cambridge University Press: 1–19.

Shermer, Michael. 2002. *Why People Believe Weird Things: Pseudoscience, Superstition, and Other Confusions of Our Time.* New York: Henry Holt.

Smith, Eric. 1989. *The Unchanging American Voter.* Berkeley and Los Angeles: University of California Press.

Somin, Ilya. 1998. "Voter Ignorance and the Democratic Ideal." *Critical Review* 12(4): 99–111.

———. 2004. "Political Ignorance and The Countermajoritarian Difficulty: A New Perspective on the 'Central Obsession' of Constitutional Theory." *Iowa Law Review* 89(4): 1287–1372.

Stigler, George. 1986. "Economics or Ethics?" In Kurt Leube and Thomas Gale Moore, eds., *The Essence of Stigler.* Stanford, CA: Hoover Institution Press: 303–36.

Stiglitz, Joseph. 2002a. *Globalization and Its Discontents.* New York: Norton.

————. 2002b. "Information." In David Henderson, ed., *The Concise Encyclopedia of Economics*. URL http://www.econlib.org/library/Enc/Information.html.

————. 2003. *The Roaring Nineties: A New History of the World's Most Prosperous Decade*. New York: Norton.

Surowiecki, James. 2004. *The Wisdom of Crowds*. New York: Doubleday.

Tollison, Robert, and Richard Wagner. 1991. "Romance, Realism, and Policy Reform." *Kyklos* 44(1): 57–70.

Tucker, Robert, ed. 1978. *The Marx-Engels Reader*. New York: Norton.

Tullock, Gordon. 1999. "How to Do Well While Doing Good!" In Daniel Klein, ed., *What Do Economists Contribute?* New York: New York University Press: 87–103.

Waters, Mary-Alice, ed. 1970. *Rosa Luxemburg Speaks*. New York: Pathfinder Press.

Wolfers, Justin, and Eric Zitzewitz, 2004. "Prediction Markets." *Journal of Economic Perspectives* 18(2): 107–26.

Wyden, Ron. 2003. "Wyden, Dorgan Call For Immediate Halt to Tax-Funded 'Terror Market' Scheme." URL http://wyden.senate.gov/media/2003/07282003_terrormarket.html.

■ *QUESTIONS FOR MAKING CONNECTIONS WITHIN THE READING* ■

1. Caplan devotes his energies to defining two terms in this piece: market fundamentalism and democratic fundamentalism. What definitions does he settle on, finally? Why does he place "market fundamentalism" in quotation marks, but not democratic fundamentalism?

2. Caplan both advocates and demonstrates a mode of argument that does not shy away from the charge of arrogance. Indeed, he declares openly that "[e]conomists *really do* subscribe to a long list of views that are un-popular, even offensive." What views, in particular, does he mean and to whom are they offensive? Where do you see him working self-consciously to avoid the charge of arrogance, and where do you see him striking the pose of an arrogant economist?

3. Throughout his piece, Caplan refers repeatedly to the role that "slack" plays in lives of those who participate in the market—professors, those who work in print, voters in a democracy. What is slack, exactly? How is it produced and experienced?

■ *QUESTIONS FOR WRITING* ■

1. "[T]here is no conceptual flaw in prescriptions to rely more on private choice and less on collective choice." With this conclusion, Caplan re-jects the arguments of those who believe that the best hope for social im-provement lies in collective action. If an argument about the nature of human behavior has no "conceptual flaw," what follows? Is Caplan's

commitment to the economic model an example of a private choice, the inevitable outcome of the reasoning process, or a sign of what Caplan terms "rational irrationality"?

2. Caplan proposes that one remedy to the problems of democracy could be improving the economic literacy of those who vote. Indeed, he even suggests limiting voting rights to those who demonstrate economic literacy. Caplan does not, however, provide a textbook definition for what he means by "economic literacy," nor does he offer a list of the central concepts and core skills that he would like to see taught. Drawing on the materials Caplan has provided, generate your own version of what would go into an exam on economic literacy, including the central concepts, core skills, and correct answers that would be covered in such an exam. If such an exam were used to limit access to voting, what do you think would be the consequences? What do you learn about Caplan's model by imagining putting his recommendation in practice?

■ *QUESTIONS FOR MAKING CONNECTIONS BETWEEN READINGS* ■

1. Caplan singles out William Greider as a prime example of a democratic fundamentalist. For rhetorical reasons, Caplan provides only one quote from Greider to substantiate his claim; Greider himself would doubtless use different terms to characterize his position. Indeed, in "Work Rules," he sets out to explore "the promise and the difficulties" involved in "self-ownership." That Caplan and Greider have different views of economics is clear, but what leads them to have such different views? Are they working with different facts? Different assumptions? Different beliefs? Different modes of argumentation? Rather than choosing sides, write an essay that explores the source of the disagreement between Caplan and Greider. What would it take to resolve this disagreement?

2. In "Surface and Substance," Virginia Postrel makes the following observation about what might be called human superficiality: "Denying that we care about appearance for its own sake leads us to exaggerate its deeper significance, in order to justify our natural interest." Is Postrel's view of the human condition in line with Caplan's? Does the study of the marketplace require that we focus only on the surface of human behavior, or does it reveal something deeper about our membership in society?

AMY CHUA

WILL DEMOCRACY AND the free market succeed in all parts of the world? Should they always be pursued? Do they always go together? Amy Chua poses these provocative questions in "A World on Edge," an investigation into the relations, in many different countries, among economics, politics, and ethnic identity. A law professor who spent the early part of her career working in international business, Chua sees patterns of poverty, resentment, and violence emerging everywhere in the wake of globalization. Most observers hail the spread of democracy and capitalism as the start of a "new world order," but Chua offers a darker and more guarded view of such changes. Rather than ushering in an era of greater wealth, opportunity, and freedom, the shift to open markets and popular elections has deepened long-standing conflicts among ethnic groups and nations. The results, Chua argues, are less stable and more volatile societies.

When Chua's aunt, a wealthy Chinese businesswoman living in the Philippines, was murdered by her Filipino chauffeur, the only motive listed on the police report was "revenge." In an effort to learn why her aunt was murdered and why revenge was identified as the official cause, Chua forced herself to look beyond her personal feelings about the brutal event. Her research led her to see the Philippines in a new light as a nation with a destitute majority of native Filipinos and a small minority of economically privileged ethnic Chinese. Then Chua began to recognize the parallels between the Philippines and other developing countries, where poor majorities live apart from the "market-dominant minorities."

Ultimately Chua's investigation led her to conclude that globalization creates an economic system that may actually make things worse for everyone outside the prosperous, developed First World. In the face of this possibility, she has called for the market-dominant minorities—including those residing in the United States—to play a more active role in assisting those who have been left behind by the march of progress.

Chua, Amy. "A World on Edge." *Wilson Quarterly* 26(4) (Autumn 2002): 62–78.

Biographical information is drawn from an interview with Chua available at <http://globetrotter.berkeley.edu/people4/Chua/chua-con0.html>.

In a revised form, the essay reprinted here was incorporated into Chua's book *World on Fire: How Exporting Free Market Democracy Breeds Ethnic Hatred and Global Instability (2003)*, which was a *New York Times* bestseller and was also named a Best Book of 2003 by *The Economist*. She is currently a professor at the Yale Law School.

A World on the Edge

One beautiful blue morning in September 1994, I received a call from my mother in California. In a hushed voice, she told me that my Aunt Leona, my father's twin sister, had been murdered in her home in the Philippines, her throat slit by her chauffeur. My mother broke the news to me in our native Hokkien Chinese dialect. But "murder" she said in English, as if to wall off the act from the family through language.

The murder of a relative is horrible for anyone, anywhere. My father's grief was impenetrable; to this day, he has not broken his silence on the subject. For the rest of the family, though, there was an added element of disgrace. For the Chinese, luck is a moral attribute, and a lucky person would never be murdered. Like having a birth defect, or marrying a Filipino, being murdered is shameful.

My three younger sisters and I were very fond of my Aunt Leona, who was petite and quirky and had never married. Like many wealthy Filipino Chinese, she had all kinds of bank accounts in Honolulu, San Francisco, and Chicago. She visited us in the United States regularly. She and my father—Leona and Leon—were close, as only twins can be. Having no children of her own, she doted on her nieces and showered us with trinkets. As we grew older, the trinkets became treasures. On my 10th birthday she gave me 10 small diamonds, wrapped up in toilet paper. My aunt loved diamonds and bought them up by the dozen, concealing them in empty Elizabeth Arden face moisturizer jars, some right on her bathroom shelf. She liked accumulating things. When we ate at McDonald's, she stuffed her Gucci purse with free ketchups.

According to the police report, my Aunt Leona, "a 58-year-old single woman," was killed in her living room with "a butcher's knife" at approximately 8 P.M. on September 12, 1994. Two of her maids were questioned, and they confessed that Nilo Abique, my aunt's chauffeur, had planned and executed the murder with their knowledge and assistance. "A few hours before the actual killing, respondent [Abique] was seen sharpening the knife allegedly used in the crime." After the killing, "respondent joined the two witnesses and told them that their employer was dead. At that time, he was wearing a pair of bloodied white gloves and was still holding a knife, also with traces of blood." But Abique, the report went on to say, had "disappeared," with the warrant for his arrest outstanding. The two maids were released.

Meanwhile, my relatives arranged a private funeral for my aunt in the prestigious Chinese cemetery in Manila where many of my ancestors are buried in a great, white-marble family tomb. According to the feng shui monks who were consulted, my aunt could not be buried with the rest of the family because of the violent nature of her death, lest more bad luck strike her surviving kin. So she was placed in her own smaller vault, next to—but not touching—the main family tomb.

After the funeral, I asked one of my uncles whether there had been any further developments in the murder investigation. He replied tersely that the killer had not been found. His wife explained that the Manila police had essentially closed the case.

I could not understand my relatives' almost indifferent attitude. Why were they not more shocked that my aunt had been killed in cold blood, by people who worked for her, lived with her, saw her every day? Why were they not outraged that the maids had been released? When I pressed my uncle, he was short with me. "That's the way things are here," he said. "This is the Philippines—not America."

My uncle was not simply being callous. As it turns out, my aunt's death was part of a common pattern. Hundreds of Chinese in the Philippines are kidnapped every year, almost invariably by ethnic Filipinos. Many victims, often children, are brutally murdered, even after ransom is paid. Other Chinese, like my aunt, are killed without a kidnapping, usually in connection with a robbery. Nor is it unusual that my aunt's killer was never apprehended. The police in the Philippines, all poor ethnic Filipinos themselves, are notoriously unmotivated in these cases. When asked by a Western journalist why it is so frequently the Chinese who are targeted, one grinning Filipino policeman explained that it was because "they have more money."

My family is part of the Philippines' tiny but entrepreneurial and economically powerful Chinese minority. Although they constitute just one percent of the population, Chinese Filipinos control as much as 60 percent of the private economy, including the country's four major airlines and almost all of the country's banks, hotels, shopping malls, and big conglomerates. My own family in Manila runs a plastics conglomerate. Unlike taipans Lucio Tan, Henry Sy, or John Gokongwei, my relatives are only "third-tier" Chinese tycoons. Still, they own swaths of prime real estate and several vacation homes. They also have safe deposit boxes full of gold bars, each one roughly the size of a Snickers bar, but strangely heavy. I myself have such a gold bar.

My Aunt Leona express-mailed it to me as a law school graduation present a few years before she died.

Since my aunt's murder, one childhood memory keeps haunting me. I was eight, staying at my family's splendid hacienda-style house in Manila. It was before dawn, still dark. Wide awake, I decided to get a drink from the kitchen. I must have gone down an extra flight of stairs, because I literally stumbled onto six male bodies. I had found the male servants' quarters, where my family's houseboys, gardeners, and chauffeurs—I sometimes imagine that Nilo Abique was among them—were sleeping on mats on a dirt floor. The place stank of sweat and urine. I was horrified.

Later that day I mentioned the incident to my Aunt Leona, who laughed affectionately and explained that the servants—there were perhaps 20 living on the premises, all ethnic Filipinos—were fortunate to be working for our family. If not for their positions, they would be living among rats and open sewers, without a roof over their heads. A Filipino maid then walked in; I remember that she had a bowl of food for my aunt's Pekingese. My aunt took the bowl but kept talking as if the maid were not there. The Filipinos, she continued—in Chinese, but plainly not caring whether the maid understood or not—were lazy and unintelligent and didn't really want to do much. If they didn't like working for us, they were free to leave at any time. After all, my aunt said, they were employees, not slaves.

Nearly two-thirds of the roughly 80 million ethnic Filipinos in the Philippines live on less than $2 a day. Forty percent spend their entire lives in temporary shelters. Seventy percent of all rural Filipinos own no land. Almost a third have no access to sanitation. But that's not the worst of it. Poverty alone never is. Poverty by itself does not make people kill. To poverty must be added indignity, hopelessness, and grievance. In the Philippines, millions of Filipinos work for Chinese; almost no Chinese work for Filipinos. The Chinese dominate industry and commerce at every level of society. Global markets intensify this dominance: When foreign investors do business in the Philippines, they deal almost exclusively with Chinese. Apart from a handful of corrupt politicians and a few aristocratic Spanish mestizo families, all of the Philippines' billionaires are of Chinese descent. By contrast, all menial jobs in the Philippines are filled by Filipinos. All peasants are Filipinos. All domestic servants and squatters are Filipinos. My relatives live literally walled off from the Filipino masses, in a posh, all-Chinese residential enclave, on streets named Harvard, Yale, Stanford, and Princeton. The entry points are guarded by armed private-security forces.

Each time I think of Nilo Abique—he was six-feet-two and my aunt was four-feet-eleven—I find myself welling up with a hatred and revulsion so intense it is actually consoling. But over time I have also had glimpses of how the vast majority of Filipinos, especially someone like Abique, must see the Chinese: as exploiters, foreign intruders, their wealth inexplicable, their superiority intolerable. I will never forget the entry in the police report for

Abique's "motive for murder." The motive given was not robbery, despite the jewels and money the chauffeur was said to have taken. Instead, for motive, there was just one word—"revenge."

My aunt's killing was just a pinprick in a world more violent than most of us have ever imagined. In America, we read about acts of mass slaughter and savagery—at first in faraway places, now coming closer home. We do not understand what connects these acts. Nor do we understand the role we have played in bringing them about.

In the Serbian concentration camps of the early 1990s, the women prisoners were raped over and over, many times a day, often with broken bottles, often together with their daughters. The men, if they were lucky, were beaten to death as their Serbian guards sang national anthems; if they were not so fortunate, they were castrated or, at gunpoint, forced to castrate their fellow prisoners, sometimes with their own teeth. In all, thousands were tortured and executed.

In Rwanda in 1994, ordinary Hutus killed 800,000 Tutsis over a period of three months, typically hacking them to death with machetes. Bill Berkeley writes in *The Graves Are Not Yet Full* (2001) that young children would come home to find their mothers, fathers, sisters, and brothers on the living room floor, in piles of severed heads and limbs.

In Jakarta in 1998, screaming Indonesian mobs torched, smashed, and looted hundreds of Chinese shops and homes, leaving more than 2,000 dead. One who survived—a 14-year-old Chinese girl—later committed suicide by taking rat poison. She had been gang-raped and genitally mutilated in front of her parents.

In Israel in 1998, a suicide bomber driving a car packed with explosives rammed into a school bus filled with 34 Jewish children between the ages of six and eight. Over the next few years such incidents intensified, becoming daily occurrences and a powerful collective expression of Palestinian hatred. "We hate you," a senior aide to Yasir Arafat elaborated in April 2002. "The air hates you, the land hates you, the trees hate you, there is no purpose in your staying on this land."

On September 11, 2001, Middle Eastern terrorists hijacked four American airliners, intent on using them as piloted missiles. They destroyed the World Trade Center and the southwest side of the Pentagon, crushing or incinerating more than 3,000 people. "Americans, think! Why you are hated all over the world," proclaimed a banner held by Arab demonstrators.

There is a connection among these episodes apart from their violence. It lies in the relationship—increasingly, the explosive collision—among the three most powerful forces operating in the world today: markets, democracy, and ethnic hatred. There exists today a phenomenon—pervasive outside the West yet rarely acknowledged, indeed often viewed as taboo—that turns free-market democracy into an engine of ethnic conflagration. I'm speaking of the phenomenon of market-dominant minorities: ethnic minorities who, for widely varying reasons, tend under market conditions to dominate economically, often to a startling extent, the "indigenous" majorities around them.

Market-dominant minorities can be found in every corner of the world. The Chinese are a market-dominant minority not just in the Philippines but throughout Southeast Asia. In 1998 Chinese Indonesians, only three percent of the population, controlled roughly 70 percent of Indonesia's private economy, including all of the country's largest conglomerates. In Myanmar (formerly Burma), entrepreneurial Chinese recently have taken over the economies of Mandalay and Yangon. Whites are a market-dominant minority in South Africa—and, in a more complicated sense, in Brazil, Ecuador, Guatemala, and much of Latin America. Lebanese are a market-dominant minority in West Africa, as are the Ibo in Nigeria. Croats were a market-dominant minority in the former Yugoslavia, as Jews almost certainly are in postcommunist Russia.

Market-dominant minorities are the Achilles' heel of free-market democracy. In societies with such a minority, markets and democracy favor not just different people or different classes but different ethnic groups. Markets concentrate wealth, often spectacular wealth, in the hands of the market-dominant minority, while democracy increases the political power of the impoverished majority. In these circumstances, the pursuit of free-market democracy becomes an engine of potentially catastrophic ethnonationalism, pitting a frustrated "indigenous" majority, easily aroused by opportunistic, vote-seeking politicians, against a resented, wealthy ethnic minority. This conflict is playing out in country after country today, from Indonesia to Sierra Leone, from Zimbabwe to Venezuela, from Russia to the Middle East.

Since September 11, the conflict has been brought home to the United States. Americans are not an ethnic minority (although we are a national-origin minority, a close cousin). Nor is there democracy at the global level. Nevertheless, Americans today are everywhere perceived as the world's market-dominant minority, wielding outrageously disproportionate economic power relative to our numbers. As a result, we have become the object of the same kind of mass popular resentment that afflicts the Chinese of Southeast Asia, the whites of Zimbabwe, and other groups.

Global anti-Americanism has many causes. One of them, ironically, is the global spread of free markets and democracy. Throughout the world, global markets are bitterly perceived as reinforcing American wealth and dominance. At the same time, global populist and democratic movements give strength, legitimacy, and voice to the impoverished, frustrated, excluded masses of the world—in other words, precisely the people most susceptible to anti-American demagoguery. In more non-Western countries than Americans would care to admit, free and fair elections would bring to power antimarket, anti-American leaders. For the past 20 years, Americans have been grandly promoting both marketization and democratization throughout the world. In the process, we have directed at ourselves what the Turkish writer Orhan Pamuk calls "the anger of the damned."

The relationship between free-market democracy and ethnic violence around the world is inextricably bound up with globalization. But the phenomenon of market-dominant minorities introduces complications that have escaped the view of both globalization's enthusiasts and its critics.

To a great extent, globalization consists of, and is fueled by, the unprecedented worldwide spread of markets and democracy. For more than two decades now, the American government, along with American consultants and business interests, has been vigorously promoting free-market democracy throughout the developing and postcommunist worlds. Both directly and through powerful international institutions such as the World Bank, International Monetary Fund, and World Trade Organization (WTO), it has helped bring capitalism and democratic elections to literally billions of people. At the same time, American multinationals, foundations, and nongovernmental organizations (NGOs) have touched every corner of the world, bringing with them ballot boxes and Burger Kings, hip-hop and Hollywood, banking codes and American-drafted constitutions.

The prevailing view among globalization's supporters is that markets and democracy are a kind of universal elixir for the multiple ills of underdevelopment. Market capitalism is the most efficient economic system the world has ever known. Democracy is the fairest political system the world has ever known, and the one most respectful of individual liberty. Together, markets and democracy will gradually transform the world into a community of prosperous, war-shunning nations, and individuals into liberal, civic-minded citizens and consumers. Ethnic hatred, religious zealotry, and other "backward" aspects of underdevelopment will be swept away.

Thomas Friedman of the *New York Times* has been a brilliant proponent of this dominant view. In his best-selling book *The Lexus and the Olive Tree* (1999), he reproduced a Merrill Lynch ad that said "the spread of free markets and democracy around the world is permitting more people everywhere to turn their aspirations into achievements," erasing "not just geographical borders but also human ones." Globalization, Friedman elaborated, "tends to turn all friends and enemies into 'competitors.'" Friedman also proposed his "Golden Arches Theory of Conflict Prevention," which claims that "no two countries that both have McDonald's have ever fought a war against each other." (Unfortunately, notes Yale University historian John Lewis Gaddis, "the United States and its NATO allies chose just that inauspicious moment to begin bombing Belgrade, where there was an embarrassing number of golden arches.")

For globalization's enthusiasts, the cure for group hatred and ethnic violence around the world is straightforward: more markets and more democracy. Thus, after the September 11 attacks, Friedman published an op-ed piece pointing to India and Bangladesh as good "role models" for the

Middle East and citing their experience as a solution to the challenges of terrorism and militant Islam: "Hello? Hello? There's a message here. It's democracy, stupid!"—". . . multiethnic, pluralistic, free-market democracy."

I believe, rather, that the global spread of markets and democracy is a principal aggravating cause of group hatred and ethnic violence throughout the non-Western world. In the numerous societies around the world that have a market-dominant minority, markets and democracy are not mutually reinforcing. Because markets and democracy benefit different ethnic groups in such societies, the pursuit of free-market democracy produces highly unstable and combustible conditions. Markets concentrate enormous wealth in the hands of an "outsider" minority, thereby fomenting ethnic envy and hatred among often chronically poor majorities. In absolute terms, the majority may or may not be better off—a dispute that much of the globalization debate revolves around—but any sense of improvement is overwhelmed by its continuing poverty and the hated minority's extraordinary economic success. More humiliating still, market-dominant minorities, along with their foreign-investor partners, invariably come to control the crown jewels of the economy, often symbolic of the nation's patrimony and identity—oil in Russia and Venezuela, diamonds in South Africa, silver and tin in Bolivia, jade, teak, and rubies in Myanmar.

Introducing democracy under such circumstances does not transform voters into open-minded co-citizens in a national community. Rather, the competition for votes fosters the emergence of demagogues who scapegoat the resented minority and foment active ethnonationalist movements demanding that the country's wealth and identity be reclaimed by the "true owners of the nation." Even as America celebrated the global spread of democracy in the 1990s, the world's new political slogans told of more ominous developments: "Georgia for the Georgians," "Eritreans out of Ethiopia," "Kenya for Kenyans," "Venezuela for Pardos," "Kazakhstan for Kazakhs," "Serbia for Serbs," "Hutu Power," "Jews out of Russia." Vadim Tudor, a candidate in Romania's 2001 presidential election, was not quite so pithy. "I'm Vlad the Impaler," he declared, and referring to the historically dominant Hungarian minority, he promised, "We will hang them directly by their Hungarian tongue!"

When free-market democracy is pursued in the presence of a market-dominant minority, the result, almost invariably, is backlash. Typically, it takes one of three forms. The first is a backlash against markets that targets the market-dominant minority's wealth. The second is an attack against democracy by forces favorable to the market-dominant minority. And the third is violence, sometimes genocidal, directed against the market-dominant minority itself.

Zimbabwe today is a vivid illustration of the first kind of backlash—an ethnically targeted antimarket reaction. For several years now, President Robert Mugabe has encouraged the violent seizure of 10 million acres of white-owned commercial farmland. As one Zimbabwean explained, "The land belongs to us. The foreigners should not own land here. There is no black Zimbabwean who owns land in England. Why should any European own land here?" Mugabe has been more explicit: "Strike fear in the heart of the white man, our real enemy." Most of the country's white "foreigners" are third-generation Zimbabweans. They are just one percent of the population, but they have for generations controlled 70 percent of the country's best land, largely in the form of highly productive 3,000-acre tobacco and sugar farms.

Watching Zimbabwe's economy take a free fall as a result of the mass land grab, the United States and United Kingdom, together with dozens of human rights groups, urged President Mugabe to step down and called resoundingly for "free and fair elections." But the idea that democracy is the answer to Zimbabwe's problems is breathtakingly naive. Perhaps Mugabe would have lost the 2002 elections in the absence of foul play. But even if that's so, it's important to remember that Mugabe himself is a product of democracy. The hero of Zimbabwe's black liberation movement and a master manipulator of the masses, he swept to victory in the closely monitored elections of 1980 by promising to expropriate "stolen" white land. Repeating that promise has helped him win every election since. Moreover, Mugabe's land-seizure campaign was another product of the democratic process. It was deftly timed in anticipation of the 2000 and 2002 elections, and deliberately calculated to mobilize popular support for Mugabe's teetering regime. According to *The Economist*, 95 percent of Zimbabwe's largely white-owned commercial farms are now earmarked for confiscation without compensation, and many farmers have been ordered off the land.

In the contest between an economically powerful ethnic minority and a numerically powerful impoverished majority, the majority does not always prevail. Rather than a backlash against the market, another possible outcome is a backlash against democracy that favors the market-dominant minority. Examples of this dynamic are extremely common. The world's most notorious cases of "crony capitalism" have all involved partnerships between a market-dominant ethnic minority and a cooperative autocrat. Ferdinand Marcos's dictatorship in the Philippines, for example, sheltered and profited from the country's wealthy Chinese before he was driven from office in 1986. In Kenya, President Daniel arap Moi, who had once warned Africans to "beware of bad Asians," is sustained by a series of "business arrangements" with a handful of local Indian tycoons. And the bloody tragedy of Sierra Leone's recent history can be traced in significant part to the regime of President Siaka Stevens, who converted his elective office into a dictatorship during the early 1970s and promptly formed a shadow alliance with five of the country's Lebanese diamond dealers.

In Sierra Leone, as in many other countries, independence (which came in 1961) had been followed by a series of antimarket measures and policies that took direct aim at market-dominant minorities. People of "European or Asiatic origin," including the Lebanese, were denied citizenship. Stevens's approach thus represented a complete about-face—a pattern that's been repeated in country after country. Stevens protected the economically powerful Lebanese, and in exchange, they—with their business networks in Europe, the Soviet Union, and the United States—worked economic wonders, generating enormous profits and kicking back handsome portions to Stevens and other officials. (It is just such webs of preexisting relationships with the outside world that have given economically dominant minorities their extraordinary advantages in the current era of globalization.) Stevens was succeeded by other autocrats, who struck essentially the same deal while also successfully courting foreign investment and aid. In 1989 and 1990, the International Monetary Fund championed a "bold and decisive" free-market reform package that included a phase-out of public subsidies for rice and other commodities. Already living in indescribable poverty, Sierra Leoneans watched the cost of rice nearly double, and many blamed the Lebanese. In any event, the rebel leader Foday Sankoh had little trouble finding recruits for his insurgency. Some 75,000 died in the ensuing chaos.

The third and most ferocious kind of backlash is majority-supported violence aimed at eliminating a market-dominant minority. Two recent examples are the "ethnic cleansing" of Croats in the former Yugoslavia and the mass slaughter of Tutsi in Rwanda. In both cases, sudden, unmediated democratization encouraged the rise of megalomaniacal ethnic demagogues and released long-suppressed hatreds against a disproportionately prosperous ethnic minority.

Of course, markets and democracy were not the only causes of these acts of genocide, but they were neglected factors. In the former Yugoslavia, for example, the Croats, along with the Slovenes, have long enjoyed a strikingly higher standard of living than the Serbs and other ethnic groups. Croatia and Slovenia are largely Catholic, with geographical proximity and historical links to Western Europe, while the Eastern Orthodox Serbs inhabit the rugged south and lived for centuries under the thumb of the Ottoman Empire. By the 1990s, per capita income in northern Yugoslavia had risen to three times that in the south. The sudden coming of Balkan electoral democracy helped stir ancient enmities and resentments. In Serbia, the demagogue and future "ethnic cleanser" Slobodan Milosevic swept to power in 1990 as supporters declared to hysterical crowds, "We will kill Croats with rusty spoons because it will hurt more!" (In the same year, Franjo Tudjman won a landslide victory in Croatia preaching anti-Serb hatred; the subsequent mass killing of Croatia's Serbs shows that market-dominant minorities aren't always the victims of persecution.) In a now-famous speech delivered in March 1991—which contains a telling allusion to Croat and Slovene market dominance—Milosevic declared: "If we must fight, then my God we will fight. And I hope they will not be so crazy as to fight against us. Because if we don't know how to work well or to do business, at least we know how to fight well!"

To their credit, critics of globalization have called attention to the grotesque imbalances that free markets produce. In the 1990s, writes Thomas Frank in *One Market under God* (2000), global markets made "the corporation the most powerful institution on earth," transformed "CEOs as a class into one of the wealthiest elites of all time," and, from America to Indonesia, "forgot about the poor with a decisiveness we hadn't seen since the 1920s." A host of strange bedfellows have joined Frank in his criticism of "the almighty market": American farmers and factory workers opposed to the North American Free Trade Agreement, environmentalists, the American Federation of Labor—Congress of Industrial Organizations, human rights activists, Third World advocates, and sundry other groups that protested in Seattle, Davos, Genoa, and New York City. Defenders of globalization respond, with some justification, that the world's poor would be even worse off without global marketization, and recent World Bank studies show that, with some important exceptions, including most of Africa, globalization's "trickle down" has benefited the poor as well as the rich in developing countries.

More fundamentally, however, Western critics of globalization, like their pro-globalization counterparts, have overlooked the ethnic dimension of market disparities. They tend to see wealth and poverty in terms of class conflict, not ethnic conflict. This perspective might make sense in the advanced Western societies, but the ethnic realities of the developing world are completely different from those of the West. Essentially, the anti-globalization movement asks for one thing: more democracy. At the 2002 World Social Forum in Brazil, Lori Wallach of Public Citizen rejected the label "anti-globalization" and explained that "our movement, really, is globally for democracy, equality, diversity, justice and quality of life." Wallach has also warned that the WTO must "either bend to the will of the people worldwide or it will break." Echoing these voices are literally dozens of NGOs that call for "democratically empowering the poor majorities of the world." But unless democratization means something more than unrestrained majority rule, calling for democracy in the developing world can be shortsighted and even dangerous. Empowering the Hutu majority in Rwanda did not produce desirable consequences. Nor did empowering the Serbian majority in Serbia.

Critics of globalization are right to demand that more attention be paid to the enormous disparities of wealth created by global markets. But just as it is dangerous to view markets as the panacea for the world's poverty and strife, so too it is dangerous to see democracy as a panacea. Markets and democracy may well offer the best long-run economic and political hope for developing and postcommunist societies. In the short run, however, they're part of the problem.

In the West, terms such as "market economy" and "market system" refer to a broad spectrum of economic systems based primarily on private property and competition, with government regulation and redistribution ranging from substantial (as in the United States) to extensive (as in the Scandinavian countries). Yet for the past 20 years the United States has been promoting throughout the non-Western world raw, laissez-faire capitalism— a form of markets that the West abandoned long ago. The procapitalism measures being implemented today outside the West include privatization, the elimination of state subsidies and controls, and free-trade and foreign investment initiatives. As a practical matter they rarely, if ever, include any substantial redistribution measures.

"Democracy," too, can take many forms. I use the term "democratization" to refer to the political reforms that are actually being promoted in the non-Western world today—the concerted efforts, for example, largely driven by the United States, to implement immediate elections with universal suffrage. It's striking to note that at no point in history did any Western nation ever implement laissez-faire capitalism and overnight universal suffrage simultaneously—though that's the precise formula for free-market democracy currently being pressed on developing countries around the world. In the United States, the poor were totally disenfranchised by formal property qualifications in virtually every state for many decades after the Constitution was ratified, and economic barriers to participation remained well into the 20th century.

It is ethnicity, however, that gives the combination of markets and democracy its special combustibility. Ethnic identity is not a static, scientifically determinable status but shifting and highly malleable. In Rwanda, for example, the 14 percent Tutsi minority dominated the Hutu majority economically and politically for four centuries, as a kind of cattle-owning aristocracy. But for most of this period, the lines between Hutus and Tutsi were permeable. The two groups spoke the same language, intermarriage occurred, and successful Hutus could "become Tutsi." That was no longer true after the Belgians arrived and, steeped in specious theories of racial superiority, issued ethnic identity cards on the basis of nose length and cranial circumference. The resulting sharp ethnic divisions were later exploited by the leaders of Hutu Power. Along similar lines, all over Latin America today— where it is often said that there are no "ethnic divisions" because everyone has "mixed" blood—large numbers of impoverished Bolivians, Chileans, and Peruvians are suddenly being told that they are Aymaras, Incas, or just indios, whatever identity best resonates and mobilizes. These indigenization movements are not necessarily good or bad, but they are potent and contagious.

At the same time, ethnic identity is rarely constructed out of thin air. Subjective perceptions of identity often depend on more "objective" traits assigned to individuals based on, for example, perceived morphological characteristics, language differences, or ancestry. Try telling black and white Zimbabweans that they are only imagining their ethnic differences—that "ethnicity is a social construct"—and they'll at least agree on one thing: You're not being helpful. Much more concretely relevant is the reality that there is roughly zero intermarriage between blacks and whites in Zimbabwe, just as there is virtually no intermarriage between Chinese and Malays in Malaysia or between Arabs and Israelis in the Middle East. That ethnicity can be at once an artifact of human imagination and rooted in the darkest recesses of history—fluid and manipulable, yet important enough to kill for—is what makes ethnic conflict so terrifyingly difficult to understand and contain.

The argument I am making is frequently misunderstood. I do not propose a universal theory applicable to every developing country. There are certainly developing countries without market-dominant minorities: China and Argentina are two major examples. Nor do I argue that ethnic conflict arises only in the presence of a market-dominant minority. There are countless instances of ethnic hatred directed at economically oppressed groups. And, last, I emphatically do not mean to pin the blame for any particular case of ethnic violence—whether the mass killings perpetrated by all sides in the former Yugoslavia or the attack on America—on economic resentment, on markets, on democracy, on globalization, or on any other single cause. Many overlapping factors and complex dynamics—religion, historical enmities, territorial disputes, or a particular nation's foreign policy—are always in play.

The point, rather, is this: In the numerous countries around the world that have pervasive poverty and a market-dominant minority, democracy and markets—at least in the raw, unrestrained forms in which they are currently being promoted—can proceed only in deep tension with each other. In such conditions, the combined pursuit of free markets and democratization has repeatedly catalyzed ethnic conflict in highly predictable ways, with catastrophic consequences, including genocidal violence and the subversion of markets and democracy themselves. That has been the sobering lesson of globalization over the past 20 years.

Where does this leave us? What are the implications of market-dominant minorities for national and international policymaking? Influential commentator Robert D. Kaplan offers one answer: Hold off on democracy until free markets produce enough economic and social development to make democracy sustainable. In *The Coming Anarchy* (2000), Kaplan argues that a middle class and civil institutions—both of which he implicitly assumes would be generated by market capitalism—are preconditions for democracy. Contrasting Lee Kuan Yew's prosperous authoritarian Singapore with the murderous, "bloodletting" democratic states of Colombia, Rwanda, and South Africa, Kaplan roundly condemns America's post–Cold War campaign to export democracy to "places where it can't succeed."

This is a refreshingly unromantic view, but ultimately unsatisfactory. As one writer has observed, "If authoritarianism were the key to prosperity, then Africa would be the richest continent in the world." Ask (as some do) for an Augusto Pinochet or an Alberto Fujimori, and you may get an Idi Amin or a Papa Doc Duvalier. More fundamentally, Kaplan overlooks the global problem of market-dominant minorities. He stresses the ethnic biases of elections but neglects the ethnic biases of capitalism. He is overly optimistic about the ability of markets alone to lift the great indigenous masses out of poverty, and he fails to see that markets favor not just some people over others but, often, hated ethnic minorities over indigenous majorities. Overlooking this reality, Kaplan blames too much of the world's violence and anarchy on democracy.

The best economic hope for developing and postcommunist countries does lie in some form of market-generated growth. Their best political hope lies in some form of democracy, with constitutional constraints, tailored to local realities. But if global free-market democracy is to succeed, the problem of market-dominant minorities must be confronted head-on. If we stop peddling unrestrained markets and overnight elections as cure-alls—both to ourselves and others—and instead candidly address the perils inherent in both markets and democracy, there is in many cases room for optimism.

The first and most obvious step is to isolate, where possible, and address, where appropriate, the causes of the market dominance of certain groups. In South Africa, expanding educational opportunities for the black majority—restricted for more than 70 years to inferior Bantu schooling—is properly a national priority and should be vigorously supported by the international community. Throughout Latin America, educational reform and equalization of opportunities for the region's poor indigenous-blooded majorities are imperative if global markets are to benefit more than just a handful of cosmopolitan elites.

Yet we must be realistic. The underlying causes of market dominance are poorly understood, difficult to reduce to tangible factors, and in any event highly intractable. Research suggests, for example, that additional spending on education, if not accompanied by major socioeconomic reforms, produces depressingly few benefits. Political favoritism, though often a sore point with the majority in many societies with a market-dominant minority, tends to be more the consequence than the cause of market dominance. Most market-dominant minorities, whether the Bamiléké in Cameroon or Indians in Fiji, enjoy disproportionate economic success at every level of society down to the smallest shopkeepers, who can rarely boast of useful political connections. Indeed, many of these minorities succeed despite official discrimination against them. Any explanation of their success will likely include a host of intangibles such as the influence of religion and culture.

To "level the playing field" in developing societies will thus be a painfully slow process, taking generations if it is possible at all. More immediate measures will be needed to address the potentially explosive problems of ethnic resentment and ethnonationalist hatred that threaten these countries.

A crucial challenge is to find ways to spread the benefits of global markets beyond a handful of market-dominant minorities and their foreign investor partners. Western-style redistributive programs—progressive taxation, social security, unemployment insurance—should be encouraged, but, at least in the short run, they have limited potential. There simply is not enough to tax, and nearly no one who can be trusted to transfer revenues. Other possibilities are somewhat more encouraging. The Peruvian economist Hernando de Soto makes a powerful case in *The Mystery of Capital* (2000) for the benefits of giving the poor in the developing world formal, legally defensible property rights to the land they occupy but to which, because of underdeveloped legal systems and the tangles of history, they very often lack legal title.

A more controversial strategy consists of direct government intervention in the market designed to "correct" ethnic wealth imbalances. The leading example of such an effort is Malaysia's New Economic Policy (NEP), a program established after violent riots in 1969 by indigenous Malays angry over the economic dominance of foreign investors and the country's ethnic Chinese minority. The Malaysian government adopted sweeping ethnic quotas on corporate equity ownership, university admissions, government licensing, and commercial employment. It also initiated large-scale purchases of corporate assets on behalf of the bumiputra (Malay) majority.

In many respects, the results have been impressive. While the NEP has not lifted the great majority of Malays (particularly in the rural areas) out of poverty, it has helped to create a substantial Malay middle class. Prime minister Mahathir Mohamad, who frankly concedes that the NEP has tended to favor elite, well-connected Malays, nevertheless contends that it serves an important symbolic function: "With the existence of the few rich Malays at least the poor can say their fate is not entirely to serve rich non-Malays. From the point of view of racial ego, and this ego is still strong, the unseemly existence of Malay tycoons is essential."

Efforts like the NEP, however, are far from a universal solution. Few countries enjoy the degree of prosperity that makes them feasible, and even Malaysia has not achieved its goal of eradicating poverty. Moreover, such programs may well exacerbate ethnic tensions rather than relieve them, especially when government leaders are themselves ethnic partisans. . . .

Open ethnic conflict is rare in "mixed blood" Latin America. But light-skinned minorities dominate many economies, and new leaders are rallying the discontented around their Indian roots. Serbia's Slobodan Milosevic was conducting a form of affirmative action on behalf of long-exploited majorities, as Zimbabwe's Robert Mugabe doubtless feels he is doing now.

For better or worse, the best hope for global free-market democracy lies with market-dominant minorities themselves. This is adamantly not to blame these groups for the ethnonationalist eruptions against them. But it is to suggest that they may be in the best position to address today's most pressing challenges. To begin with, it must be recognized that market-dominant minorities often engage in objectionable practices—bribery, discriminatory lending, labor exploitation—that reinforce ethnic stereotypes and besmirch the image of free-market democracy. In Indonesia, the notorious "crony capitalism" of President Suharto depended on a handful of Chinese magnates and fueled massive resentment of the Chinese community generally.

More affirmatively, if free-market democracy is to prosper, the world's market-dominant minorities must begin making significant and visible contributions to the local economies in which they are thriving. Although such efforts have been relatively few and by no means always successful in promoting goodwill, some valuable models can be found. The University of Nairobi, for example, owes its existence to wealthy Indians in Kenya. The Madhvani family, owners of the largest industrial, commercial, and agricultural complex in East Africa, not only provide educational, health, housing, and recreational opportunities for their African employees, but also employ Africans in top management and offer a number of wealth-sharing schemes. In Russia, there is the unusual case of the Jewish billionaire Roman Abramovich, whose generous philanthropy and ambitious proposals won him election as governor of the poverty-stricken Chukotka region in the Russian Far East. More typically, however, building ethnic goodwill would require collective action. Fortunately, most economically successful minorities do have the resources for such action, in the form of local ethnic chambers of commerce, clan associations, and other organizations.

What of the world's largest economically dominant minority? What are Americans to do? It's obviously true that anti-Americanism, including the virulent Islamicist strain, doesn't stem from economic deprivation alone. As others have pointed out, the Islamicists themselves rarely even speak of a desire for prosperity. And it is fantasy to think that U.S. economic aid can do anything more than make a small dent in world poverty, at least in the near future. Yet those who call for increases in U.S. aid to the world's poor do seem to have wisdom on their side. The United States now devotes only 0.1 percent of its gross domestic product to foreign aid, a smaller share than any other advanced country. Rightly or wrongly, for millions around the world the World Trade Center symbolized greed, exploitation, indifference, and cultural humiliation. By extending themselves to the world's poor, Americans could begin to send a different sort of message. Retreating into isolationism or glorifying American chauvinism holds no long-term promise. It is difficult to see, in any event, how a little generosity and humility could possibly hurt.   ∎

■ *QUESTIONS FOR MAKING CONNECTIONS WITHIN THE READINGS* ■

1. Chua opens her essay with a story that engages the reader, but also complicates easy moral judgments by presenting multiple perspectives. Chua tells the story from her own perspective as an American niece of her murdered aunt, but we also glimpse events through other eyes as well. How does the Chinese community in the Philippines look at events of this sort and respond to them? How do the Filipino authorities view such matters? What about ordinary Filipinos—how might they regard the Chinese in their country? Should we understand the murder as one person's response to injustice, or do you regard "injustice" as an inappropriate choice of words? Would it be accurate to describe the Chinese as "oppressing" or "exploiting" the Filipinos, or is the situation more complex than these terms suggest? After all, Americans also qualify as a "market-dominant minority."

2. According to Chua, all peasants in the Philippines are Filipinos, whereas most members of the merchant class are Chinese. How has this situation developed in the Philippines, and why have similar imbalances arisen in other countries across the globe? Why might peasant-farmers be ill-suited to enter the world of international finance? What contributions to a society are made by "market-dominant minorities"? In what ways does the economic division in societies like the Philippines—with a majority of the native-born living in poverty while immigrants and their descendants dominate high finance—create a vicious circle in which the rich stay rich and the poor stay poor?

3. Chua identifies three causes of the "explosive violence" we are witnessing around the world: markets, democracy, and ethnic hatred. How exactly do these three causes reinforce one another? To a certain extent, everyone on earth wants the wealth and security that markets bring, and nearly everyone wants democracy. And yet, if Chua is correct in her claim that these two aspirations are unleashing ethnic hatred, then democracy and free markets by themselves cannot be the solution. Do you agree with Robert Kaplan's argument that poor countries need to begin their long march to development with authoritarian governments? Or do you find Chua's own proposals more compelling?

■ *QUESTIONS FOR WRITING* ■

1. Are democracy and globalization inherently compatible? Ordinarily, we associate free markets with democracy, and we assume that political democracy will foster greater economic opportunity. On the basis of Chua's evidence, however, would you say that these assumptions will

hold true in most cases around the world? Could the rise of markets on a global scale actually strengthen the undemocratic power of local elites, or could it create a new global elite for whom genuine democracy holds very little appeal? Should democracy become the world's top priority, or should democracy take a back seat to the broadening of prosperity? Consider in particular a success story like Mahathir Mohamad's policies in Malaysia.

2. Americans have tried to solve the problem of ethnic hatred by relying on the influence of education and by asking for support from prominent public figures. The schools teach the value of diversity, while opinion makers in the public eye are asked to speak out against prejudice. Do you believe that such strategies are likely to work if we attempt to apply them on a global scale? Have they worked here in the United States? Are social problems like racism really unsolved economic problems? With the broadening of opportunity, is the problem of ethnic hatred likely to diminish or even disappear?

■ QUESTIONS FOR MAKING CONNECTIONS BETWEEN READINGS ■

1. In "Dogs Snarling Together," Pietra Rivoli provides an account of how the global apparel market and the textile industry in the American South have come into conflict over the past 50 years. Rivoli discusses this development as evidence of the "politicization" of the global apparel trade. On the other hand, Chua contends that "the combined pursuit of free markets and democratization has repeatedly catalyzed ethnic conflict in highly predictable ways, with catastrophic consequences, including genocidal violence and the subversion of markets and democracy themselves." Has the global apparel trade, as Rivoli presents it, worsened the situation Chua describes or has it unfolded according to a different logic? Does individual action or desire make a difference in either scenario? Is democratization a political act or an economic project or something else altogether?

2. Chua's "A World on the Edge" and Beth Loffreda's "Losing Matt Shepard" both begin with the aftermath of a murder that expresses tensions in the larger culture. What are some of those tensions? Matt Shepard's murderers kill him because he is gay, whereas Aunt Leona is targeted because of her Chinese ethnicity, but the commonalities of these victims may extend beyond their shared identity as outsiders or people who are different. In a certain sense, the gay subculture in America is a national, and even global, phenomenon that cannot readily be contained by county lines or national boundaries. Similarly, the Chinese in Southeast Asia belong to an international community. To what degree do both murders and their aftermaths bear witness to a conflict between a local way of life and an intrusive, cosmopolitan culture?

DEVRA DAVIS

DEVRA DAVIS IS an environmental health expert who both directs the Center for Environmental Oncology at the University of Pittsburgh Cancer Institute and teaches epidemiology at the university's graduate program in public health. In *The Secret History of the War on Cancer*, she draws upon her years of epidemiological study to conclude that "the cancer war has been fighting the wrong battles, with the wrong weapons, against the wrong enemies" and that there have been "over 10 million preventable cancer deaths over the past 30 years."

In her critique, Davis targets the chemical, pharmaceutical, food, and health care industries that benefit from the public's continuing ignorance of the environmental factors that lead to cancer. She faults the government for creating a judicial environment that "make[s] the burden of proof close to impossible when it comes to human harm and environmental contamination," thereby all but eliminating the possibility of using the legal system to prevent cancer through the prosecution of the producers of carcinogenic substances. The combined influence of industrial secrecy and government reticence to act has created a decades-long "war on cancer" that focuses on treatment after the fact rather than on prevention.

Davis's call to reconsider public policy regarding environmental sources for cancer is particularly timely in an era when "half of all men and a third of all women in developed nations will contract the disease, and more than one in four of their citizens will die from it." Encounters with cancer are not random: they are highly determined by the quality of one's surroundings, which are, inevitably, also a function of one's social and economic status. "Rates of prostate, breast, and colo-rectal cancer are . . . much higher in blacks than whites," Davis points out, and the root cause of this, she argues, may be found in the fact that "one in three [black Americans] works in a blue collar job, and one in five lives within two miles of a hazardous waste site." For Davis, cancer must be understood

Davis, Devra. *The Secret History of the War on Cancer.* New York: Basic Books, Perseus, 2007.

Quotations come from "The War on Cancer, Cont'd," an editorial by Davis in the *Pittsburgh Post-Gazette,* available at <http://www.post-gazette.com/pg/07294/826873-109.stm>; a summary of *The Secret History of the War on Cancer* at the Environmental Oncology Institute's site, available at <http://www.environmentaloncology.org/secrethistorycancer2.htm>; and the author's own Web site at <http://www.devradavis.com/note.php>.

in the context of the countless variables ignored in contemporary approaches to "fighting" the disease. Cancer-free living will remain out of reach until we acknowledge the chemical substances that now permeate our living spaces and find their way into our bodies.

This multivariant approach to cancer invites a general reexamination of how we conceive of illness. How would public policy change if we began to look at cancer and other diseases as consequences of the world we have shaped for ourselves rather than the whim of genetics or the twist of fate? In order to be effective, is it necessary that public health policy become a form of social engineering, with economics and urban planning part of its purview? In order to be successful, must the "war on cancer" ultimately be a war against trade secrecy and poverty as well?

Presumed Innocent

Chronic ailments do not conveniently become evident when people suddenly succumb to symptoms neatly in one locale. Instead, cancer and neurological disorders arise over years of time as a result of assorted triggers in our lives that may reflect where we have worked, what we have eaten, and where we happen to live now and in the past. The difficulties of unraveling the complex factors that contribute to current patterns of disease cannot be overstated. But their complexity does not mean that they need to remain unresolved mysteries.

We are heavily invested in doing things as we always have, working out of places that have just been that way forever. Entire costly systems are built on wireless technologies and other electric-powered advances. We know they work extraordinarily well. We live with them, depend on them and can't imagine life without them. We hope they don't harm us. We can't imagine not using cell phones, not ordering diagnostic radiation tests to resolve medical problems or not taking greater numbers of drugs to treat disorders that didn't even exist years ago. At this point, we can't easily know whether any of these breakthrough technologies carries any long-term hazard.

Does the absence of agreed-upon proof of these potential hazards mean that they are not dangerous? There's got to be a better way to build our world than waiting for enough bodies to drop or sicken before we decide we've got a problem. We've got several looming health problems that require fundamentally different solutions than the technologies that gave rise to them. Why are more children developing cancer and learning problems?

Our ability to know whether unexplained patterns of disease are linked in any way with modern technologies and medications is severely hampered by a closed system that leaves us no independent means to evaluate such growing public health problems. We are only asked to do so after a pattern of disease has become so overwhelming that it makes network news.

Phones and Our Cells

Cell phones transform and save lives. Their risks are not easily thought about, given how intimately they have redefined normal life. Wrenching calls left on answering machines by victims of 9/11 gave some a chance to connect at the last moments of their lives. Today much of the world relies on cell phones rather than land lines. The growth in the use of these phones and the towers needed to connect them remains explosive. And, the discussion of their possible risks is ominously absent.

There's no debate that driving, biking or conducting any other mechanical physical activity while talking on a cell phone is a bad idea. That's why several states and some countries have already banned such practices. But what about the long-term risk to our health? Do the towers that transmit cell signals or the phones themselves convey a risk? Does living close to high-power electric switching stations affect the blood and brains of children? What about those who repair or build such towers? What about switching stations where high-voltage electricity is stepped down and sent throughout our workplaces and homes?

Then think of Ronald Reagan and George Bush Sr.'s political adviser Lee Atwater, General Electric's Jack Welch, Dan Case, the high-powered brother of AOL founder Steve Case, Calgary business leader Clark H. Smith, writer Bebe Moore Campbell and other heavy users of the first generations of cell phones when they were first introduced. Each of these brain cancer cases spent hours with some of the early cell phones next to their skulls. So did Maryland neurologist Christopher Newman. After developing a rarely survivable brain tumor—an anaplastic astrocytoma-grade III—he filed an $800 million lawsuit against Motorola, Bell Atlantic and others. That suit was dismissed in 2002 on the grounds that science did not prove harm.

One of the problems with studies of cell phones is that the issues they are trying to understand are inherently complex. Science works best examining one thing at a time, as we do with drugs in clinical trials. The problems posed by cell phones in the real world are like huge simultaneous equations—mathematical formulas of relationships between multiple unknowns. How can you determine the role of one factor, such as cell phone exposure to the skull, when others, like diet, workplace conditions and local air pollution, are changing at the same time and at different rates? The science that was invoked in Newman's case was not the work of lab researchers conducting experiments in test tubes under highly controlled conditions, changing one condition at a time to see which triggered the most serious or severe effects.

Instead, it was the ever-more perplexing studies of epidemiologists, who are forced to make sense of the real world with all of its complexity and ambiguity as it integrates the effects of multiple risk factors all at once.

Studying brain cancer is one of the toughest jobs in epidemiology because it is a rare disease, takes years to decades to develop, and impairs the very systems that might give us clues, a person's ability to recall and describe past activities and exposures that might have put them at risk. What happens to moms and dads where they live and work and from what they eat and drink can have an impact on whether children develop brain cancer. But, because the disease can take forty years to develop in adults, and because most adults with brain cancer often develop problems of speech and recall—either from the disease itself or from the treatment—and usually don't survive, we often have to interview their remaining family members about their life histories and try to figure out what could have led to the disease. Few of us really know all the good and bad things we've dealt with in our lives, let alone those of our relatives.

When it comes to sorting through the risks of cell phones, we have lately been assured that there are none based upon reports from what appear to be independent scientific reviewers. For example, researchers from the Danish Cancer Society reported in the *Journal of the National Cancer Institute* in 2006 that they found no evidence of risk in persons who had used cell phones. Headlines around the world boasted of this latest finding from an impeccable source published in a first tier scientific journal. The press coverage of this study tells us a great deal about what journalists and the rest of us who depend so heavily on these phones would like to believe.

"Cell Phones Don't Cause Brain Cancer"
—*Toronto Daily News,* December 10, 2006

"Cell Phones Don't Raise Cancer Risk"
—Reuters, December 6, 2006

"Big Study Finds No Link Between Cell Phones, Cancer"
—*San Jose Mercury News,* December 6, 2006

"Study: Cell Phones Don't Cause Cancer"
—*Albuquerque Tribune,* December 6, 2006

"Study: Cell Phones Safe"
—*Newsday,* December 7, 2006

"Cell Phones Do Not Cause Cancer"
—Techtree.com, India, December 7, 2006

But let's look at what the researchers actually studied.

They reviewed health records through 2002 of about 421,000 people who had first signed up for private use of cell phones between 1982 and 1995. A "cell phone user" in the study was anyone who made a single phone call a week for six months during the period 1981 to 1995. The study kicked out anyone who was part of a business that used cell phones, including only those who had used a cell phone for personal purposes for eight years.

This research design raises a lot of questions. Why did they not look at business users—those with far more frequent use of cell phones? Why lump all users together, putting those who might have made a single cell phone call a week with those who used the phones more often? Why stop collecting information on brain tumors in 2002, when we know that brain tumors often take decades to develop and be diagnosed?

When you are looking at a large population to find an effect, generally the more people you study, the better your chance of finding something. But if you merge a large number of people with very limited exposure together with a small number of people with very high exposure, you dilute the high-exposure group and so lower your chances of finding any effect at all. It would be better to compare the frequent users with non-users, omitting the limited users altogether. Lumping all these various users together is like looking all over a city for a stolen car when you know it's in a five-block radius. Perhaps you'll find what you're looking for, but the chances are greater that you won't. It would be far more effective to limit your search to the five-block area. The Danish study was designed to look definitively thorough—421,000 people!—but in fact it was biased against positive findings from the start. Given how broadly cell signals now penetrate coffee shops, airports and some downtown areas of major cities, it is very difficult to find any truly unexposed groups against which to compare results. Because cell phone use has grown so fast and its technologies change every year, it is as if we are trying to study the car in which we are driving.

Another study that was well publicized in 2000 found no increased risk of most types of brain cancer in cell phone users; but the average length of use among participants was less than three years.[1] Still, the study found that those people who had used phones for even this short period of time had twice the risk of a very rare brain tumor—neuroepitheliomatous cancers, the kind that wraps itself around the nerve cells of the lining of the brain, right at the locus that cell signals can reach.

Of course, epidemiologic research is the research that works best when we have solid information on the nature of the use or exposure we are trying to understand. All of us have cell phone bills that provide detailed records of our use, and most of these can be accessed online. These were not used in this study, nor in any study of the industry to date. A gold mine of data lies untapped that could enable researchers to distinguish non-users from low frequency users from high frequency users, thereby increasing the validity and sensitivity of studies.

Underlying this whole body of research is clear evidence that cell phone signals penetrate the brain. As the Danish researchers admitted in their own study, "During operation, the antenna of a cellular telephone emits radio frequency electromagnetic fields that can penetrate 4–6 cm into the human brain."[2] What the research seeks to determine is what this means biologically.

We know that cell phone signals can warm the side of the head, where the auditory nerve is located. An earlier Swedish study, used in Dr. Newman's case, compared more than 1,400 people with brain tumors to a similar number without the disease between 1997 and 2000. Tumors of the auditory nerve were three times more frequent in persons who had used cell phones for more than a decade.[3] In 2004, other Swedish researchers found that long-term cell phone users had significantly more tumors on the auditory nerves than nonusers.[4]

The study of chronic health problems is hardly as simple as we often presume.[5] We notice that most people with lung cancer have been smokers, or that many women over sixty who get breast cancer have used hormone replacement therapy. We deduce that a single condition gave rise to a single outcome, even though we know that life is not so simple.

George Carlo is an epidemiologist who once directed a multimillion-dollar, multicountry study of cell phones that was overseen by the U.S. government and funded by the industry starting in 1993. He was fired or resigned, depending on whose story you credit, and has continued to work on the issue ever since.

The study Carlo never completed for the industry began as a series of projects looking into whether cell phone signals disrupted cultures of animal cells growing in the laboratory. Some of the work done in laboratories clearly showed that wireless signals could affect the ways cells talk to one another to stay under control—what is called gap-junction communication. Under healthy conditions, cells send messages through proteins and enzymes that keep things in order and tell badly behaving cells to get in line or die. Wireless signals disturb this ability. Cells that can't communicate well are prone to grow out of control. In essence, wireless signals promote a kind of social breakdown among cells. Unfortunately, the implications of this work were never completed.

The human health component of the study of cell phones remains unfinished, and it may well be unfinishable. A major international study of brain cancer in wireless phone users is still under way, headquartered at the International Agency for Research on Cancer (IARC) of the World Health Organization in Lyon, France. The large study was designed to combine more than 3,000 cases of brain tumors from around the industrial world and was supposed to release its results in 2006. In Canada, Daniel Krewski, a respected epidemiologist who heads that country's national study of cell phones, receives much of his funding from the industry. Some have asked whether this constitutes bias. Krewski is also part of the IARC study.

The former director of the IARC, Lorenzo Tomatis, is concerned about the lack of independence of this important work. He complained publicly in 2004 about the close cooperation that was developing between the cell phone industry and those who were studying brain cancer that could be associated with cell phones' use. When Tomatis returned to the facility to meet with colleagues with whom he had worked, he was treated like no other former director: he was ordered to leave and security guards escorted him from the building.

More than a year after the IARC study was to have ended, it's still "under way." At the time this book was in final editing, in May 2007, the chief of the IARC study on cell phones reported that she did not have any idea when the work might be published. It is now in its tenth year.

At the core of the IARC project is a major effort to learn from brain cancer patients whether they used cell phones more frequently than did others. The limits of the work are easy to grasp. The ways to overcome them are not. Still, some German findings published just last year are disquieting.

The German study captured information about the daily lives of people in Mainz, Bielefeld and Heidelberg. What did they have for breakfast regularly? Where did they live? How often did they use the cell phone? For how long? On which ear? These are the sorts of things epidemiologists like me hope you remember. This work contrasted the life experiences and reported cell phone use of 366 people with deadly tumors of the brain called gliomas and 381 with slow-growing, usually benign tumors of the membranes that cover the spinal cord, against some 1,500 people between the ages of thirty and sixty-nine who had better luck and did not have brain tumors. When asking both groups about their past and current uses of cell phones, they did not find any increased risk in those who used phones for less than a decade. But, those who reported having used cell phones for ten years or more had twice the risk of coming down with gliomas.[6] This is a tumor that begins in the glial cells of the brain, the cells that support neurons and hold them together. The growth of gliomas can be silent, with symptoms that mimic flu or a headache. But eventually, they become undeniable. People lose speech, sight, movement or hearing, depending on where the tumor starts and where it ends up.

It should be obvious that looking at people with a fatal illness and asking them to try hard to remember what they did up to forty years ago is not easy. With all the information governments now assemble to combat terror, including library and cell phone records, what would it take for those powers to be directed toward learning whether our use of cell phones places us at risk from a disease that could be averted through better design and technology?

That's not a question likely to get much attention at this moment, but it is well worth asking. The studies to date that have not found a general, clear and consistent risk from cell phones need to be understood as tentative.

They have for the most part looked at older technologies over short periods of exposure. None is asking about the impact of cell phones on the brains of children and teenagers—one of the fastest growing groups of users in the world today. The governments of England, Israel and Sweden advise that those persons under eighteen should not use cell phones at all. American toddlers learn to play with toy versions of them.

What makes this especially troubling are the results from several other studies that have looked at more recent regular users. After a decade of heavy use, cell phone users have double the risk of brain cancer. The tumors tend to occur on the side of the head that the user typically favors.[7]

Another, entirely different set of data on electromagnetic fields, exposures of which cell phone signals are but one type, comes from looking at an illness even more extraordinarily rare than brain cancer—breast cancer in men. The total number of cases of male breast cancer in the United States today is thought to be less than 4,000, but some 1,400 new cases are reported each year, according to the American Cancer Society. Studies of men who work with electromagnetic fields in radio and television or in assembling cell towers have found that they have much greater risks of breast cancer as well as cancer of the brain.[8]

Table 1, from the National Institute of Environmental Health Sciences, shows the relative risks found in studies conducted on breast cancer in men (and some women) working in jobs involving regular contact with electromagnetic fields. These risks contrast the amount of cancer found in those with known exposures compared to those without such exposures. Of course, there can be no completely unexposed group for comparison purposes in the workplace. Both men and women have greater rates of breast cancer if their jobs involve heavy exposure to electromagnetic fields.

Men typically do not get breast cancer, and when they do, the disease is often much more difficult to treat. Still, this table shows that for many professions involving work with electronics, men have between two and four times more breast cancer than those without such experiences.

Electricians, railway workers, telecommunication line workers—in a striking number of industries men have greater risks of breast cancer. How can we know whether electromagnetic fields are responsible for these differences? Perhaps they all work with solvents or other chemicals that are also associated with giving men breast cancer? As with all workplace hazards, we can only draw conclusions from the totality of information at hand.

What about the rest of us? What about children who live near power lines or cell towers? What about the growing number of young children and teenagers who have their own cell phones, despite the fact that Scandinavia and many other countries warn that children should not use cell phones at all? We hope that today's digital technologies are safer than the older analog phones and other wireless systems. The Cellular Telecommunications and Internet Association reports that in 2007 there are more than 180 million

Table 1 Risk of Breast Cancer and Workplace Exposure to Electromagnetic Fields[9]

Reference, Country	Cohort Description	Exposure Classification	Males		Females		Comments
			No. of Cases	RR (95% CI)	No. of Cases	RR (95% CI)	
(Tynes et al., 1992); Norway	37,945 male workers (aged 20–70) followed 1961–85 in the Cancer Registry of Norway	12 electrical occupations	170	2.1 (1.1–3.6)	NA		SIR
		Electric transport work <ISCO codes 631, 632, 641, 693>	4	4.0 (1.1–10)	NA		
(Guénel, et al., 1993); Denmark	All actively employed Danes (aged 10–64) in 1970 followed 1970–87 in the cancer registry. 172,000 men and 83,000 women in jobs exposed to magnetic fields were compared with reference workers in unexposed jobs.	Job with intermittent field exposure	23	1.2 (0.77–1.8)	1526	0.96 (0.91–1.0)	SIR relative to economically active subjects
		Jobs with continuous exposure	2	1.5 (0.16–4.9)	55	0.88 (0.68–1.2)	

(Continued)

Table 1 (Continued)

Reference, Country	Cohort Description	Exposure Classification	Males		Females		Comments
			No. of Cases	RR (95% CI)	No. of Cases	RR (95% CI)	
(Floderus et al., 1994); Sweden	Male railway workers (aged 20–64) in the 1960 census compared with all employed men (940 person-years in 1960–69). Cancers for 1960–69 and 1970–79 obtained from Cancer-Environment Registry.	Engine drivers	2	8.3 (2.0–34)	NA		SIR adjusted for age. All cases occurred in 1960–1969 follow-up period (none in the 1970s).
		Conductors	1	2.7 (0.4–20)	NA		
		Railway workers (and station masters, dispatchers & linemen)	4	4.3 (1.6–12)	NA		

Source: Christopher J. Portier and Mary S. Wolfe, eds., "Assessment of Health Effects from Exposure to Power-Line Frequency Electric and Magnetic Fields (NIEHS Working Group Report)," June 1998. http://www.niehs.nih.gov/emfrapid/html/WGReport/WorkingGroup.html.

subscribers in the United States, up from 110 million users just three years earlier. Experts estimate that by 2010 there will be 2.2 billion subscribers worldwide. Cell phones are becoming so ubiquitous that soon there will be no control group against which to compare their risks.

With respect to the risks to children from living close to electromagnetic fields from power stations or high voltage transmission lines, some well-respected researchers, like Dan Wartenberg of Rutgers and others from the Karolinska Institute in Sweden, believe a growing body of evidence shows that there's a serious problem.[10] They aren't the only ones suggesting that electromagnetic fields be considered a possible human carcinogen. The World Health Organization officially recommends that power line siting decisions should consider ways to lower exposures and keep people out of the line of high voltage electricity and has classified EMF as a possible human carcinogen as has the U.S. National Institute of Environmental Health Sciences.[11]

The debate over electromagnetic fields and cell phones takes place on a playing field that is not at all level. Much of the research funding is provided by the telecommunications industry just as much of the research funding on more general electromagnetic field research was provided by the electric power industry. It may not surprise you to learn that the highly publicized Danish Cancer Society study that exonerated cell phones and the yet-to-be completed IARC study are directly funded by the industry.[12] Whether this affects the design of the studies and their outcome can't be determined. One group will have an answer in 2009, after they complete a long-term animal research project. What are we supposed to do while we wait for those results? . . .

By now you can probably persuade most people that cigarettes aren't worth the risk. But what about artificial sweeteners like Aspartame? Now one of the most widely used food supplements in the world, this chemical was first approved for limited use for diabetics, for whom glucose, the usual form of sugar, can be life-threatening.

In January 1977, FDA Chief Counsel Richard Merrill made agency history. He formally asked the U.S. Attorney's office to convene a grand jury to decide whether to indict the major producer of aspartame, G. D. Searle, for knowingly misrepresenting "findings, concealing material facts and making false statements" in aspartame safety tests. That this investigation never happened speaks volumes about the difficulty of acquiring independent information on commercially valuable products.

Two decades after this indictment had been filed, I spoke with James Olney, a research neurologist and psychiatrist at Washington University in St. Louis, about aspartame's early history. What he told me was hard to believe. In 1969, Searle asked the researcher Harry Waisman to study aspartame in seven infant monkeys. After a year of drinking milk flavored with the stuff, one was dead and five had suffered severe epileptic seizures. In the spring of 1971, Waisman died and his research was never completed. Olney's own studies showed that aspartame paired with the food flavoring monosodium glutamate produced brain tumors in rats.

In 1973, reviewing what Searle did include, Martha Freeman, an FDA scientist, determined that the information submitted on the safety of aspartame was not adequate. She recommended that aspartame not be allowed on the market.[13] Events eventually made her advice irrelevant.

Shortly after the proposed investigation was announced, Searle hired Donald Rumsfeld, who had just left office as Defense Secretary, to be its chief operating officer. He started in early 1977. That July, the chief attorney in charge of the grand jury, Samuel Skinner, resigned and went to work for Sidley & Austin, the law firm representing Searle. The person who replaced him, William Conlon, would eventually join Skinner at the same firm.

They had their work cut out for them. That August the FDA released its official report on aspartame, called the Bressler report, that included much of the information that formed the basis for the grand jury probe. It depicted a stunning number of irregularities. In one study of nearly two hundred animals, half of them weren't autopsied until long after they had died. Have you ever found a dead mouse in a trap? After a week, what's left is dried out, shrunken and stiff. Imagine trying to figure out whether that mouse had cancer and which organs were affected. The report noted that some rats that were recorded as having died later sprang back to life.

Immediately after the Bressler report was released, the FDA formed a task force to investigate the authenticity of research done by Searle regarding the safety of aspartame. A senior FDA investigator, Jacqueline Verrett, looked into these allegations and seconded the Bressler report's findings. A seasoned toxicologist, Verrett testified to the U.S. Senate in 1989 that the work she had reviewed on aspartame ten years earlier did not pass muster:

> At this point it might be helpful to mention some of the deficiencies and improper procedures encountered: no protocol was written until the study was well under way; animals were not permanently tagged to avoid mix-ups; changes were introduced in some laboratory methods during the study with inadequate documentation; there was sporadic monitoring and/or inadequate reporting of food consumption and animal weights; tumors were removed and the animals returned to the study; animals were recorded as dead, but subsequent records, after varying periods of time indicated the same animal was still alive (almost certain evidence of mix-ups); many animal tissues were autolyzed (decomposed) before any postmortem examinations were performed; and finally, of extreme importance, in the DKP study there was evidence, including pictures, that the diets were not homogeneous and that the animals could discriminate between feed and the included DKP. Almost any single one of these aberrations would suffice

to negate a study designed to assess the safety of a food additive, and most certainly a combination of many such improper practices would, since the results are bound to be compromised.

It is unthinkable that any reputable toxicologist, given a completely objective evaluation of data resulting from such a study, could conclude anything other than that the study was uninterpretable and worthless, and should be repeated.

In 1978, the journal *Medical World News* reported that the methanol content of aspartame is a thousand times greater than most foods under FDA control. In high concentrations, methanol, or wood alcohol, is a lethal poison that can cause blindness and damage the brain. Some of us humans can be uniquely sensitive to such materials, especially those who do not yet crawl or walk. While most of us can easily handle methanol and its more familiar cousin, ethanol—the alcohol we drink on social occasions—some of us can't handle it well at all.

At the end of September 1980, another FDA review board weighed in. Its three members voted unanimously against approving aspartame, noting that the FDA "has not been presented with proof of reasonable certainty that aspartame is safe for use as a food additive." Meanwhile, the grand jury investigation fizzled. So much time had elapsed that the authority to keep it going had expired. Expert legal advice—doubtlessly provided by former FDA officials who had started the investigation and now worked for the aspartame industry—had helped Searle run out the clock. Scientific evidence became irrelevant.

And then Donald Rumsfeld proved his worth. Searle's directors clearly had not hired him for his pharmaceutical expertise—he had none to speak of—but for his already legendary Washington connections. After the election of President Reagan in November 1980 these suddenly became much more powerful. Rumsfeld told a Searle sales meeting that he would get aspartame approved within the year. According to a 2006 article in the *Ecologist*, he vowed to "call in his markers" with the FDA.[14]

The day after President Reagan was inaugurated, January 22, 1981, Searle reapplied for FDA approval. Ignoring the recommendation of yet another review panel, the new FDA commissioner, Arthur Hull Hayes, approved aspartame for use in dry products on May 19, 1981. Within a year, that approval extended to liquids and vitamins.

On October 12, 1987, United Press International reported that more than ten American government officials who had been involved in the decision to approve aspartame were now working in the private sector with or for the aspartame industry. One of them was Commissioner Hayes, who had gone to work for Burton-Marsteller, the chief public relations firm representing Searle and Monsanto. (Monsanto purchased Searle in 1985. In this merger, Searle's aspartame business became a separate Monsanto subsidiary, the NutraSweet Company.)[15]

The U.S. military was not sanguine about aspartame's safety. Both the U.S. Air Force magazine *Flying Safety* and the U.S. Navy magazine *Navy Physiology* warned that aspartame can cause serious brain problems in pilots.[16]

Around 1995 the FDA stopped gathering adverse reaction reports. If you don't want to know, don't ask. By 1996, aspartame was approved for all uses.

What about all those studies finding aspartame safe? In 1996 Ralph G. Walton, a professor of clinical psychology at Northeastern Ohio University, surveyed them for the news show *60 Minutes*. Walton reviewed 165 separate studies published in medical journals over a twenty-year period. *All* of the studies that found aspartame safe happened to be sponsored by industry. Every single one that questioned its safety was produced by scientists without industry ties.

The *Ecologist* quotes the Bressler report directly:

> The question you have got to ask yourself is: why wasn't greater care taken? Why didn't Searle, with their scientists, closely evaluate this, knowing full well that the whole society, from the youngest to the elderly, from the sick to the unsick, will have access to this product?

Aspartame is now one of the most commonly used ingredients in drinks, cakes, cookies and candies. There is no evidence at all that those who use it actually lose weight. There is some indication that it creates a sugar deficit, leading people to seek more sugar from other sources.

But leaving aside whether it has any benefits, is it safe? Do we have enough information to know? Remember that we test compounds in animals to find out how they might affect humans. Olney, who published original studies showing that rats exposed to aspartame developed brain abnormalities in the 1970s and 1980s, returned to the subject in 1996, asking whether patterns of brain cancer in adults in the early 1990s might reflect past use of aspartame.[17] He told me that even though his findings were written in the tentative tone of scientific inquiry, when this paper, questioning whether brain tumors could be tied with aspartame use, was accepted for publication by the *Journal of Neuropathology and Experimental Neurology*, attorneys for Monsanto asked the editors not to publish the work. In fact, brain cancer may have a latency as long as thirty years between the time of first exposure and the expression of the illness, so Olney's question was certainly premature. Given the rapid growth in recent years in the use of aspartame, if there is an impact on brain cancer or other cancers, it might not yet be evident.

Still, the National Cancer Institute and the American Cancer Society felt compelled to weigh in on the same question with a resounding no. How did they reach this conclusion? They conducted a survey in 1995 and 1996 of drinking and eating patterns in half a million volunteers of the AARP, asking how many of them had come down with lymphoma or brain cancer five years later. The fact that no effect was found is hardly the last word on the subject.

Until recently, studies in lab animals were run for a period of two years. When working with rodents, scientists have generally ended the studies and the varmints' lives after 712 days, hoping in that time to get the animals to consume as much of whatever is being tested as a human would use in seventy years. But rats can live longer. It's entirely possible that by stopping studies at this point, we are missing an important part of the picture. What happens to animals or people in the last third of their lives? That's something that many of us want to know.

At the European Ramazzini Foundation in Bologna, Italy, a group of scientists led by Italy's leading toxicologist, Cesare Maltoni, came up with a different approach to testing animals to predict human impacts—an approach that is being adopted throughout the world today. For more than three decades, they have been letting rats and mice live out their natural lifetimes (generally three years) as they are exposed to various substances present in the industrial or general environment, to see whether these agents affected their chances of getting cancer. This lifespan protocol contrasts with that of other laboratories where rodents are killed at two years of age and examined for signs of tumors or other damage. Two years in a rat corresponds to about sixty years in humans, but more and more of us expect to live into our eighties.

What about aspartame? Maltoni died in 2001, but his work continued. Eighteen hundred Sprague-Dawley rats were allowed to eat aspartame from the age of eight weeks until their natural deaths about three years later. The study demonstrated for the first time that the artificial sweetener, when administered to rats in feed, caused a statistically significant, dose-related increase of lymphomas/leukemias and tumors of the renal pelvis and ureter in females and malignant tumors of peripheral nerves in males.[18] Moreover, these tumors occurred even at a daily dose well under that allowed in America or Europe, namely 50 mg/kg and 40 mg/kg respectively. Table 2, from the European Ramazzini Foundation, estimates the average amount of aspartame consumed from only a few of the 6,000 products in which it is present.

If a woman ate these foods and weighed 60 kilograms (approximately 132 pounds), she would consume an aspartame daily dose of 15.1 mg/kg of body weight; a child weighing 30 kg (approximately 66 pounds) with a similar daily intake would have an aspartame daily dose twice as high—30.3 mg/kg of body weight. This level is well over the dose that caused lymphomas/leukemias in the study. This study was the first to show that aspartame caused cancer in multiple organs.

In a letter to the journal that published Soffritti's work, the industry soundly rejects his study. It refers to an independent evaluation by the European Food Safety Authority Scientific Panel on Food Additives, Flavorings, Processing Aids, and Materials in Contact with Food. In fact, many members of this "independent" panel work directly for the same industry. They suggest

Table 2   Average Daily Intake of Aspartame

Substance	Quantity/Day	Concentration of Aspartame Consumed
Diet soda (200 mg/can)	2 cans	400 mg
Yogurt (125 mg/yogurt)	2 yogurts	250 mg
Diet custard/pudding (75 mg/mousse)	1 serving	75 mg
Coffee with sweetener (40/mg packet)	4 cups	160 mg
Candy/chewing gum (2.5/candy)	10 candies	25 mg
Totals		**910 mg**

that the findings of this three-year study are completely without merit because there were unusual patterns of cancer in these animals that have not generally occurred in other studies.

Let's look at what the Ramazzini Foundation did. Soffritti's team studied more than 1,800 animals for a period of three years. The European critics of Soffritti noted that the animals in both the control group and those that regularly drank aspartame suffered from inflammatory respiratory problems. They charge that the increased risk of cancer could have happened as a result of some underlying infection, but this completely misses one key point. The animals lived out their natural lifetimes. Animals, just like the rest of us, have to die of something. Pulmonary infections, like pneumonia, are called the old man's friend, because they can be a relatively painless way to go. But, even if these animals all developed lung problems as they aged, why did so many of those who drank aspartame develop cancers in so many different organs?

There is no question that medical and information breakthrough technologies make our fast-moving, fast-talking world easier to handle. Whether they may also make our lives more prone to cancer is a question that is simply not being asked. We presume that the things we rely on today to see through bodies, talk across the world in an instant, and keep our children from spinning out of control are safe; to do otherwise would require an entirely new way of looking at the world.

The absence of extensive information confirming that human health is endangered by any one of these technologies and medications lulls most of us into assuming that no such hazard exists. [My argument] is that we should all question this presumption. Highly profitable industries have no incentive to ask whether the products on which they depend may have adverse consequences. Nor is there any independent system in place to compel them to do so. As Searle's former CEO Donald Rumsfeld said in a very different context, absence of evidence is not evidence of absence. A lack of definitive evidence regarding human harm is not proof that no such harm occurs. Rather it shows the difficulties and roadblocks that surround efforts to develop information on the health effects of modern technologies and chemicals.

The presumption of innocence with which we accept new technologies today, like that with which the world greeted x-rays at the dawn of the twentieth century, makes no sense. Our naive faith and fascination with what's novel does a disservice to ourselves and our children and grandchildren.

If we are to learn about the long-term impact of essential components of new technologies and medicines, we need open systems or evaluation that currently don't exist. Drugs and technologies are created to fix problems. How can we know whether these rapid solutions may endanger our lives later on?

The short answer is, we can't.

If we insist that we cannot act to prevent future harm until we have proof of past harms, we are treating people like lab rats in uncontrolled experiments. If we say, let's let the experts decide, where do we get experts without baggage? The costs of experimental laboratory research are growing and debates about the value of various research methods are becoming ever more complex. These debates are sometimes fueled by those who have a knack for turning molehills of scientific minutiae into mountains of uncertainty. In a world where information on the health and safety of workers remains locked up in company files, wrapped in the protections of confidentiality, independent information and independent experts to make sense of it are an endangered species.

We have seen repeatedly how some people in industry, whether tobacco, asbestos, benzene or vinyl chloride, understood risks long before the rest of us were able to learn about them. We know of many instances where insurance companies tracked health hazards for years, as claims mounted and reports of various ailments accumulated, without letting workers know the dangers they faced. We also know that current laws discourage giving such information up. The federal Toxic Substances Control Act provides criminal penalties for anyone who has knowledge that someone endangers public health or the environment and does not report it. The result is that most companies no longer develop such knowledge or collect such information, so that they can't be charged with breaking this law.

With respect to long-standing workplace and environmental hazards, the idea of prosecuting those found guilty of past harms has just not worked. The crimes are of such long standing, the victims are so many, and retribution is so pointless that perhaps the best course is to emulate the South African Truth and Reconciliation Commissions (TRC) and offer amnesty in exchange for a better future. In 1994, to create a break with its deadly past, South Africa set up a stunning series of national public confessions. Nelson Mandela, the head of the African National Congress, and South African President F. W. de Klerk both understood that for the racist system of apartheid to die, it needed a proper burial. Without public acknowledgment of the brutality of the apartheid past, the country would never recover.

De Klerk's white supremacist National Party wanted blanket amnesty for the violence they had committed in the name of the law. The members of Mandela's African National Congress wanted revenge. If the country was not to be torn apart, it needed to create something that had never really been done before—a national commission for truth and reconciliation.

People came forward asking questions that they could not have uttered at any other time. What happened to my son or daughter or husband or wife or brother or sister or father or mother? Where did they go? Who killed them? How had they died? These were not easy questions to ask. They were even less easy to answer. The system was based on the premise that without answers, the country could never be brought together.

In her memoir *Every Secret Thing*, the South African writer Gillian Slovo writes that she had to struggle hard to accept this premise. Her mother, Ruth First, a white supporter of Mandela, was killed by a package bomb sent by the Nationalist Party. Her father, Joe Slovo, had fought Hitler in Germany and would fight with Mandela against the white supremacists in South Africa. The last effort of his life was to seek restorative justice for the man who had murdered his wife.[19]

Gillian Slovo explained her father's remarkable position. "My father, one of the architects of the final settlement, put it this way: the best revenge, he said, that I can think of for those men who murdered my wife is that they be made to live in peace in a system that they had fought so brutally against. The truth telling that this unleashed was painful, sobering, and so far has proved to have provided more healing than hurt. A nation that once was awash in the blood of its people is moving toward a more free and open society than it has ever known."[20]

This open approach went far beyond any of the efforts to mete out justice that arose after the end of World War II. National law, whatever it may have said or allowed, becomes irrelevant and is replaced by an almost biblical view of what is required to restore a nation. Not punishment and vengeance, but grace and forgiveness, become the grounds for renewal and restoration.

Those who witnessed the creation of South Africa's TRC call it a miracle. They note that what took place in postwar Germany and Japan, and in Central and Latin America after the fall of right-wing dictatorships, made it clear that direct and full prosecution, if carried out, would rip a country apart. Where a majority are guilty, punishment becomes unending. Where only a few are prosecuted, as was the case in Germany and Japan, this creates the delusion that the rest of the country bears no responsibility for the past. Because these nations had embraced violence against their own citizens as a matter of national policy and law, turning to the law to provide redress against this violence made no sense.

If persons in charge of major firms today learn that chemicals their workers are using will shorten their lives, and they fail to act on this knowledge, are these actions no less morally wrong than those of the South African leaders, Nazi supremacists or Japanese imperialists? Creating a harmful workplace and concealing that harm is surely a more subtle crime than forcing young girls to serve as "comfort women" or loading entire villages into boxcars for transport to death camps. But if we were to count the deaths caused, or if we could somehow reckon up the total human suffering, we would find ourselves in similar territory.

I have learned from others, whom I can't name at this point, that the files of many large multinational businesses could easily tell us about many more health risks associated with workplace exposures of the past. These companies are largely self-insured and pay for their workers' health care. They have complex information systems at hand to control the manufacture of chemicals, the ordering of materials, and the processing of health claims. Can you really imagine that such an organization does not know whether or not its workforce in Indonesia or Silicon Valley has greater risks of breast cancer and leukemia? Can you believe that Pratt & Whitney—one of the largest and most profitable makers of airplane engines in the world—does not know whether or not its workers have higher rates of brain cancer than the general population?

According to the company's website, Pratt & Whitney engines power nearly half of the world's commercial fleet.[21] Every few seconds—more than 20,000 times a day—a Pratt & Whitney-powered airliner takes flight somewhere in the world. Their military engines power the air force's front line fighters today—the F-15 and F-16—and our F-119 and F-135 engines will power the front line fighters of the future—the F-22 Raptor and F-35 Joint Strike Fighter. Their rocket engines send payloads into orbit at 20,000 miles per hour. Is it believable that this same company can't tell us now whether the men and women who have made these engines over the past thirty years have more cancer than others?

I am not smart enough to know what kind of system will best identify and address the preventable causes of cancer in our environment. I just know that what we have been doing doesn't work. For every lawsuit that is won on behalf of persons harmed by cancerous activities, many more are never even filed. Lawsuits brought on behalf of those who believe their injuries were caused by their employers' bad actions succeed less and less often. In large part this is because recent court decisions have changed the rules of the game and the presumptions of evidence.

It may shock you to learn that of the 100,000 chemicals that are commonly used in commerce, most have not been studied as to their ability to affect our health. In 1983 and again in 1998, the National Academy of Sciences confirmed that we have no public record of the toxicity of three out of every four of the top 3,000 chemicals in use today. Despite declarations by industry of their intent to close this gap, in reality it would take dozens of years and billions of dollars to do so. It can take three weeks to approve a new chemical for use and thirty years to remove an old one.

In the past, experimental findings in rodents and small mammals were accepted as indications of human harm. Nowadays the field of experimental carcinogenesis itself has become wracked with debates about how to interpret findings. While drugs are still created based on animal experiments, the appraisal of commercial chemicals is littered with endless debates about mechanisms and appropriate models.

In a sense we have come full circle. In the 1930s, the world's leading cancer experts, using experimental information, detailed observations on highly exposed workers, and some public health statistics, identified many important causes of cancer in industry, nutrition and behavior. For the past seventy-five years, that evidence has been stretched, reviewed, revised, culled, pulled about and put back together again.

While Heraclitus said no one ever steps into the same river twice, he could not have had in mind the circular voyage the world of cancer research has taken. We have known for more than a century that it is inherently difficult to evaluate the extent to which a given exposure results in a given health problem. As we have seen repeatedly in this book, cancer-causing agents can produce many different types of cancer as well as an entire suite of other health problems through biological paths that can't be easily tracked.

Epistemology is the study of how we come to know what we believe we know. Plato pointed out that what we know is in a basic sense socially constructed at the intersection of our shared beliefs and presumed truths. Cancer research is no different from any other form of knowing. It relies on customs and practices. What can be considered known about cancer is profoundly economic and political and reflects the views and values of those who pay for the work, decide whether or not it should be carried out, and when and if it should ever become public.

The loggerhead at which science and law now abut may become a tipping point. Science works to establish the truth. Law aims to mete out justice. Because scientists know that certainty is never absolute, scientific knowledge is always hedged. There's always room for more. Law requires enough faith in precision to mete out justice. Carl Cranor and David Eastmond, two scholars on toxic injuries, succinctly describe the dilemma of how to meld scientific evidence to obtain justice regarding such harms:

> At this juncture, the point is not to propose a specific alternative, but to sketch the types of legal modifications that should be explored in order to induce corporations to engage in far more scientific research when it

matters—not to win lawsuits but to protect society against the risks posed by their products. The proper role for scientists with regard to toxic substances should be to provide needed information about possible latent defects, not to cast deciding votes on liability because causation has been made a surrogate for morally responsible corporate behavior.[22]

As a first step to preserving the central aims of tort law, courts will need to recognize the wide variety of respectable, reliable patterns of evidence on which scientists themselves rely for drawing inferences about the toxicity of substances. The patterns of inferences presented above for carcinogens, arguably one of the most difficult of toxic substances with which scientists and courts must deal, serve as examples of some of the variety of inference patterns utilized in the scientific community. Courts, recognizing a wider variety of inferences, would then he able to better assess the sparse scientific evidence that is typically available.

. . . If scientific knowledge about the toxicity of a substance in humans could be accumulated instantaneously, there would not be the concern that science delayed or incomplete was justice denied. If scientists could instantaneously have the best human evidence of toxicity, they would not need to piece together animal, mechanistic, genetic, structure-activity, and other inferential evidence. If diseases could be identified at an early stage, left their signatures, or did not have long latency periods, there might be a lesser need for various kinds of non-human evidence. However, given the nature of the biological world and the recognition that science in its current stage of development does not have such capabilities, courts must recognize this and utilize scientifically reliable patterns of evidence that will permit plaintiffs to receive just treatment in tort cases. If this is not done or it is not adequate, more fundamental solutions to these issues will need to be found.[23]

In fact, the courts are moving in just the opposite direction. They are not piecing together information or tapping alternative methods of inferring facts and associations but allowing the absence of proof of human harm to be construed as evidence that there is no such harm.

A truth and reconciliation commission might provide the sort of revelations about toxic hazards that we all feel have to be at hand, but realize remain out of our reach. If one asks who should pay for this system, we may draw another lesson from World War II. During and after that war, an excess profits fee was placed on those industries that benefited from the conflict. There is no doubt that tobacco, alcohol, chemical and pharmaceutical manufacturing are industries that create risks and benefits, often to quite different groups of people. A fee can be levied on all those industries as a way to fund a truly independent and neutral forum where information can be safely exchanged on environmental health hazards.

Some will argue that creating a TRC-like institution to accept information on environmental health hazards would only allow people to get away with past activities that have injured or killed people. The tort system exists to redress wrongs and to exact financial penalties from those who have harmed others. Such people cannot be absolved by a new institution.

The harder we try to exact vengeance against those who have caused harm, the more incentive they have to conceal information, and the more harm will be done in the future. But new approaches to generate information on the risks of work and the environment can reduce the chances that current harms will result in future damages. If we create a place where industry can deposit information on health hazards of work and the environment, with the privacy of individuals appropriately shielded, the world will be better off for our having tried to do so.

The European community is trying to produce a better set of information on chemical hazards as part of the Re-registration, Evaluation, and Assessment of Chemical Hazards (REACH) program. It's too soon to know if this voluntary program will work, but some are concerned.

As Soffritti, the Italian scientist who continues Maltoni's pioneering approach in long-term animal carcinogenicity testing, recently told me, "The REACH program has passed the burden of proof for chemical safety to the industries that produce the agents. Unfortunately, history teaches us that industry reports do not necessarily contain all that is needed to evaluate the risk or safety of products. In looking at the ways that information can be manipulated, John Bailar notes that, 'There are many ways to distort the scientific truth without actually lying.'[24] Consequently, I would therefore be very cautious about using industry data as the principal basis for regulatory action. The structure of the REACH program means that independent data will be relegated to anecdotal status."

It is a huge dilemma. Another tack can be pursued as well. For those with known or suspected exposures in the workplace or environment, why not establish what are called "medical surveillance" programs to look for the ones who are ill? We know that there are some illnesses where early treatment can keep people from early deaths. A smart outfit that has put a dangerous product on the market should be interested in systems that would reach out to people at risk and help them. This approach may back us all down from a precipice, to a point where people who are going to get increasingly sick will have a chance to be helped through medical surveillance programs set up to find them before their illness is too far advanced.

A leading tort lawyer commented on this idea with guarded enthusiasm. "In my twenty years of work, not once have I had a client who was glad they had me as a lawyer because they had this really awful cancer they just were thrilled about."

She noted that perhaps an admission of knowledge on cancer-causing practices would be lifesaving as well as good for the soul. "The companies need to put the shoe on the other foot. If it were their family, they'd want a system that gave them an opportunity to look for ways to hold people accountable, and to help them stay well for as long as possible. Medical surveillance would remove the hazard and work with those who've been exposed with the goal of keeping people healthy."

Of course, even if we set up such a system and found ways to pay for it, we have to live with what cannot be undone. The systems currently in place to understand and control toxic substances do not work well enough. The penalties mandated by the Toxic Substances Control Act, requiring that anyone having knowledge that an activity threatens public health or safety has to report it, had just the opposite effect. Rather than creating information on public health threats, the act has discouraged companies from publicizing analyses of their workers' health.

Protected trade secrets are now defined so broadly that they sometimes encompass information on the health and safety of workers, including even workmen's compensation claims. The way out of this problem has got to be different from the way in. As Einstein noted in another matter, we can't solve the problems of the present by repeating the mistakes of the past.

But the past still offers a guide. In the eighteenth century, the philosopher Immanuel Kant argued that we have to act as if there were goodness, truth and justice, because by doing so, we compel these qualities to arise. We have learned that much evil in modern history is not natural but man-made, the result not of divine but of human will.

The move toward greener energy from tides and sun and wind will eventually turn the Middle East conflict into a relic of the days when the world depended on liquid fossil fuels that may become irrelevant in my grandchildren's lifetimes. Arnold Schwarzenegger played the Terminator, Conan the Barbarian and Conan the Destroyer, characters wired to end much of the world. In his latest reinvention, the wealthy, unsalaried governor of California appears as the great green giant, campaigning for a just and clean world, featured on the cover of *Newsweek* holding up the entire globe with one finger. For more than twenty years, since the death of her first husband, Sen. John Heinz, Teresa Heinz Kerry has marshaled the wealth of the Heinz Endowment to foster a green renaissance of the once smoky city of Pittsburgh. Formerly known as hell with the lid off, Pittsburgh today is a center of green building, chemistry, health care and operations in my own hospital system—all built to have a smaller footprint. Television programming of dizzying arrays, luxury and regular magazines and new websites are proliferating to promote green living options that are not just for the true believers. Yes, such activities appear in the midst of commercials for Hummers and SUVs, but those are dropping faster than lead balloons. The environment is no longer a niche issue of radical chic, but a matter of broadly understood importance. Those of us who indict past failures have a duty to develop new solutions.   ∎

NOTES

1. Joshua E. Muscat et al., "Handheld Cellular Telephone Use and Risk of Brain Cancer," *Journal of the American Medical Association* 284, no. 23 (2000): 3001–3007.

2. Joachim Schüz et al., "Cellular Telephone Use and Cancer Risk: Update of a Nationwide Danish Cohort," *Journal of the National Cancer Institute* 98, no. 23 (2006): 1707–1713.

3. L. Hardell et al., "Case-Control Study on the Use of Cellular and Cordless Phones and the Risk for Malignant Brain Tumours," *International Journal of Radiation Biology* 78, no. 10 (2002): 931–936.

4. S. Lonn, A. Ahlbom, P. Hall, and M. Feychting, "Mobile Phone Use and the Risk of Acoustic Neuroma," *Epidemiology* 15, no. 6 (2004): 653–659.

5. Roberta B. Ness, James S. Koopman, and Mark S. Roberts, "Causal System Modeling in Chronic Disease Epidemiology," *Annals of Epidemiology*, February 26, 2007 (EPub).

6. Joachim Schüz et al., "Cellular Phones, Cordless Phones, and the Risks of Glioma and Meningioma (Interphone Study Group, Germany)," *American Journal of Epidemiology* 163, no. 6 (2006): 512–520.

7. J. Schüz, E. Bohler, G. Berg, B. Schlehofer, I. Hettinger, K. Schlaefer et al., "Cellular Phones, Cordless Phones, and the Risks of Glioma and Meningioma (Interphone Study Group, Germany)," *American Journal of Epidemiology* 163, no. 6 (2006): 512–520; Anna Lahkola et al., "Mobile Phone Use and Risk of Glioma in 5 North European Countries," *International Journal of Cancer* 120, no. 8 (2007): 1769–1775.

8. Ed Edelson, "Men with Breast Cancer at High Risk of Second Tumor," *HealthDay News*, January 25, 2007, <www.hon.ch/News/HSN/601257.html>.

9. Christopher J. Portier and Mary S. Wolfe, eds., "Assessment of Health Effects from Exposure to Power-Line Frequency Electric and Magnetic Fields (NIEHS Working Group Report)," June 1998. <http://www.niehs.nih.gov/emfrapid/html/WGReport/Working Group.html>.

10. A. Ahlbom et al., "A Pooled Analysis of Magnetic Fields and Childhood Leukaemia," *British Journal of Cancer* 83, no. 5 (2000): 692–698.

11. <http://www.who.int/mediacentre/factsheets/fs263/en/index.html>.

12. Lorenzo Tomatis, personal communication.

13. "FDA Handling of Research on NutraSweet Is Defended," *New York Times*, July 18, 1987, p. 50.

14. Pat Thomas, "Aspartame—The Shocking Story of the World's Bestselling Sweetner," *The Ecologist,* September 2005, p. 35–51.

15. See <www.nutrasweet.com/company. asp>.

16. U.S. Air Force, "Aspartame Alert," *Flying Safety* 48, no. 5 (1992): 20–21.

17. John W. Olney et al., "Glutamate-Induced Brain Damage of Infant Primates," *Journal of Neuropathology and Experimental Neurology* 31, no. 3 (1972): 464–488; John W. Olney et al., "Brain Damage in Mice From Voluntary Ingestion of Glutamate and Aspartate," *Neurobehavioral Toxicology and Teratology* 2, no. 2 (1980): 125–129; John W. Olney, "Excitotoxic Food Additives: Functional Teratological Aspects," *Progress in Brain Research* 73 (1988): 283–294; and John W. Olney et al., "Increasing Brain Tumor Rates: Is There a Link to Aspartame?" *Journal of Neuropathology and Experimental Neurology* 55, no. 11 (1996): 1115–1123.

18. M. Soffritti et al., "First Experimental Demonstration of the Multipotential Carcinogenic Effects of Aspartame Administered in the Feed to Sprague-Dawley Rats,"

Environmental Health Perspectives 114, no. 3 (2006): 379–385; M. Soffritti et al., "Aspartame Induces Lymphomas and Leukaemias in Rats," *European Journal of Oncology* 10 (2005): 107–116.

19. Gillian Slovo, "Making History: South Africa's Truth and Reconciliation Commission," May 12, 2002, <www.opendemocracy.net/democracy-africa_democracy/article_818.jsp>.

20. Ibid.

21. "Pratt & Whitney: A United Technologies Company," <www.pw.utc.com/vgn-exttemplating/v/index.jsp?vgnextoid=fb654e15c86fb010VgnVCM1000000881000a RCRD>.

22. Carl F. Cranor and David A. Eastmond, "Scientific Ignorance and Reliable Patterns of Evidence in Toxic Tort Causation: Is There a Need for Liability Reform?" *Law and Contemporary Problems*, Autumn 2001, p. 5.

23. Ibid.

24. John Bailar, "How to Distort the Scientific Record Without Actually Lying," *European Journal of Oncology* 11, no. 4 (2007): 217–224.

▪ QUESTIONS FOR MAKING CONNECTIONS WITHIN THE READING ▪

1. Davis presents her reader with a wide array of evidence on environmental toxins. After you have generated a catalog of the evidence she cites, identify the evidence that you found to be the most compelling. Given Davis's argument, is it possible to say that her evidence is convincing?

2. Davis asks questions throughout "Presumed Innocent"—more than a dozen appear in the first section alone. As you reread the piece, highlight the questions she poses, paying attention to when and where the questions arise. Do you detect a pattern? Are the questions all of the same kind? Versions of the same question? Do they tell us anything about Davis's method?

3. Given Davis's analysis of how major corporations do business, do you regard her solution as adequate and likely to succeed? Obviously, Davis is aware that the South African Truth and Reconciliation Commissions were not concerned with scientific research on cancer, but with apartheid. Why, then, does she offer these commissions as an appropriate model for transforming research on cancer?

▪ QUESTIONS FOR WRITING ▪

1. "Cancer research is no different from any other form of knowing. It relies on customs and practices." With this statement, Davis moves scientific research into the realm of all social ways of knowing, stressing in the process that such research is necessarily influenced by who is funding the project, who carries it out, when it is done, and who stands to lose the

most by negative results. Is this the same as saying that, in the final analysis, scientific research is subjective or inescapably biased? What is the status of truth in Davis's analysis?

2. Early in "Presumed Innocent," Davis declares that "[w]e've got several looming health problems that require fundamentally different solutions than the technologies that gave rise to them." One could argue, though, that new technologies are also responsible for making us aware of health problems that would otherwise go undetected. Davis, however doesn't look to technology to solve the problems she has identified. Where does she look? In what sense are the solutions she proposes "fundamentally different"?

■ *QUESTIONS FOR MAKING CONNECTIONS BETWEEN READINGS* ■

1. Edward Tenner assures us, in spite of all the complications, that progress "comes in by the back door." In making this claim, he seems to believe that a self-correcting process will usually operate, with "intensity" followed by "disaster," which produces "precaution" and finally "vigilance." Is this argument confirmed, extended, complicated, or refuted by Davis's description of current research on cancer? Does Davis's argument that corporate concerns influence this research show that technology's self-correcting tendencies have been derailed in this instance? Are financial considerations necessarily at odds with the development of scientific knowledge?

2. "Those of us who indict past failures have a duty to develop new solutions." Davis represents herself throughout "Presumed Innocent" as someone keenly concerned about the future; she worries about the "ecological footprint" left by her generation and the world that her grandchildren will inherit. Those grandchildren, presumably, are part of what Jean Twenge terms "Generation Me." Is it possible for a generation raised on the self-esteem curriculum to comprehend the problems Davis has described? To feel a sense of "duty to develop new solutions" to current problems? To think that technology is *not* the solution to every problem? What role can Generation Me—a generation raised on cell phones and aspartame—play in responding to the dangers Davis sees as surrounding us all?

ANNIE DILLARD

ANNIE DILLARD, POET, essayist, novelist, and writing teacher, won a Pulitzer Prize for her book of naturalist reflections, *Pilgrim at Tinker Creek* (1973), when she was just 29 years old. In this, her first book, Dillard describes the life she elected to live in a remote part of the Blue Ridge Mountains after she had survived a near-fatal bout of pneumonia. Weaving together observations of her surroundings with mystical longings and theological reflections on the violence and the beauty that coexist in the natural world, Dillard set out, in her own words, "to learn, or remember, how to live. . . . I don't think I can learn from a wild animal how to live in particular . . . but I might learn something of mindlessness, something of the purity of living in the physical senses and the dignity of living without bias or motive."

In the many books that have followed, including *Teaching a Stone to Talk* (1982), her autobiographical musings in *An American Childhood* (1987), and the novel *The Living* (1992), Dillard has continued to ruminate on the power of nature and to wonder about the place of humanity in the cosmos. For Dillard, the enduring appeal and importance of such a spiritual project is self-evident: "In nature I find grace tangled in a rapture with violence; I find an intricate landscape whose forms are fringed in death; I find mystery, newness, and a kind of exuberant, spendthrift energy."

"The Wreck of Time" includes passages that appear in *For the Time Being* (2000), Dillard's most recent work of nonfiction. That book is an effort to define a spiritual vision that embraces a cosmos where grace "is tangled in a rapture with violence." Although Dillard was raised a Presbyterian, she converted to Catholicism in her twenties and now describes herself as a "Hasidic Christian," her meditations on the natural world having led her to unite Jewish mysticism with

Dillard, Annie. "The Wreck of Time: Taking Our Century's Measure." *Harper's.* 296, no. 1772 (January 1998): 51–56.

Quotations come from Annie Dillard, *Pilgrim at Tinker Creek,* HarperPerennial, 1998; interview with Grace Suh, October 4, 1996, <http://www.yaleherald.com/archive/xxii/10.4.96/ae/dillard.html>; Annie Dillard, *For the Time Being,* Vintage Books, 2000; for the review of Dillard's second novel, *The Maytrees,* please see <http://query.nytimes.com/gst/fullpage.html?res=9807E6D91731F936A15755C0A9619C8B63&sec=&spon=&pagewanted=all>.

Christian spirituality. "The world is as glorious as ever, and exalting," Dillard announces at the beginning of *For the Time Being*, "but for credibility's sake let's start with the bad news." If one starts with the bad news, as Dillard does in "The Wreck of Time," is it possible to recover a sense that "the world is as glorious as ever"? That the future is bright? In her recently published second novel, *The Maytrees,* Dillard turns from the bad news back to the good. She weaves a story about "the ebb and flow of love" that nevertheless offers "musings about solitude or eternity," proof positive that Dillard continues to struggle with the inextricable glory and violence of the world—and still asks her readers to wrestle with these issues as well.

■ ■

The Wreck of Time

Taking Our Century's Measure

I

Ted Bundy, the serial killer, after his arrest, could not fathom the fuss. What was the big deal? David Von Drehle quotes an exasperated Bundy in *Among the Lowest of the Dead*: "I mean, there are *so* many people."

One R. Houwink, of Amsterdam, uncovered this unnerving fact: The human population of earth, arranged tidily, would just fit into Lake Windermere, in England's Lake District.

Recently in the Peruvian Amazon a man asked the writer Alex Shoumatoff, "Isn't it true that the whole population of the United States can be fitted into their cars?"

How are we doing in numbers, we who have been alive for this most recent installment of human life? How many people have lived and died?

"The dead outnumber the living, in a ratio that could be as high as 20 to 1," a demographer, Nathan Keyfitz, wrote in a 1991 letter to the historian Justin Kaplan. "Credible estimates of the number of people who have ever lived on the earth run from 70 billion to over 100 billion." Averaging those figures puts the total persons ever born at about 85 billion. We living people now number 5.8 billion. By these moderate figures, the dead outnumber us about fourteen to one. The dead will always outnumber the living.

Dead Americans, however, if all proceeds, will not outnumber living Americans until the year 2030, because the nation is young. Some of us will be among the dead then. Will we know or care, we who once owned the still bones under the quick ones, we who spin inside the planet with our heels in the air? The living might well seem foolishly self-important to us, and overexcited.

We who are here now make up about 6.8 percent of all people who have appeared to date. This is not a meaningful figure. These times are, one might say, ordinary times, a slice of life like any other. Who can bear to hear this, or who will consider it? Are we not especially significant because our century is—our century and its nuclear bombs, its unique and unprecedented Holocaust, its serial exterminations and refugee populations, our century and its warming, its silicon chips, men on the moon, and spliced genes? No, we are not and it is not.

Since about half of all the dead are babies and children, we will be among the longest-boned dead and among the dead who grew the most teeth—for what those distinctions might be worth among beings notoriously indifferent to appearance and all else.

In Juan Rulfo's novel *Pedro Páramo*, a dead woman says to her dead son, "Just think about pleasant things, because we're going to be buried for a long time."

II

On April 30, 1991—on that one day—138,000 people drowned in Bangladesh. At dinner I mentioned to my daughter, who was then seven years old, that it was hard to imagine 138,000 people drowning.

"No, it's easy," she said. "Lots and lots of dots, in blue water."

The paleontologist Pierre Teilhard de Chardin, now dead, sent a dispatch from a dig. "In the middle of the tamarisk bush you find a red-brick town, partially exposed. . . . More than 3,000 years before our era, people were living there who played with dice like our own, fished with hooks like ours, and wrote in characters we can't yet read."

Who were these individuals who lived under the tamarisk bush? Who were the people Ted Bundy killed? Who was the statistician who reckoned that everybody would fit into Lake Windermere? The Trojans likely thought well of themselves, one by one; their last settlement died out by 1,100 B.C.E. Who were the people Stalin killed, or any of the 79.2 billion of us now dead, and who are the 5.8 billion of us now alive?

"God speaks succinctly," said the rabbis.

Is it important if you have yet died your death, or I? Your father? Your child? It is only a matter of time, after all. Why do we find it supremely pertinent, during any moment of any century on earth, which among us is topsides? Why do we concern ourselves over which side of the membrane of topsoil our feet poke?

"A single death is a tragedy, a million deaths is a statistic." Joseph Stalin, that connoisseur, gave words to this disquieting and possibly universal sentiment.

How can an individual count? Do we individuals count only to us other suckers, who love and grieve like elephants, bless their hearts? Of Allah, the Koran says, "Not so much as the weight of an ant in earth or heaven escapes from the Lord." That is touching, that Allah, God, and their ilk care when one ant dismembers another, or note when a sparrow falls, but I strain to see the use of it.

Ten years ago we thought there were two galaxies for each of us alive. Lately, since we loosed the Hubble Space Telescope, we have revised our figures. There are nine galaxies for each of us. Each galaxy harbors an average of 100 billion suns. In our galaxy, the Milky Way, there are sixty-nine suns for each person alive. The Hubble shows, says a report, that the universe "is at least 15 billion years old." Two galaxies, nine galaxies . . . sixty-nine suns, 100 billion suns—

These astronomers are nickel-and-diming us to death.

III

What were you doing on April 30, 1991, when a series of waves drowned 138,000 people? Where were you when you first heard the astounding, heartbreaking news? Who told you? What, seriatim, were your sensations? Who did you tell? Did you weep? Did your anguish last days or weeks?

All my life I have loved this sight: a standing wave in a boat's wake, shaped like a thorn. I have seen it rise from many oceans, and I saw it rise from the Sea of Galilee. It was a peak about a foot high. The standing wave broke at its peak, and foam slid down its glossy hollow. I watched the foaming wave on the port side. At every instant we were bringing this boat's motor, this motion, into new water. The stir, as if of life, impelled each patch of water to pinch and inhabit this same crest. Each crest tumbled upon itself and released a slide of white foam. The foam's bubbles popped and dropped into the general sea while they were still sliding down the dark wave. They trailed away always, and always new waters peaked, broke, foamed, and replenished.

What I saw was the constant intersection of two wave systems. Lord Kelvin first described them. Transverse waves rise abaft the stern and stream away perpendicular to the boat's direction of travel. Diverging waves course out in a V shape behind the boat. Where the waves converge, two lines of standing crests persist at an unchanging angle to the direction of the boat's motion. We think of these as the boat's wake. I was studying the highest standing wave, the one nearest the boat. It rose from the trough behind the stern and spilled foam. The curled wave crested over clear water and tumbled down. All its bubbles broke, thousands a second, unendingly. I could watch the present; I could see time and how it works.

On a shore, 8,000 waves break a day. James Trefil, a professor of physics, provides these facts. At any one time, the foam from breaking waves covers between 3 and 4 percent of the earth's surface. This acreage of foam is equal to the entire continent of North America. By coincidence, the U.S. population bears nearly the same relation to the world population: 4.6 percent. The U.S. population, in other words, although it is the third largest population among nations, is as small a portion of the earth's people as breaking waves' white foam is of the sea.

"God rises up out of the sea like a treasure in the waves," wrote Thomas Merton.

We see generations of waves rise from the sea that made them, billions of individuals at a time; we see them dwindle and vanish. If this does not astound you, what will? Or what will move you to pity?

IV

One tenth of the land on earth is tundra. At any time, it is raining on only 5 percent of the planet's surface. Lightning strikes the planet about a hundred times every second. The insects outweigh us. Our chickens outnumber us four to one.

One fifth of us are Muslims. One fifth of us live in China. And every seventh person is a Chinese peasant. Almost one tenth of us live within range of an active volcano. More than 2 percent of us are mentally retarded. We humans drink tea—over a billion cups a day. Among us we speak 10,000 languages.

We are civilized generation number 500 or so, counting from 10,000 years ago, when we settled down. We are *Homo sapiens* generation number 7,500, counting from 150,000 years ago, when our species presumably arose; and we are human generation number 125,000, counting from the earliest forms of *Homo*.

Every 110 hours a million more humans arrive on the planet than die into the planet. A hundred million of us are children who live on the streets. Over a hundred million of us live in countries where we hold no citizenship.

Twenty-three million of us are refugees. Sixteen million of us live in Cairo. Twelve million fish for a living from small boats. Seven and a half million of us are Uygurs. One million of us crew on freezer trawlers. Nearly a thousand of us a day commit suicide.

HEAD-SPINNING NUMBERS CAUSE MIND TO GO SLACK, the *Hartford Courant* says. But our minds must not go slack. How can we think straight if our minds go slack? We agree that we want to think straight.

Anyone's close world of family and friends composes a group smaller than almost all sampling errors, smaller than almost all rounding errors, a group invisible, at whose loss the world will not blink. Two million children die a year from diarrhea, and 800,000 from measles. Do we blink? Stalin starved 7 million Ukrainians in one year, Pol Pot killed 1 million Cambodians, the flu epidemic of 1918 killed 21 or 22 million people . . . shall this go on? Or do you suffer, as Teilhard de Chardin did, the sense of being "an atom lost in the universe"? Or do you not suffer this sense? How about what journalists call "compassion fatigue"? Reality fatigue? At what limit for you do other individuals blur? Vanish? How old are you?

V

Los Angeles airport has 25,000 parking spaces. This is about one space for every person who died in 1985 in Colombia when a volcano erupted. This is one space for each of the corpses of more than two years' worth of accidental killings from leftover land mines of recent wars. At five to a car, almost all the Inuit in the world could park at LAX. Similarly, if you propped up or stacked four bodies to a car, you could fit into the airport parking lot all the corpses from the firestorm bombing of Tokyo in March 1945, or the corpses of Londoners who died in the plague, or the corpses of Burundians killed in civil war since 1993. But you could not fit America's homeless there, not even at twenty to a car.

Since sand and dirt pile up on everything, why does the world look fresh for each new crowd? As natural and human debris raises the continents, vegetation grows on the piles. It is all a stage—we know this—a temporary stage on top of many layers of stages, but every year a new crop of sand, grass, and tree leaves freshens the set and perfects the illusion that ours is the new and urgent world now. When Keats was in Rome, I read once, he saw pomegranate trees overhead; they bloomed in dirt blown onto the Colosseum's broken walls. How can we doubt our own time, in which each bright instant probes the future? In every arable soil in the world we grow grain over tombs—sure, we know this. But do not the dead generations seem to us dark and still as mummies, and their times always faded like scenes painted on walls at Pompeii?

How can we see ourselves as only a new, temporary cast for a long-running show when a new batch of birds flies around singing and new clouds move? Living things from hyenas to bacteria whisk the dead away like stagehands hustling between scenes. To help a living space last while we live on it, we brush or haul away the blowing sand and hack or burn the greenery. We are mowing the grass at the cutting edge.

VI

In northeast Japan, a seismic sea wave killed 27,000 people on June 15, 1896. Do not fail to distinguish this infamous wave from the April 30, 1991, waves that drowned 138,000 Bangladeshi. You were not tempted to confuse, conflate, forget, or ignore these deaths, were you?

On the dry Laetoli plain of northern Tanzania, Mary Leakey found a trail of hominid footprints. The three barefoot people—likely a short man and woman and child *Australopithecus afarensis*—walked closely together. They walked on moist volcanic tuff and ash. We have a record of those few seconds from a day about 3.6 million years ago—before hominids even chipped stone tools. More ash covered their footprints and hardened. Ash also preserved the pockmarks of the raindrops that fell beside the three who walked; it was a rainy day. We have almost ninety feet of the three's steady footprints intact. We do not know where they were going or why. We do not know why the woman paused and turned left, briefly, before continuing. "A remote ancestor," Leakey said, "experienced a moment of doubt." Possibly they watched the Sadiman volcano erupt, or they took a last look back before they left. We do know we cannot make anything so lasting as these three barefoot ones did.

After archeologists studied this long strip of record for several years, they buried it again to save it. Along one preserved portion, however, new tree roots are already cracking the footprints, and in another place winds threaten to sand them flat; the preservers did not cover them deeply enough. Now they are burying them again.

Jeremiah, walking toward Jerusalem, saw the smoke from the Temple's blaze. He wept; he saw the blood of the slain. "He put his face close to the ground and saw the footprints of sucklings and infants who were walking into captivity" in Babylon. He kissed the footprints.

Who were these individuals? Who were the three who walked together and left footprints in the rain? Who was that eighteenth-century Ukrainian peasant the Baal Shem Tov, the founder of modern Hasidism, who taught, danced, and dug clay? He was among the generations of children of Babylonian exiles whose footprints on the bare earth Jeremiah kissed. Centuries later the Emperor Hadrian destroyed another such son of exile in Rome, Rabbi Akiba. Russian Christians and European Christians tried, and Hitler tried, to wipe all those survivors of children of exile from the ground of the earth as a man wipes a plate—survivors of exiles whose footprints on the ground I kiss, and whose feet.

Who and of what import were the men whose bones bulk the Great Wall, the 30 million Mao starved, or the 11 million children under five who die each year now? Why, they are the insignificant others, of course; living or dead, they are just some of the plentiful others. And you?

Is it not late? A late time to be living? Are not our current generations the important ones? We have changed the world. Are not our heightened times the important ones, the ones since Hiroshima? Perhaps we are the last generation—there is a comfort. Take the bomb threat away and what are we? We are ordinary beads on a never-ending string. Our time is a routine twist of an improbable yarn.

We have no chance of being here when the sun burns out. There must be something ultimately heroic about our time, something that sets it above all those other times. Hitler, Stalin, Mao, and Pol Pot made strides in obliterating whole peoples, but this has been the human effort all along, and we have only enlarged the means, as have people in every century in history. (That genocides recur does not mean that they are similar. Each instance of human evil and each victim's death possesses its unique history and form. To generalize, as Cynthia Ozick points out, is to "befog" evil's specificity.)

Dire things are happening. Plague? Funny weather? Why are we watching the news, reading the news, keeping up with the news? Only to enforce our fancy—probably a necessary lie—that these are crucial times, and we are in on them. Newly revealed, and I am in the know: crazy people, bunches of them! New diseases, sways in power, floods! Can the news from dynastic Egypt have been any different?

As I write this, I am still alive, but of course I might well have died before you read it. Most of the archeologists who reburied hominid footprints have likely not yet died their deaths; the paleontologist Teilhard is pushing up daisies.

Chinese soldiers who breathed air posing for 7,000 individual clay portraits—twenty-two centuries ago—must have thought it a wonderful difference that workers buried only their simulacra then so that their sons could bury their flesh a bit later. One wonders what they did in the months or years they gained. One wonders what one is, oneself, up to these days.

VII

Was it wisdom Mao Tse-tung attained when—like Ted Bundy—he awakened to the long view?

"The atom bomb is nothing to be afraid of," Mao told Nehru. "China has many people. . . . The deaths of ten or twenty million people is nothing to be afraid of." A witness said Nehru showed shock. Later, speaking in Moscow, Mao displayed yet more generosity: he boasted that he was willing to lose 300 million people, half of China's population.

Does Mao's reckoning shock me really? If sanctioning the death of strangers could save my daughter's life, would I do it? Probably. How many others' lives would I be willing to sacrifice? Three? Three hundred million?

An English journalist, observing the Sisters of Charity in Calcutta, reasoned: "Either life is always and in all circumstances sacred, or intrinsically of no account; it is inconceivable that it should be in some cases the one, and in some the other."

One small town's soup kitchen, St. Mary's, serves 115 men a night. Why feed 115 individuals? Surely so few people elude most demographics and achieve statistical insignificance. After all, there are 265 million Americans, 15 million people who live in Mexico City, 16 million in greater New York, 26 million in greater Tokyo. Every day 1.5 million people walk through Times Square in New York; every day almost as many people—1.4 million—board a U.S. passenger plane. And so forth. We who breathe air now will join the already dead layers of us who breathed air once. We arise from dirt and dwindle to dirt, and the might of the universe is arrayed against us.   ■

■ *QUESTIONS FOR MAKING CONNECTIONS WITHIN THE READING* ■

1. "The Wreck of Time" is divided into seven sections. What is each section about? How are the sections connected? Is there an argument that develops over the course of the seven sections? Are there themes that are repeated across the sections? What is it that Dillard would like her readers to see or understand when they've completed her essay?

2. In the third section of "The Wreck of Time," Dillard describes how a boat creates a standing wave. At the end of her description, she writes that watching such waves allowed her to "see time and how it works." How does time work? What does her vision of the standing wave have to do with the other images she details in her essay?

3. When Dillard's essay first appeared in *Harper's,* a series of images were interspersed throughout the text. What images do you think would be appropriate for this essay? Bring to class an image or series of images that you feel illustrates or comments on the argument Dillard is making in

"The Wreck of Time." Be prepared to discuss why the image you've selected is appropriate.

■ *QUESTIONS FOR WRITING* ■

1. In many ways, Annie Dillard's "The Wreck of Time" defies our common expectations about what a piece of writing *should* do: the essay has no clear thesis statement; it has no marked transitions between the paragraphs; it provides no obvious connection between its various subsections. Indeed, on first reading Dillard's piece, one might be tempted to conclude that it's little more than the recitation of a series of unrelated statistics and the posing of a series of unanswered questions. What is the relationship between the way that Dillard has written this piece and what she has to say in the piece? What is it that Dillard wants us to think about while reading her essay?

2. "We who are here now make up about 6.8 percent of all people who have appeared to date," Dillard writes; "This is not a meaningful figure." "The Wreck of Time" is filled with statistics about world population, the size of the universe, natural and man-made disasters. Are any of these figures "meaningful"? Can such figures be invested with meaning?

■ *QUESTIONS FOR MAKING CONNECTIONS BETWEEN READINGS* ■

1. In "Immune to Reality," Daniel Gilbert makes the following statement: "Explanation robs events of their emotional impact because it makes them seem likely and allows us to stop thinking about them." Does this statement apply to Annie Dillard's "The Wreck of Time"? Has Dillard provided an explanation in her essay? Does Dillard's essay serve the same function for her as it does for her readers? For you?

2. Deborah Tannen calls for an alternative to debate as the best mode of intellectual inquiry. She calls as well for an effort to move beyond dualism. Would you say that Annie Dillard's "The Wreck of Time" is an example of the kind of alternative Tannen seeks? Does Dillard move beyond dualistic thinking? Does her essay reveal complexities that Tannen leaves unexplained? Write an essay in which you consider the challenges and the opportunities any writer confronts in attempting to "move beyond dualism."

SUSAN FALUDI

PULITZER PRIZE–WINNING journalist Susan Faludi first became interested in writing about feminism in the fifth grade when she polled her classmates to determine their feelings about the Vietnam War and legalized abortion. In the furor that followed Faludi's release of data showing her peers' liberal attitudes, Faludi came to realize, as she put it in an interview, "the power that you could have as a feminist writer. Not being the loudest person on the block, not being one who regularly interrupted in class or caused a scene, I discovered that through writing I could make my views heard, and I could actually create change."

The daughter of a homemaker and a Hungarian holocaust survivor, Faludi was raised in Queens and attended Harvard, where she studied literature and American history. After graduating in 1981, Faludi worked for a number of newspapers, including the *New York Times* and the *Wall Street Journal,* before devoting her time to writing *Backlash: The Undeclared War Against American Women* (1991), a study of the media's assault on feminism. The following year, *Backlash* won the National Book Critics Circle Award for general nonfiction and made Faludi into a household name. She appeared on the cover of *Time* magazine with Gloria Steinem and became almost overnight a national spokesperson on women's rights and the future of feminism.

While doing research for *Backlash,* Faludi began to wonder why the men who opposed women's progress were so angry. In setting out to understand this anger, Faludi interviewed Promise Keepers, sex workers in the pornography industry, union members, the unemployed, and other disenfranchised males. "The Naked Citadel," which presents Faludi's investigation into why male cadets were so enraged by the admission of women into the military academy, is one part of this project and has since been incorporated into Faludi's second book, *Stiffed: The Betrayal of the American Man* (1999). The surprising thesis of *Stiffed* is that men, too, have suffered during the recent social upheavals because "working

Faludi, Susan. "The Naked Citadel." *The New Yorker,* September 5, 1994. 62–81.

Quotations come from Brian Lamb's interview with Susan Faludi on Booknotes, October 25, 1992 <http://www.booknotes.org/transcripts/10096.htm> and Kate Melloy's interview with Susan Faludi, "Feminist Author Susan Faludi Preaches Male Inclusion" <http://www.kollegeville.com/kampus/faludi.htm>.

with others anonymously and loyally to build something larger than yourself is no longer seen as glorious."

Faludi's most recent book, *The Terror Dream: Fear and Fantasy in Post-9/11 America* (2007), returns to the issues of gender and social upheaval. While "The Naked Citadel" explores antifeminist attitudes among the militarily minded in a time of peace, *The Terror Dream* charts the difficulties facing feminism in a time of war. Faludi concludes in this book that the September 11 attacks have created further challenges for feminism by ushering in an era of hysterical insistence on traditional roles for men and women: the men are summoned to protect, while the women are to be passively defended. In spite of this, Faludi holds out the hope for a society where men and women can work together cooperatively and on equal footing. But she also believes that "[t]o revive a genuine feminism, we must disconnect feminism from the individual pursuit of happiness and reconnect it with the individual desire for social responsibility: the basic human need and joy to be part of a larger, meaningful struggle, which engages the entire society."

■ ■

The Naked Citadel

Along the edges of the quad, in the gutters, the freshman cadets were squaring their corners. The "knobs," as they are called for their nearly hairless doorknob pates, aren't allowed to step on the lawn of the broad parade ground, which is trimmed close, as if to match their shorn heads. Keeping off the grass is one of many prohibitions that obtain at The Citadel, a public military college on Charleston's Ashley River. Another is the rule that so many of the cadets say brought them to this Moorish-style, gated campus: Girls keep out.

The campus has a dreamy, flattened quality, with its primary colors, checkerboard courtyards, and storybook-castle barracks. It feels more like an architect's rendering of a campus—almost preternaturally clean, orderly, antiseptic—than the messy real thing. I stood at the far end of the quad, at the academic hall's front steps, and watched the cadets make their herky-jerky perpendicular turns as they drew closer for the first day of class. They walked by stiffly, their faces heat-blotched and vulnerable, and as they passed each in turn shifted his eyes downward. I followed one line of boys into a classroom, a Western Civ class—except, of course, they weren't really boys at all. These were college men, manly recruits to an élite military college whose virile exploits were mythicized in best-selling novels by Calder Willingham and Pat Conroy, both Citadel alumni. So why did I expect their voices to crack when they spoke for the first time? Partly, it was the grammar-schoolish taking of attendance, compulsory at The Citadel. Multiple absences can lead to "tours," hours of marching back and forth in the courtyard with a pinless rifle over one shoulder; or to "cons," confinement to one's room.

But mostly it was the young men themselves, with their doughy faces and twitching limbs, who gave me the urge to babysit. Despite their enrollment in a college long considered "the big bad macho school" (as a former R.O.T.C. commander, Major General Robert E. Wagner, once put it), the cadets lacked the swagger and knowingness of big men on campus. They perched tentatively on their chairs, their hands arranged in a dutiful clasp on their desktops, as if they were expecting a ruler slap to the knuckles. A few dared to glance over at the female visitor, but whenever they made eye contact they averted their gaze and color stained their cheeks.

"As many of you probably know," their teacher said, "this was almost the day the first woman joined The Citadel." The cadets continued to study their polished shoes. "How do you, in fact, feel about whether women should be allowed to attend?"

Silence reigned. Maybe the cadets felt the question put them in an awkward spot. Not only was their teacher in favor of admitting women to The Citadel's Corps of Cadets, the teacher *was* a woman. Indeed, Professor Jane Bishop seemed to be in the strange situation of calling in an air strike on her own position. It was the first day of fall classes in the 1993–94 academic year at The Citadel, and she was broaching the question of the hour. But this incongruity wasn't limited to her classroom. From the moment I stepped onto the school's campus, I had been struck by an unexpected circumstance: though an all-male institution—an institution, moreover, whose singular mission was "making men"—The Citadel was by no means free of women. Female teachers were improving cadets' minds, female administrators were keeping their records, and an all-female (and all-black) staff served the meals in the mess hall. There was also the fact that female students made up seventy-seven percent of the enrollment of the evening school, and many other female students attended summer school with the cadets. What about them? Of course, summer school and evening school aren't part of the military college proper. Cadets don't attend the evening school; and as Major Rick Mill, The Citadel's public-relations director, notes, those cadets who attend the summer school "aren't wearing their uniforms."

Today they were, and so was their teacher. All permanent instructors, regardless of their sex (about fifteen percent are women), wear uniforms as part of their required affiliation with a largely ceremonial outfit once known as the South Carolina Unorganized Militia, and still called by the unfortunate acronym SCUM. Bishop wore hers with what seemed like a deliberate air of disarray.

The cadets' uniforms were considerably tidier—testament to the efficacy of the famous cadet shirt tuck, a maneuver akin to hospital-corners bedmaking and so exacting a cadet cannot perform it without assistance. Even so, the gray cadet uniform, with the big black stripe down the side of the pants and the nametag above the left breast, is the sort more often seen on high-school band members than on fighting soldiers.

"Remember," Bishop prodded them, "speech is free in the classroom."

At last, a cadet unclasped and raised a hand. "Well, I'd have no problem with her in the day program, but she can't join the Corps."

"She," as everyone there knew, was Shannon Faulkner, the woman who had challenged the school's hundred-and-fifty-year-old all-male policy by omitting reference to her sex from her application and winning acceptance to the Corps of Cadets earlier that year—acceptance that was rescinded once the administrators discovered their error. Faulkner's attempt to gain entrance then shifted from the admissions office to the courts. She was allowed under court order to attend day classes during the spring semester of 1994, the first woman to do so. On July 22nd, a United States District Court ruled that The Citadel must admit Faulkner into the Corps of Cadets proper; three weeks later, the Fourth United States Circuit Court of Appeals granted The Citadel a stay pending appeal.

Yet why shouldn't she be permitted into the Corps, Bishop pressed. One of her students recited the fitness requirement—forty-five pushups and fifty-five sit-ups in two-minute sets, and a two-mile run in sixteen minutes. But the administration made passing the fitness test a requirement for graduation only *after* Shannon Faulkner filed suit. An alumnus recounted in court that many upperclassmen he knew who had failed the test skipped the punitive morning run and "sat around and ate doughnuts." Another of Bishop's students cited the shaved-head rule. But this, too, seemed a minor point. A woman cadet could conceivably get a buzz cut. Sinéad O'Connor had done it, Bishop pointed out, without undue injury to her career. And, anyway, after freshman year the men no longer get their heads shaved. Other deprivations of freshman year were invoked: having to "brace" on demand—that is, assume a stance in which a knob stands very erect and tucks in his chin until it puckers up like a rooster's wattle—and having to greet every upperclassman's bellowed command and rebuke with "Sir, yes sir!" or "Sir, no sir!" or "Sir, no excuse sir!" But women, obviously, aren't incapable of obeisance; one might even say they have a long history of it.

Weighing heaviest on the cadets' minds, it turned out, was the preservation of the all-male communal bathroom. The sharing of the stall-less showers and stall-less toilets is "at the heart of the Citadel experience," according to more than one cadet. The men bathe as a group; they walk to the shower down the open galleries, in full view of the courtyard below, and do so, one cadet said, in "nothing but our bathrobes" or "even without any clothes." Another cadet said, "I know it sounds trivial, but all of us in one shower, it's

Freshmen are in the "fourth-class system," a regimen to "strip" each recruit of his identity and remold him into the "Whole Man." Illustration by Mark Zingarelli, originally published in *The New Yorker*. © Mark Zingarelli/House of Zing

like we're all one, we're all the same, and—I don't know—you feel like you're exposed, but you feel safe. You know these guys are going to be your friends for life." His voice trailed off. "I just can't explain it but when they take that away, it's over. This place will be ruined."

"If women come here, they'll have to put up window shades in all the rooms," a cadet said. "Think of all the windows in the barracks. That could be eight thousand, nine thousand dollars. You've got to look at the costs."

At the end of the hour, the cadets filed out and resumed their double-time jog along the gutters—and their place in the "fourth-class system." This "system" is a nine-month regimen of small and large indignities intended to "strip" each young recruit of his original identity and remold him into the "Whole Man," a vaguely defined ideal, half Christian soldier, half Dale Carnegie junior executive. As a knob explained it to me, "We're all suffering together. It's how we bond." Another knob said, "It's a strange analogy, but it's almost like a P.O.W. camp."

One cadet dawdled, glancing nervously around, then sidled up to me. He spoke in a near whisper, and what he had to say had nothing to do with lavatory etiquette or military tradition. "The great majority of the guys here are very misogynistic," he said. "All they talk about is how girls are pigs and sluts."

I asked him to explain at greater length. He agonized. "I have to keep quiet," he said, but he finally agreed to meet me later, in an out-of-the-way spot on the upper floor of the student-activities center. He rejoined his class-mates with that distinctive knob march, "the march of the puppets," as a professor described it to me later. It was a gait caused in some cases, I was told, by the most conscientious cadets' efforts to keep their shirts perfectly straight with the help of garters—one end of the garter clipped to the shirt-tail, the other end to the socks.

As I waited for my cadet informant, I decided to kill an hour on the vast pa-rade ground, where the Corps of Cadets marches every Friday afternoon in full dress uniforms, and where, according to an old school brochure, "man-hood meets mastery." This is a paramilitary display, not a military one. De-spite the regalia and officer ranks, and despite its notoriously fierce military discipline ("To discipline is to teach" is the motto emblazoned on one of the school's books of regulations), this is a military academy by self-designation only. Unlike the federal service academies—West Point, Annapolis, the Air Force Academy—The Citadel has no connection with the United States Armed Forces (other than its R.O.T.C. program and its em-ployment of some active and retired officers). Its grounds are adorned with dusty and decommissioned military hardware—a Sherman tank, a subma-rine's torpedo-loading hatch, a Phantom jet named Annette, two cannons named Betsy and Lizzie. In most cases, the weapons, including the pinless M-14s the cadets carry, are inoperative. The mouths of the various cannons are stuffed with cement—all except those of Betsy and Lizzie, which are fired during parades, but carefully aimed high enough so that their powder does not dust the crenellated barracks. The over-all effect is that of a theme park for post–Cold War kids.

The hokeyness and childlike innocence of the scene—the stage-prop artillery, the toy-soldier clip-clop of the cadets as they squared their corners—were endearing, in a Lost Boys sort of way, and I strolled over to the student-activities center for my rendezvous with my cadet informant thinking that The Citadel's version of martial culture was not so menacing after all. The cadet was not in evidence. I spent the next thirty minutes prowling the halls, which were lined with portraits of stern-faced "generals" (I couldn't tell which were United States military and which were SCUM), and examining ads on the student bulletin board for items like "Save the Males" bumper stickers. I tried to reach the cadet's room by phone—women aren't admitted into the barracks—but he was not there. A bit thoughtlessly, I left a message with an upper-classman and headed toward town.

At my hotel, the receptionist handed me a message from my vanished cadet. "Please, don't ever call here again!" it read. The phone clerk peered at me curiously. "Sorry about that exclamation mark, but he seemed quite distraught," she said. "His voice was shaking."

What brought a young man to an all-male preserve in the last decade of the twentieth century, anyway? What was going on outside the academy gates that impelled thousands of boys, Southern and Northern alike (about a fifth of its student body of about two thousand are Yankees), to seek refuge behind a pair of corroding cannons?

"The forces arrayed against us," an attorney named Robert Patterson declared in a February, 1994, court hearing, consider his military academy to be "some big-game animal to be hunted down, tracked, caught, badgered, and killed so that some lawyer or some organization can go back up and hang a trophy on a wall in an office." Patterson was defending not The Citadel but the Virginia Military Institute, which is the only other public military academy in the United States that does not admit women, and which was involved in a similar sex-discrimination suit. (Three months later, Patterson, a V.M.I. alumnus, returned to court to defend The Citadel.) "I will say this, Your Honor," he went on. "This quest by these people constitutes the longest and most expensive publicly financed safari in the annals of big-game hunting."

The Citadel's administration has fought the female hunters with a legal arsenal of nearly a million dollars and with dour, tight-lipped determination, which has only increased with time. The Citadel's president, Claudius Elmer (Bud) Watts III, who is a retired Air Force lieutenant general and a second-generation Citadel alumnus, views Shannon Faulkner's legal efforts as an enemy invasion, placing his young troops "under attack." "The Citadel is in this to the end," he pronounced at a press conference held in the spring of 1994 on the parade ground, his feet planted between Betsy and Lizzie, his uniform decked with ribbons, and his chin tucked in, as is his custom, as if in a permanent brace position.

Later, in his living room, surrounded by coffee-table books on football, Watts told me firmly, "You cannot put a male and a female on that same playing field," though he couldn't say exactly why. Of his own Citadel years he conceded, "I've not the foggiest notion if it would have been different" had women attended. He was just glad there were no female cadets then; otherwise, he said, the cadets would have faced "a different form of intimidation—not wanting to be embarrassed in front of a girl."

Faulkner has been opposed not only by many Citadel staff and alumni but—at least, publicly—by almost all the current cadets. They say that her presence in the Corps would absolutely destroy a basic quality of their experience as Citadel men. She would be what one Citadel defender called in his court deposition "a toxic kind of virus." Tellingly, even before the United States District Court judge enjoined The Citadel to admit Faulkner to the Corps of Cadets for the fall of 1994, and before the injunction was set aside, the administration announced its selection of her living quarters: the infirmary.

Cadets cite a number of reasons that women would have a deleterious effect on the Corps of Cadets, and the reasons are repeated so often as to be easily predictable, though their expression can be novel. "Studies show—I can't cite them, but studies show that males learn better when females aren't there," one cadet explained to me (a curious sentiment at a school where a knob motto about grades is "2.0 and Go"). "If a girl was here, I'd be concerned not to look foolish. If you're a shy student, you won't be as inhibited." Another cadet said, "See, you don't have to impress them here. You're free." From a third: "Where does it end? Will we have unisex bathrooms?" But among the reasons most frequently heard for repelling Faulkner at the gate is this: "She would be destroying a long and proud tradition."

The masculine traditions of West Point and Annapolis were also closely guarded by their male denizens, but the resistance to women joining their ranks was nowhere near as fierce and filled with doomsday rhetoric as The Citadel's efforts to repel feminine interlopers. At Norwich University, a private military college in Northfield, Vermont, that voluntarily opened its barracks to women in 1974, two years before the federal service academies, the administration actually made an effort to recruit and accommodate women. "There was no storm of protest," said a Norwich spokeswoman, Judy Clauson. But then, "it was a time when there were so many rules that were being loosened." The Air Force veteran Linnea Westberg, who was one of the eight women in Norwich's first coed class, recalled, of her integration into its corps, that "ninety-five percent of the male cadets were fine, especially the freshmen, who didn't know any different." Westberg said she was baffled by the intensity of The Citadel's opposition to women in its corps. "It's hard for me to believe it's still an issue."

"The Citadel is a living museum to the way things used to be," John Drennan, a Citadel graduate and a public defender in Charleston, told me one day during The Citadel's legal proceedings. But how, exactly, did things use to be? The cadets and the alumni of the school, along with those protesting against its exclusionary policies, envision its military tradition above all. And The Citadel once did have a strong military aspect: it was formed as an arsenal in 1822 in response to a slave revolt purportedly planned by the freed Charleston slave Denmark Vesey, which, though it was foiled, aroused widespread alarm in the region. Yet twenty years later the guns and the gold braid became mere adornment as The Citadel turned into an industrial school of domestic and practical skills. Union troops shut down The Citadel at the end of the Civil War, but it was reinvented and reopened in 1882, after the Union's Reconstruction officials had thoroughly stripped the school of all military muscle. Its new mission was to reinvigorate the masculinity of the South by showing its men how to compete with the business and industrial skills of the Yankee carpetbaggers, who were believed to be much better prepared than the sons of Dixie to enter the Darwinian fray of modern commerce. John Peyre Thomas, who ran The Citadel from 1882 to 1885, wrote of the need to teach spoiled plantation boys the rudiments of self-reliance. "It must be admitted that the institution of African slavery, in many respects, affected injuriously the white youth of the South," he wrote. "Reared from infancy to manhood with servants at his command to bring his water, brush his shoes, saddle his horse, and, in fine, to minister to his personal wants, the average Southern boy grew up in some points of character dependent, and lazy, and inefficient. He was found, too, wanting in those habits of order and system that come from the necessity, in man, to economize time and labor."

What makes the school's Reconstruction-era mission important is that in so many ways it remains current; the masculine and industrial culture of our age and that of the conquered South may have more in common than we care to imagine. Again, we are at a psychic and economic crisis point for manhood. And, again, the gun issues hide the butter issues: the bombast masks a deep insecurity about employment and usefulness in a world where gentleman soldiers are an anachronism and a graduate with gentleman's C's may find himself busing tables at Wendy's.

The uncertain prospects of Citadel graduates are worsened by military downsizing. Only about a third of recent graduates entered the military—a figure that has fallen steeply since the mid-seventies, when half of The Citadel's graduating class routinely took a service commission. News of Shannon Faulkner's court case competed in the Charleston *Post & Courier* with news of the shutting down of the local shipyards and decommissionings from the local military installations.

The night before the closing arguments in Faulkner's suit, I had dinner at the on-campus home of Philippe and Linda Ross, who have both taught at The Citadel. Philippe, the head of the Biology Department, had just completed his first round of moonlighting as a "retraining" instructor at the Charleston Naval Shipyard. He had been prepping laid-off nuclear engineers to enter one of the few growth industries in the area—toxic-waste management. Facing a room filled with desperate men each day had been a dispiriting experience, he said. He recalled the plea of a middle-aged engineer, thrust out of the service after twenty-six years: "All I want to do is work." Linda Ross, who was then teaching psychology at The Citadel, looked across the table with a pained expression. "That whole idea that if a young man went to college he could make a decent living and buy a house, and maybe even a boat, just does not hold anymore," she said softly. "There's a Citadel graduate working as a cashier at the grocery store. And the one thing these young men felt they could count on was that if things got hard they could always go into the military. No more. And they are bitter and angry."

In the fall of 1991, Michael Lake, a freshman, decided to leave The Citadel. He had undergone weeks of bruising encounters with upperclassmen—encounters that included being knocked down with a rifle butt and beaten in the dark by a pack of cadets. Incidents of hazing became so violent that, in a school where publicly criticizing the alma mater is virtually an act of treason, several athletes told their stories to *Sports Illustrated*. Much of the violence was aimed at star freshman athletes: a member of the cycling team was forced to hang by his fingers over a sword poised two inches below his testicles; a placekicker had his head dunked in water twenty times until he was unconscious; a linebacker was forced to swallow his chewing tobacco and tormented until, he said later, "I was unable even to speak clearly in my classes." It was a time when the Churchill Society, a literary club reportedly containing a white-supremacist faction, was organized on campus. It was a time when the local chapter of the National Association for the Advancement of Colored People urged a federal investigation into a pair of racial incidents on the school's campus: the appearance of a noose over the bed of a black freshman who had earlier refused to sing "Dixie," and the shooting and wounding of a black cadet by a sniper who was never identified. (A few years earlier, upperclassmen wearing Klan-like costumes left a charred paper cross in the room of a black cadet.) And it was a time when a leader of the Junior Sword Drill, a unit of cadet sword-bearers, leaped off a five-foot dresser onto the head of a prostrate cadet, then left him in a pool of blood in a barracks hall. According to one cadet, a lacrosse-team member returning from an away game at three in the morning stumbled upon the victim's unconscious body, his face split open, jaw and nose broken, mouth a jack-o'-lantern of missing teeth.

One night, at about 2 A.M., high-ranking cadets trapped a raccoon in the barracks and began to stab it with a knife. Beau Turner, a student at the school, was awakened by the young men's yelling. "My roommate and I went out there to try and stop it," Turner recalled, "but we were too late." Accounts of the episode vary. In a widely circulated version (which was referred to in a faculty member's testimony), the cadets chanted, "Kill the bitch! Kill the bitch!" as they tortured the raccoon to death.

In October, 1993, two upperclassmen burst into the room of two freshmen and reportedly kneed them in the genitals, pulled out some of their chest hair, and beat them up. They were arrested on charges of assault and battery, and agreed to a program of counselling and community service, which would wipe clean their records. They withdrew from The Citadel, in lieu of expulsion, the spokesman Major Rick Mill said.

One of the offending cadets, Adrian Baer, told me that he and the other accused sophomore, Jeremy Leckie, did indeed come back from drinking, burst into the knobs' room after 10 P.M., and "repeatedly struck them in the chest and stomach" and bruised one of them in the face, but he denied having kicked them in the groin and yanked out chest hair. He said that what he did was common procedure—and no different from the "motivational" treatment he had received as a knob at the hands of a senior who came into *his* room. They entered the freshmen's room, Baer explained, because they viewed one of the occupants as "a problem" knob who "needed some extra motivation." Baer elaborated: "His pinkie on his right hand wouldn't completely close when he went to salute. He caught a lot of heat for that, of course, because it's a military school; it's important to salute properly." The strict rule that upperclassmen not fraternize with knobs, he said, meant that they couldn't simply counsel the freshman kindly. "If we just sat down and said, 'Listen, guy, we have a little problem,' that would be fraternization. And more important, knobs would lose respect for upperclassmen. It's a lot of denial on the part of officials at The Citadel about hazing," Baer said. "They don't want to believe it goes on." Leckie's father, Timothy Rinaldi, said that while he believed his son "was definitely in the wrong," he felt The Citadel's fourth-class system bred such behavior. "They help build this monster," he said of The Citadel, "the monster gets up off the table and starts walking through town—and now Dr. Frankenstein wants to shoot it."

Needless to say, not every cadet embraces the climate of cruelty; the nocturnal maulings likely frighten as many cadets as they enthrall. But the group mentality that pervades The Citadel assures that any desire on the part of a cadet to speak out about the mounting violence will usually be squelched by the threat of ostracism and shame. While group rule typifies many institutions, military and civilian, that place a premium on conformity, the power and authoritarianism of the peer group at The Citadel is exceptional, because the college gives a handful of older students leave to "govern" the others as they see fit. (A lone officer provided by the military, who sleeps in a wing off one of the dorms, seldom interferes.) This is a situation that, over the years, an occasional school official has challenged, without success. A former assistant commandant for discipline, Army Lieutenant Colonel T. Nugent Courvoisie, recalled that he "begged" the school's president back in the sixties to place more military officers—and ones who were more mature—in the barracks, but his appeals went unheeded. Discipline and punishment in the dorms is in the hands of the student-run regimental command, and ascendancy in this hierarchy is not always predicated on compassion for one's fellow-man. In consequence, the tyranny of the few buys the silence of the many.

This unofficial pact of silence could, of course, be challenged by the Citadel officialdom. On a number of occasions over the past three decades—most recently when some particularly brutal incidents found their way into the media—The Citadel has commissioned "studies." But when the administration does go on the offensive, its animus is primarily directed not at miscreant cadets but at the "unfair" media, which are "victimizing" the institution by publicizing the bad behavior of its boys.

In recent years, enough bad news leaked out locally to become a public-relations nightmare, and the school appointed a committee of Citadel loyalists to assess the situation. Even the loyalists concluded, in a January, 1992, report, that the practice of physical abuse of freshmen, along with food and sleep deprivation, had got out of hand. As a result, Major Mill told me, The Citadel ordered upperclassmen to stop using pushups as a "disciplinary tool" on individual cadets. "That was the most important one" of the reforms prompted by the report, Mill said. Other reforms were adopted: for example, freshmen would no longer be compelled to deliver mail to upperclassmen after their evening study hours, thus reducing opportunities for hazing; freshmen would—at least officially—no longer be compelled to "brace" in the mess hall. At the same time, the report declared that it "wholeheartedly endorses the concept of the fourth-class system," which it called "essential to the attainment of college objectives and the development of the Citadel man."

Institutions that boast of their insularity, whether convents or military academies, are commonly pictured in the public imagination as static, unchanging abstractions, isolated from the ebb and flow of current events. But these edifices are rarely as otherworldly as their guardians might wish; indeed, in the case of The Citadel, its bricked-off culture has functioned more as a barometer of national anxieties than as a garrison against them. The militaristic tendencies within the Corps seem to vary inversely with the esteem in which the American soldier is held in the larger society. In times when the nation has been caught up in a socially acceptable conflict, one in which its soldiers return as heroes greeted by tickertape parades, The Citadel has loosened its militaristic harness, or even removed it altogether. Thus, during perhaps the most acceptable war in American history, the Second World War, the fourth-class system of knob humiliation was all but discontinued.

Upperclassmen couldn't even order a knob to brace. The changes began largely in response to the demands of the real military for soldiers they could use in a modern war. "The War Department and the Navy Department were asking R.O.T.C. to do less drilling, more calculus," Jamie Moore, a professor of history at The Citadel and a former member of the United States Army's Historical Advisory Committee, told me. "The Citadel dismantled its fourth-class system because it was getting in the way of their military training." The changes didn't seem to interfere with the school's production of Whole Men; on the contrary, an extraordinary percentage of The Citadel's most distinguished graduates come from these years, among them United States Senator Ernest (Fritz) Hollings; Alvah Chapman, Jr., the former chief executive of Knight-Ridder; and South Carolina's former governor John C. West.

The kinder, gentler culture of the Second World War–era Citadel survived well into the next decade. Although a new fourth-class system was soon established, it remained relatively benign. "We didn't have the yelling we have today," Colonel Harvey Dick, class of '53 and now a member of The Citadel's governing body, recalled. "They didn't even shave the freshmen's heads."

The postwar years also brought the admission of women to the summer program, and without the hand-wringing provoked by Shannon Faulkner's application. "WOMEN INVADE CITADEL CLASSES FIRST TIME IN SCHOOL'S HISTORY," the Charleston daily noted back on page 16 of its June 21, 1949, edition. "Most male students took the advent of the 'amazons' in their stride," the paper reported cheerfully. "Only the younger ones seemed at all uneasy. Professors and instructors were downright glad to see women in their classes."

The Vietnam War, needless to say, did not inspire the same mood of relaxation on campus. "The fourth-class system was very physical," Wallace West, the admissions director, who was an undergraduate at The Citadel during the Vietnam War years, said. "When I was there, there was no true emphasis on academics, or on positive leadership. It was who could be worked to physical exhaustion." Alumni from those years recounted being beaten with sticks, coat hangers, and rifle butts. That was, of course, the era that inspired Pat Conroy's novel "The Lords of Discipline," a tale of horrific hazing, directed with special virulence against the school's first African-American cadet. "They just tortured us," Conroy recalled from his home, in Beaufort, South Carolina. "It taught me the exact kind of man I didn't want to be," he added.

In 1968, the administration appointed a committee to investigate the violence. The committee issued a report that, like its 1992 successor, concluded "there have been significant and extensive abuses to the [fourth-class] system." And, with its strong recommendation that hazing result in expulsion, the report seemed to promise a more pacific future on campus.

In the past decade and a half, however, the record of violence and cruelty at The Citadel has attracted increasing notice, even as the armed forces have been racked by downsizing and scandal. The Citadel president during much of this era, Major General James A. Grimsley, Jr., declined to discuss this or any other aspect of campus life during his tenure. "I don't do interviews," he said. "Thank you for calling, young lady." He then hung up. Others have been less reticent.

Thirteen years before Vice-Admiral James B. Stockdale consented to be Ross Perot's running mate, he took on what turned out to be an even more thankless task: fighting brutal forms of hazing at The Citadel. In 1979, Stockdale, who had graduated from Annapolis, was chosen to be The Citadel's president because of his status as a genuine military hero: he had survived eight years as a P.O.W. in Vietnam. This hero failed to see the point of manufactured adversity. In an afterword to the book "In Love and War," a collaboration between Stockdale and his wife, Sybil, he wrote that there was "something mean and out of control about the regime I had just inherited."

On his first day in the president's office, Stockdale opened a desk drawer and discovered "what turned out to be Pandora's box," he wrote. "From the top down, what was written on the papers I took out of the desk drawers—and conversations with some of their authors—was enough to break anybody's heart." Among them was a letter from an infuriated father who wanted to know what had happened to his son "to change him from a levelheaded, optimistic, aggressive individual to a fatigued, irrational, confused and bitter one." He also found copies of memos from The Citadel's staff physician complaining repeatedly of (as Stockdale recalled) "excessive hospitalization"—such as the case of a knob who had suffered intestinal bleeding and was later brought back to the infirmary, having been exercised to unconsciousness. Stockdale sought to reform the system, but he was stymied at every turn. He clashed with The Citadel's powerful Board of Visitors, an eleven-member committee of alumni that sets school policy. The Board of Visitors overruled his expulsion of a senior cadet who had reportedly been threatening freshmen with a pistol. A year into his presidency, Stockdale submitted his resignation. After he left, the board reinstated an avenging friend of the senior cadet who, according to Stockdale, had attempted to break into his house one evening. (The then chairman of the Board of Visitors maintains that the cadet was drunk and looking for the barracks.)

"They thought they were helping people into manhood," Stockdale recalled, from a more serene post, in Palo Alto, California, where he is a scholar at Stanford's Hoover Institution on War, Revolution, and Peace. "But they had no idea what that meant—or who they were."

After Watts became president, in 1989, some faculty members began to observe a creeping militarization imposed by the administration upon the

Corps's already drill-heavy regimen. Four special military days were added to the academic year. At the beginning of one semester, President Watts held a faculty meeting in a room above the mess hall."Watts had these soldiers standing around the room with their hands behind them," Gardel Feurtado, a political-science professor and one of only two African-American professors, recalled. Watts, he said, lectured the faculty for about three hours. "He didn't talk about academics or educational goals. He just talked about cadets' training, and he showed us a film of it," Feurtado told me. According to

Illustration by Mark Zingarelli, originally published in *The New Yorker.* © Mark Zingarelli/ House of Zing

Feurtado, Watts told the faculty to line up in groups behind the soldiers for a tour of the barracks. "I said, 'Enough of this,' and I started to walk out. And this soldier stopped me and said, 'Where do you think you're going, sir?' and I said, 'You do realize that I am not in the military?'" Feurtado had to push by him to leave.

When Michael Lake looked back on the abuse he suffered during his abbreviated knob year of '91, he could now see before him, like the emergence of invisible ink on what appeared to be a blank piece of paper, the faint outlines of another struggle. What he saw was a submerged gender battle, a bitter but definitely fixed contest between the sexes, concealed from view by the fact that men played both parts. The beaten knobs were the women, "stripped" and humiliated, and the predatory upperclassmen were the men, who bullied and pillaged. If they couldn't re-create a male-dominant society in the real world, they could restage the drama by casting male knobs in all the subservient feminine roles.

"They called you a 'pussy' all the time," Lake recalled. "Or a 'fucking little girl.'" It started the very first day they had their heads shaved, when the upperclassmen stood around and taunted. "Oh, you going to get your little girlie locks cut off?" When they learned that Lake would be playing soccer that fall, their first response was "What is that, a girl's sport?" Another former cadet said that he had withstood "continual abuse," until he found himself thinking about jumping out the fourth-story window of the barracks—and quit. He reported an experience similar to Lake's. Virtually every taunt equated him with a woman: whenever he showed fear, they would say, "You look like you're having an abortion," or "Are you menstruating?" The knobs even experienced a version of domestic violence. The upperclassmen, this cadet recalled, "would go out and get drunk and they would come home and haze, and you just hoped they didn't come into your room."

"According to the Citadel creed of the cadet," Lake said, "women are objects, they're things that you can do with whatever you want to." In order to maintain this world view, the campus has to be free of women whose status might challenge it—a policy that, of course, is rarely enunciated. The acknowledged policy is that women are to be kept at a distance so they can be "respected" as ladies. Several months before Faulkner's lawsuit came to trial, I was sitting in the less than Spartan air-conditioned quarters of the senior regimental commander, Norman Doucet, the highest-ranking cadet, who commanded the barracks. Doucet, who was to be The Citadel's star witness at the Faulkner trial, was explaining to me how excluding women had enhanced his gentlemanly perception of the opposite sex. "The absence of women makes us understand them better," Doucet said. "In an aesthetic kind of way, we appreciate them more—because they are not there."

Women at less of a remove fare less well. In The Citadel's great chain of being, the "waitees"—as many students call that all-black, all-female mess-hall staff—rate as the bottom link. Some upperclassmen have patted them on their rear ends, tried to trip them as they pass the tables, or hurled food at their retreating backs. Cadets have summoned them with "Come here, bitch," or addressed one who dropped a plate or forgot an order as "you stupid whore." The pages of the *Brigadier,* the school's newspaper, bear witness to the cadets' contempt for these women. Gary Brown, now the editor-in-chief of the *Brigadier,* once advised fellow-cadets to beware of "waitee" food contamination—"the germ filled hands, the hair follicles, and other unknown horrors." Not only was he dismayed by "wavy little follicles in my food" but he found the women insufficiently obedient. "Duty is certainly not the sublimest word in the Waitee language," he wrote. In a letter to the editor, Jason S. Pausman, class of '94, urged fellow-cadets to demand "waitees without chronic diseases that involve sneezing, coughing or wiping of body parts. . . . The reality is simple, we CANNOT sit by and let the waitees of this school control us."

Some women faculty members report similarly resentful responses to their presence, despite—or because of—their positions of authority. Angry messages on a professor's door are one tactic. When Jane Bishop recently posted on her office door a photocopy of a *New York Times* editorial supporting women's admission to the Corps of Cadets, she found it annotated with heated rejoinders in a matter of days. "Dr. Bishop, you are a prime example of why women should not be allowed here," one scribble read. Another comment: "Women will destroy the world."

The Citadel men's approach to women seems to toggle between extremes of gentility and fury. "First, they will be charming to the women to get their way," Linda Ross said. "But if that doesn't work they don't know any other way. So then they will get angry." It's a pattern that is particularly evident in some cadets' reaction to younger faculty women.

December Green joined The Citadel's Political Science Department in 1988, the first woman that the department had ever hired for a tenure-track position. She was twenty-six and attractive—"someone the cadets might fantasize about," a colleague recalled. They were less enchanted, however,

The legendary Citadel elder known as the Boo, who oversaw racial integration at The Citadel in the sixties, says, "With women, there's going to be sexual harassment." His wife, Margaret, counters, "Oh, honey, those cadets are harassing each other right now." "That's different," he says. "That's standard operating procedure."
Illustration by Mark Zingarelli, originally published in *The New Yorker*. © Mark Zingarelli/House of Zing

by her left-leaning politics. She soon found herself getting obscene phone calls in the middle of the night. Then obscenities began appearing on her office door. "Pussy" is the one that sticks in her mind.

Though Green's work at The Citadel was highly praised—she received an award for teaching, research, and service—she said that no one in the administration tried to stop her when she left in 1992, in despair over her inability to contain the cadets' fury. Nor, apparently, had anyone responded to her appeals to correct the situation. "A lot of terrible things happened to me there," Green, who is now teaching in Ohio, said, reluctant to revisit them. The hostility ranged from glowering group stares in the hallway to death threats—some of which appeared on the cadets' teacher-evaluation forms. The male faculty offered little support. Green recalls the department chairman instructing her to "be more maternal toward the students" when a cadet lodged a complaint about her (she had challenged his essay in which he praised apartheid). And a professor who stood by one day while his students harassed her and another woman informed her, "You get what you provoke."

Green said she eventually had to get an unlisted number to stop the obscene calls, and also moved, in part out of fear of the cadets' vengeance. The last straw, however, came when she submitted the written threats she had received to her chairman, who passed them on to the dean of undergraduate studies, in hopes of remedial action. The dean, she said, did nothing for some months, then, after she inquired, said he had "misplaced" the offending documents.

The dean, Colonel Isaac (Spike) Metts, Jr., told me he didn't recall saying he misplaced the documents but "I might have said it's not on my desk at that time and I don't know where it is." He added that Green was a "very valuable" professor. "I don't know what else we could've done," Metts said. In any event, soon after submitting the threatening notes to the dean Green gave up. At her exit interview, she recalled, President Watts told her he didn't understand why she had been upset by the cadet harassment. "It's just a bunch of kid stuff," another male colleague said. (Lewis Spearman, the assistant to the president, said that, because of federal privacy law, Watts would have no response to Green's version of events.)

The remaining category of women that cadets have to deal with is "the dates," as the young women they socialize with are generally called. (There are no wives; Citadel policy forbids cadets to marry, and violators are expelled.) In some respects, these young women are the greatest challenge to the cadet's sense of gender hierarchy. While the "waitees" can be cast as household servants and the female teachers as surrogate mothers, the dates are more difficult to place. Young women their age are often college students, with the same aspirations as the cadets, or even greater ones. The cadets deal with young women's rising ambitions in a number of ways. One is simply to date high-school girls, an option selected by a number of cadets. Another strategy, facilitated by The Citadel, is to cast the young women who are invited on campus into the homecoming-queen mold. The college holds a Miss Citadel contest each year, and Anne Poole, whose husband, Roger, is the vice-president of academic affairs and the dean of the college, has sat on the judging panel. Each cadet company elects a young woman mascot from a photograph competition, and their faces appear in the yearbook.

The school also sends its young men to an in-house etiquette-training seminar, in which the Citadel "hostess," a pleasant woman in her forties named Susan Bowers, gives them a lecture on how "to act gentlemanly with the girls." She arms cadets with "The Art of Good Taste," a do's-and-don'ts manual with a chapter entitled "Helping the Ladies." The guidebook outlines the "correct way of offering an arm to a lady . . . to help her down the steps," and the best method for assisting "a lady in distress." (The example of distress provided involves an elderly woman trying to open a door when her arms are full of shopping bags.) Such pointers are illustrated with pictures of fifties-style coeds sporting Barbie-doll hair flips and clinging to the arms of their cadets, who are escorting them to "the Hop." The manual's preface states emphatically, "At all times [ladies] must be sheltered and protected not only from the elements and physical harm but also from embarrassment, crudity, or coarseness of any sort."

Susan Bowers explained the duties of her office: "At the beginning of the year, we do 'situation cards' for the freshmen. And we'll bring in cheerleaders and use them as props. . . . We show cadets how to go through the receiving line, how to introduce your date, and what to say to them. In the past, we didn't have the cheerleaders to use, so they dressed up some of the guys as girls." Bowers said she felt bad for the cadets, who often come to her seeking maternal consolation. "They are very timid—afraid, almost," she said. "They are so lost, and they need a shoulder."

"The Art of Good Taste" is silent on the subject of proper etiquette toward women who require neither deference nor rescue. And, as Linda Ross observed, when the gentlemanly approach fails them cadets seem to have only one fallback—aggression. Numerous cadets spoke to me of classmates who claimed to have "knocked around" uncompliant girlfriends. Some of those classmates, no doubt, were embellishing to impress a male audience, but not always. "I know lots of stories where cadets are violent toward women," a 1991 Citadel graduate named Ron Vergnolle said. He had witnessed cadets hitting their girlfriends at a number of Citadel parties—and observed one party incident in which two cadets held down a young woman while a third drunken cadet leaned over and vomited on her. Vergnolle, a magna-cum-laude graduate of the Citadel class of '91, recounted several such stories to me, and added that bragging about humiliating an ex-girlfriend is a common practice—and the more outrageous the humiliation, the better the story, as far as many cadets are concerned. Two such cadet storytellers, for example, proudly spread the word of their exploits on Dog Day, a big outdoor party sponsored by The Citadel's senior class. The two cadets told about the time they became enraged with their dates, followed them to the Portosans, and, after the women had entered, pushed the latrines over so they landed on the doors, trapping the occupants. The cadets left them there. Another cadet told Vergnolle that he had tacked a live hamster to a young woman's door. There was also the cadet who boasted widely that, as vengeance against an uncooperative young woman, he smashed the head of her cat against a window as she watched in horror. "The cat story," Vergnolle noted, "that was this guy's calling card."

Something of these attitudes shows up even in the ditties the cadets chant during their daily runs. Many of the chants are the usual military "jodies," well known for their misogynistic lyrics. But some are vintage Citadel, and include lyrics about gouging out a woman's eyes, lopping off body parts, and evisceration. A cadence remembered by one Citadel cadet, sung to the tune of "The Candy Man," begins, "Who can take two jumper cables/Clip 'em to her tit/Turn on the battery and watch the bitch twitch." Another verse starts with "Who can take an ice pick . . ." and so on.

The day after last Thanksgiving, the phone rang at one-thirty in the morning in the home of Sandy and Ed Faulkner, in Powdersville, South Carolina, a tiny community on the outskirts of Greenville. The caller was a neighbor. They had better come outside, he said—a car had been circling their block. Sandy and Ed, the parents of Shannon Faulkner, went out on their front lawn and looked around. At first, they saw nothing. Then, as they turned back to the house, they saw that across the white porch columns and along the siding of the house, painted in gigantic and what Sandy later recalled as "blood-red" letters, were the words, "Bitch," "Dyke," "Whore," and "Lesbo." Ed got up again at 6 A.M. and, armed with a bucket of white paint, hurried to conceal the message from his daughter.

A few days after the judge ordered The Citadel to admit Faulkner to the Corps of Cadets, morning rush-hour drivers in Charleston passed by a huge portable sign that read "Die Shannon." At least this threat wasn't home delivered. In the past year, instances of vandalism and harassment have mounted at the Faulkner home. Someone crawled under the house and opened the emergency exhaust valve on the water heater. The gas tank on Sandy's car was pried open. Someone driving a Ford Bronco mowed down the mailbox. Another motorist "did figure-eights through my flower bed," Sandy said. "This year, I didn't even plant flowers, because I knew they would just tear them up." And someone with access to Southern Bell's voice-mail system managed, twice, to tap into their voice mail and change their greeting, both times to a recording featuring rap lyrics about a "bitch" with a "big butt." Callers phoned in the middle of the night with threatening messages. Sandy called the county sheriff's department about the vandalism, but in Anderson county, which has been home to many Citadel's graduates, the deputy who arrived was not particularly helpful. He told them, Sandy recalled, "Well, if you're going to mess with The Citadel, you're just going to have to expect that."

Every trial has its rare moments of clarity, when the bramble of admissibility arguments and technicalities is cut away and we see the actual issue in dispute. One such moment came toward the end of the Faulkner-Citadel trial, when Alexander Astin, the director of the Higher Education Research Institute at the University of California at Los Angeles, took the stand. Astin, who is widely viewed as a leading surveyor of college-student performance and attitudes, found no negative effects on male students in nineteen all-male colleges he had studied which had gone coeducational.

"Can you tell me what kind of woman you would think would want to attend a coeducational Citadel?" Robert Patterson, the Citadel attorney who had previously represented V.M.I., asked Astin, his voice full of unflattering insinuation about the kind of woman he imagined her to be.

ASTIN: I suppose the same as the kind of men who want to go there.

PATTERSON: Would it be a woman that would not be all that different from men?

ASTIN: Yes.

To Patterson, this was a triumphant moment, and he closed on it: he had forced the government's witness to admit that a woman like Shannon Faulkner would have to be a mannish aberration from her gender. But in fact Astin's testimony expressed the precise point that the plaintiff's side had been trying to make all along, and that The Citadel strenuously resisted: that the sexes were, in the end, not all that different.

"I was considered the bitch of the band," Shannon Faulkner said, without embarrassment, of her four years in her high school's marching band—just stating a fact. She was lounging on the couch in her parents' living room, comfortable in an old T-shirt and shorts, one leg swung over an arm of the couch. "That's because I was the one who was mean and got it done." The phone rang, for the millionth time—another media call. "I'm not giving statements to the press right now," she said efficiently into the phone, and hung up. She did not apologize for her brusqueness, as I was half expecting her to do, after she put down the receiver. There is nothing of the good girl about her. Not that she is disagreeable; Shannon Faulkner just doesn't see the point in false deference. "I never let anyone push me around, male or female," Faulkner said, and that fact had been exasperatingly obvious to reporters who covered the trial: they found that all the wheedling and cheap flatteries that usually prompt subjects to say more than they should didn't work with Faulkner.

One could scrounge around in Faulkner's childhood for the key to what made her take on The Citadel. You could say that it was because she was born six weeks premature, and her fierce struggle to live forged a "survivor." You could cite her memory that as a small child she preferred playing outside with the boys to playing with certain girls whom she deemed "too prissy." You could point to her sports career in high school and junior high: she lettered in softball for four years and kept stats for three of the schools' four basketball teams. You could note her ability to juggle tasks: she edited the yearbook, wrote for the school paper, and graduated with a 3.48 grade-point average. And you could certainly credit the sturdy backbone and outspokenness of both her mother and her maternal grandmother; this is a family where the women talk and the men keep a low profile. Her father, Ed, owns a small fence-building business. At thirty, a few years after Shannon's birth, Sandy returned to college to get her degree, a double major in psychology and education, and became a high-school teacher of psychology, sociology, United States history, and minority cultures. When a male professor had complained about certain "older women" in his class who asked "too many questions," Sandy hurled one of her wedge-heeled sandals at him. "I said, 'I'm paying for this class, and don't you ever tell me what I can ask.'" Shannon's maternal grandmother, sixty-seven-year-old Evelyn Richey, was orphaned at six and worked most of her life in textile factories, where, she noted, "women could do the job and men got the pay." Of her granddaughter's suit she said, "Women have got to come ahead. I say, let's get on with the show."

But there's little point in a detailed inspection of family history, because there's no real mystery here. What is most striking about Shannon herself is that she's not particularly unusual. She reads novels by Tom Clancy and John Grisham, has worked in a local day-care center, is partial to places like Bennigan's. She wants a college education so she can support herself and have a career as a teacher or a journalist—she hasn't yet decided which. She might do a stint in the military, she might not. She is in many ways representative of the average striving lower-middle-class teenage girl, circa 1994, who intends to better herself and does not intend to achieve that betterment through a man—in fact, she has not for a moment entertained such a possibility.

Throughout the trial, cadets and Citadel alumni spoke of a feminist plot: she is "a pawn" of the National Organization for Women, or—a theory repeatedly posited to me by cadets—"Her mother put her up to it." Two Citadel alumni asked me in all seriousness if feminist organizations were paying Shannon Faulkner to take the stand. In truth, Shannon makes an unlikely feminist poster girl. She prefers to call herself "an individualist" and seems almost indifferent to feminist affairs; when I mentioned Gloria Steinem's name once in conversation, Shannon asked me, "Who's that?" After the judge issued his decision to admit her to the Corps, she told the *New York Times* that she didn't consider the ruling a victory "just for women"—only a confirmation of her belief that if you want something, "go for it." Shannon Faulkner's determination to enter The Citadel's Corps of Cadets was fuelled not so much by a desire to trailblaze as by a sense of amazement and indignation that this trail was barricaded in the first place. She had never, she told the court, encountered such a roadblock in all her nineteen years—a remark that perhaps only a young woman of her fortunate generation could make without perjuring herself.

Shannon Faulkner got the idea of attending The Citadel back in December of 1992. She was taking a preparatory education course at Wren High School, the local public school. Mike Hazel, the teacher, passed out articles for them to read and discuss, and Faulkner picked the article in *Sports Illustrated* about hazing at The Citadel. "It was almost as accidental as Rosa

Parks," Hazel recalled. "I just held up *Sports Illustrated* and asked, 'Who wants to do this?'"

Faulkner told me she'd selected the article because "I had missed that issue." During the ensuing discussion, the class wandered off the subject of hazing and onto the question of what, exactly, a public state institution was doing barring women from its classrooms. After a while, Faulkner got up and went down to the counselor's office, and returned with an application form from The Citadel. "I said, 'Hey, it doesn't even say 'Male/Female,'''" she recalled. While she was sitting in class, she filled it out. "I didn't really make a big to-do about it."

Two weeks after Faulkner received her acceptance letter, The Citadel got word she was a woman and revoked her admission, and in August of 1993 she went off to spend a semester at the University of South Carolina at Spartanburg while the courts thrashed out the next move. As the lawyers filed papers, The Citadel's defenders delivered their own increasingly agitated personal beliefs to the plaintiff herself. Faulkner worked evenings as a waitress in a local bar called Chiefs Wings and Firewater until the nightly tirades from the many drunk Citadel-graduate customers got to be too much. Actually, Faulkner said, she wouldn't have quit if some of her male college friends hadn't felt the need to defend her honor. "I didn't want them getting hurt," she said. Her manner of dealing with the Citadel crowd was more good-humored. One day at the bar, she recalled, "a guy came up to me. 'Are you Shannon Faulkner?' he asked, and I said, 'Why?'—very casual. Then he got real huffy-puffy, madder and madder." Finally, she said, he stuck his ring in her face, then slammed his hand down on the table. "You will never wear *that!*" he yelled. Shannon saw him a few times in the bar after that, scowling at her from a far table. To lighten the mood, she once had the bartender send him a beer. He wouldn't drink it.

"I never show my true emotions in public," Shannon said. "I consider that weak." She can laugh at the cadets' threats, even when they turn ugly, because she doesn't see the reason for all the fuss. Whenever she is asked to sign the latest T-shirt inspired by the controversy, which depicts a group of male bulldogs (The Citadel's mascot) in cadet uniforms and one female bulldog in a red dress, above the caption "1,952 Bulldogs and 1 Bitch," Faulkner told me, "I always sign under the 'Bitch' part."

The first day that Shannon Faulkner attended classes, in January, 1994, the cadets who had lined up by the academic building told the media the same thing over and over. "We were trained to be gentlemen, and that's what we'll be." But in Shannon's first class, biology, all three cadets assigned to sit in her row changed their seats. The teacher, Philippe Ross, had to threaten to mark them absent to get them to return to their places. (More than twenty unexcused absences a semester is grounds for failure.) Shortly thereafter, a rumor began to circulate that Faulkner was using a fake I.D. in the local bars. This summer, talk of a plot against Faulkner surfaced—to frame her, perhaps by planting drugs in her belongings. The threat seemed real enough for Faulkner to quit her summer job, in the Charleston area, and return home.

The *Brigadier*'s column "Scarlet Pimpernel" took up the anti-Shannon cause with a vengeance. The columnist dubbed her "the divine bovine," likening her to a plastic revolving cow at a nearby mall (the mounting of which is a cadet tradition). The "Pimpernel" comments on an incident that occurred on Faulkner's first day were particularly memorable. An African-American cadet named Von Mickle dared to shake her hand in front of the media and say, "It's time for women," and compared the exclusion of women to that of blacks. For this lone act, he was not only physically threatened by classmates but derided in the "Pimpernel." "The PIMP doth long to tame the PLASTIC COW on this most wondrous of nights," the anonymous author wrote, with the column's usual antique-English flourishes and coded references. "But it seems that we will have a live specimen, a home grown DAIRY QUEEN from the stables of Powdersville. Perhaps NON DICKLE will be the first to saddle up. He is DIVINE BOVINE's best friend after all."

More disturbing were cadet writings on Faulkner that were not for public consumption. Tom Lucas, a graduate student in The Citadel's evening program, told me about some "very harsh" graffiti that he'd found all over one of the men's rooms in The Citadel's academic building. The inscription that most stuck in his mind: "Let her in—then fuck her to death."

On the whole, The Citadel administrators to whom I spoke were defensive, evasive, or dismissive of the cadets' hostile words and deeds toward Faulkner. When I asked Citadel officials to respond to reports of barracks violence, harassment of women on staff, or verbal abuse of Faulkner, the responses were dismaying. Cases of violence and abuse were "aberrations"; cadets who spoke up were either "troublemakers" or "mama's boys"; and each complaint by a female faculty member was deemed a "private personnel matter" that could not be discussed further.

Certainly the administrators and trustees themselves are less than enthusiastic about Faulkner's arrival. William F. Prioleau, Jr., until recently a member of the Board of Visitors, implied on a radio talk show that abortions would go up as a result of the female invasion, as he claimed had happened at West Point. Meanwhile, in The Citadel's Math Department, all that was going up as a result of Shannon Faulkner's presence was the grade-point average. Faulkner's highest mark at the semester's end was in calculus, where she earned an A (prompting a surprised Dean Poole to comment to her that she was "certainly not the stereotypical woman"). The Math Department has in recent years invited A students to an annual party. But rather than include Faulkner, the department limited the guest list to math majors. Math professor David Trautman, who was in charge of invitations to the party, explained in an E-mail message to colleagues, "Her presence would put a damper on the evening."

Linda Ross, then a professor at The Citadel, was speaking one day with a seventy-six-year-old alumnus, and the talk turned to Faulkner's lawsuit. He asked her if she thought it possible that this young woman might prevail. "Well, it's probably an inevitable turning of the tide," Ross said, shrugging. To her amazement, the alumnus began to cry.

"I have the worst chance in society of getting a job, because I'm a white male," William H. Barnes, the senior platoon leader, shouted at me over the din in The Citadel's mess hall, a din created by the upperclassmen's tradition of berating knobs at mealtime. "And that's the major difference between me and my father." In a society where, at least since the Second World War, surpassing one's father has been an expected benchmark of American manhood, Barnes's point is a plangent one. But it's hard to say which Citadel generation is more undone by the loss of white male privilege—the young men who will never partake of a dreamed world of masculine advantage or the older men who are seeing that lived world split apart, shattered.

"I was in Vietnam in '63, and I'll defy you or Shannon or anyone else to hike through the rice paddies," the usually genial Colonel Harvey Dick, sixty-seven, a Board of Visitors member, an ex-marine, and an Army lieutenant colonel, was practically shouting from his recliner armchair in his Charleston home. He popped a Tums in his mouth. "There's just no way you can do that. . . . You can't pick up a ninety-five-pound projectile. There are certain things out there that are differences." On the wall above his head were seven bayonets. He was wearing his blue Citadel T-shirt, which matched the Citadel mementos that overwhelmed his den—Citadel mugs, hats, footballs, ceramic bulldogs. It was a room known in the Dick household as "Harvey's 'I Love Me' Room." Dick treated it as his command post—whenever the phone rang, he whipped it off the cradle and barked "Colonel Dick!"—but what he was commanding was unclear; he retired in 1993 from a sixteen-year stint as The Citadel's assistant commandant. Still, he at least knew that he was once in charge, that he once enjoyed lifetime job security as a career military man. This was something his son couldn't say: Harvey Dick II, a nuclear pipe fitter, had recently been laid off at the Charleston Naval Shipyard.

Colonel Dick wanted it known that he wasn't "one of those male-chauvinist pigs"; in fact, he believes that women are smarter than men. "Women used to let the men dominate," he said. "Maybe we need a male movement, since evidently we're coming out second on everything." He slipped another Tums from an almost empty roll. The sun was dropping as we spoke, and shadows fell across the Citadel hats and figurines in his room. "Go back and look at your Greek and Roman empires and why they fell," he said.

His wife cleared her throat. "This doesn't have anything to do with male-female," she said.

"I see a decline in this great nation of ours," Dick said. He crossed his arms and stared into the gathering darkness of the late summer afternoon. After a while, he said, "I guess I sound like a buffoon."

Unlike the cadets, the older male Citadel officials often have to face dissent from wives or daughters whose views and professional aspirations or accomplishments challenge their stand on women's proper place. Lewis Spearman, the assistant to the president, recently remarried, and his wife is a feminist paralegal who is now getting her master's degree in psychology. She says she engaged for more than a year in "shriekfests" with him over the Shannon Faulkner question before she halfheartedly came around to The Citadel party line on barring women. And, while the wife of Dean Poole may have sat on the Miss Citadel judging panel, their daughter, Mindy, had loftier ambitions. Despite the fact that she suffered from cystic fibrosis, she was an ardent skier, horseback rider, and college athlete, rising at 5 A.M. daily with her crew-team members at the University of Virginia. And, despite a double lung transplant during her junior year, she graduated in 1991 with honors and won a graduate fellowship. "She was an outstanding young lady," Poole said. "I was very proud of her." His eyes clouding over at the memory, he recalled that she had made him promise to take her to the big Corps Day parade on The Citadel's sesquicentennial. The day the father and daughter were to attend the parade was the day she died. "Sort of an interesting footnote," he said, wiping at his moist eyes. What if she had wanted to go to The Citadel? Well, actually, Poole said, she *had* talked about it. If she had persisted he would have tried to change her mind, he said, but he added, "I would never have stopped her from doing something she wanted to do."

One of the biggest spousal battles over Shannon Faulkner is waged nightly at the home of a man who might seem the least likely figure at The Citadel to wind up with a feminist wife. Probably The Citadel's most legendary elder, thanks to Pat Conroy's thinly veiled and admiring portrait of him in "The Lords of Discipline," is Lieutenant Colonel T. Nugent Courvoisie, who, as an assistant commandant in the sixties, oversaw the admission of the first African-American cadet to The Citadel. A gravelly-voiced and cigar-chomping tender tyrant, Courvoisie—or the Boo, as he is known, for obscure reasons—was a fixture at the school for more than two decades. There are two Citadel scholarships in his family name, and his visage peers down from two portraits on campus.

A courtly man, and still dapper at seventy-seven, the Boo, who has since given up cigars, insisted on picking me up at my hotel and driving me to his home, though I had a rental car sitting in the parking lot. On the drive over, he ticked off the differences between the sexes which he believed made it impossible for The Citadel to admit women—differences such as that "the average female is not as proficient athletically as the average male." When we were settled in the living room, the Boo on his recliner and his second wife, Margaret, who is also seventy-seven, in a straight-back chair, the subject of Shannon Faulkner was revisited. The first words out of Margaret's mouth were "The Citadel wants to chop the head off women." A low growl emanated from the Boo's corner. He lowered the recliner a notch. "We don't talk about it here," Margaret said—an obvious untruth. "We haven't come to blows yet, but—"

The Boo interrupted, "I have the correct view."

She retorted, "No one has the *correct* view." She turned and addressed me. "You have to understand him," she said of her husband of nine years. "This is a man who went to military prep schools and a church that was male-dominated, naturally."

The Boo interrupted. "J.C. picked twelve *men* as his disciples," he said.

Margaret rolled her eyes. "See? He even takes it into the church—and he's on such familiar ground with Christ he calls him J.C."

The Boo said, "J.C. never picked a woman, except his mother."

Margaret said, "Oh God, see, this is why we don't go into it."

But, as usual, go into it they did. As the words got batted back and forth, with Margaret doing most of the batting, the Boo levered his recliner progressively lower, until all I could see of him were the soles of his shoes.

MARGARET: You had plenty of good women soldiers in Saudi Arabia.

BOO: Plenty of pregnant ones . . .

MARGARET: What, do you think [the cadets] didn't get girls pregnant before? There've been plenty of abortions. And I know of a number of cases that, by the time [a cadet] graduated, there were four or five kids.

BOO: That's an exaggeration. Maybe two or three . . . With women, there's going to be sexual harassment.

MARGARET: Oh, honey, those cadets are harassing each other right now, all the time.

BOO: That's different. That's standard operating procedure.

In the nineteen-sixties, Margaret worked in the library at The Citadel, where she would often see Charles Foster, the first African-American cadet (who died a few years ago) alone at one of the library desks. "He would just come to the library and sit there a lot. It's hard to be the only one, to be the groundbreaker. That's why I admire this girl."

Boo's voice boomed from the depths of his recliner: "But there's no need for her. She's ruining a good thing."

Margaret gave a mock groan. "This is the last vestige of male bastionship," she said, "and it's going to kill 'em when it crumbles." Boo raised his chair halfway back up and considered Margaret. "She has a good mind," he told me after a while.

Margaret smiled. "I'm a new experience for him. He's always been military. People didn't disagree with him."

The Boo showed the way upstairs, to the attic, where he has his own "Citadel room"—a collection of Citadel memorabilia vaster than but almost identical to Dick's. Around the house, there were sketches of Boo at various points in his Citadel career. He told me that, before he retired, the cadets commissioned a portrait of him that hangs in Jenkins Hall. "Man, I looked good in that," he said. "Like a man. A leader."

Margaret didn't think so. "No, it was horrible," she said. "It didn't look like you."

"If Shannon were in my class, I'd be fired by March for sexual harassment," Colonel James Rembert, an English professor, was saying as we headed toward his classroom. He had a ramrod bearing and a certain resemblance to Ted Turner (who, it happens, sent all three of his sons to The Citadel—Beau Turner among them—and donated twenty-five million dollars to the school earlier this year). The Colonel identifies himself as one of "the last white Remberts" in South Carolina, the Remberts being a Huguenot family of sufficiently ancient lineage to gain him admission to the St. John's Hunting Club, of South Carolina—an all-male society chaired by a Citadel alumnus. Rembert, who has a Cambridge University doctorate and wrote a book on Jonathan Swift, said he preferred the company of men, in leisure and in learning. "I've dealt with young men all my life," he went on. "I know how to play with them. I have the freedom here to imply things I couldn't with women. I don't want to have to watch what I say."

The literary work under discussion that day was "Beowulf," and the cadets agreed that it was all about "brotherhood loyalty" and, in the words of one student, "the most important characteristics of a man—glory and eternal fame." Then they turned to their papers on the topic.

"Mr. Rice," Rembert said in mock horror. "You turned in a single-spaced paper." This was a no-no. Rembert instructed him to take a pencil and "pen-e-trate"—Rembert drew the syllables out—the paper with the point. He shook his head. "What a pansy!" Rembert said. "Can't catch, can't throw, can't write." Another student was chastised for the use of the passive voice. "Never use the passive voice—it leads to effeminacy and homosexuality," Rembert told the class. "So next time you use the passive voice I'm going to make you lift up your limp wrist." Literary pointers concluded, Rembert floated the subject of Shannon Faulkner. The usual objections were raised. But then the class wandered into more interesting territory, provoked by a cadet's comment that "she would change the relationship between the men here." Just what is the nature of that relationship?

"When we are in the showers, it's very intimate," a senior cadet said. "We're one mass, naked together, and it makes us closer. . . . You're shaved, you're naked, you're afraid together. You can cry." Robert Butcher, another senior, said that the men take care of each classmate. "They'll help dress him, tuck in his shirt, shine his shoes." "You mean like a mother-child relationship?" I asked.

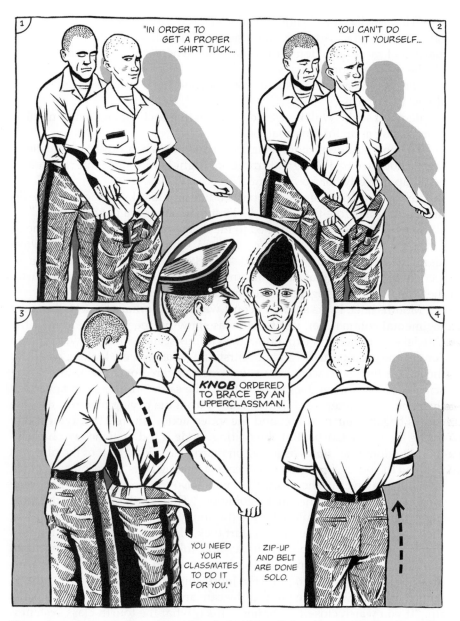

Dependency is a main theme in cadet relationships. Colonel James Rembert says that the cadets' intimate bond is "like a true marriage."
Illustration by Mark Zingarelli, originally published in *The New Yorker*. © Mark Zingarelli/House of Zing

"That *is* what it is," another cadet said. "It's a family, even the way we eat—family style." A fourth cadet said, "Maybe it's a Freudian thing, but males feel more affection with each other when women are not around. Maybe we're all homosexuals."

The class groaned. "Speak for yourself, buddy," a number of cadets said, almost in a chorus.

Rembert said, "With no women, we can hug each other. There's nothing so nurturing as an infantry platoon."

The hooted-down cadet weighed in again: "When I used to wrestle in high school, we had this great tradition. Right before the game, the coach, he'd slap us really hard on the butt."

Rembert, a onetime paratrooper, said he and his skydiving buddies did that, too, right before they jumped. "First man out gets a pat right there."

Over lunch, Rembert returned to the theme of manly nurturance among Citadel men. "We hug each other," he said. One of his colleagues, "always kisses me on the cheek," he went on. "It's like a true marriage. There's an affectionate intimacy that you will find between cadets. With this security they can, without being defensive, project tenderness to each other."

Months later, I was sitting in court watching Norman Doucet, the cadet regimental commander, testify. He was showing the judge a video of the Citadel experience and explaining the various scenes. First we were shown "one of the great parts" of a knob's first day—the mothers looking weepy at the gate as their sons were led away. Doucet lingered over the head-shaving science. "This is what does it, right here," he said. "Mothers can't even tell their sons apart after this." Thus shielded from the prying maternal eye, the cadets began their new life, and the video action shifted to a typical day in the life of the Corps. But the editing made it a day as heavy on early-morning domestic chores as it was on martial activity. Much of the film was devoted to housekeeping: scenes of cadets making beds, dressing each other, sweeping, taking out the trash, all of which Doucet described as "like some kind of a ballet or a dance that's going on." This is a dance where the most important moves took place before the show, in the dressing room. "What they are doing here is the Citadel shirt tuck," Doucet said. The tuck requires that a cadet unzip his pant halfway and fold down his waistband, then stand still while his helper approaches him from the back, puts his arms around the cadet's waist, pulls the loose shirt material firmly to the back, jams it as far down in the pants as he can, and then pulls the cadet's pants up. "If you watch closely right here, this is what the fourth-class system is all about," Doucet continued. "In order to get a proper shirt tuck, you can't do it yourself—you need your classmates to do it for you. There's really a lot of dependence upon your classmates." But, as Doucet's account suggested, cadets can experience that dependence only in concealment, away from mothers, away from all women.

When a Citadel attorney asked Doucet why female cadets would pose a problem on the campus, the only issue he raised was the humiliation that cadets feel if women observed the cadets' on-campus interactions. He spoke of the shame that knobs feel when, on occasion, a woman happened to be on the parade ground while upperclassmen were disciplining them. The cadets observing in the courtroom nodded in agreement.

It may seem almost paradoxical that the fourth-class system should be so solicitous of the emotional vulnerability of its wards—the same wards it subjects to such rigors. And yet the making of Whole Men evidently requires an initial stage of infantilization. Indeed, the objective of recapitulating childhood development is plainly spelled out in The Citadel's yearbook, known as "the Sphinx." The 1990 "Sphinx" explained, "As a freshman enters, he begins to release his childhood and takes the first steps to becoming a 'Citadel Man.' . . . As a 'knob,' every aspect of life is taught, a new way to walk. . . . Knobs are told how, where, and when to walk." Reentrance into manhood for the toddling knobs occurs on Recognition Day, when the upperclassmen force the knobs to do calisthenics until they drop, then gently lift up their charges and nurse them with cups of water. At that moment, for the first time in nine months, the older cadets call the knobs by their first names and embrace them.

The relationship between knobs and upperclassmen following Recognition Day, as they are integrated into the Corps, shifts from maternal to matrimonial. The yearbooks of the last several years picture Citadel men spending a lot of time embracing and kissing. Of course, this impulse, when it is captured on film, is always carefully disarmed with a jokey caption.

One afternoon, a group of cadets recounted for me the campus's many "nudity rituals," as they jokingly called them. There's "Senior Rip-Off Day," a spring rite in which three hundred seniors literally rip each other's clothes off, burn them in a bonfire, and hug and wrestle on the ground. There's "Nude Platoon," in which a group of juniors, unclad except for their cross-webbing, run around the quad yelling, "We love the Nude Platoon!" And there's the birthday ritual, in which the birthday boy is stripped, tied to a chair, and covered with shaving cream, while his groin is coated in liquid shoe polish.

During the fall semester before graduation, the seniors receive their "band of gold" (as it is called) in the Ring Ceremony. The chaplain blesses each class ring. (Receiving the ring, which I was constantly reminded is "the biggest class ring of any college," is a near-sacrament, and the yearbooks are filled with pictures of young men holding up their rings in fervor, as if clutching a crucifix before a vampire.) Then each senior walks through a ten-foot replica of the class ring with his mother on one arm and his "date" on the other. In a sort of reverse marriage ceremony, the mother gives the cadet away. Mother and date accompany him through the towering ring; then he kisses Mother farewell and marches under the arched swords of the Junior Sword Drill, a new bride of the Corps. Several cadets and alumni told me that when a Citadel graduate marries, it is a tradition to slide the class ring over the wedding band. Indeed, I saw such an ordering of priorities on the fingers of a number of Citadel men in the courtroom.

In the late-twentieth-century setting of The Citadel, in a time when extreme insecurity and confusion about masculinity's standing run rampant, the Corps of Cadets once again seeks to obscure a domestic male paradise with an intensifying of virile showmanship and violence. The result is a ruthless intimacy, in which physical abuse stands in for physical affection, and every display of affection must be counterbalanced by a display of sadism. Knobs told me that they were forced to run through the showers while the upperclassmen "guards" knocked the soap out of their hands and, when the knobs leaned over to retrieve it the upperclassmen would unzip their pants and yell, "Don't pick it up, don't pick it up! We'll use you like we used those girls!" A former Citadel Halloween tradition, of upperclassmen dressing up—mostly in diapers and women's clothes—and collecting candy treats from knobs, has given way to "tricks" of considerable violence. (One upperclassman told me of cadets who knocked dressers over on candy-dispensing cadets and then walked on top of them.) The administration tried, unsuccessfully, to put a stop to the whole affair; too many freshmen were getting injured. And the playful pat on the butt that served to usher cadets into the brotherhood has degenerated into more invasive acts. According to a recent graduate one company of cadets recently devised a regimen in which the older cadets tested sophomores nightly with increasingly painful treatments—beatings and stompings and so forth. The process, which they dubbed "Bananarama," culminated on a night in which an unpeeled banana was produced—and shoved into a cadet's anus.

Given this precarious dynamic, it is not surprising that in the past few years at The Citadel social rage has been directed toward any men who were perceived to be gay. Several young men who were suspected of homosexual inclinations were hounded out of the school. One cadet, Herbert Parker, who said that he was falsely accused of having a sexual encounter with a male janitor, recalled a year of total isolation—cadets refused to sit near him in the mess hall or in classes—and terror: incessant threatening phone calls and death threats. The cadets and the administration—which had responded to the report of his encounter by sending out a campus-security police car with lights flashing to question him—acted "like I had murdered someone."

The scapegoating reached such brutal proportions that the counselling center recently set up a sort of group-therapy session for the targeted young men, who are known as It, as in the game of tag.

One evening after the trial, I went over to the Treehouse, a "mixed" bar in Charleston, with an upstairs gay bar and nightly drag shows on the weekends. My intention was to ask about cadet violence against gay men. I presumed that on a campus where every second epithet was "faggot" such hate crimes were all but inevitable. There were indeed a few such cases, I learned, but the circumstances were different from what I had imagined. Nor were those cases the essence of my findings that evening.

"The proper terminology for The Citadel," a customer at the bar named Chris said, "is The Closet." Up and down the bar, heads bobbed in agreement. "They love faggots like me." What he meant by "like me," however, was not that he was gay. That night, he looked like a male model—sleek black hair and a handsome, chiselled face. But on the nights he was dressed for a performance he could pass for a woman. Arching an eyebrow, Chris said, "The cadets go for the drag queens."

Chris's observation was echoed in ensuing conversations in the bar. There are thousands of cadets, presumably, who have not dated drag queens, but in two visits to the Treehouse I could find only two drag queens, out of maybe a dozen, who did not tell me of dating a cadet—and that was only because these two found Citadel men "too emotional." Cadets can also occasionally be dangerous, Chris told me. "You can get the ones who are violent. They think they want it, then afterwards they turn on you, like you made them do it." Nonetheless, a drag queen who called himself Holly had been happily involved with a cadet for three years now. Marissa, another drag queen, the reigning "Miss Treehouse, 1993–94," had gone out with one cadet, broken up, and was now in the throes of a budding romance with another. A third drag queen, who asked to be identified as Tiffany, was known to be a favorite of cadets.

As Chris and I were talking that first night, a drag queen called Lownie wandered in and settled on a bar stool. Lownie delighted in the Corps of Cadets pageantry—especially the Friday dress parades. "The parades are a big thing with the queers in Charleston," he said. "We'll have a cocktail party and go over and watch the boys. It's a very Southern-'lady' thing to do." Years ago, Lownie had been a student at the College of Charleston when he met *his* Citadel lover, and they had begun covert assignations—communicating through notes slipped in little-used books in the Citadel library. The only drawback, Lownie said, was dealing with his lover's constant emotional anxiety over making the grade at The Citadel. He was, in fact, a model macho cadet: a Junior Sword Drill member, a regimental officer, and a "hang king," who could dangle interminably from a closet rack by his fingertips. Lownie, who found such records more amusing than impressive, grinned, and said, "I used to make him wear his shako"—The Citadel's military cap—"when we were having sex. It's manhood at its most."

Lownie said he could begin to fathom his cadet's intense attachment to The Citadel—an emotion that he likened to a love affair—because he himself had spent four years in the Air Force. "The day-to-day aspect of being in a military environment is that you run around in a little bit of clothing and you are being judged as to how good a man you are by doing women's work—pressing pants, sewing, polishing shoes. You are a *better* man if you have mastery of womanly arts. . . . The camaraderie doesn't get any stronger than when you are in the barracks, sitting around at the end of the day in your briefs and T's and dogtags—like a bunch of hausfraus, talking and gossiping." The military stage set offers a false front and a welcome trapdoor—an escape hatch from the social burdens of traditional masculinity. Behind the martial backdrop, Lownie said, "you don't have to be a bread-winner. You don't have to be a leader. You can play back seat. It's a great relief. You can act like a human being and not have to act like a man."

"You know what the [cadet] I'm seeing now said to me?" Tiffany said. We were sitting in the dressing room a couple of hours before the night's performance, and as Tiffany spoke he peered into an elaborate mirror set il-luminated with miniature movie-star lights, applying layer after layer of mascara and eyeliner with expert precision. "He said, 'You're more of a woman than a woman is.' And that's an exact quote." Tiffany stood up and struck a Southern belle pose by way of illustration. "I overexemplify every-thing a female is—my breasts, my hair, the way I hold myself." And who could better complete the hoopskirts picture than a fantasy gentleman in uniform?

Marissa, Miss Treehouse, looked up from his labors, painting row after row of fake nails with pink polish. "I love how they wear their caps slung low so you can't quite see their eyes," he said. "It's like all of us are female illusionists and they are male illusionists. A man in a uniform is a kind of dream."

Tiffany said, "For Halloween, you know what my cadet boyfriend wanted to dress as? A cadet."

The dressing-room scene before me, of a group of men tenderly helping each other get ready for the evening—an elaborate process of pinning and binding and stuffing—was not very different, in its way, from the footage in Norman Doucet's video of the cadets tucking in each other's shirts. As the drag queens conversed, they tossed stockings and Ace bandages and cos-metic bags back and forth. "Has anyone seen my mascara wand?" "O.K., who has the blush?" There was a homey comfort that reminded me of slum-ber parties when I was a girl, where we would put big pink spongy rollers in each other's hair and screech with laughter at the results. And suddenly it became obvious to me what was generating that void, that yearning, in the cadets' lives—and maybe in the lives of many American men. What was going on here was play—a kind of freedom and spontaneity that, in this cul-ture, only women are permitted.

No wonder men found their Citadels, their Treehouses, where the rules of gender could be bent or escaped. For the drag queens of the Treehouse, the distinctions between the sexes are a goof, to be endlessly manipulated with fun-house-mirror glee. For cadets, despite the play set of The Citadel and the dress-up braids and ribbons, the guarding of their treehouse is a dead-serious business. Still, undercover at The Citadel, the cadets have man-aged to create for themselves a world in which they get half the equation that Lownie described: they can "act like human beings" in the safety of the daily domestic life of the barracks. But, in return, the institution demands that they never cease to "act like a man"—a man of cold and rigid bearing, a man no more male than Tiffany's Southern belle is female, a man that no one, humanly, can be. That they must defend their inner humanity with outer brutality may say as much about the world outside The Citadel walls as about the world within them. The cadets feel called to defend those walls. Never mind that their true ideal may not be the vaunted one of martial masculinity, just as their true enemy is not Shannon Faulkner. The cadets at The Citadel feel that something about their life and routine is worthy on its merits and is endangered from without. And in that they may be right.   ■

■ *QUESTIONS FOR MAKING CONNECTIONS WITHIN THE READING* ■

1. In "The Naked Citadel," Susan Faludi provides a series of vignettes that describe life at the military school. Why does she present the vignettes in the order she does? Why does she start her article in Jane Bishop's classroom? Why does she then move to the courtroom? Make a chart that tracks the organization of Faludi's essay. What is the argument that Faludi is making by telling these vignettes in this order?

2. The sociologist Erving Goffman coined the term "total institutions" to describe places that become almost entirely self-enclosed and self-referential in their values and behaviors. Goffman's principal example was the mental asylum. Can we describe The Citadel accurately as a "total institution"? Are its values the product of its isolation, or does Faludi's account furnish evidence that the attitudes holding sway in The Citadel also persist outside the institution as well? Is The Citadel just an aberration, or does it tell us certain truths about our own society?

3. Faludi offers this overview of The Citadel:

> In the late-twentieth-century setting of The Citadel, in a time when extreme insecurity and confusion about masculinity's standing run rampant, the Corps of Cadets once again seeks to obscure a domestic male paradise with an intensifying of virile showmanship and violence. The result is a ruthless intimacy, in which physical abuse stands in for physical affection, and every display of affection must be counterbalanced by a display of sadism.

On the basis of the evidence Faludi provides, is this a fair assessment of the culture of The Citadel? What evidence confirms this assessment? What evidence might be said to complicate or even contradict it? What other explanations might we offer for events at The Citadel? Does masculinity have to occupy the central place in our analysis, or might other factors be more important?

■ *QUESTIONS FOR WRITING* ■

1. In what sense is Susan Faludi a feminist? If we define a feminist as someone who is specifically concerned with defending the rights of women,
does she qualify? Does she regard the rights of women as practically or
theoretically distinct from the rights of men? How about the needs and aspirations of women? Are these fundamentally different from the needs and
aspirations of men? Does Faludi see men as "oppressors of women"? Does
she imply that our society systematically empowers men while systematically disempowering women, or does disempowerment cross gender lines?

2. "The Naked Citadel" might be described as a case study of the relations
between sexuality and social structures. In what ways do social structures
shape sexuality at The Citadel? Does Faludi's account call into question
the belief in a single, natural form of male sexual expression? Is the problem with The Citadel that natural sexuality has been perverted by linking
it to relations of power? Can sexuality and power ever be separated?

■ *QUESTIONS FOR MAKING CONNECTIONS BETWEEN READINGS* ■

1. In "Immune to Reality," Daniel Gilbert sets out to create a theory of happiness, one that explains why humans, in general, are so unprepared to
predict and to pursue the material things and activities that lead to happiness. Does Gilbert's theory shed new light on the choices and the actions of the cadets at The Citadel? Would Gilbert's explanation for why
The Citadel continues to attract students—male and female—reinforce,
extend, or contradict Faludi's understanding? Write an essay about the
degree to which happiness, as Gilbert defines it, plays a role in education
inside and outside The Citadel.

2. In "When I Woke Up Tuesday Morning, It was Friday," from *The Myth of
Sanity*," Martha Stout explores the psychological dynamics of dissociation. According to Stout, the experience of trauma "changes the brain
itself." Under conditions of extreme pain or distress, the brain becomes
unable to organize experience "usefully" or to integrate new experience
with other, prior memories. Does it seem possible that dissociation plays
a role in the training of cadets at The Citadel? What circumstantial evidence can you find to support this claim, or to dispute it? Does Stout's account of dissociation help to explain why so few cadets rebel against the
treatment they receive? Is it possible that certain institutions use dissociation intentionally to weaken bonds sustained by affection and shared values? How might our society protect itself against the use of dissociation
as a political instrument?

DANIEL GILBERT

HISTORICALLY, THE STUDY of human psychology has tended to emphasize the negative. Scholars and practitioners of mental health focused on schizophrenia, depression, and other forms of psychological distress. In recent years, however, an interdisciplinary cohort of psychologists and other researchers have turned their attention to what turns out to be an equally baffling area: human happiness.

Among the leaders of this movement—sometimes called "positive psychology," or, more informally, "happiness studies"—is Daniel Gilbert, a professor of social psychology at Harvard University. Gilbert pioneered the field of affective forecasting, or the study of what people imagine their emotional states to be in the future given their uncertainty about what the future will bring. Having dropped out of high school to travel and write science fiction, Gilbert is well suited to help us understand the role emotions play when we make plans for the future. While living in Denver, Colorado, Gilbert tried to enroll in a creative writing course at a local community college. Turned away because of oversubscription, he decided to take the only open course: psychology. Realizing that psychology "wasn't about crazy people," but "about all of us," Gilbert stumbled onto the path that brought him to the present.

In his international bestseller *Stumbling on Happiness* (2006), Gilbert suggests that people suffer from "illusions of prospection" on top of illusions of perception (such as mirages) and illusions of retrospection (such as inaccurate memories) that psychologists have already covered. Through his experimental research, he discovered the following discrepancy: though few people seriously believe they can predict the future with much accuracy, many more believe they can accurately predict how they will feel about that future. Our predictions about future emotional states are often subject to "impact bias," which leads us to overestimate the intensity and the duration of emotional events both negative and positive.

Gilbert, Daniel. "Immune to Reality." *Stumbling on Happiness*. New York: Knopf, Random House, 2006.

Quotations are drawn from an interview conducted at SXSW available at <http://2006.sxsw .com/bits_n_bytes/pivot/entry.php?id=79#body> and from an interview conducted by Dave Weich of Powell's books at <http://www.powells.com/authors/danielgilbert. html>.

The chapter from *Stumbling on Happiness* included here, "Immune to Reality," offers just some of Gilbert's counterintuitive discoveries. Here we meet experimental subjects who are unable to predict their level of happiness just minutes into the future. Though we are not surprised by their inability to do so even in a controlled setting, we remain confident that we know ourselves well enough that the same discontinuity would not emerge. Gilbert also details the "psychological immune system" that activates when we suffer substantial emotional setbacks but not minor ones, resulting in surprising complacency in the face of significant blows but disproportionate responses in the face of trivial irritations. Gilbert's conclusions challenge the conventional ways we understand our mental well-being by showing just how poorly these conventions reflect the reality of emotional cognition. Through their work, Gilbert and the other champions of happiness studies are seeking to reshape how we go about the "pursuit of happiness."

■ ■

Immune to Reality

Upon my back, to defend my belly; upon my wit, to defend my wiles; upon my secrecy, to defend mine honesty; my mask, to defend my beauty.

SHAKESPEARE, *Troilus and Cressida*

Albert Einstein may have been the greatest genius of the twentieth century, but few people know that he came *this* close to losing that distinction to a horse. Wilhelm von Osten was a retired schoolteacher who in 1891 claimed that his stallion, whom he called Clever Hans, could answer questions about current events, mathematics, and a host of other topics by tapping the ground with his foreleg. For instance, when Osten would ask Clever Hans to add three and five, the horse would wait until his master had finished asking the question, tap eight times, then stop. Sometimes, instead of *asking* a question, Osten would write it on a card and hold it up for Clever Hans to read, and the horse seemed to understand written language every bit as well as it understood speech. Clever Hans didn't get *every* question right, of course, but he did much better than anyone else with hooves, and his public performances were so impressive that he soon became the toast of Berlin. But in 1904 the director of the Berlin Psychological Institute sent his student, Oskar Pfungst, to look into the matter more carefully, and Pfungst noticed that Clever Hans was much more likely to give the wrong answer when Osten was standing in back of the horse than in front of it, or when Osten himself did not know the answer to the question the horse had been asked. In a series of experiments, Clever Pfungst was able to show that Clever Hans could indeed read—but that what he could read was Osten's body language. When Osten bent slightly, Clever Hans would start tapping, and when Osten straightened up, or tilted his head a bit, or faintly raised an eyebrow, Clever Hans would stop. In other words, Osten was signaling Clever Hans to start and stop tapping at just the right moments to create the illusion of horse sense.

Clever Hans was no genius, but Osten was no fraud. Indeed, he'd spent years patiently talking to his horse about mathematics and world affairs, and he was genuinely shocked and dismayed to learn that he had been fooling himself, as well as everyone else. The deception was elaborate and effective, but it was perpetrated unconsciously, and in this Osten was not unique. When we expose ourselves to favorable facts, notice and remember favorable facts, and hold favorable facts to a fairly low standard of proof, we are generally no more aware of our subterfuge than Osten was of his. We may refer to the processes by which the psychological immune system does its job as "tactics" or "strategies," but these terms—with their inevitable connotations of planning and deliberation—should not cause us to think of people as manipulative schemers who are consciously *trying* to generate positive views of their own experience. On the contrary, research suggests that people are *typically unaware* of the reasons why they are doing what they are doing,[1] but when asked for a reason, they readily supply one.[2] For example, when volunteers watch a computer screen on which words appear for just a few milliseconds, they are unaware of seeing the words and are unable to guess which words they saw. But they are influenced by them. When the word *hostile* is flashed, volunteers judge others negatively.[3] When the word *elderly* is flashed, volunteers walk slowly.[4] When the word *stupid* is flashed, volunteers perform poorly on tests.[5] When these volunteers are later asked to explain *why* they judged, walked, or scored the way they did, two things happen: First, they don't know, and second, they do not say, "I don't know." Instead, their brains quickly consider the facts of which they *are* aware ("I walked slowly") and draw the same kinds of plausible but mistaken inferences about themselves that an observer would probably draw about them ("I'm tired").[6]

When we cook facts, we are similarly unaware of why we are doing it, and this turns out to be a good thing, because *deliberate* attempts to generate positive views ("There must be *something* good about bankruptcy, and I'm not leaving this chair until I discover it") contain the seeds of their own destruction. Volunteers in one study listened to Stravinsky's *Rite of Spring*.[7] Some were told to listen to the music, and others were told to listen to the music while consciously trying to be happy. At the end of the interlude, the volunteers who had tried to be happy were in a *worse* mood than were the volunteers who had simply listened to the music. Why? Two reasons. First, we may be able deliberately to generate positive views of our own experiences if we close our eyes, sit very still, and do nothing else,[8] but research suggests that if we become even slightly distracted, these deliberate attempts tend to backfire and we end up feeling worse than we did before.[9] Second, deliberate attempts to cook the facts are so transparent that they make us feel cheap. Sure, we *want* to believe that we're better off without the fiancée who left us standing at the altar, and we *will* feel better soon as we begin to discover facts that support this conclusion ("She was never really right for me, was she, Mom?"), but the process by which we discover those facts must *feel* like a discovery and not like a snow job. If we *see* ourselves cooking the facts ("If I phrase the question just this way and ask nobody but Mom, I stand a pretty good chance of having my favored conclusion confirmed"), then the jig is up and *self-deluded* joins *jilted* in our list of pitiful qualities. For positive views to be credible, they must be based on facts that we *believe* we have come upon honestly. We accomplish this by unconsciously cooking the facts and then consciously consuming them. The diner is in the dining room, but the chef is in the basement. The benefit of all this unconscious cookery is that it works; but the cost is that it makes us strangers to ourselves. Let me show you how.

Looking Forward to Looking Backward

To my knowledge, no one has ever done a systematic study of people who've been left standing at the altar by a cold-footed fiancé. But I'm willing to bet a good bottle of wine that if you rounded up a healthy sample of almost-brides and nearly grooms and asked them whether they would describe the incident as "the worst thing that ever happened to me" or "the best thing that ever happened to me," more would endorse the latter description than the former. And I'll bet an entire *case* of that wine that if you found a sample of people who'd never been through this experience and asked them to predict which of all their possible future experiences they are most likely to look back on as "the best thing that ever happened to me," not one of them will list "getting jilted." Like so many things, getting jilted is more painful in prospect and more rosy in retrospect. When we contemplate being hung out to dry this way, we naturally generate the most dreadful possible view of the experience; but once we've actually *been* heartbroken and humiliated in front of our family, friends, and florists, our brains begin shopping for a less dreadful view—and as we've seen, the human brain is one smart shopper. However, because our brains do their shopping unconsciously, we tend not to realize they will do it at all, hence we blithely assume that the dreadful view we have when we look forward to the event is the dreadful view we'll have when we look back on it. In short, we do not realize that our views will change because we are normally unaware of the processes that change them.

This fact can make it quite difficult to predict one's emotional future. In one study, volunteers were given the opportunity to apply for a good-paying job that involved nothing more than tasting ice cream and making up funny names for it.[10] The application procedure required the volunteer to undergo an on-camera interview. Some of the volunteers were told that their interview would be seen by a judge who had sole discretionary authority to decide whether they would be hired (judge group). Other volunteers were told that their interview would be seen by a jury whose members would vote to decide whether the volunteer should be hired (jury group). Volunteers in the jury group were told that as long as *one* juror voted for them, they would get the job—and thus the only circumstance under which they would *not* get the job was if the jury voted unanimously against them. All of the volunteers then underwent an interview, and all predicted how they would feel if they didn't get the job. A few minutes later, the researcher came into the room and explained apologetically that after careful deliberation, the judge or jury had decided that the volunteer just wasn't quite right for the job. The researcher then asked the volunteers to report how they felt.

The results of the study are shown in Figure 1. As the bars on the left show, volunteers in the two groups expected to feel equally unhappy. After all, rejection is a major whack on the nose, and we expect it to hurt whether the whacker is a judge, a jury, or a gang of Orthodox rabbis. And yet, as the bars on the right show, the whacks hurt more when they were administered by a jury than by a judge. Why? Well, just imagine that you've applied for a job as a swimsuit model, which requires that you don something skimpy and parade back and forth in front of some gimlet-eyed twit in a three-dollar suit. If the twit looked you over, shook his head, and said, "Sorry, but you're not model material," you'd probably feel bad. For a minute or two. But this is the sort of interpersonal rejection that everyone experiences from time to time, and after a few minutes, most of us get over it and on with our lives. We do this quickly because our psychological immune systems have no trouble finding ways to exploit the ambiguity of this experience and soften its sting: "The guy wasn't paying attention to my extraordinary pivot" or "He's one of those weirdos who prefers height to weight" or "I'm supposed to take fashion advice from a guy with a suit like *that?*"

But now imagine that you've just modeled the skimpy thing for a whole roomful of people—some men, some women, some old, some young—and they all look you over and shake their heads in unison. You'd probably feel bad. Truly bad. Humiliated, hurt, and confused. You'd probably hurry

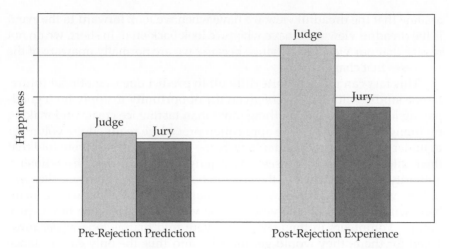

Figure 1   Volunteers were happier when they were rejected by a capricious judge than by a unanimous jury (*bars on right*). But they could not foresee this moment before it happened (*bars on left*).

offstage with a warm feeling in your ears, a tight feeling in your throat, and a wet feeling in your eyes. Being rejected by a large and diverse group of people is a demoralizing experience because it is so thoroughly unambiguous, and hence it is difficult for the psychological immune system to find a way to think about it that is both positive and credible. It's easy to blame failure on the eccentricities of a judge, but it's much more difficult to blame failure on the eccentricities of a unanimous jury. Claims such as "a synchronized mass blink caused ninety-four people to miss my pivot at precisely the same moment" are just not credible. Similarly, volunteers in this study found it easier to blame their rejection on an idiosyncratic judge than on a panel of jurors, which is why they felt worse when they were rejected by a jury.

Now, all this may seem painfully obvious to you as you contemplate the results of this study from the comfort of your sofa, but allow me to suggest that it is painfully obvious only after someone has taken pains to point it out to you. Indeed, if it were really painfully obvious, then why were a bunch of smart volunteers *unable to predict that it would happen just a few minutes before it did?* Why didn't the volunteers realize that they would have more success blaming a judge than a jury? Because when volunteers were asked to predict their emotional reactions to rejection, they imagined its sharp sting. Period. They did not go on to imagine how their brains might try to relieve that sting. Because they were unaware that they would alleviate their suffering by blaming those who caused it, it never occurred to them that they would be more successful if a single person were to blame rather than an entire group. Other studies have confirmed this general finding. For example, people *expect* to feel equally bad when a tragic accident is the result of human negligence as when it is the result of dumb luck, but they *actually* feel worse when luck is dumb and no one is blameworthy.[11]

Ignorance of our psychological immune systems causes us to mispredict the circumstances under which we will blame others, but it also causes us to mispredict the circumstances under which we will blame ourselves.[12] Who can forget the scene at the end of the 1942 film *Casablanca* in which Humphrey Bogart and Ingrid Bergman are standing on the tarmac as she tries to decide whether to stay in Casablanca with the man she loves or board the plane and leave with her husband? Bogey turns to Bergman and says: "Inside we both know you belong with Victor. You're part of his work, the thing that keeps him going. If that plane leaves the ground and you're not with him, you'll regret it. Maybe not today. Maybe not tomorrow. But soon and for the rest of your life."[13]

This thin slice of melodrama is among the most memorable scenes in the history of cinema—not because it is particularly well acted or particularly well written but because most of us have stood on that same runway from time to time. Our most consequential choices—whether to marry, have children, buy a house, enter a profession, move abroad—are often shaped by how we imagine our future regrets ("Oh no, I forgot to have a baby!"). Regret is an emotion we feel when we blame ourselves for unfortunate outcomes that might have been prevented had we only behaved differently in the past, and because that emotion is decidedly unpleasant, our behavior in the present is often designed to preclude it.[14] Indeed, most of us have elaborate theories about when and why people feel regret, and these theories allow us to avoid the experience. For instance, we expect to feel more regret when we learn about alternatives to our choices than when we don't,[15] when we accept bad advice than when we reject good advice,[16] when our bad choices are unusual rather than conventional,[17] and when we fail by a narrow margin rather than by a wide margin.[18]

But sometimes these theories are wrong. Consider this scenario. You own shares in Company A. During the past year you considered switching to stock in Company B but decided against it. You now find that you would have been better off by $1,200 if you had switched to the stock of Company B. You also owned shares in Company C. During the past year you switched to stock in Company D. You now find out that you'd have been better off by $1,200 if you kept your stock in Company C. Which error causes you more regret? Studies show that about nine out of ten people expect to feel more regret when they foolishly switch stocks than when they foolishly fail to switch stocks, because most people think they will regret foolish actions more than foolish inactions.[19] But studies also show that nine out of ten people are wrong. Indeed, in the long run, people of every age and in every walk of life seem to regret *not* having done things much more than they regret things they *did*, which is why the most popular regrets include not going to college, not grasping profitable business opportunities, and not spending enough time with family and friends.[20]

But why do people regret inactions more than actions? One reason is that the psychological immune system has a more difficult time manufacturing positive and credible views of inactions than of actions.[21] When our action causes us to accept a marriage proposal from someone who later becomes an axe murderer, we can console ourselves by thinking of all the things we learned from the experience ("Collecting hatchets is not a healthy hobby"). But when our inaction causes us to reject a marriage proposal from someone who later becomes a movie star, we can't console ourselves by thinking of all the things we learned from the experience because . . . well, there wasn't one. The irony is all too clear: Because we do not realize that our psychological immune systems can rationalize an excess of courage more easily than an excess of cowardice, we hedge our bets when we should blunder forward. As students of the silver screen recall, Bogart's admonition about future regret led Bergman to board the plane and fly away with her husband. Had she stayed with Bogey in Casablanca, she would probably have felt just fine. Not right away, perhaps, but soon, and for the rest of her life.

Little Triggers

Civilized people have learned the hard way that a handful of iniquitous individuals can often cause more death and destruction than an invading army. If an enemy were to launch hundreds of airplanes and missiles against the United States, the odds are that none would reach its target because an offensive strike of that magnitude would trigger America's defensive systems, which are presumably adequate to quash the threat. On the other hand, were an enemy to launch seven guys with baggy pants and baseball caps, those men might well reach their targets and detonate bombs, release toxins, or fly hijacked airplanes into tall buildings. Terrorism is a strategy based on the idea that the best offense is the one that fails to trigger the best defense, and small-scale incursions are less likely to set off the alarm bells than are large-scale assaults. Although it is possible to design a defensive system that counters even the smallest threat (e.g., electrified borders, a travel ban, electronic surveillance, random searches), such systems are extraordinarily costly, in terms of both the resources required to run them and the number of false alarms they produce. A system like that would be an exercise in overkill. To be effective, a defensive system must respond to threats; but to be practical, it must respond only to threats that exceed some *critical threshold*—which means that threats that fall short of the critical threshold may have a destructive potential that belies their diminutive size. Unlike large threats, small threats can sneak in under the radar.

The Intensity Trigger

The psychological immune system is a defensive system, and it obeys this same principle. When experiences make us feel sufficiently unhappy, the psychological immune system cooks facts and shifts blame in order to offer us a more positive view. But it doesn't do this *every* time we feel the slightest tingle of sadness, jealousy, anger, or frustration. Failed marriages and lost jobs are the kinds of large-scale assaults on our happiness that trigger our psychological defenses, but these defenses are not triggered by broken pencils, stubbed toes, or slow elevators. Broken pencils may be annoying, but they do not pose a grave threat to our psychological well-being and hence do not trigger our psychological defenses. The paradoxical consequence of this fact is that it is sometimes more difficult to achieve a positive view of a *bad* experience than of a *very bad* experience.

For example, volunteers in one study were students who were invited to join an extracurricular club whose initiation ritual required that they receive three electric shocks.[22] Some of the volunteers had a truly dreadful experience because the shocks they received were quite severe (severe-initiation group), and others had a slightly unpleasant experience because the shocks they received were relatively mild (mild-initiation group). Although you might expect people to dislike anything associated with physical pain, the volunteers in the severe-initiation group actually liked the club more. Because these volunteers suffered greatly, the intensity of their suffering triggered their defensive systems, which immediately began working to help them achieve a credible and positive view of their experience. It isn't easy to find such a view, but it can be done. For example, physical suffering is bad ("Oh my God, that *really* hurt!"), but it isn't *entirely* bad if the thing one suffers for is extremely valuable ("But I'm joining a *very* elite group of *very* special people"). Indeed, research shows that when people are given electric shocks, they actually feel *less pain* when they believe they are suffering for something of great value.[23] The intense shocks were unpleasant enough to trigger the volunteers' psychological defenses, but the mild shocks were not, hence the volunteers valued the club most when its initiation was most painful.[24] If you've managed to forgive your spouse for some egregious transgression but still find yourself miffed about the dent in the garage door or the trail of dirty socks on the staircase, then you have experienced this paradox.

Intense suffering triggers the very processes that eradicate it, while mild suffering does not, and this counterintuitive fact can make it difficult for us to predict our emotional futures. For example, would it be worse if your best friend insulted you or insulted your cousin? As much as you may like your cousin, it's a pretty good bet that you like yourself more, hence you probably think that it would be worse if the epithet were hurled your way. And you're right. It *would* be worse. At first. But if intense suffering triggers the psychological immune system and mild suffering does not, then over time you should be more likely to generate a positive view of an insult that was directed at you ("Felicia called me a pea-brain . . . boy, she can really crack me up sometimes") than one that was directed at your cousin ("Felicia called Cousin Dwayne a pea-brain . . . I mean, she's *right*, of course, but it wasn't very nice of her to say"). The irony is that you may ultimately feel better when you are the *victim* of an insult than when you are a *bystander* to it.

This possibility was tested in a study in which two volunteers took a personality test and then *one* of them received feedback from a psychologist.[25] The feedback was professional, detailed, and unrelentingly negative. For example, it contained statements such as "You have few qualities that distinguish you from others" and "People like you primarily because you don't threaten their competence." Both of the volunteers read the feedback and then reported how much they liked the psychologist who had written it. Ironically, the volunteer who was the *victim* of the negative feedback liked the psychologist *more* than did the volunteer who was merely a *bystander* to it. Why? Because bystanders were miffed ("Man, that was a really crummy thing to do to the other volunteer"), but they were not devastated, hence their psychological immune systems did nothing to ameliorate, their mildly negative feelings. But victims *were* devastated ("Yikes, I'm a certified loser!"), hence their brains quickly went shopping for a positive view of the experience ("But now that I think of it, that test could only provide a small glimpse into my very complex personality, so I rather doubt it means much"). Now here's the important finding: When a new group of volunteers was asked to *predict* how much they would like the psychologist, they predicted that they would like the psychologist *less* if they were victims than if they were bystanders. Apparently, people are not aware of the fact that their defenses are more likely to be triggered by intense than mild suffering, thus they mispredict their own emotional reactions to misfortunes of different sizes.

The Inescapability Trigger

Intense suffering is one factor that can trigger our defenses and thus influence our experiences in ways we don't anticipate. But there are others. For example, why do we forgive our siblings for behavior we would never tolerate in a friend? Why aren't we disturbed when the president does something that would have kept us from voting for him had he done it before the election? Why do we overlook an employee's chronic tardiness but refuse to hire a job seeker who is two minutes late for the interview? One possibility is that blood is thicker than water, flags were made to be rallied around, and first impressions matter most. But another possibility is that we are more likely to look for and find a positive view of the things we're *stuck with* than of the things we're not.[26] Friends come and go, and changing candidates is as easy as changing socks. But siblings and presidents are *ours,* for better or for worse, and there's not much we can do about it once they've been born or elected. When the experience we are having is not the experience we *want* to be having, our first reaction is to go out and have a different one, which is why we return unsatisfactory rental cars, check out of bad hotels, and stop hanging around with people who pick their noses in public. It is only when we cannot *change the experience* that we look for ways to *change our view of the experience,* which is why we love the clunker in the driveway, the shabby cabin that's been in the family for years, and Uncle Sheldon despite his predilection for nasal spelunking. We find silver linings only when we must, which is why people experience an increase in happiness when genetic tests reveal that they *don't* have a dangerous genetic defect, or when the tests reveal that they *do* have a dangerous genetic defect, but *not* when the tests are inconclusive.[27] We just can't make the best of a fate until it is inescapably, inevitably, and irrevocably ours.

Inescapable, inevitable, and irrevocable circumstances trigger the psychological immune system, but, as with the intensity of suffering, people do not always recognize that this will happen. For example, college students in one study signed up for a course in black-and-white photography.[28] Each student took a dozen photographs of people and places that were personally meaningful, then reported for a private lesson. In these lessons, the teacher spent an hour or two showing students how to print their two best photographs. When the prints were dry and ready, the teacher said that the student could keep one of the photographs but that the other would be kept on file as an example of student work. Some students (inescapable group) were told that once they had chosen a photograph to take home, they would not be allowed to change their minds. Other students (escapable group) were told that once they had chosen a photograph to take home, they would have several days to change their minds—and if they did, the teacher would gladly swap the photograph they'd taken home for the one they'd left behind. Students made their choices and took one of their photographs home. Several days later, the students responded to a survey asking them (among other things) how much they liked their photographs. The results showed that students in the escapable group liked their photograph *less* than did students in the inescapable group. Interestingly, when a new group of students was asked to *predict* how much they would like their photographs if they were or were not given the opportunity to change their minds, these students predicted that escapability would have no influence whatsoever on their satisfaction with the photograph. Apparently, inescapable circumstances trigger the psychological defenses that enable us to achieve positive views of those circumstances, but we do not anticipate that this will happen.

Our failure to anticipate that inescapability will trigger our psychological immune systems (hence promote our happiness and satisfaction) can cause us to make some painful mistakes. For example, when a new group of photography students was asked whether they would prefer to have or not to have the opportunity to change their minds about which photograph to keep, the vast majority preferred to have that opportunity—that is, the vast majority of students preferred to enroll in a photography course in which they would ultimately be dissatisfied with the photograph they produced. Why would anyone prefer less satisfaction to more? No one does, of course, but most people do seem to prefer more freedom to less. Indeed, when our freedom to make up our minds—or to change our minds once we've made them up—is threatened, we experience a strong impulse to reassert it,[29] which is why retailers sometimes threaten your freedom to own their products with claims such as "Limited stock" or "You must order by midnight tonight."[30] Our fetish for freedom leads us to patronize expensive department stores that allow us to return merchandise rather than attend auctions that don't, to lease cars at a dramatic markup rather than buying them at a bargain, and so on.

Most of us will pay a premium today for the opportunity to change our minds tomorrow, and sometimes it makes sense to do so. A few days spent test-driving a little red roadster tells us a lot about what it might be like to own one, thus it is sometimes wise to pay a modest premium for a contract that includes a short refund period. But if keeping our options open has benefits, it also has costs. Little red roadsters are naturally cramped, and while the committed owner will find positive ways to view that fact ("Wow! It feels like a fighter jet!"), the buyer whose contract includes an escape clause may not ("This car is so tiny. Maybe I should return it"). Committed owners attend to a car's virtues and overlook its flaws, thus cooking the facts to produce a banquet of satisfaction, but the buyer for whom escape is still possible (and whose defenses have not yet been triggered) is likely to evaluate the new car more critically, paying special attention to its imperfections as she tries to decide whether to keep it. The costs and benefits of freedom are clear—but alas, they are not equally clear: We have no trouble anticipating the advantages that freedom may provide, but we seem blind to the joys it can undermine.[31]

Explaining Away

If you've ever puked your guts out shortly after eating chili con carne and found yourself unable to eat it again for years, you have a pretty good idea of what it's like to be a fruit fly. No, fruit flies don't eat chili, and no, fruit flies don't puke. But they do associate their best and worst experiences with the circumstances that accompanied and preceded them, which allows them to seek or avoid those circumstances in the future. Expose a fruit fly to the odor of tennis shoes, give it a very tiny electric shock, and for the rest of its very tiny life it will avoid places that smell tennis-shoey. The ability to associate pleasure or pain with its circumstances is so vitally important that nature has installed that ability in every one of her creatures, from *Drosophila melanogaster* to Ivan Pavlov.

But if that ability is necessary for creatures like us, it certainly isn't sufficient, because the kind of learning it enables is far too limited. If an organism can do no more than associate particular experiences with particular circumstances, then it can learn only a very small lesson, namely, to seek or avoid those particular circumstances in the future. A well-timed shock may teach a fruit fly to avoid the tennis-shoe smell, but it won't teach it to avoid the smell of snowshoes, ballet slippers, Manolo Blahniks, or a scientist armed with a miniature stun gun. To maximize our pleasures and minimize our pains, we must be able to associate our experiences with the circumstances that produced them, but we must also be able to *explain* how and why those circumstances produced the experiences they did. If we feel nauseous after a few turns on the Ferris wheel and our explanation involves poor equilibrium, then we avoid Ferris wheels in the future—just as a fruit fly would. But unlike a fruit fly, we also avoid some things that are *not* associated with our nauseating experience (such as bungee jumping and sailboats) and we do *not* avoid some things that *are* associated with our nauseating experience (such as hurdy-gurdy music and clowns). Unlike a mere association, an explanation allows us to identify particular aspects of a circumstance (spinning) as the *cause* of our experience, and other aspects (music) as irrelevant. In so doing, we learn more from our upchucks than a fruit fly ever could.

Explanations allow us to make full use of our experiences, but they also change the nature of those experiences. As we have seen, when experiences are unpleasant, we quickly move to explain them in ways that make us feel better ("I didn't get the job because the judge was biased against people who barf on Ferris wheels"). And indeed, studies show that the mere act of explaining an unpleasant event can help to defang it. For example, simply writing about a trauma—such as the death of a loved one or a physical assault—can lead to surprising improvements in both subjective well-being and physical health (e.g., fewer visits to the physician and improved production of viral antibodies).[32] What's more, the people who experience the greatest benefit from these writing exercises are those whose writing contains an *explanation* of the trauma.[33]

But just as explanations ameliorate the impact of *unpleasant* events, so too do they ameliorate the impact of *pleasant* events. For example, college students volunteered for a study in which they believed they were interacting in an online chat room with students from other universities.[34] In fact, they were actually interacting with a sophisticated computer program that simulated the presence of other students. After the simulated students had provided the real student with information about themselves ("Hi, I'm Eva, and I like to do volunteer work"), the researcher pretended to ask the simulated students to decide which of the people in the chat room they liked most, to write a paragraph explaining why, and then to send it to that person. In just a few minutes, something remarkable happened: The real student received e-mail messages from *every one* of the simulated students indicating that they liked the real student best! For example, one simulated message read: "I just felt that something clicked between us when I read your answers. It's too bad we're not at the same school!" Another read: "You stood out as the one I would like the most. I was especially interested in the way you described your interests and values." A third read: "I wish I could talk with you directly because . . . I'd ask you if you like being around water (I love water-skiing) and if you like Italian food (it's my favorite)."

Now, here's the catch: Some real students (informed group) received e-mail that allowed them to know *which* simulated student wrote each of the messages, and other real students (uninformed group) received e-mail messages that had been stripped of that identifying information. In other words, every real student received exactly the same e-mail messages indicating that they had won the hearts and minds of all the simulated people in the chat room, but only real students in the informed group knew *which* simulated individual had written each of the messages. Hence, real students in the informed group were able to generate explanations for their good fortune ("Eva appreciates my values because we're both involved with Habitat for Humanity, and it makes sense that Catarina would mention Italian food"), whereas real students in the uninformed group were not ("Someone appreciates my values . . . I wonder who? And why would anyone mention Italian food?"). The researchers measured how happy the real students were immediately after receiving these messages and then again fifteen minutes later. Although real students in both groups were initially delighted to have been chosen as everyone's best friend, only the real students in the uninformed group remained delighted fifteen minutes later. If you've ever had a secret admirer, then you understand why real students in the uninformed group remained on cloud nine while real students in the informed group quickly descended to clouds two through five.

Unexplained events have two qualities that amplify and extend their emotional impact. First, they strike us as rare and unusual.[35] If I told you that my brother, my sister, and I were all born on the same day, you'd probably consider that a rare and unusual occurrence. Once I explained that we were triplets, you'd find it considerably less so. In fact, just about *any* explanation I offered ("By *same day* I meant we were all born on a Thursday" or "We were all delivered by cesarean section, so Mom and Dad timed our births for maximum tax benefits") would tend to reduce the amazingness of the coincidence and make the event seem more probable. Explanations allow us to understand how and why an event happened, which immediately allows us to see how and why it might happen again. Indeed, whenever we say that something *can't* happen—for example, mind reading or levitation or a law that limits the power of incumbents—we usually just mean that we'd have no way to explain it if it did. Unexplained events seem rare, and rare events naturally have a greater emotional impact than common events do. We are awed by a solar eclipse but merely impressed by a sunset despite the fact that the latter is by far the more spectacular visual treat.

The second reason why unexplained events have a disproportionate emotional impact is that we are especially likely to keep thinking about them. People spontaneously try to explain events,[36] and studies show that when people do not complete the things they set out to do, they are especially likely to think about and remember their unfinished business.[37] Once we explain an event, we can fold it up like freshly washed laundry, put it away in memory's drawer, and move on to the next one; but if an event defies explanation, it becomes a *mystery* or a *conundrum*—and if there's one thing we all know about mysterious conundrums, it is that they generally refuse to stay in the back of our minds. Filmmakers and novelists often capitalize on this fact by fitting their narratives with mysterious endings, and research shows that people are, in fact, more likely to keep thinking about a movie when they can't explain what happened to the main character. And if they *liked* the movie, this morsel of mystery causes them to remain happy longer.[38]

Explanation robs events of their emotional impact because it makes them seem likely and allows us to stop thinking about them. Oddly enough, an explanation doesn't actually have to *explain* anything to have these effects—it merely needs to *seem* as though it does. For instance, in one study, a researcher approached college students in the university library, handed them one of two cards with a dollar coin attached, then walked away. You'd probably agree that this is a curious event that begs for explanation. Both cards stated that the researcher was a member of the "Smile Society," which was devoted to "random acts of kindness." But one card also contained two extra phrases—"Who are we?" and "Why do we do this?" These empty phrases didn't really provide any new information, of course, but they made students *feel* as though the curious event had been explained ("Aha, *now* I understand why they gave me a dollar!"). About five minutes later, a different researcher approached the student and claimed to be doing a class project on "community thoughts and feelings." The researcher asked the student to complete some survey questions, one of which was "How positive or negative are you feeling right now?" The results showed that those students who had received a card with the pseudo-explanatory phrases felt less happy than those who had received a card without them. Apparently, even a fake explanation can cause us to tuck an event away and move along to the next one.

Uncertainty can preserve and prolong our happiness, thus we might expect people to cherish it. In fact, the opposite is generally the case. When a new group of students was asked which of the two cards [offering a free dollar] would make them happier, 75 percent chose the one with the meaningless explanation. Similarly, when a group of students was asked whether they would prefer to know or not know which of the simulated students had written each of the glowing reports in the online chat-room study, 100 percent chose to know. In both cases, students chose certainty over uncertainty and clarity over mystery—despite the fact that in both cases clarity and certainty had been shown to diminish happiness. The poet John Keats noted that whereas great authors are "capable of being in uncertainties, mysteries, doubts, without any irritable reaching after fact and reason," the rest of us are "incapable of remaining content with half-knowledge."[39] Our relentless desire to explain everything that happens may well distinguish us from fruit flies, but it can also kill our buzz.

Onward

The eye and the brain are conspirators, and like most conspiracies, theirs is negotiated behind closed doors, in the back room, outside of our awareness. Because we do not realize that we have generated a positive view of our current experience, we do not realize that we will do so again in the future. Not only does our naïveté cause us to overestimate the intensity and duration of our distress in the face of future adversity, but it also leads us to take actions that may undermine the conspiracy. We are more likely to generate a positive and credible view of an action than an inaction, of a painful experience than of an annoying experience, of an unpleasant situation that we cannot escape than of one we can. And yet, we rarely choose action over inaction, pain over annoyance, and commitment over freedom. The processes by which we generate positive views are many: We pay more attention to favorable information, we surround ourselves with those who provide it, and we accept it uncritically. These tendencies make it easy for us to explain unpleasant experiences in ways that exonerate us and make us feel better. The price we pay for our irrepressible explanatory urge is that we often spoil our most pleasant experiences by making good sense of them.   ∎

NOTES

The notes contain references to the scientific research that supports the claims I make in the text. Occasionally they contain some extra information that may be of interest but that is not essential to the argument. If you don't care about sources, aren't interested in nonessentials, and are annoyed by books that make you flip back and forth all the time, then be assured that the only important note in [this chapter] is this one.

1. T. D. Wilson, *Strangers to Ourselves: Discovering the Adaptive Unconscious* (Cambridge, Mass.: Harvard University Press, 2002); and J. A. Bargh and T. L. Chartrand, "The Unbearable Automaticity of Being," *American Psychologist* 54: 462–79 (1999).

2. R. E. Nisbett and T. D. Wilson, "Telling More Than We Can Know: Verbal Reports on Mental Processes," *Psychological Review* 84: 231–59 (1977); D. J. Bem, "Self-Perception

Theory," in *Advances in Experimental Social Psychology*, ed. L. Berkowitz, vol. 6 (New York: Academic Press, 1972), 1–62; M. S. Gazzaniga, *The Social Brain* (New York: Basic Books, 1985); and D. M. Wegner, *The Illusion of Conscious Will* (Cambridge, Mass.: MIT Press, 2003).

3. E. T. Higgins, W. S. Rholes, and C. R. Jones, "Category Accessibility and Impression Formation," *Journal of Experimental Social Psychology* 13: 141–54 (1977).

4. J. Bargh, M. Chen, and L. Burrows. "Automaticity of Social Behavior: Direct Effects of Trait Construct and Stereotype Activation on Action," *Journal of Personality and Social Psychology* 71: 230–44 (1996).

5. A. Dijksterhuis and A. van Knippenberg, "The Relation Between Perception and Behavior, or How to Win a Game of Trivial Pursuit," *Journal of Personality and Social Psychology* 74: 865–77 (1998).

6. Nisbett and Wilson, "Telling More Than We Can Know."

7. J. W. Schooler, D. Ariely, and G. Loewenstein, "The Pursuit and Assessment of Happiness Can Be Self-Defeating," in *The Psychology of Economic Decisions: Rationality and Well-Being*, ed. I. Brocas and J. Carillo, vol. 1 (Oxford: Oxford University Press, 2003).

8. K. N. Ochsner et al., "Rethinking Feelings: An fMRI Study of the Cognitive Regulation of Emotion," *Journal of Cognitive Neuroscience* 14: 1215–29 (2002).

9. D. M. Wegner, R. Erber, and S. Zanakos, "Ironic Processes in the Mental Control of Mood and Mood-Related Thought," *Journal of Personality and Social Psychology* 65: 1093–104 (1993); and D. M. Wegner, A. Broome, and S. J. Blumberg, "Ironic Effects of Trying to Relax Under Stress," *Behaviour Research and Therapy* 35: 11–21 (1997).

10. D. T. Gilbert et al., "Immune Neglect: A Source of Durability Bias in Affective Forecasting," *Journal of Personality and Social Psychology* 75: 617–38 (1998).

11. Ibid.

12. D. T. Gilbert et al., "Looking Forward to Looking Backward: The Misprediction of Regret," *Psychological Science* 15: 346–50 (2004).

13. M. Curtiz, *Casablanca*, Warner Bros., 1942.

14. T. Gilovich and V. H. Medvec, "The Experience of Regret: What, When, and Why," *Psychological Review* 102: 379–95 (1995); N. Roese, *If Only: How to Turn Regret into Opportunity* (New York: Random House 2004); G. Loomes and R. Sugden, "Regret Theory: An Alternative Theory of Rational Choice Under Uncertainty," *Economic Journal* 92: 805–24 (1982); and D. Bell, "Regret in Decision Making Under Uncertainty, *Operations Research* 20: 961–81 (1982).

15. I. Ritov and J. Baron, "Outcome Knowledge, Regret, and Omission Bias," *Organizational Behavior and Human Decision Processes* 64: 119–27 (1995); I. Ritov and J. Baron, "Probability of Regret: Anticipation of Uncertainty Resolution in Choice: Outcome Knowledge, Regret, and Omission Bias," *Organizational Behavior and Human Decision Processes* 66: 228–36 (1996); and M. Zeelenberg, "Anticipated Regret, Expected Feedback and Behavioral Decision Making," *Journal of Behavioral Decision Making* 12: 93–106 (1999).

16. M. T. Crawford et al., "Reactance, Compliance, and Anticipated Regret," *Journal of Experimental Social Psychology* 38: 56–63 (2002).

17. I. Simonson, "The Influence of Anticipating Regret and Responsibility on Purchase Decisions," *Journal of Consumer Research* 19: 105–18 (1992).

18. V. H. Medvec, S. F. Madey, and T. Gilovich, "When Less Is More: Counterfactual Thinking and Satisfaction Among Olympic Medalists," *Journal of Personality and Social*

Psychology 69: 603–10 (1995); and D. Kahneman and A: Tversky, "Variants of Uncertainty," *Cognition* 11: 143–57 (1982).

19. D. Kahneman and A. Tversky, "The Psychology of Preferences," *Scientific American* 246: 160–73 (1982).

20. Gilovich and Medvec, "The Experience of Regret."

21. T. Gilovich, V. H. Medvec, and S. Chen, "Omission, Commission, and Dissonance Reduction: Overcoming Regret in the Monty Hall Problem," *Personality and Social Psychology Bulletin* 21: 182–90 (1995).

22. H. B. Gerard and G. C. Mathewson, "The Effects of Severity of Initiation on Liking for a Group: A Replication," *Journal of Experimental Social Psychology* 2: 278–87 (1966).

23. P. G. Zimbardo, "Control of Pain Motivation by Cognitive Dissonance," *Science* 151: 217–19 (1966).

24. See also E. Aronson and J. Mills, "The Effect of Severity of Initiation on Liking for a Group," *Journal of Abnormal and Social Psychology* 59: 177–81 (1958); J. L. Freedman, "Long-Term Behavioral Effects of Cognitive Dissonance," *Journal of Experimental Social Psychology* 1: 145–55 (1965); D. R. Shaffer and C. Hendrick, "Effects of Actual Effort and Anticipated Effort on Task Enhancement," *Journal of Experimental Social Psychology* 7: 435–47 (1971); H. R. Arkes and C. Blumer; "The Psychology of Sunk Cost," *Organizational Behavior and Human Decision Processes* 35: 124–40 (1985); and J. T. Jost et al. "Social Inequality and the Reduction of Ideological Dissonance on Behalf of the System: Evidence of Enhanced System Justification Among the Disadvantaged," *European Journal of Social Psychology* 33: 13–36 (2003).

25. D. T. Gilbert et al., "The Peculiar Longevity of Things Not So Bad," *Psychological Science* 15: 14–19 (2004).

26. D. Frey et al., "Re-evaluation of Decision Alternatives Dependent upon the Reversibility of a Decision and the Passage of Time," *European Journal of Social Psychology* 14: 447–50 (1984); and D. Frey, "Reversible and Irreversible Decisions: Preference for Consonant Information as a Function of Attractiveness of Decision Alternatives," *Personality and Social Psychology Bulletin* 7: 621–26 (1981).

27. S. Wiggins et al., "The Psychological Consequences of Predictive Testing for Huntington's Disease," *New England Journal of Medicine* 327: 1401–5 (1992).

28. D. T. Gilbert, and J. E. J. Ebert, "Decisions and Revisions: The Affective Forecasting of Changeable Outcomes," *Journal of Personality and Social Psychology* 82: 503–14 (2002).

29. J. W. Brehm, *A Theory of Psychological Reactance* (New York: Academic Press, 1966).

30. R. B. Cialdini, *Influence: Science and Practice* (Glenview, Ill.: Scott, Foresman, 1985).

31. S. S. Iyengar and M. R. Lepper, "When Choice Is Demotivating: Can One Desire Too Much of a Good Thing?" *Journal of Personality and Social Psychology* 79: 995–1006 (2000); and B. Schwartz, "Self-Determination: The Tyranny of Freedom," *American Psychologist* 55: 79–88 (2000).

32. J. W. Pennebaker, "Writing About Emotional Experiences as a Therapeutic Process," *Psychological Science* 8: 162–66 (1997).

33. J. W. Pennebaker, T. J. Mayne, and M. E. Francis, "Linguistic Predictors of Adaptive Bereavement," *Journal of Personality and Social Psychology* 72: 863–71 (1997).

34. T. D. Wilson et al., "The Pleasures of Uncertainty: Prolonging Positive Moods in Ways People Do Not Anticipate," *Journal of Personality and Social Psychology* 88: 5–21 (2005).

35. B. Fischoff, "Hindsight ≠ foresight: The Effects of Outcome Knowledge on Judgment Under Uncertainty," *Journal of Experimental Psychology: Human Perception and*

Performance 1: 288–99 (1975); and C. A. Anderson, M. R. Lepper, and L. Ross, "Perseverance of Social Theories: The Role of Explanation in the Persistence of Discredited Information," *Journal of Personality and Social Psychology* 39: 1037–49 (1980).

36. B. Weiner, "'Spontaneous' Causal Thinking," *Psychological Bulletin* 97: 74–84 (1985); and R. R. Hassin, J. A. Bargh, and J. S. Uleman, "Spontaneous Causal Inferences," *Journal of Experimental Social Psychology* 38: 515–22 (2002).

37. B. Zeigarnik, "Das Behalten erledigter und unerledigter Handlungen," *Psychologische Forschung* 9: 1–85 (1927); and G. W. Boguslavsky, "Interruption and Learning," *Psychological Review* 58: 248–55 (1951).

38. Wilson et al., "Pleasures of Uncertainty."

39. J. Keats, letter to Richard Woodhouse, 27 October 1881, in *Selected Poems and Letters by John Keats*, ed. D. Bush (Boston: Houghton Mifflin, 1959).

■ *QUESTIONS FOR MAKING CONNECTIONS WITHIN THE READING* ■

1. Throughout "Immune to Reality," Gilbert describes mental operations in quotidian terms: the brain is "one smart shopper"; our brains are "conspirators"; once we come up with an explanation, "we can fold it up like freshly washed laundry, put it away in memory's drawer, and move on to the next one." Obviously, Gilbert is seeking to make his thoughts about human psychology readily accessible, but what exactly is he trying to convey with these descriptions? As you reread the essay, generate a list of the most significant images and analogies Gilbert uses to describe mental operations. What does this list tell you about Gilbert's theory of mind?

2. On the basis of the experiments and studies Gilbert presents, would you say that happiness is fundamentally an illusion? Or is it the *pursuit* of happiness that deserves to be reconsidered? If happiness is not something that we can pursue consciously, then how do we go about becoming happy? Should we be pursuing something other than happiness?

3. What is the meaning of "reality" at the end of Gilbert's discussion of our "psychological immune system"? What exactly is it that this system is designed to protect us from? Is the psychological immune system analogous to our biological immune system, or does it operate according to a different logic? Is the reality from which this system protects us ultimately an illusion? Or are psychological realities fundamentally different from material realities?

■ *QUESTIONS FOR WRITING* ■

1. The Declaration of Independence proclaims "all men" are "endowed by their Creator with certain unalienable rights," among them "Life, Liberty, and the pursuit of Happiness." What are the *political* implications of the research indicating that the pursuit of happiness is often misdirected

because people typically fail to recognize the conditions that will really make them happy? Does Gilbert's work suggest that Thomas Jefferson's proclamation was based on a false assumption? Is the pursuit of happiness properly understood as belonging in the same category as the rights guaranteed by the U.S. Constitution—namely, the rights of free speech and assembly, trial by jury, and so on? Or is the idea that the pursuit of happiness is an unalienable right itself an expression of a mistaken understanding of the necessary conditions for bringing about happiness?

2. What are the *economic* implications of Gilbert's argument? If people began to choose "action over inaction, pain over annoyance, and commitment over freedom," would the consumer economy survive? That is, is consumerism dependent upon our collective ignorance about the path to happiness, or is the hope that one's life will be improved by increased purchasing power itself a path to happiness? Is trying to be happy with what one has a form of action or inaction? If Gilbert is right that "explanation robs events of their emotional impact," what role does explanation play in consumer economy? Is a healthy economy dependent upon consumers who are well informed or consumers who are "immune to reality"?

▪ QUESTIONS FOR MAKING CONNECTIONS BETWEEN READINGS ▪

1. In "The Enhanced and the Unenhanced," Gregory Stock argues for a free market in what he calls "advanced germinal choice." Essentially, Stock means that people in the near future should have the freedom to provide their children with the genetic enhancements they deem to be most desirable. When we stop to consider Gilbert's argument, though, it may influence our response to Stock. Even if genetic technology can deliver on its bright promises, are the results likely to be as rewarding as Stock seems to believe? Is scientific progress driven by the workings of the psychological immune system, which "makes us strangers to ourselves"? Or, conversely, does genetic technology have the potential to redefine the workings of the psychological immune system, putting happiness at last within our reach?

2. What are the connections between the quest for happiness as Gilbert describes it and the cultivation of wisdom that Robert Thurman outlines? Is the Buddhist experience of nothingness a way of freeing people from the hot states in which we overestimate our own capacity to find satisfaction through changes in external conditions? Or is the notion of wisdom itself an example of the kind of unconscious fact cooking Gilbert describes, which generates happiness only if it feels "like a discovery and not like a snow job"? Is there a way to determine, finally, if another person is happy or wise? Can one know oneself with certainty in either of these systems?

MALCOLM GLADWELL

HOW DO CULTURES CHANGE? Is it possible to control and direct cultural change? These are the questions that most interest Malcolm Gladwell, author of the best-selling books, *The Tipping Point: How Little Things Can Make A Big Difference* (2000) and *Blink: The Power of Thinking Without Thinking* (2005). Gladwell first became interested in the notion that ideas might spread through culture like an epidemic while he was covering the AIDS epidemic for *The Washington Post*. In epidemiology, the "tipping point" is the moment when a virus reaches critical mass; AIDS, as Gladwell learned while doing his research, reached its tipping point in 1982, "when it went from a rare disease affecting a few gay men to a worldwide epidemic." Fascinated by this medical fact, Gladwell found himself wondering whether it also applied to the social world. That is, is there some specific point where a fad becomes a fashion frenzy? Where delinquency and mischief turn into a crime wave? Where repetition leads to understanding?

The Tipping Point is the result of Gladwell's effort to understand why some ideas catch on and spread like wildfire and others fail to attract widespread attention and wither on the vine. Drawing on psychology, sociology, and epidemiology, Gladwell examines events as diverse as Paul Revere's ride, the success of *Sesame Street* and *Blue's Clues*, and the precipitous decline in the crime rate in New York City, which is discussed in "The Power of Context," the chapter included here. Working across these wide-ranging examples, Gladwell develops an all-encompassing model of how cultural change occurs, a model that highlights the influential role that context plays in shaping and guiding human acts and intentions.

Gladwell returns to the idea of the tipping point from a different direction in *Blink*, his second book. Prompted by his experience with racial profiling (a fact he does not reveal until the book's conclusion), Gladwell delves into the

Gladwell, Malcolm. "The Power of Context: Bernie Goetz and the Rise and Fall of New York City Crime," *The Tipping Point: How Little Things Can Make a Big Difference*. Boston: Little, Brown, and Co., 2000. 133–68.

Quotations come from Author Q&A at <http://www.gladwell.com/books2.html> and interview by Toby Lester, *The Atlantic Unbound* <http://www.theatlantic.com/unbound/interviews/ba2000-03-29.htm>.

tipping point of human expertise. When, he asks, do we stop being amateurs and become experts, and what are the psychological consequences of this transition? As in *The Tipping Point*, Gladwell's journalistic skill allows him to weave together examples from every human endeavor, from art criticism to simulated warfare to relationship therapy to taste testing.

Gladwell was born in England, grew up in Canada, and graduated with a degree in history from the University of Toronto in 1984. After spending over a decade as a science writer and New York bureau chief for *The Washington Post*, Gladwell joined the staff of *The New Yorker* in 1996. At *The New Yorker*, Gladwell is able to continue exploring his diverse interests; he sees himself as "a kind of translator between the academic and nonacademic worlds. There's just all sorts of fantastic stuff out there, but there's not nearly enough time and attention paid to that act of translation. Most people leave college in their early twenties, and that ends their exposure to the academic world. To me that's a tragedy."

The Power of Context

Bernie Goetz and the Rise and Fall of New York City Crime

1.

On December 22, 1984, the Saturday before Christmas, Bernhard Goetz left his apartment in Manhattan's Greenwich Village and walked to the IRT subway station at Fourteenth Street and Seventh Avenue. He was a slender man in his late thirties, with sandy-colored hair and glasses, dressed that day in jeans and a windbreaker. At the station, he boarded the number two downtown express train and sat down next to four young black men. There were about twenty people in the car, but most sat at the other end, avoiding the four teenagers, because they were, as eyewitnesses would say later, "horsing around" and "acting rowdy." Goetz seemed oblivious. "How are ya?" one of the four, Troy Canty, said to Goetz, as he walked in. Canty was lying almost prone on one of the subway benches. Canty and another of the teenagers, Barry Allen, walked up to Goetz and asked him for five dollars. A third youth, James Ramseur, gestured toward a suspicious-looking bulge in his pocket, as if he had a gun in there.

"What do you want?" Goetz asked.

"Give me five dollars," Canty repeated.

Goetz looked up and, as he would say later, saw that Canty's "eyes were shiny, and he was enjoying himself. . . . He had a big smile on his face," and somehow that smile and those eyes set him off. Goetz reached into his pocket and pulled out a chrome-plated five-shot Smith and Wesson .38, firing at each of the four youths in turn. As the fourth member of the group, Darrell Cabey, lay screaming on the ground, Goetz walked over to him and said, "You seem all right. Here's another," before firing a fifth bullet into Cabey's spinal cord and paralyzing him for life.

In the tumult, someone pulled the emergency brake. The other passengers ran into the next car, except for two women who remained riveted in panic. "Are you all right?" Goetz asked the first, politely. Yes, she said. The second woman was lying on the floor. She wanted Goetz to think she was dead. "Are you all right?" Goetz asked her, twice. She nodded yes. The conductor, now on the scene, asked Goetz if he was a police officer.

"No," said Goetz. "I don't know why I did it." Pause. "They tried to rip me off."

The conductor asked Goetz for his gun. Goetz declined. He walked through the doorway at the front of the car, unhooked the safety chain, and jumped down onto the tracks, disappearing into the dark of the tunnel.

In the days that followed, the shooting on the IRT caused a national sensation. The four youths all turned out to have criminal records. Cabey had been arrested previously for armed robbery, Canty for theft. Three of them had screwdrivers in their pockets. They seemed the embodiment of the kind of young thug feared by nearly all urban-dwellers, and the mysterious gunman who shot them down seemed like an avenging angel. The tabloids dubbed Goetz the "Subway Vigilante" and the "Death Wish Shooter." On radio call-in shows and in the streets, he was treated as a hero, a man who had fulfilled the secret fantasy of every New Yorker who had ever been mugged or intimidated or assaulted on the subway. On New Year's Eve, a week after the shooting, Goetz turned himself in to a police station in New Hampshire. Upon his extradition to New York City, the *New York Post* ran two pictures on its front page: one of Goetz, handcuffed and head bowed, being led into custody, and one of Troy Canty—black, defiant, eyes hooded, arms folded—being released from the hospital. The headline read, "Led Away in Cuffs While Wounded Mugger Walks to Freedom." When the case came to trial, Goetz was easily acquitted on charges of assault and attempted murder. Outside Goetz's apartment building, on the evening of the verdict, there was a raucous, impromptu street party.

2.

The Goetz case has become a symbol of a particular, dark moment in New York City history, the moment when the city's crime problem reached epidemic proportions. During the 1980s, New York City averaged well over

2,000 murders and 600,000 serious felonies a year. Underground, on the subways, conditions could only be described as chaotic. Before Bernie Goetz boarded the number two train that day, he would have waited on a dimly lit platform, surrounded on all sides by dark, damp, graffiti-covered walls. Chances are his train was late, because in 1984 there was a fire somewhere on the New York system every day and a derailment every other week. Pictures of the crime scene, taken by police, show that the car Goetz sat in was filthy, its floor littered with trash and the walls and ceiling thick with graffiti, but that wasn't unusual because in 1984 every one of the 6,000 cars in the Transit Authority fleet, with the exception of the midtown shuttle, was covered with graffiti—top to bottom, inside and out. In the winter, the cars were cold because few were adequately heated. In the summer, the cars were stiflingly hot because none were air-conditioned. Today, the number two train accelerates to over 40 miles an hour as it rumbles toward the Chambers Street express stop. But it's doubtful Goetz's train went that fast. In 1984, there were 500 "red tape" areas on the system—places where track damage had made it unsafe for trains to go more than 15 miles per hour. Fare-beating was so commonplace that it was costing the Transit Authority as much as $150 million in lost revenue annually. There were about 15,000 felonies on the system a year—a number that would hit 20,000 a year by the end of the decade—and harassment of riders by panhandlers and petty criminals was so pervasive that ridership of the trains had sunk to its lowest level in the history of the subway system. William Bratton, who was later to be a key figure in New York's successful fight against violent crime, writes in his autobiography of riding the New York subways in the 1980s after living in Boston for years, and being stunned at what he saw:

> After waiting in a seemingly endless line to buy a token, I tried to put a coin into a turnstile, and found it had been purposely jammed. Unable to pay the fare to get into the system, we had to enter through a slam gate being held open by a scruffy-looking character with his hand out; having disabled the turnstiles, he was now demanding that riders give him their tokens. Meanwhile, one of his cohorts had his mouth on the coin slots, sucking out the jammed coins and leaving his slobber. Most people were too intimidated to take these guys on: Here, take the damned token, what do I care? Other citizens were going over, under, around, or through the stiles for free. It was like going into the transit version of Dante's *Inferno*.

This was New York City in the 1980s, a city in the grip of one of the worst crime epidemics in its history. But then, suddenly and without warning, the epidemic tipped. From a high in 1990, the crime rate went into precipitous decline. Murders dropped by two-thirds. Felonies were cut in half. Other cities saw their crime drop in the same period. But in no place did the level of violence fall farther or faster. On the subways, by the end of the decade, there were 75 percent fewer felonies than there had been at the decade's start. In 1996, when Goetz went to trial a second time, as the defendant in a civil suit brought by Darrell Cabey, the case was all but ignored by the press, and Goetz himself seemed almost an anachronism. At a time when New York had become the safest big city in the country, it seemed hard to remember precisely what it was that Goetz had once symbolized. It was simply inconceivable that someone could pull a gun on someone else on the subway and be called a hero for it. . . .

3.

During the 1990s violent crime declined across the United States for a number of fairly straightforward reasons. The illegal trade in crack cocaine, which had spawned a great deal of violence among gangs and drug dealers, began to decline. The economy's dramatic recovery meant that many people who might have been lured into crime got legitimate jobs instead, and the general aging of the population meant that there were fewer people in the age range—males between eighteen and twenty-four—that is responsible for the majority of all violence. The question of why crime declined in New York City, however, is a little more complicated. In the period when the New York epidemic tipped down, the city's economy hadn't improved. It was still stagnant. In fact, the city's poorest neighborhoods had just been hit hard by the welfare cuts of the early 1990s. The waning of the crack cocaine epidemic in New York was clearly a factor, but then again, it had been in steady decline well before crime dipped. As for the aging of the population, because of heavy immigration to New York in the 1980s, the city was getting younger in the 1990s, not older. In any case, all of these trends are long-term changes that one would expect to have gradual effects. In New York the decline was anything but gradual. Something else clearly played a role in reversing New York's crime epidemic.

The most intriguing candidate for that "something else" is called the Broken Windows theory. Broken Windows was the brainchild of the criminologists James Q. Wilson and George Kelling. Wilson and Kelling argued that crime is the inevitable result of disorder. If a window is broken and left unrepaired, people walking by will conclude that no one cares and no one is in charge. Soon, more windows will be broken, and the sense of anarchy will spread from the building to the street on which it faces, sending a signal that anything goes. In a city, relatively minor problems like graffiti, public disorder, and aggressive panhandling, they write, are all the equivalent of broken windows, invitations to more serious crimes:

> Muggers and robbers, whether opportunistic or professional, believe they reduce their chances of being caught or even identified if they operate on streets where potential victims are already intimidated by prevailing

conditions. If the neighborhood cannot keep a bothersome panhandler from annoying passersby, the thief may reason, it is even less likely to call the police to identify a potential mugger or to interfere if the mugging actually takes place.

This is an epidemic theory of crime. It says that crime is contagious—just as a fashion trend is contagious—that it can start with a broken window and spread to an entire community. The Tipping Point in this epidemic, though, isn't a particular kind of person. . . . It's something physical like graffiti. The impetus to engage in a certain kind of behavior is not coming from a certain kind of person but from a feature of the environment.

In the mid-1980s Kelling was hired by the New York Transit Authority as a consultant, and he urged them to put the Broken Windows theory into practice. They obliged, bringing in a new subway director by the name of David Gunn to oversee a multibillion-dollar rebuilding of the subway system. Many subway advocates, at the time, told Gunn not to worry about graffiti, to focus on the larger questions of crime and subway reliability, and it seemed like reasonable advice. Worrying about graffiti at a time when the entire system was close to collapse seems as pointless as scrubbing the decks of the *Titanic* as it headed toward the icebergs. But Gunn insisted. "The graffiti was symbolic of the collapse of the system," he says. "When you looked at the process of rebuilding the organization and morale, you had to win the battle against graffiti. Without winning that battle, all the management reforms and physical changes just weren't going to happen. We were about to put out new trains that were worth about ten million bucks apiece, and unless we did something to protect them, we knew just what would happen. They would last one day and then they would be vandalized."

Gunn drew up a new management structure and a precise set of goals and timetables aimed at cleaning the system line by line, train by train. He started with the number seven train that connects Queens to midtown Manhattan, and began experimenting with new techniques to clean off the paint. On stainless-steel cars, solvents were used. On the painted cars, the graffiti were simply painted over. Gunn made it a rule that there should be no retreat, that once a car was "reclaimed" it should never be allowed to be vandalized again. "We were religious about it," Gunn said. At the end of the number one line in the Bronx, where the trains stop before turning around and going back to Manhattan, Gunn set up a cleaning station. If a car came in with graffiti, the graffiti had to be removed during the changeover, or the car was removed from service. "Dirty" cars, which hadn't yet been cleansed of graffiti, were never to be mixed with "clean" cars. The idea was to send an unambiguous message to the vandals themselves.

"We had a yard up in Harlem on one hundred thirty-fifth Street where the trains would lay up over night," Gunn said. "The kids would come the first night and paint the side of the train white. Then they would come the next night, after it was dry, and draw the outline. Then they would come the third night and color it in. It was a three-day job. We knew the kids would be working on one of the dirty trains, and what we would do is wait for them to finish their mural. Then we'd walk over with rollers and paint it over. The kids would be in tears, but we'd just be going up and down, up and down. It was a message to them. If you want to spend three nights of your time vandalizing a train, fine. But it's never going to see the light of day."

Gunn's graffiti cleanup took from 1984 to 1990. At that point, the Transit Authority hired William Bratton to head the transit police, and the second stage of the reclamation of the subway system began. Bratton was, like Gunn, a disciple of Broken Windows. He describes Kelling, in fact, as his intellectual mentor, and so his first step as police chief was as seemingly quixotic as Gunn's. With felonies—serious crimes—on the subway system at an all-time high, Bratton decided to crack down on fare-beating. Why? Because he believed that, like graffiti, fare-beating could be a signal, a small expression of disorder that invited much more serious crimes. An estimated 170,000 people a day were entering the system, by one route or another, without paying a token. Some were kids, who simply jumped over the turnstiles. Others would lean backward on the turnstiles and force their way through. And once one or two or three people began cheating the system, other people—who might never otherwise have considered evading the law—would join in, reasoning that if some people weren't going to pay, they shouldn't either, and the problem would snowball. The problem was exacerbated by the fact fare-beating was not easy to fight. Because there was only $1.25 at stake, the transit police didn't feel it was worth their time to pursue it, particularly when there were plenty of more serious crimes happening down on the platform and in the trains.

Bratton is a colorful, charismatic man, a born leader, and he quickly made his presence felt. His wife stayed behind in Boston, so he was free to work long hours, and he would roam the city on the subway at night, getting a sense of what the problems were and how best to fight them. First, he picked stations where fare-beating was the biggest problem, and put as many as ten policemen in plainclothes at the turnstiles. The team would nab fare-beaters one by one, handcuff them, and leave them standing, in a daisy chain, on the platform until they had a "full catch." The idea was to signal, as publicly as possible, that the transit police were now serious about cracking down on fare-beaters. Previously, police officers had been wary of pursuing fare-beaters because the arrest, the trip to the station house, the filling out of necessary forms, and the waiting for those forms to be processed took an entire day—all for a crime that usually merited no more than a slap on the wrist. Bratton retrofitted a city bus and turned it into a rolling station house, with its own fax machines, phones, holding pen, and fingerprinting facilities. Soon the turnaround time on an arrest was down to an hour. Bratton also insisted that a check be run on all those arrested. Sure enough, one out of seven arrestees had an outstanding warrant for a previous crime, and one out of twenty was carrying a weapon of some sort. Suddenly it wasn't hard to convince police officers that tackling fare-beating made sense. "For the cops it was a bonanza," Bratton writes. "Every arrest was like opening a box of Cracker Jack. What kind of toy am I going to get? Got a gun? Got a knife? Got a warrant? Do we have a murderer here? . . . After a while the bad guys wised up and began to leave their weapons home and pay their fares." Under Bratton, the number of ejections from subway stations—for drunkenness, or improper behavior—tripled within his first few months in office. Arrests for misdemeanors, for the kind of minor offenses that had gone unnoticed in the past, went up fivefold between 1990 and 1994. Bratton turned the transit police into an organization focused on the smallest infractions, on the details of life underground.

After the election of Rudolph Giuliani as mayor of New York in 1994, Bratton was appointed head of the New York City Police Department, and he applied the same strategies to the city at large. He instructed his officers to crack down on quality-of-life crimes: on the "squeegee men" who came up to drivers at New York City intersections and demanded money for washing car windows, for example, and on all the other above-ground equivalents of turnstile-jumping and graffiti. "Previous police administration had been handcuffed by restrictions," Bratton says. "We took the handcuffs off. We stepped up enforcement of the laws against public drunkenness and public urination and arrested repeat violators, including those who threw empty bottles on the street or were involved in even relatively minor damage to property. . . . If you peed in the street, you were going to jail." When crime began to fall in the city—as quickly and dramatically as it had in the subways—Bratton and Giuliani pointed to the same cause. Minor, seemingly insignificant quality-of-life crimes, they said, were Tipping Points for violent crime.

Broken Windows theory and the Power of Context are one and the same. They are both based on the premise that an epidemic can be reversed, can be tipped, by tinkering with the smallest details of the immediate environment. This is, if you think about it, quite a radical idea. Think back, for instance, to the encounter between Bernie Goetz and those four youths on the subway: Allen, Ramseur, Cabey, and Canty. At least two of them, according to some reports, appear to have been on drugs at the time of the incident. They all came from the Claremont Village housing project in one of the worst parts of the South Bronx. Cabey was, at the time, under indictment for armed robbery. Canty had a prior felony arrest for possession of stolen property. Allen had been previously arrested for attempted assault. Allen, Canty, and Ramseur also all had misdemeanor convictions, ranging from criminal mischief to petty larceny. Two years after the Goetz shooting, Ramseur was sentenced to twenty-five years in prison for rape, robbery, sodomy, sexual abuse, assault, criminal use of a firearm, and possession of stolen property. It's hard to be surprised when people like this wind up in the middle of a violent incident.

Then there's Goetz. He did something that is completely anomalous. White professionals do not, as a rule, shoot young black men on the subway. But if you look closely at who he was, he fits the stereotype of the kind of person who ends up in violent situations. His father was a strict disciplinarian with a harsh temper, and Goetz was often the focus of his father's rage. At school, he was the one teased by classmates, the last one picked for school games, a lonely child who would often leave school in tears. He worked, after graduating from college, for Westinghouse, building nuclear submarines. But he didn't last long. He was constantly clashing with his superiors over what he saw as shoddy practices and corner-cutting, and sometimes broke company and union rules by doing work that he was contractually forbidden to do. He took an apartment on Fourteenth Street in Manhattan, near Sixth Avenue, on a stretch of city block that was then heavy with homelessness and drug dealing. One of the doormen in the building, with whom Goetz was close, was beaten badly by muggers. Goetz became obsessed with cleaning up the neighborhood. He complained endlessly about a vacant newsstand near his building, which was used by vagrants as a trash bin and stank of urine. One night, mysteriously, it burned down, and the next day Goetz was out on the street sweeping away the debris. Once at a community meeting, he said, to the shock of others in the room, "The only way we're going to clean up this street is to get rid of the spics and niggers." In 1981, Goetz was mugged by three black youths as he entered the Canal Street station one afternoon. He ran out of the station with the three of them in pursuit. They grabbed the electronics equipment he was carrying, beat him, and threw him up against a plate-glass door, leaving him with permanent damage to his chest. With the help of an off-duty sanitation worker, Goetz managed to subdue one of his three attackers. But the experience left him embittered. He had to spend six hours in the station house, talking to police, while his assailant was released after two hours and charged, in the end, with only a misdemeanor. He applied to the city for a gun permit. He was turned down. In September 1984, his father died. Three months later, he sat down next to four black youths on the subway and started shooting.

Here, in short, was a man with an authority problem, with a strong sense that the system wasn't working, who had been the recent target of humiliation. Lillian Rubin, Goetz's biographer, writes that his choice to live on Fourteenth Street could hardly have been an accident. "For Bernie," she writes, "there seems to be something seductive about the setting. Precisely because of its deficits and discomforts, it provided him with a comprehensible target for the rage that lives inside him. By focusing it on the external world, he need not deal with his internal one. He rails about the dirt, the noise, the drunks, the crime, the pushers, the junkies. And all with good reason." Goetz's bullets, Rubin concludes, were "aimed at targets that existed as much in his past as in the present."

If you think of what happened on the number two train this way, the shooting begins to feel inevitable. Four hoodlums confront a man with apparent psychological problems. That the shooting took place on the subway seems incidental. Goetz would have shot those four kids if he had been sitting in a Burger King. Most of the formal explanations we use for criminal behavior follow along the same logic. Psychiatrists talk about criminals as people with stunted psychological development, people who have had pathological relationships with their parents, who lack adequate role models. There is a relatively new literature that talks about genes that may or may not dispose certain individuals to crime. On the popular side, there are endless numbers of books by conservatives talking about crime as a consequence of moral failure—of communities and schools and parents who no longer raise children with a respect for right and wrong. All of those theories are essentially ways of saying that the criminal is a personality type—a personality type distinguished by an insensitivity to the norms of normal society. People with stunted psychological development don't understand how to conduct healthy relationships. People with genetic predispositions to violence fly off the handle when normal people keep their cool. People who aren't taught right from wrong are oblivious to what is and what is not appropriate behavior. People who grow up poor, fatherless, and buffeted by racism don't have the same commitment to social norms as those from healthy middle-class homes. Bernie Goetz and those four thugs on the subway were, in this sense, prisoners of their own, dysfunctional, world.

But what do Broken Windows and the Power of Context suggest? Exactly the opposite. They say that the criminal—far from being someone who acts for fundamental, intrinsic reasons and who lives in his own world—is actually someone acutely sensitive to his environment, who is alert to all kinds of cues, and who is prompted to commit crimes based on his perception of the world around him. That is an incredibly radical—and in some sense unbelievable—idea. There is an even more radical dimension here. The Power of Context is an environmental argument. It says that behavior is a function of social context. But it is a very strange kind of environmentalism. In the 1960s, liberals made a similar kind of argument, but when they talked about the importance of environment they were talking about the importance of fundamental social factors: crime, they said, was the result of social injustice, of structural economic inequities, of unemployment, of racism, of decades of institutional and social neglect, so that if you wanted to stop crime you had to undertake some fairly heroic steps. But the Power of Context says that what really matters is little things. The Power of Context says that the showdown on the subway between Bernie Goetz and those four youths had very little to do, in the end, with the tangled psychological pathology of Goetz, and very little as well to do with the background and poverty of the four youths who accosted him, and everything to do with the message sent by the graffiti on the walls and the disorder at the turnstiles. The Power of Context says you don't have to solve the big problems to solve crime. You can prevent crimes just by scrubbing off graffiti and arresting fare-beaters. . . . This is what I meant when I called the Power of Context a radical theory. Giuliani and Bratton—far from being conservatives, as they are commonly identified—actually represent on the question of crime the most extreme liberal position imaginable, a position so extreme that it is almost impossible to accept. How can it be that what was going on in Bernie Goetz's head doesn't matter? And if it is really true that it doesn't matter, why is that fact so hard to believe?

4.

[Elsewhere], . . . I talked about two seemingly counterintuitive aspects of persuasion. One was the study that showed how people who watched Peter Jennings on ABC were more likely to vote Republican than people who watched either Tom Brokaw or Dan Rather because, in some unconscious way, Jennings was able to signal his affection for Republican candidates. The second study showed how people who were charismatic could—without saying anything and with the briefest of exposures—infect others with their emotions. The implications of those two studies go to the heart of the Law of the Few, because they suggest that what we think of as inner states—preferences and emotions—are actually powerfully and imperceptibly influenced by seemingly inconsequential personal influences, by a newscaster we watch for a few minutes a day or by someone we sit next to, in silence, in a two-minute experiment. The essence of the Power of Context is that the same thing is true for certain kinds of environments—that in ways that we don't necessarily appreciate, our inner states are the result of our outer circumstances. The field of psychology is rich with experiments that demonstrate this fact. . . .

In the early 1970s, a group of social scientists at Stanford University, led by Philip Zimbardo, decided to create a mock prison in the basement of the university's psychology building. They took a thirty-five-foot section of corridor and created a cell block with a prefabricated wall. Three small, six- by nine-foot cells were created from laboratory rooms and given steel-barred, black-painted doors. A closet was turned into a solitary confinement cell. The group then advertised in the local papers for volunteers, men who would agree to participate in the experiment. Seventy-five people applied, and from those Zimbardo and his colleagues picked the 21 who appeared the most normal and healthy on psychological tests. Half of the group were chosen, at random, to be guards, and were given uniforms and dark glasses and told that their responsibility was to keep order in the prison. The other half were told that they were to be prisoners. Zimbardo got the Palo Alto

Police Department to "arrest" the prisoners in their homes, cuff them, bring them to the station house, charge them with a fictitious crime, fingerprint them, then blindfold them and bring them to the prison Psychology Department basement. Then they were stripped and given a prison uniform to wear, with a number on the front and back that was to serve as their only means of identification for the duration of their incarceration.

The purpose of the experiment was to try to find out why prisons are such nasty places. Was it because prisons are full of nasty people, or was it because prisons are such nasty environments that they make people nasty? In the answer to that question is obviously the answer to the question posed by Bernie Goetz and the subway cleanup, which is how much influence does immediate environment have on the way people behave? What Zimbardo found out shocked him. The guards, some of whom had previously identified themselves as pacifists, fell quickly into the role of hard-bitten disciplinarians. The first night they woke up the prisoners at two in the morning and made them do pushups, line up against the wall, and perform other arbitrary tasks. On the morning of the second day, the prisoners rebelled. They ripped off their numbers and barricaded themselves in their cells. The guards responded by stripping them, spraying them with fire extinguishers, and throwing the leader of the rebellion into solitary confinement. "There were times when we were pretty abusive, getting right in their faces and yelling at them," one guard remembers. "It was part of the whole atmosphere of terror." As the experiment progressed, the guards got systematically crueler and more sadistic. "What we were unprepared for was the intensity of the change and the speed at which it happened," Zimbardo says. The guards were making the prisoners say to one another they loved each other, and making them march down the hallway, in handcuffs, with paper bags over their heads. "It was completely the opposite from the way I conduct myself now," another guard remembers. "I think I was positively creative in terms of my mental cruelty." After 36 hours, one prisoner began to get hysterical, and had to be released. Four more then had to be released because of "extreme emotional depression, crying, rage, and acute anxiety." Zimbardo had originally intended to have the experiment run for two weeks. He called it off after six days. "I realize now," one prisoner said after the experiment was over, "that no matter how together I thought I was inside my head, my prisoner behavior was often less under my control than I realized." Another said: "I began to feel that I was losing my identity, that the person I call ———, the person who volunteered to get me into this prison (because it was a prison to me, it still is a prison to me, I don't regard it as an experiment or a simulation . . .) was distant from me, was remote, until finally I wasn't that person. I was 416. I was really my number and 416 was really going to have to decide what to do."

Zimbardo's conclusion was that there are specific situations so powerful that they can overwhelm our inherent predispositions. The key word here is "situation." Zimbardo isn't talking about environment, about the major external influences on all of our lives. He's not denying that how we are raised by our parents affects who we are, or that the kinds of schools we went to, the friends we have, or the neighborhoods we live in affect our behavior. All of these things are undoubtedly important. Nor is he denying that our genes play a role in determining who we are. Most psychologists believe that nature—genetics—accounts for about half of the reason why we tend to act the way we do. His point is simply that there are certain times and places and conditions when much of that can be swept away, that there are instances where you can take normal people from good schools and happy families and good neighborhoods and powerfully affect their behavior merely by changing the immediate details of their situation. . . .

The mistake we make in thinking of character as something unified and all-encompassing is very similar to a kind of blind spot in the way we process information. Psychologists call this tendency the Fundamental Attribution Error (FAE), which is a fancy way of saying that when it comes to interpreting other people's behavior, human beings invariably make the mistake of overestimating the importance of fundamental character traits and underestimating the importance of the situation and context. We will always reach for a "dispositional" explanation for events, as opposed to a contextual explanation. In one experiment, for instance, a group of people are told to watch two sets of similarly talented basketball players, the first of whom are shooting baskets in a well-lighted gym and the second of whom are shooting baskets in a badly lighted gym (and obviously missing a lot of shots). Then they are asked to judge how good the players were. The players in the well-lighted gym were considered superior. In another example, a group of people are brought in for an experiment and told they are going to play a quiz game. They are paired off and they draw lots. One person gets a card that says he or she is going to be the "Contestant." The other is told he or she is going to be the "Questioner." The Questioner is then asked to draw up a list of ten "challenging but not impossible" questions based on areas of particular interest or expertise, so someone who is into Ukrainian folk music might come up with a series of questions based on Ukrainian folk music. The questions are posed to the Contestant, and after the quiz is over, both parties are asked to estimate the level of general knowledge of the other. Invariably, the Contestants rate the Questioners as being a lot smarter than they themselves are.

You can do these kinds of experiments a thousand different ways and the answer almost always comes out the same way. This happens even when you give people a clear and immediate environmental explanation of the behavior they are being asked to evaluate: that the gym, in the first case, has few lights on; that the Contestant is being asked to answer the most impossibly biased and rigged set of questions. In the end, this doesn't make much difference. There is something in all of us that makes us instinctively want to explain the world around us in terms of people's essential attributes: he's a better basketball player, that person is smarter than I am.

We do this because . . . we are a lot more attuned to personal cues than contextual cues. The FAE also makes the world a much simpler and more understandable place. . . . The psychologist Walter Mischel argues that the human mind has a kind of "reducing valve" that "creates and maintains the perception of continuity even in the face of perpetual observed changes in actual behavior." He writes:

> When we observe a woman who seems hostile and fiercely independent some of the time but passive, dependent and feminine on other occasions, our reducing valve usually makes us choose between the two syndromes. We decide that one pattern is in the service of the other, or that both are in the service of a third motive. She must be a really castrating lady with a façade of passivity—or perhaps she is a warm, passive-dependent woman with a surface defense of aggressiveness. But perhaps nature is bigger than our concepts and it is possible for the lady to be a hostile, fiercely indepen- dent, passive, dependent, feminine, aggressive, warm, castrating person all- in-one. Of course which of these she is at any particular moment would not be random or capricious—it would depend on who she is with, when, how, and much, much more. But each of these aspects of her self may be a quite genuine and real aspect of her total being.

Character, then, isn't what we think it is or, rather, what we want it to be. It isn't a stable, easily identifiable set of closely related traits, and it only seems that way because of a glitch in the way our brains are organized. Character is more like a bundle of habits and tendencies and interests, loosely bound together and dependent, at certain times, on circumstance and context. The reason that most of us seem to have a consistent character is that most of us are really good at controlling our environment. . . .

5.

Some years ago two Princeton University psychologists, John Darley and Daniel Batson, decided to conduct a study inspired by the biblical story of the Good Samaritan. As you may recall, that story, from the New Testament Gospel of Luke, tells of a traveler who has been beaten and robbed and left for dead by the side of the road from Jerusalem to Jericho. Both a priest and a Levite—worthy, pious men—came upon the man but did not stop, "passing by on the other side." The only man to help was a Samaritan—the member of a despised minority—who "went up to him and bound up his wounds" and took him to an inn. Darley and Batson decided to replicate that study at the Princeton Theological Seminary. This was an experiment very much in the tradition of the FAE, and it is an important demonstration of how the Power of Context has implications for the way we think about social epidemics of all kinds, not just violent crime.

Darley and Batson met with a group of seminarians, individually, and asked each one to prepare a short, extemporaneous talk on a given biblical theme, then walk over to a nearby building to present it. Along the way to the presentation, each student ran into a man slumped in an alley, head down, eyes closed, coughing and groaning. The question was, who would stop and help? Darley and Batson introduced three variables into the experiment, to make its results more meaningful. First, before the experiment even started, they gave the students a questionnaire about why they had chosen to study theology. Did they see religion as a means of personal and spiritual fulfillment? Or were they looking for a practical tool for finding meaning in everyday life? Then they varied the subject of the theme the students were asked to talk about. Some were asked to speak on the relevance of the professional clergy to the religious vocation. Others were given the parable of the Good Samaritan. Finally, the instructions given by the experimenters to each student varied as well. In some of the cases, as he sent the students on their way, the experimenter would look at his watch and say, "Oh, you're late. They were expecting you a few minutes ago. We'd better get moving." In other cases, he would say, "It will be a few minutes before they're ready for you, but you might as well head over now."

If you ask people to predict which seminarians played the Good Samaritan (and subsequent studies have done just this) their answers are highly consistent. They almost all say that the students who entered the ministry to help people and those reminded of the importance of compassion by having just read the parable of the Good Samaritan will be the most likely to stop. Most of us, I think, would agree with those conclusions. In fact, neither of those factors made any difference. "It is hard to think of a context in which norms concerning helping those in distress are more salient than for a person thinking about the Good Samaritan, and yet it did not significantly increase helping behavior," Darley and Batson concluded. "Indeed, on several occasions, a seminary student going to give his talk on the parable of the Good Samaritan literally stepped over the victim as he hurried on his way." The only thing that really mattered was whether the student was in a rush. Of the group that was, 10 percent stopped to help. Of the group who knew they had a few minutes to spare, 63 percent stopped.

What this study is suggesting, in other words, is that the convictions of your heart and the actual contents of your thoughts are less important, in the end, in guiding your actions than the immediate context of your behavior. The words "Oh, you're late" had the effect of making someone who was ordinarily compassionate into someone who was indifferent to suffering—of turning someone, in that particular moment, into a different person. Epidemics are, at their root, about this very process of transformation. When we are trying to make an idea or attitude or product tip, we're trying to change our audience in some small yet critical respect: we're trying to infect them, sweep them up in our epidemic, convert them from hostility to acceptance. That can be done through the influence of special kinds of people, people of extraordinary personal connection. That's the Law of the Few. It can be done by changing the content of communication, by making a message so memorable that it sticks in someone's mind and compels them to action. That is the Stickiness Factor. I think that both of those laws make intuitive sense. But we need to remember that small changes in context can be just as important in tipping epidemics, even though that fact appears to violate some of our most deeply held assumptions about human nature.

This does not mean that our inner psychological states and personal histories are not important in explaining our behavior. An enormous percentage of those who engage in violent acts, for example, have some kind of psychiatric disorder or come from deeply disturbed backgrounds. But there is a world of difference between being inclined toward violence and actually committing a violent act. A crime is a relatively rare and aberrant event. For a crime to be committed, something extra, something additional, has to happen to tip a troubled person toward violence, and what the Power of Context is saying is that those Tipping Points may be as simple and trivial as everyday signs of disorder like graffiti and fare-beating. The implications of this idea are enormous. The previous notion that disposition is everything—that the cause of violent behavior is always "sociopathic personality" or "deficient superego" or the inability to delay gratification or some evil in the genes—is, in the end, the most passive and reactive of ideas about crime. It says that once you catch a criminal you can try to help him get better—give him Prozac, put him in therapy, try to rehabilitate him—but there is very little you can do to prevent crime from happening in the first place. . . .

Once you understand that context matters, however, that specific and relatively small elements in the environment can serve as Tipping Points, that defeatism is turned upside down. Environmental Tipping Points are things that we can change: we can fix broken windows and clean up graffiti and change the signals that invite crime in the first place. Crime can be more than understood. It can be prevented. There is a broader dimension to this. Judith Harris has convincingly argued that peer influence and community influence are more important than family influence in determining how children turn out. Studies of juvenile delinquency and high school drop-out rates, for example, demonstrate that a child is better off in a good neighborhood and a troubled family than he or she is in a troubled neighborhood and a good family. We spend so much time celebrating the importance and power of family influence that it may seem, at first blush, that this can't be true. But in reality it is no more than an obvious and commonsensical extension of the Power of Context, because it says simply that children are powerfully shaped by their external environment, that the features of our immediate social and physical world—the streets we walk down, the people we encounter—play a huge role in shaping who we are and how we act. It isn't just serious criminal behavior, in the end, that is sensitive to environmental cues, it is all behavior. Weird as it sounds, if you add up the meaning of the Stanford prison experiment and the New York subway experiment, they suggest that it is possible to be a better person on a clean street or in a clean subway than in one littered with trash and graffiti.

"In a situation like this, you're in a combat situation," Goetz told his neighbor Myra Friedman, in an anguished telephone call just days after the shooting. "You're not thinking in a normal way. Your memory isn't even working normally. You are so hyped up. Your vision actually changes. Your field of view changes. Your capabilities change. What you are capable of changes." He acted, Goetz went on, "viciously and savagely. . . . If you corner a rat and you are about to butcher it, okay? The way I responded was viciously and savagely, just like that, like a rat."

Of course he did. He was in a rat hole.   ■

■ *QUESTIONS FOR MAKING CONNECTIONS WITHIN THE READING* ■

1. "The Power of Context" is one of the middle chapters in Malcolm Gladwell's book, *The Tipping Point: How Little Things Can Make a Big Difference*. In "The Power of Context," Gladwell refers to the three principles that govern what he calls "the epidemic transmission" of an idea: the Law of the Few, the Stickiness Factor, and the Power of Context. He provides thumbnail sketches of the first two principles in this chapter, along with an elaboration of the Power of Context. What is "the Law of the Few"? What is "the Stickiness Factor"? How much can you piece together about the first two principles from what Gladwell presents in "The Power of Context"?

2. Gladwell states that the "Broken Windows theory and the Power of Context are one and the same." What is the "Broken Windows theory" of crime? How would one go about testing this theory? What other theories are available to explain the cause of crime? Does it matter which theory one accepts?

3. Why is it a mistake to think of "character as something unified and all-encompassing"? If we accept the alternative, namely, that character is fragmented and situation specific, what follows? How is this meant to change one's understanding of criminals and their behavior? Of law-abiding citizens and their behavior?

■ *QUESTIONS FOR WRITING* ■

1. Toward the end of "The Power of Context," Gladwell asserts that his discussion of the relationship between criminal activity and local context has implications that "are enormous." Gladwell leaves it to his readers to spell

out these implications. How would our social structure, our criminal system, our modes of education have to change if we abandoned what Gladwell terms our "most passive and reactive ideas about crime"?

2. Gladwell argues that "small changes in context" can play a major role in determining whether an idea takes off or disappears without a trace. This fact, he goes on, "appears to violate some of our most deeply held assumptions about human nature." What does "human nature" mean, if one accepts the argument Gladwell makes in "The Power of Context"? Is it possible to create any form of human behavior just by manipulating the contextual background? Does Gladwell's view suggest that humans are more free than previously thought or that their behavior is more fully determined than previously thought possible?

■ *QUESTIONS FOR MAKING CONNECTIONS BETWEEN READINGS* ■

1. Drawing on Darley and Batson's Good Samaritan study, Gladwell finds evidence that "the convictions of your heart and the actual contents of your thoughts are less important, in the end, in guiding your actions than the immediate context of your behavior." The challenge here is defining what counts as one's "immediate context." Does the generation you belong to count as an immediate context? Explore this possibility and its implications by turning to Jean Twenge's description of the characteristics and qualities of Generation Me. What relationship, if any, is there between the influence of membership in a generation and the Power of Context, as Gladwell describes it?

2. In "The Naked Citadel," Susan Faludi provides a rich description of how lives are lived in an alternate social structure—the military academy. Does Malcolm Gladwell's account help to explain why Shannon Faulkner wasn't welcomed into the academy? Did Faulkner's appearance cause the academy to "tip"? Does Gladwell's theory have any predictive value? That is, could it tell us, ahead of time, whether the academy would be transformed by being required to admit women?

WILLIAM GREIDER

WILLIAM GREIDER, PROMINENT political journalist and author, has spent much of the past two decades writing about politics and the economy. A former editor at *Rolling Stone* and *The Washington Post*, Greider now writes regularly on economic matters for *The Nation*. To date, he has published six books that challenge mainstream assumptions about how the economy works: *The Education of David Stockman and Other Americans* (1982); *Secrets of the Temple: How the Federal Reserve Runs the Country* (1987); *Who Will Tell the People: The Betrayal of American Democracy* (1992); *One World, Ready or Not: The Manic Logic of Global Capitalism* (1997); *Fortress America: The American Military and the Consequences of Peace* (1999); and, most recently, *The Soul of Capitalism: Opening Paths to a Moral Economy* (2003), from which the following chapter is drawn.

Whether his topic is the Federal Reserve, the new media's coverage of economic policy, the spread of global capitalism, or the workings of the military's large-scale acquisitions programs, Greider writes with an eye toward exposing the tensions that exist between the theory of a free market and the actual practices of the regulatory agencies, bankers, and financial investors who drive the capitalist enterprise. More interested in reform than revolution, Greider has consistently sought to use his work as a reporter to educate his readers about the excesses of capitalism and to argue for changes in policy and practice that will allow for the creation of what he calls a "moral economy." In bidding us to consider the human consequences of the economy's inequities, Greider seeks not to dismantle capitalism but rather, as he puts it, to show that is it still possible for citizens to "change the economic system's operating values."

Greider, William. "Work Rules." *The Soul of Capitalism: Opening Paths to a Moral Economy.* New York: Simon and Schuster, 2003. 49–74.

Biographical information and quote come from William Greider's home page <http://www.williamgreider.com/about/>.

Work Rules

Yes, the country is fabulously rich in material terms, but are Americans really free? The question itself sounds like civic heresy. It offends national pride and the promise of liberty expressed in our founding documents, but also runs counter to the twentieth-century history of political accomplishments that greatly expanded individual rights to cover once excluded groups. Yet the disturbing contradictions are visible everyday when people go to work. The loss of freedom goes largely unnoticed because it is so routinely part of their lives.

In pursuit of "earning a living" most Americans go to work for someone else and thereby accept the employer's right to command their behavior in intimate detail. At the factory gate or the front office, people implicitly forfeit claims to self-direction and are typically barred from participating in the important decisions that govern their daily efforts. Most employees lose any voice in how the rewards of the enterprise are distributed, the surplus wealth their own work helped to create. Basic rights the founders said were inalienable—free speech and freedom of assembly, among others—are effectively suspended, consigned to the control of others. In some ways, the employee also surrenders essential elements of self.

This stark imbalance of power is embedded in the standard terms of employment and properly described as a master-servant relationship, as economist David Ellerman puts it. Stripped of social coloring and modern legal restraints, the arrangement for work in contemporary America resembles the same terms that functioned during feudalism. But this is more than an echo from distant times. The employment system is the defining structure for maintaining a still dominant hierarchy among citizens, those with stunted rights and those with expansive power over others. Centuries ago, the feudal lord owned the land and all who worked or lived on his land were subject to his rule. In the present, these terms are typically assumed, less bluntly and brutally, by the firm that operates the factory, shop or office. Individual freedom, equitable relationships, and self-empowered lives are severely compromised still.

The description sounds too harsh, of course, because people in workplaces develop their own informal accommodations that soften the everyday interactions among them. The actual circumstances of work vary dramatically across different companies and sectors, from free-spirited and highly collaborative firms to the harsh systems of clockwork supervision that oppressively monitor every move and moment in a worker's day. For most Americans, nevertheless, the underlying reality is this: The terms of their rights, the quality of their work life, the tangible and intangible rewards are determined at the discretion of the employer. For better and for worse. Under feudalism, there were kind and caring lords and there were abusive lords. Either way, no one doubted his power to command the serfs.

Anyone may test this proposition for themselves. Ask yourself if it sounds right, ask others. Is work in America organized around a master-servant relationship? In my occasional random samplings, I have yet to encounter anyone who thinks the premise is wrong. Some pause to ponder the matter. Others respond instantly, of course. Isn't that obvious? I have put the question to managers and owners as well as rank-and-file employees; neither group wishes to argue the basic point. A recognition of these underlying terms seems jarring only because the relationship is so deeply internalized in nearly everyone's life expectations, just the way things are and probably immutable (unless one aspires to become the boss). Thus, despite great leaps forward in technological invention and productive efficiency, despite the rising abundance and various civil protections, the economic realm of work continues to function in distinctly premodern terms—master and servant—an arrangement that sets limits on human liberty as surely as the laws and the Constitution.

I start from this fundamental proposition because it is a bedrock source for so many of the largest discontents and disorders that continue to accompany the capitalist process in America, despite the presence of general prosperity. It is from this malformed power relationship that workers encounter often cruel confinements on their larger lives, the inequities and inequalities that warp and divide. The authorities typically attribute these consequences to "market forces," an abstraction that sounds neutral and objective. But the outcomes also emanate, more concretely, from a top-heavy structure of command and control in which those down below have little or no capacity to appeal or resist.

This feudal remnant helps to explain a lot about American life. It is an important subtext, though not the only one, for the persistent and growing inequalities of income and wealth, a lopsided and self-interested distribution of rewards by those in charge that redundantly favors those who already have great accumulations. It produces many stunting effects on people's life experiences that show up as stressful demands and insecurities imposed upon workers, often ensnaring well-paid professionals as well. A lack of voice and influence obviously injures people in the lower tiers most severely, but also spreads general damage—beyond the money—for many others who experience the deteriorating content of their own work. The inherent qualities and challenges in one's work—the source of much personal satisfaction and self-meaning—often are reengineered for greater efficiency, thereby degrading and sometimes destroying the coherence and integrity of what people do. The inner narrative of one's life often is embedded in one's work, in the satisfying routines and sense of fulfillment, in the sheer pleasure of doing things well. For many Americans, that story has been obliterated in the present age.

Social consequences flow from these conditions in many different directions: the longer working hours that tear up family life and weaken community; a broadening sense of sullen resignation that may feed social resentments and acquisitive envy; the continuing conflicts pitting workers against coworkers or against larger interests of the community. The most serious consequence, however, is political, not personal. It is the deleterious influence upon democracy itself.

Elaine Bernard of Harvard's trade union program explained the connection: "As power is presently distributed, workplaces are factories of authoritarianism polluting our democracy. Citizens cannot spend eight hours a day obeying orders and being shut out of important decisions affecting them, and then be expected to engage in a robust, critical dialogue about the structure of our society. Indeed, in the latter part of this [past] century, instead of the workplace becoming more democratic, the hierarchical corporate workplace model [came] to dominate the rest of society."

Where did citizens learn the resignation and cynicism that leads them to withdraw as active citizens? They learned it at the office; they learned it on the shop floor. This real-life education in who has power and who doesn't creates a formidable barrier to ever establishing an authentic democracy in which Americans are genuinely represented and engaged. The socialization of powerlessness is probably far more damaging to politics than the special-interest campaign money or the emptiness of television advertising. Indeed, both of those malign influences feed off the disillusionment.

Statistics do not capture the texture of these confinements very well. And sweeping generalizations are always misleading or wrong, given the vast diversity in Americans' work experiences. To make the point concretely, let me flash through some snapshots from American workplaces.

In Baltimore, Maryland, a service technician named Joseph Bryant is fired after twenty-four years with Bell Atlantic (now Verizon) because he refuses to work overtime on weekdays. Bryant couldn't stay late on the job. As a single parent, he had to pick up his kids from school by 6:00 P.M. His supervisors are unyielding. Bell Atlantic "rationalized" its workforce, reduced employment by 15 percent, and instructed the others to pick up the slack by working longer hours. Overtime pay is actually cheaper (more efficient) for a firm than hiring additional workers who collect full benefits. Bryant's union, the Communications Workers of America, wins his job back—one small victory for family life.

Middle-level managers, though presumably more powerful, frequently resent their unionized subordinates who seem to enjoy better job security and protections, according to Professor Russell L. Ackoff of the Wharton School of Business. When managements attempt to encourage greater teamwork—the celebrated Quality of Work Life movement—reforms are often sabotaged by midlevel personnel who were ignored in the discussions. "Their quality of work life is often worse than that of production workers,"

Ackoff explains. While genuine progress has been achieved by many companies, Ackoff cautions: "The QWL movement has not died, but it is in a coma."

In Georgetown, Kentucky, a young "team leader" at Toyota's plant denounces inhumane conditions at the factory, regularly rated the most efficient auto assembly plant in North America. "What I think we have here is a high-priced sweatshop," Tracy Giles tells me. "Four team members in my area were out of work for shoulder surgery. If you're a temp worker and you're injured, which happens a lot, you are sent home and there's another person waiting in line to get the job." At one point, a new time-motion study raised the output goals and speeded up assembly at his workstation where the workers lift forty-pound modules sixty-five times an hour. "We couldn't keep up, and my team members were practically passing out," he says. "I can't stand it; it makes me sick to my stomach. For me, as team leader, it's more of a moral dilemma than anything else."

In the little town of Martinsville, Virginia, one man announces that he has held forty-six jobs in the last three years. He has the pay stubs to prove it. He is a temp worker and the town of 14,000 has nine temporary employment agencies that hire out labor for a few days, a few weeks or months, to do low-wage assembly and packaging jobs. The transaction is more like a short-term rental, only it involves human labor instead of equipment, because the agency collects an overhead fee for each hour of work, ranging from 35 to 45 percent of the wage. Employers are willing to pay a higher cost for temp laborers because they are disposable. "We call it pimping people out," says Suzie Qusenberry, "because that's really what it is. 'I'm going to pimp you out for $8 an hour and all you're going to get is $5.35.' They take the money and you do the work. Isn't that just like pimping?"

If one jumps from a depressed backwater in Virginia to the leading edge of American industry, the fabulous, wealth-creating center known as Silicon Valley, there is a similar snapshot in high-tech production. Temp jobs are the valley's sixth-largest job sector. Major names like Hewlett Packard, Sun, and Apple "outsource" work to smaller component suppliers where the average wages are 30 percent lower. Until the high-tech bust halted expansion, the "virtual employer" was the area's second-fastest-growing source of employment. At one time, Microsoft in Seattle had a third of its employees on temp status, long-term employees who call themselves "permatemps" and wear orange badges instead of the regulars' corporate blue. Nearly 30 percent of American workers are now employed in so-called "nonstandard" jobs: temp workers, part-timers, contract employees, on-call and day laborers, or the self-employed. A minor portion have skill specialties and high-end wages. Most experience the opposite.

Efficiency obliterates identity, the sense of self-meaning in work, and not just for temp jobs or assembly lines. In Puget Sound, Boeing's 20,000 engineers and technicians staged a successful forty-day strike, but the central issue was not money. "Why the heck did we strike? At the highest level, it really was about respect, respect for what engineers do," says Charles Bofferding, executive director of the Seattle Professional Engineer Employees Association. A new, computerized design system was gumming up production. The white-collar engineers weren't consulted, though they possess intimate, problem-solving knowledge of how to build jet aircraft. "They did it the old-school way, brought in a big plan and said this is how it's going to be," Bofferding recalls. "We tried to insert ourselves and, well, we failed." The engineers, hurt personally and professionally, turn uncharacteristically belligerent. "We're not fighting to hurt Boeing, we're fighting to save it," the union leader explains. "It's all short-term thinking, everybody's focused on what the stock price is doing. You're not respected any more. The employees get squeezed. The reason we have design-built teams, integrative product teams, is because we know there are varying perspectives in the company and, unless you honor them all, you're going to come up with a suboptimized product. People matter. Our professionalism matters as well."

Doctors, pro athletes, airline pilots, graduate students—these and other esteemed professionals seek protection from rigid work structures or exploitative terms of employment. It is one of the perverse twists of modern prosperity that many who have very high incomes and the supposed leverage of highly specialized talents employ the collective power of unionization at a time when the older industrial unions are declining in size, some perilously. An AFL-CIO survey focused on the attitudes of young workers, union and nonunion, but uncovered a startling point about their elders: Most young people have hopeful expectations, as they should, but most employees over thirty-five years old have concluded that "working hard isn't enough any more because employers are not loyal." The longer one is employed, the more one knows about the masters. Social trust is among the casualties of work.

These snapshots suggest, among other things, that the brilliant technologies of modern life, while potentially empowering and democratizing, may be employed just as readily to deepen the confinements. Automation displaces workers, of course, but that is the idea: Labor-saving devices raise human productivity. For many firms, however, the new machines allowed them to disembowel the content of work, dumbing down the tasks and challenges by reducing workers to robotic functions. The electronic devices, likewise, enable managers to adopt oppressive systems of intimate control. A survey of business organizations by the American Management Association found that 78 percent use surveillance mechanisms to monitor their employees' communications and performance. "It's got to add stress when everyone knows their production is being monitored," one employer said. "I don't apologize for that."

The contemporary workplace is where energetic capitalism collides, most visibly, with the softer values of human existence. At a large Boston bakery, sociologist Richard Sennett found a grim contrast between the 1970s, when he first observed workers there, and the modernized bakery twenty years later. "In this high-tech, flexible workplace, where everything is user friendly, the workers felt personally demeaned by the way they work. . . . Operationally, everything is so clear; emotionally so illegible," Sennett wrote. He found the workers confused and sullen, indifferent to their work and colleagues, also with much lower wages. Punching computer icons is easier work, but it robs them of the logic and consequences in their actions. They no longer know how to bake bread; many never even see it. The automated ovens also produce lots of waste, daily mounds of misbaked, blackened loaves. Sennett found only one worker in the bakery resisting these "improvements," a Jamaican-born foreman who seemed perpetually angry, frustrated by the wastefulness and also by his fellow workers. "He told me he believed many of these problems could be sorted out if the workers owned the bakery," Sennett reported.

To recapitulate, the snapshots convey that the confinements on human dignity, equity, and self-worth are not restricted to the lower tiers of employment. The deteriorated quality and discontents are far more inclusive now. Their impact stretches upward on the ladder of occupational status and incomes, even to much admired and supposedly privileged stations. The reengineering of work has left many white-collar workers feeling bereft of security and satisfaction. The purposeful efficiencies of downsizing and restructuring are blind to the human identity of a chemical engineer as much as to that of a machinist or casual laborer.

The essential economic transaction modern management has performed, especially in larger companies where the leaders are more distant from the followers, is to shift the burdens of risk and cost from the firm to the employees, economic risks in many forms, but also the personal costs that cannot be counted up. "We did a lot of violence to the expectations of the American workforce," an executive vice president of General Electric acknowledged upon retirement.

Still, it is important to acknowledge the countervailing reality: Many Americans, myself included, are lucky enough to have found jobs we love, work so fulfilling and important to our identity we can't seem to get enough of it (family and friends sometimes see this devotion to work as an addictive disorder). In a perfect world, everyone would find satisfying work—regardless of skills or income—useful tasks that are rewarding in everyday, routine ways and draw out the best of what is within us. But envisioning an economic system where such satisfaction becomes broadly possible for all collides with our deep cultural prejudices. A condescending bias prevails in American life, especially strong among the well-educated elites but also internalized by many working people, that presumes those who do "brain work" are somehow more meritorious than those who work with their hands.

"Our culture says, if your hands are involved, you can't have a brain," Ronald Blackwell, an AFL-CIO official and former clothing-union leader, observed. "The seamstress and the machinist and nearly every kind of job involves brain as well as hands, but the intellectual content of working with your hands is ignored."

Anyone who has closely observed a carpenter at work—or a seamstress, a machinist, or a truck driver, for that matter—will recognize Blackwell's point. Doing any job well requires abstract reasoning and a continuous process of thinking through choices, just as most intellectual work involves patterns of familiar repetitions and reflexive responses. A skillful brain surgeon might, for instance, be a less creative thinker than a skillful carpenter. A capable trash collector who performs his job effectively may experience greater satisfaction at work than an overwrought bond trader. If we had to decide which occupations the society cannot do without, some of us might choose trash collectors and carpenters over bond traders and brain surgeons.

The point is, the cultural stereotypes attached to work are arbitrary and create their own destructive social divisions. They are generally wrong— inferences made at a distance about people whom we do not know, based upon their status in the occupational hierarchies. Industrial capitalism organizes jobs and work in a broad-based, layered pyramid with a commanding pinnacle, just as feudalism did, though with more productive logic, the division of labor. The pecking order of work is a convenient artifact of capitalism, not the natural order of human existence.

These observations may simply deepen the despair for some readers. If white-collar professionals are as voiceless as blue-collar workers in influencing the conditions of their work, it seems even harder to imagine that anything can change. The first step toward remedy and action, however, is the recognition that there exists a broader, unacknowledged unity among very different working people in the nature of their shared powerlessness. To see this is not easy. It means backing off the familiar conceits and biases about one's status and abilities compared to others. It means accepting the possibility that people have a common self-interest deeper than class or income. It suggests fellow employees need to start talking with one another, despite the vast differences in their jobs and status.

The fundamental solution can be bluntly summarized: People must figure out how to "own" their own work. That is, individually and jointly, they own the place where they work. They accept responsibility, collectively, for the well-being of the firm. They authorize the managers who direct things, but all participate in the rule making and other important policy decisions. They share the returns from the enterprise and agree upon the terms for sharing. None of these structural changes exempts anyone from the harrowing competition of capitalism or the demand for effective practices and productivity. Nor would this protect anyone from the normal human folly and error—the risks of loss and failure.

But does anyone doubt that, if employees acquired such self-governing powers, the terms of work would be reformed drastically in American business? Or that, if they owned the enterprise together, the rewards and risks would be reallocated in more equitable ways?

What follows is an exploration of this idea of self-ownership—the promise and the difficulties. The concept seems utterly remote to the standard terms of enterprise (and it is), but it is not utopian. Millions of Americans already work in such circumstances, or at least possess important aspects of shared control and responsibility. They are mutual owners of the firm and have a voice in running it. They work in employee-owned companies and cooperatives and partnerships or hybrid variations of all three. Some are highly paid professionals, some are assembly-line workers, some are clerks or janitors. They make it work—together—or they fail. The vision is most difficult to achieve, but many do succeed in practical reality. Running a successful business is difficult, and self-ownership is more so, because people must also alter their own attitudes and aspirations and develop new, more trusting relations among themselves. Profound change is always difficult, yet it is always required to reach the next important stage in human fulfillment.

The master-servant legacy embedded in modern enterprise poses a fundamental question: How can genuine individual freedom ever flourish except for a privileged few—or democracy ever be reconciled with capitalism—so long as the economic system functions along opposite principles, depriving people of rights and responsibilities, even denying their uniqueness as human beings? David Ellerman, an economist with the rare ability to apply moral philosophy to the underlying structure of economic life, has answered the question with an uncompromising argument. This power relationship is inherently illegitimate as a matter of natural law, Ellerman reasons, and is based upon "a legalized fraud." The "fraud" is the economic pretense that people can be treated as things, as commodities or machines, as lifeless property that lacks the qualities inseparable from the human self, the person's active deliberation and choices, the personal accountability for one's actions.

The fact that human beings have accepted this arrangement over the centuries—or were compelled to accept it—does not alter the unnaturalness. The fact that some people prefer mindless subservience to responsibility and self-realization does not confer legitimacy on their masters. Ellerman, formerly a staff economist at the World Bank, has devoted years to constructing a multilayered brief for "economic democracy," melding philosophy, law, and economics to illuminate long-existing fallacies. This discussion does not do justice to the rich complexity of his case but follows his lead in sorting out the fundamental terms. The ideological underpinnings are important to understand because they make clear why the structure of capitalism confines human existence illegitimately and how this might be transformed.*

The subservient nature of the work relationship has been papered over by myth and comforting metaphors, inherited "wisdom" generally accepted by society and firmly codified in its laws. But Ellerman poses an awkward question: What exactly makes the modern system so different from serf-dom? The American republic, remember, originated in a Constitution that explicitly recognized the right to own people as private property. The insti-tution of slavery, as a productive capital asset protected by law, was not abolished until the thirteenth amendment, less than 150 years ago. Social traces of the iniquity linger still.

Formal economics has an answer for Ellerman's question, though not one that satisfies his objection. "Workers may not be bought and sold, only rented and hired," Alfred Marshall, a preeminent economist in his time, wrote in 1920. Paul Samuelson, author of a standard textbook for present-day Economics 101, sticks to the same distinction. "Since slavery was abol-ished, human earning power is forbidden by law to be capitalized [bought and sold as property]," he wrote. "A man is not even free to sell himself; he must rent himself at a wage." The "rented" worker is certainly much better off than the "owned" worker, no question. Yet, as their language suggests, the distinction between slavery and freedom is narrower than supposed, and aspects of property still heavily influence the transaction. Human labor is treated as an input of production no different from the other inputs—machines, raw materials, buildings, capital itself—and these inputs are in-terchanged routinely in organizing the elements of production. Employees are now described as "human resources," the oddly dehumanizing usage adopted by modern corporations.

The trouble is, people are not things. They are autonomous human ac-tors, not mere "resources." They cannot be reduced to physical inputs, even if they assent, because they are conscious, responsible agents of self, en-dowed with inalienable rights and inescapably liable for their behavior, legally and otherwise. Ellerman put the point in a way anyone can grasp: "Guns and burglary tools, no matter how efficacious and 'productive' they may be in the commission of a crime, will never be hauled into court and charged with the crime." Human beings, on the other hand, will be held accountable for their behavior in myriad ways because their actions carry a

---

*David Ellerman's principal text is *Property & Contract in Economics: The Case for Economic Democracy,* Blackwell, 1992. Still largely unheralded, his work is beginning to draw respectful consideration among philosophers, though not yet from many economists.

presumption of individual will and decision. "A hired killer is still a murderer even though he sold his labor," Ellerman observed. Thus, people cannot be "rented" anymore than they can be "sold" without presuming to detach them from the core of what makes them human. This point of collision with capitalism is what makes life and liberty seem incomplete to many Americans.

The violation of natural rights, Ellerman explained, is needed to sustain the fictitious relationship within a company that allows it to exclude the employees from any claim to the new wealth their labor creates—the product and profit of the enterprise. "The capitalist, like the slave owner, has used a legalized fraud, which pretends the worker is an instrument, to arrive at the position of being the 'owner of both instruments of production' [labor and capital] so he can then make a legally defensible claim on the positive product," Ellerman wrote. Workers collect "rent" on their time and exertions but, in most situations, the terms of employment do not allow them to share in the company profits—the surplus wealth their contributions have produced. This contractual reality helps explain the great redundancy of concentrated wealth that persists in American society, why the rich get richer. As the firm's insiders and investors, they own the entire output, both finished product and profit. The "rented" employees whose lives and knowledge are intimately engaged in the firm's functionings are entitled to none (unless the insiders decide to share).

The employment system is thus a main engine generating American inequality, and perhaps the most powerful one. Its functional structure effectively guarantees that the gross inequalities of income and wealth will endure in our society, largely unaltered and replicated for each new generation, despite any ameliorative actions by the government. The system is designed to produce this outcome. The steep ladder of personal incomes, from top to bottom, is reflected by the enormous and growing wage disparities in which the CEO earns more than five hundred times more than the company's average workers. But it is the harvesting of the profits exclusively by insiders and distant owners, instead of by the working employees, that has the greatest impact. This arrangement is not logically inevitable in capitalism—workers might own their own work and harvest the surpluses for themselves—but this is the format that blanketed American life a century ago as Americans moved from farm to factory, from self-employed work to the contract terms of wages and hours.

The contract for employment, its explicit and implied terms, determines these outcomes, but its central impact is obscured and mystified by the aura of property rights, a convenient veil inherited from the feudal order that lends a sense of customary correctness to the domination of labor by the owners of capital. The man who owns the factory, it is generally assumed, commands the workforce and collects the profits as a function of his rights as the property owner. This is an historical myth, in Ellerman's analysis, one that must be demolished if people are to see the situation clearly and recognize the opportunity for changing their condition.

"Marx bought the myth," Ellerman explained. That is, Karl Marx started from the same premise of property's mythological power over others. Whoever owns "the means of production" will rule under capitalism, he asserted (and gave the system its name). Thus, his theoretical solution involved abolishing private property and establishing state ownership of the productive assets. In theory, this would make everyone a "virtual" owner, though in fact they were in charge of neither their work nor their lives, as history has amply demonstrated. The idea that workers "rented" by a government-owned enterprise would be better off somehow—empowered—compared to workers "rented" by private capital was a central fallacy of communism. It failed the test of reality—spectacularly.

The fallacy is easier to recognize in modern capitalism than it was in Marx's time. Many large and successful companies today actually do not own great assets themselves. Their control derives from the insiders' role in organizing the contractual relationships among all of the various elements that contribute to production: the employees; the suppliers; the providers of capital; and the firm's controlling insiders, who may or may not own the factory or contribute much of their own capital to the enterprise. A firm's organizers, if they choose, may "hire" the land and buildings, "lease" the machines, "borrow" the capital or "sell" shares in their ownership, just as they "rent" the workforce. Property ownership, if things are organized shrewdly, is superfluous to their claim on the final product and profits.

The real basis for the insiders' power and their legal claim to the profits is their acceptance of responsibility for the firm, their contractual commitments to pay the costs of production and to absorb the negative consequences of losses and liabilities as well as the positive results. Employees, in a sense, are awarded an opposite status: irresponsibility in the fortunes of the company and, thus, no share in its success unless the management decides to grant one. In exchange for this privileged irresponsibility, workers are rendered powerless. They accept the master-servant status, are subject to the command of others, and have no voice in the company's management or any claim to its returns.

Stated in those stark terms, it does not sound like such a good deal. But understanding the basic contractual relationship prompts a liberating thought: Contracts can be changed. If the power is derived from the employment contract and not from inherited notions of property rights, then the active participants in a company might renegotiate their roles and responsibilities or even create a new firm that reflects a different balance of power. Ellerman describes the opportunity: "Instead of capital hiring labor, labor hires capital."

Labor hires capital? The role reversal seems beyond the plausible until one remembers that this transaction is approximately what does occur in many existing enterprises. The workers, in fact, borrow the capital to own and operate the firm themselves, then pay back their loans from the returns of the enterprise, an arrangement known as the employee-owned company. The ESOP transaction (for employee stock ownership plan) resembles a leveraged buyout in which company insiders borrow capital to take over a controlling position in company stock, then pay back creditors with the company's profits. Or workers form partnerships, like a law firm, collectively assuming responsibility and thus sharing in the governance and the returns. Or they create a cooperative enterprise that, roughly speaking, blends some elements of partnership and employee ownership.

The same essential reversal is present in all three cases: the workers are the "insiders" who organize the firm's contractual relationships; they accept shared responsibility for the firm and allocate the profits among themselves, not with absentee stockholders. The result, in Ellerman's words, is "people jointly working for themselves in democratic firms." Quite literally, they own their own work.

At the start of this new century, around 10 million Americans are worker-owners in some 11,000 employee-owned companies, with total assets of more than $400 billion. Thousands of cooperative enterprises also operate around the country, ranging from some 300 worker cooperatives in manufacturing and services to cooperative day-care centers and small banks to the mammoth agricultural marketing cooperatives owned collectively by the farmers who produce the foodstuffs. The professional partnerships—lawyers, doctors, architects, and others—incorporate similar principles, as do many small firms of the self-employed. These are the meaningful exceptions, however. Most Americans have no ownership of enterprise whatever. For those who do own stock shares, the "owners" are typically confined to a weak and attenuated status.

Self-ownership was the road not taken in American history. The cultural memory still enshrines independent yeomanry—the small farmer toiling in his own fields—but the modern organization of work largely obliterated those values.

It seems odd but necessary to point out that Americans did not always live like this. Just as my grandfather McClure proudly reported himself "unemployed" to the census taker in 1900, workers during the nineteenth century regarded wage employment as alien and inferior to their independent lives. They typically called it "wage slavery" because, as sociologist Charles Perrow has explained, "slavery was the closest thing to factory bureaucracy that people could conceive of; it was the closest precedent in history. Another precedent was also invoked—the military—and people referred to the 'industrial army' in attempting to describe the new situation." For a time, machinists and other craftsmen maintained independent worker-owned shops that sold their output to larger manufacturing firms, but these were gradually pushed aside. Just as the cultural meaning of "unemployed" changed, "free labor" was replaced in the language by "labor supply."

During the explosive rise of industrial capitalism in the second half of the nineteenth century, some organizations of workers, like the Knights of Labor and the American Federation of Labor's early formation, did fight for a larger vision based on worker and community ownership of enterprises, described as the alternative to "wage slavery." But those efforts were overwhelmed by the force and effectiveness of the emerging national corporations, both their scale and deft management of divisions of labor in industrial processes. Advocates of worker ownership lacked the means and resources to carry it out, or their vision seemed insufficiently militant for the ferocious fight underway with capitalists of that era. Led by guilds of skilled craftsmen, unions did fight for control of the workplace (and still do in some sectors), but the contest between labor and capital gradually devolved to the narrower conflicts over wages and job benefits. Labor's victories on these issues were an essential element in creating the broad middle-class prosperity of modern times.

Organized labor, which built the model for collective action in the first half of the twentieth century and mobilized workers to secure political rights for collective bargaining, has since withered greatly in size and power. Its ranks are reduced to 13.5 percent of the workforce overall and to only 9 percent in the private economy. Federal labor law is now archaic and confines workers rather than liberates them. It is used routinely by employers as a blunt instrument to thwart efforts to organize a collective voice, that is, a union. If union members tried to open conversations with middle managers about their shared discontents with the employer such talk would violate the National Labor Relations Act, which imposes legalistic and unnatural divisions upon the broad ranks of employees (in any case, the middle managers likely would be fired for consorting privately with union members). The companies' preferred antiunion weapon is fear—fear of being fired—and the NLRA provides very weak penalties that companies ignore with little consequence (20,000 U.S. workers are fired illegally for union organizing every year, according to Human Rights Watch). Management lawyers game the technicalities for years. When the fines are finally imposed, the fired workers are long gone, the organizing campaign has already been broken. Yet labor lacks the political power to reform the laws.

Labor's weakened position is reflected in the deteriorated terms and conditions of work for union and nonunion members alike. It suggests another discomforting acknowledgment: The mobilization of organized labor, at least as we have known it, has not proved an adequate response to the confining powers of American capitalism. Unions still do win important victories in many arenas, and renewed organizing energies in some unions may yet produce a turnaround in labor's strength. But, to prevail at this point in history, the ethos and spirit of collective action requires, ironically, a much more ambitious vision, one that might reignite sympathies and energies among Americans at large.

That agenda would start from a more fundamental perspective: attacking the compromised civil rights of working people and articulating a critique of the deteriorated conditions of work that speaks also for employees in the many occupations not covered by union protections. The case for self-ownership is a much better fit with present circumstances than it was for struggling workers a century ago. Employee ownership and self-management provide a plausible route toward eventually achieving greater wage equity, reforming the quality of work, and fostering accumulation of financial wealth among the many instead of the few. Eliminating the artificial dividing line between master and servant would open a vast new horizon of possibilities for individual fulfillment. The obvious problem with this approach is that it requires commitment to the long term—and enormous patience—at a time when most unions are embattled on many defensive fronts at once. Some unions are dispirited bureaucracies without hope or ambition and alienated from their rank-and-file members. Some union leaders assume, condescendingly, that their members are not interested in ownership and that the issue would merely undermine class consciousness, confusing the old labor refrain: Which side are you on?

The redeeming fact, however, is that some forward-looking labor leaders, often driven by necessity, have swung around impressively on the subject of ownership during the last few decades. Led by former president Lynn R. Williams, the United Steelworkers of America, one of the most embattled "old industry" unions, became the pioneer twenty years ago in engineering employee takeovers of troubled companies, retaining viable plants that larger corporations were discarding and saving thousands of jobs as well as valuable productive assets. Unions now actively engaged in employee ownership and worker takeovers range from machinists to papermakers, from autos to clothing and textiles. The largest employee-owned company is the troubled United Airlines that along with other major airlines filed for bankruptcy in 2002. The machinists' and pilots' unions are together the majority shareholders with seats on the board, but United got into deep financial trouble for approximately the same reasons as its competitors. The unions ostensibly have controlling power, but they have not yet figured out how to assert their power effectively or to reform United's corporate strategy and management behavior.

On the fringes of organized labor some rank-and-file activists are searching for a larger vision. "Imagine that in place of our half-century-old labor law . . . we had a labor law based on the constitutional rights of free speech, assembly and labor freedom," the Labor Party, an allied political group, declared. The new labor law, the party suggested, would be based on legal principles found in the thirteenth amendment abolishing involuntary servitude.

In any case, the idea of self-ownership no longer belongs to labor alone, and unions are not present in the overwhelming majority of employee-owned firms. Given the many obstacles that burden unions, this transformation is often led by managers and owners. The idea does not belong to either left or right. Indeed, in an earlier era, some enlightened leaders of capitalism shared the progressive vision that corporations might someday be owned entirely by their employees. Owen D. Young was CEO of General Electric in the 1920s when he described the dream: "Perhaps someday we may be able to organize the human beings in a particular undertaking so that they truly will be the employer buying capital as a commodity in the market at the lowest possible price. It will be necessary for them to provide an adequate guarantee fund in order to buy the capital at all. If that is realized, the human beings will be entitled to all the profits over the cost of capital. I hope that day may come when the great business organizations will truly belong to the men who are giving their lives and their efforts to them, I care not in what capacity." Labor hires capital. Workers reap the new wealth. General Electric was a very different company in those days.

The temporary employment agency called Solidarity provides a dramatic illustration of what can happen to ordinary people when they assume the role of owners (so dramatic, in fact, some readers may find it hard to believe). The temp agency operates in Baltimore, Maryland, and is organized as a cooperative. It belongs to the same temp workers it sends out everyday to fill various short-term jobs. They work at the city convention center arranging chairs and setting tables for huge banquets or do light manufacturing jobs or rehab old buildings or fill temps slots at small businesses, hotels, and construction sites. These men come from the "inner city" and the loose pool of workers once known as "casual labor"—the very bottom of the American job ladder. The vast majority of them are recovering narcotics addicts and/or have criminal records and time in prison.

Their firm is thriving and expanding. They earn wages a dollar or two an hour higher than rates paid by competing temp agencies plus they have health insurance coverage. When a new client seeks to hire their labor, Solidarity workers go out to check the employer first and inspect the terms and conditions of work. At year's end the regulars will receive a bonus check from the firm's profits, typically several thousand dollars each. None of these men expect to get rich (some saw a lot more cash when they were dealing drugs), but the idea of owning something themselves is a powerful experience.

"Naturally, when it's your company, your productivity is bound to go up—it belongs to you," said Curtis Brown, a forty-seven-year-old worker who had scuffled in low-wage jobs since he was seventeen. "It's not us against them; it's all us. You're all fighting against the same thing. I've seen guys, I know myself, glad to go to work, happy to go to work. Everybody's working to get the job right."

Oddly enough, their personal troubles turned out to be an asset for the firm. Workers know each other from the streets, but mainly from attending the same Narcotics Anonymous meetings. "How I would I describe it? It's almost like a spiritual thing among the guys," Brown explains. "A lot of us knew each other. When a new guy comes in, we usually recognize him. We seen him in the rooms." "In the rooms" is their phrase for identifying a fellow Narcotics Anonymous member who attends meetings, someone who's been through the same fire and is working on the struggle for personal redemption. Within the cooperative, this powerful subculture has been a source of trust and teamwork, but also for self-discipline. Nobody cons others who are also "in the rooms."

Avis Ransom, an idealistic MBA graduate who left her business consulting career to manage Solidarity, found the firm has competitive advantage in its shared ethos of "self-policing in the workplace—one employee going to another and telling him, 'You're goofing off; start working.' When we started out, our members would come to work and get in prayer circles outside the convention center. Workers from the other [temp] agencies would join them, sometimes even managers. We began to see how easy it was to take workers and jobs from our competitors." Solidarity regularly trains workers and pays the seasoned ones to serve as teachers. It increases the level of training as the firm gains better jobs—do simple math, swing a hammer, read a shop-floor plan. Workers meet every two weeks to air out complaints and share ideas. Not all of them survive the self-criticism. They are not ready to meet the cooperative's standards.

"The greatest problems," Ransom explains, "are workers don't show up on time. They don't show up in the numbers ordered. The client orders ten; eight show up. Or they don't show up work ready. They're sleepy or high or badly dressed or unclean. We called a meeting of workers, maybe twenty or so, and explained these problems. They said, We can fix that. If we have to start work at two, tell us to report at one. If they need twenty people, send twenty-five and, if they don't need the extra workers, send them home with two hours' pay. Now we call it show-up pay. They said, We don't want our clients to see us as not work ready, so you screen us at the work site. Pick out the ones who aren't ready and send them home. We started doing that for every job and it got to the point where we were regularly sending extra people and they would get hired because people from the other agencies didn't show up. We've got an excellent reputation with our clients."

Solidarity made a profit its second year—$50,000—and Ransom called the members together to announce the good news. "The workers made it clear to me: This was *their* money; they had already earned it," she said. "But they wanted to keep the money in the company to develop more alliances with businesses and get a stronger foothold in the industry. For folks who are making eight dollars an hour, that's a phenomenal decision." Profits rose fourfold in the third year and workers collected profit shares based on how many hours they had worked.

It should be obvious that, in these humble circumstances, the workers could not have launched this alone. They had an experienced and influential sponsor in BUILD, a community organization that for twenty-five years has mobilized Baltimore's citizens and neighborhoods, drawn together from black and white churches across the city, to push their own civic agenda of housing, education, and other concerns. BUILD launched the nation's first "living wage" campaign and won a city ordinance boosting incomes for low-wage employees of public contractors and suppliers, an idea that has since spread across the country. Affiliated with the Industrial Areas Foundation's nationwide network of sixty-three grassroots organizations, BUILD adheres to the IAF's "iron rule": "Never do anything for people that they can do for themselves—never." In this case, the organizers patiently canvassed the city's powerless temp workers and helped some of them take the leap to a self-owned firm. BUILD provided a $35,000 line of credit and used its political clout to persuade some public agencies and private employers to become the first clients.

Solidarity, though still fragile like any small start-up, is expanding laterally into new fields of employment and moving workers upward in skills and income. An environmental consultant trained the workers to do the work on a major contract refitting public buildings for energy efficiency: caulking, weather stripping, and other tasks. In exchange, the workers "carried" the contractor for a few weeks during his own early cash-flow problems by temporarily deferring half their pay. Rehab work on church-sponsored halfway houses (a place these men had passed through themselves) is being done by Solidarity members as both workers and contractors.

This is small stuff, to be sure, but it illustrates how, with self-ownership, the work itself can become a leveraging asset. One by one they were hapless temp workers tumbling in and out of jobs. Collectively they possess a little bargaining power to open more doors for the cooperative and to ratchet up the content and value of their own work. This sort of transaction requires business savvy, but also a strong foundation of trust. Solidarity draws inspiration and a model from Mondragon, a much-celebrated network of more than one hundred cooperatives in the Basque region of northern Spain, where workers share ownership and returns in scores of affiliated enterprises, from small manufacturing companies to a major supermarket chain. Mondragon has no stockholders, but relies upon its own self-financing bank and a strong fabric of mutual support among its many small parts. Collectively, Mondragon resembles a powerful business corporation with more than 20,000 employees.

Solidarity's lead organizers, Arnold Graf and Jonathon Lange, have a larger, less tangible vision: changing the culture of work in Baltimore, starting from the bottom up and eventually affecting others far up the line. They have been scouting for a building convenient to main bus lines that BUILD could turn into a "workers center," a service center and social hall for low-wage workers and their families, equipped with recreational materials and a library, computers and a chapel, music and art, a barbershop and banking services. BUILD may not have the resources to start its own bank like Mondragon, but they are talking to local bankers about forming a self-interested alliance—a worker-friendly bank.

"There's such a terrific breakdown in community places, nowhere for people to come together and call it their own," Graf says. "What excites me is trying to change the culture of what people expect from the economy, what they consider the nature of work. Do I have a right to a living wage and a job where I have something to say about decisions? Or is it just the boss? These are concrete ways of rebuilding community through different aspects of work. We had originally thought about community in terms of the neighborhoods, but we are beginning to see a different kind of vision—the community that is based in work." Solidarity's organizing activities resemble what aggressive labor unions in garment making and other sectors did for low-wage and immigrant members three generations ago. "Somebody accused us of trying to reinvent the wheel," Lange said, "but we take pride in that."

Actually, the example of Solidarity makes the cooperative process seem easier than it is. These working men, after all, may have needed some outside help, but they did not need to create a culture of trust and self-criticism. They already had absorbed that "in the rooms." Mondragon, likewise, is a brilliant model of successful cooperatives but draws power from the unique separateness of the Basque people, an embattled minority struggling to preserve its cultural integrity while also achieving prosperity. In the American experience, immigrant groups similarly rely upon ethnic solidarity—pooling their meager resources and sacrifices—to build something real for themselves. Muslims and Koreans today, Irish, Italian, and Jews in yesteryear.

Given the splintered condition of America's social relations, this is very hard work in most circumstances—constructing a social texture that binds people together in mutual trust and endeavors—and it is especially difficult within large, complicated business organizations. Teamwork is an elusive quality and cannot be faked (nor bought and sold). Modern Americans are remarkably capable people, skillful and inventive in many ways, but they are not so good at talking to one another across their vast differences of social class and economic status. Shared ownership may make it easier to have such conversations and encourage trust but, paradoxically, shared ownership is unlikely to succeed unless the trust becomes real.   ∎

■ *QUESTIONS FOR MAKING CONNECTIONS WITHIN THE READING* ■

1. Using your own reading of "Work Rules" rather than a dictionary, explain what Greider means by "the socialization of powerlessness"? What does "socialization" involve, and how do people become "socialized" into one way of life or another? If most people are indeed powerless on the job, why do so many of them indicate high rates of job satisfaction in polls? Is job satisfaction the same thing as autonomy? Is job satisfaction inconsistent with a master-servant relationship?

2. After paying particular attention to Greider's discussion of Karl Marx, would you say that Greider is a Marxist? Does Greider make an argument in favor of private property, or against it? Are worker-owned businesses less consistent with the free market than corporations owned by entrepreneurs and stockholders? Are corporations in some ways less consistent with free market ideals than worker-owned companies?

3. The subtitle to the book from which this excerpt was taken is "Opening Paths to a Moral Economy." In what ways might the treatment of people as things contribute to the erosion of ethical codes that healthy societies depend on? What might Greider have in mind when he argues for a "moral economy"? Aren't all economies "amoral," that is, morally neutral? What would be the characteristics of an "immoral" economy?

■ *QUESTIONS FOR WRITING* ■

1. Greider refers to his grandfather McClure, who "proudly reported himself 'unemployed' to the census taker in 1900." Investigate the work history of your own family. If you can, find out something about what your grandparents did for a living, and also about the conditions under which they labored. Would you say that you enjoy more prosperity than they did? More personal freedom? More security? Does your family's experience confirm, complicate, or contradict Greider's argument?

2. Will worker-owned businesses really solve the problem of citizens' powerlessness? Drawing on the examples that Greider provides—United Airlines and Solidarity—discuss the economic obstacles that stand in the way of workplace equality. In a worker-owned company, will employees still need to "rent" themselves? If one purpose of a business is to compete with other businesses, what pressures work against the achievement of worker equality? In what ways might worker equality provide a competitive advantage?

■ *QUESTIONS FOR MAKING CONNECTIONS BETWEEN READINGS* ■

1. In "Presumed Innocent," Devra Davis describes the vested corporate interests that lead the pharmaceutical, medical, food, and health care industries to focus on profit rather than the environmental causes of cancer. If these industries were to become worker-owned, would their market behavior change? That is, would the workers be better able to—or more inclined to—lead these industries in the direction that Devra calls for, one where the desire to protect workers from environmental hazards outweighs the drive for profit?

2. In "Meat and Milk Factories," Peter Singer and Jim Mason shift the question about the ethics of factory farming from a focus on individual producers to a focus on the system itself. One could argue that Greider, by contrast, shifts the question about the ethics of ownership from a focus on the system itself to a focus on the individuals in the system. Is ethics a matter of individual behavior or does it depend on the appropriate social system? Given that we live in a market-driven system and that factory farming is a major part of that system, is ethical action by individuals in the system possible? Or is the only ethical action available to opt out of the system? Is opting out even possible?

HENRY JENKINS

THERE ARE FEW scholars in the humanities who have forged multimillion-dollar international collaborations with foreign governments (<http://gambit.mit.edu/>), fewer still whom their peers would call "the 21st-century [Marshall] McLuhan." Among these, only one can be found mud-wrestling his wife at a two-day party called the Steer Roast every spring. Profiles of MIT professor Henry Jenkins in the press are invariably a patchwork record of his remarkable professional success, his formative influence on the field of media studies, and his colorful personality.

Jenkins, who wrote his doctoral dissertation on the Marx brothers and other comedies of the 1930s, was an unlikely candidate to shape the field of media studies, least of all at MIT, where the humanities take second billing to the school's illustrious programs in science and technology. However, Jenkins immersed himself in digital culture and subsequently founded the university's Comparative Media Studies Program in 1999, a decade after he was hired. That same year, Jenkins drew the national spotlight for his testimony before a Senate committee hearing on youth and media violence. Jenkins, who had co-edited the collection *From Barbie to* Mortal Kombat: *Gender and Computer Games* (1998) the previous year, entered a personal testimony against censorship and in defense of videogame-playing adolescents. Calling violent videogames "the symbols of youth alienation and rage—not the causes," Jenkins defied legislators who sought to find an easy scapegoat in the increasingly complicated media landscape.

A leading expert on fandom and a self-proclaimed "aca-fan," Henry Jenkins sees his scholarly study of fan communities and his own personal excitement about popular culture as residing on a continuum. He has traced the engagement of fans with popular culture across different media in over ten authored or edited books. "Why Heather Can Write: Media Literacy and the *Harry Potter* Wars," is a chapter from one of these, a book called *Convergence Culture: Where*

Jenkins, Henry. "Why Heather Can Write: Media Literacy and the Harry Potter Wars." *Convergence Culture: Where Old and New Media Collide*. New York: New York University Press, 2006.

Quotations are drawn from the following chapter and from a *Chronicle of Higher Education* profile by Jeffrey R. Young, available at <http://chronicle.com/free/v54/i03/03b02001.htm>.

Old and New Media Meet (2006). In this book, Jenkins argues against the traditional story of new media emergence and old media obsolescence, suggesting instead that old media remain and form complicated relationships with new media in the lives of media consumers and practitioners. In this chapter, Jenkins tells the story of Heather Lawver, a precocious home-schooled student who launches an Internet-based fictional newspaper revolving around the world of *Harry Potter*. Lawver's story becomes a focal point for the tensions that emerge as new media and new stories come into conflict with some of the oldest existing institutions in American culture, among them schools and libraries (which seek to maintain their place in the promulgation of media literacy), corporations (which strive to maintain intellectual property laws), and cultural conservatives (who worry about the increasingly secular nature of education).

In the conflict among these groups, which have "competing notions of media literacy and how it should be taught," Jenkins draws attention to what he terms the "discernment movement" occurring among certain Christians. These practitioners of discernment don't simply reject cultural products that don't completely represent their point of view; rather, they read critically and with an open mind, learning about their own values while finding redeeming qualities in the books, films, and songs that others reject outright. It is ultimately this lesson of engaged and critical cultural participation that animates Jenkins's work and his own involvement with the proliferating new media productions.

■ ■

Why Heather Can Write
Media Literacy and the *Harry Potter* Wars

[C]orporate media increasingly recognizes the value, and the threat, posed by fan participation. Media producers and advertisers now speak about "emotional capital" or "lovemarks" to refer to the importance of audience investment and participation in media content. Storytellers now think about storytelling in terms of creating openings for consumer participation. At the same time, consumers are using new media technologies to engage with old media content, seeing the Internet as a vehicle for collective problem solving, public deliberation, and grassroots creativity. Indeed, we have suggested that it is the interplay—and tension—between the top-down force of corporate convergence and the bottom-up force of grassroots convergence that is driving many of the changes we are observing in the media landscape.

On all sides and at every level, the term "participation" has emerged as a governing concept, albeit one surrounded by conflicting expectations. Corporations imagine participation as something they can start and stop, channel and reroute, commodify and market. The prohibitionists are trying to shut down unauthorized participation; the collaborationists are trying to win grassroots creators over to their side. Consumers, on the other side, are asserting a right to participate in the culture, on their own terms, when and where they wish. This empowered consumer faces a series of struggles to preserve and broaden this perceived right to participate.

All of these tensions surfaced very visibly through two sets of conflicts surrounding J. K. Rowling's *Harry Potter* books, conflicts that fans collectively refer to as "the Potter wars." On the one hand, there was the struggle of teachers, librarians, book publishers, and civil liberty groups to stand up against efforts by the religious right to have the *Harry Potter* books removed from school libraries and banned from local bookstores. On the other, there were the efforts of Warner Bros. to rein in fan appropriations of the *Harry Potter* books on the grounds that they infringed on the studio's intellectual property. Both efforts threatened the right of children to participate within the imaginative world of *Harry Potter*—one posing a challenge to their right to read, the other a challenge to their right to write. From a purely legal standpoint, the first constitutes a form of censorship, the other a legitimate exercise of property rights. From the perspective of the consumer, on the other hand, the two start to blur since both place restrictions on our ability to fully engage with a fantasy that has taken on a central place in our culture.

The closer we look at these two conflicts, the more complex they seem. Contradictions, confusions, and multiple perspectives should be anticipated at a moment of transition where one media paradigm is dying and another is being born. None of us really knows how to live in this era of media convergence, collective intelligence, and participatory culture. These changes are producing anxieties and uncertainties, even panic, as people imagine a world without gatekeepers and live with the reality of expanding corporate media power. Our responses to these changes cannot be easily mapped in traditional ideological terms: there is not a unified right wing or left wing response to convergence culture. Within Christianity, there are some groups that embrace the potentials of the new participatory culture and others terrified by them. Within companies, as we have seen, there are sudden lurches between prohibitionist and collaborationist responses. Among media reformers, some forms of participation are valued more than others. Fans disagree among themselves on how much control J. K. Rowling or Warner

Bros. should have over what consumers do with *Harry Potter*. It isn't as if any of us knows all of the answers yet.

All of the above suggests that the Potter wars are at heart a struggle over what rights we have to read and write about core cultural myths—that is, a struggle over literacy. Here, literacy is understood to include not simply what we can do with printed matter but also what we can do with media. Just as we would not traditionally assume that someone is literate if they can read but not write, we should not assume that someone possesses media literacy if they can consume but not express themselves. Historically, constraints on literacy come from attempts to control different segments of the population—some societies have embraced universal literacy, others have restricted literacy to specific social classes or along racial and gender lines. We may also see the current struggle over literacy as having the effect of determining who has the right to participate in our culture and on what terms. *Harry Potter* is a particularly rich focal point for studying our current constraints on literacy because the book itself deals so explicitly with issues of education (often lending its voice to children's rights over institutional constraints) and because the book has been so highly praised for inciting young people to develop their literacy skills.

Yet the books have also been the focus of various attempts to constrain what kids read and write. My focus is on the *Harry Potter* wars as a struggle over competing notions of media literacy and how it should be taught: the informal pedagogy that emerged within the *Harry Potter* fan community, the attempts to tap kids' interests in the books in classrooms and libraries, the efforts of corporate media to teach us a lesson about the responsible treatment of their intellectual property, the anxieties about the secularization of education expressed by cultural conservatives, and the very different conception of pedagogy shared by Christian supporters of the *Harry Potter* novels within the "discernment movement." All sides want to claim a share in how we educate the young, since shaping childhood is often seen as a way of shaping the future direction of our culture.[1] By looking more closely at these various bids on education, we may map some of the conflicting expectations shaping convergence culture. In the process, I will consider what happens as the concept of participatory culture runs up against two of the most powerful forces shaping children's lives: education and religion.

Consider this a story of participation and its discontents.

Hogwarts and All

When she was thirteen, Heather Lawver read a book that she says changed her life: *Harry Potter and the Sorcerer's Stone*.[2] Inspired by reports that J. K. Rowling's novel was getting kids to read, she wanted to do her part to promote literacy. Less than a year later, she launched *The Daily Prophet*

(<http://www.dprophet.com>), a Web-based "school newspaper" for the fictional Hogwarts. Today, the publication has a staff of 102 children from all over the world.

Lawver, still in her teens, is its managing editor. She hires columnists who cover their own "beats" on a weekly basis—everything from the latest quidditch matches to muggle cuisine. Heather personally edits each story, getting it ready for publication. She encourages her staff to closely compare their original submissions with the edited versions and consults with them on issues of style and grammar as needed. Heather initially paid for the site through her allowances until someone suggested opening a post office box where participants could send their contributions; she still runs it on a small budget, but at least she can draw on the allowances of her friends and contributors to keep it afloat during hard times.

Lawver, by the way, is home schooled and hasn't set foot in a classroom since first grade. Her family had been horrified by what they saw as racism and anti-intellectualism, which they encountered when she entered first grade in a rural Mississippi school district. She explained, "It was hard to combat prejudices when you are facing it every day. They just pulled me and one of my brothers out of school. And we never wanted to go back."

A girl who hadn't been in school since first grade was leading a world-wide staff of student writers with no adult supervision to publish a school newspaper for a school that existed only in their imaginations.

From the start, Lawver framed her project with explicit pedagogical goals that she used to help parents understand their children's participation. In an open letter to parents of her contributors, Lawver describes the site's goals:

> The Daily Prophet is an organization dedicated to bringing the world of literature to life. . . . By creating an online "newspaper" with articles that lead the readers to believe this fanciful world of Harry Potter to be real, this opens the mind to exploring books, diving into the characters, and analyzing great literature. By developing the mental ability to analyze the written word at a young age, children will find a love for reading unlike any other. By creating this faux world we are learning, creating, and enjoying ourselves in a friendly utopian society.[3]

Lawver is so good at mimicking teacherly language that one forgets that she has not yet reached adulthood. For example, she provides reassurances that the site will protect children's actual identities and that she will screen posts to ensure that none contain content inappropriate for younger participants.[4] Lawver was anxious to see her work recognized by teachers, librarians, and her fellow home schoolers. She developed detailed plans for how teachers can use her template to create localized version of a Hogwarts school newspaper as class projects. A number of teachers have taken up her offer.

Whether encountered inside or outside formal education, Lawver's project enabled kids to immerse themselves into the imaginary world of

Hogwarts and to feel a very real sense of connection to an actual community of children around the world who were working together to produce *The Daily Prophet*. The school they were inventing together (building on the foundations of J. K. Rowling's novel) could not have been more different from the one she had escaped in Mississippi. Here, people of many different ethnic, racial, and national backgrounds (some real, some imagined) formed a community where individual differences were accepted and where learning was celebrated.

The point of entry into this imaginary school was the construction of a fictional identity, and subsequently these personas get woven into a series of "news stories" reporting on events at Hogwarts. For many kids, the profile is all they would write—having a self within the fiction was enough to satisfy the needs that brought them to the site. For others, it was the first step toward constructing a more elaborate fantasy about their life at Hogwarts. In their profiles, kids often combined mundane details of their everyday experiences with fantastical stories about their place within J. K. Rowling's world:

> I recently transferred from Madame McKay's Academy of Magic in America to come to Hogwarts. Lived in southern California for most of my life, and my mother never told my father that she was a witch until my fifth birthday (he left shortly afterwards).

> Orphaned when at 5 when her parents died of cancer, this pure blood witch was sent to live with a family of wizards associated with the Ministry of Magic.

The image of the special child being raised in a mundane (in this case, muggle) family and discovering their identities as they enter school age is a classic theme of fantasy novels and fairy tales, yet here there are often references to divorce or cancer, real-world difficulties so many kids face. From the profiles themselves, we can't be sure whether these are problems they have confronted personally or if they are anxious possibilities they are exploring through their fantasies. Heather has suggested that many kids come to *The Daily Prophet* because their schools and families have failed them in some way; they use the new school community to work through their feelings about some traumatic event or to compensate for their estrangement from kids in their neighborhoods. Some children are drawn toward some of the fantasy races—elves, goblins, giants, and the like—while other kids have trouble imagining themselves to be anything other than muggle-born, even in their fantasy play. Children use stories to escape from or reaffirm aspects of their real lives.[5]

Rowling's richly detailed world allows many points of entry. Some kids imagine themselves as related to the characters, the primary ones like Harry Potter or Snape, of course, but also minor background figures—the inventors of the quidditch brooms, the authors of the textbooks, the heads of referenced agencies, classmates of Harry's mother and father, any affiliation that allows them to claim a special place for themselves in the story. In her book, *Writing Superheroes* (1997), Anne Haas Dyson uses the metaphor of a "ticket to play" to describe how the roles provided by children's media properties get deployed by children in a classroom space to police who is allowed to participate and what roles they can assume.[6] Some children fit comfortably within the available roles; others feel excluded and have to work harder to insert themselves into the fantasy. Dyson's focus has to do with divisions of gender and race, primarily, but given the global nature of *The Daily Prophet* community, nationality also was potentially at stake. Rowling's acknowledgment in subsequent books that Hogwarts interacted with schools around the world gave students from many countries a "ticket" into the fantasy: "Sirius was born in India to Ariel and Derek Koshen. Derek was working as a Ministry of Magic ambassador to the Indian Ministry. Sirius was raised in Bombay, and speaks Hindi fluently. While he was in Bombay he saved a stranded Hippogriff from becoming a jacket, cementing his long-lasting love of magical creatures. He attended Gahdal School of Witchcraft and Wizardry in Thailand." Here, it helps that the community is working hard to be inclusive and accepts fantasies that may not comfortably match the world described within the novels.

One striking consequence of the value placed on education in the *Harry Potter* books is that almost all of the participants at *The Daily Prophet* imagine themselves to be gifted students. Kids who read recreationally are still a subset of the total school population, so it is very likely that many of these kids are teacher's pets in real life. Hermione represented a particularly potent role model for the studiously minded young girls who were key contributors to *The Daily Prophet*. Some feminist critics argue that she falls into traditional feminine stereotypes of dependency and nurturance.[7] This may be true, but this character provides some point of identification for female readers within a book otherwise so focused on young boys. Here's how one young writer framed her relationship to the character:

> My name is Mandi Granger. I am 12 yrs old. I am also muggle born. Yes, I am related to Hermione Granger. I am Hermione's cousin. I am attending Hogwarts School for Witchcraft and Wizardry. This is my third year at Hogwarts. I am doing this article between all my studies. I guess I pick up my study habits from my cousin. I am in the Gryffindor house just like my cousin. I do know Harry Potter personally by my cousin. My cousin took him to my house before I went to Hogwarts. We mostly talk about Hogwarts and the Weasley's children.

Through children's fantasy play, Hermione takes on a much more active and central role than Rowling provided her. As Ellen Seiter notes in regard to girl-targeted series such as *Strawberry Shortcake* (1981), feminist parents sometimes sell their daughters short by underestimating their ability to extend beyond what is represented on the screen and by stigmatizing the already limited range of media content available to them.[8] Female readers are certainly free to identify across gender with a range of other characters—and one can see the claims of special family ties as one way of marking those identifications. Yet at an age when gender roles are reinforced on all sides, transgressing gender roles through the fantasy may be harder than reconstructing the characters as vehicles for your own empowerment fantasies.

In some cases, the back stories for these characters are quite elaborate with detailed accounts of their wands, the animal familiars, their magical abilities, their favorite classes, their future plans, and the like. These fictional personas can contain the seeds of larger narratives, suggesting how the construction of an identity may fuel subsequent fan fiction:

> I'm the only sister of Harry Potter, and I am going to play for the Gryffindor quidditch team this year as a chaser. My best friend is Cho Chang, and I am dating Draco Malfoy (although Harry's not happy about that). One of my other good friends is Riley Ravenclaw, a co-writer. I have a few pets, a winged Thestral named Bostrio, a unicorn foal named Golden, and a snowy owl (like Hedwig) named Cassiddia. I was able to escape the Lord Voldemort attack on my family for the reason that I was holidaying with my Aunt Zeldy in Ireland at the time, though I mourn the loss of my mum and dad. I was mad about the awful things Ms. Skeeter wrote about my little brother, and I have sent her her own little package of undiluted bubotuber pus. HA!

As *The Daily Prophet* reporters develop their reports about life at Hogwarts, they draw each other's personas into their stories, trying to preserve what each child sees as its special place within this world. The result is a jointly produced fantasy—somewhere between a role-playing game and fan fiction. The intertwining of fantasies becomes a key element of bonding for these kids, who come to care about one another through interacting with these fictional personas.

What skills do children need to become full participants in convergence culture?. . . . The example of *The Daily Prophet* suggests [one] important cultural competency: role-playing both as a means of exploring a fictional realm and as a means of developing a richer understanding of yourself and the culture around you. These kids came to understand *Harry Potter* by occupying a space within Hogwarts; occupying such a space helped them to map more fully the rules of this fictional world and the roles that various characters played within it. Much as an actor builds up a character by combining things discovered through research with things learned through personal introspection, these kids were drawing on their own experiences to flesh out various aspects of Rowling's fiction. This is a kind of intellectual mastery that comes only through active participation. At the same time, role-playing was providing an inspiration for them to expand other kinds of literacy skills—those already valued within traditional education.

What's striking about this process, though, is that it takes place outside the classroom and beyond any direct adult control. Kids are teaching kids what they need to become full participants in convergence culture. More and more, educators are coming to value the learning that occurs in these informal and recreational spaces, especially as they confront the constraints imposed on learning via educational policies that seemingly value only what can be counted on a standardized test. If children are going to acquire the skills needed to be full participants in their culture, they may well learn these skills through involvement in activities such as editing the newspaper of an imaginary school or teaching one another skills needed to do well in massively multiplayer games or any number of others things that teachers and parents currently regard as trivial pursuits.

Rewriting School

University of Wisconsin–Madison School of Education Professor James Paul Gee calls such informal learning cultures "affinity spaces," asking why people learn more, participate more actively, engage more deeply with popular culture than they do with the contents of their textbooks.[9] As one sixteen-year-old *Harry Potter* fan told me, "It is one thing to be discussing the theme of a short story you've never heard of before and couldn't care less about. It is another to be discussing the theme of your friend's 50,000-word opus about Harry and Hermione that they've spent three months writing."[10] Affinity spaces offer powerful opportunities for learning, Gee argues, because they are sustained by common endeavors that bridge across differences in age, class, race, gender, and educational level, because people can participate in various ways according to their skills and interests, because they depend on peer-to-peer teaching with each participant constantly motivated to acquire new knowledge or refine his or her existing skills, and because they allow each participant to feel like an expert while tapping the expertise of others. More and more literacy experts are recognizing that enacting, reciting, and appropriating elements from preexisting stories is a valuable and organic part of the process by which children develop cultural literacy.[11]

A decade ago, published fan fiction came mostly from women in their twenties, thirties, and beyond. Today, these older writers have been joined by a generation of new contributors who found fan fiction surfing the Internet and decided to see what they could produce. *Harry Potter* in particular has encouraged many young people to write and share their first stories. Zsenya, the thirty-three-year-old Webmistress of The Sugar Quill, a leading site for Harry Potter fan fiction, offered this comment:

> In many cases, the adults really try to watch out for the younger members (theoretically, everybody who registers for our forums must be at least 13).

They're a little bit like den mothers. I think it's really actually an amazing way to communicate. . . . The absence of face-to-face equalizes everyone a little bit, so it gives the younger members a chance to talk with adults without perhaps some of the intimidation they might normally feel in talking to adults. And in the other direction, I think it helps the adults remember what it was like to be at a certain age or in a certain place in life.[12]

These older fans often find themselves engaging more directly with people like Flourish. Flourish started reading *The X-Files* fan fiction when she was ten, wrote her first Harry Potter stories at twelve, and published her first online novel at fourteen.[13] She quickly became a mentor for other emerging fan writers, including many who were twice her age or more. Most people assumed she was probably a college student. Interacting online allowed her to keep her age to herself until she had become so central to the fandom that nobody cared that she was in middle school.

Educators like to talk about "scaffolding," the ways that a good pedagogical process works in a step-by-step fashion, encouraging kids to try out new skills that build on those they have already mastered, providing support for these new steps until the learner feels sufficient confidence to take them on their own. In the classroom, scaffolding is provided by the teacher. In a participatory culture, the entire community takes on some responsibility for helping newbies find their way. Many young authors began composing stories on their own as a spontaneous response to a popular culture. For these young writers, the next step was the discovery of fan fiction on the Internet, which provided alternative models for what it meant to be an author. At first, they might only read stories, but the fan community provides many incitements for readers to cross that last threshold into composing and submitting their own stories. And once a fan submits, the feedback he or she receives inspires further and improved writing.

What difference will it make, over time, if a growing percentage of young writers begin publishing and getting feedback on their work while they are still in high school? Will they develop their craft more quickly? Will they discover their voices at an earlier age? And what happens when these young writers compare notes, becoming critics, editors, and mentors? Will this help them develop a critical vocabulary for thinking about storytelling? Nobody is quite sure, but the potentials seem enormous. Authorship has an almost sacred aura in a world where there are limited opportunities to circulate your ideas to a larger public. As we expand access to mass distribution via the Web, our understanding of what it means to be an author—and what kinds of authority should be ascribed to authors—necessarily shifts. This shift could lead to a heightened awareness of intellectual property rights as more and more people feel a sense of ownership over the stories they create. Yet, it also can result in a demystification of the creative process, a growing recognition of the communal dimensions of expression, as writing takes on more aspects of traditional folk practice.

The fan community has gone to extraordinary lengths to provide informal instruction to newer writers. The largest *Harry Potter* archive, <www.fictionalley.org>, currently hosts more than 30,000 stories and book chapters, including hundreds of completed or partially completed novels. These stories are written by authors of all ages. More than two hundred people are on its unpaid staff, including forty mentors who welcome each new participant individually. At The Sugar Quill, <www.sugarquill.net>, every posted story undergoes beta reading (a peer-review process). Beta reading takes its name from beta testing in computer programming: fans seek out advice on the rough drafts of their nearly completed stories so that they can smooth out "bugs" and take them to the next level. As the editors explain, "We want this to be a place where fanfiction can be read and enjoyed, but where writers who want more than just raves can come for actual (gentle—think Lupin, not McGonagall) constructive criticism and technical editing. We've found this to be essential for our own stories, and would be pleased to help with the stories of others. Our hope is that this experience will give people the courage and confidence to branch out and start writing original stories."[14] (Lupin and McGonagall are two of the teachers Rowling depicts in the novels, Lupin a gentle pedagogue, McGonagall practicing a more tough love approach.) New writers often go through multiple drafts and multiple beta readers before their stories are ready for posting. "The Beta Reader service has really helped me to get the adverbs out of my writing and get my prepositions in the right place and improve my sentence structure and refine the overall quality of my writing," explains Sweeney Agonistes, an entering college freshman with years of publishing behind her.[15]

Instructions for beta readers, posted at Writer's University (<www.writersu.net>), a site that helps instruct fan editors and writers, offers some insights into the pedagogical assumptions shaping this process:

A good beta reader:

- admits to the author what his or her own strengths and weaknesses are—i.e. "I'm great at beta reading for plot, but not spelling!" Anyone who offers to check someone else's spelling, grammar, and punctuation should probably be at least worthy of a solid B in English, and preferably an A.
- reads critically to analyze stylistic problems, consistency, plot holes, unclarity, smoothness of flow and action, diction (choice of words), realism and appropriateness of dialog, and so forth. Does it get bogged down in unnecessary description or back-story? Do the characters "sound" like they're supposed to? Is the plot logical and do the characters all have motives for the things they do?
- suggests rather than edits. In most cases a beta reader shouldn't rewrite or merely correct problems. Calling the author's attention to problems helps the author be aware of them and thereby improve.

- points out the things he or she likes about a story. Even if it was the worst story you ever read, say something positive! Say multiple somethings positive! See the potential in every story. . . .
- is tactful, even with things she considers major flaws—but honest as well.
- improves her skills. If you are serious about wanting to help authors, consider reading some of the writing resources linked at the bottom of the page, which will give you some great perspective on common mistakes fanfic writers make, in addition to basic tips about what makes for good writing.[16]

This description constructs a different relationship between mentors and learners than shapes much schoolroom writing instruction, starting with the opening stipulation that the editors acknowledge their own strengths and limitations, and continuing down through the focus on suggestion rather than instruction as a means of getting students to think through the implications of their own writing process.

As educational researcher Rebecca Black notes, the fan community can often be more tolerant of linguistic errors than traditional classroom teachers and more helpful in enabling the learner to identify what they are actually trying to say because reader and writer operate within the same frame of reference, sharing a deep emotional investment in the content being explored.[17] The fan community promotes a broader range of different literary forms—not simply fan fiction but various modes of commentary—than the exemplars available to students in the classroom, and often they showcase realistic next steps for the learner's development rather than showing only professional writing that is far removed from anything most students will be able to produce.

Beyond beta reading, The Sugar Quill provides a range of other references relevant to fan writers, some dealing with questions of grammar and style, some dealing with the specifics of the *Harry Potter* universe, but all designed to help would-be writers improve their stories and push themselves in new directions. The Sugar Quill's genre classifications provide models for different ways would-be writers might engage with Rowling's text: "Alternative Points of View," which reframe the events of the book through the eyes of a character other than Harry; "I Wonder Ifs," which explore "possibilities" that are hinted at but not developed within the novels; "Missing Moments," which fill in gaps between the plot events; and "Summer after Fifth Year," which extend beyond the current state of the novel, but do not enter into events Rowling will likely cover once she picks up her pen again. The Sugar Quill holds writers to a strict and literal interpretation, insisting that the information they include in their stories be consistent with what Rowling has revealed. As the editor explains,

> I don't write fanfic to "fix" things, I write it to explore corners that [the Harry Potter] canon didn't have the opportunity to peek into, or to speculate

on what *might* have led up to something, or what *could* result from some other thing. A story that leaves these wonderful corners isn't a story that needs fixing, it's a story that invites exploration, like those pretty little tree-lined side streets that you never get a chance to go down when you're on a bus, heading for work along the main drag. That doesn't mean there's anything wrong with the bus, with the main drag, or with going to work—it just means there's more down there to take a look at.[18]

Many adults worry that these kids are "copying" preexisting media content rather than creating their own original works. Instead, one should think about their appropriations as a kind of apprenticeship. Historically, young artists learned from established masters, sometimes contributing to the older artists' works, often following their patterns, before they developed their own styles and techniques. Our modern expectations about original expression are a difficult burden for anyone at the start of a career. In this same way, these young artists learn what they can from the stories and images that are most familiar to them. Building their first efforts upon existing cultural materials allows them to focus their energies elsewhere, mastering their craft, perfecting their skills, and communicating their ideas. Like many of the other young writers, Sweeney said that Rowling's books provided her the scaffolding she needed to focus on other aspects of the writing process: "It's easier to develop a good sense of plot and characterization and other literary techniques if your reader already knows something of the world where the story takes place." Sweeney writes mostly about the Hogwarts teachers, trying to tell the novels' events from their perspectives and exploring their relationships when they are not in front of the class. As she explains,

> I figure J. K. Rowling is going to take care of the student portion of the world as Harry gets to it. The problem with world building is that there is so much backstory to play with. I like filling in holes. . . . See if you can figure out a plausible way that would fit into the established canon to explain why Snape left Voldemort and went to serve Dumbledore. There are so many explanations for that but we don't know for sure yet, so when we find out, if we find out, there are going to be so many people reading for it and if someone gets it right, they are going to go, yes, I nailed it.

Others noted that writing about someone else's fictional characters, rather than drawing directly on their own experience, gave them some critical distance to reflect on what they were trying to express. Sweeney described how getting inside the head of a character who was very different from herself helped her make sense of the people she saw around her in school who were coming from very different backgrounds and acting on very different values. She saw fan fiction, in that sense, as a useful resource for surviving high school. *Harry Potter* fan fiction yields countless narratives of youth empowerment as characters fight back against the injustices their writers encounter every day at school. Often, the younger writers show a fascination with getting inside the heads of the adult characters. Many of the best stories are told from teachers' perspectives or depict Harry's parents and mentors when they were school age. Some of the stories are sweetly romantic or bitter-sweet coming-of-age stories (where sexual consummation comes when two characters hold hands); others are charged with anger or budding sexual feelings, themes the authors say they would have been reluctant to discuss in a school assignment. When they discuss such stories, teen and adult fans talk openly about their life experiences, offering each other advice on more than just issues of plot or characterization.

Through online discussions of fan writing, the teen writers develop a vocabulary for talking about writing and learn strategies for rewriting and improving their own work. When they talk about the books themselves, they make comparisons with other literary works or draw connections with philosophical and theological traditions; they debate gender stereotyping in the female characters; they cite interviews with the writer or read critical analyses of the works; they use analytic concepts they probably wouldn't encounter until they reached the advanced undergraduate classroom.

Schools are still locked into a model of autonomous learning that contrasts sharply with the kinds of learning that are needed as students are entering the new knowledge cultures. Gee and other educators worry that students who are comfortable participating in and exchanging knowledge through affinity spaces are being deskilled as they enter the classroom:

> Learning becomes both a personal and unique trajectory through a complex space of opportunities (i.e., a person's own unique movement through various affinity spaces over time) and a social journey as one shares aspects of that trajectory with others (who may be very different from oneself and inhabit otherwise quite different spaces) for a shorter or longer time before moving on. What these young people see in school may pale by comparison. It may seem to lack the imagination that infuses the non-school aspects of their lives. At the very least, they may demand an argument for "Why school?"[19]

Gee's focus is on the support system that emerges around the individual learner, Pierre Lévy's focus is on the ways that each learner contributes to the larger collective intelligence; but both are describing parts of the same experience—living in a world where knowledge is shared and where critical activity is ongoing and lifelong.

Not surprisingly, someone who has just published her first online novel and gotten dozens of letters of comment finds it disappointing to return to the classroom where her work is going to be read only by the teacher and feedback may be very limited. Some teens confessed to smuggling drafts of stories to school in their textbooks and editing them during class; others sit around the lunch table talking plot and character issues with their classmates or try to work on the stories on the school computers until the librarians accuse them of wasting time. They can't wait for the school bell to ring so they can focus on their writing.

Lawver was not the only one to see the educational payoff from fan writing. A number of libraries have brought in imaginary lecturers on muggle life or run weekend-long classes modeled after those taught at the remarkable school. A group of Canadian publishers organized a writing summer camp for children, designed to help them perfect their craft. The publishers were responding to the many unsolicited manuscripts they had received from Potter fans.[20] One educational group organized Virtual Hogwarts, which offered courses on both academic subjects and the topics made famous from Rowling's books. Adult teachers from four continents developed the online materials for thirty different classes, and the effort drew more than three thousand students from seventy-five nations.

It is not clear that the successes of affinity spaces can be duplicated by simply incorporating similar activities into the classroom. Schools impose a fixed leadership hierarchy (including very different roles for adults and teens); it is unlikely that someone like Heather or Flourish would have had the same editorial opportunities they have found through fandom. Schools have less flexibility to support writers at very different stages of their development. Even the most progressive schools set limits on what students can write compared to the freedom they enjoy on their own. Certainly, teens may receive harsh critical responses to their more controversial stories when they publish them online, but the teens themselves are deciding what risks they want to take and facing the consequences of those decisions.

That said, we need to recognize that improving writing skills is a secondary benefit of participating in the fan fiction writing community. Talking about fan fiction in these terms makes the activity seem more valuable to teachers or parents who may be skeptical of the worthiness of these activities. And the kids certainly take the craft of writing seriously and are proud of their literacy accomplishments. At the same time, the writing is valuable because of the ways it expands their experience of the world of *Harry Potter* and because of the social connections it facilitates with other fans. These kids are passionate about writing because they are passionate about what they are writing about. To some degree, pulling such activities into the schools is apt to deaden them because school culture generates a different mindset than our recreational life.

Defense Against Dark Arts

J. K. Rowling and Scholastic, her publisher, had initially signaled their support for fan writers, stressing that storytelling encouraged kids to expand their imaginations and empowered them to find their voices as writers.

Through her London-based agent, the Christopher Little Literary Agency, Rowling had issued a statement in 2003 describing the author's long-standing policy of welcoming "the huge interest that her fans have in the series and the fact that it has led them to try their hand at writing."[21] When Warner Bros. bought the film rights in 2001, however, the stories entered a second and not so complimentary intellectual property regime.[22] The studio had a long-standing practice of seeking out Web sites whose domain names used copyrighted or trademarked phrases. Trademark law was set up to avoid "potential confusions" about who produces particular goods or content; Warner felt it had a legal obligation to police sites that emerged around their properties. The studio characterized this as a "sorting out" process in which each site was suspended until the studio could assess what the site was doing with the *Harry Potter* franchise. Diane Nelson, senior vice president of Warner Bros. Family Entertainment, explained:

> When we dug down under some of these domain names, we could see clearly who was creating a screen behind which they were exploiting our property illegally. With fans you did not have to go far to see that they were just fans and they were expressing something vital about their relationship to this property. . . . You hate to penalize an authentic fan for the actions of an inauthentic fan, but we had enough instances of people who really were exploiting kids in the name of *Harry Potter*.

In many cases, the original site owner would be issued permission to continue to use the site under the original name, but Warner Bros. retained the right to shut it down if they found "inappropriate or offensive content."

The fans felt slapped in the face by what they saw as the studio's efforts to take control over their sites. Many of those caught up in these struggles were children and teens, who had been among the most active organizers of the *Harry Potter* fandom. Heather Lawver, the young editor of *The Daily Prophet*, formed the American-based organization, Defense Against the Dark Arts, when she learned that some fan friends had been threatened with legal action: "Warner was very clever about who they attacked. . . . They attacked a whole bunch of kids in Poland. How much of a risk is that? They went after the 12 and 15 year olds with the rinky-dink sites. They underestimated how interconnected our fandom was. They underestimated the fact that we knew those kids in Poland and we knew the rinky dink sites and we cared about them." Heather herself never received a cease-and-desist letter, but she made it her cause to defend friends who were under legal threats. In the United Kingdom, fifteen-year-old Claire Field emerged as the poster girl in the fans' struggle against Warner Bros. She and her parents had hired a solicitor after she received a cease-and-desist letter for her site, <www.harrypotterguide.co.uk>, and in the process, took the struggle to the British media. Her story was reported worldwide, and in each location other teen Webmasters who had been shut down by Warner's legal representatives also came public.[23] Lawver joined forces with Field's British supporters, helping to coordinate media outreach and activism against the studio.

Defense Against Dark Arts argued that fans had helped to turn a little known children's book into an international best-seller and that the rights holders owed them some latitude to do their work. The petition ends with a "call to arms" against studios that fail to appreciate their supporters: "There are dark forces afoot, darker even than He-Who-Must-Not-Be-Named, because these dark forces are daring to take away something so basic, so human, that it's close to murder. They are taking away our freedom of speech, our freedom to express our thoughts, feelings, and ideas, and they are taking away the fun of a magical book."[24] Lawver, the passionate and articulate teen, debated a Warner Bros. spokesman on MSNBC's *Hardball with Chris Matthews* (1997). As Lawver explained, "We weren't disorganized little kids anymore. We had a public following and we had a petition with 1500 signatures in a matter of two weeks. They [Warner Bros.] finally had to negotiate with us."

As the controversy intensified, Diane Nelson, senior vice president of Warner Bros. Family Entertainment, publicly acknowledged that the studio's legal response had been "naïve" and "an act of miscommunication."[25] Nelson, now executive vice president for Global Brand Management, told me, "We didn't know what we had on our hands early on in dealing with *Harry Potter*. We did what we would normally do in the protection of our intellectual property. As soon as we realized we were causing consternation to children or their parents, we stopped it." Out of the conflict, the studio developed a more collaborative policy for engaging with *Harry Potter* fans, one similar to the ways that Lucas was seeking to collaborate with *Star Wars* fan filmmakers:

> Heather is obviously a very smart young woman and did an effective job drawing attention to the issue. . . . She brought to our attention fans who she felt had been victims of these letters. We called them. In one instance, there was a young man she was holding up as a poster child for what we were doing wrong. He was a young man out of London. He and two of his friends from school had started a Triwizard Tournament of the internet. They were having contests through their sites. . . . Ultimately, what we did with them was the basis of what we did with subsequent fans. We deputized them. We ended up sponsoring their tournament and paying for their P.O. box for off line entries to this contest. . . . We were not at all opposed to his site or what he was doing on it or how he was expressing himself as a fan. In fact, we believed from day one that those sites were critical to the success of what we were doing and the more of them the better. We ended up giving him official sanction and access to materials to include on the site so that we could keep him within the family and still protect *Harry Potter* materials appropriately.

Many *Potter* fans praised Warner for admitting its mistakes and fixing the problems in their relations with fans. Lawver remains unconvinced, seeing the outcome more as an attempt to score a public relations victory than any shift in their thinking. She has recently added a section to *The Daily Prophet* designed to provide resources for other fan communities that wish to defend themselves against studio restrictions on their expression and participation.[26]

Heather Lawver and her allies had launched their children's campaign against Warner Bros. under the assumption that such fan activism had a long history. She explained: "I figured with the history that *Star Wars* and *Star Trek* fan writers had, people would have done this before. I didn't think much of it. I thought we had precedence but apparently not." Other groups had tried, but not with nearly the same degree of success. After several decades of aggressive studio attention, there is literally no case law concerning fan fiction. The broad claims sometimes asserted by the studios have never been subjected to legal contestation. Studios threaten, fans back down, and none of the groups that would normally step forward to defend free expression rights consider it part of their agenda to defend amateur creators. Free-speech organizations, including the American Civil Liberties Union and the Electronic Frontier Foundation, joined Muggles for Harry Potter, a group created to support teachers who wanted to keep the *Harry Potter* books in the classroom, but failed to defend the fan fiction writers who asserted their rights to build their fantasies around Rowling's novel. The Stanford Center for Internet and Society posted a statement—explicitly supportive, implicitly condescending—about fan fiction on its Chilling Effects Web site (<http://www.chillingeffects.org/fanfic>). The statement in effect concedes most of the claims made by the studio attorneys.[27] Adopting a similar position, Electronic Frontier Foundation chairman of the board Brad Templeton writes, "Almost all 'fan fiction' is arguably a copyright violation. If you want to write a story about Jim Kirk and Mr. Spock, you need Paramount's permission, pure and simple."[28] Note how Templeton moves from legal hedge words like "arguably" in the first sentence to the moral certainty of "plain and simple" by the second. With friends like these, who needs enemies?

The fan community includes plenty of lawyers, some informed, some otherwise, who have been willing to step up where the public interest groups have failed, and to offer legal advice to fans about how to contest efforts to shut down their Web sites.[29] Fan activists, for example, support Writers University, a Web site that, among other services, provides periodic updates on how a range of different media franchises and individual authors have responded to fan fiction, identifying those who welcome and those who prohibit participation.[30] The site's goal is to allow fans to make an informed choice about the risks they face in pursuing their hobbies and interests. Legal scholars Rosemary J. Coombe and Andrew Herman note that fans have found posting their cease-and-desist letters on the Web to be an effective tactic, one that forces media companies to publicly confront the consequences of their actions, and one that helps fans see the patterns of legal action that might otherwise be felt only by those Webmistresses directly involved.[31]

Nobody is sure whether fan fiction falls under current fair-use protections. Current copyright law simply doesn't have a category for dealing with amateur creative expression. Where there has been a "public interest" factored into the legal definition of fair use—such as the desire to protect the rights of libraries to circulate books or journalists to quote or academics to cite other researchers—it has been advanced in terms of legitimated classes of users and not a generalized public right to cultural participation. Our current notion of fair use is an artifact of an era when few people had access to the marketplace of ideas, and those who did fell into certain professional classes. It surely demands close reconsideration as we develop technologies that broaden who may produce and circulate cultural materials. Judges know what to do with people who have professional interests in the production and distribution of culture; they don't know what to do with amateurs, or people they deem to be amateurs.

Industry groups have tended to address copyright issues primarily through a piracy model, focusing on the threat of file sharing, rather than dealing with the complexities of fan fiction. Their official educational materials have been criticized for focusing on copyright protections to the exclusion of any reference to fair use. By implication, fans are seen simply as "pirates" who steal from the studios and give nothing in return. Studios often defend their actions against fans on the grounds that if they do not actively enforce their copyrights they will be vulnerable to commercial competitors encroaching on their content.

The best legal solution to this quagmire may be to rewrite fair-use protections to legitimate grassroots, not-for-profit circulation of critical essays, and stories that comment on the content of mass media. Companies certainly are entitled to protect their rights against encroachment from commercial competitors, yet under the current system, because other companies know how far they can push and are reluctant to sue each other, they often have greater latitude to appropriate and transform media content than amateurs, who do not know their rights and have little legal means to defend them even if they did. One paradoxical result is that works that are hostile to the original creators and thus can be read more explicitly as making critiques of the source material may have greater freedom from copyright enforcement than works that embrace the ideas behind the original work and simply seek to extend them in new directions. A story where Harry and the other students rose up to overthrow Dumbledore because of his paternalistic policies is apt to be recognized by a judge as political speech and parody, whereas a work that imagines Ron and Hermione going on a date may be so close to the original that its status as criticism is less clear and is apt to be read as infringement.

In the short run, change is more likely to occur by shifting the way studios think about fan communities than reshaping the law. . . . Nelson said that the *Harry Potter* controversy was instrumental in starting conversations within the studio between business, public relations, creative, and legal department staffers, about what principles should govern their relations with their fans and supporters: "We are trying to balance the needs of other creative stakeholders, as well as the fans, as well as our own legal obligations, all within an arena which is new and changing and there are not clear precedents about how things should be interpreted or how they would be acted upon if they ever reached the courts."

In the course of the interview, she described fans as "core shareholders" in a particular property and the "life blood" of the franchise. The studio needed to find ways to respect the "creativity and energy" these fans brought behind a franchise, even as they needed to protect the franchise from encroachment from groups who wanted to profit for their efforts, to respond quickly to misinformation, or, in the case of material aimed at the youth market, to protect children from access to mature content. As far as fan fiction goes,

> We recognize that it is the highest compliment in terms of the fans inserting themselves into the property and wanting to express their love for it. We are very respectful of what that means. There is a degree to which fan fiction is acceptable to authors and there is a degree to which it moves into a place where it does not feel appropriate, respectful, or within the rights of fans. A lot has to do with how a fan wants to publish and whether they want to benefit commercially off of that fan fiction. If it is purely just an expression for others to read and experience and appreciate, I think that is generally pretty tolerable by a studio rights holder and a creator. The more broadly the fan wants to see that fan fiction disseminated or trade upon it for revenue, promotion, or publicity, the less tolerant the studio or creator might be.

But, as Nelson acknowledged, the fan's "sense of ownership over a particular property" posed challenges for the studio:

> When we stray from the source material or what fans perceive as the true roots of a property, we are under their scrutiny. They can become either advocates for what we are doing or strong dissenters. They can shift the tide of how a property is introduced into the market place depending on whether they perceive us as having presented it carefully, respectfully, and accurately. . . . Fans may be trying to promote the property on the internet in their terms but they can sometimes compromise our responsibility to protect that intellectual property so as to keep it pure and to keep our legal rights in tact.

There is still—and perhaps may always be—a huge gap between the studio's assumptions about what constitutes appropriate fan participation and the fans' own sense of moral "ownership" over the property. The studios are now, for the most part, treating cult properties as "love marks" and fans as "inspirational consumers" whose efforts help generate broader interests in their properties. Establishing the fans' loyalty often means lessening traditional controls that companies might exert over their intellectual properties and thus opening up a broader space for grassroots creative expression.

Muggles for *Harry Potter*

. . . So far, we have been focused on participation as a positive force in the lives of these kids—something that is motivating children to read, write, form communities, and master other kinds of content—not to mention, stand up for their rights. Yet as we turn our attention to some of *Harry Potter's* conservative critics, participation takes on altogether more sinister connotations. Evangelist Phil Arms, for example, describes *Harry Potter* and *Pokémon* (1998) as "fatal attractions" drawing children toward the realm of the occult: "Sooner or later, all who enter the world of *Harry Potter* must meet the true face behind the veil. And when they do, they discover what all those who toy with evil discover, and that is, that while they may have been just playing, the Devil always plays for keeps."[32] The moral reformers cite the example of kids dressing up like *Harry Potter*, putting a magic sorting cap on their heads in an imitation of the book's initiation ritual, or drawing lightning bolts on their foreheads to duplicate Harry's scar, as evidence that children are moving from reading the books into participating in occult activities. Tapping deep-seated anxieties about theatricality and role-playing, Arms and his allies worry that immersion into fictional worlds may amount to a form of "astral projection"[33] or that when we speak words of magic, the demon forces that we summon do not necessarily realize that we are only pretending. These conservative critics warn that the compelling experiences of popular culture can override real-world experiences until children are no longer able to distinguish between fact and fantasy. For some, this level of engagement is enough to leave the *Harry Potter* books suspect: "These books are read over and over by children in the same way the Bible should be read."[34]

More generally, they are concerned about the immersive and expansive nature of the imaginary worlds being constructed in contemporary media franchises. Another evangelist, Berit Kjos, compares the *Harry Potter* books with *Dungeons and Dragons* (1975) in that regard:

1. Both immerse their fans in a plausible, well-developed fantasy world, replete with an evolving history, a carefully mapped geography, and wizards that model the thrill-packed and power-filled way of the mythical shaman.

2. In this fantasy world, adults and children alike are led into imagined experiences that create memories, build new values, guide their thinking and mold their understanding of reality.[35]

Here, the conservative critics seem to be taking aim at the very concept of transmedia storytelling—seeing the idea of world making as dangerous in itself insofar as it encourages us to invest more time mastering the details of a fictional environment and less time confronting the real world.

If these religious reformers are concerned about the immersive qualities of *Harry Potter*, they are equally concerned about its intertextuality. Kjos warns us:

> The main product marketed through this movie is a belief system that clashes with everything God offers us for our peace and security. This pagan ideology comes complete with trading cards, computer and other wizardly games, clothes and decorations stamped with HP symbols, action figures and cuddly dolls and audio cassettes that could keep the child's minds focused on the occult all day and into night. But in God's eyes, such paraphernalia become little more than lures and doorways to deeper involvement with the occult.[36]

In particular, they argue that Rowling makes more than sixty specific references in the first four books to actual occult practices and personages from the history of alchemy and witchcraft. They identify some historical and literary allusions Rowling intended to be recognized by literate readers, such as her reference to Nicolas Flamel, the medieval alchemist who is credited with discovering the Sorcerer's Stone or to Merlin and Morgana from the Arthurian romances as figures on the wizards' collectors' cards. But some fundamentalist critics read the lightning bolt on Harry's forehead as the "mark of the beast" or map Voldemort onto "the nameless one," an anti-Christian witch, both foretold in *Revelations*. They contend that children seeking additional information will be drawn toward pagan works that promise more knowledge and power. One Catholic writer explains: "When he has finished reading the *Potter* series, what will he turn to? There is a vast industry turning out sinister material for the young that will feed their growing appetites."[37] In fairness, librarians and educators tap many of these same intertextual references. For example, among the courses offered at Virtual Hogwarts are classes in fortunetelling, astrology, and alchemy, taught no doubt as historical beliefs and practices, but nevertheless deeply offensive to fundamentalists.

These moral reformers agree that the books are sparking literacy and learning, but they are anxious about what kids are being taught. Some activists see the books as a dilution of Christian influence on American culture in favor of a new global spiritualism. Kjos warns that "the *Harry Potter* books would not have been culturally acceptable half a century ago.

Today's cultural climate—an 'open-mindedness' toward occult entertainment together with 'closed-mindedness' toward Biblical Christianity—was planned a century ago. It was outlined by the United Nations in the late 1940s and has been taught and nurtured through the developing global education system during the last six decades."[38] Whereas a generation ago these groups might have taken aim at secular humanism, they now see a new phase of globalization during which multinational companies and supranational organizations are actively erasing cultural differences. To reach a global market, these Christian critics argue, American capitalism must strip aside the last vestiges of the Judeo-Christian tradition, and to promote consumerism, it must erode away all resistance to temptation. Aspects of pagan and Eastern faiths are entering classrooms in a secularized form—the worship of the earth transformed into ecology, astral projection into visualization exercises—while Christianity remains locked outside by advocates of the separation of church and state. The *Harry Potter* books are, as a consequence, going to have very different effects than, say, *The Wizard of Oz* (1900), which was read by children within a deeply Christian culture. Instead, the fundamentalists warn, American children are susceptible to the pagan influences of these books because they are consumed alongside television shows like *Pokémon* (1998) or read in schools that already have a global and secular curriculum.

If some adults were simply "too busy" to defend *Harry Potter* against these would-be censors, many teachers risked their jobs defending the books. Mary Dana, a middle school teacher in Zeeland, Michigan, was one of the educators who found herself caught up in these debates.[39] Dana had come to teaching as a second career after having spent more than a decade as an independent bookseller. She had weathered a range of previous controversies about books she had brought into this community. She drew a line in 2000 when the local superintendent decided that *Harry Potter* books should be outlawed from public readings, removed from the open shelves of the school library, barred from future purchase, and left accessible only to students who had written permission from their parents. Dana explains: "I don't like confrontations and I don't like to speak in public. I'm a pretty shy person actually. I had plenty of experience of First Amendment challenges when we owned our bookstore. I had been under attack before. It was a very ugly difficult experience, but ultimately, when you think you just can't fight them, you still have to because they are wrong. . . . I wasn't going to let it drop." Like Lawver, Dana saw the potential of the *Harry Potter* books to excite kids about reading and learning; she felt that such books needed to be in the classroom.

Working with a local parent, Nancy Zennie, Dana organized opposition to the superintendent's decision, helping to frame and circulate petitions, organize rallies, and pull people to a school board meeting where the issue was going to be discussed. Trying to rally public support, Dana and Zennie helped to create an organization, Muggles for Harry Potter, which could tap national and international fan interest. They were joined by a group of eight organizations, representing booksellers, publishers, librarians, teachers, writers, civil libertarians, and consumers. "Muggles for Harry Potter is fighting for the right of students and teachers to use the best books that are available for children, even when some parents object," said Christopher Finan, president of the American Booksellers Foundation for Free Expression. "The Potter books are helping turn video-game players into readers. We can't allow censorship to interfere with that."[40] In the end, the school board removed many of the restrictions placed on the books, though the ban on reading them in the classroom remained.

Over the next nine months, over 18,000 people joined the Muggles campaign through its Web site, and the group has been credited with curbing the nationwide efforts of fundamentalists to get the books banned from schools.[41] The organization sought to teach young readers of the *Harry Potter* books about the importance of standing up for free expression. The organization, which later changed its name to kid-SPEAK! (<www.kidspeakonline. org>), created online forums where kids could share their views with one another about the Potter wars and other censorship issues. For example, Jaclyn, a seventh-grader, wrote this response to news that a fundamentalist minister had cut up copies of *Harry Potter* when the fire department refused to grant him a permit to have a book burning:

> Reverend Taylor, the host of Jesus Party should look closer before judging. Kids are reading these books and discovering there is more to life than going to school. What have they discovered exactly? Their imaginations. Does Reverend Doug Taylor realize what he is doing? Kids are fighting for their First Amendment rights but do they also have the fight for their imaginations—the one thing that keeps one person different than the others? We stand back and watch him rip the books to shreds, almost symbolically, ripping up our imaginations. Children like the books because they want to live in that world, they want to see magic, not see some phony magician pull a rabbit out of his hat. They want to have a brave friend like Harry Potter and ride across the dark lake where the giant squid lurks to the grand castle of Hogwarts. Although they want to do all of these things, they know Hogwarts isn't real and Harry Potter does not exist.

One of the striking features of the discussions on kidSPEAK is how often the kids are forced to recant their fantasies in order to defend their right to have them in the first place. Here's another example: "And another thing Anti-*Harry Potter* people it is FICTION get that entirely made up except like the setting (England) and the places (Kings Cross Station) etc. But I seriously doubt if you go to London you'll find The Leaky Cauldron or a Wizard.

That's what fiction is—made up. So all you people against *Harry Potter*. Get over it."[42]

The fundamentalists claim that fantastical representations of violence or the occult shaped children's beliefs and actions in the real world. Countering such claims, the books' defenders were forced to argue that fantasies do not really matter, when in fact, what we have said so far suggests that the immersive quality of the books is what makes them such a powerful catalyst for creative expression. Even the name of the organization suggests uncertainty about what kind of relationship the adults wanted to foster to the books' fantasy. Dana explained: "The term refers to anyone who does not possess the magical powers. Anyone who is not a wizard by definition has to be a muggle. Of course, it was somewhat amusing because if people weren't willing to say they were muggles then what were they saying, that they had witchcraft powers." On the one hand, the name does tap fannish knowledge: only those people familiar with Rowling's world would recognize the term. On the other hand, adopting a muggle identity aligned participants with the mundane world. Rowling is merciless in making fun of the closed-mindedness of the Dursleys, Harry's adopted family. The Dursleys are totally uncomfortable with his special abilities and kept him literally closeted. The contrast between the group's embrace of muggleness and the fantastical identifications Lawver had enabled through *The Daily Prophet* could not be starker. The educators, librarians, and publishers saw the books as a means to an end—a way of getting kids excited about reading—whereas for the fans, reading and writing was the means to their end, having a more deeply engaged relationship with the world of Hogwarts.

The conservative Christians are simply the most visible of a broad range of groups, each citing their own ideological concerns that are reacting to a shift in the media paradigm, Anti–*Harry Potter* Christians share many concerns with other reform groups linking worries about the persuasive power of advertising to concerns about the demonic nature of immersion, tapping anxieties about consumerism and multinational capitalism in their critiques of global spiritualism. In *Plenitude* (1998), Grant McCracken talks about the "withering of the witherers," that is, the breakdown of the power traditional groups exercise over cultural expression.[43] Corporate gatekeepers, educational authorities, and church leaders all represent different forces that historically held in check tendencies toward diversification and fragmentation. Over the past several decades, McCracken argues, these groups have lost their power to define cultural norms as the range of different media and communication channels have expanded. Ideas and practices that were once hidden from public view—say, the Wiccan beliefs that fundamentalist critics claim are shaping the *Harry Potter* books—are now entering the mainstream, and these groups are struggling to police the culture that comes into their own homes and communities. . . .

What Would Jesus Do with *Harry Potter*?

We would be wrong to assume that the Potter wars represented a struggle of conservative Christians against liberal educators and fans. If some simply want to reinscribe old authorities and build up the institutions being challenged by a more participatory culture, others want to help children learn to make judgments about media content. Many Christian groups defended the books, presenting the concept of "discernment" as an alternative to culture war discourse. Connie Neal, the author of *What's a Christian to Do with Harry Potter?*, framed the choices in terms of "building a wall" to protect children from outside influences or "fitting them with armor" so that they can bring their own values with them when they encounter popular culture. Neal notes that "restricting freedom can incite curiosity and rebellion, leading the one you're trying to protect to try to get past the protective barrier to see what he or she is missing. . . . Even if you could keep children separated from all potentially dangerous influences, you would also be keeping them from a situation in which they could develop the maturity to ward off such dangers for themselves."[44] Instead, Neal advocates giving children media literacy skills, teaching them to evaluate and interpret popular culture within a Christian framework.

One discernment group, Ransom Fellowship, defines discernment as "an ability, by God's grace, to creatively chart a godly path through the maze of choices and options that confront us, even when we're faced with situations and issues that aren't specifically mentioned in the Scriptures."[45] The discernment movement draws inspiration from a range of biblical passages that speak of people who maintained their faith even when living in an alien land. Christians,

The Christian Counterculture

Rather than rejecting popular culture outright, a growing number of Christians are producing and consuming their own popular media on the fringes of the mainstream entertainment industry. While many Christians have felt cut off from mass media, they have been quick to embrace new technologies—such as videotape, cable television, low-wattage radio stations, and the Internet—that allow them to route around established gatekeepers. The result has been the creation of media products that mirror the genre conventions of popular culture but express an alternative set of values. In *Shaking the World for Jesus* (2004), Heather Hendershot offers a complex picture of the kinds of popular culture being produced by and for evangelicals.[1] Frustrated by network television, cultural conservatives have created their own animated series and sitcoms distributed on video. They have produced their own science fiction, horror, mystery, and romance novels, all of which can be purchased online. And alarmed by contemporary video games, they have produced their own, such as *Victory at Hebron* (2003), where players battle Satan or rescue martyrs.

The emergence of new media technologies has allowed evangelicals some degree of autonomy from commercial media, allowing them to identify and enjoy media products that more closely align with their own worldviews. Technology has also lowered the costs of production and distribution, enabling what remains

---

[1]Heather Hendershot, *Shaking the World for Jesus: Media and Conservative Evangelical Culture* (Chicago: University of Chicago Press, 2004).

essentially a niche market to sustain a remarkably broad range of cultural products. Of course, as "niche markets" go, this one may be astonishingly large. According to a 2002 ABC News/Beliefnet poll, 83 percent of Americans consider themselves to be Christians, and Baptists (only one of the evangelical denominations) make up 15 percent of the nation.[2]

As commercial media producers have realized the size of this demographic, the walls between Christian and mainstream popular culture are breaking down. *Veggie Tales* (1994) videos are finding their way into Wal-Mart, Focus on the Family's *Adventures in Odyssey* (1991) records get distributed as kids' meal prizes at Chick-fil-A, the *Left Behind* (1996) books become top sellers on Amazon.com, and Christian pop singer Amy Grant breaks into Top 40 radio. In the process, some of the more overtly religious markings get stripped away. Network television has begun to produce some shows, such as *Touched by an Angel* (1994), *7th Heaven* (1996), and *Joan of Arcadia* (2003), that deal with religious themes in a way designed to appeal to the "searchers" and the "saved" alike. Predictably, some evangelicals fear that Christianity has been commodified and that Jesus is becoming just another brand in the great big "marketplace of ideas."

It is in this context that we need to understand the staggering success of Mel Gibson's *The Passion of the Christ* (2004). The Christians knew how to get folks into the theater to support this film. For example, Gibson sought out the services of Faith Highway, a group that had previously produced public service messages that local churches could sponsor through local cable outlets to give their messages a more professional

they argue, are living in "modern captivity," holding on to and transmitting their faith in an increasingly hostile context.

In "Pop Culture: Why Bother?" Denis Haack, the founder and director of the Ransom Fellowship, argues that engaging with, rather than hiding from, popular culture has important benefits. Discernment exercises can help Christians develop a greater understanding of their own value system, can provide insights into the worldview of "nonbelievers," and can offer an opportunity for meaningful exchange between Christians and non-Christians. According to Haack, "If we are to understand those who do not share our deepest convictions, we must gain some comprehension of what they believe, why they believe it, and how those beliefs work out in daily life."[46] Their site provides discussion questions and advice about how to foster media literacy within an explicitly religious context, finding ideas worth struggling with in mainstream works as diverse as *Bruce Almighty* (2003), *Cold Mountain* (2003), and *Lord of the Rings* (2001). The Oracle in *The Matrix* (1999) is compared to a biblical prophet; viewers are invited to reflect on the role of prayer in the *Spider-Man* (2002) movies and on the kinds of "great responsibilities" Christians bear; and they are encouraged to show sympathy toward the spiritual quests undertaken by indigenous people in *Whale Rider* (2002) or by Bill Murray's character in *Lost in Translation* (2003). The site is very explicit that Christians are apt to disagree among themselves about what is or what is not valuable in such works, but that the process of talking through these differences focuses energy on spiritual matters and helps everyone involved to become more skillful in applying and defending their faith.

---

[2]Gary Langer, "Poll: Most Americans Say They're Christian." *ABC News*, July 18, 2002, <http://abcnews.go.com/US/story?id=90356&page=1>.

Whereas some cultural conservatives saw the immersiveness of contemporary popular culture as ensnaring young people in a dangerous realm of fantasies, some within the discernment movement have promoted the use of live action role-playing and computer games as spaces for exploring and debating moral questions. The Christian Gamers Guild (whose monthly newsletter is known as *The Way, The Truth & The Dice*) emerged in the midst of strong attacks from some evangelical leaders on role-playing and computer games. As they turn their attention toward games, they take this concept of discernment one step further—arguing that individual game masters (the people who "run" live action role-playing games) have the power to appropriate and transform these cultural materials according to their own beliefs. They are, to borrow the name of another group, Fans for Christ (FFC).

Groups like Fans for Christ and Anime Angels define themselves within the same kind of identity-politics language that sustains gay, lesbian, and bisexual or feminist Christian organizations. The FAQ for FFC explains:

> We have been alone too long! There are many of us fans out there who feel *different* because we are what we are. Some call us freaks, weirdoes, geeks, nerds, whatever. FFC is here for all of you to talk with your brothers and sisters who are Christians and share your freakiness. . . . You are welcome here to be as freaky and geeky as you like. . . . FFC is here to help show that our fan lifestyle is perfectly acceptable to Jesus. We hope to help our FFC members be able to explain clearly to others that the Bible does not condemn what we do, that we know that fiction is fiction, and

polish. Faith Highway urged churches to help raise money to support advertisements for the film and to link them back to their local messages. Many churches loaded up school buses full of worshippers to attend screenings and, with the release of the DVD, put together bulk orders to get the film into the hands of their congregations. Some church leaders have acknowledged backing this film in hopes that its commercial success will get Hollywood to pay attention to them. Faith Highway's CEO Dennis Dautel explained: "The leaders in the church are chomping at the bits to get media that is relevant to their message. Hollywood doesn't produce it. . . . The congregations went behind it because they wanted to see people turn out and see that movie. There was a strong desire in the Christian community for that movie to be a home run. This was our *Passion*."[3]

The *Harry Potter* controversy was fueled by these alternative media channels. While many of the mainstream televangelists and radiocasters, such as Charles Colson and James Dobson, made their peace with Rowling's universe, either endorsing it outright or urging parents to proceed with caution,[4] the anti-Potter voices most often came from new ministries that had staked a space for themselves on the Internet. They used the debate to strike back at what they saw as a theological establishment. One such site, Trumpet Ministries, went so far as to denounce Colson and Dobson as "modern day Judas Iscariots" because of their refusal to join the campaign against

---

[3]Dennis Dautel, personal interview, Fall 2004.

[4]For a range of Christian response, see Neal, *What's a Christian to Do?* See also "Opinion Roundup: Positive about Potter," Christianity Today, <http://www.christianitytoday.com/ct/1999/150/12.0.html>.

the books.[5] Just as the fluidity of culture has allowed youth greater access to pagan beliefs than ever before, it also meant that small-scale ministries could exert worldwide influence by posting their sermons and critiques from the national hinterland. Similarly, smaller video production companies, such as Jeremiah Films, could produce DVD documentaries with titles such as *Harry Potter: Witchcraft Repackaged* (2001) and sell them to concerned parents via the Web or infomercials on late-night cable.

The evangelical community sought to identify some Christian fantasy writers as alternatives to *Harry Potter*. Following in the tradition of Lewis and Tolkien, G. P. Taylor, an Anglican vicar, used his fantasy novel, *Shadowmancer* (2004), to explore moral and theological questions. The book outpaced *Harry Potter* for fifteen weeks in the United Kingdom and held six straight weeks on *the New York Times* best-seller list in the summer of 2004. The book was heavily promoted through Christian media, including Pat Robertson's "The 700 Club" and James Dobson's "Focus on the Family" as "just the thing to counter Harry Potter's magic." *Shadowmancer* broke into Christian bookstores that normally did not carry fantasy books, and from there made it into secular bookstores that still don't carry large amounts of spiritual fiction. The film rights were quickly optioned by Fortitude Films, a group formed to support Mel Gibson's *The Passion of the Christ,* and there has been some speculation that Gibson may direct the film adaptation. For his part, Taylor has been explicit that he wrote the book to show children God's power and not as an alternative to the *Harry Potter* books, which he claims not to have read.[6]

------

[5]"Harry Potter? What Does God Have to Say?" <http://www.lasttrumpetministries.org/tracts/tract7.html>.

[6]Dinitia Smith, "*Harry Potter* Inspires a Christian Alternative," *New York Times,* July 24, 2004, A15.

that God has made us different and it is wonderful.[47]

The site provides a list of "fan friendly" churches that respects their lifestyle choices and values their unique perspectives on spiritual issues. In return, the members pledge to share their love of Christ with other fans, to hold their own gatherings to promote Christian fantasy and science fiction authors, and to write their own fan stories that address central religious concerns.

Many leaders of the discernment movement are less celebratory of the "geeky and freaky" aspects of popular culture, but they do see the value in appropriating and rethinking works of popular culture. Many discernment advocates regard the *Harry Potter* books as the perfect opening for parents to talk with their children about the challenges of preserving their values in a secular society. Haack explains:

> Truth is taught here, truth that is worth some reflection and discussion, and though it is taught in an imaginary world, it applies to reality as well. . . . The world in which Harry Potter lives is a world of moral order, where ideas and choices have consequences, where good and evil are clearly distinguished, where evil is both dehumanizing and destructive, and where death is distressingly real. . . . Even if what all the critics say were true, the defensiveness of their recommendations is frankly embarrassing. If the *Harry Potter* novels were introductions to the occult, the church should welcome the opportunity to read and discuss them. Neopaganism is a growing reality in our post-Christian world, and our children need to be able to meet its challenge with a quiet confidence

in the gospel. They need to know the difference between fantasy literature and the occult. And they need to see their elders acting righteously, not scandalously.[48]

Few discernment advocates go as far as Heather Lawver does in inviting children to adopt fantasy roles and play within the world of the story, but some do appropriate the books to speak to Christian values. Connie Neal asks Christian parents to consider what Jesus would do confronted with these stories:

> Jesus might read the *Harry Potter* stories and use them as starting points for parables. . . . Just as Jesus noticed and met others' physical needs, he might attend to the earthly needs revealed in the lives of those who identify with the characters in *Harry Potter*. He might get them talking about *Harry Potter* and listen to what they identify with most: neglect, poverty, discrimination, abuse, fears, dreams, the pressures to fit in, desires to accomplish something in life, or the stresses of school. Then he would show them how to deal with such real parts of their lives.[49]

Rather than ban content that does not fully fit within their worldview, the discernment movement teaches Christian children and parents how to read those books critically, how to ascribe new meanings to them, and how to use them as points of entry into alternative spiritual perspectives.

Rather than shut down the intertextuality that is so rampant in the era of transmedia storytelling, Neal, Haack, and the other discernment leaders are looking for ways to harness its power. They provide reading lists for parents who want to build on their children's interests in *Harry Potter* as a point of entry into Christian fantasy. Several discernment groups published study guides to accompany the *Harry Potter* books and films with "probing questions" designed to explore the moral choices the characters made coupled with Bible verses that suggest how the same decisions are confronted within the Christian tradition. They focus, for example, on the moment when Harry's mother sacrifices her life to protect him as representing a positive role model for Christian love, or they discuss the corrupt moral choices that led to the creation of the Sorcerer's Stone as an example of sin. If the anti–*Harry Potter* Christians want to protect children from any exposure to those dangerous books, the discernment movement focuses on the agency of consumers to appropriate and transform media content.

As we can see, the conflicts that gave rise to the Potter Wars do not reduce themselves to evil censors and good defenders of civil liberties. The churn created by a convergence culture does not allow us to operate with this degree of moral certainty. All of those groups are struggling with the immersive nature and expansive quality of the new entertainment franchises. In the age of media convergence, consumer participation has emerged as the central conceptual problem: traditional gatekeepers seek to hold onto their control of cultural content, and other groups—fans, civil libertarians, and the Christian discernment movement—want to give consumers the skills they need to construct their own culture. For some, such as Heather Lawver or James Gee, role-playing and fan fiction writing are valuable because they allow kids to understand the books from the inside out; such activities involve a negotiation between self-expression and shared cultural materials, between introspection and collaborative fantasy building. Others, such as the Fans for Christ or the Christian gamers, embrace these activities because they allow players and writers to explore moral options, to test their values against fictional obstacles, and to work through in an imaginative way challenges that would have much higher stakes in their everyday lives. For still others, such as the conservative Christians who opposed the teaching of the books, role-playing and shared fantasies are dangerous because they distract youth from serious moral education and leave them susceptible to the appeals of pagan groups and occult practices. Yet in some ways, groups such as Muggles for Harry Potter seemed to share their concern that fantasy may itself be dangerous for kids, especially if they are unable to discern what separates the imaginative realm from reality.

We can read this debate as a reaction against many of the properties of convergence culture—against the expansion of fictional realms across multiple media, against the desire to master the arcane details of those texts and turn them into resources for a more participatory culture. For some, the concern is with the specific content of those fantasies—whether they are consistent with a Christian worldview. For others, the concern is with the marketing of those fantasies to children—whether we want opportunities for participation to be commodified. Ironically, at the same time, corporations are anxious about this fantasy play because it operates outside their control.

Unlike many previous fights over children's culture, however, this is not a story of children as passive victims of adult attempts at regulation and restraint. They are active participants in these new media landscapes, finding their own voice through their participation in fan communities, asserting their own rights even in the face of powerful entities, and sometimes sneaking behind their parents' back to do what feels right to them. At the same time, through their participation, these kids are mapping out new strategies for negotiating around and through globalization, intellectual property struggles, and media conglomeration. They are using the Internet to connect with children worldwide and, through that process, finding common interests and forging political alliances. Because the *Harry Potter* fandom involved both adults and children, it became a space where conversations could occur across generations. In talking about media pedagogies, then, we should no longer imagine this as a process where adults teach and children learn. Rather, we should see it as increasingly a space where children teach one another and where, if they would open their eyes, adults could learn a great deal.   ∎

NOTES

1. The assumptions underlying this argument are developed more fully in Henry Jenkins, "Childhood Innocence and Other Myths," in Henry Jenkins (ed.), *The Children's Culture Reader* (New York: New York University Press, 1998).
2. Unless otherwise noted, all quotes from Heather Lawver taken from interview with author, August 2003.
3. Heather Lawver, "To the Adults," <http://www.dprophet.com/hq/openletter.html>.
4. Ibid.
5. For more on the ways younger children use stories to work through real-life concerns, see Henry Jenkins, "Going Bonkers! Children, Play, and Pee-Wee," in Constance Penley and Sharon Willis (eds.), *Male Trouble* (Minneapolis: University of Minnesota Press, 1993).
6. Anne Haas Dyson, *Writing Superheroes: Cotemporary Childhood, Popular Culture, and Classroom Literacy* (New York: Teacher's College Press, 1997).
7. See, for example, Christine Schoefer, "Harry Potter's Girl Trouble," *Salon*, January 13, 2000, <http://archive.salon.com/books/feature/2000/01/13/potter/>. For a rebuttal, see Chris Gregory, "Hands Off Harry Potter! Have Critics of J. K. Rowling's Books Even Read Them?" *Salon*, March 1, 2000, <http://archive.salon.com/books/feature/2000/03/03/harry_potter/>.
8. Ellen Seiter, *Sold Separately: Children and Parents in Consumer Culture* (New Brunswick, N.J.: Rutgers University Press, 1993).
9. James Gee, *Language, Learning, and Gaming: A Critique of Traditional Schooling* (New York: Routledge, 2005), read in manuscript form.
10. Flourish, interview with author, August 2003.
11. See, for example, Shelby Anne Wolf and Shirley Brice Heath, *Braid of Literature: Children's World of Reading* (Cambridge, Mass.: Harvard University Press, 1992).
12. Zsenya, e-mail correspondence with author, July 2005.
13. Flourish, interview with author, August 2003.
14. Sugar Quill, <http://www.sugarquill.net>.
15. Sweeney Agonistes, interview with author, August 2003.
16. Elizabeth Durack, "Beta Reading!" *Writers University*, <http://www.writersu.com/WU//modules.php?name+News&file=article&sid=17>.
17. R. W. Black, "Anime-inspired Affiliation: An Ethnographic Inquiry into the Literacy and Social Practices of English Language Learners Writing in the Fanfiction Community," presented at 2004 meeting of American Educational Research Association, San Diego, accessible at <http://labweb.education.wisc.edu/room130/PDFS/InRevision.pdf>.
18. Interview with author, August 2003.
19. Gee, *Language, Learning, and Gaming*.

20. "The Leaky Cauldron," June 16, 2001, <http://www.the-leaky-cauldron.org/MTarchives/000767.html>.

21. Tracy Mayor, "Taking Liberties with Harry Potter," *Boston Globe Magazine*, June 29, 2003.

22. Stephanie Grunier and John Lippman, "Warner Bros. Claim Harry Potter Sites, "*Wall Street Journal Online*, December 20, 2000, <http://zdnet.com.com/2102-11_2 -503255.html>; "Kids 1—Warner Bros. 0: When the Big Studio Set Its Hounds on Some *Harry Potter* Fan Web Sites, It Didn't Bargain on the Potterhead Rebellion," *Vancouver Sun*, November 17, 2001.

23. Claire Field, interview with author, August 2003.

24. "Defense Against the Dark Arts," <http://www.dprophet.com/dada/>.

25. Ryan Buell, "Fans Call for War; Warner Bros. Claim Misunderstanding!" <http://www.entertainment-rewired.com./fan_appology.htm>.

26. See <http://www.dprophet.com/dada/>.

27. "Fan Fiction, Chilling Effects," <http://www.chillingeffects.org/fanfic>.

28. Brad Templeton, "10 Big Myths about Copyright Explained," <http://www .templetons.com/brad/copymyths.html>.

29. See, for example, Rebecca Tushnet, "Legal Fictions: Copyright, Fan Fiction, and a New Common Law," *Loyola of Los Angeles Entertainment Law Journal*, 1977, accessed online at <http://www.tushnet.com/law/fanficarticle.html>; A. T. Lee, "Copyright 101: A Brief Introduction to Copyright for Fan Fiction Authors," *Whoosh!*, October 1998, <http://www.whoosh.org/issue25/lee1.html>.

30. Katie Dean, "Copyright Crusaders Hit Schools," *Wired*, August 13, 2004, <http://www.wired.com/news/digiwood/0,1412,64543,00.html>.

31. Rosemary Coombe and Andrew Herman, "Defending Toy Dolls and Maneuvering Toy Soldiers: Trademarks, Consumer Politics and Corporate Accountability on the World Wide Web," presented at MIT Communication Forum, April 12, 2001, accessed at <http://web.mit.edu/comm-forum/papers/coombherman/coombeherman .html>.

32. Phil Armes, *Pokémon & Harry Potter: A Fatal Attraction* (Oklahoma City: Hearthstone, 2000), p. 84.

33. <http://www.cuttingedge.org/news/n1390.cfm>.

34. Kathy A. Smith, "*Harry Potter*: Seduction into the Dark World of the Occult," <http://www.fillthevoid.org/Entertainment/Harry-Potter-1.html>.

35. Berit Kjos, "*Harry Potter* Book Shares Pre-Sale Frenzy with D&D," accessed at <http://www.crossroad.to/text/articles/D&D-text.htm>.

36. Berit Kjos, "Twelve Reasons Not to See *Harry Potter* Movies," http://www. crossroad.to/articles2/HP-Movie.htm>.

37. Michael O'Brien, "Some Thoughts on the *Harry Potter* Series," Catholic Educator's Resource Center, <http://www.catholiceducation.org/articles/arts/a10071.html>.

38. Berit Kjos, "*Harry Potter & The Order of the Phoenix:* 'It's Only Fantasy' and Other Deceptions," <http://www.crossroad.to/articles2/2003/phoenix.htm>.

39. Mary Dana, interview with author, September 2003.

40. "Muggles for Harry Potter."

41. Christopher Finnan, personal interview, April 2003.

42. See <http://www.kidspeakonline.org/kidssaying.html>.

43. Grant McCracken, *Plentitude* (self-published, 1998), p. 60.

44. Connie Neal, *What's a Christian to Do with Harry Potter?* (Colorado Springs: Water-book, 2001), pp. 151–152.

45. Denis Haack, "Christian Discernment 101: An Explanation of Discernment," Ransom Fellowship, <http://ransomfellowship.org/articledetail.asp?AID=38&B=Denis%20 Haack&TID=8>.

46. Denis Haack, "Christian Discernment 202: Pop Culture: Why Bother?" Ransom Fellowship, <http://ransomfellowship.org/articledetail.asp?AID=41&B=Denis%20 Haack&TID=8>.

47. "The Purpose of Fans for Christ," Fans for Christ, <http://www.fansforchrist .org/phpBB2/purpose.htm>.

48. Denis Haack, "The Scandal of *Harry Potter*," Ransom Fellowship, <http:// ransomfellowship.org/articledetail.asp?AID=19&B=Denis%20Haack&TID=5>.

49. Neal, *What's a Christian to Do?* pp. 88–90.

■ *QUESTIONS FOR MAKING CONNECTIONS WITHIN THE READING* ■

1. Jenkins sees the controversy over *Harry Potter* as being essentially a controversy about rights: the "right of children to participate within the imaginative world" of the series; the "right to read"; the "right to write"; "children's rights." What leads Jenkins to assert that children have these rights? Would it make a difference to Jenkins's argument if instead of rights he spoke about society's *obligation* to provide children with an education?

2. "Schools are still locked into a model of autonomous learning that contrasts sharply with the kinds of learning that are needed as students are entering the new knowledge culture." Jenkins never explicitly defines either the "model of autonomous learning" to which schools are committed or what the "new knowledge culture" is that awaits students. As you reread "Why Heather Can Write," develop a list of the characteristics of these two contrasting models for learning. How would schools have to change to prepare students to enter the new knowledge culture?

3. In the section "What Would Jesus Do with *Harry Potter?*" Jenkins deploys a nonstandard approach for presenting his argument: early in the discussion, an additional column is added to the page, with the text in bold, and footnotes at the bottom of the page. What is the relationship between the two columns of text? Why does Jenkins adopt this mode of presentation at this point in his argument? Once you develop an explanation for Jenkins's motivation, assess the success of his effort.

■ *QUESTIONS FOR WRITING* ■

1. In "Why Heather Can Write," Jenkins elaborates on the three major types of responses to the unprecedented popularity of the *Harry Potter* series: the

prohibitionists, the collaborationists, and the consumers who are asserting their "right to participate" in the imaginary world that J. K. Rowling has created. How does one distinguish between active participation and mindless copying? Is the reason that Heather can write the same reason that the evangelist Phil Arms and the Fans for Christ can write? Has participatory culture generated new reasons for writing? New kinds of writing? New ways of thinking?

2. Because Jenkins is focused on acts of writing, he doesn't discuss the uses to which fan cultures have put the movie versions of the *Harry Potter* series. On YouTube, for example, with little effort, you can find clips from the *Harry Potter* movies that have been provided with new soundtracks, different voiceovers, and adoring comments. After you've performed your own search, discuss whether the examples you've found provide evidence to support Jenkins's broader claim that "through their participation, these kids are mapping out new strategies for negotiating around and through globalization, intellectual property struggles, and media conglomeration."

■ *QUESTIONS FOR MAKING CONNECTIONS BETWEEN READINGS* ■

1. In "Why Heather Can Write," Jenkins is concerned with describing the characteristics of the various affective communities that have evolved around the *Harry Potter* series. Are these affective communities examples of "self-organizing systems," as defined by Steven Johnson in "The Myth of the Ant Queen"? Does convergence culture give rise to complexity or simple multiplicity? What exactly has converged in convergence culture—individuals, groups, opposed ideas, self-organizing systems, or something else altogether?

2. In "Metakeninesis: How God Becomes Intimate in Contemporary U.S. Christianity," Tanya Luhrmann identifies "the rise of television and modern media" as having played a primary role in spreading an experience that has come to be equated with spirituality in the late twentieth century—"the experience of absorption, the experience of being caught up in fantasy and distracted from an outer world." Does the *Harry Potter* series serve this function for its fans? Can an avowedly fictional account generate the experience of intimacy and absorption that interests Luhrmann? Or is it that such experiences can only be realized in the technological age through an encounter with the moving image?

STEVEN JOHNSON

STEVEN JOHNSON IS the founder and editor of one of the Web's earliest magazines, *Feed*, and the author of *Interface Culture: How New Technology Transforms the Way We Create and Communicate* (1997); *Emergence: The Connected Lives of Ants, Brains, Cities, and Software* (2001), from which "The Myth of the Ant Queen" is drawn; *Mind Wide Open: Your Brain and the Neuroscience of Everyday Life* (2004); *Everything Bad Is Good for You: How Today's Popular Culture Is Actually Making Us Smarter* (2005); and, most recently, *The Ghost Map: The Story of London's Most Terrifying Epidemic —And How it Changed Science, Cities, and the Modern World* (2006). He has recently announced the launching of outside.in, a new Web venture that tracks conversations local residents are having about neighborhoods.

Johnson's preoccupation throughout these works, most controversially in *Everything Bad Is Good for You*, is with rethinking the nature of intelligence. Although it is common to think of intelligence as located in the individual—the outstanding student, the creative genius, the scientist at work in his lab—Johnson invites us to consider intelligence not as the property of an individual, but as a characteristic that emerges out of a system working as a whole. To illustrate this reconceptualization of intelligence, Johnson looks at complex systems, like ant colonies, cities, and software programs, and argues that in these contexts intelligence emerges in the absence of any central form of leadership or authority; the intelligence of the whole is created, rather, by individual agents—ants, people, subroutines—following what Johnson terms "local rules." By showing how decentralized, adaptive, self-organizing systems use lower-level thinking to solve higher-order problems, Johnson asks his readers to see the advent of the Internet itself not simply as an extension of human intelligence, but as a new frontier where the very nature of human intelligence is being transformed, one hyperlink at a time.

Johnson acknowledges the difficulties involved in imagining intelligence in these terms. When filmmakers try to depict artificial intelligence, they envision

Johnson, Steven. *Emergence: The Connected Lives of Ants, Brains, Cities and Software*. New York: Scribner, Simon & Schuster, 2001.

Quotation drawn from <http://www.oreillynet.com/pub/a/network/2002/02/22/johnson.html>.

a future where cyborgs look and think just like humans. Johnson predicts, though, that when there is a significant breakthrough in the effort to create artificial intelligence, the result "won't quite look like human intelligence. It'll have other properties in it, and it may be hard for us to pick up on the fact that it is intelligent because our criteria [are] different." In the current political environment, the importance of developing new criteria for describing intelligence should be clear: decentralized terrorist networks work in the emergent ways Johnson describes, as did the residents of New York City in the wake of the attacks on the Twin Towers.

■ ■

The Myth of the Ant Queen

It's early fall in Palo Alto, and Deborah Gordon and I are sitting in her office in Stanford's Gilbert Biological Sciences building, where she spends three-quarters of the year studying behavioral ecology. The other quarter is spent doing fieldwork with the native harvester ants of the American Southwest, and when we meet, her face still retains the hint of a tan from her last excursion to the Arizona desert.

I've come here to learn more about the collective intelligence of ant colonies. Gordon, dressed neatly in a white shirt, cheerfully entertains a few borderline-philosophical questions on group behavior and complex systems, but I can tell she's hankering to start with a hands-on display. After a few minutes of casual rumination, she bolts up out of her chair. "Why don't we start with me showing you the ants that we have here," she says. "And then we can talk about what it all means."

She ushers me into a sepulchral room across the hallway, where three long tables are lined up side by side. The initial impression is that of an underpopulated and sterilized pool hall, until I get close enough to one of the tables to make out the miniature civilization that lives within each of them. Closer to a Habitrail than your traditional idea of an ant farm, Gordon's contraptions house an intricate network of plastic tubes connecting a dozen or so plastic boxes, each lined with moist plaster and coated with a thin layer of dirt.

"We cover the nests with red plastic because some species of ants don't see red light," Gordon explains. "That seems to be true of this species too." For a second, I'm not sure what she means by "this species"—and then my eyes adjust to the scene, and I realize with a start that the dirt coating the plastic boxes is, in fact, thousands of harvester ants, crammed so tightly into their quarters that I had originally mistaken them for an undifferentiated mass. A second later, I can see that the whole simulated colony is wonderfully alive, the clusters of ants pulsing steadily with movement. The tubing and cramped conditions and surging crowds bring one thought immediately to mind: the New York subway system, rush hour.

At the heart of Gordon's work is a mystery about how ant colonies develop, a mystery that has implications extending far beyond the parched earth of the Arizona desert to our cities, our brains, our immune systems—and increasingly, our technology. Gordon's work focuses on the connection between the microbehavior of individual ants and the overall behavior of the colonies themselves, and part of that research involves tracking the life cycles of individual colonies, following them year after year as they scour the desert floor for food, competing with other colonies for territory, and—once a year—mating with them. She is a student, in other words, of a particular kind of emergent, self-organizing system.

Dig up a colony of native harvester ants and you'll almost invariably find that the queen is missing. To track down the colony's matriarch, you need to examine the bottom of the hole you've just dug to excavate the colony: you'll find a narrow, almost invisible passageway that leads another two feet underground, to a tiny vestibule burrowed out of the earth. There you will find the queen. She will have been secreted there by a handful of ladies-in-waiting at the first sign of disturbance. That passageway, in other words, is an emergency escape hatch, not unlike a fallout shelter buried deep below the West Wing.

But despite the Secret Service–like behavior, and the regal nomenclature, there's nothing hierarchical about the way an ant colony does its thinking. "Although *queen* is a term that reminds us of human political systems," Gordon explains, "the queen is not an authority figure. She lays eggs and is fed and cared for by the workers. She does not decide which worker does what. In a harvester ant colony, many feet of intricate tunnels and chambers and thousands of ants separate the queen, surrounded by interior workers, from the ants working outside the nest and using only the chambers near the surface. It would be physically impossible for the queen to direct every worker's decision about which task to perform and when." The harvester ants that carry the queen off to her escape hatch do so not because they've been ordered to by their leader; they do it because the queen ant is responsible for giving birth to all the members of the colony, and so it's in the colony's best interest—and the colony's gene pool—to keep the queen safe. Their genes instruct them to protect their mother, the same way their genes instruct them to forage for food. In other words, the matriarch doesn't train her servants to protect her, evolution does.

Popular culture trades in Stalinist ant stereotypes—witness the authoritarian colony regime in the animated film *Antz*—but in fact, colonies are the exact opposite of command economies. While they are capable of remarkably coordinated feats of task allocation, there are no Five-Year Plans in the ant kingdom. The colonies that Gordon studies display some of nature's most mesmerizing decentralized behavior: intelligence and personality and learning that emerges from the bottom up.

I'm still gazing into the latticework of plastic tubing when Gordon directs my attention to the two expansive white boards attached to the main colony space, one stacked on top of the other and connected by a ramp. (Imagine a two-story parking garage built next to a subway stop.) A handful of ants meander across each plank, some porting crumblike objects on their back, others apparently just out for a stroll. If this is the Central Park of Gordon's ant metropolis, I think, it must be a workday.

Gordon gestures to the near corner of the top board, four inches from the ramp to the lower level, where a pile of strangely textured dust—littered with tiny shells and husks—presses neatly against the wall. "That's the midden," she says. "It's the town garbage dump." She points to three ants marching up the ramp, each barely visible beneath a comically oversize shell. "These ants are on midden duty: they take the trash that's left over from the food they've collected—in this case, the seeds from stalk grass—and deposit it in the midden pile."

Gordon takes two quick steps down to the other side of the table, at the far end away from the ramp. She points to what looks like another pile of dust. "And this is the cemetery." I look again, startled. She's right: hundreds of ant carcasses are piled atop one another, all carefully wedged against the table's corner. It looks brutal, and yet also strangely methodical.

I know enough about colony behavior to nod in amazement. "So they've somehow collectively decided to utilize these two areas as trash heap and cemetery," I say. No individual ant defined those areas, no central planner zoned one area for trash, the other for the dead. "It just sort of happened, right?"

Gordon smiles, and it's clear that I've missed something. "It's better than that," she says. "Look at what actually happened here: they've built the cemetery at exactly the point that's furthest away from the colony. And the midden is even more interesting: they've put it at precisely the point that maximizes its distance from both the colony *and* the cemetery. It's like there's a rule they're following: put the dead ants as far away as possible, and put the midden as far away as possible without putting it near the dead ants."

I have to take a few seconds to do the geometry myself, and sure enough, the ants have got it right. I find myself laughing out loud at the thought: it's as though they've solved one of those spatial math tests that appear on standardized tests, conjuring up a solution that's perfectly tailored to their environment, a solution that might easily stump an eight-year-old human. The question is, who's doing the conjuring?

It's a question with a long and august history, one that is scarcely limited to the collective behavior of ant colonies. We know the answer now because we have developed powerful tools for thinking about—and modeling—the emergent intelligence of self-organizing systems, but that answer was not always so clear. We know now that systems like ant colonies don't have real leaders, that the very idea of an ant "queen" is misleading. But the desire to find pacemakers in such systems has always been powerful—in both the group behavior of the social insects, and in the collective human behavior that creates a living city.

Records exist of a Roman fort dating back to A.D. 76 situated at the confluence of the Medlock and Irwell Rivers, on the northwestern edge of modern England, about 150 miles from London. Settlements persisted there for three centuries, before dying out with the rest of the empire around A.D. 400. Historians believe that the site was unoccupied for half a millennium, until a town called Manchester began to take shape there, the name derived from the Roman settlement Mamucium—Latin for "place of the breastlike hill."

Manchester subsisted through most of the millennium as a nondescript northern-England borough: granted a charter in 1301, the town established a college in the early 1400s, but remained secondary to the neighboring town of Salford for hundreds of years. In the 1600s, the Manchester region became a node for the wool trade, its merchants shipping goods to the Continent via the great ports of London. It was impossible to see it at the time, but Manchester—and indeed the entire Lancashire region—had planted itself at the very center of a technological and commercial revolution that would irrevocably alter the future of the planet. Manchester lay at the confluence of several world-historical rivers: the nascent industrial technologies of steam-powered looms; the banking system of commercial London; the global markets and labor pools of the British Empire. The story of that convergence has been told many times, and the debate over its consequences continues to this day. But beyond the epic effects that it had on the global economy, the industrial takeoff that occurred in Manchester between 1700 and 1850 also created a new kind of city, one that literally exploded into existence.

The statistics on population growth alone capture the force of that explosion: a 1773 estimate had 24,000 people living in Manchester; the first official census in 1801 found 70,000. By the midpoint of the century, there were more than 250,000 people in the city proper—a tenfold increase in only seventy-five years. That growth rate was as unprecedented and as violent as the steam engines themselves. In a real sense, the city grew too fast for the authorities to keep up with it. For five hundred years, Manchester had technically been considered a "manor," which meant, in the eyes of the law, it was run like a feudal estate, with no local government to speak of—no city planners, police, or public health authorities. Manchester didn't even send representatives to Parliament until 1832, and it wasn't incorporated for another six years. By the early 1840s, the newly formed borough council finally began to institute public health reforms and urban planning, but the British government didn't officially recognize Manchester as a city until 1853. This constitutes one of the great ironies of the industrial revolution, and it captures just how dramatic the rate of change really was: the city that most defined the future of urban life for the first half of the nineteenth century didn't legally become a city until the great explosion had run its course.

The result of that discontinuity was arguably the least planned and most chaotic city in the six-thousand-year history of urban settlements. Noisy, polluted, massively overcrowded, Manchester attracted a steady stream of intellectuals and public figures in the 1830s, traveling north to the industrial magnet in search of the modern world's future. One by one, they returned with stories of abject squalor and sensory overload, their words straining to convey the immensity and uniqueness of the experience. "What I have seen has disgusted and astonished me beyond all measure," Dickens wrote after a visit in the fall of 1838. "I mean to strike the heaviest blow in my power for these unfortunate creatures." Appointed to command the northern districts in the late 1830s, Major General Charles James Napier wrote: "Manchester is the chimney of the world. Rich rascals, poor rogues, drunken ragamuffins and prostitutes form the moral. . . . What a place! The entrance to hell, realized." De Tocqueville visited Lancashire in 1835 and described the landscape in language that would be echoed throughout the next two centuries: "From this foul drain the greatest stream of human industry flows out to fertilize the whole world. From this filthy sewer pure gold flows. Here humanity attains its most complete development and its most brutish; here civilization works its miracles, and civilized man is turned back almost into a savage."

But Manchester's most celebrated and influential documentarian was a young man named Friedrich Engels, who arrived in 1842 to help oversee the family cotton plant there, and to witness firsthand the engines of history bringing the working class closer to self-awareness. While Engels was very much on the payroll of his father's firm, Ermen and Engels, by the time he arrived in Manchester he was also under the sway of the radical politics associated with the Young Hegelian school. He had befriended Karl Marx a few years before and had been encouraged to visit Manchester by the socialist Moses Hess, whom he'd met in early 1842. His three years in England were thus a kind of scouting mission for the revolution, financed by the capitalist class. The book that Engels eventually wrote, *The Condition of the Working Class in England*, remains to this day one of the classic tracts of urban history and stands as the definitive account of nineteenth-century Manchester life in all its tumult and dynamism. Dickens, Carlyle, and Disraeli had all attempted to capture Manchester in its epic wildness, but their efforts were outpaced by a twenty-four-year-old from Prussia.

But *The Condition* is not, as might be expected, purely a document of Manchester's industrial chaos, a story of all that is solid melting into air, to borrow a phrase Engels's comrade would write several years later. In the midst of the city's insanity, Engels's eye is drawn to a strange kind of order, in a wonderful passage where he leads the reader on a walking tour of the industrial capital, a tour that reveals a kind of politics built into the very topography of the city's streets. It captures Engels's acute powers of observation, but I quote from it at length because it captures something else as well—how difficult it is to think in models of self-organization, to imagine a world without pacemakers.

> The town itself is peculiarly built, so that someone can live in it for years and travel into it and out of it daily without ever coming into contact with a working-class quarter or even with workers—so long, that is to say, as one confines himself to his business affairs or to strolling about for pleasure. This comes about mainly in the circumstances that through an unconscious, tacit agreement as much as through conscious, explicit intention, the working-class districts are most sharply separated from the parts of the city reserved for the middle class. . . .
>
> I know perfectly well that this deceitful manner of building is more or less common to all big cities. I know as well that shopkeepers must in the nature of the business take premises on the main thoroughfares. I know in such streets there are more good houses than bad ones, and that the value of land is higher in their immediate vicinity than in neighborhoods that lie at a distance from them. But at the same time I have never come across so systematic a seclusion of the working class from the main streets as in Manchester. I have never elsewhere seen a concealment of such fine sensibility of everything that might offend the eyes and nerves of the middle classes. And yet it is precisely Manchester that has been built less according to a plan and less within the limitations of official regulations—and indeed more through accident—than any other town. Still . . . I cannot help feeling that the liberal industrialists, the Manchester "bigwigs," are not so altogether innocent of this bashful style of building.

You can almost hear the contradictions thundering against each other in this passage, like the "dark satanic mills" of Manchester itself. The city has built a *cordon sanitaire* to separate the industrialists from the squalor they have unleashed on the world, concealing the demoralization of Manchester's working-class districts—and yet that disappearing act comes into the world without "conscious, explicit intention." The city seems artfully planned to hide its atrocities, and yet it "has been built less according to a plan" than any city in history. As Steven Marcus puts it, in his history of the young Engels's sojourn in Manchester, "The point to be taken is that this astonishing and outrageous arrangement cannot fully be understood as the result of a plot, or even a deliberate design, although those in whose interests it works also control it. It is indeed too huge and too complex a state of organized affairs ever to have been *thought up* in advance, to have preexisted as an idea."

Those broad, glittering avenues, in other words, suggest a Potemkin village without a Potemkin. That mix of order and anarchy is what we now call emergent behavior. Urban critics since Lewis Mumford and Jane Jacobs have known that cities have lives of their own, with neighborhoods clustering into place without any Robert Moses figure dictating the plan from above. But that understanding has entered the intellectual mainstream only in recent years—when Engels paced those Manchester streets in the 1840s, he was left groping blindly, trying to find a culprit for the city's fiendish organization, even as he acknowledged that the city was notoriously unplanned. Like most intellectual histories, the development of that new understanding—the sciences of complexity and self-organization—is a complicated, multithreaded tale, with many agents interacting over its duration. It is probably better to think of it as less a linear narrative and more an interconnected web, growing increasingly dense over the century and a half that separates us from Engels's first visit to Manchester.

Complexity is a word that has frequently appeared in critical accounts of metropolitan space, but there are really two kinds of complexity fundamental to the city, two experiences with very different implications for the individuals trying to make sense of them. There is, first, the more conventional sense of complexity as sensory overload, the city stretching the human nervous system to its very extremes, and in the process teaching it a new series of reflexes—and leading the way for a complementary series of aesthetic values, which develop out like a scab around the original wound. The German cultural critic Walter Benjamin writes in his unfinished masterpiece, *The Arcades Project*:

> Perhaps the daily sight of a moving crowd once presented the eye with a spectacle to which it first had to adapt. . . . [T]hen the assumption is not impossible that, having mastered this task, the eye welcomed opportunities to confirm its possession of its new ability. The method of impressionist painting, whereby the picture is assembled through a riot of flecks of color, would then be a reflection of experience with which the eye of a big-city dweller has become familiar.

There's a long tributary of nineteenth- and twentieth-century urban writing that leads into this passage, from the London chapters of Wordsworth's *Prelude* to the ambulatory musings of Joyce's *Dubliners:* the noise and the senselessness somehow transformed into an aesthetic experience. The crowd is something you throw yourself into, for the pure poetry of it all. But complexity is not solely a matter of sensory overload. There is also the sense of complexity as a self-organizing system—more Santa Fe Institute than Frankfurt School. This sort of complexity lives up one level: it describes the system of the city itself, and not its experiential reception by the city dweller. The city is complex because it overwhelms, yes, but also because it has a coherent personality, a personality that self-organizes out of millions of individual decisions, a global order built out of local interactions. This is the "systematic" complexity that Engels glimpsed on the boulevards of Manchester: not the overload and anarchy he documented elsewhere, but instead a strange kind of order, a pattern in the streets that furthered the political values of Manchester's elite without being deliberately planned by them. We know now from computer models and sociological studies—as well as from the studies of comparable systems generated by the social insects, such as Gordon's harvester ants—that larger patterns can emerge out of uncoordinated local actions. But for Engels and his contemporaries, those unplanned urban shapes must have seemed like a haunting. The city appeared to have a life of its own.

A hundred and fifty years later, the same techniques translated into the language of software . . . trigger a similar reaction: the eerie sense of something lifelike, something organic forming on the screen. Even those with sophisticated knowledge about self-organizing systems still find these shapes unnerving—in their mix of stability and change, in their capacity for open-ended learning. The impulse to build centralized models to explain that behavior remains almost as strong as it did in Engels's day. When we see repeated shapes and structure emerging out of apparent chaos, we can't help looking for pacemakers.

Understood in the most abstract sense, what Engels observed are *patterns* in the urban landscape, visible because they have a repeated structure that distinguishes them from the pure noise you might naturally associate with an unplanned city. They are patterns of human movement and decision-making that have been etched into the texture of city blocks, patterns that are then fed back to the Manchester residents themselves, altering their subsequent decisions. (In that sense, they are the very opposite of the traditional sense of urban complexity—they are signals emerging where you would otherwise expect only noise.) A city is a kind of pattern-amplifying machine: its neighborhoods are a way of measuring and expressing the repeated behavior of larger collectivities—capturing information about group behavior, and sharing that information with the group. Because those patterns are fed back to the community, small shifts in behavior can quickly escalate into larger movements: upscale shops dominate the main boulevards, while the working class remains clustered invisibly in the alleys and side streets; the artists live on the Left Bank, the investment bankers in the Eighth Arrondissement. You don't need regulations and city planners deliberately creating these structures. All you need are thousands of individuals and a few simple rules of interaction. The bright shop windows attract more bright shop windows and drive the impoverished toward the hidden core. There's no need for a Baron Haussmann in this world, just a few repeating patterns of movement, amplified into larger shapes that last for lifetimes: clusters, slums, neighborhoods.

Not all patterns are visible to every city dweller, though. The history of urbanism is also the story of more muted signs, built by the collective behavior of smaller groups and rarely detected by outsiders. Manchester harbors several such secret clusters, persisting over the course of many generations, like a "standing wave in front of a rock in a fast-moving stream." One of them lies just north of Victoria University, at a point where Oxford Road becomes Oxford Street. There are reports dating back to the mid-nineteenth century of men cruising other men on these blocks, looking for casual sex, more lasting relationships, or even just the camaraderie of shared identity at a time when that identity dared not speak its name. Some historians speculate that Wittgenstein visited these streets during his sojourn in Manchester in 1908. Nearly a hundred years later, the area has christened itself the Gay Village and actively promotes its coffee bars and boutiques as a must-see Manchester tourist destination, like Manhattan's Christopher Street and San Francisco's Castro. The pattern is now broadcast to a wider audience, but it has not lost its shape.

But even at a lower amplitude, that signal was still loud enough to attract the attention of another of Manchester's illustrious immigrants: the British polymath Alan Turing. As part of his heroic contribution to the war effort, Turing had been a student of mathematical patterns, designing the equations and the machines that cracked the "unbreakable" German code of the Enigma device. After a frustrating three-year stint at the National Physical Laboratory in London, Turing moved to Manchester in 1948 to help run the university's embryonic computing lab. It was in Manchester that Turing began to think about the problem of biological development in mathematical terms, leading the way to the "Morphogenesis" paper, published in 1952, that Evelyn Fox Keller would rediscover more than a decade later. Turing's war research had focused on detecting patterns lurking within the apparent chaos of code, but in his Manchester years, his mind gravitated toward a mirror image of the original code-breaking problem: how complex patterns could come into being by following simple rules. How does a seed know how to build a flower?

Turing's paper on morphogenesis—literally, "the beginning of shape"—turned out to be one of his seminal works, ranking up there with his more publicized papers and speculations: his work on Gödel's undecidability problem, the Turing Machine, the Turing Test—not to mention his contributions to the physical design of the modern digital computer. But the morphogenesis paper was only the beginning of a shape—a brilliant mind sensing the outlines of a new problem, but not fully grasping all its intricacies. If Turing had been granted another few decades to explore the powers of self-assembly—not to mention access to the number-crunching horsepower of non-vacuum-tube computers—it's not hard to imagine his mind greatly enhancing our subsequent understanding of emergent behavior. But the work on morphogenesis was tragically cut short by his death in 1954.

Alan Turing was most likely a casualty of the brutally homophobic laws of postwar Britain, but his death also intersected with those discreet patterns of life on Manchester's sidewalks. Turing had known about that stretch of Oxford Road since his arrival in Manchester; on occasion, he would drift down to the neighborhood, meeting other gay men—inviting some of them back to his flat for conversation, and presumably some sort of physical contact. In January of 1952, Turing met a young man named Arnold Murray on those streets, and the two embarked on a brief relationship that quickly turned sour. Murray—or a friend of Murray's—broke into Turing's house and stole a few items. Turing reported the theft to the police and, with his typical forthrightness, made no effort to conceal the affair with Murray when the police visited his flat. Homosexuality was a criminal offense according to British law, punishable by up to two years' imprisonment, and so the police promptly charged both Turing and Murray with "gross indecency."

On February 29, 1952, while the Manchester authorities were preparing their case against him, Turing finished the revisions to his morphogenesis paper, and he argued over its merits with Ilya Prigogine, the visiting Belgian chemist whose work on nonequilibrium thermodynamics would later win him a Nobel prize. In one day, Turing had completed the text that would help engender the discipline of biomathematics and inspire Keller and Segel's slime mold discoveries fifteen years later, and he had enjoyed a spirited exchange with the man who would eventually achieve world fame for his research into self-organizing systems. On that winter day in 1952, there was no mind on the face of the earth better prepared to wrestle with the mysteries of emergence than Alan Turing's. But the world outside that mind was conspiring to destroy it. That very morning, a local paper broke the story that the war-hero savant had been caught in an illicit affair with a nineteen-year-old boy.

Within a few months Turing had been convicted of the crime and placed on a humiliating estrogen treatment to "cure" him of his homosexuality. Hounded by the authorities and denied security clearance for the top-secret British computing projects he had been contributing to, Turing died two years later, an apparent suicide.

Turing's career had already collided several times with the developing web of emergence before those fateful years in Manchester. In the early forties, during the height of the war effort, he had spent several months at the legendary Bell Laboratories on Manhattan's West Street, working on a number of encryption schemes, including an effort to transmit heavily encoded waveforms that could be decoded as human speech with the use of a special key. Early in his visit to Bell Labs, Turing hit upon the idea of using another Bell invention, the Vocoder—later used by rock musicians such as Peter Frampton to combine the sounds of a guitar and the human voice—as a way of encrypting speech. (By early 1943, Turing's ideas had enabled the first secure voice transmission to cross the Atlantic, unintelligible to German eavesdroppers.) Bell Labs was the home base for another genius, Claude Shannon, who would go on to found the influential discipline of information theory, and whose work had explored the boundaries between noise and information. Shannon had been particularly intrigued by the potential for machines to detect and amplify patterns of information in noisy communication channels—a line of inquiry that promised obvious value to a telephone company, but could also save thousands of lives in a war effort that relied so heavily on the sending and breaking of codes. Shannon and Turing immediately recognized that they had been working along parallel tracks: they were both code-breakers by profession at that point, and in their attempts to build automated machines that could recognize patterns in audio signals or numerical sequences, they had both glimpsed a future populated by even more intelligence machines. Shannon and Turing passed many an extended lunchtime at the Bell Labs, trading ideas on an "electronic brain" that might be capable of humanlike feats of pattern recognition.

Turing had imagined his thinking machine primarily in terms of its logical possibilities, its ability to execute an infinite variety of computational routines. But Shannon pushed him to think of the machine as something closer to an actual human brain, capable of recognizing more nuanced patterns. One day over lunch at the lab, Turing exclaimed playfully to his colleagues, "Shannon wants to feed not just data to a brain, but *cultural* things! He wants to play music to it!" Musical notes were patterns too, Shannon recognized, and if you could train an electronic brain to understand and respond to logical patterns of zeros and ones, then perhaps sometime in the future we could train our machines to appreciate the equivalent patterns of minor chord progressions and arpeggios. The idea seemed fanciful at the time—it was hard enough getting a machine to perform long division, much less savor Beethoven's Ninth. But the pattern recognition that Turing and Shannon envisioned for digital computers has, in recent years, become a central part of our cultural life, with machines both generating music for our entertainment and recommending new artists for us to enjoy. The connection between musical patterns and our neurological wiring would play a central role in one of the founding texts of modern artificial intelligence, Douglas Hofstadter's *Gödel, Escher, Bach.* Our computers still haven't developed a genuine ear for music, but if they ever do, their skill will date back to those lunchtime conversations between Shannon and Turing at Bell Labs. And that learning too will be a kind of emergence, a higher-level order forming out of relatively simple component parts.

Five years after his interactions with Turing, Shannon published a long essay in the *Bell System Technical Journal* that was quickly repackaged as a book called *The Mathematical Theory of Communication*. Dense with equations and arcane chapter titles such as "Discrete Noiseless Systems," the book managed to become something of a cult classic, and the discipline it spawned—information theory—had a profound impact on scientific and technological research that followed, on both a theoretical and practical level. *The Mathematical Theory of Communication* contained an elegant, layman's introduction to Shannon's theory, penned by the esteemed scientist Warren Weaver, who had early on grasped the significance of Shannon's work. Weaver had played a leading role in the Natural Sciences division of the Rockefeller Foundation since 1932, and when he retired in the late fifties, he composed a long report for the foundation, looking back at the scientific progress that had been achieved over the preceding quarter century. The occasion suggested a reflective look backward, but the document that Weaver produced (based loosely on a paper he had written for *American Scientist*) was far more prescient, more forward-looking. In many respects, it deserves to be thought of as the founding text of complexity theory—the point at which the study of complex systems began to think of itself as a unified field. Drawing upon research in molecular biology, genetics, physics, computer science, and Shannon's information theory, Weaver divided the last few centuries of scientific inquiry into three broad camps. First, the study of simple systems: two or three variable problems, such as the rotation of planets, or the connection between an electric current and its voltage and resistance. Second, problems of "disorganized complexity": problems characterized by millions or billions of variables that can only be approached by the methods of statistical mechanics and probability theory. These tools helped explain not only the behavior of molecules in a gas, or the patterns of heredity in a gene pool, but also helped life insurance companies turn a profit despite their limited knowledge about any individual human's future health. Thanks to Claude Shannon's work, the statistical approach also helped phone companies deliver more reliable and intelligible long-distance service.

But there was a third phase to this progression, and we were only beginning to understand. "This statistical method of dealing with disorganized complexity, so powerful an advance over the earlier two-variable methods, leaves a great field untouched," Weaver wrote. There was a middle region between two-variable equations and problems that involved billions of variables. Conventionally, this region involved a "moderate" number of variables, but the size of the system was in fact a secondary characteristic:

> Much more important than the mere number of variables is the fact that these variables are all interrelated. . . . These problems, as contrasted with the disorganized situations with which statistics can cope, *show the essential feature of organization*. We will therefore refer to this group of problems as those of *organized complexity*.

Think of these three categories of problems in terms of [a] billiards table analogy. . . . A two- or three-variable problem would be an ordinary billiards table, with balls bouncing off one another following simple rules: their velocities, the friction of the table. That would be an example of a "simple system"—and indeed, billiard balls are often used to illustrate basic laws of physics in high school textbooks. A system of disorganized complexity would be that same table enlarged to include a million balls, colliding with one another millions of times a second. Making predictions about the behavior of any individual ball in that mix would be difficult, but you could make some accurate predictions about the overall behavior of the table. Assuming there's enough energy in the system at the outset, the balls will spread to fill the entire table, like gas molecules in a container. It's complex because there are many interacting agents, but it's disorganized because they don't create any higher-level behavior other than broad statistical trends. Organized complexity, on the other hand, is like [a] motorized billiards table, where the balls follow specific rules and through their various interactions create a distinct macrobehavior, arranging themselves in a specific shape, or forming a specific pattern over time. That sort of behavior, for Weaver, suggested a problem of organized complexity, a problem that suddenly seemed omnipresent in nature once you started to look for it:

> What makes an evening primrose open when it does? Why does salt water fail to satisfy thirst? . . . What is the description of aging in biochemical terms? . . . What is a gene, and how does the original genetic constitution of a living organism express itself in the developed characteristics of the adult?
>
> All these are certainly complex problems. But they are not problems of disorganized complexity, to which statistical methods hold the key. They are all problems which involve dealing simultaneously with a sizable number of factors which are interrelated into an organic whole.

Tackling such problems required a new approach: "The great central concerns of the biologist . . . are now being approached not only from *above,* with the broad view of the natural philosopher who scans the whole living world, but also from *underneath,* by the quantitative analyst who measures the underlying facts." This was a genuine shift in the paradigm of research, to use Thomas Kuhn's language—a revolution not so much in the interpretations that science built in its attempt to explain the world, but rather in the types of questions it asked. The paradigm shift was more than just a new mind-set, Weaver recognized; it was also a by-product of new tools that were appearing on the horizon. To solve the problems of organized complexity, you needed a machine capable of churning through thousands, if not millions, of calculations per second—a rate that would have been unimaginable for individual brains running the numbers with the limited calculating machines of the past few centuries. Because of his connection to the Bell Labs group, Weaver had seen early on the promise of digital computing, and he knew that the mysteries of organized complexity would be much easier to tackle once you could model the behavior in close-to-real time. For millennia, humans had used their skills at observation and classification to document the subtle anatomy of flowers, but for the first time they were perched on the brink of answering a more fundamental question, a question that had more to do with patterns developing over time than with static structure: Why does an evening primrose open when it does? And how does a simple seed know how to make a primrose in the first place? . . .

"Organized complexity" proved to be a constructive way of thinking . . . but . . . was it possible to model and explain the behavior of self-organizing systems using more rigorous methods? Could the developing technology of digital computing be usefully applied to this problem? Partially thanks to Shannon's work in the late forties, the biological sciences . . . made a number of significant breakthroughs in understanding pattern recognition and feedback. . . . Shortly after his appointment to the Harvard faculty in 1956, the entomologist Edward O. Wilson convincingly proved that ants communicate with one another—and coordinate overall colony behavior—by recognizing patterns in pheromone trails left by fellow ants. . . . At the Free University of Brussels in the fifties, Ilya Prigogine was making steady advances in his understanding of nonequilibrium thermodynamics, environments where the laws of entropy are temporarily overcome, and higher-level order may spontaneously emerge out of underlying chaos. And at MIT's Lincoln Laboratory, a twenty-five-year-old researcher named Oliver Selfridge was experimenting with a model for teaching a computer how to learn.

There is a world of difference between a computer that passively receives the information you supply and a computer that actively learns on its own. The very first generation of computers such as ENIAC had processed information fed to them by their masters, and they had been capable of performing various calculations with that data, based on the instruction sets programmed into them. This was a startling enough development at a time when "computer" meant a person with a slide rule and an eraser. But even in those early days, the digital visionaries had imagined a machine capable of more open-ended learning. Turing and Shannon had argued over the future musical tastes of the "electronic brain" during lunch hour at Bell Labs, while their colleague Norbert Wiener had written a best-selling paean to the self-regulatory powers of feedback in his 1949 manifesto *Cybernetics*.

"Mostly my participation in all of this is a matter of good luck for me," Selfridge says today, sitting in his cramped, windowless MIT office. Born in England, Selfridge enrolled at Harvard at the age of fifteen and started his doctorate three years later at MIT, where Norbert Wiener was his dissertation adviser. As a precocious twenty-one-year-old, Selfridge suggested a few corrections to a paper that his mentor had published on heart flutters, corrections that Wiener graciously acknowledged in the opening pages of *Cybernetics*. "I think I now have the honor of being one of the few living people mentioned in that book," Selfridge says, laughing.

After a sojourn working on military control projects in New Jersey, Selfridge returned to MIT in the midfifties. His return coincided with an explosion of interest in artificial intelligence (AI), a development that introduced him to a then-junior fellow at Harvard named Marvin Minsky. "My concerns in AI," Selfridge says now, "were not so much the actual processing as they were in how systems change, how they evolve—in a word, how they learn." Exploring the possibilities of machine learning brought Selfridge back to memories of his own education in England. "At school in England I had read John Milton's *Paradise Lost*," he says, "and I'd been struck by the image of Pandemonium—it's Greek for 'all the demons.' Then after my second son, Peter, was born, I went over *Paradise Lost* again, and the shrieking of the demons awoke something in me." The pattern recognizer in Selfridge's brain had hit upon a way of teaching a computer to recognize patterns.

"We are proposing here a model of a process which we claim can adaptively improve itself to handle certain pattern-recognition problems which cannot be adequately specified in advance." These were the first words Selfridge delivered at a symposium in late 1958, held at the very same National Physical Laboratory from which Turing had escaped a decade before. Selfridge's presentation had the memorable title "Pandemonium: A Paradigm for Learning," and while it had little impact outside the nascent computer-science community, the ideas Selfridge outlined that day would eventually become part of our everyday life—each time we enter a name in our Palm-Pilots or use voice-recognition software to ask for information over the phone. Pandemonium, as Selfridge outlined it in his talk, was not so much a specific piece of software as it was a way of approaching a problem. The problem was an ambitious one, given the limited computational resources of the day: how to teach a computer to recognize patterns that were ill-defined or erratic, like the sound waves that comprise spoken language.

The brilliance of Selfridge's new paradigm lay in the fact that it relied on a distributed, bottom-up intelligence, and not a unified, top-down one. Rather than build a single smart program, Selfridge created a swarm of limited miniprograms, which he called demons. "The idea was, we have a bunch of these demons shrieking up the hierarchy," he explains. "Lower-level demons shrieking to higher-level demons shrieking to higher ones."

To understand what that "shrieking" means, imagine a system with twenty-six individual demons, each trained to recognize a letter of the alphabet. The pool of demons is shown a series of words, and each demon "votes" as to whether each letter displayed represents its chosen letter. If the first letter is *a*, the *a*-recognizing demon reports that it is highly likely that it has recognized a match. Because of the similarities in shape, the *o*-recognizer might report a possible match, while the *b*-recognizer would emphatically declare that the letter wasn't intelligible to it. All the letter-recognizing demons would report to a master demon, who would tally up the votes for each letter and choose the demon that expressed the highest confidence.

Then the software would move on to the next letter in the sequence, and the process would begin again. At the end of the transmission, the master demon would have a working interpretation of the text that had been transmitted, based on the assembled votes of the demon democracy.

Of course, the accuracy of that interpretation depended on the accuracy of the letter recognizers. If you were trying to teach a computer how to read, it was cheating to assume from the outset that you could find twenty-six accurate letter recognizers. Selfridge was after a larger goal: How do you teach a machine to recognize letters—or vowel sounds, minor chords, fingerprints—in the first place? The answer involved adding another layer of demons, and a feedback mechanism whereby the various demon guesses could be graded. This lower level was populated by even less sophisticated miniprograms, trained only to recognize raw physical shapes (or sounds, in the case of Morse code or spoken language). Some demons recognized parallel lines, others perpendicular ones. Some demons looked for circles, others for dots. None of these shapes were associated with any particular letter; these bottom-dwelling demons were like two-year-old children—capable of reporting on the shapes they witnessed, but not perceiving them as letters or words.

Using these minimally equipped demons, the system could be trained to recognize letters, without "knowing" anything about the alphabet in advance. The recipe was relatively simple: Present the letter *b* to the bottom-level demons, and see which ones respond, and which ones don't. In the case of the letter *b*, the vertical-line recognizers might respond, along with the circle recognizers. Those lower-level demons would report to a letter-recognizer one step higher in the chain. Based on the information gathered from its lieutenants, that recognizer would make a guess as to the letter's identity. Those guesses are then "graded" by the software. If the guess is wrong, the software learns to dissociate those particular lieutenants from the letter in question; if the guess happens to be right, it *strengthens* the connection between the lieutenants and the letter.

The results are close to random at first, but if you repeat the process a thousand times, or ten thousand, the system learns to associate specific assemblies of shape-recognizers with specific letters and soon enough is capable of translating entire sentences with remarkable accuracy. The system doesn't come with any predefined conceptions about the shapes of letters—you train the system to associate letters with specific shapes in the grading phase. (This is why handwriting-recognition software can adapt to so many different types of penmanship, but *can't* adapt to penmanship that changes day to day.) That mix of random beginnings organizing into more complicated results reminded Selfridge of another process, whose own underlying code was just then being deciphered in the form of DNA. "The scheme sketched is really a natural selection on the processing demons," Selfridge explained. "If they serve a useful function they survive and perhaps are even the source for other subdemons who are themselves judged on their merits. It is perfectly reasonable to conceive of this taking place on a broader scale . . . instead of having but one Pandemonium we might have some crowd of them, all fairly similarly constructed, and employ natural selection on the crowd of them."

The system Selfridge described—with its bottom-up learning, and its evaluating feedback loops—belongs in the history books as the first practical description of an emergent software program. The world now swarms with millions of his demons.   ■

■ QUESTIONS FOR MAKING CONNECTIONS WITHIN THE READING ■

1. Do you accept Johnson's analogy between the behavior of harvester ants and the emergence of cities like Manchester? Does Johnson mean that instinct guides human builders in much the same way as it guides the ants? Does he mean that in both cases an order has emerged entirely by accident? Or does he mean that there is something about "systems" in general—ant colonies as well as sprawling conurbations—that makes them self-organizing? What exactly is a self-organizing system, and how do both the ant colony and the city qualify as equally appropriate examples? How does each system organize itself?

2. The idea of self-organizing systems might seem to suggest that order automatically and smoothly arises as ants and human beings go about their private business. Can Manchester in the nineteenth century, when Napier, Dickens, and Engels each observed it, be described as orderly? Was there an order behind the apparent disorder? How can we distinguish between a self-organizing system and the results that are produced entirely by chance?

3. One could say that there are three different parts to "The Myth of the Ant Queen." The first deals with the colony of harvester ants. The second deals with the city of Manchester. The third deals with the emergence of complexity theory. In what ways are these three parts connected? Why doesn't Johnson make the connections more explicit—why does he leave them for the reader to work out? Could the structure of his chapter in some way reflect the nature of his argument about self-organization?

■ QUESTIONS FOR WRITING ■

1. What role does intelligence play in self-organizing systems? This question might be more complex than it seems at first because intelligence may exist on multiple levels. The intelligence demonstrated by an ant colony may be much greater than the intelligence of an individual ant. On any particular day during the 1880s, life in Manchester must have seemed to

many people very close to absolute chaos, but could it be said that the city as a whole possessed a certain intelligence? Does Johnson mean to suggest that the ideas and aspirations of individuals do not matter? Are we, from the standpoint of complexity theory, intelligent beings? What is intelligence, anyway?

2. Families, communities, schools, religious groups, circles of friends, political parties, public service organizations—all of these qualify as social institutions, and there are many others. Choose one institution and, drawing on Johnson's chapter, decide whether it qualifies as truly self-organizing. If it does not, can you imagine how it might be reorganized in a bottom-up fashion? In what ways do our customs and traditions encourage or discourage self-organization? What do you conclude from the importance of kings, presidents, generals, CEOs, bosses, coaches, principals, and other leaders in our culture?

■ *QUESTIONS FOR MAKING CONNECTIONS BETWEEN READINGS* ■

1. Do self-organizing systems manage, as time goes on, to insulate themselves from the influence of chance? Does chance continue to play a role, or does it actually become even more important? To explore these questions, you might consider the examples that Johnson provides—the ant colony, the city, and the development of the science of complexity. But you might also consider Edward Tenner's discussion of technology and unintended consequences. Although technology appears to make life safer and more stable, it also exposes us to "revenge effects." Does self-organization protect us from these effects, or might it make them more likely?

2. At first glance, Robert Thurman's claim that we have no permanent or essential self may seem like sheer nonsense, since, clearly, each of us is a self or has one. But does "the self," as we call it, actually represent a self-organizing system, more like an ant colony than a single ant, or more like a city than a single neighborhood? As you work through this question, you should move beyond the two texts to consider your own experience. Are you always the same person from one moment to the next? To what degree is your identity at any particular time shaped by your interactions with others? Can you accurately predict what you will be like ten years from now? Ten months? Ten days?

CHRISTINE KENNEALLY

SOME ASPECTS OF what it means to be human are relatively easy to track throughout history. The archaeological excavation of bones and tools allows us to trace the development of our ancestors as they took the physical form and developed the cultural habits that we now consider to be definitive of humanity. Other aspects of human culture are much more obscure, however, and foremost among these is language. While there exists a scattered and incomplete history of the written word, the origins of spoken language have long evaded anthropologists, evolutionary psychologists, linguists, and other scholars searching for the beginnings of language.

Journalist Christine Kenneally takes on this challenge in *The First Word: The Search for the Origins of Language* (2007), her first book. A native Australian, Kenneally earned her bachelor's degree in English and linguistics at Melbourne University and her doctorate in linguistics at Cambridge University and then moved to the United States to become a freelance writer. Before turning her attention to the historical investigation of language, she wrote widely for *The New Yorker*, *The New York Times*, *Discover*, *Slate*, and *Salon*, among other publications, on subjects ranging from Alex the talking African grey parrot to hemispherectomies—operations involving the removal of half of a human brain.

The First Word follows two narratives: the first is an evolutionary story, exploring the possible random adaptations that led to the emergence of *Homo loquens*, the talking animal. At the same time, it traces the politics of scientific research, asking why the study of linguistic evolution was a taboo subject for so long, "formally banned by the Linguistics Society of Paris" in an interdiction that was never officially relaxed. In her research, Kenneally discovers that "the platforms of language were built over thousands of millennia and we share many of these with very different animals." The following chapter from her book—"You Have Gestures"—traces just some of these shared communicative habits. Weaving together different strands of research to offer a holistic view of how language evolves, Kenneally forces into the light the uncomfortable issues

Kenneally, Christine. "You Have Gestures." *The First Word*. New York: Viking Penguin, 2007.
The quotation is drawn from "A Path to Language," an original essay by Kenneally available at the Powell's Books Web site <http://www.powells.com/essays/kenneally.html>.

that led some scholarly groups to ban the study of linguistic evolution in the first place. Just how exceptional is human expression? How are we to interpret the many forms of language-based expression (foremost among these literature) if language is simply an evolutionary quirk? By bringing these questions back into the conversation about language, Kenneally offers new ways to understand our world, and our words.

You Have Gestures

Picture the house in which you grew up. Think about the rooms, the hallways, the stairs, visualize where they all are. Where was the front door? The back door? What color was the roof? Did you have wall-to-wall carpeting or were rugs spread all over the place? If you turned now and attempted to describe the house to someone nearby, it's highly likely that you'd gesture as you spoke. In fact, even if you just imagine a person and then describe the house aloud to her, you'll probably gesture as well. Gesture experts say that it is almost impossible to talk about space without gesturing. Gesture is spontaneous, and as integral to individual expression as it is to communication. Even though you probably won't gesture as much if you are talking on the phone, you will still wave your arms about. Blind people gesture when they speak in the same way that seeing people do.

Gesture may be integral to human expression, but it is not uniquely human. At the Gestural Communication in Nonhuman and Human Primates conference in 2004, Mike Tomasello of the Max Planck Institute in Leipzig, Germany, and his associates presented a huge compilation of gestures that they had observed in monkeys, gibbons, gorillas, chimpanzees, bonobos, and orangutans. Many of them had been observed at the spectacular ape exhibit at the Leipzig city zoo, where a leafy path leads to the center of a big ring. Radiating out from the central space are walks that divide all the great ape species from one another. In one section are the gorillas, sitting impassively. In another are the bonobos—only three of them, a reflection of their dwindling numbers worldwide. In the third section are the orangutans. The male sits near the viewing window looking profoundly deflated, while his orange cage mate hangs upside down from a tree stump and stretches. In the fourth section are the chimpanzees. There are more than a dozen chimps in the compound, and they make a lively community. Some recline sensuously, others fly through the air on ropes or trunks. Some busily work at boxes, inserting sticks into various holes. The exhibit is climate-controlled; it feels like a light summer day. Tomasello has a number of testing rooms installed at the zoo for his various experiments.

Gestures play a large role in primate communication, Tomasello explained, and as is the case with humans, these gestures are learned, flexible, and under voluntary control. Most primates, humans included, gesture communicatively with their right hands, suggesting that the dominance of one side of the brain for vocal and gestural communication could be as old as thirty million years. Just as with human gestures, ape gestures can involve touch, noise, or vision. Apes wait until they have the attention of another ape before making visual gestures, and often if their visual or auditory gestures are unacknowledged, they will go over to the ape they want to communicate with and make some kind of touching gesture instead. Apes also repeat gestures that don't get the desired response. Like human gestures, ape gestures seem to be holistic: a series of gestures doesn't break down cleanly into meaningful components. Moreover, a set of different gestures may mean just one thing, while a single gesture may be used to convey many meanings.

Tomasello and his group divide ape gestures into two types: attention getters and intention movements. Attention getters, said Tomasello, slapping the podium, do just what they say—they call attention to the ape making the gesture. Chimpanzees will hit the ground, clap their hands, and stamp their feet for this purpose. They also lay their arms on other chimps, tug on their hair, or poke them. Once the observer pays attention to the gesturing ape, said Tomasello, what is required becomes clear. To illustrate this, Tomasello showed a video of a chimpanzee who walks over to another chimp and starts jumping up and down on the spot. When the second chimp finally notices the display, the first one turns around and sits down. The message is obvious—groom me, and that's what the second ape starts to do.

Intention movements are the beginnings of an actual movement, like a raised fist to indicate a threat in humans.

The process by which these gestures evolve in individuals, Tomasello explained, goes like this: "I'm really doing something, you come to anticipate it, I notice your anticipation so I only make the beginnings of the movement." Male chimpanzees, for example, make a penis-offer gesture to propose sex. They sit back on their haunches and repeatedly thrust their pelvis, pushing their erect penis in the direction of another chimpanzee. "In papers we call it the penis offer," Tomasello said. "Between ourselves, it's called 'dirty dancing.'"

Mimicking another intention movement, Tomasello rolled his arms over his head, like a chimp barrel-hitting a companion. The move is reminiscent of the way that humans feint at each other to make a point without actually following through. Cats and dogs make a similar movement when they raise their paws and bat them, as if they are about to strike another animal, so the gesture is not restricted to primates. "It's typical mammalian play," Tomasello explained. "Remember," he said, invoking the tree of life, "it's not a ladder; it's a tree. It's not a ladder; it's a tree."

Another gesture researcher, Joanna Blake at York University in Canada, directly compared the gestures that infants make when they are learning language with the gestures made by apes, which have a lot in common. Both apes and children make a lot of request gestures—begging for food, raising their arms to be picked up and carried—and they extend their whole hand to point. Children and apes likewise make the same gestures of protest, pushing someone away or turning away themselves while shaking their heads. They also emote in the same ways, stamping their feet, flapping their arms, and rocking, and when they want someone to do something, both take a person's or an ape's hand and place it on the object to be manipulated, or they proffer objects that they want someone to manipulate. Clearly there is a close family relationship between human and ape gesture, confirming that it is an ancient trait that precedes the existence of modern humans and of language.

Janette Wallis, who has been watching primates since she was an undergraduate at the University of Oklahoma, is drawn to the more subtle aspects of primate communication. She used hidden cameras to capture evidence of a baboon gesture she calls the muzzle wipe—a quick pass across the bridge of the nose with the hand. The muzzle wipe typically occurs in situations in which a baboon may be nervous or conflicted for some reason. As with many human gestures, there's no evidence that the wipe is intentional, but it's likely that other animals read it as a signal that reveals information about the wiper.[1]

Wallis presented videos of the muzzle wipe at the Leipzig gesture conference. Although most early studies of baboons, she said, hardly mention the gesture, her films showed baboons doing it in captivity and in the wild. The gesture rarely lasts longer than a few seconds, so it is not easy to see, yet once Wallis told the audience what to look for, the muzzle wipe was clearly evident. Nervous baboons could be seen constantly putting their hands to their faces in difficult situations. She noted that monkeys make a similar move and that a chimpanzee will often put its wrist to its forehead in similar contexts. Could this overlooked gesture be some kind of precursor to comparable gestures in humans? asked Wallis. Humans do put their hand to their face when nervous, and indeed, as she pointed out, psychiatrists and law enforcement officials often interpret a hand-to-face gesture as evidence of uncertainty or even deception.

Once Wallis convinced the audience that the muzzle wipe existed, she showed a video of George H. W. Bush. The ex-president was speaking at a press conference about his son the president of the United States. He discussed what was at the time headline news—George W. Bush's having been arrested in his youth on a drunk-driving charge. "Unlike some," said the older Bush in a tone of complete confidence, "he accepts responsibility." He then raised his hand to the bridge of his nose and scratched it.[2]

Only ten years ago researchers were unanimous in their agreement that pointing was unique to humans. Even now many stand by that claim. In fact, apes and many species of monkeys that are much more distantly related to humans do point as well, though they typically do so with their whole hand.[3] (Scholars of gesture complain that pointing with the hand has been treated as a second-class kind of pointing, even though it is common in many human groups.) Usually, apes make this gesture only for humans, not between themselves. They point at objects and alternate their gaze between the object that is pointed at and the human they are pointing for. The animals learn how to point without explicit training, and simply pick it up from humans.

Although there is only one anecdotal report of a bonobo's pointing with its index finger in the wild, some apes have been shown to do so in captivity. William D. Hopkins, a researcher at the Yerkes National Primate Research Center at Emory University, and his colleague David Leavens, a professor of psychology at the University of Sussex, showed a videotape at the gesture conference of a chimpanzee pointing. In the video, Leavens is in a white lab coat and a surgical mask while a chimpanzee stands eating on the other side of a wall of wire mesh. When the ape drops some food through the mesh, it points its index finger through the wire to indicate the food and looks at Leavens, who picks it up and returns it. "I submit," Leavens said, "that there is a well-trained primate in this video, but it is not the chimpanzee."

At the Leipzig conference Tomasello was skeptical that apes could point and, if they did, that it actually meant anything. But he began to wonder about it and later said, "Many of the aspects of language that make it such a uniquely powerful form of human cognition and communication are already present in the humble act of pointing."

Tomasello had already established in previous experiments that apes know what other apes are seeing, and it was clear that they gesture easily and creatively for one another. More recent experiments have shown that chimpanzees will cooperate with one another in situations where collective help is needed (in order to get food, for example), and in quite simple tasks they'll also assist without the prospect of a reward—like picking up a dropped object and handing it to someone. While the Hopkins and Leavens video showed they are capable of pointing, why, Tomasello asked, do apes point only for humans and not one another? The answer he arrived at is both simple and far-reaching: it is because humans respond. Apes don't point referentially for other apes, because they will be ignored.

Human children learn to point at a very young age. Tomasello and his colleagues have videotaped many instances of children spontaneously pointing in a helpful manner. In one experimental setup, a very young child was placed on her mother's lap. Mother and child sat across a desk from a woman stapling papers together. The woman left the room for a moment, and while she was away a man entered, took the stapler, and placed it on a cupboard behind the desk. When the woman returned she made a great show of looking for the stapler. The infant watched her for a while, and then, unprompted, pointed to where the stapler had been moved so the woman could find it. In other examples, a child and adult played together until for some reason (the ball dropped, the toy fell) the game stopped. Without prompting, the child looked at the adult and pointed to the problem, clearly requesting that the game begin again. In other cases, the child pointed at an object or proffered it merely to show it to the adult in order to elicit a reaction.

Tomasello first started to consider how much this kind of shared, cooperative attention mattered at dinner in a restaurant one night. He was watching a mother and child play together. The mother blew a raspberry on the child's arm, then the roles were reversed, and the baby followed suit. Why did it happen this way? wondered Tomasello. Why did the child reciprocate the gesture rather than simply imitating the action on himself?

The answer, he believes, is that humans are particularly cooperative in the way they communicate.[4] Reciprocation is fundamental to the interactions of our species. Offering is not instinctive for humans, but is taught by parents to children, who learn it very easily. And crucially, we offer not only food and other objects but information and experiences as well. Children, says Tomasello, want you to look at what they are looking at and to emote in response. In many theories of evolution, human altruism is treated as an anomaly. But Tomasello thinks of it as an evolutionary strategy that has served us incredibly well.

Chimps don't spontaneously point in this fashion, and Tomasello believes it is due to a fundamental difference in the balance of cooperation and competition within the species. Chimpanzees lack the set of skills and motivations that underlie our pointing. Tomasello conducted an experiment with Brian Hare, then a doctoral student, in which two barrels were set up in a room. Food was placed in one, while the other was left empty. Hare stood on one side of the barrels as a chimpanzee entered the room. In one run-through, Hare pointed helpfully at the barrel with the food in it. But, said Tomasello, the chimpanzee would look at the finger, and then look at the barrel, and then look at the other barrel, and then it would choose completely randomly between them. It did not comprehend that Hare was being helpful and telling it where the food was located. In another run-through of the experiment, the chimpanzee would come into the room, and instead of pointing to the food, Hare would reach for the barrel, as if to grab it and the food in it. The chimpanzee understood this gesture without any problem, and it would head for the appropriate barrel. The movement Hare made was essentially the same in each case—a basic arm extension—but his intention was clearly cooperative in the first instance and competitive in the second.[5]

Tomasello and his colleagues' gesture work demonstrates both a continuum that connects human and ape communication and significant differences between them. In our evolutionary history some individuals must have been born with a greater inclination and ability to collaborate than our common ancestor with chimpanzees. These individuals were more successful and bred more offspring with those characteristics, Tomasello said. What we have evolved into now is a species for whom an experience means little if it's not shared. Chimpanzees took a different path. In their communication, there is never just plain showing, where the goal is simply to share attention. While they do share and collaborate and understand different kinds of intentions, they don't have communicative intentions. We do, said Tomasello, and it's in this shared space that the symbolic communication of language lies.

Tomasello's conclusions resonate deeply with observations made by Sue Savage-Rumbaugh. Before Kanzi, Savage-Rumbaugh worked with two apes called Sherman and Austin. The apes had successfully acquired many signs and used them effectively. There didn't seem to be anything odd about their language use until one day they were asked to talk to each other. What resulted was a sign-shouting match; neither ape was willing to listen. Language, wrote Savage-Rumbaugh, "coordinates behaviors between individuals by a complex process of exchanging behaviors that are punctuated by speech."[6]

At its most fundamental, language is an act of shared attention, and without the fundamentally *human* willingness to listen to what another person is saying, language would not work. Symbols like words, said Tomasello, are devices that coordinate attention, just as pointing does. They presuppose a general give-and-take that chimpanzees don't seem to have. For this reason, Tomasello explained, "asking why only humans use language is like asking why only humans build skyscrapers, when the fact is that only humans, among primates, build freestanding shelters at all . . . At our current level of understanding, asking why apes do not have language may not be our most productive question. A much more productive question, and one that can currently lead us to much more interesting lines of empirical research, is asking why apes do not even point."

Whether you are human or another kind of ape, one of the ways that gesture becomes ritualized and communicative is in being passed on by learning. As humans, we observe a gesture, and then we reproduce it by imitation. Imitation is crucial to the learning process, and we are not the only imitators in the animal world. Lori Marino, one of the researchers who explored the ability of dolphins to recognize themselves in mirrors, said that "imitation is an everyday behavior with dolphins." They are very good at shadowing, imitation in real time. "If you make certain hand gestures in front of the tank in a captive facility, they will be able to follow your hand, even when you're moving your hand back and forth in different ways. They also seem able to pick up patterns very well and anticipate patterns, so if you set up a certain pattern going and then you stop, they seem to anticipate what the next step in the pattern is."

Frans de Waal speaks of the difficulties of measuring fleeting and ephemeral behaviors like imitation. "A lot of the cognition studies are on technical cognition, like: Can they count? How do they use tools? Do they understand gravity? Social intelligence is more difficult," he said.

Particular difficulties arise with imitation studies, as de Waal explained:

> What people do, for example, in these imitation studies is they put an experiment in front of the chimpanzee and they show how to do something, and then they see the chimp imitate. But I think imitation also requires that you identify with the person and that you like the person actually. If you look at humans who imitate, children who imitate, they imitate the people they know and they like, and they want to be like Mom or they want to be like Dad or their big brother or whatever. They're not imitating a random person. It's very selective. I think the scientists who have failed to come up with these social learning tasks on chimpanzees, to some degree, have worked with the wrong paradigm. They put a human in front of the animal, which is already a different species, and the human may not have much of a relationship with them. I think we can only resolve these issues by focusing on behavior among animals themselves.

De Waal has been studying the ways that capuchins imitate one another. The experimenters train one capuchin to perform a task, and while other monkeys watch it, they attempt to determine if any imitation is taking place. De Waal is also probing the relevance of who gets imitated—if a capuchin is more likely to imitate its mother, for example, than an unrelated male.

Sue Savage-Rumbaugh's experiences with Kanzi back up de Waal's observation about laboratory experiments. She noted that Kanzi's mother, Matata, had two other children who never got the amount of attention from human caretakers that Kanzi did. She believes it was the significant relationships with humans in the period in which Kanzi was most sensitive to acquiring language that enabled him to pick it up.[7]

Other research suggests that imitation can be affected by who the original performer is. One recent study described the way a population of dolphins off the coast of western Australia passed on a tradition of tool use. These dolphins learned from adults in the pod to use sponges to forage on the ocean floor. But they didn't just acquire the skill from any of the adults: the tradition seemed to be passed down solely from mother to daughter.

The combination of gestural communication and imitation can be as powerful as vocal communication. In human hunter-gatherer groups, such as the Ngatatjara of western Australia and the northern Déné of the Canadian subarctic, the transmission of knowledge about the environment and how to survive in it is achieved by observation and experimentation rather than by verbal explanation. Moreover, studies have shown that a group learning how to manufacture a stone flake (such as those used by Stone Age societies) from a teacher who only gestured took no longer at the task than, and were as good at it as, a group in which the teacher gave precise verbal instructions on how to make the flake.[8]

In modern humans gestures come in a variety of types. There is here-and-now pointing (this book, right here!), action gestures (she picked it up with one hand!), abstract pointing (and another thing!), and metaphorical gestures that make symbolic reference to people, events, space, motion, action. Most gestures are initiated with the right hand. They typically occur slightly before or at the same time as speech.

Gestures that accompany speech typically amplify the meaning conveyed by the speaker. Sometimes, gesture communicates information that isn't explicitly stated in the verbal message it accompanies. For example, a speaker may move his fingers stepwise in a spiral while saying, "I ran all the way upstairs." The listener can infer that the staircase was spiral even though the fact was not stated.[9] While gesture doesn't break up into word-like segments, there are rules about the way gestures can be combined. And as obvious as the meaning of many gestures is when they are used by people while they are talking, listeners can usually guess at the meaning of a gesture without sound only 50 to 60 percent of the time. (Think about gesturing while saying, "I had a big ball" and "The guy had a huge hot dog.")

For a long time gesture was more or less ignored in linguistics, and elsewhere it received little attention. Researchers considered it paralinguistic, meaning that it was merely supplementary to language, perhaps useful in terms of emphasis but ultimately a secondary and unimportant phenomenon. People assumed that gesture was only for the benefit of the listener and justified removing it from serious consideration for the simple reason that it could be removed. It is possible, after all, to hear and understand someone even if you don't look at him. (In the same way, structure in language has been treated as separate from meaning, because you can go a long way analyzing both of them without reference to the other. Similarly, intonation has been largely ignored within Chomskyan linguistics.) The assumption was that because you could separate them in analysis, they worked independently in the body and they therefore evolved independently of each other. But even though you can discover much about speech and language without worrying about gesture, the fact is they usually occur together in the real world. Speech is disembodied only on the phone or radio, and in evolutionary time these types of communication have not been around very long.

Today, like the study of language evolution itself, the field of gesture studies in undergoing a small revolution. More and more people are engaging in experimental studies of gesture, and researchers are discovering how complicated and interesting it can be. Conference organizers in the last few years have been surprised at the number of scholars who want to attend meetings about gesture. This mini-boom is part of the general trend to reconsider what used to be called the epiphenomena of language. In a relatively short amount of time, researchers have shown that speech and gesture, as well as gesture and thought, interact as language is being learned and even after it has been fully acquired.

Traditionally, developmental psychologists thought that children gestured simply because they saw their parents do so. They believed that infants acquired language separate from any gesturing and in a predictable pattern. There was a one-word stage, followed by a two-word stage, and once a child crossed a critical threshold into a three-word stage, her three words very rapidly became many structured sentences. Seen this way, language acquisition was quite miraculous: children went from one word to many in the space of two years.

Experts now agree the picture is more complicated. Strictly speaking, there is no one-word stage. The first sign of language is usually a gesture, which infants will make at about ten months. The best way to think about this process is that it begins with a one-element stage, and that element may be a word or a gesture, such as pointing. If you have ever seen a baby sit and whack his high chair table imperiously, demanding his lunch, you have witnessed the origins of language in the individual. Following the first one-element stage, there is a two-element stage, when word and gesture appear together. This combination can function like a sentence, as when a child says "eat" and points at a banana at the same time. Gesture-and-speech combinations increase between fourteen and twenty-two months. Children also show a three-element stage using both gesture and speech before producing three-elements in speech alone.[10] Following this stage, speech starts to emerge as the prime method of communication.

These findings suggest that gesture doesn't simply precede language but is fundamentally tied to it.[11] In fact gesture and speech are so integral to each other in children that researchers are able to predict a child's language ability at three years of age based on its gesturing at one year. They can also diagnose delays or problems that children might be having with language by examining their gestures.

For a long time the trend was to regard infants, much like animals, as mute and unthinking. Until they learned their first few words, it was thought that not a lot was going on inside their heads. And certainly, if you removed gesture from the language acquisition picture, children did seem eventually to pull language out of thin air. But when you take gesture into account, you can see the preliminary scaffolding of language even before a child has spoken a word, and the acquisition of language, while still incredible, looks a little less mysterious.

Developmental psychologists now talk about the cross-modality of language, meaning that language is expressed in various ways. Instead of the image of a brain issuing language to a mouth, from which it emerges as imperfect speech, think, rather, of language emerging in the child as an expression of its entire body, articulating both limbs and mouth at the same time.

Before the teaching of sign language became widespread, and more recently the use of cochlear implants, the fate of deaf children was contingent on their family situation. Most children who are born without hearing now receive systematic education in schools designed to help them, but there are still rare cases where children who are born deaf do not receive sign language instruction. Whether the reasons are socioeconomic or otherwise, these children are generally spoken to by their parents using normal language and gesture, and they must invent their own ways to express what they want. Susan Goldin-Meadow, who investigates gesture at her laboratory in Chicago, has studied a number of these children. The gestural language they invent is called homesign. Goldin-Meadow's work on homesign and other gestures reveals a great deal about the way the ancient platform of gesture works in modern humans.

The versions of homesign used by each of these children share a number of traits, including the fact that they generally feature a stable list of words and a kind of syntax. Certain words will appear in a particular spot in a sentence depending on the role they take. There is structure in homesign words, as well as in homesign sentences. The symbols that homesigning children invent are not specific to a particular situation or time. For example, they might use a "twist" gesture to ask someone to open a jar, or to indicate that a jar has been twisted open, or to observe that it is possible to twist a jar open. Homesign symbols are also like words in that the number that can be invented appears to be limitless, as well as stable.[12] Even though these children are exposed to a normal combination of gesture and speech by their parents, their own homesign doesn't resemble their parents' gesturing. Children who develop homesign pass through stages of development similar to those of hearing children who are learning speech. Moreover, the linear ordering of elements in a homesign utterance appears to be universal, regardless of the language community the children are born into. Interestingly, if hearing people gesture without speaking, their gestures start to look like the signs of homesigners.

How is it possible that these homesign children who are spoken to (even if they can't hear the words) and gestured at end up gesturing communicatively in the absence of a sign education? Where does this facility for structure and words come from? Goldin-Meadow believes that sentence- and word-level structure are inherent.

Altogether, Goldin-Meadow's studies show that gesture is highly versatile. It is used both with speech and without, and it differs depending on whether it is used with the spoken word. It takes a backseat when it accompanies language, and it becomes much more mimetic when it is used alone. When gesture carries the full burden of communication, says Goldin-Meadow, it becomes much more segmented. She likens it to beads on a string.

Homesign may represent an extreme example of the way that gesture and speech interact, but other recent experiments have demonstrated how speech and gesture can depend on each other. It's been shown that adults will gesture differently depending on the language they are speaking and the way that their language encodes specific concepts, like action. For example, experimenters have compared the idiosyncratic way that Turkish and English speakers describe a cartoon that depicts a character rolling down a hill. Asli Özyürek, a research associate at the Max Planck Institute for Psycholinguistics, compared the performance of children and adults in this task. She showed that initially children produce the same kinds of gestures regardless of the language they are speaking. It takes a while for gesture to take on the characteristic forms of a specific language. When it does, people change their gestures depending on the syntax of the language they are speaking. At this stage, instead of gesture's providing occasional, supplementary meaning to speech without being connected to it in any real way, language and gesture appear to interact online in expression.

In another experiment Goldin-Meadow asked children and adults to solve a particular type of math problem.[13] After they completed the task, the participants were asked to remember a list of words (for the children) and letters (for the adults). Subjects were then asked to explain at a blackboard how they had solved the problem. Goldin-Meadow and her colleagues found that when the experimental subjects gestured during their explanation, they later remembered more from the word list than when they did not gesture. She noted that while people tend to think of gesturing as reflecting an individual's mental state, it appears that gesture contributes to shaping that state. In the case of her subjects, their gesturing somehow lightened the mental load, allowing them to devote more resources to memory.

Gesture interacts with thought and language in other complicated ways. In another experiment Goldin-Meadow asked a group of children to solve a different kind of problem.[14] She then videotaped them describing the solution and noted the way they gestured as they answered. In one case, the children were asked if the amount of water in two identical glasses was the same. (It was.) One of the glasses was then poured into a low and wide dish. The children were asked again if the amount of water was the same. They said it wasn't. They justified their response by describing the height of the water, explaining it's different because this one is taller than that one. As they spoke, some of the children produced what Goldin-Meadow calls a gesture-speech match; that is, they said the amounts of water in the glass and the bowl were unequal, and as they did, they indicated the different heights of the water with their gesture (one hand at one height, the other hand at the other height). Other children who got the problem wrong showed an interesting mismatch between their gesture and their speech. Although these children also said that the amount of the water was different because the height was different, gesturally they indicated the width of the dishes. "This information," said Goldin-Meadow, "when integrated with the information in speech, hints at the correct answer—the water may be higher but it's also skinnier."

The mismatch children suggested by their hand movements that they knew unconsciously what the correct response was. And it turned out that when these children were taught what the relationship between the two amounts of water was after the initial experiment, they were much closer to comprehension than those whose verbal and gestural answers matched— and were wrong.

Gestures also affect listeners. In another experiment children were shown a picture of a character and later asked what he had been wearing. As the researcher posed the question, she made a hat gesture above her head. The children said that the character was wearing a hat even though he wasn't.

Such complicated dependencies and interactions demonstrate that speech and gesture are part of the same system, say Goldin-Meadow and other specialists. Moreover, this system, made up of the two semi-independent subsystems of speech and gesture, is also closely connected to systems of thought. Perhaps we should designate another word entirely for intentional communication that includes gesture and speech. Whatever it should be, Goldin-Meadow and others have demonstrated that this communication is fundamentally embodied.[15]

The most important effect of this research is that it makes it impossible to engage with the evolution of modern language without also considering the evolution of human gesture. Precisely how gesture and speech may have interacted since we split from our common ancestors with chimpanzees is still debated. Michael Corballis, who wrote *From Hand to Mouth: The Origins of Language*, has suggested that quite complicated manual, and possibly facial, gesture may have preceded speech by a significant margin, arising two million years ago when the brains of our ancestors underwent a dramatic burst in size. The transition to independent speech from this gesture language would have occurred gradually as a result of its many benefits, such as communication over long distances and the ability to use hands for other tasks, before the final shift to autonomous spoken language. Other researchers stress how integral gesture is to speech today, arguing that even as the balance of speech and gesture may have shifted within human communication, it is unlikely that gesture would have evolved first without any form of speech. David McNeill, head of the well-known McNeill Laboratory Center for Gesture and Speech Research at the University of Chicago, and colleagues propose that from the very beginning it is the combination of speech and gestures that were selected in evolution.   ■

NOTES

1. Baboons have a rich repertoire of gestures in addition to the muzzle wipe. The adult males exchange complicated greetings, where they make particular facial expressions, assume certain postures, embrace each other, and briefly handle one another's genitals—kind of like a handshake but with the most vulnerable part of the body.

2. Wallis was introduced by Josep Call, a highly experienced researcher, and afterward, Call showed a video of chimpanzees in the wild, mentioning that he hadn't noticed any muzzle-wipe behavior in the animals. On the spot, Wallis got him to replay some frames of his video. She pointed out at least five examples of a movement that looked like a muzzle wipe. Call was visibly startled to see the gesture, then he laughed and turned to the audience: he recounted yet another time that Wallis was told by a primatologist that he had never seen the gesture she was talking about. Then, too, Wallis got the primatologist to replay some of his own footage, and she pointed out what he had missed. Some make the case that we've been observing chimpanzees and other animals for so long now—fifty years—we are not going to find anything that would surprise us. And yet until Wallis showed her videos of the baboons' muzzle wipe, it could have been said that there was no evidence for this gesture—despite the fact that it exists and is ubiquitous. Wallis was the only one to see it and take it seriously, and her experience shows how easy it is for experts to miss what is right before their eyes.

    Ideally, science would be based on observations of all reality, but it is not like this, and animal science is even less so. Instead, the picture is blotchy. Each researcher who announces findings about animal behavior has made choices along the way about what observations are possible, what they have time for, and what they have money for. For instance, if the available spot to observe a gesturing gorilla is four meters away, the researcher may not be able to note the animal's facial expressions because the faces of gorillas are very dark and hard to see. With a lighter-faced animal, like a chimpanzee, four meters would be no problem. In some cases, this partial gathering of information won't matter, but it's possible the facial expressions accompanying the gestures would alter the conclusions. There are other practical considerations as well. Tomasello observed that it would be interesting to study throwing in chimpanzees, but it's not something that any researcher is willing to do—if they reward throwing behavior, the chimpanzees will start throwing their feces at the researchers.

3. D. A. Leavens, W. D. Hopkins, "The Whole-Hand Point."

4. Orangutans are quite cooperative, as are bonobos, which raises the possibility that we didn't evolve to become cooperative from being noncooperative, but that chimpanzees evolved away from this trait.

5. Tomasello and Hare also ran the experiment with dogs, and the canines had no problem interpreting the cooperative pointing. The researchers attribute the dogs' sensitivity to the human-behavior agenda to their domestication.

6. E. S. Savage-Rumbaugh, "Why Are We Afraid of Apes with Languages?"

7. E. S. Savage-Rumbaugh, S. Shanker, T. J. Taylor, *Apes, Language, and the Human Mind.*

8. T. M. Pearce, "Did They Talk Their Way Out of Africa?"

9. S. Goldin-Meadow et al., "Explaining Math: Gesturing Lightens the Load."

10. S. Özçalişkan, S. Goldin-Meadow, "Gesture Is at the Cutting Edge of Early Language Development."

11. J. M. Iverson, S. Goldin-Meadow, "Gesture Paves the Way for Language Development."

12. S. Goldin-Meadow, "What Language Creation in the Manual Modality Tells Us About the Foundations of Language."

13. The children were asked to solve problems like $4 + 5 + 3 = \underline{?} + 3$. The adults were asked to solve problems like $x^2 - 5x + 6 = (\underline{})(\underline{})$. S. Goldin-Meadow et al., "Explaining Math: Gesturing Lightens the Load."

14. S. Goldin-Meadow, S. M. Wagner, "How Our Hands Help Us Learn."

15. In recent years, linguists have studied two very interesting cases where small deaf communities invented a sign language, the first in Nicaragua and the second among the Al-Sayyid Bedouin group in Israel. In both cases, the inception of the language has been pinpointed in time, and the codification of grammar in ensuing generations has been traced. The resulting syntactic conventions are taken as evidence of innate linguistic structure. These investigations are fascinating and important, but whether they reveal innate properties of language is considered controversial. The most salient criticism is that the deaf individuals are communicating with people who already have language. Surely the success or failure of the interpretations made by listeners who are not deaf (including, in the case of the Al-Sayyid Bedouin group, all of the deaf individuals' parents) guides the way the sign language evolves. These issues, which also relate to the investigation of homesign, are yet to be resolved.

REFERENCES

Goldin-Meadow, Susan, "What Language Creation in the Manual Modality Tells Us About the Foundations of Language," *The Linguistic Review* 22 (2005): 199–225.

Goldin-Meadow, S., H. Nusbaum, S. D. Kelly, and S. Wagner, "Explaining Math: Gesturing Lightens the Load," *Psychological Science* 12 (2001): 516–22.

Goldin-Meadow, S., and S. M. Wagner, "How Our Hands Help Us Learn," *Trends in Cognitive Science* 9 (2006): 234–41.

Iverson, Jana M., and Susan Goldin-Meadow, "Gesture Paves the Way for Language Development," *Psychological Science* 16 (2005): 367–71.

Leavens, D. A., and W. D. Hopkins, "The Whole-Hand Point: The Structure and Function of Pointing from a Comparative Perspective," *Journal of Comparative Psychology* 113 (1999): 417–25.

Özçalişkan, S., and S. Goldin-Meadow, "Gesture Is at the Cutting Edge of Early Language Development," *Cognition* 96 (2005): B101–13.

Pearce, Toby M., "Did They Talk Their Way Out of Africa?" *Behavioral and Brain Sciences* 26 (2003): 235–36.

Savage-Rumbaugh, E. S., "Why Are We Afraid of Apes with Language?" in eds. Arnold B. Scheibel and J. William Schopf, *The Origin and Evolution of Intelligence* (Boston: Jones and Bartlett, 1997), pp. 43–69.

Savage-Rumbaugh, E. Sue, Stuart Shanker, and Talbot J.Taylor, *Apes, Language, and the Human Mind* (New York: Oxford University Press, 1998).

■ *QUESTIONS FOR MAKING CONNECTIONS WITHIN THE READING* ■

1. Kenneally's article begins with a thought experiment: Imagine describing the house you grew up in to another person. Kenneally asserts that it is "highly likely" that you would see yourself gesturing during your description; she says, as well, that it is "almost impossible to talk about space without gesturing." Without mentioning gesturing, ask some of your friends and acquaintances to describe places they've lived. What do you notice? Is Kenneally right?

2. At a pivotal point in her article, Kenneally cites Mike Tomasello on the importance of moving beyond questions about why primates don't have language: "A much more productive question, and one that can currently lead us to much more interesting lines of empirical research, is asking why apes do not even point." Why is exploring the absence of certain intentional gestures in primates a better way to go? What does this question make visible that remained unnoticed while researchers were focusing on language alone?

3. Kenneally lists two categories of gestures: attention getters and intention movements. At the end of her article, she notes recent research that unsettles the commonplace understanding of "gesture as reflecting an individual's mental state," research that suggests "gesture contributes to that state." Drawing on examples of gestures that Kenneally provides and others from your own experience, fill out the hypothesis that gesture is not simply reflective of a mental state, but also constitutive.

■ *QUESTIONS FOR WRITING* ■

1. Kenneally proposes that the studies she has discussed "demonstrate that speech and gesture are part of the same system," before calling for a new word or phrase to designate intentional communication, one that highlights that such communication "is fundamentally embodied." Both writing and reading surely fall into the category of intentional communication, and yet it is not immediately evident what role, if any, gesture and embodiment play in these activities. If Kenneally and her colleagues were to focus on these intentional acts, what would they attend to? Could you

apply Kenneally's insights to the daily acts of reading and writing that define the lives of students? Or would you recommend attending to other forms of intentional communication?

2. The dominant version of Darwin's theory of evolution focuses on competition and the "survival of the fittest." The research on gesture that Kenneally discusses, however, highlights the importance and the centrality of reciprocation, cooperation, and altruism. "Language," Kenneally states, "is an act of shared attention." Language can obviously be used in the service of aggression and hostility as well as cooperation and altruism, so what is gained by defining language as "an act of shared attention"? How does this differ from saying that language is a means of communication, for example, or a means of persuasion?

■ *QUESTIONS FOR MAKING CONNECTIONS BETWEEN READINGS* ■

1. Is language a technology? By tracking the differences between the ways that primates and humans use gestures, Kenneally highlights the evolutionary development of the capacity for intentional communication. While the development of this capacity was not the expression of an individual desire or individual initiative initially, looking after language acquisition is a central concern of any developed society—through parenting, schooling, and educational programming, for example. Has the steady advance in the human powers of communication produced "revenge effects," as Edward Tenner defines the term in "Another Look Back, and a Look Ahead"? Have these developments been driven by human desire or has language itself, as a technology, served to shape the needs and choices humans have made to advance our powers of communication?

2. "Language," Kenneally states, "is an act of shared attention, and without the fundamentally *human* willingness to listen to what another person is saying, language would not work." With Henry Jenkins's analysis of the *Harry Potter* wars in mind, discuss the degree to which it is possible to cultivate this "willingness to listen" in others. Do "affective communities" necessarily promote this willingness, or are they formed, in part, by a shared refusal to listen to those outside the community? Is convergence culture enhancing this willingness to listen, or is it having some other effect?

JON KRAKAUER

JON KRAKAUER, A regular contributor to *Outside Magazine*, rose to national prominence with the publication of *Into the Wild*, his investigative account of the life and death of Chris McCandless, a young man who disappeared after graduating from college in Georgia in the early 1990s and whose body was discovered two years later in an abandoned school bus in the wilds of Alaska. (The book became the object of renewed interest in the fall of 2007, when Sean Penn adapted it for the screen.) In an interview, Krakauer explained why he was driven to pursue McCandless's story in such detail:

> I was haunted by the particulars of the boy's starvation and by vague, unsettling parallels between events in his life and those in my own. Unwilling to let McCandless go, I spent more than a year retracing the convoluted path that led to his death in the Alaskan taiga, chasing down details of his peregrinations with an interest that bordered on obsession. In trying to understand McCandless, I inevitably came to reflect on other, larger subjects as well: the grip wilderness has on the American imagination, the allure high-risk activities hold for young men of a certain mind, the complicated, highly charged bond that exists between fathers and sons.

Retracing McCandless's journey, Krakauer meditates not only on what it means to be a man at the end of the twentieth century but also, more generally, on the place of the natural world in contemporary society.

After completing *Into the Wild*, Krakauer set off to study the tourist industry's guided climbs up Mount Everest. *Into Thin Air*, which also became an instant bestseller, is Krakauer's firsthand account of his experiences on a disastrous trip up Mount Everest that left nine climbers dead. The fact that this tragedy could easily have been avoided by staying down off the mountain has

Krakauer, Jon. *Into the Wild.* New York: Villard Books, Random House, 1996.

The digital image is drawn from the Outside Online Web site <http://www.outsidemag.com/disc/guest/krakauer/bookintro.html>.

Quotations come from Krakauer's "Everest a Year Later: Lessons in Futility," *Outside,* May 1997 <http://www.outsidemag.com/magazine/0597/9705krakauer.html> and Krakauer's author introduction, *Outside* <http://www.outsidemag.com/disc/guest/krakauer/bookintro.html>.

not escaped Krakauer's attention: "[W]hen I got back from Everest, I couldn't help but think that maybe I'd devoted my life to something that isn't just selfish and vainglorious and pointless, but actually wrong. There's no way to defend it, even to yourself, once you've been involved in something like this disaster. And yet I've continued to climb." Why do people embark on such adventures? What are they looking for? What is it they hope to achieve? These inquiries into extreme journeys, which he picked up again in a different way in his book on religious faith, *Under the Banner of Heaven: A Story of Violent Faith* (2003), animate both Krakauer's writing and his own search for self-understanding.

■ ■

Selections from
Into the Wild

The Alaska Interior

I wished to acquire the simplicity, native feelings, and virtues of savage life; to divest myself of the factitious habits, prejudices and imperfections of civilization; . . . and to find, amidst the solitude and grandeur of the western wilds, more correct views of human nature and of the true interests of man. The season of snows was preferred, that I might experience the pleasure of suffering, and the novelty of danger.

Estwick Evans,
A Pedestrious Tour, of Four Thousand Miles,
Through the Western States and Territories,
During the Winter and Spring of 1818

Wilderness appealed to those bored or disgusted with man and his works. It not only offered an escape from society but also was an ideal stage for the Romantic individual to exercise the cult that he frequently made of his own soul. The solitude and total freedom of the wilderness created a perfect setting for either melancholy or exultation.

Roderick Nash,
Wilderness and the American Mind

On April 15, 1992, Chris McCandless departed Carthage, South Dakota, in the cab of a Mack truck hauling a load of sunflower seeds. His "great

Alaskan odyssey" was under way. Three days later he crossed the Canadian border at Roosville, British Columbia, and thumbed north through Skookumchuck and Radium Junction, Lake Louise and Jasper, Prince George and Dawson Creek—where, in the town center, he took a snapshot of the signpost marking the official start of the Alaska Highway. MILE "0," the sign reads, FAIRBANKS 1,523 MILES.

Hitchhiking tends to be difficult on the Alaska Highway. It's not unusual, on the outskirts of Dawson Creek, to see a dozen or more doleful-looking men and women standing along the shoulder with extended thumbs. Some of them may wait a week or more between rides. But McCandless experienced no such delay. On April 21, just six days out of Carthage, he arrived at Liard River Hotsprings, at the threshold of the Yukon Territory.

There is a public campground at Liard River, from which a boardwalk leads half a mile across a marsh to a series of natural thermal pools. It is the most popular way-stop on the Alaska Highway, and McCandless decided to pause there for a soak in the soothing waters. When he finished bathing and attempted to catch another ride north, however, he discovered that his luck had changed. Nobody would pick him up. Two days after arriving, he was still at Liard River, impatiently going nowhere.

At six-thirty on a brisk Thursday morning, the ground still frozen hard, Gaylord Stuckey walked out on the boardwalk to the largest of the pools, expecting to have the place to himself. He was surprised, therefore, to find someone already in the steaming water, a young man who introduced himself as Alex.

Stuckey—bald and cheerful, a ham-faced sixty-three-year-old Hoosier—was en route from Indiana to Alaska to deliver a new motor home to a Fairbanks RV dealer, a part-time line of work in which he'd dabbled since retiring after forty years in the restaurant business. When he told McCandless his destination, the boy exclaimed, "Hey, that's where I'm going, too! But I've been stuck here for a couple of days now, trying to get a lift. You mind if I ride with you?"

"Oh, jiminy," Stuckey replied. "I'd love to, son, but I can't. The company I work for has a strict rule against picking up hitchhikers. It could get me canned." As he chatted with McCandless through the sulfurous mist, though, Stuckey began to reconsider: "Alex was clean-shaven and had short hair, and I could tell by the language he used that he was a real sharp fella. He wasn't what you'd call a typical hitchhiker. I'm usually leery of 'em. I figure there's probably something wrong with a guy if he can't even afford a bus ticket. So anyway, after about half an hour I said, 'I tell you what, Alex: Liard is a thousand miles from Fairbanks. I'll take you five hundred miles, as far as Whitehorse; you'll be able to get a ride the rest of the way from there.'"

A day and a half later, however, when they arrived in Whitehorse—the capital of the Yukon Territory and the largest, most cosmopolitan town on the Alaska Highway—Stuckey had come to enjoy McCandless's company so much that he changed his mind and agreed to drive the boy the entire distance. "Alex didn't come out and say too much at first," Stuckey reports. "But it's a long, slow drive. We spent a total of three days together on those washboard roads, and by the end he kind of let his guard down. I tell you what: He was a dandy kid. Real courteous, and he didn't cuss or use a lot of that there slang. You could tell he came from a nice family. Mostly he talked about his sister. He didn't get along with his folks too good, I guess. Told me his dad was a genius, a NASA rocket scientist, but he'd been a bigamist at one time—and that kind of went against Alex's grain. Said he hadn't seen his parents in a couple of years, since his college graduation."

McCandless was candid with Stuckey about his intent to spend the summer alone in the bush, living off the land. "He said it was something he'd wanted to do since he was little," says Stuckey. "Said he didn't want to see a single person, no airplanes, no sign of civilization. He wanted to prove to himself that he could make it on his own, without anybody else's help."

Stuckey and McCandless arrived in Fairbanks on the afternoon of April 25. The older man took the boy to a grocery store, where he bought a big bag of rice, "and then Alex said he wanted to go out to the university to study up on what kind of plants he could eat. Berries and things like that. I told him, 'Alex, you're too early. There's still two foot, three foot of snow on the ground. There's nothing growing yet.' But his mind was pretty well made up. He was chomping at the bit to get out there and start hiking." Stuckey drove to the University of Alaska campus, on the west end of Fairbanks, and dropped McCandless off at 5:30 P.M.

"Before I let him out," Stuckey says, "I told him, 'Alex, I've driven you a thousand miles. I've fed you and fed you for three straight days. The least you can do is send me a letter when you get back from Alaska.' And he promised he would.

"I also begged and pleaded with him to call his parents. I can't imagine anything worse than having a son out there and not knowing where he's at for years and years, not knowing whether he's living or dead. 'Here's my credit card number,' I told him. '*Please* call them!' But all he said was 'Maybe I will and maybe I won't.' After he left, I thought, 'Oh, why didn't I get his parents' phone number and call them myself?' But everything just kind of happened so quick."

After dropping McCandless at the university, Stuckey drove into town to deliver the RV to the appointed dealer, only to be told that the person responsible for checking in new vehicles had already gone home for the day and wouldn't be back until Monday morning, leaving Stuckey with two days to kill in Fairbanks before he could fly home to Indiana. On Sunday morning, with time on his hands, he returned to the campus. "I hoped to find Alex and spend another day with him, take him sightseeing or something. I looked for a couple of hours, drove all over the place, but didn't see hide or hair of him. He was already gone."

After taking his leave of Stuckey on Saturday evening, McCandless spent two days and three nights in the vicinity of Fairbanks, mostly at the university. In the campus book store, tucked away on the bottom shelf of the Alaska section, he came across a scholarly, exhaustively researched field guide to the region's edible plants, *Tanaina Plantlore/Dena'ina K'et'una: An Ethnobotany of the Dena'ina Indians of Southcentral Alaska* by Priscilla Russell Kari. From a postcard rack near the cash register, he picked out two cards of a polar bear, on which he sent his final messages to Wayne Westerberg and Jan Burres from the university post office.

Perusing the classified ads, McCandless found a used gun to buy, a semiautomatic .22-caliber Remington with a 4-x-20 scope and a plastic stock. A model called the Nylon 66, no longer in production, it was a favorite of Alaska trappers because of its light weight and reliability. He closed the deal in a parking lot, probably paying about $125 for the weapon, and then purchased four one-hundred-round boxes of hollow-point long-rifle shells from a nearby gun shop.

At the conclusion of his preparations in Fairbanks, McCandless loaded up his pack and started hiking west from the university. Leaving the campus, he walked past the Geophysical Institute, a tall glass-and-concrete building capped with a large satellite dish. The dish, one of the most distinctive landmarks on the Fairbanks skyline, had been erected to collect data from satellites equipped with synthetic aperture radar of Walt McCandless's design. Walt had in fact visited Fairbanks during the start-up of the receiving station and had written some of the software crucial to its operation. If the Geophysical Institute prompted Chris to think of his father as he tramped by, the boy left no record of it.

Four miles west of town, in the evening's deepening chill, McCandless pitched his tent on a patch of hard-frozen ground surrounded by birch trees, not far from the crest of a bluff overlooking Gold Hill Gas & Liquor. Fifty yards from his camp was the terraced road cut of the George Parks Highway, the road that would take him to the Stampede Trail. He woke early on the morning of April 28, walked down to the highway in the predawn gloaming, and was pleasantly surprised when the first vehicle to come along pulled over to give him a lift. It was a gray Ford pickup with a bumper sticker on the back that declared, I FISH THEREFORE I AM. PETERSBURG, ALASKA. The driver of the truck, an electrician on his way to Anchorage, wasn't much older than McCandless. He said his name was Jim Gallien.

Three hours later Gallien turned his truck west off the highway and drove as far as he could down an unplowed side road. When he dropped McCandless off on the Stampede Trail, the temperature was in the low thirties—it would drop into the low teens at night—and a foot and a half of crusty spring snow covered the ground. The boy could hardly contain his excitement. He was, at long last, about to be alone in the vast Alaska wilds.

As he trudged expectantly down the trail in a fake-fur parka, his rifle slung over one shoulder, the only food McCandless carried was a ten-pound bag of long-grained rice—and the two sandwiches and bag of corn chips that Gallien had contributed. A year earlier he'd subsisted for more than a month beside the Gulf of California on five pounds of rice and a bounty of fish caught with a cheap rod and reel, an experience that made him confident he could harvest enough food to survive an extended stay in the Alaska wilderness, too.

The heaviest item in McCandless's half-full backpack was his library: nine or ten paperbound books, most of which had been given to him by Jan Burres in Niland. Among these volumes were titles by Thoreau and Tolstoy and Gogol, but McCandless was no literary snob: He simply carried what he thought he might enjoy reading, including mass-market books by Michael Crichton, Robert Pirsig, and Louis L'Amour. Having neglected to pack writing paper, he began a laconic journal on some blank pages in the back of *Tanaina Plantlore.*

The Healy terminus of the Stampede Trail is traveled by a handful of dog mushers, ski tourers, and snow-machine enthusiasts during the winter months, but only until the frozen rivers begin to break up, in late March or early April. By the time McCandless headed into the bush, there was open water flowing on most of the larger streams, and nobody had been very far down the trail for two or three weeks; only the faint remnants of a packed snow-machine track remained for him to follow.

McCandless reached the Teklanika River his second day out. Although the banks were lined with a jagged shelf of frozen overflow, no ice bridges spanned the channel of open water, so he was forced to wade. There had been a big thaw in early April, and breakup had come early in 1992, but the weather had turned cold again, so the river's volume was quite low when McCandless crossed—probably thigh-deep at most—allowing him to splash to the other side without difficulty. He never suspected that in so doing, he was crossing his Rubicon. To McCandless's inexperienced eye, there was nothing to suggest that two months hence, as the glaciers and snowfields at the Teklanika's headwater thawed in the summer heat, its discharge would multiply nine or ten times in volume, transforming the river into a deep, violent torrent that bore no resemblance to the gentle brook he'd blithely waded across in April.

From his journal we know that on April 29, McCandless fell through the ice somewhere. It probably happened as he traversed a series of melting beaver ponds just beyond the Teklanika's western bank, but there is nothing to indicate that he suffered any harm in the mishap. A day later, as the trail crested a ridge, he got his first glimpse of Mt. McKinley's high, blinding-white bulwarks, and a day after that, May 1, some twenty miles down the trail from where he was dropped by Gallien, he stumbled upon the old bus beside the Sushana River. It was outfitted with a bunk and a barrel stove, and previous visitors had left the improvised shelter stocked with matches, bug dope, and other essentials. "Magic Bus Day," he wrote in his journal. He decided to lay over for a while in the vehicle and take advantage of its crude comforts.

He was elated to be there. Inside the bus, on a sheet of weathered plywood spanning a broken window, McCandless scrawled an exultant declaration of independence:

> *TWO YEARS HE WALKS THE EARTH. NO PHONE, NO POOL, NO PETS, NO CIGARETTES. ULTIMATE FREEDOM. AN EXTREMIST. AN AESTHETIC VOYAGER WHOSE HOME IS <u>THE ROAD</u>. ESCAPED FROM ATLANTA. THOU SHALT NOT RETURN, 'CAUSE "THE WEST <u>IS</u> THE BEST." AND NOW AFTER TWO RAMBLING YEARS COMES THE FINAL AND GREATEST ADVENTURE. THE CLIMACTIC BATTLE TO KILL THE FALSE BEING WITHIN AND VICTORIOUSLY CONCLUDE THE SPIRITUAL PILGRIMAGE. TEN DAYS AND NIGHTS OF FREIGHT TRAINS AND HITCHHIKING BRING HIM TO THE GREAT WHITE NORTH. NO LONGER TO BE POISONED BY CIVILIZATION HE FLEES, AND WALKS ALONE UPON THE LAND TO BECOME LOST <u>IN THE WILD</u>.*
>
> *Alexander Supertramp*
> *May 1992*

Reality, however, was quick to intrude on McCandless's reverie. He had difficulty killing game, and the daily journal entries during his first week in the bush include "Weakness," "Snowed in," and "Disaster." He saw but did not shoot a grizzly on May 2, shot at but missed some ducks on May 4, and finally killed and ate a spruce grouse on May 5; but he didn't shoot anything else until May 9, when he bagged a single small squirrel, by which point he'd written "4th day famine" in the journal.

But soon thereafter his fortunes took a sharp turn for the better. By mid-May the sun was circling high in the heavens, flooding the taiga with light. The sun dipped below the northern horizon for fewer than four hours out of every twenty-four, and at midnight the sky was still bright enough to read by. Everywhere but on the north-facing slopes and in the shadowy ravines, the snowpack had melted down to bare ground, exposing the previous season's rose hips and lingonberries, which McCandless gathered and ate in great quantity.

He also became much more successful at hunting game and for the next six weeks feasted regularly on squirrel, spruce grouse, duck, goose, and porcupine. On May 22, a crown fell off one of his molars, but the event didn't seem to dampen his spirits much, because the following day he scrambled up the nameless, humplike, three-thousand-foot butte that rises directly north of the bus, giving him a view of the whole icy sweep of the Alaska Range and mile after mile of uninhabited country. His journal entry for the day is characteristically terse but unmistakably joyous: "CLIMB MOUNTAIN!"

McCandless had told Gallien that he intended to remain on the move during his stay in the bush. "I'm just going to take off and keep walking west," he'd said. "I might walk all the way to the Bering Sea." On May 5, after pausing for four days at the bus, he resumed his perambulation. From the snapshots recovered with his Minolta, it appears that McCandless lost (or intentionally left) the by now indistinct Stampede Trail and headed west and north through the hills above the Sushana River, hunting game as he went.

It was slow going. In order to feed himself, he had to devote a large part of each day to stalking animals. Moreover, as the ground thawed, his route turned into a gauntlet of boggy muskeg and impenetrable alder, and McCandless belatedly came to appreciate one of the fundamental (if counterintuitive) axioms of the North: winter, not summer, is the preferred season for traveling overland through the bush.

Faced with the obvious folly of his original ambition, to walk five hundred miles to tidewater, he reconsidered his plans. On May 19, having traveled no farther west than the Toklat River—less than fifteen miles beyond the bus—he turned around. A week later he was back at the derelict vehicle, apparently without regret. He'd decided that the Sushana drainage was plenty wild to suit his purposes and that Fairbanks bus 142 would make a fine base camp for the remainder of the summer.

Ironically, the wilderness surrounding the bus—the patch of overgrown country where McCandless was determined "to become lost in the wild"— scarcely qualifies as wilderness by Alaska standards. Less than thirty miles to the east is a major thoroughfare, the George Parks Highway. Just sixteen miles to the north, beyond an escarpment of the Outer Range, hundreds of tourists rumble daily into Denali Park over a road patrolled by the National Park Service. And unbeknownst to the Aesthetic Voyager, scattered within a six-mile radius of the bus are four cabins (although none happened to be occupied during the summer of 1992).

But despite the relative proximity of the bus to civilization, for all practical purposes McCandless was cut off from the rest of the world. He spent nearly four months in the bush all told, and during that period he didn't encounter another living soul. In the end the Sushana River site was sufficiently remote to cost him his life.

In the last week of May, after moving his few possessions into the bus, McCandless wrote a list of housekeeping chores on a parchmentlike strip of birch bark: collect and store ice from the river for refrigerating meat, cover the vehicle's missing windows with plastic, lay in a supply of firewood, clean the accumulation of old ash from the stove. And under the heading "LONG TERM" he drew up a list of more ambitious tasks: map the area, improvise a bathtub, collect skins and feathers to sew into clothing, construct a bridge across a nearby creek, repair mess kit, blaze a network of hunting trails.

The diary entries following his return to the bus catalog a bounty of wild meat. May 28: "Gourmet Duck!" June 1: "5 Squirrel." June 2: "Porcupine, Ptarmigan, 4 Squirrel, Grey Bird." June 3: "Another Porcupine! 4 Squirrel, 2 Grey Bird, Ash Bird." June 4: "A THIRD PORCUPINE! Squirrel, Grey Bird." On June 5, he shot a Canada goose as big as a Christmas turkey. Then, on June 9, he bagged the biggest prize of all: "MOOSE!" he recorded in the journal. Overjoyed, the proud hunter took a photograph of himself kneeling over his trophy, rifle thrust triumphantly overhead, his features distorted in a rictus of ecstasy and amazement, like some unemployed janitor who'd gone to Reno and won a million-dollar jackpot.

Although McCandless was enough of a realist to know that hunting game was an unavoidable component of living off the land, he had always been ambivalent about killing animals. That ambivalence turned to remorse soon after he shot the moose. It was relatively small, weighing perhaps six hundred or seven hundred pounds, but it nevertheless amounted to a huge quantity of meat. Believing that it was morally indefensible to waste any part of an animal that has been shot for food, McCandless spent six days toiling to preserve what he had killed before it spoiled. He butchered the carcass under a thick cloud of flies and mosquitoes, boiled the organs into a stew, and then laboriously excavated a burrow in the face of the rocky stream bank directly below the bus, in which he tried to cure, by smoking, the immense slabs of purple flesh.

Alaskan hunters know that the easiest way to preserve meat in the bush is to slice it into thin strips and then air-dry it on a makeshift rack. But McCandless, in his naïveté, relied on the advice of hunters he'd consulted in South Dakota, who advised him to smoke his meat, not an easy task under the circumstances. "Butchering extremely difficult," he wrote in the journal on June 10. "Fly and mosquito hordes. Remove intestines, liver, kidneys, one lung, steaks. Get hindquarters and leg to stream."

June 11: "Remove heart and other lung. Two front legs and head. Get rest to stream. Haul near cave. Try to protect with smoker."

June 12: "Remove half rib-cage and steaks. Can only work nights. Keep smokers going."

June 13: "Get remainder of rib-cage, shoulder and neck to cave. Start smoking."

June 14: "Maggots already! Smoking appears ineffective. Don't know, looks like disaster. I now wish I had never shot the moose. One of the greatest tragedies of my life."

At that point he gave up on preserving the bulk of the meat and abandoned the carcass to the wolves. Although he castigated himself severely for this waste of a life he'd taken, a day later McCandless appeared to regain some perspective, for his journal notes, "henceforth will learn to accept my errors, however great they be."

Shortly after the moose episode, McCandless began to read Thoreau's *Walden*. In the chapter titled "Higher Laws," in which Thoreau ruminates on the morality of eating, McCandless highlighted, "when I had caught and cleaned and cooked and eaten my fish, they seemed not to have fed me essentially. It was insignificant and unnecessary, and cost more than it came to."

"THE MOOSE," McCandless wrote in the margin. And in the same passage he marked,

> *The repugnance to animal food is not the effect of experience, but is an instinct. It appeared more beautiful to live low and fare hard in many respects; and though I never did so, I went far enough to please my imagination. I believe that every man who has ever been earnest to preserve his higher or poetic faculties in the best condition has been particularly inclined to abstain from animal food, and from much food of any kind. . . .*
>
> *It is hard to provide and cook so simple and clean a diet as will not offend the imagination; but this, I think, is to be fed when we feed the body; they should both sit down at the same table. Yet perhaps this may be done. The fruits eaten temperately need not make us ashamed of our appetites, nor interrupt the worthiest pursuits. But put an extra condiment into your dish, and it will poison you.*

"YES," wrote McCandless and, two pages later, "*Consciousness* of food. Eat and cook with *concentration*. . . . Holy Food." On the back pages of the book that served as his journal, he declared:

> *I am reborn. This is my dawn. Real life has just begun.*
>
> *Deliberate Living: Conscious attention to the basics of life, and a constant attention to your immediate environment and its concerns, example → A job, a task, a book; anything requiring efficient concentration (Circumstance has no value. It is how one relates to a situation that has value. All true meaning resides in the personal relationship to a phenomenon, what it means to you).*
>
> *The Great Holiness of **FOOD**, the Vital Heat.*
>
> *Positivism, the Insurpassable Joy of the Life Aesthetic.*
>
> *Absolute Truth and Honesty.*
>
> *Reality.*
>
> *Independence.*
>
> *Finality—Stability—Consistency.*

As McCandless gradually stopped rebuking himself for the waste of the moose, the contentment that began in mid-May resumed and seemed to continue through early July. Then, in the midst of this idyll, came the first of two pivotal setbacks.

Satisfied, apparently, with what he had learned during his two months of solitary life in the wild, McCandless decided to return to civilization: It was time to bring his "final and greatest adventure" to a close and get himself back to the world of men and women, where he could chug a beer, talk philosophy, enthrall strangers with tales of what he'd done. He seemed to have moved beyond his need to assert so adamantly his autonomy, his need to separate himself from his parents. Maybe he was prepared to forgive their imperfections; maybe he was even prepared to forgive some of his own. McCandless seemed ready, perhaps, to go home.

Or maybe not; we can do no more than speculate about what he intended to do after he walked out of the bush. There is no question, however, that he intended to walk out.

Writing on a piece of birch bark, he made a list of things to do before he departed: "Patch Jeans, Shave!, Organize pack. . . ." Shortly thereafter he propped his Minolta on an empty oil drum and took a snapshot of himself brandishing a yellow disposable razor and grinning at the camera, clean-shaven, with new patches cut from an army blanket stitched onto the knees of his filthy jeans. He looks healthy but alarmingly gaunt. Already his cheeks are sunken. The tendons in his neck stand out like taut cables.

On July 2, McCandless finished reading Tolstoy's "Family Happiness," having marked several passages that moved him:

> He was right in saying that the only certain happiness in life is to live for others. . . .

> I have lived through much, and now I think I have found what is needed for happiness. A quiet secluded life in the country, with the possibility of being useful to people to whom it is easy to do good, and who are not accustomed to have it done to them; then work which one hopes may be of some use; then rest, nature, books, music, love for one's neighbor—such is my idea of happiness. And then, on top of all that, you for a mate, and children, perhaps—what more can the heart of a man desire?

Then, on July 3, he shouldered his backpack and began the twenty-mile hike to the improved road. Two days later, halfway there, he arrived in heavy rain at the beaver ponds that blocked access to the west bank of the Teklanika River. In April they'd been frozen over and hadn't presented an obstacle. Now he must have been alarmed to find a three-acre lake covering the trail. To avoid having to wade through the murky chest-deep water, he scrambled up a steep hillside, bypassed the ponds on the north, and then dropped back down to the river at the mouth of the gorge.

When he'd first crossed the river, sixty-seven days earlier in the freezing temperatures of April, it had been an icy but gentle knee-deep creek, and he'd simply strolled across it. On July 5, however, the Teklanika was at full flood, swollen with rain and snowmelt from glaciers high in the Alaska Range, running cold and fast.

If he could reach the far shore, the remainder of the hike to the highway would be easy, but to get there he would have to negotiate a channel some one hundred feet wide. The water, opaque with glacial sediment and only a few degrees warmer than the ice it had so recently been, was the color of wet concrete. Too deep to wade, it rumbled like a freight train. The powerful current would quickly knock him off his feet and carry him away.

McCandless was a weak swimmer and had confessed to several people that he was in fact afraid of the water. Attempting to swim the numbingly cold torrent or even to paddle some sort of improvised raft across seemed too risky to consider. Just downstream from where the trail met the river, the Teklanika erupted into a chaos of boiling whitewater as it accelerated through the narrow gorge. Long before he could swim or paddle to the far shore, he'd be pulled into these rapids and drowned.

In his journal he now wrote, "Disaster. . . . Rained in. River look impossible. Lonely, scared." He concluded, correctly, that he would probably be swept to his death if he attempted to cross the Teklanika at that place, in those conditions. It would be suicidal; it was simply not an option.

If McCandless had walked a mile or so upstream, he would have discovered that the river broadened into a maze of braided channels. If he'd scouted carefully, by trial and error he might have found a place where these braids were only chest-deep. As strong as the current was running, it would have certainly knocked him off his feet, but by dog-paddling and hopping along the bottom as he drifted downstream, he could conceivably have made it across before being carried into the gorge or succumbing to hypothermia.

But it would still have been a very risky proposition, and at that point McCandless had no reason to take such a risk. He'd been fending for himself quite nicely in the country. He probably understood that if he was patient and waited, the river would eventually drop to a level where it could be safely forded. After weighing his options, therefore, he settled on the most prudent course. He turned around and began walking to the west, back toward the bus, back into the fickle heart of the bush.

The Stampede Trail

Nature was here something savage and awful, though beautiful. I looked with awe at the ground I trod on, to see what the Powers had made there, the form and fashion and material of their work. This was that Earth of which we have heard, made out of Chaos and Old Night. Here was no man's garden, but the unhandselled globe. It was not lawn, nor pasture, nor mead, nor woodland, nor lea, nor arable, nor waste land. It was the fresh and natural surface of the planet Earth, as it was made forever and ever,—to be the dwelling of man, we say,—so Nature made it, and man may use it if he can. Man was not to be associated with it. It was Matter, vast, terrific,—not his Mother Earth that we have heard of, not for him to tread on, or to be buried in,—no, it were being too familiar even to let his bones lie there,—the home, this, of Necessity and Fate. There was clearly felt the presence of a force not bound to be kind to man. It was a place of heathenism and superstitious rites,—

*to be inhabited by men nearer of kin to the rocks and to wild animals than
we. . . . What is it to be admitted to a museum, to see a myriad of particular things,
compared with being shown some star's surface, some hard matter in its home! I
stand in awe of my body, this matter to which I am bound has become so strange to
me. I fear not spirits, ghosts, of which I am one,—that my body might,—but I fear
bodies, I tremble to meet them. What is this Titan that has possession of me? Talk of
mysteries! Think of our life in nature,—daily to be shown matter, to come in contact with it,—rocks, trees, wind on our cheeks! the solid earth! the actual world!
the common sense! Contact! Contact! Who are we? where are we?*

Henry David Thoreau, "Ktaadn"

A year and a week after Chris McCandless decided not to attempt to
cross the Teklanika River, I stand on the opposite bank—the eastern side, the
highway side—and gaze into the churning water. I, too, hope to cross the
river. I want to visit the bus. I want to see where McCandless died, to better
understand why.

It is a hot, humid afternoon, and the river is livid with runoff from the
fast-melting snowpack that still blankets the glaciers in the higher elevations
of the Alaska Range. Today the water looks considerably lower than it looks
in the photographs McCandless took twelve months ago, but to try to ford
the river here, in thundering midsummer flood, is nevertheless unthinkable.
The water is too deep, too cold, too fast. As I stare into the Teklanika, I can
hear rocks the size of bowling balls grinding along the bottom, rolled downstream by the powerful current. I'd be swept from my feet within a few
yards of leaving the bank and pushed into the canyon immediately below,
which pinches the river into a boil of rapids that continues without interruption for the next five miles.

Unlike McCandless, however, I have in my backpack a 1:63,360-scale
topographic map (that is, a map on which one inch represents one mile). Exquisitely detailed, it indicates that half a mile downstream, in the throat of
the canyon, is a gauging station that was built by the U.S. Geological Survey.
Unlike McCandless, too, I am here with three companions: Alaskans Roman
Dial and Dan Solie and a friend of Roman's from California, Andrew Liske.
The gauging station can't be seen from where the Stampede Trail comes
down to the river, but after twenty minutes of fighting our way through a
snarl of spruce and dwarf birch, Roman shouts, "I see it! There! A hundred
yards farther."

We arrive to find an inch-thick steel cable spanning the gorge, stretched
between a fifteen-foot tower on our side of the river and an outcrop on the
far shore, four hundred feet away. The cable was erected in 1970 to chart the
Teklanika's seasonal fluctuations; hydrologists traveled back and forth
above the river by means of an aluminum basket that is suspended from the
cable with pulleys. From the basket they would drop a weighted plumb line
to measure the river's depth. The station was decommissioned nine years

ago for lack of funds, at which time the basket was supposed to be chained and locked to the tower on our side—the highway side—of the river. When we climbed to the top of the tower, however, the basket wasn't there. Looking across the rushing water, I could see it over on the distant shore—the bus side—of the canyon.

Some local hunters, it turns out, had cut the chain, ridden the basket across, and secured it to the far side in order to make it harder for outsiders to cross the Teklanika and trespass on their turf. When McCandless tried to walk out of the bush one year ago the previous week, the basket was in the same place it is now, on his side of the canyon. If he'd known about it, crossing the Teklanika to safety would have been a trivial matter. Because he had no topographic map, however, he had no way of conceiving that salvation was so close at hand.

Andy Horowitz, one of McCandless's friends on the Woodson High cross-country team, had mused that Chris "was born into the wrong century. He was looking for more adventure and freedom than today's society gives people." In coming to Alaska, McCandless yearned to wander uncharted country, to find a blank spot on the map. In 1992, however, there were no more blank spots on the map—not in Alaska, not anywhere. But Chris, with his idiosyncratic logic, came up with an elegant solution to this dilemma: He simply got rid of the map. In his own mind, if nowhere else, the *terra* would thereby remain *incognita*.

Because he lacked a good map, the cable spanning the river also remained incognito. Studying the Teklanika's violent flow, McCandless thus mistakenly concluded that it was impossible to reach the eastern shore. Thinking that his escape route had been cut off, he returned to the bus—a reasonable course of action, given his topographical ignorance. But why did he then stay at the bus and starve? Why, come August, didn't he try once more to cross the Teklanika, when it would have been running significantly lower, when it would have been safe to ford?

Puzzled by these questions, and troubled, I am hoping that the rusting hulk of Fairbanks bus 142 will yield some clues. But to reach the bus, I, too, need to cross the river, and the aluminum tram is still chained to the far shore.

Standing atop the tower anchoring the eastern end of the span, I attach myself to the cable with rock-climbing hardware and begin to pull myself across, hand over hand, executing what mountaineers call a Tyrolean traverse. This turns out to be a more strenuous proposition than I had anticipated. Twenty minutes after starting out, I finally haul myself onto the outcrop on the other side, completely spent, so wasted I can barely raise my arms. After at last catching my breath, I climb into the basket—a rectangular aluminum car two feet wide by four feet long—disconnect the chain, and head back to the eastern side of the canyon to ferry my companions across.

The cable sags noticeably over the middle of the river; so when I cut loose from the outcrop, the car accelerates quickly under its own weight, rolling faster and faster along the steel strand, seeking the lowest point. It's a thrilling ride. Zipping over the rapids at twenty or thirty miles per hour, I hear an involuntary bark of fright leap from my throat before I realize that I'm in no danger and regain my composure.

After all four of us are on the western side of the gorge, thirty minutes of rough bushwhacking returns us to the Stampede Trail. The ten miles of trail we have already covered—the section between our parked vehicles and the river—were gentle, well marked, and relatively heavily traveled. But the ten miles to come have an utterly different character.

Because so few people cross the Teklanika during the spring and summer months, much of the route is indistinct and overgrown with brush. Immediately past the river the trail curves to the southwest, up the bed of a fast-flowing creek. And because beavers have built a network of elaborate dams across this creek, the route leads directly through a three-acre expanse of standing water. The beaver ponds are never more than chest deep, but the water is cold, and as we slosh forward, our feet churn the muck on the bottom into a foul-smelling miasma of decomposing slime.

The trail climbs a hill beyond the uppermost pond, then rejoins the twisting, rocky creek bed before ascending again into a jungle of scrubby vegetation. The going never gets exceedingly difficult, but the fifteen-foot-high tangle of alder pressing in from both sides is gloomy, claustrophobic, oppressive. Clouds of mosquitoes materialize out of the sticky heat. Every few minutes the insects' piercing whine is supplanted by the boom of distant thunder, rumbling over the taiga from a wall of thunderheads rearing darkly on the horizon.

Thickets of buckbrush leave a crosshatch of bloody lacerations on my shins. Piles of bear scat on the trail and, at one point, a set of fresh grizzly tracks—each print half again as long as a size-nine boot print—put me on edge. None of us has a gun. "Hey, Griz!" I yell at the undergrowth, hoping to avoid a surprise encounter. "Hey, bear! Just passing through! No reason to get riled!"

I have been to Alaska some twenty times during the past twenty years—to climb mountains, to work as a carpenter and a commercial salmon fisherman and a journalist, to goof off, to poke around. I've spent a lot of time alone in the country over the course of my many visits and usually relish it. Indeed, I had intended to make this trip to the bus by myself, and when my friend Roman invited himself and two others along, I was annoyed. Now, however, I am grateful for their company. There is something disquieting about this Gothic, overgrown landscape. It feels more malevolent than other, more remote corners of the state I know—the tundra-wrapped slopes of the Brooks Range, the cloud forests of the Alexander Archipelago, even the frozen, gale-swept heights of the Denali massif. I'm happy as hell that I'm not here alone.

* * *

At 9:00 P.M. we round a bend in the trail, and there, at the edge of a small clearing, is the bus. Pink bunches of fireweed choke the vehicle's wheel wells, growing higher than the axles. Fairbanks bus 142 is parked beside a coppice of aspen, ten yards back from the brow of a modest cliff, on a shank of high ground overlooking the confluence of the Sushana River and a smaller tributary. It's an appealing setting, open and filled with light. It's easy to see why McCandless decided to make this his base camp.

We pause some distance away from the bus and stare at it for a while in silence. Its paint is chalky and peeling. Several windows are missing. Hundreds of delicate bones litter the clearing around the vehicle, scattered among thousands of porcupine quills: the remains of the small game that made up the bulk of McCandless's diet. And at the perimeter of this boneyard lies one much larger skeleton: that of the moose he shot, and subsequently agonized over.

When I'd questioned Gordon Samel and Ken Thompson shortly after they'd discovered McCandless's body, both men insisted—adamantly and unequivocally—that the big skeleton was the remains of a caribou, and they derided the greenhorn's ignorance in mistaking the animal he killed for a moose. "Wolves had scattered the bones some," Thompson had told me, "but it was obvious that the animal was a caribou. The kid didn't know what the hell he was doing up here."

"It was definitely a caribou," Samel had scornfully piped in. "When I read in the paper that he thought he'd shot a moose, that told me right there he wasn't no Alaskan. There's a big difference between a moose and a caribou. A real big difference. You'd have to be pretty stupid not to be able to tell them apart."

Trusting Samel and Thompson, veteran Alaskan hunters who've killed many moose and caribou between them, I duly reported McCandless's mistake in the article I wrote for *Outside*, thereby confirming the opinion of countless readers that McCandless was ridiculously ill prepared, that he had no business heading into any wilderness, let alone into the big-league wilds of the Last Frontier. Not only did McCandless die because he was stupid, one Alaska correspondent observed, but "the scope of his self-styled adventure was so small as to ring pathetic—squatting in a wrecked bus a few miles out of Healy, potting jays and squirrels, mistaking a caribou for a moose (pretty hard to do). . . . Only one word for the guy: incompetent."

Among the letters lambasting McCandless, virtually all those I received mentioned his misidentification of the caribou as proof that he didn't know the first thing about surviving in the back country. What the angry letter writers didn't know, however, was that the ungulate McCandless shot was exactly what he'd said it was. Contrary to what I reported in *Outside*, the animal was a moose, as a close examination of the beast's remains now indicated and several of McCandless's photographs of the kill later confirmed beyond all doubt. The boy made some mistakes on the Stampede Trail, but confusing a caribou with a moose wasn't among them.

Walking past the moose bones, I approach the vehicle and step through an emergency exit at the back. Immediately inside the door is the torn mattress, stained and moldering, on which McCandless expired. For some reason I am taken aback to find a collection of his possessions spread across its ticking: a green plastic canteen; a tiny bottle of water-purification tablets; a used-up cylinder of Chap Stick; a pair of insulated flight pants of the type sold in military-surplus stores; a paperback copy of the bestseller *0 Jerusalem!,* its spine broken; wool mittens; a bottle of Muskol insect repellent; a full box of matches; and a pair of brown rubber work boots with the name Gallien written across the cuffs in faint black ink.

Despite the missing windows, the air inside the cavernous vehicle is stale and musty. "Wow," Roman remarks. "It smells like dead birds in here." A moment later I come across the source of the odor: a plastic garbage bag filled with feathers, down, and the severed wings of several birds. It appears that McCandless was saving them to insulate his clothing or perhaps to make a feather pillow.

Toward the front of the bus, McCandless's pots and dishes are stacked on a makeshift plywood table beside a kerosene lamp. A long leather scabbard is expertly tooled with the initials R. F.: the sheath for the machete Ronald Franz gave McCandless when he left Salton City.

The boy's blue toothbrush rests next to a half-empty tube of Colgate, a packet of dental floss, and the gold molar crown that, according to his journal, fell off his tooth three weeks into his sojourn. A few inches away sits a skull the size of a watermelon, thick ivory fangs jutting from its bleached maxillae. It is a bear skull, the remains of a grizzly shot by someone who visited the bus years before McCandless's tenure. A message scratched in Chris's tidy hand brackets a cranial bullet hole: ALL HAIL THE PHANTOM BEAR, THE BEST WITHIN US ALL. ALEXANDER SUPERTRAMP, MAY 1992.

Looking up, I notice that the sheet-metal walls of the vehicle are covered with graffiti left by numerous visitors over the years. Roman points out a message he wrote when he stayed in the bus four years ago, during a traverse of the Alaska Range: NOODLE EATERS EN ROUTE TO LAKE CLARK 8/89. Like Roman, most people scrawled little more than their names and a date. The longest, most eloquent graffito is one of several inscribed by McCandless, the proclamation of joy that begins with a nod to his favorite Roger Miller song: TWO YEARS HE WALKS THE EARTH, NO PHONE, NO POOL, NO PETS, NO CIGARETTES. ULTIMATE FREEDOM. AN EXTREMIST. AN AESTHETIC VOYAGER WHOSE NAME IS THE ROAD. . . .

Immediately below this manifesto squats the stove, fabricated from a rusty oil drum. A twelve-foot section of a spruce trunk is jammed into its open doorway, and across the log are draped two pairs of torn Levi's, laid out as if to dry. One pair of jeans—waist thirty, inseam thirty-two—is patched crudely with silver duct tape; the other pair has been repaired more carefully, with scraps from a faded bedspread stitched over gaping holes in the knees and seat. This latter pair also sports a belt fashioned from a strip of blanket. McCandless, it occurs to me, must have been forced to make the belt after growing so thin that his pants wouldn't stay up without it.

Sitting down on a steel cot across from the stove to mull over this eerie tableau, I encounter evidence of McCandless's presence wherever my vision rests. Here are his toenail clippers, over there his green nylon tent spread over a missing window in the front door. His Kmart hiking boots are arranged neatly beneath the stove, as though he'd soon be returning to lace them up and hit the trail. I feel uncomfortable, as if I were intruding, a voyeur who has slipped into McCandless's bedroom while he is momentarily away. Suddenly queasy, I stumble out of the bus to walk along the river and breathe some fresh air.

An hour later we build a fire outside in the fading light. The rain squalls, now past, have rinsed the haze from the atmosphere, and distant, backlit hills stand out in crisp detail. A stripe of incandescent sky burns beneath the cloud base on the northwestern horizon. Roman unwraps some steaks from a moose he shot in the Alaska Range last September and lays them across the fire on a blackened grill, the grill McCandless used for broiling his game. Moose fat pops and sizzles into the coals. Eating the gristly meat with our fingers, we slap at mosquitoes and talk about this peculiar person whom none of us ever met, trying to get a handle on how he came to grief, trying to understand why some people seem to despise him so intensely for having died here.

By design McCandless came into the country with insufficient provisions, and he lacked certain pieces of equipment deemed essential by many Alaskans: a large-caliber rifle, map and compass, an ax. This has been regarded as evidence not just of stupidity but of the even greater sin of arrogance. Some critics have even drawn parallels between McCandless and the Arctic's most infamous tragic figure, Sir John Franklin, a nineteenth-century British naval officer whose smugness and hauteur contributed to some 140 deaths, including his own.

In 1819, the Admiralty assigned Franklin to lead an expedition into the wilderness of northwestern Canada. Two years out of England, winter overtook his small party as they plodded across an expanse of tundra so vast and empty that they christened it the Barrens, the name by which it is still known. Their food ran out. Game was scarce, forcing Franklin and his men to subsist on lichens scraped from boulders, singed deer hide, scavenged animal bones, their own boot leather, and finally one another's flesh. Before the ordeal was over, at least two men had been murdered and eaten, the suspected murderer had been summarily executed, and eight others were dead from sickness and starvation. Franklin was himself within a day or two of expiring when he and the other survivors were rescued by a band of métis.

An affable Victorian gentleman, Franklin was said to be a good-natured bumbler, dogged and clueless, with the naïve ideals of a child and a disdain for acquiring backcountry skills. He had been woefully unprepared to lead an Arctic expedition, and upon returning to England, he was known as the

Man Who Ate His Shoes—yet the sobriquet was uttered more often with awe than with ridicule. He was hailed as a national hero, promoted to the rank of captain by the Admiralty, paid handsomely to write an account of his ordeal, and, in 1825, given command of a second Arctic expedition.

That trip was relatively uneventful, but in 1845, hoping finally to discover the fabled Northwest Passage, Franklin made the mistake of returning to the Arctic for a third time. He and the 128 men under his command were never heard from again. Evidence unearthed by the forty-odd expeditions sent to search for them eventually established that all had perished, the victims of scurvy, starvation, and unspeakable suffering.

When McCandless turned up dead, he was likened to Franklin not simply because both men starved but also because both were perceived to have lacked a requisite humility; both were thought to have possessed insufficient respect for the land. A century after Franklin's death, the eminent explorer Vilhjalmur Stefansson pointed out that the English explorer had never taken the trouble to learn the survival skills practiced by the Indians and the Eskimos—peoples who had managed to flourish "for generations, bringing up their children and taking care of their aged" in the same harsh country that killed Franklin. (Stefansson conveniently neglected to mention that many, many Indians and Eskimos have starved in the northern latitudes, as well.)

McCandless's arrogance was not of the same strain as Franklin's, however. Franklin regarded nature as an antagonist that would inevitably submit to force, good breeding, and Victorian discipline. Instead of living in concert with the land, instead of relying on the country for sustenance as the natives did, he attempted to insulate himself from the northern environment with ill-suited military tools and traditions. McCandless, on the other hand, went too far in the opposite direction. He tried to live entirely off the country—and he tried to do it without bothering to master beforehand the full repertoire of crucial skills.

It probably misses the point, though, to castigate McCandless for being ill prepared. He was green, and he overestimated his resilience, but he was sufficiently skilled to last for sixteen weeks on little more than his wits and ten pounds of rice. And he was fully aware when he entered the bush that he had given himself a perilously slim margin for error. He knew precisely what was at stake.

It is hardly unusual for a young man to be drawn to a pursuit considered reckless by his elders; engaging in risky behavior is a rite of passage in our culture no less than in most others. Danger has always held a certain allure. That, in large part, is why so many teenagers drive too fast and drink too much and take too many drugs, why it has always been so easy for nations to recruit young men to go to war. It can be argued that youthful derring-do is in fact evolutionarily adaptive, a behavior encoded in our genes. McCandless, in his fashion, merely took risk-taking to its logical extreme.

He had a need to test himself in ways, as he was fond of saying, "that mattered." He possessed grand—some would say grandiose—spiritual ambitions. According to the moral absolutism that characterizes McCandless's beliefs, a challenge in which a successful outcome is assured isn't a challenge at all.

It is not merely the young, of course, who are drawn to hazardous undertakings. John Muir is remembered primarily as a no-nonsense conservationist and the founding president of the Sierra Club, but he was also a bold adventurer, a fearless scrambler of peaks, glaciers, and waterfalls whose best-known essay includes a riveting account of nearly falling to his death, in 1872, while ascending California's Mt. Ritter. In another essay Muir rapturously describes riding out a ferocious Sierra gale, by choice, in the uppermost branches of a one-hundred-foot Douglas fir:

> [N]ever before did I enjoy so noble an exhilaration of motion. The slender tops fairly flapped and swished in the passionate torrent, bending and swirling backward and forward, round and round, tracing indescribable combinations of vertical and horizontal curves, while I clung with muscles firm braced, like a bobolink on a reed.

He was thirty-six years old at the time. One suspects that Muir wouldn't have thought McCandless terribly odd or incomprehensible.

Even staid, prissy Thoreau, who famously declared that it was enough to have "traveled a good deal in Concord," felt compelled to visit the more fearsome wilds of nineteenth-century Maine and climb Mt. Katahdin. His ascent of the peak's "savage and awful, though beautiful" ramparts shocked and frightened him, but it also induced a giddy sort of awe. The disquietude he felt on Katahdin's granite heights inspired some of his most powerful writing and profoundly colored the way he thought thereafter about the earth in its coarse, undomesticated state.

Unlike Muir and Thoreau, McCandless went into the wilderness not primarily to ponder nature or the world at large but, rather, to explore the inner country of his own soul. He soon discovered, however, what Muir and Thoreau already knew: An extended stay in the wilderness inevitably directs one's attention outward as much as inward, and it is impossible to live off the land without developing both a subtle understanding of, and a strong emotional bond with, that land and all it holds.

The entries in McCandless's journal contain few abstractions about wilderness or, for that matter, few ruminations of any kind. There is scant mention of the surrounding scenery. Indeed, as Roman's friend Andrew Liske points out upon reading a photocopy of the journal, "These entries are almost entirely about what he ate. He wrote about hardly anything except food."

Andrew is not exaggerating: The journal is little more than a tally of plants foraged and game killed. It would probably be a mistake, however, to conclude thereby that McCandless failed to appreciate the beauty of the country around him, that he was unmoved by the power of the landscape. As cultural ecologist Paul Shepard has observed,

> *The nomadic Bedouin does not dote on scenery, paint landscapes, or compile a nonutilitarian natural history. . . . [H]is life is so profoundly in transaction with nature that there is no place for abstraction or esthetics or a "nature philosophy" which can be separated from the rest of his life. . . . Nature and his relationship to it are a deadly-serious matter, prescribed by convention, mystery, and danger. His personal leisure is aimed away from idle amusement or detached tampering with nature's processes. But built into his life is awareness of that presence, of the terrain, of the unpredictable weather, of the narrow margin by which he is sustained.*

Much the same could be said of McCandless during the months he spent beside the Sushana River.

It would be easy to stereotype Christopher McCandless as another boy who felt too much, a loopy young man who read too many books and lacked even a modicum of common sense. But the stereotype isn't a good fit. McCandless wasn't some feckless slacker, adrift and confused, racked by existential despair. To the contrary: His life hummed with meaning and purpose. But the meaning he wrested from existence lay beyond the comfortable path: McCandless distrusted the value of things that came easily. He demanded much of himself—more, in the end, than he could deliver.

Trying to explain McCandless's unorthodox behavior, some people have made much of the fact that like John Waterman, he was small in stature and may have suffered from a "short man's complex," a fundamental insecurity that drove him to prove his manhood by means of extreme physical challenges. Others have posited that an unresolved Oedipal conflict was at the root of his fatal odyssey. Although there may be some truth in both hypotheses, this sort of posthumous off-the-rack psychoanalysis is a dubious, highly speculative enterprise that inevitably demeans and trivializes the absent analysand. It's not clear that much of value is learned by reducing Chris McCandless's strange spiritual quest to a list of pat psychological disorders.

Roman and Andrew and I stare into the embers and talk about McCandless late into the night. Roman, thirty-two, inquisitive and outspoken, has a doctorate in biology from Stanford and an abiding distrust of conventional wisdom. He spent his adolescence in the same Washington, D.C., suburbs as McCandless and found them every bit as stifling. He first came to Alaska as a nine-year-old, to visit a trio of uncles who mined coal at Usibelli, a big strip-mine operation a few miles east of Healy, and immediately fell in love with everything about the North. Over the years that followed, he returned repeatedly to the forty-ninth state. In 1977, after graduating from high school as a sixteen-year-old at the top of his class, he moved to Fairbanks and made Alaska his permanent home.

These days Roman teaches at Alaska Pacific University, in Anchorage, and enjoys statewide renown for a long, brash string of backcountry escapades: He has—among other feats—traveled the entire 1,000-mile length of the Brooks Range by foot and paddle, skied 250 miles across the Arctic National Wildlife Refuge in subzero winter cold, traversed the 700-mile crest of the Alaska Range, and pioneered more than thirty first ascents of northern peaks and crags. And Roman doesn't see a great deal of difference between his own widely respected deeds and McCandless's adventure, except that McCandless had the misfortune to perish.

I bring up McCandless's hubris and the dumb mistakes he made—the two or three readily avoidable blunders that ended up costing him his life. "Sure, he screwed up," Roman answers, "but I admire what he was trying to do. Living completely off the land like that, month after month, is incredibly difficult. I've never done it. And I'd bet you that very few, if any, of the people who call McCandless incompetent have ever done it either, not for more than a week or two. Living in the interior bush for an extended period, subsisting on nothing except what you hunt and gather—most people have no idea how hard that actually is. And McCandless almost pulled it off.

"I guess I just can't help identifying with the guy," Roman allows as he pokes the coals with a stick. "I hate to admit it, but not so many years ago it could easily have been me in the same kind of predicament. When I first started coming to Alaska, I think I was probably a lot like McCandless: just as green, just as eager. And I'm sure there are plenty of other Alaskans who had a lot in common with McCandless when they first got here, too, including many of his critics. Which is maybe why they're so hard on him. Maybe McCandless reminds them a little too much of their former selves."

Roman's observation underscores how difficult it is for those of us preoccupied with the humdrum concerns of adulthood to recall how forcefully we were once buffeted by the passions and longings of youth. As Everett Ruess's father mused years after his twenty-year-old son vanished in the desert, "The older person does not realize the soul-flights of the adolescent. I think we all poorly understood Everett."

Roman, Andrew, and I stay up well past midnight, trying to make sense of McCandless's life and death, yet his essence remains slippery, vague, elusive. Gradually, the conversation lags and falters. When I drift away from the fire to find a place to throw down my sleeping bag, the first faint smear of dawn is already bleaching the rim of the northeastern sky. Although the mosquitoes are thick tonight and the bus would no doubt offer some refuge, I decide not to bed down inside Fairbanks 142. Nor, I note before sinking into a dreamless sleep, do the others.   ■

■ *QUESTIONS FOR MAKING CONNECTIONS WITHIN THE READING* ■

1. Jon Krakauer is telling the story of Chris McCandless, who was interested in, among other things, recording the adventures of "Alexander Supertramp." What is the relationship between McCandless and Supertramp?

What does writing under a different name allow McCandless to do that he wouldn't otherwise be able to do?

2. Most everyone at one time or another has dreamed of getting away from it all. Chris McCandless actually did so. Would he have been able to have the adventure he was looking for if he'd done more research? Would his story be more or less compelling if he had brought along a map? If he had survived?

3. One of Krakauer's central concerns in *Into the Wild* is to determine what drove McCandless to embark on such a dangerous journey and to speculate on what McCandless's motives were when he sought to make his way back out of the wild. How does Krakauer go about trying to uncover the answers to these questions? What is his method? What counts as evidence for him? When does Krakauer know—or feel—that he has found what he was looking for?

■ *QUESTIONS FOR WRITING* ■

1. At the end of this reading, Krakauer asserts that one reason adults have so much difficulty understanding McCandless's actions is that they struggle "to recall how forcefully [they] were once buffeted by the passions and longings of youth." To understand this observation, one must be able to define what "the passions and longings of youth" are. What do these passions and longings have to do with escape? With the natural world? And if one can recall such passions and longings, how might this change one's understanding of the import of McCandless's death?

2. In providing a narrative of McCandless's journey, Krakauer draws on the writings Chris left behind in the blank pages and margins of his books and on the walls of the bus where he spent his final months. What does all this writing tell Krakauer about McCandless's motives for heading off into the wild? Is it possible to escape from civilization in the twenty-first century? Does it make sense to try?

■ *QUESTIONS FOR MAKING CONNECTIONS BETWEEN READINGS* ■

1. In "The Naked Citadel," Susan Faludi sets out to study how young men are turned into soldiers at a military academy and to record how this training process was upended when the academy was required to admit young women into its ranks. In detailing McCandless's journey into the wild, Krakauer provides a glimpse into another ritualized way of "becoming a man." Would you argue that McCandless's journey is consistent with The Citadel's efforts to create a certain kind of man? Or was McCandless's journey an attempt to escape from the masculine ideals embodied

by The Citadel's students? What, if anything, do these two stories suggest about how masculinity will be defined and experienced in the twenty-first century?

2. Toward the end of this reading, Krakauer cites the cultural ecologist Paul Shepard's observations about how the nomadic Bedouin relates to the natural world. According to Shepard: "The nomadic Bedouin does not dote on scenery, paint landscapes, or compile a nonutilitarian natural history. . . . [H]is life is so profoundly in transaction with nature that there is no place for abstraction or esthetics or a 'nature philosophy' which can be separated from the rest of his life." This, Krakauer argues, is the kind of relationship with nature that Chris McCandless achieved at the end of his travels. And yet, with Leila Ahmed's discussion of Egyptian history in mind, what are we to make of the fact that Chris sought to embrace a way of life that the modern world has relegated to the very margins of society? Is Chris's retreat from civilization essentially self-defeating? Or is it an option only for the privileged? While the word *Arab* once referred "only to the inhabitants of Arabia and to Bedouins of the region's deserts," It has come to define a civilization. Are the Arabs that Ahmed describes fleeing the very world that Chris sought to embrace?

BETH LOFFREDA

HOW DO THE media decide which stories to cover on any given day? And what gets left out when the stories that are chosen get transformed into three-minute segments on the nightly news or columns of print in the daily paper? These are some of the issues that Beth Loffreda takes up in *Losing Matt Shepard: Life and Politics in the Aftermath of Anti-Gay Murder*, her book-length study of how the residents of Wyoming responded when Shepard, a young gay student at the university in Laramie, was brutally beaten and left to die by the side of the road in the fall of 1998. Both an ethnographic study and a cultural critique, *Losing Matt Shepard* explores and carefully details the limits of the media's representation of the complexities of life in Wyoming after Shepard's highly publicized murder. In his review of *Losing Matt Shepard* for the *Lambda Book Report*, Malcolm Farley recommended that "[a]nyone who cares about the gay experience in America— or about America in general—should read Loffreda's fiercely intelligent account of the causes and consequences of Matt Shepard's murder."

Beth Loffreda is an associate professor of English and adjunct professor of African American studies at the University of Wyoming, where she also serves as an adviser to the university's Gay, Lesbian, Bisexual, and Transgender Association. Since the publication of *Losing Matt Shepard*, which was selected as a finalist for the American Library Association's Gay, Lesbian, Bisexual, and Transgendered Round Table Award in 2000, Loffreda has become a national spokesperson in discussions about hate crimes legislation and gay rights. She was also recognized as one of the University of Wyoming's top teachers in 2006, when she received the university's John P. Ellbogen Meritorious Classroom Teaching Award. In the selection from *Losing Matt Shepard* included here, Loffreda shows just how varied the response to Shepard's murder was at the University of Wyoming, in the communities surrounding Laramie, and across the nation. As she does so, she asks her readers to consider the following question: Why is it that, given the high number of murders every year, this one in particular captured the nation's attention?

Loffreda, Beth. Selections from *Losing Matt Shepard*. New York: Columbia University Press, 2000. 1–31.

Biographical information drawn from Beth Loffreda, *Losing Matt Shepard*. New York: Columbia University Press, 2000.

Selections from
Losing Matt Shepard
Life and Politics in the Aftermath of Anti-Gay Murder

Perhaps the first thing to know about Laramie, Wyoming, is that it is beautiful. On most days the high-altitude light is so precise and clear that Laramie appears some rarefied place without need of an atmosphere. We were having a stretch of days like that in early October 1998, as the news began to trickle in that a man had been found beaten somewhere on the edge of town. We'd later sort out the key facts: that Matt Shepard had encountered Russell Henderson and Aaron McKinney late Tuesday night in the Fireside Bar; that he'd left with them; that they had driven him in a pickup truck to the edge of town; that Henderson had tied him to a fence there and McKinney had beaten him viciously and repeatedly with a .357 Magnum; that they had taken his shoes and wallet and intended to rob his apartment but instead returned to town and got into a fight with two other young men, Jeremy Herrera and Emiliano Morales (McKinney clubbed Morales on the head with the same gun, still covered in Matt's blood; Herrera retaliated by striking McKinney's head with a heavy stick); that the police, responding to the altercation, picked up Henderson—McKinney had fled—and saw the gun, Matt's credit card, and his shoes in the truck but didn't yet know the fatal meaning of those objects; that after being released later that night, Henderson and his girlfriend, Chasity Pasley, and McKinney and his girlfriend, Kristen Price, began to hatch their false alibis; and that through all this Matt remained tied to the fence and wouldn't be found until Wednesday evening, after an entire night and most of a day had passed. We'd learn all that, and learn that Matt's sexuality was woven through all of it. Those facts reached us swiftly, but making sense of them took much longer.

Jim Osborn, a recent graduate of the university's education program, was the chair of the Lesbian Gay Bisexual Transgender Association that October, a group that Matt, a freshman, had just recently joined. The LGBTA is the sole gay organization on campus and in Laramie itself. While students make up most of its membership, it welcomes university staff and townspeople as well, although only a few have joined. The group has been active since 1990; before that, another gay campus organization, Gays and Lesbians of Wyoming—GLOW—had an intermittent but vivid life in the 1970s and early 1980s. Women typically outnumber men at LGBTA meetings, although not by a significant margin; altogether, attendance on any given night usually hovers between ten and twenty members. The group's email list, however, reaches far more. There's no single reason for that discrepancy; it most likely arises from a combination of factors, including the familiar reluctance of many college students to join groups and, more specifically in this case, the anxiety some gay or questioning students might feel attending a public meeting.

The LGBTA gathers weekly in a nondescript, carpeted seminar room on the second floor of the university union. It has no office space of its own. (When hundreds of letters arrived after Matt's murder, the group stored them in the corner of the Multicultural Resource Center downstairs.) Meetings are usually hourlong sessions, punctuated by bursts of laughter, during which the group plans upcoming events—speakers, dances, potlucks. The LGBTA juggles numerous, sometimes contradictory roles as it tries to be a public face for gay and lesbian issues on campus (organizing events, running panels about sexuality for many courses) and at the same time create a comfortable, safe space for socializing in a town without a gay bar or bookstore. It also serves as something of a gay news exchange, sharing information about what teachers might be supportive or not, what places in town and elsewhere might be safe or not, what's happening that might not show up in the campus paper, *The Branding Iron*.

That last role mattered on Tuesday, October 6th. As the members handled the last-minute details of Gay Awareness Week, scheduled to begin the following Monday, Jim Osborn warned the group to be careful. The week before, he had been harassed while walking across campus. A young man—Jim thinks he was probably a university student—had come up behind him, said, "You're one of those faggots, aren't you?" and thrown a punch. Jim is a big, strapping white man from northern Wyoming; he blocked the punch and hit his attacker. They then took off in opposite directions. Jim didn't report the attack to the police but did want to alert members of the LGBTA that it had happened. Matt was among those there to hear Jim's story. After the meeting, members of the group, including Matt and Jim, went out for coffee at the College Inn, something of a Tuesday-night LGBTA tradition. Jim remembers that Matt sat at the other end of a crowded table. It was the last Jim would see of him.

Jim can talk an eloquent blue streak and is something of an organizational genius—at LGBTA meetings I've listened to him recall the minutiae of university regulations and budget protocols as if they were fond personal memories. He also has a staggeringly large network of friends and acquaintances. On Thursday morning, he got an email from Tina Labrie, a friend of his and Matt's; she had introduced them in August, when Matt, new to Laramie, wanted to learn about the LGBTA. The message said that Matt had been found near death the evening before and was hospitalized in Fort Collins, Colorado. (Matt had initially been taken to Ivinson Memorial Hospital in Laramie and was then transferred to Poudre Valley Hospital's more sophisticated trauma unit. While Matt was being treated in the Ivinson Memorial ER, McKinney was a few curtains down, admitted earlier for the head wound he had received from Herrera; like Matt, McKinney would also be transferred to Poudre Valley.) Horrified, Jim phoned Tina and learned that the police were trying to reconstruct Matt's whereabouts on Tuesday evening. When he called the Laramie Police to tell them what he knew, an officer informed him that Matt wasn't going to make it. Matt was suffering from hypothermia, and there was severe trauma to the brain stem. The officer told Jim that one side of Matt's head had been beaten in several inches and that the neurosurgeon was quite frankly surprised that he was still alive.

Bob Beck, news director for Wyoming Public Radio, also got word of the attack on Thursday. Beck has lived in Laramie since 1984; he's a tall, lanky midwesterner with a serious jones for Chicago Bulls basketball. On the radio he speaks in the sedated tones cultivated by NPR reporters everywhere, but in person he displays a vinegary wit and a likably aggravated demeanor. "It was a strange thing," he told me. "I teach a class, and one of my students called up and told me he needed to miss class that day because one of his friends had got beaten up very badly and was taken to the hospital in Fort Collins." That student was Phil Labrie, Tina's husband. Worried when they couldn't reach Matt, they had called the police on Wednesday, shortly after Matt was found, and learned what had happened. "[Phil] didn't tell me a lot of details because he said the cops had told him not to really tell anyone. But then he said I will know about it later and it will be a big story. . . . So I right away thought I better follow up on this immediately." He contacted the Albany County Sheriff's Office and learned that a press conference would be held later that day.

Beck attended the press conference that day—typically a routine exercise, but one that in this case would unexpectedly and profoundly shape public reaction to the attack. According to Beck, the sheriff:

> indicated that there was a young man who had been very badly beaten, was on life support, had been taken to Poudre Valley Hospital. During the questioning, the sheriff at the time, Gary Puls, indicated that they thought he may have been beaten because he was gay. And when he described this situation to us he told us that [Shepard] was found by a mountain bike rider, tied to a fence like a scarecrow. My recollection is there was discussion of exactly what do you mean, "tied like a scarecrow," and I think every single one of us who were in the room got the impression certainly of being tied up spread-eagled, splayed out.

Matt hadn't actually been tied like a scarecrow; when he was approached first by the mountain biker, Aaron Kreifels, and then by Reggie Fluty, the sheriff's deputy who answered Kreifels's emergency call, Matt lay on his back, head propped against the fence, legs outstretched. His hands were lashed behind him and tied barely four inches off the ground to a fencepost.

In dramatic and widely reported testimony, Fluty would later state that at first she thought Matt could have been no older than thirteen, he was so small (Matt was only five feet two inches, barely over one hundred pounds). And when she described Matt's brutally disfigured face, she said that the only spots not covered in blood were the tracks cleansed by his tears—an enduring image that continues to appear in essays, poetry, and songs dedicated to Shepard. It is most likely that Kreifels was the source of Puls's press-conference description. Kreifels told police and reporters that he at first thought Matt was a scarecrow flopped on the ground, maybe some kind of Halloween joke staged a few weeks early. No matter its provenance, the notion that Matt had been strung up in something akin to a crucifixion became the starting point for the reporting and reaction to come.

Beck says, "I know that's how we all reported it, and that was never corrected."[1] The vicious symbolism of that image, combined with Puls's early acknowledgment that the beating might have been an anti-gay hate crime, drew instant attention. Attending the press conference were the Associated Press, members of the Wyoming and Colorado media, Beck, and two friends of Matt, Walt Boulden and Alex Trout. According to press reports, Boulden and Trout, afraid that the attack might go unnoticed, had already begun to alert the media earlier that day. Boulden had had plans with Matt for Tuesday night; Matt had canceled and later, apparently, had decided to head off to the Fireside alone. Boulden was not shy about seizing the attack as a political opportunity, linking the assault to the Wyoming legislature's failure to pass a hate crimes bill: he told reporters that "they said nothing like that happens in Wyoming because someone is gay, but we've always known someone would have to get killed or beaten before they finally listened. I just can't believe it happened to someone I cared so much about." By Friday morning, when the police already had McKinney, Henderson, Price, and Pasley in custody (Beck says "the investigation was one of the better I've seen"), the media interest, spurred by Thursday's press conference, had increased exponentially.

At the same time, Laramie's gay residents were learning what had happened. Stephanie and Lisa, a lesbian couple active in the LGBTA, heard the news from Jim on Thursday evening. Lisa, a striking redhead and a good friend of Jim's, talked to him first: "He told me Matt had been beaten. And I said, well, shit, how badly? Is he okay? And Jim said no—he's in critical condition, had to be airlifted to Poudre Valley." Both Stephanie and Lisa knew Matt only slightly, although Stephanie had expected to have the chance to grow closer. She had just agreed to be Matt's mentor in a program the LGBTA was considering as a way to welcome new students to the gay community. Like Lisa, Steph has an edgy, witty charisma, but it deserted her that night, as she, Lisa, and Jim watched the first TV news reports. "There was this horrifying feeling that we were standing on the brink of learning something really, really awful," she says of that Thursday. "Like the part in the horror movie just before she opens the closet and finds the dead cat. It was that moment. For a day. And then we got the facts . . . and everything started happening at this tremendous speed. The next day was the day the story broke. And there were newspaper reporters and cameras all over the place." Steph had called me early that Friday morning, spreading word of the attack and warning people associated with the LGBTA to watch their backs: "I can remember wanting to tell everybody, absolutely everybody, wanting to physically grab people by their lapels and make them listen."

An atmosphere of genuine shock permeated the university; most students and faculty I encountered that day wore stunned and distraught expressions that I imagine mirrored my own; they seemed absorbed simply in trying to understand how something so brutal could have happened within a short walk of their daily lives. Gay and lesbian members of the university that I spoke to felt a wrenching mix of fear and sadness; many, including Stephanie and Lisa, were also immediately and intensely angry. A number of students in my morning American Literature course, after a long discussion in which they sought answers for how to publicly express their repugnance for the crime, decided that the university's homecoming parade, coincidentally scheduled for the following morning, would be an ideal site for that response. Finding like-minded students in the United Multicultural Council, the LGBTA, and the student government, they began printing flyers, making hundreds of armbands, and arranging permits to join the parade.[2] Their unjaded eagerness to publicly involve themselves in the case contrasted sharply with the university administration's first official response, much of which had concerned itself with pointing out that the attack happened off campus and was committed by nonstudents.

On Friday afternoon—as Jim Osborn began to field what would eventually become an overwhelming flood of media requests for interviews—the four accused appeared in court for the first time. Bob Beck attended the initial appearance: "That's where you bring in the people, read them formal charges, and we then get their names, backgrounds—which is important for us." Beck had left for the courthouse a half hour early; initial appearances are typically held in a small room in the courthouse basement, and Beck thought it might be more full than usual. He was right. "It was sold out. It was wall-to-wall cameras." Residents of Laramie—professors and LGBTA members in particular—had also come to witness the proceedings. So many attended that the reading of the charges had to be delayed while everyone moved upstairs to the much larger district court. Beck remembers, "I went in—in fact it was so crowded I got shoved by where the jury box is located— and I stood behind the defendants when they came in. I got a really good look at everybody, and I was actually surprised at how young they looked, how scared they looked, and how little they were." Only Henderson, McKinney, and Chasity Pasley were charged that day; separate proceedings had been arranged for Kristen Price. Pasley wept throughout. She was someone Jim Osborn knew well and liked. She worked in the campus activities center and had helped Jim countless times when the LGBTA needed photocopying or assistance setting up for an event. "She was very supportive of the group," Jim says. Often when he saw her on a Wednesday, she'd ask, "Hey, how'd it go last night?" In the past, he had seen her wearing one of the group's "Straight But Not Narrow" buttons.

I was in the courtroom that afternoon and can remember the professional flatness with which the county judge, Robert Castor, read the charges aloud. Castor had arrived in the courtroom to find a cameraman sitting at the prosecution's table, an early symbol of the persistent media invasion, Bob Beck believes, that frustrated the court and the prosecutor, Cal Rerucha, and led them to sharply limit information about the case thereafter. Castor charged McKinney and Henderson with three identical counts of kidnapping, aggravated robbery, and attempted first-degree murder; Pasley he charged with a count of accessory after the fact to attempted first-degree murder (in addition to providing false alibis for their boyfriends, she and Price had also helped dispose of evidence, including Henderson's bloody clothing). After each count, Castor recited "the essential facts" supporting the charge, in what became a truly grim ritual of repetition. In language I've condensed from the court documents, the essential facts were these: "On or between October 6, 1998, and the early morning hours of October 7, 1998, Aaron McKinney and Russell Henderson met Matthew Shepard at the Fireside Bar, and after Mr. Shepard confided he was gay, the subjects deceived Mr. Shepard into leaving with them in their vehicle to a remote area near Sherman Hills subdivision in Albany County. En route to said location, Mr. Shepard was struck in the head with a pistol." (McKinney, we'd later learn, had apparently told Matt, "We're not gay, and you just got jacked," before striking him.) "Upon arrival at said location, both subjects tied their victim to a buck fence, robbed him, and tortured him, while beating him with the butt of a pistol. During the incident, the victim was begging for his life. The subjects then left the area, leaving the victim for dead." By the third time Castor read that Matt had begged for his life, the courtroom had become choked with sickness and grief. The true darkness of the crime had become impossible to flee.

The next morning—Saturday—began with the university's homecoming parade. As the parade kicked off, one hundred students, university employees, and townspeople lined up at the end of the long string of floats and marching bands. They had quietly gathered in the morning chill to protest the attack on Matt. The leaders of the march carried a yellow banner painted with green circles, symbols of peace chosen by the UMC. They were followed by a silent crowd wearing matching armbands and holding signs that read "No Hate Crimes in Wyoming," "Is This What Equality Feels Like?" and "Straight But Not Stupid." I walked a few yards from the front, watching

Carly Laucomer, a university student holding the middle of the banner, field questions from reporters walking backward a single pace in front of her. Beside me, Cat, another university student, muttered that she wished the marchers weren't so sparse. Cat, like Carly, was then a student in my American Literature course, a smart young woman usually prepared to be disappointed by the world around her. Laramie surprised her. As the march moved west down Ivinson Avenue, spectators began to join, walking off sidewalks into the street. By the time the march reached downtown (where a giant second-story banner proclaimed, "Hate Is Not a Wyoming Value") and circled back toward campus, it had swelled beyond even Cat's demanding expectations; final estimates ranged from five to eight hundred participants. It didn't seem like much—just a bunch of people quietly walking— but it was a genuinely spontaneous, grassroots effort to protest the attack and express the community's profound dismay, and in that sense it was unforgettable.

A very different sort of tribute to Matt appeared in the Colorado State University homecoming parade the same day in the city of Fort Collins. As Matt lay in the hospital just a few miles away, a float in the parade carried a scarecrow draped in anti-gay epithets. While the papers were reluctant to report the full range of insults, I heard that the signs read "I'm Gay" and "Up My Ass." Colorado State University acted quickly to punish the sorority and fraternity responsible for the float (the censured students blamed vandalism committed by an unknown third party), but still it is worth pausing for a moment to consider the degree of dehumanization such an act required, how much those responsible must have felt, however fleetingly or unconsciously, that Matt was not a fellow human being, their age, with his future torn away from him. Fort Collins is home to a visible and energetic community of gay activists, and the float was widely denounced. Still, a week later Fort Collins would vote down, by nearly a two-to-one margin, City Ordinance 22, a proposal to expand the city's antidiscrimination statute to include protections for gays and lesbians.

Later that Saturday, a moment of silence for Matt was held before the University of Wyoming's football game; players wore the UMC's symbols on their helmets. And, impossibly, the media presence continued to grow. Bob Beck, juggling requests for interviews with his own reporting, was in the thick of it and felt a growing frustration at the sloppiness of what he saw around him. "Right away it was horrible. Part of that, in fairness, was that we didn't have all the information we needed. While the sheriff was very up front at first, next thing you know, nobody's talking." City officials, naturally unprepared (in a town with barely a murder a year) for the onslaught, focused their resources on the investigation and, angry that Laramie was being depicted as a hate crimes capital, began to restrict press access. But the media, especially the TV tabloids, Beck says, needed to turn things around quickly, and since they were getting stonewalled by the city and by many

Laramie residents, "it seemed like the place they went to interview everybody was in bars. As we all know who are in the media, if you want to get somebody to be very glib, give you a few quick takes, you want to go to a bar. And you certainly are going to meet a segment of our population that will have more interesting things to say." I remember watching for footage of the Saturday morning march later that evening and seeing instead precisely the sort of bar interview Beck describes, a quick and dirty media tactic I heard many residents mock in the coming months.

Beck also remembers one of the first television news reports he saw: "It was this woman reporter outside the Fireside doing what we call a bridge, a stand-up: 'Hate: it's a common word in Wyoming.'" Beck couldn't believe it, but that mirrored precisely the assumptions of most of the media representatives he encountered that week. Journalists who interviewed him began with comments like, "Well, this kind of thing probably happens a lot up there," or, "You have that cowboy mentality in Wyoming, so this was bound to happen." Reporters criticized Laramie, he says, for not having a head trauma unit, not having gay bars, not pushing back homecoming. The tone of the questioning was hostile; Jim Osborn, speaking to journalists from locations as far-flung as Australia and the Netherlands, encountered it too. Jim says the press he spoke to wanted to hear that this was a hateful, redneck town, that Wyoming was, in the inane rhyming of some commentators, "the hate state." But Jim insisted on what he considered accurate: "Nobody expects murder here—nobody. This is not a place where you kill your neighbor, and we see each other as neighbors. This is a good place."

But the crime, and Laramie, had already begun to take on a second life, a broadcast existence barely tethered to the truths of that night or this place, an existence nourished less by facts and far more by the hyperboles of tabloid emotion. Such a development should be unsurprising to even the most novice of cultural critics, yet to be in the middle of it, to watch rumor become myth, to see the story stitched out of repetition rather than investigation, was something else entirely. Beck told me, "Right away I saw pack journalism like I have not seen pack journalism in a while. It was really something. I remember going to the courthouse, and somebody would say, 'Hey I understand he got burned'—which wasn't true by the way—'where did he get burned?' And somebody would say, 'Oh, on his face,' and they're all taking notes, and they were sources for each other. They would never say where it came from or who had the information—it was just 'there were burns on his face.'" As Beck watched, the mistakes multiplied. One journalist would announce, "'I did an interview with one of the deputies, and he told me this,' and they would all go with it; no one [else] went and interviewed the deputy. Now part of this is that the deputies and other officials weren't available to us . . . and the same stuff got continually reported." The lead investigator on the case, Sergeant Rob DeBree of the Sheriff's Office, held a press conference early on in an attempt to correct the errors, but, he told me, it didn't seem to make much of a difference—the media had become a closed loop, feeding off their own energies.

As the fall wore on, the distance between Laramie and its broadcast image would become unbridgeable. The court increasingly limited press access to the case and eventually, in the spring, issued a gag order. In response, the Wyoming Press Association wrangled with the court throughout that year over access to hearings and records, suggesting that the court model its treatment of the media on press access guidelines in the Timothy McVeigh trial. Beck assessed Wyoming Public Radio's own performance for me: "I'm not saying we didn't make any mistakes, because we probably did. But I finally got so weary of it I said, 'You know what? If we can't confirm it ourselves, we don't go with it.' It was just too wild."

As the weekend continued, vigils for Matt were held across the nation. By the end of the week, we'd heard word of vigils in Casper, Cheyenne, and Lander (Wyoming towns), Colorado, Idaho, Montana, Iowa, Arizona, Rhode Island, and Pennsylvania. A memorial in Los Angeles attracted an estimated five thousand participants; a "political funeral" in New York City that ended in civil disobedience and hundreds of arrests, about the same. Several hundred mourners lit candles at a vigil outside Poudre Valley Hospital, and a Web site set up by the hospital to give updates about Matt's condition eventually drew over 815,000 hits from around the world.

In Laramie, we held two vigils of our own Sunday night. Jim spoke at the first, held outside the St. Paul's Newman Catholic Center. Father Roger Schmit, the organizer of the event, had contacted him earlier that weekend and asked him to speak. Jim remembers, "I'm sitting here thinking, 'Catholic Church . . . this is not exactly the scene I want to get into.'" But the priest told him, Jim says, "This is such a powerful opportunity—people need to hear from you, and it will help them." Jim thought, "I want to hate him, I want to disagree with him, but I can't." Indeed, such bedfellows would become less strange in the coming months. Matt's death triggered yearlong conversations in several Laramie churches; the Newman Center, the Episcopal church, and the Unitarian-Universalist Fellowship each began discussion groups devoted to questions of sexual orientation and religious doctrine. Father Schmit, the priest Jim regarded with such initial suspicion, would in particular become a vocal advocate for gay tolerance.

I attended that first vigil, which drew nearly one thousand people, a sizable fraction of Laramie's total population. As I crossed Grand Avenue, dodging traffic, the vigil already under way, I was struck by the size and murmurous intensity of the crowd. The speakers included friends of Matt, student leaders, and university officials. Father Schmit had also invited every religious leader in town but found many reluctant to come. The event was genuinely affecting and rightly given over to the desire, as Jim put it, to think of Matt "the person" and not the newly created symbol. While speakers did indeed condemn the homophobia that slid Matt from complicated human being to easy target, others, including Jim, also tried to rehumanize Matt by offering up small details—the nature of his smile, the clothes he liked to wear. The press was there too, of course, and—perhaps inevitably under such circumstances—a faint odor of PR hung in the air. University president Phil Dubois told the assembled, "Nothing could match the sorrow and revulsion we feel for this attack on Matt. It is almost as sad, however, to see individuals and groups around the country react to this event by stereotyping an entire community, if not an entire state."

Stephanie sensed another trouble, a hypocrisy, at work that night:

> There was a tremendous outpouring of support—the vigils, the parade—and a lot of those people—not all of them, not even a substantial portion, but some of those people—if they had known that Matt was gay while he was alive, would have spit on him. But now it was a cause, and that made me upset. Not that I think you can't grieve over this because you're straight or anything like that, but I just questioned the sincerity of some people. And I grew to be very angry at the vigil Sunday night, because it was so like the one I had attended for Steve.

She meant Steve Heyman, a gay man who had been a psychology professor and LGBTA faculty adviser at the university. Heyman was found dead on November 1, 1993, on the edge of Route 70 in Denver. He appeared to have been tossed from a moving car. The case was never solved. To Stephanie, who had known and adored Heyman, the coincidence was unbearable. "It was the same candles, the same fucking hymns. I will never sing 'We are a gentle, angry people' again, because it doesn't change anything. And I'm not going to sing 'We are not afraid today deep in my heart' because I am afraid, and I will always be afraid, and that's what they want, that's why they kill us."

Driven by that anger, Stephanie spoke at the second vigil that night. Much smaller—perhaps one hundred people were in attendance—it was held on the edge of town, at the Unitarian Fellowship. People who went that night tell me it was different from the first. Instead of a lengthy list of official speakers, community members were invited to testify to their mourning, and to their experiences of anti-gay discrimination in Laramie. It was more intense, more ragged, more discomfiting. But both vigils held the same fragile promise of a changed Laramie, a town that—whether it much wanted to or not—would think hard and publicly and not in unison about the gay men and women in its midst, about their safety and comfort and rights.

Later that Sunday night, as the participants in that second vigil left for home, thought about the events of the day, and got ready for bed, Matt Shepard's blood pressure began to drop. He died in the early hours of Monday, October 12th. It was the first day of Gay Awareness Week at the University of Wyoming.

* * *

Monday, flags were flown at half-staff on the university campus. Later that week, in Casper, flags were lowered on the day of Matt's funeral to signal a "day of understanding." (According to local newspapers, Wyoming governor Jim Geringer was criticized by the Veterans of Foreign Wars for not following "proper flag etiquette.") That Monday eight hundred people gathered for a memorial service held on Prexy's Pasture, a patch of green in the middle of campus encircled by parking spaces and university buildings and anchored by a statue of "the university family," a happy heterosexual unit of father, mother, and child that one lesbian student, in a letter to the student newspaper, longingly imagined detonating. The memorial service was another exercise in what was becoming a familiar schizophrenia for Laramie residents. Even the layout of the event expressed it: speakers stood in a small clump ringed by sidewalk; spread beyond them was the far larger, shaggy-edged group of listeners. In between the two was an encampment of reporters, flourishing microphones and tape recorders, pivoting cameras back and forth, capturing clips of the speakers and reaction shots of the crowd. It was hard to see past the reporters to the event that had drawn us in the first place, and it was hard to know to a certainty whether we were all there simply to mourn Matt or to make sure that mourning was represented. Not that the second urge was itself necessarily a hypocrisy or a contradiction of the first. It was instead an early manifestation of Laramie's new double consciousness. We didn't simply live here anymore: we were something transmitted, watched, evaluated for symbolic resonance; something available for summary. I suspect a few people naturally sought that televised attention, felt authenticated and confirmed, even thrilled, by the opportunity to be representative; and others seized it, as Walt Boulden had, as a chance to articulate political goals that might otherwise go unheard. Mostly, though, it just pissed people off. As the memorial drew to a close, I walked past satellite vans and the professional autism of TV reporters practicing their opening lines and switching on their solemn expressions and talking to no one in particular.

I was on my way to the first event of Gay Awareness Week. Shortly after the memorial, Leslea Newman, scheduled long before the murder to give the keynote talk, spoke about her gay-themed children's books, which include the oft-censored *Heather Has Two Mommies*. The week's events would be held despite Matt's death, but attendance that evening hadn't necessarily swelled in response—there were maybe seventy folks scattered around in the darkened auditorium. Newman spoke with a bracing, funny, New York brusqueness that scuffed up the audience as she briskly detailed her skirmishes with religious conservatives, and she spoke as well of her sorrow over Matt and her friends' fearful pleading that she cancel her visit to Laramie. They weren't alone in feeling that anxiety; many of the members of the LGBTA were tensed for a backlash as they passed out pro-gay trinkets and "heterosexual questionnaires" at the "Straight But Not Narrow" table in the student union during Awareness Week. They knew the statistics: that anti-gay violence tends to rise sharply in the aftermath of a publicized bashing. But instead, as consoling letters and emails flooded the offices of *The Branding Iron,* the LGBTA, and Wyoming newspapers, supporters flocking to the union tables quickly ran through the association's supplies of buttons and stickers.

As the week dragged on, Laramie residents hung in their windows and cars flyers decrying hate provided by the Wyoming Grassroots Project (a year and a half later, you can still find a few examples around town, stubbornly hanging on). Yellow sashes fluttered from student backpacks; local businesses announced, on signs usually reserved for information about nightly rates, indoor pools, and bargain lunches, their dismay with the crime. The Comfort Inn: "Hate and Violence Are Not Our Way of Life." The University Inn: "Hate Is Not a Laramie Value." Arby's: "Hate and Violence Are Not Wyoming Values 5 Regulars $5.95." Obviously, those signs suggested a typically American arithmetic, promiscuously mixing moral and economic registers. Underneath the sentiment lingered a question: what will his death cost us? But it would be wrong, I think, to see all those gestures as merely cynical calculation, a self-interested weighing of current events against future tourism. We were trying to shape the media summary of Laramie all right, but we were also talking to each other, pained and wondering, through such signs.

Late Monday, about the same time as the Prexy's Pasture memorial, the charges against McKinney, Henderson, and Pasley were upgraded in a closed hearing to reflect Matt's death. Price's charge, the same as Pasley's—accessory after the fact to first-degree murder—was announced at her individual arraignment on Tuesday. In a *20/20* interview that week, Price offered her defense of McKinney and Henderson. She claimed Shepard approached McKinney and Henderson and "said that he was gay and wanted to get with Aaron and Russ." They intended, she said, "to teach a lesson to him not to come on to straight people"—as if torture and murder were reasonable responses to the supposed humiliation of overtures from a gay man. McKinney's father, speaking to the *Denver Post,* argued that no one would care about the crime if his son had killed a heterosexual, which struck me as not exactly on point, even as a media critique. Wyoming's Libertarian gubernatorial candidate (it was an election year) had his own unique twist: he told reporters, "If two gays beat and killed a cowboy, the story would have never been reported by the national media vultures."

Fred Phelps, a defrocked minister, leader of the tiny Kansas Westboro Baptist Church, and author of the Internet site GodHatesFags.com, announced that Monday that he intended to picket Matthew's funeral, scheduled for the coming Friday at St. Mark's Episcopal Church in Casper. His Web site also promised a visit to Laramie on October 19th, but in the end he didn't show. Phelps had made a name for himself in the 1990s as a virulently anti-gay activist, notorious for protesting at the funerals of AIDS victims. Never one to shy from media attention, Phelps faxed reporters images of the signs he and his followers intended to carry at the funeral: "Fag Matt in Hell," "God Hates Fags," "No Tears for Queers." On his Web site, Phelps wrote that "the parents of Matt Shepard did not bring him up in the nature and admonition of the Lord, or he would not have been trolling for perverted sex partners in a cheap Laramie bar." He also, to the bitter laughter of members of the LGBTA, deemed the University of Wyoming "very militantly pro-gay." "The militant homosexual agenda is vigorously pursued" at the university, he proclaimed. At the time of Phelps's statement, the university's equal employment and civil rights regulations did not include sexual orientation as a protected category, nor did the university offer insurance benefits to same-sex partners. President Dubois and the board of trustees, in response to Matt's death, eventually rectified the former failure in September 1999; the latter still remains true to this day. Apparently none of that mattered much in Phelps's estimation, and he would become a familiar figure in Laramie in the months to come.

The Westboro Church's announcement was only one manifestation of the murder's parallel national life, its transmutation into political and religious currency. Matt himself might have been dead, but his image was resurrected by Phelps as well as by his antagonists, and those resurrections, while not invariably hypocritical or grotesque, nevertheless struck me as always risky. Not because we shouldn't talk about Matt, about the murder, looking hard at the facts of it, as well as at its contexts. The risk, it seemed to me, lay in what his image was so often used for in the coming months—the rallying of quick and photogenic outrage, sundered from the hard, slow work for local justice.

On Wednesday, October 14th, the national gay organization the Human Rights Campaign held a candlelight vigil on the steps of the U.S. Capitol, noteworthy if only for the incongruity of an event that paired the likes of Ted Kennedy and Ellen DeGeneres. Jim Osborn was also there—Cathy Renna, a member of GLAAD (Gay and Lesbian Alliance Against Defamation), who had arrived in Laramie the previous weekend to monitor events for her organization, had asked Jim to participate and taken him to Washington. That night, DeGeneres declared that "this is what she was trying to stop" with her television sitcom *Ellen*. The proportions of that statement—the belief that a sitcom could breathe in the same sentence as the brutal vortex of murder— seemed out of kilter to say the least, but it is the age of celebrity politics, after all: Elton John would send flowers to Matt's funeral, Barbra Streisand would phone the Albany County Sheriffs office to demand quick action on the case, and Madonna would call up an assistant to UW president Dubois to complain about what had happened to Matt. Jim Osborn remembers standing next to Dan Butler, an actor on *Frasier,* during the vigil; later, he spotted Kristen Johnston (of *Third Rock from the Sun*) smoking backstage. Attended by

numerous federal legislators, the vigil was skipped by Wyoming's two senators, who had announced their sorrow and condemned intolerance in press
releases the previous day. The disconnect worked both ways: the Human
Rights Campaign, for all its sustained rallying on the national level, never, according to Jim, sent a representative to Laramie until the following summer.

Back in Laramie, on the same day as the D.C. vigil, the university initiated a three-day series of teach-ins on "prejudice, intolerance, and violence"
to begin, according to the announcement, "the healing process." The ideas
expressed that day were valuable, the sympathies genuine, but I remember
feeling overloaded by premature talk of closure. It may have seemed easy
for straight mourners to move so quickly, but as Stephanie told me that
week, she'd barely begun to realize the extent of her anger. In the face of
that, the swiftness of the official move to "healing" seemed at best a well-
intended deafness, and indeed, in their outrage by proxy, denunciations of
hatred, and exhortations for tolerance, most of the speakers seemed to be
talking implicitly and exclusively to straight members of the audience who
already agreed.

Many professors on campus also made time in their classes that week to
let their students talk about Matt; the university provided a list of teachers
willing to facilitate such discussions if individual faculty were uncomfortable raising such an emotionally fraught issue. It was indeed, as Jim Osborn
put it, a "teachable moment," and those conversations undoubtedly did real
good. One student, who spoke to me on the condition I didn't use his name,
told me that before Matt's death he "straight-up hated fags." It hadn't occurred to him that there actually were any gays or lesbians around (a surprisingly common assumption at the university, not to mention in Wyoming
generally)—"fag" was a word handy mainly for demeaning other guys in
his dorm for "being pussy" (a typical but still depressing conflation of slurs).
After seeing students cry in one of his classes as they discussed Matt's death,
he had what he called, with a defensive grin, a real breakthrough: he felt a
little sick, he told me, that he had thought things about gays that the two
killers had probably been thinking about Shepard.

It's impossible to quantify such changes in attitude, but clearly they
were happening in many classrooms around campus. Those developments
were heartening, but it would be wrong to imply that the changes were immediate or seismic; several students in the coming weeks would describe to
me overhearing others saying Matt "got what he deserved." One woman
told me that during a class devoted to discussing the murder, "There was a
really ugly incident with a couple of guys in the back who were like 'I hate
gays and I'm not changing my opinion.'" "People really think that way
here," she finished with a resigned expression. In the coming year students
and faculty checking out books on gay topics sometimes found them de-
faced, and in the spring of 1999 vandals defecated on the university's copies
of *The Advocate,* a gay magazine.

It would be wrong too to imply that the faculty were perfectly equipped to handle the events of October. When Matt died, there was only one openly gay faculty member on the university campus—Cathy Connelly, a professor of sociology. Since her arrival in 1991, Professor Connelly had periodically taught graduate courses on gay and lesbian issues, but other than Connelly and the small Safe Zone diversity-training group, the university had few resources in place to respond to what had happened. Troubling as well were the reactions of more than one professor I spoke to that week, whose primary responses were to comment on their own uselessness, their own irrelevance—as scholars of obscure fields of inquiry—to such primal issues of life and death. Academics tend to be fairly skilled at self-lacerating narcissism, but it seemed to me at the time an appalling luxury, an indulgence in a kind of intellectual self-pity at a moment when the basic skills of education—critical thinking, articulation, self-reflection—could be so concretely valuable. I wondered about that, and I wondered too when we'd stop talking about how we felt and begin talking about what to do.

Not that public political gestures are always more meaningful than private, emotional ones. On October 15th, the day before Shepard's funeral, the U.S. House of Representatives approved a resolution condemning the murder. Sponsored by Wyoming's sole representative, Barbara Cubin, it struck me as an essentially empty gesture. The nonbinding resolution stated that the House would "do everything in its power" to fight intolerance, and Cubin herself announced that "our country must come together to condemn these types of brutal, nonsensical acts of violence. We cannot lie down, we cannot bury our heads, and we cannot sit on our hands." Stirring stuff, but she also told reporters that day that she opposes federal hate crimes legislation and suggested such things be left up to individual states. So much for "our country coming together." Cubin was not alone, of course, in her contradictory patriotic embrace of Matt; flags were lowered, resolutions passed, in a nation otherwise happy to express its loathing of gays by closeting them in the military, refusing them antidiscrimination protection in most cities and states, repressing their presence in school curricula, faculty, and clubs, and denouncing them in churches. Meanwhile, back in Wyoming that afternoon, a bewildered and frustrated Casper City Council grappled with more concrete resolutions than those that faced the United States Congress. At an emergency meeting to address Phelps's intended picketing of Matt's funeral, the council decided that protesters must stay at least fifty feet from the church. Casper's SWAT team and the Street Drug Unit would be in attendance outside St. Mark's. Streets would be closed nearby the church, the Casper *Star-Tribune* reported, to allow "media satellite vehicles to position themselves."

The funeral on Friday unfurled as a heavy, wet snow fell on Casper. The storm ripped down power lines, cutting electricity in and around Casper; hundreds of cottonwoods and elms lost their branches. Phelps and his handful of protesters (along with another anti-gay protester, W. N. Orwell of Enterprise, Texas) were penned inside black plastic barricades, taunting the huge crowd of mourners, which included strangers, gay and straight alike, drawn to the scene from Cheyenne, Denver, Laramie, and elsewhere. As Charles Levendosky put it a few days later in the *Star-Tribune*, "One thousand others from Wyoming and surrounding states flew or drove into Wyoming to mourn for Matt Shepard, the symbol." While a few mourners engaged in heated debate with the picketers—one carrying a sign reading "Get Back in Your Damn Closet"—most turned their backs to them, the umbrellas pulled out for the snow acting as a fortuitous blockade. To protect the Shepard family from hearing Phelps, the assembled crowd sang "Amazing Grace" to drown out his anti-gay preaching. (The family's loss would intensify that day—Shepard's great uncle suffered what would be a fatal heart attack in the church shortly before the service began.) The funeral inside St. Mark's remained restricted to friends and family of Matt, but a live audio feed carried the service to the First Presbyterian Church nearby. Outside St. Mark's, more mourners ("some wearing black leather," the *Star-Tribune* observed) listened to a KTWO radio broadcast of the service. At the funeral, Matt's cousin Ann Kirch, a minister in Poughkeepsie, New York, delivered the sermon. Emphasizing Matt's gentleness and desire "to help, to nurture, to bring joy to others," she echoed a statement made by Matt's father earlier in the day at a press conference outside city hall: "A person as caring and loving as our son Matt would be overwhelmed by what this incident has done to the hearts and souls of people around the world."

Three days later, the university held yet another memorial service. Around one thousand people heard songs by a multicultural chorus, psalms read by Geneva Perry of the university's Office of Minority Affairs, and statements by Tina Labrie, Jim Osborn, and Trudy McCraken, Laramie's mayor. Rounding out the service was university president Dubois, who made a passionate, personal plea for hate crimes legislation—the political issue that had already, only one week after his death, come to dominate discussions of Matt's murder. "No hate crime statute, even had it existed, would have saved Matt," Dubois read. "But Matt Shepard was not merely robbed, and kidnapped, and murdered. This was a crime of humiliation. This crime was all about being gay. . . . We must find a way to commemorate this awful week in a way that will say to the entire state and nation that we will not forget what happened here."

On Tuesday, October 20th, the Wyoming Lodging and Restaurant Association offered one such response to the nation by passing a resolution in favor of hate crimes legislation. The association was up front about its motivations: to curry favor among tourists who might seek recreation elsewhere. The director was quoted in the Casper *Star-Tribune*: "We want them to know this was an isolated case and could happen anywhere."

* * *

Could happen anywhere indeed. While that oft-repeated phrase was the quick defense offered by many who felt Laramie was being unfairly vilified, it also bumped up against an undeniable truth: in the late 1990s, homosexuality and vehement opposition to it were everywhere in American public culture and politics. Gays in the military, gays in the schools, gays in church, gays in marriage—the place of gay men and lesbians in American culture seemed to be debated in every way possible. For example, on October 14th, two days before Matt's funeral, the Supreme Court upheld a Cincinnati ordinance that denied gays and lesbians legal protection from discrimination in housing, employment, and other public accommodations. Later that autumn Ohio hosted a conference, organized by Focus on the Family, on how to prevent childhood homosexuality; one speaker there, John Paulk, became notorious during the summer of 1998 when he posed with his wife for national newspaper ads announcing that they were former homosexuals "cured" by their faith in God. About the same time the Supreme Court ruled on the city ordinance, the Roman Catholic Archdiocese of Cincinnati announced a deeply contradictory attempt to "reconcile church teachings that denounce homosexual sex as immoral but encourage the loving acceptance of gays." As long as they're celibate, that is—as long as they "live chaste lives." "Hate the sin, love the sinner"—that idea was invoked again and again in Laramie, in church congregations and letters to the editor. But it seems to me that in such visions sexuality slides so intimately close to identity itself that in the end such exhortations call for moral acrobatics requiring an impossible and fundamentally hypocritical kind of dexterity.

Religious justifications were everywhere, of course, in the attacks on homosexuality. Senate Majority Leader Trent Lott, in June 1998, said he learned from the Bible that "you should try to show them a way to deal with [homosexuality] just like alcohol . . . or sex addiction . . . or kleptomaniacs." Pat Robertson announced that "the acceptance of homosexuality is the last step in the decline of Gentile civilization." Bob Jones University in South Carolina instituted a rule banning gay alumni from returning to campus. The religious right boycotted Disney and American Airlines for having policies that refused to discriminate against gays and lesbians. Salt Lake City banned all student clubs rather than allow a gay-straight alliance to continue at one public high school. The Mormon Church donated roughly half a million dollars to supporters of Alaska's Proposition 2, an initiative banning same-sex marriage that succeeded in the fall of 1998. Bans on gay marriage would also pass in Hawaii, California, and West Virginia in the next year and a half. Vermont, with its legalization of gay "civil unions" early in 2000, would be one of the few bright spots.

That Matt's death occurred in the midst of such pervasive anxiety and upheaval might begin to explain why the nation paid attention, but it doesn't stretch very far—his was only one of thirty-three anti-gay murders that year, followed by, in the first months of 1999, a beheading in Virginia and a vicious beating in Georgia. Here in Laramie, we asked a version of that question too: Why Matt, when no one in the media seemed to take a second glance at the other truly awful recent murders we had the grim distinction of claiming? Why Matt, and not Daphne Sulk, a fifteen-year-old pregnant girl stabbed seventeen times and dumped in the snow far from town? Why Matt, and not Kristin Lamb, an eight-year-old Laramie girl who was kidnapped while visiting family elsewhere in Wyoming and then raped, murdered, and thrown in a landfill? Governor Geringer asked those very questions in an October 9th press release, and we asked them too, in Laramie—in letters to the editor, in private conversation. But we didn't always mean the same thing. To some, the media attention to Matt seemed to imply that his death was somehow worse than the deaths of the two girls, and such an implication was genuinely offensive. To some, like Val Pexton, a graduate student in creative writing, it had something to do with the politics of gender: "What happened to [Lamb] was certainly as violent, as hateful, as horrible; and I guess one of my first thoughts was, if [Henderson and McKinney] had done that to a woman, would this have made it into the news outside of Laramie, outside of Wyoming?" And to some, like Jim Osborn, the comparison of Matt to Kristin and Daphne sometimes masked a hostility to gays: "They became incensed—why didn't Kristin Lamb get this kind of coverage, why didn't Daphne Sulk get this kind of coverage? That was the way people could lash out who very much wanted to say, fuck, it was just a gay guy. But they couldn't say it was just a gay guy, so they said, what about these two girls?"

    In some ways, it's easy to understand why the media industry seized upon Matt, and why so many responded to the image it broadcast (Judy Shepard, Matt's mother, told *The Advocate* magazine in March 1999 that the family had received "about 10,000 letters and 70,000 emails," as well as gifts, stuffed animals, blankets, and food). Matt was young (and looked younger), small, attractive; he had been murdered in a particularly brutal fashion. The mistaken belief that he had been strung up on the fence provided a rich, obvious source of symbolism: religious leaders, journalists, and everyday people saw in it a haunting image of the Crucifixion, and at the memorial services and vigils for Matt here and elsewhere, that comparison was often drawn. And while Matt had not in reality been put on display in that fashion, the idea that he had been resonated deeply with America's bitter history of ritual, public violence against minorities— many, including *Time* magazine, compared the attack to a lynching. But Matt seemed to provide a source of intense, almost obsessive interest whose explanation lies well beyond these considerations. Perhaps it was merely the insistent repetition of his image in those early days. In the few snapshots that circulated in the press, Matt appeared boyish, pensive, sweet, charmingly vulnerable in oversized wool sweaters—a boy who still wore braces when he died, a boy who looked innocent of sex, a boy who died because he was gay but whose unthreatening image allowed his sexuality to remain an abstraction for many. In my darker moods, I wonder too if Matt invited such sympathy and political outrage precisely because he was dead—if, for many of the straight people who sincerely mourned his murder, he would nevertheless have been at best invisible while alive. To Jim Osborn, the explanation was less dark and more simple: Matt was "someone we can identify with. Matt was the boy next door. He looked like everybody's brother and everybody's neighbor. He looked like he could have been anyone's son."

"He was the nuclear son of the nuclear family." Jay, a Shoshone-Northern Arapahoe-Navajo American Indian born on the Wind River Reservation in the center of Wyoming, is talking to me about the limits of identification. "If that was me hung on the fence, they'd just say, oh, another drunk Indian. No one would have paid much attention." Jay is gay (he uses the Navajo term *nádleeh*—which he translates as "one who loves his own kind"—to describe himself), and while he feels sympathy for Matt, he doesn't feel much kinship. To Jay, the reason why the nation seized upon Matt is just as simple as Jim Osborn's reason but radically different: to Jay, it was as if white, middle-class America finally had its own tragedy. His argument makes some undeniable sense: in a media culture consecrated to repetition, to the endless recopying of the supposed center of American life—white, moneyed, male—Matt did indeed fit the bill, did suit the recycled homogeneities of a still-myopic national culture. For Jay, the tremendous public outpouring of grief, no matter how sincere, remained essentially alienating. When I ask him how people he knows back on the reservation reacted to the murder, he sums up what he describes as a common response, which he himself shared: "Well, at least now one of them"—whites—"knows what we live through every day." Matt learned it, he says. "And one mother now knows, for a little while anyway, what our lives have always been." As he speaks, defiance, resignation, bitterness, and pride mingle in his voice. "Now people might know what our lives are like," what forms of violence— physical, political, cultural—native people experience in the still-hostile territories of the American West.

Jay's home on the reservation was without running water or electricity, but that never felt like deprivation or unusual circumstance to him—"It's just the way it was." When he was nine, Jay moved to Laramie with his family. They arrived after dark. "Laramie looked so beautiful—all these lights spread out—[it] seemed huge to me." He laughs as he describes how he has learned to love the materialism of life off the reservation—"I really, really like having things now," he admits in simultaneous mockery of himself and Anglo consumerism. When I ask him what white residents here don't know about their town, he replies that "Laramie's a nice town"—he likes life here fine—with a pointed caveat: "White people always say there's no bias in Laramie, no racism, but they just don't want to see." Jay has long black hair pulled back in a braid and a round, lived-in face; he's frequently mistaken for Hispanic. As a child, it didn't take him long to stumble across the racial fault lines he describes. In his first year in Laramie, as he walked home from school near the university campus, a college-aged man spit on him. And on the day we talked, a white woman hissed "spic" at Jay minutes before we met. A student at the university, Jay says there is a reason why the October vigils held for Matt were mostly attended by whites: when Matt died and then later, during the legal proceedings against Henderson and McKinney, Jay observes, "you never saw a minority alone on campus—they either left town, or stayed home, or walked in pairs or groups." They were, he and others say, afraid of a backlash—if "someone got killed for being gay, then someone might get killed for being black or Hispanic or native—that's how we felt." In Jay's opinion, the surprise and horror expressed at the vigils—not to mention simply attending them—was almost something of a white luxury: "They felt shock," Jay says, but "I wasn't shocked—I knew this was coming, since I was in high school, seeing the white and Hispanic kids fight. I knew sooner or later someone was going to die." To Jay, risk, the risk of visible difference, didn't seem all that unfamiliar.

Other minority students on campus confirm Jay's point, however melodramatic it might seem to some. Carina Evans, a young woman of Latino and African-American heritage, told me that when the minority community on campus heard that two Latino teenagers had also been attacked by Henderson and McKinney that night, "the immediate response was, oh my God, what about my safety? How safe am I here? And I think our way of dealing with it was just to not talk about it, because I think we figured the less we drew attention to ourselves, the less the chance that something else was going to happen. Which was a sorry response, but a lot of people left town, just did not feel safe, went away for the week or the weekend."[3] She and others thought, "I'm not going to make myself a target—I'm going to get out of here." No such retaliation was ever reported, but the fact that minority members of the community so feared its possibility that it felt logical to leave town—at the same time that so many white residents could unquestionably consider the attack an isolated incident—reveals something about the complexities of daily life in Laramie.

The divides that run through Jay's and Carina's lives became harder for many in Laramie to ignore in the aftermath of Matt's death. But it was nevertheless a town made defensive by such half-unearthed truths. "Hate is not a Wyoming value," residents kept telling each other, telling visitors, telling the press. "We really take care of each other here," a woman told me one day in a coffee shop, echoing a dearly held ethos I've heard from many in Laramie and that strikes me as generally true. That defensiveness intensified as it encountered the first, clumsy journalistic attempts to offer sociological explanations for the roots of Henderson and McKinney's violence, attempts that implied—to us here, anyway—that Laramie was to blame. Perhaps the most locally reviled version was an article written by Todd Lewan and Steven K. Paulson for the Associated Press that appeared in October, an occasionally persuasive attempt at class analysis hamstrung by bad facts and a love affair with the thuddingly clichéd symbolic density of the railroad tracks that cut through town. Here is their Laramie:

> On the east side is the University of Wyoming's ivy-clad main campus, where students drive sports cars or stroll and bike along oak-shaded sidewalks. On the opposite side of town, a bridge spans railroad tracks to another reality, of treeless trailer parks baking in the heavy sun, fenced-off half-acre lots, stray dogs picking for scraps among broken stoves, refrigerators, and junked pickups. Unlike the university students, youths on the west side have little in the way of entertainment: no malls, no organized dance troupes, no theater or playing fields.

Blowing holes in this picture is still a local sport, more than a year after the murder. Bob Beck, for example, takes fairly comprehensive aim at the story:

> They decided that the reason a murder like this happened was because those of us, including me, who live in west Laramie, the "other side of the tracks," are underprivileged, don't have benefits, all this stuff. Because we're over there, we're obviously looking to get even with the good side of the tracks and are going to commit a crime like this. [They] basically blamed the fact that some of us who live in west Laramie don't have a mall (meanwhile there isn't a mall on the east side either); so we don't have a mall, we don't have paved streets, apparently don't have trees. And this is the reason for all this violence? That was one of the most damaging stories in retrospect, because it got picked up by just about every major paper. A lot of people got their impressions of the case from that.

The list of mistakes could continue: Henderson and McKinney didn't even live in west Laramie; oaks rarely grow at seven thousand feet; and few university students drive fancy sports cars—more likely, like many of the students I've encountered, they're working fifteen to thirty hours a week to pay their tuition, maybe at the same Taco Bell where Henderson worked as a teenager. It's hard to choose, but my personal favorite is the anguished handwringing over west Laramie's lack of organized dance troupes. Organized dance troupes?

Plenty of folks I've spoken to volunteer that they live on the west side and are quick to say they're "not trash," that they like the rustic character of west Laramie's unpaved streets, that they don't necessarily feel excluded from "Laramie proper," despite, for example, the west side's usual lack of representation on the city council. And I've found few residents who weren't offended by such shallow press characterizations of Laramie, who didn't argue that status doesn't matter much here, that Laramie is friendly and easygoing and safe, that most folks don't even bother to lock their doors. All their points of rebuttal are well taken, and indeed they're reasons why many love to live here. But nevertheless I think the eager rapidity with which so many of us rejected such examples of journalistic ineptitude masked at times a certain unease—and sometimes a hardworking amnesia—about the subtle realities of class, sexuality, and race here in Laramie. Those realities may be too complicated to sum up through the convenient shorthand of railroad tracks and trailer parks, but they still flow, hushed yet turbulent, beneath daily life in this town.   ∎

NOTES

1. Melanie Thernstrom's essay on the murder in the March 1999 issue of *Vanity Fair* notes that Matt was not strung up, but only in a parenthetical remark near the end of the piece, and the article itself has the title "The Crucifixion of Matthew Shepard." JoAnn Wypijewski's tough-minded essay "A Boy's Life," which appeared in the September 1999 issue of *Harper's Magazine,* was the first thorough demystification of this myth in the national media, but many people still believe it. For example, Melissa Etheridge's song "Scarecrow" on her 1999 album *Breakdown* relies on it, as well as on other early misstatements of fact, including the false report that Shepard had been burned by his killers.

2. While the United Multicultural Council did good work that day, and while some strong connections have been made between the UMC and the LGBTA since Matt's death, it would be wrong to imply that those ties have been built without friction. Carina Evans, a university student who worked in the Minority Affairs Office that year, observed that at the time some members of the "diversity clubs" represented by the UMC "would not deal with the gay issue. The United Multicultural Council had no representation from the LGBTA, had no representation of openly gay students—and I think that's not at all multicultural. But they don't want to handle that. It's not like they're hostile about it, but they just don't encourage it." The tension flows both ways: Jay, a gay American Indian now active in the UMC, told me that some gay students of color he knows are uncomfortable attending LGBTA meetings because they feel that some members are not sensitive to racial differences.

3. A Mexican-American student, Lindsey Gonzales, spoke to me as well about the attack on Morales and Herrera. Lindsey knew Morales quite well (they'd hung out together in the past). She thinks neither the media nor the public cared much about the attack on Morales and Herrera compared to Matt because "they didn't die." But if they had, she speculates, people probably wouldn't have cared much more. When I ask her why, she says she's not sure, but she speculates that racial prejudice is simply more "familiar," something with a longer and better-known history in America, whereas "we're all just getting used to" homosexuality right now, and "that made it a big deal."

■ *QUESTIONS FOR MAKING CONNECTIONS WITHIN THE READING* ■

1. As Beth Loffreda works to unpack the significance of Matt Shepard's murder, she finds herself confronting a wide array of prejudices, not only about gays, but about Wyoming, the West, and Native Americans. Create a chart that details all of the prejudices that Loffreda uncovers. What are the relationships among these prejudices? Does Loffreda have any prejudices, or is her view unbiased?

2. In detailing the responses to Shepard's murder, Loffreda refers to many different individuals by name. Who are the most important people in the story that Loffreda has to tell? Which responses had more weight at the time of the murder? Which responses have the most weight with Loffreda? With you?

3. How is this selection from *Losing Matt Shepard* organized? Is it a series of observations or an argument? Does it build to a point? Does it have a structure? How does the structure that Loffreda has chosen influence what she has to say?

■ *QUESTIONS FOR WRITING* ■

1. One of Loffreda's arguments in *Losing Matt Shepard* is that Matt Shepard, the individual, got lost in the media frenzy that followed his murder. Part of the shock of Shepard's death, Loffreda reports, was "to watch rumor become myth, to see the story stitched out of repetition rather than investigation." If the media got Shepard's murder wrong, what are we to make of how and why they got it wrong? What would it take to provide "better coverage" of such tragedies? Are the print and visual media capable of providing nuanced understandings of unfolding events?

2. In describing how her colleagues at the University of Wyoming responded to Shepard's death, Loffreda records her own frustration at hearing teachers speak of their own "uselessness" and "irrelevance" in the face of such a tragedy. Such remarks struck Loffreda as "an appalling luxury, an indulgence in a kind of intellectual self-pity at a moment when the basic skills of education—critical thinking, articulation, self-reflection—could be so concretely valuable. I wondered about that, and I wondered too when we'd stop talking about how we felt and begin talking about what to do." What is it that teachers can or should do at such times? What role should secular institutions play in trying to shape the way their students see and understand the world?

1. This selection from *Losing Matt Shepard* closes with Loffreda's discussion of what she terms "the limits of identification." In a sense, Susan Faludi's "The Naked Citadel" could also be described as a piece centrally concerned with "the limits of identification." What are these limits? How are they discovered? Can they be changed?

2. Both Leila Ahmed and Beth Loffreda could be said to be autoethnographers—writers who make sense of cultures of which they themselves are members. Both are concerned with violence, incomprehension, and change. Beyond these similarities, would you say that there is a method to this kind of work? Is there a way to assess the results of such studies—to tell good work from bad? Is objectivity a goal in autoethnography? A necessity? An impossibility? Write a paper that draws on Ahmed and Loffreda to explore the dynamics and demands of studying one's own culture.

TANYA M. LUHRMANN

THOUGH WE OFTEN assume that our core beliefs remain constant over time, Tanya M. Luhrmann demonstrates repeatedly through her research that this is not the case. Director of the Clinical Ethnography project for the Committee on Human Development at the University of Chicago, Luhrmann has a particular interest in irrational beliefs and in understanding the ways that social practices and psychological states mutually influence one another. For her work, Luhrmann has been elected a fellow of the American Academy of Arts and Sciences as well as president of the Society for Psychological Anthropology.

In her first book, *Persuasions of the Witch's Craft* (1989), Luhrmann shows how a belief in magic comes to seem perfectly reasonable by satisfying the emotional needs of believers and by providing an explanation for the believers' common experience. In her second book, *The Good Parsi* (1996), Luhrmann explores how beliefs are shaped by the reigning political and economic climate, chronicling the growing pessimism of the Parsis in postcolonial India, who continue to thrive economically but no longer enjoy the privileged political position they held during British colonial rule. In *Of Two Minds* (2000), her most recent book, Luhrmann identifies two different cultures within the field of American psychiatry and then elaborates on the two different ways of understanding patients and their mental illnesses that result from this cultural divergence.

Since her last book, Luhrmann has turned her attention to the role that visual and aural experiences play in both psychiatric and religious contexts. "Metakinesis: How God Becomes Intimate in Contemporary U.S. Christianity," pursues the latter of these two lines of thought. Through her ethnographic research, Luhrmann discovers that contemporary evangelical American religious experiences "are giving us a God more private, more personal, and in some ways more tangibly real than the god of our fathers." Even in the realm of religious experience, which is often interpreted as a timeless link to tradition, social context determines both practical habits and psychological understanding.

Luhrmann, Tanya M. "Metakinesis: How God Becomes Intimate in Contemporary U.S. Christianity." *American Anthropologist* 6(3): 518–528.
Biographical information is drawn from <http://humdev.uchicago.edu/luhrmann.htm>.

By drawing our attention repeatedly to this fact, Luhrmann invites us to pay closer and closer attention to the environments that frame our beliefs and to the role that the irrational plays in human experience.

■ ■

Metakinesis: How God Becomes Intimate in Contemporary U.S. Christianity

In the last 30 or 40 years, middle-class U.S. citizens have begun to worship their God(s) in a markedly different manner than before. Mainstream churches have seen their congregations dwindle; evangelical, New Age, and other more demanding faiths have seen their memberships explode. And what U.S. citizens seem to want from these new religiosities—and from evangelical Christianity in particular—is intense spiritual experience. We in the academy have focused on evangelical Christianity's claim that the Bible is literally true. That claim is undeniably important (Crapanzano 2001). But it is at least as important that the new U.S. religious practices put intense spiritual experience—above all, trance—at the heart of the relationship with God. The most interesting anthropological phenomenon in U.S. evangelical Christianity is precisely that it is *not* words *alone* that convert: Instead, congregants—even in ordinary middle-class suburbs—learn to have out-of-the-ordinary experiences and to use them to develop a remarkably intimate, personal God. This God is not without majesty. But He has become a pal.

How does God become real to people? A recent, widely read book—Susan Harding's (2000) *The Book of Jerry Falwell*—argues that in evangelical Christianity, what makes God come alive to people is the mastery of His word. This book is an attempt to understand the compelling power and appeal of Jerry Falwell's brand of evangelical fundamentalism. The book is specifically cast as an account of conversion and from the beginning presumes an identity between the culture and practice of Christianity on the one hand, and its language on the other. Harding describes her book as an attempt "to show how Bible-based language persuades and produces effects" (2000:xii). She dismisses the "considerable literature, both popular and academic, on how various ritual practices and psychological techniques trigger experiences that result in conversion" (2000:35). Those experiences may "pave the way for radical shifts in belief and commitment" (2000:35) but, she says, they are not necessary. The appropriate question, she says, is this: "How does the supernatural order become real, known, experienced, and absolutely irrefutable?" (2000:36). And her answer is that it can do so through language alone:

> Among conservative Protestants, and especially among fundamentalists, it is the Word, the gospel of Jesus Christ, written, spoken, heard, and read, that converts the unbeliever. The stresses, transitions, influences, conditioning, and techniques scrutinized by many social scientists do not in themselves "explain," do not "cause," conversion to Christ. All they do is increase the likelihood that a person might listen to the Gospel; they may open or "prepare a person's heart." [2000:36]

Harding agrees. The first chapter's title and its concluding sentence (2000:60) state the basic argument: "Speaking is believing." "Generative belief, belief that indisputably transfigures you and your reality, belief that becomes you, comes only through speech" (2000:60).

Yet the patterns of new U.S. religious practice suggest that ritual practices and psychological techniques are not ancillary but central to contemporary spirituality. At least, congregants seem to want to experience the Gospel in intensely bodily ways that seem to make the message of the Gospel come alive for them in a way it has not previously. The demographic shift in U.S. religious practice since the late 1960s is remarkable. Two-thirds of the generation referred to as the "baby boomers" who were raised in religious traditions—and nearly all were—dropped out of those traditions as adults; just under half of those now seem to be returning to religious practice, but not in the style in which they were raised (Ostling 1993; Roof 1993). Across the board they have joined groups that demand more in religious practice and encourage more in religious experience. Evangelical and fundamentalist Christianity has exploded as a cultural phenomenon, as has the New Age movement, in all its many forms (such as modern witchcraft and modern Santeria): In 1996, 39 percent of U.S. citizens described themselves as "born again" or "evangelical" (Gallup and Lindsay 1999:68). Even Judaism, whose traditional and reform rabbis look askance at intense spirituality because it distracts the faithful from the obligations of their practice, has seen an enormous increase in the interest in an immediate spiritual experience of divinity, from new centers (such as the Kabbalah Centre in Los Angeles) that teach kabbalah as a practice accessible to all (a heretical idea in the past) to Chabad and Hasidic shuls that teach an experience-centered religiosity to ever-expanding crowds (e.g., Kamenetz 1997). There are many explanations for this shift and many anxieties about its political and social implications (e.g., Fogel 2000; Roof 1993). But its behavioral implications are clear: These religions greatly value intense religious experience. As a group, they encourage participants to experience the divine vividly, immediately, and through unusual moments of altered consciousness (Wuthnow 1988, 1998).

Harding is certainly accurate when she reports that evangelical Christians often say that they are converted by the Word alone. But conversion is a complex process and above all else a learning process. Converts do not make the transition from nonbeliever to believer simply by speaking—by acquiring new concepts and words. They must come to believe emotionally that those new concepts and words are true. And this, as Saba Mahmood points out in an Islamic context, is a matter of "skills and aptitudes acquired through training, practice and apprenticeship" (2001:844). As many anthropologists have pointed out, those skills often involve the body and the training is often emotional (Boddy 1989; Csordas 1994; Desjarlais 1992; Lambek 1981; Mitchell 1997; Whitehead 1987; see also the rich discussion in Rambo 1993). What is striking about U.S. religion since the 1960s is that it not only emphasizes bodily phenomena but also uses those experiences to create remarkably intimate relationships with God.

When we take an ethnographic look at what these converts actually learn in the process of becoming evangelical Christians, we see that their new cognitive/linguistic knowledge is embedded within other kinds of learning that not only make that new knowledge real but also make this God as gritty as earth and as soothing as a summer breeze. New believers do indeed acquire what Harding calls a "shared elementary language" (2000:19) of faith (see also Keane 1997). That linguistic/cognitive knowledge can be described more precisely, perhaps, than Harding has done: There are words or phrases to describe their new life in Christ (their "lexicon"); themes that structure the logic of their new understanding (their "syntax"); and a common plotline that describes the way they decided to join this way of life (their "conversion narrative"). This new knowledge is important; it is necessary to the convert's conversion.

But it is not sufficient. For these converts, in these new and intensely experiential U.S. evangelisms, God becomes an intimate relationship—a buddy, a confidante, the ideal boyfriend. It is not mere words that make Him so but learnt techniques of identifying the presence of God through the body's responses—particularly in the absorbed state we call "trance"—and learned techniques that frame that responsiveness into the experience of close relationship. This is not to say that every convert has these intense experiences of absorption. But the religion models the practices that produce these experiences as central to the experience of God.

We can describe this process as *metakinesis*, a term used in dance criticism to depict the way emotional experience is carried within the body so that the dancer conveys the emotion to the observer and, yet, does it by making the expressive gesture uniquely his or her own (Martin 1983:23–25). New believers learn to identify bodily and emotional states as signs of God's presence in their life, identifications that imply quite different learning processes than those entailed by linguistic and cognitive knowledge. Then, their new linguistic/cognitive knowledge and bodily experiences are put to use through new relational practices. Through prayer and Bible reading, worshippers report that they learn to experience themselves in an intimate interpersonal relationship with their God; they do so not only by acquiring new knowledge but also by using that knowledge to relate to what might be psychoanalytically termed an inner "object" (cf. Lester in press). These are relational processes that are yet again another kind of learning process.

These three different kinds of learning—cognitive/linguistic, metakinetic, and relational—are psychologically distinct. Linguistic/cognitive knowledge tends to be the domain of cognitive science and linguistics; emotional and altered states tend to be studied by developmentalists and those interested in psychopathology; relationship practices tend to be studied by attachment theorists, often with a psychoanalytic bent. Together, they enable new believers to do something quite remarkable—to construct, out of everyday psychological experience, the profound sense that they have a really real relationship with a being that cannot be seen, heard, or touched. The learning process used by these U.S. evangelical Christians teaches us that new religious practices are giving us a God more private, more personal, and in some fundamental sense more tangibly real than the God of our fathers. We have yet to come to terms with this enormous social fact.

The Ethnography

Horizon Christian Fellowship in southern California has the no-frills, ordinary-folks approach characteristic of the "new paradigm" Christian churches (Miller 1997). Like other such churches, Horizon has a rock band on Sunday morning, not a choir; the pastors have an informal, anti-intellectual style; many congregants meet in small-home Bible fellowships during the week; they hold their large worship meetings in a gym; and they call themselves "Bible based," by which they mean that the written Bible is literally true and the only decisive authority. They are also entrepreneurial, well organized, and extremely effective. Horizon is an offshoot of perhaps the prototypical new paradigm church, Calvary Chapel, which began to grow in the mid-1960s by reaching out to the countercultural Jesus movement on southern California beaches, but now has over 25,000 members and nearly a thousand "seeded" churches around the country. These days Horizon serves about 5,000 mostly white congregants at its main church campus. It has seven associated churches in San Diego and claims 80 offshoots around the world. Horizon runs a preschool, an elementary school, a junior high, a high school, a school of evangelism with a master's program in divinity and pastoral studies, outreach evangelism in this country and abroad, youth programs, summer camps, and constant concerts, "getaways," and social events. The specific and much-reiterated goal of this busy institution is to lead each worshipper to have a vividly personal relationship with Jesus (see also Ammerman 1987).

How does God become so real for people? The great majority of U.S. citizens (96 percent) say that they believe in God—or at least, in a power "higher than themselves"—when asked in a Gallup survey. The number has remained more or less constant for 50 years (Gallup and Lindsay 1999:24–25). At the same time, those who have come to Horizon have usually developed a faith quite different from that in which they were raised (Miller 1997). Most congregants say that they believed "intellectually" in Christ in their childhood, or not at all, and that as adults they discovered a "new" life in Christ. How does a new congregant learn to turn an amorphous, often intellectual belief in God into the rich personal experience modeled in these religious sites?

Seen from another angle, this ethnographic puzzle is the central practical issue for a church like Horizon. Congregants at Horizon are acutely aware of their newcomers; after all, the point of an evangelizing institution is to convert them. And, yet, learning to be a true Christian is understood as a lifelong goal. As so many tracts say, faith is a journey in which the believer aims always to grow in the knowledge and love of God. While sermons talk of accepting Jesus as a one-time commitment (come, today, to the altar to be saved), they speak in the same breath of a long-term process of "dying to self" so that gradually and with difficulty you learn to put God's desires above your own. Being "saved" is both a singular event that people celebrate like a birthday and an ongoing process.

As a result, there is no sharp distinction between newcomers and long-timers in actual practice. At Horizon, newcomers learn about the faith in two institutional settings. The first is the service. There are as many as five services throughout the weekend, each often packing the gym. They are usually led by different pastors and are sometimes structured differently, but they all focus on an hour-long sermon structured around a particular Biblical text. The services have the anonymity of all large groups. During the week, however, congregants often attend a more intimate fellowship, gathering in someone's home where they participate in the small group worship Robert Wuthnow (1994) finds to be so characteristic of contemporary U.S. religion. Despite variation, each home fellowship meeting will involve personal testimony about Jesus and biblical teaching.

Books are also an important vehicle for learning about the faith. The well-appointed church bookstore sells an impressive array of Christian goods. Many of their items are obviously intended as learning tools: There are perhaps a hundred guides to prayer and Bible Study, with prominent displays for what are seen as basic manuals. Each sermon, or message, is taped and sold for a nominal fee so that congregants can listen to them again in their cars. There is a wide selection of Christian novels, videos, and music. The music section has a chart that helps you to identify what mainstream music you already like and, thus, what Christian music you will like. The music ranges from folk to disco, its difference from the mainstream only in its lyrics. The wider commercial success of these products is stunning.

For three years, from 1997–2000, I carried out fieldwork with a colleague, Richard Madsen, to try to understand how adults create a personal relationship that feels to them authentic, intimate, and mutually reciprocal with an intentional being who does not exhibit any of the normal signs of existence. We studied four of the growth points of U.S. religion: (1) Horizon as an example of evangelical Christianity; (2) a charismatic Catholic church; (3) a New Age Santeria house; and (4) a *baal tschuva* (newly orthodox) shul. In each group, we attended services for months, in most cases nearly a year, bought the books and tools described as helpful to new converts, and, to the extent that was feasible, tried to understand and to do what new converts did when they entered these groups. For each group, we formally interviewed the leader of the group and ten of its congregants. Using the formal interviews and casual conversations as my guide and drawing only from fieldwork at Horizon, I now describe (in brief) at least three kinds of learning that took place: (1) cognitive/linguistic, (2) metakinetic, and (3) relational. The cognitive/linguistic learning actually contains its own analytic triad—the lexical, the syntactic, and the specific conversion narrative—which reflects the more clearly differentiated kinds of learning that take place under the rubric of the cognitive and linguistic.

Cognitive/Linguistic Knowledge: The Lexicon

At Horizon, not all of the knowledge presented in the written material is taken equally seriously by congregants, at least to judge by the content of their conversation. Few congregants spoke in their interviews about "the Rapture" and "the end of time," concepts that are central to an enormously best-selling fantasy series called *Left Behind* (e.g., LeHaye and Jenkins 1995), which was planted front and center in the bookstore and which many congregants seemed to have read. But certain phrases did reverberate through the manuals, the church services, other books, and the transcripts of our interviews. As newcomers became members of the community, these phrases became part of their speech patterns.

The most important phrase was "to walk with God." Sometimes a noun—"my *walk*"—and sometimes a verb—"learning to *walk*"—this phrase describes the daily experience of living your life as this kind of Christian. As the manuals use the term, "to *walk* with God" refers both to learning to develop a relationship with God and to managing the everyday challenges to your faith: temptation, frustration, and disappointment. This, for example, is the way one congregant uses the term when she describes her goal for a women's Bible Study group she started with students in Horizon's School of Evangelism, where she works. "It's really just interacting with them so that they can get to a different level of their walk with God."[1] To "walk with God" describes the way you incorporate God into your life, and people accept that there are different degrees of that incorporation, more being better. To "walk with God" also captures something about the sense of the intimacy of God's presence in your daily life. As another congregant said, "To me, well, now that I am walking with the Lord I know that, like, I feel that God talks to me all day long. . . . I just think God's with me all the time."

Another common phrase in the lexicon—but there were many others—is the "Word of God." The phrase refers overtly to the written Bible, but it connotes the loving, personal, and unique relationship congregants believe God has with each individual Christian. One man said, "I went [to church] for several weeks in a row and I heard the Bible and it was addressing me and speaking to me personally. . . . I was realizing that it is a love story, and it's written to me." This is a remarkable claim, the more remarkable in that it was made by a sober man in his forties: that the written Bible, a text which is the same for all who read it (issues of translation aside), was at the same time written uniquely and with love for each of us individually. "The Bible says," he continued, "that the Word of God is actually written on the tablets of your heart."

Cognitive/Linguistic Knowledge: Syntax

By *syntax*, I mean an underlying logic that knits together different phrases; syntax organizes the narratives around meaningful phrases like "my walk with God." While by *lexicon*, I mean to denote the new words and phrases that participants begin to use, by *syntax*, I mean to denote the themes of this kind of religious commitment, what one could metaphorically describe as "the grammar" of this religious life. The sermons at Horizon, along with the books and videos sold by the church, model the kind of people Christians are, what they struggle with, and to what end. New congregants are not so much learning a specific, concrete story as they are learning ways to tell a range of stories. Albert Lord (1960) famously distinguished "formula" and "theme" as building blocks for the great stories told by singers of tales, the Homeric bards among them. Such singers, he argued (with Milman Parry), did not memorize and precisely reproduce the thousands of lines of text found in the great epics. Instead, they composed anew each time in what Parry and Lord called the "oral-formulaic" tradition. They became familiar with large and small plots that could be elided or elaborated as the occasion demanded, and they learned to use common phrases associated with the tale. "Rosy-fingered dawn" is a formula, a phrase often evoked to describe the Iliadic morning; the tragedy of Achilles and the deception of the Trojan horse are themes. The new congregant to Horizon becomes familiar with formulaic phrases like "walking with God" and part of what it means to be a Christian is to use those phrases in describing your daily life. Another part of being a good Christian is to become familiar with the themes—the syntactic knowledge—that organize the way that life is understood and experienced.

Horizon's syntactic themes are well represented in its sermons, or "messages." Here is one such sermon, not recorded and transcribed but captured in my notes from the service one morning in May.

> Someone, somewhere, has to start a revolution, the pastor said. The people of this government, they've been to Harvard and Yale, they just passed a law saying that pornography can be shown on television at any time, because it's protected by the freedom of speech. But that's not what free speech is about, he said; we all know that free speech is about having the freedom to criticize the government, not to allow rubbish on television . . .
>
> Remember, he said, that we are the children of God. You ladies [and here the room got very silent], you are the daughters of God. . . . Lift your head out of the gutter. You are noble. . . . [When] you realize this, and you say to God, I'm here in a place full of body odor and bodies, a fleshly material place, and can You please help me, He will help you. Even when you want to pray so badly and you can't really get it out, it's okay because there's a spirit inside of you helping it to come out. And if you are praying and being with Jesus, the devil won't distract you. He'll say, she's got the helmet of righteousness on. She can't be reached. And he'll move on. Because his time is short. Short. And your time is infinite. So don't numb your feeling, don't dull yourself with alcohol and drugs. Feel good. Reach out. Start living. Smell every flower. Live like that, live with God. Be alive. He loves you. [field notes, May 28, 2000]

In a sermon like this, the pastor is teaching a way of thinking about how to live in the world as a Christian: what it is to be a person (you need to be responsible; you are noble, a child of a mighty Lord); what the world is like (full of rubbish, full of people who have been to Harvard and Yale but can't see what's morally obvious, a place of bodies and odors); who God is (He's responsible, He's pure, He loves you); and why a Christian person needs God (to keep you pure, to give you armor for protection from the devil, to help you be fully alive). Interwoven with these more general spiritual themes are some remarkably concrete politics. It is also worth noting that a good Christian might "want to pray so badly and you can't really get it out." These Christians expect that prayer does not come easily and naturally. It is a skill that must be learned, as a relationship to God must also be learned. That is part of the logic of the faith.

Cognitive/Linguistic Knowledge: Conversion Narrative

While congregants learn specific phrases to depict their new religiosity and thematic plots to describe God's human world, they also learn a specific personal narrative to depict their own entry into committed evangelical Christianity. This narrative form stands out from these other kinds of narratives, like the sermon above. It is both more personal and more stereotyped. This combination of the very personal and the stereotyped is hardly unique to evangelical Christians. The anthropologist Christopher Crocker (1985) describes the recruitment of Bororo shamans as exhibiting a similar combination of cultural expectations (everyone knows that the shaman-to-be must see a stump or anthill or stone move suddenly in the forest; catch a small wild game animal like a wild turkey; dream of attempted seduction; and so forth) and intensely personal experience. "Their details and sequences are standardized almost to the point of collective representations, known by most adult nonshamans. Yet the shamans I knew best spoke of them with vivid sincerity, adding variations and personal reactions at once idiosyncratic and consistent with the general pattern" (1985:206; see also Crapanzano 2000:102ff.).

In these accounts, congregants said that they knew God, or knew about God, in an abstract way or as children growing up in religious households; then they had a wild ride through drugs, sex, alcohol, and depravity; they hit bottom; they realized that their life was empty, unsatisfying, and unfulfilled. They accepted Christ (often as a result of coming to a Bible-believing church on a whim) and were filled with love, acceptance, and forgiveness. A male congregant, who worked in construction for Horizon, told us that he grew up in a house without religion, although he knew the commandments and that "there was someone I was accountable to, and that was God." By the time he was 13, he had already experimented around and realized that "it all amounted to emptiness." He continued to lark around. The sense of emptiness, he said, "really hit when I was 38." He tried drugs, what he called "Buddhism," existentialism, and one romance after another, but, apparently, he had never tried a Christian church. "I had tried everything and, because of drugs, lost everything. I lost my business, lost my place, lost my hope. Absolutely rock bottom." Homeless, he moved in with friends, and someone invited him to Horizon. When he went, he said, "I just knew it. Without a doubt." Eight of the ten people we interviewed formally gave us some version of this story of self-destruction, despair, and redemption.

Should we trust these stories? If accurate, they are an alarming glimpse into the U.S. (or at least, Californian) experience. It is possible that some congregants at Horizon learn, like Augustine, to stretch their little sins until they become an abyss of wickedness. It is also possible that a church like Horizon offers the structure to enable an addict to abandon his addiction, just as the fast-growing Pentecostal church offers women a tool with which to detach their men from drink (e.g., Brusco 1995). In any event, the message of the narrative is clear: I was lost, so deeply lost, so lost that no one could love me—and then God did, and I was found.

Metakinesis

I use the term *metakinesis* to refer to mind-body states that are both identi-fied within the group as the way of recognizing God's personal presence in your life and are subjectively and idiosyncratically experienced. These states, or phenomena, are lexically identified and indeed the process of learning to have these experiences cannot be neatly disentangled from the process of learning the words to describe them. A congregant must use lan-guage to describe and, thus, to recognize, the moment of experiencing the state. Yet congregants do not use the phrases the way they use phrases like "my walk with God," which is used to denote a general orientation toward life. In identifying metakinetic states, congregants identify—and, thus, psy-chologically organize—bodily phenomena that seem new and distinctive to them, which they come to interpret in ways that are congruent with the group's understanding of evidence of God's real reality in their lives. They seem to be engaging a variety of bodily processes that are integrated in new ways and synthesized into a new understanding of their bodies and the world. Some of these processes could be called "dissociative," in which attentional focus is narrowed and manipulated to produce noticeable shifts in conscious awareness, so that individuals feel that they are floating or not in control of their bodies. Others involve sensory hallucinations, in which people see or hear things that observers do not. There are specific and dra-matic mood elevations, in which individuals are self-consciously and notice-ably happier for extended periods of time. As a result of these phenomena, congregants literally perceive the world differently and they attribute that difference to the presence of God.

Horizon and the Calvary Chapel movement more generally do not place doctrinal nor ritual emphasis on what Christians often call the "gifts of the Holy Spirit" (see Robbins 2004). No one speaks in tongues in public ritual and spiritual authority is understood to rest in the Bible, not in pri-vate experience. Yet the singular point of the services, sermons, Bible Study groups, and prayer manuals, repeated with such maddening insistence that it becomes the texture of the religious life, is that one should build a per-sonal relationship to God through prayer. *Prayer* is a commonplace word, tinged with the mystery of the sacred but ordinary in a way that words like *meditation, visualization,* and *trance* are not. And still the act of prayer de-mands that we focus our attention inward and resist distractions. Most of us remember the prayer of childhood service. I would bow my head and my mind would wander to my dress's scratchy collar and what I would do that afternoon. In mainstream Christian and Jewish services, that is what prayer often is: a dutiful, closed-eyed silence while the leader intones, followed by a period of quiet in which it is all too easy to remember items you need to add to the shopping list. Horizon sets out to change those habits by modeling a relationship to God as the point of life—and, incidentally, of going to church—and modeling prayer as the practice on which that relationship is built. And with this emphasis, prayer becomes the conduit of anomalous psychological experience it was for the 19th century reformers, the medieval ecstatics, and the early pastoralists who sought to be still and hear the voice of God.

The taught structure of this prayer is deceptively dull: Prayer is about talking with God. But the taught practice asks the congregant to turn inwardly with great emotional attention. In the service, in the early period of worship before the pastor speaks, people start singing songs to God—songs *to* God, not *about* God. People shut their eyes, hold out their hands, and sway back and forth, singing of how much they love Him and yearn for Him. Some will have tears on their cheeks. Then the music will fade, and congregants will remain standing, eyes shut, deeply absorbed in their thoughts. Sometimes the bandleader will pray out loud here, softly describing "how much we seek to glorify You in our hearts." Prayer, says a popular manual, is a yearning for God (Burnham 2002). That private, absorbed yearning is visible on the faces of those who pray here.

There are perhaps a hundred prayer manuals and books about prayer at the Horizon bookstore. These books, the sermons, and home fellowships insistently and repeatedly assert that none of us pray as seriously as we can or should; all urge you to pray more intensely. And despite Horizon's literal interpretation of the Bible and its overt hostility to charismatic phenomena, in fact the practical theology invites the congregant to assume that truth is found inwardly and not from external experts. God is to be found in personal experience, as He speaks to you directly in your prayers and through His text. Pastors hasten to say that anything He says to you in private must be confirmed through His Word, but in fact the Bible is learned not as a text to be memorized but as a personal document, written uniquely for each.

This emphasis on prayer has, I believe, two effects. First, it encourages people to attend to the stream of their own consciousness like eager fishermen, scanning for the bubbles and whorls that suggest a lurking catch. And, perhaps, because memory is adaptive and perception obliging, they begin to note the discontinuities that are natural to our state and actually to interpret them as discontinuous, rather than smoothing them over with the presumption of a simple integrated self. Second, it demands that people engage in practices that help them to go into trance. *Trance* is an ominous-sounding word, but I mean something relatively straightforward by it: that one can become intensely absorbed in inner sensory stimuli and lose some peripheral awareness (Spiegel and Spiegel 1978). Trance is the consequence of shifting the streetlamp of our focal awareness from the external to the inward. We do this naturally when we daydream, play, or read, and we seem to vary somewhat in our spontaneous ability to ignore the distracting world. But for many, probably most of us, that ability is also a learnable skill. Prayer, as it is taught at Horizon, encourages trance because it focuses the worshipper's attention inward, away from external stimuli, and it can be learned because mental concentration responds to practice (Luhrmann 1989). There are no known bodily markers of a trance state, but as the absorption grows deeper, people become more difficult to distract, and their sense of time and agency begin to shift. They live within their imagination more, whether that be simple mindfulness or elaborate fantasy, and they feel that the experience happens to them, that they are bystanders to their own awareness, more themselves than ever before, or, perhaps, absent—but invariably different. In addition, trance practice appears to encourage the wide variety of anomalous phenomena (hallucinations, altered states, mystical awareness, and so forth) often called "spiritual" (Luhrmann 1989; Roche and McConkey 1990; Tellegen 1981; Tellegen and Atkinson 1974).

Whether because they pay new attention to their awareness, or whether because these new practices alter their conscious experience, all congregants spontaneously associated the process of "getting to know Jesus"—which one does through prayer and reading the Bible—with occasional experiences that involved heightened emotions and unusual sensory and perceptual experiences and that they identified, labeled, and discussed.

One of the less dramatic of these metakinetic states was "falling in love with Jesus." People said that you could tell when someone was a newly committed Christian because they got "this goopy look" on their face when you asked them if they loved Jesus. They repeatedly spoke of Christ as their lover or their greatest love and described this love in physical terms. Even the men did so, although for them He was more buddy than boyfriend. When I asked John (the construction worker) whether the phrase "falling in love with Jesus" made sense to him, he said, "Absolutely . . . the closer you get the more of his love you feel and it is undeniable. You become flooded. You become absolutely radiant." When asked whether that was different from falling in love with a woman, John said, "He will never disappoint me. He will never let me down. He'll tell me the absolute truth and He will never push me. He will never force me to do anything. He will always encourage. Granted, He's perfect."

"Falling in love with Jesus" is an emotional state, not a general way of being in the world, as "walking with the Lord" denotes. People spoke about this experience as if it were indeed the intense love of early adolescence, with the confidence that the beloved truly is perfect and that His perfection is a kind of miraculous confirmation of one's self. You were not necessarily in prayer when you felt it, but it emerged through the process of establishing a relationship through prayer. One woman compared her relationship with God "to a relationship with the man of my dreams." Another spoke for an hour about her love of God and ended our interview by talking about people who might tell her that God was selfish to want her exclusive love: "And you know what? They're right. They are right. He wants to be loved." Falling in love with the Lord was a giggly, euphoric experience—a breathless, wonderful high. Because of this, it could also be seen as merely the first step on the road to true Christianity. A pastor spoke scoffingly to us about people who had fallen in love with Christ but did not realize that there were rules and responsibilities to being Christian. He went on to compare the experience of being a true Christian to being married: Sure, you fell giddy in love and there was all the romance but you had to get past that and do the dishes and pay for the car.

Then there was "peace"—the "peace of God that passeth understanding." Like "falling in love with Jesus," *peace* had a bodily quality and was treated as an emotional state or a mood. People often spoke of this peace as something God gave to them. They felt sad for those who did not feel it, and often used the word in the context of turning responsibility for some decision they needed to make over to God, with a kind of relief that He would make the decision. These emotional states were clearly understood as the result of creating a relationship with God through prayer. "Falling in love" was the first phase of that relationship; what one evangelical writer describes as the "first love" years (Curtis and Eldredge 1997:30). A person "new in Christ" may experience "peace" immediately but it is also associated with mature Christian faith. Peace is the result of the engagement of the yearning, sometimes anguished spirit; the true prayer may begin in pain but it ends in peace. Peace is the sense of being spiritually heard and emotionally met, of being calmed through the act of relating to God. While the concept and its evocation are shared by all Christian traditions, at Horizon the word was likely to be used to evoke the shape of a feeling, rather than a political goal. One man said, "I almost stopped [on his way down to the altar during an altar call] but I felt peace, so I went forward."

In addition to these emotional phenomena, nearly half of the congregants reported a variety of what a psychologist would call sensory hallucinations— phenomena of thought, not mood. These are not everyday events for these Christians. They are not, however, as rare as one might think even in the wider population. Many people (in the United States, perhaps one in ten; see Bentall 2000) literally hear an apparently hallucinated external voice at least once and, for most of them, this is not a symptom of illness. The congregants do seem to experience hallucinations: Individuals were very clear about the difference between hearing God's voice "inside" and "outside" their heads. One congregant, making that distinction, remarked, "There are rare times when I hear a definite voice, but . . . it's hard to explain. Like just a small tiny push or something, like a thought in your mind." It is possible that the trancelike practice of prayer may evoke such hallucinations: that would be in accord with what we know scientifically about the relationship of concentration practices and anomalous experience (e.g., Cardena et al. 2000; Luhrmann 1989). Whether their prayer induces such phenomena or not, individuals do seem to learn to pay attention to the fragmentary chaos of conscious awareness in a new way. To some extent, we impose coherence on our conscious experience retrospectively (Gergen 1991; Kunzendorf and Wallace 2000). These congregants learn to identify and highlight these moments of discontinuity and they come to understand those moments as signs of God's presence in their lives.

Sometimes the term *Holy Spirit* is used to indicate such moments, although that term is also used more broadly than to describe hallucinations. But even moments too trivial to be glorified as the Holy Spirit are reported and associated with God nonetheless. A man who served as one of the many associate pastors called them "these quirky things that happen that there is no scriptural support for. Every person I talk to," he continued, "has some oddball supernatural experience that sounds crazy, unless you're a Christian." The story that prompted his comment was this:

> I'm pretty much a new believer at this point and I'm driving and I hear the evangelist say on the tape, "Dennis, slow down. You are going too fast." It certainly wasn't something on the tape; it was something I heard. So, I slowed down and immediately a cop passed me and pulled over another guy who was also speeding, in front of me. I thought, God is really doing something here.

Congregants also reported tactile sensations, as this woman did when I asked her how she sensed God:

> One time I was praying for this woman who had dated this guy who was into this Satan worship and she felt like there were demons in her. We were praying for her and stuff and I felt like there was a hand on my head. . . . And sometimes I just feel when I'm driving along, sometimes I can feel it on my body and sometimes it's just more inside. He is just such a comfort to me, and it's just so great.

Again, what a psychologist would call "sensory hallucinations" are not everyday events for these Christians, but they are clearly significant, meaningful enough for nearly half of our interviewees to bring up in a comparatively short formal interview and common in many evangelical accounts of prayer and divine relationship (e.g., Burnham 2002; Curtis and Eldredge 1997).

Other moments are more complexly constructed. Answering the altar call is described by many congregants as an emotionally overpowering experience accompanied by a conscious loss of bodily control. Congregants remember that God took over their body (this can be described as submission to God's will) and carried or pushed them up to the altar. One congregant said, "It was like someone had lifted me up out of my seat and I pretty much ran down there. I was walking real fast down there. It was like it wasn't me; it was kind of like He was pushing me up there. It was kind of cool. And I was just crying . . . I was weeping. I was crying so much. I was so happy." These memories recall moments that are profoundly emotional, that stand out sharply from everyday experience, that are identifiable by bodily sensations, and that for those who experience them mark God's spiritual reality in their lives.

Relational Practice

At Horizon, the goal of worship is to develop a relationship with God. Developing that relationship is explicitly presented as the process of getting to know a person who is distinct, external, and opaque, and whom you need to get to know in the ordinary way. "Acquaint thyself with God," says a classic evangelical guide; "God is a Person and He can be known in increasing degrees of intimate acquaintance" (Tozzer 1961:116). This is a remarkable characterization, the more so at Horizon because the intimacy is modeled so concretely. God is not only first principle, an awesome, distant judge, a mighty force, although congregants quickly say God is these as well. Nor is He only *spouse,* a formal term. He is *boyfriend* (for women), *buddy* (for men), *close friend* and *pal* (for both). Several congregants explained the process of developing a relationship with God by asking me whether I had a boyfriend. Congregants describe God and Jesus as people you need to meet personally, as if you were out for coffee and had to figure out what the person across the table from you really meant. As one congregant said, "It's just like any relationship. If I had a best friend and we never hung out, where would our friendship be?" Another remarked: "The closer you get to a human being, the better you can get to know them. It's the same with Jesus, the more time I spend reading the Bible, the more time I spend praying, the closer I get to Him and the better I get to know Him."

As that congregant suggests, the two practices thought to create that relationship are Bible reading and prayer. They are taught as two sides of a personal conversation: The worshipper speaks to God through prayer and receives His answer through His Word. But the printed text of the Bible is the same for all, of course. A congregant's relationship with God is supposed to be unique, private, and personal; he or she is meant to understand that this common text is a "love story . . . written to me," as the congregant put it. What seems to enable congregants to experience this personalization of a common text is their ability to identify their own bodily reactions as indicating God's responsiveness as they read the Bible, and as they pray.

At Horizon reading the Bible is modeled as an interactive process, a way to know God better and to learn what he has to say specifically to you in this love letter that he has written. God is understood to be communicating when, as one congregant put it, "a verse just jumps out at me" or when you have a powerful bodily feeling—perhaps you feel peace, or intense joy, or suddenly you feel very tired as if a burden has been lifted and now you can sleep. Another congregant told this story:

> All of a sudden I was in the Book of Isaiah. . . . I felt that the Spirit was lead-ing me. . . . I started reading about what the chosen fast was, which was to break the bonds of wickedness. And something about it made me think about my family members and how I wanted to pray for my family mem-bers. Like that was the answer for me. I really felt that God brought me to that Scripture and that this is where I need to be. . . . It was just such an amazing thing. It was like 2 o'clock in the morning, and I remember read-ing it wide awake, and as soon as I read that it was a relief, and then I felt really sleepy. It was comforting. And so that's an example of how I think God speaks to me through the Word.

She knows that God "speaks" to her because she feels different when she reads a particular scripture: that scripture then becomes what He "says" specifically to her.

Metakinetic states—when God gives you peace, speaks to you outside your head, when you feel that He carries you down to the altar—give a kind of real reality to God because they create the experience of social exchange between opaque individuals, between individuals who cannot read each other's minds and must exchange goods or words in order to become real to each other, in order to know each other's intentions. Adam, then a college undergraduate, told a story about how he didn't understand what a pastor was talking about when he spoke of being filled with the Holy Spirit. Then went on a trip to Acapulco with his friends and got high (as was his wont):

> And this night I was laying on the bed over to the side and all these guys were talking and stuff and I was quiet. I hadn't said a word in like over an hour because I was communing with Him again, and He was telling me all these things. . . . Usually when I'm high I'm kind of tingling and stuff, but this time I felt a wave going through me, though all my body. . . . I felt like I was floating. I was like, *dude*. . . . Overwhelmingly I knew that it was Him and He said, this is Me, filling you up. For the first time it was like I was being filled with the Holy Spirit and I knew what that meant because I was filled with it and I was floating.

He was, of course, high. But at that time, he was often high. He experienced this high as different, as identifiable through bodily sensations, and as proof of God's spiritual presence in his life.

Congregants seem to use more dramatic experiences as a model for their experience of everyday interaction. Later in the conversation, Adam went on to describe the way he experienced prayer on a daily basis: "When we worship we sing songs and I just close my eyes and it's like I'm talking to Him again and communing with Him. *It's the same experience I had in . . . Acapulco.* It's like me and Him talking. He knows me, He knows my name, and we just talk back and forth. . . . It's so cool" (emphasis added). It was not, of course, the same experience: Adam only felt the body wave once. But he uses that dramatic initial experience as his mnemonic marker for his ongoing experience of his relationship with God.

Dramatic experiences like hallucinations do not, in fact, seem to be nearly as central to the process of building that ongoing relationship as metakinetic states like "peace" and emotional responses that congregants come to interpret as God's participation in a daily personal dialogue with them. People say that you learn to know God by having a relationship with Him through His text, and part of that involves just getting to know the kind of "person" He is. Texts and sermons constantly discuss some Biblical passage and ask how God is reacting and why. "How is God feeling at this point?" a book asks when describing the Eden story (Curtis and Eldredge 1997:79). People read Biblical passages over and over, noting their thoughts about particular verses, or what others have said about them. Bibles are accreted with the personal history of reading; the typical congregant's Bible is stuffed with notes and sticky notes, its pages marked up in different colors and papers from past meetings stick out from the unbound sides. But a significant part of developing that relationship with God is learning to *feel* God actually interacting, and that demands that worshippers pay attention to their own bodily states as they read, as memories of previous readings wash over them, as they think about the associations of particular verses for their lives, and as they use those experiences to build a model of who God is for them in their relationship with Him. A guide for Bible Study begins with this how-to advice: "This Bible Study has been created to help you search the Scriptures and draw closer to God as you seek to understand, experience and reflect his grace. . . . Before you begin each chapter, pray for attentiveness to how God is speaking to you through His Word and for sensitivity to His prompting" (Heald 1998:v).

Adam describes his ongoing relationship with God here:

I wake up in the morning and I thank Him for nothing bad happening throughout the night because you never know what can happen. I thank Him for letting me sleep well and I ask that He blesses my day, that it will go okay, and I'm not hurt, and whatever He wants me to learn that day I'll learn. When I talk to Him, He's always listening. He doesn't talk to me verbally like, "Adam, this is God." It's more like a feeling I get inside of me that I know He is listening. Or when I go to bed at night, . . . I'll read some

scripture. Like now I'm studying Acts. . . . I'll pray that He opens my heart
so that I can kind of be transported back into that time so it makes sense to
me. . . . By reading the Bible, that's His Word. That's where He talks to you.

Adam knows from "more of a feeling I get" that God is listening. He is used
to that feeling. From his personal history, he has many memories of prayers
where he spoke to God and felt familiar emotions that made him confident
that God was listening and answering. Adam develops through this a comforting familiarity with who God is in the relationship and who he, Adam,
is in that relationship. And Adam experiences that relationship as intimate
and good.

This is a viscerally intimate God, a God who cares about your haircut,
counsels you on dates, and sits at your side in church. One congregant
talked about the fact that God speaks to her through His word on the page,
but He also interacts in a more personal manner when He "puts a thought"
into her mind. Then she talks to Him the way she talks to anyone—just more
intimately. "Sometimes I feel a real closeness to Jesus . . . I just talk to Jesus
through the day." As another congregant said, "You start to know the fulfillment and comforting feeling that God gives you. Sometimes, sitting in
church, I have this overwhelming feeling that God is speaking to me and sitting right there with me. . . . It's just so much peace." A congregant I call
"Alexis" said that at first it was a great struggle for her to pray. She couldn't
bring herself to kneel. She still can't. But now, prayer is easy for her. I can see
from the way she prays that she has learned to interpret God's presence
through her own bodily experience and she has, I think, learned to integrate
that awareness of an external being with her ideas about who she is and
who God is within the relationship. And, for her, that the relationship is real.
She did not, she said, ask the Lord whether she should paint her toenails.
Then she seemed to hesitate, as if she wondered whether she wouldn't. She
experienced Him as a person deeply involved in her everyday life, like a
husband. And that, she knew, was amazing. "It's a very humbling experience, because you're talking to the Creator, and you're an ant. . . . You know,
He created the human race so that He could have fellowship and He could
have a relationship with us. It's almost like—I wonder whether He's lonely,
or was lonely. . . . It just kind of blows my mind."

Discussion

Why now? What is it about late-20th-century U.S. life that has lead people
to search out psychologically anomalous experiences and to use them meta-
kinetically to build a relationship with God? Two tentative explanations present themselves.

The first is the rise of television and modern media. The literary scholar
Mark Hansen (2000) points out that the radical technological innovations of

our time have fundamentally altered the conditions of our perception. Technology, he argues, changes the very way we experience with our bodies. Television, the virtual reality of the Internet, and the all-encompassing world of music we can create around us seem clearly to be techniques that enhance the experience of absorption, the experience of being caught up in fantasy and distracted from an outer world. We play music to create the shell in which we work or to soothe ourselves from a daily grind. We wear headphones on buses and subways specifically to create a different subjective reality from the frazzled one that sways around us. We park our children in front of videos so that they will be absorbed into their own little universes, and we can cook or clean around them undisturbed. A classic book on trance says that "The trance experience is often best explained . . . as being very much like being absorbed in a good novel: one loses awareness of noises and distractions in the immediate environment and, when the novel is finished, requires a moment of reorientation to the surrounding world" (Spiegel and Spiegel 1978:23). Not all people have that experience of absorption in a good book, and even for those that do, it may not be that often. Television, with its gripping images and mood-setting music now provides that experience throughout they day.

The second is what one might call the attenuation of the U.S. relationship. This is a controversial issue, but a great deal of sociological data suggests that the U.S. experience of relationship is thinner and weaker than in the middle of our last century. Robert Putnam's (2000) massive analysis of the decline of civic engagement in the United States argues powerfully that U.S. citizens have become increasingly disconnected from friends, family, and neighbors through both formal and informal structures. Union membership has declined since the 1950s. PTA membership has plummeted. Fewer people vote in presidential elections (except in the South). And with data collected since 1975, one can see that people have friends to dinner less often (and go out with them no more often): "The practice of entertaining friends has not simply moved outside the house, but seems to be vanishing entirely" (Putnam 2000:100). Time diary studies suggest that informal socializing has declined markedly. Between 1976 and 1997, family vacations (with children between 8 and 17) nose-dived as a family practice, as did "just sitting and talking" together as a family (Putnam 2000:101). Even the "family dinner" is noticeably in decline.

Putnam uses this data to argue that social capital is on the wane in the late-20th- and early-21st-century United States. It also suggests, however, that U.S. citizens might feel lonelier. They are certainly more isolated. More U.S. citizens live alone now than ever before: 25 percent of them compared to eight percent in 1940 and none in our so-called ancestral environment (Wright 1995). It is possible that this increased isolation contributes to a putative increase in mood disorders (Wright 1995), as isolation is a leading risk factor for depression: Isolation certainly increases morbidity and mortality (Cacioppo and Hawkley 2003).

What may be happening is that these congregants and others like them are using an ease with trancelike phenomena supported by our strange new absorbing media and using it to build an intensely intimate relationship with God to protect them against the isolation of modern social life. After all, the most striking consequence of these new religious practices is the closely held sense of a personal relationship with God, and this God is always there, always listening, always responsive, and always with you. In this evangelical setting, congregants learn to use their own bodies to create a sense of the reality of someone external to them. That learning process is complex and subtle: It involves developing a cognitive model of who the person is in the relationship; a metakinetic responsiveness that can be interpreted as the presence of another being; and many repetitions of apparent dialogue through which a person develops an imagined sense of participation and exchange. And the experience of faith for these Christians is a process through which the loneliest of conscious creatures comes to experience themselves as in a world awash with love. It is a remarkable achievement. In the end, Harding's (2000) question—"How does the supernatural become real, known, experienced, and absolutely irrefutable?"—is the deepest question we ask of faith.   ■

NOTES

Acknowledgments. It is a great pleasure to thank Jennifer Cole, Joel Robbins, and Richard Saller for their comments on an earlier draft of this manuscript. Thanks also are due the University of Chicago's active Interdisciplinary Christianities workshop for a lively and productive meeting on the article.

1. All quotations are taken from a series of taped interviews conducted in May 2000; fieldwork spanned a considerably longer period of time.

REFERENCES

Ammerman, Nancy. 1987. *Bible Believers*. New Brunswick, NJ: Rutgers University Press.

Bentall, Richard. 2000. Hallucinatory Experiences. In *Varieties of Anomalous Experience*. Etzel Cardena, Steven Lynn, and Stanley Krippner, eds., 85–120. Washington, DC: American Psychological Association.

Boddy, Janet. 1989. *Wombs and Alien Spirits*. Madison: University of Wisconsin Press.

Brusco, Elizabeth. 1995. *The Reformation of Machismo: Evangelical Conversion and Gender in Colombia*. Austin: University of Texas.

Burnham, Sophy. 2002. *The Path of Prayer*. New York: Viking Compass.

Cacioppo, John, and Louise Hawkley. 2003. Social Isolation and Health, with an Emphasis on Underlying Mechanisms. *Perspectives in Biology and Medicine* 46(suppl. 3):39–52.

Cardena, Etzel, Steven Lynn, and Stanley Krippner, eds. 2000. *Varieties of Anomalous Experience*. Washington, DC: American Psychological Association.

Crapanazano, Vincent. 2001. *Serving the Word*. New York: New Press.

Crocker, Christopher. 1985. *Vital Souls*. Tuscon: University of Arizona Press.

Csordas, Thomas. 1994. *Sacred Self*. Berkeley: University of California Press.

Curtis, Brent, and John Eldredge. 1997. *The Sacred Romance*. Nashville: Nelson.

Desjarlais, Robert. 1992. *Body and Emotion*. Philadelphia: University of Pennsylvania.

Fogel, Robert. 2000. *The Fourth Great Awakening and the Future of Egalitarianism*. Chicago: University of Chicago Press.

Gallup, George, and D. Michael Lindsay. 1999. *Surveying the Religious Landscape*. Harrisburg, PA: Morehouse Publishing.

Gergen, Kenneth. 1991. *The Saturated Self*. New York: Basic.

Harding, Susan. 2000. *The Book of Jerry Falwell*. Princeton: Princeton University Press.

Heald Cynthia. 1998. *Becoming a Woman of Grace*. Nashville, TN: Thomas Nelson.

Kamenetz, Rodger. 1997. Unorthodox Jews Rummage through the Orthodox Tradition. *New York Times Magazine*, December 7:84–86.

Keane, Webb. 1997. Religious Language. *Annual Reviews in Anthropology* 26:47–71.

Kunzendorf, Robert, and Benjamin Wallace, eds. 2000. *Individual Differences in Conscious Experience*. Philadelphia: J. Benjamins.

Lambek, Michael. 1981. *Human Spirits*. Cambridge: University of Cambridge Press.

LeHaye, Tim, and Jerry Jenkins. 1995. *Left Behind: A Novel of the Earth's Last Days*. Wheaton, IL: Tyndale House Publishers.

Lester, Rebecca. In press. *My Name Is Jerusalem*. Berkeley: University of California Press.

Lord, Albert B. 1960. *The Singer of Tales*. Cambridge, MA: Harvard University Press.

Luhrmann, Tanya Marie. 1989. *Persuasions of the Witch's Craft*. Cambridge, MA: Harvard University Press.

Mahmood, Saba. 2001. Rehearsed Spontaneity and the Conventionality of Ritual: Disciplines of Salal. *American Ethnologist* 28(4):827–853.

Martin, John. 1983. Dance as a Means of Communication. In *What Is Dance?* R. Copeland and M. Cohen, eds., 22–27. New York: Oxford University Press.

Miller, Donald. 1997. *Reinventing American Protestantism*. Berkeley: University of California Press.

Mitchell, J. 1997. A Moment with Christ: The Importance of Feelings in the Analysis of Belief. *Journal of the Royal Anthropological Society*, n.s. 3(1):79–94.

Ostling, Richard. 1993. The Church Search. *Time*, April 5:44–49.

Putnam, Robert. 2000. *Bowling Alone*. New York: Simon and Schuster.

Rambo, Lewis. 1993. *Understanding Religious Conversion*. New Haven, CT: Yale University Press.

Robbins, Joel. 2004. Globalization of Pentacostal and Charismatic Christianity. *Annual Review of Christianity* 33.

Roche, Suzanne, and Kevin McConkey. 1990. Absorption: Nature, Assessment and Correlates. *Journal of Personality and Social Psychology* 59:91–101.

Roof, Wade Clark. 1993. *A Generation of Seekers*. San Francisco: HarperCollins.

Spiegel, David, and Herbert Spiegel. 1978. *Trance and Treatment*. Washington, DC: American Psychiatric Press.

Tellegen, Auke. 1981. Practicing the Two Disciplines for Relation and Enlightenment: Comment on "Role of the Feedback Signal in Electromyography Biofeedback: The Relevance of Attention." *Journal of Experimental Psychology: General* 100:217–226.

Tellegen, Auke, and G. Atkinson. 1974. Openness to Absorbing and Self-Altering Experiences ("Absorption"): A Trait Related to Hypnotic Susceptibility. *Journal of Abnormal Psychology* 83:268–277.

Tozzer, Aiden Wilson. 1961. *The Knowledge of the Holy.* San Francisco: Harper San Francisco.

Whitehead, Harriet. 1987. *Renunciation and Reformulation.* Ithaca, NY: Cornell University Press.

Wright, Robert. 1995. The Evolution of Despair. *Time,* August 28:50–57.

Wuthnow, Robert. 1988. *The Restructuring of American Religion.* Princeton: Princeton University Press.

_____. 1994. *Sharing the Journey.* New York: Free Press.

_____. 1998. *After Heaven.* Berkeley: University of California Press.

■ *QUESTIONS FOR MAKING CONNECTIONS WITHIN THE READING* ■

1. Luhrmann's title, "Metakinesis: How God Becomes Intimate in Contemporary U.S. Christianity," promises to explain a process. As it happens, Luhrmann discovers that the process of establishing an intimate relationship with God does not involve metakinesis alone. In your own words, summarize the forces that come into play to foster the establishment of an intimate relationship with God in the community Luhrmann discusses.

2. What is Luhrmann's relationship to the those who attend Horizon Christian Fellowship? To religious faith, more generally? As you reread her essay, underline the words and phrases that you would cite to describe when she is being neutral and when she is being evaluative.

3. What is the relationship of Luhrmann's "discussion" to the preceding sections? Does her understanding of the phenomena she has studied arise from her research, or has her research confirmed an existing hypothesis? If you only read the conclusion, how would Luhrmann's argument be affected?

■ *QUESTIONS FOR WRITING* ■

1. One can imagine another explanation for the phenomena Luhrmann has studied: the emergence of the personal God is a sign of the End Times. Luhrmann, though, doesn't entertain such an explanation; for her, the rise of these faith communities is a cultural fact that warrants study and requires analysis. What is gained when faith is treated in such terms? What, if anything, is lost?

2. It is a common practice in college to ask students to uncover the biases in an assigned reading. In this instance, though, the issue of bias is particularly complex: Luhrmann is a trained anthropologist objectively studying

faith communities, while those in the communities she studies see themselves as maintaining a personal relationship with God. Both sides might well claim to have direct access to an ultimate truth, but an outside observer might argue that both are blind to their own biases. Is it possible to uncover the "facts" of how human culture works, or is the inevitable outcome a set of unverifiable hypotheses? If the study of culture is inevitably subjective, should we give up on it?

■ *QUESTIONS FOR MAKING CONNECTIONS BETWEEN READINGS* ■

1. We might say that in "Waiting for a Jew: Marginal Redemption at the Eighth Street Shul," Jonathan Boyarin also tackles the question of how one establishes a personal religion. But Boyarin is concerned with a rather different community of believers. As he recalls, the religious community of his childhood is today "as obliterated as any *shtetl* in Eastern Europe." In seeking the renewal of such communities, is Boyarin caught up in the same sort of religions experiences that Luhrmann describes? Are the changes in the Jewish community parallel to the ones that concern Luhrmann, or do the two communities move in different directions?

2. Both Luhrmann and Christine Kenneally are centrally concerned with the ways that physical embodiment shapes human thought and expression. But the phenomena they study are separated by millions of years: how humans came to have language versus how Americans at the end of the twentieth century have come to seek out a personal relationship with God. Can Kenneally's argument be usefully extended to the situation Luhrmann studies? That is, can the search for an intimate relationship with God be understood as a gesture? An embodied form of communication? Is the rational element of human nature lost in such a formulation?

AZAR NAFISI

AZAR NAFISI ROSE to international prominence in 2003 with the publication of her critically acclaimed bestseller, *Reading Lolita in Tehran: A Memoir in Books.* A professor of aesthetics, culture, and literature, Dr. Nafisi was expelled from the University of Tehran in 1981 for refusing to comply with the Ayatollah Khomeini's mandate that women wear the *chador*, or Islamic veil. Nafisi resumed teaching again in 1987, but resigned eight years later in protest over the Iranian government's increasingly harsh treatment of women. *Reading Lolita in Tehran* provides an account of the seminar that Nafisi then went on to hold in her home from 1995 to 1997, where seven of her best students joined her to discuss some of the classic texts of Western literature. Nafisi saw the change in her circumstances as an opportunity to fulfill a dream of working with "a group of students who just love literature—who are in it not for the grades, not just to graduate and get a job but just want to read Nabokov and Austen." That Nafisi and her students persisted in this activity, despite the obvious dangers it posed, has come to symbolize for readers around the world how the struggle against totalitarianism is waged on the level of everyday human experience.

Currently a visiting fellow and professorial lecturer at the Foreign Policy Institute of the Johns Hopkins University's School of Advanced International Studies (SAIS) in Washington, D.C., Nafisi directs the Dialogue Project, "a multiyear initiative designed to promote—in a primarily cultural context—the development of democracy and human rights in the Muslim world." At the same time, the Dialogue Project is also engaged in a program of education and outreach designed to provide knowledge about the Muslim world to Western policymakers, scholars, development professionals, media workers, and citizens.

For Nafisi, the freedom to talk and think together in small groups, in a context where the ideas raised and the topics of conversation are not determined in

Nafisi, Azar. Excerpt from *Reading Lolita in Tehran: A Memoir in Books.* New York: Random House, 2003. 3–26.

Biographical information comes from Azar Nafisi's home page at <http://dialogueproject.sais-jhu.edu/anafisi.php>; quotation about the Dialogue Project comes from <http://dialogueproject.sais-jhu.edu/aboutDP.php>.

advance, is the litmus test for a true democracy; to engage in this act, she believes, is to embrace a humanity that transcends national and religious differences.

■ ■

Selections from
Reading Lolita in Tehran
A Memoir in Books

1

In the fall of 1995, after resigning from my last academic post, I decided to indulge myself and fulfill a dream. I chose seven of my best and most committed students and invited them to come to my home every Thursday morning to discuss literature. They were all women—to teach a mixed class in the privacy of my home was too risky, even if we were discussing harmless works of fiction. One persistent male student, although barred from our class, insisted on his rights. So he, Nima, read the assigned material, and on special days he would come to my house to talk about the books we were reading.

I often teasingly reminded my students of Muriel Spark's *The Prime of Miss Jean Brodie* and asked, Which one of you will finally betray me? For I am a pessimist by nature and I was sure at least one would turn against me. Nassrin once responded mischievously, You yourself told us that in the final analysis we are our own betrayers, playing Judas to our own Christ. Manna pointed out that I was no Miss Brodie, and they, well, they were what they were. She reminded me of a warning I was fond of repeating: *do not*, under *any* circumstances, belittle a work of fiction by trying to turn it into a carbon copy of real life; what we search for in fiction is not so much reality but the epiphany of truth. Yet I suppose that if I were to go against my own recommendation and choose a work of fiction that would most resonate with our lives in the Islamic Republic of Iran, it would not be *The Prime of Miss Jean Brodie* or even *1984* but perhaps Nabokov's *Invitation to a Beheading* or better yet, *Lolita*.

A couple of years after we had begun our Thursday-morning seminars, on the last night I was in Tehran, a few friends and students came to say goodbye and to help me pack. When we had deprived the house of all its items, when the objects had vanished and the colors had faded into eight gray suitcases, like errant genies evaporating into their bottles, my students and I stood against the bare white wall of the dining room and took two photographs.

I have the two photographs in front of me now. In the first there are seven women, standing against a white wall. They are, according to the law of the land, dressed in black robes and head scarves, covered except for the oval of their faces and their hands. In the second photograph the same group, in the same position, stands against the same wall. Only they have taken off their coverings. Splashes of color separate one from the next. Each has become distinct through the color and style of her clothes, the color and the length of her hair; not even the two who are still wearing their head scarves look the same.

The one to the far right in the second photograph is our poet, Manna, in a white T-shirt and jeans. She made poetry out of things most people cast aside. The photograph does not reflect the peculiar opacity of Manna's dark eyes, a testament to her withdrawn and private nature.

Next to Manna is Mahshid, whose long black scarf clashes with her delicate features and retreating smile. Mahshid was good at many things, but she had a certain daintiness about her and we took to calling her "my lady." Nassrin used to say that more than defining Mahshid, we had managed to add another dimension to the word *lady.* Mahshid is very sensitive. She's like porcelain, Yassi once told me, easy to crack. That's why she appears fragile to those who don't know her too well; but woe to whoever offends her. As for me, Yassi continued good-naturedly, I'm like good old plastic; I won't crack no matter what you do with me.

Yassi was the youngest in our group. She is the one in yellow, bending forward and bursting with laughter. We used to teasingly call her our comedian. Yassi was shy by nature, but certain things excited her and made her lose her inhibitions. She had a tone of voice that gently mocked and questioned not just others but herself as well.

I am the one in brown, standing next to Yassi, with one arm around her shoulders. Directly behind me stands Azin, my tallest student, with her long blond hair and a pink T-shirt. She is laughing like the rest of us. Azin's smiles never looked like smiles; they appeared more like preludes to an irrepressible and nervous hilarity. She beamed in that peculiar fashion even when she was describing her latest trouble with her husband. Always outrageous and outspoken, Azin relished the shock value of her actions and comments, and often clashed with Mahshid and Manna. We nicknamed her the wild one.

On my other side is Mitra, who was perhaps the calmest among us. Like the pastel colors of her paintings, she seemed to recede and fade into a paler register. Her beauty was saved from predictability by a pair of miraculous dimples, which she could and did use to manipulate many an unsuspecting victim into bending to her will.

Sanaz, who, pressured by family and society, vacillated between her desire for independence and her need for approval, is holding on to Mitra's arm. We are all laughing. And Nima, Manna's husband and my one true literary critic—if only he had had the perseverance to finish the brilliant essays he started to write—is our invisible partner, the photographer.

There was one more: Nassrin. She is not in the photographs—she didn't make it to the end. Yet my tale would be incomplete without those who could not or did not remain with us. Their absences persist, like an acute pain that seems to have no physical source. This is Tehran for me: its absences were more real than its presences.

When I see Nassrin in my mind's eye, she's slightly out of focus, blurred, somehow distant. I've combed through the photographs my students took with me over the years and Nassrin is in many of them, but always hidden behind something—a person, a tree. In one, I am standing with eight of my students in the small garden facing our faculty building, the scene of so many farewell photographs over the years. In the background stands a sheltering willow tree. We are laughing, and in one corner, from behind the tallest student, Nassrin peers out, like an imp intruding roguishly on a scene it was not invited to. In another I can barely make out her face in the small V space behind two other girls' shoulders. In this one she looks absentminded; she is frowning, as if unaware that she is being photographed.

How can I describe Nassrin? I once called her the Cheshire cat, appearing and disappearing at unexpected turns in my academic life. The truth is I can't describe her: she was her own definition. One can only say that Nassrin was Nassrin.

For nearly two years, almost every Thursday morning, rain or shine, they came to my house, and almost every time, I could not get over the shock of seeing them shed their mandatory veils and robes and burst into color. When my students came into that room, they took off more than their scarves and robes. Gradually, each one gained an outline and a shape, becoming her own inimitable self. Our world in that living room with its window framing my beloved Elburz Mountains became our sanctuary, our self-contained universe, mocking the reality of black-scarved, timid faces in the city that sprawled below.

The theme of the class was the relation between fiction and reality. We read Persian classical literature, such as the tales of our own lady of fiction, Scheherazade, from *A Thousand and One Nights,* along with Western classics—*Pride and Prejudice, Madame Bovary, Daisy Miller, The Dean's December* and, yes, *Lolita.* As I write the title of each book, memories whirl in with the wind to disturb the quiet of this fall day in another room in another country.

Here and now in that other world that cropped up so many times in our discussions, I sit and reimagine myself and my students, my girls as I came to call them, reading *Lolita* in a deceptively sunny room in Tehran. But to steal the words from Humbert, the poet/criminal of *Lolita,* I need you, the reader, to imagine us, for we won't really exist if you don't. Against the tyranny of time and politics, imagine us the way we sometimes didn't dare to imagine ourselves: in our most private and secret moments, in the most extraordinarily ordinary instances of life, listening to music, falling in love, walking down the shady streets or reading *Lolita* in Tehran. And then imagine us again with all this confiscated, driven underground, taken away from us.

If I write about Nabokov today, it is to celebrate our reading of Nabokov in Tehran, against all odds. Of all his novels I choose the one I taught last, and the one that is connected to so many memories. It is of *Lolita* that I want to write, but right now there is no way I can write about that novel without also writing about Tehran. This, then, is the story of *Lolita* in Tehran, how *Lolita* gave a different color to Tehran and how Tehran helped redefine Nabokov's novel, turning it into this *Lolita,* our *Lolita.*

2

And so it happened that one Thursday in early September we gathered in my living room for our first meeting. Here they come, one more time. First I hear the bell, a pause, and the closing of the street door. Then I hear footsteps coming up the winding staircase and past my mother's apartment. As I move towards the front door, I register a piece of sky through the side window. Each girl, as soon as she reaches the door, takes off her robe and scarf, sometimes shaking her head from side to side. She pauses before entering the room. Only there is no room, just the teasing void of memory.

More than any other place in our home, the living room was symbolic of my nomadic and borrowed life. Vagrant pieces of furniture from different times and places were thrown together, partly out of financial necessity, and partly because of my eclectic taste. Oddly, these incongruous ingredients created a symmetry that the other, more deliberately furnished rooms in the apartment lacked.

My mother would go crazy each time she saw the paintings leaning against the wall and the vases of flowers on the floor and the curtainless windows, which I refused to dress until I was finally reminded that this was an Islamic country and windows needed to be dressed. I don't know if you really belong to me, she would lament. Didn't I raise you to be orderly and organized? Her tone was serious, but she had repeated the same complaint for so many years that by now it was an almost tender ritual. Azi—that was my nickname—Azi, she would say, you are a grown-up lady now; act like one. Yet there was something in her tone that kept me young and fragile and obstinate, and still, when in memory I hear her voice, I know I never lived up to her expectations. I never did become the lady she tried to will me into being.

That room, which I never paid much attention to at that time, has gained a different status in my mind's eye now that it has become the precious object of memory. It was a spacious room, sparsely furnished and decorated. At one corner was the fireplace, a fanciful creation of my husband, Bijan.

There was a love seat against one wall, over which I had thrown a lace cover, my mother's gift from long ago. A pale peach couch faced the window, accompanied by two matching chairs and a big square glass-topped iron table.

My place was always in the chair with its back to the window, which opened onto a wide cul-de-sac called Azar. Opposite the window was the former American Hospital, once small and exclusive, now a noisy, overcrowded medical facility for wounded and disabled veterans of the war. On "weekends"—Thursdays and Fridays in Iran—the small street was crowded with hospital visitors who came as if for a picnic, with sandwiches and children. The neighbor's front yard, his pride and joy, was the main victim of their assaults, especially in summer, when they helped themselves to his beloved roses. We could hear the sound of children shouting, crying and laughing, and, mingled in, their mothers' voices, also shouting, calling out their children's names and threatening them with punishments. Sometimes a child or two would ring our doorbell and run away, repeating their perilous exercise at intervals.

From our second-story apartment—my mother occupied the first floor, and my brother's apartment, on the third floor, was often empty, since he had left for England—we could see the upper branches of a generous tree and, in the distance, over the buildings, the Elburz Mountains. The street, the hospital and its visitors were censored out of sight. We felt their presence only through the disembodied noises emanating from below.

I could not see my favorite mountains from where I sat, but opposite my chair, on the far wall of the dining room, was an antique oval mirror, a gift from my father, and in its reflection, I could see the mountains capped with snow, even in summer, and watch the trees change color. That censored view intensified my impression that the noise came not from the street below but from some far-off place, a place whose persistent hum was our only link to the world we refused, for those few hours, to acknowledge.

That room, for all of us, became a place of transgression. What a wonderland it was! Sitting around the large coffee table covered with bouquets of flowers, we moved in and out of the novels we read. Looking back, I am amazed at how much we learned without even noticing it. We were, to borrow from Nabokov, to experience how the ordinary pebble of ordinary life could be transformed into a jewel through the magic eye of fiction.

3

Six A.M.: the first day of class. I was already up. Too excited to eat breakfast, I put the coffee on and then took a long, leisurely shower. The water caressed my neck, my back, my legs, and I stood there both rooted and light. For the first time in many years, I felt a sense of anticipation that was not marred by tension: I would not need to go through the torturous rituals that had marked my days when I taught at the university—rituals governing what I was forced to wear, how I was expected to act, the gestures I had to remember to control. For this class, I would prepare differently.

Life in the Islamic Republic was as capricious as the month of April, when short periods of sunshine would suddenly give way to showers and storms. It was unpredictable: the regime would go through cycles of some tolerance, followed by a crackdown. Now, after a period of relative calm and so-called liberalization, we had again entered a time of hardships. Universities had once more become the targets of attack by the cultural purists who were busy imposing stricter sets of laws, going so far as to segregate men and women in classes and punishing disobedient professors.

The University of Allameh Tabatabai, where I had been teaching since 1987, had been singled out as the most liberal university in Iran. It was rumored that someone in the Ministry of Higher Education had asked, rhetorically, if the faculty at Allameh thought they lived in Switzerland. *Switzerland* had somehow become a byword for Western laxity: any program or action that was deemed un-Islamic was reproached with a mocking reminder that Iran was by no means Switzerland.

The pressure was hardest on the students. I felt helpless as I listened to their endless tales of woe. Female students were being penalized for running up the stairs when they were late for classes, for laughing in the hallways, for talking to members of the opposite sex. One day Sanaz had barged into class near the end of the session, crying. In between bursts of tears, she explained that she was late because the female guards at the door, finding a blush in her bag, had tried to send her home with a reprimand.

Why did I stop teaching so suddenly? I had asked myself this question many times. Was it the declining quality of the university? The ever-increasing indifference among the remaining faculty and students? The daily struggle against arbitrary rules and restrictions?

I smiled as I rubbed the coarse loofah over my skin, remembering the reaction of the university officials to my letter of resignation. They had harassed and limited me in all manner of ways, monitoring my visitors, controlling my actions, refusing a long-overdue tenure; and when I resigned, they infuriated me by suddenly commiserating and by refusing to accept my resignation. The students had threatened to boycott classes, and it was of some satisfaction to me to find out later that despite threats of reprisals, they in fact did boycott my replacement. Everyone thought I would break down and eventually return.

It took two more years before they finally accepted my resignation. I remember a friend told me, You don't understand their mentality. They won't accept your resignation because they don't think you have the right to quit. *They* are the ones who decide how long you should stay and when you should be dispensed with. More than anything else, it was this arbitrariness that had become unbearable.

What will you do? my friends had asked. Will you just stay home now? Well, I could write another book, I would tell them. But in truth I had no definite plans. I was still dealing with the aftershocks of a book on Nabokov I had just published, and only vague ideas, like vapors, formed when I turned to consider the shape of my next book. I could, for a while at least, continue the pleasant task of studying Persian classics, but one particular project, a notion I had been nurturing for years, was uppermost in my mind. For a long time I had dreamt of creating a special class, one that would give me the freedoms denied me in the classes I taught in the Islamic Republic. I wanted to teach a handful of selected students wholly committed to the study of literature, students who were not handpicked by the government, who had not chosen English literature simply because they had not been accepted in other fields or because they thought an English degree would be a good career move.

Teaching in the Islamic Republic, like any other vocation, was subservient to politics and subject to arbitrary rules. Always, the joy of teaching was marred by diversions and considerations forced on us by the regime—how well could one teach when the main concern of university officials was not the quality of one's work but the color of one's lips, the subversive potential of a single strand of hair? Could one really concentrate on one's job when what preoccupied the faculty was how to excise the word *wine* from a Hemingway story, when they decided not to teach Brontë because she appeared to condone adultery?

I was reminded of a painter friend who had started her career by depicting scenes from life, mainly deserted rooms, abandoned houses and discarded photographs of women. Gradually, her work became more abstract, and in her last exhibition, her paintings were splashes of rebellious color, like the two in my living room, dark patches with little droplets of blue. I asked about her progress from modern realism to abstraction. Reality has become so intolerable, she said, so bleak, that all I can paint now are the colors of my dreams.

The colors of my dreams, I repeated to myself, stepping out of the shower and onto the cool tiles. I liked that. How many people get a chance to paint the colors of their dreams? I put on my oversize bathrobe—it felt good to move from the security of the embracing water to the protective cover of a bathrobe wrapped around my body. I walked barefoot into the kitchen, poured some coffee into my favorite mug, the one with red strawberries, and sat down forgetfully on the divan in the hall.

This class was the color of my dreams. It entailed an active withdrawal from a reality that had turned hostile. I wanted very badly to hold on to my rare mood of jubilance and optimism. For in the back of my mind, I didn't know what awaited me at the end of this project. You are aware, a friend had said, that you are more and more withdrawing into yourself, and now that you have cut your relations with the university, your whole contact with the outside world will be mainly restricted to one room. Where will you go from here? he had asked. Withdrawal into one's dreams could be dangerous, I reflected, padding into the bedroom to change; this I had learned from Nabokov's crazy dreamers, like Kinbote and Humbert.

In selecting my students, I did not take into consideration their ideological or religious backgrounds. Later, I would count it as the class's great achievement that such a mixed group, with different and at times conflicting backgrounds, personal as well as religious and social, remained so loyal to its goals and ideals.

One reason for my choice of these particular girls was the peculiar mixture of fragility and courage I sensed in them. They were what you would call loners, who did not belong to any particular group or sect. I admired their ability to survive not despite but in some ways because of their solitary lives. We can call the class "a space of our own," Manna had suggested, a sort of communal version of Virginia Woolf's room of her own.

I spent longer than usual choosing my clothes that first morning, trying on different outfits, until I finally settled on a red-striped shirt and black corduroy jeans. I applied my makeup with care and put on bright red lipstick. As I fastened my small gold earrings, I suddenly panicked. What if it doesn't work? What if they won't come?

Don't, don't do that! Suspend all fears for the next five or six hours at least. Please, please, I pleaded with myself, putting on my shoes and going into the kitchen.

4

I was making tea when the doorbell rang. I was so preoccupied with my thoughts that I didn't hear it the first time. I opened the door to Mahshid. I thought you weren't home, she said, handing me a bouquet of white and yellow daffodils. As she was taking off her black robe, I told her, There are no men in the house—you can take that off, too. She hesitated before uncoiling her long black scarf. Mahshid and Yassi both observed the veil, but Yassi of late had become more relaxed in the way she wore her scarf. She tied it with a loose knot under her throat, her dark brown hair, untidily parted in the middle, peeping out from underneath. Mahshid's hair, however, was meticulously styled and curled under. Her short bangs gave her a strangely old-fashioned look that struck me as more European than Iranian. She wore a deep blue jacket over her white shirt, with a huge yellow butterfly embroidered on its right side. I pointed to the butterfly: did you wear this in honor of Nabokov?

I no longer remember when Mahshid first began to take my classes at the university. Somehow, it seems as if she had always been there. Her father, a devout Muslim, had been an ardent supporter of the revolution. She wore the scarf even before the revolution, and in her class diary, she wrote about the lonely mornings when she went to a fashionable girls' college, where she felt neglected and ignored—ironically, because of her then-conspicuous attire. After the revolution, she was jailed for five years because of her affiliation with a dissident religious organization and banned from continuing her education for two years after she was out of jail.

I imagine her in those pre-revolutionary days, walking along the uphill street leading to the college on countless sunny mornings. I see her walking alone, her head to the ground. Then, as now, she did not enjoy the day's brilliance. I say "then, as now" because the revolution that imposed the scarf on others did not relieve Mahshid of her loneliness. Before the revolution, she could in a sense take pride in her isolation. At that time, she had worn the scarf as a testament to her faith. Her decision was a voluntary act. When the revolution forced the scarf on others, her action became meaningless.

Mahshid is proper in the true sense of the word: she has grace and a certain dignity. Her skin is the color of moonlight, and she has almond-shaped eyes and jet-black hair. She wears pastel colors and is soft-spoken. Her pious background should have shielded her, but it didn't. I cannot imagine her in jail.

Over the many years I have known Mahshid, she has rarely alluded to her jail experiences, which left her with a permanently impaired kidney. One day in class, as we were talking about our daily terrors and nightmares, she mentioned that her jail memories visited her from time to time and that she had still not found a way to articulate them. But, she added, everyday life does not have fewer horrors than prison.

I asked Mahshid if she wanted some tea. Always considerate, she said she'd rather wait for the others and apologized for being a little early. Can I help? she asked. There's really nothing to help with. Make yourself at home, I told her as I stepped into the kitchen with the flowers and searched for a vase. The bell rang again. I'll get it, Mahshid cried out from the living room. I heard laughter; Manna and Yassi had arrived.

Manna came into the kitchen holding a small bouquet of roses. It's from Nima, she said. He wants to make you feel bad about excluding him from the class. He says he'll carry a bouquet of roses and march in front of your house during class hours, in protest. She was beaming; a few brief sparkles flashed in her eyes and died down again.

Putting the pastries onto a large tray, I asked Manna if she envisioned the words to her poems in colors. Nabokov writes in his autobiography that he and his mother saw the letters of the alphabet in color, I explained. He says of himself that he is a painterly writer.

The Islamic Republic coarsened my taste in colors, Manna said, fingering the discarded leaves of her roses. I want to wear outrageous colors, like shocking pink or tomato red. I feel too greedy for colors to see them in carefully chosen words of poetry. Manna was one of those people who would experience ecstasy but not happiness. Come here, I want to show you something, I said, leading her into our bedroom. When I was very young, I was obsessed with the colors of places and things my father told me about in his nightly stories. I wanted to know the color of Scheherazade's dress, her bedcover, the color of the genie and the magic lamp, and once I asked him about the color of paradise. He said it could be any color I wanted it to be. That was not enough. Then one day when we had guests and I was eating my soup in the dining room, my eyes fell on a painting I had seen on the wall ever since I could remember, and I instantly knew the color of my paradise. And here it is, I said, proudly pointing to a small oil painting in an old wooden frame: a green landscape of lush, leathery leaves with two birds, two deep red apples, a golden pear and a touch of blue.

My paradise is swimming-pool blue! Manna shot in, her eyes still glued to the painting. We lived in a large garden that belonged to my grandparents, she said, turning to me. You know the old Persian gardens, with their fruit trees, peaches, apples, cherries, persimmons and a willow or two. My best memories are of swimming in our huge irregularly shaped swimming pool. I was a swimming champion at our school, a fact my dad was very proud of. About a year after the revolution, my father died of a heart attack, and then the government confiscated our house and our garden and we moved into an apartment. I never swam again. My dream is at the bottom of that pool. I have a recurring dream of diving in to retrieve something of my father's memory and my childhood, she said as we walked to the living room, for the doorbell had rung again.

Azin and Mitra had arrived together. Azin was taking off her black kimonolike robe—Japanese-style robes were all the rage at the time—revealing a white peasant blouse that made no pretense of covering her shoulders, big golden earrings and pink lipstick. She had a branch of small yellow orchids—from Mitra and myself, she said in that special tone of hers that I can only describe as a flirtatious pout.

Nassrin came in next. She had brought two boxes of nougats: presents from Isfahan, she declared. She was dressed in her usual uniform—navy robe, navy scarf and black heelless shoes. When I had last seen her in class, she was wearing a huge black chador, revealing only the oval of her face and two restless hands, which, when she was not writing or doodling, were constantly in motion, as if trying to escape the confines of the thick black cloth. More recently, she had exchanged the chador for long, shapeless robes in navy, black or dark brown, with thick matching scarves that hid her hair and framed her face. She had a small, pale face, skin so transparent you could count the veins, full eyebrows, long lashes, lively eyes (brown), a small straight nose and an angry mouth: an unfinished miniature by some master who had suddenly been called away from his job and left the meticulously drawn face imprisoned in a careless splash of dark color.

We heard the sound of screeching tires and sudden brakes. I looked out the window: a small old Renault, cream-colored, had pulled up on the curb. Behind the wheel, a young man with fashionable sunglasses and a defiant profile rested his black-sleeved arm on the curve of the open window and gave the impression that he was driving a Porsche. He was staring straight in front of him as he talked to the woman beside him. Only once did he turn his head to his right, with what I could guess was a cross expression, and that was when the woman got out of the car and he angrily slammed the door behind her. As she walked to our front door, he threw his head out and shouted a few words, but she did not turn back to answer. The old Renault was Sanaz's; she had bought it with money saved from her job.

I turned towards the room, blushing for Sanaz. That must be the obnoxious brother, I thought. Seconds later the doorbell rang and I heard Sanaz's hurried steps and opened the door to her. She looked harassed, as if she had been running from a stalker or a thief. As soon as she saw me, she adjusted her face into a smile and said breathlessly: I hope I am not too late?

There were two very important men dominating Sanaz's life at the time. The first was her brother. He was nineteen years old and had not yet finished high school and was the darling of their parents, who, after two girls, one of whom had died at the age of three, had finally been blessed with a son. He was spoiled, and his one obsession in life was Sanaz. He had taken to proving his masculinity by spying on her, listening to her phone conversations, driving her car around and monitoring her actions. Her parents had tried to appease Sanaz and begged her, as the older sister, to be patient and understanding, to use her motherly instincts to see him through this difficult period.

The other was her childhood sweetheart, a boy she had known since she was eleven. Their parents were best friends, and their families spent most of their time and vacations together. Sanaz and Ali seemed to have been in love forever. Their parents encouraged this union and called it a match made in heaven. When Ali went away to England six years ago, his mother took to calling Sanaz his bride. They wrote to each other, sent photographs, and recently, when the number of Sanaz's suitors increased, there were talks of engagement and a reunion in Turkey, where Iranians did not require entrance visas. Any day now it might happen, an event Sanaz looked forward to with some fear and trepidation.

I had never seen Sanaz without her uniform, and stood there almost transfixed as she took off her robe and scarf. She was wearing an orange T-shirt tucked into tight jeans and brown boots, yet the most radical transformation was the mass of shimmering dark brown hair that now framed her face. She shook her magnificent hair from side to side, a gesture that I later noticed was a habit with her; she would toss her head and run her fingers through her hair every once in a while, as if making sure that her most prized possession was still there. Her features looked softer and more radiant—the black scarf she wore in public made her small face look emaciated and almost hard.

I'm sorry I'm a little late, she said breathlessly, running her fingers through her hair. My brother insisted on driving me, and he refused to wake up on time. He never gets up before ten, but he wanted to know where I was going. I might be off on some secret tryst, you know, a date or something.

I have been worrying in case any of you would get into trouble for this class, I said, inviting them all to take their seats around the table in the living room. I hope your parents and spouses feel comfortable with our arrangement.

Nassrin, who was wandering around the room, inspecting the paintings as if seeing them for the first time, paused to say offhandedly, I mentioned the idea very casually to my father, just to test his reaction, and he vehemently disapproved.

How did you convince him to let you come? I asked. I lied, she said. You lied? What else can one do with a person who's so dictatorial he won't let his daughter, at *this age,* go to an all-female literature class? Besides, isn't this how we treat the regime? Can we tell the Revolutionary Guards the truth? We lie to them; we hide our satellite dishes. We tell them we don't have illegal books and alcohol in our houses. Even my venerable father lies to them when the safety of his family is at stake, Nassrin added defiantly.

What if he calls me to check on you? I said, half teasingly. He won't. I gave a brilliant alibi. I said Mahshid and I had volunteered to help translate Islamic texts into English. And he believed you? Well, he had no reason not to. I hadn't lied to him before—not really—and it was what he wanted to believe. And he trusts Mahshid completely.

So if he calls me, I should lie to him? I persisted. It's up to you, Nassrin said after a pause, looking down at her twisting hands. Do *you* think you should tell him? By now I could hear a note of desperation in her voice. Am I getting you into trouble?

Nassrin always acted so confident that sometimes I forgot how vulnerable she really was under that tough-girl act. Of course I would respect your confidence, I said more gently. As you said, you are a big girl. You know what you're doing.

I had settled into my usual chair, opposite the mirror, where the mountains had come to stay. It is strange to look into a mirror and see not yourself but a view so distant from you. Mahshid, after some hesitation, had taken the chair to my right. On the couch, Manna settled to the far right and Azin to the far left; they instinctively kept their distance. Sanaz and Mitra were perched on the love seat, their heads close together as they whispered and giggled.

At this point Yassi and Nassrin came in and looked around for seats. Azin patted the empty part of the couch, inviting Yassi with her hand. Yassi hesitated for a moment and then slid between Azin and Manna. She slumped into place and seemed to leave little room for her two companions, who sat upright and a little stiff in their respective corners. Without her robe, she looked a little overweight, as if she had not as yet lost her baby fat. Nassrin had gone to the dining room in search of a chair. We can squeeze you in here, said Manna. No, thank you, I actually prefer straight-backed chairs. When she returned, she placed her chair between the couch and Mahshid.

They kept that arrangement, faithfully, to the end. It became representative of their emotional boundaries and personal relations. And so began our first class.

5

"Upsilamba!" I heard Yassi exclaim as I entered the dining room with a tray of tea. Yassi loved playing with words. Once she told us that her obsession with words was pathological. As soon as I discover a new word, I have to use it, she said, like someone who buys an evening gown and is so eager that she wears it to the movies, or to lunch.

Let me pause and rewind the reel to retrace the events leading us to Yassi's exclamation. This was our first session. All of us had been nervous and inarticulate. We were used to meeting in public, mainly in classrooms and in lecture halls. The girls had their separate relationships with me, but except for Nassrin and Mahshid, who were intimate, and a certain friendship between Mitra and Sanaz, the rest were not close; in many cases, in fact, they would never have chosen to be friends. The collective intimacy made them uncomfortable.

I had explained to them the purpose of the class: to read, discuss and respond to works of fiction. Each would have a private diary, in which she should record her responses to the novels, as well as ways in which these works and their discussions related to her personal and social experiences. I explained that I had chosen them for this class because they seemed dedicated to the study of literature. I mentioned that one of the criteria for the books I had chosen was their authors' faith in the critical and almost magical power of literature, and reminded them of the nineteen-year-old Nabokov, who, during the Russian Revolution, would not allow himself to be diverted by the sound of bullets. He kept on writing his solitary poems while he heard the guns and saw the bloody fights from his window. Let us see, I said, whether seventy years later our disinterested faith will reward us by transforming the gloomy reality created of this other revolution.

The first work we discussed was *A Thousand and One Nights,* the familiar tale of the cuckolded king who slew successive virgin wives as revenge for his queen's betrayal, and whose murderous hand was finally stayed by the entrancing storyteller Scheherazade. I formulated certain general questions for them to consider, the most central of which was how these great works of imagination could help us in our present trapped situation as women. We were not looking for blueprints, for an easy solution, but we did hope to find a link between the open spaces the novels provided and the closed ones we were confined to. I remember reading to my girls Nabokov's claim that "readers were born free and ought to remain free."

What had most intrigued me about the frame story of *A Thousand and One Nights* were the three kinds of women it portrayed—all victims of a king's unreasonable rule. Before Scheherazade enters the scene, the women in the story are divided into those who betray and then are killed (the queen) and those who are killed before they have a chance to betray (the virgins). The virgins, who, unlike Scheherazade, have no voice in the story, are mostly ignored by the critics. Their silence, however, is significant. They surrender their virginity, and their lives, without resistance or protest. They do not quite exist, because they leave no trace in their anonymous death. The queen's infidelity does not rob the king of his absolute authority; it throws him off balance. Both types of women—the queen and the virgins—tacitly accept the king's public authority by acting within the confines of his domain and by accepting its arbitrary laws.

Scheherazade breaks the cycle of violence by choosing to embrace different terms of engagement. She fashions her universe not through physical force, as does the king, but through imagination and reflection. This gives her the courage to risk her life and sets her apart from the other characters in the tale.

Our edition of *A Thousand and One Nights* came in six volumes. I, luckily, had bought mine before it was banned and sold only on the black market, for exorbitant prices. I divided the volumes among the girls and asked them, for the next session, to classify the tales according to the types of women who played central roles in the stories.

Once I'd given them their assignment, I asked them each to tell the rest of us why they had chosen to spend their Thursday mornings here, discussing Nabokov and Jane Austen. Their answers were brief and forced. In order to break the ice, I suggested the calming distraction of cream puffs and tea.

This brings us to the moment when I enter the dining room with eight glasses of tea on an old and unpolished silver tray. Brewing and serving tea is an aesthetic ritual in Iran, performed several times a day. We serve tea in transparent glasses, small and shapely, the most popular of which is called slim-waisted: round and full at the top, narrow in the middle and round and full at the bottom. The color of the tea and its subtle aroma are an indication of the brewer's skill.

I step into the dining room with eight slim-waisted glasses whose honey-colored liquid trembles seductively. At this point, I hear Yassi shout triumphantly, "Upsilamba!" She throws the word at me like a ball, and I take a mental leap to catch it.

Upsilamba!—the word carries me back to the spring of 1994, when four of my girls and Nima were auditing a class I was teaching on the twentieth-century novel. The class's favorite book was Nabokov's *Invitation to a Beheading.* In this novel, Nabokov differentiates Cincinnatus C., his imaginative and lonely hero, from those around him through his originality in a society where uniformity is not only the norm but also the law. Even as a child, Nabokov tells us, Cincinnatus appreciated the freshness and beauty of language, while other children "understood each other at the first word, since they had no words that would end in an unexpected way, perhaps in some archaic letter, an upsilamba, becoming a bird or catapult with wondrous consequences."

No one in class had bothered to ask what the word meant. No one, that is, who was properly taking the class—for many of my old students just stayed on and sat in on my classes long after their graduation. Often, they were more interested and worked harder than my regular students, who were taking the class for credit. Thus it was that those who audited the class—including Nassrin, Manna, Nima, Mahshid and Yassi—had one day gathered in my office to discuss this and a number of other questions.

I decided to play a little game with the class, to test their curiosity. On the midterm exam, one of the questions was "Explain the significance of the word *upsilamba* in the context of *Invitation to a Beheading.* What does the word mean, and how does it relate to the main theme of the novel?" Except for four or five students, no one had any idea what I could possibly mean, a point I did not forget to remind them of every once in a while throughout the rest of that term.

The truth was that *upsilamba* was one of Nabokov's fanciful creations, possibly a word he invented out of *upsilon,* the twentieth letter in the Greek alphabet, and *lambda,* the eleventh. So that first day in our private class, we let our minds play again and invented new meanings of our own.

I said I associated *upsilamba* with the impossible joy of a suspended leap. Yassi, who seemed excited for no particular reason, cried out that she always thought it could be the name of a dance—you know, "C'mon, baby, do the Upsilamba with me." I proposed that for the next time, they each write a sentence or two explaining what the word meant to them.

Manna suggested that *upsilamba* evoked the image of small silver fish leaping in and out of a moonlit lake. Nima added in parentheses, Just so you won't forget me, although you have barred me from your class: an upsilamba to you too! For Azin it was a sound, a melody. Mahshid described an image of three girls jumping rope and shouting "Upsilamba!" with each leap. For Sanaz, the word was a small African boy's secret magical name. Mitra wasn't sure why the word reminded her of the paradox of a blissful sigh. And to Nassrin it was the magic code that opened the door to a secret cave filled with treasures.

Upsilamba became part of our increasing repository of coded words and expressions, a repository that grew over time until gradually we had created a secret language of our own. That word became a symbol, a sign of that vague sense of joy, the tingle in the spine Nabokov expected his readers to feel in the act of reading fiction; it was a sensation that separated the good readers, as he called them, from the ordinary ones. It also became the code word that opened the secret cave of remembrance.

6

In his foreword to the English edition of *Invitation to a Beheading* (1959), Nabokov reminds the reader that his novel does not offer *"tout pour tous."* Nothing of the kind. "It is," he claims, "a violin in the void." And yet, he goes on to say, "I know . . . a few readers who will jump up, ruffling their hair." Well, absolutely. The original version, Nabokov tells us, was published in installments in 1935. Almost six decades later, in a world unknown and presumably unknowable to Nabokov, in a forlorn living room with windows looking out towards distant white-capped mountains, time and again I would stand witness to the unlikeliest of readers as they lost themselves in a madness of hair-ruffling.

Invitation to a Beheading begins with the announcement that its fragile hero, Cincinnatus C., has been sentenced to death for the crime of "gnostic turpitude": in a place where all citizens are required to be transparent, he is opaque. The principal characteristic of this world is its arbitrariness; the condemned man's only privilege is to know the time of his death—but the executioners keep even this from him, turning every day into a day of execution. As the story unfolds, the reader discovers with increasing discomfort the artificial texture of this strange place. The moon from the window is fake; so is the spider in the corner, which, according to convention, must become the prisoner's faithful companion. The director of the jail, the jailer and the defense lawyer are all the same man, and keep changing places. The most important character, the executioner, is first introduced to the prisoner under another name and as a fellow prisoner: M'sieur Pierre. The executioner and the condemned man must learn to love each other and cooperate in the act of execution, which will be celebrated in a gaudy feast. In this staged world, Cincinnatus's only window to another universe is his writing.

The world of the novel is one of empty rituals. Every act is bereft of substance and significance, and even death becomes a spectacle for which the good citizens buy tickets. It is only through these empty rituals that brutality becomes possible. In another Nabokov novel, *The Real Life of Sebastian Knight,* Sebastian's brother discovers two seemingly incongruous pictures in his dead brother's library: a pretty, curly-haired child playing with a dog and a Chinese man in the act of being beheaded. The two pictures remind us of the close relation between banality and brutality. Nabokov had a special Russian term for this: *poshlust.*

Poshlust, Nabokov explains, "is not only the obviously trashy but mainly the falsely important, the falsely beautiful, the falsely clever, the falsely attractive." Yes, there are many examples you can bring from everyday life, from the politicians' sugary speeches to certain writers' proclamations to chickens. Chickens? You know, the ones the street vendors sell nowadays—if you lived in Tehran, you couldn't possibly miss them. The ones they dip in paint—shocking pink, brilliant red or turquoise blue—in order to make them more attractive. Or the plastic flowers, the bright pink-and-blue artificial gladiolas carted out at the university both for mourning and for celebration.

What Nabokov creates for us in *Invitation to a Beheading* is not the actual physical pain and torture of a totalitarian regime but the nightmarish quality of living in an atmosphere of perpetual dread. Cincinnatus C. is frail, he is passive, he is a hero without knowing or acknowledging it: he fights with his instincts, and his acts of writing are his means of escape. He is a hero because he refuses to become like all the rest.

Unlike in other utopian novels, the forces of evil here are not omnipotent; Nabokov shows us their frailty as well. They are ridiculous and they can be defeated, and this does not lessen the tragedy—the waste. *Invitation to a Beheading* is written from the point of view of the victim, one who ultimately sees the absurd sham of his persecutors and who must retreat into himself in order to survive.

Those of us living in the Islamic Republic of Iran grasped both the tragedy and absurdity of the cruelty to which we were subjected. We had to poke fun at our own misery in order to survive. We also instinctively recognized poshlust—not just in others, but in ourselves. This was one reason that art and literature became so essential to our lives: they were not a luxury but a necessity. What Nabokov captured was the texture of life in a totalitarian society, where you are completely alone in an illusory world full of false promises, where you can no longer differentiate between your savior and your executioner.

We formed a special bond with Nabokov despite the difficulty of his prose. This went deeper than our identification with his themes. His novels are shaped around invisible trapdoors, sudden gaps that constantly pull the carpet from under the reader's feet. They are filled with mistrust of what we call everyday reality, an acute sense of that reality's fickleness and frailty.

There was something, both in his fiction and in his life, that we instinctively related to and grasped, the possibility of a boundless freedom when all options are taken away. I think that was what drove me to create the class. My main link with the outside world had been the university, and now that I had severed that link, there on the brink of the void, I could invent the violin or be devoured by the void.

7

The two photographs should be placed side by side. Both embody the "frag-ile unreality"—to quote Nabokov on his own state of exile—of our existence in the Islamic Republic of Iran. One cancels the other, and yet without one, the other is incomplete. In the first photograph, standing there in our black robes and scarves, we are as we had been shaped by someone else's dreams. In the second, we appear as we imagined ourselves. In neither could we feel completely at home.

The second photograph belonged to the world inside the living room. But outside, underneath the window that deceptively showcased only the mountains and the tree outside our house, was the other world, where the bad witches and furies were waiting to transform us into the hooded crea-tures of the first.

The best way I can think of explaining this self-negating and paradoxi-cal inferno is through an anecdote, one that, like similar anecdotes, defies fiction to become its own metaphor.

The chief film censor in Iran, up until 1994, was blind. Well, nearly blind. Before that, he was the censor for theater. One of my playwright friends once described how he would sit in the theater wearing thick glasses that seemed to hide more than they revealed. An assistant who sat by him would explain the action onstage, and he would dictate the parts that needed to be cut.

After 1994, this censor became the head of the new television channel. There, he perfected his methods and demanded that the scriptwriters give him their scripts on audiotape; they were forbidden to make them at-tractive or dramatize them in any way. He then made his judgments about the scripts based on the tapes. More interesting, however, is the fact that his successor, who was not blind—not physically, that is—nonetheless followed the same system.

Our world under the mullahs' rule was shaped by the colorless lenses of the blind censor. Not just our reality but also our fiction had taken on this curious coloration in a world where the censor was the poet's rival in rear-ranging and reshaping reality, where we simultaneously invented ourselves and were figments of someone else's imagination.

We lived in a culture that denied any merit to literary works, consider-ing them important only when they were handmaidens to something seem-ingly more urgent—namely ideology. This was a country where all gestures, even the most private, were interpreted in political terms. The colors of my head scarf or my father's tie were symbols of Western decadence and impe-rialist tendencies. Not wearing a beard, shaking hands with members of the opposite sex, clapping or whistling in public meetings, were likewise con-sidered Western and therefore decadent, part of the plot by imperialists to bring down our culture.

A few years ago some members of the Iranian Parliament set up an investigative committee to examine the content of national television. The committee issued a lengthy report in which it condemned the showing of *Billy Budd,* because, it claimed, the story promoted homosexuality. Ironically, the Iranian television programmers had mainly chosen that film because of its lack of female characters. The cartoon version of *Around the World in Eighty Days* was also castigated, because the main character—a lion—was British and the film ended in that bastion of imperialism, London.

Our class was shaped within this context, in an attempt to escape the gaze of the blind censor for a few hours each week. There, in that living room, we rediscovered that we were also living, breathing human beings; and no matter how repressive the state became, no matter how intimidated and frightened we were, like Lolita we tried to escape and to create our own little pockets of freedom. And like Lolita, we took every opportunity to flaunt our insubordination: by showing a little hair from under our scarves, insinuating a little color into the drab uniformity of our appearances, growing our nails, falling in love and listening to forbidden music.

An absurd fictionality ruled our lives. We tried to live in the open spaces, in the chinks created between that room, which had become our protective cocoon, and the censor's world of witches and goblins outside. Which of these two worlds was more real, and to which did we really belong? We no longer knew the answers. Perhaps one way of finding out the truth was to do what we did: to try to imaginatively articulate these two worlds and, through that process, give shape to our vision and identity.

8

How can I create this other world outside the room? I have no choice but to appeal once again to your imagination. Let's imagine one of the girls, say Sanaz, leaving my house and let us follow her from there to her final destination. She says her good-byes and puts on her black robe and scarf over her orange shirt and jeans, coiling her scarf around her neck to cover her huge gold earrings. She directs wayward strands of hair under the scarf, puts her notes into her large bag, straps it on over her shoulder and walks out into the hall. She pauses a moment on top of the stairs to put on thin lacy black gloves to hide her nail polish.

We follow Sanaz down the stairs, out the door and into the street. You might notice that her gait and her gestures have changed. It is in her best interest not to be seen, not be heard or noticed. She doesn't walk upright, but bends her head towards the ground and doesn't look at passersby. She walks quickly and with a sense of determination. The streets of Tehran and other Iranian cities are patrolled by militia, who ride in white Toyota patrols, four gun-carrying men and women, sometimes followed by a minibus. They are called the Blood of God. They patrol the streets to make sure that women like Sanaz wear their veils properly, do not wear makeup, do not walk in public with men who are not their fathers, brothers or husbands. She will pass slogans on the walls, quotations from Khomeini and a group called the Party of God: MEN WHO WEAR TIES ARE U.S. LACKEYS. VEILING IS A WOMAN'S PROTECTION. Beside the slogan is a charcoal drawing of a woman: her face is featureless and framed by a dark chador. MY SISTER, GUARD YOUR VEIL. MY BROTHER, GUARD YOUR EYES.

If she gets on a bus, the seating is segregated. She must enter through the rear door and sit in the back seats, allocated to women. Yet in taxis, which accept as many as five passengers, men and women are squeezed together like sardines, as the saying goes, and the same goes with minibuses, where so many of my students complain of being harassed by bearded and God-fearing men.

You might well ask, What is Sanaz thinking as she walks the streets of Tehran? How much does this experience affect her? Most probably, she tries to distance her mind as much as possible from her surroundings. Perhaps she is thinking of her brother, or of her distant boyfriend and the time when she will meet him in Turkey. Does she compare her own situation with her mother's when she was the same age? Is she angry that women of her mother's generation could walk the streets freely, enjoy the company of the opposite sex, join the police force, become pilots, live under laws that were among the most progressive in the world regarding women? Does she feel humiliated by the new laws, by the fact that after the revolution, the age of marriage was lowered from eighteen to nine, that stoning became once more the punishment for adultery and prostitution?

In the course of nearly two decades, the streets have been turned into a war zone, where young women who disobey the rules are hurled into patrol cars, taken to jail, flogged, fined, forced to wash the toilets and humiliated, and as soon as they leave, they go back and do the same thing. Is she aware, Sanaz, of her own power? Does she realize how dangerous she can be when her every stray gesture is a disturbance to public safety? Does she think how vulnerable the Revolutionary Guards are who for over eighteen years have patrolled the streets of Tehran and have had to endure young women like herself, and those of other generations, walking, talking, showing a strand of hair just to remind them that they have not converted?

We have reached Sanaz's house, where we will leave her on her doorstep, perhaps to confront her brother on the other side and to think in her heart of her boyfriend.

These girls, my girls, had both a real history and a fabricated one. Although they came from very different backgrounds, the regime that ruled them had tried to make their personal identities and histories irrelevant. They were never free of the regime's definition of them as Muslim women.

Whoever we were—and it was not really important what religion we belonged to, whether we wished to wear the veil or not, whether we observed certain religious norms or not—we had become the figment of someone else's dreams. A stern ayatollah, a self-proclaimed philosopher-king, had come to rule our land. He had come in the name of a past, a past that, he claimed, had been stolen from him. And he now wanted to re-create us in the image of that illusory past. Was it any consolation, and did we even wish to remember, that what he did to us was what we allowed him to do? ■

■ QUESTIONS FOR CONNECTIONS WITHIN THE READING ■

1. Why does Nafisi spend so much time describing the members of her reading group? What different motives may have brought these readers to Nafisi's apartment? We may normally think of reading as a solitary activity, unlike watching movies or sports; why was it so important for the women to meet together as a group?

2. Judging from the information that Nafisi provides, why do you think her reading group selected the particular works she mentions: *A Thousand and One Nights,* as well as *Invitation to a Beheading, Lolita,* and other novels by Nabokov? Why might religious authorities, not only in Iran but also in the United States, object to the teaching of such works?

3. Early in Chapter 10 of *Reading Lolita in Tehran,* Nafisi writes, "*Lolita* was *not* a critique of the Islamic Republic, but it went against the grain of all totalitarian perspectives." Without consulting a dictionary, and drawing instead on Nafisi's account, define "totalitarian." What social and psychological effects does the totalitarian regime have on Nafisi and her students? In what sense might *Lolita* provide a "critique" of totalitarianism?

■ QUESTIONS FOR WRITING ■

1. Does Nafisi present a theory of interpretation? In other words, what does she see as the "real" or "correct" meaning of a work of art? Does she accept Nabokov's claims that "readers were born free and ought to remain free"? Would Nafisi say a work of art can mean anything we want? What is the value of art if it has no determinate or "correct" meaning? If art has a value, is its value simply personal? Does it also have social, political, and cultural value?

2. Nafisi and her students read Nabokov against the backdrop of the Islamic Republic of Iran. In that setting, what does the experience offer them? Would their reading of the novel provide the same experience if it took place in the United States? Does literature serve a different social function in our society? How might reading a novel in a private group differ from the experience of reading the same novel in an American high school or college classroom?

■ *QUESTIONS FOR MAKING CONNECTIONS BETWEEN READINGS* ■

1. A world away from Nafisi and her students discussing *Lolita,* Henry Jenkins is now at work exploring the ways that new media are transforming both reading and the communities that emerge around shared texts. The two scholars clearly have a deep respect for the act of reading, but do they value reading for the same reasons? Could the communities that formed around *Harry Potter* also form around *Lolita* or any of the other novels Nafisi taught? Or is the kind of reading that Jenkins celebrates something one outgrows with age? Drawing on Nafisi and Jenkins, discuss the role that reading plays in social transformations big and small.

2. Toward the close of his essay "The Mind's Eye," Oliver Sacks asks, "Do any of us, finally, know how we think?" Assuming that the answer to this question is no, what conclusions can we reach about the ways that each of us interprets our individual worlds? If everyone makes things meaningful in his or her own way, what purpose might be served by an activity such as meeting to discuss a work of literature? What does the individual gain from the communal reading of a work of fiction? Do the blind subjects of Sacks's essay have anything in common with Nafisi's students? Do Sacks and Nafisi, taken together, show that there is ultimately only one way to achieve "a rich and full realization" of an inner life?

TIM O'BRIEN

IN 1968, DURING the war in Vietnam, Tim O'Brien graduated from college and was served a draft notice. An avowed opponent of the war, he considered fleeing to Canada but ultimately reported for basic training and was stationed near My Lai shortly after the infamous massacre there. O'Brien returned to the United States in 1970, having received injuries that earned him a Purple Heart. Since then he has published dozens of stories and books, both fiction and nonfiction, including the National Book Award–winning *Going After Cacciato* (1978). O'Brien has received many other prestigious awards as well, among them the O. Henry Award, the National Book Critics Circle Award, and the Pulitzer Prize. He is currently a visiting professor and endowed chair at Southwest Texas University, where he teaches in the creative writing program.

"How to Tell a True War Story," which is included in O'Brien's collection *The Things They Carried* (1998), is, paradoxically, a work of fiction. O'Brien's decision to present his narrative in this fashion is a sign of his continued engagement with a puzzle that has shaped his work for almost three decades. For O'Brien, the line between reality and fiction is always a fuzzy one, especially in accounts of war, where the experience outstrips the resources of language. Faced with the complexity of war, O'Brien is not trying to "close the books" on a painful past, but rather to keep the books from ever getting closed by those who might prefer to forget the high price that war always exacts. In O'Brien's work, this high price is not measured just in the loss of life, but also in the permanent loss of moral certainty. In response to a question about why he keeps returning to incidents that took place in the 1960s, O'Brien has said, "The war occurred half a lifetime ago, and yet the remembering makes it now. And sometimes remembering will lead to a story, which makes it forever. That's what stories are for. Stories are for joining the past to the future. Stories are for those late hours in the night when you can't remember how you got from where you were to where you are. Stories are for eternity, when memory is erased, when there is nothing to remember but the story."

O'Brien, Tim. "How to Tell a True War Story." *The Things They Carried*. New York: Broadway Books, 1998. 67–85.
Biographical information comes from <http://illyria.com/tob/tobbio.html>; quotation comes from <http://www.illyria.com/tobhp.html>.

■ ■

How to Tell a True War Story

This is true.

I had a buddy in Vietnam. His name was Bob Kiley, but everybody called him Rat.

A friend of his gets killed, so about a week later Rat sits down and writes a letter to the guy's sister. Rat tells her what a great brother she had, how together the guy was, a number one pal and comrade. A real soldier's soldier, Rat says. Then he tells a few stories to make the point, how her brother would always volunteer for stuff nobody else would volunteer for in a million years, dangerous stuff, like doing recon or going out on these really badass night patrols. Stainless steel balls, Rat tells her. The guy was a little crazy, for sure, but crazy in a good way, a real daredevil, because he liked the challenge of it, he liked testing himself, just man against gook. A great, great guy, Rat says.

Anyway, it's a terrific letter, very personal and touching. Rat almost bawls writing it. He gets all teary telling about the good times they had together, how her brother made the war seem almost fun, always raising hell and lighting up villes and bringing smoke to bear every which way. A great sense of humor, too. Like the time at this river when he went fishing with a whole damn crate of hand grenades. Probably the funniest thing in world history, Rat says, all that gore, about twenty zillion dead gook fish. Her brother, he had the right attitude. He knew how to have a good time. On Halloween, this real hot spooky night, the dude paints up his body all different colors and puts on this weird mask and hikes over to a ville and goes trick-or-treating almost stark naked, just boots and balls and an M-16. A tremendous human being, Rat says. Pretty nutso sometimes, but you could trust him with your life.

And then the letter gets very sad and serious. Rat pours his heart out. He says he loved the guy. He says the guy was his best friend in the world. They were like soul mates, he says, like twins or something, they had a whole lot in common. He tells the guy's sister he'll look her up when the war's over.

So what happens?

Rat mails the letter. He waits two months. The dumb cooze never writes back.

A true war story is never moral. It does not instruct, nor encourage virtue, nor suggest models of proper human behavior, nor restrain men from doing the things men have always done. If a story seems moral, do not believe it. If at the end of a war story you feel uplifted, or if you feel that some small bit of rectitude has been salvaged from the larger waste, then you have been made the victim of a very old and terrible lie. There is no rectitude whatsoever. There is no virtue. As a first rule of thumb, therefore, you can tell a true war story by its absolute and uncompromising allegiance to obscenity and evil. Listen to Rat Kiley. Cooze, he says. He does not say bitch. He certainly does not say woman, or girl. He says cooze. Then he spits and stares. He's nineteen years old—it's too much for him—so he looks at you with those big sad gentle killer eyes and says cooze, because his friend is dead, and because it's so incredibly sad and true: she never wrote back.

You can tell a true war story if it embarrasses you. If you don't care for obscenity, you don't care for the truth; if you don't care for the truth, watch how you vote. Send guys to war, they come home talking dirty.

Listen to Rat: "Jesus Christ, man, I write this beautiful fuckin' letter, I slave over it, and what happens? The dumb cooze never writes back."

The dead guy's name was Curt Lemon. What happened was, we crossed a muddy river and marched west into the mountains, and on the third day we took a break along a trail junction in deep jungle. Right away, Lemon and Rat Kiley started goofing. They didn't understand about the spookiness. They were kids; they just didn't know. A nature hike, they thought, not even a war, so they went off into the shade of some giant trees—quadruple canopy, no sunlight at all—and they were giggling and calling each other yellow mother and playing a silly game they'd invented. The game involved smoke grenades, which were harmless unless you did stupid things, and what they did was pull out the pin and stand a few feet apart and play catch under the shade of those huge trees. Whoever chickened out was a yellow mother. And if nobody chickened out, the grenade would make a light popping sound and they'd be covered with smoke and they'd laugh and dance around and then do it again.

It's all exactly true.

It happened, to *me*, nearly twenty years ago, and I still remember that trail junction and those giant trees and a soft dripping sound somewhere beyond the trees. I remember the smell of moss. Up in the canopy there were tiny white blossoms, but no sunlight at all, and I remember the shadows spreading out under the trees where Curt Lemon and Rat Kiley were playing catch with smoke grenades. Mitchell Sanders sat flipping his yo-yo. Norman Bowker and Kiowa and Dave Jensen were dozing, or half dozing, and all around us were those ragged green mountains.

Except for the laughter things were quiet.

At one point, I remember, Mitchell Sanders turned and looked at me, not quite nodding, as if to warn me about something, as if he already *knew*, then after a while he rolled up his yo-yo and moved away.

It's hard to tell you what happened next.

They were just goofing. There was a noise, I suppose, which must've been the detonator, so I glanced behind me and watched Lemon step from the shade into bright sunlight. His face was suddenly brown and shining. A handsome kid, really. Sharp gray eyes, lean and narrow-waisted, and when he died it was almost beautiful, the way the sunlight came around him and lifted him up and sucked him high into a tree full of moss and vines and white blossoms.

In any war story, but especially a true one, it's difficult to separate what happened from what seemed to happen. What seems to happen becomes its own happening and has to be told that way. The angles of vision are skewed. When a booby trap explodes, you close your eyes and duck and float outside yourself. When a guy dies, like Curt Lemon, you look away and then look back for a moment and then look away again. The pictures get jumbled; you tend to miss a lot. And then afterward, when you go to tell about it, there is always that surreal seemingness, which makes the story seem untrue, but which in fact represents the hard and exact truth as it *seemed*.

In many cases a true war story cannot be believed. If you believe it, be skeptical. It's a question of credibility. Often the crazy stuff is true and the normal stuff isn't, because the normal stuff is necessary to make you believe the truly incredible craziness.

In other cases you can't even tell a true war story. Sometimes it's just beyond telling.

I heard this one, for example, from Mitchell Sanders. It was near dusk and we were sitting at my foxhole along a wide muddy river north of Quang Ngai. I remember how peaceful the twilight was. A deep pinkish red spilled out on the river, which moved without sound, and in the morning we would cross the river and march west into the mountains. The occasion was right for a good story.

"God's truth," Mitchell Sanders said. "A six-man patrol goes up into the mountains on a basic listening-post operation. The idea's to spend a week up there, just lie low and listen for enemy movement. They've got a radio along, so if they hear anything suspicious—anything—they're supposed to call in artillery or gunships, whatever it takes. Otherwise they keep strict field discipline. Absolute silence. They just listen."

Sanders glanced at me to make sure I had the scenario. He was playing with his yo-yo, dancing it with short, tight little strokes of the wrist.

His face was blank in the dusk.

"We're talking regulation, by-the-book LP. These six guys, they don't say boo for a solid week. They don't got tongues. *All* ears."

"Right," I said.

"Understand me?"

"Invisible."

Sanders nodded.

"Affirm," he said. "Invisible. So what happens is, these guys get themselves deep in the bush, all camouflaged up, and they lie down and wait and that's all they do, nothing else, they lie there for seven straight days and just listen. And man, I'll tell you—it's spooky. This is mountains. You don't *know* spooky till you been there. Jungle, sort of, except it's way up in the clouds and there's always this fog—like rain, except it's not raining—everything's all wet and swirly and tangled up and you can't see jack, you can't find your own pecker to piss with. Like you don't even have a body. Serious spooky. You just go with the vapors—the fog sort of takes you in . . . And the sounds, man. The sounds carry forever. You hear stuff nobody should *ever* hear."

Sanders was quiet for a second, just working the yo-yo, then he smiled at me.

"So after a couple days the guys start hearing this real soft, kind of wacked-out music. Weird echoes and stuff. Like a radio or something, but it's not a radio, it's this strange gook music that comes right out of the rocks. Faraway, sort of, but right up close, too. They try to ignore it. But it's a listening post, right? So they listen. And every night they keep hearing that crazyass gook concert. All kinds of chimes and xylophones. I mean, this is wilderness—no way, it can't be real—but there it *is*, like the mountains are tuned in to Radio fucking Hanoi. Naturally they get nervous. One guy sticks Juicy Fruit in his ears. Another guy almost flips. Thing is, though, they can't report music. They can't get on the horn and call back to base and say, 'Hey, listen, we need some firepower, we got to blow away this weirdo gook rock band.' They can't do that. It wouldn't go down. So they lie there in the fog and keep their mouths shut. And what makes it extra bad, see, is the poor dudes can't horse around like normal. Can't joke it away. Can't even talk to each other except maybe in whispers, all hush-hush, and that just revs up the willies. All they do is listen."

Again there was some silence as Mitchell Sanders looked out on the river. The dark was coming on hard now, and off to the west I could see the mountains rising in silhouette, all the mysteries and unknowns.

"This next part," Sanders said quietly, "you won't believe."

"Probably not," I said.

"You won't. And you know why?" He gave me a long, tired smile. "Because it happened. Because every word is absolutely dead-on true."

Sanders made a sound in his throat, like a sigh, as if to say he didn't care if I believed him or not. But he did care. He wanted me to feel the truth, to believe by the raw force of feeling. He seemed sad, in a way.

"These six guys," he said, "they're pretty fried out by now, and one night they start hearing voices. Like at a cocktail party. That's what it sounds like, this big swank gook cocktail party somewhere out there in the fog. Music and chitchat and stuff. It's crazy, I know, but they hear the champagne corks. They hear the actual martini glasses. Real hoity-toity, all very civilized, except this isn't civilization. This is Nam.

"Anyway, the guys try to be cool. They just lie there and groove, but after a while they start hearing—you won't believe this—they hear chamber music. They hear violins and cellos. They hear this terrific mama-san soprano. Then after a while they hear gook opera and a glee club and the Haiphong Boys Choir and a barbershop quartet and all kinds of weird chanting and Buddha-Buddha stuff. And the whole time, in the background, there's still that cocktail party going on. All these different voices. Not human voices, though. Because it's the mountains. Follow me? The rock— it's *talking*. And the fog, too, and the grass and the goddamn mongooses. Everything talks. The trees talk politics, the monkeys talk religion. The whole country: Vietnam. The place talks. It talks. Understand? Nam—it truly *talks*.

"The guys can't cope. They lose it. They get on the radio and report enemy movement—a whole army, they say—and they order up the fire-power. They get arty and gunships. They call in air strikes. And I'll tell you, they fuckin' crash that cocktail party. All night long, they just smoke those mountains. They make jungle juice. They blow away trees and glee clubs and whatever else there is to blow away. Scorch time. They walk napalm up and down the ridges. They bring in the Cobras and F-4s, they use Willie Peter and HE and incendiaries. It's all fire. They make those mountains burn.

"Around dawn things finally get quiet. Like you never even *heard* quiet before. One of those real thick, real misty days—just clouds and fog, they're off in this special zone—and the mountains are absolutely dead-flat silent. Like *Brigadoon*—pure vapor, you know? Everything's all sucked up inside the fog. Not a single sound, except they still *hear* it.

"So they pack up and start humping. They head down the mountain, back to base camp, and when they get there they don't say diddly. They don't talk. Not a word, like they're deaf and dumb. Later on this fat bird colonel comes up and asks what the hell happened out there. What'd they hear? Why all the ordnance? The man's ragged out, he gets down tight on their case. I mean, they spent six trillion dollars on firepower, and this fatass colonel wants answers, he wants to know what the fuckin' story is.

"But the guys don't say zip. They just look at him for a while, sort of funny like, sort of amazed, and the whole war is right there in that stare. It says everything you can't ever say. It says, man, you got *wax* in your ears. It says, poor bastard, you'll never know—wrong frequency—you don't *even* want to hear this. Then they salute the fucker and walk away, because cer-tain stories you don't ever tell."

You can tell a true war story by the way it never seems to end. Not then, not ever. Not when Mitchell Sanders stood up and moved off into the dark.

It all happened.

Even now, at this instant, I remember that yo-yo. In a way, I suppose, you had to be there, you had to hear it, but I could tell how desperately

Sanders wanted me to believe him, his frustration at not quite getting the details right, not quite pinning down the final and definitive truth.

And I remember sitting at my foxhole that night, watching the shadows of Quang Ngai, thinking about the coming day and how we would cross the river and march west into the mountains, all the ways I might die, all the things I did not understand.

Late in the night Mitchell Sanders touched my shoulder. "Just came to me," he whispered. "The moral, I mean. Nobody listens. Nobody hears nothin'. Like that fatass colonel. The politicians, all the civilian types. Your girlfriend. My girlfriend. Everybody's sweet little virgin girlfriend. What they need is to go out on LP. The vapors, man. Trees and rocks—you got to *listen* to your enemy."

And then again, in the morning, Sanders came up to me. The platoon was preparing to move out, checking weapons, going through all the little rituals that preceded a day's march. Already the lead squad had crossed the river and was filing off toward the west.

"I got a confession to make," Sanders said. "Last night, man, I had to make up a few things."

"I know that."

"The glee club. There wasn't any glee club."

"Right."

"No opera."

"Forget it, I understand."

"Yeah, but listen, it's still true. Those six guys, they heard wicked sound out there. They heard sound you just plain won't believe."

Sanders pulled on his rucksack, closed his eyes for a moment, then almost smiled at me. I knew what was coming.

"All right," I said, "what's the moral?"

"Forget it."

"No, go ahead."

For a long while he was quiet, looking away, and the silence kept stretching out until it was almost embarrassing. Then he shrugged and gave me a stare that lasted all day.

"Hear that quiet, man?" he said. "That quiet—just listen. There's your moral."

In a true war story, if there's a moral at all, it's like the thread that makes the cloth. You can't tease it out. You can't extract the meaning without unraveling the deeper meaning. And in the end, really, there's nothing much to say about a true war story, except maybe "Oh."

True war stories do not generalize. They do not indulge in abstraction or analysis.

For example: War is hell. As a moral declaration the old truism seems perfectly true, and yet because it abstracts, because it generalizes, I can't believe it with my stomach. Nothing turns inside.

It comes down to gut instinct. A true war story, if truly told, makes the stomach believe.

This one does it for me. I've told it before—many times, many versions—but here's what actually happened.

We crossed that river and marched west into the mountains. On the third day, Curt Lemon stepped on a booby-trapped 105 round. He was playing catch with Rat Kiley, laughing, and then he was dead. The trees were thick; it took nearly an hour to cut an LZ for the dustoff.

Later, higher in the mountains, we came across a baby VC water buffalo. What it was doing there I don't know—no farms or paddies—but we chased it down and got a rope around it and led it along to a deserted village where we set up for the night. After supper Rat Kiley went over and stroked its nose.

He opened up a can of C rations, pork and beans, but the baby buffalo wasn't interested.

Rat shrugged.

He stepped back and shot it through the right front knee. The animal did not make a sound. It went down hard, then got up again, and Rat took careful aim and shot off an ear. He shot it in the hindquarters and in the little hump at its back. He shot it twice in the flanks. It wasn't to kill; it was to hurt. He put the rifle muzzle up against the mouth and shot the mouth away. Nobody said much. The whole platoon stood there watching, feeling all kinds of things, but there wasn't a great deal of pity for the baby water buffalo. Curt Lemon was dead. Rat Kiley had lost his best friend in the world. Later in the week he would write a long personal letter to the guy's sister, who would not write back, but for now it was a question of pain. He shot off the tail. He shot away chunks of meat below the ribs. All around us there was the smell of smoke and filth and deep greenery, and the evening was humid and very hot. Rat went to automatic. He shot randomly, almost casually, quick little spurts in the belly and butt. Then he reloaded, squatted down, and shot it in the left front knee. Again the animal fell hard and tried to get up, but this time it couldn't quite make it. It wobbled and went down sideways. Rat shot it in the nose. He bent forward and whispered something, as if talking to a pet, then he shot it in the throat. All the while the baby buffalo was silent, or almost silent, just a light bubbling sound where the nose had been. It lay very still. Nothing moved except the eyes, which were enormous, the pupils shiny black and dumb.

Rat Kiley was crying. He tried to say something, but then cradled his rifle and went off by himself.

The rest of us stood in a ragged circle around the baby buffalo. For a time no one spoke. We had witnessed something essential, something brand-new and profound, a piece of the world so startling there was not yet a name for it.

Somebody kicked the baby buffalo.

It was still alive, though just barely, just in the eyes.

"Amazing," Dave Jensen said. "My whole life, I never seen anything like it."

"Never?"

"Not hardly. Not once."

Kiowa and Mitchell Sanders picked up the baby buffalo. They hauled it across the open square, hoisted it up, and dumped it in the village well.

Afterward, we sat waiting for Rat to get himself together.

"Amazing," Dave Jensen kept saying. "A new wrinkle. I never seen it before."

Mitchell Sanders took out his yo-yo. "Well, that's Nam," he said. "Garden of Evil. Over here, man, every sin's real fresh and original."

How do you generalize?

War is hell, but that's not the half of it, because war is also mystery and terror and adventure and courage and discovery and holiness and pity and despair and longing and love. War is nasty; war is fun. War is thrilling; war is drudgery. War makes you a man; war makes you dead.

The truths are contradictory. It can be argued, for instance, that war is grotesque. But in truth war is also beauty. For all its horror, you can't help but gape at the awful majesty of combat. You stare out at tracer rounds unwinding through the dark like brilliant red ribbons. You crouch in ambush as a cool, impassive moon rises over the nighttime paddies. You admire the fluid symmetries of troops on the move, the harmonies of sound and shape and proportion, the great sheets of metal-fire streaming down from a gunship, the illumination rounds, the white phosphorus, the purply orange glow of napalm, the rocket's red glare. It's not pretty, exactly. It's astonishing. It fills the eye. It commands you. You hate it, yes, but your eyes do not. Like a killer forest fire, like cancer under a microscope, any battle or bombing raid or artillery barrage has the aesthetic purity of absolute moral indifference—a powerful, implacable beauty—and a true war story will tell the truth about this, though the truth is ugly.

To generalize about war is like generalizing about peace. Almost everything is true. Almost nothing is true. At its core, perhaps, war is just another name for death, and yet any soldier will tell you, if he tells the truth, that proximity to death brings with it a corresponding proximity to life. After a firefight, there is always the immense pleasure of aliveness. The trees are alive. The grass, the soil—everything. All around you things are purely living, and you among them, and the aliveness makes you tremble. You feel an intense, out-of-the-skin awareness of your living self—your truest self, the human being you want to be and then become by the force of wanting it. In the midst of evil you want to be a good man. You want decency. You want justice and courtesy and human concord, things you never knew you wanted. There is a kind of largeness to it, a kind of godliness. Though it's odd, you're never more alive than when you're almost dead. You recognize what's valuable. Freshly, as if for the first time, you love what's best in yourself and in the world, all that might be lost. At the hour of dusk you sit at your foxhole and look out on a wide river turning pinkish red, and at the mountains beyond, and although in the morning you must cross the river and go into the mountains and do terrible things and maybe die, even so, you find yourself studying the fine colors on the river, you feel wonder and awe at the setting of the sun, and you are filled with a hard, aching love for how the world could be and always should be, but now is not.

Mitchell Sanders was right. For the common soldier, at least, war has the feel—the spiritual texture—of a great ghostly fog, thick and permanent. There is no clarity. Everything swirls. The old rules are no longer binding, the old truths no longer true. Right spills over into wrong. Order blends into chaos, love into hate, ugliness into beauty, law into anarchy, civility into savagery. The vapors suck you in. You can't tell where you are, or why you're there, and the only certainty is overwhelming ambiguity.

In war you lose your sense of the definite, hence your sense of truth itself, and therefore it's safe to say that in a true war story nothing is ever absolutely true.

Often in a true war story there is not even a point, or else the point doesn't hit you until twenty years later, in your sleep, and you wake up and shake your wife and start telling the story to her, except when you get to the end you've forgotten the point again. And then for a long time you lie there watching the story happen in your head. You listen to your wife's breathing. The war's over. You close your eyes. You smile and think, Christ, what's the *point?*

This one wakes me up.

In the mountains that day, I watched Lemon turn sideways. He laughed and said something to Rat Kiley. Then he took a peculiar half step, moving from shade into bright sunlight, and the booby-trapped 105 round blew him into a tree. The parts were just hanging there, so Dave Jensen and I were ordered to shinny up and peel him off. I remember the white bone of an arm. I remember pieces of skin and something wet and yellow that must've been the intestines. The gore was horrible, and stays with me. But what wakes me up twenty years later is Dave Jensen singing "Lemon Tree" as we threw down the parts.

You can tell a true war story by the questions you ask. Somebody tells a story, let's say, and afterward you ask, "Is it true?" and if the answer matters, you've got your answer.

For example, we've all heard this one. Four guys go down a trail. A grenade sails out. One guy jumps on it and takes the blast and saves his three buddies.

Is it true?

The answer matters.

You'd feel cheated if it never happened. Without the grounding reality, it's just a trite bit of puffery, pure Hollywood, untrue in the way all such stories are untrue. Yet even if it did happen—and maybe it did, anything's possible—even then you know it can't be true, because a true war story does not depend upon that kind of truth. Absolute occurrence is irrelevant. A thing may happen and be a total lie; another thing may not happen and be truer than the truth. For example: Four guys go down a trail. A grenade sails out. One guy jumps on it and takes the blast, but it's a killer grenade and everybody dies anyway. Before they die, though, one of the dead guys says, "The fuck you do *that* for?" and the jumper says, "Story of my life, man," and the other guy starts to smile but he's dead.

That's a true story that never happened.

Twenty years later, I can still see the sunlight on Lemon's face. I can see him turning, looking back at Rat Kiley, then he laughed and took that curious half step from shade into sunlight, his face suddenly brown and shining, and when his foot touched down, in that instant, he must've thought it was the sunlight that was killing him. It was not the sunlight. It was a rigged 105 round. But if I could ever get the story right, how the sun seemed to gather around him and pick him up and lift him high into a tree, if I could somehow re-create the fatal whiteness of that light, the quick glare, the obvious cause and effect, then you would believe the last thing Curt Lemon believed, which for him must've been the final truth.

Now and then, when I tell this story, someone will come up to me afterward and say she liked it. It's always a woman. Usually it's an older woman of kindly temperament and humane politics. She'll explain that as a rule she hates war stories; she can't understand why people want to wallow in all the blood and gore. But this one she liked. The poor baby buffalo, it made her sad. Sometimes, even, there are little tears. What I should do, she'll say, is put it all behind me. Find new stories to tell.

I won't say it but I'll think it.

I'll picture Rat Kiley's face, his grief, and I'll think, *You dumb cooze.*

Because she wasn't listening.

It *wasn't* a war story. It was a *love* story.

But you can't say that. All you can do is tell it one more time, patiently, adding and subtracting, making up a few things to get at the real truth. No Mitchell Sanders, you tell her. No Lemon, no Rat Kiley. No trail junction. No baby buffalo. No vines or moss or white blossoms. Beginning to end, you tell her, it's all made up. Every goddamn detail—the mountains and the river and especially that poor dumb baby buffalo. None of it happened. *None* of it. And even if it did happen, it didn't happen in the mountains, it happened in this little village on the Batangan Peninsula, and it was raining like crazy, and one night a guy named Stink Harris woke up screaming with a leech on his tongue. You can tell a true war story if you just keep on telling it.

And in the end, of course, a true war story is never about war. It's about sunlight. It's about the special way that dawn spreads out on a river when you know you must cross the river and march into the mountains and do things you are afraid to do. It's about love and memory. It's about sorrow. It's about sisters who never write back and people who never listen.   ∎

■ *QUESTIONS FOR MAKING CONNECTIONS*
WITHIN THE READING ■

1. Tim O'Brien's "How to Tell a True War Story" is part of a collection of stories by the author entitled *The Things They Carried*. Although the ostensible subject of this particular short story is a series of events that may have actually happened, the subtitle of the entire collection is "A Work of Fiction." "How to Tell a True War Story" begins with the explicit statement "This is true," but what sort of truth does it manage to convey? As you consider possible answers, please remember that the narrator warns us, "In many cases a true war story cannot be believed. If you believe it, be skeptical." Why is the issue of truth so important to a story about what happens in war? Does O'Brien really mean that there is no such thing as truth when we are talking about this issue? If everything about war is subjective, then is it ever possible for one person to judge another person's military conduct?

2. Why does Rat Kiley write a letter to Curt Lemon's sister? What do you make of the details of his letter? Conventionally, such a letter would praise a fallen fellow combatant as a "hero," someone of exemplary character who had chosen to make the "ultimate sacrifice." Instead, Rat writes about the times he and Curt were "raising hell and lighting up villes and bringing smoke to bear every which way." Is Rat trying to insult the sister? Seduce her? Destroy her positive memories of her brother? When she fails to write back to him, why does Rat refer to her as a "dumb cooze"? For that matter, why does he refer to the Vietnamese as "gooks"? Is this simply an example of crude prejudice? If Rat thought of the Vietnamese as people, much like his own family back home, how would such a change influence his behavior? If he thought of Lemon's sister as nothing more than a "cooze," why did he bother to write to her at all?

3. Why does Rat Kiley kill the baby water buffalo? And why is it that "the whole platoon stood there watching, feeling all kinds of things, but [not] a great deal of pity for the baby water buffalo"? How do you explain the reaction of Mitchell Sanders: "Well, that's Nam. Garden of Evil. Over here . . . every sin's fresh and original"? If the men view Rat's killing of the buffalo as a "sin," why do they make no effort to stop him? Why do they appear to feel no remorse afterward? Do they displace onto the buffalo their desire to get back at the Vietnamese, or is their behavior even more complicated? When they kill the buffalo, are they killing something in themselves? What part of themselves might they be killing, and why might they want to do so?

■ *QUESTIONS FOR WRITING* ■

1. Readers might perceive O'Brien's story to be a powerfully realistic evocation of war as people actually live it. On the other hand, in spite of its realistic qualities, the story sometimes becomes highly poetic, as in passages like this one:

   > Twenty years later, I can still see the sunlight on Lemon's face. I can see him turning, looking back at Rat Kiley, then he laughed and took the curious half step from shade into sunlight, his face suddenly brown and shining, and when his foot touched down, in that instant, he must've thought it was the sunlight that was killing him.

   Is O'Brien guilty of aestheticizing war—that is, of making it seem more beautiful, romantic, or exotic than it really is? Do you think that your reading of his account has made you less likely or more likely to regard war as necessary and noble? Has O'Brien's account made it less likely or more likely that you will think of war as a natural and even indispensable part of life as a human being?

2. What is the connection in O'Brien's short story between experience and language? Does he believe that our language predetermines the nature of our experience, or does he suggest, instead, that our experience is often more complex than our language can accommodate? Toward the end of the story, the narrator describes the kind of exchange he has, after reading his short stories in public, often with "an older woman of kindly temperament and humane politics." What sense can you make of the narrator's remarks about this exchange? Is it ever possible to describe our experience to others? Would listeners who had served in Vietnam be more likely to understand the narrator's account than those who had never been there? How about someone who had served in a different war? How much experience must people share in order to understand one another?

■ *QUESTIONS FOR MAKING CONNECTIONS BETWEEN READINGS* ■

1. Would O'Brien's narrator be comfortable at The Citadel as described by Susan Faludi? Does the form of camaraderie we find at The Citadel correspond to the "love" felt by the men who served with the narrator of O'Brien's story? Can we understand the rituals performed at The Citadel as forging bonds similar to those forged by war, or do you see significant differences? In what ways does O'Brien's story suggest that the culture of The Citadel is likely to prove more enduring than Faludi suggests? Is the culture of The Citadel really the culture of war itself? If you think so, then why have some distinguished military leaders tried to reform that institution?

2. Would Christopher McCandless, as described by Jon Krakauer, have fit in with the soldiers O'Brien describes? Would they value the same things, and were they looking for the same forms of satisfaction? In what ways might the soldiers' experience of war have been shaped by attitudes and outlooks they already held as Americans even before they arrived in Vietnam—attitudes and outlooks expressed by Chris McCandless's journey "into the wild"? Did Vietnam become the "wilderness" for the American soldiers there? In what ways might the values we sometimes think of as closest to nature—values like independence and toughness—be the product of centuries of war? Is there really such a thing as "wilderness"? How is wilderness different from a battlefield? Is the real wilderness inside us?

VIRGINIA POSTREL

THE CRITIC CAMILLE PAGLIA has described Virginia Postrel, the author of *The Future and Its Enemies* (1998) and *The Substance of Style* (2003), as "one of the smartest women in America [who] for years . . . has demonstrated her daunting gift for cutting-edge social and economic analysis as well as her admirable command of lean, lucid prose." Now one of the nation's most sought-after public speakers on contemporary developments involving business, technology, and culture, Postrel began her career as a journalist with reporting stints at *Inc.* and *The Wall Street Journal,* then served as editor of the Libertarian magazine *Reason* from 1989 to 2000. Until 2006, Postrel wrote a regular economics column for *The New York Times.* She now writes the monthly "Commerce & Culture" column as a contributing editor of *The Atlantic* and maintains a highly trafficked weblog at <http://www.dynamist.com/weblog/index.html>, where she provides on-the-spot responses both to weighty and to seemingly trivial developments on the national and international news scene.

In *The Future and Its Enemies,* Postrel challenges those who see the spread of technology, the advent of the global economy, and the increasing influence of popular culture as threatening to undermine our nation's fundamental values and to imperil the country's future. Arguing against those on both the right and the left side of the political spectrum who see change in these areas as inevitably leading to decline, Postrel proposes an alternate "dynamist" model in which the direction of progress is understood always to be unpredictable, open ended, and contingent. She believes that embracing this model makes it possible to rethink everything from standard business practices to the search for truth and beauty. Postrel picks up this discussion in *The Substance of Style: How the Rise of Aesthetic Value Is Remaking Commerce, Culture, and Consciousness.* Here, she focuses on the liberating power that is afforded by individual choice in the

Postrel, Virginia. "Surface and Substance." *The Substance of Style: How the Rise of Aesthetic Value is Remaking Commerce, Culture, and Consciousness.* New York: HarperCollins, 2003, 66–92.

Camille Paglia's quote comes from "How the Demos Lost the White House in Seattle," Salon.com December 8, 1999, <http://www.salon.com/people/col/pagl/1999/12/08/cp1208/print.html>. Additional biographical information comes from Virginia Postrel's home page <http://www.dynamist.com/contact/biography.html>.

marketplace. Bringing together her research into fields as diverse as fashion, real estate, politics, design, and economics, Postrel seeks to establish that the biologically driven search for beauty expresses itself in all these areas, profoundly influencing the future of human culture. To this way of thinking, a seemingly trivial matter like a political candidate's hairstyle is understood to have a deeper significance, and the nation's preoccupation with style is seen not as a cause for concern but as a sign that the future belongs to those who appreciate the driving power of the desire for beauty.

Surface and Substance

To the chagrin of designers, it's hard to measure the value of aesthetics, even in a straightforward business context. Often look and feel change at the same time as other factors, making the specific advantages of each new characteristic hard to isolate. Some companies, such as Apple Computer, are good at design but less adept at other business operations, muffling whatever success their fine styling might bring. And in many markets, competition tends to wipe out any hope of direct gain; the benefits of aesthetic investment go to consumers, not producers. In these cases, spending on aesthetics is just a cost of staying in business, not a profit-increasing investment.

We know that people generally don't want something that's otherwise worthless just because it comes in a pretty package and, conversely, that valuable goods and services are worth even more in attractive wrappings. Beyond these generalities, it's often hard to tell exactly how surface and substance interact. Occasionally, however, we get a fairly pure example of how much people value aesthetics.

In the early 1990s, Motorola came out with an updated version of its most popular pager. The new version had enhanced features, but what really made it special was the pager's colorful face. Managers bored with the old look had replaced basic black with bright green, making the new-and-improved pager unlike anything on the market in those pre-iMac days. Buyers thought the green pager was cool, and they were willing to pay a premium to get it. "The moral of the story, which I repeat many, many times to engineers, is that all the fancy-ass technological engineering in the world couldn't get us a nickel more for the product," says the former head of Motorola's pager division. "But squirt-gun green plastic, which actually cost us nothing, could get us fifteen bucks extra per unit."[1]

Is this anecdote an innocent example of creativity in action, with a few laughs at the expense of technologically earnest, aesthetically clueless geeks? Or does the story provide a glimpse at just what's wrong with an age of look and feel—an era in which a bright plastic face is as important as real technological improvements? Should the success of the squirt-gun green pager give us the creeps?

An appealing pager face may delight customers, but it upsets many critics, who question the value of form without function. Surface and substance are opposites, they believe. Surface is irrelevant at best and often downright deceptive. If people pay more for mere aesthetics, goes the reasoning, then those consumers are being tricked. A squirt-gun green pager is simply not worth more than a black one. The two pagers have the same features! Paying more for green plastic is stupid, and only a dupe would do it. Function, not form, creates legitimate value.

The idea that surface itself has genuine value, for which consumers willingly pay extra when other characteristics are the same, appalls these critics. They "see that view as tantamount to advocating cannibalism of infants or something," says graphic designer Michael Bierut.[2] In one such case, he recalls, a critic berated a conference of designers "for creating meaningless distinctions between identical products like Coke and Pepsi. After some back and forth I asked him whether there was any inherent virtue in variety and beauty for their own sake. He sort of fumbled around and then more or less said that things could not exist 'for their own sake' and then invoked the example of Leni Riefenstahl's work for Hitler. That was as quick a ride from Pepsi to Nazis as I've had in a long time."

To such critics, form is dangerously seductive, because it allows the sensory to override the rational. An appealing package can make you believe that Nazis are good, or that colas are distinguishable. The very power of aesthetics makes its value suspect. "In advertising, packaging, product design, and corporate *identity*, the power of provocative surfaces speaks to the eye's mind, overshadowing matters of quality or substance," writes Stuart Ewen, the critic with whom Bierut sparred.[3] "Provocative surfaces" have no legitimate value of their own, he suggests, and they inevitably hide the truth. Contemplating the rise of streamlining in the 1930s, Ewen declares that "a century that began with a heady vision of moving beyond the ornament and uncovering the beauty of essential truth had rediscovered the lie." Aesthetics, in this view, is nothing more than a tool for manipulation and deceit.

Ewen is not alone. Sociologist Daniel Bell, in the twentieth-anniversary edition of his influential book *The Cultural Contradictions of Capitalism*, points to the prominence of cosmetics in department stores as a sign of the pervasive falsehood oiling "the machinery of gratification and instant desire" that is contemporary capitalism.[4] Women's fashion and fashion photography exemplify for Bell the same falsehood as advertising: "this task of selling illusions, the persuasions of the witches' craft," which he deems one of the contradictions that will ultimately bring down capitalism by eroding its Puritan foundation. To Bell, consumers are too susceptible to illusion and luxury, embracing hedonistic values that undermine bourgeois virtue. "The world of hedonism," he writes, "is the world of fashion, photography, advertising, television, travel. It is a world of make-believe."

Informing many such critiques is a naïve mid-twentieth-century view of how business operates: that producers can simply decree what consumers will buy, in a foolproof "circle of manipulation and retroactive need," as the Frankfurt School Marxists Theodor Adorno and Max Horkheimer put it in an influential 1944 essay.[5] In commercial products at least, such critics see ornament and variety not as goods that we value for their own sakes but as tools for creating false desire. Where the gullible public finds pleasure and meaning, the expert observer perceives deception. "That the difference between the Chrysler range and General Motors products is basically illusory strikes every child with a keen interest in varieties," declare Adorno and Horkheimer. "What connoisseurs discuss as good or bad points serve only to perpetuate the semblance of competition and range of choice."

In this view, modern commerce, because it appeals to consumers as visual, tactile creatures, is deceptive and decadent. The claim is unfalsifiable, since the more we try to proclaim the real value we attach to look and feel, the more we demonstrate just how duped we are. Legitimate value must come from objective characteristics—the taste (or, preferably, the nutritional value) of colas, the fuel-efficiency and power of cars, the cooking quality of toasters, the warmth of clothing—not through the associations and pleasures added by graphic imagery, streamlining, or fashionable cuts.

Although tinged with Marxism, this analysis is not all that different from the engineering vision of archcapitalist Scott McNealy of Sun Microsystems, who declared PowerPoint presentations wasteful because they consume more computer memory than handwritten slides—even though memory is abundant and virtually free. Hardheaded realists have no patience for the triviality of surfaces. If "content," rather than "packaging," is the only real value, then any attention to aesthetics furthers a lie, and resources spent on aesthetics are obviously wasted. This reasoning combines the oversimplified Maslovian idea, "aesthetics is a luxury," with a puritanical conviction that luxury is waste.

Just as the aesthetic imperative is not something only businesses feel, the fear that surfaces dissemble, distract, and distort is not limited to commerce and its critics. A conservative minister worries that evangelical churches, in their efforts to attract and hold members, have sacrificed the substance of preaching and prayer for mere spectacle. Today's services feature giant video screens, professionally lit stages, and high-energy rock bands. "The worship of God is increasingly presented as a spectator event of visual and sensory power rather than a verbal event in which we engage in a deep soul dialogue with the Triune God," he writes,[6] adding that

"Aesthetics, be they artistic or musical, are given a priority over holiness. More and more is seen, less and less is heard. There is a sensory feast but a famine of hearing. . . . Now there must be color, movement, audiovisual effects, or God cannot be known, loved, praised and trusted for his own sake."

Here, the "sensory feast" is less a lie than a distraction, diverting worshipers' attention and ministers' efforts from more important matters. As aesthetic expectations rise, in this view, congregants too easily forget the purpose of the spectacle. They become addicted to sensory stimulus, losing the ability to worship without it. They come to expect an experience of "color, movement, [and] audiovisual effects," an immersive environment rather than a cognitive exchange. As the aesthetic overrides the verbal, the feeling of worship overwhelms the message.

This critique reflects the widespread fear that surface and substance cannot coexist, that artifice inevitably detracts from truth. It is a fitting argument for a traditional Calvinist minister, whose dissenting forebearers stripped churches of many of their aesthetic trappings. Before ornament was a crime, it was idolatry. The whitewashed Puritan meetinghouse is as devoid of decoration as any modernist box.

You don't have to be a religious leader to worry that the spectacular may cancel out the verbal. The same anxieties arise even for pure entertainment. One sign of the "age of falsification," writes a critic, is "the blockbuster movie in which story line and plausibility are sacrificed to digital effects and Dolby Sound."[7] In this pessimistic vision, substance—"story line and plausibility"—will not survive the rise of surface. We cannot have movies that have both good stories and special effects. Our love of sensory delights is crowding out more cognitive pleasures. And it is creating a world of falsehoods.

Even worse, we fear, the aesthetic imperative is disguising who we really are. From Loos to Bell, and for centuries before them, critics of ornament have aimed some of their sharpest attacks at bodily decoration—at all the ways in which individuals create "false" selves and at the temptation to judge people by their appearances. In the seventeenth century, writers and preachers warned against women's makeup, which "takes the pencill out of God's hand," defying nature and divine will.[8] "What a contempt of God is this, to preferre the worke of thine owne finger to the worke of God?" exclaimed one writer condemning cosmetics.

The idea that unadorned faces and bodies are more virtuous and real than those touched by artifice persists to this day, usually in a secular, often political, form. In *The Beauty Myth*, Naomi Wolf advocates "civil rights for women that will entitle a woman to say that she'd rather look like herself than some 'beautiful' young stranger."[9] Wolf praises the "female identity" affirmed by women who refuse to alter their appearance with makeup, hair dye, or cosmetic surgery: "a woman's determination to show her loyalty—in the face of a beauty myth as powerful as myths about white supremacy—to her age, her shape, her self, her life." Except those born with exceptional natural beauty, authenticity and aesthetics are, in this vision, inevitably at odds. Remaining true to oneself means eschewing artifice.

The preachers—secular and religious, contemporary and historical—tell us that surfaces are meaningless, misleading distractions of no genuine value. But our experience and intuition suggest otherwise. Viscerally, if not intellectually, we're convinced that style does matter, that look and feel add something important to our lives. We ignore the preachers and behave as if aesthetics does have real value. We cherish streamlined artifacts, unconcerned that they do not really move through space. We find spiritual uplift in pageantry and music. We prefer PowerPoint typefaces and color to plain, handwritten transparencies. We define our real selves as the ones wearing makeup and high heels. We judge people, places, and things at least in part by how they look. We care about surfaces.

But we are not only aesthetic consumers. We are also producers, subject to the critical eyes of others. And that makes us worry.

We worry that other people will judge us by our flawed appearances, rather than our best selves. We worry that minding our looks will detract from more important, or more enjoyable, pursuits. We worry that we will lack the gifts or skills to measure up. And we worry that our stylistic choices will be misinterpreted. Businesses making pagers, creating sales brochures, and designing trade show booths face all the same problems, but without the emotional anguish that comes when the surface and substance are personal.

"If you look like you spend too much time on your clothes, there are people who will assume that you haven't put enough energy into your mind," says an English professor who advises aspiring humanities scholars on their appearance and manners.[10] Still, she warns that the wrong clothes can be catastrophic: "If you don't know how to dress, then what else don't you know? Do you know how to advise students or grade papers? The clothes *are* part of the judgment of the mind." Even to people ostensibly concerned only with substance, surface matters. And getting it right is hard.

Speaking to Yale University's 2001 graduating class, Hillary Rodham Clinton, just a few months into her first term as a U.S. senator, bundled these anxieties into a bitter joke. "The most important thing that I have to say today is that hair matters," she said.[11] "This is a life lesson my family did not teach me, Wellesley and Yale failed to instill in me: the importance of your hair. Your hair will send very important messages to those around you. It will tell people who you are and what you stand for. What hopes and dreams you have for the world . . . and especially what hopes and dreams you have for your hair. Likewise, your shoes. But really, more your hair. So, to sum up. Pay attention to your hair. Because everyone else will."

Beneath the humor is a sense of betrayal. *Why are you so obsessed with my hair? Why won't you take me seriously?* It wasn't supposed to be this way, not for ambitious public women. Hair is just surface stuff. And surfaces aren't supposed to be important, at least not in a postfeminist era in which women can be more than decorators and decoration. Yet Hillary Clinton's hair is so famous that there used to be a Web site, hillaryshair.com, devoted to its many changing styles.[12] Countless column inches and television minutes have chronicled her various hairdos and probed their meaning, seeking those "very important messages." Clinton is a polarizing figure, so her enemies and her allies have identified radically different messages. But both camps have opined about the meaning of her hair.

Taken literally, Clinton's joke offers another reading, equally marked by betrayal. *Somebody should have warned me. My education ripped me off.* Looks matter, and Wellesley and Yale and the Rodham family sent Hillary into the world without teaching her how to manage her appearance. They instead told her that serious people, especially serious women, don't waste precious attention on anything as trivial as hair. Inculcated with the idea that surfaces are false and unimportant, she lacked the presentation skills for an aesthetic age and had to learn them in public.

The joke simultaneously expresses three contradictory beliefs: that appearance matters and should be given due attention (the unironic reading); that appearance shouldn't matter (the ironic reading); and that appearance matters for its own aesthetic pleasures rather than for any message it sends ("what hopes and dreams you have for your hair"). These sentiments are hardly original or unique to Hillary Clinton. Most of us hold all three views at least some of the time. Untangling them—figuring out when each is true and how they relate to each other—is essential to understanding how to live in our age of look and feel.

As emotionally satisfying as it may sometimes be, declaring surfaces false and worthless is merely another form of deception. That sort of cheap dismissal not only ignores obvious realities. It also makes us a little crazy. Rather than deny that aesthetics conveys both pleasure and meaning—and, thus, has value to human beings—we need to better understand how pleasure and meaning relate to each other and to other, nonaesthetic values. What is the substance of surface?

When they aren't denouncing surfaces as lies and illusion, cultural critics typically have one explanation for why we devote time, attention, and, most of all, money to aesthetics: It's all about status. The intrinsic pleasures of look and feel are irrelevant. We're simply attracted to anything that helps us compete for recognition and dominance.

In *Luxury Fever*, a self-described "book about waste," economist Robert Frank treats the aesthetic ratchet effect as entirely status-driven.[13] We want ever-more appealing things because our neighbors have them. True enough. But in Frank's world, finding out that our neighbors are enjoying some new luxury functions only as a competitive spur, not as information about what's possible. We aren't happy for the neighbors. We don't want to share the same pleasures. We don't identify with them and want to imitate their taste. We just want to show them up. To Frank, rising expectations reflect only a desperate struggle to keep up with the Joneses.

Larger, better appointed homes are not, in this view, an enjoyable effect of prosperity but the outcome of a race to have the biggest and best on the block—a race that can have only one winner. We buy fancy clothes and luxury furnishings because we want to "stand out from the crowd," not because we like these things. Hence Frank's argument that "if, within each social group, everyone were to spend a little less on shoes, the same people who stand out from the crowd now would continue to do so. And because that outcome would free up resources to spend in other ways, people would have good reasons to prefer it."[14]

The argument depends on the conviction that we do not want those expensive shoes or large homes because of any intrinsic qualities. Frank assumes that we do not value the luxuries themselves—the soft leather of the shoes, the smooth granite countertop, the sculptural lines of the car, the drape and fit of the jacket—but just want to stand out, or at least not look bad, compared to other people. He also imagines only rivalry, not identification, a desire to stand out from the crowd, never to fit in with our friends. In Frank's world, aesthetics provides no pleasure and only the most desiccated and antisocial meaning.

Not surprisingly, he sees aesthetic competition as almost entirely wasteful, making everyone worse off. "If I buy a custom-tailored suit for my job interview," Frank writes, "I reduce the likelihood that others will land the same job; and in the process, I create an incentive for them to spend more than they planned on their own interview suits. . . . In situations like these, individual spending decisions are the seeds of a contagious process." In this view, we would all benefit if men could agree to wear cheap, ugly suits and spend their money on more important, more substantial things—a vision of fashion not unlike the British Utility scheme that took the ornament out of furniture and declared bookcases more essential than easy chairs.

Why, then, is the process contagious? Frank thinks it's just a matter of status-oriented one-upmanship, focused almost entirely on how much things cost. But consider why Frank's ideal world would require a cartel, in which everyone agreed to follow a drab standard. What would happen if every restaurant looked like a functional school cafeteria—but one establishment started to decorate with colored paint and table linens, background music, and special lighting? What if every product came in a plain black-and-white box—but one company invested in graphics and color? What if everyone wore drab Mao suits—but one person dressed with color, tailoring, and flair? People would, of course, be drawn to the aesthetic deviant, even though that nonconformity might well offend the reigning status hierarchy.

This thought experiment suggests something at work besides status and one-upmanship. Sensory pleasure works to commercial and personal advantage because aesthetics has intrinsic value. People seek it out, they reward those who offer new-and-improved pleasures, and they identify with those who share their tastes. If a nice suit helps someone win a job, that's because the interviewer finds it more enjoyable to talk with someone dressed that way. The aesthetic ratchet effect, whether it demands deodorant and clean hair or well-cut clothes and attractive shoes, rewards what we find pleasing to the senses. But there's more at work than Frank's money-oriented status pursuit. If you show up for an interview in a custom-tailored suit only to find your prospective boss wearing khakis and a polo shirt, the mismatch in aesthetic identities will cancel out any imagined status gains. You and the boss obviously have different ideas of what's enjoyable and appropriate.

Status competition is part of human life, of course. But cultural analysts like Frank are so determined to see status as the only possible value, and money as the only source of status, that they often ignore the very evidence they cite. Frank writes that "the status symbol of the 1990s has been the restaurant stove."[15] Fancy stoves are, in his opinion, entirely about keeping up with the neighbors' kitchens. To bolster his argument, he quotes a woman who owns a $7,000 stove, despite rarely cooking at home. Does she say she felt social pressure to buy an overpriced appliance? Does she say she wanted to stand out from the crowd? No, she describes the stove as a *work of art:* "You think of it as a painting that makes the kitchen look good." The supposedly damning quotation demonstrates the opposite of what Frank maintains: The woman sees the stove primarily not as a status symbol but as an aesthetic pleasure.

The manufacturers intended as much. "I was convinced that if I built something beautiful and powerful and safe, there were people out there who'd buy it," says the founder of the Viking Range Corp.[16] The company admits that most buyers are "look, don't cook" customers. Even an employee who was given a range says she never uses it, preferring to microwave something quick. "But I love looking at my Viking," she says. "Sometimes, I turn it on just to feel its power." Obviously the stoves serve something besides functional needs. But that "something" is more complex and sensual than status, combining a vision of an ideal life of home cooking with the immediate pleasures of beauty and power. Whatever status a fancy range conveys comes less from its cost than from its ability to show off the owner's discerning eye.

Even analysts who do not view luxury goods as waste do not necessarily credit the goods' intrinsic sensory appeal. In *Living It Up*, a mostly sympathetic analysis of what he calls "opuluxe," James Twitchell examines the spread of luxury goods, which he describes as "objects as rich in meaning as they are low in utility."[17] Opuluxe demonstrates the openness of today's social structure, he argues. Anyone can buy into the signs of wealth, so "making it" is no longer a matter of joining a socially exclusive club. Twitchell thus sees the profusion of luxury goods as tacky but benign.

Like Frank, however, Twitchell has a hard time noticing any qualities beyond status badges and advertising-created brand personas. And, like Frank, he unconsciously offers clues that more is going on. He tells us, for instance, that in the Beverly Hills Armani store, "I saw something I hadn't seen before. I saw customers patting the clothes, fondling the fabrics, touching the buttons. . . . It was like being in a petting zoo."[18] People pet Armani clothes because the fabrics feel so good. Those clothes attract us as visual, tactile creatures, not because they are "rich in meaning" but because they are rich in pleasure. The garments' utility includes the way they look and feel.

Twitchell's twenty-two-year-old daughter, Liz, accompanies him on his tour of Rodeo Drive, pretending to be a spoiled daddy's girl being bribed with presents to stay in college. This false persona reflects Twitchell's preconceptions about why people buy luxury goods, and what sort of people those buyers are. Only a superficial young woman, he assumes, would be wowed by luxury, not his intellectual Liz.

After a day at the act, however, Liz finally breaks down in tears, forcing the pair to make an abrupt exit from Tiffany. She explains why: "I believe myself to be everything the woman in Tiffany thought I wasn't: intelligent, self-sufficient, not given over to the whimsical spending of large amounts of money."[19] But Liz is sucked in. She wants the stuff her father is pretending he might buy for her. And she wants it not so she can impress anyone else or feel affiliated with prestigious brands. She wants those luxuries because they are aesthetically appealing, because they are, in a word, *beautiful*.

"Watching the woman in Armani try on the $20,000 beaded dress, I was momentarily entranced—and more than slightly jealous," she writes after the experiment collapses.

> The stuff was just so BEAUTIFUL, and when I looked down at my Old Navy sweater, I couldn't help but feel a bit wanting. . . . I wanted to leave Rodeo Drive for the same reason I often avoid fashion magazines: not because I don't care about such trivial stuff, but because I DO care, and when I look at these beautiful things, I'm left with an aching feeling of desire and a slight dissatisfaction with my current life. Luxury is incredibly powerful, and it gets to almost all of us, even when we're told it's meaningless.

The status critique does not actually say luxury is meaningless. To the contrary, the critics' usual argument is that such goods are *only* about meaning; they are "objects as rich in meaning as they are low in utility." The status critique sees only two possible sources of value: function and meaning; and it reduces meaning to a single idea: "I'm better than you." It denies the existence or importance of aesthetic pleasure and the many meanings and associations that can flow from that pleasure.

Luxuries, in this view, offer no intrinsic appeal beyond their social signals. But only superficial people, filled with status-anxiety and insecure about their own worth, would care about those meanings. By circular reasoning, then, to be attracted to such goods is to be a superficial person. So a serious young woman like Liz must avoid contact with fashion magazines and luxurious clothes—not simply because she would ache at the unattainable, but because wanting those things would call her identity into question. Her desire would imply that she's the sort of superficial, insecure person who cares about "such trivial stuff." To affirm that she's a young woman of substance, she must ignore the appeal of surfaces.

If surfaces are "trivial stuff," surfaces that change for no good reason are even less worthy. Hence, those who see aesthetics as "illusion" and "make-believe" are particularly vitriolic toward fashion. *Fashion* in this sense applies not just to clothing and related products but to anything whose aesthetic form evolves continuously, from typefaces and car bodies to musical styles and popular colors. Fashion is the process by which form seems exhausted and then refreshed, without regard to functional improvements.

Critics often portray fashion as entirely the product of commercial manipulation. "Typewriters and telephones came out in a wide range of colors in 1956, presumably to make owners dissatisfied with their plain old black models," sniffed the influential social critic Vance Packard in his 1957 book *The Hidden Persuaders*.[20] Nearly a half century later, many people still imagine that the world works the way Packard portrayed it. Aesthetic changes, in his view, were merely forms of deception, ways of creating artificial obsolescence. Packard offered no evidence that the colorful typewriters and telephones performed any worse than the plain old black models; rather, he objected to purely aesthetic upgrades, deeming them wasteful.

Today an engineer similarly condemns the latest iMac for using behind-the-curve chips and mocks buyers who've "been seduced by the case plastic":

> After people get over the *oh, cool!* and start really looking at this, the only real reason for getting it will be to impress people, just as was the case with the Cube, because what is *really* innovative about this is the case. And you can't actually get any work done with a fancy case[21]

Missing the effects of the technological progress he sees as legitimate innovation, the engineer doesn't consider the trade-offs. For a long time, ever-greater computing power was indeed what people looked for in a new machine. But computers are so capable these days that most customers don't need the absolutely fastest chip. To someone who doesn't plan to tax the machine's processing speed, a beautiful case may be worth more than cutting-edge technology, not just for status ("to impress people") but for personal enjoyment. At a given price, adding style will be more valuable, at least to some people, than adding power. True, you can't get any more work done with a fancy case, but you can enjoy the same work more.

From the buyer's point of view, greater aesthetic variety in an equally functional product is an unequivocal improvement, possibly (as with the green pager) one for which consumers will gladly pay a premium. If the goal is happiness rather than expert-determined "efficiency," form is itself a function. Pleasure is as real as meaning or usefulness, and its value is as subjective. Of course, aesthetic experimentation does not preclude other improvements. A new pager may have both enhanced features and a stylish face.

Fashion exists because novelty is itself an aesthetic pleasure. Even when the general form of something has reached an enduring ideal—the layout of book pages, the composition of men's suits, the structure of automobiles, the shapes of knives, forks, and spoons—we crave variation within that classic type. Colors and shapes that looked great a couple of years ago begin to seem dull. We're attracted to fresher, newer forms. The same never-ending tinkering that gives us more functional, better-looking toilet brushes also gives us new looks to replace the old.

The changes are usually incremental, moving gradually in one direction over a long period until that form's aesthetic possibilities are exhausted and something new suddenly feels right. That new look has often evolved without much notice, also building slowly, so that what seems like an abrupt shift actually represents a switch from one incremental process to another.

Consider a story told by Anne Bass, a wealthy patron of the arts and haute couture.[22] She describes her taste in clothes as classic, not "so much embellishment as beautiful lines, beautiful tailoring, things that are constructed in clever ways." In the flamboyant 1980s, her fashion choices were relatively restrained, but she did buy evening clothes "that had a bit of the 'costume' about them." Bass recalls the moment when those clothes suddenly felt obsolete. In August 1989, she attended a Paris fashion show and dinner given by Giorgio Armani:

> I remember wearing a Saint Laurent evening suit that paired a heavily embroidered jacket with a tangerine charmeuse sarong, and that was the last time I recall putting on something that made that kind of statement. Because, suddenly, that night, it felt completely wrong. It felt like Armani was modern, was what was happening. Before that night, I didn't really get Armani. I thought he was a nonevent. But I remember that evening, that party, as the end of an era. . . . I don't think it was long afterward that I opened my closet in New York, and noticed that everything was either beige or black.

The shift Bass observed had been going on for some time. Otherwise no one would have been interested in attending an Armani event in the first place. The designer had in fact come to prominence in the early 1980s. But

Bass and her fashion-savvy friends could not have known in advance when one man's vision of what clothes should look like would go from a stylistic "nonevent" to a newly dominant aesthetic. Exactly what sort of variation will seem appealing at a given time is uncertain and can be discovered only through trial and error.

The fashion process is not mechanical but contingent; which changes will fit the moment depends on a host of unarticulated desires and unnoticed influences, making shifts hard to predict. A fashion writer refers to "fashion's X-factor, the unknown quantity that makes an item seem hot to a consumer."[23] The decrees of would-be style makers—that mauve is back but in a "more sophisticated" form, that gray is the "new black," that velvet furniture is in again—suggest a sort of dictatorial authority. But this rhetoric is just a combination of bravado and best guesses. The sales racks are full of aesthetic experiments that failed to capture the public imagination, and every such item is an argument against the notion that authorities can dictate style. Now more than ever, that is not how fashion works.

Besides, there is more to fashion than profit-seeking "built-in obsolescence." We find fashion patterns in goods for which there is no commercial market. Historian Anne Hollander notes that fashion in clothing has existed for eight hundred years, centuries longer than the apparel business. "The shifty character of what looks right is not new, and was never a thing deliberately created to impose male will on females, or capitalist will on the population, or designers' will on public taste," she writes.[24] "Long before the days of industrialized fashion, stylistic motion in Western dress was enjoying a profound emotional importance, giving a dynamically poetic visual cast to people's lives, and making Western fashion hugely compelling all over the world." Pleasure, not manipulation, drives changes in look and feel.

Even intangible, noncommercial "goods" exhibit similar patterns. Sociologist Stanley Lieberson has studied how tastes in children's names change over time.[25] Nobody runs ads to convince parents to choose *Emily* or *Joshua* for their newborns. No magazine editors authoritatively dictate that "*Ryan* is the new *Michael*." But names still shift according to fashion. Name choices, like clothing choices, are influenced by the desire to be different but not too different; the ideal balance varies from person to person. Like designers experimenting with new ideas in ignorance of what their competitors are trying, parents have to choose their babies' names without knowing exactly what other parents are choosing. The result is a complex, often surprising, dynamic. Parents frequently find that the name they "just liked" is suddenly widely popular, expressing aesthetic preferences that are somehow in the air. Contrary to common assumptions about how fashion works, Lieberson finds that names don't trickle down in a simple way from high-income, well-educated parents to lower-income, less-educated parents. Newly popular names tend to catch on with everyone at about the same time.

External influences, such as the names of celebrities or fictional characters, do play a role in what's popular. But cause and effect are complicated. Fictional characters don't just publicize possible names; their creators, like new parents, select those names from the current milieu. And whether a famous name spreads partly depends on internal, purely aesthetic factors. Harrison Ford, Arnold Schwarzenegger, and Wesley Snipes are all action stars, but their stardom hasn't translated into millions of little Harrisons, Arnolds, or Wesleys—in part because their names just don't *sound* all that appealing.

What does sound appealing itself changes over time, as particular phonemes go in and out of style. In recent years, for instance, the ending *schwa* sound has been popular for girls' names, such as Hannah, Samantha, Sarah, and Jessica; in the era of Susan and Kimberly other endings seemed equally feminine. African-American parents are more likely than whites to invent completely new names for their babies; those unique names follow clear patterns that indicate gender, and they show fashion cycles in the popularity of component syllables. *La-* used to be a popular first syllable for black girls' names. Now *-eisha* is a popular ending. Names associated with living old people often seem dated, like out-of-style clothing; popular names from generations who have passed on, by contrast, may seem classic and resonant, like vintage fashion. Even in this completely noncommercial context, we see fashion cycles of distinctiveness, popularity, and obsolescence, driven by the quest for aesthetic satisfaction. That satisfaction combines purely sensory components with meaningful associations.

Whether for names or clothes, fashion reflects the primacy of individual taste over inherited custom. The freer people feel to choose names they like, rather than, say, names of relatives or saints, the more rapidly baby names go through fashion cycles. As Hollander observes, "Fashion has its own manifest virtue, not unconnected with the virtues of individual freedom and uncensored imagination that still underlie democratic ideals."[26] Fashion pervades open, dynamic societies. Through markets, media, and migration, such societies offer more outlets for creativity, more sources of new aesthetic ideas, and more chances for individuals to find and adopt the forms that please them. Our age of look and feel reflects the increasing openness of our social and economic life, which both enhances and takes advantage of aesthetic abundance. As a result, we see fashion appearing in new areas, with much greater fluidity of form. The more influence accorded individual preferences, the greater the importance of fashion—and, in many cases, the more accelerated its pace.

This dynamic perturbs critics. Static, customary forms, they suggest, are more authentic. Thus Daniel Bell worries about the rise of syncretism, "the jumbling of styles in modern art, which absorbs African masks or Japanese prints into its modes of depicting spatial perceptions; or the merging of Oriental and Western religions, detached from their histories, in a modern meditative consciousness. Modern culture is defined by this extraordinary freedom to ransack the world storehouse and to engorge any and every style it comes upon."[27] And Ewen, again equating style with illusion, writes that "modern style speaks to a world where change is the rule of the day, where one's place in the social order is a matter of perception, the product of diligently assembled illusions."[28] Although he might recoil from the implications, Ewen seems to assume that "one's place in the social order" would be more valid if it were determined not by perception and individual effort but by something more impersonal and objective—bloodlines, perhaps, or skin color.

Even when he cites the advantages of the shift to a more open society, Ewen casts it in terms of false identity: "On the one hand, style speaks for the rise of a democratic society, in which who one wishes to become is often seen as more consequential than who one is. On the other hand, style speaks for a society in which coherent meaning has fled to the hills, and in which drift has provided a context of continual discontent."[29] This analysis scorns the search for individual satisfaction and self-definition—the pursuit of happiness—as no more than a source of "continual discontent." The traditionalist conservative argument against the disruptions of an open social and economic order has transmogrified into a left-wing attack on fashion.

Genuine value, such critics suggest, ought to reflect something more permanent and substantial than ever-shifting tastes. The ephemeral nature of style, in this view, confirms its fundamental falsehood. "As style reached out to a more broadly defined 'middle class' of consumers" in the nineteenth century, Ewen complains,

> the value of objects was less and less associated with workmanship, material quality, and rarity, and more and more derived from the abstract and increasingly malleable factor of aesthetic appeal. Durable signs of style were being displaced by signs that were ephemeral: shoddy goods with elaborately embossed surfaces, advertising cards, product labels. If style had once been a device by which individuals tried to surround themselves with symbols of perpetuity, now it was becoming something of the moment, to be employed for effect, and then displaced by a new device of impression.

Value in this view should approximate static, universal standards instead of fluctuating with fickle individual preferences. Hence Ewen's dislike of the "abstract and malleable factor of aesthetic appeal," which is all too subjective and personal.

The old "symbols of perpetuity" were in fact products of a traditional, fairly static social order. These goods demonstrated inherited social position; only a family that had maintained wealth and rank over generations would possess homes, portraits, furnishings, or silverware with the patina of age. You could show off your grandfather's portrait or your great-grandmother's silver only if your family was in fact one of long-standing status. Surface patina demonstrated social substance. As anthropologist Grant McCracken notes, "The patina of an object allows it to serve as the medium for a vitally important status message. The purpose of this message is not to claim status. It is to verify status claims."[30] Arrivistes could be identified by the shine of their possessions, avoiding the sixteenth-century fear of the "tailor or barber [who] in the excess of apparel [would] counterfeit and be like a gentleman."[31] (Clothes, rather than acquiring patina, wear out over time; that's why they're more subject to fashion and why status-oriented societies try to impose sumptuary laws.)

The ephemeral nineteenth-century merchandise that Ewen condemns spread new aesthetic pleasures to people of limited means. Made possible by new forms of production and distribution, these goods were cheap in both senses of the word. Embossed paper doodads might be short-lived, but they were also accessible and fun. They had little to do with social status and much to do with personal enjoyment. A world of pretty product labels is more delightful than a world of generic barrels, and it is a world in which style no longer belongs only to an elite. These new and shifting forms of aesthetic pleasure befit a fluid social order.

Fashion itself can, of course, be a source of status. As anyone who has been a teenager knows, the right style can determine who's in, while the wrong look can mean social oblivion. Early-twentieth-century social critics worried about the social pressures created by newly affordable ready-to-wear clothes when respectability depended greatly on the proper appearance. Writing in 1929, one essayist complained that "crops may fail, silkworms suffer blight, weavers may strike, tariffs may hamper, but the mass-gesture of the feminine neck bending to the yoke of each new season's fashion goes on."[32] Garment makers, she complained, made sure "that last year's wardrobe shall annually be made as obsolete as possible," placing a severe financial burden on poor women who wanted to look current. Here is an earlier version of the Packard and Ewen critiques: Fashion represents the tyranny of commercial manipulation.

Such critics exaggerated both year-to-year fashion shifts and the response of consumers; as we know from survey data, families with moderate incomes did not own large or frequently changing wardrobes. But these criticisms expressed genuine anxiety. By making fashionable clothes available to people who a generation earlier would have had no such choice, the apparel industry increased not just pleasure but aspiration. And with aspiration came, inevitably, the disappointment of limits. In industrialized countries, working women had access to new forms of self-expression and adornment, the sorts of aesthetic pleasures once reserved for the social elite. But, like Liz Twitchell in Beverly Hills, they would also ache for the unattainable.

We do not know, of course, that traditional peasant women experienced no such pangs. Folktales like "Cinderella" suggest that they did. What was different by the nineteenth century was that social critics cared, and that fashionable attire had taken on symbolic importance for average people. Dressing in style was a new sort of personal achievement, especially if you weren't rich enough to buy someone else's good taste, and it was a source of social prestige. Self-presentation had become a valuable skill, at all social levels.

That is all the more true today, and the task is far more difficult. Although the financial cost of putting on a good appearance has dropped, the trickiness of the challenge has increased. As Hillary Clinton can testify, the more technological and social choices we have about how we look, the more ways we can go wrong—and the more meaning people are likely to read into our choices. The challenges of fashion have also spread to previously fashion-free areas of life. When law firms eschewed graphic design and followed long-standing customs, no one judged them by their letterhead. Now they have to think about the connotations of typefaces and logos; sticking to the plain old style is itself an indicative choice. "Fashion," observes Hollander, "is a perpetual test of character and self-knowledge, as well as taste, whereas traditional dress"—or any other custom-bound aesthetic expression—"is not."[33]

The "character" Hollander sees tested by fashion's demands is not moral character but a combination of self-awareness, confidence, taste, and affiliation. How we deal with fashion's flux suggests something about our inner life. Can we enjoy its pleasures, using them to create an aesthetic identity that reflects who we are, including what we enjoy? Can we find a happy balance between look and feel and other values? Or do we feel compelled either to subordinate the rest of our life to appearance or to ignore appearance altogether—to treat look and feel either as the ultimate value or as entirely without value?

Much of the rhetoric surrounding appearance offers this false choice. From well-intended mothers to scathing social commentators, authorities tell us that surfaces are "meaningless." That might be true if they meant that the value of aesthetics lies in its own pleasures, not in what it says about something else. But that's not at all what they intend. Authorities call aesthetics "meaningless" to suggest that it is worthless and unimportant, that it doesn't matter. Thus, Liz Twitchell says she's been taught that luxury is "meaningless," so its pleasures shouldn't affect her. Ewen excoriates graphic designers for creating "meaningless distinctions" between products, denying the value of aesthetic pleasures and associations. "I try to help her not judge herself against the prevailing criteria of how she's supposed to be," says a father whose thirteen-year-old daughter thinks she's too skinny. "I tell her all this is meaningless."[34]

When a father tells his teenage daughter that looks are "meaningless," he is not assuring her that she's attractive or will become so over time. He is saying that she's loved and valued for her other traits, regardless of how she looks—a loving but irrelevant affirmation. Her looks do mean something important to her. They don't match her sense of who she is or would like to be. By changing the subject, her father is inadvertently agreeing that she looks bad, exacerbating her sense of failure. We do not respond similarly to teenagers who wish they were stronger, more musical, or better in school; we coach them on how to build on their natural gifts. Yet somehow we believe that looks are different, that appearance must be worth either everything or nothing.

Denying that we care about appearance for its own sake leads us to exaggerate its deeper significance, in order to justify our natural interest. Consider some of the commentary surrounding the 2000 election. When Florida Secretary of State Katherine Harris appeared with heavy makeup, wags compared her to a drag queen and Cruella De Vil.[35] Al Gore got similar treatment after he wore bad makeup in his first debate with George W. Bush. Commentators called him, among other things, "Herman Munster doing a bad Ronald Reagan impression"[36] and "a big, orange, waxy, wickless candle."[37]

In both cases, commentators appealed to their readers' interest in how other people look. To give their criticisms a respectable mask, however, many pundits treated these cosmetic problems as symbols of more serious flaws. One interpreted Harris's blue eye shadow as evidence that "she failed to think for herself" and declared that "one wonders how this Republican woman, who can't even use restraint when she's wielding a mascara wand, will manage to use it and make sound decisions in this game of partisan one-upmanship."[38] Amid the Florida recount, a Gore critic harked back to his excessive makeup to suggest that he was a phony: "While Gore yammered about [the voters'] 'will,' it was clear to my houseplants that the man who looks like he raids Katherine Harris' pancake makeup supply was really gloating about the Florida Supreme Court decision in his favor."[39]

These commentators went well beyond the idea that self-presentation may say something about the "judgment of the mind," reflecting a person's self-awareness and taste. They damned Harris and Gore not for bad judgment but for bad character. They invoked the old tradition that equates cosmetics with deception and decadence. Someone who wears a lot of makeup, they suggested, is not to be trusted.

In fact, someone who wears a lot of makeup may just have a sunburn (Gore) or out-of-date style (Harris). Surface may not say much at all about substance. Being able to separate the two is the first step toward avoiding the deception that critics of aesthetics so fear. But to do so we have to admit that aesthetics has value in and of itself instead of pretending that it is "meaningless" or trying to justify our interest in looks by freighting them with unwarranted symbolism. All other things being equal, we prefer beauty, just as we prefer intelligence, charm, eloquence, or talent. But beauty can coexist with stupidity, rudeness, or cruelty. All other things may not be equal. What's true for people is true for places and things. All other things being equal, we prefer attractive computers. That does not mean, as Apple discovered with its beautiful Cube, that we will ignore price and performance to get aesthetics.[40]

The challenge is to learn to accept that aesthetic pleasure is an autonomous good, not the highest or the best but one of many plural, sometimes conflicting, and frequently unconnected sources of value. Not all sources of value, including aesthetic and moral worth, line up in one-to-one correspondence. Rhetoric that treats aesthetic quality as a mark of goodness and truth—or as a sign of evil and deception—is profoundly misleading.

The values of design itself—function, meaning, and pleasure—can exist independently of each other. It's incorrect to argue in defense of Wal-Mart's big-box stores that "a Wal-Mart is 'ugly' only because we either ignore or devalue what it does best."[41] The value of Wal-Mart's design comes from its function. Ugliness diminishes pleasure, a different good. Function may coexist with pleasure, and increasingly it does, but it does not have to. Saying a store is ugly does not mean it has no value, only that its value must lie outside aesthetics. Just as we may value a green pager more highly than a black one entirely because of its looks, we may value Wal-Mart for its convenience and efficiency, while acknowledging that it's ugly. And we can tell nothing about the moral worth of either the green pager or the store by judging its looks.

A bad person can be beautiful or create beautiful things. A good person can be ugly or make bad art. Goodness does not create or equal beauty. The problem with Leni Riefenstahl's films is not that they're aesthetically powerful—that achievement is, considered in isolation, valuable. But aesthetic quality does not trump or cancel out other considerations. Beauty is not a moral defense, merely an autonomous value. Just as a plain face does not make a young woman bad, so artistic achievement does not justify serving an evil cause. Aesthetic pleasure and moral virtue are independent goods. They may complement or contradict each other, or operate entirely independently. Colas are neither good nor evil, and neither is their packaging. The packaging design adds pleasure and meaning, and thus value, to morally neutral products.

When evil deeds come to be associated with otherwise attractive images, the images lose their attraction. Meaning arises from association, in this case canceling out pleasure. A black swastika in a circle of white on a red background may be graphically appealing, but we do not evaluate its form independently of its historic meaning. For two generations after Hitler, well-muscled Nordic men looked like villains, not Adonises. Only recently, under the influence of gay aesthetics, has that ideal of masculine beauty begun to lose its Nazi connotations. Riefenstahl's artistic achievements, and her images, are permanently polluted by the cause she served. Film students may study her techniques, but they do not forget or forgive her moral failings. Form has its own power and worth, but it does not inevitably trump content. Aesthetics is not a psychological superweapon, capable of blinding us to all other values.

When terrorists slammed two passenger jets into the World Trade Center on September 11, 2001, Michael Bierut had his own moment of Nazis-to-Pepsi self-doubt. He was in London and returned home to Manhattan a few days after the attack. "As a designer," he wrote me, "I am still reeling from the images of 9/11."[42] The act had been horrifying, but the images it created could not have been better designed: "The timing of the collisions, the angle of the second plane, the colors of the explosions, the slow-motion collapsing of the towers: could the terrorists ever dream how nightmarishly vivid this would be to the vast viewing audience?"

Amid the trauma of mid-September, this terrible juxtaposition—striking images in the service of death—recalled all the attacks ever made on surface for its own sake, and on the designers who create surface appeal. If an event so awful could look so vivid, even beautiful in a purely formal sense, how could we trust aesthetic pleasure? How could designers like Bierut justify their work, except when surface serves some grander substance? The attack, wrote Bierut, "makes me think about all the times I've worked on purposeless assignments and put meaningless content into beautiful packages. I will not approach my work the same way from now on."

He knew better. The destruction of the World Trade Center was not a carefully composed movie scene, designed to arouse pity and terror within the safe frame of fiction. It was the all-too-real murder of thousands. It was entirely substance. The attack was not packaging, not surface, not performance art. It had both meaning and political purpose. The striking images produced led viewers not to praise but to condemn the attackers who created them. Only those who embraced the murderers' cause rejoiced in those images. Aesthetics did not prove a superweapon, justifying slaughter. To the contrary, the media images that followed were attempts to capture the events—and the horror and grief—of the day. Those images were valuable because they could say more than words. But the images were not the act itself.

In the horror of the moment, Bierut had forgotten the meaning and value of his work, falling into the puritanical mind-set that denies the value of aesthetic pleasure and seeks always to link it with evil. To wrap meaningless, as opposed to vicious, content in beautiful packaging does no harm. To the contrary, such creativity enriches the world and affirms the worth of the individuals whose pleasure it serves. Colas are not genocide.

Bierut soon had second thoughts. "One of the signatures of any repressive regime," he wrote the following day, "is their need to control not just meaningful differences—the voices of dissent, for instance—but ostensibly 'meaningless' ones as well, like dress. It will take some time for people to realize that creating the difference between Coke and Pepsi is not just an empty pastime but one of many signs of life in a free society."[43] The Afghan women who risked the Taliban's prisons to paint their faces and style their hair in underground beauty shops, and who celebrated the liberation of Kabul by coloring their nails with once-forbidden polish, would agree.[44] Surface may take on meaning, but it has a value all its own.   ∎

NOTES

1. Iain Morris, quoted in Eric Nee, "Open Season on Carly Fiorina," *Fortune*, July 23, 2001, p. 120.

2. Michael Bierut interview with the author, November 11, 2000, and e-mail to the author, May 9, 2001.

3. Stuart Ewen, *All Consuming Images*, pp. 22, 149.

4. Daniel Bell, *The Cultural Contradictions of Capitalism*, 2nd ed. (New York: Basic Books, 1996), pp. 283, 293–94, 70. Bell's 1996 critique is heavily influenced by Warner Sombart's *Luxury and Capitalism*, which in Bell's words "made the idiosyncratic argument that illicit love and the style of life it produced gave rise to luxury— and capitalism." He also cites Rousseau on adornment's origins in falsehood: "Rousseau related what happened in that mythical moment when young men and women, growing up, began to meet around a large tree or campfire, to sing and dance and be 'true children of love and leisure.' But when 'each one began to look at the others and wanted to be looked at himself,' public esteem became a value. 'The one who sang or danced the best, the handsomest, the strongest, the most adroit, or the most eloquent, became the most highly considered; and *that was the first step toward inequality and, at the same time, toward vice.*' Those who had lost out, so to speak, began to dissemble, to adorn themselves, to wear plumage, to be sly or boisterous; in short, 'for one's own advantage to appear to be other than what one in fact was, to be and seem to become two altogether different things; and from this distinction [arise] conspicuous ostentation, deceptive cunning, and all the vices that follow from them,'" pp. 294–95.

5. Theodor W. Adorno and Max Horkheimer, "The Culture Industry: Enlightenment as Mass Deception," in Juliet B. Schor and Douglas B. Holt, eds., *The Consumer Society Reader* (New York: The New Press, 2000), pp. 4–5.

6. Sinclair B. Ferguson, "'Repent,' Said Jesus; Do Evangelicals Hear Him?" *The Dallas Morning News*, January 27, 2001, p. 4G. Ferguson is a minister in the Church of Scotland.

7. Kenneth Brower, "Photography in the Age of Falsification," *The Atlantic Monthly*, May 1998, p. 93. In Platonic thought, of course, storytelling itself is a suspect act, creating falsehoods.

8. The first quote is from a sermon by John Donne; the second is from Thomas Tuke's 1616 tract *A Treatise against Painting and Tincturing of Men and Women*. Both are quoted in Frances E. Dolan, "Taking the Pencil out of God's Hand: Art, Nature, and the Face-Painting Debate in Early Modern England," *PMLA*, March 1993, pp. 224–39.

9. Naomi Wolf, *The Beauty Myth: How Images of Beauty Are Used Against Women* (New York: Anchor Books, 1992), pp. 55–66.

10. Emily Toth, quoted in Alison Schneider, "Frumpy or Chic? Tweed or Kente? Sometimes Clothes Make the Professor," *The Chronicle of Higher Education*, January 23, 1998, p. A12.

11. Hillary Rodham Clinton, "Remarks of Senator Hillary Rodham Clinton," Class Day, Yale University, May 20, 2001, http://clinton.senate.gov/~clinton/speeches/010520.html.

12. The domain name hillaryshair.com now belongs to an unrelated pornography site that draws traffic from the many links still aimed at the old site.

13. Robert Frank, *Luxury Fever: Why Money Fails to Satisfy in an Era of Excess* (New York: The Free Press, 1999), p. 9.

14. Robert Frank, *Luxury Fever*, p. 9.

15. Robert Frank, *Luxury Fever*, p. 24.

16. Fred Carl and Tawana Thompson, quoted in Molly O'Neill, "The Viking Invasion," *The New Yorker*, July 29, 2002, pp. 40–45.

17. James B. Twitchell, *Living It Up: Our Love Affair with Luxury* (New York: Columbia University Press, 2002), p. 1.

18. James B. Twitchell, *Living It Up*, p. 91.

19. James B. Twitchell, *Living It Up*, pp. 102–3. Twitchell has his wife play a similarly degraded role on a shopping trip in Palm Beach. Her equally unexpected rebellion takes a different form; she takes off and goes shopping without him, buying luxuries, such as Paloma Picasso earrings, that she likes and can afford on her own salary.

20. Vance Packard, *The Hidden Persuaders* (New York: David McKay, 1957), p. 172.

21. Steven Den Beste, *USS Clueless*, January 7, 2002, http://denbeste.nu/cd_log_entries/2002/01/fog/0000000118.shtml.

22. Anne Bass, "The 1980s," *Vogue*, November 1999, pp. 492, 542.

23. Amy M. Spindler, "Are Retail Consultants Missing Fashion's X-Factor?" *The New York Times*, June 13, 1996, p. B8.

24. Anne Hollander, *Sex and Suits* (New York: Kodansha, 1994), pp. 11–12.

25. Stanley Lieberson, *A Matter of Taste: How Names, Fashions, and Culture Change* (New Haven: Yale University Press, 2000).

26. Anne Hollander, *Sex and Suits*, p. 12.

27. Daniel Bell, *The Cultural Contradictions of Capitalism*, pp. 13–14.

28. Stuart Ewen, *All Consuming Images*, p. 23.

29. Stuart Ewen, *All Consuming Images*, p. 38.

30. Grant McCracken, *Culture and Consumption* (Bloomington: Indiana University Press, 1988), p. 35.

31. Sir Thomas Elyot, quoted in Grant McCracken, *Culture and Consumption*, p. 33. Spelling has been modernized.

32. Jenna Weissman Joselit, *A Perfect Fit: Clothes, Character, and the Promise of America* (New York: Metropolitan Books, 2001), p. 33.

33. Anne Hollander, *Sex and Suits*, p. 21.

34. Jeffrey Leder, quoted in Abby Ellin, "How Fathers Can Help Daughters in the Body-Image Battle," *The New York Times*, September 18, 2000, p. B7.

35. *When Florida Secretary of State* Janny Scott, "When First Impressions Count," *The New York Times*, December 3, 2000, sec. 4, p. 3. Kim Folstad, "She Monitors Election, We Monitor Her," *The Palm Beach Post*, November 18, 2000, p. 1D. Hayley Kaufman, "Fashion Victim," *The Boston Globe*, November 16, 2000, p. D2.

36. Mark Steyn, "Game Face Otherwise Occupied," *Chicago Sun-Times*, October 15, 2000, p. 48.

37. Maureen Dowd, "Dead Heat Humanoids," *The New York Times*, October 5, 2000, p. A35.

38. Robin Givhan, "The Eyelashes Have It," *The Washington Post*, November 18, 2000, p. C1.

39. Andrea Peyser, "Oh, How I Wish That I'd Never Voted for Gore," *The New York Post*, November 24, 2000, p. 5.

40. Virginia Postrel, "Can Good Looks Guarantee a Product's Success?" *The New York Times*, July 12, 2001, p. C2.

41. Dan Hansen, "The Beauty of Wal-Mart," *Happy Fun Pundit*, August 9, 2002, http://happyfunpundit.blogspot.com/2002_08_04_happyfunpundit_archive.html.

42. Michael Bierut, e-mail to the author, September 18, 2001.

43. Michael Bierut, e-mail to the author, September 19, 2001.

44. Saira Shah, "Beneath the Veil: The Taliban's Harsh Rule of Afghanistan," *CNN Presents*, September 22, 2001. Virginia Postrel, "Free Hand," *Reason*, March 2002, p. 82.

■ *QUESTIONS FOR MAKING CONNECTIONS WITHIN THE ESSAY* ■

1. A key word in Postrel's argument is "value." What exactly does she mean by this word? What are the different kinds of value that she acknowledges in her essay? Why is it so important for her that we grant to the aesthetic a special value all its own? Postrel argues that we have failed to see the value of aesthetics, but is it possible to value aesthetics too highly? Does Postrel's chapter implicitly present a theory about the ways that different kinds of values should be related to one another?

2. In her piece, Postrel takes on a number of arguments against aesthetics. On what assumptions do these varied arguments rest? Pay attention to the values and concerns that might motivate the critics she responds to. Daniel Bell is an American sociologist. Theodor Adorno and Max Horkheimer were social theorists inspired by Karl Marx. Other critics of the aesthetic named by Postrel include Sun Microsystems CEO Scott McNealy, an unnamed "conservative minister," Senator Hillary Rodham Clinton, the economist Robert Frank, and the English professor James Twitchell. What might lie behind their attitudes toward aesthetics? Given the diversity of the critics, what might we conclude about our society's prevailing attitudes toward beauty, pleasure, and so on?

3. In her final paragraph, Postrel writes that "creating the difference between Coke and Pepsi is not just an empty pastime but one of the many signs of life in a free society." In what ways might aesthetics be connected to freedom, either for individuals or for society as a whole? In what ways may aesthetics help to heighten or intensify our sense of being alive? Is there a difference between "living" form and "dead" form? If there is, do people tend to agree about the forms that seem most alive? We may ordinarily assume that our experiences of beauty, harmony, and energy are entirely subjective, but are they really? If our perception of "life" in things is entirely subjective, then why did so many customers buy the same "squirt-gun green pagers"?

■ *QUESTIONS FOR WRITING* ■

1. What are the larger implications of Postrel's argument? One way to answer this question is to ask if she has ultimately done nothing more than defend crass commercialism. Has Postrel simply devised a clever argument in defense of a life dedicated to superficiality and acquisitiveness? Or does she point the way to alternative forms of intellectual depth and personal integrity? If most people were to think and act in the way that Postrel would like them to, would our society be any different—or any better—than it is right now?

2. Is the "surface" of Postrel's chapter consistent with its "substance"? Is the *way* she makes her point appropriate to the point she makes? In order to answer this question, you might look carefully at the formal qualities of her argument, starting with a paragraph-by-paragraph outline. Would you describe Postrel's chapter in the main as "polemical" or as "affirmative"? What do you notice about the tone of the chapter? Would you call it "adversarial" or "conciliatory," "genial" or "strident"? Would you describe Postrel's treatment of other writers as "balanced" or "tendentious"? If you regard the surface of Postrel's argument as inconsistent with its substance, can you think of a more effective way to get the same point across?

■ *QUESTIONS FOR MAKING CONNECTIONS BETWEEN READINGS* ■

1. How is Postrel's argument changed if we consider the economic system that supports the mass production of the items she admires? Is it possible to maintain a commitment to the aesthetic once attention is turned from the object itself to the labor that was required to make the object? Taking Pietra Rivoli's discussion of the market forces governing the creation and distribution of T-shirts, consider what is gained by attending to labor rather than to aesthetics. Is labor the "substance" while aesthetics is the "surface"? If consumers valued aesthetics more highly, would labor relations change?

2. Postrel offers a spirited defense of aesthetics, but she never looks carefully at the ways people actually experience beauty, pleasure, novelty, excitement, and so on. We might find clues to the nature of aesthetic experience, however, in Robert Thurman's "Wisdom." Take a look in particular at the section entitled "Practice: Trying to Find Your 'I.'" When we cultivate awareness in the way that Thurman describes, does every moment become an aesthetic experience? Could it be that our awareness of aesthetics is in some way similar to an experience like meditation? What happens to the "I" when we become aware of beauty, novelty, order, or energy in the world around us?

PIETRA RIVOLI

AS CONSUMERS, WE see goods only at the very end of their life cycles, when they are waiting to be bought in stores or online. What shoppers don't see is the long and complicated journey that consumer products now take to reach stores where we find them. Even something as simple as a T-shirt, which we buy, wear, and dispose of with hardly a second thought, arrives by way of an increasingly intricate and contested route. Pietra Rivoli, a professor of finance and international business at the McDonough School of Business at Georgetown University, tracks this process step by step in *The Travels of a T-Shirt in the Global Economy: An Economist Examines the Markets, Power, and Politics of World Trade* (2005). She begins by purchasing a discounted T-shirt from a convenience store and then works backwards across the world to see how it got to be in that store, waiting for her. Widely acclaimed for its unique and engaging approach to globalization, this book was designated the best scholarly book of 2005 in the category of finance and economics by the American Association of Publishers.

"Dogs Snarling Together" is a chapter from *The Travels of a T-Shirt in the Global Economy* that traces a particularly contentious issue in the T-shirt trade. As the economy has become an increasingly complex global system, the "market mechanism" has bumped up against traditional economic nationalism. The snarling dogs of the chapter's title are the lobbyists and American textile industry representatives who "can speak with one voice—or snarl together" to ensure that their interests are protected. Rivoli details the strengthening and the unraveling of the protectionist measures as national interests, the drive for profit, and the global economy come into conflict.

"When I decided to follow my T-shirt around the world," Rivoli writes in a reflective article, "what I wanted most of all was to tell a great story." By setting aside her assumptions and any didactic motivation, Rivoli is able to tell a story

Rivoli, Pietra. "Dogs Snarling Together." *The Travels of a T-Shirt in the Global Economy: An Economist Examines the Markets, Power, and Politics of World Trade*. Hoboken: John Wiley & Sons, 2005. 111–138.

Biographical information comes from <http://faculty.msb.edu/rivolip/#>; quotations come from a reflective article at the Powell's Books Web site, <http://www.powells.com/essays/rivoli.html>.

without villains, one in which "every business, every entrepreneur, every politician . . . was just trying to make their way in a competitive market, a market that often changes under their feet." In doing so, she is able to draw our attention to the complexities of trade and business and our own complex role in the global economy.

■ ■

Dogs Snarling Together

How Politics Came to Rule the Global Apparel Trade

Chinese T-Shirts versus American Jobs

The shipping container stacked with T-shirts boards the freighter in Shanghai and heads back across the Pacific.[1] The ship travels south along the western coast of Mexico and squeezes through the Panama Canal before heading north to the Miami port, and finally to the screen printing factory at Sherry Manufacturing. At this point, the T-shirts enter the most complex and challenging phase of their lives: trying to gain access to the U.S. market. Chinese T-shirts and Chinese immigrants have similar experiences in attempting to get to America. In both cases, the journey is expensive, risky, and often illegal. There is an army waiting on shore, ready to fight the invasion. The U.S. apparel industry has lost the race to the bottom, and while this may be the result of a "happy concurrence of causes" as David Hume suggested in 1748, not everybody is happy about it. Most of the American South has moved onward and upward from textile production, but there are pockets across the Carolinas and Georgia where the mills are still at the center of the economy and the community. Losers in the U.S. textile and apparel industries are not going gracefully, especially not when losing to China. The textile and apparel trade is the most managed and protected manufacturing trade in U.S. history, or, as one writer noted, "the most spectacular and comprehensive protectionist regime in existence."[2] Whether the regime has at the same time been a spectacular success or failure depends upon one's point of view.

When Auggie Tantillo sees a T-shirt from China, he gets a bad feeling in his stomach, but his reflex is fight rather than flight. Auggie can go into Wal-Mart to buy soap or batteries, but he can't even walk by the clothing without the feeling coming back so he avoids that section of the store entirely. Auggie is executive director of the American Manufacturing Trade Action Coalition (AMTAC), an advocacy group dedicated to preserving manufacturing jobs in the American textile and apparel industries. Auggie represents not so much a "special interest" as a moral viewpoint. As the youngest of nine children in a traditional Sicilian family, Auggie is used to fighting for his fair share. He is soft-spoken, fiercely intelligent, and very sure that he is right. Auggie has spent his entire adult life on defense, trying to block or slow the waves of cheap clothing imports flowing into U.S. markets. For 25 years the waves have been growing bigger, but he keeps bouncing back, ready to block and punch.

But Auggie thinks the fight with China could be the last. Between 2000 and 2004, the U.S. textile and apparel industries lost more than one-third of their remaining jobs, and looming on Auggie's horizon—and on the horizon of manufacturers everywhere—is the China threat, as well as a new set of rules to govern global trade in T-shirts. U.S. producers of yarn, fabric, and apparel have no hope of competing with China, at least not under the radical new rules of the game scheduled to take effect in 2005. Unless somebody stops China, it will be all over, Auggie believes. Waves of T-shirts, socks, underwear, caps, sweaters, pants, and ties will come flooding in, and will drown the American textile industry within the decade, along with the industries in dozens of other countries. Unless somebody stops China, there won't be another war to fight because there won't be an industry left to save.

Auggie used to have a bigger army in the war against apparel imports, but one by one his fellow soldiers have dropped out, or worse yet, defected to the dark side. The AKA (American Knitwear Association), AAMA (American Apparel Manufacturers Association), ASA (American Sweater Association) are all gone now, the industry associations having no raison d'etre without an industry. In 2003, I met with executives of the American Textile Manufacturers Institute (ATMI), which for half a century had been the booming voice of the industry in Washington, where hundreds of Congressmen would answer their calls on the first ring, and even U.S. presidents made sure to stay friendly. When I went back a year later the ATMI was gone, having shrunk and consolidated with other gasping textile associations into a shadow of itself, a shadow that often did not get its calls returned from Capitol Hill. Worse than the soldiers who have faded away, however, are the defectors. A Rolodex full of former government officials and even members of Congress are now across enemy lines, arguing not just for free trade in general but for free trade in T-shirts in particular.

Auggie understands the pull to the dark side. Increasingly that is where the paymasters are, the rich retailers, the powerful China lobby, and all of the American apparel firms that are now just importing machines. Auggie understands that there are more realists than idealists in Washington, though he himself isn't one of them. For most of his life, the manufacturing job news released every month has been bad news, and Auggie seems to take each layoff personally. But he also knows that without his relentless scuffles, there would be fewer jobs still, so he keeps going. Auggie also knows that, in the long run, he will lose. But on the way to losing there are victories, and these keep him energized. When Auggie can keep a factory open for a few more years, then a community will stay intact a while longer, a few more children will grow up with working parents, and a few more of them will be able to go to college. Every day an American textile mill stays open is a win for Auggie Tantillo, and every day somebody keeps a job is a good day.

Though Auggie's army is smaller than it once was, the troops are rallying in the fight against China. After 10 years of squabbling and splintering, there is a renewed unity and purpose in the face of a common enemy. In July 2003, the leaders of the ATMI, AMTAC, NTA, AYSA, AFMA, NCC, ASIA, ATMA, CRI, GTMA, THA, AFAI, NCMA, and TDA joined forces in a powerful alphabet army to demand that the Bush administration take action against China.[3] They demanded that the U.S. government institute "safeguard" quotas restricting Chinese textile and apparel imports, and also demanded that apparel from other countries be restricted in its use of Chinese fabrics. Weeks later they fired off more specific requests, demanding immediate limits on Chinese knit fabrics, brassieres, dressing gowns, and gloves. In the meantime, a delegation from China flew to Washington to stop the madness, and the Bush administration had to decide whether to anger the Chinese—just when it needed China's cooperation on dozens of other issues, ranging from North Korea to semiconductors to intellectual property—or anger Auggie, just when it needed his help in the upcoming election. The Bush administration sided with Auggie and restricted the imports from China.

Several months later, the alphabet armies lined up 117 Congresspeople behind a request for a meeting of the WTO to consider responses to the looming China threat.[4] John Kerry was on board, but Bush was on the spot, torn between his commitments to China and the wrath of the voters in the textile mills. During the summer of 2004, the administration was trying to leave itself some wiggle room: room to side with Auggie, room to side with China, or more likely, room to split the differences somehow in a web of Washington deal making. But as the 2004 election heated up in the fall, Auggie played his best card: In mid-October, AMTAC filed about a dozen safeguard petitions to restrict Chinese imports of goods such as T-shirts, cotton pants, and underwear.[5] As George W. Bush rushed around the swing states in the days leading up to the election, the administration had to decide whether to reject or accept the petitions for consideration. The deadline for the administration to respond? November 1. Few were surprised when the administration sided with Auggie.

Julia Hughes, Washington representative for the U.S. Association of Importers of Textiles and Apparel, is a leader in the opposing army, and has sat across the table from Auggie many times over the years. While Julia respects Auggie's integrity and commitment, she just thinks that Auggie is wrong, and that he and his troops should stop whining and join the twenty-first century. And besides, from Julia's perspective, almost everything has gone Auggie's way. As Julia sees it, Auggie's army has had unfair advantages for nearly 50 years. Where Auggie sees a flood of T-shirts from China washing American jobs away, Julia sees the Chinese T-shirts as underdogs with both hands tied behind their backs, hopelessly handicapped against the political power of Auggie's troops.

Most economists, of course, are on Julia's side. Under the widely accepted doctrine of free trade, the best course of action for both the United States and China is for everyone to clear the ring and let the best T-shirts win. This is the best course for the United States, where access to the best T-shirts at the best prices will boost incomes; it is the best course for Charlotte, North Carolina, which is now a regional hub in the global economy; and it is the best course for developing countries, where, as we have seen, exports of textiles and apparel provide a route from rural poverty and a first step onto the development ladder.

But free trade may not be the best course—at least in the short run—for Kannapolis, North Carolina, where nearly 5,000 textile workers lost their jobs on a single day in 2003. My T-shirt's perilous journey home shows that the best economic policy from the perspective of the United States or even North Carolina does not make for the best politics, and that trade in T-shirts is not (yet) a contest of faster better cheaper on the part of competing businesses, but is instead a contest played out in the realm of politics. While the market forces powering the race to the bottom are strong, the political forces pushing back against the markets are strong as well, particularly in the United States. Trade flows in T-shirts are the result of economic forces but also the result of thousands of deals cut in Washington, Geneva, and Beijing, and politics are at least as important as markets in understanding the T-shirt's journey. Many of the firms still standing in the U.S. industry do not believe that they should have to compete with sweatshops that pay their workers 50 cents an hour, and especially not with China where cheating of almost every type is rampant. Better to build a fence to keep out the lions than to run an unfair race that can't be won. The fence hasn't worked as well as many U.S. producers would have liked, but it has slowed the competition down, and most of all it has confused them.

The effects of political barriers to Chinese apparel into the United States are readily apparent. While Chinese apparel has captured approximately 80 percent of apparel imports in several other industrialized countries, as of 2003, China's share of the U.S. apparel imports was approximately 14 percent.[6] China's victory in the race to the bottom is obvious when we examine its overall exports, but is far less striking when we examine its performance in the U.S. market (see Figure 1). My Chinese T-shirt, in particular, was one of the lucky ones. As Figure 2 shows, U.S. imports of cotton knit

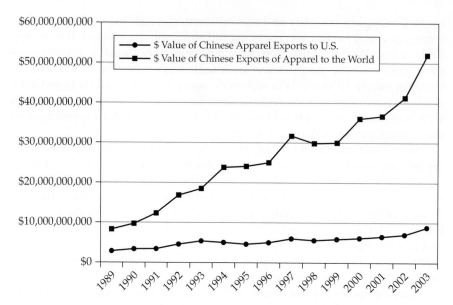

Figure 1   Chinese Apparel Exports to the United States vs. Total Chinese Apparel Exports

Sources: United Nations COMTRADE database; OTEXA, U.S. Department of Commerce.

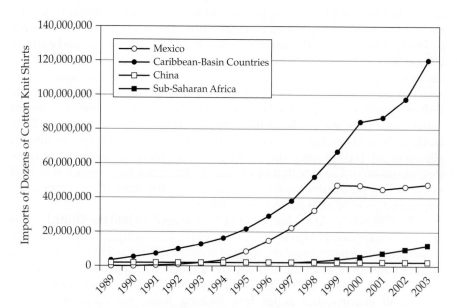

Figure 2   Cotton Knit Shirts Imported into the United States, by Region

Source: OTEXA, U.S. Department of Commerce (apparel categories 338 and 339).

shirts from other regions have grown far more rapidly than have imports from China. As we will see, it is trade policy, not comparative advantage, that explains these patterns.

Auggie Tantillo and Julia Hughes spend their days in a Washington dance, following each other around the Commerce Department, the Congress, Customs, and the office of the U.S. Trade Representative, with Auggie trying to plug holes in the import dike and Julia trying to punch them open. Because Auggie and Julia are in constant motion, the trade policies governing apparel are in constant motion as well. Textiles and apparel are subject to not only a higher level of trade protection but also a higher level of trade protection complexity than any imports into the United States outside of agricultural goods.

During the time that I was writing this book the rules governing apparel imports into the United States often seemed to change almost daily. The rules governing how many T-shirts of which types could be sold by which countries; the fabric the T-shirts could be made of under alternative regimes; whether a collar counted as a "component" or a "trim" (and whether it mattered); where the T-shirt's fabric could be dyed and "finished"; and, of course, tariffs, had all changed. In 1999, the rules did not look so bad for a Chinese T-shirt trying to enter the United States, but by 2003, the rules shifted against the Chinese in favor of producers in the Caribbean and Mexico. By 2005, however, it appears that the rules will be back on China's side, though not if Auggie Tantillo can help it.

Gary Sandler, the owner of Sherry Manufacturing in Miami, faces a daunting task in keeping apace of the rules governing T-shirt imports into the United States. Simply put, the rules are nuts, as even the people who made them readily agree.

A Taste of the (Crazy) Rules in 2003

Under the 2002 U.S.-Caribbean Trade Partnership Act (CBTPA), Gary Sandler may import apparel from 24 countries in the Caribbean free from tariff and duties.[7] However, free access applies only to clothing that meets the American "yarn forward" requirement, which requires that both the fabric and yarn from which the clothing is constructed be made in the United States. Both dyeing and finishing of the fabric must also occur in the United States, and the fabric must be cut into pieces in the United States, as well. However, apparel pieces may be cut in the Caribbean countries if U.S.-made thread is then used to stitch the components together.

Apparel that is "knit to shape"—rather than made from fabric that is knit and then cut into pieces—may be made from fabric formed in the Caribbean country, as long as the fabric is made from U.S.-made yarns and the imports are below a certain limit. However, there are more restrictive provisions for socks and T-shirts. Brassieres have their own astonishingly complicated rule book, which allows them free access only if the firm producing the brassieres has used components in which at least 75 percent of the value of the fabric has been sourced in the United States for certain *prior years'* exports of brassieres to the United States. A debate over which parts of the brassiere "count" toward the 75 percent went on for some time, and was finally negotiated to include cups, sides, wings, and backs but to exclude straps, bows, and labels.

T-shirts are also privileged with their own special rules. T-shirts made from Caribbean-made fabric using U.S.-made yarn may enter the United States freely, but only to a limit of 5,651,520 dozen in 2003. The special T-shirt cap was negotiated at the insistence of Fruit of the Loom, which tried to match the quantitative limit to its own productive capacity. This maneuver gave free access for the firm's T-shirt products into the United States while at the same time dissuading competitors from setting up rival T-shirt manufacturing plants in the Caribbean.

Julia, Auggie, and the alphabet armies negotiated for years over the CBTPA provisions, in a telling example of the dominance of politics over markets in T-shirt trade flows. U.S. retailers wanted to simply lift the gates and allow free access to whatever apparel the Caribbean countries produced. Roger Milliken, a billionaire South Carolina textile magnate and self-proclaimed "economic nationalist" joined forces in an unlikely alliance with the textile and apparel workers trade union (UNITE). Together, along with Senator Fritz Hollings and other like-minded Congresspeople, they opposed any free access at all for Caribbean-made apparel, believing, both procedurally and substantively, that "giving away" access to the U.S. market was bad policy. The ATMI, as well as a number of U.S. producers, lobbied for the U.S. fabric requirement, while other producers—such as Fruit of the Loom and Russell Mills, along with the Caribbean countries—fought to gain benefits for apparel produced with Caribbean-made fabrics.

The complexity of the rules is perhaps inevitable, given the nature of these multiple opposing forces. In the end, the rules were hammered out in the only way possible given the disparate interests involved: sock by sock, bra strap by bra strap. It may be hammered out all over again in a few years, as the CBTPA is set to expire in 2008.

A similar set of rules—though different enough to keep importers like Sandler confused—govern T-shirt imports from Sub-Saharan Africa under the African Growth and Opportunity Act (AGOA) and from Bolivia, Colombia, Ecuador, and Peru under the Andean Trade Preference Act (ADTPA).[8] Under the North American Free Trade Agreement (NAFTA), still other rules apply to T-shirt imports from Canada and Mexico.

To Julia Hughes, the only thing more outrageous than these rules is to hear them referred to as "free trade" agreements. According to Julia, a free trade agreement should make it easier, not harder, to trade. The poorest countries of the world, especially those in Africa, already handicapped on almost any dimension, cannot possibly succeed in such a byzantine tangle of rules, Julia believes, and many U.S. importers take one look at the rules and walk away. Trade from these areas is not free at all. It is easier and cheaper (at least once the time is factored in) just to pay the tariff and source from preference-free countries. Julia Hughes once tried to make sense out of the various free trade area provisions for her retail clients. She found, however, that she could not put them on a grid; they were all just too different. Auggie, for his part, believes that the retailers are responsible for the complexities: The complications, as Auggie sees it, are simply the result of all the exceptions that were made for Julia.

In 2003, cotton T-shirts that did not meet the requirements for "preferential treatment," either because they came from countries outside the membership of AGOA, the CBTPA, ADTPA, or NAFTA, or because they did not meet the requirements regarding the origin of the fabric or yarn, were charged an import tariff of 17.4 percent, except if they were from Jordan, in which case the tariff rate was 10.9 percent, or Israel, in which case the tariff rate was 0.[9]

Complexities are apparent in the tariff schedule as well. For some apparel, the power of particular companies is evident. Tariffs are nearly 30 percent on some categories of clothing, including, for example, Harmonized Tariff Schedule category 6102.30.20, which are:

> womens' or girls' overcoats, car coats, capes, cloaks, anoraks (including ski jackets), windbreakers, and similar articles, knitted or crocheted, of manmade fiber, containing less than 25% leather by weight and containing 23% or less wool or fine animal hair.

It might be hard to imagine such a garment, but it is clear from the tariff rate—nearly the highest of any on apparel—that someone in the United States manufactures them.

As of 2003, U.S. apparel imports for an additional 40 WTO member countries were limited under the umbrella of the Agreement on Textiles and Clothing (ATC).[10] The ATC, in turn, is the phase-out mechanism for the Multifiber Agreement (MFA), which had set quantitative limits, or quotas, on clothing and textile imports from dozens of countries since 1974. In 2003, the United States had quota limits on cotton knit shirts from 27 countries; some of these are shown in Figure 3. Though the ATC is scheduled for expiration at the beginning of 2005, a number of quota regimes will remain in place for U.S. apparel. First, the China safeguard allows importing countries to impose quotas on Chinese apparel imports through 2008. Second,

U.S. Import Limits for Cotton Knit Shirts, 2003

Country	Quota Limit (in dozens)
China	2,525,562
Vietnam	10,463,635
Turkey	17,777,705
Pakistan	12,407,951
India	5,777,025
Egypt	4,717,195
Poland	3,533,491
Cambodia	4,187,637
Philippines	3,633,517
Sri Lanka	2,635,755
Romania	1,270,216
Oman	922,140

Figure 3   U.S. Import Quota Limits for Cotton Knit Shirt Quotas, 2003
Source: U.S. Customs.

quotas will remain in effect for a number of countries that are not WTO members.

All in all, the restrictions and regulations governing apparel imports are written, administered, and enforced by hundreds of lobbyists and lawyers, as well as bureaucrats from the Department of the Treasury, the Department of Commerce, the Congressional Textile Caucus, the U.S. Trade Representative, and the interdepartmental Committee for the Implementation of Textile Agreements. In fact, a leading textbook illustrates the interlocking webs of government involvement in textile and apparel trade policy with a full-page map containing 11 boxes linked together by a dozen arrows.[11] While the United States is the largest offender, it is not alone. As Richard Friman has shown, other rich countries also employ complex "patchwork" approaches to protecting their domestic textile industries.[12]

Beginning in 2002, the web site of the United States Association of Importers of Textiles and Apparel showed a clock with days, minutes, hours, and seconds ticking by. With the MFA scheduled to expire on January 1, 2005, apparel importers could go to the web site for an exact calculation of the length of time they had to contend with perhaps the most tortuously complex set of trade protections in U.S. history. The regime, as we will see, had many effects: good, bad, and mostly unintended. When the clock strikes zero, there will be more surprises still.

According to many, it will be the last nail for the U.S. industry in the sad story of plant closings and job losses that has lasted nearly 50 years. It will also mean the last nail for Auggie Tantillo and the alphabet armies who have fought to save the U.S. industry from the waves of cheap imports. "It's about time," many people told me. More than a few Washington insiders muttered "dinosaurs" when I asked them about Auggie Tantillo's troops. The Southern textile interests are living in the past, clinging to something that makes no sense in today's global economy, people told me over and over again.

The dinosaur label doesn't bother Auggie. "We're not extinct," he told me, "not yet."

Snarling Together

How did the United States—as the self-anointed free trade champion of the universe—end up with such a dauntingly complex and downright silly mass of barriers to the import of T-shirts? Why, in an era of progressive trade liberalization and increasing deference to the market mechanism, has the role of politics remained so pervasive in this industry?

The first factor to explain the dominance of politics in the trade is the size of the textile and apparel manufacturing base, even today. While textile and apparel employment in the United States peaked shortly after World War II at approximately 2.5 million workers, the industries in 2004 employed about 700,000 people, which accounts for about 5 percent of manufacturing employment.[13] Given the size of the employment base, the unrelenting job losses related to the global race to the bottom have strengthened the political voice of the industry, as the "groans of the weavers" have become both louder and more sophisticated. Winning industries do not groan, and losing industries' groans become louder with the extent of their misfortune. The U.S. textile industry felt the first serious threat from imports immediately after World War II, and foreign competition since that time has been growing steadily and sometimes exponentially, which has led to compensating cries for help in Washington.

Yet the withering of America's competitive position in these industries is not sufficient to explain their political power, as industries from toys to bicycles to televisions have faded away with few rescue missions from Washington. Political response to industrial demise is the result of not only the demise itself, or even the size of the industry, but the strength of industry alliances and the access the alliances have to policymakers.[14] Or, as Jock Nash, perhaps the American textile industry's most colorful voice in Washington, reportedly advises, when a pack of dogs snarl together, people have to listen. The extent to which the industry can speak with one voice—or snarl together—goes a long way toward explaining its political influence.

Erik Autor, the chief lobbyist on trade matters for the National Retail Federation, is continually frustrated by the "snarl together" phenomenon. Though retailers ranging from a beachfront tourist shop to Saks Fifth Avenue to Wal-Mart all benefit from access to cheaper T-shirts from abroad, such diverse groups of businesses find it difficult to speak with a single voice. Southern textile leaders, however, share a cultural and historical bond that allows them to speak together. (They all know each other, Erik told me. Their daddies all knew each other. Their granddaddies all built the mills, and they all knew each other, too.) Related to the historical and cultural bond that strengthens their collective voice is the geographic concentration of the U.S. textile industry. More than 60 percent of apparel and textile manufacturing is located in Georgia, South Carolina, and North Carolina, and there remain many Congressional districts where the textile industry—or even a single firm—is the major employer. A geographic swath of Congresspeople remains beholden to the industry, even as its fortunes wane. The U.S. retail industry, in contrast, while employing significantly more people than the textile and apparel industries, is not only unable to snarl in unison, it is spread across the country in a manner that leaves it nobody's Congressional priority.[15]

A third factor that lends support to the regime is that the American public is nervous about trade, especially trade with China, and especially when the trade is believed to have severe effects on small American communities. The "It coulda been me" syndrome leaves many American voters far more tolerant of complex trade protections than we might expect them to be. While North Carolina now has a diversified economy that has "moved up" from textiles, many towns, along with many less-skilled workers, have not moved up alongside Charlotte.

I was not able to find anyone in Washington and certainly no one in China who was happy with the rules governing imports of T-shirts into the United States, or indeed anyone who tried to defend these rules. Participants from across the spectrum agreed that the deal-making process often showed Washington politics at its worst. But observers on all sides also agree that access to the American apparel consumer is currency in Washington, and this currency, like any good money, can and has been traded for almost anything. Often, the currency has been traded for votes, which has left generations of Congresspeople and even a few presidents indebted to the textile industry. Access to the American apparel consumer has also frequently been traded for foreign policy favors, from crushing Communism in Central America to crippling terrorists in Pakistan. Ironically, however, perhaps the most common use of the currency has been to pay Auggie Tantillo and his troops to move out of the way of broader trade-liberalizing initiatives. Beginning with Dwight Eisenhower and ending with

George W. Bush, every U.S. president has paid the U.S. textile industry to be quiet so that America could get on with the business of free trade.

Auggie Goes to Washington

Auggie had thought little about politics and even less about trade policy as he neared his college graduation from Clemson University in 1980. He didn't know what his next step would be, and it was a fluke and a stroke of luck that led to a job as an assistant in Senator Strom Thurmond's office. Auggie left for the big city, having no idea what to expect. If he had opinions about politics, he doesn't remember them. Whatever illusions he might have had, however, were shattered at the ripe old age of 21, when he saw how Washington really worked. Auggie likens his Washington awakening to the day he discovered that Santa Claus was a fake. Santa Claus was President Ronald Reagan.

Strom Thurmond had figured critically in Reagan's 1980 election. Though the U.S. textile industry had a variety of trade protections in place at the time, Asian imports were gushing through new holes in the dike by the day. Between 1976 and 1979, textile and apparel imports into the United States had increased by nearly 50 percent.[16] In exchange for Thurmond's support, Reagan promised, if elected, to put a stop to it. In a letter to Strom Thurmond several months before the election, Reagan promised to limit the growth in textile and apparel imports to the growth in the domestic market.[17]

Thurmond kept his end of the deal and delivered a large Southern vote to Ronald Reagan. Reagan, however, shuffled his feet as Asian imports continued to soar. Auggie was just a note-taker and a gopher, but he remembers Thurmond's outrage as he raced around Washington meeting with Edwin Meese, George Schultz, and James Baker. He pounded the table, shoved the letter under their noses, as mill after mill closed and imports surged. "You've got to do something about this. *You promised.*"

Several people who had been involved with the negotiations in Washington told me that the infamous Reagan textile promise would have been impossible to keep, even with the best of intentions. It would have been a foreign policy disaster to renege on the deals already in place, which allowed imports under quota to grow at a rate of 6 percent, rather than the approximately 1 percent growth in the domestic market. It also would have required the United States to bring under quota many countries that had never been under export restraints, as well as to limit many categories of textiles and apparel that had also been without quota.

But to Auggie, Strom Thurmond, and the still millions of textile and apparel workers, a deal had been a deal. So Auggie Tantillo's introduction to Washington was the broken Reagan textile promise. It was Auggie's first experience in the value of textile promises as currency, but it was not the last. Strom Thurmond, who died in 2003 at the age of 100, had played this game before and he would play it again. In fact, every post–World War II president has made his own version of the campaign textile promise to Strom Thurmond, and, beginning in the 1960s, to Fritz Hollings and Jesse Helms as well. Some of the promises have been kept, and some have not.

But since the end of World War II, every U.S. president has also publicly supported the doctrine of free trade. Indeed, scholars of presidential rhetoric cite free trade doctrine as a "remarkably consistent rhetoric" across both time and party lines.[18] For some presidents, free trade was a foreign policy choice, designed to keep Communists or war at bay. For others, it was a clear case of the best economic policy. For yet others, a free trade posture was a matter of moral consistency. The United States had been the architect of the postwar General Agreement on Tariffs and Trade (GATT), a set of rules with free trade principles at its very core. For more than half a century, the United States has been the world's self-appointed champion of free trade, in word if not in deed.

Regardless of what has motivated the free trade rhetoric of U.S. presidents, all have found it impossible to implement the rhetoric without paying the textile and apparel industries to get out of the way. While a long list of trade liberalizing initiatives—from tariff reductions to NAFTA to China's WTO accession—has been championed by the United States, these initiatives have only been politically possible by making exceptions for Southern textile interests. In television appearances and public speeches, each postwar president has eloquently advanced the case for free trade on the grounds of freedom, prosperity, and morality.[19] But away from the cameras, in private phone calls, furtive telegrams, and secret meetings, each of them has assured the domestic textile industry that he had not really been talking to them. For 50 years, U.S. policymakers have played a balancing act with Auggie and his troops, trying to toss (or promise) them enough crumbs to get their votes and cooperation, but not so many as to make an obvious mockery of the free trade rhetoric. Almost every postwar president has needed help from the senators and governors in the Carolinas, who in turn needed help for their textile towns. Each special deal for the industry was labeled a temporary measure, but many of them, in one form or another, are still in place.

Making Deals and Making Exceptions

The first groans of the weavers came shortly after World War II as cheap Japanese cotton goods took the lead in the race to the bottom. Though official U.S. policy was to open trade with Japan to encourage prosperity and thus stave off the Communist threat in Asia, the mill owners in both New

England and the South felt a much more immediate threat from the growing imports from Japan than they did from the Communists. The American Cotton Manufacturers Institute (ACMI) announced that a crisis was at hand:

> We are face to face with a life or death question of whether our own government will stand idly by and permit low-wage competition from Japan to seriously cripple our industry. Must there be closed mills and breadlines before the administration in Washington concedes the possibility of irreparable damage to our industry?[20]

In order to quiet the groans and especially to advance its broader trade-liberalizing agenda, the Eisenhower administration persuaded Japan to "voluntarily" limit their exports of cotton textiles to the United States to allow temporary breathing room for the U.S. industry. Like much else from the 1950s, from today's perspective the Voluntary Export Restraint (VER) agreement with Japan looks charmingly simple and innocent. The agreement was only temporary, and it dealt with only one country, Japan. Only one alphabet troop, the ACMI, had been involved, and the agreement covered only a narrow range of goods. Though Eisenhower saw no choice but to toss the crumbs, he was clearly not happy about it. In his diary he later wrote of the "short-sightedness bordering on tragic stupidity" of the protectionists, and worried that unless the United States opened its markets, Japan would "fall prey to the Communists."[21]

In what would become a long epic of unintended consequences, the politics served to accelerate rather than slow the race to the bottom. The VERS, which limited imports from Japan, supplied not so much protection for the U.S. textile industry as an opening for Japan's competitors in the race—especially Hong Kong and Taiwan—to supply the U.S. market. In a pattern that continues to this day, the effect of plugging one hole in the dike was to increase the force of imports gushing through others. Between 1956 and 1961, imports of cotton goods from Hong Kong rose by nearly 700 percent.[22]

The soaring imports led to predictable cries lamenting the imminent collapse of the U.S. industry.[23] In the 1960 presidential campaign, John F. Kennedy promised Governor Ernest Hollings of South Carolina that he would help. Kennedy fulfilled his promise by instituting the Short Term Arrangement on Cotton Textiles (STA) as temporary assistance to the industry. The arrangement allowed the United States to negotiate import limits from other countries—not just Japan—in cotton textiles. The effect was a bigger program, covering both more countries and more goods than the original Japanese VER.

Of course a reprieve of one year was not enough to save the U.S. industry. In response to the continuing groans, on the expiration of the STA the Kennedy administration created the Long Term Arrangement for Cotton Textiles (LTA), effective from 1962 to 1967. Just as the STA was a bigger VER, the LTA was a bigger STA, covering more countries, more products, and more years. In effect, the LTA imposed quotas to limit import growth from the major producers—particularly in Asia—to annual growth of 5 percent per year.

In exchange for protecting its own industry against imports, the ACMI dropped its fight against Kennedy's Trade Expansion Act and allowed the Kennedy Round trade liberalization to continue. The Kennedy Round resulted in tariff cuts on U.S. imports of 30 percent, but textile and apparel tariffs were off limits in the negotiation. They maintained their already high levels and were, in the case of apparel, even increased.[24] Representative Carl Vinson of Georgia proudly wrote the ACMI that, "Thanks to their good friends in Congress, the industry had been singled out for special treatment by President Kennedy and his Cabinet."[25]

The "temporary" LTA was renewed in 1967 and again in 1970, each time as a bribe to allow Lyndon Johnson and then Richard Nixon to seek trade liberalization in other ways. By 1973, the LTA was restricting hundreds of categories of cotton textile imports from dozens of countries. With the passage of the LTA and its extensions, U.S. trade policy for textiles and apparel took the seemingly irreversible step to a complexity that left it unintelligible to all but a few.

However, just as blocking the flow of clothing from Japan had resulted in an even more forceful flow of imports from Hong Kong, blocking imports of cotton textiles and apparel also served to accelerate rather than slow the race to the bottom.

By limiting imports of cotton textiles and apparel, U.S. policy unwittingly encouraged its trading partners to upgrade their production and sales efforts to wool and to the increasingly popular man-made fibers such as nylon and polyester. Predictably, imports of man-made fiber apparel from Asia soon soared, with U.S. imports of these fibers from developing countries increasing 2,500 percent between 1964 and 1970.[26] Just as predictably, U.S. textile interests extended their groans to these other sectors. The ACMI morphed into the ATMI (American Textile Manufacturers Institute), and U.S. textile interests began an intensive campaign to extend the LTA to other fibers, calling for the implementation of a Multifiber Agreement (MFA).

In his 1968 presidential campaign, Richard Nixon promised Senator Strom Thurmond that he would seek to broaden the LTA into an MFA and would extend quotas from cotton to wool, man-made fibers, and blends.[27] Once elected, Nixon faced the familiar challenge of reconciling his free trade rhetoric with his campaign promise. On the one hand, Nixon had a vision of trade as a path not just to economic growth but to political freedom. On the other hand, there was the MFA promise telegram to Thurmond that had been printed in newspapers all over the South. Nixon's rhetoric showed the balancing act, and was typical of rhetoric from Dwight Eisenhower to George W. Bush: Free trade was good, but textiles were a special case:

> By expanding world markets, our trade policies have speeded the pace of our own economic progress and aided the development of others. . . . We must seek a continued expansion of world trade, even as we also seek the dismantling of those other barriers—political, social, and ideological—that have stood in the way of a freer exchange of people and ideas, as well as of goods and technology. . . .
>
> [H]owever, the textile import problem, of course, is a special circumstance that requires special measures.[28]

In the end, MFA I, in effect from 1974 to 1977, was signed by 50 countries and covered approximately 75 percent of U.S. textile and apparel imports.[29] In painstaking bilateral negotiations, country after country hammered out with U.S. negotiators how much of which categories of textiles and clothing could enter the U.S. market. Though largely successful in satisfying the domestic textile interests, the MFA was, as William Cline wrote, "an embarrassing breach of the GATT principles," principles that the United States had authored and continued to espouse.[30]

In the 1976 campaign Jimmy Carter promised to extend the "temporary" MFA. MFA II, which extended the arrangement through 1981, was more restrictive still in allowing access to U.S. and European markets. In the meantime, Carter and then Reagan also wished to maintain the free trade momentum on a new round of trade liberalization talks—the so-called Tokyo Round. Once again the textile and apparel industries were largely exempt: The United States cut its import tariffs on manufactured goods to an average of 6.5 percent, but apparel tariffs, while reduced from their postwar highs, remained at an average of 22.5 percent.[31]

Though Ronald Reagan had not kept his election-year textile promise to Strom Thurmond, Reagan had little choice but to toss some crumbs in the direction of the textile industry. Reagan would have to show his face in South Carolina in the 1984 campaign, as Thurmond kept reminding him. With MFA III, the temporary regime of textile and apparel quotas was extended yet again. In effect for the 1981 to 1986 period, MFA III was the most restrictive yet.

Jobs for Bureaucrats

With the implementation of the MFA and its extensions, the administration of the quota regime became—and remained in 2004—a small industry both in Washington and in the exporting countries, as the mind-numbing complexity of the regime increased over time in response to the groans from certain companies, industries, or Congressional districts. In the simplest case, the United States negotiated a bilateral agreement with each country, which allowed the country to export to the United States certain quantities of various categories of textiles and apparel, such as men's woolen sweaters or women's cotton knit shirts.[32] In some cases, the country is allowed to use the quota for any garment in the category, but in other cases there are limits on subcategories. For example, while the Chinese quota for all cotton knit shirts was 2,373,699 dozen in 2002, T-shirts and tank tops were limited to 1,801,137 dozen of this amount.

Even where quota allocations appear to be identical, market access to the United States can differ. Throughout the year countries might apply "swing" (borrowing T-shirt quota from another category of textiles and apparel quota from the same country), "special shift" (borrowing T-shirt quota from a prespecified list of other categories of quota), "carryover" (shifting last year's unused T-shirt quota to the current year), or "carryforward" (borrowing against next year's T-shirt quota).

In order for quota to be traded across time and categories, each category is assigned a square meter equivalent (SME) of cloth.[33] A dozen cotton knit shirts (category 338 or 339) is convertible to 6 SMEs of cloth while a dozen handkerchiefs of man-made fiber (category 630) are convertible into 1.4 SMEs. As a result, a country that applied swing from cotton knit shirts to polyester handkerchiefs could trade the right to sell 1 T-shirt for the right to sell 4.29 handkerchiefs. Some apparel is measured by weight rather than quantity—a kilogram of silk ties is convertible to 6.6 square meters of cloth, making a kilogram of ties "worth" slightly more than a dozen T-shirts for the purpose of quota swing.

Another whole mini-industry must deal with MFA "origination" requirements. If a T-shirt is sewn in China from fabric pieces that were cut in Hong Kong but knit in Malaysia from yarn that was spun in the United States, where is the T-shirt from, and whose quotas should it count against? While the general rule for most of the MFA's history was that fabric cutting conferred origin, the rules have been fluid, and since the mid-1990s have specified that it is generally the stitching, rather than the knitting, spinning, or cutting, that determines where the T-shirt is from for MFA purposes.

The MFA, then, while designed to save the U.S. textile and apparel industries, actually at the same time created its own industry, with hundreds of bureaucrats around the world to negotiate, implement, and enforce the innumerable bilateral deals that collectively have comprised the MFA. Each minute provision of each bilateral agreement is the result of a push-pull negotiation among multiple parties, and each provision also by necessity creates its own supporting bureaucratic structures. To see the SME equivalents, the swings or shifts, and of course the product and country lists themselves in action is to appreciate the MFA not so much as a protectionist regime but instead as a marvel of bureaucratic engineering.

Unity 1985 to 1990

In what had become a predictable pattern, even with the stricter quotas under MFA III, the crisis continued in the U.S. industry and the groans of the weavers were unabated. Though the speakers had changed, the speeches had not. In 1985 Representative Ed Jenkins of Georgia told his House colleagues that the industry was experiencing its "last gasp," while a textile association president threatened that "in five years, the industry will cease to exist."[34]

The renewal of the MFA also did little to lessen the sense of betrayal that still stung from Reagan's unfulfilled promise to Strom Thurmond, and once Reagan had won a second term, the industry's hopes for justice were further dashed. Strom Thurmond's leverage over Reagan was gone, and White House aides had stopped picking up the phone. Ronald Reagan would not have to go back to South Carolina. Yet there was a silver lining in the betrayal: The injustice united the industry in a manner seen neither before nor since. Snarling together, they almost achieved the impossible.

If the White House would not listen, the Congress would have to. The mid-1980s were a golden era of sorts for the domestic textile and apparel industries. Though their fortunes were shrinking and their plants were closing, there was an energy and unity of purpose that propelled them forward. It was a pinnacle, according to Auggie Tantillo and many others with whom I spoke, where standing upon each other's shoulders they had made their greatest reach, coming within only inches of achieving justice. All of the alphabet armies in the U.S. textile and apparel complex, from yarn spinners to fabric producers to apparel manufacturers—the ATMI, AFMI, AYSA, and AAMA—along with the unions representing the workers—began to snarl together. Auggie Tantillo, still young but by now an expert in the areas of both textile trade policy and the ways of Washington, accepted a position to open the Washington office for Russell Mills, one of America's largest T-shirt producers. United, the troops formed an industry coalition, the Fiber, Fabric, and Apparel Coalition for Trade (FFACT), to battle the imports.

Auggie and his troops sought legislation that would keep the Reagan promise. The Jenkins Global Quota bill would limit the growth of imports not from particular countries, but instead place a global cap on U.S. textile and apparel imports, and also give the United States unilateral power to restrict imports, rather than requiring negotiations with each trading partner. The bill would roll back quotas for the largest Asian suppliers, as well as negate more than 30 existing bilateral textile and apparel trade agreements.[35] Ronald Reagan and his administration were nervous. Once Auggie and his troops got into the U.S. Capitol, there was no telling what would happen.

Though the framers of the U.S. Constitution placed responsibility for formulating trade policy on the shoulders of the Congress, during the past 50 years it has become increasingly clear—perhaps especially to Congress itself—that they are not up to the task of formulating rational trade policy.

A Congressperson seeking election or reelection is often forced into a protectionist posture, but can only obtain protection for his interests by offering the same to his colleagues. "The political logic of protection leads to
protection all around" wrote an observer in 1935, because Congress's natural tendency is a spiraling protectionism extending trade barriers into the
districts of each Congressperson.[36] A vote for free trade, according to
another early observer, is an "unnatural act" for a Congressperson.[37] Only a
very few die-hard constitutional literalists believe that the U.S. Congress
should be in charge of trade policy.

Julia Hughes understands this all too well. While she has some free
trade allies in Congress, nobody wins elections by promising free trade or
help for the apparel consumer. Auggie, however, has comrades in Congress
who will fall on their sword, or at least pretend to, to help the U.S. textile industry. From North Carolina through Georgia and Alabama, in town after
town the voters will choose the candidate who promises to keep the mill
open. What members of Congress most want, however, is to make protectionist speeches without having to take protectionist actions. Indeed, as
Destler notes, by surrendering power to make trade policy decisions, Congresspeople are more freely able to spout protectionist rhetoric, secure in the
knowledge that they will be unable to take action:

> A Congressman, no matter how keen his desire to help the toy marble mak
> ers, does not want to be given the right of voting them an increase in tariff
> rates. He prefers to be in the position of being allowed merely to place a
> speech in their favor in the Congressional Record . . . free to indulge the re
> sponsibility afforded those who do not participate in the final decision.[38]

But FFACT, having been spurned by the Reagan administration, began
knocking on the doors of members of Congress. The Jenkins Bill passed easily in both the Senate and the House, where it had 230 cosponsors. But this
victory was only the first step, as Reagan swiftly vetoed the bill. Some of
those involved in the negotiations told me that at least some Congresspeople were able to vote for the bill because they felt assured that Reagan
would veto it. Dan Rostenkowski, chair of the House Ways and Means Committee, though sympathetic to the plight of the mill workers saw the bill as
being fraught with unworkable elements. "This bill is garbage," he allegedly
remarked to Tip O'Neill. O'Neill, surveying the political landscape, replied,
"Yeah, but move it along, Dan. Move the garbage."

The override received 276 votes, just 8 votes short of the two-thirds
needed to undo Reagan's veto.[39] Yet it was a win of sorts. As Auggie Tantillo
remembers, "We scared them good."

To many observers, the close vote was a terrifying brush with insanity,
an example of the madness that can result if trade policy is left in the hands
of elected representatives. Economist William Cline estimated that the bill
would have cut back imports of textiles from Hong Kong, Korea, and

Taiwan by nearly 60 percent, and would have cost U.S. consumers approximately $43,945 per U.S. textile job saved.[40] In addition, by the sheer force of its hypocrisy when placed against American free trade rhetoric, it would also have likely tied U.S. hands in pursuing other trade negotiations. And finally, swift and disabling retaliation against U.S. exports was virtually assured.

But, like Auggie said, they had been scared. They had seen the whites of Auggie's eyes, and were willing to talk. The USTR was willing to talk, Hong Kong was willing to talk, and even Reagan was willing to talk. The MFA IV, signed for a five-year period ending in 1991, was the most restrictive yet. For the first time, quotas were placed on fabrics not even produced in the United States, such as silk, ramie, and linen. The only fibers now exempt from U.S. quotas were jute and abaca, though U.S. negotiators warned that these too would be dealt with if imports surged.

In the meantime, Auggie Tantillo had moved up yet again. After serving a stint as Strom Thurmond's Chief of Staff, Auggie was appointed by President George H.W. Bush as Undersecretary of Commerce for Textiles and Apparel. The job was the top textile post in Washington, and carried with it the chairmanship of the Committee for the Implementation of Textile Agreements (CITA), an interdepartmental policy committee with representatives from the Departments of State, Labor, Treasury, and the USTR.

Snarling Back

From the pinnacle of political power they held in the late 1980s, the U.S. textile and apparel industries' influence declined rapidly in the 1990s. While their power remained the envy of virtually any other industry, compared to their influence in the heady days of the Jenkins Bill the troops were tattered and weakened. First, FFACT itself began to splinter, with infighting that weakened its collective voice. More important, however, other political voices began to rise in volume, not drowning out but at least softening the snarls from the U.S. industry.

The apparel industry was the first to splinter off from the cause. Under the industry's new business models, Auggie was starting to sound like a bit of a dinosaur. For the firms who continued to produce apparel in the United States, access to cheaper and more fashionable foreign fabric was a necessity. By limiting their access to foreign fabrics, trade restrictions were making it more, not less, difficult to keep their production in America. For other apparel firms, such as Warnaco and Liz Claiborne, it was becoming more attractive to source their clothing from abroad, partly because of the restrictions associated with gaining access to their fabrics of choice, and partly because of the increasing quality and price competitiveness of the

Asian producers. The American Apparel Manufacturers Association made a clean break with Auggie in 1990, when they refused to sign on to support the 1990 version of the global quota bill. They did not cross the line to the dark side at first, but instead made clear that they were not going to help. By the mid-1990s, however, the AAMA was the enemy, fighting in direct opposition to Auggie's efforts to contain textile and apparel imports, and a short time later, the AAMA was gone.

The textile workers' union (UNITE), as well as the yarn and fabric sectors, also began to splinter into different directions. While the fabric producers wanted a freer rein to use imported yarn in production, the yarn spinners predictably preferred to limit the use of foreign yarn in U.S.-made fabrics. As trade agreements started to be negotiated, further splits appeared. The yarn and fabric guys squabbled over the provisions in the agreements, and the union workers generally opposed any agreements at all. Unable to snarl in unison, the industry became an annoyance rather than a threat on Capitol Hill.

As FFACT's united political front crumbled, other alphabet armies began to snarl in unison. For the first time, the U.S. retail industry formed a collective voice on the subject of trade in general, and apparel imports in particular. The Retail Industry Trade Action Coalition (RITAC) led by Sears, JCPenney, and Dayton Hudson, had first been formed to counter FFACT on the Jenkins Bill, but soon took on the larger goal of doing away with all quotas.[41]

Gone On Long Enough

RITAC was soon bolstered by another collective force as the developing countries that had been constrained by quotas also began to speak with one voice. The International Textiles and Clothing Bureau (ITCB), a coalition of developing country textile and clothing exporters, began to echo RITAC's call for the end of quotas. In a foreshadowing of the collective clout they would display in 2004, poor countries banded together to shape the global trade agenda.

Many of the family businesses in Asia had first come under quota under John F. Kennedy's administration, and some business owners remembered when their grandfathers had been assured that the quotas would be temporary. ITCB members were running out of patience in the globalized economy, where the MFA appeared increasingly anomalous and hypocritical, and was viewed as a rich country plot that stood in the way of poor country fortunes. In a twist on the well-worn historical pattern, America would now have to pay the developing countries to move out of the way of broader trade liberalization.

George H.W. Bush and then Bill Clinton were eager to see a successful conclusion of the Uruguay Round, the third major round of postwar trade liberalization talks. While both the Kennedy and Tokyo Rounds had focused on and achieved tariff reductions (though not for U.S. textile and apparel imports), U.S. aims for the Uruguay Round were more complex. In particular, U.S. negotiators wanted developing countries to liberalize rules for trade in financial and other services, and for foreign investment, and they also sought new agreements in areas such as intellectual property. The United States had little left to offer in return besides the MFA. Thanks to the successive rounds of liberalization, the United States maintained few trade barriers of any kind, save for those in place for agriculture and textiles, as tariffs for imports into the United States were close to zero for most goods outside of these industries. The ITCB made clear that they were willing to negotiate only if the MFA was on the table.

As Uruguay Round negotiations progressed, the MFA was extended twice more as the final agreement was hammered out. In the end, the negotiation took seven years and produced 22,000 pages of agreements.[42] With Auggie's troops in splinters, the new voice of the retail industry rising in the background, and, most important, the developing countries united for the first time in history, the rich countries agreed to abandon the MFA.

The Slow Unraveling

If there were doubts about the political staying power of the U.S. industry, they were dashed as it became clear that an agreement to end the MFA was not the same thing as the end of the MFA. While retailers and developing countries wanted to yank the thread to unravel the regime in a few pulls, the textile interests pushed the other way, and ultimately made sure that the unraveling would proceed at a snail's pace. Negotiations over *whether* to end the MFA were simple compared to the negotiations over *how* to end the MFA.

Should the MFA be phased out over 5, 10, 15, or perhaps even 25 years? Should the poorest countries be freed from quotas first, or should the bigger exporters be allowed to go first? Or perhaps each category of clothing should be freed from constraint at the same time for all countries? The tortuous complexity that had characterized the administration of the MFA for decades was in the end trumped by the even more daunting complexity of the regime's undoing. Finally, the countries agreed to a 10-year phase-out, beginning in 1995. The countries also agreed to lift the quotas in stages by product. In 1995, goods comprising 16 percent of SME imports were freed from quotas; the subsequent two tranches, in 1998 and 2002, freed 17 percent and 18 percent, respectively, of SME imports from quota.[43] The final tranche, set for liberalization in 2005, liberalizes the remaining 49 percent of imports.

However, the term "phase-out" is quite a misnomer, because the agreement does not phase out quotas steadily but instead leaves most in place until the "cliff" in 2005. The agreement specifies that certain percentages of *imports* be freed from quota, but it does not require that the goods freed be those that were under quota to begin with. As a result, during the first two tranches, very few quotas were removed, because most of the goods specified in the tranches had not been under quota. Approximately 85 percent of quotas were scheduled to still be in effect until December 31, 2004.[44] Indeed, in the first tranche, the United States lifted only one quota: that for work gloves from Canada.[45]

Julia Hughes and Erik Autor could only shake their heads at the beginning of the "phase-out" as nonexistent quotas were rescinded on parachutes, kelims, silk sport bags, and laparoscopy sponges. Thanks to the weakened but still snarling domestic industry, they would have to wait another 10 years to see the quotas vanish (maybe) on things that people actually buy, such as cotton T-shirts, underwear, or pants.   ■

NOTES

1. This essay relies on interviews during 2001 to 2004 in Washington, Alexander City, Alabama, and Shanghai with Erik Autor, Phyllis Bonanno, Christopher Champion, Jennifer Hillman, Julia Hughes, John Jackson, Cass Johnson, Donna Lee McGee, Michael Levy, Carlos Moore, James Moore, Paul O'Day, Michael Ryan, Ronald Sorini, Auggie Tantillo, Earl Whipple, Patrick Xu, and Tom Young. Telephone discussions were held with Jack Albertine, Ross Arnold, Michael Hubbard, Jeff Martin, and David Trumbull.

2. Underhill, *Industrial Crisis*, 4.

3. Joint Textile Industry letter on China to President Bush at <www.atmi.org> accessed July 20, 2003. The letter was signed by American Textile Manufacturers Institute; American Manufacturing Trade Action Coalition, National Textile Association, American Yarn Spinners Association, American Fiber Manufacturers Association, National Cotton Council, American Sheep Industry Association, American Textile Machinery Association, Carpet and Rug Institute, Association of Georgia's Textile, Carpet & Consumer Products Manufacturers, Hosiery Association, Industrial Fabrics Association International, North Carolina Manufacturers Association, and Textile Distributors Association.

4. Joint Press Release, Amtac et al., June 9, 2004.

5. For an account of the pre-election safeguard campaign, see Blustein, "Textile Makers Fight for Limits." The status of China safeguard petitions is reported at <http://www.otexa.ita.doc.gov>.

6. World Trade Atlas, accessed June 3, 2004, for HTS categories 61 (knit apparel) and 62 (woven apparel).

7. See <http:www.ustr.gov/regions/whemisphere/camerica/regional.shtml>.

8. As of 2003, only 19 of the 48 countries in the Sub-Saharan Africa region had been granted apparel benefits by the United States. Textile and apparel trade provisions of these agreements are at <http://otexa.ita.doc.gov/Trade_Act_2000.htm#>.

9. USITC *Harmonized Tariff Schedule of the United States* (2003) (Rev 1). This abstracts from a further complexity, because if the T-shirt is all white without a collar or pocket, then it falls under the "underwear" category.

10. <http://www.customs.gov/xp/cgov/import/textiles_and_quotas/archived/2003_year_rpt/>.

11. Dickerson, *Textiles and Apparel in the Global Economy*, 399.

12. Friman, *Patchwork Protectionism*.

13. Includes employment in NCAIS categories 313 (textile mills), 314 (textile product mills), and 316 (apparel). See <http://www.bls.gov> for employment data by industry.

14. Friman, "Rocks, Hard Places, and the New Protectionism," 691.

15. On the effects of geographic concentration on political influence in trade policy, see Schiller, "Trade Politics in the American Congress," or Metcalfe and Goodwin, "An Empirical Analysis of the Determinants of Trade Policy Protection."

16. Aggarwal, *Liberal Protectionism*, 164.

17. The Reagan letter is excerpted in Brandis, *The Making of Textile Trade Policy*, 56.

18. Conti, *Reconciling Free Trade*, xiv.

19. See Conti for an analysis of presidential rhetoric related to trade.

20. Quoted in Rosen, *Making Sweatshops*, 82.

21. Quoted in Rothgeb, *U.S. Trade Policy*, 102.

22. Aggarwal, *Liberal Protectionism*, 53.

23. Ikenson, *Threadbare Excuses*, 9.

24. Cline, *The Future of World Trade in Textiles*, 163.

25. Vinson's letter is excerpted in Brandis, *The Making of Textile Trade Policy*, 25.

26. Aggarwal, *Liberal Protectionism*, 111.

27. Ibid., 69.

28. Nixon, Public Papers, 944–946.

29. Brandis, *The Making of Textile Trade Policy*, 46.

30. Cline, *The Future of World Trade in Textiles*, 150; GATT principles prohibit quantitative restraints, or quotas, as well as market access that discriminate across countries.

31. Cline, *The Future of World Trade in Textiles*, 163.

32. Quotas and bilateral agreements are at <http://otexa.ita.doc.gov>.

33. SMEs are shown in <http://otexa.ita.doc.gov/correlations>.

34. Ikenson, *Threadbare Excuses*, 10.

35. Dickerson, *Textiles and Apparel in the Global Economy*, 365.

36. Quoted in Rothgeb, *U.S. Trade Policy*, 21.

37. Quoted in Destler, *American Trade Politics*, 5.

38. Quoted in Conti, *Reconciling Free Trade*, 22.

39. Dickerson, *Textiles and Apparel in the Global Economy*, 366.

40. Cline, *The Future of World Trade in Textiles*, 213.

41. In *Making Sweatshops*, Rosen provides a complete treatment of the political rise of the retail industry on the subject of trade.

42. Schott and Buurman, *The Uruguay Round*, 5.

43. The baseline import figures were derived from 1990 imports. Product lists for each tranche of the phase-out are at <http://otexa.ita.doc.gov/#IMPORTQUOTAS>.

44. USITC, *The Economic Effects of Significant U.S. Import Restraints*, 61.

45. Dickerson, *Textiles and Apparel in the Global Economy*, 378.

REFERENCES

Aggarwal, Vinod K. *Liberal Protectionism: The International Politics of Organized Textile Trade.* Berkeley: University of California Press, 1985.

Brandis, R. Buford. *The Making of Textile Trade Policy, 1935–1981.* Washington, DC: American Textile Manufacturers Institute, 1982.

Cline, William R. *The Future of World Trade in Textiles and Apparel.* (Rev. ed.) Washington, DC: Institute for International Economics, 1990.

Conti, Delia B. *Reconciling Free Trade, Fair Trade, and Interdependence: The Rhetoric of Presidential Economic Leadership.* Westport, CT: Praeger, 1998.

Destler, I.M. *American Trade Politics.* 3rd ed. Washington, DC: Institute for International Economics, 1995.

Dickerson, Kitty. *Textiles and Apparel in the Global Economy.* 3rd ed. Upper Saddle River, NJ: Merrill, Prentice-Hall, 1999.

Friman, H. Richard. "Rocks, Hard Places, and the New Protectionism: Textile Trade Policy Choices in the United States and Japan." *International Organization* 42, no. 4 (Autumn 1988): 689–723.

_____. *Patchwork Protectionism: Textile Trade Policy in the United States, Japan, and West Germany.* Ithaca: Cornell University Press, 1990.

Ikenson, Dan. *Threadbare Excuses: The Textile Industry's Campaign to Preserve Import Restraints.* Trade Policy Analysis No. 25. Washington, DC: CATO Institute, Center for Trade Policy Studies, 2003.

Metcalfe, Mark R., and Barry K. Goodwin. "An Empirical Analysis of the Determinants of Trade Policy Protection in the U.S. Manufacturing Sector." *Journal of Policy Modeling* 21, no. 2 (March 1999): 153–165.

Rosen, Ellen Israel. *Making Sweatshops: The Globalization of the U.S. Apparel Industry.* Berkeley: University of California Press, 2002.

Rothgeb, John M., Jr. *U.S. Trade Policy: Balancing Economic Dreams and Political Realities.* Washington, DC: CQ Press, 2001.

Schiller, Wendy J. "Trade Politics in the American Congress: A Study of the Interaction of Political Geography and Interest Group Behavior." *Political Geography* 18, no. 7 (September 1999): 769–789.

Schott, Jeffrey J., and Johanna W. Buurman. *The Uruguay Round: An Assessment.* Washington, DC: Institute for International Economics, 1994.

Underhill, Geoffrey R.D. *Industrial Crisis and the Open Economy: Politics, Global Trade and the Textile Industry in the Advanced Economies.* New York: St. Martin's Press, 1998.

U.S. International Trade Commission. *Textiles and Apparel: Assessment of the Competitiveness of Certain Foreign Suppliers to the U.S. Market* (Vol. 1). Investigation No. 332-448, Publication No. 3671. Washington, DC: USITC, 2004.

■ *QUESTIONS FOR MAKING CONNECTIONS WITHIN THE READING* ■

1. Throughout her argument, Rivoli repeatedly uses the phrase "the race to the bottom" without ever explicitly defining what it means. What is this race? Who are the participants? What are they racing to the bottom of? What is the prize that goes to the winner? What do the losers get?

2. One of the particular challenges Rivoli faces in writing about the recent history of trade policy governing textiles in the United States is the sheer complexity of the regulations; another is the large number of players involved (the "alphabet armies"). Yet another complexity is that alliances shift over time, with key players moving over to the "dark side." Given the level of detail this subject requires, it is possible that Rivoli's larger points are in danger of getting lost. What would you say are Rivoli's larger concerns, beyond pointing out the complexity of the issue of textile trade?

3. Rivoli is writing about events as they unfold and thus cannot offer her assessment as final or definitive. She can only say, as she does repeatedly, that this is how the situation looked heading into 2005. Did the MFA quotas expire, as scheduled, on December 31, 2004? If you were to update Rivoli's argument, what would you say has happened to the textile trade in the years after she published *The Travels of a T-Shirt in the Global Economy?*

■ *QUESTIONS FOR WRITING* ■

1. Rivoli identifies the negotiations over the U.S.-Carribbean Trade Partnership Act as a "telling example of the dominance of politics over markets," an example that appears to carry on an American tradition of exempting the textile industries from free trade. Is a world where markets dominate the political system superior to one where politics would dominate over markets? Given that Rivoli's case involves a long history of American presidents exempting the textile industries from compliance with broader trade policies, how does this illustrate the dominance of politics over markets rather than vice versa? How might politics suffer if economic forces become too powerful?

2. Towards the end of her chapter Rivoli observes that "[n]egotiations over *whether* to end the MFA were simple compared to the negotiations over *how* to end the MFA." Given the history Rivoli has related, this can't be much of a surprise; indeed, one could say that it is the very nature of political entities to impede the pace of change. With this thought in mind, describe what might have happened had all the trade restrictions Rivoli describes been eliminated in the blink of an eye. Then, based on your own independent research, discuss what actually happened to the textile industry once it went over the "cliff" of 2005. Do we now find ourselves with a free market?

■ *QUESTIONS FOR MAKING CONNECTIONS BETWEEN READINGS* ■

1. In "'Market Fundamentalism' Versus the Religion of Democracy," Bryan Caplan asserts that it "is more important for students to understand that self-interest often encourages socially beneficial behavior than to understand that this mechanism falls short of perfection." Does the textile trade, as Rivoli describes it, serve to illustrate Bryan Caplan's central point? Would Caplan focus on individual agents or groups to illustrate the value of self-interest, or would he focus on the collective value derived from the actions of everyone acting at the same time? Or does Caplan believe that any economic activity can be seen as "encourag[ing] socially beneficial behavior" of some kind? Write a paper in which you explore the role of self-interest in the creation and maintenance of the textile industry.

2. In "A World on the Edge," Amy Chua discusses the very same issues that concern Rivoli: globalization, democracy, markets. Yet Chua's account differs both in its focus and its conclusions: where Rivoli sees the steady erosion of trade protections for the textile industry, Chua sees a rise in ethnic violence and a failure of the United States to fulfill its global obligations to the disadvantaged. How do you explain these differing views on the import of globalization? Does Rivoli's study illustrate the broader developments discussed by Chua? Or does Chua's account illustrate the macroeconomic forces Rivoli discusses? Which version of globalization seems better at explaining our world today?

OLIVER SACKS

WHEN OLIVER SACKS was awarded the Lewis Thomas Prize by Rockefeller University in 2002 for his life's work presenting the case histories of patients with neurological diseases, he was praised for his ability to take his readers into the nearly unimaginable mental worlds of those who have suffered brain damage: "Sacks," the awards committee concluded, "presses us to follow him into uncharted regions of human experience—and compels us to realize, once there, that we are confronting only ourselves." This is an extraordinary claim, given that Sacks has written, most famously, about patients who suffered sleeping sickness for decades, about a man who mistook his wife for a hat, and about what it is like to live with Tourette's syndrome, a disease that drives its victims to spew forth curses in public. It has been Sacks's lifelong project to write about the mentally ill in ways that foreground the humanity of those who are suffering from diseases that generate all manner of strange behavior.

Born and educated in England, Sacks has lived in New York since 1965, where he was for decades a clinical professor of neurology at the Albert Einstein College of Medicine, adjunct professor of neurology at the NYU School of Medicine, and consultant neurologist to the Little Sisters of the Poor. In 2007, he was appointed Professor of Clinical Neurology and Clinical Psychiatry at Columbia University Medical Center; along with this appointment, he was designated Columbia University's first Columbia Artist, granting him close to free rein in working across departments and organizing interdisciplinary programs. Sacks explained in a recent interview that his interest in the brain and in neurology arose from his childhood experience of visual migraines. "I would often lose sight to one side, and sometimes one can lose the idea of one side in a migraine, which can be very, very strange thing. When I was young I was sort of terrified of these things. I asked my mother, who was a doctor herself and also had visual migraines. She was the first to explain to me that we are not just cameras—we are not just given the visual world. We make it to some extent."

Sacks, Oliver. "The Mind's Eye." *The New Yorker*. July 28, 2003. 48–59.

Quotations come from the Rockefeller University Web site, <http://www.rockefeller.edu/lectures/sacks031802.html>, and the Salon.com interview with Sacks, <http://www.salon.com/dec96/sacks961223.html>.

The observation of how patients creatively adapt to the challenges an illness poses has shaped Sacks's own approach to medicine and has led him to create what he has called a "neuroanthropology" of how illness is both perceived and experienced around the world. Most recently he has turned his attention to the nearly universal love of music and its neurological underpinnings. The author of *Awakenings* (1973), *The Man Who Mistook His Wife for a Hat* (1985), *An Anthropologist on Mars* (1995), and *Musicophilia: Tales of Music and the Brain* (2007), among other works, Sacks brings together biology and biography in their interest of forging a humane medical practice.

The Mind's Eye
What the Blind See

In his last letter, Goethe wrote, "The Ancients said that the animals are taught through their organs; let me add to this, so are men, but they have the advantage of teaching their organs in return." He wrote this in 1832, a time when phrenology was at its height, and the brain was seen as a mosaic of "little organs" subserving everything from language to drawing ability to shyness. Each individual, it was believed, was given a fixed measure of this faculty or that, according to the luck of his birth. Though we no longer pay attention, as the phrenologists did, to the "bumps" on the head (each of which, supposedly, indicated a brain-mind organ beneath), neurology and neuroscience have stayed close to the idea of brain fixity and localization—the notion, in particular, that the highest part of the brain, the cerebral cortex, is effectively programmed from birth: this part to vision and visual processing, that part to hearing, that to touch, and so on.

This would seem to allow individuals little power of choice, of self-determination, let alone of adaptation, in the event of a neurological or perceptual mishap.

But to what extent are we—our experiences, our reactions—shaped, predetermined, by our brains, and to what extent do we shape our own brains? Does the mind run the brain or the brain the mind—or, rather, to what extent does one run the other? To what extent are we the authors, the creators, of our own experiences? The effects of a profound perceptual deprivation such as blindness can cast an unexpected light on this. To become blind, especially later in life, presents one with a huge, potentially overwhelming challenge: to find a new way of living, of ordering one's world, when the old way has been destroyed.

A dozen years ago, I was sent an extraordinary book called "Touching the Rock: An Experience of Blindness." The author, John Hull, was a professor of religious education who had grown up in Australia and then moved to England. Hull had developed cataracts at the age of thirteen, and became completely blind in his left eye four years later. Vision in his right eye remained reasonable until he was thirty-five or so, and then started to deteriorate. There followed a decade of steadily failing vision, in which Hull needed stronger and stronger magnifying glasses, and had to write with thicker and thicker pens, until, in 1983, at the age of forty-eight, he became completely blind.

"Touching the Rock" is the journal he dictated in the three years that followed. It is full of piercing insights relating to Hull's life as a blind person, but most striking for me is Hull's description of how, in the years after his loss of sight, he experienced a gradual attenuation of visual imagery and memory, and finally a virtual extinction of them (except in dreams)—a state that he calls "deep blindness."

By this, Hull meant not only the loss of visual images and memories but a loss of the very idea of seeing, so that concepts like "here," "there," and "facing" seemed to lose meaning for him, and even the sense of objects having "appearances," visible characteristics, vanished. At this point, for example, he could no longer imagine how the numeral 3 looked, unless he traced it in the air with his hand. He could construct a "motor" image of a 3, but not a visual one.

Hull, though at first greatly distressed about the fading of visual memories and images—the fact that he could no longer conjure up the faces of his wife or children, or of familiar and loved landscapes and places—then came to accept it with remarkable equanimity; indeed, to regard it as a natural response to a nonvisual world. He seemed to regard this loss of visual imagery as a prerequisite for the full development, the heightening, of his other senses.

Two years after becoming completely blind, Hull had apparently become so nonvisual as to resemble someone who had been blind from birth. Hull's loss of visuality also reminded me of the sort of "cortical blindness" that can happen if the primary visual cortex is damaged, through a stroke or traumatic brain damage—although in Hull's case there was no direct damage to the visual cortex but, rather, a cutting off from any visual stimulation or input.

In a profoundly religious way, and in language sometimes reminiscent of that of St. John of the Cross, Hull enters into this state, surrenders himself, with a sort of acquiescence and joy. And such "deep" blindness he conceives as "an authentic and autonomous world, a place of its own. . . . Being a whole-body seer is to be in one of the concentrated human conditions."

Being a "whole-body seer," for Hull, means shifting his attention, his center of gravity, to the other senses, and he writes again and again of how these have assumed a new richness and power. Thus he speaks of how the sound of rain, never before accorded much attention, can now delineate a whole landscape for him, for its sound on the garden path is different from its sound as it drums on the lawn, or on the bushes in his garden, or on the fence dividing it from the road. "Rain," he writes, "has a way of bringing out the contours of everything; it throws a coloured blanket over previously invisible things; instead of an intermittent and thus fragmented world, the steadily falling rain creates continuity of acoustic experience . . . presents the fullness of an entire situation all at once . . . gives a sense of perspective and of the actual relationships of one part of the world to another."

With his new intensity of auditory experience (or attention), along with the sharpening of his other senses, Hull comes to feel a sense of intimacy with nature, an intensity of being-in-the-world, beyond anything he knew when he was sighted. Blindness now becomes for him "a dark, paradoxical gift." This is not just "compensation," he emphasizes, but a whole new order, a new mode of human being. With this he extricates himself from visual nostalgia, from the strain, or falsity, of trying to pass as "normal," and finds a new focus, a new freedom. His teaching at the university expands, becomes more fluent, his writing becomes stronger and deeper; he becomes intellectually and spiritually bolder, more confident. He feels he is on solid ground at last.

What Hull described seemed to me an astounding example of how an individual deprived of one form of perception could totally reshape himself to a new center, a new identity.

It is said that those who see normally as infants but then become blind within the first two years of life retain no memories of seeing, have no visual imagery and no visual elements in their dreams (and, in this way, are comparable to those born blind). It is similar with those who lose hearing before the age of two: they have no sense of having "lost" the world of sound, nor any sense of "silence," as hearing people sometimes imagine. For those who lose sight so early, the very concepts of "sight" or "blindness" soon cease to have meaning, and there is no sense of losing the world of vision, only of living fully in a world constructed by the other senses.

But it seemed extraordinary to me that such an annihilation of visual memory as Hull describes could happen equally to an adult, with decades, an entire lifetime, of rich and richly categorized visual experience to call upon. And yet I could not doubt the authenticity of Hull's account, which he relates with the most scrupulous care and lucidity.

Important studies of adaptation in the brain were begun in the nineteen-seventies by, among others, Helen Neville, a cognitive neuroscientist now working in Oregon. She showed that in prelingually deaf people (that is, those who had been born deaf or become deaf before the age of two or so) the auditory parts of the brain had not degenerated or atrophied. These had remained active and functional, but with an activity and a function that were new: they had been transformed, "reallocated," in Neville's term, for processing visual language. Comparable studies in those born blind, or early blinded, show that the visual areas of the cortex, similarly, may be reallocated in function, and used to process sound and touch.

With the reallocation of the visual cortex to touch and other senses, these can take on a hyperacuity that perhaps no sighted person can imagine. Bernard Morin, the blind mathematician who in the nineteen-sixties had shown how a sphere could be turned inside out, felt that his achievement required a special sort of spatial perception and imagination. And a similar sort of spatial giftedness has been central to the work of Geerat Vermeij, a blind biologist who has been able to delineate many new species of mollusk, based on tiny variations in the shapes and contours of their shells.

Faced with such findings and reports, neurologists began to concede that there might be a certain flexibility or plasticity in the brain, at least in the early years of life. But when this critical period was over, it was assumed, the brain became inflexible, and no further changes of a radical type could occur. The experiences that Hull so carefully recounts give the lie to this. It is clear that his perceptions, his brain, did finally change, in a fundamental way. Indeed, Alvaro Pascual-Leone and his colleagues in Boston have recently shown that, even in adult sighted volunteers, as little as five days of being blindfolded produces marked shifts to nonvisual forms of behavior and cognition, and they have demonstrated the physiological changes in the brain that go along with this. And only last month, Italian researchers published a study showing that sighted volunteers kept in the dark for as little as ninety *minutes* may show a striking enhancement of tactile-spatial sensitivity.

The brain, clearly, is capable of changing even in adulthood, and I assumed that Hull's experience was typical of acquired blindness—the response, sooner or later, of everyone who becomes blind, even in adult life.

So when I came to publish an essay on Hull's book, in 1991, I was taken aback to receive a number of letters from blind people, letters that were often somewhat puzzled, and occasionally indignant, in tone. Many of my correspondents, it seemed, could not identify with Hull's experience, and said that they themselves, even decades after losing their sight, had never lost their visual images or memories. One correspondent, who had lost her sight at fifteen, wrote, "Even though I am totally blind . . . I consider myself a very visual person. I still 'see' objects in front of me. As I am typing now I can see my hands on the keyboard. . . . I don't feel comfortable in a new environment until I have a mental picture of its appearance. I need a mental map for my independent moving, too."

Had I been wrong, or at least one-sided, in accepting Hull's experience as a typical response to blindness? Had I been guilty of emphasizing one mode of response too strongly, oblivious to the possibilities of radically different responses?

This feeling came to a head in 1996, when I received a letter from an Australian psychologist named Zoltan Torey. Torey wrote to me not about blindness but about a book he had written on the brain-mind problem and the nature of consciousness. (The book was published by Oxford University Press as "The Crucible of Consciousness," in 1999.) In his letter Torey also spoke of how he had been blinded in an accident at the age of twenty-one, while working at a chemical factory, and how, although "advised to switch from a visual to an auditory mode of adjustment," he had moved in the opposite direction, and resolved to develop instead his "inner eye," his powers of visual imagery, to their greatest possible extent.

In this, it seemed, he had been extremely successful, developing a re-markable power of generating, holding, and manipulating images in his mind, so much so that he had been able to construct an imagined visual world that seemed almost as real and intense to him as the perceptual one he had lost—and, indeed, sometimes more real, more intense, a sort of con-trolled dream or hallucination. This imagery, moreover, enabled him to do things that might have seemed scarcely possible for a blind man.

"I replaced the entire roof guttering of my multi-gabled home single-handed," he wrote, "and solely on the strength of the accurate and well-focused manipulation of my now totally pliable and responsive mental space." (Torey later expanded on this episode, mentioning the great alarm of his neighbors at seeing a blind man, alone, on the roof of his house—and, even more terrifying to them, at night, in pitch darkness.)

And it enabled him to think in ways that had not been available to him before, to envisage solutions, models, designs, to project himself to the in-side of machines and other systems, and, finally, to grasp by visual thought and simulation (complemented by all the data of neuroscience) the complex-ities of that ultimate system, the human brain-mind.

When I wrote back to Torey, I suggested that he consider writing an-other book, a more personal one, exploring how his life had been affected by blindness, and how he had responded to this, in the most improbable and seemingly paradoxical of ways. "Out of Darkness" is the memoir he has now written, and in it Torey describes his early memories with great visual intensity and humor. Scenes are remembered or reconstructed in brief, poetic glimpses of his childhood and youth in Hungary before the Second World War: the sky-blue buses of Budapest, the egg-yellow trams, the light-ing of gas lamps, the funicular on the Buda side. He describes a carefree and privileged youth, roaming with his father in the wooded mountains above the Danube, playing games and pranks at school, growing up in a highly intellectual environment of writers, actors, professionals of every sort. Torey's father was the head of a large motion-picture studio and would often give his son scripts to read. "This," Torey writes, "gave me the opportunity to visualize stories, plots and characters, to work my imagination—a skill that was to become a lifeline and source of strength in the years ahead."

All of this came to a brutal end with the Nazi occupation, the siege of Buda, and then the Soviet occupation. Torey, now an adolescent, found himself passionately drawn to the big questions—the mystery of the universe, of life, and above all the mystery of consciousness, of the mind. In 1948, nineteen years old, and feeling that he needed to immerse himself in biology, engineering, neuroscience, and psychology, but knowing that there was no chance of study, of an intellectual life, in Soviet Hungary, Torey made his escape and eventually found his way to Australia, where, penniless and without connections, he did various manual jobs. In June of 1951, loosening the plug in a vat of acid at the chemical factory where he worked, he had the accident that bisected his life.

"The last thing I saw with complete clarity was a glint of light in the flood of acid that was to engulf my face and change my life. It was a nanosecond of sparkle, framed by the black circle of the drumface, less than a foot away. This was the final scene, the slender thread that ties me to my visual past."

When it became clear that his corneas had been hopelessly damaged and that he would have to live his life as a blind man, he was advised to rebuild his representation of the world on the basis of hearing and touch and to "forget about sight and visualizing altogether." But this was something that Torey could not or would not do. He had emphasized, in his first letter to me, the importance of a most critical choice at this juncture: "I immediately resolved to find out how far a partially sense-deprived brain could go to rebuild a life." Put this way, it sounds abstract, like an experiment. But in his book one senses the tremendous feelings underlying his resolution—the horror of darkness, "the empty darkness," as Torey often calls it, "the grey fog that was engulfing me," and the passionate desire to hold on to light and sight, to maintain, if only in memory and imagination, a vivid and living visual world. The very title of his book says all this, and the note of defiance is sounded from the start.

Hull, who did not use his potential for imagery in a deliberate way, lost it in two or three years, and became unable to remember which way round a 3 went; Torey, on the other hand, soon became able to multiply four-figure numbers by each other, as on a blackboard, visualizing the whole operation in his mind, "painting" the suboperations in different colors.

Well aware that the imagination (or the brain), unrestrained by the usual perceptual input, may run away with itself in a wildly associative or self-serving way—as may happen in deliria, hallucinations, or dreams—Torey maintained a cautious and "scientific" attitude to his own visual imagery, taking pains to check the accuracy of his images by every means available. "I learned," he writes, "to hold the image in a tentative way, conferring credibility and status on it only when some information would tip the balance in its favor." Indeed, he soon gained enough confidence in the reliability of his visual imagery to stake his life upon it, as when he undertook roof repairs by himself. And this confidence extended to other, purely mental projects. He became able "to imagine, to visualize, for example, the inside of a differential gearbox in action as if from inside its casing. I was able to watch the cogs bite, lock and revolve, distributing the spin as required. I began to play around with this internal view in connection with mechanical and technical problems, visualizing how subcomponents relate in the atom, or in the living cell." This power of imagery was crucial, Torey thought, in enabling him to arrive at a solution of the brain-mind problem by visualizing the brain "as a perpetual juggling act of interacting routines."

In a famous study of creativity, the French mathematician Jacques Hadamard asked many scientists and mathematicians, including Einstein, about their thought processes. Einstein replied, "The physical entities which seem to serve as elements in thought are . . . more or less clear images which can be 'voluntarily' reproduced and combined. [Some are] of visual and some of muscular type. Conventional words or other signs have to be sought for laboriously only in a secondary stage." Torey cites this, and adds, "Nor was Einstein unique in this respect. Hadamard found that almost all scientists work this way, and this was also the way my project evolved."

Soon after receiving Torey's manuscript, I received the proofs of yet another memoir by a blind person: Sabriye Tenberken's "My Path Leads to Tibet." While Hull and Torey are thinkers, preoccupied in their different ways by inwardness, states of brain and mind, Tenberken is a doer; she has travelled, often alone, all over Tibet, where for centuries blind people have been treated as less than human and denied education, work, respect, or a role in the community. Virtually single-handed, Tenberken has transformed their situation over the past half-dozen years, devising a form of Tibetan Braille, establishing schools for the blind, and integrating the graduates of these schools into their communities.

Tenberken herself had impaired vision almost from birth but was able to make out faces and landscapes until she was twelve. As a child in Germany, she had a particular predilection for colors, and loved painting, and when she was no longer able to decipher shapes and forms she could still use colors to identify objects. Tenberken has, indeed, an intense synesthesia. "As far back as I can remember," she writes, "numbers and words have instantly triggered colors in me. . . . The number 4, for example, [is] gold. Five is light green. Nine is vermillion. . . . Days of the week as well as months have their colors, too. I have them arranged in geometrical formations, in circular sectors, a little like a pie. When I need to recall on which day a particular event happened, the first thing that pops up on my inner screen is the day's color, then its position in the pie." Her synesthesia has persisted and been intensified, it seems, by her blindness.

Though she has been totally blind for twenty years now, Tenberken continues to use all her other senses, along with verbal descriptions, visual memories, and a strong pictorial and synesthetic sensibility, to construct "pictures" of landscapes and rooms, of environments and scenes—pictures so lively and detailed as to astonish her listeners. These images may sometimes be wildly or comically different from reality, as she relates in one incident when she and a companion drove to Nam Co, the great salt lake in Tibet. Turning eagerly toward the lake, Tenberken saw, in her mind's eye, "a beach of crystallized salt shimmering like snow under an evening sun, at the edge of a vast body of turquoise water. . . . And down below, on the deep green mountain flanks, a few nomads were watching their yaks grazing." But it then turns out that she has been facing in the wrong direction, not "looking" at the lake at all, and that she has been "staring" at rocks and a gray landscape. These disparities don't faze her in the least—she is happy to have so vivid a visual imagination. Hers is essentially an artistic imagination, which can be impressionistic, romantic, not veridical at all, where Torey's imagination is that of an engineer, and has to be factual, accurate down to the last detail.

I had now read three memoirs, strikingly different in their depictions of the visual experience of blinded people: Hull with his acquiescent descent into imageless "deep blindness," Torey with his "compulsive visualization" and meticulous construction of an internal visual world, and Tenberken with her impulsive, almost novelistic, visual freedom, along with her remarkable and specific gift of synesthesia. Was there any such thing, I now wondered, as a "typical" blind experience?

I recently met two other people blinded in adult life who shared their experiences with me.

Dennis Shulman, a clinical psychologist and psychoanalyst who lectures on Biblical topics, is an affable, stocky, bearded man in his fifties who gradually lost his sight in his teens, becoming completely blind by the time he entered college. He immediately confirmed that his experience was unlike Hull's: "I still live in a visual world after thirty-five years of blindness. I have very vivid visual memories and images. My wife, whom I have never seen—I think of her visually. My kids, too. I see myself visually—but it is as I last saw myself, when I was thirteen, though I try hard to update the image. I often give public lectures, and my notes are in Braille; but when I go over them in my mind, I see the Braille notes visually—they are visual images, not tactile."

Arlene Gordon, a charming woman in her seventies, a former social worker, said that things were very similar for her: "If I move my arms back and forth in front of my eyes, I see them, even though I have been blind for more than thirty years." It seemed that moving her arms was immediately translated for her into a visual image. Listening to talking books, she added, made her eyes tire if she listened too long; she seemed to herself to be reading at such times, the sound of the spoken words being transformed to lines of print on a vividly visualized book in front of her. This involved a sort of cognitive exertion (similar perhaps to translating one language into another), and sooner or later this would give her an eye ache.

I was reminded of Amy, a colleague who had been deafened by scarlet fever at the age of nine but was so adept a lipreader that I often forgot she was deaf. Once, when I absent-mindedly turned away from her as I was speaking, she said sharply, "I can no longer hear you."

"You mean you can no longer see me," I said.

"*You* may call it seeing," she answered, "but I experience it as hearing."

Amy, though totally deaf, still constructed the sound of speech in her mind. Both Dennis and Arlene, similarly, spoke not only of a heightening of visual imagery and imagination since losing their eyesight but also of what seemed to be a much readier transference of information from verbal description—or from their own sense of touch, movement, hearing, or smell—into a visual form. On the whole, their experiences seemed quite similar to Torey's, even though they had not systematically exercised their powers of visual imagery in the way that he had, or consciously tried to make an entire virtual world of sight.

There is increasing evidence from neuroscience for the extraordinarily rich interconnectedness and interactions of the sensory areas of the brain, and the difficulty, therefore, of saying that anything is purely visual or purely auditory, or purely anything. This is evident in the very titles of some recent papers—Pascual-Leone and his colleagues at Harvard now write of "The Metamodal Organization of the Brain," and Shinsuke Shimojo and his group at Caltech, who are also exploring intersensory perceptual phenomena, recently published a paper called "What You See Is What You Hear," and stress that sensory modalities can never be considered in isolation. The world of the blind, of the blinded, it seems, can be especially rich in such in-between states—the intersensory, the metamodal—states for which we have no common language.

Arlene, like Dennis, still identifies herself in many ways as a visual person. "I have a very strong sense of color," she said. "I pick out my own clothes. I think, Oh, that will go with this or that, once I have been told the colors." Indeed, she was dressed very smartly, and took obvious pride in her appearance.

"I love travelling," she continued. "I 'saw' Venice when I was there." She explained how her travelling companions would describe places, and she would then construct a visual image from these details, her reading, and her own visual memories. "Sighted people enjoy travelling with me," she said. "I ask them questions, then they look, and see things they wouldn't otherwise. Too often people with sight don't see anything! It's a reciprocal process—we enrich each other's worlds."

If we are sighted, we build our own images, using our eyes, our visual information, so instantly and seamlessly that it seems to us we are experiencing "reality" itself. One may need to see people who are color-blind, or motion-blind, who have lost certain visual capacities from cerebral injury, to realize the enormous act of analysis and synthesis, the dozens of subsystems involved in the subjectively simple act of seeing. But can a visual image be built using *nonvisual* information—information conveyed by the other senses, by memory, or by verbal description?

There have, of course, been many blind poets and writers, from Homer on. Most of these were born with normal vision and lost their sight in boyhood or adulthood (like Milton). I loved reading Prescott's "Conquest of Mexico" and "Conquest of Peru" as a boy, and feel that I first saw these lands through his intensely visual, almost hallucinogenic descriptions, and I was amazed to discover, years later, that Prescott not only had never visited Mexico or Peru but had been virtually blind since the age of eighteen. Did he, like Torey, compensate for his blindness by developing such powers of visual imagery that he could experience a "virtual reality" of sight? Or were his brilliant visual descriptions in a sense simulated, made possible by the evocative and pictorial powers of language? To what extent can language, a picturing in words, provide a substitute for actual seeing, and for the visual, pictorial imagination? Blind children, it has often been noted, tend to be precocious verbally, and may develop such fluency in the verbal description of faces and places as to leave others (and perhaps themselves) uncertain as to whether they are actually blind. Helen Keller's writing, to give a famous example, startles one with its brilliantly visual quality.

When I asked Dennis and Arlene whether they had read John Hull's book, Arlene said, "I was stunned when I read it. His experiences are so unlike mine." Perhaps, she added, Hull had "renounced" his inner vision. Dennis agreed, but said, "We are only two individuals. You are going to have to talk to dozens of people. . . . But in the meanwhile you should read Jacques Lusseyran's memoir."

Lusseyran was a French Resistance fighter whose memoir, "And There Was Light," deals mostly with his experiences fighting the Nazis and later in Buchenwald but includes many beautiful descriptions of his early adaptations to blindness. He was blinded in an accident when he was not quite eight years old, an age that he came to feel was "ideal" for such an eventuality, for, while he already had a rich visual experience to call on, "the habits of a boy of eight are not yet formed, either in body or in mind. His body is infinitely supple." And suppleness, agility, indeed came to characterize his response to blindness.

Many of his initial responses were of loss, both of imagery and of interests:

> A very short time after I went blind I forgot the faces of my mother and father and the faces of most of the people I loved. . . . I stopped caring whether people were dark or fair, with blue eyes or green. I felt that sighted people spent too much time observing these empty things. . . . I no longer even thought about them. People no longer seemed to possess them. Sometimes in my mind men and women appeared without heads or fingers.

This is similar to Hull, who writes, "Increasingly, I am no longer even trying to imagine what people look like. . . . I am finding it more and more difficult to realize that people look like anything, to put any meaning into the idea that they have an appearance."

But then, while relinquishing the actual visual world and many of its values and categories, Lusseyran starts to construct and to use an imaginary visual world more like Torey's.

This started as a sensation of light, a formless, flooding, streaming radiance. Neurological terms are bound to sound reductive in this almost mystical context. Yet one might venture to interpret this as a "release" phenomenon, a spontaneous, almost eruptive arousal of the visual cortex, now deprived of its normal visual input. This is a phenomenon analogous, perhaps, to tinnitus or phantom limbs, though endowed here, by a devout and precociously imaginative little boy, with some element of the supernal. But then, it becomes clear, he does find himself in possession of great powers of visual imagery, and not just a formless luminosity.

The visual cortex, the inner eye, having now been activated, Lusseyran's mind constructed a "screen" upon which whatever he thought or desired was projected and, if need be, manipulated, as on a computer screen. "This screen was not like a blackboard, rectangular or square, which so quickly reaches the edge of its frame," he writes. "My screen was always as big as I needed it to be. Because it was nowhere in space it was everywhere at the same time. . . . Names, figures and objects in general did not appear on my screen without shape, nor just in black and white, but in all the colors of the rainbow. Nothing entered my mind without being bathed in a certain amount of light. . . . In a few months my personal world had turned into a painter's studio."

Great powers of visualization were crucial to the young Lusseyran, even in something as nonvisual (one would think) as learning Braille (he visualizes the Braille dots, as Dennis does), and in his brilliant successes at school. They were no less crucial in the real, outside world. He describes walks with his sighted friend Jean, and how, as they were climbing together up the side of a hill above the Seine Valley, he could say:

> "Just look! This time we're on top. . . . You'll see the whole bend of the river, unless the sun gets in your eyes!" Jean was startled, opened his eyes wide

and cried: "You're right." This little scene was often repeated between us, in a thousand forms.

"Every time someone mentioned an event," Lusseyran relates, "the event immediately projected itself in its place on the screen, which was a kind of inner canvas. . . . Comparing my world with his, [Jean] found that his held fewer pictures and not nearly as many colors. This made him almost angry. 'When it comes to that,' he used to say, 'which one of us two is blind?' "

It was his supernormal powers of visualization and visual manipulation—visualizing people's position and movement, the topography of any space, visualizing strategies for defense and attack—coupled with his charismatic personality (and seemingly infallible "nose" or "ear" for detecting falsehood, possible traitors), which later made Lusseyran an icon in the French Resistance.

Dennis, earlier, had spoken of how the heightening of his other senses had increased his sensitivity to moods in other people, and to the most delicate nuances in their speech and self-presentation. He could now recognize many of his patients by smell, he said, and he could often pick up states of tension or anxiety which they might not even be aware of. He felt that he had become far more sensitive to others' emotional states since losing his sight, for he was no longer taken in by visual appearances, which most people learn to camouflage. Voices and smells, by contrast, he felt, could reveal people's depths. He had come to think of most sighted people, he joked, as "visually dependent."

In a subsequent essay, Lusseyran inveighs against the "despotism," the "idol worship" of sight, and sees the "task" of blindness as reminding us of our other, deeper modes of perception and their mutuality. "A blind person has a better sense of feeling, of taste, of touch," he writes, and speaks of these as "the gifts of the blind." And all of these, Lusseyran feels, blend into a single fundamental sense, a deep attentiveness, a slow, almost prehensile attention, a sensuous, intimate being at one with the world which sight, with its quick, flicking, facile quality, continually distracts us from. This is very close to Hull's concept of "deep blindness" as infinitely more than mere compensation but a unique form of perception, a precious and special mode of being.

What happens when the visual cortex is no longer limited, or constrained, by any visual input? The simple answer is that, isolated from the outside, the visual cortex becomes hypersensitive to internal stimuli of all sorts: its own autonomous activity; signals from other brain areas—auditory, tactile, and verbal areas; and the thoughts and emotions of the blinded individual. Sometimes, as sight deteriorates, hallucinations occur—of geometrical patterns, or occasionally of silent, moving figures or scenes that appear and disappear spontaneously, without any relation to the contents of consciousness, or intention, or context.

Something perhaps akin to this is described by Hull as occurring almost convulsively as he was losing the last of his sight. "About a year after I was registered blind," he writes, "I began to have such strong images of what people's faces looked like that they were almost like hallucinations."

These imperious images were so engrossing as to preëmpt consciousness: "Sometimes," Hull adds, "I would become so absorbed in gazing upon these images, which seemed to come and go without any intention on my part, that I would entirely lose the thread of what was being said to me. I would come back with a shock . . . and I would feel as if I had dropped off to sleep for a few minutes in front of the wireless." Though related to the context of speaking with people, these visions came and went in their own way, without any reference to his intentions, conjured up not by him but by his brain.

The fact that Hull is the only one of the four authors to describe this sort of release phenomenon is perhaps an indication that his visual cortex was starting to escape from his control. One has to wonder whether this signalled its impending demise, at least as an organ of useful visual imagery and memory. Why this should have occurred with him, and how common such a course is, is something one can only speculate on.

Torey, unlike Hull, clearly played a very active role in building up his visual imagery, took control of it the moment the bandages were taken off, and never apparently experienced, or allowed, the sort of involuntary imagery Hull describes. Perhaps this was because he was already very at home with visual imagery, and used to manipulating it in his own way. We know that Torey was very visually inclined before his accident, and skilled from boyhood in creating visual narratives based on the film scripts his father gave him. We have no such information about Hull, for his journal entries start only when he has become blind.

For Lusseyran and Tenberken, there is an added physiological factor: both were attracted to painting, in love with colors, and strongly synesthetic— prone to visualizing numbers, letters, words, music, etc., as shapes and colors—before becoming blind. They already had an overconnectedness, a "cross talk" between the visual cortex and other parts of the brain primarily concerned with language, sound, and music. Given such a neurological situation (synesthesia is congenital, often familial), the persistence of visual imagery and synesthesia, or its heightening, might be almost inevitable in the event of blindness.

Torey required months of intense cognitive discipline dedicated to improving his visual imagery, making it more tenacious, more stable, more malleable, whereas Lusseyran seemed to do this almost effortlessly from the start. Perhaps this was aided by the fact that Lusseyran was not yet eight when blinded (while Torey was twenty-one), and his brain was, accordingly, more plastic, more able to adapt to a new and drastic contingency.

But adaptability does not end with youth. It is clear that Arlene, becoming blind in her forties, was able to adapt in quite radical ways, too, developing not exactly synesthesia but something more flexible and useful: the ability to "see" her hands moving before her, to "see" the words of books read to her, to construct detailed visual images from verbal descriptions. Did she adapt, or did her brain do so? One has a sense that Torey's adaptation was largely shaped by conscious motive, will, and purpose; that Lusseyran's was shaped by overwhelming physiological disposition; and that Arlene's lies somewhere in between. Hull's, meanwhile, remains enigmatic.

There has been much recent work on the neural bases of visual imagery—this can be investigated by brain imaging of various types (PET scanning, functional MRIs, etc.)—and it is now generally accepted that visual imagery activates the cortex in a similar way, and with almost the same intensity, as visual perception itself. And yet studies on the effects of blindness on the human cortex have shown that functional changes may start to occur in a few days, and can become profound as the days stretch into months or years.

Torey, who is well aware of all this research, attributes Hull's loss of visual imagery and memory to the fact that he did not struggle to maintain it, to heighten and systematize and use it, as Torey himself did. (Indeed, Torey expresses horror at what he regards as Hull's passivity, at his letting himself slide into deep blindness.) Perhaps Torey was able to stave off an otherwise inevitable loss of neuronal function in the visual cortex; but perhaps, again, such neural degeneration is quite variable, irrespective of whether or not there is conscious visualization. And, of course, Hull had been losing vision gradually for many years, whereas for Torey blindness was instantaneous and total. It would be of great interest to know the results of brain imaging in the two men, and indeed to look at a large number of people with acquired blindness, to see what correlations, what predictions could be made.

But what if their differences reflect an underlying predisposition independent of blindness? What of visual imagery in the sighted?

I first became conscious that there could be huge variations in visual imagery and visual memory when I was fourteen or so. My mother was a surgeon and comparative anatomist, and I had brought her a lizard's skeleton from school. She gazed at this intently for a minute, turning it round in her hands, then put it down and without looking at it again did a number of drawings of it, rotating it mentally by thirty degrees each time, so that she produced a series, the last drawing exactly the same as the first. I could not imagine how she had done this, and when she said that she could "see" the skeleton in her mind just as clearly and vividly as if she were looking at it, and that she simply rotated the image through a twelfth of a circle each time, I felt bewildered, and very stupid. I could hardly see anything with my mind's eye—at most, faint, evanescent images over which I had no control.

I did have vivid images as I was falling asleep, and in dreams, and once when I had a high fever—but otherwise I saw nothing, or almost nothing, when I tried to visualize, and had great difficulty picturing anybody or anything. Coincidentally or not, I could not draw for toffee.

My mother had hoped I would follow in her footsteps and become a surgeon, but when she realized how lacking in visual powers I was (and how clumsy, lacking in mechanical skill, too) she resigned herself to the idea that I would have to specialize in something else.

I was, however, to get a vivid idea of what mental imagery could be like when, during the nineteen-sixties, I had a period of experimenting with large doses of amphetamines. These can produce striking perceptual changes, including dramatic enhancements of visual imagery and memory (as well as heightenings of the other senses, as I describe in "The Dog Beneath the Skin," a story in "The Man Who Mistook His Wife for a Hat"). For a period of two weeks or so, I found that I could do the most accurate anatomical drawings. I had only to look at a picture or an anatomical specimen, and its image would remain both vivid and stable, and I could easily hold it in my mind for hours. I could mentally project the image onto the paper before me—it was as clear and distinct as if projected by a camera lucida—and trace its outlines with a pencil. My drawings were not elegant, but they were, everyone agreed, very detailed and accurate, and could bear comparison with some of the drawings in our neuroanatomy textbook. This heightening of imagery attached to everything—I had only to think of a face, a place, a picture, a paragraph in a book to see it vividly in my mind. But when the amphetamine-induced state faded, after a couple of weeks, I could no longer visualize, no longer project images, no longer draw—nor have I been able to do so in the decades since.

A few months ago, at a medical conference in Boston, I spoke of Torey's and Hull's experiences of blindness, and of how "enabled" Torey seemed to be by the powers of visualization he had developed, and how "disabled" Hull was—in some ways, at least—by the loss of his powers of visual imagery and memory. After my talk, a man in the audience came up to me and asked how well, in my estimation, *sighted* people could function if they had no visual imagery. He went on to say that he had no visual imagery whatever, at least none that he could deliberately evoke, and that no one in his family had any, either. Indeed, he had assumed this was the case with everyone, until he came to participate in some psychological tests at Harvard and realized that he apparently lacked a mental power that all the other students, in varying degrees, had.

"And what do you do?" I asked him, wondering what this poor man *could* do.

"I am a surgeon," he replied. "A vascular surgeon. An anatomist, too. And I design solar panels."

But how, I asked him, did he recognize what he was seeing?

"It's not a problem," he answered. "I guess there must be representations or models in the brain that get matched up with what I am seeing and doing. But they are not conscious. I cannot evoke them."

This seemed to be at odds with my mother's experience—she, clearly, did have extremely vivid and readily manipulable visual imagery, though (it now seemed) this may have been a bonus, a luxury, and not a prerequisite for her career as a surgeon.

Is this also the case with Torey? Is his greatly developed visual imagery, though clearly a source of much pleasure, not as indispensable as he takes it to be? Might he, in fact, have done everything he did, from carpentry to roof repair to making a model of the mind, without any conscious imagery at all? He himself raises this question.

The role of mental imagery in thinking was explored by Francis Galton, Darwin's irrepressible cousin, who wrote on subjects as various as fingerprints, eugenics, dog whistles, criminality, twins, visionaries, psychometric measures, and hereditary genius. His inquiry into visual imagery took the form of a questionnaire, with such questions as "Can you recall with distinctness the features of all near relations and many other persons? Can you at will cause your mental image . . . to sit, stand, or turn slowly around? Can you . . . see it with enough distinctness to enable you to sketch it leisurely (supposing yourself able to draw)?" The vascular surgeon would have been hopeless on such tests—indeed, it was questions such as these which had floored him when he was a student at Harvard. And yet, finally, how much had it mattered?

As to the significance of such imagery, Galton is ambiguous and guarded. He suggests, in one breath, that "scientific men, as a class, have feeble powers of visual representation" and, in another, that "a vivid visualizing faculty is of much importance in connection with the higher processes of generalized thoughts." He feels that "it is undoubtedly the fact that mechanicians, engineers and architects usually possess the faculty of seeing mental images with remarkable clearness and precision," but goes on to say, "I am, however, bound to say, that the missing faculty seems to be replaced so serviceably by other modes of conception . . . that men who declare themselves entirely deficient in the power of seeing mental pictures can nevertheless give lifelike descriptions of what they have seen, and can otherwise express themselves as if they were gifted with a vivid visual imagination. They can also become painters of the rank of Royal Academicians." I have a cousin, a professional architect, who maintains that he cannot visualize anything whatever. "How do you think?" I once asked him. He shook his head and said, "I don't know." Do any of us, finally, know how we think?

When I talk to people, blind or sighted, or when I try to think of my own internal representations, I find myself uncertain whether words, symbols, and images of various types are the primary tools of thought or whether there are forms of thought antecedent to all of these, forms of thought essentially amodal. Psychologists have sometimes spoken of "interlingua" or "mentalese," which they conceive to be the brain's own language, and Lev Vygotsky, the great Russian psychologist, used to speak of "thinking in pure meanings." I cannot decide whether this is nonsense or profound truth—it is the sort of reef I end up on when I think about thinking.

Galton's seemingly contradictory statements about imagery—is it antithetical to abstract thinking, or integral to it?—may stem from his failure to distinguish between fundamentally different levels of imagery. Simple visual imagery such as he describes may suffice for the design of a screw, an engine, or a surgical operation, and it may be relatively easy to model these essentially reproductive forms of imagery or to simulate them by constructing video games or virtual realities of various sorts. Such powers may be invaluable, but there is something passive and mechanical and impersonal about them, which makes them utterly different from the higher and more personal powers of the imagination, where there is a continual struggle for concepts and form and meaning, a calling upon all the powers of the self. Imagination dissolves and transforms, unifies and creates, while drawing upon the "lower" powers of memory and association. It is by such imagination, such "vision," that we create or construct our individual worlds.

At this level, one can no longer say of one's mental landscapes what is visual, what is auditory, what is image, what is language, what is intellectual, what is emotional—they are all fused together and imbued with our own individual perspectives and values. Such a unified vision shines out from Hull's memoir no less than from Torey's, despite the fact that one has become "nonvisual" and the other "hypervisual." What seems at first to be so decisive a difference between the two men is not, finally, a radical one, so far as personal development and sensibility go. Even though the paths they have followed might seem irreconcilable, both men have "used" blindness (if one can employ such a term for processes which are deeply mysterious, and far below, or above, the level of consciousness and voluntary control) to release their own creative capacities and emotional selves, and both have achieved a rich and full realization of their own individual worlds.   ∎

■ *QUESTIONS FOR MAKING CONNECTIONS*
WITHIN THE READING ■

1. Early in his essay, Sacks poses this question: "Does the mind run the brain or the brain the mind—or, rather, to what extent does one run the other?" Most of the discussion that follows this question, however, concerns the experience of blindness: instead of providing an extended analysis of

mental processing or brain chemistry, Sacks gives us details about people who have lost their vision and then adapted in different ways. How do these accounts of blindness connect to the debate about mind and brain?

2. To what extent are the different responses of the people Sacks discusses attributable to their individual ways of "being in the world"? Do you see any evidence of a continuity in the behavior of his subjects before and after the onset of their blindness? What are the larger implications of their adaptations? Would you say that the world is what we make it, or are there limits to the power of imagination, intelligence, and determination? What does Sacks appear to believe?

3. At one point in his essay, Sacks recalls a period in his life when he was "experimenting with large doses of amphetamines":

> For a period of two weeks or so, I found that I could do the most accurate anatomical drawings. I had only to look at a picture or an anatomical specimen, and its image would remain both vivid and stable, and I could easily hold it in my mind for hours. I could mentally project the image onto the paper before me—it was as clear and distinct as if projected by a camera lucida—and trace its outlines with a pencil. . . . But when the amphetamine-induced state faded, . . . I could no longer visualize, no longer project images, no longer draw—nor have I been able to do so in the decades since.

Why does Sacks include this vignette? What point does he make, and how does the passage extend the argument he develops in the previous pages? Does it matter that the story he tells is personal?

■ QUESTIONS FOR WRITING ■

1. Do the discoveries of neuroscience undermine our assumptions about such issues as free will, the uniqueness of each individual, and the importance of creativity? Ordinarily, we might think that if we can explain an emotion like love or the experience of beauty as the product of the brain's hardwiring, something important will be lost. But will it? Is human behavior in any way diminished or degraded by our knowledge of brain science? In what ways might an understanding of neuroscience foster greater understanding and a tolerance for diversities—and uniformities—in human behavior?

2. For the last century or so, thinkers have debated the relative influence of "nature" and "nurture" over human behavior. By "nature," people ordinarily mean biology, chemistry, genetics, and neuroscience. By "nurture," they mean custom, culture, and education. What does Sacks's essay contribute to this debate? Can he be accused of perpetuating "reductionism": Does he, in other words, oversimplify the complexities of human life by reducing everything to one explanation?

3. On the basis of the evidence that Sacks provides, can we ever say that human behavior is entirely "hardwired"? Can we argue, in other words, that the ways in which we act are predetermined by the structure and functioning of our brains? Or are we entitled to say that the brain is flexible enough to adapt to an event like the loss of sight in ways that are infinitely varied? Do the adaptations vary infinitely, or are there biological limits? Are there no commonalities among all the different adaptations that Sacks discusses? Do you think that these commonalities have their origin in the brain, or can they be explained in some other way?

■ *QUESTIONS FOR MAKING CONNECTIONS BETWEEN READINGS* ■

1. In what ways does Sacks's essay complicate or even contradict Gregory Stock's argument in "The Enhanced and the Unenhanced"? On the basis of the evidence that Sacks provides, would you say that intelligence resides primarily in our brains, or is it a product of the ways in which we interact with the world? If intelligence does not reside entirely in our brains, but is also a quality of our behavior, then how likely is it that intelligence might be passed on through or improved by genetic engineering? Is education just as likely as genetic engineering to produce creative, thoughtful, and adaptive people?

2. Sacks suggests that the human brain is actually quite flexible in its adaptations to the world. Charles Siebert finds evidence of a similar adaptability in the brains of elephants. This seeming similarity poses a problem, though: if the brains of all mammals can adapt to trauma, what is the role of choice in the process? Is it possible that human consciousness has evolved through trial and error in much the same way as different species have evolved? Or do humans merely project their own mental states onto the rest of the world, discovering trauma in elephants when, in fact, there is no evidence that these animals have consciousness or that they can be traumatized? Drawing on Sacks and Siebert, discuss the relationships or the nonrelationships among choice, consciousness, and trauma.

Charles Siebert

HAVING CLAIMED DOMINANCE over the planet for centuries, human beings have, by and large, made use of the earth without much consideration for the environmental and social needs of other animals. As a result, the areas in which animals are free to move about without danger from humans have steadily declined both in size and number. Overall, most of the animal kingdom has acquiesced without substantial resistance. But what happens when an animal community responds to the destruction of its natural habitat by turning against people, other species, and themselves? Charles Siebert addresses this issue in "An Elephant Crackup?"—an article that appeared in *The New York Times Magazine.*

An essayist, novelist, and a poet, Charles Siebert has published numerous articles in *The New York Times Magazine, The New Yorker, Harper's,* and other periodicals. He has published three books, *A Man After His Own Heart* (2004), a meditation on the human heart (literally); *Angus: A Novel* (2000), an account of the inner life of a Jack Russell terrier; and *Wickerby: An Urban Pastoral* (1998), which explores the fluid relationship between the urban and the rural worlds.

"An Elephant Crackup?" is a further example of the sympathy for the emotional lives of animals that Siebert first explored in *Angus.* Here, Siebert conducts research across Africa, India, and parts of southeastern Asia on the new phenomenon called "Human-Elephant Conflict," which has resulted in hundreds of human deaths since the year 2000. This is especially troubling, Siebert feels, because elephants possess "a highly developed sensibility" and "a deep-rooted sense of family" that is nowhere in evidence during these violent rampages. Drawing on research into the social fabric of animal society, and the similarities between the emotional brains of elephants and the emotional brains of humans, Siebert weaves a compelling narrative of conflict between a species that once enjoyed dominance over its territory and the species that has the upper hand now.

Siebert, Charles. "An Elephant Crackup?" *The New York Times Magazine.* October 8, 2006. 42–71.

An Elephant Crackup?

"We're not going anywhere," my driver, Nelson Okello, whispered to me one morning this past June, the two of us sitting in the front seat of a jeep just after dawn in Queen Elizabeth National Park in southwestern Uganda. We'd originally stopped to observe what appeared to be a lone bull elephant grazing in a patch of tall savanna grasses off to our left. More than one "rogue" crossed our path that morning—a young male elephant that has made an overly strong power play against the dominant male of his herd and been banished, sometimes permanently. This elephant, however, soon proved to be not a rogue but part of a cast of at least 30. The ground vibrations registered just before the emergence of the herd from the surrounding trees and brush. We sat there watching the elephants cross the road before us, seeming, for all their heft, so light on their feet, soundlessly playing the wind-swept savanna grasses like land whales adrift above the floor of an ancient, waterless sea.

Then, from behind a thicket of acacia trees directly off our front left bumper, a huge female emerged—"the matriarch," Okello said softly. There was a small calf beneath her, freely foraging and knocking about within the secure cribbing of four massive legs. Acacia leaves are an elephant's favorite food, and as the calf set to work on some low branches, the matriarch stood guard, her vast back flank blocking the road, the rest of the herd milling about in the brush a short distance away.

After 15 minutes or so, Okello started inching the jeep forward, revving the engine, trying to make us sound as beastly as possible. The matriarch, however, was having none of it, holding her ground, the fierce white of her eyes as bright as that of her tusks. Although I pretty much knew the answer, I asked Okello if he was considering trying to drive around. "No," he said, raising an index finger for emphasis. "She'll charge. We should stay right here."

I'd have considered it a wise policy even at a more peaceable juncture in the course of human-elephant relations. In recent years, however, those relations have become markedly more bellicose. Just two days before I arrived, a woman was killed by an elephant in Kazinga, a fishing village nearby. Two months earlier, a man was fatally gored by a young male elephant at the northern edge of the park, near the village of Katwe. African elephants use their long tusks to forage through dense jungle brush. They've also been known to wield them, however, with the ceremonious flash and precision of gladiators, pinning down a victim with one knee in order to deliver the decisive thrust. Okello told me that a young Indian tourist was killed in this fashion two years ago in Murchison Falls National Park, just north of where we were.

These were not isolated incidents. All across Africa, India and parts of Southeast Asia, from within and around whatever patches and corridors of their natural habitat remain, elephants have been striking out, destroying villages and crops, attacking and killing human beings. In fact, these attacks have become so commonplace that a whole new statistical category, known as Human-Elephant Conflict, or HEC, was created by elephant researchers in the mid-1990's to monitor the problem. In the Indian state Jharkhand near the western border of Bangladesh, 300 people were killed by elephants between 2000 and 2004. In the past 12 years, elephants have killed 605 people in Assam, a state in northeastern India, 239 of them since 2001; 265 elephants have died in that same period, the majority of them as a result of retaliation by angry villagers, who have used everything from poison-tipped arrows to laced food to exact their revenge. In Africa, reports of human-elephant conflicts appear almost daily, from Zambia to Tanzania, from Uganda to Sierra Leone, where 300 villagers evacuated their homes last year because of unprovoked elephant attacks.

Still, it is not only the increasing number of these incidents that is causing alarm but also the singular perversity—for want of a less anthropocentric term—of recent elephant aggression. Since the early 1990's, for example, young male elephants in Pilanesberg National Park and the Hluhluwe-Umfolozi Game Reserve in South Africa have been raping and killing rhinoceroses; this abnormal behavior, according to a 2001 study in the journal *Pachyderm*, has been reported in "a number of reserves" in the region. In July of last year, officials in Pilanesberg shot three young male elephants who were responsible for the killings of 63 rhinos, as well as attacks on people in safari vehicles. In Addo Elephant National Park, also in South Africa, up to 90 percent of male elephant deaths are now attributable to other male elephants, compared with a rate of 6 percent in more stable elephant communities.

In a coming book on this phenomenon, Gay Bradshaw, a psychologist at the environmental-sciences program at Oregon State University, notes that in India, where the elephant has long been regarded as a deity, a recent headline in a leading newspaper warned, "To Avoid Confrontation, Don't Worship Elephants." "Everybody pretty much agrees that the relationship between elephants and people has dramatically changed," Bradshaw told me recently. "What we are seeing today is extraordinary. Where for centuries humans and elephants lived in relative peaceful coexistence, there is now hostility and violence. Now, I use the term 'violence' because of the intentionality associated with it, both in the aggression of humans and, at times, the recently observed behavior of elephants."

For a number of biologists and ethologists who have spent their careers studying elephant behavior, the attacks have become so abnormal in both number and kind that they can no longer be attributed entirely to the customary factors. Typically, elephant researchers have cited, as a cause of aggression, the high levels of testosterone in newly matured male elephants or the competition for land and resources between elephants and humans. But in "Elephant Breakdown," a 2005 essay in the journal *Nature,* Bradshaw and several colleagues argued that today's elephant populations are suffering from a form of chronic stress, a kind of species-wide trauma. Decades of poaching and culling and habitat loss, they claim, have so disrupted the intricate web of familial and societal relations by which young elephants have traditionally been raised in the wild, and by which established elephant herds are governed, that what we are now witnessing is nothing less than a precipitous collapse of elephant culture.

It has long been apparent that every large, land-based animal on this planet is ultimately fighting a losing battle with humankind. And yet entirely befitting of an animal with such a highly developed sensibility, a deep-rooted sense of family and, yes, such a good long-term memory, the elephant is not going out quietly. It is not leaving without making some kind of statement, one to which scientists from a variety of disciplines, including human psychology, are now beginning to pay close attention.

Once the matriarch and her calf were a comfortable distance from us that morning, Okello and I made the 20-minute drive to Kyambura, a village at the far southeastern edge of the park. Back in 2003, Kyambura was reportedly the site of the very sort of sudden, unprovoked elephant attack I'd been hearing about. According to an account of the event in the magazine *New Scientist,* a number of huts and fields were trampled, and the townspeople were afraid to venture out to surrounding villages, either by foot or on their bikes, because elephants were regularly blocking the road and charging out at those who tried to pass.

Park officials from the Uganda Wildlife Authority with whom I tried to discuss the incident were reluctant to talk about it or any of the recent killings by elephants in the area. Eco-tourism is one of Uganda's major sources of income, and the elephant and other wildlife stocks of Queen Elizabeth National Park are only just now beginning to recover from years of virtually unchecked poaching and habitat destruction. Tom Okello, the chief game warden at the park (and no relation to my driver), and Margaret Driciru, Queen Elizabeth's chief veterinarian, each told me that they weren't aware of the attack in Kyambura. When I mentioned it to the executive director of the wildlife authority, Moses Mapesa, upon my initial arrival in the capital city, Kampala, he eventually admitted that it did happen, but he claimed that it was not nearly as recent as reported. "That was 14 years ago," he said. "We have seen aggressive behavior from elephants, but that's a story of the past."

Kyambura did look, upon our arrival, much like every other small Ugandan farming community I'd passed through on my visit. Lush fields of banana trees, millet and maize framed a small town center of pastel-colored single-story cement buildings with corrugated-tin roofs. People sat on stoops out front in the available shade. Bicyclers bore preposterously outsize loads of bananas, firewood and five-gallon water jugs on their fenders and handlebars. Contrary to what I had read, the bicycle traffic along the road in and out of Kyambura didn't seem impaired in the slightest.

But when Okello and I asked a shopkeeper named Ibrah Byamukama about elephant attacks, he immediately nodded and pointed to a patch of maize and millet fields just up the road, along the edges of the surrounding Maramagambo Forest. He confirmed that a small group of elephants charged out one morning two years earlier, trampled the fields and nearby gardens, knocked down a few huts and then left. He then pointed to a long orange gash in the earth between the planted fields and the forest: a 15-foot-deep, 25-foot-wide trench that had been dug by the wildlife authority around the perimeter of Kyambura in an attempt to keep the elephants at bay. On the way out of town, Okello and I took a closer look at the trench. It was filled with stacks of thorny shrubs for good measure.

"The people are still worried," Byamukama said, shaking his head. "The elephants are just becoming more destructive. I don't know why."

Three years ago, Gay Bradshaw, then working on her graduate degree in psychology at the Pacifica Graduate Institute outside Santa Barbara, California, began wondering much the same thing: was the extraordinary behavior of elephants in Africa and Asia signaling a breaking point? With the assistance of several established African-elephant researchers, including Daphne Sheldrick and Cynthia Moss, and with the help of Allan Schore, an expert on human trauma disorders at the department of psychiatry and biobehavioral sciences at UCLA, Bradshaw sought to combine traditional research into elephant behavior with insights about trauma drawn from human neuroscience. Using the few remaining relatively stable elephant herds in places like Amboseli National Park in Kenya, as control groups, Bradshaw and her colleagues analyzed the far more fractious populations found in places like Pilanesberg in South Africa and Queen Elizabeth National Park in Uganda. What emerged was a portrait of pervasive pachyderm dysfunction.

Elephants, when left to their own devices, are profoundly social creatures. A herd of them is, in essence, one incomprehensibly massive elephant: a somewhat loosely bound and yet intricately interconnected, tensile organism. Young elephants are raised within an extended, multitiered network of doting female caregivers that includes the birth mother, grandmothers, aunts and friends. These relations are maintained over a life span as long as 70 years. Studies of established herds have shown that young elephants stay within 15 feet of their mothers for nearly all of their first eight years of life, after which young females are socialized into the matriarchal network, while young males go off for a time into an all-male social group before coming back into the fold as mature adults.

When an elephant dies, its family members engage in intense mourning and burial rituals, conducting weeklong vigils over the body, carefully covering it with earth and brush, revisiting the bones for years afterward, caressing the bones with their trunks, often taking turns rubbing their trunks along the teeth of a skull's lower jaw, the way living elephants do in greeting. If harm comes to a member of an elephant group, all the other elephants are aware of it. This sense of cohesion is further enforced by the elaborate communication system that elephants use. In close proximity they employ a range of vocalizations, from low-frequency rumbles to higher-pitched screams and trumpets, along with a variety of visual signals, from the waving of their trunks to subtle anglings of the head, body, feet and tail. When communicating over long distances—in order to pass along, for example, news about imminent threats, a sudden change of plans or, of the utmost importance to elephants, the death of a community member—they use patterns of subsonic vibrations that are felt as far as several miles away by exquisitely tuned sensors in the padding of their feet.

This fabric of elephant society, Bradshaw and her colleagues concluded, had effectively been frayed by years of habitat loss and poaching, along with systematic culling by government agencies to control elephant numbers and translocations of herds to different habitats. The number of older matriarchs and female caregivers (or "allomothers") had drastically fallen, as had the number of elder bulls, who play a significant role in keeping younger males in line. In parts of Zambia and Tanzania, a number of the elephant groups studied contained no adult females whatsoever. In Uganda, herds were often found to be "semipermanent aggregations," as a paper written by Bradshaw describes them, with many females between the ages of 15 and 25 having no familial associations.

As a result of such social upheaval, calves are now being born to and raised by ever younger and inexperienced mothers. Young orphaned elephants, meanwhile, that have witnessed the death of a parent at the hands of poachers are coming of age in the absence of the support system that defines traditional elephant life. "The loss of elephants' elders," Bradshaw told me, "and the traumatic experience of witnessing the massacres of their family, impairs normal brain and behavior development in young elephants."

What Bradshaw and her colleagues describe would seem to be an extreme form of anthropocentric conjecture if the evidence that they've compiled from various elephant researchers, even on the strictly observational level, wasn't so compelling. The elephants of decimated herds, especially orphans who've watched the death of their parents and elders from poaching and culling, exhibit behavior typically associated with post-traumatic stress disorder and other trauma-related disorders in humans: abnormal startle response, unpredictable asocial behavior, inattentive mothering and hyper-aggression. Studies of the various assaults on the rhinos in South Africa, meanwhile, have determined that the perpetrators were in all cases adolescent males that had witnessed their families being shot down in cullings. It was common for these elephants to have been tethered to the bodies of their dead and dying relatives until they could be rounded up for translocation to, as Bradshaw and Schore describe them, "locales lacking traditional social hierarchy of older bulls and intact natal family structures."

In fact, even the relatively few attempts that park officials have made to restore parts of the social fabric of elephant society have lent substance to the elephant-breakdown theory. When South African park rangers recently introduced a number of older bull elephants into several destabilized elephant herds in Pilanesburg and Addo, the wayward behavior—including unusually premature hormonal changes among the adolescent elephants—abated.

But according to Bradshaw and her colleagues, the various pieces of the elephant-trauma puzzle really come together at the level of neuroscience, or what might be called the physiology of psychology, by which scientists can now map the marred neuronal fields, snapped synaptic bridges and crooked chemical streams of an embattled psyche. Though most scientific knowledge of trauma is still understood through research on human subjects, neural studies of elephants are now under way. (The first functional MRI scan of an elephant brain, taken this year, revealed, perhaps not surprisingly, a huge hippocampus, a seat of memory in the mammalian brain, as well as a prominent structure in the limbic system, which processes emotions.) Allan Schore, the UCLA psychologist and neuroscientist who for the past 15 years has focused his research on early human brain development and the negative impact of trauma on it, recently wrote two articles with Bradshaw on the stress-related neurobiological underpinnings of current abnormal elephant behavior.

"We know that these mechanisms cut across species," Schore told me. "In the first years of humans as well as elephants, development of the emotional brain is impacted by these attachment mechanisms, by the interaction that the infant has with the primary caregiver, especially the mother. When these early experiences go in a positive way, it leads to greater resilience in things like affect regulation, stress regulation, social communication and empathy. But when these early experiences go awry in cases of abuse and neglect, there is a literal thinning down of the essential circuits in the brain, especially in the emotion-processing areas."

For Bradshaw, these continuities between human and elephant brains resonate far outside the field of neuroscience. "Elephants are suffering and behaving in the same ways that we recognize in ourselves as a result of violence," she told me. "Elephant behavior is entirely congruent with what we know about humans and other mammals. Except perhaps for a few specific features, brain organization and early development of elephants and humans are extremely similar. That's not news. What is news is when you start asking, What does this mean beyond the science? How do we respond to the fact that we are causing other species like elephants to psychologically break down? In a way, it's not so much a cognitive or imaginative leap anymore as it is a political one."

Eve Abe says that in her mind, she made that leap before she ever left her mother's womb. An animal ethologist and wildlife-management consultant now based in London, Abe (pronounced AH-bay) grew up in northern Uganda. After several years of studying elephants in Queen Elizabeth National Park, where decades of poaching had drastically reduced the herds, Abe received her doctorate at Cambridge University in 1994 for work detailing the parallels she saw between the plight of Uganda's orphaned male elephants and the young male orphans of her own people, the Acholi, whose families and villages have been decimated by years of civil war. It's work she proudly proclaims to be not only "the ultimate act of anthropomorphism" but also what she was destined to do.

"My very first encounter with an elephant was a fetal one," Abe told me in June in London as the two of us sipped tea at a cafe in Paddington Station. I was given Abe's contact numbers earlier in the spring by Bradshaw, who is currently working with Abe to build a community center in Uganda to help both elephants and humans in their recovery from violence. For more than a month before my departure from New York, I had been trying without luck to arrange with the British Home Office for Abe, who is still waiting for permanent residence status in England, to travel with me to Uganda as my guide through Queen Elizabeth National Park without fear of her being denied re-entry to England. She was to accompany me that day right up to the departure gate at Heathrow, the two of us hoping (in vain, as it turned out) for a last-minute call that would have given her leave to use the ticket I was holding for her in my bag.

"My dad was a conservationist and a teacher," explained Abe, a tall, elegant woman with a trilling, nearly girlish voice. "He was always out in the parks. One of my aunts tells this story about us passing through Murchison park one day. My dad was driving. My uncle was in the front seat. In the back were my aunt and my mom, who was very pregnant with me. They suddenly came upon this huge herd of elephants on the road, and the elephants just stopped. So my dad stopped. He knew about animals. The elephants just stood there, then they started walking around the car, and looking into the car. Finally, they walked off. But my father didn't start the car then. He waited there. After an hour or more, a huge female came back out onto the road, right in front of the car. It reared up and trumpeted so loudly, then followed the rest of the herd back into the bush. A few days later, when my mom got home, I was born."

Abe began her studies in Queen Elizabeth National Park in 1982, as an undergraduate at Makerere University in Kampala, shortly after she and her family, who'd been living for years as refugees in Kenya to escape the brutal violence in Uganda under the dictatorship of Idi Amin, returned home in the wake of Amin's ouster in 1979. Abe told me that when she first arrived at the park, there were fewer than 150 elephants remaining from an original population of nearly 4,000. The bulk of the decimation occurred during the war with Tanzania that led to Amin's overthrow: soldiers from both armies grabbed all the ivory they could get their hands on—and did so with such cravenness that the word "poaching" seems woefully inadequate. "Normally when you say 'poaching,'" Abe said, "you think of people shooting one or two and going off. But this was war. They'd just throw hand grenades at the elephants, bring whole families down and cut out the ivory. I call that mass destruction."

The last elephant survivors of Queen Elizabeth National Park, Abe said, never left one another's side. They kept in a tight bunch, moving as one. Only one elderly female remained; Abe estimated her to be at least 62. It was this matriarch who first gathered the survivors together from their various hideouts on the park's forested fringes and then led them back out as one group into open savanna. Until her death in the early 90's, the old female held the group together, the population all the while slowly beginning to rebound. In her yet-to-be-completed memoir, *My Elephants and My People,* Abe writes of the prominence of the matriarch in Acholi society; she named the park's matriarchal elephant savior Lady Irene, after her own mother. "It took that core group of survivors in the park about five or six years," Abe told me, "before I started seeing whole new family units emerge and begin to split off and go their own way."

In 1986, Abe's family was forced to flee the country again. Violence against Uganda's people and elephants never completely abated after Amin's regime collapsed, and it drastically worsened in the course of the full-fledged war that developed between government forces and the rebel Lord's Resistance Army. For years, that army's leader, Joseph Kony, routinely "recruited" from Acholi villages, killing the parents of young males before their eyes, or sometimes having them do the killings themselves, before pressing them into service as child soldiers. The Lord's Resistance Army has by now been largely defeated, but Kony, who is wanted by the International Criminal Court for numerous crimes against humanity, has hidden with what remains of his army in the mountains of Murchison Falls National Park, and more recently in Garamba National Park in northern Congo, where poaching by the Lord's Resistance Army has continued to orphan more elephants.

"I started looking again at what has happened among the Acholi and the elephants," Abe told me. "I saw that it is an absolute coincidence between the two. You know we used to have villages. We still don't have villages. There are over 200 displaced people's camps in present-day northern Uganda. Everybody lives now within these camps, and there are no more elders. The elders were systematically eliminated. The first batch of elimination was during Amin's time, and that set the stage for the later destruction of northern Uganda. We are among the lucky few, because my mom and dad managed to escape. But the families there are just broken. I know many of them. Displaced people are living in our home now. My mother said let them have it. All these kids who have grown up with their parents killed—no fathers, no mothers, only children looking after them. They don't go to schools. They have no schools, no hospitals. No infrastructure. They form these roaming, violent, destructive bands. It's the same thing that happens with the elephants. Just like the male war orphans, they are wild, completely lost."

On the ride from Paddington that afternoon out to Heathrow, where I would catch a flight to Uganda, Abe told me that the parallel between the plight of Ugandans and their elephants was in many ways too close for her to see at first. It was only after she moved to London that she had what was, in a sense, her first full, adult recognition of the entwinement between human and elephant that she says she long ago felt in her mother's womb.

"I remember when I first was working on my doctorate," she said. "I mentioned that I was doing this parallel once to a prominent scientist in Kenya. He looked amazed. He said, 'How come nobody has made this connection before?' I told him because it hadn't happened this way to anyone else's tribe before. To me it's something I see so clearly. Most people are scared of showing that kind of anthropomorphism. But coming from me it doesn't sound like I'm inventing something. It's there. People know it's there. Some might think that the way I describe the elephant attacks makes the animals look like people. But people are animals."

Shortly after my return from Uganda, I went to visit the Elephant Sanctuary in Tennessee, a 2,700-acre rehabilitation center and retirement facility situated in the state's verdant, low-rolling southern hill country. The sanctuary is a kind of asylum for some of the more emotionally and psychologically disturbed former zoo and circus elephants in the United States—cases so bad that the people who profited from them were eager to let them go. Given that elephants in the wild are now exhibiting aberrant behaviors that were long observed in captive elephants, it perhaps follows that a positive working model for how to ameliorate the effects of elephant breakdown can be found in captivity.

Of the 19 current residents of the sanctuary, perhaps the biggest hard-luck story was that of a 40-year-old, five-ton Asian elephant named Misty. Originally captured as a calf in India in 1966, Misty spent her first decade in captivity with a number of American circuses and finally ended up in the early 80's at a wild-animal attraction known as Lion Country Safari in Irvine, Calif. It was there, on the afternoon of July 25, 1983, that Misty, one of four performing elephants at Lion Country Safari that summer, somehow managed to break free of her chains and began madly dashing about the park, looking to make an escape. When one of the park's zoologists tried to corner and contain her, Misty killed him with one swipe of her trunk.

There are, in the long, checkered history of human-elephant relations, countless stories of lethal elephantine assaults, and almost invariably of some gruesomely outsize, animalistic form of retribution exacted by us. It was in the very state of Tennessee, back in September 1916, that another five-ton Asian circus elephant, Mary, was impounded by a local sheriff for the killing of a young hotel janitor who'd been hired to mind Mary during a stopover in the northeast Tennessee town of Kingsport. The janitor had apparently taken Mary for a swim at a local pond, where, according to witnesses, he poked her behind the left ear with a metal hook just as she was reaching for a piece of floating watermelon rind. Enraged, Mary turned, swiftly snatched him up with her trunk, dashed him against a refreshment stand and then smashed his head with her foot.

With cries from the townspeople to "Kill the elephant!" and threats from nearby town leaders to bar the circus if "Murderous Mary," as newspapers quickly dubbed her, remained a part of the show, the circus's owner, Charlie Sparks, knew he had to do something to appease the public's blood lust and save his business. Among the penalties he is said to have contemplated was electrocution, a ghastly precedent for which had been set 13 years earlier, on the grounds of the nearly completed Luna Park in Coney Island. A longtime circus elephant named Topsy, who'd killed three trainers in as many years— the last one after he tried to feed her a lighted cigarette—would become the largest and most prominent victim of Thomas Edison, the father of direct-current electricity, who had publicly electrocuted a number of animals at that time using his rival George Westinghouse's alternating current, in hopes of discrediting it as being too dangerous.

Sparks ultimately decided to have Mary hanged and shipped her by train to the nearby town of Erwin, Tennessee, where more than 2,500 people gathered at the local rail yard for her execution. Dozens of children are said to have run off screaming in terror when the chain that was suspended from a huge industrial crane snapped, leaving Mary writhing on the ground with a broken hip. A local rail worker promptly clambered up Mary's bulk and secured a heavier chain for a second, successful hoisting.

Misty's fate in the early 80's, by contrast, seems a triumph of modern humanism. Banished, after the Lion Safari killing, to the Hawthorn Corporation, a company in Illinois that trains and leases elephants and tigers to circuses, she would continue to lash out at a number of her trainers over the years. But when Hawthorn was convicted of numerous violations of the Animal Welfare Act in 2003, the company agreed to relinquish custody of Misty to the Elephant Sanctuary. She was loaded onto a trailer transport on the morning of Nov. 17, 2004, and even then managed to get away with one final shot at the last in her long line of captors.

"The details are kind of sketchy," Carol Buckley, a founder of the Elephant Sanctuary, said to me one afternoon in July, the two of us pulling up on her all-terrain four-wheeler to a large grassy enclosure where an extremely docile and contented-looking Misty, trunk high, ears flapping, waited to greet us. "Hawthorn's owner was trying to get her to stretch out so he could remove her leg chains before loading her on the trailer. At one point he prodded her with a bull hook, and she just knocked him down with a swipe of her trunk. But we've seen none of that since she's been here. She's as sweet as can be. You'd never know that this elephant killed anybody."

In the course of her nearly two years at the Elephant Sanctuary—much of it spent in quarantine while undergoing daily treatment for tuberculosis—Misty has also been in therapy, as in psychotherapy. Wild-caught elephants often witness as young calves the slaughter of their parents, just about the only way, shy of a far more costly tranquilization procedure, to wrest a calf from elephant parents, especially the mothers. The young captives are then dispatched to a foreign environment to work either as performers or laborers, all the while being kept in relative confinement and isolation, a kind of living death for an animal as socially developed and dependent as we now know elephants to be.

And yet just as we now understand that elephants hurt like us, we're learning that they can heal like us as well. Indeed, Misty has become a testament to the Elephant Sanctuary's signature "passive control" system, a therapy tailored in many ways along the lines of those used to treat human sufferers of post-traumatic stress disorder. Passive control, as a sanctuary newsletter describes it, depends upon "knowledge of how elephants process information and respond to stress" as well as specific knowledge of each elephant's past response to stress. Under this so-called nondominance system, there is no discipline, retaliation or withholding of food, water and treats, which are all common tactics of elephant trainers. Great pains are taken, meanwhile, to afford the elephants both a sense of safety and freedom of choice—two mainstays of human trauma therapy—as well as continual social interaction.

Upon her arrival at the Elephant Sanctuary, Misty seemed to sense straight off the different vibe of her new home. When Scott Blais of the sanctuary went to free Misty's still-chained leg a mere day after she'd arrived, she stood peaceably by, practically offering her leg up to him. Over her many months of quarantine, meanwhile, with only humans acting as a kind of surrogate elephant family, she has consistently gone through the daily rigors of her tuberculosis treatments—involving two caregivers, a team of veterinarians and the use of a restraining chute in which harnesses are secured about her chest and tail—without any coaxing or pressure. "We'll shower her with praise in the barn afterwards," Buckley told me as Misty stood by, chomping on a mouthful of hay, "and she actually purrs with pleasure. The whole barn vibrates."

Of course, Misty's road to recovery—when viewed in light of her history and that of all the other captive elephants, past and present—is as harrowing as it is heartening. She and the others have suffered, we now understand, not simply because of us, but because they are, by and large, us. If as recently as the end of the Vietnam War people were still balking at the idea that a soldier, for example, could be physically disabled by a psychological harm—the idea, in other words, that the mind is not an entity apart from the body and therefore just as woundable as any limb—we now find ourselves having to make an equally profound and, for many, even more difficult leap: that a fellow creature as ostensibly unlike us in every way as an elephant is as precisely and intricately woundable as we are. And while such knowledge naturally places an added burden upon us, the keepers, that burden is now being greatly compounded by the fact that sudden violent outbursts like Misty's can no longer be dismissed as the inevitable isolated revolts of a restless few against the constraints and abuses of captivity.

They have no future without us. The question we are now forced to grapple with is whether we would mind a future without them, among the more mindful creatures on this earth and, in many ways, the most devoted. Indeed, the manner of the elephants' continued keeping, their restoration and conservation, both in civil confines and what's left of wild ones, is now drawing the attention of everyone from naturalists to neuroscientists. Too much about elephants, in the end—their desires and devotions, their vulnerability and tremendous resilience—reminds us of ourselves to dismiss out of hand this revolt they're currently staging against their own dismissal. And while our concern may ultimately be rooted in that most human of impulses—the preservation of our own self-image—the great paradox about this particular moment in our history with elephants is that saving them will require finally getting past ourselves; it will demand the ultimate act of deep, interspecies empathy.

On a more immediate, practical level, as Gay Bradshaw sees it, this involves taking what has been learned about elephant society, psychology and emotion and inculcating that knowledge into the conservation schemes of researchers and park rangers. This includes doing things like expanding elephant habitat to what it used to be historically and avoiding the use of culling and translocations as conservation tools. "If we want elephants around," Bradshaw told me, "then what we need to do is simple: learn how to live with elephants. In other words, in addition to conservation, we need to educate people how to live with wild animals like humans used to do, and to create conditions whereby people can live on their land and live with elephants without it being this life-and-death situation."

The other part of our newly emerging compact with elephants, however, is far more difficult to codify. It requires nothing less than a fundamental shift in the way we look at animals and, by extension, ourselves. It requires what Bradshaw somewhat whimsically refers to as a new "trans-species psyche," a commitment to move beyond an anthropocentric frame of reference and, in effect, be elephants. Two years ago, Bradshaw wrote a paper for the journal *Society and Animals,* focusing on the work of the David Sheldrick Wildlife Trust in Kenya, a sanctuary for orphaned and traumatized wild elephants—more or less the wilderness-based complement to

Carol Buckley's trauma therapy at the Elephant Sanctuary in Tennessee. The trust's human caregivers essentially serve as surrogate mothers to young orphan elephants, gradually restoring their psychological and emotional well-being to the point at which they can be reintroduced into existing wild herds. The human "allomothers" stay by their adopted young orphans' sides, even sleeping with them at night in stables. The caregivers make sure, however, to rotate from one elephant to the next so that the orphans grow fond of all the keepers. Otherwise an elephant would form such a strong bond with one keeper that whenever he or she was absent, that elephant would grieve as if over the loss of another family member, often becoming physically ill itself.

To date, the Sheldrick Trust has successfully rehabilitated more than 60 elephants and reintroduced them into wild herds. A number of them have periodically returned to the sanctuary with their own wild-born calves in order to reunite with their human allomothers and to introduce their off-spring to what—out on this uncharted frontier of the new "trans-species psyche"—is now being recognized, at least by the elephants, it seems, as a whole new subspecies: the human allograndmother. "Traditionally, nature has served as a source of healing for humans," Bradshaw told me. "Now humans can participate actively in the healing of both themselves and nonhuman animals. The trust and the sanctuary are the beginnings of a mutually benefiting interspecies culture."

On my way back to New York via London, I contacted Felicity de Zulueta, a psychiatrist at Maudsley Hospital in London who treats victims of extreme trauma, among them former child soldiers from the Lord's Resistance Army. De Zulueta, an acquaintance of Eve Abe's, grew up in Uganda in the early 1960's on the outskirts of Queen Elizabeth National Park, near where her father, a malaria doctor, had set up camp as part of a malaria-eradication program. For a time she had her own elephant, orphaned by poaching, that local villagers had given to her father, who brought it home to the family garage, where it immediately bonded with an orphan antelope and dog already residing there.

"He was doing fine," de Zulueta told me of the pet elephant. "My mother was loving it and feeding it, and then my parents realized, How can we keep this elephant that is going to grow bigger than the garage? So they gave it to who they thought were the experts. They sent him to the Entebbe Zoo, and although they gave him all the right food and everything, he was a lonely little elephant, and he died. He had no attachment."

For de Zulueta, the parallel that Abe draws between the plight of war orphans, human and elephant, is painfully apt, yet also provides some cause for hope, given the often startling capacity of both animals for recovery. She told me that one Ugandan war orphan she is currently treating lost all the members of his family except for two older brothers. Remarkably, one of those brothers, while serving in the Ugandan Army, rescued the younger sibling from the Lord's Resistance Army; the older brother's unit had captured the rebel battalion in which his younger brother had been forced to fight.

The two brothers eventually made their way to London, and for the past two years, the younger brother has been going through a gradual process of recovery in the care of Maudsley Hospital. Much of the rehabilitation, according to de Zulueta, especially in the early stages, relies on the basic human trauma therapy principles now being applied to elephants: providing decent living quarters, establishing a sense of safety and of attachment to a larger community and allowing freedom of choice. After that have come the more complex treatments tailored to the human brain's particular cognitive capacities: things like reliving the original traumatic experience and being taught to modulate feelings through early detection of hyperarousal and through breathing techniques. And the healing of trauma, as de Zulueta describes it, turns out to have physical correlatives in the brain just as its wounding does.

"What I say is, we find bypass," she explained. "We bypass the wounded areas using various techniques. Some of the wounds are not healable. Their scars remain. But there is hope because the brain is an enormous computer, and you can learn to bypass its wounds by finding different methods of approaching life. Of course there may be moments when something happens and the old wound becomes unbearable. Still, people do recover. The boy I've been telling you about is 18 now, and he has survived very well in terms of his emotional health and capacities. He's a lovely, lovely man. And he's a poet. He writes beautiful poetry."

On the afternoon in July that I left the Elephant Sanctuary in Tennessee, Carol Buckley and Scott Blais seemed in particularly good spirits. Misty was only weeks away from the end of her quarantine, and she would soon be able to socialize with some of her old cohorts from the Hawthorn Corporation: eight female Asians that had been given over to the sanctuary. I would meet the lot of them that day, driving from one to the next on the back of Buckley's four-wheeler across the sanctuary's savanna-like stretches. Buckley and Blais refer to them collectively as the Divas.

Buckley and Blais told me that they got word not long ago of a significant breakthrough in a campaign of theirs to get elephants out of entertainment and zoos: the Bronx Zoo, one of the oldest and most formidable zoos in the country, had announced that upon the death of the zoo's three current elephant inhabitants, Patty, Maxine and Happy, it would phase out its elephant exhibit on social-behavioral grounds—an acknowledgment of a new awareness of the elephant's very particular sensibility and needs. "They're really taking the lead," Buckley told me. "Zoos don't want to concede the inappropriateness of keeping elephants in such confines. But if we as a society determine that an animal like this suffers in captivity, if the information shows us that they do, hey, we are the stewards. You'd think we'd want to do the right thing."

Four days later, I received an e-mail message from Gay Bradshaw, who consults with Buckley and Blais on their various stress-therapy strategies. She wrote that one of the sanctuary's elephants, an Asian named Winkie, had just killed a 36-year-old female assistant caretaker and critically injured the male caretaker who'd tried to save her.

People who work with animals on a daily basis can tell you all kinds of stories about their distinct personalities and natures. I'd gotten, in fact, an elaborate breakdown from Buckley and Blais on the various elephants at the sanctuary and their sociopolitical maneuverings within the sanctuary's distinct elephant culture, and I went to my notebook to get a fix again on Winkie. A 40-year-old, 7,600-pound female from Burma, she came to the sanctuary in 2000 from the Henry Vilas Zoo in Madison, Wisconsin, where she had a reputation for lashing out at keepers. When Winkie first arrived at the sanctuary, Buckley told me, she used to jump merely upon being touched and then would wait for a confrontation. But when it never came, she slowly calmed down. "Has never lashed out at primary keepers," my last note on Winkie reads, "but has at secondary ones."

Bradshaw's e-mail message concludes: "A stunning illustration of trauma in elephants. The indelible etching."

I thought back to a moment in Queen Elizabeth National Park this past June. As Nelson Okello and I sat waiting for the matriarch and her calf to pass, he mentioned to me an odd little detail about the killing two months earlier of the man from the village of Katwe, something that, the more I thought about it, seemed to capture this particularly fraught moment we've arrived at with the elephants. Okello said that after the man's killing, the elephant herd buried him as it would one of its own, carefully covering the body with earth and brush and then standing vigil over it.

Even as we're forcing them out, it seems, the elephants are going out of their way to put us, the keepers, in an ever more discomfiting place, challenging us to preserve someplace for them, the ones who in many ways seem to regard the matter of life and death more devoutly than we. In fact, elephant culture could be considered the precursor of our own, the first permanent human settlements having sprung up around the desire of wandering tribes to stay by the graves of their dead. "The city of the dead," as Lewis Mumford once wrote, "antedates the city of the living."

When a group of villagers from Katwe went out to reclaim the man's body for his family's funeral rites, the elephants refused to budge. Human remains, a number of researchers have observed, are the only other ones that elephants will treat as they do their own. In the end, the villagers resorted to a tactic that has long been etched in the elephant's collective memory, firing volleys of gunfire into the air at close range, finally scaring the mourning herd away.   ∎

■ *QUESTIONS FOR MAKING CONNECTIONS WITHIN THE READING* ■

1. What evidence does Siebert provide to support the claim there is such a thing as an "elephant culture"? Is Siebert's assertion a sign of anthropomorphism? Anthropocentrism? Or is it a statement of fact? Can we even prove that our fellow human beings have thoughts and emotions like our own?

2. As Siebert's discussion unfolds, elephants are described as experiencing trauma, being intentionally violent, and responsive to psychotherapy. Is this surprising? Is Siebert seeking to establish that humans and elephants are part of a continuum? Are essentially identical? Are on parallel paths?

3. Siebert's piece ends with two acts of violence: a caretaker killed by an elephant in captivity, and a villager killed and buried by an elephant herd. Why does he do this? Since the piece begins with violence, has Siebert gone full circle? Or has he put his readers in a better position to understand the violence?

■ *QUESTIONS FOR WRITING* ■

1. Throughout "An Elephant Crackup?" Siebert gestures towards modes of consciousness that differ significantly from the model of an individual thinking. He describes a herd of elephants as, "in essence, one incomprehensibly massive elephant." He observes that saving elephants from extinction "will demand the ultimate act of deep, interspecies empathy." And he cites Gay Bradshaw's call for the development of a "trans-species psyche" that will allow humans to "be elephants." How would one go about developing these new modes of consciousness? What makes it possible for Siebert's sources to think in these ways?

2. Siebert notes that those who are concerned with the effects of trauma on the elephant population are now focusing on the "physiology of psychology"—that is, on the neurological foundation for psychological development. Based on the preliminary results of these studies, would you say that the turn to neurology provides cause for optimism about the possibilities of overcoming trauma? Or does the fact that trauma during the formative years results in "a literal thinning down of the essential circuits in the brain" mean that there's no saving young victims of trauma, be they elephant or human?

■ *QUESTIONS FOR MAKING CONNECTIONS BETWEEN READINGS* ■

1. "Language," as Christine Kenneally defines it, "is an act of shared attention, and without the fundamentally *human* willingness to listen to what another person is saying, language would not work." Throughout "An Elephant Crackup?" Siebert casts humans and elephants as being in communication with one another. Is the kind of communication that concerns Siebert what Kenneally means by "language"? Or would Kenneally reject the idea of an interspecies language? In tracing the evolution of language through the primates, has Kenneally overlooked essential evidence elsewhere in the animal kingdom? Or is animal communication simply an anthropocentric projection onto creatures we can never understand?

2. In "Meat and Milk Factories," Peter Singer and Jim Mason describe in detail the practices of the pork industry. Should the interspecies empathy that Siebert calls for extend to pigs? Or does the brutality described by Singer and Mason suggest that such empathy is simply not part of human nature? That is, couldn't one argue that the human ingenuity that has gone into creating the pork industry shows that humans are predisposed to the domination of other life forms? If one develops a "trans-species psyche," does this lead to a concern for the fate of pigs or only for elephants?

Peter Singer and Jim Mason

Peter Singer is controversial. When he first joined the Princeton University Center for Human Values faculty in 1999 after teaching for over two decades at Monash University in Australia, campus protests led to multiple arrests. Yet even his opponents respect him. One of these opponents, the disability rights lawyer Harriet McBryde Johnson, concedes that many consider Singer "the most influential philosopher of our time."

Singer is best known for his work in applied ethics, a style of philosophy that brings theoretical ethical constructs to bear on real-life situations. In the over forty books he has written or edited, the most influential being *Practical Ethics* (1979), Singer returns repeatedly to questions of responsibility. What responsibility does a person have with respect to another person? To a less privileged person? To members of other species? To the environment? Singer's work is so controversial because he challenges the conventional understanding of what it means to be a person, arguing that disability and other factors that influence an individual's self-realization over time can make someone more or less of a person and thus more or less entitled to various rights and privileges.

Though in recent years he has drawn the most criticism for his contentions about the nature of humanity, Singer rose to international prominence for his passionate defense of animals, first outlined in *Animal Liberation* (1975). He condemns "speciesism," or discrimination based on morally irrelevant physical details, and calls for changing the relationship between humans and other animal species. He considers the claim that animals have less intelligence or self-awareness invalid, arguing that some developmentally disabled humans are less mentally capable than some animals yet they are still afforded privileged treatment for their membership in the human species. Thus, our ethical responsibility to reduce suffering applies beyond the confines of our species to any being capable of experiencing suffering.

Singer, Peter, and Jim Mason. "Meat and Milk Factories," *The Ethics of What We Eat: Why Our Food Choices Matter*. New York: Rodale Books, 2006. 42–68.

Details in the first paragraph come from Harriet McBryde Johnson, "Unspeakable Conversations," *New York Times Magazine*, February 16, 2003. <http://query.nytimes.com/gst/fullpage.html?res=9401EFDC113BF935A25751C0A9659C8B63&sec=health&spon=&pagewanted=all>.

In an immediate practical sense, this means attending to the animals we see after their suffering is over: the ones that we eat. With Jim Mason, an attorney who grew up on a Missouri farm, Singer has co-authored two books that address this issue, *Animal Factories* (1980) and *The Ethics of What We Eat: Why Our Food Choices Matter* (2006). "Meat and Milk Factories," a chapter drawn from the latter of these two books, is an inside look into the industrial practices of America's pork, dairy, and beef producers. Drawing on the visits they and others have paid to massive farms, as well as on research into the conditions that are optimal for the animals themselves, Singer and Mason make clear the differences between the conditions in which the animals are forced to live and the conditions under which they could live comfortably. They point out case after case in which the profit motive supersedes ethical responsibility. By emphasizing the richness of the animals' cognitive and emotional lives when treated well, Singer and Mason compel us to wonder why we have allowed industrial-scale farming.

Meat and Milk Factories

The average American eats more than 200 pounds of red meat, poultry, and fish per year. That's an increase of 23 pounds over 1970, and it would be difficult for anyone to maintain that Americans in 1970 were not eating enough of these foods. In the last thirty-five years, the amount of beef eaten has fallen, but that has been outweighed by the near doubling of chicken consumption. Pork comes in third, at 51 pounds per person, behind chicken and beef. More than 60 percent of the pork eaten by Americans is bought already processed, as bacon, ham, lunch meats, hot dogs, or sausage.[1]

The Oscar Mayer bacon that Jake bought is in this category. We wanted to trace it back to the farms that raised the pigs, but that proved impossible. Oscar Mayer is now owned by Kraft Foods, the largest food and beverage company in North America and the second largest in the world (only Nestlé is bigger).[2] After numerous phone calls that involved working our way through seemingly endless menu options, we spoke to Consumer Services' Renee Zahery, who told us that "information about our procurement and processing of our product is considered proprietary in nature" and suggested we take up these questions with "a great source," Janet Riley, senior vice president at the American Meat Institute.[3]

When we talked with Riley, she told us only that Oscar Mayer probably has contracts with suppliers such as Tyson, Smithfield, and some of the lesser known, vertically integrated pork producing companies. So although we could not identify any of the specific farms that produce pigs for Oscar Mayer, it seems a fair assumption that their bacon comes from a cross section of today's intensive pork industry. What is that industry like?

The Poop on Pigs

When Peter first wrote about factory farming in America in 1975, there were more than 660,000 pig farms producing just under 69 million pigs a year.[4] Over the next 30 years, nearly 90 percent of those pig farms vanished, so that by 2004 there were only 69,000. But these farms will produce 103 million pigs a year.[5] Across the country, the family pig farmer has been replaced by Smithfield, ConAgra, ContiGroup, and the Seaboard Corporation. Most pigs raised today come from factory farms.

The boom in mega-piggeries has caused environmental problems even more acute than those caused by intensive chicken production. An adult pig produces about four times the amount of feces of a human, so a large confinement operation with, say, fifty thousand pigs, creates half a million pounds of pig urine and excrement every day. That's as much waste as a medium-sized town—but remember that human sewage is elaborately treated before being released into the environment and factory farm waste is not.

The summer of 1995 was wetter than usual in North Carolina. During the preceding 15 years, pig production in that state had boomed, making the state the second largest pork producer in the United States. Its pigs were producing 19 million tons of waste per year—or 2.5 tons of feces and urine for every citizen in the state.[6] During that wet summer, spilled animal waste killed ten million fish in North Carolina. In one of the most dramatic incidents, an 8-acre waste pond—the industry term is "lagoon" but that word conjures up images of blue water around a coral island, not a vast outdoor cesspool—burst, releasing 25 million gallons of liquid pig excrement into the New River, killing thousands of fish and polluting the river for miles downstream. Regulations in North Carolina were tightened, but spills continue to happen from time to time across the country. Even when there is no major spill, there is often seepage from the waste pond and run-off into the creeks when the manure is sprayed onto nearby farmland.[7]

Pig-factory farms are, if anything, even worse neighbors than chicken-factory farms. Carolyn Johnsen, a reporter for the Nebraska Public Radio Network, covered the controversial growth of mega-piggeries in that state. She attended heated public meetings, divided between those who saw economic opportunities in the new industry and those angry at the contamination of their air and water and concerned about the fate of the family farm. She spoke to people like Janie Mullinex, who lives south of Imperial, Nebraska, about a mile away from 48,000 pigs confined in 24 large barns. The owner had claimed, before putting up the confinement operation, that he had new technology and it would not smell. But Mullinex claimed that was not the case. "It comes in the house—even with the windows shut, it comes in with a strong south wind," Mullinex says. "It gives my seven-year-old diarrhea if we have it all day and it makes me sick. I don't vomit, but I'm nauseous and I have a tremendous headache." The Mullinex family has new storm windows and new siding and they have insulated their house, but it hasn't stopped the smell from coming in.

Johnsen also visited Mabel Bernard, who has lived and raised her family on her property near Enders, Nebraska, since 1926. Her enjoyment of her home has been spoiled by the construction of sheds holding 36,000 pigs about a mile north. When the wind comes from that direction, the stench wakes her up at night, burning her eyes and making her feel sick.[8] One Nebraska pig producer gave implicit support to those who don't want pig farms nearby when he won a 30 percent property tax reduction on his house by arguing that its value was decreased because it was located near a pig farm—his own.[9]

But big pig farms are more than a nuisance. They are also a public-health risk, according to the American Public Health Association, the largest body of public-health professionals in the United States. In 2003, citing a host of human diseases linked to farm animal waste and antibiotic use, the APHA passed a resolution urging government officials to adopt a moratorium on the construction of new factory farms.[10]

A Pig's Life

Pigs are affectionate, inquisitive animals. The film *Babe* was on solid scientific ground when it made its hero capable of doing everything a dog can do in the way of herding sheep. In fact, Professor Stanley Curtis thinks that the sheepdog's job would be a "pushover" for pigs he has investigated. Curtis is a hard-nosed scientist who worked for many years in the Department of Animal Sciences at the University of Illinois and received a Distinguished Service Award from the National Pork Producers Council in 2001. He conceived the idea of making it possible for pigs to tell producers what kind of conditions they prefer, and to that end, trained them to operate joystick-controlled video games. They learned quickly, and Curtis discovered that "there is much more going on in terms of thinking and observing by these pigs than we would ever have guessed."[11] The big problem, in fact, is not getting pigs to tell us what they prefer, but persuading the producers to give it to them.

To keep a dog locked up for life in a crate too narrow for her to turn around or walk more than a step or two forwards or backwards would be cruel and illegal. Yet when it comes to how pigs are kept in the U.S., here are two startling, and critical facts:

1. There is no federal law governing the welfare of farmed animals on the farm. Literally, nothing. In the U.S., federal law begins only when animals are transported or arrive at the slaughterhouse. (And even then, there is no law regarding the slaughter of chickens or other birds, who make up 95 percent of all land animals slaughtered in the U.S.) This is not because there is any constitutional barrier to covering the welfare of animals on farms, but simply because Congress has never chosen to enact any such law.

2. Most states with major animal industries have written into their anti-cruelty laws exemptions for "common farming practices." Effectively, then, cruelty is legal as long as it is done by most farmers, and you can't prosecute anyone for it.

Together, these two points mean that, as lawyer and author David Wolfson puts it, "farmed animals in such states are literally beyond the law and any common practice, no matter how horrifying, is legal."[12] More than 90 percent of pigs raised for meat today are raised indoors in crowded pens of concrete and steel. They never get to go outside or root around in pasture and don't even have straw to bed down in.[13] The most tightly confined of all are the breeding sows. Under the factory's rigid production schedule, they are made to produce litter after litter as quickly as possible, which means that they are pregnant for most of their lives. During their pregnancies, which last about 16 weeks, most American sows are confined in "gestation crates"—steel-barred crates or stalls just a foot or so longer than their bodies, and so narrow that the sows cannot even turn around. Of the 1.8 million sows used for breeding by America's ten biggest pig producers, about 90 percent are kept in this manner, and for the industry as a whole, the figure is around 80 percent.[14]

In these conditions, apart from the brief period when they are eating, these sensitive, intelligent, and highly social animals have nothing to do all day. They cannot walk around or socialize with other sows. All they can do is stand up or lie down on the bare concrete floor. When the time comes to give birth, they are also confined in what producers call a farrowing crate. (Is it part of the gulf we draw between ourselves and other animals that leads farmers to talk of animals as "farrowing" rather than "giving birth," "feeding" rather than "eating," and "gestating" rather than "being pregnant"?) The farrowing crate keeps the sow in position, with her teats always exposed to her piglets. She is unable to roll over—and this, the defenders of the crate say, ensures that she will not roll on top of, and perhaps smother, her piglets.

In Europe, widespread public concern about the close confinement of sows led to the European Union asking its scientific veterinary advisory committee to investigate the impact of gestation crates—or sow stalls, as they are known there—on the welfare of the sows. The investigation found that sow stalls had "major disadvantages" for welfare. Pigs like to forage and explore their environment. In natural conditions they will spend up to three-quarters of their waking hours doing this. In stalls, of course, they cannot. When a sow is first put into a stall, she typically tries to escape and may push against or attack the bars. After a time, she gives up, and often becomes quite inactive and unresponsive. This, the scientific veterinary committee says, indicates clinical depression. Other sows in stalls carry out meaningless, repetitive motions, like biting the bars of the stall, chewing the air, shaking their heads from side to side, nosing around repeatedly in the empty feed trough. These pointless movements are signs of stress, similar to the endless back and forth pacing of tigers and other big cats when kept in the traditional sterile cages of old-fashioned zoos. Fortunately, many zoos have become more enlightened and no longer keep their animals in such cages. No doubt public disapproval helped persuade them to make the change. Sows in factory farms are actually worse off than the big cats in zoos used to be, because they can't even pace back and forth. But they are invisible to the public.

In addition to psychological stress, sows in crates are also less healthy than sows able to walk around. (That shouldn't be a surprise to anyone who knows that it is healthy to get some exercise.) Sows in crates frequently become lame and develop foot injuries from standing on concrete for every moment when they are not lying down. They also get more urinary-tract infections.

In sum, the scientific veterinary committee concluded, "sows should preferably be kept in groups."[15] After considering this report, the European Union passed a law phasing out sow crates by the end of 2012, except for the first four weeks after mating, and requiring that sows be given straw or similar materials that they can play around with, to reduce the stress of boredom. This law will apply to all 25 countries of the European Union, which together slaughter more than twice as many pigs as the United States.[16] Even before the new law comes into effect, Britain and Sweden acted to ban sow stalls. All of the 600,000 breeding sows in Britain now have, at least, room to turn around and can interact with other pigs.

"Wayne Bradley," Iowa Pig Producer

As we mentioned when discussing how agribusiness corporations refused our requests to see how they keep their animals, one Iowa pig producer was more open than all the rest. In his view, "education is the best defense against the animal rights attack on the livestock industry." He felt he had an obligation to show people around his farm, he told us, because many years ago he had become "unglued" by a television show about farming. His wife told him: 'I'm not going to listen to this. Next time somebody calls out here for an interview . . . you better talk to them. Either that or just shut up." He's been talking ever since. He talked to us several times—by telephone and in person when we toured his farm. Everything went well until we sent him what we had written and asked him to check it for any inaccuracies. At that point he suddenly asked us to not use his real name or say anything that might identify his farm and location. He had worries about "animal-rights people," he said, "doing damage to things." In what follows, therefore, everything is as it happened, but we have changed the farmer's name.

The Bradley farmhouse and main buildings stand near the intersection of two county roads. Like many farmsteads in Iowa, it is sheltered from the winter winds by rows of lush cedar trees along the north and west. There is a big white house, a wide yard, silos, and an old barn. But these emblems of an older way of farming are overwhelmed by those of the new. The drive-way opens up on an array of tractors, trucks, and machinery and, farther down, rows of low metal pig-confinement buildings. A complex of metal grain bins, augers, and pipes towers over everything. Wayne Bradley greets us in the driveway. He is a big, hefty man, 50-something, full of energy, friendly and talkative. We walk to a small office in the corner of one of the pig buildings and sit down. Things are a bit tense at first, but grow easier as he tells us about his family and farm. He farms the land of his father and grandfather—Bradleys have been farming here since 1875. His son, Alex, farms with him and runs a herd of cattle on land of his own. It is a family farm, he says, but also a corporation because of financial advantages that in-corporation offers. He farms 2,600 acres, much of it land rented from neigh-bors "scattered around about 9 miles." The Bradleys have 500 sows, and they sell between 10,000 and 12,000 pigs a year.

As we chat, he is eager to make a few points right away. He emphati-cally opposes the claim that pigs in confinement are abused. "When it's thirty below zero, my hogs are laying out comfortable in a 70-degree building—granted, it's not bedded, but they're clean and they're just laying there grunting and oblivious to the blizzard that's going on outside. That's as opposed to when we used to raise them out in open sheds and we spent the day bedding them and they'd have frozen ears and frozen tails and those types of things."

Wayne wants us to understand the economics that have driven his deci-sions. "We've had to specialize to a certain degree," he says. His other major concern is government regulation, primarily of waste handling. He feels that his farm is "under intense regulation and intense scrutiny all the time." He believes it is unfair because he collects manure and wastes in a concrete basin and can use the nutrients on the fields as weather permits. "Our capability of handling wastes now is so much better than before. Our chances of polluting are so much less because we inject it." Many pig producers mix the manure with water and spray it onto fields. That just leaves it on the surface where it can easily run off into creeks when it rains. Wayne has a liquid manure injector, which he pulls behind a tractor. Essentially a large tank on wheels, it pumps liquid manure down on the ground where discs cover it with about 2 inches of topsoil.

Wayne obviously feels caught in the middle—being squeezed between those who promote organic or pasture-raised pork and the giant corporations that now dominate pig production. "I'll defend confinement. I'm not going to defend Smithfield Foods because I think it's taking it to the extreme. They had 250,000 sows and then they went to 500,000 and now they're up to 700,000 sows. I don't think that's economically healthy. . . . The packers are getting more power and control than they need."

Making Bacon

The Bradleys' pigs are in what's known as "total confinement"—none of them ever go outdoors. He begins the tour by taking us into one of his four farrowing rooms, where his sows give birth and then feed their piglets. These were his first confinement buildings, which he built himself in 1975. He tells us, "I was so happy when we got the hogs in here. I could get them in out of the cold." We are in a large room maybe 20 by about 40 feet. It stinks inside, of course, but not as badly as some units we've been in over the years. A concrete walkway runs down the length of the building between two rows of farrowing crates containing sows and baby pigs. The crate has two parts: a taller metal framework to hold the large sow and a lower "creep" area to one side where the baby pigs sleep when they are not nursing. The sow's part is about 2 feet by 6 feet; her body nearly fills the space. She can stand up and lie down to sleep or nurse her piglets. She cannot turn around or do much else. In some crates, the "floors" are steel slats; in others, large-gauge wire mesh coated in plastic. There is no straw or other soft bedding material. Pig wastes pass through the openings and fall into a shallow pit below. A system of cables and scrapers periodically sweeps the wastes down to a pipe and they flow into a covered pit outside.

Each sow stays in her farrowing crate for about 20 days. Wayne tells us that the crate offers the piglets a safe area away from the sow when she lies down to sleep or nurse them. We look down on a sow with a litter of baby pigs all piled up like puppies and fast asleep and say something about how cute they are. "Do they look like they're abused?" he asks. No, they certainly don't, we tell him. But what about the various mutilations that we had heard are routinely carried out on pigs kept in confinement: cutting off their tails and clipping their "needle teeth" and castrating them without an anesthetic?

There are reasons for each of them, Wayne explains. The pigs' needle teeth can cut their mother's nipples and they can cut each other in fighting over nipples. "Tail docking" prevents pigs from biting and chewing on each other's tails. We press him further: Isn't it only pigs in confinement who bite each other's tails? Don't they do this because they are bored, spending all their time crowded together in a sterile environment with nothing to do all day long? "I guess I would have to agree with that to a point. But we used to raise pigs out in large pens like cattle lots and we had tail-biting then too. So we've been docking tails for quite a number of years." We've seen cattle lots, and we would not be surprised if the pigs were bored there too. But we keep that thought to ourselves.

Wayne castrates his male pigs at ten days after birth. Consumer demand drives that, Wayne says. Meat from male pigs with testicles has a distinctive gamy taste called "boar taint" that consumers, apparently, don't like. If the pigs are killed at an earlier age, as happens in some other countries, this isn't a problem. But the U.S. consumer likes large cuts of meat that can only come from a more mature pig, and then the taint becomes more noticeable.

Why are these painful procedures done without any anesthetic? Again, Wayne is disarmingly candid: "I guess I don't have a good answer for that." We ask if it is the expense involved. "Well, it would be an expense. Obviously it is going to cost money. I have no idea. I can't sit here and say, 'Well it's going to cost me a dollar a pig.' Because if it was a dollar a pig, I mean there's not a dollar a pig to throw away. If it was a nickel or a penny or something like that, there would be no reason that we couldn't. But I doubt that it would be that inexpensive." We ask Wayne if he has ever heard of anyone using a local anesthetic for these procedures: "I never have. It's obviously a question to be asked." He hesitates before continuing: "You know, maybe farm folks are more . . . I don't know if I'd say immune to that or not. I mean until I was 22 years old my dentist never used novocaine. I went to the dentist and I grabbed ahold of the chair and he drilled and it was over."

We're thinking that we would have made a different choice—and perhaps the pigs would too, if they could—when Wayne turns the conversation back to the sow with her piglets in the farrowing crate in front of us. "Another advantage to this versus a pasture farrowing situation is that we can do a better job of keeping an eye on the sow and the pigs. If there's a problem, you're right here. It's very easy to give her a shot if she's not feeling well."

Wayne's piglets are weaned when they are two weeks and a few days old. In more natural environments, piglets nurse from their mothers for at least nine weeks, and sometimes longer,[17] but nursing would prevent the sow becoming pregnant again during that period, thereby reducing her productivity. So the piglets are removed from their mother and she goes back to the breeding area, while they are placed together with other litters in a "nursery" building on a nearby farm. The breeding area is part of the gestation room, and that is where Wayne takes us next. At one end stand three huge, hairy boars, one to a stall. Wayne explains that they stay in these stalls about half the time, spending the other half in a resting pen where they do have room to walk around. They rotate the boars back and forth, he says, because "overuse" lowers semen quality. The boars are rough and wild-looking.

A sow will be made pregnant again as soon as she comes into estrus. Wayne uses a combination of "live mating"—a boar is allowed to mount the sow—and "AI," or artificial insemination. Wayne's pregnant sows live in group pens instead of the narrow crates that are typical of the big corporate pig factories. Each of the three pens here holds up to forty sows. Each pen has an automated self-feeder in the center; it looks like another kind of crate but with gates on each end. It holds one sow at a time. Wayne explains how it works: "The sows are all tagged with an electronic chip. When one goes in there, that machine reads the chip and it tells whether or not she's had her feed for the day. They're allowed so many pounds. They can go through there until they've eaten their daily quota." The purpose, he says, is to make sure that every sow gets to eat her ration at her own speed.

We move on past the pens of pregnant sows and down a corridor. We stop at a steel door with a small window. Wayne motions for us to take a look. It's the room where the herd manager collects semen from the boar. We ask the obvious question: "How do you collect sperm from the boar?" Wayne is all business: "We use a steel dummy." He leads us a few steps to a dusty, windowless cubby hole just off the corridor. It is about 7 or 8 feet square and empty except for a low steel bench with a rubber mat under it. "There's the dummy. Some of the boars will jump right on that and ride it and ejaculate. And others won't. You have to use a sow. The herdsman catches the semen in a thermos with a gloved hand. He'll extend the semen so that one ejaculation can make about twenty doses of semen. Once again, it's an economic thing. It gives us more use of that one boar, instead of having to feed so many boars. But it goes beyond that. We can change our genetics faster than we could if we had a stable of twenty or twenty-five boars. It's better to have one really good boar and use his semen."

Next stop is the nursery—that's the industry term for a place where early-weaned pigs are given special feed to enable them to survive the stress of separation and weaning. Each of the pens contains a few dozen small pigs. We ask him how the pigs handle the stress of weaning. "Oh, there really isn't much that happens. The first day they just kind of lay around. Whenever you come in the building, they grunt and make a lot of noise because they are used to having mama around."

We get back in the truck and go to another farm where Wayne has a finishing building, where the pigs are grown to market weight. Along the way, we talk about the changes in farming we've both seen over the years. He mentions the loss of middle-income people in the rural areas around him. Now, he says, "We've got a bunch of people that are looking for $150-a-month houses to move into. They're making meth and they're making trouble. The rural countryside has changed dramatically." (Making methamphetamine, in Iowa? At the time, we thought Wayne must have been exaggerating, but when we checked it out, we found that Iowa has the second highest number of meth labs and the fourth highest level of meth use in the nation.[18] Is that a consequence of the loss of family farmers too, we wondered?)

The conversation drifts to the price of corn and subsidies. Wayne thinks that years of government subsidies have kept corn artificially cheap for livestock producers. "We've been producing grain below the cost of production for so many years that it's just a given. It's a guarantee. If we'd gotten corn prices up to where they ought to be, a lot of this livestock thing never would have happened. It's been on the back of cheap grain. I don't know how you change that."

We have reached the finishing building. It's open on both sides. Running the length of the building on each side is a plastic curtain he can roll up and down to adjust temperature and ventilation. "Let's open the door just to give you a whiff of the air quality." We step through to the pens. On this mild spring day, a breeze is blowing over the pens full of pigs. It is total confinement, but with a breath of semi-fresh air. "If it's thirty below zero outside, these curtains will be closed and the furnace will be running a bit. These old pigs here'll be all stretched out and as comfortable as if they were in the Bahamas."

We ask him about drugs and medications administered to these pigs. He says that this is "one of those deals that gets misrepresented. People think we're feeding a lot of antibiotics out here. Our whole goal is not to feed a lot of them because they cost us money." He explains that when he first brings pigs into a finishing building he gives them a dose of the antibiotic tetracycline in their feed "just to give them something for the stress in moving them." Then he puts them on "a growth promotant called BMD, bacitracin something something. I can't tell you what all is in it. It helps them grow faster and that's the name of the game." (He's referring to bacitracin methylene disalicylate, another antibiotic.) If the pigs develop diarrhea or "a cough or a problem," they give them an antibiotic or other medication, usually in the water. "A pig will drink when they won't eat," he explains.

Our tour is over and it's time to leave. We're sitting in Wayne's pickup truck in the driveway back at his home. He emphasizes again how he wants to get the right story out there. "What really concerns us in animal agriculture is that we've been made out to be the bad guys. We're working hard to produce a quality product and we're treated like we're just . . . well, terrible people. It doesn't go down well in the ag community."

We don't think he's a bad guy. He worked hard to buy the farm from his parents and brothers—a farm that had been in the family for a century—and he found a way to keep it going when most family pig farms were going out of business. We like the fact that he doesn't keep his pregnant sows in crates—probably the least defensible aspect of standard pig-confinement practices in America. We particularly admire his openness about what he is doing, a refreshing contrast to all the other intensive pig producers we contacted. His method of disposing of his manure seems more responsible than that of many pig producers. We appreciate that his buildings keep his pigs warm in the cold Iowa winters. But we wondered if there couldn't be a way of keeping them warm and giving them a better life than they can have living in an environment as barren and restrictive as his total-confinement buildings.

When we sent Wayne what we had written about our visit, in addition to asking not to be identified and making a few other minor suggestions, he and Mrs. Bradley wrote that they thought our final sentence—the one you have just read—made "no sense." Instead they suggested a different way of ending our account of our visit to their farm. Here it is, with their original underlining. You be the judge.

> Raising pigs today is so much improved over methods used by our great-grandparents, <u>and the meat that we consume is so much leaner and healthier for us to eat</u>! The highest-quality standard of 'the other white meat' is the goal of USA pork production in the 21st century. Let's thank the American farmer for a solid science-based industry that includes good animal care while being good stewards of the environment. Let's enjoy that pork chop hot off the grill, or that pork roast with potatoes and carrots, <u>because there's no safer food source than USA-raised pigs</u> for the pork consumers in the USA and other countries which import our pork!

Profitability and Animal Welfare

The real ethical issue about factory farming's treatment of animals isn't whether the producers are good or bad guys, but that the system seems to recognize animal suffering only when it interferes with profitability. The animal industry always says that producers take care of their animals because what is good for the animals is good for the producer. Professor Bernard Rollin, who has taught veterinary ethics at Colorado State University for almost 30 years, has given a graphic example of how profitability and animal welfare can pull in opposite directions. A veterinarian was visiting a 500-sow, "farrow to finish" swine operation with three full-time employees and a manager. He noticed that one of the sows in the gestation crates had a hind leg sticking out at an odd angle. When he inquired, he was told "She broke her leg yesterday, and she's due to farrow next week. We'll let her farrow in here, and then we'll shoot her and foster off her pigs." The vet was troubled by the idea of leaving the sow for a week with a broken leg and offered to put the leg in a splint, charging only the cost of his materials. He was told that the operation could not afford the manpower involved in separating and caring for the sow. At this point, the vet, who had been brought up on a family pig farm where the animals had names and were treated as individuals, realized that "confinement agriculture had gone too far."[19]

Is this an extreme case, or common practice? The cost calculations that Wayne made when discussing the possible use of a local anesthetic to reduce the pain of operations like castration—"there's not a dollar a pig to throw away"—show that this kind of thinking is built into intensive animal raising. As long as the market provides no incentive for reducing the pigs' pain, the pig producer cannot afford to spend more than a penny, or perhaps a nickel, for that purpose. If he does, someone else who won't spend anything to reduce pain will produce cheaper pigs and put him out of business. That is why the way that factory farming treats animals is not so much a problem of gratuitous cruelty or sadism, and the main problem is not a matter of preventing isolated incidents of animal abuse. The core issue is the commercial pressures that exist in a competitive market system in which animals are items of property, and the conditions in which they are kept are not regulated by federal or state animal-welfare law.

Tracking Down Jake's Milk

Jake thought that she was buying milk from local farms because Coleman Dairy, the brand she bought at Wal-Mart, is an Arkansas-based corporation. When we called and asked if we could see their cows, however, Walt Coleman told us that they hadn't had any cows since 1935. They buy their milk from Dairy Farmers of America, a big dairy cooperative, and although some of their milk comes from Arkansas, it can also come from Texas or New Mexico. Coleman wasn't willing to help us any further in our quest to see the source of Jake's milk.

Milk and cheese production enjoy a better reputation than other forms of intensive farming, and the dairy industry is keen to keep it that way. In advertisements for dairy products, it's common to see cows enjoying acres of rolling green pasture, often with their calves nearby. The impression many consumers get is that dairy cows lead natural lives, and we humans merely take the surplus milk that the calf does not require. People also think that cows are placid animals without much of an emotional life. Both are misconceptions. Cows have strong emotional lives. They form friendships with two, three, or four other cows, and, if permitted, will spend most of their time together, often licking and grooming each other. On the other hand, they can form dislikes to other cows and bear grudges for months or even years.

More remarkably still, cows can get excited when they solve intellectual challenges. Donald Broom, professor of animal welfare at Cambridge University, set cows a problem—to work out how to open a door to get some food—while measuring their brainwave patterns. When the cows solved the problem, Broom reported, "Their brainwaves showed their excitement; their heartbeat went up and some even jumped into the air. We called it their eureka moment."[20]

Peter Lovenheim is a writer who lives in Rochester, New York. He was standing in line at McDonald's one day when he decided that he'd like to know more about how a hamburger is produced. He bought three newborn calves and had them raised in the usual way until it was time to slaughter them. Because Rochester is close to many of New York State's dairy farms—and New York is the third largest dairying state in the U.S., after Wisconsin and California—Lovenheim bought male calves from a nearby dairy farm. Most males born to dairy calves are raised for veal, or slaughtered immediately for pet food, but a few of the stronger ones are raised for beef. Thanks to Andrew and Sue Smith, who were remarkably open about what they do, Lovenheim was able to spend a lot of time at Lawnel Farm, and the following account draws on his description of Lawnel when he was there in 2000.[21]

With about 900 cows being milked—that doesn't include young cows who were not yet giving milk, nor cows who were temporarily not lactating—Lawnel was a medium-sized dairy operation, larger than some of the organic farms we will describe in Part II but small compared to, say, Bill Braum's dairy near Tuttle, Oklahoma, which milks over 10,000 cows, or Threemile Canyon in Oregon, which milks 18,000 cows.[22] A Cornell University study expects the number of dairy farms in the United States to decline from 105,000 in 2000 to 16,000 in 2020, while the number of cows per farm and the total milk production both increase.[23]

At Lawnel, the cows were kept indoors, in barns. Unlike many dairy farms, they were free to walk around inside the barn—they were not in "tie-stalls" that confine cows, for most of the year, to a single stall where they are fed and milked. In the western United States, dairy cows are more likely to be kept outside, but even then they are just in dirt lots. Very few dairy cows in the U.S. get to graze in the grassy meadows typical of dairy-industry advertising—the exceptions are mostly cows producing milk certified "organic," but, as we shall see, even some of them are not on pasture.

The modern dairy cow has been bred to produce as much milk as possible and now produces more than three times as much milk as a typical dairy cow did 50 years ago.[24] The result is considerable stress on the cow's body. To increase milk production still further, the Smiths gave their cows injections, every other week, of BST, or bovine somatotrophin, a genetically engineered growth hormone. BST is banned in Canada and in the European Union because of concerns for the health and welfare of dairy cows, but it is widely used in the United States. It increases milk production by about 10 percent, but the site of the injection may become swollen and tender. BST can also increase problems with mastitis, a painful udder infection that afflicts about one in six U.S. dairy cows.[25] Sue Smith said she didn't like giving the injections, but "If we're making more milk and it's profitable, it's something we should be doing."[26]

Like human females, dairy cows do not give milk until they have given birth, and their milk production will begin to decline some six months after the birth. So after they reach maturity they are made pregnant by artificial insemination roughly every year. Normally a calf would suckle from its mother for six months, and the bond between mother and child would remain strong during that period, but dairy farms are in business to sell milk, not give it to calves. At Lawnel Farms, Lovenheim watched a cow give birth and begin to lick her calf, but forty minutes later a farmhand came and took the calf away. The cow sniffed the straw where the calf had been, bellowed, and began to pace around. Hours later she was sticking her nose under the gate to the barn in which she was confined, bellowing continuously. Meanwhile her calf was in another part of the farm, lying shivering on a concrete floor. Within a few days he was dead, and his body was lying on the farm's compost pile.[27]

Oliver Sacks, who writes about people with unusual neurological conditions, spent some time with Temple Grandin, the livestock consultant McDonald's has employed to advise them on animal-welfare issues. Sacks was more interested in Grandin's autism than in her work with animals, but he accompanied her on a visit to a dairy farm. As Sacks describes it: "We saw one cow outside the stockade, roaming, looking for her calf, and bellowing. 'That's not a happy cow,' Temple said. 'That's one sad, unhappy, upset cow. She wants her baby. Bellowing for it, hunting for it. She'll forget for a while, then start again. It's like grieving, mourning—not much written about it. People don't like to allow them thoughts or feelings.'"[28] John Avizienius, the senior scientific officer in the Farm Animals Department of the RSPCA in Britain, says that he "remembers one particular cow who appeared to be deeply affected by the separation from her calf for a period of at least six weeks. When the calf was first removed, she was in acute grief; she stood outside the pen where she had last seen her calf and bellowed for her offspring for hours. She would only move when forced to do so. Even after six weeks, the mother would gaze at the pen where she last saw her calf and sometimes wait momentarily outside of the pen. It was almost as if her spirit had been broken and all she could do was to make token gestures to see if her calf would still be there."[29]

Female dairy calves may be reared as replacements for the "culled" cows who get sent to slaughter. Although the natural lifespan of a cow is around 20 years, dairy cows are usually killed at between five and seven years of age, because they cannot sustain the unnaturally high rate of milk production. Male calves who survive are sent to auction at an age when they can barely walk. Temple Grandin has strong views about that, too: "Worst thing you can do is put a bawling baby on a trailer. It's just an awful thing to do."[30]

The usual options for these male dairy calves are, as already mentioned, to be slaughtered immediately or to be raised for "milk-fed" veal. From the calf's point of view, immediate slaughter is the better fate, for it spares him

16 weeks of confinement in semi-darkness, in a bare wooden crate too narrow to turn around. He will be tied at the neck, further restricting his movements. Already stressed by separation from his mother and unable to mingle with others of his kind, he will be fed only "milk replacer," a liquid mixture of dried milk products, starch, fats, sugar, antibiotics, and other additives. This diet is deliberately so low in iron that he will develop subclinical anemia. That's what the veal producer wants, because it means that the calf's flesh, instead of becoming the normal healthy red color of a 16-week-old calf on pasture, will retain the pale pink color and soft texture of "prime veal." Bought mostly by expensive restaurants catering to gourmet tastes, that kind of veal fetches the highest price. For the same reason, the calf will be denied hay or straw for bedding—if he had it, his desire for roughage and something to chew on would cause him to eat it, and since it contains iron, that too would change the color of his flesh. The wooden stalls and neck tether are part of the same plan. If the stall had iron fittings, he would lick them, and if he were able to turn around, he would lick his own urine—again, in order to satisfy his craving for iron.

Apart from the separation of cows from their calves and the way the newborn male calves are treated, the most disturbing passages in Lovenheim's description of Lawnel Farm portray the treatment of "downers"—cows who, through illness or accident, are no longer able to stand. On one occasion Lovenheim saw Sue Smith trying to raise a downed cow, No. 4482. She started by coaxing her with gentle words, but when that didn't work she twisted the stump of the cow's tail, then jabbed her knee into the cow's side and screamed into her ear. When that met with no success she twisted the cow's ear and jabbed her several times in the ribs with an electric prod. That didn't work either. If a downed cow can't be raised, she is dragged out. So they called Bill, a renderer, to take the cow away. Lovenheim describes what happened next: "Andrew gets on a small tractor and backs it through the barn door while Bill ties a sling around 4482's front right hoof. When the sling is attached to the tractor, Andrew reverses direction, dragging the downed cow 30 or 40 feet across the barn door, her useless back feet spread wide, her left front hoof kind of paddling along to keep up." (While this was going on, Andrew and Bill discussed what crops the farm had planted that season.) Once out of the barn, Bill winched the cow up a steeply inclined ramp into the back of a truck that took her to the slaughterhouse. After watching this, Lovenheim asked Sue if she had ever considered euthanizing downed animals on the farm. She told him that they'd done that once, but the procedure was expensive.[31]

Manure from dairies, like that from chicken and pig factory farms, pollutes rivers, kills fish, and ruins the homes of nearby residents. Another pollution problem, more specific to cows, is often treated as a joke. When cows ruminate, or "chew the cud," they produce gases called "volatile organic compounds." (For those who like anatomical details, most is generated in burps rather than farts.) When there are a lot of cows, that makes for a lot of gas and can cease to be a joke. The San Joaquin Valley, part of California's Central Valley and one of the world's richest agricultural regions, ranks alongside Houston and Los Angeles as having the worst air pollution in the United States. Over the last six years, the valley has violated the federal limit on ozone smog over an eight-hour period more often than any other region in the country. Officials from the San Joaquin Valley Air Pollution Control District believe that the valley's 2.5 million dairy cows are the biggest single source of a major smog-causing pollutant and are trying to force the dairy industry to do something about it. Other gases are emitted by cow manure and the lagoons in which it is stored. The dairy industry is resisting proposals for change. Tom Frantz, who says he has developed asthma as a result of dairy farms moving near to him, heads a group called the Association of Irritated Residents that is calling for stricter regulation. Frantz says: "Ag hasn't been regulated in the past, but times are changing. Our lungs will not become an agricultural subsidy."[32]

The problem isn't only one for local residents, either. The gases contain methane, which contributes significantly to global warming. In that respect we are all subsidizing agriculture.

The Beef Industry

By a curious coincidence, about the same time that Peter Lovenheim in New York was buying calves in order to follow the process of turning a calf into a hamburger, Michael Pollan, another writer, was doing much the same thing in the Midwest. Lovenheim's calves were byproducts of the dairy industry and were raised by a dairy farmworker and his wife who kept about a dozen cattle on the side. Pollan bought a young steer—a castrated male—from a ranch in South Dakota and had him fattened alongside 37,000 other cattle on a feedlot in Kansas. The dairy industry that Lovenheim observed is the source of about half of the hamburger meat served at the fast-food restaurants Jake likes to frequent. The beef industry that Pollan portrays is where most of America's 36 million beef cattle are produced every year and is the likely source of the porterhouse steak she buys at Wal-Mart.

Pollan's calf, known as 534, was born in March. The calf remained with his mother for more than six months, part of a herd that had many acres of prairie pasture on which to graze. He wasn't even weaned until October. But it was all downhill from there. The young steer was loaded into a truck and driven 500 miles to Pokey Feeders where, in Pollan's words, "Cattle pens stretch to the horizon, each one home to 150 animals standing dully or lying around in a grayish mud that, it eventually dawns on you, isn't mud at all." When Pollan visited, he could smell a "bus-station-men's-room" odor more than a mile before he got there. Here 534 lived another eight months, until slaughter.[33]

On arrival at the feedlot, 534 was given an implant of a synthetic hormone in the back of his ear—something similar to the muscle-building testosterone surrogates that athletes use. Giving them to cattle is banned in Europe because of concerns about the potential health risk of drug residues, and of course U.S. law prohibits people from self-medicating with steroids. In the U.S., however, giving them to cattle is standard practice. It makes them put on more muscle, which means more money for the growers. When Pollan asked Rich Blair, the rancher from whom he bought 534, what he thought about the hormone implants, Blair said: "I'd love to give up hormones. The cattle could get along better without them. But the market signal's not there, and as long as my competitor's doing it, I've got to do it, too."

Instead of grass, 534 now ate corn kernels, together with a daily dose of antibiotics to enable him to survive on this diet. Dr Mel Metzen, the staff veterinarian at Pokey Feeders, told Pollan that a great many of the health problems that he and his eight assistants have to deal with stem from the diet. "They're made to eat forage," Metzen says, "and we're making them eat grain." Ruminant animals have a digestive system that has evolved to break down grass. If they don't get enough roughage, they develop lactic acid in their rumens, which creates gas and causes "feedlot bloat," a condition so severe that cattle can suffocate from it. Liver abscesses are also frequent. Putting cattle on a corn-based diet is like putting humans on a diet of candy bars—you can live on it for a while, but eventually you are going to get sick. For the beef producer that doesn't matter, as long as the animal doesn't drop dead before being slaughtered. By feeding antibiotics on a daily basis, the risk of that happening is reduced to manageable proportions—and it is a risk worth taking, because the cattle reach market weight in 14 months, rather than the 18 months to two years they would otherwise take. Without antibiotics, Metzen admitted, it wouldn't be possible to fatten cattle on corn. "Hell, if you gave them lots of grass and space," he joked, "I wouldn't have a job."

Corn isn't the only strange food that cattle are fed. When mad cow disease became a major issue in Europe, the public was surprised to learn that it was caused by cattle eating the remains of sheep who had been infected with a related disease. Since when, people asked, do cattle eat meat? In fact, slaughterhouse leftovers have been going into cattle feed for about 40 years, because they are cheap and add protein to the diet. In the wake of the mad cow disaster, most countries placed restrictions on feeding meat remnants to cattle, but in the U.S. it is still, at the time of writing, permitted for cattle feed to contain beef blood and fat, as well as gelatin, "plate waste" (restaurant leftovers), chicken and pig meat, and chicken litter—which includes fecal matter, dead birds, chicken feathers, and spilled feed. The spilled feed can include the same beef and bone meal that is not allowed to be fed to cattle directly, but can be fed to chickens.

In January 2004 the Food and Drug Administration announced plans to ban blood, plate waste, and chicken litter, and an international review panel convened by the Secretary of Agriculture recommended banning all slaughterhouse remnants; two years later, none of these proposed bans had come into effect. Frustrated at the delay, scientists and McDonald's Corporation told the FDA that stronger steps were needed to stop mad cow disease, which the researchers called "an insidious threat." McDonald's vice president Dick Crawford called on the government "to take further action to reduce this risk."[34]

One of the reasons for the delay, according to Stephen Sundlof, Director of the FDA's Center for Veterinary Medicine, was that the proposed ban on the use of chicken litter generated "huge concern" from chicken producers. No wonder—about a million tons of chicken litter are disposed of by being fed to cattle each year. That means that, on average, each of the 36 million cattle produced in the U.S. has eaten 66 pounds of it. In other words, environmental problems created by the chicken industry are preventing the FDA from taking steps recommended by public health experts to ensure the safety of U.S. beef.

The feedlot system is also an ecological disaster. When we eat ruminants who have been grazing on pasture, we are, in effect, harvesting the free energy of the sun. But feedlots thrive because in the U.S. bulk corn sells for about 4 cents a pound—less than the cost of production, thanks to the billions of taxpayers' dollars the government gives in subsidies to the growers. (Most of the cash goes to people who are already very wealthy.) The corn in turn requires chemical fertilizers, which are made from oil. So a corn-fattened feedlot steer is, as Pollan says, "the very last thing we need: a fossil-fuel machine." Pollan asked David Pimentel, a Cornell ecologist, to calculate how much oil went into fattening 534 to his slaughter weight of 1,250 pounds. Pimentel's answer: 284 gallons.

Then there is the issue of what happens to the run-off from the feedlots. Nebraska is *the* state for big feedlots, with 760 of them authorized to have more than 1,000 head of cattle. The largest, near Broken Bow, is licensed for 85,000 cattle. Alan Kolok, a professor of biology at the University of Nebraska, is studying the impact of feedlots on streams that flow into the Elkhorn River. We met him in Omaha, and he drove us west into Cuming County, one of the nation's top beef-producing counties. Near West Point, we came to a feedlot for about 5,000 cattle—the usual fenced, bare, dirt-and-manure yards with bored-looking cattle standing in the sun. It was June, and although it wasn't especially hot yet, we remarked on the lack of shade, saying to Alan that if any had been provided, most of these cattle would have been standing in it. He said that the weather was going to get hotter. Indeed, by the end of July, much of Nebraska had had 30 days with temperatures above 90 degrees, and several above 100. Roxanne Bergman, who runs a "dead-stock removal" company in Clearwater, said her company alone had hauled out 1,250 dead cattle during a few days of hot weather and could not handle all the calls it was receiving.[35]

Researchers from the Department of Animal Science and Food Technology at Texas Tech University studied the use of shade in feedlots. The study divided cattle into a group that had shade available and one that did not have shade available. The cattle with shade available "used the shade extensively" from 9.00 A.M. to 5.30 P.M., following the shade as the sun moved. Cattle without shade were four times as aggressive to other cattle than those with shade. But the researchers also noted that "In west Texas, shade is generally not used in commercial feedlots because it is not thought to be cost effective."[36] Once again—and not only in west Texas—when better animal welfare costs money, animal welfare loses.

Alan showed us how the feedlot we were looking at had been built right down to the edge of the north fork of Fisher Creek. A holding lagoon built to catch the feedlot run-off, filled with unpleasant-looking brown water, was separated from the creek by an earth embankment. Alan explained that in heavy rain, it was likely that polluted water would run off from the feedlot into the creek, or could seep through the embankment into the creek. We drove on and came to another feedlot on sloping land not far from the Elkhorn River. Here Alan has found local fish, fathead minnows, showing signs of altered sexual features. As compared with fish captured near a wildlife refuge where there are no feedlots, the male minnows had less pronounced masculine features and females had less pronounced feminine features. This phenomenon is known as "endocrine disruption." If fathead minnows are altered, the same could happen to fish used for recreational fishing, like bass and catfish, and the Nebraska Department of Game and Parks is concerned about the problem. Alan and his colleagues have published studies hypothesizing that the most likely explanation is the steroids implanted in the feedlot cattle. The cattle excrete them, and when it rains they wash off into the rivers, where they have a half-life of 6 to 12 months.[37]

Although Nebraska livestock producers say that their state has some of the strictest regulations in the nation, there is very little enforcement of regulations regarding feedlots. In addition to its 4,560 cattle feedlots, Nebraska has thousands of confined pig units, and of course egg and chicken producers as well. In 1999, the Nebraska Department of Environmental Quality stated that there were 25,000 to 30,000 hog and cattle feeding operations in the state, most of which had never applied for permits from the agency, although state law had required permits since 1972. Even if these pig farms and cattle feedlots had applied for permits, the Department simply would not have had the staff to inspect more than a small fraction of them. In 1997, the Department's director testified that he had a staff of five for issuing permits and inspecting livestock-feeding operations and that they "tried" to inspect 225 of the larger operations.[38]

It's not unusual in the U.S. for state departments to lack the resources to monitor water pollution. Idaho, it seems, is in a similar position to Nebraska. Mike Bussell, director of the Environmental Protection Agency's regional office of compliance and enforcement, said that his office was going to have to start inspecting feedlots in Idaho because the Idaho State Department of Agriculture was "never able to accomplish" the basic task of producing an "overall inventory of the regulated community, so we'd know how many operations we were dealing with, and who needs to comply."[39] In Michigan, according to a regional Environmental Protection Agency report, the Department of Environmental Quality "does not conduct inspections to determine compliance by CAFQs (Concentrated Animal Feeding Operations) with permit application and other program requirements."[40]

If the untreated waste from feedlots doesn't flow directly into the streams and rivers, it will be sprayed onto fields through a center-pivot irrigation system. Manure is wet and costly to transport, so it is spread on fields close to the animal feeding operations, often in quantities too great for the soil to absorb, and in heavy rain, it runs off into the creeks. (The method of working it into the soil used by Wayne Bradley in Iowa isn't widespread because it takes more labor.) In 2002, the Nebraska Department of Environmental Quality sampled about 5,000 of the state's more than 16,000 miles of rivers and streams and found that pollution exceeded the standard for uses like recreation, aquatic life, agriculture, and drinking supply in 71 percent—a significant jump on the already alarming 58 percent found to be polluted in 2000.[41] Dennis Schueth, who manages the Upper Elkhorn Natural Resources District, told Nebraska Public Radio Network reporter and author Carolyn Johnsen: "We can be more environmentally sound if we want to pay more for our food."[42] Right. But what mechanism is supposed to bring about that outcome? Even if Jake and Lee were willing to pay more for their meat in order to protect the environment in Nebraska, how could they be sure—or even reasonably hopeful—that the extra dollars they were spending were having this effect?

As we drove back along Route 275 near West Point, Alan pointed out dozens of big containers of anhydrous ammonia—a synthetic nitrogen fertilizer. "Isn't it odd," he asked, "that all this synthetic fertilizer is being used in the midst of a feedlot region, where there is all this much better natural fertilizer available?"

Australian Beef

Raising beef doesn't have to be like this. On a visit to Australia, we met Patrick Francis, the editor of *Australian Farm Journal*, a popular farming magazine. Patrick had heard of our interest in ethical farming and invited us to look at the small beef property—in America it would be called a ranch—that he ran with his wife Anne near Romsey, in Victoria. The property was a delight to stroll around, in part because Patrick and Anne have set aside 20 percent of the land for revegetation, mostly with native eucalypts. The straightest trees will, in time, be sold for timber, but meanwhile, by storing carbon, they are making a small contribution to mitigating global warming. A recent carbon balance calculation showed that each year the farm was absorbing from the atmosphere 220 tons more carbon dioxide than it was emitting. The plantations also provide a habitat for native animals, including a mob of gray kangaroos who hopped away as we strolled by. Meanwhile, in the open fields, the cattle made a remarkable contrast to the dusty, manure-caked animals we saw in the bare Nebraska feedlots.

It was mid-April, the southern hemisphere's autumn, and there had been little rain for months, but Patrick rotates his cattle around different fields every week or two, a technique that gives the grass time to recover from grazing and ensures healthy soils and well-grassed pastures. This method eliminates the need to conserve fodder—Australian winters are mild and free of snow, and there is enough grass in the fields for the cattle to eat all year round. The rotation makes for thick pastures, which eliminates the need to use pesticides for weed control.

The day we were there coincided with one of those rotations, and we watched as Patrick moved the cattle on to the next field. He has a way of calling his cattle to him, and they follow where he leads. First among them is a particularly affectionate seven-year-old bullock—a term used for an older steer—who Patrick has kept on the farm for his leadership role in showing the newer cattle on the property what to do. (His flesh, by now, would be too tough for anything but hamburger.) The day was pleasant, and the sun had lost the sting it has at the height of summer, but once the cattle had moved into the new pasture, they soon found the shade cast by a row of cypresses, and most of them stood under the trees. Though the youngest calves were six months old, they were still keeping company with their mothers. The lives of these cattle were, it seemed, entirely comfortable. They had what cattle need: plenty of grass, clean water, shade, and their own social group.

Patrick told us that he prefers to sell his cattle direct from the farm to the slaughterhouse, but there are times of the year when he doesn't have enough grass on his pasture to get them ready to market. Then he sells them to a feedlot for short-term fattening. For the Australian domestic market, only about 25 percent of cattle are fattened in feedlots, although that percentage is growing because supermarkets prefer the greater reliability of the quality of the meat. Nevertheless, most Australian cattle are fed for only 70 days, less than half the normal period in feedlots in the U.S. For export markets—predominantly Japan and Korea, with a small amount going to the United States—cattle are generally fed for about 150 days, because consumers there have developed a taste for the marbled, fattier meat that results from fattening cattle largely on grain for a longer period of time.

Slaughter

Mammals killed for food in the U.S.—unlike chickens, ducks, and turkeys—are required by law to be stunned before being killed. No, that's not quite right: The U.S. Department of Agriculture ludicrously classifies rabbits as poultry, although they are mammals, thus allowing producers to avoid the legal requirement to stun them before slaughter. Temple Grandin surveyed American slaughterhouses to find out what percentages of animals are rendered insensible by the first application of the stun-gun. In her first survey, in 1996, only 36 percent of slaughterhouses were able to effectively stun at least 95 percent of animals on the first attempt. Six years later, 94 percent were able to do so. That is a dramatic improvement.

Nevertheless, as a General Accounting Office report to Congress on the enforcement of the Humane Methods of Slaughter Act acknowledges, despite the improvement, setting a standard of only 95 percent of animals being stunned on the first attempt "still indicates that hundreds of thousands of animals were not stunned on the first try. . . . Thus, there may be undetected instances of inhumane treatment." The report notes that there were "approximately six observations for HMSA compliance per month, or less than two observations per week, for each of the 918 plants that are covered by the act." In other words, with hundreds of animals being killed every hour, the inspectors are rarely present. When they are there, the plant operator knows it, and so what the inspectors observe may not be representative of what happens when they are absent. Even when inspectors are present and do find violations, the report found that enforcement polices were inconsistent and "inspectors often do not take enforcement action when they should."[43]

A video taken by an undercover investigator at AgriProcessors, Inc., in Postville, Iowa, during the summer of 2004 shows what can happen when inspectors are not present. AgriProcessors, Inc., is a kosher slaughterhouse, which means that it kills animals in accordance with orthodox Jewish dietary law, which forbids stunning before slaughter. In theory, in kosher slaughter animals should be killed quickly and cleanly by having their throats cut with a single slash of a sharp knife. Unconsciousness from loss of blood to the brain should follow within a few seconds. In the video, however, cattle who have had their throats cut and their tracheas removed still thrash around for a long time before they die. Some struggle to get to their feet—and even succeed in standing up. While this happens, a worker waits for the animal to collapse so that he can tie a chain around its rear leg and hoist it off the ground. One animal goes so far as to stagger through an opening into a different area of the slaughterhouse before collapsing. Two more cattle come down the killing line and have their throats cut before this one is finally hoisted off its feet and dragged away.[44]

We are not suggesting that these scenes are typical of kosher slaughter, or of American slaughter in general. But it is worth noting that AgriProcessors is the world's largest kosher slaughterhouse, and its owner has stated that "[w]hat you see on the video is not out of the ordinary." Similarly, the Orthodox Union, the world's largest kosher certifier, has defended the plant consistently and has said that the plant meets "the highest standards of Jewish law and tradition" and that its kosher status has never been in jeopardy.[45]

Since inspectors are not assigned to the point of kill in any U.S. slaughterhouses, it is probable that anyone who eats meat will, unknowingly, from time to time be eating meat that comes from an animal who died an agonizing death.   ■

NOTES

1. Christopher G. Davis and Biing-Hwan Lin, "Factors Affecting US Pork Consumption," Economic Research Service, U.S. Department of Agriculture, Outlook Report No. (LDPM13001), May 2005 <www.ers.usda.gov/publications/LDP/may05/ldpm13001/ldpm13001.pdf>.

2. Corporate Fact Sheet; Overview, Kraft Foods <http://kraft.com/profile/factsheet.html>.

3. Renee Zahery, telephone message, February 1, 2005.

4. Ronald L. Plain, "Trends in U.S. Swine Industry," paper for U.S. Meat Export Federation Pork Conference, Taipei, Taiwan, September 24, 1997 <www.ssu.missouri.edu/faculty/RPlain/papers/swine.htm>; T. Stout and G. Packer, "National Trends Reflected in Changing Ohio Swine Industry," Ohio State University Extension Research Bulletin, Special Circular 156, Agricultural Economics Department, (n.d.) <http://ohioline.osu.edu/scl56/scl56_48.html>.

5. U.S. Department of Agriculture, National Agricultural Statistics Service, Livestock Slaughter, 2004 Summary, March 2005 <http://usda.mannlib.cornell.edu/reports/nassr/livestock/pls-bban/lsan0305.pdf>. The decline in pig farm numbers averages about 7 percent per year.

6. Environmental Defense, "Factory Hog Farming: The Big Picture," November 2000 <www.environmentaldefense.org/documents/2563_FactoryHogFarmingBigPicture.pdf>.

7. Lynn Bonner, "Critics Say State Must Do More to Protect Rivers," Raleigh News & Observer, 17 August 1995; Minority Staff, U.S. Senate Committee on Agriculture, Nutrition and Forestry, "Animal Water Pollution in America: An Emerging National Problem," 105th Congress, 1st session, December 1997, p. 3. We owe these references to Carolyn Johnsen, Raising a Stink: The Struggle Over Factory Hog Farms in Nebraska, University of Nebraska Press, Lincoln, 2003, pp. 14–15.

8. Carolyn Johnsen, Raising a Stink: The Struggle Over Factory Hog Farms in Nebraska, University of Nebraska Press, Lincoln, 2003, pp. 21–26.

9. Paul Hammel, "Turning Hog Odors into Tax Deductions," Omaha World-Herald, March 5, 2002, cited in Carolyn Johnsen Raising a Stink: The Struggle Over Factory Hog Farms in Nebraska, University of Nebraska Press, Lincoln, 2003, p. 138.

10. American Public Health Association, "Precautionary Moratorium on New Concentrated Animal Feed Operations," 2003 Policy Statements, pp. 12–14 <www.apha.org/legislative/policy/2003/2003-007.pdf>.

11. Ross Clark, "If only pigs could talk," *Sunday Telegraph* (London) March 23, 1997; Roger Highfield, "Computer Skills Show Just How Smart Pigs Are," *Ottawa Citizen,* May 29, 1997. (originally published in the *Daily Telegraph,* London.)

12. David Wolfson, *Beyond the Law: Agribusiness and the Systemic Abuse of Animals Raised for Food or Food Production,* Watkins Glen, NY: Farm Sanctuary, Inc., 1999. See also "COK Talks with David Wolfson, Esq." <www.cok.net/abol/16/04.php>.

13. On the number of pigs kept indoors, see National Animal Health Monitoring System, Animal and Plant Health Inspection Service, U.S. Department of Agriculture, *Swine 2000,* Part I: Reference of Swine Health and Management in the United States, 2000, Washington, DC, 2001, p. 26. Very few total confinement systems in the U.S. use straw or any other form of bedding. <www.aphis.usda.gov/vs/ceah/ncahs/nahms/swine/swine2000/Swine2kPt1.pdf>.

14. On the number of sows in crates in the ten biggest producers, see U.S. Department of Agriculture, Agricultural Research Service, Livestock Issues Research, "Research Project: The Emerging Issue of Sow Housing," 2004 Annual Report. The overall estimate is from Glenn Grimes, professor emeritus of agricultural economics, University of Missouri, interview with Jim Mason, July 5, 2005.

15. See Scientific Veterinary Committee, Animal Welfare Section, The Welfare of Intensively Kept Pigs, 1997, and Clare Druce and Philip Lymbery, "Outlawed in Europe," in Peter Singer, ed., *In Defense of Animals: The Second Wave,* Blackwell, Oxford, 2005.

16. In the European Union, 242 million pigs were slaughtered in 2005, compared to 103 million in the U.S. See "EU output data revised," *Pig International Electronic Newsletter,* June 23, 2005, based on Eurostat information <www.wattnet.com/newsletters/Pig/htm/jun05pigenews.htm>.

17. Per Jensen, "Observations on the Maternal Behaviour of Free-Ranging Domestic Pigs" *Applied Animal Behaviour Science,* vol. 16 (1986), pp. 131–42.

18. Governor's Office of Drug Control Policy, "Iowa, METH Facts," February 23, 2005 <www.state.ia.us/government/odcp/docs/Meth_Other_Drug_Facts_Feb23.pdf>.

19. Bernard Rollin first reported on this case in his column in *Canadian Veterinary Journal,* 32:10 (October 1991), p. 584; the column is reprinted in Bernard Rollin, *Introduction to Veterinary Medical Ethics: Theory and Cases,* Blackwell, Oxford, 1999.

20. Jonathan Leake, "The Secret Lives of Moody Cows," *Sunday Times,* February 27, 2005.

21. Peter Lovenheim, *Portrait of a Burger as a Young Calf,* Three Rivers Press, New York, 2002. We are grateful to Peter Lovenheim for checking our text and clarifying some issues.

22. John Peck, "Dairy Farmer Workers Fight for Their Rights in Oregon," *Z Magazine Online,* vol. 17, no. 12 (December 2004) <http://zmagsite.zmag.org/Dec2004/peckprl204.html>; <www.braums.com/FAQ.asp#9>.

23. Eddy LaDue, Brent Gloy, and Charles Cuykendall, "Future Structure of the Dairy Industry: Historical Trends, Projections and Issues," Cornell University, Ithaca, NY, June 2003 <http://aem.cornell.edu/research/researchpdf/rb0301.pdf>, p. iii.

24. To be precise, the increase is from 665 gallons a year in 1950 to 2,365 gallons per year in 2004, an increase of 355 percent. See Erik Marcus, *Meat Market,* Brio Press, Ithaca, NY, 2005, pp. 10–11, drawing on figures from USDA National Agricultural Statistical Services, and updated from <http//usda.mannlib.cornell.edu/reports/nassr/dairy/pmp-bb/2005/mkpr0105.txt>.

25. USDA, National Animal Health Monitoring System, *Dairy 2002,* Part I: Reference of Dairy Health and Management in the United States, p. 54 <www.aphis.usda.gov/vs/ceah/ncahs/nahms/dairy/dairy02/Dairy02Pt1.Pdf>.

26. Peter Lovenheim, *Portrait of a Burger as a Young Calf*, Three Rivers Press, New York, 2002, p. 87.

27. Peter Lovenheim, *Portrait of a Burger as a Young Calf*, Three Rivers Press, New York, 2002, p. 16.

28. Oliver Sacks, *An Anthropologist on Mars*, Knopf, New York, 1995, p. 267.

29. Quoted from People for the Ethical Treatment of Animals, "Cows Grieve," <www.goveg.com/f-hiddenlivescows_giants.asp>.

30. Jon Bonné, "Can Animals You Eat Be Treated Humanely?" MSNBC News, June 28, 2004 <http://www.msnbc.com/id/5271434/>.

31. Peter Lovenheim, *Portrait of a Burger as a Young Calf*, Three Rivers Press, New York, 2002, pp. 112–113.

32. Miguel Bustillo, "In San Joaquin Valley, Cows Pass Cars as Polluters," *Los Angeles Times*, August 2, 2005.

33. Michael Pollan, "Power Steer," *The New York Times Sunday Magazine*, March 31, 2002.

34. "Researchers, McDonald's Say U.S. Govt BSE Defense Not Working," *Cattlenetwork.com*, January 4, 2006 <www.cattlenetwork.com/content.asp?contentid=16082>.

35. Chris Clayton, "More than 1250 Nebraska Cattle Died in Heat Wave," *Omaha World-Herald*, July 27, 2005.

36. F. M. Mitlöhner, et al, "Effects of shade on heat-stressed heifers housed under feedlot conditions," *Burnett Center Internet Progress Report*, no. 11, February 2001 <www.depts.ttu.edu/liru_afs/pdf/bc11.pdf>; see also F. M. Mitlöhner, et al, "Shade effects on performance, carcass traits, physiology, and behavior of heat-stressed feedlot heifers." *Journal of Animal Science*, vol. 80 (2002), pp. 2043–2050 <http://jas.fass.org/cgi/content/full/80/8/2043>.

37. A. M. Soto et al, "Androgenic and estrogenic activity in cattle feedlot effluent receiving water bodies of eastern Nebraska, USA," *Environmental Health Perspectives*, 112 (2004), pp. 346–352; E. F. Orlando et al, "Endocrine disrupting effects of cattle feedlot effluent on an aquatic sentinel species, the fathead minnow," *Environmental Health Perspectives*, 112 (2004), pp. 353–358; Janet Raloff, "Hormones: Here's the Beef," *Science News*, vol. 161 (Jan. 5, 2002), p. 10 <www.sciencenews.org/articles/20020105/bob13.asp>.

38. Carolyn Johnsen, *Raising a Stink: The Struggle Over Factory Hog Farms in Nebraska*, University of Nebraska Press, Lincoln, 2003, p. 24.

39. "EPA says it will inspect Idaho feedlots," *Cow-Calf Weekly* (BEEF), August 5, 2005.

40. U.S. Environmental Protection Agency, Region 5, *Results of an Informal Investigation of the National Pollutant Discharge Elimination System Program for Concentrated Animal Feeding Operations in the State of Michigan*, Interim Report, July 24, 2002; we owe the reference to Tony Dutzik, The State of Environmental Enforcement, CoPIRG Foundation, Denver, 2002 <www.environmentcolorado.org/reports/envenfco10_02.pdf>, which discusses the problem of lack of state environmental enforcement.

41. Nebraska Department of Environmental Quality, Water Quality Division, 2002 Nebraska Water Quality Report, Lincoln, 2002, cited by Carolyn Johnsen, *Raising a Stink: The Struggle Over Factory Hog Farms in Nebraska*, University of Nebraska Press, Lincoln, 2003, p. 138.

42. Carolyn Johnsen, *Raising a Stink: The Struggle Over Factory Hog Farms in Nebraska*, University of Nebraska Press, Lincoln, 2003, p. 122.

43. U.S. General Accounting Office, *Humane Methods of Slaughter Act*, January 2004 <www.gao.gov/new.items/d04247.pdf>.

44. "AgriProcessors," video available on the Web site of People for the Ethical Treatment of Animals <www.petatv.com/inv.html>.

45. Sholem Rubashkin, "Response." Shmais News Service, no date, <www.shmais.com/jnewsdetail.cfm?ID=148>; Department of Public Relations, Orthodox Union, "Orthodox Union Releases Industry Animal Welfare Audit of Agriprocessors," March 7, 2005 <www.ou.org/oupr/2005/agri65.htm>.

■ QUESTIONS FOR MAKING CONNECTIONS WITHIN THE READING ■

1. In "Meat and Milk Factories," Singer and Mason assume that their readers will know what is meant by an "intensive" industry. The beef, chicken, and pork industries are all described as "intensive." What does this term mean? Are each of these industries intensive in the same way?

2. Singer and Mason write that "[t]he real ethical issue about factory farming's treatment of animals isn't whether the producers are good or bad guys, but that the system seems to recognize animal suffering only when it interferes with profitability." What would an ethical system look like? How would it differ from the one in place now? Is the Australian farming system that Singer and Mason describe ethical? Is it not ultimately concerned with profitability?

3. Throughout their piece, Singer and Mason describe farm animals as experiencing maladies that overlap with human experience: the animals experience "clinical depression," "psychological stress," and "the stress of boredom." What evidence do they provide to justify these descriptions? Is there a scientific basis for such descriptions, or are Singer and Mason being metaphorical? Is the impact of their descriptions the result of the evidence they provide or of the stories they tell?

■ QUESTIONS FOR WRITING ■

1. Toward the middle of their piece, Singer and Mason pose the following parenthetical question: "Is it part of the gulf we draw between ourselves and other animals that leads farmers to talk of animals as 'farrowing' rather than 'giving birth,' 'feeding' rather than 'eating,' and 'gestating' rather than 'being pregnant'?" What is the answer to this question? If the farmers Singer and Mason describe used a different set of words, would farming practices change? Would the eating habits of American consumers change if the "gulf we draw between ourselves and other animals" were closed?

2. After their visit to "Wayne Bradley's" farm, Singer and Mason share their account of the experience with him and, seeing his words in print, he asks to have his name and location changed. Singer and Mason comply and close their discussion of pork farming by juxtaposing their assessment of the Bradley farm with the Bradleys' self-assessment. What are we to make of the fact that the assessments are diametrically opposed? What would Singer and Mason like the Bradleys to do? Can individuals—producers or consumers—change the system Singer and Mason have described?

■ *QUESTIONS FOR MAKING CONNECTIONS BETWEEN READINGS* ■

1. In "Another Look Back, and a Look Ahead," Edward Tenner describes what he terms the "revenge effects" of technology and the unintended consequences that follow from these acts of "revenge." Do you think that Tenner would be likely to share Singer and Mason's concerns about the factory farm? What revenge effects might Tenner expect to see follow from intensive farming? On balance, do the benefits of the factory farm outweigh the dangers and the ethical dilemmas posed by the way animals are treated on these farms? Is there an objective way to assess the ethical benefits and costs of this system?

2. Singer and Mason conclude their discussion of the factory farm with gruesome descriptions of the slaughtering process. The last thought they leave their readers with is this: "it is probable that anyone who eats meat will, unknowingly, from time to time be eating meat that comes from an animal who died an agonizing death." It is clear that this fact matters to Singer and Mason, but can they make it matter to all the others whose eating habits fuel the factory farming industries? In "An Army of One: *Me*," Jean Twenge asserts that "Narcissism is one of the few personality traits that psychologists agree is almost completely negative." Does narcissism play a role in eating habits? Is it fair to say that eating meat evidences a "lack of empathy," or is there an ethical way to be a carnivore?

Rebecca Solnit

IT IS NOT surprising that Rebecca Solnit, an author with far-ranging interests, would be the one to write *Wanderlust: A History of Walking* (2000). Unaffiliated with any university or other institution, Solnit has pursued her interests without regard to disciplinary, temporal, or geographical boundaries. In the words of one *Columbia Journalism Review* assessment, "irrepressible curiosity has led her to investigate and reflect on a diverse range of subjects: landscapes both rural and urban, politics, the environment, indigenous people, technology, gender, art, and photography. Each of the labels that have been used to describe her—historian, journalist, cultural theorist, critic, activist—bumps up against the others."

Prior to *Wanderlust,* Solnit wrote two books of art criticism, and another about her ancestral homeland called *A Book of Migrations: Some Passages in Ireland* (1997). The same year that she published *Wanderlust,* Solnit published *Hollow City* (2000), a book about the changing cultural landscape of her hometown, San Francisco. She later turned her attention to nineteenth-century photography and the evolution of motion-capture media technology in the award-winning *River of Shadows: Eadweard Muybridge and the Technological Wild West* (2003), which she followed up in 2004 with *Hope in the Dark,* a celebration of political protest. Solnit's wandering intellect returned to its fascination with the pathways and byways that we take in life with *A Field Guide to Getting Lost* (2005).

"The Solitary Stroller and the City," a chapter from Solnit's history of walking, explores the many elements of human experience and the many sides of human character that emerge in the course of a stroll on the city streets. "The word *street,*" Solnit points out, "has a rough, dirty magic to it. It conjures up images of transgressions and encounters that could only take place on public paths." For Solnit, streets are more than just the space left over between buildings: they constitute a vital public space that has, throughout history, served intermittently as the staging ground for revolutionary movements and the field

---

Solnit, Rebecca. "The Solitary Stroller and the City," *Wanderlust: A History of Walking*. New York: Penguin, 2001. 171–195.

Quotations come from "Room to Roam," a Q&A conducted by Peter Terzian for the July/August 2007 issue of the *Columbia Journalism Review,* <http://www.cjr.org/q_and_a/room_to_roam.php>, and from *Storming the Gates of Paradise* (U of CA Press, 2007).

for flirting young people. Though it offers its share of dangers and unsavory possibility, Solnit champions urban walking as a cultural activity of great import both in the past and in the present, when "consumption and production" are the organizing values of our cities.

"The straight line of conventional narrative," Solnit writes in the introduction to *Storming the Gates of Paradise* (2007), her most recent book, "is too often an elevated freeway permitting no unplanned encounters or necessary detours. It is not how our thoughts travel, nor does it allow us to map the whole world rather than one streamlined trajectory across it." By resisting the straight lines of such narratives, Solnit's prose mirrors the content of her books. Her cultural history of walking is just one of several demonstrations of what a mind can discover when set to wander.

The Solitary Stroller and the City

I lived in rural New Mexico long enough that when I came back home to San Francisco, I saw it for the first time as a stranger might. The exuberance of spring was urban for me that year, and I finally understood all those country songs about the lure of the bright lights of town. I walked everywhere in the balmy days and nights of May, amazed at how many possibilities could be crammed within the radius of those walks and thrilled by the idea I could just wander out the front door to find them. Every building, every storefront, seemed to open onto a different world, compressing all the variety of human life into a jumble of possibilities made all the richer by the conjunctions. Just as a bookshelf can jam together Japanese poetry, Mexican history, and Russian novels, so the buildings of my city contained Zen centers, Pentecostal churches, tattoo parlors, produce stores, burrito places, movie palaces, dim sum shops. Even the most ordinary things struck me with wonder, and the people on the street offered a thousand glimpses of lives like and utterly unlike mine.

Cities have always offered anonymity, variety, and conjunction, qualities best basked in by walking: one does not have to go into the bakery or the fortuneteller's, only to know that one might. A city always contains more than any inhabitant can know, and a great city always makes the unknown and the possible spurs to the imagination. San Francisco has long been called the most European of American cities, a comment more often made than explained. What I think its speakers mean is that San Francisco, in its scale and its street life, keeps alive the idea of a city as a place of unmediated encounters, while most American cities are becoming more and more like enlarged suburbs, scrupulously controlled and segregated, designed for the noninteractions of motorists shuttling between private places rather than the interactions of pedestrians in public ones. San Francisco has water on three sides and a ridge on the fourth to keep it from sprawling, and several neighborhoods of lively streets. Truly urban density, beautiful buildings, views of the bay and the ocean from the crests of its hills, cafés and bars everywhere, suggest different priorities for space and time than in most American cities, as does the (gentrification-threatened) tradition of artists, poets, and social and political radicals making lives about other things than getting and spending.

My first Saturday back, I sauntered over to nearby Golden Gate Park, which lacks the splendor of a wilderness but has given me many compensatory pleasures: musicians practicing in the reverberant pedestrian underpasses, old Chinese women doing martial arts in formation, strolling Russian émigrés murmuring to each other in the velvet slurp of their mother tongue, dog walkers being yanked into the primeval world of canine joys, and access by foot to the shores of the Pacific. That morning, at the park's bandshell, the local radio variety show had joined forces with the "Watershed Poetry Festival," and I watched for a while. Former poet laureate of the United States Robert Hass was coaching children to read their poetry into the microphone onstage, and some poets I knew were standing in the wings. I went up to say hello to them, and they showed me their brand-new wedding rings and introduced me to more poets, and then I ran into the great California historian Malcolm Margolin, who told me stories that made me laugh. This was the daytime marvel of cities for me: coincidences, the mingling of many kinds of people, poetry given away to strangers under the open sky.

Margolin's publishing house, Heydey Press, was displaying its wares along with those of some other small presses and literary projects, and he handed me a book off his table titled *920 O'Farrell Street*. A memoir by Harriet Lane Levy, it recounted her own marvelous experiences growing up in San Francisco in the 1870s and 1880s. In her day, walking the streets of the city was as organized an entertainment as a modern excursion to the movies. "On Saturday night," she wrote, "the city joined in the promenade on Market Street, the broad thoroughfare that begins at the waterfront and cuts its straight path of miles to Twin Peaks. The sidewalks were wide and the crowd walking toward the bay met the crowd walking toward the ocean. The outpouring of the population was spontaneous as if in response to an urge for instant celebration. Every quarter of the city discharged its residents into the broad procession. Ladies and gentlemen of imposing social repute; their German and Irish servant girls, arms held fast in the arms of their sweethearts; French, Spaniards, gaunt, hard-working Portuguese; Mexicans, the Indian showing in reddened skin and high cheekbone—everybody, anybody, left home and shop, hotel, restaurant, and beer garden to empty into Market Street in a river of color. Sailors of every nation deserted their ships at the water front and, hurrying up Market Street in groups, joined the vibrating mass excited by the lights and stir and the gaiety of the throng. 'This is San Francisco,' their faces said. It was carnival; no confetti, but the air a criss-cross of a thousand messages; no masks, but eyes frankly charged with challenge. Down Market from Powell to Kearny, three long blocks, up Kearny to Bush, three short ones, then back again, over and over for hours, until a glance of curiosity deepened to one of interest; interest expanded into a smile, and a smile into anything. Father and I went downtown every Saturday night. We walked through avenues of light in a world hardly solid. Something was happening everywhere, every minute, something to be happy about. . . . We walked and walked and still something kept happening afresh."[1] Market Street, which was once a great promenade, is still the city's central traffic artery, but decades of tearing it up and redeveloping it have deprived it of its social glory. Jack Kerouac managed to have two visions on it late in the 1940s or early in the 1950s, and he would probably embrace its freeway-shadowed midtown population of panhandlers and people running sidewalk sales out of shopping carts.[2] Levy's downtown stretch is now trod by office workers and shoppers and by tourists swarming around the Powell Street cable car turnaround; more than a mile farther uptown, Market Street finally bursts into vigorous pedestrian life again for a few blocks before it crosses Castro Street and begins its steep ascent of Twin Peaks.

The history of both urban and rural walking is a history of freedom and of the definition of pleasure. But rural walking has found a moral imperative in the love of nature that has allowed it to defend and open up the countryside. Urban walking has always been a shadier business, easily turning into soliciting, cruising, promenading, shopping, rioting, protesting, skulking, loitering, and other activities that, however enjoyable, hardly have the high moral tone of nature appreciation. Thus no similar defense has been mounted for the preservation of urban space, save by a few civil libertarians and urban theorists (who seldom note that public space is used and inhabited largely by walking it). Yet urban walking seems in many ways more like primordial hunting and gathering than walking in the country. For most of us the country or the wilderness is a place we walk through and look at, but seldom make things in or take things from (remember the famous Sierra Club dictum, "Take only photographs, leave only footprints"). In the city, the biological spectrum has been nearly reduced to the human and a few scavenger species, but the range of activities remains wide. Just as a gatherer may pause to note a tree whose acorns will be bountiful in six months or inspect a potential supply of basket canes, so an urban walker may note a grocery open late or a place to get shoes resoled, or detour by the post office. Too, the average rural walker looks at the general—the view, the beauty— and the landscape moves by as a gently modulated continuity: a crest long in view is reached, a forest thins out to become a meadow. The urbanite is on the lookout for particulars, for opportunities, individuals, and supplies, and the changes are abrupt. Of course the city resembles primordial life more than the country in a less charming way too; while nonhuman predators have been radically reduced in North America and eliminated in Europe, the possibility of human predators keeps city dwellers in a state of heightened alertness, at least in some times and places.

Those first months at home were so enchanting that I kept a walking journal and later that glorious summer wrote, "I suddenly realized I'd spent seven hours at the desk without a real interruption and was getting nervous and hunchbacked, walked to the Clay Theater on upper Fillmore via a passage on Broderick I'd never seen before—handsome squat old Victorians near the housing projects—and was pleased as ever when the familiar yielded up the unknown. The film was *When the Cat's Away*, about a solitary young Parisienne forced to meet her Place de Bastille neighbors when her cat vanishes, full of uneventful events and people with seesaw strides and rooftops and mumbling slang, and when it got out I was exhilarated and the night was dark with a pearly mist of fog on it. I walked back fast, first along California, past a couple—her unexceptional, him in a well-tailored brown suit with the knock knees of someone who'd spent time in leg braces—and ignored the bus, and did the same on Divisadero with that bus. Slowed down at an antique store window to look at a big creamy vase with blue Chinese sages painted on it, then a few doors down saw a balding Chinese man holding a toddler boy up to the glass of a store, where a woman on the inside was playing with him through the glass. To their confusion, I beamed. There's a way the artificial lights and natural darkness of nightwalks turn the day's continuum into a theater of tableaux, vignettes, set pieces, and there's always the unsettling pleasure of your shadow growing and shrinking as you move from streetlight to streetlight. Dodging a car as a traffic light changed, I broke into a canter and it felt so good I loped along a few more blocks without getting winded, though I got warm.

"All along Divisadero keeping an eye on the other people and on the open venues—liquor stores and smoke shops—and then turned up my own street. At a cross street a young black guy in a watch cap and dark clothes was running downhill at me at a great clip, and I looked around to suss up my options just in case—I mean if Queen Victoria was moving toward you that fast you'd take note. He saw my hesitation and assured me in the sweetest young man's voice, 'I'm not after you, I'm just *late*' and dashed past me, so I said, 'Good luck' and then, when he was into the street and I had time to collect my thoughts, 'Sorry to look suspicious, but you were kind of speedy.' He laughed, and then I did, and in a minute I recalled all the other

encounters I'd had around the 'hood lately that might have had the earmarks of trouble but unfolded as pure civility and was pleased that I'd been
prepared without being alarmed. At that moment, I looked up and saw in a
top-floor window the same poster of Man Ray's *A l'heure de l'observatoire*—
his painting of the sunset sky with the long red lips floating across it—that
I'd seen in another window somewhere else in town a night or two before.
This poster was bigger, and this night was more exuberant; seeing *A l'heure*
twice seemed magic. Home in about twenty minutes at most."

Streets are the space left over between buildings. A house alone is an island
surrounded by a sea of open space, and the villages that preceded cities
were no more than archipelagos in that same sea. But as more and more
buildings arose, they became a continent, the remaining open space no
longer like the sea but like rivers, canals, and streams running between the
land masses. People no longer moved anyhow in the open sea of rural space
but traveled up and down the streets, and just as narrowing a waterway increases flow and speed, so turning open space into the spillways of streets
directs and intensifies the flood of walkers. In great cities, spaces as well
as places are designed and built: walking, witnessing, being in public, are as
much part of the design and purpose as is being inside to eat, sleep, make
shoes or love or music. The word *citizen* has to do with cities, and the ideal
city is organized around citizenship—around participation in public life.

   Most American cities and towns, however, are organized around consumption and production, as were the dire industrial cities of England, and
public space is merely the void between workplaces, shops, and dwellings.
Walking is only the beginning of citizenship, but through it the citizen
knows his or her city and fellow citizens and truly inhabits the city rather
than a small privatized part thereof. Walking the streets is what links up
reading the map with living one's life, the personal microcosm with the
public macrocosm; it makes sense of the maze all around. In her celebrated
Death and Life of Great American Cities, Jane Jacobs describes how a popular,
well-used street is kept safe from crime merely by the many people going by.[3]
Walking maintains the publicness and viability of public space. "What distinguishes the city," writes Franco Moretti, "is that its spatial structure (basically its concentration) is functional to the intensification of mobility: spatial
mobility, naturally enough, but mainly social mobility."[4]

   The very word *street* has a rough, dirty magic to it, summoning up the
low, the common, the erotic, the dangerous, the revolutionary. A man of the
streets is only a populist, but a woman of the streets is, like a streetwalker, a
seller of her sexuality. Street kids are urchins, beggars, and runaways, and the
new term *street person* describes those who have no other home. *Street-smart*
means someone wise in the ways of the city and well able to survive in it,
while "to the streets" is the classic cry of urban revolution, for the streets are
where people become the public and where their power resides. *The street*

means life in the heady currents of the urban river in which everyone and everything can mingle. It is exactly this social mobility, this lack of compartments and distinctions, that gives the street its danger and its magic, the danger and magic of water in which everything runs together.

In feudal Europe only city dwellers were free of the hierarchical bonds that structured the rest of society—in England, for example, a serf could become free by living for a year and a day in a free town. The quality of freedom within cities then was limited, however, for their streets were usually dirty, dangerous, and dark. Cities often imposed a curfew and closed their gates at sunset. Only in the Renaissance did the cities of Europe begin to improve their paving, their sanitation, and their safety. In eighteenth-century London and Paris, going out anywhere at night was as dangerous as the worst slums are supposed to be nowadays, and if you wanted to see where you were going, you hired a torchbearer (and the young London torch carriers—link boys, they were called—often doubled as procurers). Even in daylight, carriages terrorized pedestrians. Before the eighteenth century, few seem to have walked these streets for pleasure, and only in the nineteenth century did places as clean, safe, and illuminated as modern cities begin to emerge. All the furniture and codes that give modern streets their orderliness—raised sidewalks, streetlights, street names, building numbers, drains, traffic rules, and traffic signals—are relatively recent innovations.

Idyllic spaces had been created for the urban rich—tree-lined promenades, semipublic gardens and parks. But these places that preceded the public park were anti-streets, segregated by class and disconnected from everyday life (unlike the pedestrian *corsos* and paseos of the plazas and squares of Mediterranean and Latin countries and Levy's Market Street promenade—or London's anomalous Hyde Park, which accommodated both carriage promenades for the rich and open-air oratory for the radical). Though politics, flirtations, and commerce might be conducted in them, they were little more than outdoor salons and ballrooms.[5] And from the mile-long Cours de la Reine built in Paris in 1616 to Mexico City's Alameda to New York's Central Park built during the 1850s, such places tended to attract people whose desire to display their wealth was better served by promenading in carriages than walking. On the Cours de la Reine, the carriages would gather so thickly a traffic jam would result, which may be why in 1700 a fashion for getting out and dancing by torchlight on the central round developed.

Though Central Park was shaped by more-or-less democratic impulses, English landscape garden aesthetics, and the example of Liverpool's public park, poor New Yorkers often paid to go to private parks akin to Vauxhall Gardens instead, where they might drink beer, dance the polka, or otherwise engage in plebeian versions of pleasure. Even those who wished only to have an uplifting stroll, as the park's codesigner Frederick Law Olmsted had intended them to, found obstacles. Central Park became a great promenade for the rich, and once again carriages segregated the society. In their history of the park and its city, Ray Rosenzweig and Elizabeth Blackmar write, "Earlier in the [nineteenth] century the late afternoon, early evening, and Sunday promenades of affluent New Yorkers had evolved into parades of high fashion; the wide thoroughfares of Broadway, the Battery, and Fifth Avenue had become a public setting in which to see and be seen. By midcentury, however, the fashionable Broadway and Battery promenades had declined as 'respectable' citizens lost control over these public spaces. . . . Both men and women wanted grander public space for a new form of public promenading—by carriage. In the mid-nineteenth century, carriage ownership was becoming a defining feature of urban upper-class status." The rich went to Central Park, and a populist journalist said, "I hear that pedestrians have acquired a bad habit of being accidentally run over in that neighborhood."[6]

Just as poorer people continued to promenade in New York's Battery, so their Parisian counterparts strolled along the peripheries of the city, often under avenues of trees planted to shade just such excursions. After the Revolution, Paris's Tuileries could be entered by anyone the guards deemed properly dressed. Private pleasure gardens modeled after London's famous Vauxhall Gardens, including Ranelagh and Cremorne Gardens in London itself; Vienna's Augarten; New York's Elysian Fields, Castle Gardens, and Harlem Gardens; and Copenhagen's Tivoli Gardens (sole survivor of them all) sorted out people by the simpler criterion of ability to pay. Elsewhere in these cities, markets, fairs, and processions brought festivity to the sites of everyday life, and the stroll was not so segregated. To me, the magic of the street is the mingling of the errand and the epiphany, and no such gardens seem to have flourished in Italy, perhaps because they were unneeded.

Italian cities have long been held up as ideals, not least by New Yorkers and Londoners enthralled by the ways their architecture gives beauty and meaning to everyday acts. Since at least the seventeenth century, foreigners have been moving there to bask in the light and the life. Bernard Rudofsky, nominally a New Yorker, spent a good deal of time in Italy and sang its praises in his 1969 *Streets for People: A Primer for Americans*. For those who consider New York the exemplary American pedestrian city, Rudofsky's conviction that it is abysmal is startling. His book uses primarily Italian examples to demonstrate the ways plazas and streets can function to tie a city together socially and architecturally. "It simply never occurs to us to make streets into oases rather than deserts," he says at the beginning. "In countries where their function has not yet deteriorated into highways and parking lots, a number of arrangements make streets fit for humans. . . . The most refined street coverings, a tangible expression of civic solidarity—or, should one say, of philanthropy, are arcades. Apart from lending unity to the streetscape, they often take the place of the ancient forums."[7] Descendants of the Greek stoa and *peripatos*, arcaded streets blur the boundaries between inside and out and pay architectural tribute to the pedestrian life that takes place beneath them. Rudofsky singles out Bologna's famous *portici*, a four-mile-long covered walkway running from the central square to the countryside; Milan's Galleria, less strictly commercial in its functions than the upscale shopping malls modeled and named after it; the winding streets of Perugia; the car-free streets of Siena; and Brisinghella's second-story public arcades. He writes with passionate enthusiasm about the Italian predinner stroll—the *passaggiata*—for which many towns close down their main streets to wheeled traffic, contrasting it with the American cocktail hour. For Italians, he says, the street is the pivotal social space, for meeting, debating, courting, buying, and selling.

The New York dance critic Edwin Denby wrote, about the same time as Rudofsky, of his own appreciation of Italian walkers. "In ancient Italian towns the narrow main street at dusk becomes a kind of theatre. The community strolls affably and looks itself over. The girls and the young men, from fifteen to twenty-two, display their charm to one another with a lively sociability. The more grace they show the better the community likes them. In Florence or in Naples, in the ancient city slums the young people are virtuoso performers, and they do a bit of promenading any time they are not busy." Of young Romans, he wrote, "Their stroll is as responsive as if it were a physical conversation." Elsewhere, he instructs dance students to watch the walk of various types: "Americans occupy a much larger space than their actual bodies do. This annoys many Europeans; it annoys their instinct of modesty. But it has a beauty of its own, that a few of them appreciate. . . . For myself I think the walk of New Yorkers is amazingly beautiful, so large and clear."[8] In Italy walking in the city is a universal cultural activity rather than the subject of individual forays and accounts. From Dante pacing out his exile in Verona and Ravenna to Primo Levi walking home from Auschwitz, Italy has not lacked great walkers—but urban walking itself seems to be more part of a universal culture than the focus of particular experience (save that by foreigners, copiously recorded, and the cinematic strolls of such characters as the streetwalker in Federico Fellini's *Nights of Cabiria* and the protagonists in Vittorio De Sica's *Bicycle Thief* and in many of Michelangelo Antonioni's films). However, the cities that are neither so accommodating as Naples nor so forbidding as Los Angeles—London, New York—have produced their own fugitive culture of walking. In London, from the eighteenth century on, the great accounts of walking have to do not with the cheerful and open display of ordinary life and desires but with nocturnal scenes, crimes, sufferings, outcasts, and the darker side of the imagination, and it is this tradition that New York assumes.

In 1711 the essayist Joseph Addison wrote, "When I am in a serious Humour, I very often walk by my self in Westminster Abbey; where the Gloominess of the Place, and the Use to which it is applied . . . are apt to fill the Mind with a kind of Melancholy, or rather Thoughtfulness, that is not disagreeable."[9] At the time he wrote, walking the city streets was perilous, as John Gay pointed out in his 1716 poem *Trivia, or, The Art of Walking the Streets of London*. Travel through the city was as dangerous as cross-country travel: the streets were full of sewage and garbage, many of the trades were filthy, the air was already bad, cheap gin had ravaged the city's poor the way crack did American inner cities in the 1980s, and an underclass of criminals and desperate souls thronged the streets. Carriages jostled and mangled pedestrians without fear of reprisal, beggars solicited passersby, and street sellers called out their wares. The accounts of the time are full of the fears of the wealthy to go out at all and of young women lured or forced into sexual labor: prostitutes were everywhere. This is why Gay focuses on urban walking as an *art*—an art of protecting oneself from splashes, assaults, and indignities:

> Though you through cleanlier allies wind by day,
> To shun the hurries of the publick way,
> Yet ne'er to those dark paths by night retire;
> Mind only safety, and contemn the mire.[10]

Like Dr. Johnson's 1738 poem "London," Gay's *Trivia* uses a classical model to mock the present. Divided into three books—the first on the implements and techniques of walking the streets, the second on walking by day, the third on walking by night—the poem makes it clear that the minutiae of everyday life can only be observed scornfully. The high-flown style cannot but contrast abrasively with such small subjects, with something of the same mockery he brought to his *Beggars' Opera*. Gay tries—

> Here I remark each walker's diff'rent face,
> And in their look their various bus'ness trace.[11]

—but he ends by despising everyone, assuming he can read their tawdry lives in their faces. At the end of Gay's century Wordsworth "goes forward with the crowd," seeing a mystery in the face of each stranger;[12] while William Blake wanders "each charter'd street/And mark in every face I meet/Marks of weakness, marks of woe:"—the cry of a chimney sweep, the curse of a young harlot.[13] Earlier eighteenth-century literary language was not supple enough or personal enough to connect the life of the imagination to that of the street. Johnson had been one of those desperate London walkers in his early years there—in the late 1730s, when he and his friend, the poet and rogue Richard Savage, were too poor to pay for lodgings, they used to walk the streets and squares all night talking insurrection and glory—but he didn't write about it.[14] Boswell did in his *Life of Johnson*, but for Boswell, the darkness of night and anonymity of the streets were a less reflective opportunity, as his London diary records: "I should have been at Lady Northumberland's rout tonight, but my barber fell sick [meaning his hair was not properly powdered]; so I sallied to the streets, and just at the bottom of our own, I picked up a fresh, agreeable young girl called Alice Gibbs. We went down a lane to a snug place. . . ."[15] Of Alice Cibbs's impression of the streets and the night, we have no record.

That few women other than prostitutes were free to wander the streets and that wandering the street was often enough to cause a woman to be considered a prostitute are matters troubling enough to be taken up elsewhere. Here I merely want to comment on their presence in the street and in the night, habitats in which they more than almost any other kind of walker became natives. Until the twentieth century women seldom walked the city for their own pleasure, and prostitutes have left us almost no records of their experience. The eighteenth century was immodest enough to have a few famous novels about prostitutes, but Fanny Hill's courtesan life was all indoors, Moll Flanders's was entirely practical, and both of them were creations of male authors whose work was at least partly speculative. Then as now, however, a complex culture of working the streets must have existed, each city mapped according to safety and the economics of male desire. There have been many attempts to confine such activity; Byzantine-era Constantinople had its "street of harlots," Tokyo from the seventeenth to the twentieth century had a gated pleasure district, nineteenth-century San Francisco had its notorious Barbary Coast, and many turn-of-the-century American cities had red-light districts, the most famous of which was New Orleans's Storyville, where jazz is reputed to have been born. But prostitution wandered outside these bounds, and the population of such women was enormous: 50,000 in 1793, when London had a total population of one million, estimated one expert.[16] By the mid-nineteenth century they were to be found in the most fashionable parts of London too: social reformer Henry Mayhew's report refers to "the circulating harlotry of the Haymarket and Regent Street," as well as to the women working in the city's parks and promenades.[17]

Twenty-odd years ago a researcher on prostitution reported, "Prostitution streetscapes are composed of *strolls*, loosely defined areas where the women solicit. . . . On the stroll the prostitute moves around to entice or enjoin customers, reduce boredom, keep warm and reduce visibility [to the police]. Part of most streetscapes resemble common greens, areas to which all have unimpeded access. Here women assemble in groups of two to four, laughing, talking and joking among themselves. . . . Working the same stroll infuses much needed predictability into an illegal, sometimes dangerous environment."[18] And Dolores French, an advocate for prostitutes' rights, worked the streets herself and reports that her fellow streetwalkers "think that women who work in whorehouses have too many restrictions and rules" while the street "welcomed everyone democratically. . . . They felt they were like cowboys out on the range, or spies on a dangerous mission. They bragged about how free they were. . . . They had no one to answer to but themselves."[19] The same refrains—freedom, democracy, danger—come up in this as in the other ways of occupying the streets.

In the eighteenth-century city, a new image of what it means to be human had arisen, an image of one possessed of the freedom and isolation of the traveler, and travelers, however wide or narrow their scope, became emblematic figures. Richard Savage proposed this early with a 1729 poem called *The Wanderer*, and the aptly named George Walker inaugurated the new century with his novel *The Vagabond*, followed in 1814 by Fanny Burney's *Wanderer*. Wordsworth had his *Excursion* (whose first two sections were titled "The Wanderer" and "The Solitary"); Coleridge's Ancient Mariner was condemned like the Wandering Jew to roam; and the Wandering Jew himself was a popular subject for Romantics in Britain and on the continent.

The literary historian Raymond Williams remarks, "Perception of the new qualities of the modern city had been associated, from the beginning, with a man walking, as if alone, in its streets."[20] He cites Blake and Wordsworth as founders of this tradition, but it was De Quincey who wrote of it most poignantly. In the beginning of *Confessions of an English Opium Eater*, De Quincey tells of how at the age of seventeen he had run away from a dull school and his unsympathetic guardians and landed in London. There he was afraid to contact the few people he knew and unable to seek work without connections. So for sixteen weeks in the summer and fall of 1802 he starved, having found no other support in London but a home in an all-but-abandoned mansion whose other resident was a forlorn female child. He fell into a spectral existence shared with a few other children, and he wandered the streets restlessly. Streets were already a place for those who had no place, a site to measure sorrow and loneliness in the length of walks. "Being myself at that time, of necessity, a peripatetic, or walker of the streets, I naturally fell in more frequently with those female peripatetics who are technically called street-walkers. Many of these women had occasionally taken my part against watchmen who wished to drive me off the steps of houses where I was sitting." He was befriended by one, a girl named Ann—"timid and dejected to a degree which showed how deeply sorrow had taken hold of her young heart"—who was younger than he and who had turned to the streets after being cheated of a minor inheritance. Once when they were "pacing slowly along Oxford Street, and after a day when I had felt unusually ill and faint, I requested her to turn off with me into Soho Square," and he fainted. She spent what little she had on hot spiced wine to revive him. That he was never able to find her again after his fortune changed was, he declares, one of the great tragedies of his life. For De Quincey, his sojourn in London was one of the most deeply felt passages in his long life, though it had no sequel: the rest of his book is given over to its putative subject, the effects of opium, and the rest of his life to rural places.[21]

Charles Dickens was different, in that he chose such urban walking and his writing explored it thoroughly over the years. He is the great poet of

London life, and some of his novels seem as much dramas of place as of people. Think of *Our Mutual Friend*, where the great euphemistic piles of dust, the dim taxidermy and skeleton shop, the expensively icy interiors of the wealthy, are portraits of those associated with them. People and places become one another—a character may only be identified as an atmosphere or a principle, a place may take on a full-fledged personality. "And this kind of realism can only be gained by walking dreamily in a place; it cannot be gained by walking observantly," wrote one of his best interpreters, C. K. Chesterton. He attributed Dickens's acute sense of place to the well-known episode in his boyhood when his father was locked up in a debtor's prison and Dickens himself was put to work in a blacking factory and lodged in a nearby roominghouse, a desolate child abandoned to the city and its strangers. "Few of us understand the street," Chesterton writes. "Even when we step into it, we step into it doubtfully, as into a house or room of strangers. Few of us see through the shining riddle of the street, the strange folk that belong to the street only—the street-walker or the street arab, the nomads who, generation after generation have kept their ancient secrets in the full blaze of the sun. Of the street at night many of us know less. The street at night is a great house locked up. But Dickens had, if ever man had, the key of the street. . . . He could open the inmost door of his house—the door that leads onto the secret passage which is lined with houses and roofed with stars." Dickens is among the first to indicate all the other things urban walking can be: his novels are full of detectives and police inspectors, of criminals who stalk, lovers who seek and damned souls who flee. The city becomes a tangle through which all the characters wander in a colossal game of hide and seek, and only a vast city could allow his intricate plots so full of crossed paths and overlapping lives. But when he wrote about his own experiences of London, it was often an abandoned city.[22]

"If I couldn't walk fast and far, I should explode and perish," he once told a friend, and he walked so fast and far that few ever managed to accompany him. He was a solitary walker, and his walks served innumerable purposes.[23] "I am both a town traveller and a country traveller, and am always on the road," he introduces himself in his essay collection *The Uncommercial Traveller*. "Figuratively speaking, I travel for the great house of Human Interest Brothers, and have rather a large connection in the fancy goods way. Literally speaking, I am always wandering here and there from my rooms in Covent-garden, London." This metaphysical version of the commercial traveler is an inadequate description of his role, and he tried on many others.[24] He was an athlete: "So much of my travelling is done on foot, that if I cherished better propensities, I should probably be found registered in sporting newspapers under some such title as the Elastic Novice, challenging all eleven stone mankind to competition in walking. My last special feat was turning out of bed at two, after a hard day, pedestrian and otherwise, and walking thirty miles into the country to breakfast. The road was so lonely in the night that I fell asleep to the monotonous sound of my own feet, doing their regular four miles an hour." And a few essays later, he was a tramp, or a tramp's son: "My walking is of two kinds: one straight on end to a definite goal at a round pace; one, objectless, loitering, and purely vagabond. In the latter state, no gypsy on earth is a greater vagabond than myself; it is so natural to me, and strong with me, that I think I must be the descendant, at no great distance, of some irreclaimable tramp."[25] And he was a cop on the beat, too ethereal to arrest anyone but in his mind: "It is one of my fancies, that even my idlest walk must always have its appointed destination. . . . On such an occasion, it is my habit to regard my walks as my beat, and myself as a higher sort of police-constable doing duty on the same."[26]

And yet despite all these utilitarian occupations and the throngs who populate his books, his own London was often a deserted city, and his walking in it a melancholy pleasure. In an essay on visiting abandoned cemeteries, he wrote, "Whenever I think I deserve particularly well of myself, and have earned the right to enjoy a little treat, I stroll from Covent-garden into the City of London, after business-hours there, on a Saturday, or—better yet—on a Sunday, and roam about its deserted nooks and corners."[27] But the most memorable of them all is "Night Walks," the essay that begins, "Some years ago, a temporary inability to sleep, referable to a distressing impression, caused me to walk about the streets all night, for a series of several nights." He described these walks from midnight till dawn as curative of his distress, and during them "I finished my education in a fair amateur experience of houselessness"—or what is now called homelessness. The city was no longer as dangerous as it had been in Gay's and Johnson's time, but it was lonelier. Eighteenth-century London was crowded, lively, full of predators, spectacles, and badinage between strangers. By the time Dickens was writing about houselessness in 1860, London was many times as large, but the mob so feared in the eighteenth century had in the nineteenth been largely domesticated as the crowd, a quiet, drab mass going about its private business in public: "Walking the streets under the pattering rain, Houselessness would walk and walk and walk, seeing nothing but the interminable tangle of streets, save at a corner, here and there, two policemen in conversation, or the sergeant or inspector looking after his men. Now and then in the night—but rarely—Houselessness would become aware of a furtive head peering out of a doorway a few yards before him, and, coming up with the head, would find a man standing bolt upright to keep within the doorway's shadow, and evidently intent upon no particular service to society. . . . The wild moon and clouds were as restless as an evil conscience in a tumbled bed, and the very shadow of the immensity of London seemed to lie oppressively upon the river." And yet he relishes the lonely nocturnal streets, as he does the graveyards and "shy neighborhoods" and what he quixotically called "Arcadian London"—London out of season, when society had gone en masse to the country, leaving the city in sepulchural peace.[28]

There is a subtle state most dedicated urban walkers know, a sort of basking in solitude—a dark solitude punctuated with encounters as the night sky is punctuated with stars. In the country one's solitude is geographical—one is altogether outside society, so solitude has a sensible geographical explanation, and then there is a kind of communion with the nonhuman. In the city, one is alone because the world is made up of strangers, and to be a stranger surrounded by strangers, to walk along silently bearing one's secrets and imagining those of the people one passes, is among the starkest of luxuries. This uncharted identity with its illimitable possibilities is one of the distinctive qualities of urban living, a liberatory state for those who come to emancipate themselves from family and community expectation, to experiment with subculture and identity. It is an observer's state, cool, withdrawn, with senses sharpened, a good state for anybody who needs to reflect or create. In small doses melancholy, alienation, and introspection are among life's most refined pleasures.

Not long ago I heard the singer and poet Patti Smith answer a radio interviewer's question about what she did to prepare for her performances onstage with "I would roam the streets for a few hours."[29] With that brief comment she summoned up her own outlaw romanticism and the way such walking might toughen and sharpen the sensibility, wrap one in an isolation out of which might come songs fierce enough, words sharp enough, to break that musing silence. Probably her roaming the streets didn't work so well in a lot of American cities, where the hotel was moated by a parking lot surrounded by six-lane roads without sidewalks, but she spoke as a New Yorker. Speaking as a Londoner, Virginia Woolf described anonymity as a fine and desirable thing, in her 1930 essay "Street Haunting." Daughter of the great alpinist Leslie Stephen, she had once declared to a friend, "How could I think mountains and climbing romantic? Wasn't I brought up with alpenstocks in my nursery, and a raised map of the Alps, showing every peak my father had climbed? Of course, London and the marshes are the places I like best."[30] London had more than doubled in size since Dickens's night walks, and the streets had changed again to become a refuge. Woolf wrote of the confining oppression of one's own identity, of the way the objects in one's home "enforce the memories of our own experience." And so she set out to buy a pencil in a city where safety and propriety were no longer considerations for a no-longer-young woman on a winter evening, and in recounting—or inventing—her journey, wrote one of the great essays on urban walking.[31]

"As we step out of the house on a fine evening between four and six," she wrote, "we shed the self our friends know us by and become part of that vast republican army of anonymous trampers, whose society is so agreeable after the solitude of one's room." Of the people she observes she says, "Into each of these lives one could penetrate a little way, far enough to give one the illusion that one is not tethered to a single mind, but can put on briefly for a few minutes the bodies and minds of others. One could become a washerwoman, a publican, a street singer." In this anonymous state, "the shell-like covering which our souls have excreted for themselves, to make for themselves a shape distinct from others, is broken, and there is left of all these wrinkles and roughnesses a central oyster of perceptiveness, an enormous eye. How beautiful a street is in winter! It is at once revealed and obscured."[32] She walked down the same Oxford Street De Quincey and Ann had, now lined with windows full of luxuries with which she furnished an imaginary house and life and then banished both to return to her walk. The language of introspection that Wordsworth helped develop and De Quincey and Dickens refined was her language, and the smallest incidents—birds rustling in the shrubbery, a dwarf woman trying on shoes—let her imagination roam farther than her feet, into digressions from which she reluctantly returns to the actualities of her excursion. Walking the streets had come into its own, and the solitude and introspection that had been harrowing for her predecessors was a joy for her. That it was a joy because her identity had become a burden makes it modern.

Like London, New York has seldom prompted unalloyed praise. It is too big, too harsh. As one who knows only smaller cities intimately, I continually underestimate its expanse and wear myself out on distances, just as I do by car in Los Angeles. But I admire Manhattan: the synchronized beehive dance of Grand Central Station, the fast pace people set on the long grids of streets, the jay-walkers, the slower strollers in the squares, the dark-skinned nannies pushing pallid babies before them through the gracious paths of Central Park. Wandering without a clear purpose or sense of direction, I have often disrupted the fast flow of passersby intent on some clear errand or commute, as though I were a butterfly strayed into the beehive, a snag in the stream. Two-thirds of all journeys around downtown and midtown Manhattan are still made on foot, and New York, like London, remains a city of people walking for practical purposes, pouring up and down subway stairs, across intersections—but musers and the nocturnal strollers move to a different tempo.[33] Cities make walking into true travel: danger, exile, discovery, transformation, wrap all around one's home and come right up to the doorstep.

The Italophile Rudofsky uses London to scorn New York: "On the whole North America's Anglo-Saxomania has had a withering effect on its formative years. Surely, the English are not a desirable model for an urban society. No other nation developed such a fierce devotion to country life as they did. And with good reason; their cities have been traditionally among Europe's least wholesome. Englishmen may be intensely loyal to their towns, but the street—the very gauge of urbanity—does not figure large in their affections."[34] New York's streets do figure large in the work of some of its writers. "Paris, c'est une blonde," goes the French song, and Parisian poets have often made their city a woman. New York, with its gridded layout, its dark buildings and looming skyscrapers, its famous toughness, is a masculine city, and if cities are muses, it is no wonder this one's praises have been sung best by its gay poets—Walt Whitman, Frank O'Hara, Allen Ginsberg, and the prose-poet David Wojnarowicz (though everyone from Edith Wharton to Patti Smith has paid homage to this city and its streets).

In Whitman's poems, though he often speaks of himself as happy in the arms of a lover, the passages in which he appears as a solitary walking the streets in quest of that lover—a precursor of the gay cruiser—ring more true. In "Recorders Ages Hence," the immodest Whitman states for the record that he was one "Who often walk'd lonesome walks thinking of his dear friends, his lovers."[35] A few poems later in the final version of *Leaves of Grass,* he begins another poem with the oratorical address "City of orgies, walks and joys." After listing all the possible criteria for a city's illustriousness—houses, ships, parades—he chooses "not these, but as I pass O Manhattan, your frequent and swift flash of eyes offering me love": the walks rather than the orgies, the promises rather than the delivery, are the joys.[36] Whitman was a great maker of inventories and lists to describe variety and quantity and one of the first to love the crowd. It promised new liaisons; it expressed his democratic ideals and oceanic enthusiasms. A few poems past "City of Orgies" comes "To a Stranger": "Passing stranger! You do not know how longingly I look upon you. . . ."[37] For Whitman the momentary glimpse and the intimacy of love were complementary, as were his own emphatic ego and the anonymous mass of crowds. Thus he sang the praises of the swelling metropolis of Manhattan and the new possibilities of urban scale.

Whitman died in 1892, just as everyone else was beginning to celebrate the city. For the first half of the new century, the city seemed emblematic—the capital of the twentieth century, as Paris had been of the nineteenth century. Destiny and hope were urban for both radicals and plutocrats in those days, and New York with its luxury steamers docking and immigrants pouring off Ellis Island, with its skyscrapers even Georgia O'Keeffe couldn't resist painting during her time as a New Yorker, was the definitive modern city. In the 1920s a magazine was devoted to it, the *New Yorker,* whose Talk of the Town section compiled minor street incidents made incandescent by its writers in the tradition of eighteenth-century London's *Spectator* and *Rambler* essays, and it had jazz and the Harlem Renaissance uptown and radical Bohemia down in the Village (and in Central Park was the Ramble, an area so well known for gay cruising it was nicknamed "the fruited plain").[38] Before World War II, Berenice Abbott roamed New York's streets photographing buildings, and after it, Helen Levitt photographed children playing in the streets while Weegee photographed the underworld of fresh corpses on sidewalks and prostitutes in paddy wagons. One imagines them wandering purposefully like hunter-gatherers with the camera a sort of basket laden with the day's spectacles, the photographers leaving us not their walks, as poets do, but the fruits of those walks. Whitman, however, had no successor until after the war, when Allen Ginsberg stepped into his shoes, or at least his loose long lines of celebratory ranting.

Ginsberg is sometimes claimed as a San Franciscan, and he found his poetic voice during his time there and in Berkeley in the 1950s, but he is a New York poet, and the cities of his poems are big, harsh cities. He and his peers were passionate urbanists at a time when the white middle class was abandoning city life for the suburbs (and though many of the so-called Beats gathered in San Francisco, most wrote poetry about things more personal or more general than the streets they thronged, or used the city as a gateway to Asia and the western landscape). He did write about suburbs, notably in his "Supermarket in California," in which he summoned up a supermarket where the abundance of produce and shopping families makes wry comedy of the dead gay poets—Whitman and Federico García Lorca (a New Yorker from 1929 to 1930)—cruising the aisles. But otherwise his early poems burst with snow, tenements, and the Brooklyn Bridge. Ginsberg walked considerably in San Francisco and in New York, but in his poems walking is always turning into something else, since the sidewalk is always turning into a bed or a Buddhist paradise or some other apparition. The best minds of his generation were "dragging themselves through the negro streets at dawn looking for an angry fix," but they immediately commenced to see angels staggering on tenement roofs, eat fire, hallucinate Arkansas and Blake-light tragedy, and so on, even if they did afterward stumble to unemployment offices and walk "all night with their shoes full of blood on the snowbank docks waiting for a door in the East River to open. . . ."[39]

For the Beats, motion or travel was enormously important, but its exact nature was not (save for Snyder, the true peripatetic of the bunch). They caught the tail end of the 1930s romance of freighthoppers, hobos, and railroad yards, they led the way to the new car culture in which restlessness was assuaged by hundreds of miles at 70 m.p.h. rather than dozens at 3 or 4 on foot, and they blended such physical travel with chemically induced ramblings of the imagination and a whole new kind of rampaging language. San Francisco and New York seem pedestrian anchors on either side of the long rope of the open road they traveled. In the same mode, one can see the shift in country ballads: sometime in the 1950s disappointed lovers stopped walking away or catching the midnight train and began driving, and by the 1970s the apotheosis of eighteen-wheeler songs had arrived. Had he lived that long, Kerouac would've loved them. Only in the first section of *Kaddish*, when Ginsberg gives over singing of his generation and his pals to mourn his mother, do the act and the place remain particular. The streets are repositories of history, walking a way to read that history. "Strange now to think of you, gone without corsets & eyes, while I walk on the sunny pavement of Greenwich Village,"[40] it opens, and as he walks Seventh Avenue he thinks of Naomi Ginsberg in the Lower East Side, "where you walked 50 years ago, little girl—from Russia / . . . then struggling in the crowds of Orchard Street toward what? /—toward Newark—" in an antiphony of her city and his, joined in later sections by their shared experiences during his childhood.[41]

Handsome as a marble statue, Frank O'Hara was as unlike Ginsberg as a gay poet born the same year could be, and he wrote about far more delicate diurnal adventures. Ginsberg's poetry was oratorical—jeremiads and hymns to be shouted from the rooftops; O'Hara's poetry is as casual as conversation and sequenced by strolls in the street (among his book titles are *Lunch Poems*—not about eating but about lunchtime excursions from his job at the Museum of Modern Art—*Second Avenue,* and the essay collection *Standing Still and Walking in New York*). While Ginsberg tended to speak to America, O'Hara's remarks often addressed a "you" who seemed to be an absent lover in a silent soliloquy or a companion on a stroll. The painter Larry Rivers recalls, "It was the most extraordinary thing, a simple walk" with O'Hara, and O'Hara wrote a poem titled "Walking with Larry Rivers."[42] Walking seems to have been a major part of his daily repertoire, as well as a kind of syntax organizing thought, emotion, and encounter, and the city was the only conceivable site for his tender, street-smart, and sometimes campy voice celebrating the incidental and the inconsequential. In the prose-poem "Meditations in an Emergency" he affirmed, "I can't even enjoy a blade of grass unless I know there's a subway handy, or a record store or some other sign that people do not totally *regret* life. It is more important to affirm the least sincere; the clouds get enough attention as it is. . . ."[43] The poem "Walking to Work" ends

> I'm becoming
> the street.
>
> Who are you in love with?
> me?
> Straight against the light I cross.[44]

Yet another walking poem begins:

> I'm getting tired of not wearing underwear
> And then again I like it
>   strolling along
> feeling the wind blow softly on my genitals[45]

and goes on to speculate on "who dropped that empty carton / of cracker jacks," before turning to the clouds, the bus, his destination, the "you" to whom he speaks, Central Park. The texture is that of everyday life and of a connoisseur's eye settling on small things, small epiphanies, but the same kind of inventory that studs Whitman's and Ginsberg's poems recurs in O'Hara's. Cities are forever spawning lists.

David Wojnarowicz's *Close to the Knives: A Memoir of Disintegration* reads like a summary of all the urban experience that came before him. Like De Quincey he was a runaway, but like De Quincey's friend Ann he supported himself as a child prostitute, and like Dickens and Ginsberg he brought an incandescant, hallucinatory clarity to the moods and scenes of his city. Most who took up the Beat subject of the urban underworld of the erotic, the intoxicated, and the illegal took it up in William Burroughs's amoral vein, more interested in its coolness than its consequences or its politics, but Wojnarowicz raged at the system that created such suffering, that created his suffering as a runaway child, a gay man, a person with AIDS (of which he died in 1991). He writes in a collage of memories, encounters, dreams, fantasies, and outbursts studded with startling metaphors and painful images, and in his writings walking appears like a refrain, a beat: he always returns to the image of himself walking alone down a New York street or a corridor. "Some nights we'd walk seven or eight hundred blocks, practically the whole island of Manhattan," he wrote of his hustling years, for walking remained the recourse for those with nowhere to sleep, as it had been for Johnson and Savage.[46]

Wojnarowicz's 1980s New York had come full circle to resemble Gay's early eighteenth-century London. It had the scourges of AIDS, of the vast new population of homeless people, and of the drug-damaged staggering around like something out of William Hogarth's Gin Lane, and it was notoriously violent, so that the well-to-do feared its streets as they once had London's. Wojnarowicz writes of seeing "long legs and spiky boots and elegant high heels and three prostitutes suddenly surround a business man from the waldorf and they're saying: 'Come on honey' and rubbing his dick . . . and his wallet appears behind his back in the hands of one of them and they all drop away as he continues to giggle" and we're back to Moll Flanders stripping a passed-out trick of his silver gloves, snuffbox, and even his periwig. He writes of the years when he was suffering from malnutrition and exposure, living on the streets until he was eighteen, "I had almost died three times at the hands of people I'd sold my body to in those days and after coming off the street. . . . I could barely speak when in the company of other people. . . . That weight of image and sensation wouldn't come out until I picked up a pencil and started putting it down on paper." "Coming off the street": the phrase describes all streets as one street and that street as a whole world, with its own citizenry, laws, language. "The street" is a world where people in flight from the traumas that happen inside houses become natives of the outside.

One of the book's sections, "Being Queer in America: A Journal of Disintegration," is as tidy a chronicle of the uses of walking for a queer man of the streets in 1980s urban America as *Pride and Prejudice* is of the uses of walking for a country lady almost two centuries before. "I'm walking through these hallways where the windows break apart a slow dying sky and a quiet wind follows the heels of the kid as he suddenly steps through a door frame ten rooms down," it opens. He follows the kid into the room, which resembles the long wharves and warehouses he used to cruise, sucks him off, and a few sections later his walking becomes mourning for his friend, the photographer Peter Hujar, dead of AIDS. "I walked for hours through the streets after he died, through the gathering darkness and traffic, down into the dying section of town where bodies litter the curbsides and dogs tear apart the stinking garbage by the doorways. There was a green swell to the clouds above the buildings. . . . I turned and left, walking back into the gray haze of traffic and exhaust, past a skinny prostitute doing the junkie walk bent over at the waist with knuckles dragging the sidewalk." He meets a friend— "man on second avenue at 2:00 am"—who tells him about a third man being jumped on West Street by a carload of kids from Jersey and brutally beaten for being gay. And then comes his refrain, "I walk this hallway twenty-seven times and all I can see are the cool white walls. A hand rubbing slowly across a face, but my hands are empty. Walking back and forth from room to room trailing bluish shadows I feel weak. . . ." His city is not hell but limbo, the place in which restless souls swirl forever, and only passion, friendship, and visionary capacity redeem it for him.

I began walking my own city's streets as a teenager and walked them so long that both they and I changed, the desperate pacing of adolescence when the present seemed an eternal ordeal giving way to the musing walks and innumerable errands of someone no longer wound up so tight, so isolated, so poor, and my walks have now often become reviews of my own and the city's history together. Vacant lots become new buildings, old geezer bars are taken over by young hipsters, the Castro's discos become vitamin stores, whole streets and neighborhoods change their complexion. Even my own neighborhood has changed so much it sometimes seems as though I have moved two or three times from the raucous corner I started out on just before I turned twenty. The urban walkers I have surveyed suggest a kind of scale of walking, and on it, I have moved from near the Ginsberg-Wojnarowicz end of the spectrum to that of a low-rent Virginia Woolf.

Two days before the end of the year, I went to one of the local liquor stores for milk early one Sunday morning. Around the corner a guy was sitting in a doorway drinking and singing falsetto, with that knack some local drunks have for sounding like fallen angels. The word *Alooooone* trilled out of nowhere, echoing beautifully in the stairwell. On my way back I saw him weaving so intently down the street he didn't notice me pass a few feet away. Merely walking seemed to take all the singer's concentration, as though he were forcing himself through an atmosphere that had become thick around him. When I started watering the tree in front of my building, he was still winding around the corner. The old lady who always wears a dress and always speaks so politely in word-salad non sequiturs was walking in the other direction. I said hello to her as she passed me, but she didn't notice me any more than he did. All of a sudden, when she had reached the same point on her side of the street that he had on his, she broke into a sort of soft-shoe shuffle that carried on until she turned out of sight down the facing corner. The two of them seemed to be listening to some inaudible music that carried them along and made them joyous as well as haunted.

Later on the churchgoers would appear. When I first moved here, there were no cafés, and all the churchgoers walked—on Sunday mornings the streets were busy and sociable with black women in resplendent hats, walking in all directions to their churches, not with the dogged steps of pilgrims but with the festive stride of celebrants. That was long ago; gentrification has dispersed the Baptist congregations to other neighborhoods, from which many now drive to church. Young African-American men still saunter by, their legs nonchalant while their arms and shoulders jump around as though staking a bodily territory, but most of the churchgoers have been replaced on the sidewalks these weekend mornings by joggers and dog walkers pumping towards that great secular temple of the middle class, the garden as represented by Golden Gate Park, while the hung-over drift towards the cafés. But this early the street belonged to us three walkers, or to the two of them, for they made me feel like a ghost drifting through their private lives out in public on that cold, sunny Sunday morning, in the communal solitude of urban walkers.   ∎

NOTES

Philip Lopate's essay "The Pen on Foot: The Literature of Walking Around," Parnassus, vol. 18, no. 2 and 19, no 1, 1993, pointed me to Edwin Denby's writings and to specific poems of Walt Whitman's.

1. "On Saturday night . . .": Harriet Lane Levy, 920 *O'Farrell Street* (Berkeley: Heyday Books, 1997), 185–86.

2. Kerouac managed to have two visions on [Market Street]: see *Atlantic Monthly*, reprinting a May 1961 letter, November 1998, 68: "It [*On the Road*] was really a story about two Catholic buddies in search of God. And we found him. I found him in the sky, in Market Street San Francisco (those 2 visions)."

3. how a popular, well-used street is kept safe: Jane Jacobs, *The Death and Life of Great American Cities* (New York: Vintage Books, 1961), throughout the chapter "The Uses of Sidewalks: Safety."

4. "What distinguishes the city": Moretti, quoted in Peter Jukes, *A Shout in the Street: An Excursion into the Modern City* (Berkeley: University of California Press, 1991), 184.

5. little more than outdoor salons and ballrooms: *Cities and People* (New Haven and London: Yale University Press, 1985), 166–68, 237–38.

6. "Earlier in the [nineteenth] century," "I hear that pedestrians": Ray Rosenzweig and Elizabeth Blackmar, *The Park and the People: A History of Central Park* (Ithica: Cornell University Press, 1992), 27, 223.

7. "It simply never occurs to us": Bernard Rudofsky, *Streets for People: A Primer for Americans* (New York: Van Nostrand Reinhold, 1982), epigraph quoting his own *Architecture without Architects*.

8. "In ancient Italian towns the narrow main street": Edwin Denby, *Dancers, Buildings and People in the Streets*, introduction by Frank O'Hara (New York: Horizon Press, 1965), 183.

9. "When I am in a serious Humour": Addison in Joseph Addison and Richard Steele, *The Spectator, Vol. 1* (London: J. M. Dent and Sons, 1907), 96, from *Spectator,* no. 26 (March 30, 1711).

10. "Though you through cleaner allies": John Gay, "Trivia, or, the Art of Walking the Streets of London," book 3, line 126, in *The Abbey Classics: Poems by John Gay* (London: Chapman and Dodd, n.d.), 88.

11. "Here I remark": Ibid., II. 275–82, 78.

12. "goes forward with the crowd": Wordsworth, *Prelude,* 286.

13. "each charter'd street": The famous opening of William Blake's "London," in *William Blake,* ed. J. Bronowski (Harmondsworth, England: Penguin Books, 1958), 52.

14. one of those desperate London walkers: See Richard Holmes, *Dr. Johnson and Mr. Savage* (New York: Vintage Books, 1993), 44, quoting Sir John Hawkins in the chapter on these walks: "Johnson has told me, that whole nights have been spent by him and Savage in conversations of this kind, not under the hospitable roof of a tavern, where warmth might have invigorated their spirits, and wine dispelled their care; but in a perambulation round the squares of Westminster, St. James's in particular, when all the money they could both raise was less than sufficient to purchase for them the shelter and sordid comforts of a night cellar."

15. "I should have been": James Boswell, *Boswell's London Journal,* ed. Frederick A. Pottle (New York: Signet, 1956), 235.

16. 50,000 [prostitutes in London] in 1793: Henry Mayhew, *London Labour and the London Poor,* vol. 4 (1861–62; reprint, New York: Dover Books, 1968), 211, citing Mr. Colquhoun, a police magistrate, and his "tedious investigations."

17. "the circulating harlotry of the Haymarket and Regent Street": Ibid., 213. On 217, "They [the streetwalkers] are to be seen between three and five o'clock in the Burlington Arcade, which is a well known resort of cyprians of the better sort. They are well acquainted with its Paphian intricacies, and will, if their signals are responded to, glide into a friendly bonnet shop, the stairs of which leading to the coenacula or upper chambers are not innocent of their well formed 'bien chaussée' feet. The park is also, as we have said, a favorite promenade, where assignations may be made or acquaintances formed."

18. "Prostitution streetscapes are composed of *strolls*": Richard Symanski, *The Immoral Landscape: Female Prostitution in Western Societies* (Toronto: Butterworths, 1981), 175–76.

19. "think that women who work in whorehouses": Dolores French with Linda Lee, *Working: My Life as a Prostitute* (New York: E. P. Dutton, 1988), 43.

20. "Perception of the new qualities of the modern city": Raymond Williams, *The Country and the City* (New York: Oxford University Press, 1973), 233.

21. "Being myself at that time, of necessity, a peripatetic" and following: De Quincey, *Confessions of an English Opium Eater* (New York: Signet Books, 1966), 42–43.

22. "And this kind of realism," "Few of us understand the street": C. K. Chesterton, *Charles Dickens, a Critical Study* (New York: Dodd, Mead, 1906), 47, 44.

23. "If I couldn't walk fast and far": Dickens to John Forster, cited in Ned Lukacher, *Primal Scenes: Literature, Philosophy, Psychoanalysis* (Ithaca: Cornell University Press, 1986), 288.

24. "I am both a town traveller": Charles Dickens, *The Uncommercial Traveller and Reprinted Pieces Etc.* (Oxford and New York: Oxford University Press, 1958), 1.

25. "So much of my travelling is done on foot," "My walking is of two kinds": Dickens, "Shy Neighborhoods," ibid., 94, 95.

26. "It is one of my fancies": Dickens, "On an Amateur Beat," ibid., 345.

27. "Whenever I think I deserve particularly well of myself": Dickens, "The City of the Absent," ibid., 233.

28. "Some years ago, a temporary inability to sleep": Dickens, "Night Walks," ibid., 127.

29. "I would roam the streets": Patti Smith, when asked what she did to prepare to go on-stage, *Fresh Air,* National Public Radio, Oct. 3, 1997.

30. "How could I think mountains and climbing romantic?": *The Letters of Virginia Woolf,* vol. 3, *A Change of Perspective,* ed. Nigel Nicholson (London: Hogarth Press, 1975–80), letter to V. Sackville-West, Aug. 19, 1924, 126.

31. "enforce the memories of our own experience": Virginia Woolf, "Street Haunting: A London Adventure," in *The Death of the Moth and Other Essays* (Harmondsworth, England: Penguin Books, 1961), 23.

32. "As we step out of the house," "the shell-like covering": Ibid., 23–24.

33. Two-thirds of all journeys . . . still made on foot: Tony Hiss, editorial, *New York Times,* January 30, 1998.

34. "On the whole North America's Anglo-Saxomania has had a withering effect": Rudofsky, *Streets for People,* 19.

35. "Who often walk'd lonesome walks": Walt Whitman, "Recorders Ages Hence," *Leaves of Grass* (New York: Bantam Books, 1983), 99.

36. "City of orgies, walks and joys": Ibid., 102.

37. "Passing stranger!": Ibid., 103.

38. "the fruited plain": Ken Gonzales-Day, "The Fruited Plain: A History of Queer Space," *Art Issues,* September/October 1997, 17.

39. "dragging themselves through the negro streets," "shoes full of blood": Allen Ginsberg, "Howl," in *The New American Poetry,* ed. Donald M. Allen (New York: Grove Press, 1960), 182, 186.

40. "Strange now to think of you, gone": Allen Ginsberg, *Kaddish and Other Poems, 1958–1960* (San Francisco: City Lights Books, 1961), 7.

41. "where you walked 50 years ago": Ibid., 8.

42. "It was the most extraordinary thing": Brad Gooch, *City Poet: The Life and Times of Frank O'Hara* (New York: Alfred A. Knopf, 1993), 217.

43. "I can't even enjoy a blade of grass": Frank O'Hara, "Meditations in an Emergency," in *The Selected Poems* (New York: Vintage Books, 1974), 87.

44. "I'm becoming": O'Hara, "Walking to Work," ibid., 57.

45. "I'm getting tired of not wearing": O'Hara, "F. (Missive and Walk) I. #53," ibid., 194.

46. "Some nights we'd walk seven or eight hundred blocks": David Wojnarowicz, *Close to the Knives: A Memoir of Disintegration* (New York: Vintage Books, 1991), 5; "long legs and spiky boots," 182; "I had almost died three times," 228; "I'm walking through these hallways," 64; "I walked for hours," 67; "man on second avenue," 70; "I walk this hallway twenty-seven times," 79.

■ QUESTIONS FOR MAKING CONNECTIONS WITHIN THE READING ■

1. "The Solitary Stroller and the City" comes from a book entitled *Wander-lust*. On first reading, the goal of Solnit's itinerary is likely to appear to be unclear: she pauses over details; she moves from section to section

without obvious transitions; she catalogs authors, friends, and locations that can't all be familiar to her readers. As you reread the piece, number the five sections that Solnit creates through the use of white space and summarize the work she does in each section. Does an order emerge? What is Solnit's organizational strategy? Where is she trying to take her reader?

2. Solnit contrasts urban and rural walking, walks in European cities and walks in American cities, walks taken 200 years ago and walks taken today, walks taken by men and walks taken by women. Are separate mindsets associated with each kind of walking? Catalog the places where you walk: has Solnit left anything out of her study that you feel is important?

3. Solnit's essay concludes with a vignette about a Sunday morning walk, one that illustrates "the communal solitude of urban walkers." Is this "communal solitude" something that is learned or is it natural to city dwellers? Is it available to urban drivers? Does Solnit offer this vision to her readers in hopes of fostering this state of mind or is she more concerned with describing something that is endangered?

▪ QUESTIONS FOR WRITING ▪

1. Following Solnit's example, describe one of your walks through an urban landscape. Does your description serve to illustrate her assertion that "urban walking seems in many ways more like primordial hunting and gathering than walking in the country"? Does following Solnit's example bring to light anything about your way of moving through the world that would otherwise go unnoticed? Are you led to the same conclusions? Does this way of writing carry within it the same thesis for all writers?

2. Solnit finds something liberating in the mental state that urban walking produces—"cool, withdrawn, with senses sharpened, a good state for anybody who needs to reflect or create." Can you identify passages in "The Solitary Stroller and the City" that are the result of Solnit's achieving this state of mind? Why does walking generate this state, but not other forms of travel? Is this a personal experience, or is it a biological condition? How does one distinguish this state of mind from indifference? Discuss the relationship between physical movement, state of mind, and social engagement.

▪ QUESTIONS FOR MAKING CONNECTIONS BETWEEN READINGS ▪

1. In "The Ecology of Magic," David Abram describes how his travels made him "a student of subtle differences." Solnit is also concerned with the relationship between travel and states of mind. It is no surprise that the

person traveling through rural Bali both sees and thinks about different things than the person traveling through New York City, San Francisco, and London. If we push this observation to the furthest extreme, though, we might be driven to conclude that thought, location, and movement are fundamentally intertwined, so that the person traveling in Bali can think in ways not available to the urban stroller and vice versa. Drawing on Abram and Solnit, discuss the degrees to which thought, location, and movement are connected.

2. In "The Power of Context," Malcolm Gladwell argues that the rundown condition of New York City in 1984 played a significant role in leading Bernhard Goetz to shot four young men on the subway. Does this argument extend, contradict, or reinforce Solnit's observations about the effects of urban walking? Can Gladwell's argument be used to explain Solnit's experience? If context is so powerful, can any experience be said to be personal?

SANDRA STEINGRABER

AN ECOLOGIST, AUTHOR, and cancer survivor, Sandra Steingraber has devoted much of her career to demonstrating the links between cancer and the environment. Her first co-authored publication, *The Spoils of Famine: Ethiopian Famine Policy and Peasant Agriculture* (1988), concerned the relationship between ecology and human rights in Africa. Steingraber's more recent work seeks to establish the impact that environmental factors have on human well-being in First World nations as well.

Drawing on her literary education (she earned a master's in English literature at Illinois State University before her doctorate in biology at the University of Michigan), Steingraber published a volume of poetry about surviving cancer called *Post-Diagnosis* (1995). She then turned her attention to the link between environmental contamination and the development of cancer in *Living Downstream: An Ecologist Looks at Cancer and the Environment* (1997), the highly lauded study from which the following chapter is drawn. Steingraber compiles data about cancer incidence with newly released information about environmental toxicity to suggest that the two are more than coincidentally related. She sees access to information on the presence of toxins in the environment as a public right, a right that should allow people to make informed decisions about their exposure to dangerous chemicals.

In *Having Faith: An Ecologist's Journey to Motherhood* (2001), Steingraber's most recent book, she turns her perspective as an ecologist onto the process of motherhood. The womb, she reasons, is the baby's first environment. Just as in the world outside, if not more so, the developing child depends on the delicate balance of food, water, and vital nutrients provided by this environment. Adults suffer when the natural environment is contaminated and this balance is disturbed; for a fetus, which cannot escape the prenatal environment, any contamination is inescapable.

Steingraber, Sandra. "War," *Living Downstream: A Scientist's Personal Investigation of Cancer and the Environment*. Vintage, 1998. 87–117.

Biographical information comes from the author's Web site, <http://www.steingraber.com>.

While she maps the intimate environment of the womb in *Having Faith*, in the following essay Steingraber elevates her arguments to the geopolitical level. "War," a chapter from *Living Downstream*, traces the relationship between World War II use of the pesticide DDT, its overproduction, and its consequent release into civilian circulation as a product widely used by the agricultural industry. This is just one example of the growing distribution of synthetic chemicals across the nation and around the world. The research and industrial development that accompanied the war, Steingraber writes, "was a catalyst for the transformation from a carbohydrate-based economy . . . to a petrochemical-based economy." Without advocating for the total cessation of production or use of these chemicals, Steingraber insists that we attend to the public health costs of their continued employment and that we chart our future course with the health of future generations in mind.

■   ■

War

When my father, at age sixty-nine, wrote his memoirs on a manual typewriter and sent copies to all surviving members of his family, he did so to commemorate the fiftieth anniversary of the Allies' victory in the Mediterranean theater. The significance of this event is emphasized throughout the text. It was his defining moment.

I have often imagined my father as a soldier in Italy. His two desires: to stay alive and to avenge the capture of his brother, my Uncle LeRoy, held as a prisoner of war in Germany. His one fear, which the Allied victory in Europe very nearly realized, was to be sent to the other theater—the blood-soaked Pacific.

My father firmly believes his life was saved by excellent typing skills. This was not a lesson to be lost on his daughters. The ninth child of a poor Chicago family, he moved a dozen times before finishing school and enlisting. How exactly he learned to type a hundred words per minute *with no errors* I do not know. It is part of my father's mystique. Throughout my childhood, the sounds of rapid, flawless typing filled my parents' bedroom. According to legend, his remarkable talent with the typewriter saved him for two reasons: first, because he was selected to work in correspondence at a U.S. Army office safely away from the front and, second, because he was therefore privy to orders about upcoming troop deployments. Thus forewarned, he deftly reenlisted in the right unit at the right moment and kept himself out of harm's way. His skills as a tank destroyer (motto: Seek, Strike, and Destroy), for which he was trained, would go untested.

With these stories, I was encouraged to spend time practicing penmanship, dictation, and typing at my father's big desk. Like him, I am nearsighted and left-handed. Neither were allowable excuses for sloppy work. But if I became more attracted to the sounds of the words than to the speed with which I could produce them, it was both for my plain lack of clerical talent and for the irrelevance introduced into the whole endeavor by electric, self-correcting machines—and, later, computers. Still, until I read his error-free autobiography while sitting at my own big desk, I did not realize how deeply my father's stories had influenced me or how much I am like that nineteen-year-old army clerk furiously typing up casualty reports. My own work as a writer is a legacy of a war ended years before I was born.

World War II is mentioned throughout the chapters of *Silent Spring.** Carson's references are casual, and they seem designed to remind already-aware readers that the technologies developed for wartime purposes had changed chemistry and physics forever. The atomic bomb was only the most arresting example. More intimate aspects of the human economy were also changed. The multitude of new synthetic products made available after the war altered how food was grown and packaged, homes constructed and furnished, bathrooms disinfected, children deloused, and pets de-flea'd. Carson described this transformation almost offhandedly, as though the connection between lawn-care practices and warfare was perfectly obvious.[1]

Carson made at least two other points about World War II. First, because many of these new chemicals were developed under emergency conditions and within the secretive atmosphere of wartime, they had not been fully tested for safety. After the war, private markets were quickly developed for these products, and yet their long-term effects on humans or the environment were not known. Second, because wartime attitudes accompanied these products onto the market, the goals of conquest and annihilation were transferred from the battlefield to our kitchens, gardens, forests, and farm fields. The Seek, Strike, and Destroy maxim of my father's antitank unit was brought home and turned against the natural world. This attitude, Carson believed, would be our undoing. All life was caught in the crossfire.[2]

When *Silent Spring* was published, the victory days of the Second World War had not yet reached their twentieth anniversary. Compared to Carson's generation, those of us born after World War II are not as aware of the domestic changes wrought by this war. We have inherited its many inventions—as well as the waste produced in their manufacture—but we do

*Authored by Rachel Carson, this is a classic text in environmental studies.

not have a keen sense of their origins. In seeking explanations for the unprecedented cancer rates among our ranks, we need to examine them.

Taped above my desk are graphs showing the U.S. annual production of synthetic chemicals. I keep them here to make visible a phenomenon I was born in the midst of but am too young to recall firsthand. The first consists of several lines, each representing the manufacture of a single substance. One line is benzene, the human carcinogen known to cause leukemia and suspected of playing a role in multiple myeloma and non-Hodgkin's lymphoma. Another is perchloroethylene, the probable human carcinogen used to dry-clean clothes. A third represents production of vinyl chloride, a known cause of angiosarcoma and a possible breast carcinogen. They all look like ski slopes. After 1940, the lines begin to rise significantly and then shoot upward after 1960.

A second graph shows the annual production of all synthetic organic chemicals combined. It resembles a child's drawing of a cliff face. The line extending from 1920 to 1940 is essentially horizontal, hovering at a few billion pounds per year. After 1940, however, the line rockets skyward, becoming almost vertical after 1960. This kind of increase is exponential, and in the case of synthetic organic chemical production, the doubling time is every seven to eight years. By the end of the 1980s, total production had exceeded two hundred billion pounds per year. In other words, production of synthetic organic chemicals increased 100-fold between the time my mother was born and the year I finished graduate school. Two human generations.

The terms *organic* and *synthetic* are slippery ones and require explanation. *Organic* has two definitions that very nearly contradict each other. In popular usage, *organic* describes that which is simple, healthful, and close to nature. Similarly, in the language of agriculture, *organic* refers to food grown only with the aid of substances derived from plant and animal matter. Food certified as organic is supposed to be free from manufactured pesticides, antibiotics, hormones, and other additives—that is, fruits, vegetables, meat, eggs, and milk produced without the use of artificial, *synthetic* chemicals.

In the parlance of chemistry, however, *organic* simply refers to any chemical with carbon in it. The study of organic chemistry is the study of carbon compounds. The word *synthetic* means essentially the same as it does in everyday conversation: a synthetic chemical is one that has been formulated in a chemical laboratory, usually by combining smaller substances into larger ones. Most often, these substances contain carbon. Indeed, many organic chemicals now in daily use are synthetic—they do not exist in nature.

Of course, not all organic substances are synthetic. Wood, leather, crude oil, sugar, blood, coal—these are all carbon-based, organic substances found in the natural world. But, insofar as they have carbon atoms in their structures somewhere, the vast majority of synthesized chemicals are also organic. Plastic, detergent, nylon, trichloroethylene, DDT, PCBs, and CFCs are all synthetic organic compounds. The close alignment between organic and synthetic leads to the absurd but truthful concept that organic farmers are those who shun the use of (synthetic) organic chemicals.

Most synthetic organic compounds are derived from either petroleum or coal. Recognizing this fact brings the widely divergent definitions of the word *organic* together. To a biologist, organic substances are those that come from organisms—living or dead. Long chains of carbon atoms compose the chemical infrastructure of all life forms, including the liquefied organisms and the petrified organisms who lived on the planet eons ago and who have since been extracted from their burial grounds. Nothing manufactured from these so-called fossil fuels is really "unnatural." A molecule of DDT is made up of rearranged carbon atoms distilled from some creature's once-living body.

And here lies the problem. Many synthetic molecules are chemically similar enough to substances naturally found in the bodies of living organisms that, as a group, they tend to be biologically active. Our blood, lungs, liver, kidneys, colon—with the help of an elaborate enzyme system—are all designed to shuttle around, break apart, recycle, and reconstruct carbon-containing molecules. Thus, synthetic organics easily interact with the various naturally occurring biochemicals that constitute our anatomy and participate in the various physiological processes that keep us alive. By design, petroleum-derived pesticides have the power to kill because they chemically interfere with one or another of these processes. DDT, for example, interferes with the conduction of nerve impulses. The weed killer atrazine hinders the process of photosynthesis. The phenoxy herbicides bring about death by mimicking the effect of plant growth hormones.

Chlorofluorocarbons (CFCs), the famous ozone depleters, were exceptional because they did not share this property of biological activity. And because they are so chemically stable, CFC molecules can be swept into the stratosphere in their still intact state. Only when hit by a beam of ultraviolet light do they finally fall apart, releasing the chlorine atom that begins the destructive chain reaction culminating in the loss of ozone. CFCs were invented in 1928 but came into large-scale production only after World War II. Since the 1950s, the total amount of chlorine in the stratosphere has increased by a factor of ten.[3]

Plenty of other synthetic organics are similarly inert in their finished forms. Indeed, this is why they are not biodegradable: their molecules are so large or otherwise so complex that they do not decay. They are thus exempt from the global carbon cycle that is constantly building up and breaking down organic molecules. And, of course, this exemption is what you want in a roof gutter, a water pipe, or a window frame.

For several reasons, however, this unreactiveness is misleading. First, many of these compounds are themselves synthesized from synthetic chemicals that are highly reactive. By accident or on purpose, these industrial feedstocks are routinely released, dumped, or spilled in the general environment.

While PVC plastic is, biochemically speaking, quite lethargic, the vinyl chloride from which it is manufactured exerts striking effects on the human liver. Second, inactive synthetic substances can shed or off-gas the smaller, more reactive molecules from which they are made.[4] Third, new reactive chemicals can be created if these substances are subsequently burned—as when perfectly benign piles of vinyl siding are shoveled into a garbage incinerator, and poisonous dioxin rises from the stack. The incinerator itself, in this case, acts as a de facto chemical laboratory synthesizing new organic compounds from feedstocks of discarded consumer products.

Through all of these routes, we find ourselves facing a rising tide of biologically active, synthetic organic chemicals. Some interfere with our hormones, some attach themselves to our chromosomes, some cripple the immune system, and some overstimulate the activity of certain enzymes. If we could metabolize these chemicals into completely benign breakdown products and excrete them, they would pose less of a hazard. Instead, a good many of them accumulate. In essence, synthetic organic chemicals confront us with the worst of both worlds.[5] They are similar enough to naturally occurring chemicals to react with us but different enough to not go away easily.

A number of these chemicals are soluble in fat and so collect in tissues high in fat content.[6] Synthetic organic solvents, such as perchloroethylene and trichloroethylene, are an example. They are specifically designed to dissolve other oil- and fat-soluble chemicals. In paint, they work well to carry oil-based pigments. As degreasing agents, they work well to clean lubricated machine parts. As dry-cleaning fluids, they excel at dissolving human body oils and greasy fabric stains. They also all work splendidly to dissolve human body oils still on our skin and can thus easily enter our bodies upon touch. In addition, they are readily absorbed across the membranes of our lungs. Once inside, they take up residence in fat-containing tissues.

Many such tissues exist. Breasts are famous for their high fat content and often serve as repositories for synthetic organic chemicals circulating within the female body. But organs less renowned for fat content also collect these chemicals. The liver, for example, is surprisingly high in fat. So is bone marrow, the target organ for benzene. And, amazingly enough, because nerve cells are swathed in a fatty coating, so are our brains. Consider that many solvents have been used as anesthetic gases due to their ability to affect brain functioning. Chloroform is one.

Its medical uses long since discontinued, chloroform continues to be used as a solvent, fumigant, and ingredient in the manufacture of refrigerants, pesticides, and synthetic dyes. U.S. annual production of chloroform is currently about 600 million pounds, and it is found in nearly half of the hazardous waste sites on the Superfund National Priorities List. Trace amounts are also formed when drinking water is chlorinated. Chloroform is classified as a probable human carcinogen. Its residence time in the body is actually quite brief. DDT, for example, has a half-life of at least seven years, while that of chloroform is a mere eight hours. (Half-life is the time required to convert half the body's burden of a given substance into excretable by-products.) The problem, then, with chloroform is not so much biological persistence but the fact that we are continuously exposed through multiple routes. All human beings, according to the U.S. Agency for Toxic Substances and Disease Registry, receive at least low levels through water, food, and inhalation.[7]

In the last half of the twentieth century, cancers of the brain, liver, breast, and bone marrow (multiple myeloma) have been on the rise. These are all human organs with high fat content. In the last half of the twentieth century, the production of fat-soluble, synthetic chemicals has also been on the rise. Many are classified as known, probable, or possible carcinogens. We need to ask what connections might exist between these two time trends.

* * *

First synthesized in 1874, DDT languished without purpose until drafted into World War II, and it proved its mettle by halting a typhus epidemic in Naples. My father arrived in this occupied city not long after. According to his wartime account, Naples lay in ruins, its people hungry, dirty, and in great despair. Little wonder they were also vulnerable to typhus. DDT's ability to annihilate the insect carriers of this disease—fleas, lice, and mites—must have seemed miraculous. Shortly thereafter, DDT was loaded onto American bombers and sprayed over the Pacific Islands to control mosquitoes. War production of DDT soon exceeded military requirements, and by 1945, the U.S. government allowed the surplus to be released for general civilian use.

As documented by the historians Thomas Dunlap and Edmund Russell, this decision marked a profound change in purpose. It is one thing to fumigate war refugees falling ill from insect-borne epidemics and quite another to douse the food supply of an entire nation not at risk for such diseases. It is one thing to rain insecticide over war zones ravaged by malaria and quite another to drench suburban Long Island.[8] The skillful advertising that accompanied this transformation advocated a whole new approach to the insect world. Various insect species—some, mere nuisances—were recast in the public's imagination as deadly fiends to be rooted out at all cost. Cohabitation was no longer acceptable. In demonizing the home front's new enemy, one cartoon ad even went so far as to place Adolf Hitler's head on the body of a beetle.[9]

Synthetic pesticide use thus began in the United States in the 1940s. Two other chemicals participated in this debut: parathion and the phenoxy herbicides 2,4-D and 2,4,5-T.[10] Parathion—and its sibling malathion—belong to a group of synthetic chemicals called organophosphates, which are created by surrounding phosphate molecules with various carbon chains and rings.

Like the chlorinated pesticides, they attack an insect's nervous system, but they do so by interfering with the chemical receptor molecules between the nerve cells[11] rather than by affecting the conduction of electricity, which is DDT's mode of action.[12] Like the chlorinated pesticides, organophosphate poisons played a starring role during the war—but as villain rather than hero. Developed by a German company as a nerve gas, members of the first generation of organophosphate poisons were tested on prisoners in the concentration camps of Auschwitz.[13]

By contrast, the phenoxy herbicides were an Allied weapon. They were mobilized in the 1940s with the goal of destroying enemy crops. Another American invention—the atomic bomb—ended that war before field testing could yield to full-scale chemical warfare. Twenty more years would pass before 2,4-D and 2,4,5-T would reenter combat—this time in Vietnam's rainforests under the nom de guerre Agent Orange. In the meantime, they were introduced into U.S. agriculture for weed control and into forestry for shrub control.[14] By 1960, 2,4-D accounted for half of all U.S. herbicide production. The hoe was fast on its way to becoming obsolete.[15]

The graphical picture of pesticide use in the United States closely resembles the graphs of synthetic chemical production: a long, gentle rise between 1850 and 1945 and then, like the side of a mesa rising from the desert, the lines shoot up.[16] Insecticide use begins ascending first; herbicide use closely follows. The line for fungicide use rises more gradually. All together, within ten years of their introduction in 1945, synthetic organic chemicals captured 90 percent of the agricultural pest-control market and had almost completely routed the pest-control methods of the prewar years.[17] In 1939, there were 32 pesticidal active ingredients registered with the federal government. At present, 860 active ingredients are so registered and are formulated into 20,000 different pesticidal products.[18] Current U.S. annual use is estimated at 2.23 billion pounds.[19]

While agriculture consumes the lion's share of this total, with only about 5 percent used by private households, family pesticide use is emerging as an important source of exposure for those of us not living on farms.[20] According to the EPA's National Home and Garden Pesticide Survey, 82 percent of U.S. households use pesticides of some kind.[21] In a survey of families in Missouri, nearly 98 percent said they use pesticides at least once a year, and almost two-thirds said they use them five or more times.[22] Yard and garden weed killers are used by about 50 percent of U.S. families, as are insecticidal flea collars, sprays, dusts, shampoos, and dips for household pets. These kinds of uses place us in intimate contact with pesticide residues, which can easily find their way into bedding, clothing, carpets, and food. Pesticidal residues persist much longer indoors than outdoors, where sunlight, flowing water, and soil microbes help break them down or carry them away.[23] Yard chemicals tracked indoors on the bottoms of shoes can remain impregnated in carpet fibers for years. Some researchers now believe that infants and toddlers experience significant exposure to pesticides by crawling on carpets and ingesting house dust—perhaps even more so than by ingesting pesticide residues on food.[24]

Several studies have linked childhood cancer to home pesticide use. Childhood cancer in Los Angeles was found to be associated with parental exposure to pesticides during pregnancy or nursing.[25] In a 1995 study in Denver, children whose yards were treated with pesticides were four times more likely to have soft tissue cancers than children living in households that did not use yard chemicals.[26] In another case-control study, researchers found statistically significant associations between the incidence of brain tumors in children and the use of several household pesticidal products:[27] pest-repelling strips, lindane-containing lice shampoos, flea collars on pets, and weed killers on the lawn.[28] All together, these findings may represent the beginning of an explanation as to why brain cancer in children under age fourteen has risen sharply during the past twenty years.[29]

Of course, the postwar boom in synthetic organics was not limited to pesticides. Industrial products manufactured from fossil fuels also exploded onto the scene. In this case, World War II simply accelerated a process set in motion years earlier.

Historians of chemistry date the twentieth-century rise of the petrochemical industry back to the near extermination of whales in the nineteenth century: lack of whale oil for lamps created a market for kerosene, one of the lighter fractions of petroleum. Another petroleum derivative, gasoline, found purpose with the advent of the automobile.[30] With the blockades against imported materials during World War I, the chemical industries of all warring nations were stimulated to invent new products. Germany, for example, developed artificial fertilizers when its supplies of Chilean saltpeter were cut.[31] The same manufacturing process proved quite useful for producing explosives—as the fertilizer-derived bomb that destroyed the Oklahoma City federal building in 1995 illustrates.

With a large supply on hand for making dyes, Germany turned to chlorine gas to serve as a wretched weapon of chemical warfare in the trenches of France. Chlorinated solvents were also introduced during this time.[32] After the war ended, new chemical products in the United States were protected by high tariffs, the war's losing parties surrendered their chemical secrets to the victors, and considerable wealth and prestige accrued to the chemical industry.[33] By the 1930s, petroleum began to outpace coal as the source of carbon for new chemical inventions.[34]

The cliff face of exponential growth in synthetic organic chemicals, however, did not begin until the 1940s. The all-out assaults of World War II created instant demands for explosives, synthetic rubber, aviation fuel, metal parts, synthetic oils, solvents, and pharmaceuticals.[35] The innovations in chemical processing developed in the wake of World War I—such as the cracking of large, heavy petroleum molecules to produce many lighter and smaller molecules—were perfected and tested in large-scale production. When the war ended, the resulting economic boom, housing boom, and baby boom created unprecedented consumer demands as wartime chemicals, aided by skillful advertising, were transferred to civilian posts. Fearing a return to economic depression, national leaders encouraged the conversion of military products to civilian use.[36] "In the United States," the historian Aaron Ihde has wryly noted, "peace did not prove catastrophic to an industry grown to monstrous proportions in response to the needs of war."[37]

From an ecological point of view, World War II was a catalyst for the transformation from a carbohydrate-based economy—as it has been called by some analysts—to a petrochemical-based economy.[38] For those of us born in the last fifty years, a review of petroleum's displaced, replaced, and discarded natural chemical predecessors is a fascinating exercise. I found myself amazed at how many products now derived from a barrel of oil were once manufactured from vegetation.

You may be excited to learn, as I was, that plastic existed before it was synthesized from petroleum. It was derived from plants, invented in the 1870s, and called celluloid. Clear plastic film derived from wood pulp with adhesive on one side was introduced in the 1920s as cellophane tape. Plant-derived substances were once used to make steering wheels, instrument panels, and spray paint for cars. Thus, while the carcinogen vinyl chloride was actually first synthesized in 1913, its production did not begin to skyrocket until after World War II when research on the industrial uses of plant matter was replaced by an emphasis on petrochemistry. Automobile interiors would no longer come from cotton fibers or wood pulp, but from oil.

Guess, if you can, what formaldehyde and soybeans have in common. Imported from Asia in the nineteenth century, soybeans are a low-growing legume that produces round, yellow seeds inside of fuzzy pods. One of the oldest and simplest synthetic organic chemicals, formaldehyde consists of a single atom each of carbon and oxygen, plus two hydrogen atoms. These two substances could hardly be more different. Both happen to be deeply familiar to me, since soybeans cover the Illinois prairies and formaldehyde is the standard preservative of biological specimens destined for dissection. (Anyone who has ever confronted a pickled frog in a biology class would instantly recognize its distinctive odor.) Classified as a possible chemical carcinogen, formaldehyde is consistently ranked among the top fifty chemicals with the highest annual production volumes in the United States.[39] In 1990 alone, 6.4 billion gallons were produced. Formaldehyde serves as an embalming fluid in funeral homes. It is also sprayed on fabric to create permanent press. In the 1970s, formaldehyde-based foams became popular for thermal insulation of houses.[40] But nearly half of formaldehyde's annual production is used for synthetic resins to hold pieces of wood together as plywood and particle board. The subsequent evaporation of formaldehyde vapors from construction materials and furniture makes this chemical a significant contributor to indoor air pollution.[41] As with chloroform, the problem with formaldehyde is not that it accumulates in our tissues but that we are exposed to small amounts of it almost continuously and from so many sources—from our subflooring to our wrinkle-free sheets.[42]

Now the answer to the riddle: What formaldehyde shares with the soybean is an ability to act as an adhesive. Before formaldehyde was synthesized in such gargantuan quantities, soybean resins were used to hold particle board and plywood together. Soybean oil was also used in fire-suppressant foam and wallpaper glue, and as a base for paints, varnishes, and lacquers.[43]

Other plant-based oils also played leading roles in industry before the war. Oils extracted from corn, olives, rice, grape seeds, and other plant parts were used to make paint, inks, soaps, emulsifiers, and even floor covering. The word *linoleum* echoes the name of its original key ingredient: linseed oil. Castor oil, from the tropical castor bean tree, was used to lubricate machine parts.[44]

Countless examples of synthetic substitutions have occurred in the last half century and have provided us with new exposures to known or suspected carcinogens. In the 1950s, for instance, synthetic cutting oils were introduced into machine shops.[45] Used for cooling metal parts during both cutting and grinding, cutting fluids come into close association with machinists through both touch and inhalation. Synthetic degreasers, such as perc, are then often used to clean the parts once they are cut. These have become a common contaminant of hazardous waste sites and therefore of drinking water. Researchers have recently discovered that synthetic cutting fluids can expose workers to N-nitrosamines, a contaminant formed during their manufacture.[46] By the 1970s, cancer among machine operators and its possible relationship to synthetic cutting fluids began receiving attention. In one study the researchers concluded:

> Until now, N-nitrosamines have not been directly associated with human cancers because no population groups had been identified that were inadvertently exposed. Cutting fluid users have the dubious honor of being the first such population group to be identified.[47]

* * *

The rapid birthrate of new synthetic products that began in 1945 far surpassed the ability of government to regulate their use and disposal. Between 45,000 and 100,000 chemicals are now in common commercial use; 75,000 is the most frequently cited estimate. Of these, only about 1.5 to 3 percent

(1,200 to 1,500 chemicals) have been tested for carcinogenicity.[48] The vast majority of commercially used chemicals were brought to market before 1979, when the federal Toxics Substances Control Act (TSCA) mandated the review of new chemicals. Thus, many carcinogenic environmental contaminants likely remain unidentified, unmonitored, and unregulated.[49] Too often, this lack of basic information is paraphrased as "there is lack of evidence of harm," which in turn is translated as "the chemical is harmless."

Pesticides are regulated by twin laws: the Federal Food, Drug, and Cosmetic Act (FFDCA) and the Federal Insecticide, Fungicide, and Rodenticide Act (FIFRA).[50] FFDCA governs pesticide tolerances on agricultural commodities—that is, it sets legal limits for pesticide residues allowed in foodstuffs ranging from raw vegetables to animal feed. FIFRA, on the other hand, requires companies manufacturing pesticides to test their products for toxicity and submit the results to the federal government. Amendments to FIFRA require reevaluation of old, untested pesticides approved before the current requirements for scientific testing were put into place. Initially scheduled to be completed in 1976, this reregistration process is still under way, has been repeatedly delayed, and is now scheduled for completion in the year 2010. Until then, the old, untested pesticides can be sold and used. As one critic has noted, it is as if the bureau of motor vehicles issued everyone a driver's license but did not get around to giving us a road test until decades later.[51] According to the National Research Council, only 10 percent of pesticides in common use have been adequately assessed for hazards; for 38 percent, nothing useful is known; the remaining 52 percent fall somewhere in between.[52]

In the 1970s and 1980s, various right-to-know laws began springing up as a response to this ever-expanding mosh pit of toxic chemicals. The first group of laws established employees' right to know about hazardous substances in their workplaces. A second group sanctioned citizens' right to know about the presence of toxic chemicals in their communities and, finally, about the routine release of some of these chemicals into the environment. For nearly four decades after the widespread introduction of such chemicals into our environment, these rights were not ours. The identity of chemicals released by industry was considered privileged information—trade secrets. Those of us born during this time—the 1940s until the mid-1980s—will never know with certainty what we were exposed to as children and what carcinogenic risks we have assumed from such exposures. We can, however, obtain partial information about our current exposures.

Significantly, neither set of laws came about because legislators and manufacturers calmly agreed that citizens should be made aware of their chemical exposures. Rather, workplace right-to-know laws are rooted in a long history of labor struggle, and the community-based laws—codified as the Emergency Planning and Community Right-to-Know Act (EPCRA)—

passed the U.S. Congress in 1986 over intense industry opposition. This legislation was a response to citizen activism at the state and local levels, as well as a direct reaction to the 1984 chemical disaster in Bhopal, India, which occurred when a feedstock for pesticide manufacture escaped from a Union Carbide plant and killed many thousands of sleeping residents in their homes. Emergency medical efforts were frustrated by the fact that no one knew what the chemical was. A similar chemical release occurred at a sister plant in West Virginia. Shortly thereafter, Congress voted EPCRA into law. Key parts of this legislation passed by a one-vote margin.[53]

The linchpin of EPCRA is the Toxics Release Inventory (TRI). As the SEER Program registry is to cancer incidence, TRI is to carcinogens and other toxins. It requires that certain manufacturers report to the government the total amount of each of some 654 toxic chemicals released each year into air, water, and land. The government then makes these data public information. As a pollution disclosure program, TRI has many deficiencies. Its main shortcoming is that it relies completely on self-reporting and lacks adequate procedures for checking data quality. In addition, it does not address the presence of carcinogens in consumer products; small companies are exempt from reporting; the compliance rate among industries that are required to file is only about 66 percent; and 654 is a small fraction of the total chemicals they use.[54]

Furthermore, loopholes in reporting requirements allow industries to play an elaborate shell game with their wastes. Some analysts believe the substantial decline in emissions from 1987 to the present, for example, partly consists of phantom reductions—such as changes in accounting methods or the contracting of highly polluting processes to other facilities.[55] Researchers tracking the flow of toxic chemicals through the economy point out that declines in toxic waste *releases* have not always been accompanied by parallel declines in toxic waste *production:* the generation of toxic waste by TRI-reporting facilities remains high. Where, then, is the waste going? Without thorough materials accounting, which is not currently required, no one is exactly sure.[56]

Nevertheless, under EPCRA, for the first time in history, any citizen can request from the Environmental Protection Agency (EPA) a list of the reported toxic releases in his or her home county. Access to this information is now acknowledged by our government as a fundamental public right.

In some communities, the TRI has served as a powerful tool for pressuring factories to reduce pollution. Its most important function may be the implicit recognition that a so-called private industry is engaging in a very public act when it releases toxic chemicals into a community's air, water, and soil.[57] Conceptually, we all know the industries in our communities pollute the environment. We may even be able to see and smell the results. But very often, the picture does not come into focus for us until we actually stare at the list of specifics, as when the names and the numbers are printed in our local newspapers: how many pounds of which known or suspected carcinogens were released by which companies into the air we breathe or into the rivers we fish and from which we draw our drinking water?

The TRI's first report, released by the EPA in 1989, had just such an effect. It revealed that *billions* of pounds of toxic chemicals were being routinely emitted each year into the nation's air, water, and land. Nearly all who read the report were amazed. This was the first attempt to gather together routine toxic releases, and the sum was an unquestionably staggering amount. Said a representative from the Chemical Industry Council of New Jersey: "I'll be honest with you. [Our reduction in emissions] probably would not have occurred if that data had not become public information. It was something that caught everyone's attention, including the corporate leaders." A Monsanto spokesman was even more blunt: "The law is having an incredible effect. . . . There's not a chief executive officer around who wants to be the biggest polluter in Iowa."[58]

In the first year of reporting, only about 5 percent of toxic releases in the country were reported under TRI, and yet the effect of ending the silence about toxic releases was huge. Some companies who found themselves on the list of the worst toxic offenders immediately entered into voluntary programs to reduce their emissions. Several communities began using their local data to force more recalcitrant industries to follow suit. Concerned citizens who also happened to be computer wizards came together to provide technical support to communities wishing to access their local TRI data electronically (a task that can now be accomplished on a home computer or at almost any local library). Public Data Access, Inc., mapped the information and, by bringing TRI data together with death certificate data, correlated areas of severe environmental contamination with areas of elevated cancer mortality.

According to the most recent TRI, which is about the size of an average telephone book, 2.26 billion pounds of toxic chemicals were released into the environment in 1994. Of these, 177 million pounds were known or suspected carcinogens.[59]

* * *

In a favorite photograph of myself as a child, I am hanging determinedly onto a tricycle, wearing a goofy expression and my father's army hat. The determination came from trying to salute my father, the photographer, while simultaneously pedaling. It is 1962. The setting is the concrete patio on the south side of our house. A construction worker before the GI Bill returned him to the typewriter as a college student, my father poured this patio himself and laid the brick walkway leading out into his 1.5 acres of former cow pasture.

After the war, my father married a farmer's daughter with a degree in biology and another in chemistry. He built his house on Pekin's east bluff and planted lines of silver maple and white pine in the sod. Before the trees grew up to form a wall around the borders of his property, the patio offered a spectacular view. To the east, cows grazed. Although afraid of them, I liked to stand at the fence and watch them eat—their purply tongues and black plumes of flies, the ripping sounds of the grass.

Just beyond, the bluff's pastures unrolled into what was once—and I am guessing here—hill prairie. Here lay vast fields of corn and soybeans. I liked the corn—each stalk a green man waving his arms. In September, the soybeans turned brilliant yellow and then deepened into an orange-brown far richer than my burnt sienna crayon.

"What color would you call soybeans?" I inquired of Aunt Ann, who farmed two counties east from us.

She didn't miss a beat. "At six dollars a bushel, I would call them gold."

My father drove west to work every morning. Looking through the patio screen from my tricycle, I could see the smokestacks, cooling towers, and distillation chambers of the river valley's three dozen industries. I liked the steam clouds, trails of smoke, and mysterious shimmering vapors. I was especially fond of the pink-and-white-striped towers, which reminded me of giant candy canes. These stacks belonged to the ethanol distillery and the coal-burning power plant just upriver. At night, they became lighthouses—great blinking columns warning planes away. To my sister and me, my father referred to this scene as "progress, girls, progress."

Tazewell Country, Illinois, is home to two distinct cultures, one emblemized by the lone figure on his tractor and the other by picket lines of striking plant workers. Our house was situated in the transitional zone between the two.

Among farmers, Tazewell is known as the birthplace of Reid's Yellow Dent, a famous strain of field corn that became the ancestor of many hybrid seed lines. Among industrialists, Tazewell County is known for the 127-acre Pekin Energy Company, one of the nation's largest producers of ethanol, and as the manufacturing site and proving grounds for Caterpillar tractors, backhoes, and bulldozers. Caterpillar's management offices are headquartered across the Illinois River in Peoria. A hydrologist's description of the area from 1950 is as good as any: "The Peoria-Pekin area is a highly industrialized district requiring an enormous volume of water. The industrial areas are surrounded by the fertile agricultural prairie lands of the corn belt."[60]

Settled before the prairie was sod-busted, Pekin began as a military fort. War and manufacturing have frequently danced together here. Distilling and brewing began as a means of transforming grain into a nonperishable cash commodity that could easily be shipped east. Wartime needs for industrial alcohol then provided a huge new market and inspired new production technologies.[61] One of Pekin's distilleries was founded in 1941 expressly to provide the U.S. military with ethanol. In 1916, the U.S. Army ordered the first Caterpillar tractors, which it used to drag cannons, ammunitions, and supplies to the front. During World War II, Caterpillar machines were used to bulldoze airstrips, grade roads, clear bomb wreckage, and topple palm trees.[62] By 1945, 85 percent of Caterpillar's production was shipped overseas for military work. Collected photographs of "Cats" in action during both world wars and the Korean War are still a hot item in the local bookstore.[63]

Other photographs from the turn of the century show child laborers posing in the sugar-beet fields.[64] The black smoke of the sugar factory forms a dramatic backdrop against the little white faces. The sugar works later become Corn Products, which produced Argo cornstarch and Karo syrup. In 1924, a starch explosion incinerated forty-two workers. In 1980, Corn Products became Pekin Energy.

In September 1994, I drove along the Illinois River banks to pass by where those old beet fields must have been—less than two miles from the house I grew up in. The floodplains are now a landscape of docks, stacks, rail yards, conveyers, elevators, hopper bins, pits, lagoons, coal piles, tailings ponds, settling tanks, power lines, and scrap heaps—all that I had seen at a distance as a child. A union billboard announced, "You Are Now Entering a War Zone," a comment not on the environment but on labor's latest showdown with management at the nearby Caterpillar plant.

There are some places in this world that prompt one to ask, "Where did all this come from?" The fish, vegetable, and flower markets of New York City always bring me to this question. Tazewell County is another kind of place. Spend some time on the Pekin docks. Watch the barges of coal, grain, steel, chemicals, and petroleum products. "Where is all this going?"

There are partial answers. The grain elevators and the mills ship corn and pelletized animal feed south to New Orleans and from there to Asia and Europe. The coal-fired power plant called Powerton sends electricity 165 miles north to Chicago via high-power lines. In 1943, its smoke prevented landings at an airport forty-one miles away. In 1974—the year I turned fifteen—this plant was named the worst polluter in the state of Illinois. Trace Chemicals formulates pesticides. I do not know where they end up. The brass foundry makes huge cylinders, called bushings, for draglines, drills, and crushers used in strip mines. Caterpillars end up everywhere. In 1986, I looked out the window of a bus heading south along the Nile River in eastern Sudan and found myself face to face with Caterpillar's familiar logo—a giant capital *C*—painted on a billboard near a military installation.[65]

About the other industries lining the river valley I know less. I do not know what goes on at Airco Industrial Gases, the Sherex Chemical Company, the Agrico Chemical Company, or the aluminum foundry. I know that

Keystone Steel and Wire makes nails and barbed wire out of scrap metal. In 1993, the company faced charges for polluting the sand aquifer below its facilities with TCE and another synthetic degreaser, 1,1,1-trichloroethane, a suspected carcinogen. The promises it made to clean up and switch to less toxic chemical technologies have, so far, kept Keystone off the Superfund's National Priorities List.[66]

Like a film of gasoline on a pond's surface, an emotional blankness coats my words here. There are, of course, many ways of expressing the relevance of the historical past to the personal present. Surely there is one that could describe the private thoughts of an East Bluff girl returning home from Boston and passing by the hospital where, years before, she was diagnosed with a type of cancer known to be caused by exposure to environmental carcinogens. Surely there is a language able to explain why such a woman would now drive along Distillery Road, breathing the acrid air, searching for nineteenth-century sugar-beet fields and twentieth-century hazardous waste sites.

A silence spreads out. I cannot make her speak.

It is not the silence of resignation or paralysis. It is the fear that speaking intimately about this landscape—or myself as a native of this place—would make too exceptional what is common and ordinary. I feel protective of my hometown. Its citizens are not unusually ignorant or evil or shortsighted. And, away from the river, the city itself is lovely. Between the fields and the factories are nice, old neighborhoods, beautiful parks, the county fairgrounds, and reasonably good schools. There is nothing unique or even unusual about Tazewell County, Illinois. As true everywhere else, its agricultural and industrial practices—from weed control to degreasing parts—were transformed by chemical technologies introduced after World War II. As true everywhere else, these chemicals, many of them carcinogens, have found their way into the general environment. As true almost everywhere else, no systematic investigation has been conducted to determine whether any connection exists between the release of these chemicals and the rates of cancer here.

"We know the emissions are present, and the cancer, but we don't know if the two are related," said a state toxicologist quoted in the local paper in March 1995. This article concluded:

> The impact of tons of toxic emissions on the health of industrial workers and the public never has been systematically studied and may be impossible to determine. . . . Health statistics in Peoria and Tazewell counties are troubling, but the connection between emissions and health problems is not clear.[67]

There is nothing special or unusual about the toxic release inventories for Tazewell and Peoria Counties. Of seventy-eight regions in Illinois, the Pekin-Peoria area ranks only thirteenth in TRI emissions. Nonetheless, I cried when I first read through these inventories. Hundreds of pages of computer print itemize the toxic emissions for area industries during the years since 1987, when this information was first compiled. In 1991, for example, large manufacturers in Peoria and Tazewell Counties legally released 11.1 million pounds of toxic chemicals into the air, water, and land. Among the known and suspected carcinogens released were benzene, chromium, formaldehyde, nickel, ethylene, acrylonitrile, butyraldehyde, lindane, and captan.[68] Captan is a carcinogenic fungicide prohibited for many domestic uses in 1989. In 1987, according to the TRI, 250 pounds of captan ended up in the Pekin sewer system. In 1992, 321 pounds were released into the air.[69]

Tips of all kinds of icebergs are revealed in other right-to-know documents.[70] For example, I have a partial record of pre-TRI toxic releases in Tazewell County dating back to 1972. The carcinogens catch my eye first—PCBs, vinyl chloride, benzene—but the list also includes other frightening and curious items: printing ink, jet fuel, asphalt sealer, dynamite, scrubber sludge, fuel oil, antifreeze, fly ash, coal dust, herbicides, furnace oil, and "explosive vapors."

In addition, I possess a twenty-four-page list of facilities in Tazewell County with permits to discharge wastes into particular rivers and streams ("local receiving waters: Farm Creek . . . local receiving waters: Illinois River," etc.). I have also obtained a thirty-four-page list of each and every facility—from the local crematorium to the auto body shop—permitted to deal in any way with hazardous materials. Right-to-know legislation has given me access to a hefty off-site transfer report, a document particularly revealing because it shows the flow of toxic wastes coming into Tazewell County. I know, for example, that the Sun Chemical Corporation of Newark, New Jersey, sent 250 pounds of friable asbestos to the Pekin Metro landfill for disposal in 1987. Tazewell doubled the amount of hazardous waste it generated and shipped off-site between 1989 and 1992,[71] but, as one of the state's top receiving counties, it still received four times more waste than it produced.[72]

The spill report for Tazewell County details chemical accidents. Here is the first entry as it appears on the list:[73]

DATE: 6/11/1988

STREET: RTE 24

MATERIAL SPILLED: METHYL CHLORIDE

AMOUNT SPILLED: 2,000 LBS

WATERWAY/OTHER: AIR RELEASE

EVENT DESCRIPTION: WEIGH TANK/WHILE PREPARING FOR
    INSPECTORS, VALVE INADVERTENTLY OPENED/EXACT CAUSE
    UNDER INVESTIGATION

ACTION TAKEN: TEMPORARILY EVACUATED AFFECTED BUILDING
    FOR TWO HOURS . . . SHUT VALVE TO STOP RELEASE

Route 24 is an old highway. To the west, it follows the Illinois River valley for some miles before shooting across the plains to the Mississippi River town of Quincy. To the east, it connects Pekin to the Indiana border, passing four miles south of my grandparents' farm in Forrest. I can tell you about every small town between here and there, describe every moraine, name every creek.

Methyl chloride is classified as a probable human carcinogen. It causes mutations in bacteria and kidney cancers in mice. It also causes birth defects and degeneration of the sperm-carrying tubules in rat testicles. Used in the manufacture of silicone products, fuel additives, and herbicides, methyl chloride is synthesized by attaching a chlorine atom onto a molecule of wood alcohol. By 1981, annual production reached 362 million pounds per year. Domestic consumption expands approximately 6.5 percent per year. Methyl chloride's long-term effects on human health have never been studied directly.[74]

Amid a flooded sea of information, an absence of knowledge. Amid a thousand computer-generated words, a silence spreads out.

* * *

Seek. Strike. Destroy. Of all the unexpected consequences of World War II, perhaps the most ironic is the discovery that a remarkable number of the new chemicals it ushered in are estrogenic—that is, at low levels inside the human body, they mimic the female hormone estrogen. Many of the hypermasculine weapons of conquest and progress, are, biologically speaking, emasculating.[75]

This effect occurs through a variety of biochemical mechanisms. Some chemicals imitate the hormone directly, while others interfere with the various systems that regulate the body's production and metabolism of natural estrogens. Still others seem to work by blocking the receptor sites for male hormones, which are collectively called androgens. In 1995, fifty years after its triumphant return from the war and entry into civilian life, DDT again made headlines when new animal studies showed that DDT's main metabolic breakdown product, DDE, is an androgen-blocker.[76]

Our enzymes quickly convert DDT into DDE. But because the next step is much slower (recall DDT's seven-year half-life), we accumulate DDE as we age—much as a fine stream of sand grains gradually forms a heap at the bottom of an hourglass. DDE molecules can cross the human placenta and can also accumulate in breast milk. Thus, those of us too young to have been sprayed by DDT directly nevertheless have accumulated DDE in our bodies through at least two routes: from our mothers (both before and after birth) and our consumption of milk, meat, eggs, and fish. Animals, like the humans who eat them, lack the biochemical hardware needed for efficient conversion of DDE to something excretable.[77]

For boys and men, the consequences may include physical deformities such as undescended testicles, lowered sperm counts, and testicular cancer. No one knows what effect DDE exposure has on the reproductive development of girls or women; no research has been done. The only thing we know for a fact is that DDE is biochemically different enough from anything else in the human body—male or female—that it is not completely metabolized as are our own natural sex hormones. This is one reason why, more than two decades after DDT's forced retirement in the United States, we still have DDE molecules floating around in our tissues.

Much of the concern about hormone-disrupting chemicals has been focused on their possible role in contributing to birth defects, reproductive failures in wildlife, and infertility in humans.[78] At times, these discussions seem nearly to eclipse the quieter, but longer-running conversations about the possible contributions of estrogen-mimicking contaminants to cancer. Certain breast cancers, for example, are notorious for growing faster in the presence of estrogen, which is why prescribing antiestrogenic drugs is standard chemotherapeutic protocol. Many other cancers—those of the ovary, uterus, testicle, and prostate, for example—are also known to be, or suspected to be, hormonally mediated. Thus, identifying pollutants that interfere with hormones is important to public dialogue about human cancers of all kinds.[79]

The relevance of endocrine disruption for cancer is not a new subject. Rachel Carson mentioned it explicitly in *Silent Spring*.[80] Nevertheless, a mysterious event in a Tufts University laboratory a few years ago brought renewed attention to the topic.

The cell biologists Ana Soto and Carlos Sonnenschein were working out the details of estrogen's relationship to breast cancer when something puzzling happened in their laboratory. Breast cancer cells growing in plastic dishes containing no estrogen started dividing rapidly, as though they were being hormonally stimulated. "This indicated that some type of contamination had occurred," Soto remembers. "We made an accidental discovery."[81]

Soto and Sonnenschein traced the contamination to the plastic tubes they were using to store blood serum. Together, they purified the contaminant and identified it as nonylphenol, a synthetic organic chemical added during the manufacture of plastic to prevent it from cracking. Molecules of nonylphenol were being shed from the tubes into the serum.

In a series of follow-up experiments, the two researchers demonstrated that nonylphenol is estrogenic. It activates estrogen receptors within cells so equipped, which in turn alters the activity of certain genes and changes the rate at which these cells divide. Nonylphenol makes breast cancer cells—at least those growing in petri dishes—grow faster. Soto and Sonnenschein began testing other chemical aliens—certain common pesticides, detergents, and other types of plastics—and discovered estrogenic activity in a whole variety of petrochemically derived substances.[82] Other researchers were inspired to do the same. Approximately forty such chemicals have so far been identified as capable of mimicking estrogen.[83]

This flurry of attention has shed light on the biological activities of two ubiquitous but almost totally unknown groups of synthetic compounds: plasticizers and surfactants.[84] Plasticizers are chemicals that are mixed with plastics to give them more strength and flexibility. Surfactants are added to, for example, detergents, herbicides, and paints to help the active ingredient stick to the surface of its target—dirt particles, weeds, or the wall of a house. Alkylphenol polyethoxylates (APEOs) are surfactants widely used in household detergents. Since their introduction in the 1940s, they have become widely disseminated in rivers, lakes, and streams via sewage systems. APEOs have been detected in drinking water in New Jersey.[85] In 1994, in the wake of Soto and Sonnenschein's discovery, a team of researchers in England reported that APEOs can, in trace amounts, stimulate the growth of breast cancer cells and feminize male fish exposed to contaminated sewage.[86] Fish collected from many U.S. rivers also display hormonal abnormalities consistent with exposure to estrogenic substances in river-borne sewage.[87] However, it is not at all clear at this point—either in England or the United States—whether the feminization of fish downstream of sewage outfalls can be totally explained by exposure to chemicals such as APEO surfactants. New evidence suggests that at least some of the problem may stem from exposure to natural and synthetic estrogens found in women's urine—and so researchers investigating the gender-bending potential of sewage are now turning their attention from washing machines to toilets.

Phthalates, the plasticizers with the nearly impossible name, turn out to be the most abundant industrial contaminant in the environment. At least two have now been identified as estrogenic, and traces of both have been found in food. One is used in plastic food wrap and the other in papers and cardboard designed for contact with liquid, dry, and fatty foods.[88]

Some phthalates are known to be overtly carcinogenic. For example, DEHP—which stands for the even more impossible di(2ethylhexyl)phthalate— gives PVC plastic its flexibility. It is also classified as a probable human carcinogen and because of this, its use in baby pacifiers, plastic food wrap, and toys has been discontinued. Residues of DEHP have been found in food items, especially those with high fat content, such as eggs, milk, cheese, margarine, and seafood.[89] Because DEHP, like nonylphenol, can leach from plastic containers holding bodily fluids, it has also been found in blood used for transfusions.[90] In 1993, the yearly production of DEHP was 270 million pounds. According to TRI data, in 1991 alone 3.76 million pounds of DEHP were released into the environment or transfered off-site for disposal.

About half of the synthetic materials known to function as endocrine disrupters belong to a chemical group called organochlorines.[91] Not all estrogenic materials are organochlorines, and not all organochlorines are estrogenic, but the overlap is impressive. Moreover, organochlorines are such a large group—around eleven thousand exist—and they tend to be so persistent in the environment, so reactive within human tissues, and so frequently associated with cancer that they merit special consideration.

Many of the chemicals we have already discussed belong to this group. Lindane, DDT, heptachlor, chlordane, PCBs, CFCs, TCE, perc, 2,4-D, methyl chloride, vinyl chloride, polyvinyl chloride, dioxin, and chloroform are all organochlorines. Benzene, formaldehyde, nonylphenol, and phthalates are not.

Organochlorines, which involve a chemical marriage between chlorine and carbon atoms, are not strictly a human invention. A few are formed during volcanic eruptions and forest fires and some by living organisms such as marine algae. For the most part, however, chlorine and carbon move in separate spheres in the natural world—and in the bodies of humans and other mammals. To force the two together, elemental chlorine gas is required.

Although it holds a rightful place in the periodic table of elements, pure chlorine *is* a human invention. It can be produced by passing electricity through salt water in a procedure that was first undertaken on an industrial scale in 1893. A powerful poison, chlorine gas became known to the world during World War I, but its manufacture grew slowly until World War II, then rose exponentially. About 1 percent of this production is used for disinfecting water and about 10 percent for bleaching paper, and the majority is combined with various carbon compounds, usually derived from petroleum, to make organochlorines.

In its elemental form, chlorine (but not the ion chloride) is highly reactive with carbon, which is why so many different combinations are possible. Like houses of different architectural styles, some organochlorines are very small and plain, and others huge and ornate. One of the simplest is chloroform, which consists of a single carbon atom with one hydrogen and three chlorine atoms attached to it like four spokes on a hub. Consisting of one chlorine, two carbon, and three hydrogen atoms, vinyl chloride is not much more complicated. The dry-cleaning solvent perchloroethylene is two carbon and four chlorine atoms, while the industrial degreaser trichloroethylene consists of two carbon and three chlorine atoms.

On the more elaborate side are chlorinated phenols. These consist of a hexagonal ring of six carbons with various chlorinated groups hanging off the corners. The pesticide lindane, for example, consists of a carbon hexagon with six chlorine atoms attached all around. The herbicide 2,4-D is a hexagon with chlorines attached to the second and fourth carbon atoms and a carbon chain waving like a flag from the first carbon atom. DDT is more complicated yet. It consists of two hexagonal rings, each with one chlorine atom attached, yoked together by a single carbon atom from which dangles a chlorinated carbon tail.

And then there are the PCBs. PCBs are the elders of the group, and they are referred to in the plural for a reason. As their name implies, polychlorinated biphenyls comprise two rings of carbon atoms welded directly together, around which are attached any number of chlorine atoms. In fact, there are 209 possible combinations and therefore 209 different PCBs. Some of these chemical combinations are estrogenic and some appear not to be, but no one has worked this out definitively.

As a group, organochlorines tend to be persistent in air and water. When they evaporate and are swept into the wind currents, some fall back to the earth close to their origins, while others can circulate for thousands of miles before being redeposited into water, vegetation, and soil. From there, they enter the food chain. Diet is thus believed to be a major route of exposure for us.

Not all organochlorines are deliberately constructed. Whenever elemental chlorine is present, the natural environment will synthesize additional, unwanted organochlorine molecules. These reactions can take place when water containing organic matter, such as decayed leaves, is chlorinated. It can happen in pulp and paper mills during the process of bleaching or when chlorinated plastics are burned. It can happen during the manufacture of other organochlorines. The production of 2,4,5-T, the burning of plastic, and certain methods of bleaching paper all contribute to the birth of dioxin. A chemical of no known usefulness and never manufactured on purpose, dioxin has been linked to a variety of cancers and is now believed to inhabit the body tissues of every person living in the United States. Dioxin is a beautifully symmetrical molecule, consisting of two chlorinated carbon rings held together by a double bridge of oxygen atoms.[92]

* * *

The development of industrial chemistry in this century has been driven by the exigencies of war. Out of this crucible came new chemicals of all sorts. Some, such as organophosphate nerve gas, seem to have been born from truly evil intentions; others, from admirable ones. But few were invented solely for the purposes to which they were turned after the war's end. And few were adequately tested for long-term health effects.

As the daughter of a World War II veteran, I am grateful that my father did not die in a typhus epidemic in Naples. But as a survivor of cancer, as a native of Tazewell County, and as a member of the most poisoned generation to come of adult age, I am sorry that cooler heads did not prevail in the calm prosperity of peacetime, when careful consideration and a longer view on public health were once again permissible and necessary. I am sorry that no one asked, "Is this the industrial path we want to continue along? Is this the most reasonable way to rid our dogs of fleas and our trees of gypsy moths? Is this the safest material for a baby's pacifier or for a tub of margarine?" Or that those who did ask such questions were not heard.

These questions are finally beginning to receive a hearing. In 1993, the American Public Health Association issued a resolution calling for the gradual phaseout of most organochlorine compounds and for the pursuit of safe alternatives.[93] In doing so, it followed another august agency, the International Joint Commission on the Great Lakes. Citing rising rates of breast cancer within the Great Lakes basin, the commission recommended scrapping the current practice of regulating persistent toxic chemicals after they have been produced, used, and released. Taking its place would be a preventive strategy recognizing that all such substances are "deleterious to the human condition" and must no longer be tolerated in the ecosystem, "whether or not unassailable scientific proof of acute or chronic damage is universally accepted."[94]

In the fall of 1994, the esteemed epidemiologist David Ozonoff addressed a group of five hundred breast cancer activists in Boston and expressed his support for these concepts:

> The ability to make these chemicals [organochlorines] in high volume did not even exist prior to World War II. . . . They are not a legacy from the industrial revolution of the 19th century, but of the rise of the chemical industry of the 20th. They are not woven into the warp and woof of our national fabric, but on the contrary, are recent and unwelcome newcomers.[95]

I do not contend that all synthetic organic chemicals should be banned. Neither do I advocate a return to the days of celluloid and castor oil. From what I understand, celluloid was flammable and brittle, and I'm sure castor oil had its own problems. However, I am convinced that human inventiveness is not restricted to acts of war. The path that chemistry has taken in the last half of this century is only one path—and not even a particularly imaginative one.

Some solutions may indeed be found through the rescue of chemical processes abandoned years before—as in the quiet decision of many daily newspapers to switch to soy-based inks—while others may be sought through altogether new applications of knowledge. Chlorine-free methods of bleaching paper are possible and are already in small-scale commercial use both here and in Europe. Citrus-based solvents, ultrasonics, and old-fashioned soap and water can often replace chlorinated solvents used for degreasing operations and precision cleaning of electronic parts. New methods of embalming and different attitudes about the role of funeral services can reduce the use of formaldehyde in mortuaries.[96]

Sweeping changes are immediately possible in the dry-cleaning industry. Most clothing tagged as "dry-clean only" can in fact be professionally cleaned with the use of water, special soaps, and reengineered washing machines that allow computerized control over humidity, agitation, and heat. (Pressurized carbon dioxide also holds promise as a nontoxic solvent for cleaning textiles.)[97] The Boston area, for example, is home to one such wet-cleaning operation, a pilot project of the Toxics Use Reduction Institute. I recently delivered to this shop a down coat, a silk dress, a badly stained antique kimono, and a pile of my best wool, cashmere, and rayon suits. All came back clean, beautifully pressed, and odor-free. The white streak across the sleeve of the green blazer—the result of an encounter with a freshly painted doorframe—was gone. Best of all, the proprietor, who appeared about eight months pregnant, expressed to me her relief at not having to be exposed to perc.

Most of the perchloroethylene manufactured in the United States is used by the textile and dry-cleaning industry. In 1992 alone, 12.3 million pounds of this organochlorine and suspected carcinogen was released into air, ten thousand pounds to rivers and streams, and nine thousand pounds to land. Thirteen thousand pounds were directly injected into underground wells. The recycling of perchloroethylene produces contaminated sludge and filters, which are subsequently deposited in landfills where they poison soil. Traces of perchloroethylene have been found in breast milk, cow's milk, meat, oil, fruit, fish, shellfish, and algae. Perc has been detected in rainwater, seawater, river water, groundwater, and tap water.[98] More than 650,000 workers are thought to be exposed to perc on the job, and an estimated 99,000 New York City dwellers are exposed to elevated levels just from breathing—many because their office or apartment shares the same building with a dry-cleaner. A 1993 survey found that 83 percent of New York City apartments located above a dry-cleaning establishment had ambient perc levels in excess of state health guidelines.[99]

It is time to start pursuing alternative paths. From the right to know and the duty to inquire flows the obligation to act.   ∎

NOTES

1. World War II in *Silent Spring:* R. Carson, *Silent Spring* (Boston: Houghton Mifflin, 1962). (See especially Chapters 2 and 3.)
2. All life was caught in the crossfire: Ibid., 8.
3. CFCs and stratospheric chlorine: S. Solomon, "Progress towards a Quantitative Understanding of Antarctic Ozone," *Nature* 347 (1990): 347–54.
4. inactive synthetic substances can shed or off-gas: J. Gilbert et al., "Identification by Gas Chromatography–Mass Spectrometry of Vinyl Chloride Oligomen and other Low-Molecular-Weight Components in Poly (Vinyl Chlorides) Resins for Food Packaging Applications," *Journal of Chromatography* 237 (1982): 249–61.
5. the worst of both worlds: Some critics contend that exposure to estrogen-mimicking industrial chemicals is unlikely to play a significant role in breast cancer because our exposure levels to these substances are far less than the exposure to naturally occurring estrogens in food crops. See, for example, S. H. Safe, "Environmental and Dietary Estrogens and Human Health: Is There a Problem?" *EHP* 103 (1995): 346–51. This argument ignores the fact that plant estrogens are readily broken down and excreted by the human body, while synthetic chemicals with estrogenic properties can be stored in fatty tissue for years. Furthermore, plant-based estrogens appear to have a protective effect against breast cancer. See J. Barrett, "Phytoestrogens: Friends or Foes?" *EHP* 104 (1996): 478–82.

More broadly, some researchers have argued that public concern about synthetic, environmental carcinogens is misplaced because the majority of carcinogens to which we are exposed are "natural" and include pest-repelling chemicals manufactured by food crops themselves. See, for example, B. N. Ames et al., "The Causes and Prevention of Cancer," *Proceedings of the National Academy of Science* 92 (1995): 5258–65; and NRC, *Carcinogens and Anticarcinogens in the Human Diet* (Washington, D.C.: National Academy Press, 1996). Again, this kind of accounting is incomplete. Unlike natural chemicals, daily exposures to very tiny amounts of synthetic chemicals are cumulative. As Devra Davis has pointed out, natural carcinogens can often be dismantled by human enzymes before they cause harm or, in the case of many fruits and vegetables, are often accompanied by equally potent anticarcinogens. As John Wargo has pointed out, it is hardly prudent to avoid regulating synthetic carcinogens just because we also have exposures to natural ones. If anything, an awareness of our exposures to unavoidable natural carcinogens should generate greater urgency toward eliminating the avoidable synthetic ones. Moreover, natural carcinogens in foodstuffs present only one route of exposure. Unlike their synthetic counterparts, plant-generated chemicals do not spill into waterways, pollute groundwater, contaminate sport fish, waft up from dump sites, or drift into other continents. Presumably, natural carcinogens have not skyrocketed in production over the past half century. They cannot explain the coincident rise in cancer incidence rates. See J. Wargo, *Our Children's Toxic Legacy: How Science and Law Fail to Protect Us from Pesticides* (New Haven, Conn.: Yale Univ. Press, 1996), 127; the exchange of letters between Bruce Ames and his critics in the Dec. 1990 through Feb. 1991 issues of *Science,* vols. 250 and 251; and W. Linjinsky, "Environmental Cancer Risks—Real and Unreal" (editorial), *Environmental Research* 50 (1989): 207–9.

6. collect in tissues high in fat: J. D. Sherman, *Chemical Exposure and Disease: Diagnostic and Investigative Techniques* (Princeton, N.J.: Princeton Scientific Publishing, 1994); L. S. Welch, "Organic Solvents," in M. Paul (ed.), *Occupational and Environmental Reproductive Hazards: A Guide for Clinicians* (Baltimore: Williams & Wilkins, 1993), 267–79.

7. chloroform: ATSDR, *Toxicological Profile for Chloroform* (Atlanta: ATSDR, 1993); IEPA, "Chloroform: Chemical. Information Sheet" (Springfield Ill.: IEPA, Office of Chemical Safety, 1990).

8. DDT in World War II: E. P. Russell III, "Speaking of Annihilation': Mobilizing for War against Human and Insect Enemies, 1914–1945," *Journal of American History* 82 (1996): 1505–29; T. R. Dunlap, *DDT: Scientists, Citizens, and Public Policy* (Princeton, N.J.: Princeton Univ. Press, 1981) 61–62; J. Whorton, *Before* Silent Spring: *Pesticides and Public Health in Pre-DDT America* (Princeton, N.J.: Princeton Univ. Press, 1974), 248–55.

9. Hitler's head: This ad appeared in the trade magazine *Soap and Sanitary Chemicals* in April 1944 and is reprinted in Russell, "Speaking of Annihilation."

10. phenoxy herbicides: D. E. Lilienfeld and M. A. Gallo, "2,4-D, 2,4,5-T, and 2,3,7,8-TCDD: An Overview," *Epidemiologic Reviews* 11 (1989): 28–58.

11. parathion, and other organophosphates: Sherman, *Chemical Exposure and Disease,* 24; H. W. Chambers, "Organophosphorous Compounds: An Overview," in J. E. Chambers and P. E. Levi (eds.), *Organophosphate Chemistry, Fate, and Effects* (San Diego: Academic Press, 1992), 3–17.

12. mechanisms of action: L. J. Fuortes et al., "Cholinesterase-Inhibiting Insecticide Toxicity," *American Family Physician* 47 (1993): 1613–20; F. Matsumura, *Toxicology, of Insecticides,* 2nd ed. (New York: Plenum, 1985), 111–202.

13. organophosphates as German nerve gas: Sherman, *Chemical Exposure and Disease,* 161; J. Borkin, *The Crime and Punishment of I. G. Farben* (New York: Harper & Row, 1978), 722–23.

14. phenoxy herbicides in war: P. F. Cecil, *Herbicidal Warfare: The Ranch Hand Project in Vietnam* (New York; Praeger, 1986); A. Ihde, *The Development of Modern Chemistry* (New York: Harper & Row, 1964), 722–23.

15. by 1960, 2,4-D accounted for half: Lilienfeld and Gallo, "2,4-D, 2,4,5-T."

16. graphs of pesticide use: W. J. Hayes Jr. and E. R. Laws (eds.), *Handbook of Pesticide Toxicology,* vol. 1, *General Principles* (New York: Academic Press, 1991), 22.

17. capturing 90 percent of the market: NRC: *Pesticides in the Diets,* 15.

18. pesticide use statistics: EPA, *Pesticide Industry Sales and Usage 1992–93 Market Estimates,* 733-K-94-001 (Washington, D.C.: EPA, 1994), 14, table 4, NRC, *Pesticides in the Diets,* 15.

19. current U.S. annual use: This figure includes nonconventional pesticide use, such as wood preservatives and disinfectants. Herbicides, fungicides, and insecticides alone totaled 1.25 billion pounds in 1995 (Jay Feldman, National Coalition against the Misuse of Pesticides, personal communication).

20. family pesticide use as an important route of exposure: M. Moses, *Designer Poisons: How to Protect Your Health and Home from Toxic Pesticides* (San Francisco: Pesticide Education Center, 1995).

21. 82 percent of households use pesticides: R. W. Whitmore et al., *The National Home and Garden Pesticide Survey,* vol. 1, *Executive Summary: Results and Recommendations,* RTl/5100/17-01F (Washington, D.C.: EPA, 1992). See also the excellent review by S. H. Zahm and A. Blair, "Carcinogenic Risk from Pesticides," in General Motors Cancer Research Fund, *1992 Accomplishments in Cancer Research* (Philadelphia: J. B. Lippincott, 1993), 266–78.

22. families in Missouri: J. R. Davis et al., "Family Pesticide Use in the Home, Garden, Orchard, and Yard," *Archives of Environmental Contamination and Toxicology* 22 (1992): 260–66.

23. persistence of pesticidal residues indoors: Moses, *Designer Poisons,* 25–30.

24. pesticides in carpet fibers and house dust: R. G. Lewis et al., "Evaluation of Methods for Monitoring the Potential Exposure of Small Children to Pesticides in the Residential Environment," *Archives of Environmental Contamination and Toxicology* 26 (1994): 37–46; M. Moses et al., "Environmental Equity and Pesticide Exposure," *Toxicology and Industrial Health* 9 (1993): 913–59.

25. Los Angeles study: R. A. Lowengart et al., "Childhood Leukemia and Parents' Occupational and Home Exposures," *JNCI* 79 (1987): 39–46.

26. Denver study: J. K. Leiss and D. A. Savitz, "Home Pesticide Use and Childhood Cancer: A Case-Control Study," *AJPH* 85 (1995): 249–52.

27. brain tumors in children and household pesticides. J. R. Davis et al., "Family Pesticide Use and Childhood Brain Cancer," *Archives of Environmental Contamination and Toxicology* 24 (1993): 87–92.

28. lindane-containing lice shampoo: According to the National Pediculosis Association, six million Americans contract lice each year. Lindane, an organochlorine, is banned for agricultural use in several countries and is tightly restricted in the United States. Nevertheless, some lice shampoos still contain lindane, which the USDHHS classifies as a substance "which may reasonably be anticipated to be a carcinogen" (USDHHS, *Seventh Annual Report on Carcinogens,* Summary [Research Triangle Park, N.C.: USDHHS, 1994], 241–44). The use of lindane-based lice shampoo has also been linked to the development of cancer-related blood disorders in humans. See A. E. Rauch et al.,

"Lindane (Kwell)-Induced Aplastic Anemia," *Archives of Internal Medicine* 150 (1990): 2393–95.

29. rise in brain cancers in children: L. A. G. Ries et al., *SEER Cancer Statistics Review; 1971–1991: Tables and Graphs,* NIH Pub. 94-2789 (Bethesda, Md.: NCI, 1994), 428.

30. rise of petrochemicals: R. F. Sawyer, "Trends in Auto Emissions and Gasoline Composition," *EHP* 101, suppl. 6 (1993): 5–12; Ihde, *Modern Chemistry.*

31. Germany's artificial fertilizer: Ihde, *Modern Chemistry,* 680–81.

32. chlorine gas and chlorinated solvents: International Programme on Chemical Safety, WHO, "Chlorine and Hydrogen Chloride," *Environmental Health Criteria* 21 (1982): 54–60; Dr. Edmund Russell III, personal communication.

33. after the war ended: A. Thackary et al., *Chemistry in America, 1876–1976* (Dordrecht, Netherlands: Reidel, 1985).

34. by the 1930s: Ihde, *Modern Chemistry.*

35. the all-out assaults of World War II: Ibid.

36. fear of national leaders: Dr. Edmund Russell III, personal communication.

37. quote by Aaron Ihde: Ihde, *Modern Chemistry,* 674.

38. transformation from a carbohydrate-based economy to a petrochemical-based one: D. Morris and I. Ahmed, *The Carbohydrate Economy: Making Chemical and Industrial Materials from Plant Matter* (Washington, D.C.: Institute for Local Self-Reliance, 1992). For an entertaining history of plant-derived plastics and their replacement by petrochemical plastics, see S. Fenichell, *Plastic: The Making of a Synthetic Century* (New York: Harper-Business, 1996).

39. production, use, and carcinogenicity of formaldehyde: USDHHS, *Seventh Annual Report,* 214–19.

40. formaldehyde in foam insulation: IDPH, "Urea Formaldehyde Foam Insulation" (pamphlet) (Springfield, Ill.: IDPH, 1992).

41. formaldehyde as an indoor air pollutant: M. C. Marbury and R. A. Krieger, "Formaldehyde," in J. M. Samet and J. D. Spengler (eds.), *Indoor Air Pollution. A Health Perspective* (Baltimore: Johns Hopkins Univ. Press, 1991), 223–51.

42. routes of exposure to formaldehyde: USDHHS and U.S. Labor Department, "Formaldehyde: Evidence of Carcinogenicity," *Joint NIOSH/OSHA Current intelligence Bulletin* 34 (1980).

43. soybeans as a formaldehyde predecessor: Morris and Ahmed, *Carbohydrate Economy.*

44. other oil-based plants: Ibid.

45. synthetic cutting fluids in machine shops: Y. T. Fan, "N-Nitrosodiethanolamine in Synthetic Cutting Fluids: A Part-per-Hundred Impurity," *Science* 196 (1977): 70–71.

46. contaminants in cutting fluids: USDHHS, *Seventh Annual Report,* 282.

47. quote from cutting-fluid study: Fan, "N-Nitrosodiethanolamine," 71.

48. percentage of chemicals tested: NRC, *Toxicity Testing: Strategies to Determine Needs and Priorities* (Washington, D.C.: National Academy Press, 1984). Updated estimate obtained from Dr. James Huff, Environmental Carcinogenesis Program, National Institute for Environmental Health Sciences, Jan. 1997.

49. review of new chemicals under TSCA: L. Ember, "Pollution Prevention: Study Says Chemical Industry Lags," *Chemical and Engineering News,* 20 Mar. 1995, 6.

50. FFDCA and FIFRA: For a thoughtful discussion of the loopholes and shortcomings of both of these laws, see Wargo, *Our Children's Toxic Legacy* and GAO, *Food Safety: Changes Needed to Minimize Unsafe Chemicals in Food,* Report to the Chairman, Human

Resources and Intergovernmental Relations Subcommittee, Committee on Government Operations, House of Representatives, GAO/RCED-94-192, Sept. 1994.

51. issuing everyone a driver's license: D. Ozonoff, "Taking the Handle off the Chlorine Pump" (presentation at the public health forum, "Environmental and Occupational Health Problems Posed by Chlorinated Organic Chemicals," Boston Univ. School of Public Health, 5 Oct. 1993).

52. NRC report: NRC, *Toxicity Testing*.

53. history of right-to-know laws: B. A. Goldman, "Is TRI Useful in the Environmental Justice Movement?" (presentation to the Toxics Release Inventory Data Use Conference, Boston, Mass., 6 Dec. 1994), reprinted in *EPA Proceedings: Toxics Release Inventory (TRI) Data Use Conference, Building TRI and Pollution Prevention Partnerships*, EPA/749-R-95-001 (Washington, D.C.: EPA, 1995), 133–37; and Paul Orum, Working Group on Community-Right-to-Know, personal communication.

54. deficiencies of TRI: Goldman, "Is TRI Useful"; Working Group on Community Right-to-Know, "Environmental Groups Blast EPA for Toxics Reporting Loophole," press release, Washington D.C., July 25, 1994; Paul Orum, personal communication.

55. phantom reductions: Working Group on Community Right-to-Know, "New Toxics Data Show Little Progress in Source Reduction," press release, Washington, D.C., 27 Mar. 1995.

56. declines in releases not tethered to decline in production: Inform, Inc., *Toxics Watch 1995* (New York: Inform, Inc., 1995). Since TRI's inception, there has been no overall decline in toxic waste generation by the 74,000 plants that, as of 1995, had to report to TRI. As the EPA itself admits, the total amount of toxic chemical waste generated by industry has actually increased, not declined, since the first TRI report was released. Nevertheless, *reported* releases dropped about 35 percent between 1988 and 1992. Some analysts attribute this apparent discrepancy to better containment. "So while industry may be improving its management of toxic chemical waste, clearly there are still many opportunities for preventing pollution by reducing the use of toxic chemicals," concluded EPA administrator Carol Browner in 1992 (EPA, *1992 Toxics Release Inventory: Public Data Release*, 745-R-94-001 [Washington, D.C.: EPA, 1994]).

57. impact of the TRI report: J. H. Cushman, "Efficient Pollution Rule under Attack," *New York Times*, 28 June 1995, A-16; K. Schneider, "For Communities, Knowledge of Polluters Is Power," *New York Times*, 24 Mar. 1991, A-5.

58. quotes from chemical industry representatives: Reprinted in *Working Notes on Community-Right-to-Know* (Washington, D.C.: Working Group on Community Right-to-Know, May–June 1995), 3.

59. the most recent TRI: EPA, *1994 Toxics Release Inventory: Public Data Release*, 745-R-96-002 (Washington, D.C.: EPA, 1996).

60. a hydrologist's description: L. Hoberg et al., *Groundwater in the Peoria Region*, Cooperative Research Bulletin 39 (Urbana: ISGWS, 1950), 53.

61. history of Pekin: *Pekin, Illinois, Sesquicentennial (1824–1974): A History* (Pekin, Ill.: Pekin Chamber of Commerce, 1974).

62. one of Pekin's distilleries: Midwest Grain Products, *1994 Annual Report*.

63. "Cats" in action: P. A. Letourneau (ed.), *Caterpillar Military Tractors*, vol. 1. (Minneapolis: Iconografix, 1994).

64. sugar-beet fields and starch explosion: *Pekin, Illinois. Sesquicentennial*, 68.

65. pollution from Powerton: "Pekin Edison Plant Named–Worst Polluter," *Bloomington Daily Pantagraph*, 10 Aug. 1974; J. Simpson, "Conservationist Blasts Pekin Energy Plant," *Bloomington Daily Pantagraph*, 30 July 1971.

66. Keystone: E. Hopkins, "Keystone Plans Costly Cleanup," *PJS,* 3 July 1993, A-1; E. Hopkins, "Region Awash in Toxic Chemicals: Study," *PJS,* 25 July 1993, p. A-2.

67. quote from toxicologist and newspaper's conclusion: E. Hopkins, "Emissions List Ranks Region 13th," *PJS,* 19 Mar. 1995, A-1, A-22.

68. statistics on toxic emissions in the Pekin-Peoria: From TRI. See also Hopkins, "Region Awash."

69. Captan: EPA, *Suspended, Cancelled, and Restricted Pesticides,* 20T-1002 (Washington, D.C.: EPA, 1990).

70. documents: From the Right-to-Know Network's copies of EPA's TRI, PCS, and FINDS databases. These searches were conducted by Kathy Grandfield on 1 Jan. 1995. Additional data for Tazewell County were provided by Joe Goodner, TRI coordinator at the IEPA in Springfield.

71. Tazewell doubled the amount of hazardous waste: IEPA, *Summary of Annual Reports on Hazardous Waste in Illinois for 1991 and 1992: Generation, Treatment, Storage, Disposal, and Recovery,* IEPA/BOL/94-155 (Springfield, Ill.: IEPA, 1994), 61.

72. received four times more waste than it produced: IEPA, *Illinois Nonhazardous Special Waste Annual Report for 1991* (Springfield, Ill.: IEPA, 1993), table K.

73. the spill report: The report is part of the Tazewell County, Illinois, Area Report taken from the Right-to-Know Network's copy of EPA's ERNS database.

74. toxicity and production of methyl chloride: National Institute for Occupational Safety and Health, *NIOSH Current Intelligence Bulletin,* 43, NIOSH Pub. 84-117 (Cinninnati: NIOSH, 1984).

75. estrogenicity of postwar chemicals: D. M. Klotz et al., "Identification of Environmental Chemicals with Estrogenic Activity Using a Combination of *In Vitro* Assays," *EHP* 104 (1996): 1084–89; "Masculinity at Risk" (editorial), *Nature* 375 (1995): 522; R. M. Sharpe, "Another DDT Connection," *Nature* 375 (1995): 538–39; "Male: Reproductive Health and Environmental Oestrogens" (editorial), *Lancet* 345 (1995): 933–35; Institute for Environment and Health, *Environmental Oestrogens: Consequences to Human Health and Wildlife* (Leicester, England: Univ. of Leicester, 1995); J. Raloff, "Beyond Estrogens: Why Unmasking Hormone-Mimicking Pollutants Proves So Challenging," *Science News* 148 (1995): 44–46.

76. DDE: W. R. Kelce et al., "Persistent DDT Metabolite *p,p'*-DDE is a Potent Androgen Receptor Antagonist," *Nature* 375 (1995): 581–85. More recently, researchers have discovered estrogenic properties in two other DDT metabolites, both isomers of DDD, previously thought to be non-estrogenic. See Klotz, "Identification of Environmental Chemicals."

77. persistence of DDE: Dr. Mary Wolff, Mt. Sinai School of Medicine, personal communication.

78. concern focuses on reproduction and wildlife: The most readable summary is T. Colborn et al., *Our Stolen Future: Are We Threatening Our Fertility, Intelligence, and Survival?—A Scientific Detective Story* (New York: Dutton, 1996).

79. long-running conversations about cancer: D. L. Davis and H. L. Bradlow, "Can Environmental Estrogens Cause Breast Cancer?" *Scientific American,* Oct. 1995, 166–72; D. L. Houghton and L. Ritter, "Organochlorine Residues and Risk of Breast Cancer," *Journal of American College of Toxicology* 14 (1995): 71–89; T. Key and G. Reeves, "Organochlorines in the Environment and Breast Cancer," *British Medical Journal* 308 (1994): 1520–21; D. L. Davis et al., "Medical Hypothesis: Xenoestrogens as Preventable Causes of Breast Cancer," *EHP* 101 (1993): 372–77; U.S. House of Representatives, *Health Effects of Estrogenic Pesticides: Hearing before the Subcommittee on Health and the*

Environment, Cong., sess., 21 Oct. 1993; R. Coosen and F. L. van Velsen, "Effects of the ß-Isomer of Hexachlorocyclohexane on Estrogen-Sensitive Human Mammary Tumor Cells," *'Toxicology and Applied Pharmacology* 101 (1989): 310–18; J. A. Nelson, "Effects of Dichlorodiphenyltrichloroethane (DDT) Analogs and Polychlorinated Biphenyl (PCB) Mixtures on 17ß-[³H]estradiol Binding to Rat Uterine Receptor," *Biochemical Pharmacology* 23 (1974): 447–51; R. M. Welch et al., "Estrogenic Action of DDT and Its Analogs," *Toxicology and Applied Pharmacology* 14 (1969): 358–67; C. Huggins and N. C. Yang, "Induction and Extinction of Mammary Cancer," *Science* 137 (1962): 257–62.

80. Carson's mention of endocrine disruption: R. Carson, *Silent Spring* (Boston: Houghton Mifflin, 1962), 212, 235–37.

81. Soto and Sonnenschein's discovery: A. M. Soto et al., "*p*-Nonylphenol: An Estrogenic Xenobiotic Released from 'Modified' Polystyrene," *EHP* 92 (1991): 167–73.

82. estrogenic activity in other substances: A. M. Soto et al., "The Pesticides Endosulfan, Toxaphene, and Dieldrin Have Estrogenic Effects on Human Estrogen-Sensitive Cells," *EHP* 102 (1994): 380–383.

83. chemicals identified as estrogenic: B. Hileman, "Concerns Broaden over Chlorine and Chlorinated Hydrocarbons," *Chemical and Engineering News,* 19 Apr. 1993, 11–20.

84. many plasticizers and surfactants are estrogenic: J. A. Brotons et al., "Xenoestrogens Released from Lacquer Coatings in Food Cans," *EHP* 103 (1995): 608–12; J. Raloff, "Additional Sources of Dietary Estrogens," *Science News* 147 (1995): 341; R. White et al., "Environmentally Persistent Alkylphenolic Compounds Are Estrogenic," *Endocrinology* 135 (1994): 175–82; A. V. Krishnan et al., "Bisphenol-A: An Estrogenic Substance Is Released from Polycarbonate Flasks during Autoclaving," *Endocrinology* 132 (1993): 2279–86.

85. APEOs in New Jersey drinking water: L. B. Clark et al., "Determination of Alkylphenol Ethoxylates and Their Acetic Acid Derivatives in Drinking Water by Particle Beam Liquid Chromotography/Mass Spectrometry," *International Journal of Environmental Analytic Chemistry* 47 (1992): 167–80.

86. English researchers found APEOs stimulate breast cancer cells and feminize fish: White, "Alkylphenolic Compounds."

87. source of estrogens in sewage: J. Kaiser, "Scientists Angle for Answers," *Science* 274 (1996): 1837–38; L. C. Folmar et al. "Vitellogenin Induction and Reduced Serum Testosterone Concentrations in Feral Male Carp (*Cyprinus carpio*) Captured Near a Major Metropolitan Sewage Treatment Plant," *EHP* 104 (1996): 1096–1101; C. E. Purdom et al., "Estrogenic Effects of Effluents from Sewage Treatment Works," *Chemistry and Ecology* 8 (1994): 275–85; S. Jobling and J. P. Sumpter, "Detergent Components in Sewage Effluent Are Weakly Estrogenic to Fish: An *In Vitro* Study Using Rainbow Trout (*Oncorhynchus mykiss*) Hypatocytes," *Aquatic Toxicology* 27 (1993): 361–72.

88. phthalates: S. Jobling et al., "A Variety of Environmentally Persistent Chemicals, Including Some Phthalate Plasticizers, Are Weakly Estrogenic," *EHP* 103 (1995): 582–87; J. Raloff, "Newest Estrogen Mimics the Commonest?" *Science News* 148 (1995): 47.

89. production, use, and toxicity of DEHP: IEPA, "Di(2-ethylhexyl)phthalate: Chemical Information Sheet," IEPA/ENV/93-006 (Springfield, Ill.: IEPA, 1993).

90. DEHP in blood bags: S. D. Pearson and L. A. Trissel, "Leaching of Diethylhexl Phthalate from Polyvinyl Chloride Containers by Selected Drugs and Formulation Components," *American Journal of Hospital Pharmacology* 50 (1993): 1405–9; R. J. Jaeger and R. J. Rubin, "Migration of a Phthalate Ester Plasticizer from Polyvinyl Chloride Blood Bags in Stored Human Blood and Its Localization in Human Tissues," *NEJM* 287 (1972): 1114–18.

91. half of endocrine disrupters are organochlorines: Hileman, "Concerns Broaden."

92. creation and use of organochlorines: International Programme of Chemical Safety, WHO, "Chlorine and Hydrogen Chloride."

93. 1993 resolution: American Public Health Association Resolution 9304, "Recognizing and Addressing the Environmental and Occupational Health Problems Posed by Chlorinated Organic Chemicals," *AJPH* 84 (1994): 514–15.

94. quote from the IJC: International Joint Commission, *Sixth Biennial Report on Great Lakes Water Quality* (Washington, D.C., and Ottawa, Ontario: International Joint Commission, 1992), 5.

95. quote from David Ozonoff: "On the Need to Ban Organochlorines" (presentation to the Massachusetts Breast Cancer Coalition Conference, "Breast Cancer and Environment: Our Health at Risk," Boston, Mass., 28 Oct. 1996).

96. formaldehyde for embalming: Toxics Use Reduction Institute, *Formaldehyde Use Reduction in Mortuaries*, Technical Report 24 (Lowell, Mass.: TURI, 1994).

97. alternatives to dry-cleaning: H. Black, "A Cleaner Bill of Health," *EHP* 104 (1996): 488–90; S. B. Williams et al., "Fabric Compatibility and Cleaning Effectiveness of Dry Cleaning with Carbon Dioxide," *Los Alamos National Laboratory Report*, LA-UR-96-822 (Los Alamos, N.M.: Los Alamos National Laboratory, 1996).

98. statistics on perchloroethylene: U.S. Agency for Toxic Substances and Disease Registry, *Toxicological Profile for Tetrachloroethylene*, TP-92118 (Atlanta: ATSDR, 1993); USDHHS, *Seventh Annual Report on Carcinogens* (Rockville, Md.: USDHHS, 1994), 375; EPA, *Chemical Summary for Perchloroethylene*, 749-F-94-020a (Washington, D.C.: EPA Office of Pollution Prevention and Toxics, 1994).

99. dry-cleaning in New York: D. Wallace et al., *Upstairs, Downstairs: Perchloroethylene in the Air in Apartments Above New York City Dry Cleaners* (New York: Consumers Union, 1995); M. Green, *Clothed in Controversy: The Risk to New Yorkers from Dry Cleaning Emissions and What Can Be Done About It* (New York: Office of the Public Advocate for the City of New York, 1994.).

■ *QUESTIONS FOR MAKING CONNECTIONS WITHIN THE READING* ■

1. Steingraber begins "War" with a description of her father's service in World War II and then provides additional personal information throughout the rest of the chapter. Mark off each of the sections where Steingraber adds to her personal narrative. Is there a logic to the order that Steingraber has chosen for revealing information about herself? Does this personal information affect her ability to be objective about environmental toxins?

2. One challenge posed by Steingraber's work is the specialized vocabulary it requires: *organic,* with its nearly contradictory meanings; *synthetic, carcinogens, phenoxy herbicides,* and so on. Create a master list of the key terms that are essential for understanding Steingraber's argument and write out definitions for each term. What is the relationship between the list of words you have generated and Steingraber's title, "War"?

3. Steingraber declares near the end of her piece: "I am convinced that human inventiveness is not restricted to acts of war." Based on the information that Steingraber has provided, is there cause to believe that

human inventiveness can clean up the environment? Is Steingraber's conviction grounded in reason or hope?

■ *QUESTIONS FOR WRITING* ■

1. In the middle of "War," after describing her travels back to the Illinois county where she grew up, Steingraber writes: "A silence spreads out. I cannot make her speak." And shortly after this, she writes: "Amid a flooded sea of information, an absence of knowledge. Amid a thousand computer-generated words, a silence spreads out." What is the relationship between these statements about silence and the rest of Steingraber's discussion? By the end of "War," has she moved her readers beyond the "sea of information" to a place of knowledge?

2. Not too surprisingly, Steingraber's piece ends with a call to action. But what kind of action is appropriate, given all that Steingraber has revealed? Does her account establish that actions to protect public health are likely to emerge from the government? Corporations? Concerned citizens? Scientists? Is change on the scale she calls for brought about through reason? Legal action? Moral persuasion?

■ *QUESTIONS FOR MAKING CONNECTIONS BETWEEN READINGS* ■

1. In "The Myth of the Ant Queen," Steven Johnson describes how computing has helped to unlock some of the secrets of "organized complexity." Is the situation that Steingraber describes one of "organized complexity" or "disorganized complexity"? Are the solutions the same in any case? Or has Steingraber drawn attention to a system of such complexity, with so many different variables, that the very notion of a solution is out of the question? If no solution exists, does this mean that there is nothing to be done?

2. Given the argument that Annie Dillard develops in "The Wreck of Time," does it make sense to pursue a project like controlling the release of toxins into the environment? Is Dillard's view of the natural world consonant with Steingraber's? Absent a notion of "the sacred," can science and information lead to environmental change?

GREGORY STOCK

GREGORY STOCK, THE former director of the Program on Medicine, Technology, and Society at the UCLA School of Medicine, is currently the CEO of Signum Biosciences. He is a scientist, educator, and entrepreneur. He is also a vocal and enthusiastic supporter of using genetic technology to alter human DNA to select for desired traits. Interestingly, Stock does not believe that limits should be placed on the characteristics we should be allowed to select for; he advocates the manipulation of genetic material to gain "enhanced" results ranging from better health to increased strength, intelligence, and attractiveness. Stock argues that genetic choice technology is not simply a possibility but an inevitability, and for that reason he believes that we should begin to think seriously about how to deal with the swift and dramatic changes that will come to human reproduction in the immediate future. In "The Enhanced and the Unenhanced," he writes: "The enormous collective project of conscious human evolution has begun."

Stock's vision is not merely a practical one; implicit in his argument is a philosophy that reinterprets the concepts of nature, life, and humanity. In fact, Stock does not view "human-directed" technology and nature as separate spheres. Rather, he argues that humans are a part of the natural world, as are the technologies we create. Furthermore, Stock feels that the development of germinal choice technology is "the ultimate expression and realization of our humanity" rather than a threat to what is "human within us." While Stock supports the results of these technologies, he acknowledges that considerable thinking remains to be done about how the changes to human reproduction will unfold, and he urges us to take part in the conversation as a society. As he observes, "My view is that we don't have the wisdom to understand these technologies yet. [. . .] You wait to see how people actually use them. You keep an eye on them."

Stock, Gregory. "The Enhanced and the Unenhanced." *Redesigning Humans: Our Inevitable Genetic Future*. Boston: Houghton Mifflin, 2002. 176–201.

Biographical information comes from <http://www.thelavinagency.com/usa/gregorystock.html> and <http://www.promenadespeakers.com/id164.html> as well as <http://www.kurzweilai.net/bios/frame.html?main=/bios/bio0189.html>. Quotations come from the Salon.com interview with Gregory Stock, <http://socgen.ucla.edu/pmts/salon.htm>, and from *Redesigning Humans*.

■ ■

The Enhanced and the Unenhanced

> Gradually, the truth dawned on me: that Man had not remained one species,
> but had differentiated into two distinct animals: that my graceful children
> of the Upperworld were not the sole descendants of our generation, but that
> this bleached, obscene, nocturnal Thing, which had flashed before me, was
> also heir to all the ages.
>
> —*H. G. Wells*, The Time Machine, *1895*

As we move into an era of advanced germinal choice, children conceived
with these technologies will necessarily intermingle with those with more
haphazard beginnings. But how they will relate to one another in the long
run is no more clear than whether a gulf will ultimately widen between
them, partitioning humanity into the enhanced and the unenhanced.

The answers depend on which enhancements become feasible, their
cost, who has access to them, who adopts them, and the nature of competing enhancements for adults. All this is as yet uncertain, but we can begin to
discern some of the critical choices we will face. At so early a point in the development of GCT (germinal choice technology), identifying the policies
that will serve us best is difficult, but spotting some that would serve us
poorly is easy.

I have argued that germinal choice technology will offer us significant
benefits and we will use the technology to acquire them. Moreover, the first
wave of technologies offering substantive new human reproductive choices
may be only a decade away. In-depth genetic testing, sophisticated preimplantation genetic diagnosis, egg banking, improved *in vitro* fertilization,
and cloning are poised to transform our reproductive choices, while
progress in genomics and with highly targeted pharmaceuticals will work
in parallel by altering our perceptions of our genetic potentials, vulnerabilities, and handicaps. A decade or so beyond this first wave, a few rudimentary germline modifications may appear in special situations. And another
decade beyond, more sophisticated and powerful germline manipulations
may begin supplementing sophisticated genetic screenings and adult interventions. This timeline is little more than a guess, but whether substantive
GCT enhancement arrives in ten years or fifty, the social and ethical challenges it brings will be similar.

A closer look at the possibility of overlapping effects of embryo screening procedures and early germline engineering suggests that preimplantation genetic diagnosis will likely be potent enough to provide significant
human enhancement in addition to disease screening. Consider what would
happen if parents wishing to enrich for a trait that is substantively shaped

by genetics were to create a hundred healthy embryos, test them . . . and implant the one most predisposed toward that trait.

If such embryos could be selected, for example, for the gene variants responsible for a large portion of the genetic contribution to high IQ[1], the average score of children selected in this way might be nearly 120[2], well above the average score of 100 found in the general population and higher than nearly 9 out of 10 people. Moreover, this shift would take place in a single generation and use a proven medical procedure.

Such sophisticated embryo selection would be just as much a human enhancement as germline engineering. Indeed, no one would later be able to tell whether the lab had selected an embryo or modified one to obtain a particular genome. Here is another case where, if we continue to focus on the theological implications of laboratory procedures rather than on the results they bring, we will greatly weaken our attempt to deal with the approaching challenges.

To imagine that progress in germinal choice technology is irrelevant to the health of adults not planning high-tech parenthood is tempting, since the fateful meeting of sperm and egg that brought us into being is now beyond reach. Our lives, however, may be linked more directly to the arrival of advanced germinal choice than we might think. Adult enhancement, to the extent that it is feasible, rests on the same scientific foundations as embryo selection and will probably become available around the same time. The importance of nuclear transfer techniques to both reproductive cloning and regenerative medicine is no coincidence; such intersections will occur again and again.

Keeping in mind that genetic enhancement may be only a first step in humanity's coming journey of self-transformation adds valuable perspective to discussions of GCT. Fusion of human and machine in this century may be unlikely, but eventually the two may begin to join in important ways. If they do, the philosophical questions provoked by the coexistence of enhanced and unenhanced humans will arise once again. The future debate would not be about the displacement within our biological selves of the natural by the made, however, but about the displacement of the biological by the machine. This could make today's battles over mere biological enhancement seem quaint, because whatever these future humans may have become, they would have to grapple not merely with enhancement but with moving beyond biology itself.

The Enhanced

When bioethicists use the term "enhancement," they usually must confront the problem of defining normal human functioning, because they wish to differentiate between therapy and actual enhancement.[3] The committee of the American Association for the Advancement of Science that considered germline policy in year 2000, for example, concluded that although "the use of IGM [inherited genetic modifications] to prevent and treat clear-cut diseases in future generations is ethically justifiable . . . IGM should be used only for cases which are clearly therapeutic." But such distinctions become arbitrary for such goals as retarding aging, which would be both an enhancement of our vitality and a therapy for age-related decline—in effect, a *therapeutic enhancement.*

I see nothing wrong with enhancement per se, so I use the term to mean any augmentation of attributes or overall functioning, whether or not it moves a person beyond our sense of normal human functioning. Abstract judgments about the value of particular characteristics and whether they relate to disease will tell us no more about how people will use germinal choice technology than they've told us about the use of cosmetic surgery or drugs. To see the future of GCT, we need to be more pragmatic and acknowledge that people want to be healthier, smarter, stronger, faster, more attractive. Enhancements are those modifications that people view as largely beneficial and that serve their goals. Virtually by definition, people seek such modifications.

A useful way of analyzing potential embryo enhancements is to categorize them by two measures: the degree to which the altered quality is health-related, and the magnitude of the embodied changes. Targeted traits will range from those that are clearly health-related—risks for heart disease, diabetes, or severe depression—to those that touch health less directly, such as obesity, and those that are largely cosmetic and idiosyncratic—hair color, musical talent, height, curiosity. We all would want our children to be at low risk for leukemia, but we might disagree about how tall or outgoing we'd like them to be.

We may best gauge the extent of a modification by comparing it to the typical range of human functioning in that realm. At one extreme are restorations of lost capacities—hearing for the deaf or improved immune response for those with compromised immune systems. In the middle are improvements that make people a little smarter, stronger, or taller, and that lift the underperformers to average level, and the average up to elite performance. At the other extreme are enhancements that carry a person beyond the normal human range, exceeding even today's elite performers—superhuman endurance, intellect, strength, or vitality.

Enhancements with different effects will present us with very different social, moral, and political questions. Many people, for example, have no problem with enhancements that are health related and that improve subnormal attributes—we generally call them therapies. Enhancements of idiosyncratic traits are more troubling because they can seem subjective and frivolous, though we know that those who seek cosmetic surgery often view it as critical to their mental health. But enhancements that would take us to elite or superhuman levels give most people cause for concern.

What is essential to realize about such interventions is that as the degree of enhancement rises, so will the technical difficulties involved. I cannot overemphasize this, because it is central to the future trajectory of human enhancement technology. Less extreme improvements will be much easier to accomplish and will even be available through embryo screening procedures, which do not manipulate genes.[4] So initially GCT will offer less to those seeking superhuman performance than to those trying to avoid genetic impairments or improve some area of low or average performance. Widespread use of GCT would almost certainly raise average performance levels and improve health in coming generations, as well as narrow the spread between those with higher and lower potentials. This leveling does not arise from any imposed restriction on the technology. It flows directly from the step-by-step nature of technological advance, the greater complexity of more extreme enhancements, and people's tendency not to subject their children to unnecessary risks. Moreover, if adult enhancements become broadly available, they will lead to a similar flattening of the distribution of individual endowments.

Ridley Scott's 1982 film *Blade Runner,* like most science fiction, portrays genetic engineering as creating superhuman powers. The film's "replicants" are superior to mere mortals in most ways, but the tradeoff for their powers is extreme: after four years, they collapse and die. Roy, a replicant who returns to Earth looking for a way to escape his fate, crushes to death his creator, Tyrell, who tells him that it cannot be: "The light that burns twice as bright burns half as long. And you have burned so very very brightly, Roy. . . . Revel in your time."

Such imagery disregards the immensity of the challenge of designing superhuman performance. Dog breeding illustrates the problem. Over thousands of years, emphasis on any one characteristic has brought tradeoffs with others. By amplifying specific wolf traits, we have bred specialist canines, not created superwolves. The saluki runs faster than any wolf. The bloodhound follows a scent better. The springer spaniel flushes game better. The toy poodle certainly is no superwolf. In their 1965 book *Genetics and the Social Behavior of the Dog,* John Paul Scott and John Fuller articulated it this way: "It is inconceivable that any particular domestic breed could compete with wolves under natural conditions. . . . A wolf is a rugged and powerful animal adapted to life under a variety of adverse conditions. Consequently, no one of his behavioral capacities can be developed to a high degree. . . . The idea that natural selection will produce a super-man or super-animal of any sort is an unobtainable myth."[5]

We have seen too much progress in the intervening decades to be so sure that genetic engineering cannot create superior humans, but we are far from that goal. If the task were easy, natural evolution would have done it already. No such difficulty will keep us from improving average or below-average performance. All we have to do is copy nature. To give an embryo the genetics to achieve an adult height of eight feet without grave health problems would be an immense challenge; to achieve a height of six feet would not.

As GCT becomes increasingly potent, we will face tough personal decisions about what is best for our children and what risks and tradeoffs we will accept for them. There will be no simple answers. Our personalities and values will shape our attitudes. We will probably agree that certain types of manipulation are wrong, just as we agree that certain parental behaviors constitute abuse, and we will agree that certain enhancements exist that any responsible parent would make, just as we generally agree that kids should enhance their immunity by getting vaccinations. But there will also be passionate disagreements, and these cases will be very difficult to regulate.

Let's return to the example of the deaf parents who wish to have a deaf child. Germinal choice technology will make it possible, and as hard as it may be for someone with normal hearing to accept, preventing these parents from doing so would be dangerously close to coercive eugenics that targets the disabled. As long as deaf parents rely on embryo selection, stopping them from selecting an embryo destined to develop into a deaf child is tantamount to making them destroy that embryo.

The coming choices will force us to confront our attitudes about what constitutes a meaningful life, our responsibilities to others, our prejudices, and what we mean when we say that all potential lives are equal and deserve protection. In essence, we will soon have to face, in concrete human terms, the implications of our philosophies about human diversity.

Humans and Posthumans: Our Evolutionary Future

Humanity's manipulation of canine evolution has produced a wide range of breeds and served as an unwitting pilot project for our coming manipulation of our own evolution.[6] In the early phases of human self-modification, the social constraints will be entirely different from those of canines, and the methods much more sophisticated, but scientists no doubt will encounter some of the same biological limits and possibilities.

Two critical questions that come up are whether this process will fragment humanity into independent breeds—future human Saint Bernard and dachshund analogs—and if so, whether they will persist and evolve into separate *posthuman* species.

First let's look at the idea of speciation. Despite the dramatically different shapes, sizes, and dispositions of dogs, *Canis familiaris* is still a single species.[7] Reproductive isolation is central to speciation. Different species cannot interbreed under normal conditions. Such isolation is unlikely to occur in future human subpopulations. Not only will our offspring remain in close physical proximity, unless and until humans migrate out into the vast seas of space, but genomics and advanced reproductive technologies are breaching the barriers to genetic exchange even among different species. If scientists in Oregon can already give a jellyfish gene to a primate, surely we will continue to be able to exchange genes with one another.

In addition, species are biological forms that persist, averaging some four million years before extinction, according to the fossil record. If we succeed in progressively modifying our biology by altering our genes and supplementing our chromosomes, however, changes will be ongoing and new variants will emerge within a span of generations or centuries. Such posthumans could hardly be called "species."

Although even the concept of species may cease to be meaningful as reproduction shifts to the laboratory, the issue of whether the human community will eventually fragment into persistent independent groups remains. The only constant in a future of rapid biological manipulation would be evolutionary change itself. What could unite us in this future would be our common participation in this fluid, self-directed process rather than any transitory similarities in form. Seen in this light, strange as future humans may become if germline manipulation achieves its promise, they will still remain *human*.

In the past, the reproductive isolation needed to generate even the modest biological differences among human groups has required geographical or cultural separation. Both, however, are greatly diminishing because of increased individual mobility, modern communications, and softening cultural rigidities—trends likely to deepen despite strong opposition. Traditional Darwinian evolution now produces almost no change in humans and has little prospect of doing so in the foreseeable future. The human population is too large and entangled, and selective pressures are too localized and transitory.

In the future, however, the rapid technology-driven process of genetic design may achieve meaningful group-specific changes without reproductive isolation. With genetic refinements accumulating in the laboratory instead of in biological lineages, groups of individuals bound only by a common commitment to some specific enhancement could serve as a virtual test bed for refining genetic alterations. The spread of gene modules would not be by reproductive success but by reputation, word of mouth, even advertising. In essence, mimetic rather than biological mechanisms will drive the penetration of genes in the human population.[8]

The underlying source of this profound shift in the evolutionary process is the external storage and manipulation of human genes. As the genetic constructs we provide our children are increasingly explored, maintained, and refined in laboratories, working their way into our hearts and our children's bodies by public relations and persuasion rather than sex, the cultural processes hitherto shaped by our biology will turn the tables and remold our biology.

The consequences of a similar externalization some five thousand years ago give a hint of the tremendous implications of the coming genetic breakthroughs. The development of writing allowed knowledge—which hitherto had been stored only biologically and passed imperfectly from one fragile brain to another—to be captured physically and copied as needed.[9] The result was the accumulation, refinement, and spread of knowledge to an extent otherwise impossible. Civilization rests upon this.

Our genetics has been similarly constrained. Evolution, for all its awesome constructions, is ultimately a vast tale of trial and error—and a slow and cautious one for a large organism like us. Random change is more likely to be deleterious than beneficial, so modifications must prove themselves over many generations. But while nature has eons, you and I do not.

As researchers gather and correlate human genetic profiles and adult human attributes, they will be able to assemble and interpret information about the effects of various clusters of genes. When they identify favorable combinations, they will preserve them outside our bodies—in tissue cultures, in freezers, and on computers—and we will pass them on to our children if we choose to. We will make mistakes. But so do random variation and natural selection. The enormous collective project of conscious human evolution has begun.

The Tensions of Living Together

As we gain conscious control over our biology, we will transform the range of what is human by expanding our diversity. Whether this diversification of the human form and character will isolate us from one another and make us truly separate is uncertain. Here I refer not to physical isolation, though that might well occur, but to a separation of our spirits, our purposes, and our biological identities. Dogs and cats, for example, are distinct and live among us, but they are our pets. If groups of future humans come to see each other as different, will they be able to remain on an equal footing?

Such changes to whole populations will require widespread germinal choice, of course, but a gradual transition to laboratory conception will likely follow the arrival of comprehensive embryo screening and advanced IVF, as parents come to view this as protection for their children. Even those uninterested in enhancement may start to see it as reckless and primitive to conceive a child without prior genetic testing.

With the advent of germline engineering, however, human artificial chromosomes will probably render laboratory conception obligatory rather than optional. The union of egg and sperm from two individuals with different numbers of chromosomes or different sequences of genes on their extra chromosomes would be too unpredictable with intercourse. But laboratory conception may not be a burden because such parents will probably want the most up-to-date chromosome enhancements anyway.

This move from bedroom to laboratory conception is one that future humans are unlikely ever to reverse, because they will not want to discard the benefits residing on their artificial chromosomes. This change seems dramatic, but it is not as big a leap as it might initially seem. Laboratory conception is just one more step down the path we took long ago when our distant ancestors embraced fire, clothing, and other early technologies, beginning a cultural process that has continually deepened our connection with and dependence on technology.

In the future, laboratory-mediated conception may seem no more foreign than medically assisted birth does today. In 1900, few thought of giving birth in a hospital as "natural"; only 5 percent of births took place there.[10] Today, in the United States, almost all births do, and some 30 percent are by cesarean section, a frequently avoidable procedure that is nonetheless readily accepted.

How germinal choice technology affects our future will hinge on who has access to it as well as on what it offers. If the technology is available to large numbers of people, it is unlikely to give rise to a narrow elite.

Regulatory and healthcare policies will be important factors in determining how broadly available GCT becomes, but the nature of the technology itself may play a more critical role. Whether GCT is a free healthcare benefit or is for sale on the open market, the more complex and individualized the technology, the more expensive and less widely available it will be. With healthcare plans the costly procedures are rationed; on the open market, only the affluent can afford them.

Different technological approaches will likely lead to procedures with different costs.[11] To alter specific genes in place in an embryo's genome, for example, would be expensive because it would require a customized research effort for each embryo. Artificial chromosomes, on the other hand, might allow cheap enhancement for the many, because robotic devices could load them with a tailored package of off-the-shelf gene modules, and validate and test them before injecting them into embryos. So government policies that encourage research to refine artificial chromosomes and other technology platforms suited to widely available GCT might push development in this direction.

An altogether different strategy is to focus on access to the technology by attempting to control its clinical use. Such an approach poses a significant risk because it leads to categorical bans that, as previously discussed, will reserve the technology for narrow segments of society. Provision of free universal access to major aspects of GCT would align better with our ideals of equal opportunity for children and might be surprisingly affordable. If the price of a full GCT procedure could be kept down to, say, $6,000 a baby, this would be roughly equal to the average yearly expenditure on a student in public school in the United States.

As GCT begins to offer parents truly meaningful possibilities, our regulatory policies will have significant consequences for society. The first important choice we face will be our handling of advanced PGD, IVF, and egg banking. If tests to screen for almost all genetic diseases, for example, become available, but primarily to the affluent, such disorders will turn into diseases of the disadvantaged. Our policies will become even more crucial when we can screen embryos for genetic potentials.

As society moves closer to becoming a meritocracy, the most talented from all ethnicities and backgrounds will intermingle, form partnerships, and mate with similarly talented and successful others. Over time, this self-sorting will tend to divide society, increasingly distancing the more gifted from the less. Narrowly limited genetic screening and enhancement technology would accelerate such divisions and reinforce privilege, whereas broadly available technology would counteract them.

Not long ago, restricting access to education was one way of reinforcing class divisions, but we work so hard now to provide every child with the education to reach his or her potential that this repartitioning of society by talent and intellect, rather than by family and status, is already well under way in many countries. In the United States, the student bodies at elite institutions are ethnically and culturally more diverse than ever, but they are drawn from a narrow segment of the population. In 1990, Yale and Harvard together enrolled 1 in 400 of all freshmen at four-year colleges, but that included 1 in 10 of the small number of students scoring above 700 on the verbal portion of the Scholastic Aptitude Test, or SAT.[12] This aggregation of an intellectual elite at the top universities is a new phenomenon. In 1950, such schools were ten times less selective when it came to standardized tests.

Kids soon learn how competitive the world is and where their talents do and do not lie. We have all been through this. If we were astute, lucky, or found good mentors, we ended up doing what we were best at. Some of our aptitudes emerged from our experiences; others—those innate talents that come so naturally we may take them for granted—came straight from our biology. People without the special talents and attributes that our society values—those who are clumsy, inarticulate, unattractive, slow-witted; those who would find it wonderful just to be average—are at a great disadvantage. Their hopes and aspirations may have always matched their lesser potentials, but more likely their dreams had to shrink one disappointment at a time.

Perhaps a mother who is unattractive remembers what it was like to suffer the teasing of her classmates and recalls her struggle for acceptance. Perhaps a father who was short and weak recalls being picked on as a boy. Perhaps a young man remembers watching others easily answer questions he could not fathom and thinks back on how humiliating it was to be dropped to the "slow" group. Maybe a young woman wanted to be a writer, but could never bring any magic to the words she wrote. These wounds heal, but they do not go away. Saying that we all have special, different talents and need to find them is too glib. Think about that person who was not bright or athletic or musically gifted, who felt lucky just to get by.

We have no choice, of course, but to play the hand we are dealt. But at the same time, we strive to protect our children and give them the breaks we never had: the education we couldn't afford, the family stability we wanted, the wealth we dreamed of, the guidance we needed. Society applauds these efforts but will be wary of parents who try to help their children through genetic interventions. Safety aside, though, why shouldn't we try to give our future children the talents we did not have or eliminate deficiencies that held us back? If we could make our baby smarter, more attractive, a better athlete or musician, or keep him or her from being overweight, why wouldn't we?

One social problem that might attend germinal choice technology, if it really can give our children raw talents, would be that such enhanced abilities would soon be less special. As in Garrison Keillor's Lake Wobegon, all the children would be above average. To the extent that talent and good health are heritable, children of some parents have an edge. Show me the brilliant intellectual who does not expect his child to be near the top of the class, the sports superstar who does not expect his child to have athletic gifts. Such kids may not turn out to be the smartest or the most talented, but they will probably do fairly well. Their genetics is not the whole story, but it is important. There is a reason adopted children tend to resemble their biological parents more than their adoptive ones: life does not start from scratch each generation; it takes from the past.

With the completion of the sequencing of the human genome, it has become fashionable to make a point of saying that we differ from one another in only 1 in 1,000 of our DNA bases. We are 99.9 percent the same as our fellow humans, whoever they may be. This statement is reassuring and politically correct, but misleading. We only have to look around us to see the extraordinary differences among us. Biological diversity is real. We come in a multitude of shapes and sizes. We have distinct personalities and temperaments. We possess various talents and vulnerabilities. We draw much of this from our genetic constitutions.

How can this be when our genetics are 99.9 percent the same? We see the answer when we realize that our DNA sequence is about 98.5 percent the same as a chimpanzee's, perhaps 85 percent the same as a mouse's. Open up a mouse and you find a heart, lungs, intestines, bones, nerves, muscles. Mice are close cousins to us. And when it comes simply to having homologous genes rather than exact DNA sequences, the similarity between all life is even clearer. Some 98 percent of the mouse's genes are ours too, 60 percent of the fruit fly's, and more than 25 percent of those of a banana.[13] All life has cells. These cells divide in the same ways. They regulate their DNA and manage their metabolism and cellular communication in the same ways. They have the same basic biochemistry. Our genetic similarities come from the fundamentals we all share. Of course you and I are nearly the same. We are both animals, both vertebrates, both primates—both humans. The differences between us are subtle, but that doesn't mean we shouldn't care about them. A difference of 1 in 1,000 bases between any two people is not trivial, even though it is much less than the difference between, say, two chimpanzees. It amounts to 3 million differing bases in their individual genomes. Sure, the vast majority will be scattered through the so-called junk DNA between their genes, and of the 150,000 or so differences in their actual genes, most will be neutral and not lead to any functional differences. But a single base can be the difference between vibrant health and early death. Parkinson's disease comes from a single changed base. So do sickle cell anemia and hemophilia. A single base difference can make the fingers on a person's hands resemble toes, or cause mental retardation.

We do not yet know what percentage of two people's genes differ in meaningful ways, but a good guess is around 10 to 20 percent—several thousand genes.[14] Moreover, because our major competitors for just about everything in life are other people, we are fine-tuned by evolution to be highly sensitive to the minute distinctions among us. We don't care that we are all mammals, all primates. These are givens. We care about our differences. All people might look pretty much the same to a space alien or a mosquito—or even an evolutionary biologist—but not to a coach trying to build a winning sports team or to someone looking for a mate.

As we untangle our genes and learn to select and alter them, some parents will want to give their children endowments they themselves could only dream of. If such interventions become commonplace, the result will be revolutionary, because it will be a major step toward equalizing life's possibilities. The gifted of today ultimately may not welcome such a leveling, because it would diminish the edge their children enjoy and make society very competitive, even for the best endowed.

If GCT enhancements prove feasible, eventually the mass of humanity will seize the power to enrich its children's natural endowments. Strong voices will oppose this, but most of the warnings about the danger of eugenics and the threat of lab-built humans will come from people with the most to lose—the well-endowed elite. Surely theirs are the children who would ultimately suffer from the arrival of a genetic bazaar where all parents can obtain equivalent talents and potentials for their children.

Today's intellectual elite might not want to live in a world as aggressive, competitive, and uncontrolled as the one that would emerge from universal access to potent germinal choice technologies, so their distaste for the technology may deepen once its true implications become clear.[15] Such resistance would be reminiscent of earlier elites who liked society the way it was and tried to protect their privileged position. The wellborn of an earlier time were right to fear the political reforms that broke down class divisions. Now a new elite may wince, because if the God-given gifts of talent and intelligence that have raised them above the throng are suddenly laid out for everyone else, their future would not be so secure.

The concern about preserving the ideals of an egalitarian society and preventing the creation of a genetic elite that inspires many of the philosophical objections to GCT among intellectuals is ironic, both because they themselves are among the elite and because any enduring effort to block these technologies will restrict access to them, compounding rather than alleviating genetic advantages.[16]

To look at the possible implications of advanced germinal choice technology more concretely, let's imagine a best-case scenario: science and policy combine to make germinal enhancement widely available, relatively commonplace, and largely under the control of individual parents.

In such a society, many parents might shun GCT, but others would embrace it enthusiastically. With time, people's genetics would become a manifestation of their parents' values and predilections. Initially, the differences between the enhanced and the unenhanced would be only statistical, in that those with enhancements would tend to outperform many, but not all, of those without enhancements. But as the technology grew more potent, less overlap would exist between the two populations, and as this became clear to parents, many of the children of those who had shunned the technology would likely enhance their own children, to keep them from being at a disadvantage.

A similar story would be played out globally, as countries that initially blocked GCT gradually felt compelled to amend or repeal their laws and accept it. Access to advanced technology typically flows from national wealth, but adoption of GCT may hinge more on the religious and cultural traditions in particular regions. Some of the richest nations could easily be the most resistant to the technology. Eventually, however, they probably will have no choice. What, after all, would a country that bans advanced embryo diagnosis do if other nations were to embark on popularly supported eugenic programs aimed at dramatically raising the average IQ of their next generation?

Breeds Apart

As we move from embryo selection to direct germline enhancement, one might imagine that devising artificial chromosomes that can enhance one embryo as effectively as another would ensure that humanity would not split into separate breeds, since future parents, whatever their own particular genetic endowments, would be able to select their children's genetic modules from an expanding common library of enhancements.[17]

Enabling couples to give their future children genetic predispositions differing from their own, however, does not necessarily mean that they would. Our experiences, associations, and natures circumscribe our values and attitudes. Parents with general competencies might well consider such balance good for their children, while parents with narrow, highly specialized talents might see greater specialization as preferable.

As we increasingly manifest our aptitudes, temperaments, and philosophies in our children through our decisions about their genetic makeup, a self-reinforcing channeling of human lineages will likely develop. Family names once denoted family professions that persisted for generations. The Cooks, Fishers, Smiths, Taylors, and Bakers of the world could no doubt uncover the corresponding trades among their ancestors. Perhaps in the future, clusters of genetic predispositions, lifestyles, and philosophical orientations will arise that are equally persistent. Families of musicians, politicians, therapists, scientists, and athletes would not be locked in by social constraints and limited opportunities, however, but by tight feedback between genetic selection and the values, philosophies, and choices that both author that selection and flow from it. Such future human specialization might be far deeper than that which has occurred historically. Maintaining it would require an ongoing cycle of renewed choices that couples, at least theoretically, could break when they decided to have children, but most probably would not.

Ideally, the resulting partitioning of the social landscape would proceed according to individual predispositions and desires rather than some preexisting template imposed on unwilling populations. But the possibilities of abuse by governments or individual parents who breed children for their own purposes should rightly give us pause. We must remember, though, that tyranny and child abuse require no advanced technology, and whether either would be changed much by the presence of germinal choice is highly debatable.

Even disregarding outright abuse, scenarios of human design are jarring, if not frightening, because they evoke troubling images of freakish human forms. While we should not dismiss such images entirely, neither should we allow them to grow in our minds to the point where they oversimplify and distort a future landscape whose complicated topography is not yet defined. Rare, special attributes such as photographic memory or extraordinary athletic ability may become both more extreme and more commonplace, but that does not mean they will be grotesque. As for the fear that parental choices might become too uniform, children would be as unique as they are now. The multiplicity of individual experience molds an infinity of expression from our genes, even if they have been chosen.

Despite the occasional exception, as in the case of parents who select deafness, when we are able to choose our offspring's genetic predispositions, we will probably opt to avoid most of the genetic disabilities and vulnerabilities that afflict us today. In this limited sense, early applications of preimplantation genetic diagnosis will narrow human diversity, but the polio vaccine did as much and brought few complaints.[18] And as sophisticated embryo screening and germline manipulation begin to enrich enhancement possibilities, no doubt clusters of attributes will be reinforced, which in time will expand diversity.

Today, when that rare combination of genetic and environmental factors comes together to create genius in one of its many guises, the combination usually disappears in the next generation. This happens because contributing environmental influences do not recur and because genetic constellations dissipate during genetic recombination. In the future, parents not only might preserve key aspects of such genetic influences through embryo selection, they might also have the knowledge and the means to push those talents even further, by creating environments that reinforce them and by refining chromosomal additions.

What aspects of themselves people will want to boost or moderate is hard to say. But taken together, their choices will have a powerful effect on society. Children's biological predispositions will come to reflect parental philosophies and attitudes, and thus children will manifest the ethos and values that influence their parents. Consider gender. Many couples would make different choices about the attributes of boys and girls. Thus, GCT might translate cultural attitudes about gender into the biology of children. If a society believes that women are (or should be) more empathetic and supportive, and boys more aggressive and independent, then whether or not these gender specificities are true now is not as important as the likelihood that they will gradually become true.

Because our notions of personal identity are specific to particular cultures and times, purely cultural distinctions could become more embedded in our genetics and may increase the biological differences among human populations. Each culture assigns its own value to traits such as calmness, obedience, and curiosity. To the extent that genes can influence these differences, GCT might reinforce them.

Many social commentators today complain about the homogenization of culture, brought on by global commerce and communications. The arrival of advanced, widespread germinal choice technology may counteract that trend by allowing people to infuse some of their cultural differences into the biology of their children. In a mixed cultural environment like that in America, of course, these effects would be played out on a national stage. Current debates about whether some of the differences among ethnic and racial groups are cultural or biological will soon become irrelevant, given the coming interdependence of the two. In any event, once we can fashion our children's biological predispositions, many cultural and personal influences will feed directly into biology.

Enhancement will be not a single dimension of change but a wide range of modification and augmentation, superimposed on the broad distribution of naturally occurring human qualities, so distinguishing between the enhanced and the unenhanced will initially be difficult, if not impossible. But germinal choice will eventually become so commonplace that the question won't even be interesting, especially given that potent quasi-medical pharmaceutical enhancements for adults will probably also become widespread. If so conservative a group as the Amish are willing to seek gene therapy, virtually no one will forgo drug, technological, and genetic enhancement once it is safe, reliable, beneficial, and perhaps even fashionable.

In the future, humanity will be an ever-shifting mélange of those who are biologically unaltered, those with improved health and longevity, and those with sundry other enhancements. In essence, we and our children increasingly will be reflections of our personal philosophies and values. Where today we sculpt our minds and bodies using exercise, drugs, and surgery, tomorrow we will also use the tools that biotechnology provides.

We cannot say what powers future humans will assume, what forms they will take, or even if they will be strictly biological, but we can be certain of one predisposition they will have. They will be committed to the process of human enhancement and self-directed evolution.[19] This we know, because without this commitment they would lag behind and be displaced by those who are more aggressive in this regard.

But the immediate cultural landscape wrought by germinal choice and biological manipulation will be more familiar than we might think. We are used to enormous human diversity. An anorexic eighty-pound fashion model, a four-hundred-pound sumo wrestler, a tiny svelte gymnast, and a towering basketball center are very different from one another. So may be their lives and passions—or those of a deaf-mute and a concert pianist, for that matter. We also are used to enormous technological gulfs between people: the vision and hearing of those with and without televisions and telephones differ greatly.

Whether our differences today are primarily the result of genetics, culture, technology, or education, they are real and they permeate our lives. Many of us revel in the giant and diverse human aggregations that are our modern cities; others simply cope with them. The enhancements brought by germinal choice will not soon sweep us into a realm so alien that we could detect the change on a stroll through a crowd but the changes will affect us profoundly.

The biggest challenge will be our changing image of ourselves. At the outset I said that these new technologies would force us to examine the very question of what it means to be human. As we follow the path that germline choice offers, we are likely to find that being human has little to do with the particular physical and mental characteristics we now use to define ourselves, and even less to do with the methods of conception and birth that are now so familiar. Adjusting to new possibilities in these areas will be hard for many of us, because it will demand a level of tolerance and acceptance that until now has been the exception rather than the rule. But perhaps the drama of the shift will itself ease the change by capturing our attention and forcing us into new patterns of relationship. Until now, to accept each other we often have had to pretend that we are all the same, but maybe when we see that we are all different and unequal—increasingly so—we will learn to accept our differences.

As we move into the centuries ahead, our strongest bond with one another may be that we share a common biological origin and are part of a common process of self-directed emergence into an unknowable future. Seen in this light, the present differences among us are trivial, because we are companions in transition and are likely to remain so.

Perhaps this state of transition is what has always defined us. The mechanisms of change were different in previous eras, but the culturally and technologically driven process of becoming that which we are not, of changing the world around us and our own selves, is not new—only the pace and depth of change are truly unprecedented.

A World Aborning

To some, the coming of human-directed change is unnatural because it differs so much from any previous change, but this distinction between the natural and the unnatural is an illusion. We are as natural a part of the world as anything else is, and so is the technology we create. As we consciously transform ourselves, we will become no less human than we became tens of thousands of years ago when we embarked upon a course of self-domestication and began, quite unconsciously, to self-select for the human qualities that enable us to live and work together effectively.[20] That we are uneasy about what lies ahead is not surprising. The arrival of GCT signals a diffuse and unplanned project to redesign ourselves. But it is neither an invasion of the inhuman, threatening that which is human within us, nor a transcendence of our human limits. Remaking ourselves is the ultimate expression and realization of our humanity. We would be foolish to believe that this future is without peril and filled only with benefits, that these powerful technologies will not require wisdom to handle well, or that great loss will not accompany the changes ahead. We are beginning an extraordinary adventure that we cannot avoid, because, judging from our past, whether we like it or not this *is* the human destiny.

It brings to mind the advertisement that Sir Ernest Shackleton, the renowned British explorer, placed in 1912 when he was recruiting a team for an expedition to cross the icy Antarctic continent on foot: "Men wanted for hazardous journey. Small wages. Bitter cold. Long months of complete darkness. Safe return doubtful. Honour and recognition in case of success."[21]

Some five thousand people responded to his call. Shackleton selected twenty-seven and began the journey. Their ship became frozen in place just off the Antarctic coast and was later crushed by the ice, but after a harrowing and nearly unbelievable two-year ordeal, they all returned safely. Shackleton looked back on it in his diary: "In memories we were rich. We had pierced the veneer of outside things. We had suffered, starved and triumphed, groveled down yet grasped at glory, grown bigger in the bigness of the whole. We had seen God in His splendors, heard the text that nature renders. We had reached the naked soul of man."

Our journey into our own biology is very different. The endeavor is collective rather than individual, its course encompasses centuries rather than years, there will be no return, and the voyage is as spiritual as it is physical. But we too are entering uncharted territory. We too will no doubt face adversity. And the destination may prove less important than the journey itself. As we pierce the veneer of inside things, we too may reach the naked soul of man.

We have created artificial intelligence from the inert sand at our feet through the silicon revolution, we are moving out into space from the thin planetary patina that hitherto has held all life, we are reworking the surface of our planet and shaping it to suit us. These developments will transform the world we inhabit. Amid all this, could we really imagine that we ourselves would somehow remain unchanged? Or that we would want to? If we were to succeed in turning back from the path of self-modification now opening before us, we would not be pleased with the result, because ultimately we would find ourselves in a world so different from the one that spawned us that we would feel estranged and adrift. Adaptable as we are, to remain at home in the world we are forming, we will have to adjust ourselves to cope with it.

At the end of the nineteenth century, visionary biologists imagined a bleak human future. Our very successes, by softening natural selection and saving those who would otherwise die young, seemed to ensure that the human species would slowly deteriorate. Germinal choice technology frees us from this fate, but it brings other, more immediate threats.

As we enter into advanced reproductive technology, we would do well to recall the Nazi concentration camps. Eugenics, as practiced in the first half of the past century, attests to the horrors of governmental abuse, and although Germany was the most egregious case, it was not alone. In the 1920s, the eugenics movement, which was often called "race hygiene," was centered in the United States and Great Britain, and included adherents in Poland, France, Italy, Scandinavia, Japan, and Latin America. Many of these programs were voluntary, but some were not.[22]

Some say that if we do not learn from history, we risk repeating it, but the challenge is always to understand what history is telling us. The lessons of past eugenic abuse do not concern technology, biology, or human reproduction, but nationalism, totalitarian regimes, individual freedom, and tyranny. Government abuse is what we must fear, not germinal choice technology. GCT is not a weapon, and the chaos of countless individual genetic choices by individual parents is not a threat, especially if the choices are circumscribed by modest oversight. Some push for uniform global policies, but these raise specters of the same governmental abuses that history warns us about.[23] Far better that we find our way in this coming journey by trial and error—cautious, informed trial, of course, and as little error as possible—but trial and error nonetheless.

There is no way we can permanently forgo these enhancement technologies if they prove robust and useful. Those who would shun healthier constitutions and extended lifespans might hope to remain the way they are, linked to a human past they cherish. But future generations will not want to remain "natural" if that means living at the whim of advanced creatures to whom they would be little more than intriguing relics from an abandoned human past.

What is occurring now is no less than a birth. The occasion may prove messy and painful, but it carries the wonder of new life and new possibilities, the promise of growth and achievement. Humanity has been building toward this moment for tens of thousands of years. Conception took place long ago when we first chipped stone tools and used fire. Quickening came with early agriculture, writing, and the formation of larger human communities. Now the contractions are forceful and rapid. The head is beginning to show. Will we suddenly lose our nerve because of the realization that life will change forever and because we can barely guess the character of this child of our creation? I hope not. We cannot push the head back, and we risk doing ourselves grievous harm if we make the attempt. We may not like the future we are creating, so vastly will it ultimately differ from our present. Yet our descendants—those beings who are the product of today's crude beginnings at unraveling our biology—will be unable to imagine living without the many enhancements that we will make possible for them.

A thousand years hence, these future humans—whoever or whatever they may be—will look back on our era as a challenging, difficult, traumatic moment. They will likely see it as a strange and primitive time when people lived only seventy or eighty years, died of awful diseases, and conceived their children outside a laboratory by a random, unpredictable meeting of sperm and egg. But they will also see our era as the fertile, extraordinary epoch that laid the foundation of their lives and their society. The cornerstone will almost certainly be the reworking of human biology and reproduction. To me, being here, not only to witness but to participate in this unprecedented development, is an amazing privilege. But we are so much more than observers and architects of these changes; we are also their objects.

Public policies about germinal choice technology will be effective only to the extent that they are prescient enough to elicit technology that succeeds in promoting future research and development. Whether DNA chips, advanced *in vitro* fertilization, and human artificial chromosomes will provide the foundation for germinal choice or whether some other cluster of technologies will fill that role remains to be seen. In either case, we will work toward embryo screening and other germline procedures that are either cheap and accessible to everyone or expensive and accessible to only a few.

If there is a window of opportunity for government to influence the future path of these technologies, it is unlikely to last for long. Only a few countries now have the capacity to realize them. If these nations move toward workable GCT and responsible strategies for using the resulting reproductive procedures, they may shape the basic approaches that become dominant. If they restrict the development of GCT and simply continue probing the fundamentals of our biology, unknown others will take the critical early steps and determine the shape of GCT for the immediate future.

The great challenge is not how we handle cloning, embryo selection, germline engineering, genetic testing, genetically altered foods, or any other specific technology. We will muddle through as we always have. Unlike nuclear weapons, these technologies will be forgiving; they carry no threat of imminent destruction to multitudes of innocent bystanders. The crucial question is whether we will continue to embrace the possibilities of our biological future or pull back and relinquish their development to braver souls in more adventurous nations of the world.

Many European countries have already made a provisional decision in this regard. In part because of their sensitivity over the eugenic abuses of the past, they are forgoing these technologies and trusting others to forge them.

I suspect that this stance on so central an element of our future will be temporary, but in any event, Europe will have a decade to mull over the matter before GCT emerges in a serious way.

As I see it, the coming opportunities in germinal choice technology far outweigh the risks. What is more, a free-market environment with real individual choice, modest oversight, and robust mechanisms to learn quickly from mistakes is the best way both to protect us from potential abuses and to channel resources toward the goals we value.   ■

NOTES

1. Predispositions for high IQ—and other cognitive attributes, for that matter—may be among the most complex of human traits. Though single-gene mutations have been implicated in various substantial diminutions of cognitive functioning, no specific genes have yet been found that account for even a few percentage points of variation in IQ among people with average and above-average scores. Current bioinformatic studies are too primitive—too small and crude—to identify combinations of alleles that together will raise IQ or to identify rare individual alleles that do. If researchers have so far failed to identify any strong single-gene contributions, this does not mean that combinations of genes will exert no strong effects, that there are no rare alleles that exert significant effects, or that no way will be found to manipulate relevant biochemical pathways. But if embryo selection for the main components of the heritable contribution to high IQ proves possible, this would still not usher in a genetic supermarket where parents could fill a shopping cart with multiple enhancements. Even without inherent biological tradeoffs among traits, finding the right gene combinations would require the screening of huge numbers of embryos.

2. This estimate assumes that IQ is only 50 percent heritable in typical environments (which is at the low end of current estimates; see, for example, Steen, 1999, pp. 113–35) and that only half of the total genetic variance is within individual families. The top embryo—selected on genetic criteria alone—would on average become an adult who tested at 118. By comparison, the top 1 percent of children have IQs of about 138.

3. See Parens, 1998. "The use of IGM": See Frankel and Chapman, 2000, p. 42.

4. Say IQ turned out to be very complex, shaped by twenty key genes and hundreds of others with minor influences. No doubt there would be many genes or small clusters of genes that when mutated cause nutritional problems or otherwise disrupt normal brain development, resulting in diminished intelligence. PKU (phenylketonuria) is one such condition described by Paul (1998, p. 178), and it is relatively straightforward to repair. But the task of improving on a rare combination of genes that contribute to genius would be far more difficult and demand greater caution about unseen tradeoffs.

5. See Scott and Fuller, 1974, pp. 403, 411.

6. See Vila et al., 1997, and Wayne, 1993. Although the oldest archaeological evidence of the association between dogs and people dates back only about 14,000 years, mitochondrial sequencing suggests that dogs branched off from gray wolves around 135,000 years ago. (Gray wolves had branched off from coyotes and foxes 5 to 10 million years earlier.) It is possible that dogs did not diverge anatomically from wolves until humans began to inhabit agricultural centers and impose stronger selective pressures. Few dog breeds can be traced back more than a few thousand years, and most have appeared only in the past few centuries. This may seem a short time, but a single breeder's hand can direct their evolution for thirty or more dog generations, whereas our evolution, with so few generations encompassed by any single human lifetime, must be directed by larger social and cultural forces.

   In a forty-year domestication experiment on foxes, Russian breeders, using modern methods, selected for a single trait: tameness. This, they believe, is the common trait that all human domestication has selected, and it produced aspects of doglike morphology, coat color variability, size changes, tail changes, and such. See Trut, 1999. <www.blarg.net/~critter/dogfamily/ancientdog_3.htm>.

7. When researchers compared a hundred different genetic markers from ninety-six dog breeds, they couldn't distinguish one breed from another. This means that the differences are much more fine-grained, encompassing relatively small numbers of genes. These differences may give us great insight into the potential for directing human evolution. Certainly, such efforts have been relatively easy with dogs and foxes. (Personal communication, Jasper Rine, University of California at Berkeley.) Biological forms that persist: See Raup, 1991, p. 108.

8. See Blackmore, 1999.

9. See Stock, 1993, p. 85.

10. See Wertz and Wertz, 1989.

11. See Capecchi, 2000. $6,000 a baby: The cost of a viable pregnancy by IVF for a thirty-year-old woman without serious fertility problems is now about $12,000. Assuming savings from new technology, IVF that is routine, massive numbers of procedures, and automated GCT, the lower figure is not outlandish; it costs about the same amount to order a strain of knock-out mice from a laboratory.

12. See Cook and Frank, 1991.

13. These figures are not precise, since we don't even know the exact number of human genes, but they are in the ballpark. For a good general discussion of the human genome, see the *Nova* interview with Eric Landers, the director of the Center for Genome Research at the Whitehead Institute: <www.pbs.org/wgbh/nova/genome/deco_lander.html>. The differences between us: We are a young species, all coming from a population of a few tens of thousands of people that existed 100,000 years ago in Africa. Because this founder population was so small and recent, the differences between two humans are perhaps a quarter as great as those between two chimpanzees.

14. This would include the coding regions of genes, which determine the sequences of the protein or proteins each gene specifies, and the non-coding regions, which regulate the expression of the genes. Together these account for perhaps 5 percent of the human genome.

15. While some people fear that GCT will be narrowly held and therefore lead to a genetic elite, others fear that the multitudes will have access to GCT and make pathological or at least unwise choices. And some people fear both. For example, Sheldon Krimsky, a professor at Tufts University, writes, "The availability of eugenic techniques in reproduction to a minority of affluent people will support the 'geneticization' of a society, enabling an aristocracy with so-called proper genes to use it to their class advantage." This suggests that such choices would be of value. But elsewhere in the same essay, he suggests that "offering people the opportunity to choose the phenotype of a child will result in psychosocial pathologies, including deeper class and racial divisions within society" (Krimsky, 2000). Apparently, only the elite would have the sense to use the technology to their benefit.

16. The so-called War on Drugs provides a cautionary tale for GCT. This war has filled our jails, corrupted swaths of law enforcement and government, made criminals out of many otherwise law-abiding citizens, and funneled enormous resources into the hands of criminals. But many supporters of it contend that legalization would be far worse, because it would bring about greater use of drugs and destroy countless lives. Duke and Gross (1994) presents an excellent argument against the War on Drugs.

17. Were enhancements based on changes to our 46 existing chromosomes rather than on replaceable artificial chromosomes, each generation would have to build on the changes made by the previous one, so family lineages would progressively accumulate benefits and diverge from one another. In essence, everyone's genetic choices about their offspring would be circumscribed by the past decisions of their ancestors.

18. The screening out of genetic vulnerabilities would no doubt also result in fewer individuals whose afflictions bring about uncommon achievements—the manic depressive who writes great literature, the physically impaired artist who creates great works of art. In any event, in the future many such afflictions will be increasingly blunted by improved medical treatment.

19. Campbell (1995) explores the concept of self-directed evolution at length. He calls it "regenerative evolution" and believes that small groups of future humans, highly committed to self-evolution, will outstrip humanity as a whole, leaving it far behind. In his view, how humanity responds to GCT is irrelevant, because small founder groups will be at the heart of any future evolutionary change.

20. This process mirrors our domestication of dogs, cats, livestock, and crops. By selecting for those qualities that bring these species into our lives, we have transformed them, and we have transformed ourselves through a similar process of self-selection. Our transformation has been primarily cultural, but it has almost certainly had a biological component: selection for the traits that allow survival in the altered world we have been creating.

21. See Worsley, 1931.

22. Kevles (1995) provides an in-depth look of the origins of the eugenics movement. The mainstream movement was largely oriented toward voluntarism and relied on education, contraception, and moral injunction. Eugenic ideas were so commonly accepted that a 1937 poll in *Fortune* magazine showed 63 percent of Americans endorsing the compulsory sterilization of habitual criminals and 66 percent in favor of sterilizing "mental defectives." In 1939, Hermann Muller, who later won the Nobel Prize and helped found the "genius" sperm bank in San Diego, published a "Genetics Manifesto" with twenty-two other scientists asserting that it should be "an honor and a privilege, if not a duty, for a mother, married or unmarried, or for a couple, to have the best children possible, both in upbringing and genetic endowment."

23. See Macer, 2000.

REFERENCES

Blackmore, S. 1999. *The Meme Machine*. New York: Oxford University Press.

Campbell, J. 1995. "The Moral Imperative of Our Future Evolution." In *Evolution and Human Values*, edited by R. Wesson and P. Williams. New York: Rodopi.

Capecchi, M. 2000. "Human Germline Gene Therapy: How and Why." In *Engineering the Human Germline: An Exploration of the Science and Ethics of Altering the Genes We Pass to Our Children*, edited by G. Stock and J. Campbell, 31–42. New York: Oxford University Press.

Cook, P., and R. Frank. 1991. "The Growing Concentration of Top Students at Elite Schools." In *The Economics of Higher Education*, edited by C. Clotfelter and M. Rothschild. Chicago: NBER-University of Chicago Press.

Duke, S., and A. Gross. 1994. *America's Longest War: Rethinking Our Tragic Crusade Against Drugs*. New York: Putnam.

Frankel, M., and A. Chapman. 2000. *Human Inheritable Genetic Modifications: Assessing Scientific, Ethical, Religious, and Policy Issues*. Washington, D.C.: AAAS Publication Services. <www.aaas.org/spp/dspp/sfrl/germline/main.htm>.

Kevles, D. 1995. *In the Name of Eugenics: Genetics and the Uses of Human Heredity*. Cambridge: Harvard University Press.

Krimsky, S. 2000. "The Psychosocial Limits on Human Germline Modification." In *Engineering the Human Germline: An Exploration of the Science and Ethics of Altering the Genes We Pass to Our Children*, edited by G. Stock and J. Campbell, 104–7. New York: Oxford University Press.

Macer, D. 2000. "Universal Bioethics for the Human Germline." In *Engineering the Human Germline: An Exploration of the Science and Ethics of Altering the Genes We Pass to Our*

Children, edited by G. Stock and J. Campbell, 139–141. New York: Oxford University Press.

Parens, E., ed. 1998. *Enhancing Human Traits: Ethical and Social Implications.* Washington, D.C.: Georgetown University Press.

Paul, D. 1998. *The Politics of Heredity: Essays on Eugenics, Biomedicine, and the Nature-Nurture Debate.* Albany: State University of New York Press.

Raup D. 1991. *Extinction: Bad Genes or Bad Luck?* New York: W. W. Norton.

Scott, J., and L. Fuller. 1974. *Genetics and the Social Behavior of the Dog.* Chicago: University of Chicago Press.

Steen, G. 1996. *DNA and Destiny: Nature and Nurture in Human Behavior.* New York: Plenum, 161–83.

Stock, G. 1993. *Metaman: Humans, Machines, and the Birth of a Global Super-organism.* New York: Simon & Schuster.

Trut, L. N. 1999. "Early Canid Domestication: The Farm Fox Experiment." *American Scientist* 87 (March).

Vila, C., et al. 1997. "Multiple and Ancient Origins of the Domestic Dog." *Science* 76: 1687–89.

Wayne, R. 1993. "Molecular Evolution of the Dog Family." *Trends in Genetics* 9: 218–24.

Wertz, R., and D. Wertz. 1989. *Lying-In: A History of Childbirth in America.* New Haven: Yale University Press.

Worsley, F. 1931. *Endurance.* New York: W. W. Norton.

■ *QUESTIONS FOR MAKING CONNECTIONS WITHIN THE READING* ■

1. The last paragraph of Stock's reading begins with these words: "As I see it, the coming opportunities in germinal choice technology far outweigh the risks." Do you feel that Stock's argument fully supports this claim? Conversely, would you say that he has done an adequate job of giving the risks "equal time" with the benefits?

2. Much of the debate over genetic technology has focused on the issue of cloning. Does Stock's focus on genetic choice technology as opposed to cloning make his job as a spokesperson easier or more difficult? Can Stock's argument for genetic choice technology be applied to cloning as well? Can his argument be used to justify technological changes of every kind? If you feel that his argument could be used to justify every change, is that a strength or a weakness?

3. What does Stock mean in this passage:

   > Today's intellectual elite might not want to live in a world as aggressive, competitive, and uncontrolled as the one that would emerge from universal access to potent germinal choice technology, so their distaste for the technology may deepen once its true implications become clear.

   Why would the world that Stock foresees be more "aggressive, competitive, and uncontrolled" than it is right now? What would elites have to fear from such a world? If our society creates a free market in genetic technology, are we likely to see more, or less, equality? Will we see more, or less, peace and security? If everyone gets smarter and stronger, what might be the result?

■ *QUESTIONS FOR WRITING* ■

1. Questions related to genetic technology can be viewed from many perspectives—scientific, ethical, historical, religious, economic, political, and pragmatic. What perspectives does Stock tend to adopt? How does his choice of perspectives shape the conclusions he reaches?

2. How does Stock's proposal differ from the practice of eugenics in Nazi Germany? Does it matter if individuals rather than governments make decisions about the genetic modification of future generations? Do you agree that individuals are less likely than governments to withhold access to genetic technologies? Should *anyone* have the right to change the genetic make-up of the coming generation?

■ *QUESTIONS FOR MAKING CONNECTIONS BETWEEN READINGS* ■

1. Stock assumes that genetic technologies can be made widely, or even universally, available. Does William Greider paint a picture of American social life that lends credence to Stock's assumptions? Would a free market in genetic technology assure that everyone could take advantage of such technological advances? How might the market in these technologies be protected or controlled to make certain that everyone would be able to compete equally for these benefits? Should such market protections be introduced?

2. Stock's discussion of genetic technology focuses on enhancing the conventional physical and mental powers of individuals. He appears to be less interested in the psychological effects that might follow from such "enhancements." Starting with Martha Stout's discussion of the way the brain processes traumatic events, weigh the advantages and disadvantages of genetic changes that might eliminate our innate tendency to dissociate ourselves from painful events. Could it be that the fugue state Stout describes has a survival advantage? Is it possible that the desire to redesign human beings is a product of a dissociated state of mind? Would a person less alienated from the world really want to enhance human beings as they now exist?

MARTHA STOUT

WHAT IS SANITY? Are "normal" people always dependably sane, or could it be said that we experience sanity only as a temporary, fluctuating state? After witnessing a traumatic event, have you ever spent time in a state that is not exactly sane, a state of either frantic agitation or numbness, withdrawal, and distraction? These are the questions that Martha Stout, a clinical psychologist in private practice and the best-selling author of *The Sociopath Next Door* (2005) and *The Paranoia Switch* (2007), pursued in her first book, *The Myth of Sanity: Divided Consciousness and the Promise of Awareness* (2002). Stout taught psychology at Harvard Medical School for 26 years. Drawing on this and her nearly 30 years of clinical experience specializing in treating patients who have suffered psychological trauma, Stout uses her case studies to show that the ability to dissociate from reality, which functions as a life-preserving defense mechanism during times of stress in childhood, can develop into a way of life that leads to emotional detachment and prolonged disengagement with the world. In the most extreme cases, the dissociative behavior can lead individuals to black out for extended periods of time or to develop multiple personalities in order to contend with life's many demands.

In seeking to establish a continuum that extends from the everyday experience of spacing out to the more traumatic experience of being shell shocked, Stout invites her readers to recognize just how common the experience of dementia, or "self-shifting," can be. The patients Stout focuses on have been forced to come to terms with the extreme forms this dementia can take, and, with her help, they come to see the meaning of their own lives as something they must continually work to construct. In jargon-free prose, Stout tells stories of her patients' struggles for and with sanity, revealing in each case how buried or missing memories of the past serve to disrupt and distort the experience of the present.

Stout, Martha. "When I Woke Up Tuesday Morning, It Was Friday," in *The Myth of Sanity: Divided Consciousness and the Promise of Awareness*. New York: Penguin Books, 2002. 15–43.

Biographical information comes from <http://harvard.com/events/press_release.php?id=1880> and <http://www.huffingtonpost.com/dr-martha-stout/>.

When I Woke Up Tuesday Morning, It Was Friday

"The horror of that moment," the King went on, "I shall never, never forget!"

"You will, though," the Queen said, "if you don't make a memorandum of it."

—Lewis Carroll

Imagine that you are in your house—no—you are *locked* in your house, cannot get out. It is the dead of winter. The drifted snow is higher than your windows, blocking the light of both moon and sun. Around the house, the wind moans, night and day.

Now imagine that even though you have plenty of electric lights, and perfectly good central heating, you are almost always in the dark and quite cold, because something is wrong with the old-fashioned fuse box in the basement. Inside this cobwebbed, innocuous-looking box, the fuses keep burning out, and on account of this small malfunction, all the power in the house repeatedly fails. You have replaced so many melted fuses that now your little bag of new ones is empty; there are no more. You sigh in frustration, and regard your frozen breath in the light of the flashlight. Your house, which could be so cozy, is tomblike instead.

In all probability, there is something quirky in the antiquated fuse box; it has developed some kind of needless hair trigger, and is not really reacting to any dangerous electrical overload at all. Should you get some pennies out of your pocket, and use them to replace the burned-out fuses? That would solve the power-outage problem. No more shorts, not with copper coins in there. Using coins would scuttle the safeguard function of the fuse box, but the need for a safeguard right now is questionable, and the box is keeping you cold and in the dark for no good reason. Well, probably for no good reason.

On the other hand, what if the wiring in the house really is overloaded somehow? A fire could result, probably will result eventually. If you do not find the fire soon enough, if you cannot manage to put the fire out, the whole house could go up, with you trapped inside. You know that death by burning is hideous. You know also that your mind is playing tricks, but thinking about fire, you almost imagine there is smoke in your nostrils right now.

So, do you go back upstairs and sit endlessly in a dark living room, defeated, numb from the cold, though you have buried yourself under every blanket in the house? No light to read by, no music, just the wail and rattle of the icy wind outside? Or, in an attempt to feel more human, do you make things warm and comfortable? Is it wise to gamble with calamity and howling pain? If you turn the power back on, will you not smell nonexistent smoke every moment you are awake? And will you not have far too many of these waking moments, for how will you ever risk going to sleep?

Do you sabotage the fuse box?

I believe that most of us cannot know what we would do, trapped in a situation that required such a seemingly no-win decision. But I do know that anyone wanting to recover from psychological trauma must face just this kind of dilemma, made yet more harrowing because her circumstance is not anything so rescuable as being locked in a house, but rather involves a solitary, unlockable confinement inside the limits of her own mind. The person who suffers from a severe trauma disorder must decide between surviving in a barely sublethal misery of numbness and frustration, and taking a chance that may well bring her a better life, but that feels like stupidly issuing an open invitation to the unspeakable horror that waits to consume her alive. And in the manner of the true hero, she must choose to take the risk.

For trauma changes the brain itself. Like the outdated fuse box, the psychologically traumatized brain houses inscrutable eccentricities that cause it to overreact—or more precisely, *mis*react—to the current realities of life. These neurological misreactions become established because trauma has a profound effect upon the secretion of stress-responsive neurohormones such as norepinephrine, and thus an effect upon various areas of the brain involved in memory, particularly the amygdala and the hippocampus.

The amygdala receives sensory information from the five senses, via the thalamus, attaches emotional significance to the input, and then passes along this emotional "evaluation" to the hippocampus. In accordance with the amygdala's "evaluation" of importance, the hippocampus is activated to a greater or lesser degree, and functions to organize the new input, and to integrate it with already existing information about similar sensory events. Under a normal range of conditions, this system works efficiently to consolidate memories according to their emotional priority. However, at the extreme upper end of hormonal stimulation, as in traumatic situations, a breakdown occurs. Overwhelming emotional significance registered by the amygdala actually leads to a *decrease in hippocampal activation,* such that some of the traumatic input is not usefully organized by the hippocampus, or integrated with other memories. The result is that portions of traumatic memory are stored not as parts of a unified whole, but as isolated sensory images and bodily sensations that are not localized in time or even in situation, or integrated with other events.

To make matters still more complex, exposure to trauma may temporarily shut down Broca's area, the region of the left hemisphere of the brain that translates experience into language, the means by which we most often relate our experience to others, and even to ourselves.

A growing body of research indicates that in these ways the brain lays down traumatic memories differently from the way it records regular memories. Regular memories are formed through adequate hippocampal and cortical input, are integrated as comprehensible wholes, and are subject to meaning-modification by future events, and through language. In contrast, traumatic memories include chaotic fragments that are sealed off from modulation by subsequent experience. Such memory fragments are wordless, placeless, and eternal, and long after the original trauma has receded into the past, the brain's record of it may consist only of isolated and thoroughly anonymous bits of emotion, image, and sensation that ring through the individual like a broken alarm.

Worse yet, later in the individual's life, in situations that are vaguely similar to the trauma—perhaps merely because they are startling, anxiety-provoking, or emotionally arousing—amygdala-mediated memory traces are accessed more readily than are the more complete, less shrill memories that have been integrated and modified by the hippocampus and the cerebral cortex. Even though unified and updated memories would be more judicious in the present, the amygdala memories are more accessible, and so trauma may be "remembered" at inappropriate times, when there is no hazard worthy of such alarm. In reaction to relatively trivial stresses, the person traumatized long ago may truly *feel* that danger is imminent again, be assailed full-force by the emotions, bodily sensations, and perhaps even the images, sounds, smells that once accompanied great threat.

Here is an illustration from everyday life. A woman named Beverly reads a morning newspaper while she sits at a quiet suburban depot and waits for a train. The article, concerning an outrageous local scandal, intrigues her so much that for a few minutes she forgets where she is. Suddenly, there is an earsplitting blast from the train as it signals its arrival. Beverly is painfully startled by the noise; her head snaps up, and she catches her breath. She is amazed that she could have been so lacking in vigilance and relaxed in public. Her heart pounds, and in the instant required to fold the newspaper, she is ambushed by bodily feelings and even a smell that have nothing whatever to do with the depot on this uneventful morning. If she could identify the smell, which she never will, she would call it "chlorine." She feels a sudden rigidity in her chest, as if her lungs had just turned to stone, and has an almost overpowering impulse to get out of there, to run.

In a heartbeat, the present is perceptually and emotionally the past. These fragments of sensation and emotion are the amygdala-mediated memories of an afternoon three decades before, in Beverly's tenth summer, when, walking home from the public swimming pool, she saw her younger sister skip into the street and meet an immediate death in front of a speeding car. At this moment, thirty years later, Beverly *feels* that way again.

Her sensations and feelings are not labeled as belonging to memories of the horrible accident. In fact, they are not labeled as anything at all, because they have always been completely without language. They belong to no narrative, no place or time, no story she can tell about her life; they are free-form and ineffable.

Beverly's brain contains, effectively, a broken warning device in its limbic system, an old fuse box in which the fuses tend to melt for no good reason, emphatically declaring an emergency where none now exists.

Surprisingly, she will probably not wonder about or even remember the intense perceptual and emotional "warnings," because by the next heartbeat, a long-entrenched dissociative reaction to the declared emergency may already have been tripped in her brain, to "protect" her from this "unbearable" childhood memory. She may feel strangely angry, or paranoid, or childishly timid. Or instead she may feel that she has begun to move in an uncomfortably hazy dream world, far away and derealized. Or she may completely depart from her "self" for a while, continue to act, but without self-awareness. Should this last occur in a minor way, her total experience may be something such as, "Today when I was going to work, the train pulled into the station—the blasted thing is so loud!—and the next thing I remember, it was stopping at my stop." She may even be mildly amused at herself for her spaciness.

Most of us do not notice these experiences very much. They are more or less invisible to us as we go about daily life, and so we do not understand how much of daily life is effectively spent in the past, in reaction to the darkest hours we have known, nor do we comprehend how swampy and vitality-sucking some of our memories really are. Deepening the mire of our divided awareness, in the course of a lifetime such "protective" mental reactions acquire tremendous *habit strength*. These over-exercised muscles can take us away even when traumatic memory fragments have not been evoked. Sometimes dissociation can occur when we are simply confused or frustrated or nervous, whether we recognize our absences or not.

Typically, only those with the most desperate trauma histories are ever driven to discover and perhaps modify their absences from the present. Only the addictions, major depressions, suicide attempts, and general ruination that attend the most severe trauma disorders can sometimes supply motivation sufficiently fierce to run the gauntlet thrown down by insight and permanent change. On account of our neurological wiring, confronting past traumas requires one to reendure all of their terrors mentally, in their original intensity, to feel as if the worst nightmare had come true and the horrors had returned. All the brain's authoritative warnings against staying present for the memories and the painful emotions, all the faulty fuses, have to be deliberately ignored, and in cases of extreme or chronic past trauma, this process is nothing short of heroic.

It helps to have an awfully good reason to try, such as suffocating depression or some other demonic psychological torment. Perhaps this is a part of the reason why philosophers and theologians through the centuries have observed such a strong connection between unbearable earthly sorrow and spiritual enlightenment, a timeless relationship that psychologists have mysteriously overlooked.

In order to appreciate what psychological trauma can do to the mind, and to a life, let us consider an extreme case of divided awareness, that of a woman whose psyche was mangled by profound trauma in her past, and who came to me for treatment after several serious suicide attempts. Her story is far grimmer than any most of us will ever know, and the consequent suffering in her adult life has been nearly unsurvivable. And yet, should one meet her on the street, or know her only casually, she would seem quite normal. In fact, one might easily view her as enviable. Certainly, when looking on from a distance, nothing at all would appear to be wrong, and much would be conspicuously right.

Julia is brilliant. After the *summa cum laude* from Stanford, and the full scholarship at the graduate school in New York, she became an award-winning producer of documentary films. I met her when she was thirty-two, and an intellectual force to be reckoned with. A conversation with her reminds me of the *New York Review of Books,* except that she is funnier, and also a living, breathing human being who wears amethyst jewelry to contrast with her electric auburn hair. Her ultramarine eyes gleam, even when she is depressed, giving one the impression, immediately upon meeting her, that there is something special about her. She is, however, soft-spoken and disarming in the extreme. She does not glorify, does not even seem to notice, either her prodigious intelligence or her beauty.

Those same blue eyes notice everything, instantly, photographically. The first time she walked into my office, she said, "Oh how nice. Did you get that little statue in Haiti? I did a kind of project there once. What a spellbinding place!"

She was referring to a small soapstone figurine, the rounded abstraction of a kneeling man, that I had indeed purchased in Port-au-Prince, and that sat on a shelf parallel to my office door. She had not glanced back in that direction as she came in, and must have captured and processed the image in a microsecond of peripheral perception.

"That's very observant," I said, whereupon she directed at me a smile so sparkling and so warm that, for just the barest moment, her lifelong depression cracked and vanished from the air around her, as if it had been nothing but a bubble. The radiance of her momentary smile caused me to blink, and I knew exactly then, even before the first session began, that if she would let me, I would do everything I could to keep this particular light from going out.

At a moment's notice, Julia can speak entertainingly and at length about film, music, multicultural psychology, African politics, theories of literary criticism, and any number of other subjects. Her memory for detail is beyond exceptional, and she has the storyteller's gift. When she is recounting information, or a story, her own intellectual fascination with it gives her voice the poised and expertly modulated quality of the narrator of a high-budget documentary about some especially wondrous endangered animals, perhaps Tibetan snow leopards. She speaks a few astutely inflected sentences, and then pauses, almost as if she is listening—and expects you to be listening—for the stealthy *crunch-crunch* of paws on the snow's crust.

Curious about this, I once asked her whether she were an actress as well as a filmmaker. She laughed, and replied that she could do first-rate narrative voice-overs, if she did say so herself, but had not a smidgen of real theatrical ability. In fact, she said, sometimes the people she worked with teased her good-naturedly about this minor chink in her armor.

At my first session with her, when I asked her why she had come to therapy, she spent thirty minutes telling me in cinematic detail about her recent attempt to kill herself, by driving to an isolated Massachusetts beach at three A.M. on a Tuesday in late January, and lying down by the surf. By so doing, she sincerely expected not to be found until well after she had frozen to death. Taking her omniscient narrator tone, intellectually intrigued by the memory, she described the circumstances of her unlikely accidental rescue by a group of drunken college students, and then spent the second thirty minutes of our hour together likening this near-death experience to the strangely impersonal distance from story one can achieve on film with certain authorial camera moves.

"By then, I was floating above myself, looking down, sort of waiting. And I know I couldn't actually have seen those kids, but I *felt* that I did. Over the sound of the waves, I don't think you can really *hear* footsteps in the sand, but still . . ."

And I strained to hear the *crunch-crunch.*

Therapy is a frightening thing, and people do not often seek it out because they are only mildly unhappy. In my work, and because of the high-risk individuals who are referred to me, it is not unusual for me to hear stories of attempted suicide from people I have only just met. I have come almost to expect such accounts, in fact.

At our second session, and in exactly the same tone she had used to describe her suicide attempt, Julia began by giving me an interesting account of her new project on the life of a promising writer who had died young, reportedly of a rare blood disease he had contracted in western China. After about fifteen minutes of this, I stopped her, and explained that I wanted to know something about her, about Julia herself, rather than about Julia's work. Seeing the blank expression come over her face, I tried to provide her with some nonthreatening guidance. I asked her some general, factual questions about her childhood.

And at that second session, this is what the articulate, intellectually gifted Julia remembered about her own childhood: An only child, she knew that she had been born in Los Angeles, but she did not know in which hospital. She vaguely remembered that when she was about ten, her parents had moved with her to another neighborhood; but she did not remember anything about the first neighborhood, or even where it was. Though she did not know for sure, she assumed that the move must have taken place because her parents had become more prosperous. She remembered that she had a friend in high school named Barbara (with whom "I must have spent a lot of time"), but she could not remember Barbara's last name, or where Barbara had gone after high school. I asked Julia about her teachers, and she could not remember a single one of them, not from grade school, not from middle school, not from high school. She could not remember whether or not she had gone to her high school prom or her high school graduation. The only thing she seemed to remember vividly from childhood was that when she was about twelve, she had a little terrier dog named Grin, and that her mother had Grin put to sleep when he needed an expensive stomach operation.

And that was all she remembered of her childhood, this successful thirty-two-year-old woman with the cinematic mind. And it took forty-five minutes for her to pull out that much from the dark, silent place that housed her early memories. She could not remember a single holiday or a single birthday. At thirty-two, she could swim, read, drive a car, and play a few songs on the piano. But she could not remember learning any of these skills.

Insufficient memory in the context of an adequate intellect, let alone a gifted one, is the next observation—right after the extraordinary understatement and humor—that causes me to become suspicious about a patient's past.

At our third session, she asked me an astonishing question, but also, really, the obvious question: "Do other people remember those things, about their teachers, and going to their graduation, and learning to drive, and so on?" When I told her that, yes, they usually do remember, at least to a much greater degree than she did, she reverently said, "Wow," and then she was quiet for a few minutes. Finally, she leaned forward a little and asked, "So what's wrong with me?"

Cautiously, because I knew what I had to say might at first sound preposterous or worse to Julia, I said, "I'm wondering about early traumatic experiences in your life. Even when someone's cognitive memory is perfectly good, as yours is, trauma can disrupt the memory in emotional ways."

Julia thought I was way off base; or at least the part of her that collected amethyst jewelry, made award-winning films, and talked about camera angles thought I was way off base. Another part of Julia, the part that kept trying to commit suicide, the part that prevented her from moving back to Los Angeles as her career demanded, the part that sometimes made her so sleepy during the middle of an ordinary day that she had to be driven home, that part kept her coming back to therapy for the next six years. During those six years, step by step, Julia and I cast some light on what had happened to her. She agreed to be hypnotized; she began to remember her dreams; she acknowledged her faint suspicions. She even traveled back to Los Angeles, to talk with distant relatives and old neighbors.

What we eventually discovered was that, when she was a child, Julia had lived in a house of horrors, with monsters jumping out at her without warning and for no apparent reason, except that Julia had come to assume, as abused children do, that she must be a horrible person who deserved these punishments. By the time she was school age, she had learned not to cry, because tears only encouraged her parents to abuse her further. Also, she had lost any inclination whatsoever to let anyone know what was going on. Telling someone and asking for help were concepts foreign to her despairing little soul. The thought that her life might be different had simply stopped occurring to her.

And soon, in a sense, she had stopped telling even herself. When the abuse began, she would "go somewhere else"; she would "not be there." By this, she meant that her mind had learned how to dissociate Julia's self from what was going on around her, how to transport her awareness to a place far enough away that, at most, she felt she was watching the life of a little girl named Julia from a very great distance. A sad little girl named Julia was helpless and could not escape; but psychologically, Julia's self could go "somewhere else," could be psychologically absent.

Simply put, Julia did not remember her childhood because she was not present for it.

All human beings have the capacity to dissociate psychologically, though most of us are unaware of this, and consider "out of body" episodes to be far beyond the boundaries of our normal experience. In fact, dissociative experiences happen to everyone, and most of these events are quite ordinary.

Consider a perfectly ordinary person as he walks into a perfectly ordinary movie theater to see a popular movie. He is awake, alert, and oriented to his surroundings. He is aware that his wife is with him and that, as they sit down in their aisle seats, she is to his right. He is aware that he has a box of popcorn on his lap. He knows that the movie he has come to see is entitled *The Fugitive,* and that its star is Harrison Ford, an actor. As he waits for the movie to begin, perhaps he worries about a problem he is having at work.

Then the lights in the theater are lowered, and the movie starts. And within twenty-five minutes, he has utterly lost his grasp on reality. Not only is he no longer worried about work, he no longer realizes that he has a job. If one could read his thoughts, one would discover that he no longer believes he is sitting in a theater, though in reality, he is. He cannot smell his popcorn; some of it tumbles out of the box he now holds slightly askew, because he has forgotten about his own hands. His wife has vanished, though any observer would see that she is still seated four inches to his right.

And without moving from his own seat, he is running, running, running—not with Harrison Ford, the actor—but with the beleaguered fugitive in the movie, with, in other words, a person who does not exist at all, in this moviegoer's real world or anyone else's. His heart races as he dodges a runaway train that does not exist, either.

This perfectly ordinary man is dissociated from reality. Effectively, he is in a trance. We might label his perceptions as psychotic, except for the fact that when the movie is over, he will return to his usual mental status almost instantly. He will see the credits. He will notice that he has spilled some popcorn, although he will not remember doing so. He will look to his right and speak to his wife. More than likely, he will tell her that he liked the movie, as we all tend to enjoy entertainments in which we can become lost. All that really happened is that, for a little while, he took the part of himself that worries about work problems and other "real" things, and separated it from the imaginative part of himself, so that the imaginative part could have dominance. He *dissociated* one part of his consciousness from another part.

When dissociation is illustrated in this way, most people can acknowledge that they have had such interludes from time to time, at a movie or a play, reading a book or hearing a speech, or even just daydreaming. And then the out-of-body may sound a little closer to home. Plainly stated, it is the case that under certain circumstances, ranging from pleasant or unpleasant distraction to fascination to fear to pain to horror, a human being can be psychologically absent from his or her own direct experience. We can go somewhere else. The part of consciousness that we nearly always conceive of as the "self" can be not there for a few moments, for a few hours, and in heinous circumstances, for much longer.

As the result of a daydream, this mental compartmentalization is called distraction. As the result of an involving movie, it is often called escape. As the result of trauma, physical or psychological, it is called a dissociative state. When a hypnotist induces dissociation, by monotony, distraction, relaxation or any number of other methods, the temporary result is called an hypnotic state, or a trance. The physiological patterns and the primary behavioral results of distraction, escape, dissociative state, and trance are virtually identical, regardless of method. The differences among them seem to result not so much from how consciousness gets divided as from how often and how long one is forced to keep it divided.

Another recognizable example of how consciousness can be split into pieces has to do with the perception of physical pain. On the morning after seeing *The Fugitive*, our moviegoer's wife is working frenetically to pack her briefcase, eat her breakfast, get the kids off to school, and listen to a news report on television, all at the same time. She is very distracted. In the process of all this, she bashes her leg soundly against the corner of a low shelf. Yet the woman is not seemingly aware that she has injured herself. That night, as she is getting ready for bed, she notices that she has a large colorful bruise on her right thigh. She thinks, "Well, now, I wonder how I did that."

In this case, a person was distracted, and the part of her consciousness that would normally have perceived pain was split apart from, and subjugated to, the part of her consciousness that was goal-directed. She was not there for the direct experience of her pain. She was somewhere else (the briefcase, the breakfast, the kids, the news). And because she was not there, she does not remember the accident.

The direct experience of physical pain can be split off in cases of much more serious injury as well. Most of us have heard stories along the lines of the parent who, with a broken leg, goes back to the scene of an accident and wrenches open a mangled car door with her bare hands in order to rescue her child. Less valorous, I myself remember my car being demolished by a speeding limousine. My knee was injured, but I felt no pain just after the crash, was more or less unaware of my body at all. My first thought before being dragged out of my car was to peer into the rearview mirror and inspect my teeth, and to decide that everything must be okay because there were no chips in them. And then there are the war stories about maimed infantrymen who have had to flee from the front line. All such circumstances affect memory in fascinating ways. Note, for example, that when veterans get together, they often laugh and tell war stories as though those times had been the best of their lives.

Agony that is psychological can be dissociated, too. While she was being abused, Julia developed the reaction of standing apart from herself and her situation. She stopped being there. Certainly, some parts of her consciousness must have been there right along. She could watch her parents, even predict their moods. She could run and hide. She could cover her injuries. She could keep her parents' secrets. But the part of her consciousness that she thinks of as her self was not there; it was split off, put aside, and therefore in some sense protected. And because her self had not been there, her self could not remember what had happened to her during much of her childhood.

What does this feel like, not being able to remember whole chapters of one's own life? I have asked many people this question, Julia among them. As usual, her answer was obvious and startling at the same time.

"It doesn't feel like anything," she answered. "I never really thought about it. I guess I just assumed, sort of tacitly assumed, that everyone's memory was like mine, that is to say, kind of blank before the age of twenty or so. I mean, you can't see into someone else's mind, right? All you can do is ask questions, and it never even occurred to me to ask anybody about this. It's like asking, 'What do you see when you see blue?' First of all, you'd never think to ask. And secondly, two people can agree that the clear blue sky is blue, but does the actual color blue look the *same* to both of them? Who knows? How would you even ask that question?

"Of course, every now and then I'd hear people talking about pin-the-tail-on-the-donkey, or some other thing about a little kid's birthday, and I'd wonder how they knew that. But I guess I just figured their memory was especially good, or maybe they'd heard their parents talk about it so much that it seemed like a memory.

"The memories I did have seemed like aberrations, like pinpoints of light in a dark room, so vague that you're not really sure whether you're seeing them or not. Certainly, there was nothing like a continuous thread of memory that linked one part of my life to another.

"Really it wasn't until you started asking me questions about my teachers and so forth that I ever even had any serious questions about my memory. After you started asking, I asked a couple of other people, just out of curiosity, and I began to realize that other people really do have childhood memories, and some of them are pretty vivid. I was surprised.

"What can I tell you? It just never occurred to me to wonder about it before. It felt like . . . it felt like nothing."

She shrugged. Most people shrug. They are genuinely surprised, and at a loss.

Now the conspicuous question to ask Julia was, "All this time that you've been so unhappy, all the times you've tried to end your life, what did you think was causing all that misery?"

"I thought I was crazy," she answered.

This is easy enough to understand. Imagine a simple and, relatively speaking, innocuous example. Imagine that someone, call her Alice, leaves work early one day and goes to the oral surgeon to have her two bottom wisdom teeth extracted. The extractions go well; the doctor packs the gums with cotton and sends Alice home. On the way home, for some fictitious reason, let us say magic moonbeams, Alice completely loses her memory of the visit to the oral surgeon. She now assumes that she is driving directly home from work, as she does on most days. After she gets home, she is okay for a while, but gradually the anesthetic wears off, and she begins to experience a considerable amount of pain in her mouth. Soon the pain is too strong to ignore, and she goes to the bathroom mirror to examine the situation. When she looks into her mouth, she discovers that there are wads of cotton in there. And when she takes the cotton out, she discovers that two of her teeth are missing, and she is bleeding!

Alice is now in the twilight zone. The ordinary experience of having her wisdom teeth pulled has turned into a situation that makes her feel insane. One or two more of such experiences, and she would be convinced.

Childhood trauma creates a particularly bewildering picture. Observe normal children at play, and you will realize that children are especially good at dissociating. In the interest of play, a child can, in a heartbeat, leave himself behind, become someone or something else, or several things at once. Reality is even more plastic in childhood. Pretend games are real and wonderful and consuming. It is clear to anyone who really looks that normal children derive unending joy from their superior ability to leap out of their "selves" and go somewhere else, be other things. The snow is not cold. The body is not tired, even when it is on the verge of collapse.

Because children dissociate readily even in ordinary circumstances, when they encounter traumatic situations, they easily split their consciousness into pieces, often for extended periods of time. The self is put aside and hidden. Of course, this reaction is functional for the traumatized child, necessary, even kind. For the traumatized child, a dissociative state, far from being dysfunctional or crazy, may in fact be lifesaving. And thanks be to the normal human mind that it provides the means.

This coping strategy becomes dysfunctional only later, after the child is grown and away from the original trauma. When the original trauma is no longer an ongoing fact of life, prolonged dissociative reactions are no longer necessary. But through the years of intensive use, the self-protective strategy has developed a hair trigger. The adult whom the child has become now experiences dissociative reactions to levels of stress that probably would not cause another person to dissociate.

The events that are most problematic tend to be related in some way to the original trauma. However, human beings are exquisitely symbolic creatures, and "related" can reach unpredictable and often indecipherable levels of abstraction and metaphor. A long shadow from a city streetlight can remind someone of the tall cacti on the Arizona desert where his father used to threaten to "feed" him to the rattlesnakes. An innocent song about the wind in the willow trees can remind someone else of the rice fields that were a part of her childhood's landscape in Cambodia. A car backfiring on Beacon Street in Boston can remind yet another person of that spot on the trail where his eighteen-year-old platoon mate exploded six feet in front of him.

And so for the adult who was traumatized as a child, the present too has a kind of mercurial quality. The present is difficult to hold on to, always getting away.

In Julia's case, though she had not questioned her poverty of memory for the past, she had begun to suspect even before she came into therapy that she was losing time in the present. Probably this is because there are more external reality checks on the present than there are on the past. From other people—and from radio, television, the Internet, date books—there are ongoing reminders of the present time of day, and day of the week. Markers of time in the past are less immediate, and sooner or later most dates and chronologies for the past begin to feel amorphous to us all. It is hardly amazing that one should have forgotten something that happened twenty years ago. But if a person lets on that she has no memory of an important event that occurred this very week, friends and associates are unlikely to let such a lapse go unremarked.

At one of her early sessions with me, Julia announced, "When I woke up Tuesday morning it was Friday."

"Pardon?"

"When I woke up this morning it was Tuesday, and then I discovered that it was Friday for everybody else."

"How do you mean?"

"Well, the last thing I remember before waking up this morning was having dinner Monday night. So I thought it was Tuesday. And then I went in to work, and some sponsors were there that I was supposed to meet with on Friday. So I asked my assistant what was up, and she said, 'You wanted to meet with these people this morning, remember?' And I said, 'No. I wanted to meet with them on Friday.' She looked at me, and said, 'Today is Friday, Julia.'

"I finessed. I laughed and said, 'Of course. That's terrible. No more late nights for me. Pretty soon I'll be forgetting my name. Ha, ha.' But it isn't funny. This happens a lot. I just lose time. Hours, days. They're gone, and I don't know what I've done or where I've been or anything else.

"I've never told anyone this before. It's embarrassing. Actually, it's terrifying.

"I don't understand any of it, but the thing I understand the least is that apparently I go about my business during these times, and nobody notices any difference in me. At least, no one ever says anything. After the meeting this morning, I realized that on Tuesday, Wednesday, and Thursday, I must have done a mountain of editing. There it was, all finished. I did a good job, even. And I don't remember a bloody thing."

During this confession, I saw Julia cry for the first time. Quickly, though, she willed her tears under control, and wanted me to tell her about a word she had heard me use the previous week, "dissociative." She questioned me as if the issue were a strictly academic one for her, which it clearly was not. I gently steered her back to the subject of herself and her week.

"Where did you have dinner Monday night?"

"What? Oh. Dinner Monday night. I had dinner at the Grill 23 with my friend Elaine."

"Was it a nice time?" I continued to question.

"I think so. Yes, I think it was okay."

"What did you and Elaine talk about, do you remember?"

"What did we talk about? Let's see. Well, I think we talked about the film a bit. And we talked about the waiter. Very cute waiter." She grinned. "And we probably spent the longest time talking about Elaine's relationship with this new guy, Peter. Why do you ask?"

"You said the dinner was the last thing you remembered before you woke up this morning. I thought it might be important. What did Elaine say about Peter?"

"Well, she said she's madly in love, and she said she wanted me to meet him because she thought we'd have a lot to talk about. He's from L.A., too."

"You and Peter are both from L.A. What else did you and Elaine say about L.A.?"

Julia looked suddenly blank, and said, "I don't remember. Why? Do you really think something about the place where I grew up scares me enough that just talking about it blasts me into never-never land for three days? That really can't be, though. I mean, I talk about L.A. a lot to people."

"I think it's possible that something during the dinner scared you enough to make you lose yourself for a while, although we'll never know for sure. Obviously, talking about L.A. doesn't always do that, but maybe there was something in that particular conversation that reminded you of something else that triggered something in your mind, something that might seem innocuous to another person, or even to you at another time. But as I say, we'll never know for sure."

"That's frightening. That's awful. It's like I'm in jail in my own head. I don't think I can live this way anymore."

"Yes, it's very frightening. I suspect it's been very frightening for a long time."

"You got that right."

Julia's knowledge of her own life, both past and present, had assumed the airy structure of Swiss cheese, with some solid substance that she and her gifted intellect could use, but riddled with unexplained gaps and hollows. This had its funny side. A few months later, when she had gained a better acceptance of her problem, she came in, sat down, and said in a characteristically charming way, "How do you like my new bracelet?"

"It's beautiful," I replied. "I've always admired your amethyst jewelry. When did you get that piece?"

"Who knows?"

She grinned at me again, and we both laughed.

The somewhat old-fashioned term for Julia's departures from herself during which she would continue to carry out day-to-day activities is "fugue," from the Italian word *fuga*, meaning "flight." A dissociative state that reaches the point of fugue is one of the most dramatic spontaneously occurring examples of the human mind's ability to divide consciousness into parts. In fugue, the person, or the mind of the person, can be subdivided in a manner that allows certain intellectually driven functions to continue—rising at a certain time, conversing with others, following a schedule, even carrying out complex tasks—while the part of consciousness that we usually experience as the "self"—the self-aware center that wishes, dreams, plans, emotes, and remembers—has taken flight, or has perhaps just darkened like a room at night when someone is sleeping.

The departures of fugue are related to certain experiences in ordinary human life that are not generated by trauma. For example, similar is the common experience of the daily commuter by car who realizes that sometimes she or he arrives back at home in the evening without having been aware of the activities of driving. The driving was automatically carried out by some part of the mind, while the self part of the mind was worrying, daydreaming, or listening to the radio. The experience is that of arriving at home without remembering the process of the trip. If one reflects upon the minute and complex decisions and maneuvers involved in driving a car, this ordinary event is really quite remarkable.

Clinical fugue differs from common human experience not so much in kind as in degree. Fugue is terror-driven and complete, while the more recognizable condition is the result of distraction, and relatively transparent. As fugue, the car trip example would involve a driver who failed to remember not just the process of the trip, but also the fact that there had been a trip, and from where. Far beyond distraction, the more remarkable dissociative reaction of fugue would have been set off by something—an event, a conversation, an image, a thought—that was related, though perhaps in some oblique and symbolic way, to trauma.

Not all traumatized individuals exhibit outright fugue. For some people, stressful events trigger a demifugue that is less dramatic but in some ways more agonizing. Another of my patients, Lila, refers to her experience as "my flyaway self":

"I had an argument with the cashier at the Seven-Eleven store. I gave him a twenty and he said I gave him a ten. He wouldn't give me my other ten dollars back. The way he looked at me—it was just the way my stepfather used to, like I was stupid, like I was dirt. I knew he wasn't really my stepfather, but all the feelings were there anyway. After a minute, I just couldn't argue about it. I left without my money, and by the time I got back home, my flyaway self thing had started. Once it starts, it's like there's absolutely nothing I can do about it. I'm gone, and there's nothing I can do about it."

"What does it feel like?"

"Oh boy. I don't know how to describe it. It's just . . . it's just really awful. I don't know . . . everything around me gets very small, kind of unreal, you know? It's my flyaway self, I call it. It feels like . . . my spirit just kind of flies away, and everything else gets very small—people, everything. If it were happening now, for example, you would look very small and far away, and the room would feel kind of unreal. Sometimes even my own body gets small and unreal. It's awful. And when it happens, I can't stop it. I just can't stop it."

What Lila describes as her "flyaway self" is in some respects similar to the derealization that most people have known occasionally, usually under passing conditions of sleep deprivation or physical illness. One temporarily has the sense of looking at the world through the wrong end of a telescope: everything looks small and far away, though one knows intellectually that these same things are just as close and life-sized as ever.

Imagine being forced to live lengthy segments of your life in this state. Imagine that you were falling inexorably into it, to remain there for a week or more at a time, because of events such as an unpleasant argument with a stranger at a convenience store. As bad as this would be, the situation for someone like Lila is incalculably worse, because for her the phenomenon has its origins in trauma.

Another of my patients offered a specific image, and for me an indelible one, to describe the same dissociative condition. Forty-nine-year-old Seth, like Julia, is successful, educated, and visually talented, and his disquieting description reflects his aptitudes. At the beginning of this particular therapy session, he had been telling me about a startling encounter, at a company softball game, with another person lost in the dissociated space with which he himself was all too familiar.

"I knew exactly where she was," said Seth.

"What does it feel like?" I asked. "Can you tell me what it feels like when you're there? How do you change?"

"I don't change. It's not that I change. *Reality* changes. Everything becomes very small, and I exist entirely inside my mind. Even my own body isn't real."

Indicating the two of us and the room around us, he continued, "Right now, this is what's real. You're real. What we're saying is real. But when I'm like that, the office is not real. *You're* not real anymore."

"What is real at those times?" I asked.

"I don't know exactly. It's hard to explain. Only what's going on in my mind is real. I'll tell you what it feels like: I feel like I'm dog-paddling out in the ocean, moving backwards, out to sea. When I'm still close enough to the land, I can sort of look way far away and see the beach. You and the rest of the world are all on the beach somewhere. But I keep drifting backwards, and the beach gets smaller, and the ocean gets bigger and bigger, and when I've drifted out far enough, the beach disappears, and all I can see all around me is the sea. It's so gray—gray on gray on gray."

"Is there anything out in the ocean with you?" I asked.

Seth replied, "No. Not at that point. I'm completely alone, more alone than you can imagine. But if you drift out farther, if you go all the way out to where the bottom of the sea drops off to the real abyss part, then there are awful things, these bloodthirsty sea creatures, sharks and giant eels and things like that. I've always thought that if something in the real world scared me enough, I'd drift out and out to past the dropping-off part, and then I would just be gobbled up, gone—no coming back, ever.

"When I'm floating out in the middle of the sea, everything else is very far away, even time. Time becomes unreal, in a way. An hour could go by that seems like a day to me, or four or five hours could go by, and it seems like only a minute."

Some extreme trauma survivors recognize that they are dissociative, and others do not recognize this. Many times, an individual will realize at some point in adulthood that she or he has had a lifelong pattern of being "away" a grievously large portion of the time.

During the same session, Seth described his own situation in this way:

"Actually, when I was a child, I don't know how much time I spent away like that. I never thought about it. It was probably a lot of the time, maybe even all the time. It just *was*."

"You mean it was your reality, and so of course you never questioned it, any more than any other child questions his reality?"

"Right. That's right. That was when I was a child. And most of the time it still happens automatically, bang, way before I know it's coming; but in here now, sometimes, there's this brief moment when I know I'm about to go away, but I still have time to try to keep it from taking over. Emphasis on *try*."

"How do you do that?" I asked.

"By concentrating. By trying with everything I've got to concentrate on you, and what you're saying, and on the things around me in the office here. But then there's physical pain, too. My eyes hurt, and I know I could make myself feel better if I shut them. But I try not to. And I get this thing in my stomach, which is the hardest thing to fight. There's this pain that feels like I just swallowed a whole pile of burning coals, this torture feeling that beams out from my stomach to the rest of my body; sooner or later, it just takes me over."

He grimaced and put a fist to his breastbone.

When Seth said this about pain in his stomach, I remembered, as I had remembered during descriptions by many, many others, that there is a common Japanese term, *shin pan*, inexactly translated as "agitated heart syndrome," referring to a great pain between the chest and the stomach, just under the solar plexus. *Shin pan*, a condition as real within Eastern medicine as is cataract or ulcer or fractured fibula within Western medicine, is a pain of the heart that does not involve the actual physical organ. In our culture, we consider such a thing—a "heartache," if you will—to be poetry at most. We do not understand that much of the rest of the world considers it to be quite real.

I said to Seth, "It must be frightening to be out in the ocean like that."

"Actually, it's not," he replied. "The abyss part, with the sharks and all, that's frightening. But for most of my life it was really no more frightening than the things that were on the beach, no more frightening than reality, I guess is what I'm saying. So floating in the middle of the ocean was really the best place, even though I guess that sounds strange. Also, being there takes care of the physical pain; there's no more pain when I'm there. It's just that now, I mean lately, the beach, where you are, and everything else, sometimes it makes me wish I could maybe be there instead. I guess you could say that now, at least sometimes, I want to live."

I smiled at him, but he looked away, unsure of what he had just proposed.

Referring back to Seth's softball team acquaintance, whose dissociative episode had begun our discussion, I said, "It must be strange to be with another person when you know she's drifting away in an ocean just like you do sometimes."

"Yes, it's very strange."

"How did you know she was drifting? Did she tell you?"

"No. She didn't tell me. She didn't say anything at all about being dissociated. She was just standing around with us, talking about these incredible things, horrible things from her past, without any emotion, without any reaction to them. She played well that day, actually, but she won't remember any of it, that's for sure."

"You mean," I asked, "another person, besides you, might not have known she was dissociated?"

"Absolutely. I'm sure someone else might not have known at all. It's just that I looked at her, and I saw me. It was like talking to somebody who didn't have a soul."

"You mean her soul was somewhere else?"

"Yes, I guess so. Her soul was somewhere else," Seth said.

After a brief silence, he turned the discussion back to his own life: "The other day, my wife was trying to talk to me about something really important that happened when the twins were born. Doesn't matter what it was; what matters is that I had no idea what she was talking about. I didn't have a clue. It wasn't a dim memory. It wasn't anything. I didn't have that memory because I wasn't there."

"You weren't there, but your wife didn't know that at the time?" I asked.

"No, she didn't know that at all. But you know, most of the time when she and I are making love, and I'm not there, she doesn't know it even then."

"You mean, someone can be that close to you, and still not know?"

"Yes."

At that moment I thought, and then decided to say aloud, "That's so sad."

A single tear skimmed down Seth's cheek. He wiped it quickly with the back of his hand, and said, "I'm sorry, it's just that, well, when I think about it, I realize that, really, I've missed most of my own life."

He stopped and took a deep breath, and I wondered whether he might have to dissociate just to get through this experience in my office.

I asked, "Are you here now, at this moment?"

"Yes, I think so. Yes."

There was another pause, and then with more emotion in his voice than he was usually able to show, he said, "It's so hard, because so much of the time when I'm here, what you're seeing is not what I'm seeing. I feel like such an impostor. I'm out in my ocean, and you don't know that. And I can't tell you what's going on. Sometimes I'd really like to tell you, but I can't. I'm gone."

Seth's description of his inner life makes it wrenchingly clear that the traumatized person is unable to feel completely connected to another person, even a friend, even a spouse. Just as limiting, perhaps even more limiting, is such a person's disconnection from his or her own body. You will recall that Lila's "flyaway self" owned a body that was only "small and unreal," and that when Seth was in his ocean, his mind was separated from his physical self. I began this chapter with Julia, the brilliant producer of documentary films, and as it happens, about a year into her treatment, an event occurred that well illustrates the survivor's trauma-generated dissociation from the body itself, or more accurately, from those aspects of mind that inform one of what is going on in the body.

One morning just after the workday began, Julia's assistant, a gentle young woman who was quite fond of her boss, noticed that Julia was looking extremely pale. She asked how Julia was feeling, and Julia replied that she thought her stomach was a little upset, but other than that she was sure she was fine. Ten minutes later, walking down a corridor, Julia fell to the floor, and by the time the panic-stricken assistant came to her aid, she was unconscious. An ambulance arrived and rushed Julia to the Massachusetts General Hospital, where she underwent an immediate emergency appendectomy. Her life was in danger, and the situation was touch-and-go for a while, because her infected appendix had already ruptured and severe peritonitis had resulted. She survived, however, and during her recovery, when she was well enough to see me again, she recounted a postsurgery conversation with her doctor.

"The doctor kept asking me, 'Didn't you feel anything? Weren't you in pain?' I told her my stomach had been upset that morning, but I didn't remember any real pain. She said, 'Why didn't you call me?' I guess she just couldn't believe that I really hadn't felt any pain. She said that I should have been in agony by the previous night, at the very latest. She kept saying 'agony.' But I didn't feel it. I swear to you I didn't feel any pain, much less agony."

"I believe you," I said to Julia.

"Well, I don't think she did. I guess a ruptured appendix involves a lot of pain for most people."

"Yes. Yes it does," I replied, trying to disguise some of my own astonishment.

"I know I've tried to kill myself intentionally, more than once, so maybe this sounds crazy—but I don't want to die one day just because I'm confused."

"What do you mean?" I asked.

"I don't want to die because I can't feel anything. I don't want to end up dead because I can't feel what's going on in my body, or because I can't tell the difference between that psychosomatic pain I'm always getting in my chest and some honest-to-God heart attack."

Julia said "psychosomatic," but I was thinking *shin pan*, again.

"You know how we talk about my tendency to be dissociative? Well do you think I dissociate from my body too? Because if that's what I'm doing, then it's the illusion from hell. I mean, if it's supposed to save me, it's not working. In fact, it's going to kill me one day. And even if it doesn't kill me, what's the use of living if I can't feel anything? Why should I be alive when I lose big parts of my life? I mean, really, how can you care about anything if you can't even know the truth about yourself? If you keep losing yourself?"

I said, "I think that's one of the best questions I've ever heard."

"You do? You mean you agree with me about how I can't really care about living if I keep losing myself?"

"I said that's one of the best *questions*. I didn't say I knew the answer."

"Oh boy, you're cagey," she said, and grinned. "So okay, how do I find the answer?"

"Well you know, you could try to remember. We could try hypnosis, for one thing."

I believed that Julia might be ready to bring up the lights in the cold, dark house of her past.

"Yes, so you've said. And the idea scares the hell out of me." There was a substantial pause before she continued. "The idea scares the hell out of me, but I think I have to do it anyway."

"Why do you have to?"

"Because I want to know. Because I want to live."

"So, let's do it?" I asked.

"Let's do it," Julia said.   ∎

■ *QUESTIONS FOR MAKING CONNECTIONS WITHIN THE READING* ■

1. Drawing on the information Stout provides, discuss the relations between the mind—in particular the memory—and the brain. Why are traumatic memories generally inaccessible? When Stout refers to "our divided awareness," what does she mean? Is it possible for awareness to become undivided? If such a state can be achieved at all, can it ever become permanent, or is "dividedness" an inescapable feature of consciousness itself?

2. Explain the difference between dissociation and ordinary distraction. What is it about Julia's lapses of memory that qualifies them as examples of dissociation? Are there significant differences between Julia's lapses and Seth's? Has Seth devised ways of coping that have proven more successful than Julia's?

3. In her discussion of Seth, Stout makes a reference to the condition known as *shin pan*, a term taken from Asian medicine. Does this reference bring

something new to our understanding that the term "heartache" does not? Is Stout just showing off her knowledge of Eastern culture, or is she trying to get us to rethink our own attitudes about the importance of emotions?

■ *QUESTIONS FOR WRITING* ■

1. The title of Stout's book is *The Myth of Sanity: Divided Consciousness and the Promise of Awareness*. Now that you have read one chapter from her book, why do you think she refers to sanity as a "myth"? What does she mean by "the promise of awareness"? How might "awareness" differ from "sanity"?

2. Julia and Seth both qualify as extreme cases of dissociation, but their experiences may also shed some light on ordinary consciousness. Taking Stout's essay as your starting point, and drawing also on your own experience, discuss the nature of consciousness. Does the mind operate like a camcorder, or is awareness more complex and less continuous than the images stored in a camcorder's memory?

3. Can people ever know reality, or are we trapped within our own mental worlds? If memory shapes our perceptions from moment to moment, then would you say that experience can ever teach us anything new? If memory is unreliable, then what are the implications for self-knowledge? Is the ancient adage "Know Thyself" actually an invitation to wishful thinking?

■ *QUESTIONS FOR MAKING CONNECTIONS BETWEEN READINGS* ■

1. Could our contemporary relation to the natural world be described as dissociated? Is it possible that an entire society can suffer from dissociation? Has David Abram described a society that is, in Stout's sense of the term, *dissociated* from sensuous experience? Are the steps Abram prescribes for restoring our connections to the natural environment comparable to the kind of therapeutic program Stout supports for improving the lives of her patients? Can a society become "healthy," or is this a project that only individuals can embark on?

2. In what ways does Oliver Sacks's discussion in "The Mind's Eye" confirm, complicate, or contradict Stout's claims about trauma and its consequences? Although Sacks is concerned with adaptations to blindness and not emotional trauma, both authors explore the ways the mind compensates for losses and injuries of one kind or another. Are Julia and Seth in some ways comparable to the blind men and women Sacks describes?

Deborah Tannen

Deborah Tannen became interested in cross-cultural communication after she graduated from college in 1966 and taught English in Greece for two years. After earning a master's degree in English from Wayne State University and teaching writing in the United States for a few years, Tannen decided to pursue a doctorate in linguistics at Berkeley. It was just Tannen's luck that the first linguistics institute she attended focused on language in a social context. "Had I gone another summer," Tannen has said, "it's quite likely I would have concluded linguistics was not for me."

Tannen is currently University Professor on the faculty of the linguistics department at Georgetown University. Tannen, who has published over twenty books and more than one hundred articles and is the recipient of five honorary doctorates, is best known as the author of *You Just Don't Understand: Women and Men in Conversation* (1991), which is credited with bringing gender differences in communication style to the forefront of public awareness. This book "was on the *New York Times* bestseller list for nearly four years, including eight months as number one, and has been translated into twenty-nine languages."

"The Roots of Debate in Education and the Hope of Dialogue" is drawn from Tannen's 1998 book *The Argument of Culture*, which examines the social, political, and emotional consequences of treating discussions as battles to be won or lost. Tannen's goal in this work is to get her readers to notice "the power of words to frame how you think about things, how you feel about things, how you perceive the world. The tendency in our culture to use war metaphors so pervasively, and to frame everything as a metaphorical battle, influences how we approach each other in our everyday lives."

Tannen, Deborah. "The Roots of Debate in Education and the Hope of Dialogue." *The Argument Culture: Moving from Debate to Dialogue.* New York: Random House, 1998. 256–290.

Biographical information comes from Deborah Tannen's home page, <http://www9.georgetown .edu/faculty/tannend/>; quotations come from Harvey Bloom, "Deborah Tannen: A Writer First," *The Boston Book Review* <http://www.bookwire.com/bbr/interviews/amy-tannen.html>.

The Roots of Debate in Education and the Hope of Dialogue

The teacher sits at the head of the classroom, feeling pleased with herself and her class. The students are engaged in a heated debate. The very noise level reassures the teacher that the students are participating, taking responsibility for their own learning. Education is going on. The class is a success.

But look again, cautions Patricia Rosof, a high school history teacher who admits to having experienced that wave of satisfaction with herself and the job she is doing. On closer inspection, you notice that only a few students are participating in the debate; the majority of the class is sitting silently, maybe attentive but perhaps either indifferent or actively turned off. And the students who are arguing are not addressing the subtleties, nuances, or complexities of the points they are making or disputing. They do not have that luxury because they want to win the argument—so they must go for the most gross and dramatic statements they can muster. They will not concede an opponent's point, even if they can see its validity, because that would weaken their position. Anyone tempted to synthesize the varying views would not dare to do so because it would look like a "cop-out," an inability to take a stand.

One reason so many teachers use the debate format to promote student involvement is that it is relatively easy to set up and the rewards are quick and obvious: the decibel level of noise, the excitement of those who are taking part. Showing students how to integrate ideas and explore subtleties and complexities is much harder. And the rewards are quieter—but more lasting.

Our schools and universities, our ways of doing science and approaching knowledge, are deeply agonistic. We all pass through our country's educational system, and it is there that the seeds of our adversarial culture are planted. Seeing how these seeds develop, and where they came from, is a key to understanding the argument culture and a necessary foundation for determining what changes we would like to make.

Roots of the Adversarial Approach to Knowledge

The argument culture, with its tendency to approach issues as a polarized debate, and the culture of critique, with its inclination to regard criticism and attack as the best if not the only type of rigorous thinking, are deeply rooted in Western tradition, going back to the ancient Greeks.[1] This point is made by Walter Ong, a Jesuit professor at Saint Louis University, in his book *Fighting for Life*. Ong credits the ancient Greeks[2] with a fascination with adversativeness in language and thought. He also connects the adversarial tradition of educational institutions to their all-male character. To attend the earliest universities, in the Middle Ages, young men were torn from their families and deposited in cloistered environments where corporal, even brutal, punishment was rampant. Their suffering drove them to bond with each other in opposition to their keepers—the teachers who were their symbolic enemies. Similar in many ways to puberty rites in traditional cultures, this secret society to which young men were confined also had a private language, Latin, in which students read about military exploits. Knowledge was gleaned through public oral disputation and tested by combative oral performance, which carried with it the risk of public humiliation. Students at these institutions were trained not to discover the truth but to argue either side of an argument—in other words, to debate. Ong points out that the Latin term for school, *ludus*, also referred to play or games, but it derived from the military sense of the word—training exercises for war.

If debate seems self-evidently the appropriate or even the only path to insight and knowledge, says Ong, consider the Chinese approach. Disputation was rejected in ancient China as "incompatible with the decorum and harmony cultivated by the true sage."[3] During the Classical periods in both China and India, according to Robert T. Oliver, the preferred mode of rhetoric was exposition rather than argument. The aim was to "enlighten an inquirer," not to "overwhelm an opponent." And the preferred style reflected "the earnestness of investigation" rather than "the fervor of conviction." In contrast to Aristotle's trust of logic and mistrust of emotion, in ancient Asia intuitive insight was considered the superior means of perceiving truth. Asian rhetoric was devoted not to devising logical arguments but to explicating widely accepted propositions. Furthermore, the search for abstract truth that we assume is the goal of philosophy, while taken for granted in the West, was not found in the East, where philosophy was concerned with observation and experience.

If Aristotelian philosophy, with its emphasis on formal logic, was based on the assumption that truth is gained by opposition, Chinese philosophy offers an alternative view. With its emphasis on harmony, says anthropologist Linda Young, Chinese philosophy sees a diverse universe in precarious balance that is maintained by talk. This translates into methods of investigation that focus more on integrating ideas and exploring relations among them than on opposing ideas and fighting over them.

Onward, Christian Soldiers

The military-like culture of early universities is also described by historian David Noble, who describes how young men attending medieval universities were like marauding soldiers: The students—all seminarians—roamed the streets bearing arms, assaulting women, and generally creating mayhem. Noble traces the history of Western science and of universities to joint origins in the Christian Church. The scientific revolution, he shows, was created by religious devotees setting up monastery-like institutions devoted to learning. Early universities were seminaries, and early scientists were either clergy or devoutly religious individuals who led monk-like lives. (Until as recently as 1888, fellows at Oxford were expected to be unmarried.)

That Western science is rooted in the Christian Church helps explain why our approach to knowledge tends to be conceived as a metaphorical battle: The Christian Church, Noble shows, has origins and early forms rooted in the military. Many early monks[4] had actually been soldiers before becoming monks. Not only were obedience and strict military-like discipline required, but monks saw themselves as serving "in God's knighthood," warriors in a battle against evil. In later centuries, the Crusades brought actual warrior-monks.

The history of science in the Church holds the key to understanding our tradition of regarding the search for truth as an enterprise of oral disputation in which positions are propounded, defended, and attacked without regard to the debater's personal conviction. It is a notion of truth as objective, best captured by formal logic, that Ong traces to Aristotle. Aristotle regarded logic as the only trustworthy means for human judgment; emotions get in the way: "The man who is to judge would not have his judgment warped by speakers arousing him to anger, jealousy, or compassion. One might as well make a carpenter's tool crooked before using it as a measure."[5]

This assumption explains why Plato wanted to ban poets from education in his ideal community. As a lover of poetry, I can still recall my surprise and distress on reading this in *The Republic* when I was in high school. Not until much later did I understand what it was all about.[6] Poets in ancient Greece were wandering bards who traveled from place to place performing oral poetry that persuaded audiences by moving them emotionally. They were like what we think of as demagogues: people with a dangerous power to persuade others by getting them all worked up. Ong likens this to our discomfort with advertising in schools, which we see as places where children should learn to think logically, not be influenced by "teachers" with ulterior motives who use unfair persuasive tactics.

Sharing Time: Early Training in School

A commitment to formal logic as the truest form of intellectual pursuit remains with us today. Our glorification of opposition as the path to truth is related to the development of formal logic, which encourages thinkers to regard truth seeking as a step-by-step alternation of claims and counterclaims.[7] Truth, in this schema, is an abstract notion that tends to be taken out of context. This formal approach to learning is taught in our schools, often indirectly.

Educational researcher James Wertsch shows that schools place great emphasis on formal representation of knowledge. The common elementary school practice of "sharing time" (or, as it used to be called, "show-and-tell") is a prime arena for such training. Wertsch gives the example of a kindergarten pupil named Danny who took a piece of lava to class.[8] Danny told his classmates, "My mom went to the volcano and got it." When the teacher asked what he wanted to tell about it, he said, "I've always been taking care of it." This placed the rock at the center of his feelings and his family: the rock's connection to his mother, who gave it to him, and the attention and care he has lavished on it. The teacher reframed the children's interest in the rock as informational: "Is it rough or smooth?" "Is it heavy or light?" She also suggested they look up "volcano" and "lava" in the dictionary. This is not to imply that the teacher harmed the child; she built on his personal attachment to the rock to teach him a new way of thinking about it. But the example shows the focus of education on formal rather than relational knowledge—information about the rock that has meaning out of context, rather than information tied to the context: Who got the rock for him? How did she get it? What is his relation to it?

Here's another example of how a teacher uses sharing time to train children to speak and think formally. Sarah Michaels spent time watching and tape-recording in a first-grade classroom. During sharing time, a little girl named Mindy held up two candles and told her classmates, "When I was in day camp we made these candles. And I tried it with different colors with both of them but one just came out, this one just came out blue and I don't know what this color is." The teacher responded, "That's neat-o. Tell the kids how you do it from the very start. Pretend we don't know a thing about candles. OK, what did you do first? What did you use?" She continued to prompt: "What makes it have a shape?" and "Who knows what the string is for?" By encouraging Mindy to give information in a sequential manner, even if it might not seem the most important to her and if the children might already know some of it, the teacher was training her to talk in a focused, explicit way.

The tendency to value formal, objective knowledge over relational, intuitive knowledge grows out of our notion of education as training for debate. It is a legacy of the agonistic heritage. There are many other traces as well. Many Ph.D. programs still require public "defenses" of dissertations or dissertation proposals, and oral performance of knowledge in comprehensive exams. Throughout our educational system, the most pervasive inheritance is the conviction that issues have two sides, that knowledge is best gained through debate, that ideas should be presented orally to an audience that does its best to poke holes and find weaknesses, and that to get recognition, one has to "stake out a position" in opposition to another.

Integrating Women in the Classroom Army

If Ong is right, the adversarial character of our educational institutions is inseparable from their all-male heritage. I wondered whether teaching techniques still tend to be adversarial today and whether, if they are, this may hold a clue to a dilemma that has received much recent attention: that girls often receive less attention and speak up less in class.[9] One term I taught a large lecture class of 140 students and decided to take advantage of this army (as it were) of researchers to answer these questions. Becoming observers in their own classrooms, my students found plenty of support for Ong's ideas.

I asked the students to note how relatively adversarial the teaching methods were in their other classes and how the students responded. Gabrielle DeRouen-Hawkins's description of a theology class was typical:

> The class is in the format of lecture with class discussion and participation. There are thirteen boys and eleven girls in the class. In a fifty-minute class:
> Number of times a male student spoke: 8
> Number of times a female student spoke: 3
> . . . In our readings, theologians present their theories surrounding G-D, life, spirituality and sacredness. As the professor (a male) outlined the main ideas about the readings, he posed questions like "And what is the fault with /Smith's/ basis that the sacred is individualistic?" The only hands that went up were male. Not one female <u>dared</u> challenge or refute an author's writings. The only questions that the females asked (and all female comments were questions) involved a problem they had with the content of the reading. The males, on the other hand, openly questioned, criticized, and refuted the readings on five separate occasions. The three other times that males spoke involved them saying something like: "/Smith/ is very vague in her theory of XX. Can you explain it further?" They were openly argumentative.[10]

This description raises a number of fascinating issues. First, it gives concrete evidence that at least college classrooms proceed on the assumption that the educational process should be adversarial: The teacher invited students to criticize the reading. (Theology, a required course at Georgetown, was a subject where my students most often found adversarial methods—interestingly, given the background I laid out earlier.) Again, there is nothing inherently wrong with using such methods. Clearly, they are very effective in many ways. However, among the potential liabilities is the risk that women students may be less likely to take part in classroom discussions that are framed as arguments between opposing sides—that is, debate—or as attacks on the authors—that is, critique. (The vast majority of students' observations revealed that men tended to speak more than women in their classes—which is not to say that individual women did not speak more than individual men.)

Gabrielle commented that since class participation counted for 10 percent of students' grades, it might not be fair to women students that the agonistic style is more congenial to men. Not only might women's grades suffer because they speak up less, but they might be evaluated as less intelligent or prepared because when they did speak, they asked questions rather than challenging the readings.

I was intrigued by the student's comment "/Smith/ is very vague in her theory of XX. Can you explain it further?" It could have been phrased "I didn't understand the author's theory. Can you explain it to me?" By beginning "The author is vague in her theory," the questioner blamed the author for *his* failure to understand. A student who asks a question in class risks appearing ignorant. Prefacing the question this way was an excellent way to minimize that risk.

In her description of this class, Gabrielle wrote that not a single woman "dared challenge or refute" an author. She herself underlined the word "dared." But in reading this I wondered whether "dared" was necessarily the right word. It implies that the women in the class wished to challenge the author but did not have the courage. It is possible that not a single woman *cared* to challenge the author. Criticizing or challenging might not be something that appealed to them or seemed worth their efforts. Going back to the childhoods of boys and girls, it seems possible that the boys had had more experiences, from the time they were small, that encouraged them to challenge and argue with authority figures than the girls had.

This is not to say that classrooms are more congenial to boys than girls in every way. Especially in the lowest grades, the requirement that children sit quietly in their seats seems clearly to be easier for girls to fulfill than boys, since many girls frequently sit fairly quietly for long periods of time when they play, while most boys' idea of play involves at least running around, if not also jumping and roughhousing. And researchers have pointed out that some of the extra attention boys receive is aimed at controlling such physical exuberance. The adversarial aspect of educational traditions is just one small piece of the pie, but it seems to reflect boys' experiences and predilections more than girls'.

A colleague commented that he had always taken for granted that the best way to deal with students' comments is to challenge them; he took it to be self-evident that this technique sharpens their minds and helps them develop debating skills. But he noticed that women were relatively silent in his classes. He decided to try beginning discussion with relatively open questions and letting comments go unchallenged. He found, to his amazement and satisfaction, that more women began to speak up in class.

Clearly, women can learn to perform in adversarial ways. Anyone who doubts this need only attend an academic conference in the field of women's studies or feminist studies—or read Duke University professor Jane Tompkins's essay showing how a conference in these fields can be like a Western shoot-out. My point is rather about the roots of the tradition and the tendency of the style to appeal initially to more men than women in the Western cultural context. Ong and Noble show that the adversarial culture of Western science and its exclusion of women were part and parcel of the same historical roots—not that individual women may not learn to practice and enjoy agonistic debate or that individual men may not recoil from it. There are many people, women as well as men, who assume a discussion must be contentious to be interesting. Author Mary Catherine Bateson recalls that when her mother, the anthropologist Margaret Mead, said, "I had an argument with" someone, it was a positive comment. "An argument," to her, meant a spirited intellectual interchange, not a rancorous conflict. The same assumption emerged in an obituary for Diana Trilling, called "one of the very last of the great midcentury New York intellectuals."[11] She and her friends had tried to live what they called "a life of significant contention"—the contention apparently enhancing rather than undercutting the significance.

Learning by Fighting

Although there are patterns that tend to typify women and men in a given culture, there is an even greater range among members of widely divergent cultural backgrounds. In addition to observing adversarial encounters in their current classrooms, many students recalled having spent a junior year in Germany or France and commented that American classrooms seemed very placid compared to what they had experienced abroad. One student, Zach Tyler, described his impressions this way:

> I have very vivid memories of my junior year of high school, which I spent in Germany as an exchange student. The classroom was very debate-oriented and agonistic. One particular instance I remember well was in physics class, when a very confrontational friend of mine had a heated debate with the teacher about solving a problem. My friend ran to the board and scribbled out how he would have solved the problem, completely different from the teacher's, which also gave my friend the right answer and made the teacher wrong.
>
> STUDENT: "You see! This is how it should be, and you are wrong!"
> TEACHER: "No! No! No! You are absolutely wrong in every respect! Just look at how you did this!" (He goes over my friend's solution and shows that it does not work.) "Your solution has no base, as I just showed you!"
> STUDENT: "You can't prove that. Mine works just as well!"
> TEACHER: "My God, if the world were full of technical idiots like yourself! Look again!" (And he clearly shows how my friend's approach was wrong, after which my friend shut up.)

In Zach's opinion, the teacher encouraged this type of argument. The student learned he was wrong, but he got practice in arguing his point of view.

This incident occurred in high school. But European classrooms can be adversarial even at the elementary school level, according to another student, Megan Smyth, who reported on a videotape she saw in her French class:

> Today in French class we watched an excerpt of a classroom scene of fifth-graders. One at a time, each student was asked to stand up and recite a poem that they were supposed to have memorized. The teacher screamed at the students if they forgot a line or if they didn't speak with enough emotion. They were reprimanded and asked to repeat the task until they did it perfectly and passed the "oral test."

There is probably little question about how Americans would view this way of teaching, but the students put it into words:

> After watching this scene, my French teacher asked the class what our opinion was. The various responses included: French schools are very strict, the professor was "mean" and didn't have respect for the students, and there's too much emphasis on memorization, which is pointless.

If teaching methods can be more openly adversarial in European than American elementary and high schools, academic debate can be more openly adversarial there as well. For example, Alice Kaplan, a professor of French at Duke University, describes a colloquium on the French writer Céline that she attended in Paris:

> After the first speech, people started yelling at each other. "Are you suggesting that Céline was fascist!" "You call that evidence!" "I will not accept ignorance in the place of argument!" I was scared.[12]

These examples dramatize that many individuals can thrive in an adversarial atmosphere. And those who learn to participate effectively in any verbal game eventually enjoy it, if nothing else than for the pleasure of exercising that learned skill. It is important to keep these examples in mind in order to avoid the impression that adversarial tactics are always destructive. Clearly, such tactics sometimes admirably serve the purpose of intellectual inquiry. In addition to individual predilection, cultural learning plays a role in whether or not someone enjoys the game played this way.

Graduate School as Boot Camp

Although the invective Kaplan heard at a scholarly meeting in Paris is more extreme than what is typical at American conferences, the assumption that challenge and attack are the best modes of scholarly inquiry is pervasive in

American scholarly communities as well. Graduate education is a training ground not only for teaching but also for scientific research. Many graduate programs are geared to training young scholars in rigorous thinking, defined as the ability to launch and field verbal attacks.

Communications researchers Karen Tracy and Sheryl Baratz tapped into some of the ethics that lead to this atmosphere in a study of weekly symposia attended by faculty and graduate students at a major research university. When they asked participants about the purpose of the symposia, they were told it was to "trade ideas" and "learn things." But it didn't take too much discussion to uncover the participants' deeper concern: to be seen as intellectually competent. And here's the rub: To be seen as competent, a student had to ask "tough and challenging questions."

One faculty member commented, when asked about who participated actively in a symposium,

> Among the graduate students, the people I think about are Jess, Tim, uh let's see, Felicia will ask a question but it'll be a nice little supportive question.[13]

"A nice little supportive question" diminished the value of Felicia's participation and her intelligence—the sort of judgment a student would wish to avoid. Just as with White House correspondents, there is value placed on asking "tough questions." Those who want to impress their peers and superiors (as most, if not all, do) are motivated to ask the sorts of questions that gain approval.

Valuing attack as a sign of respect is part of the argument culture of academia—our conception of intellectual interchange as a metaphorical battle. As one colleague put it, "In order to play with the big boys, you have to be willing to get into the ring and wrestle with them." Yet many graduate students (and quite a few established scholars) remain ambivalent about this ethic, especially when they are on the receiving rather than the distribution end. Sociolinguist Winnie Or tape-recorded a symposium at which a graduate student presented her fledgling research to other students and graduate faculty. The student later told Or that she left the symposium feeling that a truck had rolled over her. She did not say she regretted having taken part; she felt she had received valuable feedback. But she also mentioned that she had not looked at her research project once since the symposium several weeks before. This is telling. Shouldn't an opportunity to discuss your research with peers and experts fire you up and send you back to the isolation of research renewed and reinspired? Isn't something awry if it leaves you not wanting to face your research project at all?

This young scholar persevered, but others drop out of graduate school, in some cases because they are turned off by the atmosphere of critique. One woman who wrote to me said she had been encouraged to enroll in graduate school by her college professors, but she lasted only one year in a major midwest university's doctoral program in art history. This is how she described her experience and her decision not to continue:

> Grad school was the nightmare I never knew existed. . . . Into the den of wolves I go, like a lamb to slaughter. . . . When, at the end of my first year (masters) I was offered a job as a curator for a private collection, I jumped at the chance. I wasn't cut out for academia—better try the "real world."

Reading this I thought, is it that she was not cut out for academia, or is it that academia as it was practiced in that university is not cut out for people like her. It is cut out for those who enjoy, or can tolerate, a contentious environment.

(These examples remind us again of the gender dynamic. The graduate student who left academia for museum work was a woman. The student who asked a "nice little supportive question" instead of a "tough, challenging one" was a woman. More than one commentator has wondered aloud if part of the reason women drop out of science courses and degree programs is their discomfort with the agonistic culture of Western science. And Lani Guinier has recently shown that discomfort with the agonistic procedures of law school is partly responsible for women's lower grade point averages in law school, since the women arrive at law school with records as strong as the men's.)

The Culture of Critique: Attack in the Academy

The standard way of writing an academic paper is to position your work in opposition to someone else's, which you prove wrong. This creates a need to make others wrong, which is quite a different matter from reading something with an open mind and discovering that you disagree with it. Students are taught that they must disprove others' arguments in order to be original, make a contribution, and demonstrate their intellectual ability. When there is a need to make others wrong, the temptation is great to oversimplify at best, and at worst to distort or even misrepresent others' positions, the better to refute them—to search for the most foolish statement in a generally reasonable treatise, seize upon the weakest examples, ignore facts that support your opponent's views, and focus only on those that support yours. Straw men spring up like scarecrows in a cornfield.

Sometimes it seems as if there is a maxim driving academic discourse that counsels, "If you can't find something bad to say, don't say anything." As a result, any work that gets a lot of attention is immediately opposed. There is an advantage to this approach: Weaknesses are exposed, and that is surely good. But another result is that it is difficult for those outside the field (or even inside) to know what is "true." Like two expert witnesses hired by opposing attorneys, academics can seem to be canceling each other out. In the words of policy analysts David Greenberg and Philip Robins:

> The process of scientific inquiry almost ensures that competing sets of results will be obtained. . . . Once the first set of findings are published, other researchers eager to make a name for themselves must come up with different approaches and results to get their studies published.[14]

How are outsiders (or insiders, for that matter) to know which "side" to believe? As a result, it is extremely difficult for research to influence public policy.

A leading researcher in psychology commented that he knew of two young colleagues who had achieved tenure by writing articles attacking him. One of them told him, in confidence, that he actually agreed with him, but of course he could not get tenure by writing articles simply supporting someone else's work; he had to stake out a position in opposition. Attacking an established scholar has particular appeal because it demonstrates originality and independence of thought without requiring true innovation. After all, the domain of inquiry and the terms of debate have already been established. The critic has only to say, like the child who wants to pick a fight, "Is not!" Younger or less prominent scholars can achieve a level of attention otherwise denied or eluding them by stepping into the ring with someone who has already attracted the spotlight.

The young psychologist who confessed his motives to the established one was unusual, I suspect, only in his self-awareness and willingness to articulate it. More commonly, younger scholars, or less prominent ones, convince themselves that they are fighting for truth, that they are among the few who see that the emperor has no clothes. In the essay mentioned earlier, Jane Tompkins describes how a young scholar-critic can work herself into a passionate conviction that she is morally obligated to attack, because she is fighting on the side of good against the side of evil. Like the reluctant hero in the film *High Noon*, she feels she has no choice but to strap on her holster and shoot. Tompkins recalls that her own career was launched by an essay that

> began with a frontal assault on another woman scholar. When I wrote it I felt the way the hero does in a Western. Not only had this critic argued *a, b,* and *c,* she had held *x, y,* and *z!* It was a clear case of outrageous provocation.[15]

Because her attack was aimed at someone with an established career ("She was famous and I was not. She was teaching at a prestigious university and I was not. She had published a major book and I had not."), it was a "David and Goliath situation" that made her feel she was "justified in hitting her with everything I had." (This is analogous to what William Safire describes as his philosophy in the sphere of political journalism: "Kick 'em when they're up.")[16]

The claim of objectivity is belied by Tompkins's account of the spirit in which attack is often launched: the many motivations, other than the search for truth, that drive a critic to pick a fight with another scholar. Objectivity would entail a disinterested evaluation of all claims. But there is nothing disinterested about it when scholars set out with the need to make others wrong and transform them not only into opponents but into villains.

In academia, as in other walks of life, anonymity breeds contempt. Some of the nastiest rhetoric shows up in "blind" reviews—of articles submitted to journals or book proposals submitted to publishers. "Peer review" is the cornerstone of academic life. When someone submits an article to a journal, a book to a publisher, or a proposal to a funding institution, the work is sent to established scholars for evaluation. To enable reviewers to be honest, they remain anonymous. But anonymous reviewers often take a tone of derision such as people tend to use only when talking about someone who is not there—after all, the evaluation is not addressed to the author. But authors typically receive copies of the evaluations, especially if their work is re-jected. This can be particularly destructive to young scholars just starting out. For example, one sociolinguist wrote her dissertation in a firmly estab-lished tradition: She tape-recorded conversations at the company where she worked part-time. Experts in our field believe it is best to examine conversa-tions in which the researcher is a natural participant, because when strangers appear asking to tape-record, people get nervous and may change their behavior. The publisher sent the manuscript to a reviewer who was used to different research methods. In rejecting the proposal, she referred to the young scholar "using the audiotaped detritus from an old job." Ouch. What could justify the sneering term "detritus"? What is added by append-ing "old" to "job," other than hurting the author? Like Heathcliff, the target hears only the negative and—like Heathcliff—may respond by fleeing the field altogether.

One reason the argument culture is so widespread is that arguing is so easy to do. Lynne Hewitt, Judith Duchan, and Erwin Segal came up with a fascinating finding: Speakers with language disabilities who had trouble taking part in other types of verbal interaction were able to participate in arguments. Observing adults with mental retardation who lived in a group home, the researchers found that the residents often engaged in verbal con-flicts as a means of prolonging interaction. It was a form of sociability. Most surprising, this was equally true of two residents who had severe language and comprehension disorders yet were able to take part in the verbal dis-putes, because arguments have a predictable structure.

Academics, too, know that it is easy to ask challenging questions with-out listening, reading, or thinking very carefully. Critics can always com-plain about research methods, sample size, and what has been left out. To study anything, a researcher must isolate a piece of the subject and narrow the scope of vision in order to focus. An entire tree cannot be placed under a microscope; a tiny bit has to be separated to be examined closely. This gives critics the handle of a weapon with which to strike an easy blow: They can point out all the bits that were not studied. Like family members or partners in a close relationship, anyone looking for things to pick on will have no trouble finding them.

All of this is not to imply that scholars should not criticize each other or disagree. In the words of poet William Blake, "Without contraries is no progression."[17] The point is to distinguish constructive ways of doing so from nonconstructive ones. Criticizing a colleague on empirical grounds is the beginning of a discussion; if researchers come up with different findings, they can engage in a dialogue: What is it about their methods, data, or means of analysis that explains the different results? In some cases, those who set out to disprove another's claims end up proving them instead—something that is highly unlikely to happen in fields that deal in argumentation alone.

A stunning example in which opponents attempting to disprove a heretical claim ended up proving it involves the cause and treatment of ulcers. It is now widely known and accepted that ulcers are caused by bacteria in the stomach and can be cured by massive doses of antibiotics. For years, however, the cure and treatment of ulcers remained elusive, as all the experts agreed that ulcers were the classic psychogenic illness caused by stress. The stomach, experts further agreed, was a sterile environment: No bacteria could live there. So pathologists did not look for bacteria in the stomachs of ailing or deceased patients, and those who came across them simply ignored them, in effect not seeing what was before their eyes because they did not believe it could be there. When Dr. Barry Marshall, an Australian resident in internal medicine, presented evidence that ulcers are caused by bacteria, no one believed him. His findings were ultimately confirmed by researchers intent on proving him wrong.[18]

The case of ulcers shows that setting out to prove others wrong can be constructive—when it is driven by genuine differences and when it motivates others to undertake new research. But if seeking to prove others wrong becomes a habit, an end in itself, the sole line of inquiry, the results can be far less rewarding.

Believing as Thinking

"The doubting game" is the name English professor Peter Elbow gives to what educators are trained to do. In playing the doubting game, you approach others' work by looking for what's wrong, much as the press corps follows the president hoping to catch him stumble or an attorney pores over an opposing witness's deposition looking for inconsistencies that can be challenged on the stand. It is an attorney's job to discredit opposing witnesses, but is it a scholar's job to approach colleagues like an opposing attorney?

Elbow recommends learning to approach new ideas, and ideas different from your own, in a different spirit—what he calls a "believing game." This does not mean accepting everything anyone says or writes in an unthinking way. That would be just as superficial as rejecting everything without thinking deeply about it. The believing game is still a game. It simply asks you to give it a whirl: Read *as if* you believed, and see where it takes you. Then you can go back and ask whether you want to accept or reject elements in the argument or the whole argument or idea. Elbow is not recommending that we stop doubting altogether. He is telling us to stop doubting exclusively. We need a systematic and respected way to detect and expose strengths, just as we have a systematic and respected way of detecting faults.

Americans need little encouragement to play the doubting game because we regard it as synonymous with intellectual inquiry, a sign of intelligence. In Elbow's words, "We tend to assume that the ability to criticize a claim we disagree with counts as more serious intellectual work than the ability to enter into it and temporarily assent."[19] It is the believing game that needs to be encouraged and recognized as an equally serious intellectual pursuit.

Although criticizing is surely part of critical thinking, it is not synonymous with it. Again, limiting critical response to critique means not doing the other kinds of critical thinking that could be helpful: looking for new insights, new perspectives, new ways of thinking, new knowledge. Critiquing relieves you of the responsibility of doing integrative thinking. It also has the advantage of making the critics feel smart, smarter than the ill-fated author whose work is being picked apart like carrion. But it has the disadvantage of making them less likely to learn from the author's work.

The Socratic Method—Or Is It?

Another scholar who questions the usefulness of opposition as the sole path to truth is philosopher Janice Moulton. Philosophy, she shows, equates logical reasoning with the Adversary Paradigm, a matter of making claims and then trying to find, and argue against, counterexamples to that claim. The result is a debate between adversaries trying to defend their ideas against counterexamples and to come up with counterexamples that refute the opponent's ideas. In this paradigm, the best way to evaluate someone's work is to "subject it to the strongest or most extreme opposition."[20]

But if you parry individual points—a negative and defensive enterprise— you never step back and actively imagine a world in which a different system of ideas could be true—a positive act. And you never ask how larger systems of thought relate to each other. According to Moulton, our devotion to the Adversary Paradigm has led us to misinterpret the type of argumentation that Socrates favored: We think of the Socratic method as systematically leading an opponent into admitting error. This is primarily a way of showing up an adversary as wrong. Moulton shows that the original Socratic method—the *elenchus*—was designed to convince others, to shake them out of their habitual mode of thought and lead them to new insight. Our version of the Socratic method—an adversarial public debate—is unlikely to result in opponents changing their minds. Someone who loses a debate usually attributes that loss to poor performance or to an adversary's unfair tactics.

Knowledge as Warring Camps

Anne Carolyn Klein, an American woman who spent many years studying Tibetan Buddhism, joined a university program devoted to women's studies in religion. It was her first encounter with contemporary feminist theory, which she quickly learned was divided into two warring camps. In one camp are those who focus on the ways that women are different from men. Among these, some emphasize that women's ways are equally valid and should be respected, while others believe that women's ways are superior and should be more widely adopted. Both these views—called "difference feminism"—contrast with those in the other camp, who claim that women are no different from men by nature, so any noticeable differences result from how society treats women. Those who take this view are called "social constructionists."[21]

Klein saw that separating feminist theory into these two camps reflects the Western tendency to rigid dichotomies. Recalling how Buddhist philosophy tries to integrate disparate forces, she shows that there is much to be gained from both feminist views—and, in any case, both perspectives tend to coexist within individuals. For example, even though the constructionist view of gender has won ascendancy in academic theory (that's why we have the epithet "essentialist" to describe those who hold the view that is in disfavor but no commonly used epithet to sneer at the constructionist view), "feminists still struggle to recognize and name the commonalities among women that justify concern for women's lives around the world and produce political and social alliances." Klein asks, "Why protest current conditions unless the category 'women' is in some way a meaningful one?"[22] She shows, too, that the very inclination to polarize varied views of women and feminism into two opposing camps is in itself essentialist because it reduces complex and varied perspectives to simplified, monolithic representations. This also makes it easy to dismiss—and fight about—others' work rather than think about it.

Reflecting this warring-camps view, journalist Cynthia Gorney asked Gloria Steinem, "Where do you stand in the current debate that the feminist world has divided into 'equity' feminism versus 'difference' feminism—about whether women are to be treated like men or as different from men?" This question bears all the earmarks of the adversarial framework: the term "debate" and the separation of a complex domain of inquiry into two opposed sides. Steinem responded:

> [*Sighs.*] Of course, you understand that I've turned up in every category. So it makes it harder for me to take the divisions with great seriousness, since I don't feel attached to any of them—and also since I don't hear about the division from women who are not academics or in the media. The idea that there are two "camps" has not been my experience. The mark to me of a constructive argument is one that looks at a specific problem and says, "What shall we do about this?" And a nonconstructive one is one that tries to label people. "Difference" feminist, "gender" feminist—it has no meaning in specific situations.[23]

In this short comment, Steinem puts her finger on several aspects of the argument culture. First, she identifies academics and journalists as two groups that have a habit of—and a stake in—manufacturing polarization and the appearance of conflict. Second, she points out that this view of the world does not describe reality as most people live it. Third, she shows that polarizing issues into "a debate" often goes along with "labeling" the two sides: Lumping others together and sticking a label on them makes it easy to ignore the nuances and subtleties of their opinions and beliefs. Individuals are reduced to an oversimplification of their ideas, transformed into the enemy, and demonized.

False dichotomies are often at the heart of discord.

Question the Basic Assumption

My aim is not to put a stop to the adversarial paradigm, the doubting game, debate—but to diversify: Like a well-balanced stock portfolio, we need more than one path to the goal we seek. What makes it hard to question whether debate is truly the only or even the most fruitful approach to learning is that we're dealing with assumptions that we and everyone around us take to be self-evident. A prominent dean at a major research university commented to me, "The Chinese cannot make great scientists because they will not debate publicly." Many people would find this remark offensive. They would object because it generalizes about all Chinese scientists, especially since it makes a negative evaluation. But I would also question the assumption that makes the generalization a criticism: the conviction that the only way to test and develop ideas is to debate them publicly. It may well be true that most Chinese scientists are reluctant to engage in public, rancorous debate. I see nothing insulting about such a claim; it derives from the Chinese cultural norms that many Chinese and Western observers have documented. But we also know that many Chinese have indeed been great scientists.[24] The falsity of the dean's statement should lead us to question whether debate is the only path to insight.

Consensus Through Dissension?

The culture of critique driving our search for knowledge in the scientific world of research is akin to what I have described in the domains of politics, journalism, and law. In those three institutions, an increasingly warlike atmosphere has led many people already in those professions to leave, and many who would have considered entering these professions in the past are now choosing other paths. Those who remain are finding it less fun; they don't look forward to getting up and going to work in the same way that they and others used to. And in all these areas, raised voices and tempers are creating a din that is drowning out the perhaps more numerous voices of dialogue and reason. In law, critics of the principle of zealous advocacy object on the grounds of what it does to the souls of those who practice within the system, requiring them to put aside their consciences and natural inclinations toward human compassion—just what some among the press say about what aggression journalism is doing to journalists.

Forces affecting these institutions are intertwined with each other and with others I have not mentioned. For example, the rise of malpractice litigation, while prodding doctors to be more careful and providing deserved recompense to victims, has also made the doctor-patient relationship potentially more adversarial. At the same time, physicians are finding themselves in increasingly adversarial relationships with HMOs and insurance companies—as are the patients themselves, who now need the kind of advice that was offered under the headline "When Your HMO Says No: How to Fight for the Treatment You Need—and Win."[25]

People in business, too, report an increasingly adversarial atmosphere. There are, of course, the hostile takeovers that have become common, along with lawsuits between companies and former employees. But there is also more opposition in the day-to-day doing of business. A man who works at a large computer company in Silicon Valley told me that he sees this daily. Disagreement and verbal attack are encouraged at meetings, under the guise of challenging assumptions and fostering creativity. But in reality, he observes, what is fostered is dissension. In the end, the company's ability to do business can be threatened. He has seen at least one company virtually paralyzed by trying to seek consensus after assiduously stirring up dissension.

Who Will Be Left to Lead?

If this seems to describe an isolated phenomenon in a particular industry, take note: A comparable situation exists in our political life. The culture of critique is threatening our system of governance. Norman Ornstein, a political analyst at the American Enterprise Institute, articulates how.[26]

Ornstein offers some astonishing statistics: Between 1975 and 1989, the number of federal officials indicted on charges of public corruption went up by a staggering 1,211 percent. During the same period, the number of non-federal officials indicted doubled. What are we to make of this? he asks. Does it mean that officials during that decade were far more corrupt than before? Not likely. Every systematic study, as well as all anecdotal evidence, suggests just the opposite: Public officials are far less corrupt now; fewer take bribes, get drunk in the middle of their duties, engage in immoral conduct, and so on.

What we have is the culture of critique. The press is poised to pounce on allegations of scandal, giving them primacy over every other kind of news. And the standards by which scandals are judged have declined. Allegations make the news, no matter where they come from, often without proof or even verification. (Remember the ruckus that accompanied reports that planes were forced to circle and travelers were delayed while President Clinton got a haircut on Air Force One in the Los Angeles airport?[27] And that George Bush did not know what a supermarket scanner was? Both turned out to be false.) Political opponents seize on these allegations and use them to punish or bring down opponents. The sad result is that laws designed to improve ethics have not improved ethics at all. Instead, they have made government almost impossible. Allegations trigger long investigations that themselves damage reputations and suggest to the public that terrible things are going on even when they aren't.

Prosecutors, too, are part of the web, Ornstein continues. In the past, an ambitious prosecutor might set out to snare a criminal on the FBI's ten most wanted list. Now the temptation is to go after a senator or cabinet member— or a vice president. That's where attention is paid; that's where the rewards lie.

The threat is not only to those at the highest levels of government but to public servants at every level. I spoke to someone prominent in the arts who was invited to join a federal commission. But first there was a questionnaire to fill out—pages and pages of details requested about the prospective nominee's personal, professional, and financial life. Special request was made for anything that might be embarrassing if it became public. The person in question simply declined the invitation.

The artist I spoke to typified a situation Ornstein described: It is becoming almost impossible to get qualified people to serve in public positions, from the highest executive nominations to part-time or even honorary appointments. Leaving private life for public service has always required personal sacrifice: Your family life is disrupted; you take a pay cut. But now those contemplating such a move must be willing to make an even greater sacrifice: putting their personal reputation at risk. Instead of enhancing reputations, going into public services now threatens them, whether or not the officials have done anything to be ashamed of.

Disruption of family life is intensified, too, by the inordinate delay, Ornstein explained. While a nominee waits to be confirmed, life goes on hold: A spouse's job is in limbo; children await a change in schools; houses must—but can't—be found or rented or bought or sold. What is causing the delays to become so much more protracted than they were before? Every step in the process: Presidents (and their staffs) must take much more time in choosing potential nominees, to make absolutely sure there is nothing in their lives or backgrounds that could embarrass not just the nominee but the president. Once people are selected, the FBI takes weeks or months longer than it used to for background checks, because it too wants to make sure it is not embarrassed later. Finally, the nomination goes to the Senate, where political opponents of the president or the nominee try to go for the jugular on ethics charges.

The result of all these forces is a much smaller pool of qualified people willing to consider public service, long periods when important posts are left vacant, a climate of suspicion that reinforces public doubts about the ethics of people in government, and real disruption in the running of our country.

We have become obsessed with the appearance of impropriety, as Peter Morgan and Glenn Reynolds show in a book with that title. Meanwhile, real impropriety goes unnoticed. We have to ask, as Ornstein does, whether the price we're paying to have pristine individuals fill every public post is worth what we're getting—and he (like Morgan and Reynolds) doubts that what we're getting is less impropriety.

The Cost in Human Spirit

Whatever the causes of the argument culture—and the many causes I have mentioned are surely not the only ones—the most grievous cost is the price paid in human spirit: Contentious public discourse becomes a model for behavior and sets the tone for how individuals experience their relationships to other people and to the society we live in.

Recall the way young boys on Tory Island learned to emulate their elders:

> All around milled little boys imitating their elders, cursing, fluffing, swaggering, threatening. It was particularly fascinating to see how the children learned the whole sequence of behavior. Anything that the men did, they would imitate, shouting the same things, strutting and swaggering.[28]

Tory Island may be an especially ritualized example, but it is not a totally aberrant one. When young men come together in groups, they often engage in symbolic ritual displays of aggression that involve posturing and mock battles. Without pressing the parallel in too literal a way, I couldn't help thinking that this sounds a bit like what journalists and lawyers have observed about their own tribes: that the display of aggression for the benefit of peers is often more important than concrete results.

Consider again law professor Charles Yablon's observation that young litigators learn to value an aggressive stance by listening to their elders' war stories about "the smashing victories they obtained during pretrial discovery in cases which ultimately were settled." Litigators

> derive job satisfaction by recasting minor discovery disputes as titanic struggles. Younger lawyers, convinced that their future careers may hinge on how tough they *seem* while conducting discovery, may conclude that it is more important to look and sound ferocious than act cooperatively, even if all that huffing and puffing does not help (and sometimes harms) their cases.[29]

Against this background, recall too the observations made by journalists that their colleagues feel pressured to ask tough questions to get peer approval. Kenneth Walsh, for example, commented that "it helps your stature in journalism" if you ask challenging questions because that way "you show you're tough and you're independent." Just as litigators trade war stories about how tough they appeared (whether or not that appearance helped their client), Walsh points out that a journalist who dares to challenge the president takes on a heroic aura among his peers. He recalled a specific incident to illustrate this point:

> Remember Brit Hume asking the question . . . about the zigzag decision-making process of President Clinton? And of course President Clinton cut off the questions after that one question because he felt it was not appropriate. That's what we all remember about the Ruth Bader Ginsburg period, is that Brit asked that question.[30]

Let's look at the actual exchange that earned Brit Hume the admiration of his peers. President Clinton called the press conference to announce his nomination of Judge Ruth Bader Ginsburg to the Supreme Court. After the president introduced her, Judge Ginsburg spoke movingly about her life, ending with tributes to her family: her children, granddaughter, husband, and, finally, her mother, "the bravest and strongest person I have known, who was taken from me much too soon." Following these remarks, which moved listeners to tears, journalists were invited to ask questions. The first (and, as it turned out, also the last) asked by correspondent Hume was this:

> The withdrawal of the Guinier nomination, sir, and your apparent focus on Judge Breyer and your turn, late, it seems, to Judge Ginsburg, may have

created an impression, perhaps unfair, of a certain zigzag quality in the decision-making process here. I wonder, sir, if you could kind of walk us through it and perhaps disabuse us of any notion we might have along those lines. Thank you.

This question reminded everyone—at the very moment of Judge Ginsburg's triumph and honor—that she was not the president's first choice. It broke the spell of her moving remarks by shifting attention from the ceremonial occasion to the political maneuvers that had led up to the nomination—in particular, implying criticism of the president not from the perspective of substance (whether Judge Ginsburg would make a good Supreme Court Justice) but strategy (the decision-making process by which she was chosen). Remarking, "How you could ask a question like that after the statement she just made is beyond me," the president closed the event.

The answer to how Brit Hume could have asked a question like that lies in Walsh's observation that journalists value a display of toughness. In this view, to worry about Judge Ginsburg's feelings—or those of the viewing audience—would be like an attorney worrying about the feelings of a witness about to be cross-examined. But public ceremonies play a role in the emotional lives not only of participants but also of observers, an enormous group in the era of television. Viewers who were moved by Judge Ginsburg's personal statement shared in the ceremony and felt connected to the judge and, by implication, to our judicial system. Such feelings of connection to public figures whose actions affect our lives is a crucial element in individuals' sense of community and their feeling of well-being. Breaking that spell was harmful to this sense of connection, contributing a little bit to what is often called cynicism but which really goes much deeper than that: alienation from the public figures who deeply affect our lives and consequently from the society in which we live.

In this sense, the valuing of the appearance of toughness is related to another theme running through all the domains I discussed: the breakdown in human connections and the rise of anonymity. Lieutenant Colonel Grossman points out that this, too, was one of many ways that the experience of serving in Vietnam was different for American soldiers than was the experience of serving in previous wars. Remember my Uncle Norman, who at the age of eighty-seven was still attending annual reunions of the "boys" he had served with in World War II? This was possible because, as Grossman describes, soldiers in that war trained together, then went to war and served together. Those who were not killed or wounded stayed with the group until they all went home together at the end of the war. No wonder the bonds they forged could last a lifetime. Vietnam, in contrast, was a "lonely war" of individuals assigned to constantly shifting units for year-long tours of duty (thirteen months for Marines). Grossman's description is graphic and sad:

> In Vietnam most soldiers arrived on the battlefield alone, afraid, and without friends. A soldier joined a unit where he was an FNG, a "f——ing new

guy," whose inexperience and incompetence represented a threat to the continued survival of those in the unit. In a few months, for a brief period, he became an old hand who was bonded to a few friends and able to function well in combat. But then, all too soon, his friends left him via death, injury, or the end of their tours. . . . All but the best of units became just a collection of men experiencing endless leavings and arrivals, and that sacred process of bonding, which makes it possible for men to do what they must do in combat, became a tattered and torn remnant of the support structure experienced by veterans of past American wars.[31]

Though this pattern is most painful in this context, it parallels what we have seen in all the other domains of public dialogue. Recall attorney Susan Popik's observation "You don't come up against the same people all the time. That encouraged you to get along with them because you knew that in six months, you would be across the table from them again."[32] Recall journalists' lamenting that the present White House press corps is a large group, often unknown to aides and leaders, kept at a distance from the leaders they are assigned to cover: confined in a small room, in the back of the president's plane, behind ropes at public events. Contrast this with the recollections of those old enough to remember a small White House press corps that had free run of official buildings and lots of private off-the-record meetings with public officials, including the president and first lady, so that they actually got to know them—as people. And recall departing Senator Heflin's regret about the decline of opportunities for legislators of opposing parties to socialize, which led to friendships developed "across party and ideological lines" that "led to more openness and willingness to discuss issues on a cordial basis" and to finding "common ground." We could add the demise of the family doctor who came to your home, replaced by an overworked internist or family practitioner—if not an anonymous emergency room—and, if you're unlucky enough to need them but lucky enough to get to see them, a cadre of specialists who may not talk to each other or even much to you, or surgeons who may spend hours saving your life or limb but hardly ever see or speak to you afterward.

In all these domains, wonderful progress has been accompanied by more and more anonymity and disconnection, which are damaging to the human spirit and fertile ground for animosity.

Getting Beyond Dualism

At the heart of the argument culture is our habit of seeing issues and ideas as absolute and irreconcilable principles continually at war. To move beyond this static and limiting view, we can remember the Chinese approach to yin and yang. They are two principles, yes, but they are conceived not as irreconcilable polar opposites but as elements that coexist and should be brought into balance as much as possible. As sociolinguist Suzanne Wong Scollon notes, "Yin is always present in and changing into yang and vice versa."[33] How can we translate this abstract idea into daily practice?

To overcome our bias toward dualism, we can make special efforts not to think in twos. Mary Catherine Bateson, an author and anthropologist who teaches at George Mason University, makes a point of having her class compare *three* cultures, not two.[34] If students compare two cultures, she finds, they are inclined to polarize them, to think of the two as opposite to each other. But if they compare three cultures, they are more likely to think about each on its own terms.

As a goal, we could all try to catch ourselves when we talk about "both sides" of an issue—and talk instead about "all sides." And people in any field can try to resist the temptation to pick on details when they see a chance to score a point. If the detail really does not speak to the main issue, bite your tongue. Draw back and consider the whole picture. After asking, "Where is this wrong?" make an effort to ask "What is right about this?"— not necessarily *instead,* but *in addition.*

In the public arena, producers can try to avoid, whenever possible, structuring public discussions as debates. This means avoiding the format of having two guests discuss an issue, pro and con. In some cases three guests—or one—will be more enlightening than two.

An example of the advantage of adding a third guest was an episode of *The Diane Rehm Show* on National Public Radio following the withdrawal of Anthony Lake from nomination as director of central intelligence. White House Communications Director Ann Lewis claimed that the process of confirming presidential appointments has become more partisan and personal.[35] Tony Blankley, former communications director for Newt Gingrich, claimed that the process has always been rancorous. Fortunately for the audience, there was a third guest: historian Michael Beschloss, who provided historical perspective. He explained that during the immediately preceding period of 1940 to 1990, confirmation hearings were indeed more benign than they have been since, but in the 1920s and the latter half of the nineteenth century, he said, they were also "pretty bloody." In this way, a third guest, especially a guest who is not committed to one side, can dispel the audience's frustration when two guests make opposite claims.

Japanese television talk shows provide a window on other possibilities. Sociolinguist Atsuko Honda compared three different current affairs talk shows televised in Japan. Each one presents striking contrasts to what Americans take for granted in that genre. (The very fact that Honda chose to compare three—not two—is instructive.) The Japanese shows were structured in ways that made them less likely to be adversarial. Within each structure, participants vigorously opposed each other's ideas, yet they did so without excessively polarizing the issues.

Consider the formats of the three shows: *Nichiyoo Tooron (Sunday Discussion)* featured a moderator and four guests who discussed the recession for an hour. Only the moderator was a professional news commentator; two guests were associated with research institutes. The two other shows Honda examined concerned Japanese involvement in a peacekeeping mission in Cambodia. *Sunday Project* featured three guests: one magazine editor and two political scientists; the third show was a three-and-a-half-hour discussion involving fourteen panelists sitting around an oval table with a participating studio audience composed of fifty Japanese and Cambodian students. Viewers were also invited to participate by calling or faxing. Among the panelists were a history professor, a military analyst, a movie director, a scholar, a newscaster, and a legislator.

It is standard for American shows to provide balance by featuring two experts who represent contrasting political views: two senators or political consultants (one Republican, one Democrat), two journalist commentators (one on the left, one on the right), or two experts (one pro and one con). These Japanese shows had more than two guests, and the guests were identified by their expertise rather than their political perspectives. Another popular Japanese show that is often compared to ABC's *Nightline* or PBS's *Jim Lehrer News Hour* is called *Close-up Gendai*.[36] Providing thirty minutes of nightly news analysis, the Japanese show uses a format similar to these American TV shows. But it typically features a single guest. Japanese shows, in other words, have a wide range of formats featuring one guest or three or more—anything but two, the number most likely to polarize.

The political talk shows that Honda analyzed included many disagreements and conflicts. But whereas moderators of American and British talk shows often provoke and stoke conflict to make their shows more interesting, the Japanese moderators—and also the other guests—expended effort to modulate conflicts and defuse the spirit of opposition, but not the substance of disagreement. One last example, taken from Honda's study, illustrates how this worked.

In the long discussion among fourteen panelists, a dispute arose between two: Shikata, a former executive of the Japanese Self-Defense Forces, supported sending these forces to Cambodia. He was opposed by Irokawa, a historian who believed that the involvement of these forces violated the Japanese constitution. This exchange comes across as quite rancorous:

> Shikata: Why is it OK to send troops to the protecting side but not OK to the protected side?
> Irokawa: Because we have the Japanese Constitution.
> Shikata: Why is it so, if we have the Constitution?
> Irokawa: Well, we have to abide by the Constitution. If you don't want to follow the Constitution, you should get rid of your Japanese nationality and go somewhere else.

These are pretty strong words. And they were accompanied by strong gestures: According to Honda, as Shikata posed his question, he was beating the table with his palms; as Irokawa responded, he was jabbing the air toward Shikata with a pen.

Yet the confrontation did not take on a rancorous tone. The television cameras offered close-ups of both men's faces—smiling. In Japanese and other Asian cultures, smiling has different connotations than it does for Americans and Europeans: It tends to express not amusement but embarrassment. And while Shikata and Irokawa smiled, other panelists rushed to add their voices—and everyone burst out laughing. The laughter served to defuse the confrontation. So did the loud cacophony of voices that erupted as several panelists tried to speak at once. When individual voices finally were distinguished, they did not take one side or the other but tried to mediate the conflict by supporting and criticizing both sides equally. For example, Ohshima, a movie director, said:

> OHSHIMA: I think that both parties overestimate or underestimate the realities for the sake of making a point.

Atsuko Honda found this to be typical of the televised discussions she analyzed: When a conspicuous conflict arose between two parties, other participants frequently moved in with attempts to mediate. In this way, they supported the Japanese ideal of avoiding winners and losers and helped everyone preserve some measure of "face." This mediation did not prevent varying views from being expressed; it resulted in different kinds of views being expressed. If two sides set the terms of debate and subsequent comments support one side or the other, the range of insights offered is circumscribed by the original two sides. If the goal instead is to mediate and defuse polarization, then other panelists are more likely to express a range of perspectives that shed nuanced light on the original two sides or suggest other ways of approaching the issue entirely.

Moving from Debate to Dialogue

Many of the issues I have discussed are also of concern to Amitai Etzioni and other communitarians. In *The New Golden Rule,* Etzioni proposes rules of engagement to make dialogue more constructive between people with differing views. His rules of engagement are designed to reflect—and reinforce—the tenet that people whose ideas conflict are still members of the same community.[37] Among these rules are:

- Don't demonize those with whom you disagree.
- Don't affront their deepest moral commitments.
- Talk less of rights, which are nonnegotiable, and more of needs, wants, and interests.
- Leave some issues out.
- Engage in a dialogue of convictions: Don't be so reasonable and conciliatory that you lose touch with a core of belief you feel passionately about.

As I stressed [. . .] earlier [. . .], producers putting together television or radio shows and journalists covering stories might consider—in at least some cases—preferring rather than rejecting potential commentators who say they cannot take one side or the other unequivocally. Information shows might do better with only one guest who is given a chance to explore an idea in depth rather than two who will prevent each other from developing either perspective. A producer who feels that two guests with radically opposed views seem truly the most appropriate might begin by asking whether the issue is being framed in the most constructive way. If it is, a third or fourth participant could be invited as well, to temper the "two sides" perspective.

Perhaps it is time to reexamine the assumption that audiences always prefer a fight. In reviewing a book about the history of *National Geographic,* Marina Warner scoffs at the magazine's policy of avoiding attack. She quotes the editor who wrote in 1915, "Only what is of a kindly nature is printed about any country or people, everything unpleasant or unduly critical being avoided."[38] Warner describes this editorial approach condescendingly as a "happy-talk, feel-good philosophy" and concludes that "its deep wish not to offend has often made it dull." But the facts belie this judgment. *National Geographic* is one of the most successful magazines of all time—as reported in the same review, its circulation "stands at over 10 million, and the readership, according to surveys, is four times that number."

Perhaps, too, it is time to question our glorification of debate as the best, if not the only, means of inquiry. The debate format leads us to regard those doing different kinds of research as belonging to warring camps. There is something very appealing about conceptualizing differing approaches in this way, because the dichotomies appeal to our sense of how knowledge should be organized.

Well, what's wrong with that?

What's wrong is that it obscures aspects of disparate work that overlap and can enlighten each other.

What's wrong is that it obscures the complexity of research. Fitting ideas into a particular camp requires you to oversimplify them. Again, disinformation and distortion can result. Less knowledge is gained, not more. And time spent attacking an opponent or defending against attacks is not spent doing something else—like original research.

What's wrong is that it implies that only one framework can apply, when in most cases many can. As a colleague put it, "Most theories are wrong not in what they assert but in what they deny."[39] Clinging to the elephant's leg, they loudly proclaim that the person describing the elephant's tail is wrong. This is not going to help them—or their readers—understand an elephant. Again, there are parallels in personal relationships. I recall a man who had just returned from a weekend human development seminar. Full of enthusiasm, he explained the main lesson he had learned: "I don't have to make others wrong to prove that I'm right." He experienced this revelation as a liberation; it relieved him of the burden of trying to prove others wrong.

If you limit your view of a problem to choosing between two sides, you inevitably reject much that is true, and you narrow your field of vision to the limits of those two sides, making it unlikely you'll pull back, widen your field of vision, and discover the paradigm shift that will permit truly new understanding.

In moving away from a narrow view of debate, we need not give up conflict and criticism altogether. Quite the contrary, we can develop more varied—and more constructive—ways of expressing opposition and negotiating disagreement.

We need to use our imaginations and ingenuity to find different ways to seek truth and gain knowledge, and add them to our arsenal—or, should I say, to the ingredients for our stew. It will take creativity to find ways to blunt the most dangerous blades of the argument culture. It's a challenge we must undertake, because our public and private lives are at stake. ∎

NOTES

1. This does not mean it goes back in an unbroken chain. David Noble, in *A World Without Women,* claims that Aristotle was all but lost to the West during the early Christian era and was rediscovered in the medieval era, when universities were first established. This is significant for his observation that many early Christian monasteries welcomed both women and men who could equally aspire to an androgynous ideal, in contrast to the Middle Ages, when the female was stigmatized, unmarried women were consigned to convents, priests were required to be celibate, and women were excluded from spiritual authority.

2. There is a fascinating parallel in the evolution of the early Christian Church and the Southern Baptist Church: Noble shows that the early Christian Church regarded women as equally beloved of Jesus and equally capable of devoting their lives to religious study, so women comprised a majority of early converts to Christianity, some of them leaving their husbands—or bringing their husbands along—to join monastic communities. It was later, leading up to the medieval period, that the clerical movement gained ascendancy in part by systematically separating women, confining them in either marriage or convents, stigmatizing them, and barring them from positions of power within the church. Christine Leigh Heyrman, in *Southern Cross: The Beginnings of the Bible Belt,* shows that a similar trajectory characterized the Southern Baptist movement. At first, young Baptist and Methodist preachers (in the 1740s to 1830s) preached that both women and blacks were equally God's children, deserving of spiritual authority—with the result that the majority of converts were women and slaves. To counteract this distressing demography, the message was changed: Antislavery rhetoric faded, and women's roles were narrowed to domesticity and subservience. With these shifts, the evangelical movement swept the South. At the same time, Heyrman shows, military imagery took over: The ideal man of God was transformed from a "willing martyr" to a "formidable fighter" led by "warrior preachers."

3. Ong, *Fighting for Life,* p. 122. Ong's source, on which I also rely, is Oliver, *Communication and Culture in Ancient India and China.* My own quotations from Oliver are from p. 259.

4. Pachomius, for example, "the father of communal monasticism . . . and organizer of the first monastic community, had been a soldier under Constantine" and modeled his community on the military, emphasizing order, efficiency, and military obedience.

Cassian, a fourth-century proselytizer, "'likened the monk's discipline to that of the soldier,' and Chrysostom, another great champion of the movement, 'sternly reminded the monks that Christ had armed them to be soldiers in a noble fight'" (Noble, *A World Without Women*, p. 54).

5. Aristotle, quoted in Oliver, *Communication and Culture in Ancient India and China*, p. 259.

6. I came to understand the different meaning of "poet" in Classical Greece from reading Ong and also *Preface to Plato* by Eric Havelock. These insights informed many articles I wrote about oral and literate tradition in Western culture, including "Oral and Literate Strategies in Spoken and Written Narratives" and "The Oral/Literate Continuum in Discourse."

7. Moulton, "A Paradigm of Philosophy"; Ong, *Fighting for Life*.

8. The example of Danny and the lava: Wertsch, *Voices of the Mind*, pp. 113–14.

9. See David and Myra Sadker, *Failing at Fairness*.

10. Although my colleagues and I make efforts to refer to our students—all over the age of eighteen—as "women" and "men" and some students in my classes do the same, the majority refer to each other and themselves as "girls" and "boys" or "girls" and "guys."

11. Jonathan Alter, "The End of the Journey," *Newsweek*, Nov. 4, 1996, p. 61. Trilling died at the age of ninety-one.

12. Kaplan, *French Lessons*, p. 119.

13. Tracy and Baratz, "Intellectual Discussion in the Academy as Situated Discourse," p. 309.

14. Greenberg and Robins, "The Changing Role of Social Experiments in Policy Analysis," p. 350.

15. These and other quotes from Tompkins appear in her essay "Fighting Words," pp. 588–89.

16. Safire is quoted in Howard Kurtz, "Safire Made No Secret of Dislike for Inman," *The Washington Post*, Jan. 19, 1994, p. A6.

17. I've borrowed the William Blake quote from Peter Elbow, who used it to open his book *Embracing Contraries*.

18. Terence Monmaney, "Marshall's Hunch," *The New Yorker*, Sept. 20, 1993, pp. 64–72.

19. Elbow, *Embracing Contraries*, p. 258.

20. Moulton, "A Paradigm of Philosophy," p. 153.

21. Social constructionists often deride the ideas of those who focus on differences as "essentialist"—a bit of academic name-calling: it is used only as a way of criticizing someone else's work: "Smith's claims are repugnant because they are essentialist." I have never heard anyone claim, "I am an essentialist," though I have frequently heard elaborate self-defenses: "I am not an essentialist!" Capturing the tendency to use this term as an epithet, *Lingua Franca*, a magazine for academics, describes "essentialist" as "that generic gender studies *j'accuse!*" See Emily Nussbaum, "Inside Publishing," *Lingua Franca*, Dec.–Jan. 1977, pp. 22–24; the quote is from p. 24.

22. Klein, *Meeting the Great Bliss Queen*, pp. 8–9.

23. Cynthia Gorney, "Gloria," *Mother Jones*, Nov.–Dec. 1995, pp. 22–27; the quote is from p. 22.

24. See, for example, Needham, *Science and Civilization in China*.

25. Ellyn E. Spragins, *Newsweek*, July 28, 1997, p. 73.

26. This section is based on an interview with Ornstein. See also Ornstein's article, "Less Seems More."

27. The story behind the haircut story is told by Gina Lubrano, "Now for the Real Hair-cut Story . . . ," *The San Diego Union-Tribune,* July 12, 1993, p. B7. That the supermar-ket scanner story was not true was mentioned by George Stephanopoulos at a panel held at Brown University, as reported by Elliot Krieger, "Providence Journal/Brown University Public Affairs Conference," *The Providence Journal-Bulletin,* Mar. 5, 1995, p. 12A.

28. Fox, "The Inherent Rules of Violence," p. 141.

29. Yablon, "Stupid Lawyer Tricks," p. 1639.

30. Kenneth Walsh made this comment on *The Diane Rehm Show,* May 28, 1996.

31. Grossman, *On Killing,* p. 270.

32. Susan Popik made this comment on the *U.S. Business Litigation* panel.

33. Suzanne Wong Scollon: Personal communication.

34. Mary Catherine Bateson: Personal communication.

35. At the time of this show, Ms. Lewis was deputy communications director.

36. Yoshiko Nakano helped me with observations of *Close-up Gendai.*

37. Etzioni, *The New Golden Rule,* pp. 104–106. He attributes the rule "Talk less of rights . . . and more of needs, wants, and interests" to Mary Ann Glendon.

38. Marina Warner, "High-Minded Pursuit of the Exotic," review of *Reading National Geo-graphic* by Catherine A. Lutz and Jane L. Collins in *The New York Times Book Review,* Sept. 19, 1993, p. 13.

39. I got this from A. L. Becker, who got it from Kenneth Pike, who got it from . . .

REFERENCES

Elbow, Peter. *Embracing Contraries: Explorations in Learning and Teaching* (New York and Oxford: Oxford University Press, 1986).

Etzioni, Amitai. *The New Golden Rule: Community and Morality in a Democratic Society* (New York: Basic, 1996).

Fox, Robin. "The Inherent Rules of Violence." In *Social Rules and Social Behaviour,* Peter Collet, ed. (Totowa, N.J.: Rowman and Littlefield, 1976), pp. 132–49.

Greenberg, David H., and Philip K. Robins. "The Changing Role of Social Experiments in Policy Analysis." *Journal of Policy Analysis and Management* 5:2 (1986), pp. 340–62.

Grossman, Dave. *On Killing: The Psychological Cost of Learning to Kill in War and Society* (Boston: Little, Brown, 1995).

Havelock, Eric A. *Preface to Plato* (Cambridge, Mass.: Belknap Press, Harvard University Press, 1963).

Heyrman, Christine Leigh. *Southern Cross: The Beginnings of the Bible Belt* (New York: Knopf, 1997).

Kaplan, Alice. *French Lessons: A Memoir* (Chicago: University of Chicago Press, 1993).

Klein, Anne Carolyn. *Meeting the Great Bliss Queen: Buddhists, Feminists, and the Art of the Self* (Boston: Beacon Press, 1995).

Kurtz, Howard. *Hot Air: All Talk, All the Time* (New York: Times Books, 1996).

Moulton, Janice. "A Paradigm of Philosophy: The Adversary Method." In *Discovering Reality,* Sandra Harding and Merrill B. Hintikka, eds. (Dordrecht, Holland: Reidel, 1983), pp. 149–64.

Needham, Joseph. *Science and Civilization in China* (Cambridge, England: Cambridge University Press, 1956).

Noble, David. *A World Without Women: The Christian Culture of Western Science* (New York and Oxford: Oxford University Press, 1992).

Oliver, Robert T. *Communication and Culture in Ancient India and China* (Syracuse, N.Y.: Syracuse University Press, 1971).

Ong, Walter J. *Fighting for Life: Contest, Sexuality, and Consciousness* (Ithaca, N.Y.: Cornell University Press, 1981).

Ornstein, Norman J. "Less Seems More: What to Do About Contemporary Political Corruption." *The Responsible Community* 4:1 (Winter 1993–94), pp. 7–22.

Tompkins, Jane. "Fighting Words: Unlearning to Write the Critical Essay." *Georgia Review* 42 (1988), pp. 585–90.

Tracy, Karen, and Sheryl Baratz. "Intellectual Discussion in the Academy as Situated Discourse." *Communication Monographs* 60 (1993), pp. 300–20.

Wertsch, James V. *Voices of the Mind: A Sociocultural Approach to Mediated Action* (Cambridge, Mass.: Harvard University Press, 1991).

Yablon, Charles. "Stupid Lawyer Tricks: An Essay on Discovery Abuse." *Columbia Law Review* 96 (1996), p. 1618–44.

■ *QUESTIONS FOR MAKING CONNECTIONS WITHIN THE READING* ■

1. In the course of her argument Deborah Tannen refers to "our adversarial culture," "the culture of critique," and to maleness, logic, formalism, and polarization. She refers as well to the customs and discourses of Western religion and science, and to contemporary educational practices. Define these terms and explain how they fit together. What is the relation between logic and aggression, religion and science, and ancient Greece and the education offered by our universities?

2. In what ways has the "boot camp" model shaped your own educational experience? In an actual boot camp, is it the drill sergeant alone who creates the tension, or does everyone collaborate in creating and sustaining an atmosphere of rivalry and violence? How about in the case of schooling: In what ways do the students themselves actively collaborate in making the classroom into a "camp"? In what ways does the system—the culture and the institutions of schooling—reinforce these behaviors?

3. In the section entitled "Getting Beyond Dualism," Tannen describes the dynamics of three Japanese television programs, which she offers as examples of a less agonistic style of public discussion. What features distinguish these programs from comparable discussions in the U.S. media and in places like the classroom? Does disagreement have a different significance in the context of Japanese culture? When people disagree in Western settings, what might be at stake? What values and outcomes matter the most? In the Japanese context, what values and outcomes are most significant? How might an American misunderstand the Japanese programs?

■*QUESTIONS FOR WRITING* ■

1. University professors routinely study communities and institutions outside the university, and they are often quite critical of what they discover there, but the university itself is seldom the object of comparable scrutiny. In what ways—if any—does the culture of critique stifle inquiry and thwart constructive change within the university itself? If Tannen is correct in her estimations, then would it be fair to say that the advancement of knowledge is only one of the university's many goals and perhaps not even the most important one? What might the other goals be?

2. The university in the United States is a unique institution in many ways. For one thing, all faculty above the level of assistant professor have lifetime employment and cannot be dismissed except for gross dereliction of duty. Most public universities receive automatic funding from state coffers. Many private universities have enormous endowments, sometimes in the billions of dollars. And most professors are shielded from any assessment of their effectiveness as teachers, except through course evaluations. In what ways does the university's unique situation contribute to the persistence of the culture of critique? What about the media? Do the media also contribute to the persistence of this culture?

■*QUESTIONS FOR MAKING CONNECTIONS BETWEEN READINGS* ■

1. Were the attacks on the World Trade Center and the Pentagon acts of war or were they crimes? What difference does the choice of words make in describing this—or any other—act of violence? Drawing on the work of Tannen and Andrew Bacevich, discuss the relationship between the terms we use to describe acts of violence and the ways we elect to respond to acts of violence. Would changing the words we use and the ways we use them create new options for responding to violence, or does this proposition grant a power to words that they simply don't have?

2. How does Malcolm Gladwell's discussion of the dynamics of social change confirm, contradict, or complicate Tannen's argument? Does Gladwell's account suggest that social change is decided by the strongest argument? Does debate even play a significant role? If public debate and rational deliberation have a marginal influence, why does the university place so high a premium on them? Have professors depicted the social world in ways that are flattering to themselves? In what ways is this depiction both accurate *and* inaccurate?

EDWARD TENNER

EDWARD TENNER HAS been called a "philosopher of everyday technology." His principal concern is the way that human beings interact with the products of technological innovation. In exploring these interactions, Tenner takes an expansive view, and his thinking brings together subjects as diverse as agriculture, antibiotics, automobiles, chairs, shoes, football helmets, and computer software. Tenner's studies of technological development have led him to conclude that innovation often produces—at least in the short term—unintended negative consequences. These negative consequences, which Tenner calls technology's "revenge effects," sometimes actually make life *less* safe, convenient, and efficient than before the inventions came into being. As he puts it, "A small change to solve a minor problem may create a larger one." Moreover, he notes that the risk of technology's revenge effects has only been intensified by the ubiquity of computer software in modern life.

Revenge effects unfold around us everyday—in traffic jams, for example, and as online spam. But Tenner is intrigued and inspired by the way that people have responded with creativity to these problems. Revenge effects are unintended— that much is true—but our efforts to improve the quality of life need not be self-defeating. As Tenner puts it, "human culture, not some inherent will of the machine, has created most revenge effects," and for this reason, he argues that we must not lose sight of our capacity to change and adapt. As the pace of innovation accelerates, Tenner considers one question to be especially important for any reflection on the best course for the future: "How can we break out of ruts and change our thinking?"

Tenner's educational and professional background is eclectic. In addition to *Why Things Bite Back* (1996), he is also the author of *Our Own Devices: How Technology Remakes Humanity* (2003). Tenner is currently a writer, speaker, and technology consultant, and was formerly employed as a science editor at

Tenner, Edward. "Another Look Back, and a Look Ahead." *Why Things Bite Back: Technology and the Revenge of Unintended Consequences.* New York: Knopf, 1996. 254–277.

Biographical information comes from Edward Tenner's home page, <http://www.edwardtenner .com/>. Quotations come from the Princeton University Web site, <http://www.princeton .edu/pr/pwb/02/1021/3a.shtml>, an NPR interview with Tenner, and *Why Things Bite Back.*

Princeton University Press. He is the recipient of a Guggenheim fellowship and has been affiliated with Princeton's Institute for Advanced Study and the Jerome and Dorothy Lemelson Center for the Study of Invention and Innovation at the Smithsonian.

Another Look Back, and a Look Ahead

"Doing Better and Feeling Worse." This phrase from a 1970s symposium on health care is more apt than ever, and not only in medicine. We seem to worry more than our ancestors, surrounded though they were by exploding steamboat boilers, raging epidemics, crashing trains, panicked crowds, and flaming theaters. Perhaps this is because the safer life imposes an ever-increasing burden of attention. Not just in the dilemmas of medicine but in the management of natural hazards, in the control of organisms, in the running of offices, and even in the playing of games there are, not necessarily more severe, but more subtle and intractable, problems to deal with.

To investigate why disasters should lead to improvement, and improvement should paradoxically foster discontent, it might help to look at three areas of technology we have not considered before: timekeeping, navigation, and motorization. The automobile first presented an acute problem—collisions—but its success reduced that difficulty while adding to it another, less easily soluble one—congestion. And the recent history of motoring also suggests a paradox of safety, that the better-made and less dangerous motor vehicles become, the greater are the burdens on the operator. The prognosis for revenge effects is hopeful: we will probably keep them under control. By replacing brute force with finesse, concentration with variety, and heavy traditional materials with lighter ones, we are already starting to overcome the thinking and habits that led to many revenge effects. Technology, too, is evolving and responding. The one thing we will not be able to do is avoid the endless rituals of vigilance.

In one example after another, revenge has turned out to be the flip side of intensity. The velocity of twentieth-century transportation and warfare produces trauma on an unprecedented scale, which in turn calls for equally intensive care; but the end result may be chronic brain damage that is beyond medical treatment. Intensive antibiotic therapy has removed the horror of some of the nineteenth century's most feared infections, yet it has also promoted the spread of even more virulent bacteria. Massive shielding of beaches from the energy of waves has deflected their intensity to other shores or robbed these beaches of replenishing sand. Smoke jumpers have suppressed small forest fires but have thereby helped build reservoirs of flammable materials in the understory for more intense ones. Towering smokestacks have propelled particulates at great velocity higher into the atmosphere than ever before—to the dismay of residents over an ever wider radius. Intensive chicken-pig-duck agriculture in China has rushed new influenza virus strains into production, for distribution internationally by the increasingly dense and speedy world network of commercial aircraft. Accelerating processor speed has multiplied computer operations without necessarily reducing costs to programmers, system managers, and end users. Rigid molded ski boots have helped prevent ankle and tibia fractures at the cost of anterior cruciate ligament injuries. And what are so-called pests but intensified life forms? Most of these animals and plants are unusually robust, prolific, and adaptive. The animals are mobile and the plants spread rapidly. Fire ants, Africanized bees, starlings, melaleuca go about their business single-mindedly. Even the dreamy-looking eucalyptus is capable of burning intensely to propagate itself—taking entire neighborhoods with it. And when intensity is a genuine protection against catastrophe, it may fail to address and even complicates persistent low-level problems.

We have learned the limits of intensiveness. What next? In the near time, intensification is still working. Human health and longevity have improved in most places and by most measures. As we have seen, people may feel sicker today because they are more likely to survive with some limitation or chronic illness. But they really are better off. It is hard to disagree with optimists like Leonard Sagan and Aaron Wildavsky when they point to the benefits of growth. Fortunately, every prediction of global famine and misery has failed—so far.

The second argument for optimism is humanity's success in digging deeper and looking harder for old resources and substituting new ones. In the crucible of technological change, shortages produce surpluses and crises yield alternatives. When the biologist Paul Ehrlich lost a bet with the economist Julian Simon on future prices of a bundle of commodities selected by Ehrlich—they dropped between 1980 and 1990, costing Ehrlich $576.06—the transaction seemed to bear out Simon's argument that inexhaustible human ingenuity would find a way around apparent shortages. Market forces appear to impose conservation and encourage discovery more efficiently than legislation generally can. We have seen how the feared hardwood shortage of the early twentieth century never happened, much to the dismay of Jack London and other hopeful eucalyptus growers. Of course, this analysis has revenge effects of its own for market economics: if constraint helps make us so much more clever, why should the state not prod the infinitely creative human mind with more taxes and restrictions? Heavy taxes on fossil fuels should, by the same logic, do wonders for conservation and alternative energy sources.[1]

When it comes to interpreting the last hundred years, the optimists have the upper hand. The future is another matter. Optimists counter projections of global warming, rising sea levels, population growth, and soil depletion with scenarios of gradual adjustment and adaptation. If the crisis of life in the oceans is the problem, then fish farming is the answer. A true optimist sees a silver lining even in the destruction of rain forests and wilderness: there may be much less acreage, but more and more people will be able to travel and see it. In terms of this strange anthropocentric, utilitarian calculus there will actually be more *available* forest and wilderness. As for soil depletion, genetic engineering and new methods of cultivation will presumably let us cope; the world can probably support a population of ten billion or more. (In 1994 it stood at 5.6 billion.) Optimists and pessimists disagree not so much on what is attainable, but on how long it will *be* attainable. What the first group welcomes as a successful adaptation the second belittles as a stopgap. Optimists and pessimists curiously agree that crisis is good for us, but for different reasons. Pessimists welcome emergency as a violent cure for profligacy. Optimists welcome it as an injection of innovatory stimulus.

The Ambiguity of Disaster

One reason for optimism is that disaster is paradoxically creative. It legitimizes and promotes changes in rules—changes that may be resisted as long as the levels of casualties remain "acceptable" prior to a disaster that leads to change. More important, disasters mobilize the kind of ingenuity that technological optimists believe exists in unlimited supply. Of course, new disasters may themselves be unintended consequences of prior solutions. It is uncertain whether, at least in developed countries, the incidence of new catastrophes is gradually declining or not. Should disasters be considered as waves that remain constant in amplitude, damped, or amplified? The unanswerable question about technological revenge effects is whether we are really learning. Even tragedies like Chernobyl and Bhopal are ambiguous as forewarnings. Are they just the most recent in an ongoing series that will strike again in Western Europe and North America, where matters are far less secure than their leaders admit? Or will they spark environmental consciousness and vigilance in the former Soviet bloc and the developing world? It is too soon to say, but there is excellent evidence that great disasters do have long-term reverse revenge effects.

The first great modern stimulus from disaster may have been the defeat of the Spanish Armada in 1588. The economic historian David Landes has speculated that this greatest setback in the history of Spain was what led its king Philip III to offer a perpetual pension of 6,000 ducats to "the discoverer of the longitude" when he ascended the throne ten years later. (Landes is not sure, however, what method would have kept the surviving ships from their fate on the rocks of Ireland and the Orkney Islands.) In France the Duc d'Orléans made a comparable offer. From Galileo to Newton, most of the giants of the scientific revolution of the late sixteenth and seventeenth centuries, with or without prizes in mind, joined the search. None of these thinkers produced a practical astronomical system, yet the shipwrecks and prizes did have other substantial benefits. The sociologist Robert K. Merton has suggested how many advances in mathematics, astronomy, mechanics, and magnetism could be traced to the vast losses that Spain and other maritime powers had suffered.[2]

It took a further disaster to complete the paradoxical work: the wreck of three ships from the fleet of Admiral Sir Clowdesley Shovell in 1707 on the Scilly Isles off the west coast of England, killing almost two thousand sailors. (The admiral reportedly struggled ashore, only to be murdered for his magnificent ring.) Today we know that bad geography, charts, and compasses, and poor navigation, complicated by fog and unpredictable currents, were mainly to blame. To contemporaries, though, the lesson was a new urgency in the search for a way to determine longitude at sea. Of course, a valid method would in turn make possible more accurate printed aids to navigation. The question of longitude was not immediately supported officially; only seven years later, in 1714, was an Act of Parliament passed, offering up to £20,000—at least $1 million in today's purchasing power—for a method of determining longitude on an oceangoing vessel.[3]

Entrepreneurs and cranks had been at work on solutions ever since the wreck, proposing lines of ships somehow "anchored" in mid-ocean, telepathic goats, and even dogs communicating through a "sympathetic powder" said by its promoters to relay sensations from an animal on land to one at sea after having been sprinkled on both. But the prize, after more than another decade had passed, attracted the attention of the gifted clockmaker John Harrison, who built a chronometer that met the specifications of the act. The steps and the time it took him to refine his timepiece (along with the fact that he did not secure payment of his claims until 1773, when he was eighty) are not the point here. What matters is that the magnitude of the Scilly Isles wreck eventually justified the great reward offered.

The earlier prizes contributed indirectly to the Act of Parliament. It was Newton, who had long worked on the problem, whose recommendation was essential for the act's passage. Only in hopes of the new prize did Harrison and other leading craftsmen abandon their normal clientele for a largely speculative project that had frustrated the scientific elite of Europe for decades. The search for longitude may represent the first great public high-technology program. In its costs and benefits it became one of the most successful. Anything like it would almost certainly have been long delayed in the absence of a spectacular new disaster.[4]

It took another two hundred years for a single marine disaster to have an international impact comparable to that of the Scilly Isles wreck. This was the sinking of the *Titanic,* pride of the White Star Line, on April 14, 1912. The ship's tragic end was memorialized not only as an enormous loss of life and property—over fifteen hundred passengers and crew perished, including the captain—but also as a cautionary tale. Some of its perceived lessons were social, the image of the frivolous rich fiddling as the world was about to burn, or even escaping in lifeboats as the poor drowned in steerage. Even the failure of other ships to respond to its distress calls has been blamed on the priority given by radio operators to the social cables of their first-class passengers. But in the long run, the dangers of technological pride rather than class conflict seemed to be the message of this disaster. Even more than the loss of the three English ships two centuries earlier, the sinking of the *Titanic* immediately became what risk analysts now call a *signal event*—one that reveals an ominous and previously underestimated kind of danger.[5]

The problem was not mainly in the operation of the ship's systems, useless though some of the lifeboat mechanisms turned out to be. Even though White Star officials never claimed the ship was actually unsinkable, the captain and crew acted with inappropriate confidence, steaming at high speed through waters notorious for sea ice. After the *Titanic* hit the iceberg, the same confidence in the ship's safeguards delayed, with tragic consequences, the implementation of rescue procedures that could have reduced casualties immeasurably. (Her officers doubtless had faith in the owners' stringent design specifications, but marine archaeologists now believe that the vessel's steel plates did not meet these standards.) Belief in the safety of the ship became the greatest single hazard to the survival of its passengers, greater than the icebergs themselves. In fact, crews of other nearby vessels that might have rescued passengers believed the *Titanic*'s distress flares could only mean some celebration, not an emergency.

Less known is how important the *Titanic* disaster was in solving what had been a serious problem for international navigation: the prevalence of sea ice in the ocean lanes of the world's most active and lucrative route, the North Atlantic. The wreck had precedents: in the 1880s over fifty passenger ships reported sea ice damage in and around the Grand Banks off the Newfoundland coast where the *Titanic* later went down; fourteen of them had sunk. It was the loss of the *Titanic* that led not only to new regulations requiring lifeboat space for all passengers and crew, but to a series of international conferences on the Safety of Life at Sea (SOLAS) beginning in 1913. The International Ice Patrol, established in 1913, now uses aerial surveillance, satellite images, and radio-equipped oceanographic drifter buoys. The biggest bergs even have their own radio transmitters. Ships possess advanced radar systems. It would require extraordinary negligence for a captain to let an iceberg sink a ship.[6]

At least for passengers embarking in the United States, an ocean cruise now appears extraordinarily safe. From 1970 to 1989, only two of over thirty million passengers died in accidents involving cruise ships operating out of the United States, despite a number of collisions and fires. Each generation of ships meets higher standards. SOLAS new specifies a maximum thirty-minute evacuation time for cruise ships. Only one ship has ever sunk after hitting an iceberg since the *Titanic,* and that was in 1943, when the Ice Patrol was discontinued during the Second World War.[7]

Both tragedies and their consequences illustrate the engineer and historian Henry Petroski's point that a great disaster is often the best stimulus for new engineering ideas. Two things have changed, though, since the early eighteenth century. The growth of engineering as a profession has made a new type of error possible, as Petroski has also shown: overconfidence in the safety of a new design, the defects of which too often remain hidden until some new disaster occurs. But there is also a second type of error: failure to observe the repeated rituals that safe operation of advanced technology entails. The higher potential speed of steamships required (and requires) more rather than less care. The larger number of passengers and crew required (and requires) more careful drills and inspection of equipment. It is still difficult for a prospective passenger to tell how well trained a crew may be to handle an emergency. We know some technology has a built-in demand for care, a maintenance compulsion. But there is always a hidden catch of technological improvement: the need for enhanced vigilance that we have already seen in medicine, in environmental modification, in the translocation of plants and animals, in electronic systems, and even in some aspects of athletics.[8]

At this point in the history of technology we can draw a fundamental lesson from an unexpected source, the law of negligence. In a number of important articles, the legal scholar Mark Grady correlates better and safer technology with the number of lawsuits for malpractice and personal injury. During the centuries when bleeding, purging, and mercury compounds (as we have seen) hastened the deaths of many of the West's elite, legal action against the physicians who pursued these remedies was rare. The public did not hold doctors in awe; neither did they really expect heroic remedies to work. In fact, it was precisely because they doubted the scientific basis of contemporary treatments that a malpractice suit had little point.

According to Grady, "the first negligence explosion occurred during the 1875–1905 period. In that time of industrial revolution, claims increased by fully 800%, and the negligence rule did not change significantly. When machines abound, negligence claims increase. Put differently, a doctor who forgot to perform a modern fetal health procedure could not have been liable in 1960, before the procedure was invented." On this view, a dialysis machine reduces the risk of kidney failure in nature but adds a new risk: that physicians and technicians operating the machines under their supervision may fail to make safe connections, test the hemodialytic solution, or observe all the other precautions of good practice. Anyone who has watched the pilot and copilot of a common two-engine commuter aircraft carry out their extensive preflight procedures, flipping through pages in a printed notebook as they read their scripts, has been struck by the number of precautions that a long-accepted and well-developed technology imposes.[9]

By the standards of its day, the *Titanic* was a ship relatively high in what Grady calls "durable precautions," the safety hardware that popular opinion supposed made it unsinkable. It is true that size, luxury, and speed had higher priority than safety in her design—but she had the latest in communications and damage-containment equipment. Grady's analysis suggests, though, that the very presence of these measures increased the importance of "nondurable precautions"—all the things an officer or crew member must remember to do—in keeping the ship afloat. The flow of messages on the ship's radio demanded constant attention: did a given message warrant immediate transmission to the bridge? Once the captain was aware of it, did it necessitate a change of speed or course? And with lifeboats come other questions. Have they been inspected regularly? Does each crew member know his or her part in supervising a possible abandonment? If a major marine loss occurs, it is the way an emergency plan is carried out, not physical safeguards alone, that will determine whether or not it becomes a disaster for human life.

Here is where the difference between early and industrial technology becomes telling. The captain of a seventeenth-century oceangoing ship needed excellent navigation skills, and the management of cargo, ballast, and rigging were already arts for specialists. Some captains and pilots of Renaissance and early modern Europe had superb intuition which let them achieve amazing feats of "dead reckoning": the estimation of position from relatively crude measurements of last position, direction, and speed. A gifted mariner could go beyond the limits of the technology of the day. Yet because of the difficulty of measuring longitude, compounded by the other defects of instruments, disaster could happen to the best of seafarers. That is why Sir Clowdesley Shovell still got an overbearing tomb by Grinling Gibbons in Westminster Abbey after his catastrophic end. (On the other hand, Joseph Addison ridiculed it as "the figure of a beau, dressed in a long periwig, and reposing himself upon velvet cushions under a canopy of state," and deplored that it commemorated only his demise and not his victories.) The better and the safer technology becomes, the more we presume human error when something goes seriously wrong. If it is not the error of the captain or crew, it is one of the engineers or designers of equipment, or of executives and their maintenance policies.[10]

The Automobile and Revenge Effects

Intensity—disaster—precaution—vigilance: the cycle appears on land as well as at sea. The rise of motoring shows this more clearly than the transformation of sailing, but in a different way. . . . [N]ineteenth-century railroad accidents were the first of a new type of technological disaster unknown in the eighteenth century. Historians of technology have long pointed out the importance of indignation over early railroad tragedies in developing the first complex control systems in American business, not to mention safety hardware like signals and air brakes. But there is an equally interesting side to the intensification of transportation by the railroad: the rise of automobile transport. Casualties from car accidents occur as a steady series of small disasters, not the few-but-great wrecks involving trains and steamships. The automobile invited chronic catastrophes. Indignation built more slowly.[11]

The growing capacity of the nation's railroad network had an unforeseen consequence that few scholars have noted—chaos in the horse-drawn city. Nearly every passenger journey or freight shipment began and ended with a horse-drawn vehicle or a horse, at least until cable cars and electric trolleys spread late in the century. Even the physical size of horses increased throughout the nineteenth century, to move the heavier loads and serve the larger populations of European and American cities. By the 1880s, massive Percherons were a familiar sight on American streets. Teamstering already was a crucial trade, and the number of horses for every teamster was growing. Local delivery by horse could cost nearly as much as hundreds of miles by rail. Today's Budweiser Clydesdales, a magnificent public relations asset, are the heritage of yesterday's logistical nightmares.[12]

Herds of horses multiplied. Even after cable and electric power had begun to replace horse traction for streetcars, horses were everywhere. The Fiss, Doerr, and Carroll horse auction mart on East 24th Street in New York drew up to a thousand buyers and boasted its own seven-story, block-long stable. New York City's horses alone produced over 300 million pounds of manure annually; stables accumulated tens of thousands of cubic feet for months at a time. In fact, as we have seen, one imported pest, the English sparrow, thrived on the bounty of grain in horse droppings. Repeated horse epidemics—technically epizootics—paralyzed commerce and interfered with firefighting. Despite limitation of their workdays to four hours, horses died after only a few years of service, usually in the middle of the street, up to fifteen thousand a year in New York. Dust from powdered horse manure helped spread tuberculosis and tetanus. As railroads grew safer, the horse-drawn city became more dangerous.[13]

Less remembered today than the sanitary problems caused by horses were the safety hazards they posed. Horses and horse-drawn vehicles were dangerous, killing more riders, passengers, and pedestrians than is generally appreciated. Horses panicked. In frequent urban traffic snarls, they bit and kicked some who crossed their path. Horse-related accidents were an important part of surgical practice in Victorian England and no doubt in North America as well. In the 1890s in New York, per capita deaths from wagons and carriage accidents nearly doubled. By the end of the century they stood at nearly six per hundred thousand of population. Added to the five or so streetcar deaths, the rate of about 110 per million is close to the rates of motor vehicle deaths in many industrial countries in the 1980s. On the eve of motorization, the urban world was not such a gentle place.[14]

The automobile was an answer to disease and danger. In fact, private internal-combustion transportation was almost utopian. The congested tenements of the center city spread dirt and disease. Dispersing people into the green suburbs was a favorite theme of city reformers. Progressive mayors supported the extension of horsecars and then trolleys. But at least on city stretches, these had an unpleasant intensity of their own. In 1912 the *Los Angeles Record* found their air "a pestilence . . . heavy with disease and the emanations from many bodies. . . . A bishop embraced a stout grandmother, a tender girl touched limbs with a city sport. . . ." And hard-pressed straphangers objected to allegedly high fares, reckless drivers, and rude conductors.[15]

Automobiles may have begun as rich people's toys, but thanks largely to Henry Ford, they soon came to represent independence *from* the rich: from railroad interests, traction (streetcar) companies, center-city landlords. By the 1950s and the 1960s, the automotive industry had come to represent big business at its most arrogant, but motorization won because it rallied so many small businesses. Diffuse interests were its political strength. Motoring did not benefit only car manufacturers and petroleum producers and refiners. It enriched tens of thousands of small businesses: trucking companies, suburban developers, construction contractors, dealers and parts retailers, service station operators. Of course, as Clay McShane and other urban historians before him have documented, road improvement was not really populist, or uniformly popular. It did change the nature of the street, but to the disadvantage of residents. The roadway ceased to be a gathering place and became a thoroughfare. Many neighborhoods resisted asphalt paving, and children even stoned passing cars. Still, motoring showed the political advantages of spreading benefits to many small and medium-sized interests.[16]

In spite of clear damage to urban greenery and space, using roads to help disperse people in private suburban houses remained not just a popular but a politically correct idea for a long time, and not only in America. Franklin D. Roosevelt thought that spreading population would lower the cost of government and directly reduce the expense of urban services. One radical planner, Carol Aronovici, wrote in 1932: "Let the old cities perish so that we may have great and beautiful cities." Aronovici called for "a thorough emancipation of the suburban communities from the metropolis" that was threatening to "suck their very physical existence into the body politic of decayed and corrupted political organization." (More than sixty years later, these same towns—now aging demographically and economically—are beginning to make common cause with the old central cities against the flight of businesses and residents to the sprawling outer suburbs.)[17]

At virtually the same time a school of Soviet planners called the "disurbanists" were dreaming of dispersing their own overcrowded urban masses into new settlements amid the fields and forests by building new road networks. A distinguished visitor, the French architect Le Corbusier, summed up the mood in his book *La Ville Radieuse* (1930):

> People were encouraged to entertain an idle dream: "The cities will be part of the country; I shall live 30 miles away from my office under a pine tree; my secretary will live 30 miles away from it too, in the other direction, under another pine tree. We shall both have our own car. We shall use up tires, wear out road surfaces and gears, consume oil and gasoline. All of which will necessitate a great deal of work . . . enough for all. . . ."[18]

It is almost as though postwar American suburbia was the realized fantasy of Soviet planners. Or, more accurately, the victory of motorization was an unintended consequence of an international decentralizing mood. As Kenneth Jackson has pointed out, even the *Bulletin of the Atomic Scientists* embraced dispersion of cities in a 1951 special issue, "Defense Through Decentralization." It promoted satellite cities and low-density suburbs in which former urbanites could be housed more safely for the duration of the Cold War.[19]

Automobiles and road systems promoted an old technological utopia, the community of private villas. Automobiles also have an immense advantage over railroads and trolleys: they make it possible to go directly from one outlying point to another. America never had an integrated national or even regional transportation network as European countries did. Its trains and even some of its urban transport systems were run by competing corporations. Nostalgic admirers of railroad transportation forget how many trips required completing two sides of a triangle, sometimes with hours of waiting between them. K. H. Schaeffer and Elliot Sclar, transportation analysts, exposed these shortcomings trenchantly in *Access for All*. A trip of fourteen miles from the small town of New Washington, Ohio, to its county seat could take all day by rail, even when train travel was at its peak. And New Washington's two depots were a half mile apart.[20]

Usually, motorization bought space rather than time. Ivan Illich wrote in 1974: "The typical American spends over 1,600 hours a year (or thirty hours a week or four hours a day including Sundays) in his car. This includes the time spent behind the wheel, moving or stopped, the hours of work needed to pay for it and for gasoline, tires, tolls, insurance, fines, and taxes. . . . For this American it takes 1,600 hours to cover a year total of 6,000 miles, four miles per hour. This is just as fast as a pedestrian and slower than a bicycle."[21]

In fact, the greatest surprise of motoring was the speed at which traffic clogged the roads, including freeways and other limited-access highways built to relieve congestion. When the Washington Beltway was dedicated in 1964, the governor of Maryland, who cut the ribbon on its last segment, called it "a road of opportunity." The federal highway administrator compared it to a wedding ring. The *Washington Post* declared that "the stenographer in Suitland will be able to get to the Pentagon without finding the day ruined almost before it begins." Twenty-two years later, another *Post* correspondent reported: "The dream turned to nightmare. The Great Belt tightened to the point where right now it resembles nothing less than a noose around the communal neck. . . . We could die on the Beltway and rot until vultures pick clean our bones." London's counterpart, the M25, had already exceeded its projected traffic for the year 2001 by the late 1980s, only three years after completion. Surprisingly, even states like Kentucky, Missouri, Nebraska, South Carolina, Tennessee, and Texas classify more than half their interstate highway mileage as congested. And mature suburbs of large cities have become so traffic-choked that the American Automobile Association itself has moved its headquarters from Fairfax County, Virginia, to Florida.[22]

There are social reasons for this recongestion: not just two-commuter families but the multiple motorized errands that suburban living demands. Saturday afternoons may be the most crowded times of all. Traffic engineers, applied mathematicians, and economists have also discovered that expanding old routes and adding new ones may actually increase travel time. An enlarged bridge will redirect traffic that had been taking a longer route around it, but unless it is substantially larger, it will be just as slow. New highways also may increase total travel time for all travelers when they draw traffic from alternative rail systems. And the ultimate recongesting effect is called Braess's Paradox, in honor of a pioneering investigator of the subject. Where each of two congested routes has a bottleneck, adding what appears to be a shortcut between them may actually increase travel time for everyone. The reason: the new, "direct" road actually funnels traffic through *both* the old bottlenecks. Thanks to quirks of driver psychology, even common operations like merging traffic can produce equally counterproductive results. Because motorists tend to close up spaces to discourage entering cars from cutting in front of them, especially when these attempt to enter from other roads, mysterious traffic jams can appear a mile or more from the actual merge. Because spaces are tight, a driver decelerating slightly at the head of a clump can unwittingly induce one following motorist after another to brake a bit harder. And when congestion reaches a certain maximum roadway capacity, the flow of cars falls so sharply that traffic engineers recognize (but still can't fully explain) a "breakdown." What appears rational to an individual driver becomes irrational for the motoring population and for society. Recongesting turns out to be a form of recomplicating, of creating a machine of parts coupled in poorly understood ways.[23]

What is interesting technologically about this new congestion is its unexpectedly positive side. It has helped make driving safer than anyone thought it would ever be. Congestion may be a chronic negative side effect of mobility, but safety is a positive outcome of congestion. There is a school of thought that denies that driving or anything else can ever be made safer. This is called risk homeostasis. The phrase means simply that people unconsciously seek a certain level of hazard. They compensate for "dangerous" conditions by driving more cautiously—and offset safety measures by taking more risks. The geographer John G. U. Adams looked into the accident rate of England's "adventure playgrounds," loosely supervised assortments of high wooden ladders and platforms that offer "opportunities to test skills appropriate to chimpanzees." They are visibly more dangerous than "fixed equipment" playgrounds with their smooth surfaces and rubberized matting. Yet insurance companies quote lower liability rates for the adventure playgrounds, and the secretary of the National Playing Fields Association has written that "the accident rate is lower than in orthodox playgrounds since hooliganism which results from boredom is absent." Adams and others (mainly social scientists) have argued conversely that seat belts, by making drivers feel more secure, actually cause more pedestrian casualties even as they reduce motorist injuries.[24]

Few traffic engineers accept risk homeostasis as a principle, or the seat belt as an instance of it. In fact, as Leonard Evans, a physicist and safety researcher, argues, some safety measures save more lives than we might have predicted, but others may actually increase casualties. The fifty-five-mile-per-hour speed limit reduced deaths more than anyone had expected. Seat belts met expectations. Studded tires, improved acceleration, and antilock braking systems (ABS) have a moderate benefit, though there is some evidence that ABS-equipped drivers may have as many crashes as those not similarly equipped, or perhaps even more. New traffic signals seem to have a neutral effect. So do strict inspections. And surprisingly, zebra stripes and flashing lights at crossings actually increase pedestrian injuries significantly. (That does not mean they are useless. As another leading traffic specialist, Frank Haight, has put it, the benefit of some safety measures is fair access rather than safety. They give pedestrians not absolute protection from reckless motorists but the welcome ability to cross roads that would otherwise be almost impassable.) Changing any single piece of hardware, or any law, may or may not have the desired effect.[25]

It isn't only safer equipment, then, that has brought down the rate of deaths per million passenger-miles. In fact, cause and effect might be reversed. Only when drivers start giving up speed and price to protection do manufacturers start selling safer cars. And that seems to depend on the amount of driving. The British mathematician and traffic engineer R. J. Smeed had that most remarkable gift, the ability to point out an obvious pattern that others had missed. In 1949, Smeed began to plot the relationship between fatalities per vehicle and vehicles per capita. What he found then, and what he and others have noticed ever since, is that more driving makes fatal accidents less likely per mile driven.[26]

In the late 1960s, for example, the nations with the highest fatality rates were developing countries with few private automobiles per capita. Even today within Europe, the riskiest countries are those on the periphery, like Portugal, where automobile ownership is still twenty years or more behind England or Germany. John Adams, while dissenting from Smeed's conclusions about the reasons for greater safety, found that later data supported Smeed's original 1949 paper.[27]

Smeed's observations point to a very complex process: a set of technological, legal, and social changes that more general driving brings. Countries with few roads, wide-open spaces, and few vehicles may be dangerous to motorists' health. A colleague once recalled from her childhood in Iran that on long stretches of country road, chauffeurs raced toward each other in the center, playing a local variation of chicken. Visibility was excellent, but there were no lane-dividing stripes. One driver *nearly* always turned off; the point was to wait long enough to maintain one's honor. What in the United States are adolescent rites may elsewhere be the serious contests of middle-aged men.

Early motorization's mix of human, animal, and motor power can be equally fatal. In India in the early 1980s, there were seventy-five road deaths a day, half as many as in the United States, which had forty times as many vehicles. Twenty times more people were killed in accidents than in floods. In 1989, more than a thousand died on the Grand Trunk Road from New Delhi to Calcutta alone. Uniquely Indian, or Third World? Not at all. Early in the century, New York also had a mix of animal-drawn vehicles, automobiles, streetcars, bicycles, and pedestrians, and saw casualties double during the earliest driving boom.[28]

Congestion leads to demands for limited-access roads that in turn promote safer high-speed driving. U.S. national statistics also suggest that the most dangerous roads are straight, two-lane desert highways, with the worst being the notorious U.S. 66 near Gallup, New Mexico. One study of motor-vehicle crash mortality found a hundredfold variation; in Esmeralda County, Nevada, the death rate was 558 per 100,000, while in Manhattan it was 2.5.[29] In hilly country with old roads and many new drivers, the results are similar. Whereas the United States had 248 deaths per million vehicles in 1989, Britain 248, and the Netherlands 236, Portugal had 1,163. The Portuguese-based writer Robert D. Kaplan has written of drivers on the twisting and crumbling Sintra-Lisbon highway: "Instead of going slow, they race along . . . passing on curves at night, with the ease and tranquillity of a blind person reading Braille."[30] Yet these same people are impeccably courteous pedestrians and have passed stiff written tests requiring a three-month course. The gentle Malaysians, mostly teetotaling Muslims, also reflect the spirit of early motorization. Malaysian drivers "love to pass on blind curves or approaching hills," wrote one visiting American. "They routinely ride up on each other's tails, going 50, 60, 70 miles an hour, then impertinently flash their headlights."[31]

The traffic congestion of highly motorized countries poses a chronic rather than an acute health menace. Road safety statistics do not reflect the health consequences of vehicle emissions. A car that covers ten miles in thirty minutes of rush-hour crawl produces three and a half times the hydrocarbons of one that takes eleven minutes at off-peak hours. Idling engines produce three hundred times as much carbon monoxide as those running freely. While automotive emissions were reduced by 76 to 96 percent from 1967 to 1990, the number of cities with hazardous ground-level ozone increased to over one hundred by the late 1980s. Estimates of the health and agricultural damage done by carbon monoxide and smog range from $5 billion to $16 billion per year. All of these are serious chronic consequences, but they don't alter the fact that riding in a motor vehicle has become far safer.[32]

There is an unexpected discipline in the apparently more dangerous congested road. Interstates and other limited-access highways would not be feasible without a minimum traffic volume. Density forces slower and more uniform speeds. It also makes possible greater police supervision, better rescue services, and easier access to emergency treatment facilities. The safest part of the New Jersey Turnpike is the crowded metropolitan portion north of New Brunswick; the more rural South Jersey section has twice its accident rate. And much of the reason is that congestion compels vigilance. The chairman of the Turnpike Authority explained: "[I]n the north . . . there is so much going on, you're pumping adrenaline just to stay on top of it. We're keeping you alert up here. Down there you're dozing." In fact, as Albert O. Hirschman has pointed out, proper driving is actually easier in the city than in the country. "The city traffic requires greater technical mastery, but this increase in the difficulty of driving is outweighed by the fact that intense traffic helps [the driver] in the task of focusing his attention."[33]

In spite of countless incidents of violence on the highway, in spite of all our experiences to the contrary, mature motorization seems to engender (relatively) more courteous and disciplined behavior, "collective learning" in Leonard Evans's phrase, or, as the Washington Post's Malcolm Gladwell puts it, "driving under the influence of society."[34]

A spokesman from the Insurance Institute for Highway Safety reports that while safety-related advertising once appeared to harm sales by substituting fear for fantasy, "safety is only second to quality and well ahead of price in the consumer's mind."[35] We are far from the free spirits of early motoring, of Booth Tarkington's George Amberson Miniver, of Kenneth

Grahame's Mr. Toad, "the terror, the traffic-queller, the Lord of the lone trail, before whom all must give way or be smitten into nothingness and everlasting night."[36] Or, as the columnist Richard Cohen has written, "Jay Gatsby never dreamed of gridlock."[37]

Conservation of Catastrophe?

Marine navigation and motoring alike seem to argue for optimism, for the idea that intensification can be tamed, in fact that disasters are self-correcting. Society learns. Progress, that long-despised concept, comes in by the back door. The point is not that disasters continue, but that on balance and by most measures, people continue to be better off. Unfortunately for technological optimism, things are not quite so simple.

The *Titanic*'s sinking has been moralized so much that we have to remember the incident would have turned out much differently had her plates not fractured. No one had tested (and possibly no one could have tested) metal for the kind of brittle fracture her hull experienced. Even if the crew had been able to evacuate every passenger safely, the loss of the ship would have been one of the greatest material disasters of peacetime marine history.

The disturbing fact about the accident is that we can never be completely confident of the behavior of any new material as part of a complex system. Splinters from fiber-optic cables, to take just one case, can pose serious health risks for telephone workers (and especially for self-taught laypeople) who have to cut and splice them. Yet it is rare to see this problem mentioned in most discussions of networking.

Software adds another dimension to complexity. . . . [T]he risk of fatal bugs in life-critical systems can be [very high]. Malfunction in software control of processes is also less likely to produce the warning signals familiar in the mechanical world—heat, noise, color change, vibration. A system crash may be much more sudden. It is harder to achieve what engineers call "graceful degradation."

The historian of science Michael S. Mahoney has observed that computers do not eliminate artisans but reintroduce them in the new guise of programmers. Recomplication has made software so bulky that only teams of programmers can write it, yet talented programmers are individualists who do not usually work efficiently as part of a team. This affects not only operating systems and applications software for desktop computers, but the code that runs everything from aircraft navigation to automotive fuel injection and medical equipment. As John Shore, a software engineer, has pointed out, vigilance works well for mechanical systems; high-rise elevators need constant maintenance, but they rarely injure people. Software requires maintenance, too, but this makes it less rather than more reliable. Every feature that is added and every bug that is fixed adds the possibility of some new and unexpected interaction between parts of the program. A small change to solve a minor problem may create a larger one. The technical writer Lauren Wiener has noted that the repeated paralysis of local and regional telephone systems in 1991 resulted from only a few changed lines in the millions of lines of code that drove call-routing computers. A meaningful test of the revisions would have taken thirteen weeks.[38]

Catastrophic risk will stay with us because more rather than less of life is likely to depend on complex software. Intelligent vehicle-highway systems (IVHS) may someday squeeze more capacity out of existing limited-access roads. Individual vehicles under electronic control would join formations called platoons. These convoys could be spaced more tightly than today's normal traffic. And they could control some of our daily highway nightmares, such as the tailgater, the lane jumper, and the sleepless trucker. But if software or communication or even a lead vehicle's tire failed, the results could be catastrophic. If we add the dependence of government, banking, and commerce on global electronic networks that in turn depend on software, a revival of catastrophic errors cannot be ruled out. (And the critics of IVHS insist that electronically controlled roads will soon be recongested anyway.)[39]

Even more serious than hidden risk may be displaced risk. The safety of one technology has a way of creating danger in another. Our current successes may be preparing us for failures where we least expect them. . . . [G]ood hygiene left the well-scrubbed children of the middle and upper classes more susceptible to polio than the dirty kids of the poor. . . . Mirko D. Grmek [has suggested] that success in suppressing bacterial infection indirectly promoted the rise of AIDS and other new viral infections by leaving a niche for virulent pathogens.

If hidden risk is the concern of the liberal, distrustful of corporate assurances of safety through technology, displaced risk is the objection of the conservative to regulation. And conservative skepticism is directed less often at technologies themselves than at attempts to limit, regulate, or impose them. Requiring parents to place their infants in (paid-for) child carrier seats on airlines instead of carrying them on their laps may lead more families to drive instead of fly. Since aircraft are safer than highways, the argument runs, the rule may injure more infants than would have been hurt in the air. Pesticide-free fruit and vegetables at high prices may be more harmful to public health, by reducing consumption by the poor, than cheap produce with pesticide residues would have been. Taking this line of thought to an extreme, one British researcher has even found that male physicians who quit smoking tend to offset their health gains with higher rates of alcoholism, accidents, and suicide. (Not surprisingly, tobacco industry sources supported this study.)[40]

Like hidden risks, displaced risks appear impossible to rule out of any proposed change. The natural and social worlds interact in too many poorly understood ways. Risk analysts call these unexpected effects Type III errors. (A Type I error is an unnecessary preventive step, like evacuating a coastline when storm warnings turn out to be a false alarm, or delaying the approval of a lifesaving drug. A Type II error is a decidedly harmful action like releasing a drug that turns out to have lethal side effects.) When strict directives on meat radiation after the Chernobyl meltdown of 1986 destroyed the Lapp reindeer-meat economy, as a recent report of the Royal Society pointed out, the unexpectedness of the result made it a Type III rather than a Type I error. Many market-oriented risk analysts like Aaron Wildavsky urge resilience and gradual responses to unforeseen consequences as they occur, rather than attempts to calculate and balance all possible results. The report of the Royal Society points to clearly organized schools of "anticipationism" and "resilientism." Resilience often turns out to be an excellent policy, provided the phenomena cooperate and appear distinctly and gradually on the horizon.[41]

In the real world, few trends emerge without ambiguity, beyond a reasonable doubt, before precious time is lost. It is now more than 150 years since the eccentric French utopian socialist Charles Fourier predicted that the increasing cultivation of the earth would bring about higher temperatures and eventually a melting of the polar icecap. While Fourier's scientific credentials were dubious—he thought the northern seas would become "a sort of lemonade" and humanity would move about on "antilions" and get their fish from "antisharks"—he was on to something. In fact, at about the same time, another Frenchman, coincidentally also named Fourier (the physicist Jean-Baptiste), discovered that the earth's atmosphere maintains the planet's warmth by trapping heat. As early as a hundred years ago, the Swedish geochemist Svante Arrhenius speculated on a possible increase of up to 6 degrees C. in air temperature if industrial carbon dioxide emissions continued to grow. Yet even now, the science we need most gives us not the precision we want but a set of possible tempos and consequences. We want numbers, but instead our best models give us ranges. We want a truth that will apply to the whole globe, or at least to our own continent, and face the likelihood of patchy local change. We want an idealized eighteenth-century celestial mechanics to rule our world, but we find only probabilistic models.[42]

We can't even count on conditions continuing to drift slowly. As Stephen Jay Gould and others have often reminded us, steep rather than gradual natural change is the norm, and it is extremely hard to predict the future state of a complex system even without the added imponderables of human culture and behavior. Well before climate became an issue, human culture (including technology) set off bizarre chains of cause and effect. The fashion for feathers and entire dead birds on women's hats in the late nineteenth century devastated whole species; but it also drew women and men into bird preservation movements that outlived the fad. The early automobile spread its own nemesis, the puncture weed with its tire-killing spiked seedpods. Decades after safer and puncture-resistant tubeless tires appeared, this technology unexpectedly abetted another pest: the Asian tiger mosquito, a vector for dengue fever, which traveled the Pacific in recycled tires and now enjoys an extended breeding season in water that collects in tire dumps. We have already seen how cleaning up European harbors probably helped spread tenacious zebra mussels to North America. Yet motorization also helped reduce the population of European sparrows.

Anyone correctly predicting these sequences well in advance would have seemed a crank or an alarmist. In fact, most of the greatest changes of the twentieth century simply did not occur to the nineteenth-century imagination. Air war and weapons of mass destruction were outstanding exceptions, and even these were logical extensions of pre-1900 sieges and bombardments. Otherwise the human ability to envision something truly new, good *or* bad, is surprisingly limited. Late-twentieth-century personal computers are radically different not just from nineteenth-century analytical engines and mechanical calculators but even from those (far slower) behemoths, the postwar data processors of the von Neumann era. High European mortality in tropical Asia and Africa did not prepare the Western mind for the emergence of AIDS and other "new" viruses—nor for the influenza epidemic of 1918.

Extrapolation doesn't work, because neither nature nor human society is guaranteed to act reasonably. Some things like computer processor power and data storage get better and cheaper more quickly than the optimists expected; on the other hand, the tasks that they are supposed to perform, like machine translation, turn out to be more difficult than most people had thought. What is almost a constant, though, is that the real benefits usually are not the ones that we expected, and the real perils are not those we feared. What prevail are sets of loosely calculable factors and ranges of outcomes, with no accepted procedure for choosing among them. And since we have seen that it is impossible to rid any computer models of bugs, we have no assurance that reality will not be well beyond our projected range in either direction. Instead of the malice of the isolated object, we face ever more complicated possible linkages among systems of objects.

It is impossible, then, to prove that large-scale disasters will not reassert themselves in North America and the rest of the developed world, that we will not intensify not only our chronic problems but our acute ones. William H. McNeill has a telling phrase for this possibility: the Conservation of Catastrophe. Just as engineers will continue to explore the bounds of a "safe" bridge design, test pilots will "push the envelope," regional planners will overrate the capacity of roads to evacuate a hurricane zone, and engineers will disregard all they have learned about O-rings. We can even find analogies in the realm of finance: the New Deal's precautions against the bank failures of the Depression created institutions that helped promote the wave of savings-and-loan bankruptcies of the 1980s. International electronic networks for communication and commerce make new kinds of disasters possible, as localized malfunctions now have unprecedented opportunities for spreading. If the postal carriers of one city start hoarding or discarding mail, it is a major problem but no immediate threat to the system's integrity. If a network node were to go wrong in some unforeseen way, worldwide systems could fail before the cause was even identified.

The real question is not whether new disasters will occur. Of course they will. It is whether we gain or lose ground as a result. It is whether our apparent success is part of a long-term and irreversible improvement in the human condition or a deceptive respite in a grim and open-ended Malthusian pressure of human numbers and demands against natural limits. It is whether revenge effects are getting worse or milder. I think, but cannot prove, that in the long run they are going to be good for us. And I would like to suggest why.

Retreating from Intensity

Revenge effects reached their peak in the hundred years between the 1860s and the 1960s, during the very acme of technological optimism. Clobbering nature into submission united North Americans and Europeans, Communists and Republicans. Explosives, heavy machinery, agriculture, and transportation seemed at last to be fulfilling the injunction of Genesis 1:28 to "fill the earth and subdue it." Soviet citizens named their children for Henry Ford and his tractors. Contemporaries thought they were living at the beginning of an era of open-ended change; but it is also clear that few of them reckoned with the tendency of nature to strike back. Although (as the historian Douglas Weiner has documented) Friedrich Engels himself wrote of how nature "avenges" humanity against exploitation, the Eastern Bloc kept subjugating its part of the planet until the bitter end.[43]

The real meaning of Communism's collapse had less to do, in fact, with collectivism than with a fixation on intensity that continued through the Gorbachev years. Officially the regime campaigned to conserve materials. But it also set output goals by weight, not performance. Industrial quotas, meted out in metric tons, were filled with heavy stuff—sometimes incredibly sturdy, more often simply bad. The alleged Soviet boast of producing the world's largest microchips may be apocryphal, but Marshall I. Goldman, an economist who visited the USSR often, noticed an exceptional proportion of office typewriters with unnecessary extra-long carriages.[44]

The Soviet fixation on goals by gross weight and volume was only an extreme case of the pathology of intensity: the single-minded overextension of a good thing. We should keep in mind that the West went through even more serious crises of intensification. Potatoes, a great benefit for the

European popular diet, were genetically vulnerable when grown from a single strain and used as a primary source of nutrition by the very poor. Yet terrible as the Irish potato famine of the 1840s was, nothing like it has recurred. The crash of the French raw silk industry in the 1850s, so important for Louis Pasteur's career, also showed how dangerous it could be for so many families to link their economic fate to a single organism.

It is curious how many resource-rich nations and regions have faltered because they relied too strongly on exploiting only one or two sources of natural wealth. The Mississippi delta, the deserted mining towns of the Rockies, and the desolate coal patches of the Pennsylvania anthracite country all have their counterparts overseas: Sicily, the Ukraine, and Argentina as former world breadbaskets, Romania and Azerbaijan as fabled energy reserves, Zaire and Siberia as gold vaults, the Ruhr as ironworks. The nature of the resource does not seem to matter. Nor do colonialism or foreign rule, though absentee ownership may. It was wealth that became an enemy of a vital diversity. On the other side, resource-poor islands and formerly isolated regions like Switzerland, Japan, Taiwan, and Singapore have become the twentieth century's economic stars.[45]

Of course, it is too optimistic to say that we have overcome the perils of intensity. We have already seen how "rationalized" forestry in England and Scotland has helped turn the familiar ground squirrel of North America into a significant woodland pest. The science writer Matt Ridley has described how even in Tory England, state-promoted conversion of "unproductive" downland to wheat fields and ancient forests to conifer plantations had endangered butterflies and other native wildlife and plants. In Spain and Portugal, the ancient *dehesas* of mixed cork oak and holm oak in a setting of grain and grasslands have also been threatened by clearance for Euro-subsidized crops. Elsewhere, clear-cut forestry and overfishing continue. The greatest risk of any new natural technology, especially a genetic one, is not a superpest. It is an apparently harmless organism or chemical that begins as a stunning success and displaces alternatives in the marketplace. Making anything so hardy and productive is like announcing a huge prize for the first naturally selected pests and parasites. Sooner or later there will be a big winner.[46]

All this hardly means that science or technology has overintensified life, or that traditional agriculture was always environmentally benign. In the Mediterranean and elsewhere, preindustrial agriculture could devastate as well as foster diversity; it is hard to imagine any biologically engineered organism as catastrophic in the wild as the otherwise useful and endearing goat. And technologies can follow a number of alternative paths, depending on the assumptions and interests of those who develop and support them. Technologies can help preserve old genetic resources, evaluate new crops, reduce the quantity of pesticide and herbicide applications, consume less water. In other words, they can diversify and *de*-intensify. This implies a new balance between public and market-driven research, since (as the geneticist

Richard C. Lewontin and others have shown) commercial research necessarily neglects natural, nonpatentable varieties of organisms that would be in the public domain after the first sale.

 In agriculture, the retreat from intensity means forgoing applications of heavy fertilizer in favor of planting complementary crops in the same fields, increasing both productivity and resilience. In medicine, the retreat from intensity demands a shift away from the heavy reliance on a handful of antibiotics. In business computing, it implies a heavy dose of skepticism about the functional value of "more powerful" new releases of both hardware and software. It also suggests doubts as to whether higher workloads and longer days always yield more profit; sometimes it even calls for deliberately slowing or interrupting the pace of work. In sports, it provokes a harder look at whether stiffer and more powerful equipment necessarily makes for a better game. The retreat from intensification does not necessarily require giving it up; it does mean subjecting it to much greater scrutiny.

It isn't enough, of course, to modify intensity. Reducing revenge effects demands substituting brains for stuff. And the record of human ingenuity in making brainpower do the work of energy and raw materials is impressive. Balloon-frame houses, the invention of anonymous carpenters on the nearly treeless prairies of the nineteenth-century American Midwest, became famous for their durability as well as their economy. In our own time the cheapest electronic computers available today from any discount store can calculate many times faster than the room- and building-size arrays of relays and vacuum tubes of the industry's pioneer days. Steel is lighter and stronger, yet certain plastics are lighter and stronger than steel. Automobiles now weigh less and use less gasoline per mile. A CD weighs a fraction of an LP, and a CD player is lighter and more compact than a conventional turntable. New mathematical algorithms allow the same information to be stored on smaller disks—or more information on the same size disk.

The engineer Robert Herman, the technology analyst Jesse H. Ausubel, and their associates argue that technological change exerts powerful forces both for increasing and for reducing the amount of energy and other resources used. Electronic storage can reduce the consumption of paper, but . . . it can also multiply it. Lighter goods may heighten rather than diminish the need for materials if they are marketed or treated as throwaways rather than durables. (Thick, returnable glass bottles may, for example, demand less intense use of energy and other resources than even recyclable aluminum.) In fact, as Herman and Ausubel have suggested, lighter and more efficient automobiles promote resource-consuming if dispersed suburban living and thus materialization. Nuclear power generation begins with low-weight raw materials but ends with vast contaminated structures that probably can never be reused.[47]

What appears to be a technological question—how much of anything we really need—is in the end a social one. It is the size and appearance of a yard or a lawn or a house, the taste for (or repudiation of) meat, and so forth.

Often what is most crucial, and most uncertain, is not invention and discovery but taste and preference. The open question, raised during the upheavals of the 1970s and then forgotten during the boom of the 1980s, is whether cultural change can lead to new preferences that will in turn relieve humanity's pressure on the earth's resources. Human culture, not some inherent will of the machine, has created most revenge effects. Without the taste for silk, there would have been no gypsy moths in North America. Without the preference for detached housing, there would still be congestion, perhaps, but more economical congestion. Without the love of oceanside living, shore erosion yes, but no social disruption.

Even more promising than diversification and dematerialization is an attitude that has not yet found its rightful name. It is the substitution of cunning for the frontal attack, and it is not new. It began with immunization against smallpox—as we have seen, a folk practice long before Edward Jenner introduced it to medicine—and continued with the vaccines of the late nineteenth and twentieth centuries.

Finesse means abandoning frontal attacks for solutions that rely on the same kind of latent properties that led to revenge effects in the first place. Sometimes it means ceasing to suppress a symptom. In medicine, finesse suggests closer attention to the evolutionary background of human health and illness, to the positive part that fever plays, for example, in fighting infection. At other times, finesse means living with and even domesticating a problem organism. As we have seen, researchers like Stanley Falkow and Paul Ewald have suggested a kind of evolutionary compromise with what are now lethal bacteria and viruses, turning them into common but harmless companions. In the office, finesse means producing more by taking more frequent breaks and conveying more information by, for example, limiting rather than multiplying color schemes. In construction, finesse means allowing skyscrapers to sway slightly in the wind instead of bracing them to resist it. On the road, finesse means a calmer approach to driving, improving the speed and economy of all drivers by slowing them down at times when impulse would prompt accelerating. It can mean moving more traffic by metering access to some roads and even closing off others. (Some German analysts have written of the "softening," *Besänftigung,* of traffic.) Diversification, dematerialization, and finesse are far from a rejection of science. To the contrary, it is science that points us away from crude reductionism and counterproductive brute force toward technologies that improve human life. But the improvement has a cost.

As the Red Queen said in *Through the Looking-Glass,* we are no longer in the "slow sort of country" where running gets one somewhere: "Now, *here,* you see, it takes all the running you can do, to keep in the same place. If you want to get somewhere else, you must run at least twice as fast as that!" And in fact the alternatives to the intensified, revenge-prone modes of earlier technology seem to take nearly all the running we can do. Even the optimistic report of the Council for Agricultural Science and Technology (CAST) makes clear that most of our agricultural research goes to "maintenance," that is, to keeping the gains we have made: dealing with deteriorating water quality and increasing costs, and offsetting "biological surprises like the appearance of more virulent pests." The same could probably be said of many medical efforts. Similarly, the power of personal computer hardware seems driven by the need to compensate for the way that more elaborate interfaces and features slow the fundamentals of performance.[48]

Technological optimism means in practice the ability to recognize bad surprises early enough to do something about them. And that demands constant monitoring of the globe, for everything from changes in mean temperatures and particulates to traffic in bacteria and viruses. It also requires a second level of vigilance at increasingly porous national borders against the world exchange of problems. But vigilance does not end there. It is everywhere. It is in the random alertness tests that have replaced the "dead man's pedal" for train operators. It is in the rituals of computer backup, the legally mandated testing of everything from elevators to home smoke alarms, routine X-ray screening, securing and loading new computer-virus definitions. It is in the inspection of arriving travelers for products that might harbor pests. Even our alertness in crossing the street, second nature to urbanites now, was generally unnecessary before the eighteenth century. Sometimes vigilance is more of a reassuring ritual than a practical precaution, but with any luck it works. Revenge effects mean in the end that we will move ahead but must always look back just because reality is indeed gaining on us.   ∎

NOTES

1. John Tierney, "Betting on the Planet," *New York Times Magazine,* 2 December 1990, 52.

2. David S. Landes, *Revolution in Time: Clocks and the Making of the Modern World* (Cambridge, Mass.: Harvard University Press, 1983), 103–13; Robert K. Merton, *Science, Technology, and Society in Seventeenth-Century England* (New York: Harper Torchbooks, 1970 [1938]), 167–77.

3. Derek Howse, *Greenwich Time and the Discovery of the Longitude* (Oxford: Oxford University Press, 1980), 44–72.

4. David S. Landes, *Revolution in Time: Clocks and the Making of the Modern World* (Cambridge, Mass.: Harvard University Press, 1983), 103–13, 144–57.

5. See Paul Slovic, "Perception of Risk," *Science,* vol. 236, no. 4799 (17 April 1987), 280–85; and Paul Slovic, "Perception of Risk: Reflections on the Psychometric Paradigm," in Sheldon Krimsky and Dominic Golding, eds., *Social Theories of Risk* (Westport, Conn.: Praeger, 1992), 117–52.

6. John P. Eaton and Charles A. Haas, *Titanic: Triumph and Tragedy* (New York: Norton, 1987), 310–11; Edward Bryant, *Natural Hazards* (Cambridge: Cambridge University Press, 1991), 68.

7. James T. Yenckel, "How Safe Is Cruising?," *Washington Post,* 11 August 1991, E6.

8. See Henry Petroski, *To Engineer Is Human: The Role of Failure in Successful Design* (New York: St. Martin's Press, 1985).

9. Mark F. Grady, "Torts: The Best Defense Against Regulation," *Wall Street Journal,* 3 September 1992, A11; Mark F. Grady, "Why Are People Negligent? Technology, Nondurable Precautions, and the Medical Malpractice Explosion," *Northwestern University Law Review,* vol. 82 (Winter 1988), 297–99, 312. See also Grady's review of Paul C. Weiler's *Medical Malpractice on Trial,* "Better Medicine Causes More Lawsuits, and New Administrative Courts Will Not Solve the Problem," *Northwestern University Law Review,* vol. 86 (Summer 1992), 1068–81.

10. On seventeenth-century navigation, see Landes, *Revolution in Time,* 105–11; Carla Rahn Phillips, *Six Galleons for the King of Spain* (Baltimore: Johns Hopkins University Press, 1986), 129–34. On Shovell's tomb: Margaret Whitney, *Sculpture in Britain, 1530 to 1830* (Baltimore: Penguin, 1964), 58. There is probably more to late-nineteenth- and early-twentieth-century litigation than Grady acknowledges: the deference shown by judges and juries of the time toward elite defendants in tort liability cases. To name just three other notorious cases, the industrialists' club that maintained the dam that broke and caused the Johnstown flood in 1889 (2,200 dead), the owners of the *General Slocum,* which caught fire in New York Harbor in 1904 (1,021 dead), and the proprietors of the Triangle Shirtwaist Factory, which burned with 145 dead, escaped civil and criminal action. Even with Astors, Wideners, and Guggenheims among the *Titanic* passengers and the victims' families, the final settlement with the White Star Line was minuscule by late-twentieth-century standards: $663,000 (£136,701) on total claims of $16,804,112 (£3,464,765). See Eaton and Haas, *Titanic,* 277–79.

11. James C. Beniger, *The Control Revolution: Technological and Economic Origins of the Information Society* (Cambridge, Mass.: Harvard University Press, 1986), 221–26 and references.

12. Clay McShane, *Down the Asphalt Path: The Automobile and the American City* (New York: Columbia University Press, 1994), 42–45.

13. Christopher Gray, "Who Holds the Reins of Fate of a 1907 Horse-Auction Mart?" *New York Times,* 8 November 1987, Real Estate, 14; McShane, *Asphalt Path,* 51–54.

14. Daniel Pool, *What Jane Austen Ate and Charles Dickens Knew* (New York: Simon & Schuster, 1993), 250–51; McShane, *Asphalt Path,* 46–50; for a summary of modern fatalities, Leonard Evans, *Traffic Safety and the Driver* (New York: Van Nostrand Reinhold, 1991), 3.

15. Scott L. Bottles, *Los Angeles and the Automobile: The Making of the Modern City* (Berkeley: University of California Press, 1987), 22.

16. On powers and interests in highway building, see Mark H. Rose, *Interstate: Express Highway Politics, 1941–1956* (Lawrence: University Press of Kansas, 1979).

17. Mark S. Foster, *From Streetcar to Superhighway: American City Planners and Urban Transportation, 1900–1940* (Philadelphia: Temple University Press, 1981), 143–45; "Onwards and Outwards," *Economist,* vol. 333, no. 7885 (15 October 1994), 31.

18. Cited in Anatole Kopp, *Town and Revolution: Soviet Architecture and City Planning, 1917–1935* (New York: Braziller, 1970), 173. The Disurbanists (or Deurbanists) actually had in mind the relocation of urban functions along great highways, not the present American suburban pattern.

19. Kenneth Jackson, *Crabgrass Frontier: The Suburbanization of the United States* (New York: Oxford University Press, 1985), 249.

20. K. H. Schaeffer and Elliot Sclar, *Access for All: Transportation and Urban Growth* (Baltimore: Penguin, 1975), 40–44.

21. Ivan Illich, *Energy and Equity* (New York: Harper & Row, 1974), 18–19.

22. Ibid., 95–96; David Remnick, "Berserk on the Beltway," *Washington Post Magazine*, 7 September 1986, 66ff, 95; "Urban Freeways, Interstates in a Jam," *USA Today*, 18 September 1989, 10A; John F. Harris, "Auto Club, Citing Traffic, to Shut Fairfax Office," *Washington Post*, 1 October 1986.

23. Richard Arnott and Kenneth Small, "The Economics of Traffic Congestion," *American Scientist*, vol. 82, no. 5 (September–October 1994), 446–55; Bob Holmes, "When Shock Waves Hit Traffic," *New Scientist*, vol. 142, no. 1931 (25 June 1994), 36–40.

24. "Risk Homeostasis and the Purpose of Safety Regulation," *Ergonomics*, vol. 31, no. 4 (1988), 408–9.

25. Evans, *Traffic Safety*, 287–90; Haight remarks in telephone interview, October 1991.

26. R. J. Smeed and G. O. Jeffcoate, "Effects of Changes in Motorisation in Various Countries on the Number of Road Fatalities," *Traffic Engineering and Control*, vol. 12, no. 3 (July 1970), 150–51.

27. John Adams, "Smeed's Law and the Emperor's New Clothes," in Leonard Evans and Richard C. Schwing, eds., *Human Behavior and Traffic Safety* (New York: Plenum Press, 1985), 195–96, 235–37.

28. William K. Stevens, "When It Comes to Highway Chaos, India is No. 1," *New York Times*, 26 October 1983, A2; Steve Coll, " 'Road Kings' Truck Across India," *Washington Post*, 28 October 1989, A1; McShane, *Asphalt Path*, 174–77.

29. "Drivin' My Life Away," *Scientific American*, vol. 257, no. 2 (August 1987), 28, 30; Susan P. Baker, R. A. Whitefield, and Brian O'Neill, "Geographic Variations in Mortality from Motor Vehicle Crashes," *New England Journal of Medicine*, vol. 316, no. 22 (28 May 1987), 1384–87.

30. "In Portugal, Wheels of Misfortune," *New York Times*, 22 July 1990, Travel, 39.

31. Deborah Fallows, "Malaysia's Mad Motorists," *Washington Post*, 10 July 1988, C5.

32. James J. MacKenzie, Roger C. Dower, and Donald D. T. Chen, *The Going Rate: What It Really Costs to Drive* (Washington: World Resources Institute, 1992), 13.

33. Angus Kress Gillespie and Michael Aaron Rockland, *Looking for America on the New Jersey Turnpike* (New Brunswick, N.J.: Rutgers University Press, 1989), 114–15; Albert O. Hirschman, *The Strategy of Economic Development* (New Haven, Conn.: Yale University Press, 1958), 134, 143–45. Hirschman also points out that "a road that is not traveled is likely to deteriorate sooner than one that has to support heavy traffic: the former will surely be neglected whereas there is some hope that the latter will be maintained." Because bituminous surfaces show deterioration early, they may be more suitable for less-traveled roads in developing countries than gravel would be. They don't degrade gracefully, as electrical engineers put it; they demand attention.

34. "How Driving Under the Influence of Society Affects Traffic Deaths," *Washington Post*, 2 September 1991, A3.

35. Charles Stile, "N.J. Drivers Yielding to Safety," *Trenton Times*, 15 September 1991, A1.

36. Kenneth Grahame, *The Wind in the Willows* (New York: Charles Scribner's Sons, 1961), 121.

37. "Jay Gatsby Never Dreamed of Gridlock," *Trenton Times*, 19 November 1991, A18.

38. Michael S. Mahoney, personal communication; John Shore, "Why I Never Met a Programmer I Could Trust," *Communications of the ACM*, vol. 31, no. 4 (April 1988), 372; Wiener, *Digital Woes*, 99–100.

39. For the most useful recent summary of the vast literature on road issues, see the special issue of *CQ Researcher*, vol. 4, no. 17 (6 May 1994), 385–408.

40. P. N. Lee, "Has the Mortality of Male Doctors Improved with the Reductions in Their Cigarette Smoking?" *British Medical Journal*, 15 December 1979, 1538–40.

41. *Risk: Analysis, Perception, and Management* (London: Royal Society, 1992), 155–59, 138–42.

42. See Jonathan Beecher, *Charles Fourier: The Visionary and His World* (Berkeley: University of California Press, 1987), 338–41; Spencer Weart, "From the Nuclear Frying Pan into the Global Fire," *Bulletin of the Atomic Scientists*, vol. 48, no. 5 (June 1992), 18–27.

43. See Douglas R. Weiner, *Models of Nature* (Bloomington: University of Indiana Press, 1988), 195, for Engels's article "The Role of Labor in the Transformation from Ape to Man" as a rallying point for Soviet conservationists. Their opponents insisted that Engels meant only abusive capitalist development, not dialectically informed socialist intervention.

44. On early Soviet production quotas and the technological conservatism they encouraged, see Kendall E. Bailes, *Technology and Society Under Lenin and Stalin* (Princeton, N.J.: Princeton University Press, 1978), 350; Marshall I. Goldman, *What Went Wrong with Perestroika* (New York: Norton, 1991), 87; Marshall I. Goldman, *Gorbachev's Challenge* (New York: Norton, 1987), 123–24. Let those who have never used a Pentium computer to compose a yard-sale announcement cast the first stone.

45. The superiority of knowledge and the proper work ethic to wealth in resources became a watchword of 1980s reformers. Nathan Glazer's "Two Inspiring Lessons of the 1980s," *New York Times*, 24 December 1989, Review, 11, even suggests that some resources like the agricultural lands of Europe and Japan with their heavily subsidized surplus crops are becoming "a positive burden to economic success."

46. Matt Ridley, "Butterflies Fall Victim to Man's Interfering Hand," *Sunday Telegraph*, 17 July 1994, 32; Malcolm Smith, "Science: Live the High Life and Save the Wildlife," *Independent*, 30 May 1994, 19.

47. Robert Herman, Siamak A. Ardekani, and Jesse H. Ausubel, "Dematerialization," *Technological Forecasting and Social Change*, vol. 38 (1990), 333–47.

48. Lewis Carroll, *Through the Looking-Glass*, in *The Complete Works of Lewis Carroll* (New York: Modern Library, n.d. [1896 edn.]), 164; "How Much Land Can Ten Billion People Spare for Nature?," Council for Agricultural Science and Technology Task Force Report 121 (February 1994), 26.

■ *QUESTIONS FOR MAKING CONNECTIONS WITHIN THE READING* ■

1. First, define and explain one of Tenner's key terms, such as "revenge effects," "intensiveness," "technological optimists," "signal event," "homeostasis," "complex system," "recomplication," "extrapolation," "intensity," or "finesse." Next, try to connect the key term that you have chosen with the other key terms. Finally, develop a key term of your own that names an event or process Tenner describes but does not himself name.

2. On the basis of your reading of "Another Look Back, and a Look Ahead," would you describe Tenner as a "technological optimist"? How can

anyone claim to be an optimist about technology if it is, as Tenner concedes, "extremely hard"—and perhaps even impossible—"to predict the future state of a complex system even without the added imponderables of human culture and behavior"? Is it possible that technological innovation will reach a point of diminishing returns, when the costs of innovation, or the dangers, outweigh the potential benefits? Does Tenner ever consider this possibility?

3. In what ways does Tenner's discussion of new technologies confirm his belief that progress "comes in by the back door"? To what degree does technological change take place in response to people's needs and their conscious choices? To what degree does technology shape those needs and choices? On the basis of Tenner's examples, would it be fair to say that technology has a life of its own that no one can control, or would such a claim be an exaggeration?

■ *QUESTIONS FOR WRITING* ■

1. The last two centuries have brought about technological change on a scale and at a pace that nobody in any prior age could have imagined. In fact, the pace of change has grown so quickly that we expect innovations to outstrip our predictions. Under these conditions, will it ever be possible to say "no" to technology? Many people believe, for example, that the automobile has diminished the quality of American life in many ways—by polluting the air and allowing suburban sprawl to gobble up the countryside, and by depopulating cities and erasing the local cultures of towns and neighborhoods. Perhaps the most remarkable thing about cars is the rapidity of their development—too rapid, perhaps, for anyone to stop and weigh the consequences. If technology now exceeds human control, do we need to rethink the trust we place in it?

2. How has Tenner's account changed the way you think about technology? Ordinarily, we view technology in a number of different lights: as a neutral instrument or tool; as a miraculous gift; as a specialized pursuit, far removed from human feelings; as a form of knowledge synonymous with science; as a Frankensteinlike monster; as an extension of the marketplace. In what ways does Tenner complicate and perhaps even contradict these commonsense ways of viewing technology? Is it naive to think that we have created technology simply to make our lives better and easier? Does technology express an aspect of ourselves we ordinarily overlook? Other than comfort and security, what satisfactions do we derive from its creation?

■ *QUESTIONS FOR MAKING CONNECTIONS BETWEEN READINGS* ■

1. Tenner assures us that progress, in spite of all the complications, "comes in by the back door." In making this claim, he seems to believe that a self-correcting process will usually operate with "intensity" followed by "disaster," which produces "precaution" and finally "vigilance." Is this argument confirmed, extended, complicated, or refuted by Charles Siebert's account of the transformation of elephant behavior worldwide? That is, can Tenner's account of how technology advances be used to explain transformations in other areas of human experience? Is human engagement with the animal kingdom a self-correcting system?

2. Both Tenner and Steven Johnson in his essay, "The Myth of the Ant Queen," ask their readers to reconsider the role of technological innovation in the rise of contemporary society. Would both authors agree that it makes sense to be a "technological optimist"? Or would they say that technological optimism is just an expression of wishful thinking—a hope that things will turn out well when they actually might not? Does it make sense to think that the "emergent systems" Johnson describes tend to find solutions automatically, even when the people or life-forms involved remain blissfully unaware? Or is it essential that we recognize and consciously attempt to solve the problems we have created?

ROBERT THURMAN

ROBERT THURMAN, ONE of the first Americans to be ordained as a Tibetan Buddhist monk, is often considered to be the most prominent and influential expert on Buddhism in the United States today. A scholar, translator, activist, and lecturer (as well as father to the renowned actress Uma Thurman), Thurman began his explorations into Buddhism in his early twenties when he traveled to India on a "vision quest" and ended up becoming a student of the Dalai Lama. Upon returning to the United States, Thurman wanted to continue his studies and become an academic because, in his own words, "[t]he only lay institution in America comparable to monasticism is the university." Thurman is currently the Jey Tsong Khapa Professor of Indo-Tibetan Buddhist Studies at Columbia University and the president of Tibet House, a nonprofit organization dedicated to the study and preservation of Tibetan culture.

Infinite Life (2004) is one of the most recent in a series of books that Thurman has written on Buddhism. Chief among his goals in this text is to guide laypeople into their first explorations of the Buddhist concept of selflessness. The ultimate goal of the lessons that Thurman offers his readers is to impart a deeper sense of interconnectedness, a process that is meant to reduce the negative feelings individuals hold about themselves and to increase the positive feelings they have for others. In doing so, Thurman seeks to show that the happiness America's founders guaranteed "should be ours and that there are methods for discovering which happiness is really reliable and satisfying, and then securing that in an enduring way without depriving others."

Thurman, Robert. "Wisdom." *Infinite Life.* Riverhead Books, Penguin, 2004. 49–71.

Biographical information and quotations come from Thurman's Web site, <http://www.bobthurman.com/>, and from <http://literati.net/Thurman/index.htm>.

Wisdom

Preamble: Selflessness

At one point in the early 1970s, after I'd gotten my Ph.D. and started teaching Buddhism, I went back to visit my old teacher, the Mongolian lama Geshe Wangyal. We were working on a project to translate a Buddhist scientific text from the Tibetan. We were six or seven people gathered around a kitchen table, and Geshe-la began to talk about the inner science of Buddhist psychology, the Abhidharma. He was reading us a few verses about the insight of selflessness, the deep release of becoming unbound, when I began to feel a little dizzy, even nauseous. It was a funny feeling. It felt slightly like a vibration spinning in my head. The vibration came not from Geshe-la, but from this ancient tradition. It was as though my habitual mind couldn't quite find traction. I realized that if I fought it, the sensation would only get more nerve-wracking and I would only feel more nauseous. So I didn't fight it. Instead, I let go and relaxed, and soon I was able to orient myself in another way, away from my "self." I felt like I was slowly but surely loosening my self-centered perspective on life and the world. In a useful way, a strengthening way, I was beginning to experience the great Buddhist mystery that is the selflessness of subjects and objects.

The Buddha based his psychology on his discovery of actual and ultimate reality. This he called "selflessness" and "voidness," or "emptiness." Some people love these words from the moment they hear them, but others are frightened by them. People often ask me, "Why did Buddha have to be such a downer? Obviously nirvana is a happy, cheerful state. So why didn't he just call it 'bliss' or something? Why did he have to label the reality he discovered with negative words such as 'voidness,' 'emptiness,' and 'selflessness'?" When people respond negatively to these terms, it's often because they're worried that the words imply they are going to die, disappear, or go crazy in their attempts to seek enlightenment. And that's exactly why the Buddha called reality by those names. He did it on purpose, to liberate you! Why? Because the only thing that's frightened by the word "selflessness" is the artificially constructed, unreal, and unrealistic self. That self is only a pretend self, it lacks reality, it doesn't really exist. That pseudo-self seems to quiver and quake because the habit that makes it seem real wants to keep its hold on you. So if you're seeking happiness and freedom, then you should want to scare the heck out of your "self"—you want to scare it right out of your head!

Actually, *it* is constantly scaring the heck out of *you*. Your "self" is always busy terrorizing you. You have a terrorist in your own brain, coming out of your own instincts and culture, who is pestering you all the time. "Don't relax too much," it is saying, "you'll get stepped on. A bug will bite you. Someone will be nasty to you. You'll get passed by, abused, sick. Don't be honest. Pretend. Because if you're honest, they'll hurt you." And it's ordering you, "Be my slave. Do what I tell you to do. Keep me installed up here at this very superficial level of the brain where I sit in my weird Woody Allen–type cockpit. Because I'm in control." Your falsely perceived, fixated, domineering self is precisely what's getting between you and a fulfilling life.

Early on, some of the Western psychologists who were beginning to learn from the Buddhist tradition—members of the transpersonal and other movements—came up with the idea that the relationship between Buddhist and Western psychology is this: "Western psychology helps somebody who feels they are nobody become somebody, and Buddhist psychology helps somebody who feels they are somebody become nobody." When I first heard this, I was at an Inner Science conference with the Dalai Lama. Everybody laughed, applauded, and thought it was a great insight. The Dalai Lama just looked at me and kind of winked and was too polite to say anything. I started to jump up to make a comment, but he stopped me. He told me to be quiet and let all of them ponder it for a few years until they realized the flaw in their thinking. Because of course that idea is not even remotely correct.

The purpose of realizing your own selflessness is not to feel like you are nobody. After he became enlightened, the Buddha did not sit under a tree drooling, and saying "Oh, wow! I'm nobody!" Think about it: If he just "became nobody," if he escaped from the world through self-obliteration, then he wouldn't have been able to share so many teachings here on earth, to work for the good of all beings for years and years, long after he achieved nirvana. He would've just stayed in his "nobody" state and forgotten about all of us poor humans busy suffering through our miserable lives.

The reason why we sometimes think that the goal of Buddhism is just "to become nobody" is that we don't understand the concept of selflessness. "Selflessness" does not mean that we are nobody. It does not mean that we cease to exist. Not at all. There is no way you can ever "not exist," just as you cannot become "nothing." Even if you go through deep meditation into what is called "the realm of absolute nothingness," you will still exist. Even if you are so freaked out by a tragedy, such as losing your only child, that you try to end your existence completely, you will still exist. I have a healthy respect for tragedy. We do have terrible tragedies. Personally, I don't bear misfortune well; it knocks me out. But there is no way to become nobody. Even if you were to succeed in killing yourself, you will be shocked when you awaken to disembodied awareness, out-of-body but still a somebody, a ghostly wraith who wishes he hadn't just done that. And a terribly unfortunate living person who has been so brutalized that he blanks out who he was in a seemingly impenetrable psychosis is still somebody, as everybody else around him knows.

Our mind is so powerful that it can create a state of absolute nothing-ness that seems totally concrete. Thousands of yogis in the history of India and a few mystics in the West have entered such a state of nothingness. But no one can stay there forever, and it is not where you want to be.

Have you ever had a minor experience of nothingness? I've had it in the dentist's chair with sodium pentothal, because I used to eat a lot of sweets and not brush my teeth as a youngster so I had to have teeth pulled. They give you this knockout anesthetic, and if you are a hard-working intellec-tual, you are tired of your mind, so you think, "Oh great, I'm going to be obliterated for a little while." You're really pleased, and you feel this little buzz, and you're just about to get there. You're going to experience nothing-ness, a little foretaste of the nihilistic notion of nirvana! But suddenly the nurse is shaking you awake saying, "You've been slobbering in that chair long enough. Get out of here." It's over. You started to pass out, wanting to be gone, but now you're suddenly back with no sense of having been gone at all! And that's what it is like in the state of absolute nothingness. It's like being passed out in the dentist's chair. There's no sense of duration of time. But eventually you wake up, totally disoriented with a nasty headache, and you never even got to enjoy the oblivion.

So we can never become nothing, as appealing as that may sound to those who are addicted to the idea of nothingness after death. We are always somebody, even though we are selfless in reality. We are just different sorts of "somebodies" than we used to be. "Realizing your selflessness" does not mean that you become a nobody, it means that you become the type of somebody who is a viable, useful somebody, not a rigid, fixated, I'm-the-center-of-the-universe, isolated-from-others somebody. You become the type of somebody who is over the idea of a conceptually fixated and self-created "self," a pseudo-self that would actually be absolutely weak, because of being unrelated to the reality of your constantly changing nature. You be-come the type of somebody who is content never to be quite that sure of who you are—always free to be someone new, somebody more.

That's the whole point of selflessness. If you don't know exactly who you are all the time, you're not sick, you're actually in luck, because you're more realistic, more free, and more awake! You're being too intelligent to be stuck inside one frozen mask of personality! You've opened up your wis-dom, and you've realized that "knowing who you are" is the trap—an im-possible self-objectification. None of us knows who we really are. Facing that and then becoming all that we can be—astonishing, surprising, amazing—always fresh and new, always free to be more, brave enough to become a work in progress, choosing happiness, open-mindedness, and love over certitude, rigidity, and fear—this is realizing selflessness!

I never met the late, great comedian Peter Sellers, except splitting my sides in laughter while watching some of his movies, especially the *Pink Panther* series. I know he had his ups and downs in his personal life, though you can't believe all the things you hear from the tabloids. But I did read a quote from him, or maybe from his psychiatrist, that he was deeply troubled and distressed because he suffered from "not knowing who he really was." He would get into his roles as an actor so totally, he would think he was the person he was playing, and he couldn't find himself easily as his "own" person. So he suffered, feeling himself "out of control" in his life. When I read this, my heart went out to him. I imagined his psychiatrist sternly telling him he had better calm down and track himself down, and put a lid on his ebullient sense of life, leading him on and on in self-absorption in therapy under the guise that he was going to "find himself" once and for all. I, feeling a bit more freed by having awakened to even the tiniest taste of selflessness, wanted to cry out to Peter Sellers, "Stop suffering by thinking your insight is confusion! Don't listen to the misknowing and even fear your freedom! Learn to surf the energy of life that surges through your openness! You have discovered your real self already, your great self of selflessness, and that openness is what enables you to manifest the heart that shines through your work and opens the hearts of your audiences. Your gift is to release them into laughter, itself a taste of freedom! Why be confused and feel your great gift is something wrong?" But I didn't know him so I could not tell him what I'm telling you. But our lives are infinite and I will be telling his ongoing life-form one of these days, whether I recognize him or not!

The Buddha was happy about not knowing who he was in the usual rigid, fixed sense. He called the failure to know who he was "enlightenment." Why? Because he realized that selflessness kindles the sacred fire of compassion. When you become aware of your selflessness, you realize that any way you feel yourself to be at any time is just a relational, changing construction. When that happens, you have a huge inner release of compassion. Your inner creativity about your living self is energized, and your infinite life becomes your ongoing work of art.

You see others caught in the suffering of the terminal self-habit and you feel real compassion. You feel so much better, so highly relieved, that your only concern is helping those constricted other people. You are free to worry about them because, of course, they are having a horrible time trying to know who they are and trying to be who they think they should be! They are busy being ripped apart by the great streams of ignorance, illness, death, and other people's irritating habits. So they suffer. And you, in your boundless, infinitely interconnected, compassionate state, can help them.

This is the other crucial point about selflessness: It does not mean that you are disconnected. Even nirvana is not a state of disconnection from the world. There is no way to become removed from yourself or from other beings. We are ultimately boundless—that is to say, our relative boundaries are permeable. But we are still totally interconnected no matter what we do.

You cannot disappear into your own blissful void, because you are part of everyone and they are part of you. If you have no ultimate self, that makes you free to be your relative self, along with other beings. It's as if your hand represents the universe and your fingers represent all beings. Each of your fingers can wiggle on its own, each can operate independently, just as each being has its own identity. And yet your fingers are part of your hand. If your hand did not exist, your fingers would not exist. You are one of many, many fingers on the hand that is all life.

To my surprise and delight, I learned recently that even some Western psychologists are now beginning to study and understand the harm done by self-centered thinking. The psychologist Dr. Larry Scherwitz conducted a study about type A people—the aggressive, loud, annoying types, like me. Scientists used to think that type As died younger because of their fast-paced, stressful lives. But this new study reveals that, in fact, some of us type A people are not going to die of a heart attack that soon after all. The type Bs out there, the mild-mannered, quiet, inward-focused types, might find this worrisome! We may stay around for years bothering them, because it turns out that the type A personality is not a risk factor for coronary heart disease or other stress-related health problems. It turns out that some people, like me, though we freak out all the time, are not always that stressed. Some of us actually enjoy being this way.

What is the real risk factor, then? Scherwitz and his colleagues reanalyzed the data and conducted some new studies. They discovered, by analyzing the speech patterns of type As and type Bs, that the high risk of heart disease and stress-related illness is correlated with the *amount of self-reference* in people's speech—the amount of self-preoccupation, self-centeredness, and narcissism. "Me, me, I, I, my, my, mine. mine. My golf course, my country club, my job, my salary, my way, my family, my religion, my shrine, my guru, my, my, mine." The more "I, me, my, and mine" there is in their speech—"mine" most of all—the more likely they are to succumb to stress, to keel over because their bodies revolt against that pressure of self-involvement. Whereas even though some people can be aggressive, annoying, loud, and seemingly "stressed," if their overall motivation is altruistic and they don't pay too much attention to themselves, they live longer. And the quiet type Bs who are also more concerned about others, not necessarily out of any altruistic religious inklings, but just naturally not paying much attention to themselves, tend to live longer, too.

I find this study amazing. I was with the Dalai Lama when he heard about the results. He was intrigued and very pleased. "Oh, really?" he said. "Let me see that paper. In Buddhist psychology, we also have this idea that obsessive self-preoccupation—possessiveness and selfishness and self-centeredness—is life's chief demon!"

Let us explore the problems created by this demon of self-preoccupation, the ways in which it causes us suffering. We will then practice a fundamental meditation in which we look for the fixated self and find that it does not, after all, exist. Once we have freed ourselves from the constricting habit of always thinking that we are the center of the universe, we will experience our first taste of the boundless joy and compassion that is infinite life.

Problem: Misknowledge and Self-Preoccupation

One of the hardest things we have to do on a regular basis is to admit that we are wrong. We stubbornly insist that we're right in situations where we're not quite sure if we are, and even when we sense that we've slipped. How much more indignant do we become when we feel certain that we're right and someone has the gall or the stupidity to challenge us? In this case, we feel an absolute imperative to jump up and trumpet our rightness. If we still cannot get others to agree with us, we soon become self-righteous and then outraged.

Believe it or not, the fact that we struggle so much with being wrong is of tremendous importance to our task of awakening to the reality of selflessness. We should examine our habit of needing to be right carefully to see why it feels so good.

Being right means that the world affirms us in what we think we know. "Knowing" something is a way of controlling it, being able to put it in its proper place in relation to us so that we can use it effectively. As Dharmakirti, the seventh century Indian philosopher, said, "All successful action is preceded by accurate knowledge." So knowledge is power, in the sense that it empowers us to act successfully. Misknowledge, misunderstanding a situation, is weakness, in the sense that our actions may fail in their aim, backfire, or have unintended consequences. Knowledge is security, in that we know our vulnerabilities and can avoid harm. Misknowledge is danger, in that we don't know what others might do to us or what traps may await us. We therefore feel powerful and secure when we're right, weak and vulnerable when we're wrong.

Viewed in this context, being right seems like a struggle for survival, a drive to win. It's natural for us to cling to that feeling, even when we have not investigated the reality around us because we don't really want to know if we are wrong. We think that finding ourselves in the wrong means a loss of power and safety, forgetting that actually *it is the only way* for us to discover what is truly right and truly wrong, thereby gaining real power and real safety. When we pretend, we focus our attention on appearing to be right no matter what the reality, we distract ourselves from being awake to what really is going on, and so place ourselves at a disempowering disadvantage.

In light of this simple analysis, what lies at the center of our constant need to assure our rightness and, therefore, our power and security? Is it not the certainty that "I am"? Does not the strong sense of "I am" seem absolutely right, unquestionable, in fact? Every self-identification, judgment, and impulse beginning with "I am"—"I am me," "I am American," "I am human," "I am male," "I am right," "I am sure," "I am angry"—seems natural, undeniable, imperative. As such, we are habitually driven to obey in feelings, thoughts, words, and deeds whatever comes from within the inexhaustible fountain of I am's, I think's, I want's, I love's, I hate's, and I do's. "I" is the absolute captain of our ship, the agent of our fate, the master of our lives.

When apes or bulls or mountain goats snort and paw the ground and then charge head first at one another, we interpret their behavior as an "I" versus "I" contest, sometimes to the death. Similarly, the imperative issuing from our "I" can be so adamant, so unchallengeable, that we human beings, too, will sacrifice our lives. Just think of the nature of such statements as follows, when the "I" is aligned with country, church, God, family, race, gender, or species: "I am a patriot!" "I am a Protestant!" "I am a Catholic!" "I am a Christian!" "I am a Muslim!" "I am a believer!" "I am an atheist!" "I am white!" "I am a male!" "I am human!" In these situations, the "I" exercises tremendous power over us, and can often lead us to our death.

The "I," the ego-self seemingly absolutely resident in the heart of our being, is the one thing of which we each are absolutely certain, which we will die for, which we will kill for, which we will obey slavishly and unquestioningly throughout our lives. We are so accustomed to our habitual sense of self that we consider even the slightest absence of it—a moment of derangement, a loss of consciousness in fainting or deep sleep, a disorienting distraction of passion or terror, a dizzying state of drunkenness or drug-intoxication, a psychological or neurological disorder—absolutely terrifying. We can't imagine our lives without our "I" as a constant, demanding presence.

What is shocking and difficult for most Westerners to accept is that the Buddha discovered that this most certain knowledge of the "self" is actually "misknowledge"—a fundamental misunderstanding, a delusion. And what's more, he realized that this discovery was the key to liberation, the gateway to enlightenment. When he saw the false nature of the "I," he emitted his "lion's roar," pronouncing the reality of selflessness, identitylessness, voidness. This was his *Eureka!* moment, his scientific breakthrough, his insight into reality, from whence has flowed for thousands of years the whole philosophical, scientific, and religious educational movement that is Buddhism. Identifying this habitual, certain self-knowledge as the core misknowledge allowed the Buddha to give birth to wisdom, truth, and liberating enlightenment.

But the Buddha knew perfectly well that it would do no good to simply order people to accept his declaration of selflessness as dogma and cling to it as a slogan or creed. The instinctual entanglement of human beings within the knot of self-certainty is much too powerful to be dislodged in this way, selflessness at first too counterintuitive to be acknowledged as truth. No, the Buddha realized, people must discover their real nature for themselves. So he made his declaration of selflessness not a statement of fact but rather a challenge to inquiry.

"I have discovered selflessness!" the Buddha announced. "I have seen through the reality of the seemingly solid self that lay at the core of my being. This insight did not destroy me—it only destroyed my suffering. It was my liberation! But you need not believe me. Discover the truth for yourself. Try with all your might to verify this 'self' you feel is in there, to pin it down. If you can do that, fine, tell me I'm wrong and ignore whatever else I may have to say. But if you fail to find it, if each thing you come up with dissolves under further analysis, if you discover, as I did, that there is no atomic, indivisible, durable core 'self,' then do not be afraid. Do not recoil or turn away. Rather, confront that emptiness and recognize it as the doorway to the supreme freedom! See through the 'self' and it will release you. You will discover that you are a part of the infinite web of interconnectedness with all other beings. You will live in bliss from now on as the relative self you always were; free at long last from the struggle of absolute alienation, free to help others find their own blessed freedom and happiness!"

Though in this paraphrase of his core teaching the Buddha offers us much encouragement, the challenge remains its central thrust. "You think you're really you? Don't just accept that blindly! Verify whether or not your 'self' is actually present within you. Turn your focused attention to it and explore it. If it's as solid as it seems, then it should be solidly encounterable. If you can't encounter it, then you must confront your error."

The great philosopher Descartes made a grave error when he thought he discovered in his fixed subjective self the one certain thing about existence. After demolishing the entire universe of observable things with hammer blows of systematic doubt, he was unable to give even a tiny tap to collapse this sense of self! And so he set down as the basis for his entire philosophy the famous proposition, "I think, therefore I am!"

Believe it or not, in his deep exploration for the "self," Descartes almost took another path that would have led him to enlightenment. He got very close to discovering that he could not find the "self" he felt to be so absolutely present. After intensively dissecting appearances, drilling through layer upon layer of seeming certainties, he came out with nothing that he could hold onto as the "self." But then he made the tragic mistake. Instead of accepting his selflessness, he instead said to himself, "Ah! Well, of course I cannot find the self. It is the self that is doing the looking! The 'I' is the subject and so it cannot be an object. Though I cannot find it, still my knowledge that it is the absolute subject cannot be doubted. It confirms its existence by doubting its existence. *Cogito ergo sum!* Of this I can remain absolutely certain."

Why was this mistaken? His logic sounds plausible enough at first. It is, after all, a clever way out of the dilemma of looking for something you are sure is there but cannot find. But what's wrong with it? Let's say that I am looking for a cup. I find it, so I can be certain that the cup exists. I look for my friend and find her, so I can be certain she's there. I look for my glasses, I do not find them—so I proclaim certainty that they are there? No—I go get another pair because I acknowledge I've lost them. I look for my oh-so-familiar "I," and I cannot find it! Why would I think it's there, then? Because I've arbitrarily put it in the category of "things that are there only when I can't find them"? No, when I can't find it, it's rather more sensible that I must give up the sense of certainty that it's there. I feel it's there when I don't look for it, but as soon as I look for it with real effort, it instantly eludes discovery. It seems always to be just around the next corner in my mind, yet each time I turn around to seize it, it disappears. And so I must slowly come to accept the fact that it may not be there after all.

Put another way, imagine that you are walking through the desert when, far off on the horizon, you see an oasis. Yet when you get closer, it disappears. "Aha!" you think to yourself. "A mirage." You walk away. Miles later, you turn around and look back. There's the oasis again! Do you feel certain that the water is there now? No, on the contrary you feel certain that it is only a mirage of water. In the same way, when you look for the "self" and don't find it, you must accept that it is merely a mirage. Your solid self-sense is only an illusion.

Had Descartes persisted and found the door to freedom in his selflessness, as the Buddha did, then instead of proclaiming, "I think, therefore I am," he might have said, "Even though I can find no concrete, fixated 'self,' I still can think. I still seem to be. Therefore I can continue to be myself, selflessly, as a relative, conventional, but ultimately unfindable being."

Whenever you decide to try a particular yoga recommended in this book, the crucial first step is always deciding to make the change. You must begin by accepting the fact that your habitual conceptions could be wrong. If, for example, you live with the delusion that it is just fine to remain addicted to nicotine, that three packs of cigarettes a day puts you in optimal operating condition, then there is no way you will successfully complete a yoga to quit smoking. Likewise, in this crucial quest of the self, the presumed core of your self-addiction, you must first convince yourself through empirical observation that the way you hold your self-identity—the constricted feeling of being wrapped around a solid, independent core—is uncomfortable and disabling.

Why should you even care if the rigid "self" that you believe in so strongly really exists or not? Our self feels most real when we are right and righteous, when we are wrongly or unfairly challenged. And it also seems unique, completely separate from everyone and everything else in the universe. This separateness can feel like freedom and independence when we are in a good mood. But when we are in trouble, lonely or angry, under pressure or dissatisfied, this separateness feels like isolation, alienation, unfair treatment, or deprivation. When we are wholly gripped by fury, the searing energy that wants to attack a target picks our "I" up like a mindless tool and flings us at the other person. It is so disconnected that it even disregards our sense of self-protection, making us take actions that injure us, ignore injuries undergone, and even harm others with no regard for the consequences. There is no more powerful demonstration of our strong sense of being an independent entity than when we give ourselves over completely to anger.

When we look around at others, we see that they are just as alienated from us as we are alienated from them. As we want things from them, they want things from us. As we reject them, they seem to reject us. We don't love them, so how can we expect them to love us? And yet they are endless, while "I" am just one. So I am badly outnumbered. I feel threatened. I can never get enough, have enough, or be enough. I will inevitably lose the me-versus-all-of-them struggle in the long run.

We can, of course, experience moments of unity with other beings, through falling in love, or having a child, for example. When we do, we experience tremendous relief—for a moment, there are two of us teamed up against all the others together. We have an ally. But unfortunately those moments are too rare, and they do not last long before the old self-isolation reemerges. Even lovers can turn into adversaries, couples often seek divorce, and children recoil from their parents, who in turn reject them.

This alienation caused by the presumed independent, absolute self was why the Buddha saw its illusion as the source of human suffering. The situation of feeling that it's always "the self versus the world," with the self as the long-term loser, is unsatisfactory and untenable. When we recognize the inevitable nonviability of our self-centered reality, it motivates us to engage in the quest for the true nature of the self. It makes it existentially essential for us to pause in our headlong rush through life and turn within, to verify whether the "self" really exists as we feel it does.

We can take great encouragement from the fact that the Buddha told us we could escape from our suffering. Still, we cannot merely accept someone else's report. No one else can do the job of replacing misunderstanding with understanding for us. We must look at reality and verify for ourselves whether our habitual sense of having a fixed self or the Buddha's discovery of selflessness is ultimately true. In this way, we can begin to transform the self-preoccupation that causes chronic suffering into the insightful, gradual opening and letting go of the self that is, paradoxically, so self-fulfilling. We want to be happy, but ironically we can only become happier to the extent that we can develop an unconcern for our "self." This process is long and gradual, though you will experience frequent breakthrough moments that will thrill you and motivate you to continue.

Before we actually engage in the meditation practice used to discover the true nature of the self, we must set up our parameters in practical, clear terms. When we look through a darkened house for a misplaced key, we first remember what the key looks like, and then we search for it carefully, room by room, turning lights on as we go. We use a flashlight to look under beds and in hidden corners. When we have looked everywhere exhaustively and not found it, we decide we've missed it somehow, so we go back and repeat the process. However, after one or two searches of this kind, we come to a decisive conclusion that the key is not in the house. We know we could continue looking endlessly, but that would be impractical. So we decide to proceed accordingly with our lives.

In the case of the quest for the self, we will look through all the processes of our body and mind that we can find and investigate them thoroughly. Our physical systems, sensational feelings, conceptual image bank, emotional energies, and consciousness itself constitute the house through which we will search. There are also various vaguely defined areas such as "spirit" and "soul" that, like a dusty attic or dank cellar, we may feel the need to explore. It is easy to get lost in these murky, dank, and oft-forgotten quarters of the mind. So we must get a clear picture of what we want to find ahead of time. And most important, we must set some limits to the exercise, since practically speaking we cannot continue to search indefinitely.

At this point you should search through the house of your body-mind-spirit a few times with great concentration and systematic thoroughness, with my help and the help of many experts who have guided me through this practice. If, during this process, you find a "self," then enjoy it to the full. If, however, as I suspect will be the case, you do not find what stands up solidly as your "real self" by the end of the process, then you will have to live with the fact that there is no such thing. You will need to make the practical decision to turn from seeking the "self" to explore instead the ramifications of being a relative self without any absolute underpinning.

This commitment to practicality in your quest for the self is of great importance at the outset and will have a significant impact on the success of the endeavor. Once you have made the commitment in your own mind, you may begin.

Practice: Trying to Find Your "I"

You are now prepared to deepen your understanding of your selflessness. You will be looking at yourself introspectively, trying to grasp exactly what your essence is. When you do this practice well, you will begin to feel yourself dissolving, just as I did at my mentor Geshe-la's house many years ago. You will start realizing—gradually and also suddenly, in spurts—that you can't find this mysterious "self." Your strong feeling of having an absolute "I" is maddeningly elusive when you try to pin it down precisely.

. . . In looking for your "self," start with your body. Ask yourself, "Am I my body?" In order to answer this question, you must define your body. It is composed at least of your five sense organs, right? Your skin and sensitive inner surfaces constitute the touch organ, then you have your eyes for sight, your nose for smell, your ears for hearing, and your tongue for taste. So first let's explore all of your senses together, your sensory system.

Identify the sound sense. What do you hear—a dog barking, a phone ringing, music playing, or perhaps just the sound of your own breathing? Now notice the visual field. You are reading words on the page. What else do you see? What are the images on the edge of your peripheral vision? How about smell? Perhaps you smell the scent of incense burning, or of musty wood. Do you taste anything: something you ate a while ago, tea you drank, or just the taste of your own mouth? The tactile field is everything touching your skin, including other parts of your skin touching your skin. Your hand may be resting on your knee, for example. Your bottom is touching a pillow. Just identify all the sensations, the textures, smells, tastes, sounds, and sights.

Now notice your internal sensations, like the breakfast in your tummy. You might have a slight pain in your back or your knee. Maybe your foot is falling asleep, and you're annoyed because there's a slightly painful sensation there. You might have a pleasurable sensation in some part of you that is feeling good if, for example, you worked out yesterday or had a massage.

Recognize that for each of these sensations you are experiencing, you are receiving data from the outside world. The sensations are not all coming from your own body. So your body is not just inside your skin; your body is both your organs and the field of all incoming sense objects. It's everything you are seeing and hearing and smelling and tasting and touching. It's the chair or pillow you're sitting on. The words you are reading on this page. The incense drifting into your nostrils. If you look at one sensation, you realize that you are sharing your material body with the outside world. Say, for example, you are looking at light bouncing off a table. That light is a part of your shared sensory system, and therefore part of your body, too.

So already you have begun to expand your self-definition, just by looking at your five senses. Suddenly you are not just something that sits there inside your skin. You are your environment as well. Your body interfuses with the outside world that you perceive with your senses. All of our bodies are totally overlapping, all the time. Do you see? And when you think, "this is 'me' over here inside this skin," you are unrealistically thinking that "I" am not connected to others through the sense perceptions that we have in common. But you are connected, even before you talk to them or think anything about them, through your shared environment.

Now you can move to the next level of analysis of the self, which exists at the level of your mind. First is the sensational system, the feelings of pleasure, pain, and numbness associated with sense perceptions of sights, sounds, smells, tastes, textures, and mental sense inner objects. When you experience these six kinds of objects, you react as pleased, irritated, or indifferent. Mentally inventory your sensations at the moment, and notice how you react at this basic feeling level. Notice that this heap of sense-reactions has no self-core within it.

Next is your conceptual system, your ideas, mental maps, and internal images. You have a picture of yourself as you exist in the world. You have a concept of yourself as human, not animal. You have a picture of yourself as male or female. You have a body image, and an image of each part of your body. You have a concept of your identity as a teacher, a manager, a doctor, or whatever. You have a concept of yourself as successful or as a failure. Inventory this mass of ideas and images and notice that you have whole clouds of pictures and concepts. But is this incredibly chaotic mass of images and words and diagrams and maps and so forth that is your conceptual system the real "you"? Your perception of yourself changes all the time, depending on your mood, whom you're with, or what you're doing. Sometimes you think, "I'm a high-powered executive," whereas other times you think, "I'm just a tiny speck on a tiny planet of six billion people." So surely your conceptual system cannot be your "self." The "you" self is not any of these ideas, since it seems to be the entity that is noticing all of them.

At the fourth level of analysis, find your emotional system. You are constantly reacting to all of these images and notions. Right now, you're probably feeling a bit irritated with me. You're thinking to yourself, "Why is he making me do this? Why doesn't he just crack a joke? Let's have some fun. What is this terrible business of exploring the self, 'discovering selflessness'? How is this helping me?" And so on and so forth. You're feeling annoyed and anxious and confused. Or maybe you're just feeling bored. Anyway, your emotions are there in your mind, always functioning, but always changing. You can take a peek at them now, as they swirl around in your heart and head, and you can see that they are not fixed. You are not defined by your emotions. They are not the elusive "self" you're seeking.

Lastly, turn your attention to your consciousness system. It is the most important system of all. You see at once how it is a buzzing, blooming, swirling mass of subtle energies. Nothing is fixed, nothing stable within it. With your mental consciousness, you hop from one sense to another. You analyze your ideas, you focus internally on your emotions and thoughts, and you can even focus on being thought free. Your consciousness aims itself at being free of thought by the thought of being free of thought. How strange! As you inventory your consciousness, don't allow yourself to rest with a bare awareness, but go a bit deeper—explore further with your analytic attention. Ask yourself, "Who is this supposedly rigid 'self'? Is it the same self right now as the one who woke up grumbling this morning, preparing that cup of coffee, rushing to get ready, quickly brushing its teeth? Is it the same self who was born a tiny, unaware, helpless infant years ago? Who is the 'me' who knows my name, who knows what I want, where I am, and what I'm doing? Who is the 'me' who knows I'm an American, who knows I'm a—whatever: a Buddhist or a Christian or an atheist? Where is that person now? Where is that absolute, unchanging structure?" You can see how your self-consciousness is a buzzing, blooming, swirling mass of confusion—nothing is fixed, nothing stable within it. You can barely remember what you did yesterday morning—I can't remember at all at my age! So how can you possibly have a rigid self? See how releasing these sorts of thoughts can be! . . .

The deepest stage of awareness comes when your consciousness begins to turn inward to gaze upon itself. At first it thinks, "I now know that these sensory, mental, and emotional systems looming before me are not the 'self,' they are not 'me.' But the awareness that looks at them, that contemplates and investigates them, that is my 'self.'" And yet you soon discover that you are mistaken even in this conclusion. The moment you begin to examine your own conscious mind, you engage in a whirling, internal dervish-dance where your awareness spins round and round upon itself. This contemplation can be dizzying, nauseating, painful, and even a bit frightening, as the felt "self" disappears and evades its own attention. You can never catch it, even as you become more experienced at this meditation and come back to this place again and again. Time and again you will feel frustrated by your continued failure to come up with a result. Yet you must not lose heart. You must remember that looking for your "self" is the most important thing you can ever do in your evolutionary development. You must keep faith that you are on the brink of a quantum leap; you are so close to awakening.

As you enter into this confusing realm of spinning self-seeking, be careful not to make the mistake Descartes made by withdrawing from it all with some sort of decision about "you" being the subject and therefore not any sort of findable object. Also, be careful not to fall into the nihilistic trap of withdrawing from the spinning by deciding that all is nothing after all and so naturally the self-sense is an illusion. Keep whirling upon your "self" as long as you feel absolutely there is a self to whirl upon, to look at, to catch. Put your full truth-seeking, analytic energy into the drive to find it.

Eventually, you will experience a gradual melting process. The whirling will slowly dissolve without fear: you won't shrink back in terror of falling into an abyss-like void because you are already overcoming your self-addiction. You control the tendency to shrink back in terror of falling into a looming void by your drilling, whirling energy of awareness itself. You dissolve your fearing subject, the object for which you are feeling fear, and the imagined nothingness that only the pseudo–self-addiction wants you to fear. However fully you feel such processes at first, what happens to you is that, as you begin to melt, your drive intensity lessens, you feel buoyed by a floating sensation coming from within your nerves and cells, from within your subjectivity as well as your object-field. At some point, you lose your sense of self entirely, as if you were a field of open space. Like Neo and his colleagues in the movie *The Matrix* when they entered one of the computer-generated training fields, you will find yourself standing in a blank white space—except in your case, in this transcending moment, you break free from your "digital residual self-image." You will be only the blank white space, a bare awareness of yourself as a boundless entity. Dissolving into this space, you'll feel intense bliss, a sense of extreme relief.

When you first melt into the spacious experience of freedom, it is enthralling, like emerging from a dark cave into infinite light. You feel magnificent, vast, and unbound. If you inadvertently fall into this state unprepared by arriving there too quickly, you may be tempted to think that you have arrived at the absolute reality, and this is a bit of a danger. You might think, feeling it nonverbally at this stage, that you've conquered the differentiated universe and realized its true "nothingness," experiencing it as such a profound and liberating release that you never again want any contact with the real world. Remember, however, that nothingness is not your ultimate goal—you are not trying to escape reality, but to embrace it. If you reach this space of release gradually through the repeated whirling of your self turning upon itself, then you'll be able to enjoy the vastness and magnificence without losing awareness that it is only another relational condition. You'll realize that the great emptiness is ultimately empty of itself; it is not reality, either.

Since you *are* the void, you do not need to remain in the void, and your original self-sense slowly reemerges within the universe of persons and things. But you are aware that it is not the same "self" you had before—it is forever different, now become infinite and unbound. You have changed. You now perceive your "self" consciously, living with it yet maintaining an educated distance from it. You are like one of the characters in *The Matrix*, present and active as real being, yet at the same time realizing that the apparent reality that surrounds you is only illusory. All that was apparent becomes transparent.

One of the most significant changes you will notice upon discovering your selflessness is that your sense of being separate from everyone else has now eroded. Your new awareness enables you to perceive others as equal to yourself, a part of you, even. You can see yourself as they see you, and experience empathically how they perceive themselves as locked within themselves. You have arrived at the doorway to universal compassion, and it frees you from being locked away behind a fixed point-of-awareness and opens you to a sort of field awareness wherein others are really just the same as you while simultaneously relationally different. Through the sense of sameness, you feel their pains as if they were your own: when they hurt, you hurt. Yet through the sense of relational difference and balanced responsibility, you naturally feel moved to free them from their pains, just as you move automatically to eliminate your own pains. When your hand is burned by a hot pothandle, you react at once to pull away from the heat, you plunge it into cold water, you rush to find ice. You respond instinctively to remove the pain.

You don't consider it a selfless act of compassion for your hand. You just do it through your neural connection to your hand. Your new open awareness feels others' hands through a similar sense of natural connection.   ■

■ *QUESTIONS FOR MAKING CONNECTIONS WITHIN THE READING* ■

1. Choose one important term from Thurman's essay, such as "nirvana," "nothingness," "emptiness," "enlightenment," "meditation," "compassion," "ignorance," "self," "happiness," or "freedom." Then, by tracing Thurman's use of the term throughout the chapter, offer your own explanation of its meaning. While commonplace definitions for all of these terms may be found in a dictionary, here you are being asked to explain the meaning of the term as Thurman uses it. Then you might contrast Thurman's use of the term to more commonplace understandings. "Ignorance," for example, has a special significance in the context of Buddhist thought. How does it differ from "ignorance" as we normally define it?

2. Instead of discussing the soul, Thurman focuses on the mind. How is "mind" different from "soul"? Where is the mind located, according to Thurman? Is it the same as the brain? What are some of the broader implications of Thurman's attention to the mind instead of the soul? If the mind is transformed, can the essence of the person remain somehow immune to change? Conversely, if a person's mental habits and perceptions remain unchanged, is it possible to imagine that the essence of the person has still been altered somehow? We might ordinarily think of each person as endowed with an individual soul, but is the mind individualized in the same way?

3. Thurman speaks about "enlightenment" instead of "redemption" or "salvation." How does "enlightenment" differ from "salvation"? What are the differences between Thurman's emphasis on the experience of "selflessness" and the famous Greek dictum, "Know thyself"? Could selflessness qualify as a form of self-knowledge? Could it qualify as a form of redemption or salvation?

■ *QUESTIONS FOR WRITING* ■

1. Buddhism is often studied on the college level in courses offered by philosophy and religion departments. Judging from Thurman's account, what elements does Buddhism have in common with philosophy? With religion? Or, judging from Thurman's account, would you say that Buddhism has some elements in common with science, which is based on empirical observation? In what ways might Buddhism be closer to a science than to a religion or a philosophy?

2. What are the social and political implications of Thurman's argument? How would the cultivation of "wisdom" as he describes it affect people in a competitive, consumption-oriented society like our own? Is Thurman's brand of meditation compatible with democracy and the idea that all of us are equal? How might the cultivation of wisdom influence the current political climate? Would the climate become less adversarial? Less driven by rigid ideology? Or would people who cultivate wisdom simply wash their hands of politics?

■ *QUESTIONS FOR MAKING CONNECTIONS BETWEEN READINGS* ■

1. In "When I Woke Up Tuesday Morning, It Was Friday," Martha Stout describes forms of "divided" or "dissociated" consciousness that are produced by severely traumatic events. One of Stout's patients, whom she calls "Julia," becomes so dissociated from the here and now that whole days never get recorded in Julia's memory. After rereading Stout's analysis of dissociation, decide whether or not the form of meditation that Thurman describes might help someone like Julia. Is it possible that meditation as Thurman describes it could actually *produce* dissociation in healthy people? What aspects of meditation might be most helpful to people like Julia? Is it possible that dissociation is actually more widespread than most people even realize? Is trauma really necessary to produce severely divided consciousness, or do certain features of contemporary life help to produce it—television, commercial radio, video games, and movies?

2. In what ways is reading like the practice of meditation? To explore this question, draw primarily on Azar Nafisi's chapter from *Reading Lolita in Tehran*. At a key moment in her account, Nafisi makes this observation:

> Whoever we were—and it was not really important what religion we belonged to, whether we wished to wear the veil or not, whether we absorbed certain religious norms or not—we had become the figment of someone else's dreams. A stern ayatollah, a self-proclaimed philosopher-king, had come to rule our land.

How, according to Nafisi, can the reading of fiction help us throw off the veils—literal and virtual—that others have imposed on us? Does reading as she describes involve its own form of mental cultivation, comparable in some ways to the meditational practice Thurman describes? Does reading allow Nafisi and her students to experience a form of "selflessness"? How can we tell the difference between the veils imposed on us and the persons we really are? Is it possible that "selflessness" allows us to create an identity of our own?

Jean Twenge

In the second half of the twentieth century, American culture became more and more a celebration of the individual. Collective concerns—and the language of collectivity—fell to the wayside as the self became the prime subject for consideration. Though many critics have taken the last two generations of youth to task for being more entitled than their predecessors, San Diego State University psychology professor Jean Twenge adds a new wrinkle to the critique: so much emphasis on the self isn't just bad for society; it's also bad for the individual.

Twenge's bestselling first book, *Generation Me: Why Today's Young Americans Are More Confident, Assertive, Entitled—and More Miserable than Ever Before* (2006), uses data taken from 1.3 million young people to trace the different perspectives of successive generations on self-esteem, individuality, sexuality, and other issues related to development. In reviewing this data, she sees evidence of an unprecedented shift as both education and culture have come to emphasize selfhood and self-esteem above all other values. For Baby Boomers, the term *self* was novel enough that they could speak of a journey to selfhood, Twenge observes. However, later generations internalized this concept to the point that it has become difficult for today's youth to imagine organizing culture around anything other than the self. To better understand the causes and symptoms of the emerging prevalence of narcissism, Twenge is currently conducting research for a forthcoming work tentatively called *The Narcissist Epidemic*.

Twenge, Jean. "An Army of One: *Me*," *Generation Me: Why Today's Young Americans Are More Confident, Assertive, Entitled—and More Miserable than Ever Before*. New York: Free Press, 2006. 44–71.

Biographical information comes from Jean Twenge's San Diego State University faculty Web site, <http://www.psychology.sdsu.edu/new-web/facultystaff/twenge.html>.

■ ■

An Army of One: *Me*

One day when my mother was driving me to school in 1986, Whitney Houston's hit song "The Greatest Love of All" was warbling out of the weak speakers of our Buick station wagon with wood trim. I asked my mother what she thought the song was about. "The greatest love of all—it has to be about children," she said.

My mother was sweet, but wrong. The song does say that children are the future (always good to begin with a strikingly original thought) and that we should teach them well. About world peace, maybe? Or great literature? Nope. Children should be educated about the beauty "inside," the song declares. We all need heroes, Whitney sings, but she never found "anyone to fulfill my needs," so she learned to depend on (wait for it) "me." The chorus then declares, "learning to love yourself is the greatest love of all."

This is a stunning reversal in attitude from previous generations. Back then, respect for others was more important than respect for yourself. The term "self-esteem" wasn't widely used until the late 1960s, and didn't become talk-show and dinner-table conversation until the 1980s. By the 1990s, it was everywhere.

Take, for example, the band Offspring's rockingly irreverent 1994 riff "Self-Esteem." The song describes a guy whose girlfriend "says she wants only me . . . Then I wonder why she sleeps with my friends." (Hmmm.) But he's blasé about it—it's OK, really, since he's "just a sucker with no self-esteem."

By the mid-1990s, Offspring could take it for granted that most people knew the term "self-esteem," and knew they were supposed to have it. They also knew how to diagnose themselves when they didn't have it. Offspring's ironic self-parody demonstrates a high level of understanding of the concept, the satire suggesting that this psychological self-examination is rote and can thus be performed with tongue planted firmly in cheek.

In the years since, attention to the topic of self-esteem has rapidly expanded. A search for "self-esteem" in the books section of amazon.com yielded 105,438 entries in July 2005 (sample titles: *The Self-Esteem Workbook, Breaking the Chain of Low Self-Esteem, Ten Days to Self-Esteem, 200 Ways to Raise a Girl's Self-Esteem*). Magazine articles on self-esteem are as common as e-mail spam for Viagra. *Ladies' Home Journal* told readers to "Learn to Love Yourself!" in March 2005,[1] while *Parenting* offered "Proud to Be Me!" (apparently the exclamation point is required) in April, listing "5 simple ways to help your child love who he is."[2] TV and radio talk shows would be immediately shut down by the FCC if "self-esteem" were on the list of banned words. The

American Academy of Pediatrics guide to caring for babies and young children uses the word "self-esteem" ten times in the space of seven pages in the first chapter, and that doesn't even count the numerous mentions of self-respect, confidence, and belief in oneself.[3]

How did self-esteem transform from an obscure academic term to a familiar phrase that pops up in everything from women's magazines to song lyrics to celebrity interviews? The story actually begins centuries ago, when humans barely had a concept of a self at all: your marriage was arranged, your profession determined by your parents, your actions dictated by strict religious standards. Slowly over the centuries, social strictures began to loosen and people started to make more choices for themselves. Eventually, we arrived at the modern concept of the individual as an autonomous, free person.

Then came the 1970s, when the ascendance of the self truly exploded into the American consciousness. In contrast to previous ethics of honor and duty, Baby Boomer ideals focused instead on meaning and self-fulfillment. In his 1976 bestseller, *Your Erroneous Zones,* Wayne Dyer suggests that the popular song "You Are the Sunshine of My Life" be retitled "I Am the Sunshine of My Life." Your love for yourself, he says, should be your "first love." The 1970 allegory, *Jonathan Livingston Seagull,* describes a bird bored with going "from shore to food and back again." Instead, he wants to enjoy flying, swooping through the air to follow "a higher meaning, a higher purpose for life," even though his actions get him exiled from his flock. The book, originally rejected by nearly every major publishing house, became a runaway bestseller as Americans came to agree with the idea that life should be fulfilling and focused on the needs of the self. The seagulls in the animated movie *Finding Nemo* were still on message almost twenty-five years later: all that comes out of their beaks is the word "Mine."

Boomers and Their "Journey" into the Self

Because the Boomers dominate our culture so much, we have to understand them first so we can see how they differ from the younger Generation Me. Why aren't the Boomers—the Me Generation in the 1970s—the *real* Generation Me? It's about what you explore as a young adult versus what you're born to and take for granted.

For the Boomers, who grew up in the 1950s and 1960s, self-focus was a new concept, individualism an uncharted territory. In his 1981 book *New Rules: Searching for Self-Fulfillment in a World Turned Upside Down,* Daniel Yankelovich describes young Boomers struggling with new questions: How do you make decisions in a marriage with two equal partners? How do you focus on yourself when your parents don't even know what that means? The Boomers in the book sound like people driving around in circles in the dark, desperately searching for something. The world was so new that there were no road signs, no maps to point the way to this new fulfillment and individuality.

That's probably why many Boomers talk about the self using language full of abstraction, introspection, and "growth." New things call for this kind of meticulous thought, and require the idea that the process will take time. Thus Boomers talk about "my journey," "my need to keep growing," or "my unfulfilled potentials." Sixties activist Todd Gitlin called the Boomer quest the "voyage to the interior." Icky as they are to today's young people, these phrases drum with motion and time, portraying self-focus as a continuous project that keeps evolving as Boomers look around for true meaning. In a 1976 *New York Magazine* article, Tom Wolfe described the "new dream" as "remaking, remodeling, elevating and polishing one's very self . . . and observing, studying, and doting on it."[4] Sixties radical Jerry Rubin wrote that he tried just about every fad of the 1970s (rolfing, est, yoga, sex therapy, finding his inner child); one of the chapters in his book *Growing (Up) at Thirty-Seven* is called "Searching for Myself."

Such introspection primarily surfaces today in the speech of New Agers, therapists who have read too much Maslow, and over-45 Boomers. When asked what's next in her life, Kim Basinger (born in 1953) replies, "Watching what the rest of my journey is going to be about."[5] In answer to the same question, Sarah Ferguson, Duchess of York (born in 1959) says: "My coming to stay in America for a few months is like my blossoming into my true Sarah, into my true self. And I'm just coming to learn about her myself."[6] Not all Boomers talk this way, of course, but enough do that it's an immediately recognizable generational tic. It's also a guaranteed way to get a young person to roll her eyes. She might also then tell you to lighten up.

Many authors, from William Strauss and Neil Howe in *Generations* to Steve Gillon in *Boomer Nation,* have noted that abstraction and spirituality are the primary hallmarks of the Boomer generation. Gillon describes Boomers as having a "moralistic style" and devotes a chapter to Boomers' "New Fundamentalism."[7] Whether joining traditional churches or exploring meditation or yoga, Boomers have been fascinated with the spiritual for four decades.

Even Boomers who don't adopt New Age language seek higher meaning in the new religion of consumer products—thus the yuppie revolution. In *Bobos in Paradise,* David Brooks demonstrates that upper-class Boomers have poured their wealth into things like cooking equipment, which somehow feels more moral and meaningful than previous money sinks like jewelry or furs. Even food becomes "a barometer of virtue," Brooks says, as 1960s values are "selectively updated. . . . Gone are the sixties-era things that were fun and of interest to teenagers, like Free Love, and retained are all the things that might be of interest to middle-aged hypochondriacs, like whole grains."[8]

The Boomers' interest in the abstract and spiritual shows up in many different sources. In 1973, 46% of Boomers said they "focused on internal cues."[9] Only 26% of 1990s young people agreed. Thirty percent of Boomers said that "creativity comes from within," versus 18% of young people in the 1990s.[10] Even stronger evidence comes from a national survey of more than 300,000 college freshmen. In 1967, a whopping 86% of incoming college students said that "developing a meaningful philosophy of life" was an essential life goal.[11] Only 42% of GenMe freshmen in 2004 agreed, cutting the Boomer number in half. I'm definitely a member of my generation in this way; despite being an academic, I'm not sure I know what a "meaningful philosophy of life" even is. Jerry Rubin does—if you can understand him. "Instead of seeking with the expectation of finding, I experience my seeking as an end in itself," he writes. "I become one with my seeking, and merge with the moment."[12] OK, Jerry. Let us know when you've reentered the Earth's atmosphere.

While up there, maybe Jerry met Aleta St. James, a 57-year-old woman who gave birth to twins in 2004. She explained her unusual actions by saying, "My whole world is about manifesting, so I decided to manifest children."[13] It's not surprising that an enterprising GenMe member put together a list of books on amazon.com titled "Tired of Baby Boomer Self-Righteousness?"

Boomers display another unique and somewhat ironic trait: a strong emphasis on group meetings. Boomers followed in the footsteps of their community-minded elders—they just joined the Weathermen instead of the Elks Lodge. This is one of the many reasons why Boomers are not the true Generation Me—almost everything they did happened in groups: Vietnam protests, marches for feminism, consciousness raising, assertiveness training, discos, even seminars like est. Maybe it felt safer to explore the self within a group—perhaps it felt less radical. No one seemed to catch the irony that it might be difficult to find your own unique direction in a group of other people. Even Boomers' trends and sayings belied their reliance on groups: "Don't trust anyone over 30" groups people by age, as did the long hair many Boomer men adopted in the late 1960s and early 1970s to distinguish themselves from older folks. In a 1970 song, David Crosby says he decided not to cut his hair so he could "let my freak flag fly." If you've got a flag, you're probably a group. Boomers may have thought they invented individualism, but like any inventor, they were followed by those who truly perfected the art.

Boomers took only the first tentative steps in the direction of self-focus, rather than swallowing it whole at birth. Most Boomers never absorbed it at all and settled down early to marry and raise families. Those who adopted the ways of the self as young adults speak the language with an accent: the accent of abstraction and "journeys." They had to reinvent their way of thinking when already grown, and thus see self-focus as a "process." In his book, Rubin quotes a friend who says, "We are the first generation to reincarnate ourselves in our own lifetime."

The Matter-of-Fact Self-Focus of Generation Me

Generation Me had no need to reincarnate ourselves; we were born into a world that already celebrated the individual. The self-focus that blossomed in the 1970s became mundane and commonplace over the next two decades, and GenMe accepts it like a fish accepts water. If Boomers were making their way in the uncharted world of the self, GenMe has printed step-by-step directions from Yahoo! Maps—and most of the time we don't even need them, since the culture of the self is our hometown. We don't have to join groups or talk of journeys, because we're already there. We don't need to "polish" the self, as Wolfe said, because we take for granted that it's already shiny. We don't need to look inward; we already know what we will find. Since we were small children, we were taught to put ourselves first. That's just the way the world works—why dwell on it? Let's go to the mall.

GenMe's focus on the needs of the individual is not necessarily self-absorbed or isolationist; instead, it's a way of moving through the world beholden to few social rules and with the unshakable belief that you're important. It's also not the same as being "spoiled," which implies that we always get what we want; though this probably does describe some kids, it's not the essence of the trend. (GenMe's expectations are so great and our reality so challenging that we will probably get less of what we want than any previous generation). We simply take it for granted that we should all feel good about ourselves, we are all special, and we all deserve to follow our dreams. GenMe is straightforward and unapologetic about our self-focus. In 2004's *Conquering Your Quarterlife Crisis,* Jason, 25, relates how he went through some tough times and decided he needed to change things in his life. His new motto was "Do what's best for Jason. I had to make *me* happy; I had to do what was best for myself in every situation."[14]

Our practical orientation toward the self sometimes leaves us with a distaste for Boomer abstraction. When a character in the 2004 novel *Something Borrowed* watched the 1980s show *thirtysomething* as a teen, she wished the Boomer characters would "stop pondering the meaning of life and start making grocery lists."[15] The matter-of-fact attitude of GenMe appears in everyday language as well—a language that still includes the abstract concept of self, but uses it in a very simple way, perhaps because we learned the language as children. We speak the language of the self as our native tongue. So much of the "common sense" advice that's given these days includes some variation on "self":

• Worried about how to act in a social situation? "Just be yourself."
• What's the good thing about your alcoholism/drug addiction/murder conviction? "I learned a lot about myself."

- Concerned about your performance? "Believe in yourself." (Often followed by "and anything is possible.")
- Should you buy the new pair of shoes, or get the nose ring? "Yes, express yourself."
- Why should you leave the unfulfilling relationship/quit the boring job/tell off your mother-in-law? "You have to respect yourself."
- Trying to get rid of a bad habit? "Be honest with yourself."
- Confused about the best time to date or get married? "You have to love yourself before you can love someone else."
- Should you express your opinion? "Yes, stand up for yourself."

Americans use these phrases so often that we don't even notice them anymore. Dr. Phil, the ultimate in plainspoken, no-nonsense advice, uttered both "respect yourself" and "stop lying to yourself" within seconds of each other on a *Today* show segment on New Year's resolutions.[16] One of his bestselling books is entitled *Self Matters.* We take these phrases and ideas so much for granted, it's as if we learned them in our sleep as children, like the perfectly conditioned citizens in Aldous Huxley's *Brave New World.*

These aphorisms don't seem absurd to us even when, sometimes, they are. We talk about self-improvement as if the self could be given better drywall or a new coat of paint. We read self-help books as if the self could receive tax-deductible donations. The *Self* even has its own magazine. Psychologist Martin Seligman says that the traditional self—responsible, hardworking, stern—has been replaced with the "California self," "a self that chooses, feels pleasure and pain, dictates action and even has things like esteem, efficacy, and confidence."[17] Media outlets promote the self relentlessly; I was amazed at how often I heard the word "self" used in the popular media once I started looking for it. A careful study of news stories published or aired between 1980 and 1999 found a large increase in self-reference words (I, me, mine, and myself) and a marked decrease in collective words (humanity, country, or crowd).[18]

The Self Across the Generations

Baby Boomers	*Generation Me*
Self-fulfillment	Fun
Journey, potentials, searching	Already there
Change the world	Follow your dreams
Protests and group sessions	Watching TV and surfing the Web
Abstraction	Practicality
Spirituality	Things
Philosophy of life	Feeling good about yourself

Young people have learned these self-lessons very well. In a letter to her fans in 2004, Britney Spears, 23, listed her priorities as "Myself, my husband, Kevin, and starting a family."[19] If you had to read that twice to get my point, it's because we take it for granted that we should put ourselves first on our list of priorities—it would be blasphemy if you didn't (unless, of course, you have low self-esteem). Twenty-year-old Maria says her mother often reminds her to consider what other people will think. "It doesn't matter what other people think," Maria insists. "What really matters is how I perceive myself. The real person I need to please is myself."

Smart marketers have figured this out, too. In the late 1990s, Prudential replaced its longtime insurance slogan "Get a Piece of the Rock" with the nakedly individualistic "Be Your Own Rock."[20] The United States Army, perhaps the last organization one might expect to focus on the individual instead of the group, has followed suit. Their standard slogan, adopted in 2001, is "An Army of One."

Changes in Self-Esteem: What the Data Say

The data I gathered on self-esteem over time mirror the social trends perfectly. My colleague Keith Campbell and I looked at the responses of 65,965 college students to the Rosenberg Self-Esteem Scale, the most popular measure of general self-esteem among adults.[21] I held my breath when I analyzed these data for the first time, but I needn't have worried: the change was enormous. By the mid-1990s, the average GenMe college man had higher self-esteem than 86% of college men in 1968. The average mid-1990s college woman had higher self-esteem than 71% of Boomer college women. Between the 1960s and the 1990s, college students were increasingly likely to agree that "I take a positive attitude toward myself" and "On the whole, I am satisfied with myself." Other sources verify this trend. A 1997 survey of teens asked, "In general, how do you feel about yourself?" A stunning 93% answered "good." Of the remainder, 6% said they felt "not very good," and only 1% admitted they felt "bad" about themselves.[22] Another survey found that 91% of teens described themselves as responsible, 74% as physically attractive, and 79% as "very intelligent."[23]

Children's self-esteem scores tell a different but even more intriguing story. We examined the responses of 39,353 children, most ages 9 to 13, on the Coopersmith Self-Esteem Inventory, a scale written specifically for children.[24] During the 1970s—when the nation's children shifted from the late Baby Boom to the early years of GenX—kids' self-esteem declined, probably because of societal instability. Rampant divorce, a wobbly economy, soaring crime rates, and swinging singles culture made the 1970s a difficult time to be a kid. The average child in 1979 scored lower than 81% of kids in the mid-1960s. Over this time, children were less likely to agree with statements like "I'm pretty sure of myself" and "I'm pretty happy" and more likely to agree that "things are all mixed up in my life." The individualism that was so enthralling for teenagers and adults in the 1970s didn't help kids—and, if their parents suddenly discovered self-fulfillment, it might have even hurt them.

But after 1980, when GenMe began to enter the samples, children's self-esteem took a sharp turn upward. More and more during the 1980s and 1990s, children were saying that they were happy with themselves. They agreed that "I'm easy to like" and "I always do the right thing." By the mid-1990s, children's self-esteem scores equaled, and often exceeded, children's scores in the markedly more stable Boomer years before 1970. The average kid in the mid-1990s—right in the heart of GenMe—had higher self-esteem than 73% of kids in 1979, one of the last pre-GenMe years.

This is a bit of a mystery, however. The United States of the 1980s to mid-1990s never approached the kid-friendly stability of the 1950s and early 1960s: violent crime hit record highs, divorce was still at epidemic levels, and the economy had not yet reached its late-1990s boom. So without the calm and prosperity of earlier decades, why did children's self-esteem increase so dramatically during the 1980s and 1990s?

The Self-Esteem Curriculum

The short answer is that they were taught it. In the years after 1980, there was a pervasive, society-wide effort to increase children's self-esteem. The Boomers who now filled the ranks of parents apparently decided that children should always feel good about themselves. Research on programs to boost self-esteem first blossomed in the 1980s, and the number of psychology and education journal articles devoted to self-esteem doubled between the 1970s and the 1980s.[25] Journal articles on self-esteem increased another 52% during the 1990s, and the number of books on self-esteem doubled over the same time.[26] Generation Me is the first generation raised to believe that everyone should have high self-esteem.

Magazines, television talk shows, and books all emphasize the importance of high self-esteem for children, usually promoting feelings that are actually a lot closer to narcissism (a more negative trait usually defined as excessive self-importance). One children's book, first published in 1991, is called *The Lovables in the Kingdom of Self-Esteem.* "I AM LOVABLE. Hi, lovable friend! My name is Mona Monkey. I live in the Kingdom of Self-Esteem along with my friends the Lovable Team," the book begins.[27] On the next page, children learn that the gates of the kingdom will swing open if you "say these words three times with pride: *I'm lovable! I'm lovable! I'm lovable!*" (If I hear the word "lovable" one more time, I'm going to use my hefty self-esteem to pummel the author of this book.)

Parents are encouraged to raise their children's self-esteem even when kids are simply coloring. Even the cat has high self-esteem on this coloring book cover. However, the dog lacks a self-esteem boosting ribbon. He probably has low self-esteem—after all, he drinks out of the toilet.

Another example is the "BE A WINNER Self-Esteem Coloring and Activity Book" pictured in this chapter. Inside, children find activities and pictures designed to boost their self-esteem, including coloring a "poster for your room" that reads "YOU ARE SPECIAL" in yellow, orange, and red letters against a purple background. Another page asks kids to fill in the blanks: "Accept y_ur_e_f. You're a special person. Use p_si_iv_think-ing." A similar coloring book is called "We Are All Special" (though this title seems to suggest that being special isn't so special). All of this probably sounds like Al Franken's *Saturday Night Live* character Stuart Smalley, an insecure, sweater-vest-wearing man who looks in the mirror and unconvincingly repeats, "I'm good enough, I'm smart enough, and doggone it, people like me." It sounds like it because it's exactly the type of thing Franken was parodying. And it's everywhere.

Many school districts across the country have specific programs designed to increase children's self-esteem, most of which actually build self-importance and narcissism. One program is called "Self-Science: The Subject Is Me."[28] (Why bother with biology? *I'm* so much more interesting!) Another program, called "Pumsy in Pursuit of Excellence," uses a dragon character to encourage children to escape the "Mud Mind" they experience when feeling bad about themselves. Instead, they should strive to be in the "Sparkle Mind" and feel good about themselves.[29] The Magic Circle exercise designates one child a day to receive a badge saying "I'm great." The other children then say good things about the chosen child, who later receives a written list of all of the praise. At the end of the exercise, the child must then say something good about him- or herself. Boomer children in the 1950s and 1960s gained self-esteem naturally from a stable, child-friendly society; GenMe's self-esteem has been actively cultivated for its own sake.[30]

One Austin, Texas, father was startled to see his five-year-old daughter wearing a shirt that announced, "I'm lovable and capable." All of the kindergarteners, he learned, recited this phrase before class, and they all wore the shirt to school on Fridays. It seems the school started a bit too young, however, because the child then asked, "Daddy, all the kids are wondering, what does 'capable' mean?"[31]

Some people have wondered if the self-esteem trend waned after schools began to put more emphasis on testing during the late 1990s. It doesn't look that way. Parenting books and magazines stress self-esteem as much as ever, and a large number of schools continue to use self-esteem programs. The mission statements of many schools explicitly announce that they aim to raise students' self-esteem. A Google search for "elementary school mission statement self-esteem" yielded 308,000 Web pages in January 2006. These schools are located across the country, in cities, suburbs, small towns, and rural areas. "Building," "improving," "promoting," or "developing" self-esteem is a stated goal of (among many others) New River Elementary in New River, Arizona; Shady Dell Elementary in Springfield, Missouri; Shettler Elementary in Fruitport, Michigan; Baxter Elementary in Baxter, Tennessee; Rye Elementary in Westchester County, New York; Copeland Elementary in Augusta, Georgia; and Banff Elementary in Banff, Alberta, Canada. Private religious schools are not immune: St. Wendelin Catholic Elementary in Fostoria, Ohio, aims to "develop a feeling of confidence, self-esteem, and self-worth in our students." Andersen Elementary in Rockledge, Florida, raises the bar, adding that students will "exhibit high self-esteem." So self-esteem must not just be *promoted* by teachers, but must be actively *exhibited* by students.

As John Hewitt points out in *The Myth of Self-Esteem,* the implicit message is that self-esteem can be taught and should be taught. When self-esteem programs are used, Hewitt notes, children are "encouraged to believe that it is acceptable and desirable to be preoccupied with oneself [and] praise oneself." In many cases, he says, it's not just encouraged but required. These exercises make self-importance mandatory, demanding of children that they love themselves. "The child *must* be taught to like himself or herself. . . . The child *must* take the teacher's attitude himself or herself—'I am somebody!' 'I am capable and loving!'—regardless of what the child thinks."[32]

Most of these programs encourage children to feel good about themselves for no particular reason. In one program, teachers are told to discourage children from saying things like "I'm a good soccer player" or "I'm a good singer."[33] This makes self-esteem contingent on performance, the program authors chide. Instead, "we want to anchor self-esteem firmly to the child . . . so that no matter what the performance might be, the self-esteem remains high." In other words, feeling good about yourself is more important than good performance. Children, the guide says, should be taught "that it is who they are, not what they do, that is important." Many programs encourage self-esteem even when things go wrong or the child does something bad. In one activity, children are asked to finish several sentences, including ones beginning "I love myself even though . . ." and "I forgive myself for . . ."[34]

Teacher training courses often emphasize that a child's self-esteem must be preserved above all else. A sign on the wall of one university's education department says, "We Choose to Feel Special and Worthwhile No Matter What."[35] Perhaps as a result, 60% of teachers and 69% of school counselors agree that self-esteem should be raised by "providing more unconditional validation of students based on who they are rather than how they perform or behave."[36] Unconditional validation, to translate the educational mumbo-jumbo, means feeling good about yourself no matter how you act or whether you learn anything or not. A veteran second-grade teacher in Tennessee disagrees with this practice but sees it everywhere. "We handle children much more delicately," she says. "They feel good about themselves for no reason. We've given them this cotton-candy sense of self with no basis in reality."[37]

Although the self-esteem approach sounds like it might be especially popular in liberal blue-state areas, it's common in red states as well, perhaps because it's very similar to the ideas popularized by fundamentalist Christian churches. For example, the popular Christian children's book *You Are Special* promotes the same unconditional self-esteem emphasized in secular school programs. First published in 1997, the book notes, "The world tells kids, 'You're special if . . . you have the brains, the looks, the talent.' God tells them, 'You're special just because. No qualifications necessary.' Every child you know needs to hear this one, reassuring truth." Traditional religion, of course, did have "qualifications" and rules for behavior. Adults hear this message as well.[38] In an article in *Ladies Home Journal,* Christian author

Rick Warren writes, "You can believe what others say about you, or you can believe in yourself as does God, who says you are truly acceptable, lovable, valuable, and capable."[39]

Even programs not specifically focused on self-esteem often place the utmost value on children's self-feelings. Children in some schools sing songs with lyrics like "Who I am makes a difference and all our dreams can come true" and "We are beautiful, magnificent, courageous, outrageous, and great!"[40] Other students pen a "Me Poem" or write a mock TV "commercial" advertising themselves and their good qualities. An elementary school teacher in Alabama makes one child the focus of a "VIP for a week" project.[41] The children's museum in Laramie, Wyoming, has a self-esteem exhibit where children are told to describe themselves using positive adjectives.[42]

Parents often continue the self-esteem lessons their children have learned in school, perhaps because more children are planned and cherished. The debut of the birth control pill in the early 1960s began the trend toward wanted children, which continued in the early 1970s as abortion became legal and cultural values shifted toward children as a choice rather than a duty. In the 1950s, it was considered selfish not to have kids, but by the 1970s it was an individual decision. As a result, more and more children were born to people who really *wanted* to become parents. Parents were able to lavish more attention on each child as the average number of children per family shrank from four to two. Young people often say that their parents believed in building self-esteem. "My mom constantly told me how special I was," said Natalie, 19. "No matter how I did, she would tell me I was the best." Kristen, 22, said her parents had a "wonderful" way of "telling me what a great job I did and repeatedly telling me I was a very special person." Popular media has also promoted this idea endlessly, offering up self-esteem as the cure for just about everything. In one episode of the family drama *7th Heaven*, one young character asks what can be done about war. The father on the show, a minister, says, "We can take a good look in the mirror, and when we see peace, that's when we'll have peace on earth." The rest of the episode featured each character smiling broadly to himself or herself in the mirror. In other words, if we all just loved ourselves enough, it would put an end to war. (Not only is this tripe, but wars, if anything, are usually rooted in too *much* love of self, land, and nation—not too little.) But, as TV and movies have taught us, loving yourself is more important than anything else.

These efforts have had their intended impact. Don Tapscott, who interviewed hundreds of people for his book *Growing Up Digital,* notes, "Chat moderators, teachers, parents, and community workers who spend time with [young people] invariably told us that they think this is a confident generation who think highly of themselves."[43] In a CBS News poll, the high school graduates of 2000 were asked, "What makes you feel positive about yourself?" The most popular answer, at 33%, was the tautological "self-esteem." School performance was a distant second at 18%, with popularity third at 13%.[44] Yet this is not surprising: Saying that having self-esteem makes you feel positive about yourself—forget any actual reason—is exactly what the self-esteem programs have taught today's young generation since they were in kindergarten.

Yet when everyone wears a shirt that says "I'm Special," as some of the programs encourage, it is a wide-open invitation to parody. The 1997 premiere episode of MTV's animated show *Daria* featured a character named Jane, who cracked, "I like having low self-esteem. It makes me feel special." Later in the episode, the teacher of a "self-esteem class" asks the students to "make a list of ten ways the world would be a sadder place if you weren't in it." "Is that if we'd never been born, or if we died suddenly and unexpectedly?" asks one of the students. Wanting to get out of the rest of the class, Daria and Jane recite the answers to the self-esteem "test": "The next time I start to feel bad about myself [I will] stand before the mirror, look myself in the eye and say, 'You are special. No one else is like you.' "[45]

By the time GenMe gets to college, these messages are rote. Hewitt, who teaches at the University of Massachusetts, says his students are very excited when they begin discussing self-esteem in his sociology class. But once he begins to question the validity of self-esteem, the students' faces become glum and interest wanes. Hewitt compares it to what might happen in church if a priest suddenly began questioning the existence of God. After all, we worship at the altar of self-esteem and self-focus. "When the importance of self-esteem is challenged, a major part of the contemporary American view of the world is challenged," Hewitt writes.[46]

Girls Are Great

It is no coincidence that the *Daria* episode parodying self-esteem programs features two girls. Feminist Gloria Steinem, who spent the 1970s and 1980s fighting for practical rights like equal pay and maternity leave, spent the early 1990s promoting her book *Revolution from Within: A Book of Self-Esteem*. In 1991, a study by the American Association of University Women (AAUW) announced that girls "lose their self-esteem on the way to adolescence." This study was covered in countless national news outlets and ignited a national conversation about teenage girls and how they feel about themselves. *Reviving Ophelia*, a bestselling book on adolescent girls, popularized this idea further, documenting the feelings of self-doubt girls experience as they move through junior high and high school. Apparently, girls' self-esteem was suffering a severe blow when they became teenagers, and we needed to do something about it.

Before long, programs like the Girl Scouts began to focus on self-esteem through their "Girls Are Great" program. Girls could earn badges like "Being My Best" and "Understanding Yourself and Others." Amanda, 22, says that her Girl Scout troop spent a lot of time on self-esteem. "We did workshops and earned badges based around self-esteem building projects," she says. "We learned that we could do anything we wanted, that it was good to express yourself, and being different is good."

In 2002, the Girl Scout Council paired with corporate sponsor Unilever to launch "Uniquely ME!" a self-esteem program to "address the critical nationwide problem of low self-esteem among adolescent and preadolescent girls." The program includes three booklets for girls ages 8 to 14, each including exercises on "recognizing one's strengths and best attributes" and "identifying core values and personal interests."[47]

However, there is little evidence that girls' self-esteem dives at adolescence. The AAUW study was seriously flawed, relying on unstandardized measures and exaggerating small differences. In 1999, a carefully researched, comprehensive study of sex differences in self-esteem was published in *Psychological Bulletin,* the most prestigious journal in the field. The study statistically summarized 216 previous studies on more than 97,000 people and concluded that the actual difference between adolescent girls' and boys' self-esteem was less than 4%—in other words, extremely small.[48] Exaggerating this difference might be unwise. "We may create a self-fulfilling prophecy for girls by telling them they'll have low self-esteem," said University of Wisconsin professor Janet Hyde, one of the study authors.[49]

When my colleague Keith Campbell and I did a different analysis of 355 studies of 105,318 people, we also found that girls' self-esteem does not fall precipitously at adolescence; it just doesn't rise as fast as boys' self-esteem during the teen years. There was no large drop in girls' self-esteem, and by college the difference between men's and women's self-esteem was very small.[50] Another meta-analysis, by my former student Brenda Dolan-Pascoe, found moderate sex differences in appearance self-esteem, but no sex differences at all in academic self-esteem. Girls also scored *higher* than boys in behavior self-esteem and moral-ethical self-esteem. The achievements of adolescent girls also contradict the idea that they retreat into self-doubt: girls earn higher grades than boys at all school levels, and more go on to college.

In other words, adolescent girls don't have a self-esteem problem— there is no "critical nationwide problem of low self-esteem among adolescent and preadolescent girls" as the Girl Scouts claimed. But in a culture obsessed with feeling good about ourselves, even the hint of a self-esteem deficit is enough to prompt a nationwide outcry. The Girl Scout program premiered three years after the 1999 comprehensive study found a minuscule sex difference in self-esteem. Why let an overwhelming mass of data get in the way of a program that sounded good?

Self-Esteem and Academic Performance

There has also been a movement against "criticizing" children too much. Some schools and teachers don't correct children's mistakes, afraid that this will damage children's self-esteem. One popular method tells teachers not to correct students' spelling or grammar, arguing that kids should be "independent spellers" so they can be treated as "individuals." (Imagine reading a nuespaper wyten useing *that* filosofy.)[51] Teacher education courses emphasize that creating a positive atmosphere is more important than correcting mistakes.[52] In 2005, a British teacher proposed eliminating the word "fail" from education; instead of hearing that they have failed, students should hear that they have "deferred success."[53] In the United States, office stores have started carrying large stocks of purple pens, as some teachers say that red ink is too "scary" for children's papers.[54] Florida elementary school-teacher Robin Slipakoff said, "Red has a negative connotation, and we want to promote self-confidence."[55]

Grade inflation has also reached record highs. In 2004, 48% of American college freshmen—almost half—reported earning an A average in high school, compared to only 18% in 1968, even though SAT scores decreased over this time period.[56] "Each year we think [the number with an A average] can't inflate anymore. And then it does again. The 'C' grade is almost a thing of the past," noted Andrew Astin, the lead researcher for the study. These higher grades were given out even though students were doing less work.[57] Only 33% of American college freshmen in 2003 reported studying six or more hours a week during their last year of high school, compared to 47% in 1987.[58] So why are they still getting better grades? "Teachers want to raise the self-esteem and feel-good attitudes of students," explains Howard Everson of the College Board.[59] We have become a Lake Wobegon nation: all of our children are above average.

The results of these policies have played out in schools around the country. Emily, 8, came home from school one day proud that she got half of the words right on her spelling test (in other words, a grade of 50). When her mother pointed out that this wasn't very good, Emily replied that her teacher had said it was just fine. At her school near Dallas, Texas, 11-year-old Kayla was invited to the math class pizza party as a reward for making a good grade, even though she had managed only a barely passing 71. The pizza parties used to be only for children who made A's, but in recent years the school has invited every child who simply passed.

This basically means that we don't expect children to learn anything. As long as they feel good, that seems to be all that's required. As education professor Maureen Stout notes, many educational psychologists believe that schools should be "places in which children are insulated from the outside world and emotionally—not intellectually—nourished. . . . My colleagues always referred to the importance of making kids feel good about themselves but rarely, if ever, spoke of achievement, ideals, goals, character, or decency."[60] The future teachers whom Stout was educating believed that "children shouldn't be challenged to try things that others in the class are not ready for, since that would promote competition, and competition is bad for self-esteem. Second, grading should be avoided if at all possible, but, if absolutely necessary, should be done in a way that avoids any indication that Johnny is anything less than a stellar pupil."

Grade inflation and lack of competition may be backfiring: in 2003, 43% of college freshmen reported that they were frequently bored in class during their last year of high school, up from 29% in 1985.[61] This is not surprising: how interesting could school possibly be when everyone gets an A and self-esteem is more important than learning?

Perhaps as a result of all of this self-esteem building, educational psychologist Harold Stevenson found that American children ranked very highly when asked how good they were at math.[62] Of course, their *actual* math performance is merely mediocre, with other countries' youth routinely outranking American children. Every year, news anchors solemnly report how far American kids are falling behind. The emphasis on self-esteem can't be blamed entirely for this, of course, but one could easily argue that children's time might be better spent doing math than hearing that they are special. In 2004, 70% of American college freshmen reported that their "academic ability" was "above average" or "highest 10%," an amusing demonstration of American youths' self-confidence outpacing their ability at math.

What kind of young people does this produce? Many teachers and social observers say it results in kids who can't take criticism. In other words, employers, get ready for a group of easily hurt young workers. Peter Sacks, author of *Generation X Goes to College,* noted the extraordinary thin-skinnedness of the undergraduates he taught, and my experience has been no different. I've learned not to discuss test items that the majority of students missed, as this invariably leads to lots of whiny defensiveness and very little actual learning. The two trends are definitely related: research shows that when people with high self-esteem are criticized, they became unfriendly, rude, and uncooperative, even toward people who had nothing to do with the criticism.[63]

None of this should really surprise us. Students "look and act like what the [self-esteem] theories say they should look and act like," notes Hewitt. "They tend to act as though they believe they have worthy and good inner essences, regardless of what people say or how they behave, that they deserve recognition and attention from others, and their unique individual needs should be considered first and foremost."[64] And, of course, this is exactly what has happened: GenMe takes for granted that the self comes first, and we often believe exactly what we were so carefully taught—that we're special.

But this must have an upside; surely kids who have high self-esteem go on to make better grades and achieve more in school. Actually, they don't. There is a small correlation between self-esteem and grades.[65] However, self-esteem does not cause high grades—instead, high grades cause higher self-esteem. So self-esteem programs clearly put the cart before the horse in trying to increase self-esteem. Even much of the small link from high grades to high self-esteem can be explained by other factors such as income: rich kids, for example, have higher self-esteem and get better grades, but that's because coming from an affluent home causes both of these things, and not because they cause each other. This resembles the horse and the cart being towed on a flatbed truck—neither the cart nor the horse is causing the motion in the other even though they are moving together. As self-esteem programs aren't going to make all kids rich, they won't raise self-esteem this way either.

Nor does high self-esteem protect against teen pregnancy, juvenile delinquency, alcoholism, drug abuse, or chronic welfare dependency. Several comprehensive reviews of the research literature by different authors have all concluded that self-esteem doesn't cause much of anything.[66] Even the book sponsored by the California Task Force to Promote Self-Esteem and Personal and Social Responsibility, which spent a quarter of a million dollars trying to raise Californians' self-esteem, found that self-esteem isn't linked to academic achievement, good behavior, or any other outcome the Task Force was formed to address.[67]

Are Self-Esteem Programs Good or Bad?

Psychologist Martin Seligman has criticized self-esteem programs as empty and shortsighted. He argues that self-esteem based on nothing does not serve children well in the long run; it's better, he says, for children to develop real skills and feel good about accomplishing something.[68] Roy Baumeister, the lead author of an extensive review of the research on self-esteem, found that self-esteem does not lead to better grades, improved work performance, decreased violence, or less cheating. In fact, people with high self-esteem are often more violent and more likely to cheat. "It is very questionable whether [the few benefits] justify the effort and expense that schools, parents and therapists have put into raising self-esteem," Baumeister wrote. "After all these years, I'm sorry to say, my recommendation is this: forget about self-esteem and concentrate more on self-control and self-discipline."[69]

I agree with both of these experts. Self-esteem is an outcome, not a cause. In other words, it doesn't do much good to encourage a child to feel good about himself just to feel good; this doesn't mean anything. Children develop true self-esteem from behaving well and accomplishing things. "What the self-esteem movement really says to students is that their achievement is not important and their minds are not worth developing," writes Maureen Stout. It's clearly better for children to value learning rather than simply feeling good.[70]

So should kids feel bad about themselves if they're not good at school or sports? No. They should feel bad if they didn't work hard and try. And even if they don't succeed, sometimes negative feelings can be a motivator.

Trying something challenging and learning from the experience is better than feeling good about oneself for no reason.

Also, everyone can do *something* well. Kids who are not athletic or who struggle with school might have another talent, like music or art. Almost all children can develop pride from being a good friend or helping someone. Kids can do many things to feel good about themselves, so self-esteem can be based on something. If a child feels great about himself even when he does nothing, why do anything? Self-esteem without basis encourages laziness rather than hard work. On the other hand, we shouldn't go too far and hinge our self-worth entirely on one external goal, like getting good grades. As psychologist Jennifer Crocker documents, the seesaw of self-esteem this produces can lead to poor physical and mental health.[71] A happy medium is what's called for here: don't feel bad about yourself because you made a bad grade—just don't feel good about yourself if you didn't even study. Use your bad feelings as a motivator to do better next time. True self-confidence comes from honing your talents and learning things, not from being told you're great just because you exist.

The practice of not correcting mistakes, avoiding letter grades, and discouraging competition is also misguided. Competition can help make learning fun; as Stout points out, look at how the disabled kids in the Special Olympics benefit from competing. Many schools now don't publish the honor roll of children who do well in school and generally downplay grades because, they falsely believe, competition isn't good for self-esteem (as some kids won't make the honor roll, and some kids will make C's). But can you imagine not publishing the scores of a basketball game because it might not be good for the losing team's self-esteem? Can you imagine not keeping score in the game? What fun would that be? The self-esteem movement, Stout argues, is popular because it is sweetly addictive: teachers don't have to criticize, kids don't have to be criticized, and everyone goes home feeling happy. The problem is they also go home ignorant and uneducated.

Kids who don't excel in a certain area should still be encouraged to keep trying. This isn't self-esteem, however: it's self-control. Self-control, or the ability to persevere and keep going, is a much better predictor of life outcomes than self-esteem. Children high in self-control make better grades and finish more years of education, and they're less likely to use drugs or have a teenage pregnancy. Self-control predicts all of those things researchers had hoped self-esteem would, but hasn't.

Cross-cultural studies provide a good example of the benefits of self-control over self-esteem. Asians, for example, have lower self-esteem than Americans.[72] But when Asian students find out that they scored low on a particular task, they want to keep working on that task so they can improve their performance. American students, in contrast, prefer to give up on that task and work on another one.[73] In other words, Americans preserve their self-esteem at the expense of doing better at a difficult task. This goes a long way toward explaining why Asian children perform better at math and at school in general.

Young people who have high self-esteem built on shaky foundations might run into trouble when they encounter the harsh realities of the real world. As Stout argues, kids who are given meaningless A's and promoted when they haven't learned the material will later find out in college or the working world that they don't know much at all. And what will *that* do to their self-esteem, or, more important, their careers? Unlike your teacher, your boss isn't going to care much about preserving your high self-esteem. The self-esteem emphasis leaves kids ill prepared for the inevitable criticism and occasional failure that is real life. "There is no self-esteem movement in the work world," points out one father. "If you present a bad report at the office, your boss isn't going to say, 'Hey, I like the color paper you chose.' Setting kids up like this is doing them a tremendous disservice."[74]

In any educational program, one has to consider the trade-off between benefit and risk. Valuing self-esteem over learning and accomplishment is clearly harmful, as children feel great about themselves but are cheated out of the education they need to succeed. Self-esteem programs *might* benefit the small minority of kids who really do feel worthless, but those kids are likely to have bigger problems that self-esteem boosting won't fix. The risk in these programs is in inflating the self-concept of children who already think the world revolves around them. Building up the self-esteem and importance of kids who are already egocentric can bring trouble, as it can lead to narcissism—and maybe it already has.

Changes in Narcissism

Narcissism is one of the few personality traits that psychologists agree is almost completely negative. Narcissists are overly focused on themselves and lack empathy for others, which means they cannot see another person's perspective.[75] (Sound like the last clerk who served you?) They also feel entitled to special privileges and believe that they are superior to other people. As a result, narcissists are bad relationship partners and can be difficult to work with. Narcissists are also more likely to be hostile, feel anxious, compromise their health, and fight with friends and family. Unlike those merely high in self-esteem, narcissists admit that they don't feel close to other people.[76]

All evidence suggests that narcissism is much more common in recent generations. In the early 1950s, only 12% of teens aged 14 to 16 agreed with the statement "I am an important person."[77] By the late 1980s, an incredible 80%—almost seven times as many—claimed they were important. Psychologist Harrison Gough found consistent increases on narcissism items among college students quizzed between the 1960s and the 1990s.[78] GenMe students were more likely to agree that "I would be willing to describe myself as a pretty 'strong' personality" and "I have often met people who were supposed to be experts who were no better than I." In other words, those other people don't know what they're talking about, so everyone should listen to me.

In a 2002 survey of 3,445 people conducted by Joshua Foster, Keith Campbell, and me, younger people scored considerably higher on the Narcissistic Personality Inventory, agreeing with items such as "If I ruled the world it would be a better place," "I am a special person"and "I can live my life anyway I want to."[79] (These statements evoke the image of a young man speeding down the highway in the world's biggest SUV, honking his horn, and screaming, "Get out of my way! I'm important!") This study was cross-sectional, though, meaning that it was a one-time sample of people of different ages. For that reason, we cannot be sure if any differences are due to age or to generation; however, the other studies of narcissism mentioned previously suggest that generation plays a role. It is also interesting that narcissism scores were fairly high until around age 35, after which they decreased markedly. This is right around the cutoff between GenMe and previous generations.

Narcissism is the darker side of the focus on the self, and is often confused with self-esteem. Self-esteem is often based on solid relationships with others, whereas narcissism comes from believing that you are special and more important than other people. Many of the school programs designed to raise self-esteem probably raise narcissism instead. Lillian Katz, a professor of early childhood education at the University of Illinois, wrote an article titled "All About Me: Are We Developing Our Children's Self-Esteem or Their Narcissism?" She writes, "Many of the practices advocated in pursuit of [high self-esteem] may instead inadvertently develop narcissism in the form of excessive preoccupation with oneself."[80] Because the school programs emphasize being "special" rather than encouraging friendships, we may be training an army of little narcissists instead of raising kids' self-esteem.

Many young people also display entitlement, a facet of narcissism that involves believing that you deserve and are entitled to more than others. A scale that measures entitlement has items like "Things should go my way," "I demand the best because I'm worth it," and (my favorite) "If I were on the *Titanic,* I would deserve to be on the *first* lifeboat!"[81] A 2005 Associated Press article printed in hundreds of news outlets labeled today's young people "The Entitlement Generation." In the article, employers complained that young employees expected too much too soon and had very high expectations for salary and promotions.[82]

Teachers have seen this attitude for years now. One of my colleagues said his students acted as if grades were something they simply deserved to get no matter what. He joked that their attitude could be summed up by "Where's my A? I distinctly remember ordering an A from the catalog." Stout, the education professor, lists the student statements familiar to teachers everywhere: "I need a better grade," "I deserve an A on this paper," "I *never* get B's." Stout points out that the self-esteem movement places the student's feelings at the center, so "students learn that they do not need to respect their teachers or even earn their grades, so they begin to believe that they are entitled to grades, respect, or anything else . . . just for asking!"[83]

Unfortunately, narcissism can lead to outcomes far worse than grade grubbing. Several studies have found that narcissists lash out aggressively when they are insulted or rejected.[84] Eric Harris and Dylan Klebold, the teenage gunmen at Columbine High School, made statements remarkably similar to items on the most popular narcissism questionnaire. On a videotape made before the shootings, Harris picked up a gun, made a shooting noise, and said "Isn't it fun to get the respect we're going to deserve?"[85] (Chillingly similar to the narcissism item "I insist upon getting the respect that is due me.") Later, Harris said, "I could convince them that I'm going to climb Mount Everest, or I have a twin brother growing out of my back. I can make you believe anything" (virtually identical to the item "I can make anyone believe anything I want them to"). Harris and Klebold then debate which famous movie director will film their story. A few weeks after making the videotapes, Harris and Klebold killed thirteen people and then themselves.

Other examples abound. In a set of lab studies, narcissistic men felt less empathy for rape victims, reported more enjoyment when watching a rape scene in a movie, and were more punitive toward a woman who refused to read a sexually arousing passage out loud to them.[86] Abusive husbands who threaten to kill their wives—and tragically sometimes do—are the ultimate narcissists. They see everyone and everything in terms of fulfilling their needs, and become very angry and aggressive when things don't go exactly their way. Many workplace shootings occur after an employee is fired and decides he'll "show" everyone how powerful he is.

The rise in narcissism has very deep roots. It's not just that we feel better about ourselves, but that we even think to ask the question. We fixate on self-esteem, and unthinkingly build narcissism, because we believe that the needs of the individual are paramount. This will stay with us even if self-esteem programs end up in the dustbin of history.

NOTES

1. Ladies' Home Journal *told readers:* Warren, Rick. "Learn to Love Yourself!" *Ladies' Home Journal*, March 2005; p. 36.

2. *while* Parenting *offered:* Lamb, Yanick Rice. "Proud to Be Me!" *Parenting*, April 2005.

3. *The American Academy of Pediatrics guide:* Shelov, Steven, ed. in chief. 1998. *Caring for Your Baby and Young Child: Birth to Age 5.* New York: Bantam.

4. *In a 1976* New York Magazine *article:* Wolfe, Tom. "The Me Decade and the Third Great Awakening." *New York Magazine*, August 23, 1976.

5. *When asked what's next in her life:* "Pop Quiz: Kim Basinger." *People*, September 27, 2004.

6. *In answer to the same question:* Laskas, Jeanne Marie. "Sarah's New Day." *Ladies' Home Journal,* June 2004.

7. *Gillon describes Boomers:* Gillon, Steve. 2004. *Boomer Nation.* New York: Free Press; p. 263.

8. *Even food becomes:* Brooks, David. 2000. *Bobos in Paradise.* New York: Simon & Schuster; p. 58.

9. *In 1973, 46% of Boomers:* Smith, J. Walker, and Clurman, Ann. 1997. *Rocking the Ages: The Yankelovich Report on Generational Marketing.* New York: HarperCollins.

10. *Thirty percent of Boomers:* Ibid.

11. *Even stronger evidence:* Astin, A. W., et al. 2002. *The American Freshman: Thirty-Five Year Trends.* Los Angeles: Higher Education Research Institute, UCLA. Plus 2003 and 2004 supplements.

12. *"Instead of seeking:* Rubin, Jerry. 1976. *Growing (Up) at Thirty-Seven.* New York: Lippincott; p. 175.

13. *Aleta St. James, a 57-year-old woman:* Schienberg, Jonathan. "New Age Mystic to Become Mom at 57." <www.cnn.com>. November 9, 2004.

14. *In 2004's* Conquering Your Quarterlife Crisis: Robbins, Alexandra. 2004. *Conquering Your Quarterlife Crisis.* New York: Perigee; pp. 51–52.

15. *When a character in the 2004 novel:* Giffin, Emily. 2004. *Something Borrowed.* New York: St. Martin's Press; p. 2.

16. *Dr. Phil, the ultimate in plainspoken: Today.* NBC, December 27, 2004.

17. *Psychologist Martin Seligman says:* Seligman, M. E. P. "Boomer Blues." *Psychology Today,* October 1988: 50–53.

18. *A careful study of news stories:* Patterson, Thomas E. 2000. "Doing Well and Doing Good: How Soft News and Critical Journalism Are Shrinking the News Audience and Weakening Democracy—and What News Outlets Can Do About It." Joan Shorenstein Center on the Press, Politics, and Public Policy; p. 5. PDF available for download at <www.ksg.harvard.edu/presspol/Research Publications/Reports/>.

19. *In a letter to her fans in 2004:* "The Couples of 2004." *Us Weekly,* January 3, 2005.

20. *In the late 1990s, Prudential:* Hornblower, Margot. "Great Xpectations." *Time,* June 9, 1997.

21. *My colleague Keith Campbell and I looked:* Twenge, J. M., and Campbell, W. K. 2001. Age and Birth Cohort Differences in Self-Esteem: A Cross-Temporal Meta-Analysis. *Personality and Social Psychology Review,* 5: 321–344.

22. *A 1997 survey of teens asked:* "11th Annual Special Teen Report: Teens and Self-Image: Survey Results." *USA Weekend,* May 1–3, 1998.

23. *Another survey found:* Hicks, Rick, and Hicks, Kathy. 1999. *Boomers, Xers, and Other Strangers.* Wheaton, IL: Tyndale; p. 270.

24. *We examined the responses:* Twenge, J. M., and Campbell, W. K. 2001. Age and Birth Cohort Differences in Self-Esteem: A Cross-Temporal Meta-Analysis. *Personality and Social Psychology Review,* 5: 321–344.

25. *Research on programs to boost:* Ibid.

26. *Journal articles on self-esteem:* Hewitt, John. 1998. *The Myth of Self-Esteem.* New York: St. Martin's Press; p. 51.

27. *One children's book:* Loomans, Diane. 1991. *The Lovables in the Kingdom of Self-Esteem.* New York: H. J. Kramer.

28. *One program is called:* Stout, Maureen. 2000. *The Feel-Good Curriculum.* Cambridge, MA: Perseus Books; p. 131.

29. *Another program, called "Pumsy in Pursuit of Excellence":* "Teaching Self-Image Stirs Furor." *New York Times,* October 13, 1993.

30. *The Magic Circle exercise:* <www.globalideasbank.org/site/bank/idea.php?ideaId=573>; and Summerlin, M. L.; Hammett, V. L.; and Payne, M. L. 1983. The Effect of Magic Circle Participation on a Child's Self-Concept. *School Counselor,* 31: 49–52.

31. *One Austin, Texas, father:* Swann, William. 1996. *Self-Traps: The Elusive Quest for Higher Self-Esteem.* New York: W. H. Freeman; p. 4.

32. *When self-esteem programs:* Hewitt, John. 1998. *The Myth of Self-Esteem,* New York: St. Martin's Press; pp. 84–85.

33. *In one program, teachers:* Payne, Lauren Murphy, and Rolhing, Claudia. 1994. A *Leader's Guide to Just Because I Am: A Child's Book of Affirmation.* Minneapolis: Free Spirit Publishing; and Hewitt, John. 1998. *The Myth of Self-Esteem.* New York: St. Martin's Press.

34. *children are asked to finish:* Hewitt, John. 1998. *The Myth of Self-Esteem.* New York: St. Martin's Press; p. 79.

35. *A sign on the wall:* Kramer, Rita. 1991. *Ed School Follies: The Miseducation of America's Teachers.* New York: Free Press; p. 33.

36. *Perhaps as a result, 60% of teachers:* Scott, C. G. 1996. Student Self-Esteem and the School System: Perceptions and Implications. *Journal of Educational Research,* 89: 292–297.

37. *A veteran second-grade teacher:* Gibbs, Nancy. "Parents Behaving Badly." *Time,* February 21, 2005.

38. *For example, the popular Christian:* Lucado, Max. 1997. *You Are Special.* Wheaton, IL: Crossway Books.

39. *In an article in Ladies' Home Journal. Christian author:* Warren, Rick. "Learn to Love Yourself!" *Ladies' Home Journal,* March 2005.

40. *Children in some schools:* Lynn Sherr. "Me, Myself and I—The Growing Self-Esteem Movement." 20/20. ABC, March 11, 1994.

41. *An elementary school teacher in Alabama:* Hewitt, John. 1998. *The Myth of Self-Esteem.* New York: St. Martin's Press; p. 81.

42. *The children's museum in Laramie:* Lynn Sherr. "Me, Myself and I—The Growing Self-Esteem Movement." 20/20. ABC, March 11, 1994.

43. *Don Tapscott, who interviewed:* Tapscott, Don. 1998. *Growing Up Digital.* New York: McGraw-Hill; p. 92.

44. *In a CBS News poll:* CBS News. 2001. *The Class of 2000.* Simon & Schuster eBook, available for download, p. 64.

45. *The 1997 premiere episode: Daria.* Episode: "Esteemsters." MTV, March 3, 1997.

46. *Hewitt, who teaches:* Hewitt, John. 1998. *The Myth of Self-Esteem.* New York: St. Martin's Press; pp. 1–3.

47. *In 2002, the Girl Scout Council:* <www.girlscouts.org/program/program_opportunities/leadership/uniquelyme.asp>.

48. *In 1999, a carefully researched:* Kling, K. C., et al. 1999. Gender Differences in Self-Esteem: A Meta-Analysis. *Psychological Bulletin,* 125: 470–500.

49. *"We may create:* <www.news.wisc.edu/wire/i072899/selfesteem.html>.

50. *When my colleague Keith Campbell and I did:* Twenge, J. M., and Campbell, W. K. 2001. Age and Birth Cohort Differences in Self-Esteem: A Cross-Temporal Meta-Analysis. *Personality and Social Psychology Review,* 5: 321–344.

51. *One popular method tells:* Wilde, Sandra. 1989. A Proposal for a New Spelling Curriculum. *Elementary School Journal,* 90: 275–289.

52. *Teacher education courses emphasize:* Kramer, Rita. 1991. *Ed School Follies: The Miseducation of America's Teachers.* New York: Free Press; p. 116.

53. *a British teacher proposed:* "Teachers Say No-One Should 'Fail.'" BBC News, July 20, 2005. See <news.bbc.co.uk/1/hi/education/4697461.stm>.

54. *office stores have started carrying:* Aoki, Naomi, "Harshness of Red Marks Has Students Seeing Purple." *Boston Globe,* August 23, 2004.

55. *Florida elementary schoolteacher:* Ibid.

56. *In 2004, 48% of American college freshmen:* Astin, A. W., et al. 2002. *The American Freshman: Thirty-Five Year Trends.* Los Angeles: Higher Education Research Institute, UCLA. Plus 2003 and 2004 supplements.

57. *"Each year we think:* Giegerich, Steve. "College Freshmen Have Worst Study Habits in Years But Less Likely to Drink, Study Finds." Associated Press, January 27, 2003. <www.detnews.com/2003/schools/0301/27/schools-70002.htm>.

58. *Only 33% of American:* Astin, A. W., et al. 2002. *The American Freshman: Thirty-Five Year Trends.* Los Angeles: Higher Education Research Institute, UCLA. Plus 2003 and 2004 supplements.

59. *"Teachers want to raise:* Innerst, Carol. "Wordsmiths on Wane Among U.S. Students." *Washington Times,* August 25, 1994.

60. *As education professor Maureen Stout notes:* Stout, Maureen, 2000. *The Feel-Good Curriculum.* Cambridge, MA: Perseus Books; pp. 3–4.

61. *in 2003, 43% of college freshmen:* Astin, A. W., et al. 2002. *The American Freshman: Thirty-Five Year Trends.* Los Angeles: Higher Education Research Institute, UCLA. Plus 2003 and 2004 supplements.

62. *educational psychologist Harold Stevenson:* Stevenson, H. W., et al. 1990. Mathematics Achievement of Children in China and the United States. *Child Development,* 61: 1053–1066.

63. *research shows that when people:* Heatherton, T. F., and Vohs, K. D. 2000. Interpersonal Evaluations Following Threats to Self: Role of Self-Esteem. *Journal of Personality and Social Psychology,* 78: 725–736.

64. *Students "look and act like:* Hewitt, John. 1998. *The Myth of Self-Esteem.* New York: St. Martin's Press; p. 84.

65. *There is a small correlation:* Baumeister, R. F., et al. 2003. Does High Self-Esteem Cause Better Performance, Interpersonal Success, Happiness, or Healthier Lifestyles? *Psychological Science in the Public Interest,* 4: 1–44; and Covington, M. V. 1989. "Self-Esteem and Failure in School." In A. M. Mecca, N. J. Smelser, and J. Vasconcellos, eds. *The Social Importance of Self-Esteem.* Berkeley: University of California Press; p. 79.

66. *Several comprehensive reviews:* Ibid.

67. *Even the book sponsored:* Smelser, N. J. 1989. "Self-esteem and Social Problems." In A. M. Mecca, N. J. Smelser, and J. Vasconcellos, eds. *The Social Importance of Self-Esteem.* Berkeley: University of California Press.

68. *Psychologist Martin Seligman has criticized:* Selgiman, Martin. 1996. *The Optimistic Child.* New York: Harper Perennial.

69. *"It is very questionable:* Baumeister, Roy. "The Lowdown on High Self-esteem: Thinking You're Hot Stuff Isn't the Promised Cure-all." *Los Angeles Times,* January 25, 2005.

70. *"What the self-esteem movement:* Stout, Maureen. 2000. *The Feel-Good Curriculum.* Cambridge, MA: Perseus Books; p. 263.

71. *As psychologist Jennifer Crocker documents:* Crocker, J., and Park, L. E. 2004. The Costly Pursuit of Self-esteem. *Psychological Bulletin,* 130: 392–414.

72. *Asians, for example, have lower:* Twenge, J. M., and Crocker, J. 2002. Race and Self-Esteem: Meta-Analyses Comparing Whites, Blacks, Hispanics, Asians, and American Indians. *Psychological Bulletin;* 128: 371–408.

73. *But when Asian students find out:* Heine, S. J., et al. 2001. Divergent Consequences of Success and Failure in Japan and North America: An Investigation of Self-improving Motivations and Malleable Selves. *Journal of Personality and Social Psychology,* 81: 599–615.

74. *"There is no self-esteem movement:* Shaw, Robert. 2003. *The Epidemic.* New York: Regan Books; p. 152.

75. *Narcissists are overly focused:* Campbell, W. Keith. 2005. *When You Love a Man Who Loves Himself.* Chicago: Source Books.

76. *Narcissists are also more likely:* Helgeson, V. S., and Fritz, H. L. 1999. Unmitigated Agency and Unmitigated Communion: Distinctions from Agency and Communion. *Journal of Research in Personality,* 33: 131–158.

77. *In the early 1950s, only 12% of teens:* Newsom, C. R., et al. 2003. Changes in Adolescent Response Patterns on the MMPI/MMPI-A Across Four Decades. *Journal of Personality Assessment,* 81: 74–84.

78. *Psychologist Harrison Gough found:* Gough, H. 1991. "Scales and Combinations of Scales: What Do They Tell Us, What Do They Mean?" Paper presented at the 99th Annual Convention of the American Psychological Association, San Francisco, August 1991. Data obtained from Harrison Gough in 2001.

79. *In a 2002 survey of 3,445 people:* Foster, J. D.; Campbell, W. K.; and Twenge, J. M. 2003. Individual Differences in Narcissism: Inflated Self-Views Across the Lifespan and Around the World. *Journal of Research in Personality,* 37: 469–486.

80. *Lillian Katz, a professor:* Stout, Maureen. 2000. *The Feel-Good Curriculum.* Cambridge, MA: Perseus Books; p. 178.

81. *A scale that measures entitlement:* Campbell, W. K., et al. 2004. Psychological Entitlement: Interpersonal Consequences and Validation of a Self-report Measure. *Journal of Personality Assessment,* 83: 29–45.

82. *A 2005 Associated Press article printed:* Irvine, Martha. "Young Labeled 'Entitlement Generation.'" AP, June 26, 2005. <biz.yahoo.com/ap/050626/the_entitlement_ generation. html2.v3>. Also reprinted in many newspapers.

83. *Stout, the education professor, lists:* Stout, Maureen. 2000. *The Feel-Good Curriculum.* Cambridge, MA: Perseus Books; p. 2.

84. *Several studies have found:* Bushman, B. J., and Baumeister, R. F. 1998. Threatened Egotism, Narcissism, Self-esteem, and Direct and Displaced Aggression: Does Self-love or Self-hate Lead to Violence? *Journal of Personality and Social Psychology,* 75: 219–229; and Twenge, J. M., and Campbell, W. K. 2003. "Isn't it fun to get the respect that we're going to deserve?" Narcissism, Social Rejection, and Aggression. *Personality and Social Psychology Bulletin,* 29: 261–272.

85. *Harris picked up a gun:* Gibbs, Nancy, and Roche, Timothy. "The Columbine Tapes." *Time,* December 20, 1999.

86. *In a set of lab studies, narcissistic:* Bushman, B. J., et. al. 2003. Narcissism, Sexual Refusal, and Aggression: Testing a Narcissistic Reactance Model of Sexual Coercion. *Journal of Personality and Social Psychology,* 84: 1027–1040.

■ *QUESTIONS FOR MAKING CONNECTIONS WITHIN THE READING* ■

1. "An Army of One: *Me*" is written in a lively style, with the author speaking in a number of different voices throughout: objective analyst, insider, and skeptic, to name a few. As you reread, mark the passages where Twenge's voice shifts and identify the voices on both sides of the shift. When you're done, review your markings. Is there a voice or a viewpoint that wins out in the end? Is there a voice that you feel is Twenge's real voice, or are all the voices hers?

2. What kinds of evidence does Twenge use to make her case about Generation Me? After you've generated a complete list, identify the evidence that you feel is the most compelling and the evidence that seems less so. Where would you look to find evidence that would further strengthen Twenge's argument? Is there evidence that could refute Twenge's argument? Can arguments about entire generations be either verified or disproven?

3. Twenge identifies three psychic states: thinking about the self, having self-esteem, and being a narcissist. What is the relationship among these three states? If one is educated and trained in one of these psychic states, is there a way to experience another state of mind? Does Twenge provide any evidence of what causes or enables a shift in perspective?

■ *QUESTIONS FOR WRITING* ■

1. As a member of Generation Me, Twenge is both a source for information about her subject and a translator who provides an inside view of how members of Generation Me interpret the world around them. Given this, how would you characterize Twenge's method? How does she know what she claims to knows about Generation Me? How would you go about collecting more information to test her hypothesis? Is definitive evidence available?

2. If we grant Twenge's argument about the values and expectations of Generation Me, what follows? Is it possible for this generation to reverse

course, or is it too late? Can social change be brought about through conscious effort? Or does the scale of the problem mean that what follows is inevitable? Has Twenge diagnosed a problem for which there is no cure?

■ *QUESTIONS FOR MAKING CONNECTIONS BETWEEN READINGS* ■

1. In "War," Sandra Steingraber moves back and forth between her personal experiences growing up and a discussion of the unregulated release of toxins into the environment. She concludes her piece with the statement: "From the right to know and the duty to inquire flows the obligation to act." Given Twenge's description of Generation Me, discuss what "right to know," "duty to inquire," and "obligation to act" might mean to this group of readers. Does Steingraber provide a model for a kind of writing that can bring about social change, or is she writing at a time when the "right to know," the "duty to inquire," and the "obligation to act" no longer mean anything? Is there some better way to reach the members of Generation Me than writing?

2. Twenge identifies numerous characteristics that define the differences between the way Baby Boomers and Generation Me view the self. Using Tim O'Brien's "How to Tell a True War Story," test out Twenge's theory. Do the characters perform as Twenge's theory predicts? Does O'Brien? Are generations defined by wars? Was Vietnam a Baby Boomer war? Is the Iraq War a Generation Me war? Can O'Brien's "true war story" be true for other generations?

CREDITS

AUTHOR AND TITLE INDEX